NW0 3000955   MANA/04   £25.00

KT-375-603

WITHDRAWN

N 0115229 7

The
Competitive Advantage
of Nations

About the Author

MICHAEL E. PORTER, one of the world's leading authorities on competitive strategy and international competitiveness, is the C. Roland Christensen Professor of Business Administration at the Harvard Business School. In 1983, Professor Porter was appointed to President Reagan's Commission on Industrial Competitiveness, the initiative that triggered the competitiveness debate in America. He serves as an advisor to heads of state, governors, mayors, and CEOs throughout the world. The recipient of the Wells Prize in Economics, the Adam Smith Award, three McKinsey Awards, and honorary doctorates from the Stockholm School of Economics and six other universities, Porter is the author of fourteen books, among them *Competitive Strategy, Competitive Advantage,* and *Cases in Competitive Strategy,* all published by The Free Press. He lives in Brookline, Massachusetts.

The Competitive Advantage of Nations

With a New Introduction

Michael E. Porter

NEWMAN COLLEGE
BARTLEY GREEN
BIRMINGHAM B32 3NT
CLASS 338-9
BARCODE 01152297
AUTHOR POR

palgrave

© Michael Porter 1990, 1998

All rights reserved. No reproduction, copy or transmission of
this publication may be made without written permission.

No paragraph of this publication may be reproduced, copied or
transmitted save with written permission or in accordance with
the provisions of the Copyright, Designs and Patents Act 1988,
or under the terms of any licence permitting limited copying
issued by the Copyright Licensing Agency, 90 Tottenham Court
Road, London W1P 0LP.

Any person who does any unauthorised act in relation to this
publication may be liable to criminal prosecution and civil
claims for damages.

The author has asserted his right to be identified as the author of
this work in accordance with the Copyright, Designs
and Patents Act 1988.

First edition 1990
Reprinted 10 times
New edition with updates in an Introduction by the author 1998

Published by
PALGRAVE
Houndmills, Basingstoke, Hampshire RG21 6XS and
175 Fifth Avenue, New York, N.Y. 10010
Companies and representatives throughout the world

PALGRAVE is the new global academic imprint of
St. Martin's Press LLC Scholarly and Reference Division and
Palgrave Publishers Ltd (formerly Macmillan Press Ltd).

ISBN 0–333–73642–7

This book is printed on paper suitable for recycling and
made from fully managed and sustained forest sources.

A catalogue record for this book is available
from the British Library.

10   9   8   7   6
07   06   05   04   03

Printed and bound in Great Britain by
Creative Print and Design (Wales), Ebbw Vale

For Deborah

Contents

Preface

Why do some social groups, economic institutions, and nations advance and prosper? This subject has fascinated and consumed the attention of writers, companies, and governments for as long as there have been social, economic, and political units. In fields as diverse as anthropology, history, sociology, economics, and political science, there have been persistent efforts to understand the forces that explain the questions presented by the progress of some entities and the decline of others.

In recent years, much of the work on this subject has been concerned with nations, examined under the standard of what is commonly called "competitiveness." The striking internationalization of competition in the decades after World War II has been accompanied by major shifts in the economic fortunes of nations and their firms. Governments and firms have inevitably been drawn into a heated debate about what to do.

I have come to this question somewhat reluctantly, having spent most of my professional career to date concentrating not on nations but on companies. My central concern has been with the nature of competition in industries and the principles of competitive strategy. My early research, summarized in *Competitive Strategy* (1980), was on the structure of industries and the choice of position within them. The book *Competitive Advantage* (1985) presented a framework for understanding a company's sources of competitive advantage and how competitive advantage could be enhanced. In *Competition in Global Industries* (1986), I extended the framework to address the challenges of international competition. Though strategy for competing internationally has been an essential part of the equation, my principal units of analysis have been the industry and the firm. The nation, and its government, had a role in my framework, but a limited one.

This began to change when I was appointed by President Ronald Reagan to the President's Commission on Industrial Competitiveness, a group of business executives, labor leaders, academics, and former government officials charged with examining the competitiveness of the United States. The Commission, appointed amidst a highly politicized debate about the need for "industrial policy" in America, studied the question for over a year and issued a considered and balanced report.[1]

What became clear to me during the term of the Commission was that there was no accepted definition of competitiveness. To firms, competitiveness meant the ability to compete in world markets with a global strategy. To many members of Congress, competitiveness meant that the nation had a positive balance of trade. To some economists, competitiveness meant a low unit cost of labor adjusted for exchange rates. Partly because of these differences, much energy has been expended in the United States debating whether there is a competitiveness problem at all. The Commission's report, instead of providing a consensus for action, had little effect. The debate about competitiveness raged on, and still does today.

Whichever the definition of competitiveness adopted, an even more serious problem has been that there is no generally accepted theory to explain it. Innumerable characteristics of nations and firms have been proposed as important, but there has been no way of isolating and integrating the most salient ones. In addition, many explanations are based on assumptions far removed from actual competition, raising questions about their relevance and generality. It was difficult to reconcile many of the explanations with my own experience in studying and working with international companies.

Nor has there been a shortage of recommendations for improving competitiveness through both company strategy and government policy. These recommendations have been as diverse and inconsistent as the implicit or explicit views of competitiveness on which they are based. Many of these recommendations seemed to me, again from the perspective of one with close familiarity with firms, to be counterproductive.

Having said all this, however, I developed a strong conviction that the national environment does play a central role in the competitive success of firms. With striking regularity, firms from one or two nations achieve disproportionate worldwide success in particular industries. Some national environments seem more stimulating to advancement and progress than others. I became convinced that understanding the role of the nation in international competition would be as valuable for firms as it would be for governments, because it would yield some fundamental insights into how competitive advantage was created and sustained.

In this book, I have set out to make my contribution to understanding the competitive advantage of nations, or the national attributes that foster competitive advantage in particular industries, and the implications both for firms and for governments. At the core of my theory are the principles of competitive strategy in individual industries. This should come as no surprise to those familiar with my previous work. While we can identify national characteristics that apply to many industries, my experience has been that these are overshadowed in actual competition by particular and often industry-specific circumstances, choices, and outcomes.

While much can be learned through an aggregate, economy-wide approach to understanding the competitive success of a nation, I seek here a different starting point. My theory begins from individual industries and competitors and builds up to the economy as a whole. The particular industry—passenger cars, facsimile machines, accounting services, ball bearings—is where competitive advantage is either won or lost. The home nation influences the ability of its firms to succeed in particular industries. The outcome of thousands of struggles in individual industries determines the state of a nation's economy and its ability to progress. There are some intellectual pitfalls in moving from industries to the entire economy that we must be careful to avoid, but the approach offers, I believe, an enriched understanding of a nation's economic progress.

The theory presented in this book attempts to capture the full complexity and richness of actual competition, rather than abstract from it. I have sought here to integrate the many elements which influence how companies behave and economies progress. The result is a holistic approach whose level of complexity may be uncomfortable to some. I believe, however, that greater simplification would obscure some of the most important parts of the problem, such as the interplay among the individual influences and their evolution over time.

The theory draws on and spans several fields. At its core is the theory of competitive strategy, but there are also important insights to be gained from ongoing research in such fields as technological innovation, industrial economics, economic development, economic geography, international trade, political science, and industrial sociology, that are not usually combined.

Given the large number of disciplinary literatures that bear in some way on my subject, it was simply not possible to provide complete references. Nor can I attempt here a full intellectual history of my subject. I have, however, noted some of the most important antecedents to my approach in various fields, as well as some of the individual works I found most compelling.

In order to develop a comprehensive theory of the competitive advantage of nations and to demonstrate its relevance, I set out to study a wide range of nations and, within each of them, to investigate the details of competition in many industries. Research based on only one or two nations or a handful of industries runs the risk of mistaking what may be exceptional for general principles. I selected ten nations for my research with widely differing characteristics and institutions.

One outcome of both the nature of my theory and the approach I have taken to present and verify it is a very long book. Its length is something I regret inflicting on the reader but found I could not avoid if I were to test my theory against sufficient evidence and develop its implications for business practitioners and policymakers. Part I of the book presents the theory itself, providing enough of an overview of the principles of competitive strategy to establish the needed background. In Part II, I apply the theory to explain the histories of four representative industries selected from the many we studied. I also apply the theory to the service sector, long an important sector but one where international competition has been little studied but is of growing importance. In Part III, I apply the theory to nations. For eight of the ten nations investigated, I provide a detailed profile of the internationally successful industries in the economy and how the pattern has been changing. I use my theory to explain both successes and failures as well as the evolution of the nation's economy in the postwar period. The collective experience of the nations allows me to extend the theory to explain how entire national economies advance. Part IV develops some of the implications of the theory for company strategy and government policy. The final chapter illustrates how the theory can be used to identify some of the issues that will govern the future development of each nation's economy.

Readers may, however, wish to take shorter paths through the book depending on their particular appetites. Most readers should cover the first four chapters, at a level of detail that will depend on their background and degree of comfort with theory. Part II will be of greatest interest to those seeking a demonstration of the theory in particular industries. Business executives should read most of Part II, and the general reader should at least dip into it. Understanding the process by which a national industry is formed and achieves international competitive success, in at least a few specific cases, is an important frame of reference for later chapters.

Part III offers the opportunity to select from among the nations I discuss according to the reader's particular interests. All readers, however, should look at the introduction to Chapter 7, which explains the methodology and the structure of each country description, as well the concluding section of Chapter 9, which compares the nations as a group. Readers can then select their home nations, nations where important competitors are located, or other nations of interest for study. After reading about some or all the nations, all readers should look at Chapter 10, which extends the argument to develop a theory of how entire national economies progress. The concepts in Chapter 10 will be particularly important in considering the agendas facing each nation, the subject of Chapter 13.

Part IV can also be traversed in a way that reflects the reader's frame of reference, though the implications of the theory for business executives will inform policy makers and vice versa. Business executives will want to read Chapter 11, which is about the implications of my theory for company strategy. Those readers concerned with or participating in public policy formulation should read Chapter 12. Chapter 13, which sets forth some of the issues facing each nation if its economy is to progress further, can be read selectively depending on the reader's interests. Since an important purpose of Chapter 13 is to illustrate how to apply the theory to identify constraints to national economic advancement, however, readers will benefit from not only the discussion of their own nation but also from understanding the problems facing other nations with differing circumstances. The book concludes with a brief Epilogue which contains some of my personal reflections on the study.

The text of the book contains the basic argument and my empirical findings presented in a form accessible to the serious reader. Scholars will find most of the references to literature, as well as the more technical commentary on the theory and its relationship to previous work, in footnotes. The methodology is described in Chapter 1, Chapter 7, and Appendix A.

My aim here is not a book about any single nation but one about a set of principles that apply more broadly. Though some readers may feel that an American bias may be found, I have tried to avoid this. I hope too that no reader will focus exclusively on what I have to say about particular nations, especially in Chapter 13. As I have tried to make clear, my knowledge of any one nation cannot approach that of an expert. Nor would I presume to claim a comprehensive understanding of all of the complex political and social trade-offs that guide individual policy choices. The purpose here is not to provide authoritative detailed recommendations for each nation or to discuss every relevant problem but to illustrate a useful way of thinking that can be applied to any particular nation. My hope is that readers, with their various backgrounds and perspectives, will be able to go further in drawing implications in their areas of interest.

This book is being completed during a period of exciting and unusually significant developments within individual nations and across groups of nations that bear importantly on the issues discussed here. Among the most notable are the measures designed to introduce greater European economic unification in 1992, a free trade agreement between Canada and the United States, a stream of new policy initiatives in Britain, proposed taxation changes in Japan and Germany, a controversial new American trade bill, and the social and political upheavals in Eastern Europe with their as yet unpredictable economic consequences.

My purpose here, however, is not to analyze current events but to create a theory that can be used to do so. Indeed, one of the findings from our historical research is that there has been more stability in the determinants of national competitive advantage than I originally supposed, even though the extent of internationalization has grown. Many of the principles are independent of the concerns of the moment. I will make references to implications of my theory for important developments such as Europe 1992 where they arise, but will leave a full analysis of current developments to other forums.

Some will find the views presented here controversial. My purpose has not been to seek nor to shy away from controversy but to develop a robust theory backed by a broad array of evidence. Upon completion, I must note that my findings cut across positions conventionally associated with such labels as liberal and conservative, whose view of the problem tends to reflect particular philosophical positions. I find, consistent with the traditional liberal position, for example, that strict antitrust laws, tough health and safety regulations, and heavy investment in training human resources are beneficial. But my evidence seriously questions the wisdom of intervention to resurrect sick industries, regulation that limits competition, most efforts to restrict imports, and policies to tax long-term capital gains. While I suspect that few readers will be entirely happy with my findings, I am hopeful that many will be persuaded.

*   *   *

This study could not have been completed without an extraordinary amount of assistance from a wide variety of individuals and institutions. It has truly been a global study, involving a breadth of industries and nations that sought to represent the richness of international competition. The working seminar of my project team held at Harvard in 1987 to discuss our preliminary findings provides some indication. There were twenty-four attendees representing nine nationalities. The Korean team and the Japanese team competed to see who could work later into the night. The Swedish and Danish teams traded insights about the similarities and differences of their neighboring countries. The German, Swiss, and Italian researchers traded data and discussed the differing positions of their nations in industries such as printing and packaging machinery. All the participants learned much about their nation by learning about others that had been studied using a common methodology.

Michael J. Enright served as the overall project coordinator. He helped structure and organize the entire project, and spent one year abroad shuttling among nations providing supervision and critique for the individual country efforts. He conducted a great deal of research personally and was a source of ideas, comments, and counsel throughout the research phase as well as during the preparation of the manuscript. He is a gifted researcher in his own right, and a study of this magnitude would simply not have been possible without him. He is completing his doctorate now at Harvard and promises to make important contributions to this subject through his own research.

A U.S.-based research team was involved not only in the U.S. portion of the study but played a broader and essential role in other phases of the project. I am grateful to Cheng Gaik Ong for her prominent role throughout the study and also to William McClements, Thomas Lockerby, Thomas Wesson, and Mari Sakakibara. Alice Hill also deserves my thanks for providing research assistance.

Local research teams based in many of the nations conducted much of the country-based research and contributed significantly to the findings and conclusions about their country. I am especially grateful to the team leaders for their energy and insight. The Japanese team was led by Professor Hirotaka Takeuchi of Hitotsubashi University. Team members were Hiroshi Kobayashi, Hiroshi Okamoto, Laura Rauchwarg, and Ryoko Toyama. The Swedish team was led by Professor Örjan Sölvell of the Institute of International Business of the Stockholm School of Economics. Ivo Zander was the principal Swedish researcher and also spent a period in residence at Harvard. Also contributing to the Swedish research were Thomas Gyllenmo, Maria Lundqvist, and Ingela Sölvell. The Korean team was led by Professor (and Dean) Dong-Sung Cho of Seoul National University. Researchers who contributed to the study were Chol Choi, In-Chul Chung, Dong-Jae Kim, Junsoo Kim, Sumi Kim, Dae-Won Ko, Seung Soo Lee, Ho-Seung Nam, Ki-Min Nam, Gyu Seok Oh and Joo-chol Om. The Danish team was led by Henrik Pade, in collaboration with Kim Møller and Klaus Møller Hanson (both associate professors at the Copenhagen School of Business). Other Danish researchers contributing to the study were Claus Bayer, Bent Dalum, Birgitte Gregersen, Patrick Howald, Henrik Jensen, Frederik Pitzner Jørgensen, Ulrik Jørgensen, Bodil Kühn, Morten Kvistgaard, Mogens Kühn Pedersen, Bent Petersen, Henrik Schaumberg-Müller, Jesper Strandskov, and Finn Thomassen. Much of the Swiss research was conducted by Edi Tschan, then performing doctoral studies at the University of St. Gallen, in collaboration with Michael Enright. Professor Silvio Borner of the University of Basel took over leadership of the Swiss effort, and additional Swiss research was performed by Rolf Weder.

The German research was most ably conducted by Claas van der Linde, who also contributed to the data analysis in the broader study. He is continuing to apply the theory to the West German economy in his Ph.D. dissertation at the University of St. Gallen. Dennis deCrombrugghe also contributed to the Swiss and German research. The Italian research was the responsibility of Paolo Tenti, who was a source of insight throughout the study. Michael Enright also participated heavily in both the German and Italian research. The British research was conducted largely by myself and Michael Enright and was assisted by Terry Phillips. In a number of nations, country-specific publications are in preparation which describe the research in greater detail.

I received the extremely generous assistance and support of the Harvard Business School in carrying out this study. The School offers a unique environment for carrying out large-scale, multidisciplinary research projects and for gaining access to institutions and companies throughout the world. Dean John McArthur, a friend and a source of counsel and support for many years, deserves my special thanks. I also received a great deal of help and financial backing from Jay Lorsch and his staff at the Division of Research. Funds provided by the Shell Companies Foundation constituted part of the budget for this study, for which I am grateful.

One or more cooperating institutions in each nation provided assistance in obtaining infrastructure, help in gaining access to companies and government officials, and in some cases financial support. I am extremely grateful for their contribution, though they bear no responsibility for my findings and conclusions:

Denmark	Copenhagen School of Economics and Business Administration, Henrik Pade & Associates[2]
Germany	Deutsche Bank
Italy	Ambrosetti Group
Japan	Ministry of International Trade and Industry, Hitotsubashi University, Industrial Bank of Japan
Korea	Seoul National University
Singapore	Economic Development Board
Sweden	Institute of International Business, Stockholm School of Economics
Switzerland	University of Basel, University of St. Gallen, Union Bank of Switzerland
United Kingdom	*The Economist*
United States	Harvard Business School

Particular individuals in these institutions and others to whom I bear a special debt are Hans-Peter Ferslev and Dr. Jürgen Bilstein (Deutsche Bank), Alfredo Ambrosetti and Giovanna Launo (Ambrosetti Group), Shinji Fukukawa, Wataru Aso, Hirobumi Kawano, and Shin Yasunobe (MITI), Yoh Kurasawa, A. Yatsunami, Naoya Takebe (Industrial Bank of Japan), Professors Ken-ichi Imai, Ikujiro Nonaka (Hitotsubashi University), Philip Yeo and Tan Chin Nam (Singapore Economic Development Board), Dean Staffan Burenstam Linder and Professor Gunnar Hedlund (Stockholm School of

Economics), Dr. Werner Rein and Dr. Beat Schweizer (Union Bank of Switzerland), and David Gordon and Rupert Pennant-Rea (*The Economist*). I would also like to thank Databank and the Istituto per la Ricerca Sociale (Italy) for assistance in providing Italian data, and Nixdorf Corporation for help in securing company access in Germany.

A number of colleagues at Harvard and elsewhere gave generously of their time in reading and critiquing the entire manuscript or large portions of it. In addition to Michael Enright, I would like to thank Richard Caves, David Collis, Herman Daems, Pankaj Ghemawat, Thomas McCraw, Richard Tedlow, and David Yoffie, all at or visiting Harvard. In addition, I would like to thank Silvio Borner, Thomas Craig, Roger Martin, Richard Rawlinson, Peter Schwartz, Paul Schwarzbaum, James Stone, and Mark Thomas.

Others provided valuable suggestions on portions of the manuscript or to presentations about it. I would like to thank Roger Bohn, Alfred D. Chandler, Jr., Joseph Fuller, Mark Fuller, David Gordon, Heather Hazard, Steve Kelman, Donald Lessard, John Nathan, Fabrizio Onida, Cuno Pümpin, Rupert Pennant-Rea, Garth Saloner, and Malcolm Salter. Seminars at Northwestern, MIT, Stockholm School of Economics, University of Zurich, the Japanese Ministry of International Trade and Industry, the Forum for Structural Reform (Japan), the German Council of Economic Advisors, a special policy forum organized by the Danish sponsor, and Harvard yielded useful comments, as did presentations at meetings of the Strategic Management Society, the Planning Forum, and other business groups. The members and staff of the President's Commission on Industrial Competitiveness and the Council on Competitiveness provided a valuable education in economic policy issues.

Literally hundreds of other business executives, labor leaders, academics, consultants, industry experts, bankers, and policy makers gave freely of their time. They consented to interviews and provided valuable insights into their industries and countries. Some provided extensive comments on individual case studies or country write-ups. This project could not have been carried out without their help and cooperation. It is unfortunate that space precludes acknowledging each one individually. I am most appreciative of all of their help.

Administering this large multinational study and preparing such a bulky manuscript involved unusual challenges. I want especially to thank Lyn Pohl, my assistant, for shepherding this long project from start to finish. Her help in planning, scheduling, organizing meetings, preparing the manuscript, and editing has been invaluable. I would also like to thank Denise Zaccagnino, Kathleen Kenahan, and especially Linda Estes for their fine work in production, chart preparation, and editing.

I benefited greatly from a good deal of help in crafting the manuscript and improving its clarity. Erwin Glikes, President of The Free Press and my editor, was a source of friendship, inspiration, and countless suggestions and insights. I am also grateful to Robert Wallace and Barbara Ankeny for thoughtful reviews of the entire manuscript and to Ann Hirst for her careful copyediting.

Finally, I would like to thank my wife Deborah, to whom this book is dedicated. She has been involved in this all-consuming project since its inception. She accompanied me during an extended period of residence abroad, and provided ideas, encouragement, and moral support throughout this effort. I simply could not have done it without her.

Introduction

In *The Competitive Advantage of Nations* (1990), I undertook to explain the sources of sustained prosperity in the modern global economy. While the book is set at the level of the nation, the same framework can and has been readily applied at the regional, state, and city level. While most thinking and policy had focused on the macroeconomic conditions for growth and prosperity, my focus was on the microeconomic foundations. While government was the central actor in most literature, I sought to highlight the role played by companies.

I argue that wealth is governed by productivity, or the value created per day of work, dollar of capital invested, and unit of the nation's physical resources employed. The roots of productivity lie in the national and regional environment for competition, captured in a framework graphically depicted as a diamond made up of four primary facets; the diamond metaphor has become common in referring to the theory. The diamond addresses the information, incentives, competitive pressures, and access to supporting firms, institutions, infrastructure, and pools of insight and skill in a location that support productivity and productivity growth in particular fields.

I titled the book *The Competitive Advantage of Nations* to highlight the crucial distinction between my broader concept of competitive advantage as a source of wealth and the notion of comparative advantage which had long dominated thinking about international competition. Comparative advantage, as it had come to be understood, rests on endowments of inputs such as labor, natural resources, and financial capital. I argue that factor inputs themselves have become less and less valuable in an increasingly global economy. Neither is competitiveness secured by size or military might, because neither is decisive for productivity. Instead, prosperity depends on creating a business environment, along with supporting institutions, that enable the nation to productively *use* and *upgrade* its inputs.

Beginning in the mid-1980s when I served on President Ronald Reagan's Commission on Industrial Competitiveness, I developed the growing conviction that failure to understand the distinction between comparative advantage and the new competitive advantage of nations is one of the root causes of problems in economic development. Merely using the resources available, or assembling more resources, is not enough for prosperity. Neither is redistribution of a nation's wealth between interest groups.

In my theory, competitiveness and prosperity are not a zero-sum game. Many nations can simultaneously improve their productivity, and with it their wealth. Yet wealth is not assured. The inability to improve productivity in an economy, because of poor policies, insufficient investments, or other reasons, can make wages and national income hard to sustain, let alone grow.

In the modern global economy, prosperity is a nation's *choice.* Competitiveness is no longer limited to those nations with a favorable inheritance. Nations choose prosperity if they organize their policies, laws, and institutions based on productivity. Nations choose prosperity if, for example, they upgrade the capabilities of all their citizens and invest in the types of specialized infrastructure that allow commerce to be efficient. Nations choose poverty, or limit their wealth, if they allow their policies to erode the productivity of business. They limit their wealth if skills are reserved only for a few. They limit their wealth when business success is secured by family connections or government concessions rather than productivity. War or ineffective government can derail prosperity, but these are often under the collective control of citizens.

Productivity and competitive advantage in an economy require specialization. In *The Competitive Advantage of Nations,* I introduced the concept of *clusters,* or groups of interconnected firms, suppliers, related industries, and specialized institutions in particular fields that are present in particular locations. The agglomeration of firms has long been recognized in literatures such as economic geography and regional science. However, the phenomenon was viewed narrowly, and not related to international competition in which inputs are widely accessible from many locations and reductions in transportation costs have eliminated the need to locate near supply sources or near large markets. The connection between agglomeration and a sophisticated view of competition and strategy was yet to be explored, as was its seemingly paradoxical role at a time when location is widely seen as less important.

The Competitive Advantage of Nations seeks to bridge these gaps. It shows how clusters not only reduce transaction costs and boost efficiency but improve incentives and create collective assets in the form of information, specialized institutions, and reputation, among others. More importantly, clusters enable innovation and speed productivity growth. They also ease the formation of new businesses. This powerful role of location in sophisticated competition is not inconsistent with globalization; indeed, globalization makes such locational advantage *more* important by removing artificial barriers to trade and investment and nullifying traditional input advantages. Firms no longer need to locate near raw material sources or markets, but can choose the best location for productivity and dynamism.

The Competitive Advantage of Nations advocates new, constructive, and actionable roles for government and business in the pursuit of competitiveness and prosperity. For government, old distinctions between *laissez-faire* and intervention are obsolete. Government, first and foremost, must strive to create an environment that supports rising productivity. This implies a minimalist government role in some areas (e.g., trade barriers, pricing) and an activist role in others (e.g., ensuring vigorous competition, providing high-quality education and training). Government can influence all parts of the diamond, and this influence is the best way to understand the role of government on competition rather than see government as an entity unto itself.

Government must strive to improve the business environment in many ways. It must not, however, limit competition or ease standards for safety and environmental impact. Such "help" actually retards competitiveness by stunting innovation and slowing productivity improvement.

Artificial distinctions between social and economic policy must fall away, because the two are inextricably tied in defining the environment for productive competition. Educated citizens who are healthy and work in a safe environment are necessary for productivity. Diamond theory offers a positive and constructive role for virtually all of a nation's institutions in competitiveness, whether they be schools, universities, standard-setting agencies, consumer societies, professional societies, or the judicial system. All have a role in creating the conditions for higher productivity.

For companies, a central message of *The Competitive Advantage of Nations* is that many of a company's competitive advantages lie *outside* the firm and are rooted in locations and industry clusters. This defines an agenda for companies that has been largely absent from the literature on management. Alongside government, the private sector has a role to play in investing in some of the collective assets or public goods that reside in particular locations. *The Competitive Advantage of Nations* also argues for a far more tangible and proactive role for industrial associations and other business institutions in making such investments.

More broadly, there is an inevitable mutual dependence between government and business in national productivity. An ongoing dialog is needed to remove obstacles, lower unnecessary business costs, and create appropriate inputs, information, and infrastructure. The tension, distrust, and paternalism that characterize the relationship in many countries are counterproductive and a hidden cost of doing business.

EMBEDDING THE IDEAS
IN THEORY AND PRACTICE

The diffusion of ideas is a process that can often take decades, especially with theories that are not part of a well-established tradition. *The Competitive Advantage of Nations* has this characteristic, in view of its microeconomic approach to competitiveness and economic development.

I have a strong personal conviction that real learning in social science involves not only theory but immersion in the effort to translate theory into practice. Even before the book was published, I had the privilege of personally leading major national economic policy reviews in New Zealand (beginning in 1989),[1] Canada (1990),[2] and Portugal (1991).[3] Constructive changes, and debate, continue in all three nations.[4] The book drew on research in ten leading trading nations. Follow-on books and national dialogs have occurred in Sweden, Denmark, Switzerland, Germany, and Korea.[5] Other major national assessments in advanced economies employing diamond theory, in which I was not involved, have taken place in Norway,[6] Finland,[7] the Netherlands,[8] and Hong Kong,[9] among others. Similar research has taken place at the state, provincial, and autonomous region level.[10] The ideas have been debated and played a role in policy in other advanced nations, states, and regions that have not undertaken a formal project.

The application of the principles of *The Competitive Advantage of Nations* to developing countries has also spread widely. In order to deepen my knowledge of earlier-stage economic development, I conducted a major project together with colleagues in India.[11] The book has also helped motivate important national projects or studies in Bermuda, Bolivia, Botswana, Bulgaria, Estonia,[12] Colombia, El Salvador, Peru, South Africa, Tartarstan, and Venezuela,[13] among others.

The cluster is becoming a new way of thinking about economies and organizing economic development efforts. Prominent cluster-based initiatives, spanning a significant part of the economy, have occurred or are underway in Arizona, California, Catalonia, Chihuahua, Connecticut, Costa Rica, Massachusetts, Minnesota, Morocco, the Netherlands, North Carolina, Norway, Ohio, Oregon, Scotland, and Quebec, among other locations.

The ideas in *The Competitive Advantage of Nations* have begun to be applied to cities and metropolitan regions.[14] I have also extended the ideas to the question of economic development in distressed inner city areas.[15] I argue that the problems of inner cities are as much economic as social, and that an economic strategy is needed to complement the wide array of other programs. Instead of seeing inner cities as full of disadvantages for business, however, we must reframe our thinking around the potential competitive advantages of inner cities in the metropolitan economy. This work has led to studies in an array of U.S. cities, and an active dialog about new directions in urban policy.[16]

More recently, the ideas in *The Competitive Advantage of Nations* have been applied in groups of neighboring countries. Most regional initiatives (e.g., Mercusor, NAFTA) have been focused largely on opening up trade and investment within the region, a worthy goal. However, diamond theory provides a systematic framework for thinking about the areas where cooperation among neighbors can enhance the productivity of the national business environment. This is the case because there are important externalities in the diamond that cross national borders, such as the interconnections among transportation systems, alignment of customs procedures, and strategies to improve public safety. Since 1994, I have been working with leaders in the nations of Central America on such a regional economic plan.[17] More recently, a similar project has begun in the Middle East, involving national teams from Egypt, Israel, Jordan, and the Palestinian Authority, with other nations gearing up as well. That this initiative has continued despite the political upheavals that have occurred in the region is testimony to the power of economics to forge common ground.

At the level of theory and scholarship, productivity is now an accepted definition of competitiveness, and the role of location is becoming more and more recognized. *The Competitive Advantage of Nations* has contributed to a revival of interest in economic geography.

The books already cited constitute a growing literature on applying these ideas at various geographic levels. There is a growing body of literature that tests the propositions in *The Competitive Advantage of Nations* statistically, with encouraging results.[18] There is a growing literature on clusters, and two international conferences on the subject were held in 1997.[19] Scholars in marketing are thinking about the marketing of locations.[20] The World Bank has made cluster work part of its core strategy. A body of work on the relationship between competitiveness and environmental quality, which shows how the two can be compatible, has grown out of the book.[21] This raises interesting research questions about appropriate environmental approaches in business and government in developing countries, among other topics. Finally, another book stimulated by mine—Fairbanks and Lindsay, *Plowing the Sea*—presents new learning about the impediments to putting the new theory of competitiveness into practice in developing nations.[22] This is a research area of great importance.

HITTING A RESPONSIVE CHORD

This heartening attention that *The Competitive Advantage of Nations* has received stems from a number of reasons. First, the book appeared at a time of growing competition in virtually every nation. Trade barriers were falling, and markets were opening. Socialism was collapsing (the Soviet Union dissolved in 1991; in China, accelerated economic reform began in 1992). Nations were shifting their focus away from international politics and toward improving the prosperity of their citizens. These developments continue today unabated.

Whether prosperous or mired in poverty, nations, states, and regions all over the world were searching for ways of coping. *The Competitive Advantage of Nations* offered a systematic and actionable framework for understanding competitiveness and how to improve it. It was especially welcomed by practitioners in government and business who were looking for guidance on questions unaddressed in most theoretical work.

Second, while much progress had been made in understanding the macroeconomic side of competitiveness and economic development, there was an increasing recognition that macroeconomic reform is necessary but not sufficient. As important—or even more so—are the *microeconomic* foundations of development, rooted in the nature of firm strategies and in the institutions, infrastructure, and policies that constitute the environment in which firms compete. My book filled a gap in its focus on the microeconomic side of competitiveness. It addressed the question: What next? What to do *after* macroeconomic stabilization and adjustment—a central question facing many governments.

Third, the book offered a way to bridge the gap between business and government in addressing competitiveness. *The Competitive Advantage of Nations*, by bringing to bear a rich and textured approach to competition, offers a set of ideas and examples that are far more persuasive to companies. In government, the prevailing thinking beyond macroeconomic policies was the controversial notion of industrial policy, advocating intervention to shape the outcome of competition. Industrial policy was based on a highly simplified and questionable view of competition in which scale and spending were decisive. In those nations most associated with industrial policy—France, Japan, Korea—serious difficulties have arisen which raise grave doubts about whether industrial policy, and its core practices of targeting, subsidies, and cooperative activity, ever worked. All along, companies were deeply skeptical of industrial policy, concerned about government's capacity to second-guess markets, eager for other approaches.

The Competitive Advantage of Nations rejected industrial policy. All clusters can support prosperity if they can be productive. Instead of targeting particular industries, all a nation's existing and emerging clusters deserve attention. Government should not get involved in the competitive process—its role is to improve the environment for productivity, for example, by improving the quality and efficiency of business inputs and infrastructure and creating policies and a regulatory context that stimulate upgrading and innovation. While industrial policy seeks to distort competition in favor of a particular location, diamond theory seeks to remove constraints to productivity growth. While industrial policy rests on a zero-sum view of international competition, diamond theory is based on a positive-sum world in which productivity improvement will expand the market and in which many nations can prosper if they can become more productive and innovative.

The book also provided the basis for constructive dialog about how the business environment could be improved. The concept of clusters has proven to be particularly powerful. Clusters were both a way of thinking about the economy and a means for catalyzing change. Unlike traditional groupings such as industries or sectors, which were associated with intervention and subsidy, the concept of clusters focuses thinking on productivity and cross-company linkages. Clusters bring government entities, companies, suppliers, and local institutions together around a common agenda which is constructive and actionable.

UNFINISHED AGENDAS

This re-issue of *The Competitive Advantage of Nations* is an important milestone. As heartening as the response has been, the ideas in the book remain complex, and the volume itself is formidable. The examples and country profiles are voluminous, in part because I felt that without them the book would be less convincing on such an emotionally charged subject. All this means that the book is still broadening its audience, and I am hopeful that its re-issue will bring it to the attention of new readers.

It is also clear, at this writing, that there is still much to learn. My own recent work is focused in a number of directions. One is further empirical testing within and across groups of countries. For example, a recent paper on Japan shows that international competitiveness in a broad sample of Japanese industries is strongly influenced by the intensity of local rivalry in Japan, measured by market share fluctuations. The presence of a cartel in an industry dampens rivalry and is associated with lower competitiveness. Traditional measures of comparative advantage contribute little to explanatory power.[23] Hopefully, the accumulation of such statistical evidence will make the ideas in *The Competitive Advantage of Nations* more persuasive to a wider group of scholars.

Another new direction in my work is theoretical and empirical research to develop a better understanding of clusters, and appropriate forms of public and private action to enhance cluster productivity. Third, I am deepening my knowledge about the challenges facing developing countries as they try to move away from dependence on cheap labor and natural resources. Fourth, I am involved in thinking and writing about the appropriate roles of cities, states, nations, and groups of neighboring countries in competitiveness. Fifth, I am seeking to forge tighter connections between *The Competitive Advantage of Nations* and my work on company strategy. It is clear that location affects industry structure and competitive advantage. At the industry level, intense rivalry can erode local profits but propel the local industry ahead of foreign competitors. At the firm level, it is clear that many of the resources and skills that have been a focus of the recent strategy literature reside in the local environment. There is also a strong connection between the achievement of supplier linkages, product complementarity, and the presence of a cluster. Location, then, deserves a prominent place in core strategy thinking.

Finally, my personal experience in working with government and business leaders has led to a strong interest in the reasons why some nations (or other jurisdictions) can actually change in positive ways while others, armed with the same level of knowledge, cannot. If *The Competitive Advantage of Nations* is to achieve its ultimate purpose, my own research will be just a part of a much broader agenda that unites macroeconomics, microeconomics, and the study of management in an integrated understanding of competition and the influence on location.

As I reflect on the years since the book was published, and especially on the many occasions I have had to talk and work with government and business leaders, I am struck again and again by the power of ideas to shape outcomes. It was flawed ideas about competitiveness and prosperity that doomed countless millions to poverty in the post-World War II period. It is confusion about the true causes of competitiveness today that continues to slow progress, both in governments and in companies.

At the government level, discussions of competitiveness are still too focused on macroeconomic policy, when microeconomic issues are often the real constraints to progress. Governments still mistake devaluation and currency policies as a means to increase "competitiveness" rather than see currency as the tail, not the dog, and recognize that the need for devaluation is a reflection of failed policies. Governments look to foreign investments attracted by subsidies to solve their problems, rather than tackle the weaknesses in their national business environment that will determine the nation's standard of living. Countries mistake trade deals and regional pacts with the steps required to achieve real improvements in productivity.

In companies, a profound misunderstanding of the implications of globalization continues. Companies still think they can solve their competitive problems through outsourcing. They see being global as good for its own sake, and often ignore their home business environment. Locational choices diminish productivity and retard the capacity for innovation. Companies also ask government for the wrong kind of "help" in enhancing competitiveness.

More and more countries will have to confront the question of what to do after economic stabilization and liberalization. More and more companies will have to face the consequences of real competition. We will need more and more clarity on the appropriate roles of various levels of government.

My hope is that *The Competitive Advantage of Nations* can help cut through the confusion about what to do, and provide leaders with the tools and confidence to forge ahead. If it does, it will have met my ultimate test of true scholarship.

Michael E. Porter
Brookline, Massachusetts
January 1998

Notes

1. M.E. Porter with G.T. Crocombe and M.J. Enright, *Upgrading New Zealand's Competitive Advantage,* Oxford University Press, Auckland, 1991.

2. M.E. Porter with Monitor Company, *Canada at the Crossroads: The Reality of a New Competitive Environment,* Business Council on National Issues and Minister of Supply and Services, Ottawa, Canada, 1992. See also M.E. Porter and J.H. Armstrong, unpublished working paper, September 1997.

3. M.E. Porter with Monitor Company, "Construir as Vantagens Competitivas de Portugal," Forum Para a Competitividade, Lisbon, Portugal, 1994.

4. See, for example, M.E. Porter and J.H. Armstrong, "Canada Revisited," unpublished working paper, August 1997.

5. M.E. Porter with Ö. Sölvell and I. Zander, *Advantage Sweden,* Norstedts Förlag AB, Stockholm, SWEDEN, 1991; *Vaekst og dynamik i dansk erhvervsliv,* H. Pade (editor), J.H. Schultz Information A/S, København, Denmark, 1991; *Internationale Wettbewerbsvorteile: Ein Strategisches Konzept fur die Schweiz* (International Competitive Advantage: A New Strategic Concept for Switzerland), with Silvio Borner, Rolf Weder, and Michael J. Enright, Campus Verlag, Frank-

furt/New York, 1991; C. van der Linde, *Deutsche Wettbewerbsvorteile,* Econ, Düsseldorf, Wein, New York, Moscow, 1992; *Korean Competitiveness: A Shortcut to an Advanced Nation,* Dong-Sung Cho, 1992.

6. M.E. Porter, "Applying the Competitive Advantage of Nations Paradigm to Norway," in PRAKTISK ØKONOMI & LEDELSE: ET KONSURRANSEDYK-TIGNORGE, Number 1, February 1993, Bedrifsøkonomens Forlag A/S, Oslo, Norway.

7. "Finnish Industrial Clusters," in *National Industrial Strategy for Finland,* Ministry of Trade and Industry in Finland, Industry Department, 1993; *Advantage Finland: The Future of Finnish Industries,* Hannu Hernesniemi, Markku Lammi, and Pekka Ylä-Anttila, ETLA, Taloustieto Oy, Helsinki 1996; *Finland: A Knowledge-Based Society,* Science and Technology Policy Council of Finland, EDITA, Helsinki, Finland, 1996.

8. F.A.J. van den Bosch and A.P. de Man (eds.), *Perspective on Strategy: Contributions of Michael E. Porter,* Kluwer Academic Publishers, Boston/Dordrecht/London, 1997.

9. M. J. Enright, E.E. Scott, and D. Dodwell, *The Hong Kong Advantage,* Oxford University Press, New York, 1997.

10. For example, see M.E. Porter and Monitor Company, *The Competitive Advantage of Massachusetts,* Office of the Secretary of State, Boston, MA, 1991; "The Competitive Advantage of Euskadi," Monitor Company, Cambridge, MA, 1992; and *The Quebec Industrial Atlas,* produced by P. Gagné and M. Lefèvre with the cooperation of G. Tremblay, Publi-Relais, Montréal, 1993.

11. M.E. Porter with P. Ghemawat and U. Srinivasa Rangan, "A New Vision for Indian Economic Development: The Corporate Agenda," working paper, October, 1995; M. Porter with P. Ghemawat and U. Srinivasa Rangan, "A New Vision for Indian Economic Development," working paper, March 1995.

12. J. Hyvärinen and J. Borsos, *Emerging Estonian Industrial Transformation: Towards a Dual Industrial Strategy for Estonia,* Taloustieto Oy, Helsinki, 1994.

13. *Venezuela: The Challenge of Competitiveness,* Michael J. Enright, Antonio Francés, and Edith Scott Saavedra, St. Martin's Press, New York, 1996.

14. See, for example, R.M. Smit, "Rotterdam seen through Porter-colored glasses," in F.A.J. van den Bosch and A.P. de Man (eds.), *Perspectives on Strategy: Contributions of Michael E. Porter,* Kluwer Academic Publishers, Boston/Dordrecht/London, 1997.

15. "The Competitive Advantage of the Inner City," *Harvard Business Review,* May-June 1995; "New Strategies for Inner-City Economic Development," *Economic Development Quarterly,* Volume 11, Number 1, Sage Periodicals Press, February 1997.

16. A new organization, the Initiative for a Competitive Inner City, has been founded to pursue this agenda. A full bibliography of its research is available from the author.

17. The Latin American Center for Competitiveness and Sustainable Development has been established at INCAE, the region's leading school of business, economics, and government, to support this effort. See "Project Overview and

Update," Latin American Center for Competitiveness and Sustainable Development, INCAE, Costa Rica, August 1997.

18. L.G. Thomas, "Industrial Policy and International Competitiveness in the Pharmaceutical Industry," in *Competitive Strategies in the Pharmaceutical Industry,* R.B. Helms (ed.), American Enterprise Institute for Public Policy Research, 1996; A. Shleifer, E. Glaeser, H. Kallal, and J. Scheinkman, "Growth in Cities," *Journal of Political Economy,* December 1992; V. Henderson, A. Kuncoro, and M. Turner, "Industrial Development in Cities," *Journal of Political Economy,* 1995.

19. For a bibliography of literature and cluster initiatives, see "Clusters and Competition: The New Agenda for Companies, Governments, and Institutions," in *Michael Porter on Competition,* Harvard Business School Press, Boston, forthcoming, 1998.

20. P. Kotler, S. Jatusripitak, S. Maesincee, and S. Jatusri, *The Marketing of Nations: A Strategic Approach to Building National Wealth,* The Free Press, New York, 1997.

21. M.E. Porter and C. van der Linde, "Green *and* Competitive: Ending the Stalemate," *Harvard Business Review,* September-October 1995; M.E. Porter and C. van der Linde, "Toward a New Conception of the Environment-Competitiveness Relationship," *The Journal of Economic Perspectives,* Volume 9, Number 4, Fall 1995; S. Schmidheiny with the Business Council for Sustainable Development, *Changing Course: A Global Perspective on Development and the Environment,* The MIT Press, Cambridge, Massachusetts/London, England, 1992; A.B. Jaffe, S. Peterson, P. Portney, and R.N. Stavins, "Environmental Regulation and International Competitiveness: What Does the Evidence Tell Us," draft, January 13, 1994; W. Oates, K.L. Palmer, and P. Portney, "Environmental Regulation and International Competitiveness: Thinking about the Porter Hypothesis," Resources for the Future Working Paper 94-02, 1993; R. Schmalensee, "The Costs of Environmental Regulation," Massachusetts Institute of Technology, Center for Energy and Environmental Policy Research Working Paper 93-015, 1993; T. Panayotou and J.R. Vincent, "Environmental Regulation and Competitiveness," *The Global Competitiveness Report 1997,* World Economic Forum, Geneva, Switzerland, 1997.

22. M. Fairbanks and S. Lindsay, *Plowing the Sea: Nurturing the Hidden Sources of Growth in the Developing World,* Harvard Business School Press, 1997.

23. M. Sakakibara and M.E. Porter, "Competing at Home to Win Abroad: Evidence from Japanese Industry," unpublished working paper, September 1997.

1

The Need for a New Paradigm

Why do some nations succeed and others fail in international competition? This question is perhaps the most frequently asked economic question of our times. Competitiveness has become one of the central preoccupations of government and industry in every nation. The United States is an obvious example, with its growing public debate about the apparently greater economic success of other trading nations. But intense debate about competitiveness is also taking place today in such "success story" nations as Japan and Korea.[1] Socialist countries such as the Soviet Union and others in Eastern Europe and Asia are also asking this question as they fundamentally reappraise their economic systems.

Yet although the question is frequently asked, it is the wrong question if the aim is to best expose the underpinnings of economic prosperity for either firms or nations. We must focus instead on another, much narrower one. This is: why does a nation become the home base for successful international competitors in an industry? Or, to put it somewhat differently, why are firms based in a particular nation able to create and sustain competitive advantage against the world's best competitors in a particular field? And why is one nation often the home for so many of an industry's world leaders?

How can we explain why Germany is the home base for so many of the world's leading makers of printing presses, luxury cars, and chemicals? Why is tiny Switzerland the home base for international leaders in pharmaceuticals, chocolate, and trading? Why are leaders in heavy trucks and mining equipment based in Sweden? Why has America produced the preeminent international competitors in personal computers, software, credit cards, and movies? Why are Italian firms so strong in ceramic tiles, ski boots, packaging machinery, and factory automation equipment? What makes Japanese firms so dominant in consumer electronics, cameras, robotics, and facsimile machines?

The answers are obviously of central concern to firms that must compete in increasingly international markets. A firm must understand what it is about its home nation that is most crucial in determining its ability, or inability, to create and sustain competitive advantage in international terms. But the same question will prove to be a decisive one for national economic prosperity as well. As we will see, a nation's standard of living in the long term depends on its ability to attain a high and rising level of productivity in the industries in which its firms compete. This rests on the capacity of its firms to achieve improving quality or greater efficiency. The influence of the home nation on the pursuit of competitive advantage in particular fields is of central importance to the level and rate of productivity growth achievable.

But we lack a convincing explanation of the influence of the nation. The long-dominant paradigm for why nations succeed internationally in particular industries is showing signs of strain. There is an extensive history of theories to explain the patterns of nations' exports and imports, dating back to the work of Adam Smith and David Ricardo in the eighteenth century. It has become generally recognized, however, that these theories have grown inadequate to the task. Changes in the nature of international competition, among them the rise of the multinational corporation that not only exports but competes abroad via foreign subsidiaries, have weakened the traditional explanations for why and where a nation exports. While new rationales have been proposed, none is sufficient to explain why firms based in particular nations are able to compete successfully, through both exporting *and* foreign investment, in particular industries. Nor can they explain why a nation's firms are able to sustain their competitive positions over considerable periods of time.

Explaining the role played by a nation's economic environment, institutions, and policies in the competitive success of its firms in particular industries is the subject of this book. It seeks to isolate the competitive advantage of a nation, that is, the national attributes that foster competitive advantage in an industry. Drawing on my study of ten nations and the detailed histories of over one hundred industries, I will present in Part I a theory of the competitive advantage of nations in particular fields. In Part II, I will illustrate how the theory can be employed to explain the competitive success of particular nations in a number of individual industries. In Part III, I will use the theory to shed light on the overall patterns of industry success and failure in the economies of the nations we studied and how the patterns have been changing. This will serve as the basis for presenting a framework to explain how entire national economies advance in competitive terms. Finally, in Part IV, I will develop the implications of my theory for both company strategy and government policy. The book concludes with a chapter entitled "National Agendas," which illustrates how the theory can be used to identify some of the most important issues that will shape future economic progress in each of the nations I studied.

Before presenting my theory, however, I must explain why efforts to explain the competitiveness of *an entire nation* have been unconvincing, and why attempting to do so is tackling the wrong question. I must demonstrate that understanding the reasons for the ability of the nation's firms to create and sustain competitive advantage in particular industries is addressing the right question, not only for informing company strategy but also for achieving national economic goals. I must also describe why there is a growing consensus that the dominant paradigm used to date to explain international success in particular industries is inadequate, and why even recent efforts to modify it still do not address some of the most central questions. Finally, I will describe the study that was conducted so that the reader will understand the factual foundations of what follows.

CONFLICTING EXPLANATIONS

There has been no shortage of explanations for why some nations are competitive and others are not.[2] Yet these explanations are often conflicting, and there is no generally accepted theory. It is far from clear what the term "competitive" means when referring to a nation. This is a major part of the difficulty, as we will see. That there has been intense debate in many nations about whether they have a competitiveness problem in the first place is a sure sign that the subject is not completely understood.

Some see national competitiveness as a macroeconomic phenomenon, driven by such variables as exchange rates, interest rates, and government deficits. But nations have enjoyed rapidly rising living standards despite budget deficits (Japan, Italy, and Korea), appreciating currencies (Germany and Switzerland), and high interest rates (Italy and Korea).

Others argue that competitiveness is a function of cheap and abundant labor. Yet nations such as Germany, Switzerland, and Sweden have prospered despite high wages and long periods of labor shortage. Japan, with an economy supposedly built on cheap, abundant labor, has also experienced pressing labor shortages. Its firms have succeeded internationally in many industries only after automating away much of the labor content. The ability to compete *despite* paying high wages would seem to represent a far more desirable national target.

Another view is that competitiveness depends on possessing bountiful natural resources. Recently, however, the most successful trading nations, among them Germany, Japan, Switzerland, Italy, and Korea, have been countries with limited natural resources that must import most raw materials. It is also interesting to note that within nations such as Korea, the United Kingdom, and Germany, it is the resource-poor regions that are prospering relative to the resource-rich ones.

More recently, many have argued that competitiveness is most strongly influenced by government policy. This view identifies targeting, protection, export promotion, and subsidies as the keys to international success. Evidence is drawn from the study of a few nations (notably Japan and Korea) and a few large, highly visible industries such as automobiles, steel, shipbuilding, and semiconductors. Yet such a decisive role for government policy in competitiveness is not confirmed by a broader survey of experience. Many observers would consider government policy toward industry in Italy, for example, to have been largely ineffectual in much of the postwar period, but Italy has seen a rise in world export share second only to Japan along with a rapidly rising standard of living.

Significant government policy intervention has occurred in only a subset of industries, and it is far from universally successful even in Japan and Korea. In Japan, for example, government's role in such important industries as facsimile, copiers, robotics, and advanced materials has been modest, and such frequently cited examples of successful Japanese policy as sewing machines, steel, and shipbuilding are now dated. Conversely, sustained targeting by Japan of industries such as aircraft (first targeted in 1971) and software (1978) has failed to yield meaningful international positions. Aggressive Korean targeting in large, important sectors such as chemicals and machinery has also failed to lead to significant market positions. Looking across nations, the industries in which government has been most heavily involved have, for the most part, been unsuccessful in international terms. Government is indeed an actor in international competition, but rarely does it have the starring role.

A final popular explanation for national competitiveness is differences in management practices, including labor-management relations. Japanese management has been particularly celebrated in the 1980s, just as American management was in the 1950s and 1960s.[3] The problem with this explanation, however, is that different industries require different approaches to management. What is celebrated as good management practice in one industry would be disastrous in another. The small, private, and loosely organized family firms that populate the Italian footwear, textile, and jewelry industries, for example, are hotbeds of innovation and dynamism. Each industry has produced a positive trade balance for Italy in excess of $1 billion annually. However, these same structures and practices would be a disaster in a German chemical or automobile company, a Swiss pharmaceutical producer, or an American commercial aircraft manufacturer. American-style management, with all the flaws now attributed to it, produces highly competitive firms in such industries as software, medical equipment, consumer packaged goods, and business services. Japanese-style management, for all its strengths, has produced little international success in large portions of the economy such as chemicals, consumer packaged goods, or services.

Nor is it possible to generalize about labor-management relations. Unions are very powerful in Germany and Sweden, with representation by law in management (Germany) and on boards of directors (Sweden). Despite the view by some that powerful unions undermine competitive advantage, however, both nations have prospered and contain some of the most internationally preeminent firms and industries of any country.

Clearly, none of these explanations for national competitiveness, any more than a variety of others that have been put forward, is fully satisfactory. None is sufficient by itself in rationalizing the competitive position of a nation's industries. Each contains some truth but will not stand up to close scrutiny. A broader and more complex set of forces seems to be at work.

The numerous and conflicting explanations for competitiveness highlight an even more fundamental problem. That is, just what is a ''competitive'' nation in the first place? While the term is frequently used, it is unusually ill defined. Is a ''competitive'' nation one in which every firm or industry is competitive? If so, no nation comes close to qualifying. Even Japan, as we will see, has large sectors of its economy that fall far behind the world's best competititors. Is a ''competitive'' nation one whose exchange rate makes its goods price competitive in international markets? But surely most would agree that nations such as Germany and Japan, that have experienced sustained periods of a strong currency and upward pressure on foreign prices, have enjoyed remarkable gains in standard of living in the postwar period. The ability of a nation's industry to command *high* prices in foreign markets would seem to be a more desirable national target.

Is a ''competitive'' nation one with a large positive balance of trade? Switzerland has roughly balanced trade and Italy has had a chronic trade deficit, but both nations have enjoyed strongly rising national income. Conversely, many poor nations have balanced trade but scarcely represent the sorts of economies most nations aspire to. Is a ''competitive'' nation one with a rising share of world exports? A rising share is often associated with growing prosperity, but nations with stable or slowly falling world export shares have experienced strong per capita income growth so that world export share clearly does not tell the whole story. Is a ''competitive'' nation one that can create jobs? Clearly, the ability to do so is important, but the *type* of jobs, not merely the employment of citizens at low wages, seems more significant for national income. Finally, is a ''competitive'' nation one whose unit labor costs are low? Low unit labor costs can be achieved through low wages such as those in India or Mexico, but this hardly seems an attractive industrial model. Each of these measures says something about a nation's industry, but none relates clearly to national economic prosperity.[4]

ASKING THE RIGHT QUESTION

The search for a convincing explanation of both national and firm prosperity must begin by asking the right question. We must abandon the whole notion of a ''competitive nation'' as a term having much meaning for economic prosperity. The principal economic goal of a nation is to produce a high and rising standard of living for its citizens. The ability to do so depends not on the amorphous notion of ''competitiveness'' but on the productivity with which a nation's resources (labor and capital) are employed. Productivity is the value of the output produced by a unit of labor or capital.[5] It depends on both the quality and features of products (which determine the prices they can command) and the efficiency with which they are produced.[6]

Productivity is the prime determinant in the long run of a nation's standard of living, for it is the root cause of national per capita income. The productivity of human resources determines their wages, while the productivity with which capital is employed determines the return it earns for its holders.[7] High productivity not only supports high levels of income but allows citizens the option of choosing more leisure instead of long working hours. It also creates the national income that is taxed to pay for public services which again boosts the standard of living. The capacity to be highly productive also allows a nation's firms to meet stringent social standards which improve the standard of living, such as in health and safety, equal opportunity, and environmental impact.

The only meaningful concept of competitiveness at the national level is national productivity. A rising standard of living depends on the capacity of a nation's firms to achieve high levels of productivity and to increase productivity over time. Our task is to understand why this occurs. Sustained productivity growth requires that an economy continually *upgrade* itself. A nation's firms must relentlessly improve productivity in existing industries by raising product quality, adding desirable features, improving product technology, or boosting production efficiency. Germany has enjoyed rising productivity for many decades, for example, because its firms have been able to produce increasingly differentiated products and introduce rising levels of automation to boost the output per worker. A nation's firms must also develop the capabilities required to compete in more and more sophisticated industry segments, where productivity is generally higher. At the same time, an upgrading economy is one which has the capability of competing successfully in entirely new and sophisticated industries.[8] Doing so absorbs human resources freed up in the process of improving productivity in existing fields.[9] All this should make it clear why cheap labor and a ''favorable'' exchange rate are not meaningful definitions of competitiveness. The aim is to support high wages and command premium prices in international markets.

If there were no international competition, the level of productivity attainable in a nation's economy would be largely independent of what was taking place in other nations. International trade and foreign investment, however, provide both the opportunity to boost the level of national productivity and a threat to increasing or even maintaining it. International trade allows a nation to raise its productivity by eliminating the need to produce all goods and services within the nation itself. A nation can thereby specialize in those industries and segments in which its firms are relatively more productive and import those products and services where its firms are less productive than foreign rivals, in this way raising the average productivity level in the economy. Imports, then, as well as exports are integral to productivity growth.

Establishment of foreign subsidiaries by a nation's firms can also raise national productivity, provided it involves shifting less productive activities to other nations or performing selected activities abroad (such as service or modifying the product to address local needs) that support greater penetration of foreign markets. A nation's firms can thus increase exports and earn foreign profits that flow back to the nation to boost national income. An example is the move in the last decade of less sophisticated electronics assembly activities by Japanese firms first to Korea, Taiwan, and Hong Kong, and now to Malaysia and Thailand.

No nation can be competitive in (and be a net exporter of) everything. A nation's pool of human and other resources is necessarily limited. The ideal is that these resources be deployed in the most productive uses possible. The export success of those industries with a competitive advantage will push up the costs of labor, inputs, and capital in the nation, making other industries uncompetitive. In Germany, Sweden, and Switzerland, for example, this process has led to a contraction of the apparel industry to those firms in specialized segments that can support very high wages.[10] At the same time, the expanding exports of competitive industries put upward pressure on the exchange rate, making it more difficult for the relatively less productive industries in the nation to export.[11] Even those nations with the highest standards of living have many industries in which local firms are uncompetitive.

The process of expanding exports from more productive industries, shifting less productive activities abroad through foreign investment, and importing goods and services in those industries where the nation is less productive, is a healthy one for national economic prosperity. In this way, international competition helps upgrade productivity over time.[12] The process implies, however, that market positions in some segments and industries must necessarily be lost if a national economy is to progress.[13] Employing subsidies, protection, or other forms of intervention to maintain such industries only slows down the upgrading of the economy and limits the nation's long-term standard of living.[14]

While international trade and investment can lead to major improvements in national productivity, however, they may also threaten it. This is because exposure to international competition creates for each industry an *absolute* productivity standard necessary to meet foreign rivals, not only a relative productivity standard compared to other industries within its national economy. Even if an industry is relatively more productive than others in the economy, and can attract the necessary human and other resources, it will be unable to export (or even, in many cases, to sustain position against imports) unless it is *also* competitive with foreign rivals. The American automobile industry produces more output per man hour (and pays higher wages) than many other U.S. industries, for example, but America has experienced a growing trade deficit (and a loss of high-paying jobs) in automobiles because the level of productivity in the German and Japanese industries has been even higher. American productivity in producing automobiles has also not been sufficiently greater than that of Korean firms to offset lower Korean wages. Similar tests vis-à-vis foreign rivals must be met by more and more activities and industries.[15]

If the industries that are losing position to foreign rivals are the relatively more productive ones in the economy, a nation's ability to sustain productivity growth is threatened. The same is true when activities involving high levels of productivity (such as sophisticated manufacturing) are transferred abroad through foreign investment because domestic productivity is insufficient to make performing them in the nation efficient, after taking foreign wages and other costs into account. Both limit productivity growth and result in downward pressure on wages. If enough of a nation's industries and activities within industries are affected, there may also be downward pressure on the value of a nation's currency. But devaluation, too, lowers the nation's standard of living by making imports more expensive and reducing the prices obtained for the nation's goods and services abroad.[16] Understanding why nations can or cannot compete in sophisticated industries and activities involving high productivity, then, becomes central to understanding economic prosperity.

The preceding discussion should also make it clear why defining national competitiveness as achieving a trade surplus or balanced trade *per se* is inappropriate. The expansion of exports because of low wages and a weak currency, at the same time as the nation imports sophisticated goods that its firms cannot produce with sufficient productivity to compete with foreign rivals, may bring trade into balance or surplus but lowers the nation's standard of living. Instead, the ability to export many goods produced with high productivity, which allows the nation to import many goods involving lower productivity, is a more desirable target because it translates into higher national productivity.[17] Japan, which exports many manufactured goods in which it has high productivity and imports raw materials and components involving less skilled labor and lower levels of technology, illustrates a nation where the mix of trade bolsters productivity. Similarly, it should be clear that defining national competitiveness in terms of jobs *per se* is misleading. It is high productivity jobs, not any jobs, that translate into high national income. What is important for economic prosperity is national productivity. The pursuit of competitiveness defined as a trade surplus, a cheap currency, or low unit labor costs contains many traps and pitfalls.

A rising national share of world exports is tied to living standards when rising exports from industries achieving high levels of productivity contribute to the growth of national productivity. A fall in overall world export share because of the inability to successfully increase exports from such industries, conversely, is a danger signal for a national economy. However, the particular mix of industries that are exporting is more important than a nation's average export share. A rising sophistication of exports can support productivity growth even if overall exports are growing slowly.

Seeking to explain "competitiveness" at the national level, then, is to answer the wrong question. What we must understand instead is the determinants of productivity and the rate of productivity growth. To find answers, we must focus not on the economy as a whole but on *specific industries and industry segments*. While efforts to explain aggregate productivity growth in entire economies have illuminated the importance of the quality of a nation's human resources and the need for improving technology, an examination at this level must by necessity focus on very broad and general determinants that are not sufficiently complete and operational to guide company strategy or public policy.[18] It cannot address the central issue for our purposes here, which is *why and how* meaningful and commercially valuable skills and technology are created. This can only be fully understood at the level of particular industries. The human resources most decisive in modern international competition, for example, possess high levels of specialized skills in particular fields. These are not the result of the general educational system alone but of a process closely connected to competition in particular industries, just as is the development of commercially successful technology. It is the outcome of the thousands of struggles for competitive advantage against foreign rivals in particular segments and industries, in which products and processes are created and improved, that underpins the process of upgrading national productivity I have described.

COMPETITIVE ADVANTAGE IN INDUSTRIES

Our central task, then, is to explain why firms based in a nation are able to compete successfully against foreign rivals in particular segments and industries. Competing internationally may involve exports and/or locating some company activities abroad. We are particularly concerned with the determinants of international success in relatively sophisticated industries and segments of industries involving complex technology and highly skilled human resources, which offer the potential for high levels of productivity as well as sustained productivity growth.

To achieve competitive success, firms from the nation must possess a competitive advantage in the form of either lower costs or differentiated products that command premium prices. To sustain advantage, firms must achieve more sophisticated competitive advantages over time, through providing higher-quality products and services or producing more efficiently. This translates directly into productivity growth.

When one looks closely at any national economy, there are striking differences in competitive success across industries. International advantage is often concentrated in narrowly defined industries and even particular industry segments.[19] German exports of cars are heavily skewed toward high-performance cars, while Korean exports are all compacts and subcompacts. Denmark's modest share of world exports in vitamins consists of a substantial share in vitamins based on natural substances and virtually no position in synthetic vitamins. Japan's strong position in machinery comes mostly from general-purpose varieties, such as CNC machine tools, while Italy's is derived from often world-leading positions in highly specialized machines for particular end-user applications such as leather working or cigarette manufacturing. Increased trade has led to increased specialization in narrowly defined industries and in segments within industries. Were it not for protection, which sustains firms and entire national industries with no real competitive advantage, the differences among nations in competitive position would be even more apparent.[20]

Moreover, in many industries and especially in distinct segments of industries, competitors with true international competitive advantage are *based in only a few nations*. The influence of the nation seems to apply to industries and segments, rather than to firms *per se*. Most successful national industries comprise groups of firms, not isolated participants, as my earlier examples illustrate. Leading international competitors are not only frequently located in the same nation but are often found in the same city or region within the nation. National positions in industries are often strikingly stable, stretching over many decades and, in some of our case studies, for over a century. Isolated successes can often be explained by different target segments, or by government subsidy or protection that means that the isolated national producer is not a real success at all (as in automobiles, aerospace, and telecommunications). Industries and segments of industries, then, will be the focus of our enquiry. Clearly, powerful influence of the nation is apparent in international competition in particular fields, which is important not only to firms but to national economic prosperity.

CLASSICAL RATIONALES FOR INDUSTRY SUCCESS

There is a long history of efforts to explain international success in industries in the form of international trade. The classical one is the theory of comparative advantage. Comparative advantage has a specific meaning to economists.[21] Adam Smith is credited with the notion of absolute advantage, in which a nation exports an item if it is the world's low-cost producer. David Ricardo refined this notion to that of comparative advantage, recognizing that market forces will allocate a nation's resources to those industries where it is relatively most productive. This means that a nation might still import a good where it could be the low-cost producer if it is even more productive in producing other goods. As I have discussed, both absolute and relative advantage are necessary for trade.

In Ricardo's theory, trade was based on labor productivity differences between nations.[22] He attributed these to unexplained differences in the environment or "climate" of nations that favored some industries. While Ricardo was on the right track, however, the focus of attention in trade theory shifted in other directions. The dominant version of comparative advantage theory, due initially to Heckscher and Ohlin, is based on the idea that nations all have equivalent technology but differ in their endowments of so-called factors of production such as land, labor, natural resources, and capital.[23] Factors are nothing more than the basic inputs necessary for production. Nations gain factor-based comparative advantage in industries that make intensive use of the factors they possess in abundance. They export these goods, and import those for which they have a comparative factor disadvantage.[24] Nations with abundant, low-cost labor such as Korea, for example, will export labor-intensive goods such as apparel and electronic assemblies. Nations with rich endowments of raw materials or arable land will export products that depend on them. Sweden's strong historical position in the steel industry, for example, developed because Swedish iron ore deposits have a very low content of phosphorous impurities, resulting in higher-quality steel from blast furnaces.

Comparative advantage based on factors of production has intuitive appeal, and national differences in factor costs have certainly played a role in determining trade patterns in many industries. This view has informed much government policy toward competitiveness, because it has been recognized that governments can alter factor advantage either overall or in specific sectors through various forms of intervention.[25] Governments have, rightly or wrongly, implemented various policies designed to improve comparative advantage in factor costs. Examples are reduction of interest rates, efforts to hold down wage costs, devaluation that seeks to affect comparative prices, subsidies, special depreciation allowances, and export financing addressed at particular sectors. Each in its own way, and over differing time horizons, these policies aim to lower the relative costs of a nation's firms compared to those of international rivals.

THE NEED FOR A NEW PARADIGM

There has been growing sentiment, however, that comparative advantage based on factors of production is not sufficient to explain patterns of trade.[26] Evidence hard to reconcile with factor comparative advantage is not difficult to find. Korea, having virtually no capital after the Korean War, was still able eventually to achieve substantial exports in a wide range of relatively capital-intensive industries such as steel, shipbuilding, and automobiles. Conversely, America, with skilled labor, preeminent scientists, and ample capital, has seen eroding export market share in industries where one would least expect it, such as machine tools, semiconductors, and sophisticated electronic products.

More broadly, much of world trade takes place between advanced industrial nations with similar factor endowments. At the same time, researchers have documented the large and growing volume of trade in products whose production involves similar factor proportions. Both types of trade are difficult to explain with the theory. A significant amount of trade also involves exports and imports between the different national subsidiaries of multinational firms, a form of trade left out of the theory.

Most important, however, is that there has been a growing awareness that the assumptions underlying factor comparative advantage theories of trade are unrealistic in many industries.[27] The standard theory assumes that there are no economies of scale, that technologies everywhere are identical, that products are undifferentiated, and that the pool of national factors is fixed. The theory also assumes that factors, such as skilled labor and capital, do not move among nations.[28] All these assumptions bear little relation, in most industries, to actual competition. At best, factor comparative advantage theory is coming to be seen as useful primarily for explaining broad tendencies in the patterns of trade (for example, its average labor or capital intensity) rather than whether a nation exports or imports in individual industries.

The theory of factor comparative advantage is also frustrating for firms because its assumptions bear so little resemblance to actual competition. A theory which assumes away a role for firm strategy, such as improving technology or differentiating products, leaves firms with little recourse but to attempt to influence government policy. It is not surprising that most managers exposed to the theory find that it assumes away what they find to be most important and provides little guidance for appropriate company strategy.

CHANGING COMPETITION

The assumptions underlying factor comparative advantage were more persuasive in the eighteenth and nineteenth centuries, when many industries were fragmented, production was more labor- and less skill-intensive, and much trade reflected differences in growing conditions, natural resources, and capital. America was a leading producer of ships, for example, in no small part because of an ample wood supply. Many traded goods were such products as spices, silk, tobacco, and minerals whose availability was limited to one or a few regions.

Factor costs remain important in industries dependent on natural resources, in those where unskilled or semiskilled labor is the dominant portion of total cost, and in those where technology is simple and widely available. Canada and Norway are strong in aluminum smelting, for example, largely because of a geography that allows the generation of cheap hydroelectric power. Korea rose to prominence in the international construction of simple infrastructure projects because of its pool of low-cost, highly disciplined workers.

In many industries, however, factor comparative advantage has long been an incomplete explanation for trade. This is particularly true in those industries and segments of industries involving sophisticated technology and highly skilled employees, *precisely those most important to national productivity.* Ironically, just as the theory of comparative advantage was being formulated, the Industrial Revolution was making some of its premises obsolete. As more and more industries have become knowledge-intensive in the post–World War II period, the role of factor costs has weakened even further.

Technological Change. More and more industries do not resemble those that the theory of comparative advantage was built on. Economies of scale are widespread, most products are differentiated, and buyer needs vary among countries. Technological change is pervasive and continuous. Widely applicable technologies such as microelectronics, advanced materials, and information systems have rendered obsolete the traditional distinction between high and low technology industries. The level of technology employed in an industry often differs markedly between firms in different nations.

Technology has given firms the power to circumvent scarce factors via new products and processes. It has nullified, or reduced, the importance of certain factors of production that once loomed large. Flexible automation, which allows for small lot sizes and easy model changes, is reducing the labor content of products in many industries. Access to state-of-the-art technology is becoming more important than low local wage rates. In the 1980s, manufacturing firms often moved production to high labor cost locations (to be close to markets), not the reverse. The usage of materials, energy, and other resource-based inputs has been substantially reduced or synthetic substitutes developed. Modern materials such as engineering plastics, ceramics, carbon fibers, and the silicon used in making semiconductors are made from raw materials that are cheap and ubiquitous.

Access to abundant factors is less important in many industries than the technology and skills to process them effectively or efficiently. For example, Sweden's low phosphorous content iron ores were an advantage as long as the technology of steelmaking had difficulty dealing with impurities. As steelmaking technology improved, however, the phosphorous problem was solved, nullifying Sweden's factor advantage.

Comparable Factor Endowments. Most of world trade takes place among advanced nations with broadly similar endowments of factors. Many developing nations have also achieved a level of economic development that means that they too possess comparable endowments of many factors. Their workforces have the education and basic skills necessary to work in many industries. The United States, for example, certainly no longer occupies the unique position in skilled labor that it once did. Many other nations now also have the basic infrastructure, such as telecommunications, road systems, and ports, required for competition in most manufacturing industries.[29] Traditional sources of factor advantage favoring advanced nations have been diminished in the process.

Globalization. Competition in many industries has internationalized, not only in manufacturing industries but increasingly in services. Firms compete with truly global strategies involving selling worldwide, sourcing components and materials worldwide, and locating activities in many nations to take advantage of low cost factors. They form alliances with firms from other nations to gain access to their strengths.

Globalization of industries decouples the firm from the factor endowment of a single nation. Raw materials, components, machinery, and many services are available globally on comparable terms. Transportation improvements have lowered the cost of exchanging factors or factor dependent goods among nations. Having a local steel industry, for example, is no longer an advantage in buying steel. It may well be a disadvantage if there are national policies or pressures that promote purchasing from high-cost domestic suppliers.

Capital flows internationally to credit-worthy nations, which are not restricted to locally available funds. Korea, as I noted earlier, has achieved an international position in a range of capital-intensive industries such as steel, automobiles, and memory chips, despite beginning with virtually no capital in the 1950s. Similar inflows of funds characterized such nations as Britain, the United States, Switzerland, and Sweden many years earlier.[30] Even technology trades on global markets, though usually with a lag. Where specific factor advantages are difficult to access via markets, multinational firms can locate subsidiaries there.

While many factors are increasingly mobile, however, trade persists. This apparent paradox provides an important insight that will be developed in what follows. It is where and how effectively factors are deployed that proves more decisive than the factors themselves in determining international success.

FLEETING ADVANTAGES

The same forces that have made factor advantages less decisive have also made them often exceedingly fleeting. Competitive advantage that rests on factor costs is vulnerable to even lower factor costs somewhere else, or governments willing to subsidize them. Today's low labor cost country is rapidly displaced by tomorrow's. The lowest-cost source for a natural resource can shift overnight as new technology allows the exploitation of resources in places heretofore deemed impossible or uneconomical. Who would think, for example, that Israel, mostly desert, could become an efficient agricultural producer? In factor cost-sensitive industries, leadership often shifts rapidly as such industries as apparel and simple electronic goods attest.

Those industries in which labor costs or natural resources are important to competitive advantage also often have industry structures that support only low average returns on investment. Since such industries are accessible to many nations seeking to develop their economies because of relatively low barriers to entry, they are prone to too many competitors (and too much capacity). Rapidly shifting factor advantage continually attracts new entrants who bid down profits and hold down wages. (Incumbents are disadvantaged but locked in by specialized assets.)

Developing nations are frequently trapped in such industries. Nearly all the exports of less developed nations tend to be tied to factor costs and to competing on price. Development programs often target new industries based on factor cost advantages, with no strategy for moving beyond them. Nations in this situation will face a continual threat of losing competitive position and chronic problems in supporting attractive wages and returns to capital. Their ability to earn even modest profits is at the mercy of economic fluctuations.[31]

If factor comparative advantage does not explain national success in most industries, policies based on altering factor costs will often prove ineffective. Managing industry wage rates is irrelevant in industries where labor content is small. Subsidies of any kind will have little leverage where competition is based on quality, rapid product development, and advanced features rather than price.[32]

THE THREADS OF A NEW EXPLANATION

While the insufficiency of factor advantage in explaining trade is widely accepted, what should replace or supplement it is far from clear. A range of new explanations for trade has been proposed. One is economies of scale, which give the nation's firms that are able to capture them a cost advantage that allows them to export. The presence of economies of scale provides a rationale for trade, even in the absence of factor advantages. Economies of scale in producing individual product varieties can also explain trade in similar goods. The same basic reasoning can be applied to other market imperfections such as technological change requiring substantial R&D and a learning curve in which costs decline with cumulative volume. The nation's firms that can exploit these imperfections will export.[33]

Economies of scale and other market imperfections are indeed important to competitive advantage in many industries. However, present theory leaves the most significant question for our purposes unanswered. *Which nation's firms* will reap them and in what industries?

For example, in global competition, firms from any nation can gain scale economies by selling worldwide. It is not at all clear which nation's firms will do so.[34] The evidence on actual industries confirms this indeterminacy: Italian firms reaped the economies of scale in appliances, German firms in chemicals, Swedish firms in mining equipment, and Swiss firms in textile machinery. Having a large home market, often cited as an advantage, offers little explanation; none of these countries had the largest home demand for the products involved, though the firms became world leaders. Even in large nations, any simple connection between economies of scale and international success is tenuous. In Japan, for example, there are numerous competitors in most scale-sensitive industries (there are nine Japanese automobile producers, for example), fragmenting the home market. But many of these firms have reached substantial scale by selling abroad.[35] This sort of indeterminacy applies to all types of market imperfections.

Other efforts to go beyond comparative advantage have been based, in one way or another, on technology. Ricardian theory, in which trade is based on differing labor productivity among nations in producing particular goods, rests on technology differences in a broad sense. A more recent version of this line of thinking is the so-called "technology gap" theories of trade.[36] According to these theories, nations will export in industries in which their firms gain a lead (gap) in technology. Exports will then fall as technology inevitably diffuses and the gap closes.

Technological differences are indeed central to competitive advantage, but Ricardian and technology gap theories again leave unanswered the questions that most concern us here. *Why* does a productivity difference or technology gap emerge? *Which* nation's firms will gain it? And why do certain firms from a certain nation often preserve technological advantages for many decades in an industry, instead of inevitably losing their lead as technology gap theories would suggest?

Other promising lines of inquiry have suggested a role for a nation's home market in explaining success in trade. The most comprehensive is Raymond Vernon's "product cycle" theory.[37] Vernon set out to explain why the United States was a leader in so many advanced goods. He argued that early home demand for advanced goods meant that U.S. firms would pioneer new products.[38] American companies would export during the early phases of industry development and then establish foreign production as foreign demand grew. Eventually, foreign firms would enter the industry as technology diffused, and both foreign firms and the foreign subsidiaries of American companies would export to the United States.

The product cycle notion represents the beginnings of a truly dynamic theory and suggests how the home market can influence innovation. However, it still leaves many questions of central importance to us here unanswered. As Vernon himself has recognized, the United States no longer corners the market for advanced goods, nor has it ever. The more general question is why firms from particular nations establish leadership in particular new industries. What happens when demand originates simultaneously in different nations, as is common today? Why do nations with a more slowly developing or small home market for a product often emerge as world leaders? Why is innovation continuous in many national industries and not a once-and-for-all event followed by inevitable standardization of technology as the product cycle theory implies? Why does the inevitable loss of advantage in Vernon's theory not take place in many industries? How can we explain why some nations' firms are able to sustain advantage in an industry and others are not?[39]

A final important line of inquiry has sought to explain the emergence of the multinational corporation, or company with operations in more than one nation. Multinationals compete internationally not only by exporting but through foreign investment. Their prominence means that trade is no longer the only important form of international competition. Multinationals produce and sell in many countries, employing strategies that combine trade and dispersed production. Recent estimates suggest that a significant portion of world trade is between subsidiaries of multinationals, and that a meaningful fraction of the imports of advanced nations is accounted for by imports from the subsidiaries of a nation's *own* multinationals. National success in an industry increasingly means that the nation is the home base for leading multinationals in the industry, not just for domestic firms that export. In computers, for example, America is home base for IBM, DEC, Prime, Hewlett-Packard, and other U.S. companies that have facilities and subsidiaries spread widely in Europe and elsewhere.

Multinational status is a reflection of a company's ability to exploit strengths gained in one nation in order to establish a position in other nations.[40] Multinationals are most common, outside of natural resources involving scarce deposits, in industries with differentiated products and high research intensity, where successful firms have skills and know-how that can be exploited abroad. Multinationals are frequently described as companies without countries. They can and do operate (and produce goods) anywhere it suits them.

The role of multinationals must indeed be integral to any comprehensive effort to explain competitive success in an industry. Yet explaining the existence of multinationals, the focus of much previous work, leaves the essential questions for our purposes unanswered. Multinationals that are the leading competitors in particular segments or industries are often based in only one or two nations. The important questions are *why and how* do multinationals from a particular nation develop unique skills and know-how in particular industries? Why do some multinationals from some nations sustain and build on these advantages and others do not?

TOWARD A NEW THEORY
OF NATIONAL COMPETITIVE ADVANTAGE

The central question to be answered is why do firms based in particular nations achieve international success in distinct segments and industries? The search is for the decisive characteristics of a nation that allow its firms to create and sustain competitive advantage in particular fields, that is, the competitive advantage of nations.

The globalization of industries and the internationalization of companies leaves us with a paradox. It is tempting to conclude that the nation has lost its role in the international success of its firms. Companies, at first glance, seem to have transcended countries. Yet what I have learned in this study contradicts this conclusion. As earlier examples have suggested, the leaders in particular industries and segments of industries tend to be concentrated in a few nations and sustain competitive advantage for many decades. When firms from different nations form alliances, those firms based in nations which support true competitive advantage eventually emerge as the unambiguous leaders.

Competitive advantage is created and sustained through a highly localized process. Differences in national economic structures, values, cultures, institutions, and histories contribute profoundly to competitive success. The role of the home nation seems to be as strong as or stronger than ever. While globalization of competition might appear to make the nation less important, instead it seems to make it more so. With fewer impediments to trade to shelter uncompetitive domestic firms and industries, the home nation takes on growing significance because it is the source of the skills and technology that underpin competitive advantage.

Any new theory of national advantage in industries must start from premises that depart from much previous work. First, firms can and do choose strategies that differ. A new theory must explain why firms from particular nations choose better strategies than those from others for competing in particular industries.

Second, successful international competitors often compete with global strategies in which trade and foreign investment are integrated. Most previous theories have set out to explain either trade or foreign investment. A new theory must explain instead why a nation is *home base* for successful global competitors in a particular industry that engage in both.[41] Many of the underlying causes of exports and foreign investment prove to be the same.

The home base is the nation in which the essential competitive advantages of the enterprise are created and sustained. It is where a firm's strategy is set and the core product and process technology (broadly defined) are created and maintained. Usually, though not always, much sophisticated production takes place there.[42] Firms often perform other activities in a variety of other nations.[43]

The home base will be the location of many of the most productive jobs, the core technologies, and the most advanced skills. The presence of the home base in a nation also stimulates the greatest positive influences on other linked domestic industries, and leads to other benefits to competition in the nation's economy I will explore. The nation that is the home base will also usually enjoy positive net exports.

While the ownership of firms is often concentrated at the home base, the nationality of shareholders is secondary. As long as the local company remains the true home base by retaining effective strategic, creative, and technical control, the nation still reaps most of the benefits to its economy even if the firm is owned by foreign investors or by a foreign firm.[44] Explaining why a nation is the home base for successful competitors in sophisticated segments and industries, then, is of decisive importance to the nation's level of productivity and its ability to upgrade productivity over time.

A new theory must move beyond the comparative advantage to the competitive advantage of a nation. It must explain why a nation's firms gain competitive advantage in all its forms, not only the limited types of factor-based advantage contemplated in the theory of comparative advantage. Most theories of trade look solely at cost, treating quality and differentiated products in a footnote.[45] A new theory must reflect a rich conception of competition that includes segmented markets, differentiated products, technology differences, and economies of scale. Quality, features, and new product innovation are central in advanced industries and segments. Moreover, cost advantage grows as much out of efficient-to-manufacture product designs and leading process technology as it does out of factor costs or even economies of scale. We must understand why firms from some nations are better than others at creating these advantages, so essential to high and rising productivity.

A new theory must start from the premise that competition is dynamic and evolving. Much traditional thinking has embodied an essentially static view focusing on cost efficiency due to factor or scale advantages. Technological change is treated as though it is exogenous, or outside the purview of the theory. As Joseph Schumpeter recognized many decades ago, however, there is no "equilibrium" in competition. Competition is a constantly changing landscape in which new products, new ways of marketing, new production processes, and whole new market segments emerge. Static efficiency at a point in time is rapidly overcome by a faster rate of progress. But Schumpeter, like the other researchers I have noted, stopped short of answering the central question that concerns us here. Why do some firms, based in some nations, innovate more than others?

A new theory must make improvement and innovation in methods and technology a central element.[46] We must explain the role of the nation in the innovation process. Since innovation requires sustained investment in research, physical capital, and human resources, we must also explain why the rate of such investments are more vigorous in some nations and not others. The question is how a nation provides an environment in which its firms are able to improve and innovate faster than foreign rivals in a particular industry. This will also be fundamental in explaining how entire national economies progress, because technological change, in the broad sense of the term, accounts for much of economic growth.[47]

In a static view of competition, a nation's factors of production are fixed. Firms deploy them in the industries where they will produce the greatest return. In actual competition, the essential character is innovation and change. Instead of being limited to passively shifting resources to where the returns are greatest, the real issue is how firms increase the returns available through new products and processes. Instead of simply maximizing within fixed constraints, the question is how firms can gain competitive advantage from changing the constraints. Instead of only deploying a fixed pool of factors of production, a more important issue is how firms and nations improve the quality of factors, raise the productivity with which they are utilized, and create new ones.[48] Where factors are mobile and can be tapped through global strategies, moreover, the efficiency and effectiveness with which factors can be used become even more central. Answers to these questions will emerge as decisive in understanding why nations succeed in particular industries.

Finally, since firms play a central role in the process of creating competitive advantage, the behavior of firms must become integral to a theory of national advantage. A good test of a new theory is that it makes sense to managers as well as to policy makers and economists. From a manager's perspective, much of trade theory is too general to be of much relevance. A new theory must give firms insight into how to set strategy to become more effective international competitors. It is these challenges that I have set out to meet.

THE STUDY

To investigate why nations gain competitive advantage in particular industries and the implications for firm strategy and for national economies, I conducted a four-year study of ten important trading nations:

· Denmark	· Singapore
· Germany	· Sweden
· Italy	· Switzerland
· Japan	· United Kingdom
· Korea	· United States

Included were the three leading industrial powers, the United States, Japan, and Germany, as well as several other nations chosen to vary widely in size, government policy toward industry, social philosophy, geography, and region. Much attention has been directed at Asian nations in recent years, and Japan, Korea, and Singapore were investigated here. However, European nations provide equally interesting and important insights. An array of European nations was included in the study, among them several nations such as Switzerland and Sweden engaged in a remarkable amount of international trade for their size. The study was limited to ten nations solely because of time and resource constraints. Together, the ten nations studied accounted for fully 50 percent of total world exports in 1985. An overview of some of their salient features is provided in Table 1–1.

TABLE 1-1 Selected Economic and Demographic Characteristics of the

	Denmark	Germany	Italy
Population in 1987 (millions)	5.1	61.2	57.3
Land Area (sq. mi.)	16,638	96,030	116,324
Population Density in 1987 (persons/sq. mi.)	307	637	493
Gross Domestic Product (GDP) in 1987 at 1980 prices and exchange rates (billions $ U.S.)	$77.2	$899.1	$525.9
Compound Annual Growth in GDP in 1980 prices, 1950–87	3.2%	4.6%	4.5%
Compound Annual Growth in industrial production, 1950–87	2.5%e	4.6%	5.3%
Compound Annual Population Growth, 1950–87	0.5%	0.7%	0.5%
Compound Annual Workforce Growth (number of employed persons), 1950–87	1.0%a	0.8%	0.1%
GDP per capita in 1987 at 1980 prices in $ U.S.	15,137	14,691	9,178
Compound Annual Growth in GDP per capita in 1980 prices, 1950–87	2.7%	4.0%	3.9%
Compound Annual Productivity Growth (GDP per employee), 1950–87	2.4%a	3.8%	4.4%
Net National Investment (Gross fixed capital formation less depreciation as % of GDP), 1950–87 average	11.6%	11.8%	10.9%
Exports as % of GDP (1987)	25.2%	26.2%	14.7%
Imports as % of GDP (1987)	25.1%	20.3%	16.5%
Unemployment in 1987	8.1%	8.9%	11.9%
Average Unemployment, 1951–87	6.4%	3.5%	5.4%

SOURCES: International Monetary Fund, *International Financial Statistics,* Yearbook, September 1988
National Bureau of Economic Research, *Foreign Trade Regimes and Economic Development: South Korea,* 1975
OECD Economic Outlook, *Historical Statistics,* 1960–86
United Nations, *Statistical Yearbook,* various years, and *Monthly Bulletin of Statistics*
U.S. Department of Labor, *Comparative Real GDP Figures,* unpublished data.

NOTE: Macroeconomic indicators are reported by many different organizations and employ statistics gathered from various sources using various methods. The indicators presented here have been based on standard sources and methods as much as possible in order to facilitate

The focus of the research was on the process of gaining and sustaining competitive advantage in relatively sophisticated industries and industry segments. These hold the key to high and rising productivity in a nation, and are the least understood using established theory. The nations chosen for study were ones that already compete successfully in a range of such industries or, in the case of Korea and Singapore, show signs of an improving ability to do so.[49] Korea and Singapore were selected from the group of rapidly

Nations Studied

Japan	Korea	Singapore	Sweden	Switzer-land	United Kindgom	United States
122.1	42.1	2.6	8.4	6.5	56.9	243.8
145,870	38,279	240	173,732	15,943	94,251	3,679,192
837	1,100	10,833	48	408	604	66
$1,370.6	$62.8[h]	$15.3[h]	$140.5	$114.4	$628.7	$3,301.3
7.2%[a]	7.9%[a]	8.3%[b]	3.0%	3.2%	2.5%	3.2%
9.7%	14.1%[a]	9.7%[f]	3.3%	2.6%[b]	2.2%	3.8%
1.1%	2.0%	2.6%	0.5%	0.9%	0.3%	1.3%
1.4%	3.2%[c]	3.6%[e]	0.6%[b]	0.2%[e]	0.3%	1.7%
11,225	1,528[h]	5,885[h]	16,726	17,600	11,049	13,541
6.2%[a]	5.7%[a]	6.5%[b]	2.6%	2.2%	2.2%	1.9%
5.9%[a]	5.8%[c]	4.8%[e]	2.3%[b]	1.2%[e]	2.2%	1.4%
17.6%	14.7%[g]	NA	11.0%	13.7%	7.7%	7.1%
10.7%	39.0%	143.9%	27.9%	35.6%	19.6%	5.6%
6.9%	33.8%	163.3%	25.5%	37.2%	23.0%	9.5%
2.8%	3.1%	4.7%	1.9%	0.8%	10.5%	6.2%
1.7%	5.0%[d]	4.1%[e]	2.1%	0.3%	4.7%	5.7%

international comparisons. Figures expressed in terms of 1980 prices and exchange rates have been employed. While comparisons using different base years or exchange rates sometimes differ, the ranking among nations does not change significantly except for absolute measures, notably GDP per capita. Use of purchasing power parity exchange rates makes the United States the leading nation in terms of absolute GDP per capita, though its rate of growth in GDP per capita over the postwar period still ranks last as does its growth in GDP per employed person.

[a] 1955–87   [c] 1963–87   [e] 1970–87   [g] 1955–85
[b] 1960–87   [d] 1961–87   [f] 1966–86   [h] 1985

NA = Not Available

growing, newly industrialized countries (NICs) because they have very different patterns of industry success and different mixes of government policies.[50] Korea, in particular, has enjoyed the most rapid and sustained upgrading of competitive positions of any NIC.

Most studies of national competitiveness have focused on a single nation or have relied on bilateral comparisons, often with Japan.[51] While much has been learned from this research, such an approach can only take us so far and can be misleading. The findings of bilateral comparisons often prove to be lacking in robustness when a third or fourth nation is added to the investigation. In studies that compare the United States and Japan, for example, Japanese cooperative research projects are frequently identified as an essential factor underpinning Japanese competitive success. Such studies have served as the justification for suggesting the practice elsewhere. Yet Germany and Switzerland, among other nations, seem to sustain competitive advantage in all sorts of industries without cooperative research. Also, Japanese cooperative projects, as I will describe later, are important for reasons different from those often supposed.[52] By studying nations with widely different circumstances, I hope to isolate the fundamental forces underlying national competitive advantage from the idiosyncratic ones.

The research was conducted by a group of over thirty researchers, most of whom were natives of, and based in, the nation they were studying. A common methodology was employed in each nation. The study was conducted with the assistance and support of the cooperating organizations that have been identified in the Preface. They included government entities such as the Japanese Ministry of International Trade and Industry, private financial institutions like the Deutsche Bank, educational institutions such as the Institute of International Business of the Stockholm School of Economics, and a publication, *The Economist*. Cooperating organizations provided needed infrastructure, assistance in gaining access to companies and other institutions within the nation, and sometimes also local research help.

MAPPING THE SUCCESSFUL INDUSTRIES IN NATIONAL ECONOMIES

In each nation, the study consisted of two parts. The first was to identify all (or as many as possible) of the industries in which the nation's firms were internationally successful, using available statistical data, supplementary published sources, and field interviews. We were concerned with all types of industries in the economy, including agricultural, manufacturing, and service industries. Most previous studies have excluded services, but international competition in them is increasingly prevalent and important. Though data on services are still scarce and much about national competitive positions had to be gleaned from interviews and fragmentary published sources, service industries were included both in the national profiles as well as among the industries chosen for detailed study.

The basic unit of analysis was the narrowly defined industry or distinct segment within an industry. National advantage is increasingly concentrated in particular industries and even industry segments, reflecting their specific and differing sources of competitive advantage. Within the limits of available data, we sought the least aggregated industry definitions.[53]

We defined international success by a nation's industry as *possessing competitive advantage relative to the best worldwide competitors*. Because of the existence of protection, subsidy, differing accounting conventions, and the prevalence of border trade with neighboring countries, many potential measures of competitive advantage can be misleading. Neither domestic profitability, nor the size of the industry or the leading company, nor the existence of some exports is a reliable indicator of competitive advantage. Measuring the presence of true competitive advantage statistically is challenging.

We chose as the best measures of international competitive advantage either (1) the presence of substantial and sustained exports to a wide array of other nations and/or (2) significant outbound foreign investment based on skills and assets created in the home country for the statistical phase of our research.[54] Foreign investment and trade are both integral to global strategies, and measures of international success must encompass both. For example, Swiss pharmaceutical companies and American consumer packaged goods producers have international strength that goes well beyond that measured in the trade data. In practice, however, exports and foreign investment tend to occur together. The details of how we designated competitive industries are discussed in Appendix A.[55]

The nation was treated as the home base for a firm if it was either a locally owned, indigenous firm, or a firm that was managed autonomously though owned by a foreign company or investors. A ski boot manufacturer headquartered in Italy that developed and produced substantially all its products in Italy was treated as a case of Italian competitive advantage even if it had been acquired by a foreign company. If the nation's industry consisted largely of production subsidiaries of foreign companies, however, the nation was not deemed competitive in that field.

We created a profile of all the industries in which each nation was internationally successful at three points in time: 1971, 1978, and 1985.[56] The larger nations exhibit international positions in hundreds of industries. The pattern of successful industries in each economy was far from random, and the task was to explain the pattern and how it had changed over time.[57] Of particular interest were the connections or relationships among the nation's competitive industries. We employed a tool called a cluster chart to map successful industries in each economy, described beginning in Chapter 7.[58]

HISTORIES OF SUCCESSFUL INDUSTRIES

In the second part of the study, we examined the history of competition in particular industries to understand the dynamic process by which competitive advantage was created. Based on the national profiles, we selected over

TABLE **1–2** **Industry Case Studies**

DENMARK	rubber, plastic working machinery	microwave and satellite communications equipment
agricultural machinery	X-ray apparatus	musical instruments
building maintenance services	ITALY	optical elements and instruments
consultancy engineering	ceramic tiles	robotics
dairy products	dance club and theater equipment	semiconductors
food additives	domestic appliances	sewing machines
furniture	engineering/construction	shipbuilding
industrial enzymes	factory automation equipment	tires for trucks and buses
pharmaceuticals	footwear	trucks
specialty electronics	packaging and filling equipment	typewriters
telecommunications equipment	ski boots	videocassette recorders
waste treatment equipment	wool fabrics	watches
GERMANY	JAPAN	KOREA
automobiles	air-conditioning machinery	apparel
chemicals	home audio equipment	automobiles
cutlery	car audio	construction
eyeglass frames	carbon fibers	footwear
harvesting/threshing combines	continuous synthetic weaves	pianos
optical instruments	facsimile	semiconductors
packaging, bottling equipment	forklift trucks	shipbuilding
pens and pencils		steel
printing presses		travel goods

one hundred industries or groups of industries, listed in Table 1–2, for detailed study. Many more industries were examined in less detail.

For each nation, the sample of industries was chosen to be representative of the most important groups of competitive industries in the economy. In Denmark, for example, we examined the dairy industry, one of a group of agricultural end-product industries in which Denmark is strong; food additives and agricultural machinery, examples of a group of agricultural inputs; and furniture, one of a series of household products. In the United States, American strength in business services is represented by advertising, construction engineering, and waste management; clusters of manufacturing strength by commercial aircraft, commercial refrigeration and air-conditioning equipment, and construction equipment; dominance in computing by software; the medical sector by patient monitoring equipment and syringes; consumer packaged goods by detergents; and the entertainment sector by motion pic-

video and audio
  recording tape
wigs

SINGAPORE

airlines
apparel
beverages
ship repair
trading

SWEDEN

car carriers
communication products
  for handicapped
  persons
environmental control
  equipment
heavy trucks
mining equipment
newsprint
refrigerated shipping
rock drills
semihard wood flooring

teller-operated cash
  dispensers

SWITZERLAND

banking
chocolate
confectionery
dyestuffs
fire protection equipment
freight forwarding
hearing aids
heating controls
insurance
marine engines
paper product manufactur-
  ing machinery
pharmaceuticals
surveying equipment
textile machinery
trading
watches

UNITED KINGDOM

auctioneering
biscuits

chemicals
confectionery
electrical generation
  equipment
insurance
pharmaceuticals

UNITED STATES

advertising
agricultural chemicals
commercial aircraft*
commercial refrigeration
  and air-conditioning
computer software
construction equipment
detergents
engineering/construction
motion pictures
patient monitoring equip-
  ment
syringes
waste management
  services

---

* Case study prepared by M. Yoshino. See Yoshino in Porter (1986).

---

tures. Agricultural chemicals represented the chemical sector and served as an example of an input to the large group of American agricultural industries. The industries studied accounted for a significant share of total exports in each nation, including more than 20 percent of total exports in Japan, Germany, and Switzerland and over 40 percent of exports in Korea.

All the industries selected for study were ones in which the nation had a significant international market position as of 1985. Some of the industries were still gaining international strength in 1985, while others were maintaining their position or in decline. The industries we studied include some of the most famous and important international success stories (German high-performance autos and chemicals, Japanese semiconductors and VCRs, Swiss banking and pharmaceuticals, Italian footwear and textiles, American commercial aircraft and motion pictures, and so on). Our aim, however, was to represent the entire economy and avoid a bias toward the highly visible industries so prominent in previous research. We selected some relatively obscure but highly competitive industries (such as Korean pianos, Italian ski boots, and British biscuits). A few industries were also added because they appeared to be paradoxes. In Western character typewriters, for example, Japanese home demand is all but nonexistent, yet Japan holds a strong export and foreign investment position in this industry. We avoided industries that were highly dependent on natural resources: such industries do not form the backbone of advanced economies, and the capacity to compete in them is more explicable using classical theory. We did, however, include a number of more technologically intensive, natural-resource-related industries such as newsprint and agricultural chemicals.

In order to understand the dynamic process by which national advantage was gained in an industry, it was necessary to study the industry's history. We went back as far as necessary (centuries in the cases of German cutlery and Italian fabrics, decades for U.S. software and Japanese robotics, for example) to understand how and why the industry began in the nation, how it grew, when and why firms from the nation developed international competitive advantage, and the process by which competitive advantage had either been sustained or lost.[59] The resulting case histories fall short of the work of a good historian in their level of detail, but provide much insight into the development of both the industry and the national economy.

Each case study considered the entire global industry, including both winning and losing nations. We examined the pattern of competitive advantage among firms based in different nations and how it had shifted over time. The most significant competitors from other nations were identified, along with the segments in which they were strongest and their sources of competitive advantage. In printing presses, for example, we sought to understand why Germany and Switzerland had sustained advantage but also why the United States had lost ground and Japan was gaining. In a few instances, the same broad industry was studied from the perspective of more than one nation in cases where the industry was an important source of exports in each of the nations and where firms based in each nation had been internationally successful in very different segments. Packaging machinery, for example, was studied as part of both the Italian and German research. In so doing, we also investigated the success in some segments of firms from Switzerland and Sweden as well as the reasons for the relatively poor position of the United States and other nations.

The industries were chosen to be representative of those in which each of the nations we studied was or had been strong, or the success cases. By studying some formerly successful industries in which the nation was now declining, as well as the reasons its firms were not succeeding in many other industries through the global case studies, however, we were able to examine a relatively broad cross-section of both successful and unsuccessful industries in each nation's economy. In its coverage of both nations and industries, the study sought a more comprehensive sample than previous research.

A BROADER CONCEPT
OF COMPETITIVE ADVANTAGE

This book is about why nations succeed in particular industries, and the implications for firms and for national economies. Its concepts and ideas, however, can be readily applied to political or geographic units smaller than a nation. Successful firms are frequently concentrated in particular cities or states *within* a nation. In the United States, for example, many of the nation's leading real estate developers are based in Dallas, Texas; oil and gas equipment suppliers in Houston; hospital management chains in the south central region encompassing Nashville, Tennessee; carpet producers in Dalton, Georgia; running shoe manufacturers in Oregon; mobile home producers in Elkhart, Indiana; and minicomputer companies in Boston. Something about these locations provides a fertile environment for firms in these particular industries. While my discussion is framed in terms of nations, the geographic concentration of industries within nations will be important to explain. Government policy at the state and local level has an important role to play in shaping national advantage.

Yet the underlying issues are even broader than the role of nations (or locales). What I am really exploring here is the way in which a firm's proximate "environment" shapes its competitive success over time. Or, even more broadly, why some organizations prosper and others fail. Part of a company's environment is its geographic location, with all that implies in terms of history, costs, and demand. However, a company's environment includes more than just this; also important are such things as where managers and workers were trained, and the nature of the company's early or most important customers.

Much is known about what competitive advantage is and how particular actions create or destroy it. Much less is known about *why* a company makes good choices instead of bad choices in seeking bases for competitive advantage, and why some firms are more aggressive in pursuing them. This study will shed some light on these broader and exciting questions.

In studying national economic success, there has been the tendency to gravitate to clean, simple explanations and to believe in them as an act of faith in the face of numerous exceptions. The growing specialization of disciplines has only reinforced such a perspective. More can be done. Researchers in many fields of study are just beginning to recognize that traditional boundaries between fields are limiting. It should be possible to cut across disciplines and examine more variables in order to understand how complex and evolving systems work. To do so, mathematical models limited to a few variables, and statistical tests constrained by available data, need to be supplemented by other types of work.

I have taken such an approach in this study. My theory seeks to be comprehensive and integrate many variables instead of concentrating on a few important ones. Sifting through over one hundred historical case studies is messy and not amenable to statistical analysis. Some will bemoan the judgments I made to chart national economies comprehensively. These choices reflect my conviction that understanding so complex and important a subject demands at least some research of this character. While I am sure errors and omissions remain, I am persuaded that I have identified many of the important variables that shape the competitive advantage of nations as well as some of the most significant ways they work together as a system.

My aim is to help firms and governments, who must act, choose better strategies and make more informed allocations of national resources. What I have found is that firms will not ultimately succeed unless they base their strategies on improvement and innovation, a willingness to compete, and a realistic understanding of their national environment and how to improve it. The view that globalization eliminates the importance of the home base rests on false premises, as does the alluring strategy of avoiding competition.

National governments, for their part, must set the appropriate goal, productivity, which underpins economic prosperity. They must strive for its true determinants, such as incentive, effort, and competition, not the tempting but usually counterproductive choices such as subsidy, extensive collaboration, and "temporary" protection that are often proposed. Government's proper role is to push and challenge its industry to advance, not provide "help" so industry can avoid it. At this time when much of the world is reexamining its economic structures, the need for proper choices has never been greater. National economic prosperity need not come at the expense of other nations, and many nations can enjoy it in a world of innovation and open competition.

As globalization of competition has intensified, some have begun to argue a diminished role for nations. Instead, internationalization and the removal of protection and other distortions to competition arguably make nations, if anything, more important. National differences in character and culture, far from being threatened by global competition, prove integral to success in it. Understanding the new and different role of nations in competition will be a task which occupies much of what follows.

PART I

Foundations

PART 1

Foundations

2

The Competitive Advantage of Firms in Global Industries

Firms, not nations, compete in international markets. We must understand how firms create and sustain competitive advantage in order to explain what role the nation plays in the process.[1] In modern international competition, firms need not be confined to their home nation. They can compete with global strategies in which activities are located in many countries. We must pay particular attention to how global strategies contribute to competitive advantage, because they recast the role of the home nation.

I will begin with the basic principles of competitive strategy. Many of the principles are the same whether competition is domestic or international. Having set this foundation, I will turn to the ways in which firms enhance their competitive advantage through competing globally. The principles of strategy will define what attributes of a nation are relevant.

COMPETITIVE STRATEGY

The basic unit of analysis for understanding competition is the industry. An industry (whether product or service) is a group of competitors producing products or services that compete directly with each other.[2] A strategically distinct industry encompasses products where the sources of competitive advantage are similar. Examples are facsimile machines, low-density polyethylene, heavy on-highway trucks, and plastic injection molding equipment. There may be related industries that produce products that share customers, technologies, or channels, but they have their own unique requirements for competitive advantage. In practice, drawing industry boundaries is inevitably a matter of degree.

Many discussions of competition and international trade employ overly broad industry definitions such as banking, chemicals, or machinery. These are not strategically meaningful industries because both the nature of competition and the sources of competitive advantage vary a great deal within them. Machinery, for example, is not one industry but dozens of strategically distinct industries such as weaving machinery, rubber processing equipment, and printing machinery (all of which we studied), each with its own unique requirements for competitive success.

The industry is the arena in which competitive advantage is won or lost. Firms, through competitive strategy, seek to define and establish an approach to competing in their industry that is both profitable and sustainable. There is no one universal competitive strategy, and only strategies tailored to the particular industry and to the skills and assets of a particular firm succeed.

Two central concerns underlie the choice of a competitive strategy. The first is the *industry structure* in which the firm competes. Industries differ widely in the nature of competition, and not all industries offer equal opportunities for sustained profitability. The average profitability in pharmaceuticals and cosmetics is extremely high, for example, while it is not in many kinds of apparel and steel. The second central concern in strategy is *positioning within an industry*. Some positions are more profitable than others, regardless of what the average profitability of the industry may be.

Neither concern by itself is sufficient to guide the choice of strategy. A firm in a highly attractive industry, for example, may still not earn satisfactory profits if it has chosen a poor competitive positioning.[3] Both industry structure and competitive position are dynamic. Industries can become more (or less) attractive over time, as barriers to entry or other elements of industry structure change. Competitive position reflects an unending battle among competitors.

Industry attractiveness and competitive position can both be shaped by a firm. Successful firms not only respond to their environment but also attempt to influence it in their favor. Indeed, it is changes in industry structure, or the emergence of new bases for competitive advantage, that underlie substantial shifts in competitive position. Japanese firms became international leaders in television sets, for example, on the strength of a shift toward compact, portable sets and the replacement of vacuum tubes with semiconductor technology. One nation's firms supplant another's in international competition when they are in a better position to perceive or respond to such changes.

THE STRUCTURAL ANALYSIS OF INDUSTRIES

Competitive strategy must grow out of a sophisticated understanding of the structure of the industry and how it is changing. In any industry, whether it is domestic or international, the nature of competition is embodied in five competitive forces: (1) the threat of new entrants, (2) the threat of substitute products or services, (3) the bargaining power of suppliers, (4) the bargaining power of buyers, and (5) the rivalry among the existing competitors (see Figure 2–1).[4]

The strength of the five forces varies from industry to industry and determines long-term industry profitability. In industries in which the five forces are favorable, such as soft drinks, mainframe computers, database publishing, pharmaceuticals, and cosmetics, many competitors earn attractive returns on invested capital. Industries in which pressure from one or more of the forces is intense, such as rubber, aluminum, many fabricated metal products, semiconductors, and small computers, are ones where few firms are very profitable for long periods.

The five competitive forces determine industry profitability because they shape the prices firms can charge, the costs they have to bear, and the investment required to compete in the industry. The threat of new entrants limits the overall profit potential in the industry, because new entrants bring new capacity and seek market share, pushing down margins. Powerful buyers or suppliers bargain away the profits for themselves. Fierce competitive rivalry erodes profits by requiring higher costs of competing (such as for advertising, sales expense, or R&D) or by passing on profits to customers in the form of lower prices. The presence of close substitute products limits the price competitors can charge without inducing substitution and eroding industry volume.

The strength of each of the five competitive forces is a function of *industry structure,* or the underlying economic and technical characteristics of an industry. Buyer power, for example, is a function of such things as the number of buyers, how much of a firm's sales are at risk to any one buyer,

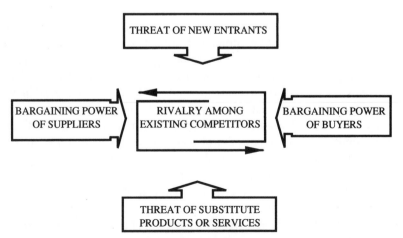

FIGURE 2–1 **The Five Competitive Forces that Determine Industry Competition**

and whether a product is a significant fraction of buyers' own costs which leads to price sensitivity.[5] The threat of entry depends on the height of barriers to entry, such as brand loyalty, economies of scale, or the need to penetrate distribution channels.

Every industry is unique and has its own unique structure. In pharmaceuticals, for example, barriers to entry are high because of the need for huge fixed research and development costs and economies of scale in selling to physicians. Substitutes for an effective drug are slow to develop, and buyers have not historically been price sensitive. Suppliers, who provide mostly commodities, have little clout. Finally, rivalry has been moderate and focused not on price cutting that erodes industry profits but on other variables such as R&D that tend to expand overall industry volume. The existence of patents has also slowed competitive imitation. Industry structure in pharmaceuticals has been highly favorable to profitability, supporting sustained returns on investment among the highest of any major industry.

Industry structure is relatively stable but can change over time as an industry evolves. The consolidation of distribution channels that is taking place in a number of European countries, for example, is increasing buyer power. The industry trends that are the most important for strategy are those affecting its underlying structure. Firms, through their strategies, can also *influence* the five forces for better or for worse. The introduction of computer information systems in the airline industry, for example, is raising barriers to entry by requiring investments in the hundreds of millions of dollars.

Industry structure is significant in international competition for a number of reasons. First, it creates differing requirements for success in different industries. Competing in a fragmented industry such as apparel requires greatly differing resources and skills from competing in commercial aircraft. A nation provides a better environment for competing in some industries than others.

Second, industries important to a high standard of living are often those that are structurally attractive. Structurally attractive industries, with sustainable entry barriers in such areas as technology, specialized skills, channel access, and brand reputation, often involve high labor productivity and will earn more attractive returns to capital. Standard of living will depend importantly on the capacity of a nation's firms to successfully penetrate structurally attractive industries. The attractiveness of an industry is not reliably indicated by size, rapid growth, or newness of technology, attributes often stressed by executives and by government planners, but by industry structure. By targeting entry into structurally unattractive industries, developing nations have frequently made poor use of scarce national resources.

A final reason why industry structure is important in international competition is that *structural change* creates genuine opportunities for competitors from a nation to penetrate new industries. Japanese copier companies, for example, successfully challenged American dominance (notably that of Xerox and IBM) by stressing an underserved product segment (small copiers), employing a new approach to the buyer (the use of dealers instead of direct sale), altering the manufacturing process (mass production versus batch), and modifying the approach to pricing (outright sale versus capital-intensive copier rental). The new strategy reduced entry barriers and nullified the previous leader's advantages. How a nation's environment points the way or pressures its firms to perceive and respond to such structural changes is of central importance to understanding the patterns of international success.

POSITIONING WITHIN INDUSTRIES

In addition to responding to and influencing industry structure, firms must choose a position within the industry. Positioning embodies the firm's overall approach to competing. In the chocolate industry, for example, American firms (such as Hershey and M&M/Mars) compete by mass-producing and mass-marketing relatively limited lines of standardized candy bars. In contrast, Swiss firms (such as Lindt and Sprüngli and Tobler/Jacobs) sell mainly premium products at higher prices through more limited and specialized distribution channels. They produce hundreds of separate items, employ top-quality ingredients, and manufacture using longer processing times. As this example illustrates, positioning involves a firm's total approach to competing, not just its product or target customer group.

At the heart of positioning is *competitive advantage*. In the long run, firms succeed relative to their competitors if they possess sustainable competitive advantage. There are two basic types of competitive advantage: *lower cost* and *differentiation*. Lower cost is the ability of a firm to design, produce, and market a comparable product more efficiently than its competitors. At prices at or near competitors, lower cost translates into superior returns. Korean steel and semiconductor producers, for example, have penetrated against foreign competitors using this strategy. They produce comparable products at very low cost, employing low-wage but highly productive labor forces and modern process technology purchased or licensed from foreign suppliers.

Differentiation is the ability to provide unique and superior value to the buyer in terms of product quality, special features, or after-sale service. German machine tool producers, for example, compete with differentiation strategies involving high product performance, reliability, and responsive service. Differentiation allows a firm to command a premium price, which leads to superior profitability provided costs are comparable to those of competitors.

Competitive advantage of either type translates into higher productivity than that of competitors. The low-cost firm produces a given output using fewer inputs than competitors require. The differentiated firm achieves higher revenues per unit than competitors. Thus competitive advantage is directly linked to the underpinning of national income.

It is difficult, though not impossible, to be both lower-cost and differentiated relative to competitors.[6] Achieving both is difficult because providing unique performance, quality, or service is inherently more costly, in most instances, to seeking only to be comparable to competitors on such attributes. Firms can improve technology or methods in ways that simultaneously reduce cost and improve differentiation. In the long run, however, competitors will imitate and force a choice of which type of advantage to emphasize.

Any successful strategy, however, must pay close attention to *both* types of advantage while maintaining a clear commitment to superiority on one. A low-cost producer must offer acceptable quality and service to avoid nullifying its cost advantage through the necessity to discount prices, while a differentiator's cost position must not be so far above that of competitors as to offset its price premium.

The other important variable in positioning is *competitive scope,* or the breadth of the firm's target within its industry. A firm must choose the range of product varieties it will produce, the distribution channels it will employ, the types of buyers it will serve, the geographic areas in which it will sell, and the array of related industries in which it will also compete.

One reason that competitive scope is important is because industries are *segmented.* In nearly every industry, there are distinct product varieties, multiple distribution channels, and several different types of customers. Segments are important because they frequently have differing needs; an unadvertised basic shirt and a designer shirt are both shirts, but are sold to buyers with very different purchasing criteria. Serving different segments requires different strategies and calls for different capabilities. The sources of competitive advantage, then, are frequently rather different in different segments, even though they are part of the same industry.[7] It is quite typical for firms from one nation to achieve success in one industry segment (Taiwan in inexpensive leather footwear) while those from a different nation are successful in another (Italy in fashion leather footwear).

Competitive scope is also important because firms can sometimes gain competitive advantage from breadth through competing globally or from exploiting interrelationships by competing in related industries. Sony, for example, gains important advantages from sharing its brand name, distribution channels, and technological skills across a wide range of electronic products on a worldwide basis. Interrelationships among distinct industries arise from the ability to share important activities or skills in competing in them. I will explore the sources of competitive advantage from competing globally below.

Firms in the same industry can choose different competitive scopes. Indeed, such differences are typical among firms from different nations. The most basic choice is between a broad scope and focusing on a particular segment. In the packaging machinery industry, for example, German firms offer wide product lines while Italian firms tend to focus on specialized end-use segments. In automobiles, leading American and Japanese companies have wide product lines, while BMW and Daimler-Benz (Germany) emphasize high-performance cars and Hyundai and Daewoo (Korea) focus on compacts and subcompacts.[8]

The type of advantage and the scope of advantage can be combined into the notion of *generic strategies,* or different approaches to superior performance in an industry. Each of these archetypical strategies, illustrated in Figure 2–2, represents a fundamentally different conception of how to compete. In shipbuilding, for example, Japanese firms follow the *differentiation* strategy, offering a wide array of high-quality vessels at premium prices. Korean shipyards pursue the *cost leadership* strategy, also offering many types of vessels but ones of good not superior quality. Korean firms, however, can produce vessels at lower cost than can Japanese firms. Successful Scandinavian yards are *focused differentiators,* concentrating on specialized types of ships such as icebreakers and cruise ships that involve specialized technology and which command prices high enough to offset higher Scandinavian labor costs. Finally, Chinese shipyards (*cost focus*), the emerging competitors in the industry, offer relatively simple, standard vessel types at even lower costs (and prices) than the Koreans.

The generic strategies make it clear that there is no one type of strategy that is appropriate for every industry. Indeed, different strategies can coexist successfully in many industries. While industry structure constrains the range of strategic options available, I have yet to encounter an industry in which only one strategy can be successful. There may also be different possible variations of the same generic strategy, involving different ways to differentiate or focus.

COMPETITIVE ADVANTAGE

		Lower Cost	Differentiation
COMPETITIVE SCOPE	Broad Target	**Cost Leadership**	**Differentiation**
	Narrow Target	**Cost Focus**	**Focused Differentiation**

FIGURE 2–2 **Generic Strategies**

Underlying the concept of generic strategies is that competitive advantage is at the heart of any strategy, and that achieving advantage requires a firm to make choices. If a firm is to gain advantage, it must choose the type of competitive advantage it seeks to attain and a scope within which it can be attained.

The worst strategic error is to be *stuck in the middle,* or to try simultaneously to pursue all the strategies. This is a recipe for strategic mediocrity and below-average performance, because pursuing all the strategies simultaneously means that a firm is not able to achieve any of them because of their inherent contradictions. The shipbuilding industry also illustrates this problem. Spanish and British shipyards have been declining because they have higher costs than the Koreans, lack any basis for differentiation relative to the Japanese, and have failed to identify particular segments (such as Finnish yards have in icebreakers) in which they can gain competitive advantage in a narrower arena. They lack any competitive advantage and exist mainly on captive government orders.

SOURCES OF COMPETITIVE ADVANTAGE

Competitive advantage grows out of the way firms organize and perform discrete activities. The operations of any firm can be divided into a series of activities such as salespeople making sales calls, service technicians performing repairs, scientists in the laboratory designing products or processes, and treasurers raising capital.

Firms create value for their buyers through performing these activities. The ultimate value a firm creates is measured by the amount buyers are willing to pay for its product or service. A firm is profitable if this value exceeds the collective cost of performing all the required activities. To gain competitive advantage over its rivals, a firm must either provide comparable buyer value but perform activities more efficiently than its competitors (lower cost), or perform activities in a unique way that creates greater buyer value and commands a premium price (differentiation).

The activities performed in competing in a particular industry can be grouped into categories as shown in Figure 2–3, in what I call the value chain. All the activities in the value chain contribute to buyer value. Activities can be divided broadly into those involved in the ongoing production, marketing, delivery, and servicing of the product (primary activities) and those providing purchased inputs, technology, human resources, or overall infrastructure functions to support the other activities (support activities). Every activity employs purchased inputs, human resources, some combination of technologies, and draws on firm infrastructure such as general management and finance.

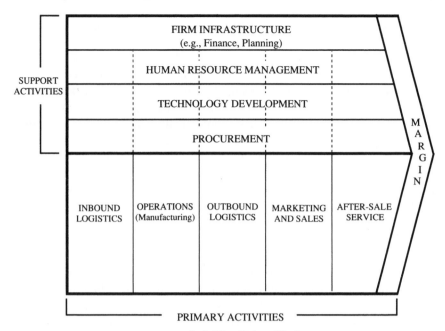

FIGURE **2–3 The Value Chain**

Strategy guides the way a firm performs individual activities and organizes its entire value chain. Activities vary in their importance to competitive advantage in different industries. In printing presses, technology development, assembly (part of operations), and after-sale service are essential to success. In detergents, advertising is crucial while manufacturing is uncomplicated and after-sale service is next to nonexistent.

Firms gain competitive advantage from conceiving of new ways to conduct activities, employing new procedures, new technologies, or different inputs. Makita (Japan) emerged as a leading competitor in power tools because it was the first to employ new, less expensive materials for making tool parts and to produce standardized models in a single plant that it sold worldwide. Swiss chocolate companies rose to prominence by pioneering new product formulations (among them milk chocolate) and the use of new processing methods such as conging (continuous stirring) that substantially improved product quality.

A firm is more than the sum of its activities. A firm's value chain is an interdependent system or network of activities, connected by *linkages*. Linkages occur when the way in which one activity is performed affects the cost or effectiveness of other activities. Linkages often create trade-offs in performing different activities that must be optimized. For example, a more costly product design, more expensive components, and more thorough inspection can reduce after-sale service costs. A company must resolve such trade-offs, in accordance with its strategy, to achieve competitive advantage.

Linkages also require activities to be coordinated. On-time delivery requires that operations, outbound logistics, and service activities such as installation should function smoothly together. Good coordination allows on-time delivery without the need for costly inventory. Coordinating linked activities reduces transaction costs, allows better information for control purposes, and substitutes less costly operations in one activity for more costly ones elsewhere. Coordinating linked activities is also an important way to reduce the combined time required to perform them, increasingly important to competitive advantage. For example, dramatic time savings are being achieved through such coordination in the design and introduction of new products and in order processing and delivery.

Careful management of linkages can be a decisive source of competitive advantage. Many linkages are not obvious, and rivals often have difficulty perceiving them. Obtaining the benefits of linkages requires both complex organizational coordination and resolution of difficult trade-offs across organizational lines, which is rare. Japanese firms have been particularly adept at managing linkages; they popularized such practices as overlapping the steps in the new product development process to improve ease of manufacturing and reduce development time, as well as more careful inspection to reduce after-sale service costs.

Gaining competitive advantage requires that a firm's value chain is managed as a system rather than a collection of separate parts. Reconfiguring the value chain, by relocating, reordering, regrouping, or even eliminating activities is often at the root of a major improvement in competitive position. A good example is in appliances, where Italian firms transformed manufacturing and exploited an entirely new channel of distribution to become world export leaders in the 1960s and 1970s. In cameras, Japanese firms became world leaders by simultaneously commercializing single lens reflex technology, transforming manufacturing into automated mass production, and pioneering mass marketing.

A company's value chain for competing in a particular industry is embedded in a larger stream of activities that I term the *value system* (see Figure 2–4). The value system includes suppliers, who provide inputs (such as raw materials, components, machinery, and purchased services) to the firm's value chain. On its way to the ultimate buyer, a firm's product often passes through the value chains of distribution channels. Ultimately, products become purchased inputs to the value chains of their buyers, who use the products in performing activities of their own.

Competitive advantage is increasingly a function of how well a company can manage this entire system. Linkages not only connect activities inside a company but also create interdependencies between a firm and its suppliers

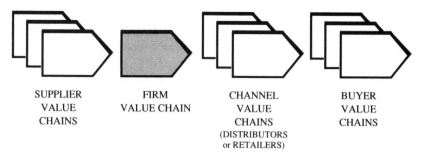

SUPPLIER VALUE CHAINS   FIRM VALUE CHAIN   CHANNEL VALUE CHAINS (DISTRIBUTORS or RETAILERS)   BUYER VALUE CHAINS

FIGURE 2–4 **The Value System**

and channels. A company can create competitive advantage by better optimizing or coordinating these links to the outside. Frequent and timely deliveries by suppliers (a practice now widely termed *kanban* after its Japanese innovators), for example, can lower a firm's handling costs and reduce the required level of inventory. But the opportunities for savings through coordinating with suppliers and channels go far beyond logistics and order processing, and encompass R&D, after-sale service, and many other activities. A company, its suppliers, and its channels can all benefit from better recognition and exploitation of such linkages.[9] The ability of a nation's firms to exploit linkages with home-based suppliers and customers will prove important to explaining the nation's competitive position in an industry.

The value chain provides a tool for understanding the sources of cost advantage.[10] A firm's cost position is its collective cost of performing all the required activities relative to competitors, and cost advantage can occur in any activity. Many managers view cost too narrowly and concentrate on manufacturing. Successful cost leaders, however, are often also low-cost product developers, low-cost marketers, and low-cost service providers. They draw cost advantage from throughout the value chain. Gaining cost advantage also usually requires optimizing the linkages among activities as well as close coordination with suppliers and channels.

The value chain also exposes the sources of differentiation. A firm creates value for its buyer (and hence meaningful differentiation) if it lowers its buyer's cost or raises the buyer's performance in ways the buyer cannot match by purchasing from competitors. Differentiation results, fundamentally, from the way a firm's product, associated services, and other activities affect its buyer's activities. There are many points of contact between a firm and its buyers, each of which represents a potential source of differentiation. The most obvious is the impact of the firm's product itself on the buyer activity in which it is used; for example, a computer used by the buyer for order processing or a detergent used in washing clothes. Creating value at this level can be called first-order differentiation. But virtually all products have more complex influences on their buyers. A component assembled into a buyer's product, for example, must be handled in incoming inventory and repaired as part of the buyer's product if it fails. Each of these more indirect product impacts leads to further opportunities for differentiation. In addition, almost any other firm activity can affect the buyer as well. For example, the supplier's engineering group can assist in designing the supplier's product into the buyer's product. Such higher-order connections between a firm and its buyer are potentially additional sources of differentiation.

The varying bases for differentiation in different industries will prove to be important to national competitive advantage. There are systematic differences in the types of buyer relationships in which particular nations' firms excel. Swiss, German, and Swedish firms are often successful in industries where close collaboration with buyers is required and after-sale service requirements are substantial. Japanese and American firms tend instead to prosper when products are more standardized.

The value chain allows a deeper look not only at the types of competitive advantage but also at the role of competitive scope in gaining competitive advantage. Scope is important because it shapes the nature of a firm's activities, the way they are performed, and how the value chain is configured. By selecting a narrow target segment, for example, a firm can tailor each activity precisely to the segment's needs and potentially achieve lower cost or differentiation compared to the broader-line competitors. Alternatively, broad scope may lead to competitive advantage if the firm can share activities across industry segments or even when competing in related industries. German chemical companies such as BASF, Bayer, and Hoechst, for example, compete in many chemical product industries but employ common sales forces and common production facilities across certain product groups. Similarly, Japanese consumer electronics producers like Sony, Matsushita, and Toshiba reap advantages from competing in related industries such as television sets, audio equipment, and VCRs. These firms use the same brand names and international marketing networks, take advantage of common product and process technologies, and employ joint purchasing.

A prominent reason why firms gain competitive advantage is that they choose a *different* scope from competitors, by focusing on a different segment, altering geographic breadth, or combining the products of related industries. Swiss hearing-aid producers, for example, concentrated on high amplification units for patients with severe hearing problems, achieving superior performance compared to less focused American and Danish competitors. Becoming one of the first companies to compete globally against domestic competitors still concentrating on their home nation is another common means of bolstering competitive advantage. The home nation plays an important role in how these differences in scope emerge.

CREATING ADVANTAGE

Firms create competitive advantage by perceiving or discovering new and better ways to compete in an industry and bringing them to market,[11] which is ultimately an act of innovation. *Innovation* here is defined broadly, to include both improvements in technology and better methods or ways of doing things. It can be manifested in product changes, process changes, new approaches to marketing, new forms of distribution, and new conceptions of scope.[12] Innovators not only respond to possibilities for change, but force it to proceed faster. Much innovation, in practice, is rather mundane and incremental rather than radical. It depends more on a cumulation of small insights and advances than on major technological breakthroughs. It often involves ideas that are not "new" but have never been vigorously pursued. It results from organizational learning as much as from formal R&D. It always involves investment in developing skills and knowledge, and usually in physical assets and marketing effort.

Innovations shift competitive advantage when rivals either fail to perceive the new way of competing or are unwilling or unable to respond. This can be the result of many causes, among them complacency, inertia, inflexible or specialized assets, or mixed motives. For example, Swiss watch producers had mixed motives in responding to Timex's (United States) inexpensive, disposable watch, for fear of undermining the Swiss image of quality and precision. They also had production facilities totally unsuited to mass-producing low-priced watches. Without a new approach to competing, however, the challenger will rarely succeed. Unless the innovator alters the nature of competition, retaliation by established leaders will usually be vigorous and effective.

In international markets, innovations that yield competitive advantage anticipate both domestic and foreign needs. For example, as international concern for product safety has grown, Swedish companies like Volvo, Atlas Copco, and AGA have succeeded by being early to anticipate the market opportunity in this area. On the other hand, innovations that respond to concerns or circumstances that are peculiar to the home market can actually retard international competitive success.

The possibilities for new ways of competing usually grow out of some discontinuity or change in industry structure. Sometimes, such changes have long presented an opportunity that has gone unnoticed. The most typical causes of innovations that shift competitive advantage are the following:

1. *New technologies.* Technological change can create new possibilities for the design of a product, the way it is marketed, produced, or delivered, and the ancillary services provided. It is the most common precursor of

strategic innovation. Industries are born when technological change makes a new product feasible. Germany first became the leader in medical imaging products, for example, after the discovery of X-rays in Germany. Leadership is most likely to change in industries when a nonincremental technological change makes obsolete or nullifies the knowledge and assets of existing leaders. For example, Japanese firms have gained a position in medical imaging (vis-à-vis German and American firms) due to the emergence of new electronics-based technologies that substitute for traditional X-rays in some applications.

It is hard for firms steeped in an old technological paradigm to perceive the significance of a new one. It is often even harder for them to respond to it. The leading American vacuum tube competitors (RCA, General Electric, GTE-Sylvania) all entered the semiconductor industry, for example, but none succeeded. Newly started competitors in semiconductors such as Texas Instruments were more committed to the new technology and had organizations with people, attitudes, and management systems better able to develop it.

2. *New or shifting buyer needs.* Competitive advantage is often created or shifts when buyers develop new needs or their priorities change significantly. Established competitors may fail to perceive the new needs or be unable to respond because meeting them demands a new value chain. American fast-food firms gained advantage internationally, for example, as buyers in many nations came to value convenience and consistency, and local restaurants were slow to adapt. The operation of a fast-food chain is radically different from that of a traditional restaurant.

3. *The emergence of a new industry segment.* The opportunity for creating advantage arises when a new distinct segment of an industry emerges or a new way is conceived to regroup existing segments. The possibilities encompass not only new customer segments but also new ways of producing particular items in the product line or new ways to reach a particular group of customers. A good example is the lift truck industry, where Japanese firms perceived an underserved segment in small lift trucks for general-purpose applications. By focusing on this segment, they were able to standardize designs and transform the manufacturing process into one employing much higher levels of automation. This example illustrates how serving a new segment frequently creates the potential to substantially reconfigure the value chain, something established competitors may find difficult.

4. *Shifting input costs or availability.* Competitive advantage frequently changes when a significant change occurs in the absolute or relative costs of inputs such as labor, raw materials, energy, transportation, communications, media, or machinery. This may reflect new conditions in supplier industries, or perhaps the possibility of using a new or different type or quality of input. A firm gains competitive advantage by optimizing based

on the new conditions while competitors are saddled with assets and approaches tailored to the old ones.

A classic example is the shift in relative labor cost among nations. Korea and now other Asian nations have become competitive in relatively simple international construction projects as wages in more industrialized countries have risen. More recently, a steep fall in the cost of transportation and communications is allowing new ways of organizing and managing firms that lead to competitive advantage, such as the ability to rely more on specialist outside suppliers and the ability to operate a truly global production system.

5. *Changes in government regulations.* Adjustments in the nature of government regulation, in areas such as product standards, environmental controls, restrictions on entry, and trade barriers, are another common stimulus to innovations which result in competitive advantage. Existing industry leaders have tailored their activities to one regulatory regime, and a shift in that regime may find them unable to respond. American securities firms are benefiting from a reduction in financial market regulation around the world, for example, because American regulators pioneered this trend and U.S. firms have already learned to deal with it.

MOVING EARLY TO EXPLOIT STRUCTURAL CHANGE

These triggers result in competitive advantage for those companies who can perceive their significance early and move aggressively to exploit them. In a remarkable number of industries, early movers sustained position for decades. The German and Swiss dye companies (Bayer, Hoechst, BASF, Sandoz, Ciba, and Geigy, later merged into Ciba-Geigy) have sustained their positions as international leaders since before World War I. Procter & Gamble, Unilever, and Colgate have been international leaders in detergents since the 1930s.

Early movers gain advantages such as being first to reap economies of scale, reducing costs through cumulative learning, establishing brand names and customer relationships without direct competition, getting their pick of distribution channels, and obtaining the best locations for facilities or the best sources of raw materials or other inputs. Moving early can allow a firm to translate an innovation into advantages of other sorts that may well be more sustainable. The innovation itself may be copied but the other competitive advantages often remain.

Early movers gain the greatest competitive advantage in those industries where economies of scale are significant and where customers are most conservative about switching suppliers. Here, entrenched positions are the most difficult to challenge. The longevity of early mover advantages depends on whether there are subsequent industry structural changes that nullify them. In many branded consumer packaged goods, for example, brand loyalties are long lived and technical change has been incremental. Brands like Ivory Soap, M&M/Mars, Lindt, Nestlé, and Persil have preserved leadership for generations.

Every significant structural change in an industry creates opportunities for *new* early movers. In watches, for example, the emergence of mass distribution channels, mass marketing, and mass production in the 1950s and 1960s allowed Timex and Bulova (both American) to overtake the Swiss in unit sales. Later, the shift from mechanical to electronic technology in watches provided the discontinuity that made it possible for Seiko, Citizen, and later Casio (all Japanese) to achieve leading positions. The early movers in one technological or product generation may well face disadvantages in moving to the next one, because their assets and skills are specialized.

Yet the watch case illustrates another important principle; early movers will not succeed unless they correctly forecast industry changes. American companies (for example, Pulsar, Fairchild, and Texas Instruments) were early entrants into electronic watches, often from positions as semiconductor producers. However, they bet heavily on light emitting diode (LED) displays. This technology proved inferior to liquid crystal displays (LCD) for less expensive watches and traditional (analog) displays combined with quartz movements for watches in higher price ranges. Seiko chose not to introduce an LED watch at all, but moved early to emphasize LCD and quartz analog technology. The introduction of LCD and quartz paved the way for Japanese firms to take over industry leadership in mass-marketed watches, and for Seiko to become the world leader.

PERCEIVING AND PURSUING INNOVATION

Information plays a large role in the process of innovation–information that is not sought or available to competitors, or information available to others that is interpreted in new ways. Sometimes it results from sheer investment in market research or R&D. It is striking, though, how often innovators are those firms that are simply looking in the right place, unencumbered by or unconcerned with conventional wisdom.

Often, innovators are "outsiders," in some way, to the existing industry. Innovation may come from a new company, whose founder has a nontraditional background or was simply not appreciated in an older, established company. Or the capacity for innovation may come into an existing company through senior managers who are new to the industry and thus more able to perceive opportunities and are bolder in pursuing them. Or innovation may occur as a company diversifies, bringing new resources, skills, or perspectives to another industry. Or innovations may come from another nation with different circumstances or ways of competing.

Outsiders may be better able to perceive new opportunities. Or they may possess the different expertise and resources required to compete in a new way. Leaders of innovating companies are frequently also outsiders in a more intangible, social sense. They are not part of the industrial elite nor are they viewed as accepted participants in the industry. This makes such companies less concerned with violating established norms or engaging in unseemly competition.

With few exceptions, innovation is the result of unusual effort. The firm that successfully implements new or improved ways of competing is the one that doggedly pursues its approach, often in the face of obstacles. The strategy is the personal crusade of an individual or group. As a consequence, innovation often results from pressure, necessity, or even adversity. The fear of loss often proves more powerful than the hope of gain.

Companies that innovate are frequently not established leaders, or even large companies, for many of these reasons. Any economies of scale in R&D that would favor large firms are outweighed by the fact that many innovations do not involve complicated technology, and large firms face many barriers to perceiving and acting on discontinuities. In our research, larger companies were often supplanted by smaller ones. Where the innovators were large firms, they were often new entrants to the industry from an established position in another industry.[13]

Why are some companies able to perceive new ways to compete and others are not? Why do some companies do so earlier than others? What makes some companies able to better anticipate the proper directions of change? Why is unusual effort applied? These fascinating questions will prove to be central ones in the chapters that follow. The answers lie in such areas as the directions in which companies' attention is focused, the possession of the proper types of resources and skills, and the *pressures* faced to change. The national environment plays an important role in all these things. In addition, the degree to which the national environment supports the emergence of "outsiders" from within the nation, preventing the loss of positions in established and new industries to firms from some other nation, will be an important influence on national prosperity.

SUSTAINING ADVANTAGE

The sustainability of competitive advantage depends on three conditions. The first is the particular *source* of the advantage. There is a *hierarchy* of sources of competitive advantage in terms of sustainability. Lower-order advantages, such as low labor costs or cheap raw materials, are relatively easy to imitate. Competitors can often readily duplicate such advantages by finding another low-cost location or source of supply, or nullify them by producing or sourcing in the same place. In consumer electronics, for example, Japan's labor cost advantage has long since been lost to Korea and Hong Kong. Firms based in these nations, in turn, are already being threatened by even lower-cost labor in Malaysia and Thailand. Japanese consumer electronics producers have established overseas production that follows this progression. Also at the lower end of the hierarchy of advantage are cost advantages due solely to economies of scale using technology, equipment, or methods sourced from or also available to competitors. Such economies of scale are nullified when new technology or methods make the old ones obsolete, or new product designs have the same effect.

Higher-order advantages, such as proprietary process technology, product differentiation based on unique products or services, brand reputation based on cumulative marketing efforts, and customer relationships protected by high customer costs of switching vendors, are more durable. Higher-order advantages are marked by a number of characteristics. The first is that achieving them requires more advanced skills and capabilities such as specialized and highly trained personnel, internal technical capability, and, often, close relationships with leading customers.

Second, higher-order advantages usually depend on a history of *sustained and cumulative investment* in physical facilities and specialized and often risky learning, research and development, or marketing.[14] Performing some activities such as advertising, selling, and R&D creates tangible and intangible *assets* in the form of a reputation, customer relationships, and a pool of specialized knowledge. Frequently, moving early means that the firm has invested longer in building them than competitors. Competitors must invest as much or more to replicate such advantages, or find ways to invent around them. Finally, the most durable advantages combine larger cumulative investment with superiority in performing the activities involved, that gives the advantages a dynamic character. Ongoing rapid investment in process technology, marketing, global service networks, or rapid new product introduction often makes it even more difficult for competitors to respond.[15] Higher-order competitive advantages are not only more sustainable but are associated with higher levels of productivity.

Pure cost advantages are frequently less sustainable than differentiation. One reason is that any new source of lower cost, even one less sophisticated, can nullify a firm's cost advantage. If labor is cheap enough, for example, even much higher efficiency can be nullified, unlike the case with differentiation advantages which normally must be matched to be exceeded. In addition, pure cost advantages are more vulnerable because new product designs or other forms of differentiation can eliminate a cost advantage in delivering old ones.

The second determinant of sustainability is the *number of distinct sources* of advantage a firm possesses. If a firm rests on only one advantage, such as an inherently less costly product design or access to a cheap raw material, competitors will concentrate on nullifying or overcoming this advantage. Firms with histories of sustained leadership tend to proliferate advantages throughout the value chain. Japanese small copier producers, for example, have advanced features, low manufacturing costs because of flexible automation, extensive dealer networks providing wider sales coverage than the traditional direct sale approach, and high levels of reliability that reduce after-sale service costs. Numerous advantages raise the ante for competitors who seek to imitate.

The third, and most important, reason competitive advantage is sustained is *constant improvement and upgrading*. Virtually any advantage can be replicated sooner or later if a leader rests on its laurels. In order to sustain advantage a firm must become a moving target, creating new advantages at least as fast as competitors can replicate old ones.

The first task is to improve relentlessly the firm's performance against its existing advantages—for example, more efficient operation of its production facilities or more responsiveness in terms of customer service. This makes it more difficult for competitors to nullify them without extraordinary rates of improvement.

In the long run, however, sustaining advantage demands that its sources be expanded and upgraded, by moving up the hierarchy to more sustainable types. This is precisely what Japanese automakers have done. They initially penetrated foreign markets with inexpensive compact cars of adequate quality, and competed on the basis of lower labor costs. Even while their labor-cost advantage persisted, however, the Japanese companies were upgrading. They invested aggressively to build large modern plants to reap economies of scale. Then they became innovators in process technology, pioneering just-in-time production and a host of other quality and productivity practices. This led to better product quality, repair records, and customer satisfaction ratings than foreign rivals. Most recently, Japanese automakers have advanced to the vanguard of product technology and are introducing new, premium brand names.

Sustaining advantage requires change. It demands that a company exploit, rather than ignore, industry trends. It also demands that a company invest to close off the avenues along which competitors could attack. If biotechnology threatens to change the nature of pharmaceutical research, for example, a pharmaceutical company seeking to sustain advantage must move early to develop superior biotechnology capability. Sure signs of waning competitive advantage are hoping that a new technology will disappear, dismissing a new buyer segment, or ignoring a new distribution channel—responses that are all too common.

To sustain its position, a firm may have to destroy old advantages to create new, higher-order ones. For example, Korean shipbuilding firms did not become international leaders until they aggressively expanded the scale of their shipyards, moved to adopt new building techniques that substantially boosted productivity by reducing labor content, and developed the technical capabilities to build more sophisticated vessels. All these steps reduced the importance of labor costs at a time when Korean firms still enjoyed a labor cost advantage. The apparent paradox involved in nullifying old advantages often deters firms from upgrading. If firms fail to take the painful and seemingly counterintuitive step of doing so, however, competitors will do it for them. How a firm's national environment influences the likelihood of this sort of behavior is a subject that will occupy us later.

The reason so few firms sustain their position is that change is extraordinarily painful and difficult for any successful organization. Complacency is much more natural. The past strategy becomes ingrained in organizational routines. Information that would modify or challenge it is not sought or filtered out. The past strategy takes on an aura of invincibility and becomes rooted in company culture. Suggesting change is tantamount to disloyalty.[16] Successful companies often seek predictability and stability. They become preoccupied with defending what they have, and any change is tempered by the concern that there is much to lose. Supplanting or superseding old advantages to create new ones is not considered until the old advantages are long gone. The past strategy becomes ossified, and structural change in the industry then leads to shifting market leadership. Smaller firms or those new to the industry, not bound by history and past investments, become the innovators and the new leaders.

The ability to modify strategy is also blocked by the fact that a company's past strategy becomes embodied in skills, organizational arrangements, specialized facilities, and a reputation that may be inconsistent with a new one. Indeed, such specialization is integral to gaining advantage in the first place. Reconfiguring the value chain is difficult and costly. In large firms, sheer scale also makes altering the strategy difficult. The process of modifying strategy frequently involves a sacrifice in financial performance and unsettling, sometimes wrenching, organizational adjustments. Firms without the legacy of a past strategy and past investments may well face lower costs of adopting a new strategy, not to mention fewer organizational difficulties. This is one reason why "outsiders," as I have defined them, are often the innovators.[17]

The behavior required to sustain advantage, then, is in many respects an unnatural act for established firms. Companies that manage to overcome inertia and the barriers to changing and upgrading advantage are most often those that have been stimulated by competitive pressure, buyer demands, or technical threats. Few companies make significant improvements and strategy changes voluntarily; most are forced to. The pressure to change is more often environmental than internal.

The managements of companies that sustain competitive advantage always run a little scared. They acutely sense external threats to competitive position and respond to them. How such behavior is catalyzed by circumstances within a nation is an important theme in subsequent chapters.

COMPETING INTERNATIONALLY

These basic principles of competitive strategy apply whether a firm is competing domestically or internationally. To understand the role of the nation in competitive advantage, however, we are particularly concerned with industries in which competition is international. We must understand how firms create competitive advantage through international strategy, and how this reinforces competitive advantages gained at home.

The pattern of international competition differs markedly from industry to industry. At one end of the spectrum, international competition takes a form that can be termed *multidomestic*. Competition in each nation (or small group of nations) is essentially independent. The industry is present in many nations (there is a consumer banking industry in Korea, one in Italy, and one in the United States, for example), but competition takes place on a country-by-country basis. A bank's reputation, customer base, and physical assets in one nation, for example, have little or no impact on its success in consumer banking in other nations. Some competitors may be multinational firms, but their competitive advantages are largely confined to each country in which they compete. The international industry is a collection of essentially domestic industries, hence the term multidomestic. Industries in which competition has traditionally taken this form include many types of retailing, many consumer food products, wholesaling, life insurance, consumer finance, simple metal fabrication, and caustic chemicals.

At the other end of the spectrum are *global* industries, in which a firm's competitive position in one nation significantly affects (and is affected by) its position in other nations. Rivals compete against each other on a truly worldwide basis, drawing on competitive advantages that grow out of their entire network of worldwide activities.[18] Firms combine advantages created at their home base with others that result from a presence in many nations, such as economies of scale, the ability to serve multinational customers, and a transferable brand reputation. Global competition occurs in such industries as commercial aircraft, television sets, semiconductors, copiers, automobiles, and watches. Industries have increasingly become global in the post–World War II period.

In the extreme case of a multidomestic industry, there is no issue of national advantage or international competitiveness. Virtually every nation will have such industries. Many, if not most, of the firms that compete in them will tend to be owned locally, because country-by-country competition makes it difficult for foreign firms to gain a competitive advantage. International trade in such industries will be modest or nonexistent. Foreign ownership, to the extent that it does occur, will'tend to be largely passive and involve only modest control from central headquarters. Local jobs, local corporate citizenship, and the location of research will not be major issues, because the national subsidiary will control most if not all of the important activities necessary to compete. There are few debates about trade problems in industries such as retailing and metal fabrication.

Global industries, in contrast, are the battleground on which firms from different nations compete in ways that significantly affect national economic prosperity. The ability to achieve competitive advantage in global industries carries high stakes for both international trade and investment.

In global industries, firms are compelled to compete internationally in order to achieve or sustain competitive advantage in the most important industry segments. There may well be segments in such industries that are domestic because of unique national needs, in which purely domestic firms can prosper. But choosing a domestic focus in a global industry is perilous, no matter what the firm's home nation.

COMPETITIVE ADVANTAGE THROUGH GLOBAL STRATEGY

A global strategy is one in which a firm sells its product in many nations and employs an integrated worldwide approach to doing so.[19] Just being a multinational does not imply a global strategy if the multinational has free-standing subsidiaries that operate independently in each nation. For example, many European (for example, Brown Boveri, now Asea-Brown Boveri, and Philips) and some American multinationals (such as General Motors and ITT) have historically competed in this way, diminishing their competitive advantage and providing an opportunity for competitors to overtake them.

In a global strategy, a firm sells in many if not all of the nations that represent significant markets for its product. This creates scale to amortize R&D costs and to allow the use of advanced production technology. The question becomes how to locate and manage the value chain for selling worldwide.

A global approach to strategy provides two distinctive ways in which a firm can gain competitive advantages or offset domestic disadvantages. The first is in the way a global firm can spread activities among nations to serve the world market. The second is via the ability of a global firm to coordinate among the dispersed activities.[20] The location of activities in the value chain most related to the buyer, such as marketing, physical distribution, and after-sale service, is usually tied to where the buyer is located. Selling in Japan, for example, usually requires a firm to have salespeople or distributors stationed in Japan and to provide for after-sale service in Japan. The location of other activities may also be tied to the buyer's location because of high transportation costs or the need for close interchange. In many service industries, for example, the production, delivery, and marketing of the service must take place near the buyer. Usually, the firm must physically locate the capability to perform such activities in each of the nations in which it operates.

In contrast, activities such as manufacturing and in-bound logistics as well as support activities such as technology development and procurement can be frequently decoupled from the buyer's location. They can be performed anywhere. In a global strategy, a firm locates such activities to optimize its cost position or differentiation from a worldwide perspective. A firm may establish one large plant from which it serves the world market, for example, reaping economies of scale. Few activities need, as a matter of necessity, to be performed in the home nation.

The strategic choices unique to global strategy can be summarized in two essential dimensions.

- *Configuration:* Where, and in how many nations, each activity in the value chain is performed. For example, do Sony or Matsushita produce VCRs in one large plant in Japan or establish additional plants in the United States and the United Kingdom?
- *Coordination:* How dispersed activities, or activities performed in several different nations, are coordinated. Is the same brand name or sales approach used in each nation, for example, or does each marketing subsidiary choose a separate brand or sales channel tailored to its local circumstances?

In multidomestic competition, multinationals have largely autonomous subsidiaries in each nation and manage them like a portfolio. In global competition, firms seek to gain much greater competitive advantage from their international presence, through locating activities with a global perspective and coordinating actively among them.

GLOBAL CONFIGURATION

In configuring its worldwide activities in an industry, a firm faces two broad choices. One is whether to concentrate activities in one or two nations or disperse them to many nations. The second is the choice of nations in which to locate particular activities.

Concentrating Activities. In some industries, competitive advantage arises from concentrating activities in one nation and exporting components or finished goods to foreign markets. This occurs where there are significant economies of scale in performing an activity, a steep learning curve that creates advantages from having only one location, or advantages in locating linked activities in the same place to allow better coordination. Concentrated, or export-based, global strategies are typical in industries such as aircraft, machinery, materials, and agriculturally related products. Normally, activities are concentrated at the firm's home base.

Concentrated global strategies are more typical in some nations than others. They are common in Korea and Italy, where today most products are designed and produced at home and only marketing takes place abroad. In Japan, this has also been the pattern in most internationally successful industries, though Japanese firms are rapidly dispersing activities such as purchasing and assembly for various reasons. The types of international strategies that are encouraged or supported in a nation influence the nature of industries in which the nation competes successfully.

Dispersing Activities. In other industries, competitive advantages arise (or home-base disadvantages are overcome) from dispersing activities to several or many nations. Dispersing activities involves foreign direct investment (FDI). It is favored in industries where there are high transportation, communication, or storage costs that make it inefficient to operate from a central location, and by the presence of risks of performing an activity in one location: exchange rate risks, political risks, and risks of supply interruption.

Dispersed activities are also favored where local product needs differ substantially. The resulting need to tailor products extensively to national markets reduces the scale or learning advantages of operating a single large plant or research laboratory. Another important motivation for dispersing activities is to enhance local marketing in a foreign nation, by signaling commitment to local buyers and/or providing greater local responsiveness. Dispersing an activity to many nations can also allow a firm to accumulate expertise in the activity via information gained from several locations (provided the firm can coordinate across subsidiaries).

Government is a powerful force in some industries for dispersing activities, through tariffs, nontariff barriers, and nationalistic purchasing. Government typically wants a firm to locate an entire value chain in its nation, because this is seen as creating benefits and spillovers to the nation that extend beyond local content.[21] Finally, dispersing some activities may sometimes allow the benefits of concentrating others to be gained. For example, placating the national government by performing final assembly in a nation may allow freer import of components from large-scale, centralized component plants located elsewhere.

The choice of concentrating or dispersing activities depends ultimately on the particular activity. In the truck industry, leaders such as Daimler-Benz, Volvo, and Saab-Scania conduct most R&D and component production at home but assemble products in a number of countries. The best configuration will differ from industry to industry. It may also differ among segments in the same industry.

Some examples will illustrate a number of these points. Swedish firms have highly dispersed strategies in a number of industries related to mining. Buyers in this sector value an extensive local presence by suppliers to provide service and technical assistance. In addition, local government ownership or involvement in the mining sector is nearly universal. Political considerations demand a local presence to respond to government's preference for a local supplier. Swedish firms such as SKF (ball bearings) and Electrolux (appliances) also tend to have highly dispersed strategies involving extensive FDI and relatively autonomous foreign subsidiaries, a function of differences in product needs among nations, the need for close proximity to buyers in marketing and service, and government pressures. Swiss firms also tend to have dispersed configurations in many industries, among them trading, pharmaceuticals, food, and dyes. Dispersed global strategies, involving substantial foreign direct investment, are also typical in such sectors as consumer packaged goods, health care, telecommunications, and many services.

Locating Activities. Along with a choice about the number of sites for an activity is the nation(s) in which to locate it. Activities are usually all located initially in the home nation. In a global strategy, however, a firm can choose any nation in which to assemble products, fabricate components, or even conduct research, *wherever* advantage lies.

Locational advantages often apply to individual activities. One of the potent benefits a global firm enjoys is the ability to spread different activities among nations to reflect *different* preferred locations. Thus, components can be produced in Taiwan, software written in India, and basic R&D performed in Silicon Valley.

The classic reason for locating an activity in a particular nation is factor costs. Assembly takes place in Taiwan or Singapore to take advantage of a pool of educated, motivated, but inexpensive labor. Capital is raised wherever it is available on the best terms. To fund crucial capacity additions in semiconductors, for example, NEC Corporation (Japan) financed convertible debt not in Japan (where this instrument was rare) but in Europe. Indeed, global competition has led to a growing dispersion of activities reflecting such considerations. Many American firms produce in the Far East (virtually all American disk drives are produced there, for example) while Japanese competitors in the sewing machine, sporting goods, electronic components, and other industries are active investors in Korean, Hong Kong, Taiwanese, and now Thai production.

More recently, firms have become more prone to locate activities in other nations not only to tap local factor costs but to perform R&D, gain access to specialized local skills, or develop relationships with pivotal customers. German plastics processing machinery companies and Swiss surveying equipment firms have both, for example, located research units in the United States to develop electronic controls. SKF (Sweden), a world leader in ball bearings, has a major production and R&D base in Germany, in close proximity to the many world-leading German machinery industries and the German automotive sector, important ball-bearing users.

Firms also locate activities in nations if doing so is a condition for operating there. Locating assembly, marketing, or service activities in a nation is important in some industries to the ability to sell and service more effectively to that nation's customers. A good example is highly engineered commercial air-conditioning equipment, where U.S. leaders such as Carrier and Trane maintain operations in many international locations to support the customization and heavy servicing requirements of this industry.

Government mandates also influence location. For example, many Japanese production investments in the United States and Europe today (such as in cars, auto parts, and consumer electronics) reflect actual or potential import restraints. Similarly, many Swedish, Swiss, and American multinationals moved abroad before World War II when trade barriers as well as transport costs were more significant, one reason they often have widely dispersed activities compared to Japanese or German firms in the same industry. A dispersed configuration is frequently hard to integrate and consolidate once in place, because local country managers desire to retain power and autonomy. The inability to shift to more concentrated and coordinated strategies necessary for competitive advantage is one reason why firms lose advantage in some industries.

My discussion of locating activities, however, must at this stage remain incomplete. The best location for the activities that constitute a firm's home base, particularly strategy development, R&D, and the more sophisticated portions of production, is after all one of the principal subjects of this book. Suffice it to say that the motivations for locating in a nation go far beyond the classical explanations outlined here.

GLOBAL COORDINATION

The other important means by which firms gain competitive advantage through a global approach to strategy is by coordinating among activities located in different nations. Coordination involves sharing information, allocating responsibility, and aligning efforts. It can lead to a number of benefits. One is accumulating knowledge and expertise gained at dispersed sites. If a firm learns how to operate the production process better in Germany, transferring that learning may also make the process run smoother in U.S. and Japanese plants. Different countries, with their inevitably differing conditions, provide a basis for comparison as well as opportunities for arbitraging knowledge obtained in different sites about different aspects of the business.

Knowledge accumulates in different countries not only about product or process technology but also about buyer needs and marketing techniques. A firm with a truly global outlook, coordinating among all its marketing units around the world, can receive an early warning of industry changes by spotting industry trends before they become broadly apparent. Coordination among dispersed activities may also lead to economies of scale by allocating subtasks among locations to allow specialization. For example, SKF (Sweden) produces a different range of bearings in each of its foreign plants and transships products among nations to allow each national marketing subsidiary to offer the full line.

Dispersed activities, if they are coordinated, may allow a firm to respond to *shifting* exchange rates or factor costs. For example, incrementally increasing the production volume at the location that currently enjoys favorable exchange rates can lower overall costs, something that Japanese firms in a variety of industries were pursuing in the late 1980s because of the high value of the Japanese yen.

Coordination can also enhance a firm's differentiation with internationally mobile or multinational buyers. Consistency in product positioning and its approach to doing business on a worldwide basis reinforces a company's brand reputation. The ability to serve multinational or mobile customers wherever they have the need is often valued. Coordination among national subsidiaries can also enhance leverage with local governments if the firm is able to grow or shrink activities in one country at the expense of others.

Finally, coordination across countries yields flexibility in responding to competitors. A global firm can choose where and how to fight a competitor. It might decide to wage a battle in the nation from which a competitor draws its greatest volume or cash flow in order to reduce the competitor's resources for competing in other countries. IBM and Caterpillar have practiced this sort of defensive behavior in their Japanese operations. A competitor with a solely domestic outlook has none of this flexibility.

Large national differences in buyer needs and local business conditions work against coordination. They make learning from one nation inapplicable in other nations. Where such conditions are present, an industry is multidomestic.

Even when there are significant benefits to coordination, however, achieving coordination among subsidiaries in a global strategy involves formidable organizational challenges because of sheer complexity, linguistic differences, cultural differences, and the need for high levels of open and credible information exchange. Another serious difficulty is aligning the interests of subsidiary managers with those of the firm as a whole. The German branch does not necessarily want to tell the U.S. branch about their latest breakthroughs in production technology, because it may make it harder for them to outdo the Americans in the annual comparison of plant operating efficiency. These vexing organizational problems mean that country subsidiaries often view each other more as competitors than collaborators, and that full and open coordination is the exception rather than the rule in global companies.[22]

LOCATION-BASED AND SYSTEM-BASED ADVANTAGES

The competitive advantages of a global firm can be usefully separated into those growing out of location (or nations) and those independent of location and arising from the firm's overall global network of activities.

Nation- or location-based advantages may arise from either the firm's *home base* or from other nations in which the firm locates particular activities. The global firm employs advantages from its home base to penetrate foreign markets. It is also able to seek out location-based advantages in performing particular activities in other nations to reinforce home advantages or offset home disadvantages.

System-based advantages are a function of the firm's total worldwide sales volume, its cumulative rate of learning in all its facilities, and the ability to coordinate across foreign and domestic locations. Economies of scale in production or R&D are in and of themselves country neutral, for example, because a large-scale plant or research center can, in principle, be located anywhere.

Global competition will not begin initially unless some firms gain an advantage at home that allows them to penetrate foreign markets. Competitive advantage drawn solely from the home base is sufficient to lead to global competition. Over time, however, successful global firms usually combine advantages drawn from their home base with those resulting from locating particular activities in other nations and those emerging from the overall worldwide network. These other advantages add to and upgrade home-based advantages to make them more sustainable, as well as offset home-based disadvantages. Advantages from each of these sources can be mutually reinforcing. The overall scale resulting from a worldwide position, for example, has allowed such German firms as Zeiss (optical instruments) and Schott (glass) to afford more R&D to better exploit the technical and demand advantages of a German home base.

In practice, firms that do not exploit and extend their home-based advantages through competing globally are vulnerable. The combination of home base advantages, the benefits of locating selected activities in foreign locations, and advantages growing out of the worldwide system, not each alone, underpins international success. As the globalization of competition has become widely recognized, attention has been focused on system advantages and on the benefits of locating in other nations. In fact, home-based advantages are usually more significant to competitive advantage, a recurring theme of later chapters.

CHOOSING A GLOBAL STRATEGY

There is no one type of global strategy, but numerous ways of competing globally involving choices about where to locate and how to coordinate activities. The best pattern depends on the particular industry. Most global strategies involve an integrated combination of trade and foreign direct investment. Finished products are exported from some nations that import components produced elsewhere, and vice versa. Foreign investment reflects the dispersion of production and marketing activities. Trade and foreign investment are complementary, not necessarily substitutes.

Segments of an industry frequently differ in the extent of globalization and in the appropriate global strategy. In lubricants, for example, automotive motor oil tends toward multidomestic competition. Countries have different driving standards, weather conditions, and local laws. Production involves blending various kinds of base oils and additives. It is subject to few economies of scale, and involves high shipping costs. Retail distribution channels, very important to competitive success, differ markedly from country to country. Domestic firms, such as Quaker State and Pennzoil in the United States, or multinationals with highly autonomous country subsidiaries such as Castrol (United Kingdom), are the leaders in most countries. Marine engine lubricant, in contrast, is a global industry. Ships move freely around the world and require that the same oil be available everywhere they stop. Brand reputations become global. Successful marine engine lubricant competitors, such as Shell, Exxon, and British Petroleum, are global.

Another example is lodging, where many segments are multidomestic because the majority of activities in the value chain are tied to buyer location and because differences among national needs and circumstances lead to few benefits from coordination. In business-oriented or luxury hotels, however, competition is more global. Global competitors such as Hilton, Marriott, and Sheraton have many dispersed properties but employ common brand names, common formats, common service standards, and worldwide reservation systems to gain marketing advantages in serving highly mobile business travelers.[23]

Vertical stages of an industry also frequently vary in the extent and pattern of globalization. In aluminum, the upstream (alumina and ingot) stages are global industries. The downstream stage, semifabrication (for example, castings, extrusions), consists of a number of multidomestic industries. Product needs vary by country, transport costs are high, and intensive local customer service is required. Scale economies in the value chain are modest. In general, components and raw materials tend to be more global than finished goods.

Variation in the pattern of globalization among segments, vertical stages, and groups of countries creates the opportunity for global focus strategies. These involve serving a particular industry segment worldwide. Daimler-Benz and BMW adopted this approach in high-performance automobiles, as have Japanese firms such as Toyota, Isuzu, and Hino in small trucks.

The global focuser concentrates worldwide on a segment of the industry that is poorly served by broad-line competitors. Competing globally can make entirely new segmentations of an industry possible, because serving a segment on a worldwide basis provides enough volume to capture economies of scale. High costs may have rendered serving the segment in one country impractical. In some industries, global focus is the only feasible international strategy because the advantages of globalization exist only in particular segments (for example, high-priced business hotels).

Global focus can be the first step toward a broad-line global strategy. A firm begins to compete globally in a segment where its home base provides a unique advantage. In industries such as cars, lift trucks, and television sets, for example, Japanese firms established initial beachheads by focusing on the compact, and neglected, end-of-the-product range. They later broadened their lines and gained commanding worldwide positions.

Smaller companies, not just large ones, can compete globally. Small- and medium-sized companies account for a substantial portion of international trade, especially in nations such as Germany, Italy, and Switzerland. They often focus on narrow segments or compete in relatively small industries. The global focus strategy is also quite common among multinationals from smaller countries such as Finland and Switzerland and among small- and medium-sized firms from all countries. Montblanc (Germany) competes globally in high-priced pens, for example, while nearly all of the many Italian companies in footwear, apparel, and furniture compete internationally in a narrow segment.

Small- and medium-sized companies tend to employ export-based strategies with only modest foreign direct investment. Yet there is a growing number of modest-sized multinationals. Denmark, Switzerland, and Germany, for example, have many relatively modest-sized multinationals, focused in particular segments. With limited resources, smaller firms face challenges in gaining foreign market access, understanding foreign market needs, and providing after-sale support. These problems are solved in different ways in different industries. One is to deal through agents or importers (typical for Italian firms), distributors, or trading companies (typical in Japan and Korea). Another approach is the use of industry associations to create a common marketing infrastructure, organize trade shows and fairs, and conduct market research. Cooperatives, for example, have been integral to the export success of Danish agriculturally based industries. More recently, smaller firms have been turning to alliances with foreign firms in order to compete globally.

THE PROCESS OF INDUSTRY GLOBALIZATION

Industries globalize because shifts in technology, buyer needs, government policy, or country infrastructure create major differences in competitive position among firms from different nations or make the advantages of a global strategy more significant. In automobiles, for example, the industry has been globalizing as Japanese companies have gained substantial competitive advantages in quality and productivity, demand for cars in different nations has become more similar (an important reason being rising fuel costs in the United States), and transportation costs have fallen, among other reasons.

An act of strategic innovation often unlocks the potential for globalization. International industry leadership frequently results from discovering how to make a global strategy feasible. For example, a firm may discover a means of reducing the cost of modifying a centrally designed and manufactured product to meet differing local country needs, such as modularizing the power supply in an otherwise standard product. In central office switching equipment used in telecommunications, for example, Northern Telecom, NEC Corporation, and Ericsson have benefited from product architectures that permit modularization of software and relatively low-cost modification to fit the needs of different national telephone systems. Or a firm may develop a new product variety or marketing approach that has universal appeal, or an innovation that overcomes impediments to competing globally. In disposable plastic syringes, for example, American companies not only pioneered a product with universal appeal but reduced transport costs compared to glass syringes, unlocking possibilities for reaping economies of scale from a single world-scale plant.

Nascent global industry leaders always begin with some advantage created at home, whether it be a preferred product design, a higher level of product quality, a new marketing concept, or a factor cost advantage. However, sustained success usually requires that the firm not stop there. The home-based advantage must then become the lever to enter foreign markets. Once there, the successful global competitor complements the initial home-base advantage with the economies of scale or reputation advantages of worldwide sales. Over time, competitive advantage is supplemented (or home-based disadvantages are offset) by locating selected activities in foreign nations.

Even if the initial home-base advantage is hard to sustain, a global strategy can contribute to supplementing and upgrading it. A good example is in consumer electronics, where Matsushita, Sanyo, Sharp, and other Japanese firms initially competed on cost in selling simply designed, portable televisions. As they began penetrating foreign markets, they gained economies of scale and further reduced cost by moving down the learning curve. Worldwide volume then helped to support aggressive investments in marketing, new production equipment, and R&D and to achieve proprietary technology. Japanese firms have long since graduated from cost focus to producing broader lines of increasingly differentiated televisions, VCRs, and other items, using world-class product and process technology. Today, the Korean competitors such as Samsung and Gold Star have taken over the cost focus position, competing in less sophisticated, standardized products based on low labor costs.

Factor costs, a lower-order advantage, are an elusive and often fleeting source of competitive advantage for an international competitor just as they are for a domestic one. This has been apparent, for example, in apparel and construction. The global competitor, through locating activities abroad, can nullify or even exploit shifts in factor costs that work against its home country. Swedish heavy truck producers (Volvo and Saab-Scania), for example, moved some production years ago to countries such as Brazil and Argentina. Firms whose *only* advantage is lower factor costs, moreover, rarely supplant previous industry leaders. A strategy of imitating leaders is too easily matched via offshore production or offshore sourcing. Firms possessing low factor costs will be able to supplant established industry leaders only if they combine such advantages with focus on a market segment that has been ignored or vacated by established leaders and/or investment in large-scale facilities employing the best technology available on world markets. They will sustain their advantage only if they compete globally and upgrade it over time. The role of national circumstances in influencing a firm's initial advantage, the ability to exploit it through a global strategy, and the capacity and will to upgrade it over time will be central concerns in later chapters.

MOVING EARLY IN GLOBAL COMPETITION

Moving early to address each structural change is as important in global competition as it is in domestic competition, if not more so. The ultimate leaders in many global industries often are among the first firms to perceive a new strategy and implement it globally. For example, Boeing was the first global competitor in aircraft, Honda in motorcycles, IBM in computers, and Kodak in film. American and British firms persist as leaders in a wide range of consumer packaged goods in no small part because they pioneered global strategies.

Benefits to moving early are extended by global competition. Early movers reap the additional benefit of being the first to establish a worldwide network. This, in turn, can lead to reputation, scale, and learning advantages. Positions resting on such advantages can be held for decades if not longer. In tobacco, whiskey, and bone china, for example, British firms have sustained leadership for over a century despite the general decline in British industry. Similar examples of long-lived international leadership can be found in Germany (printing presses, chemicals), America (soft drinks, movies, computers), and virtually all other advanced nations.

The reasons for shifts in international competitive position are no different from the more general ones I discussed earlier. Established international leaders lose position if they stand still while industry structural change provides the opportunity for new firms to leapfrog to a new generation of products or process technology. The international scale economies, reputations, and relationships with distribution channels of established leaders are thereby nullified. For example, traditional leaders have lost out to Japanese competitors in a number of industries that were transformed by electronics (such as machine tools) or where mass-production techniques superseded traditional batch production (such as cameras or forklift trucks). Entrenched leaders are also overcome if new firms perceive and exploit new market segments that have been ignored. Italian companies saw the opportunity in domestic appliances, for example, to produce compact, standardized models using mass-production methods and to sell them to the emerging retail chains in Europe under the retailers' private labels. By aggressively developing this rapidly growing new segment, Italian appliance companies became the European leaders. Firms that move first to capitalize on the structural changes often become the new leaders because they reap the next round of early mover advantages. There are strong national influences on the ability of firms to do so, and firms from one or two nations frequently emerge as global leaders in an industry, as I have discussed earlier.

The ability to sustain leadership gained from past strategy is sometimes the result of the good fortune that there is little industry change. More likely, however, it results from constant innovation to adapt to changing circumstances. In subsequent chapters, I will explore in detail the national characteristics that cause this to happen. The forces that propel a nation's firms to sustain their positions once achieved are at the heart of national competitive advantage.

ALLIANCES AND GLOBAL STRATEGY

Strategic alliances, which I also term coalitions, are a prominent tool in carrying out global strategies. These are long-term agreements between firms that go beyond normal market transactions but fall short of merger. I use

the term alliance here to encompass a whole variety of arrangements that
include joint ventures, licenses, long-term supply agreements, and other
kinds of interfirm relationships.[24] They exist in many industries and are
particularly common in automobiles, aircraft, aircraft engines, robotics, consumer electronics, semiconductors, and pharmaceuticals.

International alliances, between firms in the same industry that are based
in different countries, are one means of competing globally. They divide
the activities in the value chain on a worldwide basis with a partner. While
they have long been employed, their character has been changing. Historically, firms from developed countries formed alliances with firms in lesser-
developed countries to perform marketing activities (often required to gain
market access). Today, more and more alliances involve firms from developed countries who team up to serve whole regions or the entire world.
Alliances also increasingly extend beyond marketing to encompass multiple
activities. All the U.S. auto companies, for example, have alliances with
Japanese companies (and in several cases with Korean firms as well) to
produce cars for sale in the United States.

Companies enter into alliances to gain a number of benefits. One is
economies of scale or learning, achieved by joining forces in marketing,
component production, or assembly of particular models. A second benefit
is access to local markets, needed technologies, or to meet government
requirements for local ownership. General Motors' alliance with Toyota
(NUMMI), for example, was principally designed, from General Motors'
perspective, to gain manufacturing expertise. A third benefit of alliances
is to spread risk. A number of pharmaceutical firms have entered into cross-
licensing agreements on new drug discoveries, for example, to hedge the
risks that their own research will prove to be unsuccessful. Finally, sophisticated competitors often employ alliances to shape the nature of competition
in an industry by, for example, licensing a technology widely in order to
promote standardization. Alliances can offset competitive disadvantages,
whether they be in factor costs or technology, while preserving independence
and foregoing the need for a costly merger.

However, alliances carry substantial costs in strategic and organizational
terms. The very real problems of coordinating with an independent partner,
who often has different and conflicting objectives, are just the start. Coordination difficulties impede the ability to gain the benefits of a global strategy.
Today's partners also often become tomorrow's competitors, especially partners with more robust competitive advantages or that are more dynamic.
Japanese firms have demonstrated this in countless industries. In addition,
partners obtain a share of profits which can be substantial. Alliances are
unstable, and many dissolve or fail. After a hopeful start, the relationship
falls apart or evolves into a merger.

Alliances are frequently transitional devices. They proliferate in industries undergoing structural change or escalating competition, where managers fear that they cannot cope. They are a response to uncertainty, and provide comfort that the firm is taking action. Alliances appear to be most common among second-tier competitors or companies trying to catch up. Alliances offer initial hope in weaker competitors of preserving independence, though ultimately a sale or merger may well follow.

Alliances are no panacea. Sustaining and improving competitive position ultimately requires that a firm develop its internal capability in areas important to competitive advantage. In the long term, global leaders rarely if ever rely on a partner for assets and skills essential to competitive advantage in their industry.

The most successful alliances are highly specific in character. The alliances employed by such worldwide leaders as IBM, Novo Industri (insulin), and Canon tend to be narrow in focus and oriented toward access to particular country markets or to particular technologies. Alliances are a tool for extending or reinforcing competitive advantage but rarely a sustainable means for creating it.

THE ROLE OF NATIONAL CIRCUMSTANCES IN COMPETITIVE SUCCESS

These principles of competitive strategy in global industries highlight the perspective we must take in isolating the role of the home nation in international competition. Different strategies are appropriate for different industries, because industry structure as well as the sources of competitive advantage are different. Within the same industry, firms can choose, and succeed with, different strategies if they are seeking different competitive advantages or targeting different industry segments.

Nations succeed where country circumstances support the pursuit of the proper strategy for a particular industry or segment. What works well in the country must lead to competitive advantage in the industry. Many national attributes affect the ease or difficulty of pursuing a particular strategy, from the norms of behavior that shape the way firms are managed to the availability of certain types of skilled personnel, the nature of home demand, and the goals of local investors.[25]

Creating competitive advantage in sophisticated industries demands improvement and innovation—finding better ways to compete and exploiting them globally, and relentlessly upgrading the firm's products and processes. Nations succeed in industries if their national circumstances provide an environment that supports this sort of behavior. Creating advantage requires insight into new ways of competing and the willingness to take risks and to invest in implementing them. Nations succeed where the national environment uniquely enables firms to perceive new strategies for competing in an industry. Nations succeed where local circumstances provide an impetus for firms to pursue such strategies early and aggressively. Nations fail where firms do not receive the right signals, are not subject to the right pressures, and do not have the right capabilities.

Sustaining competitive advantage for very long demands that its sources be *upgraded*. Upgrading advantage demands more sophisticated technology, skills and methods, and sustained investment. Nations succeed in industries where the skills and resources necessary to modify strategies are present. Firms that rest on a static conception of advantage are eventually imitated, and they lose market position.

Sustaining advantage demands continual change which is uncomfortable and organizationally difficult. Nations succeed in industries where *pressures* are created that overcome inertia and promote ongoing improvement and innovation instead of an easy life. Nations fail in industries where firms stop the upgrading process.

Nations succeed in industries where their home base advantages are valuable in other nations, and where their innovations and improvements foreshadow international needs. Success in international competition demands that firms translate domestic positions into international positions. This allows advantages from the home base to be levered and reinforced by a global strategy. Nations succeed in industries where domestic firms are pushed (or encouraged) to compete globally. The search for the determinants of national competitive advantage in industries must isolate these circumstances.

3

Determinants of National Competitive Advantage

The ways that firms create and sustain competitive advantage in global industries provide the necessary foundation for understanding the role of the home nation in the process. Yet this role is far from a simple one. Our search for a new way of understanding national advantage must begin from a number of premises.

First, the nature of competition and the sources of competitive advantage differ widely among industries and even industry segments. We must isolate the influence of the nation on the firm's ability to compete in specific industries and industry segments, and with particular strategies, rather than in broad sectors. We must allow for different sources of competitive advantage in different industries rather than rely on any single, overarching one such as labor costs or economies of scale. Since products are differentiated in many industries, we must explain why some nations' firms are better able to differentiate than others and not focus only on cost differences.

Second, global competitors often perform some activities in the value chain outside their home country. The globalization of competition does not negate the role of the home nation in competitive advantage but does change its character. It means that the task is not to explain why a firm operating exclusively in the nation is internationally successful, but why the nation is a more or less desirable *home base* for competing in an industry. The home base is where strategy is set, core product and process development takes place, and the essential and proprietary skills reside. The home base is the platform for a global strategy in the industry in which advantages drawn from the home nation are supplemented by those from an integrated, worldwide position.

Third, firms gain and sustain competitive advantage in international competition through improvement, innovation, and upgrading. Innovation, as I described earlier, includes both technology and methods, encompassing new products, new production methods, new ways of marketing, identification of new customer groups, and the like. The innovations that lead to competitive advantage involve an accumulation of small steps and protracted effort as much as dramatic breakthroughs.[1]

Firms gain advantage initially through altering the basis of competition. They sustain it through improving fast enough to stay ahead. This involves not only progress in executing existing advantages but also widening and upgrading the bases of competitive advantage over time. Often this involves the move to more sophisticated industry segments. Innovation and upgrading demand sustained investment both to perceive the appropriate directions of change and to carry them out.

As Schumpeter emphasized many decades ago, competition is profoundly dynamic in character. The nature of economic competition is not "equilibrium" but a perpetual state of change. Improvement and innovation in an industry are never-ending processes, not a single, once-and-for-all event. Today's advantages are soon superseded or nullified. At the core of explaining national advantage in an industry must be the role of the home nation in stimulating competitive improvement and innovation.[2] We must explain why a nation provides an environment in which firms improve and innovate and continue to do so faster and in the proper directions compared to their international rivals. The behavior required to create and especially to sustain competitive advantage is an unnatural act in many companies, as I emphasized in the previous chapter. We must understand what it is about a national environment that overcomes the natural desire for stability and jars firms into advancing.

Finally, firms that gain competitive advantage in an industry are often those that not only perceive a new market need or the potential of a new technology but move early and most aggressively to exploit it. Each significant structural change has the potential to nullify the competitive advantages of previous leaders, creating a new opportunity for shifting competitive position through an early response. We must explain why firms from particular nations move early and aggressively to exploit change in particular industries that foreshadows international needs.

Our task is to go beyond simply recognizing differences in competitive advantage among nations. The challenge is to explain them convincingly. It is now widely recognized that economies of scale, technological leads, and differentiated products create the conditions for trade: the nation whose firms gain them in an industry are able to export.[3] However, the ability to gain these advantages and sustain them is not a cause but an effect. The real question is *which firms* from *which nations* will reap them. We know that some nations' firms achieve technological superiority, produce more differentiated or higher-quality products, or products which are more attuned to customer needs than others. The question we must answer is why.

DETERMINANTS OF NATIONAL ADVANTAGE

Why does a nation achieve international success in a particular industry? The answer lies in four broad attributes of a nation that shape the environment in which local firms compete that promote or impede the creation of competitive advantage (see Figure 3–1):

1. *Factor conditions.* The nation's position in factors of production, such as skilled labor or infrastructure, necessary to compete in a given industry.

2. *Demand conditions.* The nature of home demand for the industry's product or service.

3. *Related and supporting industries.* The presence or absence in the nation of supplier industries and related industries[4] that are internationally competitive.

4. *Firm strategy, structure, and rivalry.* The conditions in the nation governing how companies are created, organized, and managed, and the nature of domestic rivalry.

The determinants, individually and as a system, create the context in which a nation's firms are born and compete: the availability of resources and skills necessary for competitive advantage in an industry; the information that shapes what opportunities are perceived and the directions in which resources and skills are deployed; the goals of the owners, managers, and employees that are involved in or carry out competition; and most importantly, the *pressures* on firms to invest and innovate.[5]

Firms gain competitive advantage where their home base allows and supports the most rapid accumulation of specialized assets and skills, sometimes due solely to greater commitment. Firms gain competitive advantage in industries when their home base affords better ongoing information and insight into product and process needs.[6] Firms gain competitive advantage when the goals of owners, managers, and employees support intense commitment and sustained investment. Ultimately, nations succeed in particular industries because their home environment is the most dynamic and the most challenging, and stimulates and prods firms to upgrade and widen their advantages over time.

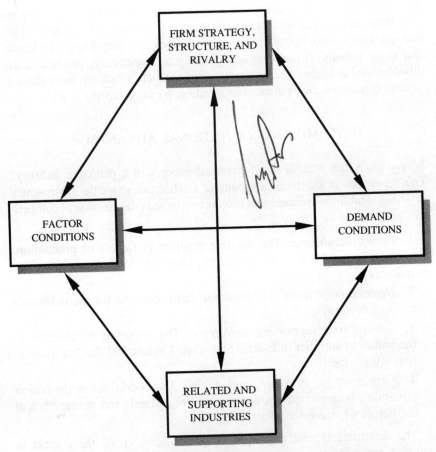

FIRM STRATEGY,
STRUCTURE, AND
RIVALRY

FACTOR
CONDITIONS

DEMAND
CONDITIONS

RELATED AND
SUPPORTING
INDUSTRIES

FIGURE 3–1 The Determinants of National Advantage

Nations are most likely to succeed in industries or industry segments where the national "diamond," a term I will use to refer to the determinants as a system, is the most favorable. This is not to say that all a nation's firms will achieve competitive advantage in an industry. In fact, the most dynamic the national environment, the more likely it is that some firms will fail, because not all have equal skills and resources nor do they exploit the national environment equally well. Yet those companies that emerge from such an environment will prosper in international competition.

The "diamond" is a mutually reinforcing system. The effect of one determinant is contingent on the state of others. Favorable demand conditions, for example, will not lead to competitive advantage unless the state of rivalry is sufficient to cause firms to respond to them. Advantages in one determinant can also create or upgrade advantages in others.[7]

Competitive advantage based on only one or two determinants is possible in natural resource-dependent industries or industries involving little sophisticated technology or skills. Such advantage usually proves unsustainable, however, because it shifts rapidly and global competitors can easily circumvent it. Advantages throughout the "diamond" are necessary for achieving and sustaining competitive success in the knowledge-intensive industries that form the backbone of advanced economies. Advantage in every determinant is not a prerequisite for competitive advantage in an industry. The interplay of advantage in many determinants yields self-reinforcing benefits that are extremely hard for foreign rivals to nullify or replicate.

Two additional variables can influence the national system in important ways, and are necessary to complete the theory. These are chance and government. Chance events are developments outside the control of firms (and usually the nation's government), such as pure inventions, breakthroughs in basic technologies, wars, external political developments, and major shifts in foreign market demand. They create discontinuities that can unfreeze or reshape industry structure and provide the opportunity for one nation's firms to supplant another's. They have played an important role in shifting competitive advantage in many industries.

The final element necessary to complete the picture is government. Government, at all levels, can improve or detract from the national advantage. This role is seen most clearly by examining how policies influence each of the determinants. Antitrust policy affects domestic rivalry. Regulation can alter home demand conditions. Investments in education can change factor conditions. Government purchases can stimulate related and supporting industries. Policies implemented without consideration of how they influence the entire system of determinants are as likely to undermine national advantage as enhance it.

The balance of this chapter will explore the influence of the determinants individually and jointly on the ability of a nation's firms to achieve competitive advantage in a particular industry. In the next chapter, I will turn to the way the determinants affect each other as a dynamic and evolving system.[8]

The basic unit of analysis for understanding national advantage is the industry. Nations succeed not in isolated industries, however, but in *clusters* of industries connected through vertical and horizontal relationships. A nation's economy contains a mix of clusters, whose makeup and sources of competitive advantage (or disadvantage) reflect the state of the economy's development. How entire national economies develop in international competitive terms will be a subject I will return to later.

FACTOR CONDITIONS

Each nation possesses what economists have termed *factors of production*. Factors of production are nothing more than the inputs necessary to compete in any industry, such as labor, arable land, natural resources, capital, and infrastructure. While the terminology may be awkward to some, it is so deeply embedded in the language of economics, and so vital to the theory of trade, that I will adopt it throughout this book.

The standard theory of trade rests on factors of production. According to the theory, nations are endowed with differing stocks of factors. A nation will export those goods which make intensive use of the factors with which it is relatively well endowed.[9] The United States, for example, has been a substantial exporter of agricultural goods, reflecting in part its unusual abundance of large tracts of arable land.

A nation's endowment of factors clearly plays a role in the competitive advantage of a nation's firms, as the rapid growth of manufacturing in low-wage countries such as Hong Kong, Taiwan, and more recently, Thailand attests. But the role of factors is different and far more complex than is often understood. The factors most important to competitive advantage in most industries, especially the industries most vital to productivity growth in advanced economies, are not inherited but are created within a nation, through processes that differ widely across nations and among industries. Thus, the stock of factors at any particular time is less important than the rate at which they are created, upgraded, and made more specialized to particular industries. More surprising, perhaps, is that an abundance of factors may undermine instead of enhance competitive advantage. Selective disadvantages in factors, through influencing strategy and innovation, often contribute to sustained competitive success.

FACTOR ENDOWMENT

To explore the role of factors in the competitive advantage of a nation, the concept must be made more meaningful to industry competition. Factors of production are often described in very broad terms such as land, labor, and capital, which are too general to bear on competitive advantage in strategically distinct industries.[10] Factors can be grouped into a number of broad categories:

- *Human resources:* the quantity, skills, and cost of personnel (including management), taking into account standard working hours and work ethic. Human resources can be divided into a myriad of categories, such as toolmakers, electrical engineers with PhDs, applications programmers, and so on.
- *Physical resources:* the abundance, quality, accessibility, and cost of the nation's land, water, mineral, or timber deposits, hydroelectric power sources, fishing grounds, and other physical traits. Climatic conditions can be viewed as part of a nation's physical resources,

as can a nation's location and geographic size. Location, relative to other nations that are suppliers or markets, affects transportation costs and the ease of cultural and business interchange. For example, proximity to Germany has had an important historical influence on Swedish industry. The time zone of a nation relative to other nations may also be significant in a world of instantaneous global communications. London's position between the United States and Japan is often identified as an advantage in financial service industries, because London-based firms can do business with both Japan and the United States during a normal working day.

- *Knowledge resources:* the nation's stock of scientific, technical, and market knowledge bearing on goods and services. Knowledge resources reside in universities, government research institutes, private research facilities, government statistical agencies, business and scientific literature, market research reports and databases, trade associations, and other sources. A nation's scientific and other knowledge resources can be subdivided into a myriad of disciplines, such as acoustics, materials science, and soil chemistry.

- *Capital resources:* the amount and cost of capital available to finance industry. Capital is not homogeneous, but comes in various forms such as unsecured debt, secured debt, "junk" (high-risk, high-yield) bonds, equity, and venture capital. There are varying terms and conditions attached to each form. The total stock of capital resources in a country, and the forms in which it is deployed, are affected by the national rate of savings and by the structure of national capital markets, both of which vary widely among nations. The globalization of capital markets, and the large capital flows among nations, is slowly making national conditions more similar. However, substantial differences remain and are likely to do so indefinitely.

- *Infrastructure:* the type, quality, and user cost of infrastructure available that affects competition, including the transportation system, the communications system, mail and parcel delivery, payments or funds transfer, health care, and so on. Infrastructure also includes such things as the housing stock and cultural institutions, which affect the quality of life and the attractiveness of a nation as a place to live and work.

The mix of factors employed (known as factor proportions) differs widely among industries. A nation's firms gain competitive advantage if they possess low-cost or uniquely high-quality factors of the particular types that are significant to competition in a particular industry. Singapore's location on a major trading route between Japan and the Middle East has made it a center for ship repair. Swiss ability to deal with different languages and cultures (Switzerland contains German-, French-, and Italian-speaking regions) is an advantage in services such as banking, trading, and logistics management. Germany and Switzerland have pools of workers uniquely skilled in optics-related fields. Such a match between industries and the factors present in a nation is what the standard theory of comparative advantage is all about.

Yet the role of factor endowment is more complicated. Competitive advantage from factors depends on *how efficiently and effectively they are deployed*. This reflects the choices made by a nation's firms about how to mobilize factors as well as the technology (including procedures and routines) used to do so.[11] Indeed, the value of particular factors can be dramatically altered by the choice of technology. Not only how but *where* factors are deployed in an economy is crucial, because technological expertise and the most capable human resources can often be utilized in a variety of industries. The mere availability of factors is not sufficient to explain competitive success; indeed, virtually all nations have some attractive factor pools that have never been deployed in appropriate industries or have been deployed poorly. Other determinants in the "diamond" will be necessary to explain where factor advantage translates into international success, because these shape the way factors are deployed.

As I discussed earlier, most advanced and even newly industrialized nations today have comparable factor endowments in terms of infrastructure; many also have similar pools of high school- and even university-educated workers (Korea, for example, has nearly 100 percent literacy and over two hundred institutions of higher learning). At the same time, globalization has made local availability of some factors less essential. The modern global corporation can source factors from other nations by purchasing from them or locating activities there. Once again, it is not mere access to factors but the ability to deploy them productively that takes on central importance to competitive advantage.

A final point is that human resources, knowledge, and capital factors can be mobile among nations. Skilled people move among nations, as does scientific and technical knowledge. This mobility has been enhanced by greater international communication and easier movement.[12] Factor availability in a nation is not an advantage if the factors leave. Other determinants will be necessary to explain those nations to which mobile factors are attracted and where they can be most productively deployed.

HIERARCHIES AMONG FACTORS

To understand the enduring role of factors in competitive advantage, it is increasingly necessary to discriminate among types of factors. Two particularly important distinctions stand out. The first is that between basic and advanced factors. *Basic factors* include natural resources, climate, location, unskilled and semiskilled labor, and debt capital. *Advanced factors* include modern digital data communications infrastructure, highly educated personnel such as graduate engineers and computer scientists, and university research institutes in sophisticated disciplines.

Few factors of production are truly inherited by a nation. Most must be developed over time through investment, and the extent and difficulty of the required investment varies dramatically. The distinction between basic and advanced factors, while inevitably a matter of degree, seeks to capture these distinctions. Basic factors are passively inherited, or their creation requires relatively modest or unsophisticated private and social investment. Increasingly, such factors are either unimportant to national competitive advantage or the advantage they provide for a nation's firms is unsustainable.

The importance of basic factors has been undermined by either their diminished necessity, their widening availability, or ready access to them by global firms through foreign activities or sourcing on international markets. These same considerations make the returns available to basic factors low, irrespective of their location. An unskilled worker is increasingly vulnerable to pressures on wages, even if the worker is American or German. Basic factors may explain some of the trade *within* firms, reflecting the location of selected activities in various nations to tap into low factor costs. But they do not explain the location of the home base in most industries.[13]

Basic factors remain important in extractive or agriculturally based industries (such as timber and soybeans) and in those where technological and skill requirements are modest and technology is widely available. An example is the construction of civil projects (such as apartments and schools) with a low engineering content. Korean firms have enjoyed international success in such projects, based in part on the availability of low-cost and disciplined Korean labor. However, firms from nations with even lower wages are supplanting Korean firms, and competitors from more advanced nations such as Italy are sourcing cheap labor pools locally in nations where they bid on international contracts or from other developing countries (for instance, India), nullifying the Korean advantage. The result, combined with the decline in Middle East projects, is that the Korean construction industry is in sharp decline, an indication of how advantages due only to basic factors are often fleeting.

Advanced factors are now the most significant ones for competitive advantage. They are necessary to achieve higher-order competitive advantages such as differentiated products and proprietary production technology. They are scarcer because their development demands large and often sustained investments in both human and physical capital. The institutions required to create truly advanced factors (such as educational programs) themselves require sophisticated human resources and/or technology. Advanced factors

are also more difficult to procure in global markets or to tap from afar via
foreign subsidiaries. They are integral to the design and development of a
firm's products and processes as well as its capacity to innovate, which
best takes place at the home base and must be closely connected to the
firm's overall strategy.

An important role for advanced factors is evident in numerous industries.
Denmark's success in enzymes reflects a base of sophisticated scientific
knowledge in fermentation, for example, and its success in furniture reflects
a pool of university-trained furniture designers. America's unique stock of
skilled personnel and scientific expertise in both computer hardware and
software has yielded significant advantage not only in these industries but
also in other U.S. industries such as medical electronics and financial services.
Since the 1950s, Japan's large pool of engineers (reflecting a much higher
number of engineering graduates per capita than almost any other nation)
has been more important to success in numerous Japanese industries than
the low wages of Japanese production workers.

It is important to recognize that a nation's advanced factors are often
built upon basic factors. A supply of doctoral-level biologists, for example,
requires a pool of talented university graduates in the field. This means
that basic factor pools, while rarely a sustainable advantage in and of themselves, must be of sufficient quantity and quality to allow for the creation
of related advanced factors.

The second important distinction among factors of production is their
specificity. *Generalized* factors include the highway system, a supply of
debt capital, or a pool of well-motivated employees with college educations.
They can be deployed in a wide range of industries. *Specialized* factors
involve narrowly skilled personnel, infrastructure with specific properties,
knowledge bases in particular fields, and other factors with relevance to a
limited range or even to just a single industry. Examples would be a scientific
institute with expertise in optics, a port specialized in handling bulk chemicals,
a cadre of skilled model makers for automobiles, or a pool of venture
capital seeking to fund software companies.[14] More advanced factors tend
also to be more specialized, though not in all cases. For example, highly
skilled computer programmers, while an advanced factor pool, can be deployed in a wide range of industries.

Specialized factors provide more decisive and sustainable bases for competitive advantage than generalized factors. Generalized factors support
only more rudimentary types of advantage. They are usually available in
many nations, and tend to be more easily nullified, circumvented, or
sourced through global corporate networks. Activities dependent on generalized factors (such as labor-intensive assembly operations requiring semiskilled employees) can often be readily performed at a distance from the
home base.

Specialized factors require more focused, and often riskier, private and social investment. They depend in many cases on already having a base of generalized factors. Both of these things make them scarcer. Specialized factors are usually necessary in the more complex or proprietary company activities, and they are necessary for more sophisticated forms of competitive advantage. This makes them integral to innovation. Specialized factors are necessary at a firm's home base and less effective at a foreign site. It is also frequently difficult for foreign firms to gain equal access to specialized factors (as well as to advanced ones). Non-Japanese firms, for example, have difficulty hiring the top Japanese engineering graduates or gaining equivalent access to local university research programs.

The most significant and sustainable competitive advantage results when a nation possesses factors needed for competing in a particular industry that are both advanced and specialized. The availability and quality of advanced and specialized factors determine the sophistication of competitive advantage that can potentially be achieved and its rate of upgrading. In optics, for example, an important reason why German firms have been able to steadily improve product performance and quality is the availability of graduates from special university programs in optical physics and a pool of highly skilled workers trained in specialized apprenticeship programs.

In contrast, competitive advantage based on basic/generalized factors is unsophisticated and often fleeting. It lasts only until some new nation, often one advancing up the development ladder, is able to match them.[15] These considerations help explain the apparent paradox I noted in the previous chapter. To sustain international competitive advantage, a nation's firms often must deliberately nullify or supplant today's basic factor advantages even though they still persist. What jars a nation's firms away from resting on basic/generalized factors becomes an important question we must address; other determinants in the "diamond" provide some of the answers.

There is an important dynamic character to factor advantage. The standard for what constitutes an advanced factor rises continually, as the state of knowledge, the state of science, and the state of practice improve. The knowledge of an electrical engineer who graduated in 1965, for example, is nearly obsolete today. Only through continuous training and upgrading of skills could the 1965 graduate have the same capability as one in 1990. Over time, master's and even doctoral training in the field have become necessary to work on frontier problems.

The standard for specialization also tends to rise continuously, as today's specialized factors tend to become tomorrow's generalized factors. A college graduate in electrical engineering was once a specialized factor, finding employment in relatively few industries. Today, these skills are needed in many industries and subfields have proliferated. The tendency for factors to lose specialization over time is particularly evident in scientific disciplines where subspecialties emerge, but is apparent as well in human resources, infrastructure, and even sources of capital.[16]

A factor pool is a depreciating basis for sustainable advantage unless it is constantly upgraded and specialized. Skilled human resources and knowledge resources, perhaps the two most important categories of factors for upgrading competitive advantage, are particularly depreciating assets, though infrastructure is not far behind. This suggests that possessing factor advantage at any one point in time is far from sufficient to explain sustained national success.

FACTOR CREATION

Another important distinction among factors, apparent in my earlier discussion, is whether they are inherited by a nation, such as its natural resources or location, or were created. Those factors most important in achieving higher-order and more sustainable competitive advantage, the more advanced and specialized ones, are created. A nation's telecommunications system or pool of microbiologists is created through *investments* made by individuals seeking to develop their skills, firms seeking the tools necessary for competing, and social institutions or governments hoping to benefit society or the economy.[17] Factor-creating mechanisms include public and private educational institutions, apprenticeship programs, government and private research institutes, and bodies providing infrastructure such as government-owned port authorities or community hospitals. The rising world standard for factors means that deriving competitive advantage from factors requires not just one-time investment but continual reinvestment to upgrade their quality, not to mention keeping the current pool of factors from depreciating.[18] Advanced and specialized factors demand the greatest, most sustained investment in the most difficult-to-make forms.

Nations succeed in industries where they are particularly good at creating and, most importantly, upgrading the needed factors. Thus nations will be competitive where they possess unusually high quality institutional mechanisms for specialized factor creation.[19] The factor-creating mechanisms in a nation are more important to competitive advantage than the nation's current factor pool, as numerous examples I will discuss will illustrate.

Furthermore, a *private sector* role in factor creation is necessary to attain factor advantage in most industries. Advanced and specialized factors are the most important to competitive advantage, and firms are best positioned to know which of these are necessary to compete in their industries. Government investments in factor creation usually concentrate on more basic and generalized factors. For example, investments in basic research, while important in seeding possibilities for commercial innovation, will not lead to competitive advantage unless transmitted to and further developed by industry. Government efforts to create advanced and specialized factors often fail unless they are closely coupled to industry, because government entities are notoriously slow or unable to identify new fields or the specialized needs of particular industries. A significant direct investment by firms, trade associations, and individuals in factor creation, as well as close coupling of private and public investments, are characteristic of internationally successful national industries.

There are sharp differences among nations in the areas in which investments in factor creation are made, as well as in the nature and quality of the factor-creating mechanisms. In Denmark, for example, there are two hospitals that specialize in treating patients and conducting research in diabetes. They are owned by the two world-ranking Danish insulin producers, Novo Industri and Nordisk Insulin. In Germany, apprenticeship programs exist in such specialized fields as printing, automotive assembly, and toolmaking. America has a highly developed network of agricultural colleges and an Agricultural Extension Service that widely disseminates improvements in agricultural technology. Computer science is another field in which there are numerous educational programs and research efforts.

Some national differences in the mechanisms for factor creation extend to many industries. In Japan, for example, factor creation tends to be private while in Sweden the public role is much greater. In Italy, much factor creation is informal through transfers of knowledge within extended families. The character of the institutional mechanisms prevalent in a nation for factor creation, which is partly a function of its social and political values and history, constrains to some extent the range of industries in which a nation can compete, as we will see.

No nation can possibly create and upgrade all types and varieties of factors. Which types are created and upgraded, and how effectively, depends heavily on the other determinants, such as home demand conditions, the presence of related and supporting industries, company goals, and the nature of domestic rivalry. Even the direction of government investments is strongly influenced by the other determinants. The presence of advanced and specialized factors in a nation is often not only a cause of national advantage but, at least in part, an effect.

SELECTIVE FACTOR DISADVANTAGES

Competitive advantage can grow out of *disadvantage* in some factors. In a narrow conception of international competition, competitive advantage results from factor abundance and disadvantages in factors cannot be overcome because technology is taken as a given. In actual competition, however, the abundance or low cost of a factor often leads to its inefficient deployment.[20] In contrast, disadvantages in *basic* factors, such as labor shortages, lack of domestic raw materials, or a harsh climate, create pressures to innovate around them. A steady rise in the nation's exchange rate can have the same effect.[21] The result is that the firm's competitive advantage can be upgraded and made more sustainable. What is a disadvantage in a narrow conception of competition can become an advantage in a more dynamic one.

Italian steel producers, for example, faced high capital costs, high energy costs, and no local raw materials. Privately owned firms (such as Grupo Lucchini) were concentrated in the area around Brescia in northern Lombardy, while state-owned producers were mostly in the south, near major ports. Private firms faced high logistical costs, due to distance from ports and an inefficient (and state-owned) Italian transportation system. The result was the pioneering of mini-mill technology, in which Brescia-area steel producers have emerged as perhaps the world leaders. Mini-mills require modest capital investment, use less energy, and employ scrap metal as the feedstock. They are efficient at small scale and allow producers to locate production facilities close to buyers and sources of scrap. Italian firms (such as Danieli) are not only important mini-mill operators but have also become world leaders in selling equipment for mini-mills.

The need for factors, particularly basic and generalized factors such as semiskilled labor or local raw materials, can often be circumvented, eliminated, or reduced through innovation. Automation reduces labor content, for example, while new materials eliminate the need for other materials. The returns from factor-saving innovations frequently far exceed their cost,[22] sometimes by yielding second-order benefits (for example, reducing labor content may well reduce the rate of defects and raise product quality) that are sometimes hard to anticipate.

Innovations to circumvent selective disadvantages not only economize on factor utilization but can create new factor advantages, because a nation's firms will innovate to offset selective disadvantages in ways that play to local strength, such as using available local infrastructure, materials, or types of labor. Most importantly, however, innovating around basic factor disadvantages leads firms to *upgrade* by developing more sophisticated competitive advantages (such as proprietary technology or economies of scale due to more automated facilities) that can be sustained longer and which may also support higher prices. At the same time, pressures are created to upgrade and specialize more rapidly other factors such as skilled human resources or infrastructure in order to keep pace.

A sports analogy illustrates some of these points. Some nations that have excelled in slalom skiing, such as Sweden, do not have large mountains at home with long ski runs. Instead, they have relatively small mountains and short runs. Aspiring skiers, to make such hills more interesting, make many turns and are pushed to refine their technique.

The role of selective factor disadvantages results from the fact that the rate and direction of improvement and innovation is a function of attention and effort. Firms have numerous avenues for innovation and face much uncertainty about all the possible directions and their payoffs. Innovation is disruptive. Firms concentrate their attention on those avenues they perceive to be the most promising, and particularly on those that address problems seen as the most pressing.

Innovation to offset selective weaknesses is more likely than innovation to exploit strengths. Selective disadvantages create visible bottlenecks, obvious threats, and clear targets for improving competitive position. They prod or force a nation's firms into new solutions.[23] This theme, that pressure instead of abundance or a comfortable environment underpins true competitive advantage, will resonate throughout this book.

Disadvantages in basic factors are part of what jars firms away from resting on basic factor costs and into seeking higher-order advantages. In contrast, local abundance of basic factors lulls firms into complacency and deters the application of advanced technology. The resulting competitive advantages are often fleeting as so is productivity growth.

Factor disadvantages that stimulate innovation must be *selective* to motivate and not discourage, involving some but not all factors. A lack of pressure means there is rarely progress, but too much adversity leads to paralysis. An intermediate level of pressure, involving a balance of advantage in some areas and disadvantage in selected others, seems to be the best combination for improvement and innovation.[24]

Selective disadvantages best contribute to competitive advantage when they *send the proper signals* about circumstances that will ultimately confront firms elsewhere. A nation's firms then become early and aggressive movers in dealing with problems that will be widespread. A good example is Switzerland. It was the nation that experienced perhaps the first labor shortages in the post–World War II period and was reluctant to allow immigration. This led Swiss firms earlier than most to upgrade labor productivity and seek higher value, and more sustainable, market segments. Firms from other nations had access to more ample supplies of workers and placed their attention elsewhere.

The most obvious case of selective disadvantage is where local firms experience high absolute cost of a factor compared to foreign rivals. Japanese firms in a variety of industries, for example, faced extremely high land cost and severe factory space constraints. To circumvent these difficulties, they created just-in-time and other space-saving production techniques that also dramatically reduced needed inventory. Factor shortages, unavailability, or strong restrictions on the use of particular factors are as or more stimulating to innovation as high factor costs.

Innovation will also be stimulated if a nation's firms experience trends in factor costs early, even if other nations catch up. Particularly rapid or visible changes in the cost or availability of factors in a nation compared with others will also lead local firms to act earlier, since the importance of selective disadvantages lies in focusing attention and effort on addressing important perceived problems or constraints. Finally, high *relative* cost of a factor in a nation may stimulate innovations that circumvent it, even if the absolute cost of the factor is comparable to that in other nations. If a nation faces a high relative cost of unskilled to skilled labor, for example, local firms may place more attention on eliminating unskilled labor even if wage rates are lower than elsewhere. This has taken place, for example, in a variety of Italian industries where firms are among the most automated in the world (Italy is also a leader in factory automation equipment).

Selective factor disadvantages were prevalent in the industries we studied, and were important to the process by which nations' firms gained competitive advantage. Around the turn of the twentieth century, for example, BASF and Hoechst (Germany) spent many years developing a synthetic indigo dye to reduce dependence on imported natural dye unavailable at home. There was less pressure to innovate in Britain because of large supplies of natural indigo in the colonies. Lack of domestic raw materials was a frequent spur to innovate in a national industry.

Scarce, expensive, or difficult-to-fire labor was another prominent driver of innovation, especially in German, Swiss, Swedish, Japanese, and Italian industries. Lifetime employment, or constraints on firing workers, made Japanese, Swedish, and Italian firms careful about hiring and prone to automate. They also moved rapidly toward more differentiated market segments.

Selective disadvantages in climate or geography were also common stimuli to innovation. Swedish firms are leaders in prefabricated housing, for example, in part because of a short building season and very high wages for construction workers. This put a premium on designs that were efficient to construct. Distance from markets has led to a disproportionate rate of innovation in logistical methods in Japan and Sweden.

The positive role of selective disadvantages in stimulating innovation, however, depends on the other determinants. Firms must have access to appropriate human resources to support innovation in the industry, for example, and supportive home demand conditions. Another precondition is goals that lead to sustained commitment to the industry. Without commitment, firms will harvest or cede competitive position in the face of disadvantages rather than innovate. Also particularly significant is the presence of active domestic rivalry, which pressures firms to seek more durable advantages over their local rivals.

Other parts of the "diamond," then, influence whether a nation's firms innovate around selective factor disadvantages rather than take the easy but less desirable solution (for competitive advantage) of sourcing factors abroad. When these broader conditions for innovation are not present, selective factor disadvantages will not work. Faced with high relative labor costs, for example, American consumer electronics firms moved to locate labor-intensive activities in Taiwan and other Asian countries, leaving the product and production process essentially the same. This response led only to labor cost parity, instead of upgrading the sources of competitive advantage. Japanese rivals, facing intense domestic rivalry and a mature home market, set out instead to eliminate labor through automation. Doing so involved reducing the number of components which further lowered cost and improved quality. Japanese firms were soon building assembly plants in the United States, the place American firms had sought to avoid.

The example of the Dutch cut flower industry, while drawn from a nation we did not study in depth, is so clear an example summarizing the influence of selective factor disadvantage that I could not resist including it.[25] Holland, by far the world leader, exports over $1 billion of cut flowers per year despite its cold, grey climate. This selective disadvantage has led to innovations in glass house growing techniques, new strains of flowers, energy conservation, and other techniques that have created sustainable competitive advantages in the industry. Dutch innovation proceeded in a direction that took advantage of Holland's large supply of natural gas, illustrating how the directions of innovation around disadvantages in one factor often reflect the supply of others.

The impetus of an inhospitable climate forced an approach to competing in the industry that is much more favorable to upgrading advantage than traditional cultivation techniques. It has allowed the Dutch industry to achieve differentiation based on freshness, quality, and variety. Yet the Dutch success and ability to upgrade advantage have also depended heavily on the other determinants. One is the existence of highly specialized research organizations in flower cultivation, packaging, and shipping (such as the Sprenger Institute and the Aalsmeer Research Station). Holland has developed a highly efficient infrastructure in flower handling and air freight.[26] A strong home demand was present in Holland for fresh flowers year-round that triggered initial interest in the industry by entrepreneurs. Active domestic rivalry has taken place at the grower, auction house (there are ten in Holland), and marketer levels. Finally, specialized home-based suppliers of important inputs such as glass houses, who also sell internationally, have contributed to upgrading.

DEMAND CONDITIONS

The second broad determinant of national competitive advantage in an industry is home demand conditions for the industry's product or service. Home
demand conditions had some influence in nearly every industry we studied.[27]
While home demand, through its influence on economies of scale, can
confer static efficiencies, its far more important influence is dynamic. It
shapes the rate and character of improvement and innovation by a nation's
firms. Three broad attributes of home demand are significant: the composition
(or nature of buyer needs) of home demand, the size and pattern of growth
of home demand, and the mechanisms by which a nation's domestic preferences are transmitted to foreign markets. The significance of the latter two
is contingent on the first. The *quality* of home demand, in terms that I
will describe, is more important than the *quantity* of home demand in determining competitive advantage.

HOME DEMAND COMPOSITION

The most important influence of home demand on competitive advantage
is through the mix and character of home buyer needs.[28] The composition
of home demand shapes how firms perceive, interpret, and respond to buyer
needs. Nations gain competitive advantage in industries or industry segments
where the home demand gives local firms a clearer or earlier picture of
buyer needs than foreign rivals can have.[29] Nations also gain advantage if
home buyers *pressure* local firms to innovate faster and achieve more sophisticated competitive advantages compared to foreign rivals. Dissimilarities
among nations in the nature of home demand underlie these benefits.

It might seem that home demand would be rendered less significant by
the globalization of competition, but this is not the case. The home market
usually has a disproportionate impact on a firm's ability to perceive and
interpret buyer needs for a number of reasons.[30] The first is simply attention.
Attention to nearby needs is the most sensitive, and understanding them is
the least costly. Product development teams, as well as the managers who
approve new products, are based with rare exceptions in the home market.
Pride and ego also focus attention on success in meeting needs in the home
market. Finally, pressures from buyers to improve products are most acutely
felt in the home market, where proximity and cultural similarity make for
clearer communications.

The importance of the home market goes beyond greater attention, however. Firms are better able to perceive, understand, and act on buyer needs
in their home market and tend to be more confident in doing so. Understanding
needs requires access to buyers, open communication between them and a
firm's top technical and managerial personnel, and an intuitive grasp of
buyers' circumstances. This is hard enough with home buyers. It is extremely

difficult to achieve, in practice, with foreign buyers because of distance from headquarters and because the firm is not truly an insider with full acceptance and access.[31] Even if a subsidiary is able to gain sufficient access to fully understand foreign buyer needs and how they are changing, it is a daunting task to communicate them credibly to headquarters. Where foreign and home market needs diverge, signals from the home market usually dominate. A product's fundamental or core design nearly always reflects home market needs.[32] All these considerations make proximity to the right type of buyers of decisive importance in national competitive advantage. Selling to foreign buyers is not a good substitute. There are three characteristics of the composition of home demand particularly significant to achieving national competitive advantage:

Segment Structure of Demand. The first is the segment structure of home demand, or the distribution of demand for particular varieties. In most industries, demand is segmented. In commercial aircraft, for example, there is a range of aircraft sizes and configurations which appeals to airlines with differing route structures and other circumstances. Some segments are more global than others.

A nation's firms are likely to gain competitive advantage in global segments that represent a large or highly visible share of home demand but account for a less significant share in other nations. In electrical transmission equipment, for example, Sweden is a leader in high voltage distribution (HVDC) equipment, used for transporting high voltage over long distances. This reflects large relative demand in this segment in Sweden because of the remoteness of Sweden's energy-intensive steel and paper industries as well as the fact that sources of electric power in Sweden are far removed from southern population centers.

It has been recognized that size of segments may be important to national advantage where there are significant economies of scale or learning.[33] Nations in which a segment is largest in absolute terms may gain advantages in reaping economies of scale. However, the absolute size of segments within a nation plays a complicated role in competitive national advantage, because firms compete globally and can achieve a large scale even if their home market is small.[34]

The more significant role of segment structure at home is in shaping the attention and priorities of a nation's firms. The relatively large segments in a nation receive the greatest and earliest attention by the nation's firms. Smaller segments, or those perceived as less desirable, are frequently accorded lower priority in allocating product design, manufacturing, and marketing resources, especially in a new or developing industry where firms are preoccupied with creating and perfecting the basic product and keeping up with growth in demand. Segments that are deemed less profitable (for example, those at the low end of the market, those perceived as oddball or unusual or those without the possibility for selling profitable ancillary services) will also be ignored. Such segments in the nation are prone to being preempted by foreign competitors. Even if they are not preempted, firms are more likely to cede such "less desirable" segments to foreign rivals over time.

A good example of these considerations is Airbus Industries' entry into commercial airliners. Airbus identified a segment of the market that had been ignored by Boeing and other U.S. manufacturers, a relatively large-capacity plane for short hauls. Such a need was quite significant in Europe with its numerous capital cities within short flying distances and served by few national airlines. American cities are more widely dispersed and the volume of traffic between most city pairs spread over a generally larger number of competitors could be met with a 100- to 200-seat aircraft. The attention of the European consortium was focused heavily on a segment which U.S. manufacturers viewed as secondary.

Another example is microwave equipment, where Japan's mountainous terrain makes microwave transmission an attractive alternative to copper cables. Japan had to rebuild its infrastructure after World War II, and Nippon Telephone and Telegraph aggressively built microwave capacity. Microwave technology was not well developed before the war, and nations whose infrastructure had not been severely damaged were heavily invested in cable. The large relative Japanese home demand for microwave led to intense attention to this technology and, ultimately, to a strong international position. Similarly, hydraulic excavators represent by far the most widely used type of construction equipment in the Japanese home market, whereas in other advanced nations its share of sales volume is far lower. Excavators are one of the few segments where Caterpillar does not hold a major share of the world market, and there is a large group of vigorous Japanese international competitors.

One implication of the importance of segment structure is that small nations can be competitive in segments which represent an important share of local demand but a small share of demand elsewhere, even if the *absolute* size of the segment is greater in other nations. Swiss firms, for example, have long held a leading position in equipment and services for tunnelling, where unusual Swiss needs are obvious. Similarly, Swedish firms have long been leaders in equipment and rock drills for mining in very hard rock, the dominant geology encounterd in Swedish mining. American firms lead in rotary mining equipment, used principally for oil and gas exploration and production. This is the dominant segment in the United States. Firms from smaller nations often employ global focus strategies in which they concentrate on such a segment of the market worldwide.

In some industries, the *range* of segments in the home market influences competitive advantage. In highly engineered or tailored products and services, exposure to a wide range of significant segments at home provides experience that can be used in entering foreign markets. In commercial air-conditioning equipment, there are many segments reflecting differences in climate, building type, and end-user industry. One of the advantages of U.S. firms was that almost every climatic and industry condition encountered in other countries in commercial air-conditioning had already been experienced somewhere in the United States.

Particularly valuable in a nation is the presence of large segments that require more sophisticated forms of competitive advantage. Their presence provides a visible path for local firms to upgrade their competitive advantage over time, and positions in such segments are more sustainable.

Sophisticated and Demanding Buyers. More important than the mix of segments *per se* is the nature of home buyers. A nation's firms gain competitive advantage if domestic buyers are, or are among, the world's most sophisticated and demanding buyers for the product or service. Such buyers provide a window into the most advanced buyer needs. Proximity, both physical and cultural, to these buyers helps a nation's firms perceive new needs. It also allows close contact in the development process and, when buyers are companies, creates opportunities to engage in joint development work in ways that are difficult for foreign firms to match.

Sophisticated and demanding buyers pressure local firms to meet high standards in terms of product quality, features, and service. In Japan, for example, consumers are highly sophisticated and knowledgeable in purchasing audio equipment. Audio equipment is a status item, and Japanese consumers gather extensive product information and want the latest, best models. Their desire for quality leads to rapid improvement by manufacturers, and their desire to have the latest features leads to rapid saturation of new models.[35] The presence of sophisticated and demanding buyers is as, or more, important to sustaining advantage as to creating it. Local firms are prodded to improve and to move into newer and more advanced segments over time, often upgrading competitive advantage in the process.

Buyers are demanding where home product needs in an industry are especially stringent or challenging because of local circumstances. In very large diesel truck engines, America's vast road network and spread-out population creates unique needs for performance. Cummins, Caterpillar, and Detroit Diesel are strong international competitors. In residential air-conditioning, Japanese firms have penetrated international markets with their compact, quiet units. Air-conditioning is much needed in Japan because of the hot and humid summers. Japanese homes are small and tightly packed together, however, and a bulky, noisy air-conditioner is simply unacceptable. This, along with high energy costs, pushed Japanese firms to pioneer energy-saving rotary compressors. This example can be extended to a number of other Japanese industries. Japanese home market conditions lead to an intense effort to innovate by producing products that are *kei-haku-tan-sho* (light, thin, short, small). The result is a constant stream of compact, portable, multifunctional products that are well accepted internationally.

Industrial buyers sometimes are unusually demanding because they face *selective factor disadvantages* in competing in their own industry. A good example is the American oil industry. The continental United States has been intensely drilled, and wells are being drilled in increasingly difficult and marginal fields. The pressure has been unusually great for American oil field equipment suppliers to perfect techniques that minimize the cost of difficult drilling and ensure full recovery from each field. This has pushed them to advance the state of the art and sustain strong international positions. The challenge of helping home buyers surmount such factor disadvantages begets competitive advantage in the nation's industries that supply them.

A nation's buyers can have unusually stringent needs for a wide variety of other reasons as well, including geography, climate, natural resource availability, taxation, tough regulatory standards, and social norms. High taxes on gasoline in Europe, for example, have contributed to strength in high-horsepower, low-displacement engines which are fuel-efficient compared to larger engines of equal horsepower. Buyers also tend to be more demanding when facing competition than if they are tightly regulated or hold a monopoly. Competitive pressure stimulates more attention to new products and creates greater efforts to control costs, reflected in demands placed on suppliers. The heavily private and decentralized health care delivery system in the United States, for example, has, by stimulating innovation, been a major advantage for American suppliers of medical equipment and supplies. Privatization of state-owned firms often stimulates them to experiment more in purchasing.

The role of sophisticated and demanding buyers can be played by *distribution channels* as well as by end users.[36] In the United States, for example, the presence of large powerful chains of eyewear stores has stimulated American contact lens producers to cut costs, create new forms of customer service, and rapidly introduce new product varieties. Italy is another good case. There, such products as shoes, clothing, furniture, and lighting are sold in greater proportion through specialty stores than in other nations. These sophisticated retailers are a major force pressuring Italian manufacturers to constantly introduce new models and reduce prices and thus costs.

One important clue to where a nation's buyers are sophisticated and demanding is national passions. Japanese have long been particularly oriented toward using pictures to record travels and family events, dating back well before World War II. They are also very sophisticated camera buyers, and the Japanese camera industry now leads the world. Japanese also pay great attention to writing instruments, because nearly all documents have until recently been handwritten in Japan due to the impracticality of typewriters in reproducing Japanese characters; penmanship is an important indication of education and culture. Japanese firms have been the innovators and have become world leaders in pens.

Germans cherish their cars and polish them on Sunday between bouts of high-speed driving on the autobahns, which have no speed limit because Germans would not tolerate one. The popular slogan is "free speed for free people." Success in durable, high-performance cars is no surprise. Americans have an unusual interest in popular entertainment (sports, movies, television, records), contributing to American world leadership in these industries. The British are known for gardening, and British firms are world class in garden tools. Italians are known for their sophistication about clothes, food, and fast cars, all areas of Italian international success. National passions translate into internationally competitive industries with striking regularity. Sometimes these passions are not only the cause but also an effect of the presence of a highly competitive national industry. More on this in Chapter 4.

Anticipatory Buyer Needs. A nation's firms gain advantages if the needs of home buyers anticipate those of other nations. This means that home demand provides an early warning indicator of buyer needs that will become widespread. The benefit is important not only for new products but on an ongoing basis, because it stimulates continuous upgrading of products over time and the ability to compete in emerging segments. Anticipatory demand is sometimes another benefit of having the world's most sophisticated buyers at home, because sophisticated buyers are often (though not always) early adopters of new product and service varieties that will come to be demanded elsewhere.

Japanese firms in a variety of industries, for example, were confronted early with buyers very concerned about energy costs, a concern elevated by a stream of government reports, widespread publicity, and some early regulations governing the allowable energy consumption of products. Japanese firms began working early to improve the energy efficiency of products, well in advance of the rest of the world which woke up after the first oil shock (U.S. energy costs were held artificially low, in contrast).

Stringent home needs benefit national competitive advantage *only if* they anticipate needs elsewhere. If they are idiosyncratic to the nation, they will undermine the competitive advantage of local firms. If home demand is slow to reflect new needs, particularly sophisticated needs, a nation's firms are at a disadvantage.

Anticipatory buyer needs may arise because a nation's political or social values foreshadow needs that will ultimately emerge elsewhere. Sweden's long-standing high level of concern for handicapped persons, for example, has spawned an industry supplying products for them that is becoming a world-class industry. A nation's home demand anticipates or lags behind world demand in part because the values embodied in its culture are spreading or are in retreat. American desire for convenience is spreading, benefiting international success in fast food, consumer packaged goods, and other industries. American appetite for credit (coupled with strengths in important technologies such as information technology used in credit scoring and validations) has led to commanding international leadership in credit cards with the likes of American Express, Visa, MasterCard, and Diners Club. Conversely, Scandinavian concern for social welfare and the environment tends today to be ahead of that in the United States. Swedish and Danish firms have achieved success in a variety of industries where this heightened environmental concern anticipates foreign needs, such as in water pollution control equipment.

Factor conditions sometimes play a role in the timing of demand. Danish dependence on imported energy, coupled with prevailing climatic conditions and government support for alternative energy sources, are important reasons why Denmark developed early demand for windmills. Danish firms have emerged as early leaders in producing and exporting them.

Regulations which lead those of other nations can also benefit competitive advantage. For example, Swedish regulations have long permitted very large and heavy trucks. Sweden has internationally prominent forestry and mining sectors located in the rugged northern regions of the nation. The prevalence of hauling timber and other materials over long distances necessitates large, extremely durable trucks. This is a typical example of how local regulations often strongly reflect local needs and values. Sweden has two leading international competitors in heavy trucks, Volvo and Saab-Scania, who have benefited from the Swedish context because large size and durability have been increasingly demanded abroad. At the same time, regulations in other nations limiting the size and weight of trucks have eased.

DEMAND SIZE AND PATTERN OF GROWTH

Provided that its composition is sophisticated and anticipates international and not just domestic needs, the size and pattern of growth of home demand can reinforce national advantage in an industry. The size of the home market has been prominent in discussions of national competitiveness,[37] though there is little agreement about the direction of causality or the reasoning. Some authors argue that a large home market is a strength, because of the existence of economies of scale. Other commentators see it as a weakness, reasoning that limited local demand forces firms to export, important to competitive advantage in global industries. Switzerland, Sweden, Korea, and even Japan are often-noted examples of nations where limited local demand led to pressures to export.[38] Home market size proves to play a complex role in national advantage, and other aspects of home demand are as or more important.

Size of Home Demand. Large home market size can lead to competitive advantage in industries where there are economies of scale or learning, by encouraging a nation's firms to invest aggressively in large-scale facilities, technology development, and productivity improvements. One must be careful, however, because global firms sell in many nations. Investments in large-scale plants or substantial R&D need not rely only on local demand, unless there is widespread protection that limits exports. The many world-class Swiss and Swedish industries attest to the ability of highly international firms to obtain scale from many different foreign markets.

The most important question in industries characterized by substantial economies of scale is which nation's firms will move first to reap them in producing products that will also meet foreign buyer needs. This is a function of the other determinants, especially home demand composition. The size of home demand may be significant in some industries, however. Local firms often enjoy some natural advantages in serving their home market compared to foreign firms, a result of proximity as well as language, regulation, and cultural affinities (even, frequently, if foreign firms are staffed with local nationals). Preferred access to a large domestic customer base can be a spur to investment by local firms. Home demand may be perceived as more certain and easier to forecast, while foreign demand is seen as more uncertain even if firms think they have the ability to fill it. In our case studies, there was nearly universal emphasis in investment decisions on domestic demand, especially early in an industry's development.

Home market size is most important to national competitive advantage in certain kinds of industries (or segments), notably those with heavy R&D requirements, substantial economies of scale in production, large generational leaps in technology, or high levels of uncertainty. In such industries, the proximity of large home demand is particularly comforting in making investment decisions.

Large home demand is not an advantage, however, unless it is for segments that are demanded in other nations. For example, the vast U.S. agricultural sector has led to a large home demand for harvesting combines. Because of differences in climate, terrain, and farming practices as well as American regulations which allowed wider combines on public streets, however, combines designed for the United States were not practical in Europe. Claas, a German firm, was the pioneer in introducing more efficient and narrower combines that could work in the more varied (and difficult) conditions in Europe. It became the European leader, despite the European presence of established U.S. firms. In the highly scale-sensitive commercial aircraft industry, in contrast, the large U.S. home demand (due to a large and dispersed population) yielded a substantial advantage because American needs were similar but arguably more advanced that those elsewhere in most segments.

Sometimes, smaller countries represent very large markets for particular products, given local conditions. For example, demand for icebreakers and cargo vessels with icebreaking capacity in Finland is disproportionately high due to Finnish weather conditions, its dependence on trade, and its special access to the nearby Russian market (with its own icebreaker demand). While local demand for ships in Finland is insignificant in world terms, such is not at all the case in the segment where Finnish yards concentrate. Since home demand for icebreakers is also stringent and sophisticated, Finnish shipbuilders are strong internationally in this area.

Home market size is an advantage if it encourages investment and reinvestment, or dynamism. Because a large home market can also provide such ample opportunities that firms see little need to pursue international sales, however, it may undermine dynamism and become a disadvantage. Other determinants, notably the intensity of domestic rivalry, are decisive in whether a large home market proves to be a strength or a weakness.

Number of Independent Buyers. The presence of a number of independent buyers in a nation creates a better environment for innovation than is the case where one or two customers dominate the home market for a product or service. A number of buyers, each with its own ideas about product needs and ideally under competitive pressure itself, expands the pool of market information and motivates progress. Serving one or two dominant customers, in contrast, may provide some static efficiencies but will rarely create the same level of dynamism.

A number of independent home buyers also stimulates entry and investment in the industry by reducing the perceived risk that a firm will be shut out of the market and limiting the power of a dominant buyer to bargain away all profits. I will discuss these issues further in the next chapter.

Rate of Growth of Home Demand. The rate of growth of home demand can be as important to competitive advantage as its absolute size. The rate of investment in an industry is as much or more a function of how rapidly the home market is growing as its size. Rapid domestic growth leads a nation's firms to adopt new technologies faster, with less fear that they will make existing investments redundant, and to build large, efficient facilities with the confidence that they will be utilized.[39] Conversely, in nations where the rate of growth of demand is more moderate, individual firms tend to expand only incrementally and are more resistant to embrace new technologies that make existing facilities and people redundant. Rapid home demand growth is especially important during periods of technological change, when firms need the conviction to invest in new products or new facilities.

A good case in point is the Italian appliance industry. The industry, less established in Italy right after World War II than it was in a number of other European countries, grew in the space of little more than a decade to be the European export leader. One of the reasons was the boom in appliance demand in Italy during the 1950s. Rapid growth led Italian producers to build uniquely large-scale, automated plants focused on individual types of appliances. Italian firms also began to supply the emerging private label segment throughout Europe, under the brand names of the newly powerful European chain stores. Other European appliance producers, with established facilities and less buoyant home market growth, tended to expand incrementally and therefore did not fundamentally alter the production methods employed. Combined with this was the fact that Italian firms produced low-cost, relatively compact appliances that fit the needs of the Italian market. This segment was growing and underserved by European competitors. Demand growth, like all aspects of demand quantity, is not an advantage unless demand composition is favorable.

Japan is another country where rapid home market growth stimulated aggressive investment in a number of industries. In steel, tires, lift trucks, and many other industries, Japan experienced rapid home market growth somewhat later than in the United States and leading European countries. Rapid growth spurred Japanese firms to invest aggressively in automated facilities of the latest vintage. Western producers, facing more mature home markets and stuck with older facilities, were unwilling to do so.

Early Home Demand. Provided it anticipates buyer needs in other nations, early local demand for a product or service in a nation helps local firms to move sooner than foreign rivals to become established in an industry.[40] They get the jump in building large-scale facilities and accumulating experience. The product varieties demanded early by local buyers are particularly important to competitive advantage because they are where a nation's firms cut their teeth. Competitive strategies are established with these segments in mind, and investments are often directed toward them. Once again, however, the composition of home demand is more important than its size. Only if home demand is anticipatory of international needs will early home demand contribute to advantage.

These considerations find an interesting application in analyzing the impact of defense spending in promoting American competitive advantage. The defense sector has been the first market in the United States for many advanced goods, and the uniquely large U.S. defense budget has been viewed as an advantage to American firms. It is indeed an advantage if defense demand mirrors civilian demand both in the United States and abroad, because firms develop assets and skills that can be transferred to meeting civilian needs. In the case of jet aircraft, defense demand for the first military jet transport was an important advantage to Boeing in becoming world leader in civilian transports—the 707 was essentially the same plane. The 747 was also originally a military aircraft design that lost out to the Lockheed C5A in the competition for a large military transport plane.

In many other industries, however, early defense demand has not necessarily been an advantage for U.S. firms. In computer-controlled machine tools, for example, defense needs were for product varieties with only modest applications in the civilian market. Japanese machine tool producers, without this distraction, concentrated on numerically controlled machine tools for general-purpose applications and became world leaders.

Whether defense demand is a strength or a weakness for U.S. firms depends on its composition—how accurately defense needs reflect or anticipate later civilian needs and how transferable skills are from defense to civilian applications. This will vary greatly from industry to industry, but it appears that the similarity between military and civilian needs has diminished.

Early Saturation. As significant as early home market penetration is early or abrupt saturation. Early penetration helps local firms become established. Early saturation forces them to continue innovating and upgrading. A saturated home market creates intense pressures to push down prices, introduce new features, improve product performance, and provide other incentives for buyers to replace old products with newer versions. Saturation escalates local rivalry, forcing cost cutting and a shakeout of the weakest firms. The result is often the emergence of fewer but stronger, more innovative local rivals.

Another frequent result of home market saturation is vigorous efforts by a nation's firms to penetrate foreign markets, in order to sustain growth and even to fill capacity. It was striking how many of the industries we studied began their first significant international activity after the home market saturated. This was particularly true in Japan and the United States, but there were examples in virtually every country. The abrupt end of the post–World War II reconstruction of Italy was an important impetus that propelled Italian construction firms to become successful international competitors, for example.[41]

Home market saturation is particularly beneficial if it is combined with buoyant growth in foreign markets. If foreign demand is surging while home demand is maturing, a nation's firms have strong incentives to sell abroad just at the time when foreign firms lack the capacity to meet booming demand or are complacent because of the absence of domestic rivalry. In many industries, such periods have been seminal ones in determining eventual leadership.

An extreme example is the rise to world prominence of U.S. engineering and construction firms in the years following World War II. The American industrial base and infrastructure were largely intact, while much of the rest of the world's were destroyed and needed rebuilding. With available capacity and skills gained in working on wartime projects, American firms were swept into the vacuum created by the foreign reconstruction boom and the absence of qualified foreign firms. That U.S. aid was partially funding the reconstruction did not hurt. Similarly, Japanese firms got their break in semiconductors when American firms could not meet demand in the economic upturn of the late 1970s. Combined with heavy investment in newer metal oxide (MOS) technology when American firms were still committed to bipolar technology, this catapulted the Japanese to industry leadership.

Another good example is consumer electronics. In consumer electronic products, saturation in the Japanese home market is rapid and product life cycles are extremely short because of homogeneity of tastes combined with the sophistication and status-consciousness of the buyers I described earlier. The result is that Japanese consumer electronics firms are scrambling to find the next product when foreign consumers are just beginning to buy the generation that is already passé in Japan. This rapid saturation is a potent advantage because home buyers are picky and seek light, compact, multifeatured products that suit Japanese living conditions. Here, rapid saturation pushes producers to innovate in ways that are valued by foreign buyers and which tend to be neglected by foreign rivals.

Like early penetration, early saturation is an advantage only if home demand composition directs a nation's firms to products and product features that are desired abroad.

INTERNATIONALIZATION OF DOMESTIC DEMAND

The composition of home demand is at the root of national advantage, while the size and pattern of growth of home demand can amplify this advantage by affecting investment behavior, timing, and motivation. But there is a third way in which home demand conditions contribute, through mechanisms by which a nation's domestic demand internationalizes and *pulls* a nation's products and services abroad.

Mobile or Multinational Local Buyers. If the nation's buyers for a product or service are mobile or are multinational companies, an advantage is created for the nation's firms because the domestic buyers are also foreign buyers.

Mobile consumers, who travel extensively to other nations, provide a base of often loyal customers in foreign markets. More important in many ways, however, is that their existence highlights the *opportunity* of establishing an overseas presence to a nation's firms and may well provide the conviction to pursue such a presence by lowering the perceived risk. This effect is quite apparent in travel-related industries, where U.S. hotel, rent-a-car, and credit card firms have benefited. It is also significant in such other industries as fast food.

A similar set of arguments applies where home buyers are multinationals, with subsidiaries or operations in many other nations. Multinationals frequently prefer to deal with suppliers of products and services based in their home nation, particularly in the early years of operating abroad but often long after their international position is established. These preferences stem from ease of communication, a desire to reduce risk, and the efficiencies of employing consistent inputs everywhere. Buyers' preference for home-grown suppliers provides an early impetus for suppliers to move abroad and a base of foreign demand.

A good example is the earthmoving equipment industry, where U.S. firms such as Caterpillar were encouraged overseas by preeminent American construction firms, mining companies, and forest products producers. In turn, U.S. oil drilling, mining, and construction equipment pulled heavy engine manufacturers, such as Cummins, abroad. American auto parts suppliers followed U.S. auto companies to Canada, Europe, and elsewhere. More recently, Japanese auto parts suppliers are following the foreign operations of the Japanese car companies.

Influences on Foreign Needs. Another way in which domestic demand conditions can pull through foreign sales is when domestic needs and desires get transmitted to or inculcated in foreign buyers. One obvious way is when foreigners come to a nation for training. They are taught approaches and values reflecting local conditions, and have a tendency to carry them back home. A typical result is the desire to use the same goods and services they were trained on. A good example is the extensive training of foreign doctors in the United States, which has aided U.S. medical equipment firms who find a receptive audience when they seek to sell abroad.

The same general phenomenon occurs because of a demonstration effect, often present in the scientific community. Foreign scientists seek to emulate the practices of those nations' scientists that are perceived as the world leaders. The leaders' procedures and equipment are often reported in technical journals as well as disseminated by word of mouth. A good example of a product that benefited from such a process is microscopes, where German firms (notably Zeiss) prospered internationally in part because of an association with world-class German researchers. A similar demonstration effect may surround any world-class national industry: foreign competitors will have a tendency to emulate the machinery and other inputs that industry employs.

Domestic buyer needs are also transmitted abroad through exports that disseminate culture, such as movies and television programs. Also significant is emigration, which creates a base of foreign demand and a demonstration effect for certain types of products, and tourism, which exposes foreigners to national tastes and norms that may prove appealing. None of these is significant to competitive advantage, however, unless home demand is advanced and sophisticated.

Another means by which home demand is transmitted is via political alliances or historical ties. This embeds in foreign nations such things as the legal system, product or technical standards, and preferences in purchasing. Britain gained enormously through such links in the 1800s through the mid-1900s. Foreign aid and special political relationships among nations are having less dramatic but similar effects today. Nations such as Italy and Japan, for example, are adept at using foreign aid to increase demand for their firms' products and services. Too much ''captive'' foreign business can undermine competitive advantage, however, by reducing the pressure to improve and innovate.

THE INTERPLAY OF DEMAND CONDITIONS

It should be clear already that the various home demand conditions can reinforce each other and have their greatest significance at different stages of an industry's evolution. The television set industry (see insert) provides a good example. The most important attributes of home demand are those that provide initial and ongoing stimulus for investment and innovation as well as for competing over time in more and more sophisticated segments. Examples are especially demanding local buyers, needs that anticipate those of other nations, rapid growth, and early saturation. The resulting advantages are more decisive and enduring than one-time advantages from demand size and mix. Some aspects of home demand are important in initially establishing advantage, while others reinforce that advantage or help sustain it.

The effect of demand conditions on competitive advantage also depends on other parts of the ''diamond.'' Without strong domestic rivalry, for example, rapid home market growth or a large home market may induce complacency rather than stimulate investment. Without the presence of appropriate supporting industries, firms may lack the ability to respond to demanding home buyers. The ''diamond'' is a system in which the role of any determinant cannot be viewed in isolation.

Demand Conditions in the Television Set Industry

Television sets provide a good example of the interplay of demand conditions that are working in tandem and are mutually reinforcing. Japanese home demand was primarily for small, compact, portable televisions because of lower per capita income and because Japanese homes are small and television sets are often put away after use. The American firms that had pioneered the industry were busy meeting home demand, which was primarily for large sets with fine furniture styling and large picture tubes. American firms spent relatively little effort designing small picture tubes and making sets compact. Japanese firms devoted most of their effort in these directions, content to license large set technology and purchase large tubes from the United States.

Japanese home demand for television sets, even though it took off somewhat later, was a much better mirror of world demand than was early American home demand because television sets became part of everyday life instead of something to put in the living room, and compact sets proved to be the global product. Also, as described earlier, Japanese buyers are extremely knowledgeable and demanding about consumer electronics, which led to intense efforts to improve quality, features, and price.

Although television set demand took off earlier in the United States than in Japan, the Japanese market reached saturation sooner. As American firms continued earning record profits, Japanese television set producers scrambled to deal with falling domestic demand. They reduced costs, introduced sets with new features, and moved aggressively to serve export markets. At the end of the 1980s, the Japanese firms were commanding world leaders, especially in differentiated segments.

RELATED AND SUPPORTING INDUSTRIES

The third broad determinant of national advantage in an industry is the presence in the nation of supplier industries or related industries that are internationally competitive.[42] Japanese machine tool producers drew on world-class suppliers of numerical control units, motors, and other components. Swedish strength in fabricated steel products (for example, ball bearings, cutting tools) has drawn on strength in specialty steels. Swiss firms are leaders in embroidered goods and also embroidery machines. Figure 3–2 illustrates how internationally competitive supplier industries underpin Italian success in footwear. Competitive advantage in some supplier industries confers potential advantages on a nation's firms in many other industries, because they produce inputs that are widely used and important to innovation or to internationalization. Semiconductors, software, and trading, for example, are industries that have important impacts on many others.

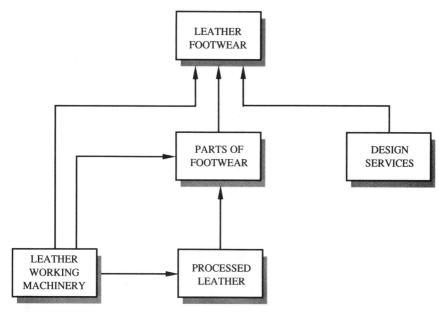

FIGURE 3–2 **Internationally Successful Italian Supplier Industries to Footwear**

The presence of competitive industries in a nation that are related is no less common or significant. The Swiss success in pharmaceuticals was closely connected to previous international success in the dye industry. Japanese leadership in facsimile owes much to the Japanese strength in copiers, while Japanese dominance in electronic musical keyboards grows out of success in acoustic instruments combined with a strong position in consumer electronics. Figure 3–3 illustrates that the Italian footwear industry is also linked to a wide variety of related industries that are competitive.

The mechanisms by which competitive advantage in supplier and related industries benefit other industries are similar. The direct effects on competitive advantage are described below. Those that work through other determinants will be discussed in Chapter 4.

COMPETITIVE ADVANTAGE IN SUPPLIER INDUSTRIES

The presence of internationally competitive supplier industries in a nation creates advantages in downstream industries in several ways. The first is via efficient, early, rapid, and sometimes preferential access to the most cost-effective inputs. Italian world leadership in gold and silver jewelry has been sustained, for example, in part because other Italian firms produce two-thirds of the world's jewelry-making machinery and are also world

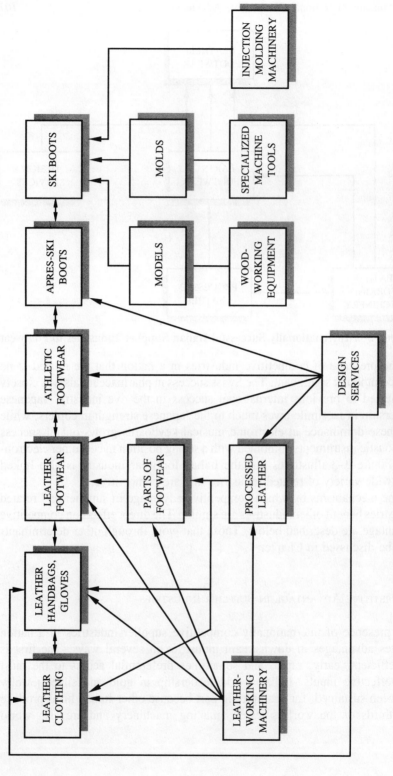

FIGURE 3–3 Internationally Successful Italian Industries Related to Footwear

leaders in equipment for recycling precious metals. The Italian jewelry industry is quick to obtain new equipment models. Italian equipment suppliers compete intensely to serve their home market, for reasons I described earlier. The result is attractive prices and responsive service.

Mere access or availability of machinery or inputs, however, is not the most significant benefit of having a home-based supplier industry that is internationally successful, even if it is early. In global competition, components, machinery, and other inputs are available on global markets, and availability is much less important than how effectively inputs are utilized.

More significant than access to machinery or other inputs is the advantage that home-based suppliers provide in terms of ongoing coordination. I described in the previous chapter how linkages between the value chains of firms and their suppliers are important to competitive advantage. Establishing such linkages is facilitated by having the essential activities and senior management of suppliers nearby. Foreign suppliers are rarely a complete substitute, even if they have local subsidiaries.

Perhaps the most important benefit of home-based suppliers, however, is in the *process of innovation and upgrading*. Competitive advantage emerges from close working relationships between world-class suppliers and the industry. Suppliers help firms perceive new methods and opportunities to apply new technology. Firms gain quick access to information, to new ideas and insights, and to supplier innovations. They have the opportunity to influence suppliers' technical efforts as well as serve as test sites for development work. The exchange of R&D and joint problem solving lead to faster and more efficient solutions. Suppliers also tend to be a conduit for transmitting information and innovations from firm to firm. Through this process, the pace of innovation within the entire national industry is accelerated. All these benefits are enhanced if suppliers are located in proximity to firms, shortening the communication lines.

Italy provides many examples of this sort of interchange. In the leather footwear industry (Figure 3–2), for example, producers interact regularly with leather manufacturers on new styles and manufacturing techniques. Footwear manufacturers learn about the new textures and colors of leather on the drawing board. Leather manufacturers, in turn, gain early insights into fashion trends which help them plan new products. As this example illustrates, however, gaining the benefits of home-based suppliers *does not happen automatically*. Both firms and their suppliers must work to do so, a theme of later chapters.

Having a competitive domestic supplier industry is far preferable to relying even on well-qualified foreign suppliers. The home market is highly visible to domestic suppliers, and success there is a matter of pride. Proximity of managerial and technical personnel, along with cultural similarity, tends to facilitate free and open information flow. Transaction costs are reduced.

Without the presence of a supplier's core research facilities in the home nation, it is unlikely that buyers will get information as early or have the same opportunities for joint development and other forms of deep interchange.[43] Foreign suppliers are also less desirable for the entire national industry because they rarely spawn new domestic entry (see Chapter 4).

A nation's firms receive maximum benefit when their suppliers are themselves global competitors. Only then will they possess the wherewithal to best upgrade their own advantages, thereby providing the needed technology flow to their home-based customers. Home-based suppliers with international positions are also more valuable sources of information and insights. Pressuring local suppliers not to serve foreign competitors is ultimately self-defeating. "Captive" suppliers, dependent solely on a firm or the national industry, will provide less impetus to improve and upgrade.

Local suppliers that are strong by world standards still bolster competitive advantage in downstream industries even when they are not in industries that compete globally. A good case in point is the advertising media. Most media industries (television, radio, and magazines) are still multidomestic, though there are some signs of globalization. The United States has long been the home of some of the most innovative and sophisticated media companies in the world, and new forms of media such as television and magazine formats have been pioneered in the United States. American marketers benefited from close and ongoing interaction with sophisticated American media providers (as well as world-leading advertising agencies), and often were the first to exploit new media forms that ultimately diffused around the world. The importance of advanced media as suppliers to companies in marketing-intensive industries is such that it is rare to find internationally competitive consumer goods industries in nations that do not have well-developed private media. Germany and Sweden, in particular, are nations whose firms have had to learn modern marketing abroad because of restrictions on advertising. International success in marketing-intensive consumer goods is rare in both nations.

A nation need not possess national advantage in all supplier industries in order to gain competitive advantage in an industry. Inputs without a significant effect on innovation or on the performance of an industry's products and processes can be readily sourced from abroad. So may other generalized technologies where the industry represents a narrow application area. In a variety of Swiss and German industries such as hearing aids and plastics processing machinery, for example, firms successfully established subsidiaries in the United States to tap into electronics or software expertise. Here, their in-depth knowledge of the user industry was more important than lack of expertise in supplier technologies. Compensating for the lack of a critical supplier industry in a nation is also feasible where the user industry is already well-developed and represents a specialized use of the supplier industry's product.

COMPETITIVE ADVANTAGE IN RELATED INDUSTRIES

The presence in a nation of competitive industries that are related often leads to new competitive industries. Related industries are those in which firms can coordinate or share activities in the value chain when competing, or those which involve products that are complementary (such as computers and applications software). Sharing of activities can occur in technology development, manufacturing, distribution, marketing, or service. For example, copiers and facsimile machines employ many of the same technologies and components and can be distributed and serviced through the same channels.

Cases where nations are internationally competitive in related industries are pervasive. A few examples drawn from our case studies are shown in Table 3–1.

TABLE **3–1 Internationally Competitive Related Industries**

Nation	Industry	Related Industry
Denmark	Dairy products, brewing	Industrial enzymes
Germany	Chemicals	Printing ink
Italy	Lighting	Furniture
Japan	Cameras	Copiers
Korea	VCRs	Videotape
Singapore	Port services	Ship repair
Sweden	Automobiles	Trucks
Switzerland	Pharmaceuticals	Flavorings
United Kingdom	Engines	Lubricants, antiknock preparations
United States	Electronic test and measuring equipment	Patient monitoring equipment

Figure 3–4 charts a group of related Japanese industries in more detail. Japan's strength in long-filament synthetic textile fibers reflects a long tradition of success in silk, as does a leading export position in silk-like continuous synthetic weaves, woven from long-filament synthetic fibers. Carbon fibers employ technology closely related to synthetic filament fibers and many of the same competitors participate in both. Also, while not overall leaders in textile machines, Japanese firms are leaders in water jet weaving machines, used to weave long-filament synthetic fibers into synthetic weaves. Such groups of linked competitive industries in a nation are common.

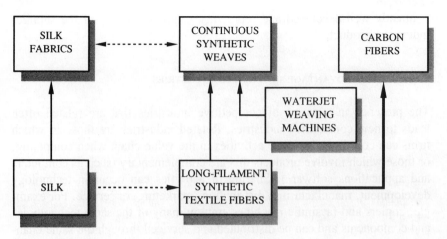

NOTE: Broken lines refer to related industries
         Solid lines represent supplier relationship

FIGURE 3–4 **Related Japanese Industries in Fibers and Fabrics**

The presence of an internationally successful related industry in a nation provides opportunities for information flow and technical interchange, much like the case with home-based suppliers. Proximity and cultural similarity make such interchange easier than is the case with foreign firms. The presence of a related industry also raises the likelihood that new opportunities in industry will be perceived. It also provides a source of new entrants who bring a new approach to competing (see Chapter 4).

Domestic companies in related industries often share activities and sometimes forge formal alliances.[44] In Switzerland, for example, the herbal candy firm Ricola accelerated its international expansion through employing the foreign distribution channels of the Swiss chocolate company, Tobler/Jacobs. In Sweden, Atlas Copco (mining machinery) and Sandvik (rock drills) have a history of formal and informal contacts including a formal marketing alliance. The presence of successful related industries in a nation may also hasten the development of supplier industries that serve both.

International success in one industry can also pull through demand for complementary products or services. The sale of American computers abroad, for example, has led to overseas demand for American computer peripherals, American software, and American database services. Service industries pull through sales of linked manufactured goods from that nation and vice versa (see Chapter 6). Complementary products or services provided by firms based in the same nation may be, or may be perceived to be, more cost effective. Companies contribute to this perception by actively recommending other firms from their home nation, because they are used to dealing with them and have confidence that their products or services will not undermine the performance of their own. Close working relationships between firms producing complementary goods may also lead to product performance that is actually better.

The strength of this pull-through effect varies by industry, in rough proportion to the extent of technical interdependencies between the products involved. Pull through tends to be strongest early in the life cycle of the industries involved. However, the link between complementary goods can create first mover advantages that persist long after the link fades. Britain, for example, gained strong international positions in many services connected with trading because it was an early, powerful trading nation. The foreign infrastructure and brand franchises created through this process have proved to be quite a durable competitive advantage for some British service providers.

National success in an industry is particularly likely if the nation has competitive advantage in a number of related industries. The most significant are those important to innovation in the industry or those that provide the opportunity to share critical activities. Prior to the emergence of the facsimile industry, for example, Japan had leading positions in copiers, other office machines, photographic equipment, and some strong competitors in telecommunications equipment, covering all essential technologies important to facsimile.

The benefits of both home-based suppliers and related industries, however, depend on the rest of the "diamond." Without access to advanced factors, home demand conditions that signal appropriate directions of product change, or active rivalry, for example, proximity to world-class domestic suppliers may provide few advantages. In the television set industry, for example, American competitors were concentrating on the home market and on segments less demanded elsewhere. They lacked the pressure to shift to solid state technology and to automate manufacturing. Proximity to then-preeminent U.S. semiconductor companies did not compensate.

FIRM STRATEGY, STRUCTURE, AND RIVALRY

The fourth broad determinant of national competitive advantage in an industry is the context in which firms are created, organized and managed as well as the nature of domestic rivalry. The goals, strategies, and ways of organizing firms in industries vary widely among nations. National advantage results from a good match between these choices and the sources of competitive advantage in a particular industry. The pattern of rivalry at home also has a profound role to play in the process of innovation and the ultimate prospects for international success.

STRATEGY AND STRUCTURE OF DOMESTIC FIRMS

The way in which firms are managed and choose to compete is affected by national circumstances. While no nation exhibits uniformity across all firms, the national context creates tendencies that are strong enough to be readily noticeable by any observer. In Italy, many successful international competitors are relatively small- or medium-sized firms that are privately owned and run like extended families. In Germany, the top management of many companies consists of individuals with technical backgrounds, and companies are hierarchical in organization and management practices. Efforts to explain why one nation's managerial system is superior have a long tradition; attention was once focused on American management, while in the 1980s it has been on Japan.

No one managerial system is universally appropriate. Nations will tend to succeed in industries where the management practices and modes of organization favored by the national environment are well suited to the industries' sources of competitive advantage. Italian firms, for example, are world leaders in a range of fragmented industries (such as lighting, furniture, footwear, woolen fabrics, and packaging machines) in which economies of scale are either modest or can be overcome through cooperation among loosely affiliated companies. Italian companies most often compete by employing focus strategies, avoiding standardized products and operating in small niches with their own particular style or customized product variety. Often dominated by a single individual, these firms rapidly develop new products and can adapt to market changes with breathtaking flexibility.

In Germany, in contrast, the engineering and technical background of many senior executives produces a strong inclination toward methodical product and process improvement. Intangible bases of competitive advantage are rarely pursued. These characteristics lead to the greatest success in industries with a high technical or engineering content (for example, optics, chemicals, complicated machinery), especially where intricate and complex products demand precision manufacturing, a careful development process, after-sale service, and hence a highly disciplined management structure. German success is much rarer in consumer goods and services where image marketing and rapid new feature and model turnover are important to competition. In Japan, a number of studies have stressed unusual cooperation across functions and the management of complex assembly operations.[45]

Important national differences in management practices and approaches occur in such areas as the training, background, and orientation of leaders, group versus hierarchical style, the strength of individual initiative, the tools for decision making, the nature of the relationships with customers, the ability to coordinate across functions, the attitude toward international activities, and the relationship between labor and management.[46] These differences in managerial approaches and organizational skills create advantages and disadvantages in competing in different types of industries.[47] Labor management relationships are particularly significant in many industries because they are so central to the ability of firms to improve and innovate.

Many aspects of a nation, too numerous to generalize, influence the ways in which firms are organized and managed. Some of the most important aspects are attitudes toward authority, norms of interpersonal interaction, attitudes of workers toward management and vice versa, social norms of individualistic or group behavior, and professional standards. These in turn grow out of the educational system, social and religious history, family structures, and many other often intangible but unique national conditions. For example, Italy's small-sized firms and family ownership reflect, among other things, a high degree of individualism and a suspicion of authority unless coming from the family or extended family. Italy is a country in which family ties are strong, and even today people prefer to remain near their birthplace. Situations where family members all work in the same firm are very common, and rather than enlarging the existing firm beyond a certain level, new firms are created for sons and daughters.[48]

The orientation of firms toward competing globally (Chapter 2) takes on unusual significance in international competition and deserves more extended treatment here. The willingness and ability of firms to compete globally is partly a function of other determinants such as pressure from domestic market saturation or local rivalry and the pull through of international demand. However, managerial attitudes play an important role as well. Several aspects of the national environment affect the international outlook of firms, or their ease and willingness to operate globally. One is attitudes toward travel. Travel has a long tradition and is a way of life in countries such as Sweden and Switzerland. In several of the Swiss industries I studied, for example, founders of important companies had been trained or had lived for a long time outside Switzerland before returning home. Inevitably, one of the founder's first acts was to establish a foreign subsidiary in the country where he or she had lived. Both Swedish and Swiss firms do well competing in industries requiring far-flung global strategies and involving sensitive relations with local governments and buyers.

Language skills and attitudes toward learning new languages are also significant in influencing whether firms adopt a global outlook. However, the Japanese case illustrates that other determinants are more important causal factors. Japanese, who have difficulty learning Western languages and whose culture is not outwardly oriented, have mastered foreign languages because they have expended great effort to do so. Driven by intense rivalry and domestic market saturation, they found exporting a necessity.

Government policy frequently plays a role in influencing the ease or difficulty of internationalization of domestic firms and, hence, the type of industries in which they succeed. A straightforward example is in the area of foreign exchange controls that limit foreign direct investment. Because of a history of such restrictions, for example, Italian firms are rarely successful in industries in which foreign direct investment is essential to competing. A nation's political stance also plays a material role in promoting globalization in certain industries. Swiss and Swedish neutrality has been an important advantage in establishing international networks, particularly in politically sensitive industries. Other policies that bear on a local firm's ability to operate abroad include controls on the movement of domestic or foreign managerial personnel.

GOALS

Sharp differences exist within and among nations in the goals that firms seek to achieve as well as the motivations of their employees and managers.[49] Nations will succeed in industries where these goals and motivations are aligned with the sources of competitive advantage. In many industries, one component of achieving and sustaining advantage is sustained investment. More broadly, nations succeed in industries where there is unusual commitment and effort.

Company Goals. Company goals are most strongly determined by ownership structure, the motivation of owners and holders of debt, the nature of the corporate governance, and the incentive processes that shape the motivation of senior managers. The goals of publicly held corporations[50] reflect the characteristics of the nation's public capital markets. Capital markets vary a great deal across nations, along such dimensions as the identity of shareholders, the local tax regime, and the prevailing standards for rate of return. In addition, the role of shareholders and debtholders in corporate governance also varies. In Germany and Switzerland, for example, most shares are held by institutions for extended periods and are rarely traded. Banks are important holders of equity shares and play a prominent role on boards of directors, guiding corporate investments. Long-term capital gains have been exempt from taxation, reinforcing a perspective to hold shares for sustained periods. Management pays attention to the board, but day-to-day stock price movements are not viewed as particularly important. Because of local accounting rules, companies can establish substantial reserves to shelter income and provide a cushion in hard times. Norms for reported profitability are modest. Companies do well in mature industries requiring ongoing investment in research and new facilities, even where industry average returns are moderate.

The United States is at the other extreme. Most shares are held by institutional investors, but institutions are measured on quarterly and annual share price appreciation. Lacking full information about companies' long-term prospects and seeking stocks which will soon appreciate, investment choices stress quarterly earnings growth. Institutions trade frequently in order to realize capital appreciation, and account for most trading in larger company stocks. Long-term capital gains of investors are taxed at the same rate as ordinary income, shortening the time horizon of investment. Many institutions, because they are managing pension assets, take no account of taxes in investment choices. When coupled with low transaction costs in the efficient U.S. market, more rapid trading is encouraged.

Shareholders have little direct influence in the management of American companies because boards play little role in corporate governance. In practice, the only effective way to remove underperforming management or affect corporate direction is through takeover. Management responds to stock price movements because of the takeover threat and the prevalence of stock options. In the United States, executive compensation is strongly influenced by overall company size and also involves a high bonus component compared to other nations, usually based on the current year's profits. Since the average tenure in management positions is short, foregoing this year's bonus for a higher one next year is unusual. The lack of effective shareholder governance means that there is little to counteract such behavior. For these reasons and others, the rate of return standards for evaluating investments are higher in America than in any other advanced nation we studied.

Coexisting in the United States with this capital market and governance structure for mature companies is a well-functioning public and quasi-public market for risk capital. This market is much less developed in most other nations. Start-ups and emerging growth companies can be readily funded, particularly if they are in glamorous industries or are viewed as "high tech." The rewards to founders are often substantial. In such industries, companies can and do show losses for five years or more. The biotechnology industry is a good example: few firms have ever made a profit in any year, yet billions of dollars of public equity have flowed into the industry over the last decade.

Britain's situation is closer to America's, while Sweden and Japan are closer to Germany and Switzerland. In both Sweden and Japan, large industrial groups (which include banks) play significant roles as long-term investors. In Germany, large banks themselves are cast in this role. In Italy, public capital markets are of less importance and many internationally successful companies are privately owned. In Korea, the public capital markets have been inefficient and poorly developed. Government policy is the decisive factor in capital allocation, based on considerations other than short-term rate of return.

While I have concentrated on the goals of investors in public companies and their influence on management, private companies play an important role in many national economies. The goals of privately owned firms are more complex. Often pride and the desire to provide continuity to employees is important. Private owners frequently have a very long time horizon, are intensely committed to the industry, and operate with different profitability thresholds. In our research, it was striking how many internationally successful companies were either privately held, effectively private because of a controlling or *de facto* controlling equity block, or owned by a nonprofit foundation (for example Zeiss, Novo Industri, and Carlsberg). The sustained investment of such companies and their close identification with and commitment to their industry were palpable.

The attitudes of debt holders also influence company goals. An important difference among nations is the extent to which debt holders also hold equity. In nations such as Japan, Germany, and Switzerland, regulations allow banks to hold corporate equity. Major lenders hold significant equity stakes and play an important role in corporate governance. By holding both, banks are motivated to be concerned with long-term company health rather than short-term cash flow and interest coverage.

Ownership structures, capital market conditions, and the nature of corporate governance in a nation have two broad influences on national advantage. The first grows out of the fact that industries have different appetites for funds, different risk profiles, different investment time horizons, and different average sustained rates of return. National capital markets will also set different goals for different types of industries. Nations will succeed in industries where the goals of owners and managers match the needs of the industry. A given institutional structure can benefit competitive advantage in some industries and impede it in others.

German and Swiss circumstances favor industries requiring modest initial risk capital but a need for heavy and sustained investment and reinvestment. American conditions favor entry into new industries requiring risk capital and competing in industries where strong incentives for annual profitability are consistent with competitive advantage (for example, in many services) because of the nature of their investment needs. The United States does well in relatively new industries (such as computers, software, and new forms of services) or ones in which equity funding of many new companies feeds active domestic rivalry (such as specialty electronics and consumer packaged goods). In more mature and less glamorous industries, however, capital market pressures and the governance process will be prone to lead to harvesting of competitive positions and an inadequate level of investment to sustain improvement and innovation. Companies in mature industries are motivated instead to seek mergers, unrelated diversification, and other actions that can quickly affect size, financial results, and investor perceptions.[51]

Second, the influence of the capital markets varies with the need for funds. In industries where private ownership is feasible, for example, a nation can succeed despite public capital markets that set counterproductive goals. Other parts of the "diamond" govern in such cases.

Goals of Individuals. The motivations of the individuals who manage and work in firms can enhance or detract from success in particular industries. The central concern is whether both are motivated to develop their skills as well as expend the effort necessary for creating and sustaining competitive advantage.

One important determinant of individual behavior and effort is the reward systems under which employees operate. An aspect of this is social values which influence attitudes toward work and the extent to which individuals are motivated by financial gain, which vary a great deal across nations. Also significant is the nation's tax structure. In Sweden, marginal tax rates are extremely high. People do not work primarily to enhance income but to contribute to the company and enhance their status. This facilitates coordination but slows decision making and limits risk taking, skewing success toward certain types of industries. Also important are pay and promotional practices. Bonus compensation based on individual performance and rapid promotion of the most outstanding employees, both typical in America, reinforce competitive advantage in some types of industries but detract from it in others, especially those requiring long accumulation of skills and complex coordination.

The attitude toward wealth also varies across nations. It is a big motivator in the United States, while looked on with some suspicion in Sweden. Swedes are less motivated than Americans to seek a fortune on a new start-up. Sweden is rarely successful in industries where this behavior is important to competitive advantage.

Another important dimension is the relationship between the manager or employee and the company. Creating and especially sustaining competitive advantage in many industries requires ongoing investments to upgrade skills, better understand the industry, and exchange ideas across functions. In industries where these attitudes are present, often because of a norm of virtually permanent employment, nations are successful. In the absence of such a relationship, national success will gravitate toward industries where competitive advantage is more a function of the brilliance or performance of a small group of individuals, such as professional and financial services, movies and other entertainment products, and specialty products based on advanced technology like software and specialized integrated circuits.

Individuals' attitudes toward skill development and toward company activities also stem from professional or technical training and pride. In Germany, employees (including managers) have often invested their entire careers training in a field or profession. The possibility that a firm cannot match its rivals' technical achievements is unthinkable, and this promotes relentless advance in industries amenable to incremental technical improvement. Another influence on individuals' goals in some nations is geographic preference. The desire to live in a particular area is the strongest in Italy of any of the nations we studied. Staying in an area often means working in the local industry, and finding a way to sustain it is tantamount to defending the home.

Attitude toward risk taking is a final important aspect of personal goals that influences the ability to achieve success in particular industries. I have discussed how "outsiders" often are prominent in innovation because of their willingness to take risk. Attitudes toward wealth affect risk taking, but so do other social and historical factors. In some nations, such as Germany, Switzerland, and Singapore, failure is viewed as personally catastrophic. In other nations, a failure or two are acceptable. The types of industries entered and the nature of the strategies chosen reflect these differences.

Also quite significant to risk taking is immigration, the ultimate source of outsiders. Nations such as America, Britain, and Switzerland, which have a history of immigration, have seen an unusual proportion of new firms emerge from newcomers.

The Influence of National Prestige/Priority on Goals. The quality of human resources attracted to particular industries and the motivation of individuals and even shareholders are affected by prestige or national priority. Unusual effort is often the result of such prestige or a sense of broader mission. Where an industry becomes a notable occupation or takes on national importance, competitive advantage often results.

Outstanding talent is a scarce resource in any nation, though the size of the pool may vary. In no small part, a nation's success depends on the types of education this talent chooses to obtain and where it chooses to work. Training the most promising young people in science and engineering is unusually beneficial to an economy because it provides the greatest spur to innovation. When an industry takes on the status of a national priority and/or a prestigious place to work, talented people flow into it and demonstrate unusual commitment and effort.

In the United States, for example, responding to Sputnik became an important stimulus to the aerospace sector. Outstanding people were attracted, and firms viewed their work as more than just business. Another good example is the German chemical sector. The sector has long been prestigious in Germany, based on early groundbreaking chemistry research. Prior to World War II, the drive for self-sufficiency in materials elevated the industry to a vital national priority. Remarkable accomplishments took place in a short span of time. In Japan, the steel and consumer electronics industries were the most prestigious in the period just after World War II.

Sometimes it is difficult to distinguish between cause and effect. The attainment of international success can make an industry prestigious. Prestige then becomes a powerful reinforcing mechanism for sustaining advantage in an industry, even if it was not decisive in creating it initially.

National priority can be attached not only to industries but to particular issues that affect many industries. This can have the same supercharging effect on motivation. In Japan, national campaigns to improve product quality and reduce energy consumption had strong impacts on a number of industries. Japanese firms moved early and aggressively to confront these problems with techniques that helped them succeed internationally.

Industries become celebrated in a nation for reasons that can be deeply rooted in history, geographic location, social structure, and many other things. If prestige and national priority favor an industry, the ripple effect on competitive advantage can be enormous. However, the reverse is true as well. If a nation's priorities shift away from success in an industry or toward an idiosyncratic conception of economic progress, competitive advantage can be systematically undermined. Working in the manufacturing industry has long been seen as low in status in Britain where the higher callings were the church, the civil service, the military, and academia. Many British manufacturing industries suffered from a lack of talented people and a lack of mission.

The role of national prestige in stimulating national competitive advantage can be extended to make a broader point: nations tend to be competitive in activities that are admired or depended upon; that is, where the heroes come from. In Italy, it is fashion and furnishings, among others. In Switzerland, it is banking and pharmaceuticals. In the United States, it is finance and anything to do with entertainment, including movies, popular music, professional sports, and related fields. In Israel, the highest callings have been defense-related endeavors and agriculture. National passions not only affect demand conditions, as I have discussed, but also how firms compete. Competitive advantage often results because celebrated professions or industries attract the most talented people as well as a steady stream of new entrants.

The Importance of Sustained Commitment. The goals of firms and individuals are reflected in the nature of the commitment of capital and human resources to an industry, to a firm, and, for employees, to a profession.

The economist's ideal is freely mobile resources, which move quickly and fluidly from one industry to another based on what is their most productive use. This view is too simple, and our research suggests that easily movable resources are far from ideal for success in international competition.

The flaw in traditional thinking about resource mobility is that it assumes that the productivity of resource utilization in an industry is given. Under these circumstances, it is sensible for resources to flow to industries where the productivity is higher. In reality, however, innovation can often boost the productivity of the resources employed in an industry much more than the gains from reallocating them. At the same time, the knowledge and expertise built up in the industry are preserved, and the competitive advantage of firms is upgraded and made more sustainable. Innovation, though, requires sustained investment in terms of both capital and human resources.

Those national industries we studied in which employees and shareholders had the most sustained commitment to the firm and the industry were often those with competitive advantage, provided other determinants were favorable. Preserving advantage may well require reinvesting all available profits in a major restructuring despite low current returns and in the face of substantial risk. Innovations are frequently most necessary at times when current profitability is down. The alternative, giving up, must be unthinkable if improvement and innovation are to take place. In contrast, nations in which resources were rapidly redeployed from one industry to another whenever conditions became difficult were rarely internationally successful in that industry.

A good case in point is the history of Italian firms in woolen cloth. As firms from other nations fled this industry in the face of competition from newly industrializing countries, Italian family firms reinvested everything to upgrade technology and try to preserve position. A long tradition in the industry, family ownership, and commitment to the local community were some of the reasons.

Not all such efforts succeed, and committed firms fail. Technological skills or appropriate human resources may be lacking. While commitment does not ensure success, however, the lack of it makes success highly unlikely.

Company diversification patterns are an important indication of commitment to industries as well as of how resources are redeployed. Focus on a single business, or tightly related diversification, are both signs of commitment as well as causes of it. Related diversifiers are also able in many instances to redeploy resources within the firm, a reflection of commitment to employees. Unrelated diversification, conversely, had a strong negative correlation with national competitive advantage in the industries we studied. Corporate parents harvested subsidiaries instead of investing to preserve their competitive advantage.[52]

Of course, some mobility of resources is a *sine qua non* of an upgrading economy, so that resources do not stay locked into hopeless situations indefinitely. Yet sustaining competitive advantage requires that resources flow only after a fight. The ideal is adjustment, not abandonment, in which committed resources are recombined or reconfigured to boost productivity instead of being frozen in their current modes of deployment by management lethargy or restrictive union agreements.

DOMESTIC RIVALRY

Among the strongest empirical findings from our research is the association between vigorous domestic rivalry and the creation and persistence of competitive advantage in an industry. It is often argued that domestic competition is wasteful, because it leads to duplication of effort and prevents firms from gaining economies of scale. The right solution is seen as nurturing one or two firms who become "national champions," with the scale and strength to compete against foreign rivals or, alternatively, to promote interfirm cooperation. Some also take the related view that domestic rivalry is unimportant in global industries.[53]

A look at the successful industries in the ten nations we studied casts grave doubts on this viewpoint. Nations with leading world positions often have a number of strong local rivals, even in small countries such as Switzerland and Sweden.[54] This is true not only in fragmented industries but also industries with substantial economies of scale. The Swiss in pharmaceuticals (Hoffmann-LaRoche, Ciba-Geigy, Sandoz), Sweden in both cars and trucks (Saab-Scania, Volvo), and Germany in chemicals (BASF, Hoechst, Bayer, and numerous others) and the United States in computers and software are illustrative. Nowhere is the extent of domestic rivalry greater than in Japan, as Table 3–2 illustrates.[55]

These examples belie the simple notion that world leadership grows out of one or two firms who reap economies of scale in the home market. In global competition, successful firms compete vigorously at home and pressure each other to improve and innovate. Additional scale is obtained by selling worldwide. The scale of the entire national industry is as important as that of individual firms.

We found, in contrast, few "national champions," or firms with virtually unrivaled domestic positions, that were internationally competitive. Instead, most were uncompetitive though often heavily subsidized and protected.[56] In many of the prominent industries in which there is only one national rival, such as in aerospace and telecommunications, government has played a major role in distorting competition.

Domestic rivalry becomes superior to rivalry with foreign competitors

TABLE 3–2 **Estimated Number of Japanese Rivals in Selected Industries, 1987**

Air conditioners	13	Motorcycles	4
Audio equipment	25	Musical instruments	4
Automobiles	9	Personal computers	16
Cameras	15	Semiconductors	34
Car audio	12	Sewing machines	20
Carbon fibers	7	Shipbuilding	33**
Construction equipment	15*	Steel	5***
Copiers	14	Synthetic fibers	8
Facsimile machines	10	Television sets	15
Lift trucks	8	Truck and bus tires	5
Machine tools	112	Trucks	11
Mainframe computers	6	Typewriters	14
Microwave equipment	5	Videocassette recorders	10

SOURCES: Field interviews; *Nippon Kōgyō Shinbun, Nippon Kōgyō Nenkan,* 1987; Yano Research, *Market Share Jiten,* 1987; researchers' estimates.

* The number of firms varied by product area. The smallest number, ten, produced bulldozers. Fifteen firms produced shovel trucks, truck cranes, and asphalt paving equipment. There were twenty companies in hydraulic excavators, a product area where Japan is particularly strong.

** Six firms had annual production exports in excess of 10,000 tons.

*** Integrated companies.

when improvement and innovation, rather than static efficiency, are recognized as the essential ingredients for competitive advantage in an industry. Rivalry among a group of domestic competitors is different from and often takes forms far more beneficial to the nation than rivalry with foreign firms. In a closed economy, monopoly is profitable. In global competition, monopolies or cartels will lose to firms from more competitive environments.

Domestic rivalry, like any rivalry, creates pressure on firms to improve and innovate. Local rivals push each other to lower costs, improve quality and service, and create new products and processes. While firms may not preserve advantages for long periods, active pressure from rivals stimulates innovation as much from fear of falling behind as the inducement of getting ahead.[57]

Domestic rivalry need not be restricted to price; in fact, rivalry in other forms such as technology may well lead to more sustainable national advantage. In Germany, for example, price competition is not typical, but active rivalry on product performance, features, and service have sustained strong competitive advantages in many German industries.

Rivalry among firms with the same home base is particularly beneficial for a variety of reasons. First, strong domestic competitors create particularly visible pressures on each other to improve. One domestic rival's success signals or proves to others that advancement is possible. It also often attracts new rivals to the industry.

Rivalry among domestic firms often goes beyond the purely economic and can become emotional and even personal. Active feuds between domestic rivals are common, and often associated with an internationally successful national industry. Local competitors received special attention in most of the industries we studied. Pride drives managers and workers to be highly sensitive to other companies in the nation, and the national press and investment analysts constantly compare one domestic competitor with the others. Domestic rivals fight not only for market share but for people, technical breakthroughs, and, more generally, "bragging rights." Foreign rivals, in contrast, tend to be viewed more analytically. Their role in signaling or prodding domestic firms is less effective, because their success is more distant and is often attributed to "unfair" advantages. With domestic rivals, there are no excuses.

Vigorous local competition not only sharpens advantages at home but pressures domestic firms to sell abroad in order to grow. Particularly when there are economies of scale, local competitors force each other to look outward in the pursuit of greater efficiency and higher profitability. In pencils, for example, the number two German competitor, Staedtler, concentrated very early on foreign markets because the industry leader, Faber-Castell, had a strong hold on the domestic market. Faber-Castell was, in turn, motivated by Staedtler's success to expand internationally as well. With little domestic rivalry, firms are more content to rely on the home market.

Toughened by domestic rivalry, the stronger domestic firms are equipped to succeed abroad. It is rare that a company can meet tough foreign rivals when it has faced no significant competition at home. If Digital Equipment can hold its own against IBM, Data General, Prime, and Hewlett-Packard, dealing with Siemens, ICL, or Machines Bull does not seem so daunting. Though some local rivals may go bankrupt and some mergers and consolidation may take place, the process of domestic rivalry produces stronger survivors.

Domestic rivalry not only creates pressures to innovate but to innovate in ways that *upgrade* the competitive advantages of a nation's firms. The presence of domestic rivals nullifies the types of advantage that come simply from being in the nation, such as factor costs, access to or preference in the home market, a local supplier base, and costs of importing that must be borne by foreign firms. If there are a number of Korean competitors in an industry, for example, none gets an advantage simply because of low labor costs or low-cost debt financing. This forces a nation's firms to seek *higher-order* and ultimately more sustainable sources of competitive advantage. Firms must find proprietary technologies, reap economies of scale, create their own international marketing networks, or exploit national advantages more effectively than the competitor down the street. Intense domestic rivalry helps break the attitude of dependence on basic factor advantages because local rivals have them as well. Without local rivals, a firm in a nation with factor advantages tends to rely on them and, worse yet, to deploy factors less efficiently.

The process of domestic rivalry also creates advantages for the entire national industry that are external to any particular firm. A group of domestic rivals tries alternative approaches to strategy and creates a range of products and services that cover many segments. This enhances innovation, and a breadth of products and approaches builds defenses against foreign penetration. The national industry's advantage is made more sustainable by removing some avenues for entry by foreign competitors. Good ideas are imitated and improved upon by local competitors, raising the overall rate of industry innovation. The stock of knowledge and skill in the national industry accumulates as firms imitate each other and as personnel move among firms. While a particular firm cannot keep all the knowledge and skills to itself, the whole national industry benefits through faster innovation. Ideas diffuse faster within the nation than across nations, because it is difficult for firms from other countries to tap into such a process.[58] Though individual firms cannot keep innovations proprietary for long, the entire national industry progresses faster than foreign rivals, and this supports profitability for many of the nation's firms.

Geographic concentration of rivals in a single city or region within a nation both reflects and magnifies these benefits. It is strikingly common around the world. Many of the Italian jewelry firms, for example, are located around two towns, Arezzo and Valenza Po, whose streets are lined with hundreds of companies. Similar concentrations of firms in successful industries are numerous, for example, Solingen, West Germany and Seki, Japan (cutlery); Basel, Switzerland (pharmaceuticals); Hamamatsu, Japan (motorcycles, musical instruments); Route 128 in Boston (minicomputers); and Madison Avenue, New York (advertising). In such an environment, popular luncheon spots are patronized by executives from several companies, who eye each other and trade the latest gossip. Information flows with enormous speed. Though any one firm must move fast to sustain its advantage, the whole national industry is dynamic and sustains, or even widens, its advantage over foreign rivals who lack the same structure.

Domestic rivalry not only creates advantages but helps to avoid some disadvantages. With a group of domestic rivals following various competitive strategies, there is a check against forms of government intervention that stifle innovations or blunt competition. When there are only one or two domestic rivals in a nation, in contrast, pressures are created for all sorts of "assistance" that undermines dynamism, such as subsidies, guaranteed home demand, or favoritism of a local firm. None of this "help" is conducive to innovation and ultimately to competitive advantage (see Chapter 12).

Competing domestic rivals keep each other honest in obtaining government support. Government contracts do not become a guaranteed market for one company. Differences in international strategy work against protection. At the same time, the presence of rivals channels government support into more constructive forms that will benefit the entire industry, such as assistance in opening foreign markets and investments in specialized factor creation.

The phenomenon I have described is not confined to business competition. In the arts, in science, and even in sporting competition, there are many examples where one nation achieved disproportionate international success for a period of time, often involving a group of artists, scientists, or athletes who were working in the same city. In tennis, for example, Sweden has achieved unusual success in the 1980s, as Australia did in the 1960s. A group of strong young players pushes and challenges each other. One player's success attracts and encourages new aspirants. One player's entry into international competition gives others the courage to try.

A group of capable domestic rivals, then, creates a fertile environment for creating and sustaining competitive advantage that is difficult to replicate through competition with foreign rivals. The role of selective factor disadvantages, sophisticated buyers, and world-class suppliers in stimulating improvement and innovation is accentuated by the active domestic rivalry. The benefits of domestic rivalry are greater still when account is taken of the ways in which a group of domestic rivals can favorably affect the availability of home-based suppliers, the pool of skilled human resources, and other parts of the "diamond" (see Chapter 4).

Nowhere is the role of domestic rivalry more evident than in Japan, where it is all-out warfare in which many companies fail to achieve profitability. With goals that stress market share, Japanese companies engage in a continuing struggle to outdo each other. Shares fluctuate markedly. The process is prominently covered in the business press. Elaborate rankings measure which companies are most popular with university graduates. The rate of new product and process development is breathtaking.

The number of domestic competitors required for effective rivalry rests on the underlying scale economies in the industry. The need for numerous competitors in all types of industries is not implied. However, the need for static economies of scale is tempered by the importance for competitive advantage of the rate of innovation. Dominant firms are not the innovators in many industries, as I discussed in the previous chapter.[59] They experience inertia and ties to old ways of competing. Many of the technologies of the 1980s and 1990s are also less scale-sensitive than earlier generations.

A completely open home market along with extremely global strategies can partially substitute for the lack of domestic rivals in a smaller nation.[60]

The number of rivals may also fall gradually as an industry matures; more local rivals tend to be optimal in the earlier stages of an industry's development. But strong domestic rivalry is a national asset whose value is hard to overstate.[61]

A number of domestic competitors is not itself sufficient to determine success. If there is no effective rivalry among the competitors, the advantages of domestic competition are nullified.[62] Moreover, the nation must have other advantages in the "diamond" or competitive success is unlikely. In insulin, for example, there have been two British insulin competitors, Wellcome and Boots, but insulin represents a small fraction of their business and neither is committed to the industry. British demand conditions also tend to be less favorable because of tight cost controls on health care spending and the fact that most purchases are funneled through only one buyer, the National Health Service. Neither British competitor became significant internationally, and Boots exited the industry in the early 1980s.

Direct cooperation among competitors, an approach advocated as a means of avoiding duplication and reaping economies of scale, undermines competitive advantage unless it takes some limited and specific forms. It eliminates diversity, saps incentives, and slows the rate of industry improvement. There is a role for cooperation through trade associations and other independent entities to which many firms have access. I will discuss guidelines for beneficial cooperative activity in Chapter 12.

New Business Formation. Intense domestic rivalry depends on new business formation to create new competitors. New business formation is also vital to the upgrading of competitive advantage, because it feeds the process of innovation in an industry. New companies serve new segments and try new approaches that older rivals fail to recognize or to which they are too inflexible to respond. New entrants are often the "outsiders," willing to take unconventional approaches to competing for reasons I discussed in the previous chapter. New business formation is also integral to the way in which one determinant reinforces others (Chapter 4). For example, aggressive rivalry among competitors leads to entry into supplier or related industries. The active formation of new competitors in the industry, by one means or another, was part of the history of virtually every internationally successful industry we studied.

The process by which new businesses are created in a nation bears importantly on the competitive advantage of national industries. There are two basic mechanisms by which new businesses are formed. One is the establishment of entirely new companies, whether they are spin-offs from established firms, are founded by employees of suppliers and customers, or are the result of ideas gleaned during academic training or university research. The national circumstances that promote this form of new business formation are varied.

One local rival in a nation frequently leads to others through the mechanism of spin-offs. Frustrated (or ambitious) employees with good ideas leave to form their own company, often nearby. One spin-off encourages others. The dynamic of spin-offs is often healthy for the national industry. It creates more rivalry. It also unlocks new product and process innovations that were stifled by inertia or conflicts with existing strategies. It leads to the serving of new segments or segments that were ignored.

Spin-offs are not equally prevalent in every nation, nor during every phase of industry development.[63] However, they were common in the internationally competitive industries we studied. Many of America's minicomputer firms are descendants of a company called General Automation (GA). For example, Digital Equipment grew out of GA, and Data General emerged out of Digital. Control Data, the early leader in what are now called supercomputers, gave birth to the current world leader, Cray Research. In the Italian packaging machinery industry, one firm (ACMA) led directly or indirectly to more than two hundred competitors, all located near Bologna.

Each of the other determinants plays some role in determining those industries in which new companies appear. Factor conditions, in the form of a pool of skilled and specially trained personnel, are a prerequisite for founding new businesses. So is access to risk capital, especially in industries where capital requirements cannot be met with individual savings and internally generated funds. Favorable demand conditions attract new entrants. The motivation of individuals is also important. National prestige and priorities can influence the industries to which outstanding people are attracted. The existence in the nation of the institutions from which new businesses typically emerge in a particular industry is also important: America has many start-ups in industries where new ideas grow out of university research laboratories, while Japan has but a few. Japanese researchers typically join the research staffs of larger companies. Finally, the nature of buyer, supplier, and related industries is also important because they are sources of personnel and ideas to form new companies.

The other mechanism for new business formation is internal diversification into new industries by established firms (acquisition is rarely new business formation, because no new entity is created).[64] National success in an industry benefits from active internal entry by firms from related industries. Diversification through internal development is almost always through related diversification, because creating a new entry from scratch almost demands that a company possess a base of relevant skills. Knowledge and assets are transferred from the existing to the new business, enhancing the prospects for competitive advantage. Conditions which foster active internal entry into an industry by firms from related fields are a potent source of national competitive advantage.

The prevalence of internal development in a nation is most affected by the goals of firms (see earlier) but also reflects other institutional characteristics. Internal entry is very common in Japan, Korea, and Germany where much diversification has historically been by means of start-ups, and acquisitions are rare. In Japan, for example, a long time horizon, the desire to redeploy employees freed up by productivity improvements, and historical difficulty in making acquisitions has led to widespread internal development by established firms. Internal development used to be commonplace in America and continues in a few sectors such as consumer packaged goods, business services, and health care (all areas of national advantage). By and large, however, shifting goals have led American companies to focus on acquisitions, many unrelated to their core businesses.

The industries in which internal development occurs, as in the case of start-ups, is a function of the "diamond." I will have more to say about these connections in Chapter 4.

THE ROLE OF CHANCE

The determinants of national advantage shape the environment for competing in particular industries. In the histories of most of the successful industries we studied, however, chance events also played a role. Chance events are occurrences that have little to do with circumstances in a nation and are often largely outside the power of firms (and often the national government) to influence. Some examples which are particularly important in influencing competitive advantage are the following:

- Acts of pure invention
- Major technological discontinuities (for example, biotechnology, microelectronics)[65]
- Discontinuities in input costs such as the oil shocks
- Significant shifts in world financial markets or exchange rates
- Surges of world or regional demand
- Political decisions by foreign governments
- Wars

Chance events are important because they create discontinuities that allow shifts in competitive position. They can nullify the advantages of previously established competitors and create the potential that a new nation's firms can supplant them to achieve competitive advantage in response to new and different conditions. The advent of microelectronics, for example, was enormously important in neutralizing American and German dominance in numerous electromechanically based industries. It provided an opportunity for Japanese firms (and others) to gain position. Similarly, a surge in demand for ships gave Korea the opportunity to enter the shipbuilding industry against Japan. The apparel industry developed in Singapore after Western nations placed quotas on apparel imports from Hong Kong and Japan, while the world-leading Korean wig industry prospered only after America banned imports from China during the cold war.

The determinants of national advantage work together as a powerful system for sustaining advantage. However, this system is to some extent specialized to a particular industry structure. A discontinuity is necessary to alter the bases of advantage enough to allow a new specialized national "diamond" to supplant another.

Chance events play their role partly by altering conditions in the "diamond." Major shifts in input costs or exchange rates, for example, create selective factor disadvantages that catalyze periods of significant innovation. Wars viewed from this perspective can raise the level and urgency of local scientific investments (factor creation) and disrupt customer relationships (demand conditions). World War I caused the loss of foreign assets and trademarks (including Bayer aspirin) of German chemical companies. It also provided a dramatic stimulus for the chemical industries in the United States, the United Kingdom, and Switzerland. Because of their neutrality in World War II, Switzerland and Sweden benefited enormously in many industries.

Chance events have asymmetric impacts on different nations. The two oil shocks hit energy-dependent nations earlier and harder. Wars often have very different effects on winners and losers. It is interesting that the defeated powers, Germany, Japan, and Italy, are perhaps the three most successful nations in the postwar period in terms of broadly based success in international competition.[66] Nations that feel the effect of a chance event first, or most severely, may move early to deal with it. The oil shocks ultimately helped upgrade Japanese industry, because Japan was especially vulnerable to energy costs and took aggressive steps toward energy conservation.

While chance events can allow shifts in competitive advantage in an industry, national attributes play an important role in *what nation exploits them*. The nation with the most favorable "diamond" will be most likely to convert chance events into competitive advantage. This will reflect an environment aligned to the new sources of advantage and firms pressured to move most aggressively to seize them.

page 108.

INVENTION, ENTREPRENEURSHIP, AND CHANCE

Invention and entrepreneurship are at the heart of national advantage. Some believe these acts are largely random; a visionary or inventor might be located in any nation, which means that the birth of a world-class industry can take place anywhere. If we accept this view, the determinants become important in developing an industry but its initial formation is a chance event.

Our research shows that neither entrepreneurship nor invention is random; assigning a role to chance does not mean that industry success is wholly unpredictable. For example, the United States is such a favorable environment for commercializing medical innovations that dozens of American entrepreneurs sprang up in most new product and service areas. In fact, foreign entrepreneurs have come to the United States to start their medical products companies because it is such a hospitable environment for this particular sector.

The determinants play a major role in locating where invention and entrepreneurship are most likely to occur in a particular industry. Demand conditions signal needs better in some nations than others. National factor creation mechanisms affect the pool of knowledge and talent. Supplier industries provide crucial help or are the source of new entrants. And so on. What looks like chance is actually the result of differences in national environments. The particular firm or individual that will do the innovating is less predictable, though, than the nation or nations in which they are likely to be located.

Sometimes the act of invention is indeed wholly decoupled from other national characteristics. For example, insulin was first isolated in Canada despite the lack of particularly favorable demand, scientific infrastructure, or other national circumstances bearing on insulin. Whether such pure inventions, or isolated acts of entrepreneurship, develop into a competitive industry, however, is again not random. The "diamond" has a major influence on the ability to convert an invention or insight into an internationally competitive industry. If a nation has only the invention, other nations' firms will be likely to appropriate it. Insulin, for example, was turned into an international commercial success by companies based in Denmark and the United States, not in Canada. Both Denmark and the United States possessed favorable demand conditions, specialized factor pools, and other advantages. Therefore, the invention, once the basic technology was known, took root and prospered elsewhere.

THE ROLE OF GOVERNMENT

Having described the determinants of national competitive advantage, a final variable is the role of government. Government is prominently discussed in treatments of international competitiveness. Many see it as a vital, if not the most important, influence on modern international competition. Government policy in Japan and Korea is particularly associated with the success these nations' firms have enjoyed.

It is tempting to make government the fifth determinant. Yet this is neither correct nor the most useful way to understand government's role in international competition. Government's real role in national competitive advantage is in influencing the four determinants. This is illustrated schematically in Figure 3–5, which now reflects the complete system.

Government can influence (and be influenced by) each of the four determinants either positively or negatively, as should be evident from some of my earlier examples. Factor conditions are affected through subsidies, policies toward the capital markets, policies toward education, and the like. Government's role in shaping local demand conditions is often more subtle. Government bodies establish local product standards or regulations that mandate or influence buyer needs. Government is also often a major buyer of many products in a nation, among them defense goods, telecommunications equipment, aircraft for the national airline, and so on. The way this role as a buyer is played can either help or hurt the nation's industry.

Government can shape the circumstances of related and supporting indus-

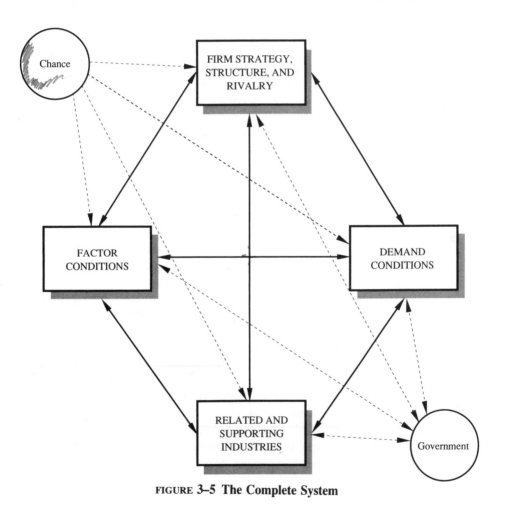

FIGURE 3–5 The Complete System

tries in countless other ways, such as control of advertising media or regulation of supporting services. Government policy also influences firm strategy, structure, and rivalry, through such devices as capital market regulations, tax policy, and antitrust laws.

Government policy, in turn, can be influenced by the determinants. Choices about where educational investments are made, for example, are affected by the number of local competitors (see Chapter 4). Strong home demand for a product may lead to early introduction of government safety standards.

It is evident that the influence of government on the underlying determinants of national competitive advantage can be positive or negative. By stimulating early demand for facsimile machines, for example, the Japanese government aided competitive advantage. Facsimile documents were approved as legal documents by the Japanese Ministry of Justice, and Japan was among the first nations to allow the connection of facsimile machines to normal telephone lines. Yet if government regulation or purchases lead to unusual or anachronistic early demand that distracts local firms from serving international markets, the role of government is negative. For example, the highly restrictive Italian regulation of local financial markets has contributed to the inability of Italian financial institutions to compete internationally.

/The positive and negative roles of government in the process of creating competitive advantage are highlighted and clarified by viewing government as an influencer of the national "diamond."/ A far broader array of public policy options and outcomes is possible than is normally explored. The determinants suggest government policies that are starkly different in some cases from those suggested by a less holistic conception of national advantage. Attempting to hold down the value of a nation's currency, for example, appears desirable if factor costs are seen as the dominant determinant of national advantage in a static world in which technology and skills are constant. My theory emphasizes that market pressures and resulting innovations can overcome factor costs, however, so that undervaluation can slow the upgrading of competitive advantage and direct firms to less sustainable, price-sensitive market segments. The result is a long-term loss of competitive advantage. Government "help" that removes the pressures on firms to improve and upgrade is counterproductive.

Government has an important influence on national competitive advantage, though its role is inevitably *partial*.[67] Government policy will fail if it remains the only source of national competitive advantage. Successful policies work in those industries where underlying determinants of national advantage are present and where government reinforces them. Government, it seems, can hasten or raise the odds of gaining competitive advantage (and vice versa) but lacks the power to create advantage itself. I will return to all these issues when I discuss government policy (Chapter 12).

THE DETERMINANTS IN PERSPECTIVE

In this chapter I have described the determinants of national advantage in an industry and the role of chance and government in affecting them. The determinants measure the extent to which the national environment is a fertile one for competing in an industry. I described earlier the forces that lead firms to create and sustain competitive advantage. The "diamond," reflecting many diverse elements of a nation, measures how well the nation creates and transmits these forces to its firms, as well as the presence of the insight and tools needed for competitive advantage.

The individual determinants that define the national environment are mutually dependent because the effect of one often depends on the state of others. Sophisticated buyers will not translate into advanced products unless, for example, the quality of human resources is sufficient to act on meeting buyer needs. Selective factor disadvantages will not motivate innovation unless rivalry is healthy and company goals support sustained investment. At the broadest level, weaknesses in any one determinant will constrain an industry's potential for advancement and upgrading.

As I have described the "diamond," I have touched on many examples of the role of social and political history and values in influencing competitive success. Social norms and values affect the nature of home demand, for example, as well as the goals of managers and the way firms are organized. Social and political history influence the skills that have been accumulated in a nation and the institutional structure within which competition operates. These aspects of a nation, which some called cultural, cannot be separated from economic outcomes. Also, "cultural factors" are, upon close inspection, often closely intertwined with economic factors. For example, Japanese management-labor relations are not particularly cultural but a function of lifetime employment, the nature of incentive systems, and management behavior toward workers. These practices all grew out of bitter labor strife in Japan both before and immediately after World War II.

Cultural factors are important as they shape the environment facing firms; they work through the determinants, not in isolation from them. Such influences are important ones to competitive advantage, however, because they change slowly and are difficult for outsiders to tap or emulate. Social and political history and values create persistent differences among nations that play a role in competitive advantage in many industries. They will be apparent when I turn to individual nations in Part III.

I have had little to say in this chapter about leaders, a popular subject in historical analyses of industrial or national success. This is not to diminish the importance of leaders but to suggest that they too do not work separately from the determinants I have described. Leaders confront problems, challenges, and opportunities that are produced by their national environments. Leaders are attracted to different problems in different nations, a function of the determinants. In Japan, revered leaders such as Akio Morita and Konosuke Matsushita work in consumer electronics. In America, individuals such as Thomas J. Watson, Jr., Seymour Cray, Kenneth Olson, and Steve Jobs work or have worked in computers. These are both instances of industries where the national environment is particularly favorable for competitive advantage. The success of leaders depends on possessing insights into opportunities and the tools to exploit them, about which this chapter has had much to say.

Indeed, one definition of a leader is someone who understands and believes in the determinants more than other individuals. Leaders believe in dynamics and change. They do not accept constraints, and know that they can change the nature of outcomes. They are in a position to perceive something about reality that has escaped others, and have the courage to act. It is often leadership that determines *which* of the firms from a favorably situated nation will succeed and fail.

So far, I have described the determinants of national advantage singly and jointly. But the "diamond" is an interactive system in which the parts reinforce each other. These dynamics will be the subject of the next chapter, along with their implications for the emergence and development of competitive industries and their eventual loss of competitive advantage.

4

The Dynamics of National Advantage

In the preceding chapter, I described how each of the determinants singly and jointly contributes to or detracts from national advantage. The effect of one determinant often depends on the state of others. Sophisticated home buyers will not translate into advanced products, for example, unless the quality of human resources permits companies to meet buyer needs. The determinants of national advantage constitute a complex system, through which a great many national characteristics influence competitive success. Yet the system is an evolving one, in which one determinant influences others. Sustained competitive advantage in an industry grows out of the self-reinforcing interplay of advantages in several areas, creating an environment which is difficult for foreign competitors to replicate. The national system is as, or more, important than the individual parts.

My purpose here is to show how the individual determinants combine into a dynamic system. I will begin by describing how each determinant is influenced by the others. Two elements—domestic rivalry and geographic industry concentration—have especially great power to transform the "diamond" into a system, domestic rivalry because it promotes upgrading of the entire national "diamond," and geographic concentration because it elevates and magnifies the interactions within the "diamond."

A consequence of the system of determinants is that a nation's competitive industries are not spread evenly through the economy but are connected in what I term *clusters* consisting of industries related by links· of various kinds. In Italy, for example, over 40 percent of total exports are due to clusters of industries all connected to food, fashion, or the home. In Sweden, over 50 percent of total exports are industry clusters in transportation, forest products, and metals. The operation and interplay of the determinants allow us to explore how competitive industries and industry clusters are born and evolve in a process in which the role of individual determinants shifts and changes. They also provide a framework for understanding why national industries wither and die.

RELATIONSHIPS AMONG THE DETERMINANTS

The determinants of national advantage reinforce each other and proliferate over time in fostering competitive advantage in an industry. As this mutual reinforcement proceeds, the cause and effect of individual determinants becomes blurred. The "diamond" that I use to illustrate the determinants, with its two-way arrows connecting them, is symbolic of these relationships. In reality, every determinant can affect every other determinant, though some interactions are stronger and more important than others.

PATTERNS OF FACTOR CREATION

The types of factors that are created in a nation are influenced by the other determinants, particularly those types of factors most decisive for national competitive advantage. Investments in generalized factors, such as transportation infrastructure and the secondary school system, are made in virtually every nation, normally as a natural outcome of public policy at various levels of government.[1] What varies is a nation's rate of investment, its desired standard of performance, and how well the institutions involved in creating factors are administered. Though generalized factors are not a sufficient basis for national advantage in advanced industries, they serve as the foundation from which advanced and specialized factors are created. Sustained national investment in generalized factors is therefore essential to national economic progress.

What is important for competitive advantage is unusually effective mechanisms for creating and upgrading factors that are advanced and specialized, such as a world-class research institute in composite materials technology. Investments in advanced and specialized factors are governed in more complicated ways. Unlike generalized factors, investments in them are far from evenly spread across national economies. Nations differ widely in the industries and sectors in which private and social investments in factor creation are made. In Denmark, for example, there are eleven agricultural colleges, the world-renowned Carlsberg Institute engaged in fermentation and biologi-

cal research, and several professorships of furniture design,[2] all in a nation
of only five million inhabitants. In the last half of the nineteenth century
and the first part of the twentieth century, when the German chemical industry
was building its advantage, German factor creation mechanisms in chemistry
were unparalleled. Germany was the home of the finest university chemistry
programs, the Kaiser Wilhelm (later Max Planck) Institutes, the most advanced scientific journals in chemistry, and numerous factor creation investments undertaken by firms, including several apprenticeship programs for
workers. I discussed in the previous chapter the plethora of specialized
research institutions in flower growing, packaging, and handling in Holland.

Where do advanced and specialized factors get created and upgraded in
a nation? The other determinants of national competitive advantage have
an important if not decisive role. Figure 4–1 illustrates several of the most
important influences.

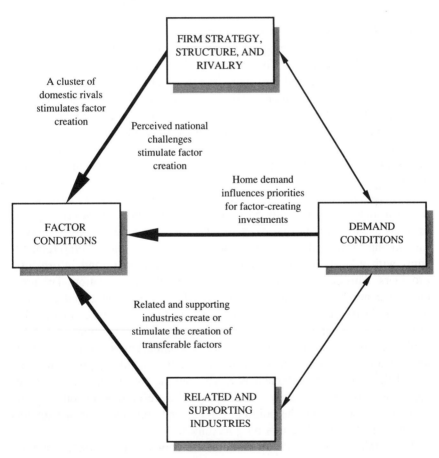

FIGURE **4–1 Influences on Factor Creation**

Factor creation is perhaps most strongly influenced by *domestic rivalry*. A number of local competitors in vigorous competition stimulates the rapid development of skilled human resources, related technologies, market-specific knowledge, and specialized infrastructure. Firms invest in factor creation themselves, singly or via trade associations, under pressure not to fall behind. As important, however, is that a group of domestic rivals also triggers special programs in local schools and universities, government-supported technical institutes and training centers, specialized apprenticeship programs, industry-specific trade journals and other information providers, and other types of investment in factors by government and other institutions. Such considerations explain the Danish agricultural colleges and furniture design professorships as well as the German investment in factors underpinning the chemical sector. A group of domestic rivals also stimulates job seekers to invest in gaining specialized skills. Factor creation will be unusually rapid in industries viewed as prestigious or as national priorities, because the attention of individuals, institutions, and government entities is most attracted.[3]

These effects will be most pronounced if the rivals are all located in one city or region. The number of degree programs, data bases, and research efforts in and around New York related to Wall Street is a typical example. There are four specialized university research institutes catering to the auto industry in southern Germany. The University of California at Davis, in the heart of California wine country, is another good example. It has become perhaps the world's leading center of wine-making research in close and active interchange with the California wine industry. This combination has engendered many of the innovations in wine making in recent years.

A single large firm can have some effect on factor creation, particularly if it is a major economic influence on a town or region. However, a group of rivals usually provides far more stimulation for several reasons. Competition among local rivals spills over into efforts to court and develop relationships with educational institutions, research institutions, and information providers. This competition will boost the rate of factor creation. The presence of a number of rivals not only signals the importance and potential of the industry, causing individuals and institutions to take notice,[4] but also reduces the risk of investing in creating specialized facilities and skills. With a group of rivals, there are a number of potential employers for graduates and several supporters and users of specialized facilities, programs, and knowledge. Rivals mitigate each other's bargaining power in sourcing specialized factors, promoting an expanded supply. The presence of several domestic rivals may also elevate the political support and consensus for investments in creating specialized factors by government.

These influences of a group of domestic competitors on factor creation are important and common, but far from automatic. Local firms must perceive the need for constantly upgrading the pool of factors, and work actively to stimulate investments in them. Vigorous domestic rivalry plays a special role in encouraging such an outlook, as does pressure from buyers.

The pool of factors and the rate at which they are created are also shaped by the presence of *related and supporting industries*. Such industries possess or stimulate their own mechanisms for creating and upgrading specialized factors. Some of the factors are usually transferable. The educational programs, skilled personnel, and research capabilities in biology resulting from the Danish food and brewing industries, for example, have been a source of advantage in Denmark's insulin, industrial enzyme, and food additives industries.

The existence of a cluster of several industries that draws on common inputs, skills, and infrastructure also further stimulates government bodies, educational institutions, firms, and individuals to invest in relevant factor creation or factor-creating mechanisms. Specialized infrastructure is enlarged, and spillovers are generated that upgrade factor quality and increase supply. Sometimes, whole new industries spring up to supply specialized infrastructure to such clusters. Such a mutually reinforcing process is occurring in the United States, where the existence of world-class industries in mainframe computers, minicomputers, microcomputers, software, and logic circuits has sent public and private institutions scrambling to create software training centers and courses. The resulting pool of skilled human resources, knowledge, scientific centers, and specialized infrastructure is benefiting the whole group of industries and is spilling over to benefit other industries that depend on information technology.

Another influence on the particular types of factors that are created is *demand conditions*. A disproportionate level of demand for a product, or unusually stringent or sophisticated demand, tends to channel social and private investments into related factor creation. Advanced and specialized factors of production grow up to help meet pressing local needs. For example, nations depending heavily on sea transport such as Sweden and Norway have well-developed specialized educational and scientific institutions geared toward oceanography and shipping. In the United States, both government and private investments are substantial in defense-related technologies and skills. High or stringent local demand raises the likelihood of a consensus in government for making factor-creating investments. It also focuses the attention of individuals and firms on the need for making private investments.

Factor-creating investments in a nation cumulate over time. The role of the other determinants in influencing educational, research, and other institutions provides an ongoing and additive stimulus for specialized factor creation. Over time, differences in the rate and direction of such investments among

nations can lead to wide national differences in the stock of specialized
factors relevant to an industry.

INFLUENCES ON DEMAND COMPOSITION AND SIZE

Home demand conditions for an industry reflect many national attributes
such as population, climate, social norms, and the mix of other industries
in the economy. Yet the other determinants play an important role as well,
as illustrated in Figure 4–2.

Perhaps the most important influence is again *domestic rivalry*. A group
of local rivals invests in marketing, driven by an intense commitment and
attention to the home market that I have described. Pricing is aggressive

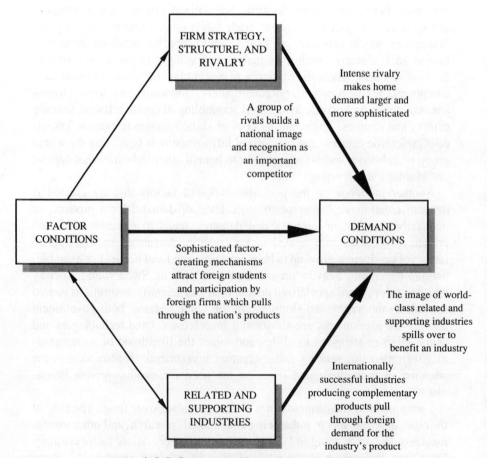

FIGURE **4–2 Influences on Home Demand Conditions**

to gain or hold local market share. Products are introduced earlier at home, and the available product variety is greater. The very presence of competitive local rivals builds awareness of the industry. Primary demand in the home market is stimulated. Not only is home demand expanded, but saturation occurs sooner and leads to aggressive efforts to internationalize. A good example is the wine industry, where high per capita consumption in wine-producing countries such as Italy and France is due in large part to the presence of local production that is associated with wide local availability of wine and greater product awareness by local consumers.

The soft drink industry illustrates some additional points. Per capita consumption of soft drinks in the United States is the highest in the world, driven by the aggressive local rivalry between Coca-Cola, Pepsi Cola, Seven Up, and others. Though these firms are global competitors, the intensity of competition in America is greater than elsewhere. Pride and proximity are just two of the reasons, which I discussed more fully in the previous chapter. The result is that advertising rates are extremely high and new products are introduced first in the United States. Here and in other industries, intense domestic rivalry not only stimulates but, in effect, *creates* home demand through product and marketing innovation.

Active domestic rivalry also upgrades home demand. The presence of a number of aggressive local rivals works to educate local buyers, make them more sophisticated, and make them more demanding because they come to expect a lot of attention. In furniture and shoes, for example, Italian demand has been upgraded by the rapid pace of new product introduction in the home market by the hundreds of Italian companies. Not all Italian firms export, and those that do rarely offer their full line abroad. The net result is that Italian consumers see and learn more and become more discriminating. (In other nations, less competitive local manufacturers offer less choice and quality.) The sophisticated, specialized retailers of furniture and shoes in Italy that I have described earlier reflect intense domestic rivalry in shoe and furniture manufacturing, because local firms were looking for distribution outlets. Retailers compete vigorously and display a wide variety of products for Italian consumers to choose from, educating the consumer in the process. An industry, once internationally competitive, creates conditions domestically which reinforce that competitiveness.

Vigorous domestic rivalry can also enhance *foreign* demand. A group of domestic rivals builds a national image in the industry. Foreign buyers take notice and include the nation in their review of potential sources. Their perceived risk in sourcing from the nation is reduced by the availability of alternative suppliers. A good example is in cosmetic pencils, where foreign cosmetic companies sought out German suppliers for a new type of pencil because of the group of world-leading German pencil manufacturers in Nuremberg.[5]

The presence of successful *related and supporting industries* can also enhance international demand for an industry's products. One way is through transferability of reputation. The image of Swiss watches carried over in the 1950s and 1960s to other Swiss precision mechanical goods, for example. The same thing has happened in the 1980s in consumer electronics, where "Made in Japan" has come to signify quality and sophistication in a widening range of product lines often produced by different Japanese companies. Another way that competitiveness in related industries improves demand conditions is through the "pull through" of complementary products, as I described earlier.

Internationalization of home demand is also influenced by *factor conditions,* especially factor-creating mechanisms. A nation with sophisticated factor-creating mechanisms connected to a particular industry will attract foreign students and firms, who will learn and observe. These students and firms often provide foreign demand for a nation's goods and services. The role of foreign doctors trained in the United States, discussed earlier, is a good example.

DEVELOPMENT OF RELATED AND SUPPORTING INDUSTRIES

The presence, breadth, and international success of related and supporting industries in a nation is influenced by other determinants. Some of the most important relationships are shown in Figure 4–3.

Factor conditions in an industry, especially factor-creating mechanisms, can also influence the development of related and supporting industries. Skills, knowledge, and technology created in an industry spill over to benefit them.

The breadth and specialization of supporting industries is enhanced by the *size and growth of home demand* for a product.[6] Where home demand is significant, more and specialized suppliers emerge to address unmet needs, replace imports, or perform activities previously carried out in-house more efficiently or effectively. The efficiency of domestic suppliers frequently rises with increasing industry scale.

Once again, the most potent influence on the development of related and supporting industries is aggressive *domestic rivals.* A group of internationally successful domestic firms, selling worldwide, channels global demand to the domestic supplier industry. For example, the world-leading group of Japanese semiconductor firms has triggered the emergence of world-leading Japanese semiconductor manufacturing equipment suppliers.

While an isolated company has to clamor for attention from suppliers of machinery, equipment, or services that also serve other industries, a group of domestic rivals begins to be noticed. Existing supplier industries create

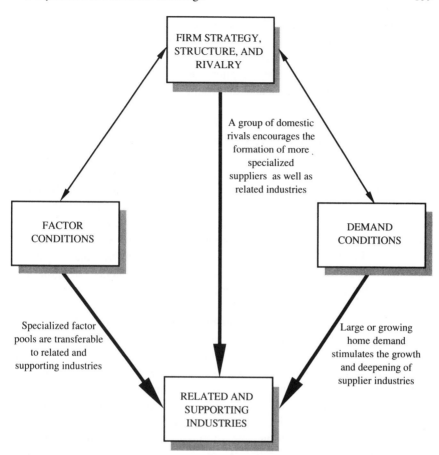

FIGURE 4–3 Influences on the Development of Related and Supporting Industries

products and services tailored to the industry. Broad-line suppliers establish special divisions to serve the industry. For example, the concentration of rivals in movie and television production in Hollywood has led to the growth of a thriving and highly specialized group of supplier industries, ranging from special effects firms, to costume designers, to firms providing production insurance. Their quality and proximity to the studios only enhance Hollywood's competitiveness.

A group of internationally successful home-based rivals challenges and pushes the supplier industry to develop. Under the pressure that grows out of aggressive competition among their customers, suppliers must innovate and improve or be replaced. The proximity of home bases facilitates interchange and collaboration on research. The supplier industry is also able to follow its customers abroad to serve their international operations, speeding its own globalization.

A group of strong domestic rivals, locked in active competition, not only helps attract and upgrade established suppliers but can raise the standard of competition in supplier industries via entry. Internationally successful firms in one industry often enter supplier industries. They also are the source of spin-offs, as employees leave to produce components, machinery, or services.

A group of domestic rivals is far superior to one dominant firm for encouraging and upgrading home-based supporting industries. The presence of competing home customers reduces the risk of selling to the industry and the bargaining power of any individual buyer, encouraging more entry into supplier industries as well as greater investment and specialization.[7] In addition, the existence of a number of domestic customers, each with some differences in needs, widens the technical avenues explored by suppliers and creates more potential centers of development that speed the rate of innovation. Finally, the existence of a group of customers creates greater odds that some will backward integrate to enter the industry, invigorating rivalry, or that a spin-off will emerge from one of them that brings a new way of competing.

Cases where internationally competitive supplier industries emerged out of competitive customer industries are numerous. In Denmark, for example, the large export-oriented dairy and fishing sectors have stimulated dozens of supporting industries in areas such as food processing machinery, fishing boats, varnish for boats, and radiotelephone communications equipment. A number of these industries are internationally competitive. In Germany, a world-leading chemical industry has led to the development of world-class suppliers of pumps, liquid measurement and control equipment, and numerous other products for the chemical sector. In America, the early success in electronics gave birth to international leadership in such supplier industries as test and measurement equipment.

Active domestic rivalry also frequently leads to entry and ultimately international positions in related industries. Many of the leading Japanese camera companies, for example, diversified into small copiers. Their transferable technical expertise in optics, along with established international distribution networks, accelerated the process by which Japan achieved world leadership. Similar cases are numerous. Italian machine tool producers moved into factory automation, for example, while Korean television set producers moved into videotape recorders.

INFLUENCES ON DOMESTIC RIVALRY

Domestic industry structure is also influenced by other determinants. Particularly important is the role of other determinants in affecting the number, skills, and strategies of domestic rivals (see Figure 4–4).

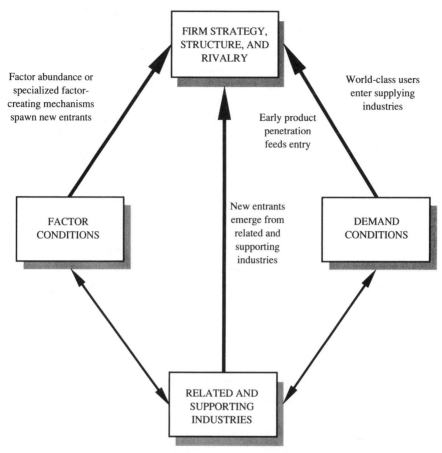

FIGURE 4–4 **Influences on Domestic Rivalry**

Demand conditions enhance domestic rivalry when demanding home buyers seek multiple sources and encourage entry. Highly sophisticated buyers based in a nation may also themselves enter the industry. This is particularly significant when they have relevant skills and view the upstream industry as strategic. A good example is the Japanese robotics industry. Many of the early and leading robotics competitors, such as Matsushita and Kawasaki, are major robot users. They initially designed robots for internal consumption but then began to sell to others. This example illustrates how sophisticated users who enter an industry can bring an acute understanding of buyer needs as well as a pool of expertise and thus enhance the prospects for competitive advantage. The response of other industry participants to their entry further upgrades the entire domestic industry. Spin-offs founded by ex-employees of sophisticated users lead to many of the same effects. Early market penetration by a product in a nation also stimulates entry, not only by users but from other industries and via start-ups.

New entry into an industry is also encouraged directly or indirectly by strong national positions in *related or supporting industries*. Entry by established firms in downstream or related industries, which often occurs along with start-ups, produces a domestic industry structure that can be especially conducive to investment and innovation. Suppliers, particularly those that are internationally successful, often enter user industries. In Sweden, for example, Sandvik moved from specialty steel into rock drills, while SKF moved from specialty steel into ball bearings. Supplier strengths in the base industry often provide a competitive advantage in entering downstream industries. Entrants from supplier industries bring with them skills and resources from their core businesses that can reshape competition in the new industry, providing the foundation for competitive advantage. They can frequently share brand names, distribution channels, and technological know-how.

Entry by suppliers into downstream industries provides a ready means for transmitting information and skills and thus supports the sort of vertical interchange so important to competitive advantage. Entrants from supplier industries in a nation also have a level of commitment to the new industry that may be unmatched by start-up entrants in other nations. Suppliers view the new industry as strategic because it is interrelated with their base business, and their brand reputations may well be at stake. The time horizon for decisions is lengthened, and short-term profitability diminishes in importance.

Even if world-class suppliers themselves do not enter the user industry, they are frequently a source of spin-offs or of other entrants. Supplier employees frequently leave to enter the industries they serve when an opportunity is seen to transfer skills or to exploit better the technology. Such entrants possess skills and relationships that can be important advantages. A well-developed supplier (subcontractor) industry also lowers barriers to entry into the downstream industry by firms who compete as assemblers. The presence of many parts suppliers, for example, facilitated new entry into the Japanese sewing machine and car audio equipment industries.

Many of the same reasons explain why competitive advantage in a related industry leads to entry into an industry. A high-profile industry often draws attention to industries that are related to it. In Italy, for example, world prominence in ski boots (centered in the Montebelluna area) led to entry by firms from the same region in aprés-ski boots. The timing of entry from one national industry into a related industry is not random. Often related diversification takes place when the base industry either becomes saturated or declines. Because this tends to affect all competitors in a nation at about the same time, it is typical to see a number of local companies simultaneously diversify into a related industry. Imitation merely compounds the process.

Entrants from a related industry, like entrants from buyer and supplier industries, are particularly desirable types of entrants for purposes of upgrading competitive advantage in a nation. They often possess transferable strengths that lead to higher-order advantages. Many Japanese competitors in personal computers, for example, began as consumer electronics companies. While Japan's overall international position in personal computers is modest, strength is now growing in laptops where compact size and liquid crystal display technology are essential to competitive success. These are areas where Japanese firms bring unique and transferable strengths not present in American and European competitors.

The most vibrant competitive advantage often comes when entrants from a number of different supplier and related industries converge in a new industry. Here a variety of approaches to competing are brought to bear and innovation often flourishes. Entrants from related industries also have the same high stakes in succeeding in the new industry as was the case with entry by suppliers. Japanese office machine companies who entered facsimile, for example, had brand reputations to protect and were anxious to have a full line of products to gain greater clout with distribution channels.

A third influence on domestic structure is the role of *specialized factor creation mechanisms* in spawning new entrants, usually start-ups, into an industry. There are countless examples where a world-class laboratory, academic department, or educational institution was the source of entrepreneurs who entered an industry. The U.S. biotechnology industry, for example, has been built by scientists from top university departments who formed companies.

DOMESTIC RIVALRY AND THE NATIONAL "DIAMOND"

Among the most striking findings from our research, as I have already discussed, is the prevalence of several domestic rivals in the industries in which the nation had international advantage. Rivalry has a direct role in stimulating improvement and innovation. Its significance is enhanced because rivalry is so important in stimulating firms to reap the benefits of other determinants, such as demanding buyers or sophisticated suppliers. But these benefits of domestic rivalry, described in the previous chapter, are only the most direct and more obvious ones. The discussion here makes it clear that domestic rivalry spills over to benefit the nation in many other and important ways that are usefully summarized:

- stimulating new rivals through spin-offs
- creating and attracting factors
- upgrading and expanding home demand

- encouraging and upgrading related and supporting industries
- channeling government policy in more effective directions.

The broader effects of domestic rivalry are closely related to an old but often neglected notion in economics known as external economies. These are economies that accrue beyond the individual firm but within the group of firms in a locality or nation. External economies arise in classic treatments because of spillovers of technology and the benefits of specialization that accrue to a large industry (though individual firms may be small).[8]

External economies within a nation of a much broader sort are a central feature of competition, and their role is more pervasive than generally supposed. Some of the most important external economies have to do with the process of innovation and upgrading competitive advantage that I have described. A group of domestic rivals draws attention to the industry, encourages investments by individuals, suppliers, and institutions that improve the national environment, and creates diversity and incentives to speed the rate of innovation, among other benefits.[9] External economies not only benefit the national industry but often extend to related industries within the nation, and their strength is heightened by geographic proximity. Many of the most important benefits do not cross national boundaries easily, however, and are difficult for foreign firms to tap even with a local subsidiary.

THE DETERMINANTS AS A SYSTEM

Nations achieve success in international competition where they possess advantages in the "diamond." Because the requirements for success in industries and industry segments differ widely, and because a limited pool of resources precludes success in all industries, nations can enjoy dominance in one industry and fail miserably in another. Nations can also prosper in one industry segment and lack competitive advantage in another.

In the most successful national industries, it is often hard to know where to start in explaining competitive advantage: the interplay and self-reinforcement of the determinants are so complex as to obscure cause and effect. The national environment becomes a more favorable one for competing over time as the "diamond" restructures itself. The system is also constantly in motion. The national industry continually evolves to reflect shifting circumstances, or it falls into decline.

Advantages in the entire "diamond" are not always necessary for competitive advantage in simple or resource-intensive industries and in the standardized, lower-technology segments of more advanced industries. In natural resource-intensive industries and those with low levels of technology, factor costs are frequently decisive. In standardized, price-sensitive segments of more sophisticated industries, technology obtainable through licenses or by purchasing foreign machinery may be sufficient and home demand advantages unnecessary because models and features are well-established and easy to copy. Industries and segments such as these offer the best prospects for nations earlier in the development process, as I will discuss below.

Competitive advantage in more sophisticated industries and industry segments, however, rarely results from only a single determinant. Usually, advantages in several combine to create self-reinforcing conditions in which a nation's firms succeed internationally. This is because competitive advantage in sophisticated industries depends fundamentally on the rate of improvement and innovation. A nation's firms which lack sophisticated home buyers, capable suppliers, or other favorable determinants face grave difficulties in innovating more rapidly than rivals who possess them. Also important, as was emphasized in the previous chapter, is that the beneficial effect of one determinant often depends on the state of others. The ability of Japanese consumer electronics firms to capitalize on demanding home buyers and rapid saturation, for example, depends on the presence of a pool of highly skilled workers and electronics engineers, goals that foster aggressive investment, and fierce domestic rivalry. Broad advantages in the "diamond" are also important because the interactions among the determinants introduce new information, new skills, and new players into industry competition, leading to more rapid innovation and competitive upgrading. While a nation's firms may initially draw their competitive advantage from just one determinant, sustaining it will usually be difficult unless advantages expand to include others.

Even in more advanced segments and industries, a nation need not always have advantages in *all* determinants to succeed internationally. Japanese firms, for example, have succeeded in typewriters despite little domestic demand. The Swiss firm Cerberus is a world leader in fire detection despite no domestic rivals. Where a nation has a disadvantage in one determinant, national success normally reflects unusual advantage in others and some way of compensating for the disadvantage. In Japanese typewriters, for example, early competitors were well-established companies, such as Brother, that were diversifying out of the related sewing machine industry. They drew on transferable technology, a ready pool of efficient parts suppliers, relatively low wage costs for skilled labor, and established distribution networks. The sewing machine companies were later joined by a number of other entrants, some of whom were Japanese electronics companies seeking a broader position in office automation. The result was fierce rivalry among a large group of diverse domestic rivals. In America and Europe, in contrast, the number of competitors was small, production technology not highly automated, and rivalry muted. Unusual advantages in related and supporting industries, coupled with fierce rivalry, allowed Japanese typewriter firms to succeed without any home demand advantages.

Demand characteristics did, however, play an interesting role. In the decade after World War II, scarce foreign exchange was used for imports of food and materials into Japan. It was impossible to obtain foreign exchange to import typewriters. Japanese companies needed typewriters to type letters in foreign languages to overseas customers and to correspond with the American occupation authorities. This demand, though small, could only be satisfied through domestic typewriter production. As a result, Brother and other sewing machine producers, who were used to producing complex mechanical products, entered the typewriter industry. Upon close scrutiny, we found that each of the four determinants had some role in creating advantage in the great majority of the successful national industries we studied.

The Cerberus case illustrates how a missing determinant is compensated for. The founder of Cerberus invented the ionization smoke detector while doing physics research at the Zurich Polytechnic Institute. The company's dynamism, despite little domestic rivalry, was a function of demand-side pressures. Swiss risk aversion (the Swiss are the most highly insured people in the world) and the presence in Switzerland of several industries sensitive to fire risk such as banking, hotels, and chemicals have resulted in Switzerland's having by far the highest penetration of fire detection equipment in the world. Substitute products, including sprinkler systems, security guards, and no formal fire detection at all, played the role of domestic rivals. Cerberus was forced to aggressively market the benefits of fire detection to its Swiss customers, lobbied local government agencies to make fire detection equipment mandatory, and persuaded insurance companies to provide incentives for installation.

In small nations, missing domestic rivalry may sometimes be offset by openness to international competition and global strategies in which the nation's firms meet foreign rivals in many countries. Both conditions apply to Cerberus. Yet the cases in which a nation is successful in an industry where there was *never* domestic rivalry are comparatively rare. More generally, compensating for a missing determinant is most likely once a nation's firms have achieved international leadership. Here, global strategies may be employed to tap selectively into advantages in other nations, and firms can command the attention and support of foreign buyers and suppliers.

Some of the determinants of national advantage are specific to a single industry, such as the presence of sophisticated customers for a product or the existence of particular related and supporting industries. Other national attributes may be more broadly applicable and may potentially affect competitive success in a range of industries. Swiss language skills, notoriously picky Japanese consumers, and U.S. strength in software have potential benefits for many industries.

While broadly applicable sources of competitive advantages bode well for success in a number of industries provided the nation has real superiority, no single source of national advantage is meaningful or significant in an entire economy or even a fraction of one. Moreover, generalized national characteristics are seldom unique and may be more easily accessed by foreign firms with narrower, industry-specific local circumstances.

In most industries, a nation succeeds because it combines some broadly applicable advantages with advantages that are specific to a particular industry or small group of industries. In facsimile, for example, Japan combined a broadly applicable pool of skilled and motivated workers and a generalized advantage in complex automation and mass production with unique demand conditions for facsimile machines (such as an inability to use telex machines and a group of established multinationals with a strong need for international communications) and strong positions in a number of vital related and supporting industries (such as small motors, cameras, copiers, and office automation equipment). Conversely, the United States has failed repeatedly to capitalize on basic research strength in important generalized technologies because other more industry-specific determinants were not in place.

SUSTAINABILITY

Advantage is sustained because its sources are widened and upgraded. Some determinants provide a more sustainable basis for advantage than others. The current pool of factors, for example, is less important than the presence of specialized and preeminent institutions for factor creation. More broadly, conditions that provide dynamic advantages (faster innovation, early mover advantages, pressures for upgrading) are more important than those conferring static advantages (such as factor costs and a large home market). Hence, demand composition is frequently more important than demand size, while the intensity of domestic rivalry is more important than whether firms have an international outlook.

While disadvantages in one or two determinants do not necessarily prevent a nation from gaining competitive advantage, the most robust competitive advantage tends strongly to be associated with widespread and self-reinforceing advantage in many determinants. Foreign competitors can sometimes duplicate one advantage or another, especially factor costs (through foreign sourcing) or sometimes demand conditions (by selling in another nation's home market). Moreover, a nation's position vis-à-vis some determinants may not be unique. However, national advantage arises when the *system* is unique. The entire system is difficult and time-consuming to duplicate. The mutual dependence and reinforcement of the determinants are essential to upgrading, and the system is hard to penetrate from another home base.

The process of building the system in a nation is also often protracted. Once in place, it allows the entire national industry to progress faster than foreign rivals can.

The important role of the interaction among the determinants means that the likelihood of achieving and sustaining advantage in an industry depends in part on how effectively the interactions work in a nation. Nations succeed in industries in which they work particularly well. How rapidly and well do rivals upgrade their suppliers? How quickly and completely do educational institutions and other factor-creating mechanisms respond to the needs of an emerging industry? How fast do buyers gain sophistication? How many new entrants emerge out of factor-creating institutions, suppliers, or customers?

The effectiveness of these interactions depends in part on other determinants such as the capacity for new business formation. It also depends on the fluidity and responsiveness of the institutions, individuals, and firms in the nation that relate to a particular industry. Geographic concentration of firms, customers, suppliers, and institutions that create factors also plays a role as I will discuss subsequently.

Similar considerations also bear on the ability of a nation to widen and upgrade its advantages in an industry over time. There may be several nations with comparable positions in one or two determinants. The speed and efficacy with which the entire "diamond" develops will determine which nation gains advantage.

A multinational with its home base in another nation faces great difficulties in replicating a national "diamond," even if it establishes a subsidiary in the nation and competes with a coordinated global strategy. Coordination costs and information failures raise the odds against a foreign multinational gaining the full benefit of national advantages from afar. Firms with their home base in the nation will have more fluid and open access to local markets, and be more sensitive to local buyers. They will also communicate with and tap into advantages from local suppliers more easily, draw more readily on local factor creation mechanisms, and be more stimulated and invigorated by local rivals. To beat the odds, a foreign multinational's local subsidiary must in effect become its "home base." But this requires that it is given worldwide strategic control of the business as well as core R&D facilities, effectively transforming the subsidiary into a local company.

CLUSTERING OF COMPETITIVE INDUSTRIES

The competitive industries in a nation will not be evenly distributed across the economy, as emerges clearly from the analysis of individual nations in Part III. The systemic nature of the "diamond" promotes the *clustering* of a nation's competitive industries. A nation's successful industries are usually linked through vertical (buyer/supplier) or horizontal (common customers, technology, channels, etc.) relationships.

A particularly striking example is in Denmark. Figure 4–5, which includes a number of the industries in which Denmark is internationally competitive, illustrates how these industries are all connected. Within Denmark there are also clusters of competitive industries related to the home (household products and furnishings) and to health (pharmaceuticals, vitamins, medical equipment, and the like). The health cluster is linked to the agricultural cluster by technology and raw material requirements.

Sweden is competitive not only in pulp and paper but in wood-handling machinery, sulphur boilers, conveyor systems, pulp-making machinery, control instruments, paper-making machinery, and paper-drying machinery. While it is generally uncompetitive in chemicals, Sweden is also internationally successful in chemicals used in pulp and paper making. In Italy, important clusters relate to fashion, furnishings, and food. In larger nations, the number of clusters is larger, but clustering is no less distinct. In Germany, for example, important clusters relate to chemicals, metalworking, transportation, and printing. In each case the nation is internationally successful in finished goods, machinery used in producing the goods, specialized inputs, and often related services. The phenomenon of clustering seems to occur in all nations, including those not part of my sample. In Israel, for example, principal clusters are related to agriculture (crops, fertilizers, irrigation equipment, other specialized equipment and machinery) and defense.[10]

The patterns of national competitive advantage in each of the nations we studied, which I will discuss fully in Part III, all exhibit extensive clustering. The phenomenon of industry clustering is so pervasive that it appears to be a central feature of advanced national economies.[11,12]

The reasons for clustering grow directly out of the determinants of national advantage and are a manifestation of their systemic character. One competitive industry helps to create another in a mutually reinforcing process. Such an industry is often the most sophisticated buyer of the products and services it depends on. Its presence in a nation becomes important to developing competitive advantage in supplier industries.[13] American leadership in consumer packaged goods and consumer durables contributed to American pre-eminence in advertising. The Japanese strength in consumer electronics meant that Japanese success in semiconductors has been skewed toward memory chips and integrated circuits that are used heavily in these types of products, while America retains leadership in complex logic chips used in computers, telecommunications equipment, and defense electronics, all industries where U.S. firms are competitive. More recently, the strong international position of Japanese automobile companies has gradually been elevating Japanese automotive suppliers to international stature. The presence of a

FIGURE 4–5 Partial Clustering of Competitive Industries in the Danish Economy

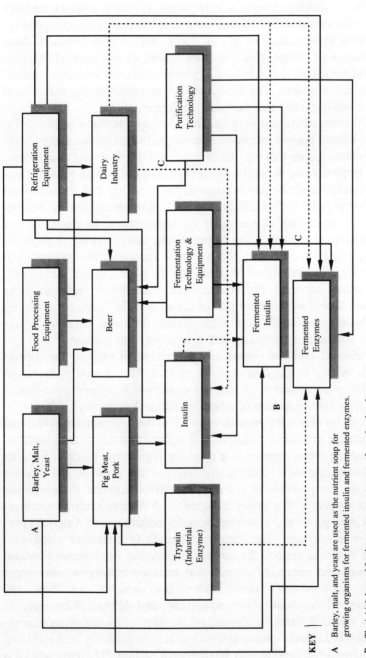

KEY

A   Barley, malt, and yeast are used as the nutrient soup for
     growing organisms for fermented insulin and fermented enzymes.

B   The initial demand for detergent enzymes comes from slaughter houses.

C   Insulin and enzyme producers sourced skilled workers from the dairy industry.

Solid line = Supply Relationship
Broken line = Common Technologies or Common Inputs

world-class buyer industry at home not only benefits suppliers domestically but can help pull these suppliers abroad; Japanese auto parts suppliers are rapidly building overseas plants today as Japanese automakers have established foreign production.

Competitive supplier industries in a nation also help encourage world-class downstream industries. They provide technology, stimulate transferable factor creation, and become new entrants. One internationally competitive industry also creates new related industries, through providing ready access to transferable skills, through related entry by already established firms, or by stimulating entry indirectly through spin-offs.

Once a cluster forms, the whole group of industries becomes mutually supporting. Benefits flow forward, backward, and horizontally. Aggressive rivalry in one industry tends to spread to others in the cluster, through the exercise of bargaining power, spin-offs, and related diversification by established firms. Entry from other industries within the cluster spurs upgrading by stimulating diversity in R&D approaches and providing a means for introducing new strategies and skills. Information flows freely and innovations diffuse rapidly through the conduits of suppliers or customers who have contact with multiple competitors. Interconnections within the cluster, often unanticipated, lead to the perception of new ways of competing and entirely new opportunities. People and ideas combine in new ways. Silicon Valley provides a good example.

The cluster becomes a vehicle for maintaining diversity and overcoming the inward focus, inertia, inflexibility, and accommodation among rivals that slows or blocks competitive upgrading and new entry. The presence of the cluster helps increase information flow, the likelihood of new approaches, and new entry from spin-offs, downstream, upstream, and related industries. It plays, in a sense, the role of creating "outsiders" from within the nation that will compete in new ways. National industries are thus more able to sustain advantage instead of losing it to other nations who innovate.

The presence of an entire cluster of industries magnifies and accelerates the process of factor creation that is present where there is a group of domestic rivals. Firms from an entire group of interconnected industries *all* invest in specialized but related technologies, information, infrastructure, and human resources, and numerous spillovers occur. The scale of the entire cluster encourages greater investment and specialization. Joint projects by trade associations involving firms from different industries are common. Government and university attention is heightened. The pull of size and prestige in attracting talent to the cluster becomes stronger. The nation's international reputation in the field grows.

The cluster of competitive industries becomes more than the sum of its parts. It has a tendency to expand as one competitive industry begets another.

The directions of expansion depend on the cluster formation processes that are most prevalent in the nation. Two examples are illustrative. In Japan, clusters tend to widen horizontally as established Japanese companies aggressively enter related industries, driven by the nature of their goals and a proclivity for internal diversification. In Italy, clusters have a tendency to deepen vertically, as new companies spin off to serve ever more specialized niches and enter supplier industries. Related diversification by established companies is more unusual.

As clusters develop, resources in the economy flow toward them and away from isolated industries that cannot deploy the resources as productively. As more industries are exposed to international competition in the economy, the more pronounced the movement toward clustering will become.

National competitive advantage, then, resides as much at the level of the cluster as it does in individual industries.[14] This carries important implications for government policy and company strategy.

INTERCHANGE WITHIN CLUSTERS

Underlying the operation of the national "diamond," and the phenomenon of clustering, is the exchange and flow of information about needs, techniques, and technology among buyers, suppliers, and related industries. When such interchange occurs *at the same time that active rivalry is maintained in each separate industry,* the conditions for competitive advantage are the most fertile. I have described some of the reasons why such interchange bolsters competitive advantage but have said little so far about the mechanisms through which it occurs. These are important, because effective interchange among independent firms in a nation is far from assured (though far more likely than interchange among firms with home bases in different nations). Firms in a national cluster have different and sometimes conflicting economic interests. Suppliers and buyers, for example, face conflicts over prices and the resulting division of profits. This may bias or restrict information flow among them because of a desire to keep information proprietary.[15] The fact that fluid interchange may benefit all the local firms in competing with foreign rivals does not wholly mitigate their concerns about relative bargaining position.

We observed sharp differences across nations, as well as across industries within nations, in how, and how well, clusters work. Nations gain an important national advantage where national attributes are supportive of intracluster interchange. The presence of especially effective interchange in a particular industry or sector, such as in Swedish mining and mining equipment, is a potent predictor of sustained national success.

Mechanisms that facilitate interchange within clusters are conditions that help information to flow more easily, or which unblock information as well as facilitate coordination by creating trust and mitigating perceived differences in economic interest between vertically or horizontally linked firms.[16] Some examples are the following:

Facilitators of Information Flow

- Personal relationships due to schooling, military service
- Ties through the scientific community or professional associations
- Community ties due to geographic proximity
- Trade associations encompassing clusters
- Norms of behavior such as a belief in continuity and long-term relationships

Sources of Goal Congruence or Compatibility Within Clusters[17]

- Family or.quasi-family ties between firms
- Common ownership within an industrial group
- Ownership of partial equity stakes
- Interlocking directors
- National patriotism

Japan provides an interesting example of well-functioning clusters (see Chapter 8). The operation of Japanese clusters is encouraged by an array of circumstances. The most obvious are the large groups, or *keiretsu,* which are loose groupings of firms with shareholding connections, remnants of much tighter pre–World War II industrial holding companies. At the center of each group is a major bank, such as the Sumitomo Bank or the Mitsubishi Bank.

It is widely perceived that these groups are important to decision making and that firms in the group represent guaranteed markets for each other. But, in fact, the group (or the mother bank) has relatively little influence on strategic or even tactical decisions. Yet these group ties are important principally for their role in the functioning of clusters. Companies consult each other and work well together because of their "special" relationship. They cooperate on technological development and send clear signals to each other about market needs. In fiber optics, for example, NEC Corporation and Sumitomo Cable (both Sumitomo Group companies) have worked closely for many years on developing fiber optics technology. NEC specializes in electronics and Sumitomo Cable on optical fiber and cable—a business with very different sources of competitive advantage.[18] The prevalence of related diversification through internal development by Japanese companies also leads to the presence of an entire array of business units competing in vertically and horizontally linked industries within a single firm. Because they were start-ups instead of acquired, exchange of information and skills among these units is remarkably fluid.

Other important facilitating mechanisms within clusters exist in Japan. One is the partial equity stakes that larger Japanese firms sometimes have in their suppliers. Another is geographic proximity of firms. Interchange within clusters is also promoted by personal relationships. Japanese develop lifelong relationships with others in the same university class, and classmates often meet regularly for decades. This creates a network for interchange among related firms. Japanese trade associations also provide a conduit for information and technical exchange, often legitimized by government sponsorship. Trade associations often encompass a group of related industries and their supplier industries.

Japanese clusters also illustrate another important point. At the same time as these mechanisms to promote interchange among linked industries are present, rivalry within each individual industry remains intense. Hard bargaining also occurs between buyers and suppliers, a function of the large number of rivals in most industries and the competitive pressure they face.

In Italy, very different but often equally effective mechanisms underlie the workings of clusters. The most important are the family or quasi-family ties that frequently link firms together. Italian industry is also particularly concentrated geographically. Many industries are centered in one or two towns. Swiss-style clustering works in yet other ways. For example, compulsory military service is an important creator of a network of relationships. In Sweden, financial groups and interlocking directorships are prominent mechanisms. In Germany, the large banks play a broadly similar role.

Mechanisms that facilitate interchange within clusters are generally strongest in Japan, Sweden, and Italy and generally weakest in the United Kingdom and United States (see Chapters 7, 8, and 9).[19] Yet one cannot generalize across industries in a nation, and understanding national advantage requires a deeper look at individual sectors. It is interesting, for example, that in the United States clusters seem to work best in health care and computing. Here, scientific ties often overcome the natural reticence of American managers toward interchange. These sectors contain some of the most internationally successful industries in the United States.

THE ROLE OF GEOGRAPHIC CONCENTRATION

Competitors in many internationally successful industries, and often entire clusters of industries, are often located in a single town or region within a nation. The vast majority of Italy's woolen textile producers, for example, are located in two towns. While geographic concentration of Italian industries is widely recognized, however, what is less understood is how prevalent the phenomenon is.[20] British auctioneers are all within a few blocks in London. Basel is the home base for all three Swiss pharmaceutical giants. Danish windmill producers are centered in Herning. In America, many leading U.S. advertising agencies are concentrated on Madison Avenue in New York City. Large-scale computer manufacturers Control Data, Cray Research, Burroughs (now part of Unisys) and Honeywell are all headquartered in or near Minneapolis, Minnesota. Pharmaceutical and related companies, among them Merck, SmithKline, American Cyanamid, Squibb, Becton-Dickinson, and C. R. Bard, are based in the New Jersey/Philadelphia area. General aviation aircraft producers are concentrated in Wichita, Kansas, and minicomputer producers in Boston.

Figures 4–6 and 4–7 show maps of Italy and Germany, respectively,

FIGURE **4–6 Geographic Concentration in Selected Italian Industries**

FIGURE 4–7 Geographic Concentration in Selected German Industries

illustrating just a selection of the industries that are grouped around one or a few small geographic areas. Concentrations of domestic rivals are frequently surrounded by suppliers, and located in areas with concentrations of particularly sophisticated and significant customers. The city or region becomes a unique environment for competing in the industry. The information flow, visibility, and mutual reinforcement within such a locale give meaning to Alfred Marshall's insightful observation that in some places an industry is "in the air."[21] Though not all industries are as striking as these, the physical proximity of world-class rivals is so common across nations as to hold important insights into the process of competition.[22]

Geographic concentration of firms in internationally successful industries often occurs because the influence of the individual determinants in the "diamond" and their mutual reinforcement are heightened by close geographic proximity within a nation. A concentration of rivals, customers, and suppliers will promote efficiencies and specialization.[23] More important, however, is the influence of geographic concentration on improvement and innovation. Rivals located close together will tend to be jealous and emotional competitors. Universities located near a group of competitors will be most likely to notice the industry, perceive it to be important, and respond accordingly. In turn, competitors are more likely to fund and support local university activity. Suppliers located nearby will be best positioned for regular interchange and cooperation with industry research and development efforts. Sophisticated customers located nearby offer the best possibilities for transmitting information, engaging in regular interchange about emerging needs and technologies,[24] and demanding extraordinary service and product performance. Geographic concentration of an industry acts as a strong magnet to attract talented people and other factors to it. Similar arguments apply to many of the other determinants.

Geographic concentration is also encouraged by the processes of entry I have described. Spin-offs have a tendency to locate near the original company, because entrepreneurs not only live there but have established relationships. Entry from supplier, user, or related industries also frequently occurs in the same location.

Proximity increases the concentration of information and thus the likelihood of its being noticed and acted upon. Proximity increases the speed of information flow within the national industry and the rate at which innovations diffuse. At the same time, it tends to limit the spread of information outside because communication takes forms (such as face to face contact) which leak out only slowly. Proximity raises the visibility of competitor behavior, the perceived stakes of matching improvements, and the likelihood that local pride will mix with purely economic motivations in energizing firm behavior. The process of clustering, and the interchange among industries in the cluster, also works best when the industries involved are geographically concentrated.[25] Proximity leads to early exposure of imbalances, needs, or constraints within the cluster to be addressed or exploited. Proximity, then, elevates the separate influences in the "diamond" into a true system.

Geographic concentration does carry with it some long-term risks, however, especially if most buyers, suppliers, and rivals do not operate internationally. I will return to these issues below.

THE COMPETITIVE ADVANTAGE OF CITIES AND REGIONS

The importance of geographic concentration raises interesting questions about whether the nation is a relevant unit of analysis. The conditions that underlie competitive advantage are indeed often localized *within* a nation, though at different locations for different industries. Indeed, the reasons why a *particular* city or region is successful in a particular industry are captured by the same considerations embodied in the "diamond"; for example, the location of the most sophisticated buyers, possession of unique factor-creating mechanisms, and a well-developed local supplier base.[26] The theory can be readily extended to explain why some cities or regions are more successful than others. The London region is prospering in the United Kingdom, for example, because of its advanced demand for many goods and services, its clusters of supporting industries, and the presence of highly skilled labor pools, among other considerations.

Locational effects are powerful ones even if cultural, political, or cost differences between locations are small. A good example is the United States. Geographic concentration of industries within the United States persists despite linguistic, cultural, and legal homogeneity, open and efficient internal transportation and communication, a common currency and capital markets, and virtually no internal trade barriers.

But nations are still important. Many of the determinants of advantage are more similar within a nation than across nations. Government policy (such as tax policy and regulation), legal rules, capital market conditions, factor costs, and many other attributes that are common to a country make national boundaries important. Social and political values and norms are linked to nations and slow to change. Yet it is the *combination* of national and intensely local conditions that fosters competitive advantage. National policies will be inadequate in and of themselves. State and local government can play a prominent role in industry success.

Indeed, falling communication and transportation costs and the reduction in barriers to trade and international competition make locational advantages for industry innovation even more significant, because firms with true competitive advantages are more able to penetrate other markets. While classical factors of production are more and more accessible because of globalization, competitive advantage in advanced industries is increasingly determined by differential knowledge, skills, and rates of innovation which are embodied in skilled people and organizational routines. The process of creating skills and the important influences on the rate of improvement and innovation are intensely local. Paradoxically, then, more open global competition makes the home base more, not less, important.

The U.S. case suggests, moreover, that cultural interchange among nations will not overcome the differences among them that underpin competitive advantage. Efforts at European unification are raising questions about whether the influence of nations on competition will diminish. Instead, freer trade will arguably make them more important. While the effective locus of competitive advantage may sometimes encompass regions that cross national borders, such as the region including southern Germany and German-speaking Switzerland, Europe is unlikely to become a "nation" from a competitive perspective. National differences in demand, factor creation, and other determinants will persist, and rivalry within nations will remain vital.

THE GENESIS AND EVOLUTION OF A COMPETITIVE INDUSTRY

Though sustained national advantage in an industry is a reflection of a well-functioning "diamond," the whole system is rarely in place at the start. An advantage in a single determinant often provides the initial impetus for an industry's formation in a nation, not infrequently around a single firm. Sometimes chance also plays a role. Once begun, a process is set in motion in which competitors are attracted, other determinants become significant, and advantages accumulate provided the potential is present.

In practice, the formation of a local industry is normally triggered by one of three determinants. An initial advantage in *factors of production* often provides the seeds for an internationally competitive industry or a predecessor industry in the cluster. The Swedish specialty steel industry grew initially out of deposits of low phosphorous content iron ore in Sweden. The local availability of factors, particularly natural factors, is what often attracts initial attention to an industry.

In more advanced industries, early competitors may emerge out of specialized factor-creating mechanisms. Personnel trained in particular fields will apply their knowledge and skills to enter an industry where there is actual or potential domestic demand. University research will lead to promising ideas that form the basis of one or more companies. The presence of a foreign company operating in the nation may lead to spin-offs by citizens of the host nation who have gained specialized knowledge in the industry. Sometimes, particularly unique factor pools will lead to entry into industries even if most demand is international. In Denmark, for example, a top professor in physical chemistry trained a number of students who set out looking for fields in which to apply their skills. The result was Haldor Topsoe, a leading supplier of catalysts used in the oil and chemical industries, where there was (and still is) little Danish demand.

The seeds of competitive industries are also found in *related and supporting industries*. The Italian ski boot industry grew out of a local industry producing climbing and hiking shoes in the mountainous northeastern region of Italy. The Italian factory automation industry emerged out of the machine tool industry. The Japanese lift truck industry is directly descended from the truck industry. Initial entrants may be firms from supplier or related industries, or start-ups by employees that have left them.

Demand conditions provide another common foundation for a competitive industry. Substantial or distinctive local demand is an early stimulus to the formation of local firms. Air-conditioning equipment was developed in the hot and humid eastern United States in the early 1900s, at a time when American prosperity made the luxury of air-conditioning more affordable than in other warm regions. Hard rock mining equipment producers grew up in Sweden to serve the needs of mining companies exploiting large (though difficult to mine) Swedish ore deposits. Supercomputers developed initially in the United States because of extraordinary demand for computer power in U.S. government defense and scientific programs.

In developing nations, the genesis of most competitive industries is basic factor conditions or unusually heavy local demand. In more advanced nations, the sources of initial industry formation are more numerous. New industries are far more likely to emerge out of related and supporting industries or from university laboratories or specialized schools. Demand stimuli for new industries are more likely to reflect unusually early, segmented, or sophisticated demand than merely demand quantity.

Alternatively, an initial company may form in a nation essentially by chance. An entrepreneur will get an idea largely through serendipity, unconnected to any unusual factor pool or related industry. Or a scientist will make an important breakthrough that could have occurred in a number of nations. Such examples occurred in our research, but more often the genesis of an industry could be traced to one of the determinants. As I discussed earlier, much invention or entrepreneurship is influenced by the "diamond" though its predictability is less than the process that occurs once the initial foundation for an industry is in place.

The ability of an initial seed from whatever source to grow into a competitive industry in the nation will be a function of whether advantages in other determinants are already present or can be created. To get beyond the initial period of industry formation, domestic rivalry is nearly always necessary. Spin-offs, and/or entry from vertically or horizontally related industries, transform a nascent industry into one with international potential. Rivalry spurs firms to move beyond the initial advantage that led to the formation of the industry and begin the process of upgrading.

To sustain advantage, the nation's bases for advantage in the industry must normally broaden and cumulate, particularly where the initial advantage is in basic factors of production. I have described how the determinants reinforce each other and how advantages in them widen. An important missing determinant, most notably the absence of competitive rivalry or unavailability of skilled personnel or technical knowledge, will normally stall the process of upgrading competitive advantage. The promising industry will not achieve its potential.

Sustainable competitive advantage can come quickly if a nation either possesses advantages in several determinants right from the start or rapidly develops them. In facsimile, for example, Japan had unique demand conditions and a group of well-established, international companies already competing in essential related and supporting industries. Especially if a nation starts with little more than a basic factor advantage, however, the path to sustained competitive advantage may be a longer one. The nation's firms must obtain the technology, assets, and global network to compete with higher-order advantages and in advanced segments.

In cars, for example, Japan began exporting in the 1950s, only to reach international prominence in the late 1970s. Initial success reflected low-cost skilled labor and cheap steel, home demand conditions that led Japanese firms to concentrate on small cars (a segment ignored by most foreign rivals), an emphasis on "fits and finishes" to satisfy Japanese consumers who are very sensitive to external appearance, surface defects, and proper initial functioning, and a succession of entrants that resulted by the 1960s in intense domestic rivalry. Japanese auto firms then moved to achieve world-class status in process technology, spurred by rising labor costs and labor shortages. They also encouraged the formation and growing sophistication of Japanese parts suppliers, located in close proximity to their assembly facilities. More recently, Japanese auto producers have become product innovators and offered increasingly broad lines of differentiated products. As the sources of advantage in the nation broaden, causality often becomes blurred as the determinants mutually reinforce each other.

As advantages are developed in several parts of the "diamond" and especially as the mutual reinforcement within the "diamond" begins to take place and cumulate, a national industry can achieve *remarkable rates of improvement and innovation* for a period of years or even decades. New domestic rivals spin off which open up new industry segments. Suppliers develop whose capabilities and resources allow more rapid improvement in process technology than firms themselves could support. Buyers with growing sophistication open up more new product avenues to pursue. This surge of rapid upgrading continues until the possibilities using then available basic technologies become exhausted or, more likely, when constraints to industry dynamism begin to emerge, many times created from within the industry itself (see below).

Nations frequently gain their initial advantage in an industry in one or two segments, as the Japanese auto case illustrates. If an initial factor advantage has triggered the industry, the early segment is often a price-sensitive one. Upgrading competitive advantage requires that firms compete in more advanced segments. The ability to do so depends on broadening the bases of national advantage to include such things as demand advantages, the presence of sophisticated supplier and related industries, and the development of specialized factor-creating mechanisms. Ironically, success in sustaining competitive advantage often requires that local firms deliberately undermine the initial bases for their success in the process of upgrading. Only intense domestic rivalry (or the threat of entry) can pressure such behavior.

The loss of competitive position in some industry segments is often a sign of healthy upgrading. The need to overcome selective factor disadvantage will push a nation's firms out of standardized, lower technology, and price-sensitive segments over time. Selective disadvantages in factor costs also influence the directions taken by improvements and innovation. The shift to newer, higher technology and more differentiated segments over time means that the process of innovation is occurring. In contrast, the loss of competitive position in new or differentiated segments, something that has occurred in many U.S. industries such as machine tools and ceramics, is a serious concern.

Chance is often involved in helping to accelerate the process by which an industry upgrades and penetrates international markets. A chance event, such as a demand surge, an input price shift, or a major technological shift, creates a discontinuity that nullifies the advantages of traditional leaders and allows a nation's firms to leap ahead. Japanese TV set manufacturers, for example, capitalized on booming demand and capacity shortages among U.S. manufacturers of color sets to gain a foothold in the vital U.S. market.

It should be clear from this discussion that a nation's basis for competitive advantage in an industry can move around the "diamond" as the industry evolves, shifting and often cumulating. Figure 4–8 illustrates the process in the Italian ski boot industry. Ski boots were initially made of leather. The Italian ski boot industry grew out of the local hiking shoe industry. Growing Italian home demand during the postwar boom provided the impetus for industry development. The 1956 Winter Olympics in Cortina, Italy, provided a major stimulus. Because of a ready pool of labor with skills in footwear and the fertile environment in Italy for starting family firms, many companies soon entered the Italian industry. Nearly all were located in the same town, Montebelluna, in northeastern Italy, where hiking boot production took place. Growing rivalry among the Italian companies led to continuous advances, encouraged by the needs of sophisticated, fast-skiing Italian consumers. When the principle of the plastic shell for a ski boot was developed by a small U.S. company, the Italian industry (led by Nordica) leapt to perfect the idea. An internationally successful Italian plastic injection molding machinery industry grew up nearby to supply the industry. Internationalization was driven by the saturation of the home market and increasing economies of scale in production and design. Eventually, a world-ranking après-ski boot industry developed in the same region, widening the cluster further.

A nation that begins such a process early gains the types of early mover advantages I described earlier, such as economies of scale, customer relationships, and a brand name established without the need to sell against rivals.

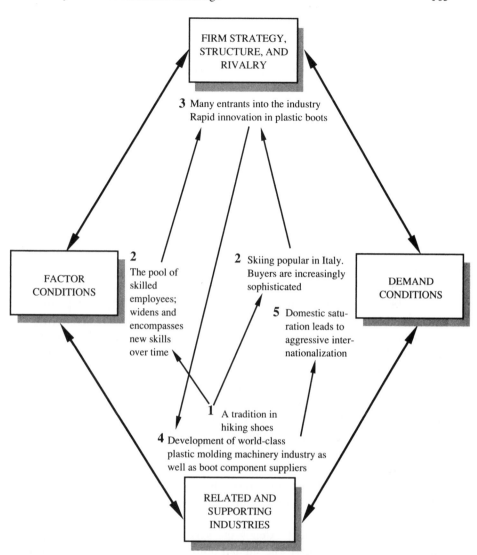

FIGURE **4–8 The Evolution of National Advantage in the Italian Ski Boot Industry**

Even more significant, however, may be the opportunity to be the *first to create a national ''diamond.''* The diamond establishes the conditions for higher-order advantage and is slow and extremely hard to replicate. Once one nation has it, the cost of entry rises substantially.

The process of gaining national advantage is one where history matters and where cause and effect become increasingly difficult to separate over time. The seed of a competitive industry may have been sown by chance. Or other nations may have been in a similar position initially. From there, though, the process of building a competitive industry takes on a momentum of its own. This momentum, fueled by the widening and self-reinforcement of the determinants, moves the industry toward broader and more robust advantages. The nation where this process takes place the most rapidly is the one that becomes successful.

THE DEVELOPMENT OF CLUSTERS

The process of industry evolution often breeds new competitive industries and hence builds or extends a cluster. Thus portions of a nation's economy develop a momentum that extends beyond individual industries and is a powerful force for economic development.

Nations differ in the typical path by which clusters emerge, a function of the types of firms in the economy, among other considerations. In Italy, the force behind many competitive industries is sophisticated consumer demand conditions for end products. A vibrant environment for entrepreneurship leads to the rapid proliferation of competitors and intense rivalry. End product industries then spawn competitive supporting industries. Clusters of competitive industries that achieve success are thus vertically deep, involving many stages of the vertical chain and industries providing machinery and other specialized inputs.

In Japan, as I discussed earlier, many competitive industries grow instead out of related industries. Because of the desire to redeploy employees and the prevalence of abrupt home market saturation, Japanese companies from one industry frequently enter an upstream, downstream, or related industry *en masse*. Where demand and factor conditions are supportive, intense domestic rivalry propels investment and innovation, and another competitive industry is born. In Japan, clusters of competitive industries are often quite wide horizontally and widen over time. Other nations fall somewhere in between these two extremes.

The formation of clusters extends the surges of progress in individual industries I spoke of earlier. The mutual reinforcement within clusters also leads to surges in innovation (and international competitive position) in whole sectors of a national economy. This is evident today in the consumer related electronics sector in Japan, where waves of innovation are spreading from traditional industries such as television sets, calculators, and audio equipment to new industries such as laptop personal computers and facsimile, and back again.

In an upgrading economy, rising factor costs due to opportunities in more productive industries will inevitably lead to a thinning of some clusters. The sustainability of a nation's position in particular industries within the cluster will vary because their competitive advantage is based on different determinants. Those industries (and segments) in which resources are employed least productively, because technology is the least sophisticated or products are the least differentiated, will lose competitive advantage. Activities in the value chain which are least productive relative to foreign firms will get relocated abroad. In the apparel sector, for example, Britain is highly competitive in thread though many other British apparel-related industries have lost international position. Other apparel industries were sensitive to labor costs. In thread, British companies were early movers and upgraded advantages. They established close relationships very early with customers around the world and gained economies of scale, substantial in the industry due to the need for a wide line of colors and varieties. Rapid service and color matching are essential to competitive advantage in the industry, since thread is a small cost item. British firms differentiated themselves along these dimensions and also established international production sites to offset labor cost disadvantages. The thread industry illustrates that an established industry can sustain position even if one determinant is lacking. Apparently isolated competitive industries in a nation were often part of an old cluster.

As an industry matures and the pace of innovation slows down or stops, the operative determinant of competitive advantage can shift back again toward basic factor costs. Yet the onset of factor disadvantages, if they are selective, should trigger upgrading. The national position in the industry may shrink but can be maintained in the more sophisticated segments provided that rivalry is healthy.

The mobility of technology has led some observers to argue that factor costs are becoming more important in international competition. While the mobility of technology may shorten the imitation lag, firms sourcing technology from other nations are always a generation behind. Moreover, the capacity to deploy technology is what leads to advantage, not mere access. The ability to employ and improve upon imported technology is powerfully influenced by the national "diamond." Competitive advantage is increasingly a function not of factors but of the ability to create and apply knowledge and technology to industry competition. Developments in information technology, new materials, and bioengineering are creating the conditions for waves of innovation and change in virtually every industry. Even in "traditional" or seemingly simple industries, "maturity" can be a false fear.

Italy has been able to exploit this situation repeatedly, as it has firms that have upgraded competitive advantage in such traditional industries as furniture, shoes, and cloth. Italian firms employ modern process technology and benefit from demanding and forward-looking local buyers. Part of the reason Italy has succeeded is that firms from other advanced nations have "written off" many of these industries to developing countries.[27] Sweden is another nation that has prospered in "mature" industries such as appliances, trucks, and mining equipment.

THE LOSS OF NATIONAL ADVANTAGE

As industries evolve, a nation's firms risk the loss of competitive advantage. The ability of a nation's firms to adapt successfully to industry changes is a function of the national "diamond." Where there are sophisticated home buyers, an improving pool of technical knowledge and skilled personnel, and intense local rivalry combined with accumulated competitive advantages such as economies of scale, brand reputation, and established global networks, a nation's firms can change and adapt to retain competitive advantage for many decades. Factor disadvantages that cannot be handled through innovation can be offset through dispersing activities in the value chain to other countries.

National competitive advantage in an industry is lost, however, when conditions in the national "diamond" no longer support and stimulate investment and innovation to match the industry's evolving structure. The national industry may not perceive needed change, may fail to invest aggressively enough to advance, or may be blocked by having assets and skills that are specialized to outmoded ways of competing and that make responding to change more profitable to newcomers. Some of the most important reasons for eroding advantage are the following:

Factor Conditions Deteriorate. Factor conditions can deteriorate for a variety of reasons. Most troubling is if a nation falls behind in the rate of creation and upgrading of factors. If the skills of specialized human resources or the base of science and technology related to an industry deteriorate relative to another nation, then competitive advantage will usually fade. Rising factor costs are also a common threat to competitive advantage. They should lead to efforts to innovate, greater focus on more advanced industry segments, and further globalization. With a proper response, pressure from rising factor costs can lead to more sustainable competitive advantage. Loss of competitive advantage in some segments and even industries is inevitable, however, because improvement and innovation cannot outrun cost increases. In machine tools, for example, simple, manual varieties are now made in Taiwan and other NICs. Where a nation's firms make little effort to upgrade competitive position, however, the loss of advantage will be rapid, and serious concerns are raised about the long-term health of the economy.

Local Needs Fall Out of Synch With Global Demand. Competitive advantage is threatened if home demand conditions begin to diverge from those in other advanced nations. Local buyers thus pull a nation's firms in the wrong directions (or fail to push them in the right new directions). New buyer needs or new channels emerge elsewhere that are slow to appear in the nation, such as desire for new features, customization, or health concerns. As world demand for cars shifted toward smaller, fuel-efficient, and reliable varieties, U.S. preferences for larger cars delayed the American industry response. A nation may also erode home demand conditions by enacting unusual local regulations, or failing to deregulate an industry that has been deregulated elsewhere.

Home Buyers Lose Sophistication. A nation's firms will face grave difficulties in maintaining advantage if foreign buyers become more sophisticated than domestic ones. In factory automation equipment, for example, the early, advanced buyers for the most advanced equipment were once American, pioneers in mass production technology. In the last decade, Japanese, German, or Italian companies have been the process innovators in many industries, early to install such new technologies as robotics and flexible manufacturing systems. The difference is particularly noticeable among medium- and small-sized companies. American process equipment companies have faced growing difficulty competing with rivals from these nations, whose home buyers are more receptive to new technology. A specific case is automatic testing equipment for semiconductor manufacturing and electronic assembly. Here Japanese suppliers such as Advantest have captured strong positions, challenging American leaders.

Home buyers lose sophistication for a variety of reasons. They can become complacent if rivalry in their industry is diminished. Trade barriers can blunt the pace of innovation, or government regulations may skew buyer needs away from those in other international markets. Whatever the cause, loss of pressure from innovative local customers makes it difficult for a nation's firms to win the innovation race with foreign rivals.

Technological Change Leads to Compelling Specialized Factor Disadvantages or the Need for New and Missing Supporting Industries. Technological change is often a trigger for shifts in national competitive advantage because it can nullify old competitive advantages and create the need for new ones. A nation's firms, far advanced along one technological track, may find it difficult or unprofitable to jump to another one. Sometimes the effect of new technology is to shift the required factors, creating a major disadvantage in terms of available human resources, knowledge, or infrastructure. Other nations' firms may gain competitive advantage before readjustment can take place.

Technological change may also create the need for new supporting industries that a nation does not possess, such as software, biotechnology, new materials, or electronic components. Another nation where leading suppliers of the new inputs already exist may take over competitive advantage. In medical imaging, for example, Japanese firms have emerged as formidable competitors in new electronics-based segments where Japan has strong positions in supporting industries, though Japan had a weak position in traditional X-ray equipment.

The risk to competitive advantage is greatest where a new technology is integral to the industry and the industry represents a substantial application. Where new technologies only affect a small part of the total product and the industry represents a narrow application, the new technologies can often be sourced from abroad. For example, German and Swiss optical manufacturers have successfully obtained electronics technology through foreign subsidiaries and licensing, because applying electronics to optics requires deep and highly specialized knowledge. No electronics firm had the incentive to enter, given the moderate size of the industry.

Goals Limit the Rate of Investment. The rate of investment in R&D, marketing, information, and physical assets is influenced by corporate and managerial goals. These are a function of the national capital markets, ownership structure, tax policy, managerial incentives, social norms, and other influences I have described.

If goals in a national industry are inconsistent with sustained investment, competitive advantage will be lost to national industries that are more willing or better able to invest. If investors penalize the firm for making the investment necessary to maintain advantage, the national industry will fall behind in technology and productivity. If firms in an industry are owned by diversified corporations seeking steady cash flow, for example, harvesting of competitive advantage is a likely result. If high wages reduce the motivation of employees to improve their circumstances, the rate of investment in training often slows, and labor-management relations shift to preservation of the *status quo*. If a new generation of managers assume company leadership but lack commitment to the technology and industry, and are instead financial stewards of what has been inherited, the rate of improvement and innovation will inevitably slacken and decline.

Firms Lose the Flexibility to Adjust. Even if a nation's firms know how they must change to sustain competitive advantage, they may lose it if there are barriers to adjustment. Often barriers to adjustment are internal. Entrenched management may grow complacent or find it difficult or unsettling to change. Management practices or forms of organization may become rigid and counterproductive in new circumstances. Union restrictions can prevent process innovations or block investment in foreign subsidiaries needed for sourcing new technologies or factors. Local regulations may have frozen product standards or impeded the introduction of new technologies. Shifts in the perceived prestige of the industry can make it impossible for firms to attract the talent necessary to deal with foreign rivals.

Often there is an unwillingness to tamper with past success or redirect key personnel. In the Danish furniture industry, for example, an important advantage has been Danish design. Yet evolving market needs have dictated that the original design concept be updated. Firms and designers have been unwilling to do so.

Sometimes a nation's firms fail to innovate not because of inertia or complacency but because doing so would make their current asset base obsolete. This is true when the fixed costs of changing, including the necessary reconfiguration of facilities and internal organization and the retraining of personnel, will not be recovered. The fundamental problem is that a firm's assets and skills are specialized to its past strategy and technology. The new competitor, without such a legacy, has lower costs of innovating. The position of the established competitor is made more difficult when following foreign rivals will hasten the rate at which its assets lose value.

In many industries, however, innovation is profitable but firms are deterred by the short-term cost or organizational disruption of supplanting their current assets. American semiconductor firms, for example, were slow to abandon bipolar technology in favor of the newer metal oxide semiconductor (MOS) technology, allowing Japanese firms to gain position. Failure to innovate may preserve competitive position tied to a particular asset base in the short run but often will ensure that a firm's assets will have little value in the long run. Sustaining competitive advantage demands that firms make their own assets obsolete with new technology or methods before someone else does it for them. The will to do this usually grows out of intense competitive pressure, demanding local customers, and goals that support investment and reflect an intense commitment to the industry.

Domestic Rivalry Ebbs. One of the most common, and often the most fatal, causes of lost national advantage is the ebbing of domestic rivalry, since pressure to improve and adjust is often lost with it. While some local industry consolidation is often part of the process of gaining or sustaining competitive advantage, consolidation often proceeds too far. One or two firms come to dominate the industry. Alternatively, market sharing, informal agreements, or widespread cooperation can turn a group of aggressive rivals into a club. The Swiss watch industry of the 1950s and 1960s is a good case in point: a tight cartel froze industry structure.

There is also a natural and sometimes fatal tendency for successive generations of managers to want to eliminate "excessive" competition in order to make life more predictable. The resulting mergers or informal agreements undermine the process of innovation in the industry. Sustained financial success can also undermine rivalry, as firms become so self-satisfied as to not want to rock the boat. The German camera industry was supplanted by the Japanese in no small part because of self-satisfaction and a lack of real local competition.

A diminished taste for rivalry is also sometimes reflected in efforts to enlist government support or intervention.[28] Successful national industries often gain some political power, and the temptation is great to exercise it. If protection or insulation from competition is the result, a slowing rate of improvement and upgrading often leads to loss of competitive position. This then results in more calls for government intervention.

Loss of domestic rivalry is a dry rot that slowly undermines competitive advantage by slowing the pace of innovation and dynamism. Its effects are initially invisible. In fact, its onset may well be associated with *higher* domestic profitability because of the low rate of investment and self-satisfaction all around. Yet the rot begins undermining the foundation of the industry.

THE PROCESS OF DECLINE

A certain momentum governs the loss of competitive advantage that mirrors the positive momentum I described earlier. Momentum first works to mask decline, because of customer loyalties and the profit-enhancing role of under-investment. Decline once begun, however, is hard to arrest because the mutual reinforcement of the "diamond" works in reverse. For example, a loss of rivalry erodes the quality of the nation's buyers and suppliers, reducing buyer-side pressure, raising input costs, stunting the development of supplier technology, and slowing innovation even further or channeling it in the wrong directions. The industry's problems widen and compound.

The loss of competitive advantage may occur quickly if a major technological change or significant shift in buyer needs occurs. A different nation's firms can quickly surge to leadership, as Japanese firms did in television sets and cameras. Yet the loss of advantage is often a slow and sometimes nearly imperceptible process. The erosion of the American steel industry took decades, for example. Especially where there are early mover advantages (such as brand name, years of accumulated learning in product and process technology, and established global sales and service networks), the process can take many years, particularly if buyers in the industry are conservative in shifting suppliers because of high risks of product failure. The lack of innovation leads to a slow retreat into segments less interesting to foreign rivals or most protected by customer inertia. Profitability often remains artificially high for a time as firms fail to invest in R&D, marketing, and new facilities.

Regaining position in an industry where the loss of advantage has gathered momentum is, based on our research, exceedingly rare. The decline may be slowed or stopped by shrinking to the least exposed segments or instituting trade protection, but we found few examples where an industry regained its former strength. Much government policy aimed at "revitalizing" industries has failed. It is doomed because it does not address the determinants of competitive advantage and is therefore not directed at the true cause of decline. In Japan, for example, numerous "recession cartels" and "restructuring cartels" to assist troubled industries have rarely resulted in a significant international competitive position. Government can legitimately assist in helping resources to flow out of an industry. However, there is little likelihood that preserving firms and capacity will lead to a turnaround.

The low- and medium-priced Swiss watch industry is one of the few cases where an industry has truly rebounded, but even here the industry is much smaller and the period of decline was about thirty years. (Note that in the early years during which competitive advantage was declining, the Swiss industry was still growing.)[29] The principal cause of the rebound, Swatch, involved innovations in design, the use of plastic for cases and bands, and the automation of the production process. These innovations came only after the industry had shrunk for decades and firms reached near desperation. Interestingly, Hattori-Seiko and other Japanese firms that had risen to industry leadership based on the aggressive development of quartz and particularly quartz analog technology were slow to recognize the potential of plastic cases.

THE INSULAR CLUSTER

Complacency and an inward focus often explain why nations lose competitive advantage. Lack of pressure and challenge means that firms fail to look constantly for and interpret new buyer needs, new technologies, and new processes. They lose the stomach to make old competitive advantages obsolete in the process of creating new ones. They hesitate to employ global strategies to offset local factor disadvantages, or to tap selectively into advantages available in other nations. They are deterred by arrogance, lack of rivalry, and an unwillingness to upset the *status quo* and sacrifice current profits. The determinants of national advantage measure how likely it is that the national environment will allow its firms to succumb to these risks.

The cluster itself, particularly if it is geographically concentrated, may contain the seeds of its own demise. If rivalry ebbs and home buyers become pliant or lose sophistication, there is a tendency for the local cluster to become insular,[30] a closed and inward-looking system. The problem is exacerbated if most firms lack significant international activities and their primary commercial relationships are with each other (for example, suppliers sell almost exclusively to a single domestic industry). Firms, customers, and suppliers all talk only to each other. None brings fresh perspectives. The histories of Sheffield (British cutlery industry) and Lancashire (British cotton industry)[31] are good cases in point. Detroit may well prove to be another.

Such clusters are vulnerable to structural change and to chance events. Moreover, national clusters often have skills, assets, and strategies that

are specialized to a particular industry structure. Firms can adapt incrementally but may have difficulty dealing with radical innovation. The result of
significant structural change in the industry becomes a loss of position.

DECLUSTERING

The loss of national competitive advantage in one important industry creates
forces that can erode advantage in other industries in the cluster. Complacency
spreads from one industry to another. The loss of competitive advantage
in one industry reduces the quantity and sophistication of demand for the
industries that supply it. Conversely, the loss of competitive advantage in
local supplier industries diminishes the flow of state-of-the-art technology,
information, and stimulation to the industries they support. It also elevates
the cost of inputs during the unavoidable time lag before the buyers shift
their business to foreign suppliers.

While it is not inevitable, there is a tendency for a cluster of competitive
industries to begin to unravel if one or two industries within the cluster
that are important to innovation lose competitive advantage. In Sweden,
for example, the loss of market position in shipbuilding has led to the
erosion or demise of positions in many supplier industries, such as ship
brokers, marine engines, and steel. Those supplier industries that are still
strong, such as welding products (ESAB), shipboard fire detection equipment
(Consilium Systems), and shipboard cranes (Hägglunds), were ones that
had already established strong global positions and were organizationally
able to make major adjustments.

Clusters are most vulnerable if many firms lack global strategies and do
not have significant activities located in other nations. If most firms are
primarily suppliers to, or otherwise connected to, the one or two industries
in the cluster that are truly international, the loss of one of these industries
may well have a severe impact on the entire cluster. This was the case,
for example, in the British shipping cluster around Glasgow, where the
failure of the shipbuilding industry led to severe consequences for most of
the supporting industries. Competitive advantage is more sustainable in the
cluster if *many* of the industries have global positions. The Swedish shipping
cluster, in this respect, was in a somewhat better position.

Those industries in the cluster that have the most vigorous rivalry and
the most global outlook and customer base will have the greatest likelihood
of avoiding the domino effect, because their contacts with foreign buyers
or suppliers can partially replace or offset a diminished national environment.
The industries that enjoy the strongest early mover advantages may also
persist. In Britain, industries such as tobacco, whiskey, and confectionery
have sustained position, for example, because of well-established brand

names, global marketing presence, and the absence of any significant shifts in technology or buyer needs that would provide new competitors with the ability to overcome them.

The systemic character of national advantage carries both a blessing and a curse. The blessing is that positive reinforcement among the determinants creates momentum to upgrade an economy as well as to widen and deepen clusters.[32] The curse is that the same momentum works in reverse. Once begun, the loss of advantage in an economy seems to spread almost inevitably for some time. Loss of advantage in a range of advanced industries frees up resources and lowers factor costs, creating competitive advantage in other industries. The problem is that these other industries are prone to deploy the resources with lower productivity and the rate of productivity growth slows down. The negative spiral is hard to arrest unless the nation has the capacity to create advantage in new, high-productivity industries. Nations, in an important sense, are either moving ahead or falling behind in the upgrading of competitive advantage. Standing still is difficult.

THE DIAMOND IN PERSPECTIVE

At its core, the system of determinants of national competitive advantage I have described is a theory of investment and innovation. Internationally competitive industries are those whose firms have the capacity and will to improve and innovate in order to create and sustain a competitive advantage. Both improvement and innovation, in the broad sense that I use the terms, require investment in such areas as R&D, learning, modern facilities, and sophisticated training.

Gaining advantage in the first place requires a new approach to competing, whether it is perceiving and then exploiting a factor advantage, discovering an underserved segment, creating new product features, or changing the process by which a product is made. Sustaining advantage requires still further improvement and innovation to broaden and upgrade the sources of competitive advantage through advancing the product, the production process, marketing methods, and service.

The determinants in the "diamond" and the interactions among them create the forces that shape the likelihood, direction, and speed of improvement and innovation by a nation's firms in an industry.[33] They elucidate the conditions that provide the will of firms to make sustained investments.[34] My perspective is Ricardian, in that I view trade (and foreign investment) as determined most importantly by productivity differences, here broadened from Ricardo's theory to include differences in technology, factor quality, and methods of competing.

The availability and interpretation of information are central to the process of gaining competitive advantage, and the "diamond" captures some of the salient aspects. National competitive advantage grows out of conditions in a nation that signal, channel, or steer its firms to perceive opportunities for improvement and innovation and move early and in the proper directions to capitalize on them. This may mean concentrating first on the product variety most demanded, pursuing process innovation that yields the best process (for example, flexible automation versus automation of a standardized variety), or supplying a market segment others have ignored. Nations succeed in industries for which the national environment helps local firms perceive opportunities more clearly and/or see into the future. Selective factor disadvantages are valuable, for example, because they highlight problems that will become widespread. Similarly, the extent to which local demand anticipates demand elsewhere is a central concern.

Competitive advantage emerges from pressure, challenge, and adversity, rarely from an easy life. Selective factor disadvantages, powerful local buyers, stringent local needs, early saturation, capable and international suppliers, and intense local rivalry can all be essential to creating and sustaining advantage. Pressure and adversity are powerful motivators for change and innovation.[35] A nation's firms succeed in an industry because pressures are juxtaposed with some advantages in responding to them, such as sophisticated local demand, a highly developed supplier base, and specialized factor pools.

An analogy to biological evolution can be drawn. This literature stresses selective survival rates of species confronted with a given environment. In international competition, however, success grows out of the ability of firms to innovate and effective firms sustain advantage for decades in the face of external change. There are subenvironments in different nations (and in cities or regions within nations) that are more favorable ones for innovation. In biological terms, some habitats lead to stronger and more resilient species that are able to roam. They prosper in other habitats compared to those species that have evolved there.

Evolutionary biology stresses the role of diversity in the advancement of species. Diversity, in the sense of new and different approaches to competing, is also important to competition. I have stressed here how diversity is not innate but encouraged by the environment. Diversity is encouraged by the "diamond" and by clusters. Creating diversity is part of the role of clusters in accelerating innovation.

In this chapter I have shown how the determinants of national advantage are a dynamic system. The self-reinforcement of the "diamond," as an industry evolves, holds the key to upgrading and sustaining competitive advantage. The influence and reinforcement of the determinants leads to the phenomenon of clustering, and to the prevalence and importance of geographic concentration. I have described how the extent of mutual reinforcement is itself a function of particular determinants and of the presence of mechanisms in a nation that facilitate interchange within clusters.[36]

The process of creating and sustaining competitive advantage is one where history matters. The base of already-established industries, institutions, and values affects the process of industry development, as do chance events.[37] The occurrence of chance events is partly influenced by the determinants, however, and the path of development toward or away from a competitive industry is foreseeable as a function of the national "diamond."

While the examples I have discussed have emphasized the explanation of past competitive advantage, the "diamond" is also a tool for *predicting* future industry evolution. A nation has the prospects for competitive advantage if the underlying determinants are favorable or can be developed. Nations lose advantage, for example, if home buyers have lost sophistication, demand is evolving away from global needs, technological change is exposing missing supplier industries, institutions for factor creation do not respond by providing training in relevant skills, and so on. While unpredictable chance events such as acts of invention are also important to industry development, the "diamond" influences their likelihood of occurring in a nation. More importantly, the diamond allows predictions about whether chance events will result in a competitive industry.[38]

To understand more fully the competitive advantage of nations, we must move from broad theory to concrete examples. The theory can and must be applied at two levels, the industry and the nation. Part II of the book, to which I now turn, treats the first. In the next chapter, I will describe the process by which four different nations became international leaders in four different industries. In Chapter 6, I will move from individual industries to the service sector, an increasingly important class of industries where international competition has not been widely studied. Part III will apply the theory to explain the patterns of international industry success in the nations we studied and provide the foundation for extending the theory to explain the development of entire national economies.

PART II

Industries

5

Four Studies in National Competitive Advantage

The determinants of national advantage are a self-reinforcing system. They create an environment in a nation in which innovation is rapid and continuous. In such an environment, cause and effect relationships among the determinants become blurred. The dynamic and interconnected character of national advantage can be better understood if we examine particular industries in particular countries. The working of the "diamond" can be revealed only by closely examining an industry over time and understanding the process by which it emerges in a nation and achieves and sustains international success.

This chapter describes the historical development of four such industries, based in four different nations, that have achieved international leadership. They are chosen from the many we studied to illustrate the process of creating advantage in very different industry structures, in nations with widely divergent circumstances, and at various times.[1] Printing presses are a German success story dating back to the nineteenth century. Patient monitoring equipment, where the United States leads, emerged in the 1930s and 1940s. Ceramic tiles is an industry where Italy became world leader in the 1960s. Finally, robotics is a relatively new industry that is still developing rapidly, and Japan is the leader.

Every industry is unique, with its own sources of competitive advantage and its own evolutionary path. These four cases are no exception. Yet the broader process at work is strikingly similar. National advantage grows out of an environment in which all the determinants play some role.

THE GERMAN PRINTING PRESS INDUSTRY[2]

Printing presses were invented in Germany by Johannes Gutenberg around 1440, and the dominance of the printing press industry by German firms dates from the nineteenth century. Such well-known companies as Heidelberger Druckmaschinen (the industry leader), Koenig & Bauer, MAN-Roland, and Albert-Frankenthal have been world leaders for, in some cases, over one hundred years. German firms account for an estimated 35 percent of world printing press production. In 1985, Germany's world export share was 50.2 percent, and exports went to some 122 countries.[3]

THE PRINTING PRESS INDUSTRY

There were three principal printing techniques at the time of our study. Letterpress used a raised negative to transfer an image to paper, gravure employed a recessed negative, and offset was a chemical process. Offset presses accounted for about 80 percent of printing press demand in 1985 (see Table 5–1). Both letterpress and offset presses could be divided into two basic types. Sheet-fed presses are smaller, standardized units, in which single sheets are fed into the press at high speed. A typical black and white sheet-fed press sells for about $85,000 while a six-color, high-speed machine might cost $550,000.[4] Web-fed presses, developed in the late nineteenth century, are much larger and more complex machines and could cost up to $70 million. Fed by a continuous roll of paper, they are designed for extremely high printing speed and are used primarily for printing newspapers and magazines. Web-fed presses are heavily customized to the individual buyer and require two to three years between order and delivery.

The printing press is the single largest capital investment for its users. The most important buyer purchase criteria are machine throughput, reliabil-

TABLE 5–1 Estimated World Printing Press Sales by Press Technology, 1985 (in billions of DM)

Offset		9.5
sheet-fed	5.0	
web-fed	4.5	
Non-offset		2.5
(roto-gravure, silk-screen, and letterpress)		
Total		12.0

SOURCE: Estimates by company executives.

ity, service, printing quality (sharpness), versatility, degree of customization, ease of maintenance, ability to control, and delivery time. Reliability is particularly important because downtime is unacceptable in many printing applications; a newspaper, for example, has to be printed on time. Manufacturers have to provide for 24-hour-per-day, 365-day-per-year service wherever their machines are in use. The need for reliability and the long useful life of a press (about twenty years) causes buyers to be conservative about new press designs. The development cycle for new generations of presses is long, measured in decades. Efficiency is important because press operating costs have a major influence on the buyer's cost structure. Price is significant, but only if these other parameters are comparable. World printing press demand has grown steadily, though demand is cyclical.

After World War II, technology shifted from letterpress to offset. Offset presses offer greater overall quality, higher speed, and lower cost than letterpress. While the first offset presses date back to the 1920s, it was not until after World War II that the new technology began to make inroads on a large scale, initially in sheet-fed machines. By the late 1960s, the substitution to sheet-fed offset was largely complete. The late 1960s saw the beginning of a move to offset technology in web-fed presses. This substitution was still under way in the late 1980s, leading to a strong demand for web-offset machines for newspaper printing.

A number of other technological developments have taken place in recent decades. One was the ability to print in multiple colors. By the early 1980s, many machines had two- or four-color capability. Another development was the replacement of mechanical with electronic controls. The first electronically controlled inking units were introduced in the 1970s, automating the inking process. Next came computerized scanners that automatically determined the amount of ink necessary under different printing conditions. Electronics also allowed advances in pre-print preparation, such as modern phototypeset techniques.

EARLY INDUSTRY HISTORY

Johannes Gutenberg came from an area that had a long tradition in wine making. It is probable that he had seen presses used for grapes and adapted them to make his book printing press.[5] Until the early 1800s, printing press designs changed little from the wooden platen press that Gutenberg had developed. Paper was fed by hand, and two or more printers worked a press that printed one side of the page at a time.

The beginning of industrialization shifted industry leadership to England and the United States. Improved presses made of steel and cast iron were developed in England at the beginning of the eighteenth century, where machinery design skills were the most advanced in the world. Friedrich Koenig, a German who was to become the pioneer of modern printing press technology, served an apprenticeship as a printer and typesetter in Leipzig (later part of East Germany) working on Gutenberg-type equipment. Later, Koenig attended lectures in mathematics and mechanics at Leipzig University, though not as a formal student.[6]

Koenig developed a plan to build an improved printing press without the many weaknesses of the equipment he had used in his apprenticeship. Unable to find support in Germany, however, he was forced in 1806 to move to England to pursue his idea. England was the world's most advanced industrial country. Printers' wages in England were much higher than on the Continent, giving print shops a greater incentive to buy an improved printing press design.[7] Steam engine technology, important for improving press productivity, was also most advanced in England. The first automated paper-making machines had been developed in England by Bryan Donkin of Frogmore, Kent, in 1803–1804.[8] These machines soon began penetrating the English market, and the uniform paper quality they produced was necessary for Koenig's high-speed printing press to work. The new paper-making machines also reduced the price of paper, leading to higher sales of newspapers and heightened interest in improved printing presses. England, then, offered advantages to a printing press manufacturer in terms of demand conditions, related and supporting industries, and risk capital for entry.

In 1809, Koenig signed an agreement with a group of London printshop owners and publishers. In return for a share of future profits from his new machine, they were to finance its construction. This illustrates how local buyers can stimulate new entry into a supplier industry.

As he was working on his idea in London, Koenig met Andreas Bauer, another German expatriate, who was an optician and precision mechanic. The two decided to join forces. The breakthrough came in 1812, when Koenig and Bauer (K&B) developed the first rotary press that printed by using a rotating cylinder instead of a platen. The publisher of the London *Times* ordered two machines.[9] In 1814, a K&B press printed a complete edition of the *Times* at the rate of 1,100 copies per hour. K&B's next advances were in "perfecting" (which allowed printing on both sides of the paper in a single pass) and the addition of a steam engine to power the press. The new K&B presses were operated by a single printer and an apprentice and could print at a rate that had previously required twenty-five printers.[10]

K&B began to prosper, but the company soon ran into a dispute with its financial backers who were also the firm's major customers. They did not want K&B to sell presses to competitors either within or outside of England. After a period of turmoil, Koenig and Bauer decided to leave England in 1818.

After searching for a new location, the company settled in Oberzell, near the Bavarian town of Würzburg. Returning to Germany appealed to Koenig and Bauer, not only because it was home but also because a recession in England had dried up the market for presses.[11] The choice of Oberzell, an unlikely place to locate because there was little industry there at the time, was the result of more curious circumstances. The king of Bavaria was actively trying to attract industry to the region and helped K&B in locating and purchasing an abandoned monastery for use as a factory. Other incentives provided to locate in the region included: financial assistance in the early years; a tax exemption for the first ten years; ten years' protection on all inventions and trades that Koenig was first to bring to Bavaria; no obligatory military service for company workers during the early years; and no tariffs on imports of machinery and other necessary raw materials. Except for this initial support of K&B, German government assistance to the printing press industry had been nonexistent.

The Oberzell location had advantages and disadvantages. In addition to the government incentives, Koenig estimated that production costs were only one-third of English costs due to lower wages and other costs. However, raw materials were difficult to obtain, and most local labor was unskilled and unfamiliar with industrial production. The skilled workers that were available in the area, as elsewhere in Germany, were still organized into guilds; those that K&B hired attempted to impose unacceptable conditions of employment on K&B. After a difficult period, Koenig fired all of its employees except for a British foreman and a German blacksmith. Local apprentices were hired and trained in-house.[12]

In 1819, K&B completed its first machine built in Germany. It had been ordered by the London *Times* before Koenig left England, and was installed in early 1820.[13] The next machine, the first for a German customer, was not finished until 1822. Three more machines were completed soon after and installed in Berlin. Over the next several years, K&B built presses for printshops in Augsburg and Hamburg (Germany), Copenhagen (Denmark), and several locations in France.

K&B took an active role in developing a related German industry in 1827, when the company founded a paper manufacturing firm. Koenig recognized that a prerequisite for the successful penetration of printing presses in Germany and elsewhere was the availability of uniform high-quality paper. With financial backing from a German printshop owner, K&B established one of the first paper-making plants in Germany. It used an English machine bought from Donkin.

THE EMERGENCE OF DOMESTIC RIVALRY

While the seed for the German printing press industry was planted in an unlikely place through circumstances hard to anticipate, the process by which it grew into a world-leading industry is much more predictable. A number of other German competitors (and one Austrian) entered the industry, starting in the 1830s. All their founders had either worked at K&B or had some other connection with the firm (Figure 5–1). In a series of spin-offs, a number of capable domestic rivals for K&B were formed and concentrated in south-central Germany.

Helbig & Müller was established in 1836 by an ex-K&B foreman. Müller developed a number of important machine improvements that he offered to share with K&B's owners in return for equity participation. When his proposal was declined, he set up production in Vienna. His improved, and more standardized, machine was highly successful. Another firm was founded in Berlin in 1840 by Georg Sigl. He had spent two years as a mechanic at Helbig & Müller.

The origin of Maschinenfabrik Augsburg Nürnberg, or MAN (now one of Germany's foremost diversified machinery firms), was a printing press company founded in 1840 in Augsburg. It was sold four years later to Koenig's nephew, Carl Reichenbach, who had worked for two decades at K&B, and Reichenbach's brother-in-law. In 1845, they began production of an improved version of the Helbig & Müller machine. The company built the first German web-fed press in 1872 and subsequently was an important innovator in web-fed and, later, offset printing. The company eventually merged with a machinery maker from Nuremberg in 1898 to become MAN.

The firm that became Miller-Johannisberg was founded in 1848 by machine mechanic Johann Klein, who had previously worked for Helbig & Müller. In 1861, Albert-Frankenthal (located in Frankenthal, Baden-Württemberg, a town with a long machinery tradition) was established by Andreas Hamm and Andreas Albert, who had worked for K&B for ten years and then for Reichenbach.

Heidelberger Druckmaschinen (Heidelberg) was founded in 1850 by the brother of Andreas Hamm. Heidelberg concentrated on sheet-fed presses, introducing a web-fed press considerably later than its competitors. The company rose to prominence when it introduced a significantly improved sheet-fed press in 1914, known as the Heidelberger Tiegel. The press, the first with fully automated paper handling, achieved an output of 2,600 sheets per hour. Printing quality was also improved by the use of a device that allowed higher printing pressure. The superior quality and performance of the Tiegel, Heidelberger's pioneering of assembly line production of printing presses (in 1926), and the early establishment of a worldwide marketing and service network led to success unparalleled in the industry. It sold more than 165,000 units by the time the model was discontinued in 1985; one Tiegel was even worshipped in the Senshu-den shrine in the Japanese city of Kobe.

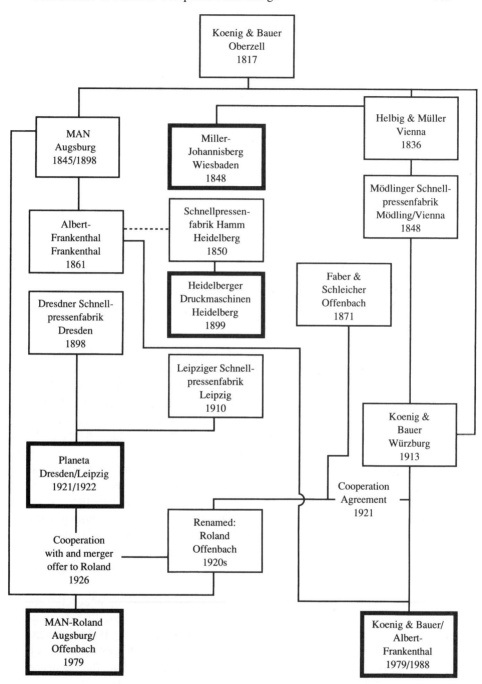

NOTE: Bold boxes identify leading competitors in 1988.

FIGURE 5–1 Family Tree of the German Printing Press Industry

By the late 1800s, these and other German firms had emerged as world leaders. A gradual process of consolidation began during the world economic downturn following World War I. In 1921, K&B acquired Mödlinger Schnell-pressenfabrik and signed a cooperation agreement with Faber & Schleicher, an Offenbach-based firm that had been established in 1871. About the same time, Dresdner Schnellpressenfabrik merged with Leipziger Schnellpressen-fabrik to become Planeta. A few years later, Faber & Schleicher (renamed Roland after its successful machine) began cooperation with Planeta that would continue for some years. Planeta exited letterpress production in order to concentrate on sheet-fed offset presses. It offered to merge with Roland in 1926, though the offer was declined.

By the 1930s, the six leading German printing press producers were Heidelberg, MAN, Roland, K&B, Albert-Frankenthal, and Planeta. They were all located in a radius of about 150 miles (see Figure 5–2). This group of companies was to sustain its industry leadership for many decades.

THE STRATEGIES OF GERMAN COMPETITORS

Heidelberg, the world leader, produced primarily small- and medium-sized sheet-fed offset presses. The firm was one of the most profitable in the German machinery sector. Roland also concentrated on sheet-fed presses, as did the East German firm Planeta. MAN concentrated on large newspaper web-fed presses. K&B was also among the world-leading producers of news-paper web-offset presses, while Albert-Frankenthal was known primarily for its line of large web-fed gravure presses.

German printing press firms competed with differentiation strategies, based on high quality and reliability, high performance, and punctual delivery. German presses often sold at premium prices compared with those from other nations. The early entry and international focus of the German firms allowed them to create extensive worldwide service networks and to develop premier international reputations. German firms maintained their strong market positions throughout the twentieth century, with only brief interruptions because of the two world wars.

German printing press firms conducted research and development activities in Germany. Most production took place in Germany, but both K&B and MAN had production facilities in the United States where they had assembled machines since the early 1980s. K&B had an alliance with Sumitomo Heavy Industries of Japan because of the difficulty of penetrating the Japanese market independently. Other firms had similar arrangements.

German firms were leaders for over a century in refining and perfecting printing techniques. Some early German innovations have already been described here, and this record continued. During the 1960s, for example,

FIGURE 5–2 Locations of World's Leading Printing Press Producers

Albert-Frankenthal pioneered the world's first press that could print on 8.5-foot-wide paper. In 1985, it introduced the world's first 9.8-foot press.[14] K&B was credited with the world's largest web-offset newspaper press[15] and the world's fastest sheet-fed offset press[16] (15,000 sheets per hour) as of the early 1980s.

Germany had a unique concentration of rivals in the industry. Its leading companies comprised nearly half of the world's significant competitors. Domestic rivalry went beyond competition for customers. German firms competed strongly not only for orders but for technical achievements and top graduates. Competition was based more on performance than price, reflecting the purchase criteria of buyers. Throughout the post–World War II period, tariffs for printing press imports into Germany were very low.

German press makers continually had to improve their machines in the face of actual and potential foreign competition.

SPECIALIZED FACTOR CREATION

The ability of German firms to advance both products and manufacturing techniques was due in part to the presence of specialized mechanisms for creating and upgrading both technology and human resources. German printing press firms all had active apprenticeship programs for workers and also provided training for newly hired engineers. Every major firm had founded its own vocational school many decades earlier to provide its workers with training specific to the printing machinery. For example, K&B's school was founded in 1870, Albert-Frankenthal's in 1873, and MAN's in 1911.[17] These schools were later accredited by the German government and became part of the German apprenticeship system. The printing press industry also drew from a ready supply of well-trained engineers. German university training was strong in all technical fields, and programs in machinery engineering were uniquely well developed compared with those in other nations. Machinery engineers were recruited from such universities as Aachen, Darmstadt, and Braunschweig, all located in centers of machinery production.

Direct research links were present between printing press firms and university institutes. The German Printing Machines Research Association (Forschungsgesellschaft Druckmaschinen) was founded in 1955 by a number of leading German printing press makers. Its aims were to conduct basic research on the physical, chemical, and cybernetic processes in printing, to provide for trial arrangements for printing machinery, and to contribute to the training of engineers.[18] It acted as a coordinating and co-financing body in joint research at Darmstadt Technical University and other research institutes.

While specialized factors were continually upgraded, German firms had to cope with high factor costs. Wages and social benefit costs were higher and working hours were shorter than those in competitor nations. These selective factor disadvantages led German firms continually to rationalize production as well as to develop the highest-technology machines.[19] A strong currency reinforced these pressures. The emphasis on highly productive and high-quality machines anticipated evolving demand patterns, as printers all around the world sought to increase automation and printing quality.

SOPHISTICATED HOME DEMAND

German demand conditions stimulated both the rate and direction of innovation in the industry. The German printing press market was not among the world's largest; it was estimated to be sixth in size behind the United States, Japan, Britain, and several other nations.[20] What was more important than size was that the German home market for printing presses had long been one of the world's most sophisticated.

Sophistication began with the ultimate consumer, the buyer of a newspaper, magazine, or book. German buyers of printed matter were unusually quality conscious. For example, a German reader would call a newspaper to complain if his or her copy was smeared or smudged, an unlikely event in most other nations. Printshops were forced by German readers to employ high-quality presses.

German printshop owners were also highly demanding buyers. High local wages led to the desire for highly productive machines, requiring fewer operating personnel. Many printing techniques involve toxic materials, and stringent technical requirements in terms of machine safety and pollution controls had been established in Germany. They had often anticipated regulations in other nations and had been a spur to product improvement.

Also important was the sophistication of the printers themselves. Education for printers had a long tradition in Germany, and German printers were thought to be the world's best trained. Special vocational schools for printers, so-called *Meisterschulen für Buchdrucker,* were established in Germany beginning in the 1920s.[21] A printer could apprentice in specialties such as sheet-fed, web-fed, flexo (flexographic printing), packaged goods, wallpaper, or silkscreen printing. The thorough training in Germany was in stark contrast to the situation in the United States, where printers received only on-the-job training. The sophistication of German printers led to a receptivity to new innovations as well as a continual dialog with manufacturers on technical matters.

The printing trade in Germany was also active in research, which had many direct spillover benefits to the printing press industry. German printers had their own research organization, Deutsche Forschungsgesellschaft für Druck- und Reproduktionstechnik (FOGRA). FOGRA research was concerned with issues such as standardization and phototypeset methods. FOGRA also engaged in collaborative projects with universities. In 1985, for example, FOGRA asked Stuttgart University to investigate the fundamentals of designing the most effective rotogravure cylinders.[22]

Paper-folding procedures as well as newspaper sizes were different in the United States from those in Europe. Machines built in the United States had to be modified to work in Europe and vice versa, and American manufacturers, who for decades were content selling primarily to their own large domestic market, experienced difficulty selling in Europe. Also, American buyers were less demanding in terms of printing quality and sought presses that were simpler to run because of less skilled personnel. It proved difficult for American firms to meet higher European standards, while German firms had a much easier time adapting to American standards. German firms had been forced early, because of a limited home market, to sell to foreign customers with differing needs.

THE GERMAN PRINTING CLUSTER

The printing press industry had long-standing links with a number of other strong German industries besides printing. Paper-making machinery was an important related industry, because the properties of paper were important to the operation of a printing press. J. M. Voith GmbH Maschinenfabrik, together with its subsidiary O. Dörries, was the world's leading paper press maker (see Table 5–2). Another world-renowned paper machine producer was Sulzer-Escher-Wyss, Swiss-owned but with its home base in Germany.[23] The close proximity of internationally successful German paper machine and printing press companies facilitated active interaction between the designers of both products.

German printing press companies also benefited from the presence of strong paper producers like Feldmühle AG, E. Holtzmann & Cie. AG, M.D. Papierfabriken Heinrich Nicolaus, and Zanders AG. The rapid increases in paper throughput would have been impossible without both the cooperation

TABLE 5–2 German Competitors in Related Industries

Company	Location	Date Founded	Revenues in 1985 (DM milllion)
Paper			
Feldmühle	Düsseldorf	1885	2,980
E. Holtzmann	Weisenbach	1883	633
Papierfabriken Heinrich Nicolaus	Dachau	1862	719
Zanders	Bergisch Gladbach	1829	838
Paper Machines			
Voith/Dörries	Heidenheim/Düren	1867/1885	1,005
Sulzer-Escher-Wyss*	Ravensburg	1856	300
Printing Ink			
BASF	Ludwigshafen	1865	1,000**
Michael Huber Farben- fabriken	Munich	1765	115
Hartmann Druckfarben	Frankfurt	1905	100
Siegwerk Farbenfabrik Keller	Siegburg	1905	250

* Owned by Sulzer of Switzerland.
** Sales of printing ink and related items.

of paper makers who had developed paper that could withstand speeds of up to thirty-five feet per second as well as the paper machine producers who developed the necessary machinery to produce it.

Internationally prominent German printing ink producers also benefited the German press industry. Printing ink became especially important to the development of multicolor web-fed presses at the beginning of the twentieth century. Advancements in presses and printing ink had been self-reinforcing. Machine improvements required improved inks that led to further machine improvements.

The success of German printing ink producers was closely related to the preeminent German chemical industry. An early breakthrough was the development in 1880 of a laboratory process to produce synthetic indigo by the German Adolf von Baeyer, and its commercialization around the turn of the century by the German chemical firms Hoechst and BASF. Synthetic inks were an offshoot of dyes. Prior to the development of synthetic inks, printing ink had been produced primarily in-house by the printshops.[24] World-famous German printing ink producers were BASF's Printing Systems division,[25] Michael Huber Farbenfabriken, Hartmann Druckfarben, and Siegwerk Farbenfabrik Keller.

Another important product related to printing presses was typesetting systems. The two world leaders were Linotype and Monotype, both founded in the United States. The typesetting systems industry had begun in the 1880s in the United States with the invention of the first mechanized typesetting machine that could set a whole line of type (hence the name linotype) by German-born O. Mergenthaler. A slightly different system that set single letters (hence monotype) was invented in 1885 by the American, T. Lanston. Even though the two leading firms were American, both had major German subsidiaries. The base for new product development had long been in Germany, reflecting the existence of the German printing cluster. Interestingly, Linotype had moved its headquarters to Eschborn, Germany, in the early 1980s,[26] illustrating the movement of a company's official home base to the location of the most favorable national "diamond," a practice that is taking place with growing frequency.

SHIFTING COMPETITIVE POSITIONS

Switzerland had maintained a position as an exporter of printing presses. The principal Swiss producer was Maschinenfabrik Wifag AG, based in Berne. It was the third-leading European producer of web-offset presses for newspaper printing. Wifag, located not far from the German border, was effectively part of the German cluster. Like its German competitors, Wifag presses were differentiated by high quality and technical innovation.

Wifag viewed Germany as its key market. It was especially proud of having sold a press in Augsburg, MAN's home town.

Two other printing press exporting nations, the United States and Britain, were steadily losing position. Britain's world export share fell from 9.2 percent in 1975 to 5.9 percent in 1985, and Baker-Perkins was the only significant producer remaining. It produced web-offset presses for newspapers, where the British home market was substantial. The United States was the second-largest exporter of printing presses, holding 19.7 percent of the world printing press exports in 1975. By 1985, the U.S. share of world exports had sunk to 3.9 percent, and the United States ran the world's largest printing press trade deficit of $330 million.

While there were several viable American sheet-fed machine producers until the early 1970s, by 1988 American firms produced only web-fed presses. Harris[27] and Goss-Rockwell were the leading competitors. Both were part of diversified companies. American technology was simpler to operate but also less sophisticated than that of European machines. American-built machines were also said to suffer more breakdowns and to rank lower in quality than German or Swiss machines. American firms maintained position vis-à-vis foreign competitors in the U.S. market in part because of its special requirements in terms of paper size and folding procedures.

Meanwhile, Japan was enjoying a growing position in the industry. The nation was a relative newcomer to international printing press competition. The Japanese industry was established in the twentieth century, only after the introduction of offset techniques had made possible the reproduction of Japanese writing. Letterpress techniques had been impractical because of the thousands of Chinese ideograms (Kanji) used in Japanese writing. This was also an important reason why modern printing techniques had been developed in Europe and the United States, despite the fact that the printing principle had been known in Asia before Gutenberg's invention.

Japanese home demand for offset printing was substantial because typing was impractical and thus all formal documents had to be printed. From the late 1970s, Japanese home demand became aligned with international demand that also moved to offset printing. This marked the beginning of inroads by Japanese press makers into foreign markets. By 1985, Japan had become the world's second-largest printing press exporter. Its world export share increased to 19.1 percent from 2.9 percent in 1975. During the same period, Japan's trade balance in presses rose from negative to $296 million, the world's second highest after Germany.

Japanese firms concentrated on smaller sheet-fed offset machines. The leading producer was Komori. Other competitors were Mitsubishi, Akiyama, Ryobi, Fuji, and Sumitomo, K&B's Japanese partner. Japanese firms stressed electronic add-ons and features, a function of the cluster of successful Japanese industries in electronics.

DANGER SIGNALS

Flexographic printing (flexo) was the newest printing technology under development and achieved some market penetration in the 1980s, especially for newspaper printing. Flexo, also called aniline printing, was a variation of the old letterpress technique but made use of aniline (water-based) inks and flexible rubber plates instead of cast metal letters. It was developed first for the food packaging industry, because aniline inks could be used on nonabsorbent surfaces and were safe for use on food wrappers. Its quality for paper printing was not as high as offset, but the investment and operating costs were lower.

Flexo was first applied to newspaper printing by American firms in the late 1970s and early 1980s.[28] The highest penetration of flexo presses was in the United States. By 1988, however, German firms were the preeminent suppliers. The leading producer of flexo presses in Germany was K&B, which built them in cooperation with Windmöller & Hölscher, a prominent German packaging machinery producer that supplied the basic flexo printing unit. Germany's strong international packaging machinery industry had been drawn by evolving technology into the printing cluster.

In 1988, the German printing press industry was enjoying growth and worldwide success despite high labor costs and rising currency exchange rates. Most producers were recording record profits. Printing press companies ranked among the most profitable firms in Germany.

Record profits, however, carried danger signals for the future. Since the 1970s, the number of German competitors had decreased substantially through consolidation. K&B acquired a 49 percent interest in Albert-Frankenthal in 1979, which was increased to a majority interest in 1988. The two firms agreed to coordinate their production programs. In 1979, MAN and Roland merged to become MAN-Roland. Some gradual consolidation is characteristic of many well-established industries, but consolidation in the German printing equipment industry had reached a point where price competition had all but disappeared and domestic rivalry was no longer assured. A more vigorous group of Japanese competitors represented a growing threat, especially in sheet-fed presses. Komori, the Japanese leader, had made an unsuccessful bid to acquire AM International (United States) in 1987, Harris' parent company.

SUMMARY

The German printing press industry is a remarkable story of competitive advantage sustained for more than 160 years. The early history of the industry shows how the international mobility of technology and skilled personnel is far from a new phenomenon. This mobility underscores the importance of understanding the reasons why some national environments allow or force factors to be mobilized the most effectively to lead to a world-class industry.

The initial seed for the industry was planted by a remarkable German, Friedrich Koenig, who became interested in presses because of his training and work as a printer. To pursue his development, he was forced to go to England, the nation with the most favorable national "diamond" for the industry at that time. Driven out of England by attempts by his buyers/ investors to limit industry growth to protect their interests, he was drawn back to his native Germany. The particular location he chose was influenced by an early example of government efforts to attract investments. What is more striking is how K&B's presence soon started a process which made Germany a more favorable environment for competitive advantage in the industry. A large group of German rivals emerged directly or indirectly out of the industry pioneer. Specialized factor-creation mechanisms were established and widened over time. As demand for presses developed in Germany, the high standards and sophistication of German printers and end users spurred innovation, reinforced by pressures from selective factor disadvantages. German demand anticipated needs for quality and productivity that would spread worldwide. All the related and supporting industries essential to innovation (paper, paper machinery, ink, typesetting systems) grew up with the printing press industry and achieved world-class status in their own right.

The organizational approach required to manage product development, production, and service in such a highly technical, complex industry fit well with German strengths. The uniquely large group of domestic competitors, located in the southern part of Germany, were each others' most important rivals. Domestic rivalry not only stimulated innovation directly but had beneficial effects on German factor creation and on related industries.

The successful Swiss firm, Wifag, was a *de facto* part of the German cluster. Firms from other nations did not challenge Germany because they lacked essential elements of the "diamond." America had poor demand quality and less domestic rivalry. England had no base of competitors, and strong unionism froze innovation for many years among English printers, eroding demand quality. Japan was a late entrant into the industry because of home demand that diverged sharply from most world demand. German firms, in contrast, enjoyed early mover advantages from having established worldwide brand reputations and service networks in an industry where buyers are conservative and loyal.

The printing press industry illustrates not only the "diamond" at work but the phenomenon of clustering. Germany is the world leader, or among the leaders, not only in printing presses but in printing, fine paper, paper machines, typesetting systems, printing inks, and packaging machinery. The last related industry became important only recently with the emergence of flexo presses. The German printing cluster is mutually reinforcing, and the industries have developed together. Relationships among companies are close and in some cases formal.

The printing press case is a vivid illustration of another even broader point. In printing presses, the entire "diamond" was important to German success and factor costs played a modest role, even though the industry developed in the nineteenth century. A similar story could be told in optical goods, cutlery, textile machinery, mining equipment, advertising agencies, motion pictures, and countless other German and non-German cases. Though postwar globalization has diminished the role of factor endowment, especially the role of basic factors, the full story of national competitive advantage has for at least a century involved much more. Factor conditions have long since been less important than commonly perceived.

Even though the German printing press industry was enjoying record profits in the late 1980s, however, there were signs that German dominance of world printing press markets might wane. Japanese printing press firms rose from nowhere to a major position within ten years. Japanese home demand, which strongly favored offset printing, had moved from out of step to perhaps ahead of demand in the rest of the world. Japanese firms are now competing with a formidable "diamond" of their own. Flexo printing was not developed in Germany. An indication that German demand is becoming less anticipatory of future world demand is that demand for this new technology is taking off first abroad.

Most significant in many ways, however, is that domestic rivalry in Germany may be eroded to the point where it is no longer sufficient to motivate constant innovation. Current profitability and market position can be misleading in any industry, particularly one such as printing presses. The printing press industry is one where early mover advantages are particularly strong, especially in large web-fed presses. Without aggressive domestic rivalry, German firms may think they are holding market position when in fact the underpinnings of future competitive advantage are already lost.

THE AMERICAN PATIENT MONITORING EQUIPMENT INDUSTRY[29]

Patient monitors measure bodily functions such as heart rate and wave form, blood pressure, temperature, and respiration rates. Since World War II, American firms have been world leaders in the patient monitoring equipment industry. Hewlett-Packard (HP) was the leading worldwide competitor, and several other U.S. firms ranked high on the list of international rivals. It was forecast that U.S. exports would exceed imports by $76.4 million in 1988.[30] The position of American firms was even stronger than suggested by the trade figures, because a number of U.S. firms also had extensive manufacturing operations overseas.

PATIENT MONITORS

Patients are monitored to track bodily functions over a period of time and to assure prompt medical reaction in case of a drastic change in condition. Measurements are taken via sensors placed on or in the patient's body. The monitor's controls select the parameters for measurement, and a screen presents one or more measurements graphically and/or alphanumerically. Modern patient monitors are equipped with alarms to alert medical personnel when measurements deviate from a predetermined range of acceptability. Monitors are also equipped with recording devices to print measurements when requested. The most advanced equipment employs microprocessor technology that allows the instantaneous calculation of trends in patient activity. Advanced monitors are modular rather than configured, allowing flexibility in the parameters to be measured. Configured monitors, which measure set parameters, are more popular in price-sensitive markets.

The world market for patient monitoring equipment reached approximately $1 billion by the mid-1980s. The United States represented at least half of the market; Europe accounted for approximately a third; while the rest was scattered around the world, with some concentration in the Far East.

INDUSTRY HISTORY

Europe was the source for many of the early advances in medical technology. Crude methods for measuring the functions of the heart were developed as early as the nineteenth century. In 1905, Einthoven of Holland developed the string galvanometer cardiograph, a bulky instrument that recorded electrical currents from the heart on photographic film. This innovation marked a breakthrough in the study of the heart, but its bulkiness and cost limited its early appeal.

Cambridge Instruments (United Kingdom) began selling cardiographs commercially soon after the Einthoven invention. In the early 1920s, Cambridge established a U.S. marketing subsidiary, and Sanborn (United States) also began producing cardiographs domestically. The cost of early models was over one thousand dollars. Efforts during this period focused on making the instruments more portable and easier to use. As portable models (about

50 pounds) were introduced in the late 1920s, demand for cardiographs from major research hospitals accelerated.

The application of amplifier and vacuum tube technology in the 1930s marked the next important development in the industry and the beginning of U.S. leadership. Amplifiers greatly reduced the size of instruments, and vacuum tubes allowed a new means for transferring electrical signals. Sanborn acquired the rights to a monitor using these concepts, along with a primitive design of a machine using both technologies, from an American inventor in 1935 and hired an electrical engineering student from MIT to improve the product. An active research program was underway at several U.S. universities on the new electronics technologies. In the late 1930s, cathode-ray tubes for real-time visual display of electrocardiographs (EKGs) were developed but did not come into common use until the 1950s.

World War II diverted attention from the development of patient monitors. However, the rapid development of electronics during the war for purposes such as radar led to a boom after the war in many electronics-related industries. Both factor creation in electronics and the development of related U.S. industries spurred progress in monitors. Technological development in EKG and related products burgeoned.

Sanborn Company developed a new recording method soon after World War II which used a heated stylus to melt the coating from white-coated paper to expose a black line corresponding to the instrument's measurement. The new method meant that the paper did not have to be photographically developed. The direct recording system also had advantages over previous methods that wrote on a curved surface. In 1948, Sanborn introduced one-, two-, and four-channel monitor/recorders with the new recording system. Cambridge Instruments was slow to move away from galvanometers and the traditional recording techniques. The company's position in the market suffered as a result.

Several new companies appeared in the United States during the early postwar period, most located near major areas of medical research or hospitals. A prominent example was Electronics for Medicine (E for M), founded by Martin Scheiner (United States). Scheiner was an electrical engineer who developed a new EKG/heart rate monitor using a cathode-ray tube in 1947 while working for Electrophysical Labs (United States), an EKG manufacturer. He published a joint paper on the new instrument with Dr. Aaron Himmelstein of New York's Bellevue Hospital. Interest in the monitor was sufficient for Scheiner to start his own company, Instrument Labs, in 1950 (its name was changed to Electronics for Medicine in 1955).

Another innovation by Scheiner and an important example of contributions made by related U.S. industries was the unbonded strain gauge transducer, which had been invented by Statham Instrument Company (United States). This device was designed to measure strains in metals used for aircraft. In the early 1950s, the gauge was adapted by Martin Scheiner to allow the measurement of blood pressure; it marked a quantum improvement in pressure measurement technology.

ANTICIPATORY U.S. DEMAND

The widening application of electronics technology to medicine in the postwar period can be divided into four areas: research equipment, patient monitoring, diagnostic equipment, and therapeutic products. The United States played a prominent role in all four fields, whose markets developed at different rates. The research devices of the 1950s were the precursors of the patient monitors of the 1960s and 1970s. Different competitors emerged in each field, but entry into related fields was common.

Most medical instruments developed during the 1950s were oriented toward research. The great majority were developed by U.S. companies, reflecting the priority placed on medical research and medical care in the United States (see Figure 5–3). Funding by government for medical research through the National Institutes of Health and the universities was the highest of any nation. This led to early and strong demand for the most advanced health care equipment in medical research institutions across the United States.

Spending on medical research in the United States benefited the American patient monitor manufacturers in several ways. Medical researchers sought out and often participated in designing new monitors, because monitoring new variables with ever-greater precision was essential to advancing the state of knowledge about a disease or a treatment. Pharmaceutical companies also spent heavily on testing new drugs, and highly sophisticated equipment was required to monitor the physiological changes that the drugs induced.

By the mid-1950s, demand began to shift from monitors solely for research applications to monitors that would be used more widely in patient care. Instead of customized monitors for individual researchers, demand was emerging for standard products manufactured on a large scale. Again, the United States was by far the largest, earliest, and most sophisticated market.

Demand for monitors used in operating rooms was the first to grow. Early monitors were tools for the anesthesiologist to keep track of the patient's condition. Products were developed by several companies, including Electronics for Medicine (United States), Sanborn (United States), and Corbin Farnsworth (United States). Cambridge Instruments (United Kingdom) was also an early participant. Aside from compactness and ease of use, hospitals sought monitors that were explosion proof and did not emit dangerous sparks that could ignite the flammable gases used as anesthetics. Electronics for Medicine took the lead with a compact, explosion-proof operating room

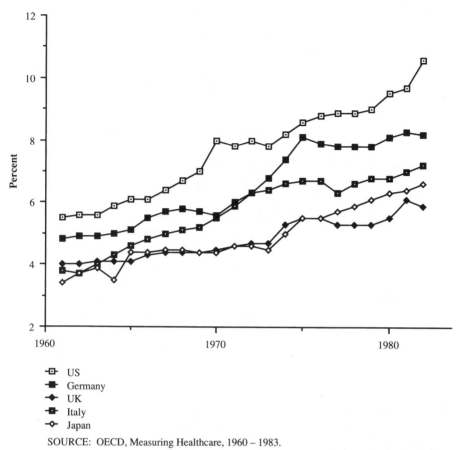

SOURCE: OECD, Measuring Healthcare, 1960 – 1983.

FIGURE 5–3 Total Health Care Expenditures as a Percentage of GDP, 1960–1983

monitor in 1957. At $575, the product was less expensive than competitive monitors and proved extremely popular. A complementary monitor for measuring blood pressure was introduced as well. Sanborn received a contract to equip two open-heart and two neurosurgical operating rooms for the National Institutes of Health in the early 1960s.

Another major application for monitoring equipment was its use for keeping track of patients in extremely unstable condition. Monitors that could display four or more bodily functions at once were developed, allowing medical personnel to become quickly aware of emerging problems. Early buyers were hospitals engaged in clinical research, but demand soon spread.

The development of solid-state technology in the late 1950s, and its subsequent replacement of the vacuum tube, was another spur to industry development. The new technology allowed products to be smaller and to generate less heat. Solid-state technology was developed in the United States, and U.S. companies were in the forefront of applying it to monitors in the early 1960s. Mennen-Greatbatch, whose name later changed to Mennen Medical (United States), was founded in 1963 and introduced the first solid-state monitor.

The idea of monitoring unstable patients was developed further in the 1960s, and again the United States was the lead market. Around 1961, Dr. Hugh Day of Kansas City began to implement his concept of a centralized critical care unit.[31] Day's idea was to establish an area in the hospital designed for patients in unstable condition. The practice spread, and the U.S. government helped speed it by sponsoring the installation of centralized intensive care systems in several medical centers across the country. During the 1960s, U.S. companies developed more and more sophisticated monitoring products for the critical care market. Alarms were added for use with unstable patients. By 1967, "central station" monitors were introduced that could simultaneously monitor up to eight patients from one location.

The growing acceptance of intensive care applications and the widening use of monitors for normal patient care marked the takeoff of the monitoring industry. Later in the 1960s, doctors began to use monitors to track patients in order to prevent crisis situations. For example, equipment was developed to detect heart arrhythmias. Monitors were also increasingly used to judge better the effects of treatment. The spread of complex monitoring systems for intensive care units made customer training and service a much more important part of the monitor equipment business. At some large installations, manufacturers kept service personnel on site. In the early 1960s, firms began in earnest to build sales and service networks. The need for service became a stumbling block to new entrants.

While the sales process in the 1950s was based on close relationships with physicians and researchers, marketing in the 1960s focused increasingly upon developing relationships with hospitals. Within the hospital, purchasing decisions were made by doctors, nurses, administrators, and later biomedical engineers, who were added in larger hospitals to help with the purchasing and maintenance of electronic equipment.

The patient monitoring equipment industry entered a period of explosive growth in the 1960s, led by the U.S. market, because American doctors and hospitals tested patients more extensively than those in other countries. American doctors were very aggressive in gathering information for their diagnoses and in devising new forms of treatment. A greater willingness to try new treatments, particularly in cardiology, led to much greater demand for more sophisticated monitors in the United States.

Cardiac care was the focus for much of early patient monitoring in the United States. Heart-related health problems were given particular attention in the United States, more so than in other countries, leading to a greater demand for cardiac care-related products. Also, U.S. doctors were much more willing to experiment with invasive techniques in surgery (such as coronary bypasses) and in patient monitoring.

The Swan-Ganz catheter, invented in the mid-1970s by American physicians, was an example of U.S. leadership in invasive cardiac technology. The catheter was capable of measuring blood flows in three of the heart's four chambers at the same time. American Edwards Company purchased the rights to the invention. Nearly a million Swan-Ganz catheters were sold from the mid-1970s to the mid-1980s. Europe lagged about five years behind the United States in the implementation of the Swan-Ganz technology.[32]

In most countries, the demand for sophisticated monitors was lower than in the United States. In countries with socialized medicine, hospitals ran fewer tests than in the United States; highly sophisticated tests were seen as unnecessary and expensive. In Europe, monitors tended to be simpler, measured fewer functions, and were designed for less complicated tasks. Outside of Europe, some wealthy private hospitals bought state-of-the-art equipment, but most hospitals got by with much less sophisticated equipment. Cost was a major concern.

Exceptions to this pattern had occurred in some segments. One was fetal monitoring, where Europeans had always been very aggressive. In 1968, Dr. Konrad Hammacher, a German physician, approached Hewlett-Packard's German subsidiary with an idea for a fetal monitor that was subsequently developed by HP in Germany. A U.S. producer of fetal monitors, Corometrics, was started around the same time by Dr. Edward Hahn of Yale, but electronic fetal monitoring was adopted faster in Europe. This was in part due to concerns over lower birth rates in Europe and a greater perceived need for close attention.

In the United States, each hospital was quite autonomous in purchasing monitors. Government involvement in the industry in the United States was limited to product testing. With freedom to purchase from any supplier and with many alternatives, U.S. hospitals pressured American monitor companies to improve products and service. The greater competition in U.S. health care led hospitals to invest aggressively in equipment. Typically, the best doctors and equipment were critical to building a reputation as a leading hospital. The best doctors were attracted in part with the best equipment. Doctors themselves competed for patients as well, and provided further impetus for more advanced monitors.

Overseas, governments played a more active role in the national health care systems. Purchases were often centralized, which slowed the process of introducing new products. Competition among health care providers was often nonexistent.

By the early 1970s, the basic technology for patient monitors was well established. Improvements shifted to enhancing the ease of use through applying new technologies such as microprocessors, computers, and telemetry, of which microprocessor technology was the most important. Microprocessors gave monitors the ability to generate numerical data and instantaneously calculate trends in measurements. Instead of generating raw data, monitors could give highly processed information in a more usable form. With the advent of microprocessors, products could also be adjusted by software rather than hardware modifications; this led to a major shift in the focal areas for product development.

In 1975, Spacelabs (United States) was the first company to use microprocessors in bedside monitors. American semiconductor firms (a supporting industry) were world leaders in the microprocessor segment and provided a source for this technology. The United States also led the world in software, another supporting industry, particularly in the 1970s. Most developments of microprocessor technology in monitors were pioneered by American firms.

American patient monitoring firms also benefited from the internationalization of U.S. medical practices. Beginning in the earliest phases of the industry, the close links between medical researchers around the world helped bolster foreign demand for American equipment. Foreign buyers sought to obtain top-of-the-line equipment being used by the top researchers in a field, often American. The advanced nature of American health care led many foreigners to study the U.S. system, U.S. methods, and U.S. products, leading to foreign demand for the same products used by American doctors. Also, in the 1960s and particularly in the 1970s, the American government established quotas to encourage foreign enrollment in U.S. medical schools in order to improve the quality of health care in developing countries. More and more foreign students were exposed to the American health care system and health care products.

A final factor that drove American demand for patient monitors was the increasingly litigious nature of U.S. medicine. Doctors were inclined to run as many tests as might be deemed necessary and monitor as many variables as possible so that they would be able to defend themselves in court. In Europe, in the absence of such a risk of lawsuits, some claimed that the physician was more free to think clearly about what was necessary and best for the patients.[33]

DEVELOPMENT OF THE U.S. INDUSTRY

The majority of competitors in the patient monitoring industry had been American since the 1940s. Aside from many small American start-ups, other companies entered the emerging patient monitoring industry from related businesses. Defibrillator manufacturers, such as American Optical and

Electrodyne, developed EKGs as complementary products in their line and gradually moved up into more sophisticated monitors. Companies tended initially to focus on a particular product type, such as operating room or cardiac-related products, and then broaden their line over time.

International sales during the 1950s were not uncommon but tended to occur more from chance than as a result of concerted marketing. Generally, a foreign doctor would see a piece of equipment during training or would hear about a monitor from another doctor. In 1960, however, Electronics for Medicine established its first overseas licensed distributorship in Italy. A local doctor had requested some equipment through a local dealer, and the company followed up the sale with a trip to Italy to make a permanent agreement with the dealer. E for M did not give the relationship very much attention, but it did represent their first step overseas.

An important milestone in the industry occurred when Sanborn, one of the initial developers of patient monitoring equipment, was acquired by Hewlett-Packard (HP) in 1961. Hewlett-Packard was a competitor in related electronic products, including testing and measuring equipment (such as oscilloscopes). From this union, Sanborn enjoyed immediate benefits of access to technology as well as a national and international sales and service network.

In the late 1960s, more hospitals began to hire biomedical engineers to cope with the growing number of electronic products. They sought products that were of top quality and well documented. Many engineers around the world were familiar with Hewlett-Packard, and this reputation helped boost market share in patient monitoring equipment during the late 1960s and early 1970s. Also, HP stressed compatibility of its products and provided thorough documentation of specifications, which allowed the engineers to maintain them more easily. Hewlett-Packard eventually emerged as the industry leader.

The patient monitoring equipment industry grew rapidly in the 1960s, and many small start-up companies entered the industry. The market segments that attracted the most attention were the intensive care and coronary care markets. Market share was evenly distributed, and rivalry was intense. New companies, such as Mennen-Greatbatch, embraced solid-state circuitry early and helped advance the state of the art. Other major competitors during the 1960s were Electrodyne, American Optical, General Electric, Spacelabs, and Electronics for Medicine. Companies emerged from a variety of related industries. Spacelabs, for example, which was founded in the late 1950s, had initially developed products to assist the National Aeronautics and Space Administration (NASA) in monitoring the bodily functions of astronauts in space. The company was quick to recognize that a larger market for their products existed in hospitals. Groups of competitors were located in close proximity to major medical research centers and locations of electronics clusters such as Boston, Massachusetts; California; and Portland, Oregon.

During the late 1960s and early 1970s, patient monitoring became more computer- and system-oriented. Monitors had to link up with central stations and central computers for information processing, and HP reaped advantage from this shift.

By 1970, the U.S. market was saturating, and from this point forward, American firms began more aggressive efforts to sell abroad. Instead of relying on word of mouth or on foreign distributors, they established sales and service branches or increased their level of investment in overseas distributorships through greater training and more sales incentives.

THE EMERGENCE OF FOREIGN COMPETITORS

Foreign firms began entering the patient monitoring industry in the early 1960s. They tended to be small and were oriented to their domestic markets, which led them to design and produce less sophisticated products than their American counterparts. Siemens (West Germany) entered in 1962, creating a monitoring company out of its related X-ray business. Hellige (Germany) entered the industry in the late 1960s. Germany had a long tradition of research in the biomedical field and international positions in a number of health care-related industries. Philips (Holland) also entered in the late 1960s, building on its strength in electronics. Simonson and Weel (Denmark) had a strong position in Scandinavia and sold some equipment in the United States under private brand to Narco, an American incubator manufacturer.

None of these firms had achieved significant penetration of the U.S. market by the mid-1970s. However, Siemens (Germany) had emerged as a significant competitor, holding a large share of the German market.[34] In 1973, Siemens attempted to enter the American market with a "European-style" monitor. This attempt failed because the product was not sophisticated enough for the U.S. market. Siemens' strength in other industries, such as computers and X-ray, yielded advantages but not enough to overcome the American "diamond."

In 1978, Siemens tried again. This time, it began by establishing a joint venture with Analogic of Danvers, Massachusetts, a company expert in digital processing techniques. This agreement gave Siemens both technical and manufacturing capacity in the United States as well as specialized skilled employees who were easier to find in the United States.[35] The U.S. market also supported innovation, and this time Siemens' entry proved to be a success. The joint company became, in effect, Siemens' global home base for patient monitoring operations, housing R&D as well as manufacturing facilities. In 1988, Siemens purchased Analogic's stake in the company.

Japanese firms produced mostly basic, single-channel cardiac monitors during the 1970s. In the early 1980s, Nihon Kohden began an effort to establish itself as a global player in the market for larger monitoring systems. It attempted to differentiate itself through the use of technological innovations such as telemetry as well as other less substantial changes in product design. It was moderately successful but lagged in service in foreign markets.

The Japanese market embraced transmission of information without wires (telemetry) faster than any other market in the world. This was due in large part to hospitals' desire to eliminate wires and clutter from the patients' bedside. It is also partially explained by the focus of Japanese medicine on cancer rather than on cardiac care. Cancer is a serious problem in Japan, while cardiac problems are rare in comparison to the United States. Cancer patients tend to be more mobile, and telemetry allowed the patient greater freedom. Telemetry applications initially were more specialized in the United States. As a result, Japanese companies tended to be leaders in telemetry applications, despite the early introduction of telemetry to patient monitoring by Spacelabs in the late 1960s.

Imports into Japan were slowed by the practice of "type acceptance," which required testing before imports were allowed. Japan's Pharmaceutical Affairs Law (PAL) did not accept foreign clinical testing data and required that foreign companies obtain marketing approval through a Japanese importer (the latter provision was removed in 1983). Product approval in Japan generally took more than twice as long as in the United States.

Changing U.S. Competition

Beginning in the 1970s, a wave of acquisitions, mostly involving U.S. companies, swept the patient monitoring industry. Pharmaceutical companies were particularly attracted. Companies including Abbott (United States), Becton Dickinson (United States), Squibb (United States), and Hoffmann-LaRoche (Switzerland) entered the industry, usually by buying existing American firms.

These arrangements proved, by and large, to be disappointing. Patient monitors were more electronic than other medical products. Although marketing relationships with hospitals could be helpful, the skills required to manufacture, sell, and service monitors effectively were entirely different from those required for other medical products. As the business became more systems oriented, the skills of the pharmaceutical firms were even less applicable. In some cases, the patient monitoring divisions became low-priority business units in the overall corporation, causing them to fall behind competitors that placed greater emphasis on the business and invested more heavily.

As Figure 5–4 indicates, many companies changed ownership. For example, Electrodyne was purchased by Becton Dickinson, who sold it to Litton,

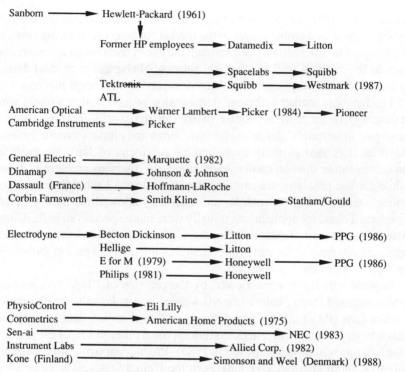

FIGURE 5–4 Acquisitions in the Patient Monitoring Industry

who in turn sold it to PPG Industries. Electronics for Medicine was purchased by Honeywell and later sold to PPG. Tektronix sold its division to Spacelabs, which was purchased by Squibb and later spun off to Westmark. The turnover and consolidation benefited HP, which was committed to the industry and possessed technological interrelationships with other business units. American Optical and Becton Dickinson were strong in the early 1970s but faded as the decade continued. By the 1980s, HP had achieved a dominant position in the United States and a worldwide leadership position, as Figure 5–5 indicates.

The estimated worldwide market share of leading competitors in the patient monitoring industry in the mid-1980s is shown in Figure 5–5. Production took place in a variety of industrialized countries. Major production bases were the United States, Germany, and Japan. Local content facilities were set up in countries that had such requirements. Some U.S. firms, including HP, had manufacturing affiliates in Europe, while Siemens, the leading European competitor, manufactured its monitors in the United States.

Suppliers of higher technology components such as semiconductors and cathode ray tubes were concentrated in the United States and Japan. However, there was no significant backward integration by either U.S. or Japanese

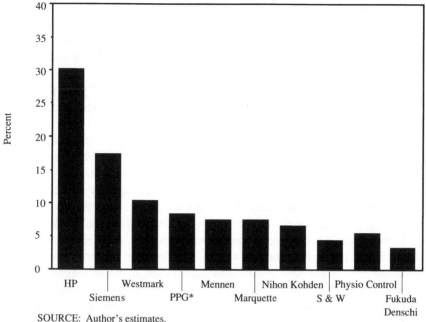

SOURCE: Author's estimates.

* Includes all of Litton and Honeywell acquisitions.

FIGURE 5–5 Estimated Global Market Shares of Patient Monitoring Equipment Companies in the Mid-1980s

monitor competitors, and the components could be sourced easily anywhere in the world. Software was a major component of modern monitors, and software engineers were most plentiful in the United States, giving U.S.-based firms a decided advantage.

Innovations during the 1980s often involved noninvasive or more convenient means of measurement, and most were pioneered by U.S. firms. For example, Dinamap, a small American start-up, developed a noninvasive cuff that intermittently measured blood pressure. Nellcor developed a method for measuring blood gases via a small sensor on the end of the patient's finger. Both of these inventions utilized microprocessor technology. Other innovations in monitors included the addition of brighter numeric readings to improve the visibility of the monitor screen from greater distances. Most innovations were part of a general effort to make the products as attractive and easy to use as possible. Because the products became quite similar to one another in function and appearance, attempts at differentiation were also based upon the addition of small, relatively superficial features that added to the aesthetic value of the product.

Many new innovative products came from entrepreneurs or smaller players.

Larger companies had more difficulty focusing on often small new segments and in pursuing potentially risky product innovations. Generally, these innovations were either acquired by other monitoring companies in licensing agreements or were standardized to allow their use with other companies' monitoring systems.

The broader use of computers in medicine was an area of great potential. Hewlett-Packard pioneered a product that could feed monitoring data directly into a computer to establish an up-to-date patient database to replace the traditional chart at the foot of the patient's bed. The penetration of patient data management systems was gradual, but the area was seen as a major source of future growth in an otherwise highly staturated market.

However, a more significant change in industry demand was occurring, especially in the United States. Most industrialized countries attempted to hold back increases in the cost of providing health care during the 1980s. In Europe, where socialized medicine was prevalent, this control was relatively direct. Throughout the postwar period, European countries were slower to spend money on new innovations and tended to be less aggressive in patient testing than the United States. A stricter cost-benefit approach to equipment purchases was well engrained in the European medical system. In the 1980s, economic slowdowns further restricted spending. In Japan, the government reallocated and reduced its financial support for hospitals in the early 1980s, leading to a much more conservative approach toward equipment purchases.

In the United States, intense pressures to curb medical spending developed in the 1980s as well. At the same time, the federal government tried to reduce its financial burden, and hospitals felt pressure from insurers and employers to control costs. Alternative forms of medical care such as health maintenance organizations (HMOs) proliferated, putting competitive pressure on hospitals. These pressures began to affect purchasing criteria for monitors by increasing emphasis on productivity enhancement and the potential for upgrading.

There was some concern that lower-priced foreign monitors might gain popularity, particularly as their capabilities approached those of U.S. companies. Nihon Kohden's and other Japanese products were configured rather than modular, which made them less expensive than most U.S. designs. Given the cost concerns in the early 1980s, industry participants felt that Nihon Kohden had a golden opportunity to win market share in the United States based on a good reputation for product reliability. It lacked adequate marketing and support, however, and its level of penetration remained limited.[36] Growing cost pressures at home could reduce this threat to U.S. firms, which had to design less expensive monitors of their own.

Another more radical change was the concept of "closed-loop" monitoring. A closed-loop system would adjust aspects of treatment (such as IV drug dosage) according to the patient's vital signs, eliminating the doctor from some immediate decisions. Closed-loop systems were gaining popularity in Europe. Such systems were going nowhere in the United States because of potential product liability problems. While the threat of lawsuits encouraged monitoring that reduced risk and did not involve treatment, it was beginning to impede innovation in monitors as well as other medical areas.

SUMMARY

The patient monitoring equipment industry first emerged and developed in the United States for several reasons that reflect the determinants. The most important were demand conditions, factor creation, and related and supporting industries. State-of-the-art medical research, where the United States led, was the impetus for creating many new monitoring products. The United States was also the early center of the electrical and electronics industry. This combination led to technology transfer and a growing cadre of American electrical engineers. These developments created a favorable environment for start-up companies, that encouraged numerous new entrants. The flood of entrants created new niches and led to active rivalry. The United States also had strong positions in related industries, such as computers and testing and measuring equipment, that spawned other entrants (such as HP).

The growth of the U.S. industry and its emergence as world leader was powered by early and sophisticated American demand, coupled with active domestic rivalry. The U.S. market was much more receptive to innovation in most segments than the markets in other countries. The many independent American hospitals and researchers made independent purchase decisions and had a history of less cost pressure. Continued innovation was also stimulated by leading U.S. positions in important supplier industries. American firms dominated the semiconductor industry in the 1950s and 1960s, and American firms still dominate microprocessors. Also significant were U.S. firms' commanding positions in computers and software.

American firms were the early international competitors in monitors. Initially, they were pulled abroad by internationalization of U.S. needs through the research community and doctors trained in America. Later, domestic market saturation, coupled with aggressive home market rivalry, led to stepped-up efforts to export. Overseas manufacturing followed to help penetrate foreign markets.

The United States represents a system for creating and sustaining advantage in this industry (and a variety of other medically related industries) that has been unmatched. Siemens is the only really successful foreign firm, but only by moving its effective home base to America has Siemens been able to gain position. American firms have been the source of nearly all the innovations in the industry, driven by sophisticated buyers, world-class supplier industries, domestic rivalry, and a heavy investment in factor creation (particularly in medical knowledge and specialized personnel). However, the American position is not without challenges: for instance, U.S. firms have been distracted and set back by repeated waves of acquisitions. As in the German printing press industry, consolidation may ultimately sap the innovativeness of what has been a group of dynamic competitors. American demand conditions have also been less anticipatory in areas such as telemetry and closed-loop systems, partly because of product liability concerns. Cost pressures are also making the U.S. market more like the foreign markets. Japanese competitors, enjoying a strong domestic electronics cluster and skills in producing standardized units, may become a growing threat. Yet as long as U.S. health care spending remains uniquely high and the American delivery system remains the most subject to competitive pressures, a major shift of international leadership in advanced monitor segments is hard to foresee.

THE ITALIAN CERAMIC TILE INDUSTRY[37]

Italian firms were by far the world leaders in the production and export of ceramic tiles, a $10 billion industry, in 1987. Italian producers accounted for about 30 percent of world production and almost 60 percent of world exports.[38] In 1987, the Italian trade surplus in ceramic tiles was 1,864 billion lire (or about $1.4 billion). Sales of foreign subsidiaries of Italian firms amounted to about $100 million, up significantly from 1980.

Italy's ceramic tile production was concentrated in the Emilia-Romagna region, in and around the small town of Sassuolo.[39] In the Sassuolo area, literally hundreds of firms were involved in the ceramic tile industry. The area was also home to world-leading producers of glazes, enamels, and ceramic tile production equipment.

Italian tiles were known throughout the world for superior mechanical and aesthetic qualities. Yet Italy's success had been as much, if not more, a function of production technology than design. In the post–World War II period, Italian firms had made the most important breakthroughs in tile production technology, including the first continuous production process and the commercialization of the single-firing technique.

PRODUCTS AND PROCESSES

Ceramic tiles were building materials used to cover and finish flat surfaces. The main applications were in flooring (60 to 65 percent of the total market) and wall covering (35 to 40 percent). Floor tiles were usually simpler in design, while wall tiles were often of higher aesthetic quality. Ceramic tiles competed with wood, vinyl tiles, marble, carpeting, and other building materials in various applications.

There were three basic processes used to produce ceramic tiles in 1987. In the first of these, the "double-firing method," clays were mixed and pressed into shape by special presses. The tiles were next fired in kilns at temperatures of approximately 1,000 degrees centigrade to harden and transform the clay into a ceramic. The hard, fired forms, or *bisque,* were then decorated with glazes and enamels and fired for a second time ("double-firing") to vitrify the glaze and make it adhere to the tile surface.

In the single-firing method, glaze was applied directly to the pressed clay form. A single firing was then employed to harden the tile and vitrify the glaze. Single-fired tiles were mostly used for floor tiles since the technique did not generally produce tiles of an aesthetic quality high enough for wall tiles.

The triple-fired technique was essentially an artisan technique in which special enamels, paints, and metal leafing were applied to double-fired tiles. The third firing was used to fix these materials to the tiles. The triple-fired technique produced expensive, highly decorative tiles.

Early Industry History

The ceramic tile industry in Sassuolo grew out of a related industry, earthenware and crockery, whose history in the area can be traced back to the thirteenth century. The first ceramic tiles in the area were used as street signs, house numbers, and on cemetery vaults in the nineteenth century. Immediately after World War II, there were only a handful of ceramic tile manufacturers in the Sassuolo area.

Demand for ceramic tiles within Italy grew dramatically in the early postwar years. The reconstruction of Italy after the war created an unprecedented boom in building materials of all kinds, including ceramic tiles. Italian demand for ceramic tiles was especially high. One reason was the nation's Mediterranean climate; ceramic tiles were cool in warm weather. There was also a tradition in Italy of using natural stone materials rather than vinyl or carpeting. Ceramic tiles fit closely with local taste. Wood was scarce and expensive in Italy, giving tiles a price/performance advantage over wood flooring. Finally, Italian buildings were generally made of concrete, which made laying tiles relatively easy. Wood buildings sometimes could not take the weight of tiles and required extra base materials.

Sassuolo was in a relatively prosperous area of the country with many well-to-do farmers and well-paid workers from the machinery industries located nearby. Many local citizens were able to put together the modest amount of capital and organizational skills required to operate a tile company at the time. A running joke was, "With four people you can play cards. With three you can start a tile company." New firms flooded into the business, many with the help of local banks. Once in the industry, firms generally financed their operations with internally generated funds.[40] In 1955, there were fourteen tile firms in and around Sassuolo. By 1962, the number was 102. Outside of Sassuolo, lack of information about the industry led to the emergence of few new competitors.[41] Assopiastrelle, the Italian ceramic tile industry association, was founded in 1964. Most Italian firms became members.

The tile industry benefited from a pool of mechanically trained workers. Emilia-Romagna, and Modena in particular, was home to Ferrari, Maserati, Lamborghini, and other firms with a long tradition of technical sophistication. Many engineers and others gravitated to the tile industry as established firms prospered and demand grew.[42] The president of Assopiastrelle in 1986, for example, started as a technician with Ferrari. In 1959, as the ceramic tile sector was booming, he formed a company to supply machinery to tile manufacturers. Not long after, he managed to purchase a tile company and began manufacturing tiles.

FOREIGN DEPENDENCE

Italian firms were initially dependent on foreign sources of raw materials and production technology. The principal raw materials used in making tiles in the 1950s were kaolin (white) clays. There were no white clay deposits near Sassuolo, so Italian producers had to import white clays from the United Kingdom. White clays, though much more expensive than more widely available (including around Sassuolo) red clays, were far easier to fire with the prevailing equipment.[43]

In the 1950s and 1960s, the production equipment used by Italian tile producers was mostly imported. Kilns came from Germany, the United States, and France; presses for forming tiles came from Germany. Even simple glazing machines had to be imported. Some of the equipment used in the Italian industry was originally designed for the food industry and modified for use in tile production.

Ceramic tiles is an industry that requires technical knowledge in design, production, and overall operations management. The raw materials vary in their physical and chemical properties. Experience and a feel for the material transformation process are essential to produce high-quality products with a minimum of waste. Italian firms developed their own technical know-how as their production experience accumulated. Information diffused rapidly through the Sassuolo area due to worker mobility and the proximity of the tile producers.

THE EMERGING ITALIAN TILE CLUSTER

Italian tile producers learned how to modify imported equipment for use with locally available red clays and natural gas (as opposed to heavy oil). A local tile equipment industry soon grew in Sassuolo as process technicians from the tile companies left to start their own equipment firms. By the mid-1960s, Italian tile firms were no longer dependent on foreign equipment producers. By 1970, Italian firms had emerged as world-class producers of kilns and presses and had begun to export. Whereas Sassuolo-area tile firms once used machinery optimized for white clays on red clays, now foreigners used Italian equipment optimized for red clays on their white clays.

The relationship between Italian tile and equipment manufacturers was a close one, made even more so because equipment manufacturers and tile manufacturers were often located next door to each other. In the mid-1980s, there were some 200 Italian equipment manufacturers; more than 60 percent were located in the Sassuolo area.[44] Italian equipment manufacturers competed fiercely for local business, and Italian tile manufacturers often received better equipment prices than foreign firms. In addition, the latest equipment was often made available to Italian firms a year or so before it was made available to foreign firms.[45] Sassuolo-area tile manufacturers could also get rapid maintenance and service on their equipment due to the proximity of suppliers. The information flow between suppliers and tile producers also favored Italian firms. Italian equipment manufacturers worked continuously with tile manufacturers to improve production machinery.

As the industry grew and concentrated around Sassuolo, a pool of specialized workers and technicians developed, including engineers, production specialists, maintenance workers, service technicians, and design personnel. New firms found it easy to hire the requisite expertise locally. A Sassuolo manufacturer also had a whole array of knowledgeable specialists in the area on whom he could call to solve production or design problems.[46]

The geographic concentration of the Italian industry encouraged the formation of other Italian firms around Sassuolo that supplied other inputs and services such as molds, glazes, packaging materials, and transportation. An array of small, specialized consulting firms emerged to give advice to tile producers on plant design, logistics, commercial, advertising, and fiscal matters. Third-party service firms were able to operate at peak efficiency due to the geographic concentration of their customer base.

GROWING SOPHISTICATION OF ITALIAN DEMAND

Home demand for tiles continued to grow rapidly, as the building boom continued through the 1960s and the Italian economy expanded, particularly in the north. By the mid-1960s, the Italian market for ceramic tiles became the single largest in the world.[47] In 1976, the Italian market accounted for some 23 percent of world consumption, followed by Germany (10 percent), France (8 percent), and Spain (7 percent).[48] In 1987, the Italian market was still the single largest in the world (see Table 5–3).

Per capita tile consumption in Italy was considerably higher than in the rest of the world. In 1976, per capita consumption of ceramic tiles was 2.68 square meters in Italy, 1.26 in Spain, 1.06 in Germany, and 1.03 in France. At 3.33 square meters, Italian per capita consumption was still the highest in the world in 1987 (see Table 5–4).

The Italian market was also considered the most sophisticated tile market in the world. Observers placed Italian market sophistication first, followed by Spain, France, and Germany.[49] Italian customers were generally the first to adopt new designs and features. The quality of Italian demand rose

TABLE 5–3 World Consumption of Ceramic Tiles by Nation, 1987 (% of volume)

Italy	15.0
Brazil*	12.6
Spain	7.7
Germany	7.2
United States	7.2
France	6.1
Japan*	4.9
Benelux	2.9
United Kingdom	2.7
Australia	1.2
Portugal	1.0
Greece	0.9
Switzerland	0.9
Finland	0.4
Sweden	0.3
Other European Countries*	6.6
Other Countries*	22.4
TOTAL	100.0

SOURCE: Based on Assopiastrelle data.
* Estimates.

TABLE 5–4 Per Capita Consumption of Ceramic Tiles, 1987 (square meters/capita)

Italy	3.33
Spain	2.55
Switzerland	1.81
Germany	1.54
Benelux	1.50
France	1.40
Portugal	1.25
Greece	1.21
Brazil	1.21
Australia	0.97
Finland	0.91
United Kingdom	0.60
Japan	0.52
Sweden	0.39
United States	0.38

SOURCE: Based on Assopiastrelle data.

in a mutually reinforcing process in which high demand and market sophistication created pressures to improve manufacturing methods and design that further boosted consumption and market sophistication. In the United Kingdom, in contrast, producers tended to make the same styles and patterns each year, and demand was relatively unsophisticated and stagnant.

The uniquely sophisticated and demanding character of Italian home demand extended to retail outlets. In the formative period of the Italian industry, ceramic tiles were sold like bricks in Italy through building material distributors. In response to strong demand in the 1960s, specialized tile showrooms began to open in Italy. Italy was characterized by a high proportion of tile sales through retail outlets, because of the importance of the housing rehabilitation market, which was served almost exclusively by retailers. Rehabilitation and remodeling were important markets in Italy in part because of the great difficulty in obtaining permission to tear down old buildings and the tendency of Italians to invest in improving their homes.

By 1985, there were some 7,600 specialized showrooms in Italy that handled approximately 80 percent of sales in the Italian market (serving the renovation and small contractor segment), while distributors handled about 9 percent of sales; some 11 percent of sales was distributed directly (mostly to construction and installation firms).[50] Italian speciality tile retailers carried several lines of competitive brands and showed little loyalty to any particular producer. It was estimated that some 49 percent of Italian retailers carried more than ten competitive lines; 29 percent carried six to ten lines, 19 percent carried three to five lines, and only 3 percent carried two lines or less.[51]

Retailers had considerable power in the relationship with manufacturers, because it was difficult to create brand awareness among consumers. End buyers were influenced in the purchase decision by the following factors, in descending order of importance: aesthetic qualities (25 percent), technical features (24 percent), price (21 percent), brand name (16 percent), and designer name (14 percent).[52] Only a small percentage of end customers were familiar with any tile brands. Tile showrooms sometimes combined tile with related products such as bathroom fixtures and building materials. Italy was also internationally competitive in these industries.

Italian tile manufacturers competed vigorously to get into retail outlets. Competition took the form of a stream of new designs and substantial promotional efforts directed at the retailer (consumers did not see designs that retailers had rejected). Manufacturers were forced continually to invent new ideas in order to get retailers and distributors to carry or continue to carry their lines. The move by Italian firms to pioneer tiles by famous designers was aimed at gaining distribution outlets and building brand awareness on the part of consumers. This stimulating interaction between manufacturers and retailers was unique to Italy, where the specialized tile retailing industry was by far the best developed. Showrooms were eventually opened in Germany and France. In both cases, the retailers did not acquire the same power as Italian retailers, because French and German outlets were generally more loyal to particular manufacturers.

SASSUOLO RIVALRY

Rivalry among Italian ceramic tile companies was intense. The sheer number of Sassuolo-area firms led to a fluid situation in which firms constantly sought to gain an edge on the others in technology, design, and distribution. News of product and process innovations spread rapidly. Innovations were usually known in days or weeks and copied in a few months. Firms seeking technical leadership had to improve constantly to stay ahead. Similarly, firms specializing in aesthetic design had to turn over their product line rapidly to stay ahead of imitators. This was especially true because copyrights and patents were generally hard to enforce. (In Germany, where the tile firms were not so concentrated, firms were able to protect company secrets longer and were under less pressure to improve continuously.)

Competition among Italian tile producers was intensely personal. All of the producers were located close together. Virtually all were privately held, and most were family run. The owners were committed to their businesses and the community. They lived in the area, knew each other, and were the leading citizens of the same towns.

Assopiastrelle, the ceramic tile industry association, with membership concentrated in the Sassuolo area, gradually began offering services in areas of common interest including bulk purchasing, foreign market research, and consulting on fiscal and legal matters. The association also took the lead in government and union relations. The growing Italian tile cluster stimulated wider mechanisms for factor creation. In 1976, a consortium of the University of Bologna, regional agencies, and various ceramic industry associations founded the *Centro ceramico di Bologna*. Its functions included research on ceramic raw materials, production processes, and chemical and mechanical analyses of finished products.

PRESSURES TO UPGRADE ADVANTAGE

By the early 1970s, Italian tile firms were struggling to reduce labor and gas costs in the face of intense domestic rivalry and pressure from retail customers. Italian producers believed their total labor costs per square meter of tile to be the highest in the world. They estimated that for each 1,000 lire in wages, total labor costs, including benefits and social security payments, ran more than 2,000 lire.[53] Italy also imported much of its natural gas from Algeria and the Soviet Union and had a cost disadvantage relative to U.S. firms (where gas prices were controlled and below market prices); at best, Italy was at parity with other European producers. The energy crisis of 1973 hit Italian producers particularly hard.

A typical cost structure for a ceramic tile producer was as follows: raw materials, 35 to 40 percent of sales; fuel (principally natural gas), 10 to 15 percent; labor costs, 20 to 30 percent; and depreciation of fixed assets, approximately 15 percent. Tile manufacture was capital intensive, requiring about 65 cents in assets for each dollar in sales.[54]

Highly visible energy and labor cost pressures led to the next major breakthrough by the Italian industry, the rapid single-firing process, in which hardening, material transformation, and glaze-fixing all took place in a single pass through the kiln. The first efforts at single-firing had taken place in the United States in the late 1950s, using white clays. Italian companies began experimenting with the technique in the early 1960s. By 1969, there were five Sassuolo-area firms using the single-firing method with local red clays. The aesthetic and technical qualities of these tiles were, however, still very low.[55]

Continued rivalry led to a breakthrough in 1972–1973 with the introduction of the rapid single-firing process by Marazzi. This required an improvement in kiln design. In the early postwar period, tunnel kilns were first introduced in England and then in the United States, Germany, and France.[56] Tunnel kilns were brickwork structures, 45 to 100 meters long. Tiles were carried through the kiln by means of automated refractory undercarriages. Tunnel kilns began to replace the prevailing Hoffman kilns which were large, ovenlike structures divided into several sections, each with an opening through which tiles were introduced. Sassuolo firms began to install tunnel kilns in the mid-1950s, and by the mid-1960s there were no Hoffman kilns left in the area.

In the early 1970s, Marazzi, in conjunction with the Italian equipment manufacturer SITI, developed roller kilns that eliminated the need for the refractory carriages that carried tiles through the kiln. Roller technology, adapted from the glass industry, resulted in a substantial decrease in energy utilization (heating the carriages wasted energy) and allowed for the full exploitation of the single-firing technology.

Rapid single-firing greatly reduced natural gas costs and improved productivity. What required 225 employees to produce using the double-firing method could be produced by only 90 employees using single-firing roller kilns in 1975.[57] The cycle time dropped from sixteen to twenty hours to fifty to fifty-five minutes.[58]

The rapid single-firing method was first employed for floor tiles with a relatively low decorative content. By the late 1970s, process improvements allowed single-fired production of tiles with a higher decorative content. By the mid-1980s, it was possible to produce even wall tiles, using the new method.

The diffusion of the rapid single-firing technology was very fast in the Italian industry, as manufacturers rushed to avoid a competitive disadvantage. In 1976, some 13 percent of total production of glazed ceramic tiles was manufactured using the single-firing method. The share of single-fired tiles in total production reached 39 percent in 1982 and 59 percent in 1987.[59]

Italian tile-making equipment manufacturers found it easier to export the new small and lighter single-firing equipment than the old double-firing equipment. By the early 1980s, exports of Italian equipment manufacturers exceeded their sales to Italian tile companies. Exports represented 75 to 80 percent of total sales in 1988.

INTERNATIONALIZATION

In the period from 1958 to 1961, sales of ceramic tiles on the domestic market more than doubled (from 21.5 to 44.1 million square meters). A sharp temporary slowdown occurred in the domestic market in the period from 1963 to 1964; however, Italian producers, faced with the prospect of cutting production, increased exports from 1.7 percent of production in 1958 to 16.0 percent in 1964 (see Table 5–5). Italian salespeople initially went from country to country with cases of samples to show to prospective customers (mostly building material distributors). Italian firms also used agents and distributors to sell abroad.

By 1970, Italian home demand had matured. The stagnant domestic market led Italian firms to step up their efforts to pursue foreign markets. Innovations in production technology raised productivity but also led to excess capacity, further stimulating efforts to sell overseas. Exports relative to production rose from 21.7 percent in 1971 to 54.0 percent in 1979.

The move to greater exports was facilitated by the presence of related and supporting Italian industries. Individual tile manufacturers began advertising in Italian and foreign high-quality home and architectural magazines. Italian home design and decorating magazines had a wide circulation around the world among architects, designers, and consumers. This heightened awareness and reinforced the image of Italian tiles.

Italian furniture and furnishings had also gained a strong international position, further upgrading the reputation of Italian tile. Italy was, or was among, the world export leaders in such related industries as marble and building stone, sinks and washbasins, furniture, lamps, and domestic appliances.

A key push in the mid-1980s was an attempt to achieve higher penetration

TABLE 5.5 Number of Firms, Employment, Production, and Exports in the Italian Ceramic Tile Industry, 1960–1987

Year	Number of Firms	Number of Employees	Employees per Firm	Production (Million Sq. Meter)	Production per Employee (Sq. Meter)	Total Sales (Million Sq. Meter)	Domestic Sales (Million Sq. Meter)	Exports (Million Sq. Meter)	Exports/ Production (%)	Share of World Exports (%)
1960	55	8,906	162	37.8	4,244	37.7	36.4	1.3	3.5	*
1962	115	14,000	122	51.5	3,679	51.5	47.8	3.7	7.2	*
1964	111	14,669	132	34.6	2,359	34.5	29.0	5.5	16.0	*
1966	115	15,450	134	78.9	5,107	78.9	61.5	17.4	22.0	*
1968	179	20,950	117	107.7	5,141	107.7	85.0	22.7	21.1	*
1970	316	30,550	97	150.0	4,910	139.7	104.0	35.7	23.8	*
1972	413	36,500	88	181.0	4,959	167.9	117.0	50.9	28.1	*
1974	465	44,823	96	230.1	5,134	211.2	137.5	73.7	32.0	*
1976	509	48,115	95	255.6	5,312	245.0	153.6	91.4	35.8	*
1978	470	43,650	93	273.7	6,271	267.1	132.6	134.5	49.1	58.6
1979	470	44,650	95	291.0	6,517	310.1	153.0	157.1	54.0	62.3
1980	470	45,880	98	335.6	7,314	330.6	181.2	149.4	44.5	59.2
1981	468	43,642	93	339.0	7,768	309.5	166.2	143.3	42.3	55.1
1982	433	40,708	94	323.3	7,942	303.5	165.4	138.1	42.7	54.2
1983	420	38,000	90	305.0	8,026	306.8	150.0	156.8	51.4	58.1
1984	413	34,469	83	334.9	9,717	329.0	154.7	174.3	52.0	50.7
1985	374	31,500	84	311.0	9,873	314.9	157.3	157.6	50.7	57.1
1986	360	29,303	81	329.0	11,228	323.2	163.0	160.2	48.7	59.1
1987	356	29,500	83	350.0	11,864	350.0	185.0	165.0	47.1	N/A

SOURCE: Based on Assopiastrelle data.
* Comparable data unavailable.

of untapped markets like the United States, while retaining or increasing share in European markets. Italian producers had to overcome a 19 percent import duty plus significant transportation costs in order to export to the United States. A few Italian producers moved to offset these disadvantages through direct investment in the United States. For example, Marazzi U.S.A. was founded in 1982 with production facilities in Texas. By 1987, it was the fourth-largest American producer.

The ceramic tile industry received help in export promotion from ICE, a government agency set up to facilitate trade between Italy and the rest of the world. However, this aid was rather minor in scope and dollar value. The great majority of financing and organizational work for export promotion came from industry.

Assopiastrelle established trade promotion offices in the United States (New York in 1980), in Germany (Düsseldorf in 1984), and in France (Paris in 1987). It also organized elaborate trade shows in locations ranging from Bologna (Italy) to Miami (Florida) and ran sophisticated advertising. Assopiastrelle spent some $8 million in promoting Italian tiles in the United States in the period from 1980 to 1987. The collective promotions attempted to enhance the overall image of Italian tiles by emphasizing their superior physical and aesthetic qualities. Such a concerted effort to promote foreign sales was unique to the Italian industry.

Italy was also home to the major trade show for ceramic tiles, CERSAIE. This exhibition was held annually in Bologna and was considered the most important industry event in the world by international buyers and manufacturers. In 1988, CERSAIE attracted almost all of the Italian producers and some ninety foreign producers.[60]

CONTINUED INNOVATION

Working together, Sassuolo tile companies and equipment manufacturers made the next important breakthrough during the mid- and late 1970s. Italian firms pioneered the development of material-handling equipment that turned tile manufacture from a batch process into a continuous process. The pioneering of continuous process technology by Italian firms seems counterintuitive given the common perception that Italian labor costs were lower during this period than those in the United States and Germany. In the United States and Germany, however, there were wide differences in labor rates for different jobs. American tile producers used minimum wage labor for material-handling duties while German firms often used low-paid immigrant workers. The U.S. and German firms also generally employed multiple shifts. In Italy, however, work rules constrained manufacturers from using overtime or multiple shifts, especially beginning in the early 1970s. Firms were restricted to eight-hour days with multiple rest periods for workers. This restriction was debilitating, because kilns are extremely costly to reheat once they cool down and are best run twenty-four hours per day.

This new selective factor disadvantage facing Italian manufacturers created strong, and highly visible, pressures to automate the production process. Italian firms were the first to develop continuous, automated production. In Germany and the United States, in contrast, little effort was placed on developing continuous processes.

The next important innovation pioneered by the Italian industry was the introduction of *designer tiles* by Piemme in 1976. This innovation drew on another related Italian industry, design services. Italy was world leader in this industry, with exports estimated at over $10 billion.[61] Marazzi had attempted to team up with architects and designers to design tiles in the early 1970s, but the collaboration resulted in some abstract tile designs that did not catch on. In 1976, Piemme contracted with the Italian designer Valentino for a series of decorated tiles. The Valentino line was a success. Many other manufacturers soon enlisted the aid of other Italian designers (Missoni, Ferré, Krizia, Biagiotti, and Versace, among others). By 1987, designer tiles accounted for some 10 percent of Italian tile sales.[62]

Another significant innovation by Italian tile producers was third-firing, or the adaptation on a large scale of the old artisan tradition of decorating ceramics by hand. Decorations were applied directly to the vitrified form that was in turn passed through small kilns for a third time (or a second time for single-fired tiles). This innovation was stimulated by the introduction of single-firing, since it was still impossible to obtain a wide range of colors or sophisticated decorations via single-firing. Third-firing was usually subcontracted by major companies to small specialized producers. Tile companies used third-fired tiles to complete the top end of their product line. In the mid-1980s, there were more than sixty small firms in the Sassuolo area specializing in third-firing.[63]

THE ITALIAN INDUSTRY IN THE 1980s

In 1987, sales of Italian ceramic tile producers amounted to 4,010 billion lire (or $3.2 billion), some 47 percent of which was exported. Some 58.6 percent of total production was single-fired tiles, 28.0 percent was double-fired tiles, and the remaining 13.4 percent was other types of tiles (*gres, cotto,* etc.). In the same year, there were 356 Italian companies, down from the peak reached in 1976. The Italian industry was quite fragmented. In 1986, the largest firm accounted for only 5.3 percent of total sales, and the top twenty firms for only 37.2 percent.[64]

There were three major groups of Italian firms.[65] Firms such as Marazzi,

222   **Industries**

Iris, Cisa-Cerdisa, and Floor Gres were investing heavily in technology to
improve productivity or product quality and aesthetics. These firms generally
had strong relationships with equipment producers and jointly developed
new equipment and improved existing machinery. The firms in this group
tended to be larger and more export oriented than average.

A small group of firms (including Piemme and Atlas Concorde) attempted
to compete on image and design in the sophisticated, highly design-sensitive
end of the market. These firms advertised heavily and invested substantial
amounts in showroom expositions.

A third group included a large number of smaller firms, who competed
largely on price. They tended to rapidly imitate successful technological
improvements and were also quick to imitate new designs, especially those
of the expensive designer tiles.[66]

Improvements in production equipment helped create overcapacity and
severe price competition in the Italian industry in the early 1980s. The
great majority of Sassuolo firms were privately owned and managed by
the owners. This, coupled with strong ties to the community, led to intense
commitment to succeed in the industry even during difficult times. Sassuolo
firms did not hesitate to invest large sums in the latest generation of kilns
or other equipment. Efforts to export also intensified. To give up and leave
the industry without a fight was unthinkable.

The ceramic tile industry had recently benefited from *cassa integrazione,*
a program in which the Italian government paid employees dismissed by
their companies. Italy did not have a formal unemployment insurance program, and each appeal for the *cassa integrazione* was considered independently. In March 1984, some 3,500 employees laid off by Italy's top fifty
ceramic tile manufacturers were being paid through this program, representing
about 10 percent of employment in the sector.[67] Some American producers
claimed this form of aid allowed Italian firms to maintain high capacity
utilization by paying wages during work reductions or plant shutdowns
and represented an unfair subsidy.[68] Italian firms counterclaimed that the
program served the same purpose as American unemployment insurance.

THE ITALIAN COMPETITIVE POSITION

Sustained innovation allowed Italian firms to hold and even increase market
position in the 1980s. Spain was the world's second-largest exporter of
ceramic tiles, with a world export share of 11 percent in 1986. The Spanish
industry, 170 producers as of 1987, exported some 37 percent of its production. The growth of the industry had been initially favored by a strong
Spanish tradition in ceramics and a high per capita consumption of ceramic

tiles, reflecting climatic conditions and aesthetic traditions that favored tiles coupled with relatively high duties on imported tiles. This constraint on imports had been partially lifted with the entry of Spain into the European Community and would be completely eliminated in 1992.

The Spanish market for ceramic tiles was the third largest in the world in volume and the second largest in terms of value. Observers estimated that the sophistication of Spanish buyers was high, second only to that of Italian buyers. It was estimated that there were more than 10,000 specialized tile retailers. A peculiar trait of the Spanish industry was that a number of Spanish firms had invested in proprietary showrooms. Starting from the mid-1980s, there was also increased advertising on television and in magazines that stimulated local demand.

A major constraint facing the Spanish industry was the unavailability of natural gas as an energy source until 1980. This had impeded the adoption of rapid single-firing techniques, because roller kilns had to be fired with natural gas. When natural gas became available, Spanish firms started to invest heavily in the latest technology, buying the most advanced equipment from Italian suppliers. By 1987, approximately half of Spanish production was single-fired.

Spanish firms were favored by local red clay deposits containing less organic residuals than the Italian clays. Better-quality clays allowed Spanish firms to be very competitive in the production of large-size tiles, due to fewer production defects and to shorter firing times. Spanish firms were also particularly advanced in the production of *monoporosa* (single-fired wall tiles with a high degree of water absorption).[69]

Approximately 90 percent of Spanish production was concentrated in the Castellan Plain, in the northeastern part of Spain north of Valencia. The ten largest Spanish companies in the industry accounted for some 40 percent of production, and some of these companies had common shareholders. However, the intensity of rivalry among the ten largest companies (and also among smaller companies) was very high. Spain had a number of elements of the "diamond" for ceramic tiles, notably demand conditions and some factor advantages, but lacked the base of related and supporting industries and rivalry as intense as in Italy. Its threat to the Italian industry was not yet imminent.

Germany was the third-largest exporter of ceramic tiles, with a world export share of 10.4 percent in 1986. German success was concentrated in a number of segments. German producers generally manufactured high-priced tiles with excellent mechanical properties. German tiles were resistant to scratching, wear, and freezing, qualities especially suited for northern European applications. German tile producers were exceptionally strong in the production of extruded tiles, an alternative to pressed tiles. The German market was the fourth largest in the world. Production was concentrated in roughly ten large firms that employed Italian and German production equipment.[70]

Brazil did not export significant quantities of ceramic tiles outside of South America, and Brazil's world export share was 1.8 percent in 1986. Brazilian firms employed Italian production equipment to manufacture tiles which were low in price and considered low in quality.[71]

There were concerns in the Italian industry in 1988 that the export of Italian ceramic tile-making equipment was creating foreign competitors. In the mid-1980s, there were new competitors emerging in Thailand and Korea that employed Italian equipment. Nevertheless, no nation could yet match Italy in either technology or quality in a broad range of tiles.

SUMMARY

Several conditions fostered the initial growth of the ceramic industry in the Sassuolo area. A tradition in a closely related industry led to initial interest in the industry. Unusually high per capita consumption and the postwar construction boom attracted competitors. A number of factors of production (capital, skilled and unskilled labor) were locally available. An imitation effect led to a flood of entries.

Vigorous domestic rivalry led Sassuolo-area firms first to modify imported equipment to process cheaper and locally available clays. The tile industry then spawned an indigenous tile-making equipment industry that became the world leader. Other supplier and support industries grew up in the area to serve tile manufacturers. The industry association performed some useful infrastructure functions. The geographic concentration both of firms and suppliers led to intensely personal rivalry, rapid advancement of knowledge, and local efforts to create a basic research infrastructure.

Distinctive Italian circumstances made home demand the largest and most sophisticated in the world. Powerful and knowledgeable retailers added to the pressure to innovate. Retail showrooms, linking tiles with other dynamic Italian industries such as furniture, fixtures, and kitchen appliances, led to further innovation.

Intense rivalry powered continuous and important innovation in the industry. The first rapid single-firing and the first continuous production process were the most important in a stream of new ideas. Italian process innovations were triggered by visible selective factor disadvantages. Under competitive pressure, Italian firms struggled early and hard with local problems that signaled fruitful directions of innovation.

As Italian demand hit a cyclical trough in the early 1960s and leveled off around 1970, Italian ceramic tile producers looked to export markets.

They had become the leading producers and exporters of ceramic tiles by the 1970s. By the early 1980s, overcapacity at home made Italian firms even more aggressive exporters. They mounted increasingly sophisticated marketing campaigns to promote Italian tiles abroad. The strength of Italian related and supporting industries (design services, other furnishing-related industries, and related media) led to further innovation as well as advantages in international marketing.

Many of the advantages which brought about the initial success of the Italian industry were not sustainable. A tradition of producing ceramic products was not a lasting advantage in the capital-intensive, technology-intensive industry that tile production became. Clay deposits were widely available either from local sources or through trade. Italy imported most of its natural gas. Even Italian-developed production technology became widely disseminated by equipment manufacturers and through specialized consultants and trade journals.

Sassuolo's sustainable competitive advantage in ceramic tiles grew not from any static or historical advantage but from dynamism and change. Constant pressure for innovation was present, due to sophisticated and demanding local buyers, strong and unique distribution channels, and intense rivalry among local firms. Private ownership of firms and loyalty to the community created intense commitment to invest and to the industry.

Knowledge grew rapidly due to cumulative production experience and continuous experimentation. A highly developed set of suppliers, support industries, services, and infrastructure benefited tile producers. The presence of world-class Italian related industries served to reinforce Italian strength in tiles. Finally, the geographic concentration of the entire cluster supercharged the whole process; the ceramic tile industry is "in the air" in Sassuolo.

The Sassuolo tile industry represents a system in which each determinant of national competitive advantage is present and self-reinforcing. The complex interactions among the determinants, taking place in the midst of the world's largest and most sophisticated tile market, gave Sassuolo-area firms unique advantages over their foreign competitors. Foreign firms must compete not with a single firm, or even a group of firms, but with an entire subculture. The organic nature of this system is the hardest to duplicate and therefore the most sustainable advantage of Sassuolo firms.

THE JAPANESE ROBOTICS INDUSTRY[72]

Japan was the world's leading producer and exporter of industrial robots in 1987. Approximately 300 Japanese firms produced 300 billion yen (about $2.3 billion) worth of robots.[73] Japanese companies produced over 50 percent of the world's industrial robots in the mid-1980s. Japanese exports of robots were by far the largest of any nation and were growing rapidly. Some 20 percent of production, or 60 billion yen, was exported. Other major robot-producing countries included the United States, Germany, Sweden, and Italy, but none approached Japan in the depth or breadth of production.

Types of Robots

Industrial robots are used primarily to perform manufacturing operations or to transport materials to and from manufacturing equipment in a factory setting. Robots can be divided into six different categories, characterized by the method of control. *Manual manipulators* are robots that need a human to control them throughout their operation. Motions of the human operator are translated directly into mechanical actions of the robot. *Fixed sequence control robots* operate sequentially in compliance with preset information that cannot be readily modified or changed. *Variable sequence control robots* can be readily reprogrammed, greatly enhancing flexibility. *Playback robots* repeat operations on the basis of instructions concerning sequence, condition, position, and other information imparted by moving the robot under operator control. *Numerically controlled robots* execute operations loaded numerically or by a program, without being taught or moved by a human operator. Numerically controlled robots generally employ computer controllers that are similar to those used in numerically controlled machine tools. *Intelligent robots* can modify their own operation through the use of artificial intelligence.

Most industrial robots were designed for particular uses, such as arc welding, spray painting, and insertion of electronic components onto circuit boards. Other robots, such as materials handling robots, light assembly robots, and machining robots were less specialized. The programmable feature of industrial robots allowed a robot to perform a variety of activities within its scope of operation. Manufacturing systems that employed a number of robots were invariably custom engineered, though often from standardized building blocks.

Buyers sought industrial robots to boost productivity, raise quality, allow more stable employment levels, or perform hazardous tasks. Gaining the full benefits of robots required significant changes in a company's approach to manufacturing compared to more conventional production equipment. Direct cost savings were often not the most important benefit, and therefore adoption of robots was a slow process in most nations.

The design of an industrial robot included specification of the mechanical, electronic, and software systems required for the robot to perform its appointed tasks. Software development was a particularly important part of the process and was beginning to dominate development cost as complex factory automation systems (in which many machines had to work together) came into being.

The manufacturing process for robots was similar to that for other complicated pieces of machinery. Metal castings were machined and finished according to specification and then assembled. The robot was then fitted with motors and the drive system that would govern its motions, and the controller was installed. Finally, robots were tested extensively to make sure they conformed to specification.

INDUSTRY HISTORY

Robots were first conceived of in the United States in the 1950s at a time when the United States was the leading nation in terms of manufacturing technology and American wages were the highest in the world. George C. Devol of the United States was credited with the first robot-related patent in 1954. Consolidated Control Inc., an American firm, developed a digitally controlled robot in 1958. In 1962, the first robots were developed by the American firms Unimation and AMF. These remained the prototypes of the most popular robots for decades. It was not until the late 1960s, however, that significant commercial production of industrial robots began.

The first robots used in Japan were imported from the United States in 1967. The Japanese robotics industry had its beginning in 1968, when Kawasaki Heavy Industries signed a licensing agreement with Unimation. Kawasaki was both a major potential user of robots as well as a producer of related products and services. It produced a broad range of machinery and parts, including engines, motorcycles, aircraft, machinery, complete plants, and ships. In 1969, Kawasaki began to sell Unimate robots, the first robots produced in Japan. Kobe Steel was also an early licensee of American robot designs.

The early Japanese robots produced results that were somewhat less than expected. They were often referred to as "expensive fools," and many were relegated to the corners of factories to collect dust.[74] However, Japanese firms began to improve upon the robots they had imported. Kawasaki redesigned some of the parts of the Unimation machine and upgraded its quality. In the late 1960s, the mean time between failures (MTBF) of an imported robot was less than 300 hours. By 1974, Kawasaki had achieved an MTBF of 800 hours. By 1975, this figure was 1,000 hours, or over 100 hours better than the best result then achieved by Unimation (900 hours). Kobe Steel made several improvements to operating speed, lowered the weight of the robot designs it had licensed, and also adapted them for use in conveyor systems.[75]

Other Japanese electrical and machinery manufacturers began to develop robot technology on their own soon after Kawasaki's agreement with Unimation. Some of the most prominent entrants were Ishikawajima-Harima Heavy Industries, Hitachi, and Toshiba Precision Machinery. All were among Japan's leading diversified manufacturing companies.

In 1971, only three years after the founding of the Japanese industry, an informal meeting among manufacturers helped lay the groundwork for the formation of the Japanese Industrial Robotics Association in 1972. This organization soon became involved in programs to promote the industry and handle relations with government.

EARLY AND SOPHISTICATED HOME MARKET DEMAND

The automotive and domestic appliance industries were the principal early markets for industrial robots in Japan. Nissan was an important early customer. It cooperated with Kawasaki to help design and provide software for automotive robots and became the first Japanese auto company to install industrial robots on a large scale, installing Kawasaki robots as early as 1970. The difficulties encountered were initially so great that Kawasaki's engineers were at Nissan nearly every day to repair leaking hydraulic lines, failed electronic circuits, and faulty mechanical parts. Eventually, the problems were solved and the auto workers themselves became adept at operating the robots and performing minor repairs.[76] Soon other companies in the highly competitive Japanese auto industry installed robots so as not to fall behind Nissan in manufacturing technology.

Japanese industries that were rapidly growing, such as autos and electronics, faced a shortage of skilled workers. In 1965, it was estimated that there was a shortfall of some 1.8 million skilled workers in Japan, and the shortages persisted into the 1980s. Capacity utilization was also affected by changing work patterns. As Japanese workers became more affluent, they became less willing to work second and third shifts. Robots represented an important solution to both problems.

In 1973, the first oil crisis led to a sharp recession in Japan and to cutthroat domestic rivalry to fill unused capacity. The inflation of 1974–1975 that followed the first oil shock drove up wage rates dramatically. Both raised cost consciousness. Combined with lifetime employment policies in major companies, these pressures also made Japanese firms more cautious in hiring new workers who could be difficult to lay off in downturns. Japanese manufacturers, under severe competitive pressure, turned to robots to increase productivity and conserve energy.

In contrast to the situation in the United States and Europe, the supportive posture of Japanese labor unions aided the rapid penetration of robots. Japanese unions, generally single-company unions, were willing to cooperate with robot introduction. Jobs in the larger companies were protected by lifetime employment policies. In addition, the industries that were the major users of robots in Japan were growing rapidly throughout the late 1970s and early 1980s and had difficulty obtaining workers. In contrast, the introduction of robots met with severe resistance in many unionized companies in America and Europe, particularly in industries such as the auto industry that were not growing.

Japanese management also appeared far more willing to install industrial robots than their foreign counterparts. A high proportion of Japanese managers were engineers. They seemed more at home with new technologies than American managers. Japanese managers were also under little pressure to produce short-term results and were better able to make long-term strategic manufacturing decisions. Robots were often hard to justify on short-term cost savings alone. Japanese firms were more confident in achieving other benefits such as improved quality and applied different investment criteria.

A final development, whose importance is hard to overestimate, was the emergence of Japanese companies as the premier manufacturing companies in the world in a wide range of industries. Through high levels of automation, reorganization of work flow, and extreme attention to quality, Japanese companies redefined manufacturing practice. Cutting-edge Japanese manufacturers were sophisticated and anticipatory buyers for the growing Japanese robotics industry and a spur to continual innovation.

All these factors combined to accelerate the development and installation of industrial robots. Japan developed the earliest, largest, and most sophisticated market for industrial robots in the world. By the early 1970s, Japan's installed base of robots was by far the largest in the world, representing over 60 percent of the world total. The number of robots produced in Japan reached 7,200 (14.1 billion yen) in 1976; 10,100 (27.3 billion yen) in 1978; 19,900 (78.4 billion yen) in 1980; 24,800 (148.4 billion yen) in 1982; and 48,500 (over 300 billion yen) in 1985. Over the same time period, the product mix within the industry moved to more sophisticated robots. By 1984, Japan's installed base of industrial robots accounted for over 66 percent of the world total compared to 14.9 percent for North America. The size of the installed base of industrial robots in the major industrialized countries is shown in Table 5–6.

Japanese buyers of robots included not only large but also small- and medium-sized Japanese companies. The network of subcontractors employed in the Japanese automotive and machinery industries was an important market for Japanese robot manufacturers. Subcontractors valued the flexibility, economy, and quality improvements that robots afforded. In addition, the shortage of skilled workers had hit small firms particularly hard, because they were generally considered less desirable places to work than the large companies.

TABLE 5–6 Industrial Robots in Operation by Country

Country	1984	1980
Japan	67,300	15,250
United States	14,500[1]	4,700[1]
Canada	700[2]	250[3]
Belgium	775[8]	58[8]
Denmark	114[13]	38[13]
Finland	187[7]	20[7]
France	2,700[5]	580[5]
Germany	6,600[4]	1,255[4]
Italy	2,585[6]	353[6]
Netherlands	213[2]	56[1]
Norway	250[14]	210[1]
Sweden	2,400[12]	940[9]
Switzerland	110[2]	50[1]
United Kingdom	2,623[12]	371[12]
Spain	516[12]	284[10]
Austria	80[11]	
Total	101,703	23,415

SOURCE: Japan Industrial Robot Association, July 1985.
NOTE: This data excludes manual manipulators and fixed sequence control machines.

[1] RIA Survey
[2] RIA Survey (1983)
[3] National Research Council (1981)
[4] IPA
[5] AFRI
[6] Italian Industrial Robotics Society
[7] Robotics Society of Finland
[8] BIRA-Robotics Survey
[9] Swedish Computers and Electronics Commission, Ministry of Industry (1979)
[10] BRA (1982)
[11] Technical University of Vienna (March 1983)
[12] BRA
[13] Danish Industrial Robot Association
[14] MVL (Norway)

RIA = Robotic Industries Association
IPA = Fraunhofer Institut für Produktionstechnik und Automatisierung
AFRI = Association Française de Robotique Industrielle
BIRA = Belgisch Institut voor Regeltechniek en Automatizering
BRA = British Robot Association

Many of these firms had to automate in order to grow. One industry expert estimated that 20 percent of the industrial robots sold in Japan in 1986 went to small- and medium-sized companies, and this figure was growing rapidly.[77] The attention to this segment was uniquely great in Japan and to a lesser extent in Italy.

By 1980, the largest users of industrial robots in Japan were the electronics industry (36 percent of the installed base), the automotive industry (29 percent), the plastic processing industry (10 percent), general machinery industries (7 percent), and the metal working industry (5 percent). This pattern had not changed much by 1985, when the household electrical machinery and automotive markets accounted for 49 percent of total Japanese robot sales and over 61 percent of domestic sales.[78]

In 1980, the Japanese government enacted several policies to stimulate robot demand:[79]

- Establishment of a leasing system and the Japan Robot Leasing Company, designed to popularize industrial robots among small- and medium-sized enterprises
- Special financing from the Small Business Finance Corporation and the People's Finance Corporation to small- and medium-sized enterprises in introducing industrial robots designed to ensure worker safety
- Establishment of a special depreciation system for high-performance industrial robots that included computers
- Loans and leasing programs covering industrial robots at the local government level to help smaller enterprises in modernizing their equipment

Two additional policies were implemented in 1984:

- Establishment of a leasing system for flexible manufacturing systems at special interest rates (special loans from the Japanese Development Bank to the Japan Robot Leasing Company)
- Establishment of tax incentives for promoting investment in advanced equipment provided with electronics for smaller enterprises, involving special depreciation allowances or special deduction of corporate taxes

All these measures were limited in scope, though they did serve the useful purpose of stimulating demand for robots in small- and medium-sized companies. The robot leasing program financed foreign as well as Japanese robots and covered only around 1 percent of total robot shipments. The special depreciation allowances reached a peak in 1978–1979 when buyers could write off 25 percent of the value of a purchased robot in the first year. This was decreased to 10 percent in the first year in 1982–1983 and was later phased out altogether. It was generally felt that these measures were not very important to the growth of the industry.

THE GROWING JAPANESE CLUSTER

Other important Japanese companies entered the robotics industry in the mid 1970s. Most were from buyer, supplier, or related industries. FANUC, the world's leading producer of numerical controls for machine tools (with about 50 percent of the world market) and a leading manufacturer of servo motors, entered in 1974. FANUC's first robots were produced for internal use.

FANUC became the leading Japanese producer of robots (in terms of number produced). The auto industry soon became the largest customer for FANUC robots, with the company itself second. FANUC's main manufacturing facility near Mt. Fuji was one of the most highly automated facilities in the world. FANUC's plant employed one hundred workers during the day and was supervised by a single guard at night. FANUC estimated that using conventional manufacturing techiques would have required ten times the capital investment and ten times as many employees.

Matsushita Denki, a unit of the large consumer electronics firm, entered in 1971. Matsushita developed its first *Panasert* automatic electronic parts mounting machine in 1967 to automate the component insertion process in electronic assembly. Matsushita installed the first Panasert machines in its own factories. In 1975, Matsushita founded a separate precision machinery division to further develop its manufacturing equipment expertise. The firm began to sell polar coordinate robots for welding in 1980 and assembly robots in 1982.

Yaskawa Electric Manufacturing Company was an example of an entrant during the second half of the 1970s. Yaskawa produced computer numerical controls (CNC) and heavy electrical products and was a major producer of electrical motors. The firm introduced its first line of robots in 1977. Arc welding robots dominated Yaskawa's line, though it also supplied robots for materials handling, machining, and assembly. The firm began to produce assembly cells in 1986. The first application of the Yaskawa assembly cell was to assemble components for the company's own popular L10W welding robot. The company planned to use its in-house system to gain experience and as a demonstration unit for buyers. Yaskawa claimed to be the largest Japanese supplier of industrial robots to the open market by the mid-1980s.

Kawasaki, initially producing American designs under license, went on to develop its own robot technology. In 1982, it began selling its *Puma* series of welding robots. In 1985, it formed a technical relationship with Adept Technology (United States) to develop direct drive robots. Kawasaki robots were used in a variety of applications including spot welding, arc welding, machining, palletizing, materials handling, sealing, and coating.

By 1980, there were no less than 130 robot manufacturers in Japan. They could be divided into four major groups. First was the producers of electrical appliances (including Hitachi, Toshiba, Nihon Electric, Mitsubishi Electric, Yaskawa, and Fuji Electric). A second group consisted of producers of machinery (including FANUC, Toyota Machine Works, Komatsu, and Toshiba Seiki). A third group was producers of transportation equipment (including Kawasaki Heavy Industries, Mitsubishi Heavy Industries, Ishikawajima-Harima Heavy Industries, and Mitsui Engineering and Shipbuilding). The fourth and final group was steelmakers (including Kobe Steel and Daido Steel).[80]

Under the Temporary Measures Law for Machinery and Electronics Industries (1971–1978) and the Temporary Measures Law on the Machinery and Information Industries, robot manufacturers could qualify for low-interest government loans from the Japan Development Bank. Few companies availed themselves of these loans, however, partly because the interest rate differential was small and partly because the competitors in robotics were significant companies with adequate resources.

Japanese producers adopted differing degrees of vertical integration that depended on the industries in which they had historically competed. Kawasaki, with expertise in hydraulics gained through its activities in the defense sector, produced hydraulic systems in-house but bought motors, gears, and small parts. Matsushita produced motors but bought gears and hydraulic parts. FANUC produced its own motors and controllers.

Japanese robot producers drew on strong domestic suppliers of all important components. Japanese firms were world leaders in virtually all of the technologies employed in industrial robots. This included numerical controllers, machine tools, motors, optical sensors, electronic components, and other electrical equipment. Many leading competitors in these related technologies had entered the robotics industry.

Many of the Japanese robotics manufacturers were also diversified companies experienced in electronics and machinery. Not only did they have in-house experience in many of the separate technologies that went into industrial robots, but they were also major users. They thus had the advantage of possessing considerable application knowledge, which was important to success in the industry.[81]

Japanese robotics competitors were also more likely to have a background in electronics and computers than their foreign rivals. Most of the American robotics firms were start-ups, users, or machinery producers, while the leading European firms were often automotive companies with the exception of ASEA (now ABB), Olivetti, and Siemens. Japanese electronics companies had an advantage over purely machinery companies in incorporating sophisticated electronics and controls in their machines.

INTERNATIONALIZATION

Exports of robots from Japan began around 1975, though at low levels. By 1981, exports still accounted for only 5 percent, by value, of industry sales. Rapid adoption of robots in Japan dwarfed demand in most foreign markets. By 1985, exports had grown to account for 20 percent of sales, with automotive companies and their suppliers representing the major market.

Robots were sold directly to end users. Selling robots was highly technical and frequently required a detailed engineering knowledge of a customer's production process. Significant efforts were usually necessary to educate the prospective buyer about the capabilities and advantages of robots and other factory automation equipment. Purchase decisions were often made at high levels. The slow growth of exports was partly explained by the high service content of the products and the need to provide the customer with maintenance, service, and training. Sales were further complicated if robots were part of a fully automated production system.

Many Japanese robot manufacturers formed links with foreign firms in order to gain access to foreign marketing, sales, and service capability, or to obtain specialized technology. The best known was General Motors-FANUC, formed in 1982. Here, General Motors supplied software, marketing strength, and a captive market, while FANUC supplied robots and robot-related hardware. Product development was carried out jointly. By 1986, some 20 percent of FANUC's robots were manufactured for General Motors. The joint venture had an approximate 27 percent share of the U.S. robot market in 1985, by far the largest of any company. FANUC also joined forces with General Electric in 1986 to develop factory automation systems.

Both ventures were widely viewed as admissions by the American companies that they could not match FANUC's robot expertise. The other ties between Japanese and U.S. firms were mostly sales agreements, in which American companies marketed Japanese-made robots.[82] No Japanese robot producer was engaged in U.S. production and all Japanese robots sold in the United States were imported, except for those produced in the General Motors-FANUC joint venture.

In the mid-1980s, Japanese firms were more successful in the U.S. market than in the European market. They had focused on supplying the domestic market first, then the U.S. market, and only then the European market. Japanese firms were just beginning to gear up for large-scale sales efforts in Europe in the mid-1980s. They had also found it easier to find American firms willing to market and resell Japanese robots than to find European firms to take on these functions.

DOMESTIC RIVALRY IN THE 1980s

By 1986, the number of Japanese robot producers had swelled to approximately 300, up from 204 in 1983 and 279 in 1985. About 100 produced robots solely for their own use. Local rivalry was fierce. Industry participants generally felt that the Japanese market was easily the world's toughest market in terms of competition. Price competition was keen. By 1986, prices for small assembly robots had fallen to 3 to 4 million yen from a level of 6 to 8 million yen only a few years before.

The pace of innovation and new product introduction among the Japanese firms was feverish. Product innovations were soon imitated or upstaged by other producers. For example, the American firm Adept Technology introduced the world's first commercially successful direct-drive robot near the end of 1984. Less than a year later, seven Japanese firms, including Yamaha, Matsushita, and FANUC, introduced direct-drive robots. In 1986, several Japanese firms, including Yaskawa, Seiko Instruments and Electronics, and Seiko-Epson, introduced special robots for use in clean rooms.

Japanese firms were willing to invest consistently and heavily in robotics. Robotics was not the largest product line of any of the major participants, but most firms saw the industry as a major area for growth. Robotics research was funded out of overall corporate earnings. One reason for the willingness to invest heavily in robotics was because internal sales were significant for most of the leading robot producers, who sought state-of-the-art technology in their own plants. Companies released designs for external sale only after they had proven successful in their own factories. It was difficult to determine the profitability of the Japanese robotics industry, but it was generally accepted that profits on sales of robots to buyers besides sister divisions were still modest.

The concentration of Japanese robotics companies spawned active efforts at factor creation. Some 180 Japanese universities and colleges had robotics labs. The Japanese government sponsored research in the field of robotics. Starting in 1983, the Ministry of International Trade and Industry (MITI) sponsored a program to develop special-purpose robots for use in space, under water, and in nuclear power plants. MITI's contribution in the eight-year period 1983–1991 was to be 20 billion yen, or about $20 million a year. The AIST (Agency of Industrial Science and Technology, a semi-independent organization under MITI) Electrotechnical Lab began a seven-year 30 billion yen research program (about $34 million per year) to develop intelligent robots. Leading robot, computer, and machinery manufacturers joined in the program and provided half of the funding.

While government support was present, it was far below the investment made by companies themselves. The relatively small influence of government in robotics contrasted sharply with that in the related machine-tool industry, where government targeting has been quite important.

RELATIVE POSITION IN 1988

Japanese firms held by far the leading position in robotics in the 1980s. Foreign firms were successful in some segments, reflecting areas where their national circumstances were particularly favorable. There were some seventy robot producers in the United States in 1986, with the top ten producers controlling 81 percent of the market. Imports of robots and parts were approximately $160.6 million, or about 25 percent of the market. American exports totaled $33.7 million, mostly to European customers.[83] Most U.S. firms tended to specialize in producing highly sophisticated, multipurpose (and expensive) robots (in contrast, Japanese firms tended to specialize in simpler, limited-purpose machines). This reflected unique demand in aerospace and defense applications as well as strengths in software design. As of 1986, most U.S. robot manufacturers were operating at a loss. Many of the American firms that sold robots engaged in little or no domestic production, preferring to source robots from offshore manufacturers, often in Japan.

The leading Swedish producers of industrial robots were ASEA (now ABB) and ESAB (welding robots). ASEA accounted for over 70 percent of Swedish production and had production or assembly facilities in the United States, Spain, France, and Japan. It was a major force in world robotics markets and, along with Cincinnati Milacron, was one of only two foreign firms to achieve a measure of success in the Japanese market. In the mid-1980s, Swedish success reflected early home market robot penetration and the presence in Sweden of important robot-using industries. ASEA provided a broad range of robots to the automotive and auto-related industries. Volvo and Saab-Scania were two important home market customers.

The most important German producers of industrial robots were Kuka, Volkswagen, Bosch, Reis, Cloos, Duer, Mautec, and Jung Heinrich. The most important foreign vendors in Germany were ASEA (now ABB), Cincinnati Milacron, Unimation, and Trallfa (Norway). The installed base of industrial robots in Germany was 8,800 at the end of 1985, of which approximately 45 percent had been imported, with 23 percent of total imports coming from other European countries, 12 percent from the United States, and 10 percent from Japan. The automotive industry was by far the leading user of industrial robots in Germany, accounting for approximately 40 percent of robot sales in 1986.[84] The relatively weak Japanese presence in the German market was partly due to the fact that many of the Japanese firms had yet to gear up to sell there. In addition, many of the robot customers in Germany, such as Volkswagen and Bosch, preferred to produce their own robots.

There were more than 50 robot producers in Italy in the mid-1980s. In 1985, Italian robot production was 111.0 billion lire; exports accounted for 43.8 billion lire, or nearly 40 percent. Italy had two centers of robotics and factory automation technology, the Turin area and the Piacenza area. Leading Italian robot firms included Comau (with a 27.3 percent share of total 1985 Italian sales), DEA (14.2 percent), and Prima Industrie (10.0 percent).[85] Comau, the machine-tool and factory automation subsidiary of

Fiat, was formed in the late 1970s out of a number of firms that had previously been independent suppliers to Fiat. Fiat was believed to be the most automated automobile manufacturer in the world, largely due to its difficult Italian labor environment. DEA was founded in 1963 by two engineers who were former Fiat employees. DEA's first product line was a series of automatic measuring devices for use on auto assembly lines, and it later began to produce assembly robots. Prima Industrie was started in 1977 by a small group of engineers, some of whom had been employed at DEA.

By early 1987, some robot applications had saturated in the Japanese home market. One expert estimated that 80 to 90 percent of Japan's auto assembly lines had already been automated. Robot penetration in electronic assembly applications was also high, as Japanese electronics manufacturers rushed to incorporate assembly robots in order to improve productivity and to combat foreign competitors (notably from Korea and Taiwan) and a rising yen. Rapid saturation also reflected the intense rivalry in Japanese user industries. When one customer installed robots, others tended to follow closely behind. The saturation of Japanese markets caused the Japanese robot manufacturers to look overseas for additional sales, and exports were growing. However, the prevailing sentiment in the Japanese industry was that the domestic market would continue to hold the largest opportunities for growth.

Saturation at home was creating pressures to find new and more advanced robot uses, making Japanese demand even more anticipatory compared to that in other nations. Growth was forecast to come through expanding the areas of application of robots to new industries or new uses within existing industries.

Japanese firms were upgrading their skills in sophisticated software that would run not only robots but entire production facilities. Japanese firms were generally viewed as lagging behind the American and European firms in this area. Observers noted that most programming languages for writing software were English-based and therefore more difficult for non-Westerners to learn. Another major thrust in the Japanese industry was to develop robots for use in entirely new fields that were not related to factory production, including robots to perform dangerous tasks, to work undersea, and in construction. As for applications for robots, there was no end in sight.

SUMMARY

America pioneered the robotics industry and made important early inventions. Yet Japan has come to dominate this vital industry since the 1960s. Japan's ascendance illustrates vividly that invention without the presence of a favorable "diamond" will fail to translate into industrial success.

American firms were the earliest entrants. Notable among the American entrants were start-up companies, reflecting the vibrant American environment for new business formation. Yet that was where the American competitive advantage largely ended. Demand was earlier, far more sophisticated, and more globally representative in Japan. Selective factor disadvantages in buyer industries (labor shortages, wage escalation, yen appreciation) widened and upgraded Japanese home demand continuously. Japanese firms proliferated models for many applications, while American firms were drawn to complex robots for a few unusual user industries.

Japanese entrants poured into the industry from buyer industries, supplier industries, and related industries. Small start-up companies entered as well. Most entrants were also sophisticated robot users, committed to mastering this important manufacturing technology in-house.

The Japanese industry drew on world-class domestic positions in virtually every important supplier industry to robotics. No other nation could approach the cluster of such industries in Japan. Close contact between robot manufacturers, their suppliers, and their customers, often because they were one and the same, only helped accelerate innovation in the Japanese industry.

Domestic rivalry was intense and stimulated rapid product improvement, cost reduction, and product line extension into new markets. The presence of so many domestic rivals forced Japanese firms to innovate as well as to upgrade rapidly into more sophisticated robots. It also stimulated active efforts at factor creation both inside and outside the industry.

Demand conditions have been so favorable in Japan that exports have only recently become a priority. But domestic market saturation had the predictable effect of directing more attention overseas. The appreciation of the yen in recent years only led Japanese firms to redouble their efforts in manufacturing. Japanese robotics producers are also actively searching out new segments. In contrast, American manufacturers are still in the early stages of adopting advanced manufacturing techniques in the first place, hardly an environment conducive to the success of American factory equipment producers.

The Japanese government had a modest role in this important industry. This is typical of the modern Japanese success stories. In innovation-driven competitive advantage, government's proper role is indirect. In robotics, government policy concentrated on improving demand conditions and stimulating factor creation, two appropriate roles.

Today, Japanese robotics firms compete in an environment so stimulating to innovation in robotics that challenges to their leadership are nowhere in sight.

6

National Competitive Advantage in Services

The most visible form of international competition is in manufactured goods. Automobiles, VCRs, and machine tools are symbols of the new international order among nations. Trade in manufactured goods has grown much more rapidly than world GNP in the postwar period, and available data show that manufactured goods account for the great majority of overall trade. Consequently, most discussions of national competitive advantage are preoccupied with manufacturing.

Yet services have long represented a significant proportion of most national economies. Indeed, the development of services such as finance, transportation, and communications was an essential part of the Industrial Revolution. Moreover, there has always been some international competition in service industries. Companies have been competing internationally in shipping, insurance, tourism, and many other service industries since at least the turn of this century. Overall, however, service industries have been largely domestic in character and trade in services relatively small.

Attitudes about services have undergone a remarkable shift in recent years, however. The service sector has been growing markedly as a proportion of the national economies of all advanced nations. It is just beginning to reach the consciousness of governments as an important component of the economy. At the same time, international competition in services is on the rise. Large, international service organizations, such as McDonald's and Servicemaster (United States), Saatchi & Saatchi and Hawley Group (United Kingdom), Adia (Switzerland), and International Service System (Denmark), have emerged in increasing numbers. Recent estimates indicate that the official government statistics on services trade seriously understate the true extent of international competition in this broad area of the economy.[1]

Nations differ markedly in their patterns of national competitive advantage in service industries, just as they do in manufacturing. Swiss firms are strong in banking, trading, logistical services, temporary help, security services, consulting, and training. British firms hold important positions in insurance, auctioneering, money management, and various types of consulting. Swedish firms are leaders in specialized shipping and environmental engineering. Singaporean firms are strong in ship repair, airlines, port and terminal services, and printing. And American firms are leaders in hotel management, accounting, advertising, and a wide variety of other service industries. Just as interesting is that a number of important nations, among them Germany, Japan, and Italy, have few leading international positions in service industries. Each of these nations, however, has a large domestic services sector. As international competition in services grows and services become more sophisticated, national competitive advantage in services, or the lack of it, is assuming growing importance to firms and nations alike.

Little is known about international competition in services, and much less about why nations succeed internationally in particular service industries. As a result, my research placed special emphasis on identifying and studying the internationally successful service industries that were present in each of the ten nations. I will begin by describing the forces underlying services demand and the sources of competitive advantage in service firms. Both are important to understanding the nature of international competition in service industries. I will then show how the tools of the previous chapters can be used to explain why nations succeed internationally in particular service industries. Applying the determinants in the context of service industries will further develop the theory and lay important groundwork for subsequent chapters in which I describe the patterns of international success in national economies.

THE GROWING ROLE OF SERVICES IN NATIONAL ECONOMIES

In order to understand why service industries are becoming more important and more international, we must take a deeper look at services and their role in an economy. The term services encompasses a wide range of industries that perform various functions for buyers but do not involve, or only involve incidentally, the sale of a tangible product.[2] Services can be broadly divided into those provided to individuals and households and those provided to businesses and institutions. Given the enormous breadth and variety of service industries, there is no generally accepted taxonomy of services. Most treatments of the service sector are highly aggregated. As with manufactured goods, however, national competitive advantage in services can only be understood at the level of the individual service industry, because the sources of competitive advantage differ widely among them.

The definition of a service industry is sometimes imprecise,[3] and the ambiguities are becoming greater as the nature of service competition evolves. If maintenance is performed in-house by a manufacturing firm, for example, the employees involved are counted as manufacturing employees, and no service revenue is recorded in national income accounts. If the same maintenance is provided by a contract maintenance company, however, both the employees and revenues are assigned to services. Part of the growth in the service sector is the result of such anomalies in national accounting.

But there is something much more significant going on in services than quirky accounting. To understand the role of services in the economy as well as the reasons for such ambiguities, the role of services in both firms and households must be understood. The tool for doing so is the value chain. I introduced the value chain in Chapter 2 to show how firms gain competitive advantage and how they compete internationally. It is obvious that buyers who are firms or institutions (for example, hospitals and schools) have value chains, just as do the firms that sell to them. Households also have value chains, because they perform discrete activities on a more or less regular basis. In households, the names of the activities are different, but many analogies can be drawn with the value chains of firms.

Service activities permeate the value chain of every manufacturing (and service) firm. Equipment maintenance services are performed in the operations category; temporary help services are part of human resource management. These services can be performed in-house or contracted out to independent service providers. Figure 6–1 shows a taxonomy of services arrayed by their role in the buyer value chain.

Service activities also permeate the activities of a household. Typical examples are food preparation, automobile maintenance, and entertainment. Households, like firms, face the choice of performing the service functions themselves or hiring an outside party. A car owner can change his or her own oil, for example, or patronize one of the new quick lube companies. The same applies to child care, income tax preparation, hairdressing, and transportation.

Services provided to both firms and households are growing rapidly. There are three basic drivers of this growth: a growing underlying need for service functions, many of which are increasingly sophisticated; de-integration of service activities formerly performed in-house to specialized outside service vendors; and the privatization of public services, which is sometimes a result of the other two drivers.[4]

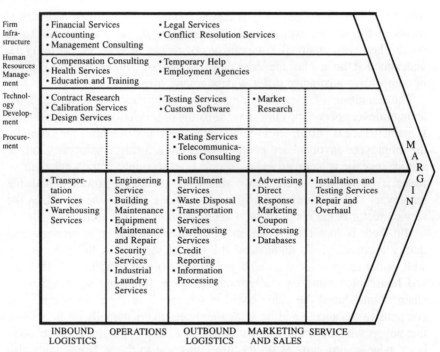

Firm Infra-structure	• Financial Services • Accounting • Management Consulting	• Legal Services • Conflict Resolution Services			
Human Resources Management	• Compensation Consulting • Health Services • Education and Training	• Temporary Help • Employment Agencies			
Technology Development	• Contract Research • Calibration Services • Design Services	• Testing Services • Custom Software	• Market Research		
Procurement		• Rating Services • Telecommunications Consulting			
	• Transportation Services • Warehousing Services	• Engineering Service • Building Maintenance • Equipment Maintenance and Repair • Security Services • Industrial Laundry Services	• Fullfillment Services • Waste Disposal • Transportation Services • Warehousing Services • Credit Reporting • Information Processing	• Advertising • Direct Response Marketing • Coupon Processing • Databases	• Installation and Testing Services • Repair and Overhaul
	INBOUND LOGISTICS	OPERATIONS	OUTBOUND LOGISTICS	MARKETING AND SALES	SERVICE

FIGURE 6–1 **Illustrative Business Services in the Value Chain**

A countervailing tendency is for what were formerly separate services to be embodied in or bundled with goods. Repairs, for example, may be performed without the need for a service call by the self-diagnostic capability of a product. Or a specialized analytical technique is programmed into packaged software that is bought instead of hiring a consultant. The embodiment of services into goods is significant in some service industries, particularly traditional household services such as laundries, beauty shops, and movie houses whose demand is actually shrinking in many nations. However, the forces causing services to grow far outweigh those leading to decline.

THE GROWING NEED FOR SERVICES

Households and firms are demanding more services as well as services of increasing quality and sophistication. Growing household service demand reflects a variety of factors. These all apply to the United States, the world's most advanced market for services, and to a lesser extent to other advanced nations:

- greater affluence
- desire for a better quality of life

- more leisure time
- urbanization, making some new services necessary (for instance, security)[5]
- demographic changes that are increasing the numbers of children and older people who consume many services
- socioeconomic changes such as dual-career families, pressures on personal time, and fewer joint family activities such as meals
- rising buyer sophistication, leading to more and broader service requirements (such as in personal financial services)
- technological changes that have upgraded service quality or made entirely new services feasible (such as in medical care, cable television, and on-line data bases for personal computers)

In firms and institutions, growth in the underlying need for services is driven by the increasing sophistication, internationalization, and complexity of management. Specialized forms of services have proliferated (for example, temporary help, coupon processing, conflict resolution) as has the complexity of needs in such established service industries as advertising, accounting, consulting, information systems, investment banking, and market research. More complex products and more sophisticated technologies throughout the value chains of firms require more design, operational, and maintenance services. The internationalization of competition is powering the growth of services needed to support trade and the management of dispersed corporate facilities (such as communications and executive recruiting). Technological and regulatory changes are opening up entirely new service fields, such as hazardous waste disposal and nondestructive testing.

DE-INTEGRATION OF SERVICE ACTIVITIES

Firms and households are increasingly hiring specialized service suppliers to perform services they used to perform themselves.[6] Once again, the United States is the leading market. Specialization and sophistication often increase as services are de-integrated, due to the greater attention and investment of specialized providers. The result is a net increase in service provision and not simply a shift in where service activity is recorded. The trend in some service industries (for instance, some legal services) is toward more integration (in-house provision), but these are in the minority.

The de-integration of service activities by firms and households is a reflection of a growing ability or necessity to de-integrate, combined with rising competitive advantages of specialized service providers compared to in-house units.

The Imperative to De-integrate. For households, growing affluence, life-style changes, and sometimes necessity are driving de-integration. Many households can afford to hire someone to perform services they once performed themselves. The need for convenience and time saving is also forcing choices to allow someone else to perform many services. For example, single parents and dual-career families buy services that they are no longer able to perform. Urbanization makes other services that were once performed at home impractical (for example, car washing).

In firms, busy managers no longer want to worry about noncritical activities, even if the services could be performed equally well in-house. Building maintenance services, order processing, payroll processing, and direct marketing are just some examples of service industries where this motivation is at work. Each involves many hard-to-recruit, hard-to-retain, hard-to-supervise employees and can consume a great deal of management time.

Advantages of Outside Service Providers. At the same time as individuals and firms are receptive to outside providers, the specialized service firm has growing advantages in many cases over in-house service provision. The reasons can perhaps best be understood by considering the value chain of a specialized service firm and how it has been changing.

In most (though not all) service industries, many of the activities performed have been labor intensive, particularly in crucial activities such as branch operations in a bank, auditing functions in an accounting firm, and cleaning activities in a building maintenance company. Today, however, the capital intensity of service firms is growing.

The most important reason for the transformation of service firm value chains is information technology. Service firms use computers or computerized techniques to perform old (and new) functions, control operations better, and make employees more productive. Garages have diagnostic computers, accounting firms use personal computers to perform audit functions, and airlines have automated much of the reservations and ticketing process. Information technology is permeating every activity in service company value chains. In temporary help firms, for example, employee testing and training are done with personal computers and videotapes.

The growing capital intensity and rising productivity of services is also due to the introduction of specialized equipment that automates service firm activities. Specialized vehicles and containers have transformed waste disposal, for example. Industrial cleaning machines have raised productivity in building maintenance services.

The introduction of new technology is both a cause and an effect of changes in industry structure and the source of competitive advantage in many service industries. Economies of scale have traditionally been modest in most services, in part because the service had to be performed at or near the buyer's location and was labor intensive. As a result, most service industries were highly fragmented, with numerous small firms providing services on a localized basis. Today, however, many service industries are rapidly consolidating. Large multi-unit service firms have emerged in fields as disparate as laundry and dry cleaning, hotels, hospital management, and mortuaries. This, in turn, has accelerated the internationalization of service competition.

The Growth of the Multi-unit Service Firm. At the root of the growth of the large, multi-unit service firm is *systematization* and in some cases *standardization* of the process of delivering services. The firm is able to replicate services consistently and efficiently at many locations because it creates standardized facilities, methodology, and procedures to guide the behavior of employees, and automates individual service delivery tasks.[7] The ability to systematize service delivery is partly a function of the tendency toward more *narrow specialization* in the services provided in an individual establishment. Instead of garages, for example, we now have quick oil change centers, muffler shops, transmission centers, and a number of other specialized car care establishments. The broad consulting firm has given way to increasingly specialized services in fields such as executive compensation, direct marketing, strategy, and assistance in the selection of investment advisors. Specialization leads to further possibilities to systematize, automate, and tailor the value chain to narrow service functions.

By proliferating standardized units at many locations, a multi-unit firm can gain substantial competitive advantages over single-unit firms, both in the service delivery process and especially in support activities (procurement, human resource management, technology development, and infrastructure). The multi-unit firm gains greater leverage through group purchasing for all its units. It reaps economies of scale in recruiting, training, and motivation (such as by creating central training schools, developing standardized training materials, and providing a career progression for employees). The multi-unit firm can spread the cost of support activities such as real estate development and accounting over its many units. It also has the scale and growth potential to tap the public capital markets. Most importantly, the multi-unit firm can afford to conduct substantial informal and formal R&D to systematize the service delivery process and to introduce more and more specialized technology. This leads to advantages in primary activities. The multi-unit service firm is the spearhead of improving technology in services; such innovation was simply beyond the capacity of individual service providers.

The multi-unit firm can also afford large-scale local and even national advertising. It gains economies of geographic scope in activities such as marketing, billing, and logistics from having several units in a particular geographic area. Wal Mart, for example, has grouped its discount stores around regional warehouses that allow a streamlined and low-cost physical distribution function compared to independent outlets. Marriott uses a common food procurement and distribution system to serve its many hotel and food service locations. Similar examples are numerous.

In some service industries, economies of scale in operating single units can be created through increasing capital intensity. Economies of scale are also being enhanced by the decoupling, to a greater or lesser extent, of the location where the service is performed and the buyer's location. The advent of more efficient logistics and telecommunications systems, combined with the introduction of information technology in the value chain and into many physical products, has meant that some service functions can be performed at a location remote from the buyer. Diagnostic programs, run over the telephone, can check and sometimes repair products. Enhanced communications make remote data processing, telemarketing, and answering services possible. Closely related is the centralization of particularly scale-sensitive activities to serve regions, nations, or even worldwide needs. Clinical laboratories perform some tests in dispersed local units but perform others involving expensive equipment or skilled personnel in regional centers, for example. All these factors have led to a growing disparity between the capabilities of in-house service departments and specialized service firms.

To these we must add two final, potent advantages of a specialized provider over an in-house unit—competition and focus. The specialized provider faces competition for the account and has incentives to raise productivity and boost quality. The captive in-house service department is a cost center. It can and should be measured against outside vendors, but replicating the pressures and incentives of competition is difficult in practice.

The specialized service firm can often hire and train people better, employ better methods, use better equipment, and perform a service cheaper or better. The specialized service firm concentrates all its management attention on a service activity that often represents a peripheral concern of the management of a company performing the service in-house as well as a low status job for employees. At the same time, an in-house service department faces some inherent constraints. There are barriers in tailoring physical facilities, policies, and procedures of in-house service units to the requirements of a particular service. In-house service units are housed at expensive locations, subject to corporate salary structures and benefit plans, constrained in some cases from using part-time workers, and live under other guidelines that are inappropriate for the nature of the service function provided. The independent service provider, conversely, tailors every aspect of its value chain to the particular service involved.

Under intense competition themselves, many firms find it harder and harder to justify inefficient or ineffective in-house service departments. Those services maintained in-house are increasingly those involving proprietary technology, services highly specialized to the particular firm, and those involving especially complex coordination with other activities. As specialized service firms have become more professional and communication has become more instantaneous, the difficulties of dealing with an outside service supplier have fallen and more firms are recognizing the benefits of greater cooperation and coordination with outside suppliers.

The increased cyclicality of many industries has also hastened de-integration. Cyclicality increases the inefficiency of maintaining permanent service capability in-house. Firms are turning to maintenance companies, specialized consultants, public relations firms, and other outside service firms whom they can call on only when they need them, converting a fixed cost into a variable one.

PRIVATIZATION OF PUBLIC SERVICES

A final reason for service sector growth, though less pervasive than the other two, is the trend in some nations for public services to be privatized. Services thus shift from a cost within government organizations to revenue in the private service sector. Privatization of public services is probably best viewed as a form of de-integration. In this light, many of the same forces described earlier can be seen to be at work. The inefficiencies of public institutions are widely recognized. In many service industries, there has been a movement to let private companies become involved in order to enjoy their growing efficiencies and the benefits of competition. Conservative doctrine, on the rise in many nations during the past decade, has been an important trigger. Some of the service industries where privatization is most widespread are waste disposal, telecommunications, health care, education, and even the management of prisons and correctional facilities. Privatization not only can improve service, cost, and quality but also promotes internationalization. With rare exceptions, government-owned service organizations do not compete globally.[8]

INTERNATIONAL COMPETITION IN SERVICES

The net result of all these developments is a large and rapidly growing services sector in most nations, a proliferation of new types of services, and the emergence of a new breed of larger, more sophisticated service companies. Modern technology and modern management techniques are now penetrating services, at an arguably faster rate than they penetrated manufacturing some time ago. Not only has the service landscape changed markedly within national economies, but the foundations have been laid for a new era of international service competition.

International competition in services takes a variety of forms. To understand these forms, we must draw on the ideas of Chapter 2 about the nature of international competitive strategy. A service firm, like a manufacturing firm, competes internationally through the manner in which it spreads activities on a regional or worldwide basis and coordinates activities dispersed in different nations. Due to the nature of most services, many of the activities in a service firm's value chain must be performed where the buyer is. As a result, the firm often establishes offices or units in each nation that actually deliver the service. The "Big Eight" accounting firms, for example, have headquarters in the United States but their offices are spread all over the world. More discretion is possible about the location of support activities, such as technology development, training, and procurement. Many are typically performed in the home nation.

TYPES OF INTERNATIONAL SERVICE COMPETITION

International competition in service industries takes one of three pure forms. It is common to see hybrids of two or sometimes all three forms in a particular service industry.[9]

1. *Mobile buyers travel to a nation to have services performed.* One solution to the need to perform a service where the buyer is located is for the buyer to come to the service provider. This is the predominant pattern of international competition in many traditional services as well as some newer services, among them tourism, most education, most health care, ship repair, warehousing or distribution for a group of countries, airport services for connecting passengers and freight, regional headquarters for companies,[10] and headquarters for international organizations. A variation of this form of international service competition is the choice by multinational firms to have services that benefit the entire enterprise performed in one of the nations in which they have operations. The mobile buyer will travel to a particular country to consume a service because it is differentiated or costs less than the service available at home or elsewhere, even when the cost of traveling to the service-providing nation is taken into account.

2. *Firms from one nation provide services in other nations using domestically based personnel and facilities.* Some services can be performed for foreign buyers using domestic personnel and facilities; for example, in management consulting and architecture, where professionals travel to the client's location to gather data or present results. Another example is in engineering, where the primary staff is located at home and a team is dispatched temporarily

abroad to gather data, work with the client, or supervise construction of facilities.

This form of international service competition is prevalent where frequent customer contact is not required, services are provided for a fixed time period, or where the buyer can readily interact with the service firm from a distance. Reinsurance is an example of a service where contracts are agreed to over the telephone or through brokers located in foreign countries. Lloyd's of London does the majority of its business overseas, for example, though nearly all of its staff and facilities are located in or near London. Other examples of this type of service are specialized testing services, computer processing, leasing, and money management.

3. *A nation's firms provide services in other countries via foreign service locations, staffed with either expatriates or local nationals.* Perhaps the most common pattern of international service competition is that in which service firms from one nation provide services in other nations through a network of foreign offices or facilities. Typically, some, if not many, of the support activities are performed at the home base, but the actual delivery of the service is in the buyer's country, reflecting the need for ongoing, close contact with the buyer in providing the service as well as savings in time and cost of travel. Personnel from the home country are sent abroad to start up foreign locations, but local nationals are hired and trained to take a broader and broader role over time. This form of international competition is predominant in accounting, advertising, hotels, fast food, car rental, temporary help, and industrial laundry services, as well as such traditional services as shipping and banking.

The first two types of international service competition are typically classified as international trade. The third shows up as foreign investment. The distinction between the forms is often a matter of degree—testing services can be viewed either as the buyer coming to the service firm with a sample to be tested, or a service which is provided for an overseas buyer using domestic personnel and facilities.

More important than fuzzy boundaries, however, are hybrids which combine forms, either in the entire service industry or for particular companies. In accounting, for example, the bulk of the foreign work is performed by locally based personnel, but specialists are dispatched from the home office to deal with some specialized problems or to supervise especially complex projects. In the same industry, competitors may employ different hybrids. In consulting, for example, large firms often have foreign offices, while smaller, more specialized firms dispatch personnel abroad to meet with clients. International trade and foreign investment are closely intertwined in many service industries, just as they often are in manufacturing industries.

In competing internationally, service firms sometimes also form alliances with firms from other countries. Almost always, these alliances bring an international service firm into partnership with local firms where the service is provided. In construction, for example, American firms such as Bechtel and Fluor might act as project manager, employ Italian and German firms as partners responsible for particular specialty areas, and use a Korean or Philippine firm to supply the bulk of the labor and first-level supervision. In effect, different activities in the construction value chain are often divided among firms from different nations according to their competitive advantages.

International competitors coexist with local competitors in most service industries, with local firms often accounting for the bulk of industry sales. Because of this, various forms of protectionism are common in service industries. These impediments to imports range from differences in treatment (such as differing regulations like reserve requirements for banks) that give domestic firms advantage over foreign ones, to outright prohibition of foreign firms in some industries (for example, foreign firms are unable to participate in some Japanese and U.S. government construction projects). Trade barriers have been one of the reasons for the prevalence of Type 3 international service competition.

The international competition in service industries is often concentrated in certain industry segments, frequently those serving affluent or sophisticated buyers, involving particularly complex service requirements, or where needs are especially internationalized. In hotels, for example, international competition is primarily in the luxury and business travel segments. In insurance, international competition is predominantly in specialized property and casualty insurance and reinsurance. International competition is most prevalent, naturally enough, in those services (and those segments) where the global firm gains the greatest advantages or faces the least resistance from local firms.

The Internationalization of Competition in Service

The extent and significance of international competition in services continues to grow. Professionally managed, multi-unit service firms increasingly have gained the capacity and vision to seek international business. Armed with a perspective on the changes under way in service industries and the types of international service competition, we are in a position to understand why.

In recent decades, growing international competition in services has been driven by a number of forces:

· *Similarity of service needs.* Many service needs are similar in most of the world, if not overall in particular segments. A client in any nation wants similar service from a temporary help agency, for example, though some local conditions or regulations will vary. As competition globalizes, firms from many nations also demand sophisticated business services. The character of many services also allows them to be tailored to local circumstances at relatively low cost. Thus, the global service firm gives up little to the domestic competitor.

· *More mobile and more informed buyers of services.* More fluid movement of information around the world, fast transportation, and increasing ease and familiarity with international travel are making buyers more likely to seek out the world's best service firms. Buyers with a more international outlook are increasingly willing to hire leading foreign firms operating in their nation instead of relying only on domestic firms. Buyers are also in a better position to know where the best services are available. Easing foreign exchange restrictions makes paying for services in another country easier as well.

· *Rising economies of scale and geographic scope.* The same advantages that have brought about the emergence of multi-unit domestic service firms have encouraged the establishment of international offices. Economies of scale allow the global service firm to spread the cost of technology development, training infrastructure, and other activities over worldwide sales revenue, as well as to enjoy even greater clout in purchasing. The global firm gains other advantages as well. It can service multinational clients anywhere, differentiating itself from the local competition. Worldwide brand reputations can be built that overshadow those of local firms. Specialized personnel and facilities can be better utilized, by employing them in whatever nation in which they are needed, often to supplement local operations.

· *Greater mobility of service personnel.* The ability to reap economies of scale has increased because service firm employees are now able to travel to foreign nations to deliver services, provided the necessary period of customer contact is relatively short. Jet aircraft and norms of heavy travel are two of the reasons.

· *Greater ability to interact with remote buyers.* Through telephone, on-line data communications, rapid parcel delivery, and a variety of other means, it is increasingly possible to communicate and engage in needed interchange with buyers of services even though they are located in foreign countries. This is true, for example, in computer processing and testing services. Automation of service functions reduces the personnel content per unit of service, thereby lowering the need to travel, and also makes interaction with remote buyers more feasible.

· *Continued wide disparities among nations in the cost, quality, and range of services available from local firms.* Wide differences remain in the quality and cost of services available in different nations. Even more importantly, the state of development of the service sector is very different in different countries, much more so in many respects than the state of development in manufacturing. The development of large, multiunit service firms is much further advanced in nations such as the United States and Britain than in most others. These differences create incentives for buyers to travel to obtain services in the best location, and for advanced service firms to attempt to serve foreign customers. For example, large temporary help firms initially developed in the United States, giving American firms such as Kelly Services and Manpower a head start in establishing overseas operations.

These forces have brought about growing internationalization of services despite the relatively high trade barriers present in many service industries. There is some movement toward international agreements to reduce service trade barriers, and this area is high on the agenda in the Uruguay Round of GATT. Though the rate of progress is slow, it is quite likely that the forces internationalizing service competition will continue.

THE RELATIONSHIP BETWEEN SERVICES AND MANUFACTURING

As the previous discussion amply illustrates, there is a close connection between service and manufacturing industries. This link has received greater attention in recent years, as some nations face competitive challenges in manufacturing industries and services grow to represent a large part of national economies. The manufacturing-services link is becoming an important part of the argument that a nation cannot afford to ignore its international competitive position in manufacturing. If services and manufacturing are linked, a nation cannot expect its service sector to replace lost manufacturing exports. What is less clear in the debate is the nature of the manufacturing-service link.

The link between manufacturing and services is important to national competitive advantage in service (and manufacturing) industries. There is not one type of link, but three distinctly different ones that affect different service industries.

Buyer/supplier relationship. The first type of link has already been extensively discussed, the connection between a service and the buyer's value chain. As we have seen, many service industries have been created through the de-integration of service activities by manufacturing (and service) firms. This has two implications. One is that without local manufacturing firms, the demand for services is limited. Though service firms also buy services, many service industries depend on manufacturing firms for a significant share of their sales.

The second implication is that the structure of the manufacturing sector in a nation can strongly influence the types and amounts of services demanded as well as the sophistication of these services. Without advanced and progressive-thinking manufacturing firms, for example, it is difficult for sophisticated custom software companies or specialized consulting firms to become established.

Services tied to the sale of manufactured goods. The second type of link between manufacturing and services occurs when the sale of a manufactured good creates demand for associated services. The sale of computers, for example, can lead to demand for custom programming services, data communication services, and training services. The sale of some equipment (for example, elevators) leads to ongoing needs for servicing. Another even more straightforward example is the link between export of nearly any manufactured good from a nation and the sales of insurance, trade financing services, and transportation services.

The international success of a nation's firms in manufactured goods can help that nation's service firms sell abroad, as I discussed in Chapter 3. Services provided by firms of the same nation may be, or may be perceived to be, more cost effective because the service firm is familiar with or has experience with the particular variety of manufactured goods. Manufacturing firms may contribute to this perception, by actively recommending service providers from their home nation.

Manufactured goods tied to the sale of services. The third type of link between manufacturing and services is the reverse of the previous one. The sale of some services, such as engineering or management consulting, can lead to demand for equipment and other associated manufactured goods. Successful international service providers from a nation may thus pull through sales of manufactured goods from that nation. This has long been the case in engineering and heavy construction, where the overseas success of leading U.S. engineering and construction companies has been important to overseas sales of such disparate products as Caterpillar tractors, Carrier, York, and Trane heating, ventilating, and air-conditioning equipment, and GE and Westinghouse electrical equipment. Swedish engineering consultants have also helped pull through Swedish products in the construction of such projects as harbors, water towers, and underground oil storage facilities, all areas of Swedish technical strength.[11]

The manufacturing-service links differ in strength and permanence. The buyer/seller relationship is a necessary one, while the other two links vary in signficance by service industry as well as in their durability over time. The link is strongest when there is a technical connection between a manufactured good and the associated services, or convenience in purchasing both together.

The tie between manufactured goods and services tends to be strongest early in the evolution of the manufacturing and service industries involved. Early U.S. exports of computers, for example, had a stronger pull-through effect on associated services than later exports. Early on, American service firms had an edge in experience working with American equipment compared to foreign vendors, due to the installed base of machines in the United States. This edge declined over time, however, as compatibility with IBM and DEC hardware became more achievable by foreign vendors.

As buyers become more knowledgeable and sophisticated, they tend to recognize that service providers from a nation may have few advantages in servicing that nation's goods unless the product involved is complex and the technical connection between the goods and services is strong. However, early mover advantages are often created by the link between manufacturing and services, which persist for some services after the link fades. Britain, for example, gained a strong international position in many services connected with trading because of its early prominence as a trading nation. The foreign infrastructure and brand franchises developed through this process have proven quite a durable competitive advantage for some British service providers.

NATIONAL COMPETITIVE ADVANTAGE IN SERVICES

Nations exhibit strikingly different patterns of national competitive advantages in services, as they do in manufactured goods. Figure 6–2 employs the best available information to show patterns of international leadership among the nations we studied in those service industries exhibiting significant international competition. Data on international competition in services are highly imperfect.[12] Figure 6–2 is a composite of many sources, including available government statistics, directories of companies, published articles, extensive field interviews, and the judgments of local research teams. It should be interpreted as a series of well-informed estimates. Some errors and, more likely, omissions remain.

The United States, United Kingdom, and Switzerland are the nations with the greatest number of *international* positions in service industries; this position remains the same if all nations are included, not only those treated here. Important nations such as Germany, Japan, and Italy, in contrast, have international positions in few service industries though their domestic services sectors are large and growing.

The same determinants of national competitive advantage in manufacturing

INDUSTRY	Denmark	Germany	Italy	Japan	Korea	Singapore	Sweden	Switzerland	U.K.	U.S.
FOOD										
Fast food										XX
Food service/vending										X
RETAILING										
Convenience stores										X
Specialty stores			X						XX	
EDUCATION AND TRAINING										
Secondary and university education		X						X	X	XX
Graduate education										XX
Corporate training										XX
LEISURE										
Entertainment								X		XX
Auctioneering									XX	
MEDICAL										
Health care services								X	X	XX
Hospital management										XX
TRAVEL RELATED[1]										
Hotels			X					X		XX
Car rentals										XX
Airlines		X				X		X	X	X
GENERAL BUSINESS										
Accounting									X	XX
Legal services									X	XX
Advertising									XX	XX
Public relations									X	X
Mgt. consulting		X						X	X	XX
Engineering/architectural[2]	X	X	X	X	X		X		X	XX
Construction				X		X		X	X	XX
Contract research									X	X
Design services			XX							
Temporary help								X		XX
Industrial laundry/apparel supply	X								X	XX
Industrial cleaning (facilities, tools, equipment)						X				X
Security services						X	X	X		X
Building maintenance services	X					X		X		X
Equipment maintenance and repair						X				
Waste disposal & management										XX
TRADING				X				XX	XX	XX
FINANCIAL										
Credit card										XX
Consumer finance										XX
Credit reporting										XX
Merchant/investment banking									X	XX
Commercial banking				X				XX	X	XX
Leasing									X	XX
Money management		XX						XX	XX	XX
Reinsurance			X					X	XX	
INFORMATION										
Information processing										XX
Custom software[3]									X	XX
Information/data									X	XX
TRANSPORT										
Air cargo		X								X
Airport terminal		X				X	X	X		
Shipping	X			X			X			
Port services		X				X				
Ship repair						X				
Logistics management								X		
Service stations									X	X

XX = leading position

X = position

[1]Excludes tourism attracted to a nation

[2]National positions in engineering tend to be in different types of projects.

[3]France also had a significant position in custom software.

Source: Author's estimates based on field interviews, case studies, and a composite of published sources.

FIGURE 6–2 Estimated Patterns of National Competitive Advantage in International Service Industries

apply to service industries.[13] My purpose here is not to repeat the discussion of earlier chapters, but to highlight those national characteristics that have particular salience for services. More importantly, I will use the theory to analyze two particular service industries.

FACTOR CONDITIONS

The role of factor conditions in service competition depends on the form of international competition in the particular service industry. In services where the buyer is attracted to a nation (Type 1), factor conditions are usually important to success. For example, tourism depends heavily on climate and geography, and education and health services depend on the training and skill of local personnel. Services that are delivered primarily by domestic facilities and personnel (Type 2) are obviously also sensitive to domestic factor conditions.

In services delivered through a network of foreign offices (Type 3), however, other determinants of national competitive advantage besides factor conditions are often decisive. In this type of service competition, most of the personnel employed are located in the nations where the service is delivered. Success here depends more on the techniques, technology, and service features that have been developed at home. Demand conditions and related and supporting industries prove in many such service industries to have been the decisive determinants.

Geographic location plays a significant role in some service industries. Singapore's strength in ship repair benefits from its location on important shipping lanes between the Middle East and Japan. Switzerland's position astride European trade routes is part of its success in a number of trade-related services. Akin to a nation's location is its time zone. London's status as a financial and trading center is aided by its location between America and Asia, which means that personnel based in London can communicate with both regions during the normal workday.

By and large, unskilled and semiskilled labor cost at home is *not* a significant source of competitive advantage in most service industries. Labor-intensive services are usually performed through local offices in other nations. However, in a few industries, notably construction services, there are large-scale exports of workers from low-wage countries. This is one of the reasons why Korean construction firms became internationally successful in some market segments.

While less-skilled labor is usually unimportant, a nation's stock of specialized, skilled professional and technical personnel is frequently vital in international service competition. Business services, in particular, demand highly trained personnel in management disciplines, engineering, or scientific fields.

The growing complexity and specialization of many service industries mean that advanced factor creation mechanisms are becoming vital to service competition. In the United States, for example, the strong international accounting, management consulting, and advertising industries draw on a large pool of graduating MBAs. Few other countries have extensive graduate business training. The United States also has specialized hotel schools and trains large numbers of computer programmers. Extensive research in health-related fields benefits the medical services industries. In the United Kingdom, there is a well-educated but relatively low-cost pool of engineers and other skilled personnel, an important reason why Britain is strong in engineering, consultancy, and contract research services for foreign clients.

A nation's language and the language skills of its citizens can play an important role in many service industries. Many services demand extensive communication with buyers, not to mention the need for communication between different offices of the firm. English as a native language is a significant benefit to service firms, because English is spoken in many parts of the world and is a second language in most others. Swiss fluency in languages, which I spoke of earlier, is one of the important reasons why Switzerland ranks with the United States and Britain as an important international service competitor. Singapore's emergence as a growing center for services also reflects in part its English-speaking population.

Also significant in many services is the ability to interact easily with many different cultures. This is another Swiss advantage. Not only do Swiss often have language skills, but their familiarity with multiple cultures yields advantages in client relations, as does Swiss neutrality. Sweden, which shares some of the same advantages as Switzerland, has not been nearly as successful in services because of a narrower base of industry, a stifling government involvement in providing services (demand conditions), and a poor climate for start-ups (firm strategy, structure, and rivalry), among other reasons.

Labor shortages or expensive labor is a spur to automation and upgrading of service industries, just as it is in manufacturing. Many service industries are being revolutionized by new technology, much of it related to information systems. This technology reduces the labor content of services and makes service delivery personnel more productive. High wages in a nation prompt service firms to employ such modern methods. This was an early advantage for the United States and is still true in many American service industries, where firms have introduced new technology to cope with the high costs of making service calls and of keeping personnel in the field.

However, a bulge of new people entering the workforce in the last decade seems to have been one of the important reasons why U.S. firms have lost dynamism relative to foreign firms in some service industries. In Sweden, for example, service workers are paid about the same as manufacturing workers, and average wages are high. In some industries, firms are far ahead of the United States or United Kingdom in automating services. Totally automated gas stations, involving no personnel, are common in Sweden. A heavy government role in services in nations such as Sweden and Germany (see below) has so far blunted the drive to translate these advantages into international positions.

DEMAND CONDITIONS

Demand conditions are perhaps the single most powerful determinant of national competitive advantage in services today, akin in many ways to their role in manufactured consumer goods in the 1950s and early 1960s. The services sector is in a period of rapid growth and advancement. Many new service industries are being created, and established service industries are being restructured and revolutionized. Demand conditions are driving this process to a considerable degree. Early mover advantages were essential to national advantage in many traditional service industries. The recent period of change and restructuring in services has elevated their importance again.

Demand Composition. Some nations are more fertile incubators of internationally transferable services than others because of the composition of home demand. The segment structure of service demand is a prominent influence. A nation benefits if its home demand is for service varieties or approaches that are demanded in other countries. A large number of business travelers within the spread-out borders of the United States, for example, helped American hotel chains learn to serve this global market segment. The American chains then became leaders worldwide.

This case also illustrates a more general point. Most service industries require firms to locate offices or branches near buyers. Providing coverage of a nation thus requires multiple locations. Where a nation has dispersed population centers, service firms gain experience managing dispersed multi-unit networks within their own country. It is a relatively simple step to add foreign locations, compared to firms with only a few viable locations in their home country.

In such service industries as hotels, car rental, industrial laundry, and others, for example, American firms developed far-flung networks within the nation consisting of dozens, if not hundreds, of offices or locations. Once they gained the experience of running a network of U.S. locations, the next step for many was to establish foreign networks. For the United Kingdom, the former colonies played a similar role.

If a large segment of the home market for a particular service is a small segment elsewhere, a nation's firms will often be internationally successful because of greater attention to the segment and faster innovation. A good example is that of Italian construction firms. Italy's hilly terrain creates the need for extensive tunnelling and bridging in road construction. Italian contractors have well-developed skills in this field and are quite successful in overseas projects of this character. In Finland and Sweden, the forest products sector is among the most significant in the economy. Consulting services related to forestry management and the operation of pulp and paper plants are areas of international strength.

The segment structure of home demand has another less straightforward influence on international service success. A paradox provides a good way to introduce the reasoning. Many international travelers would agree that the level of personal service in the United States and the United Kingdom is among the lowest in the advanced nations, certainly much lower than in Germany, Switzerland, and Japan. Why, then, are U.S. and British firms so strong internationally in many services, though somewhat different ones?

An important reason for this discrepancy lies in the conception of services in different nations.[14] In the United States, self-service, fast turnaround, relatively low levels of personal attention, and frequent turnover of service delivery personnel fit well with the American lifestyle and informal social structure. These demand characteristics, though, make services more amenable to systematization, standardization, and branding than is the case where services are seen as requiring high levels of personal attention, unhurried service delivery, and continuity of personnel who are in contact with the customer. This applies to both personal and business services.[15] A high incidence of travel and moving within the United States also supports standardization and branding, by making the assurance of a consistent service everywhere more valuable.

As I discussed earlier, systematization and standardization are the keys that unlock economies of scale and other advantages of the large, multi-unit service firm. They also make it possible to duplicate a service in another nation. McDonald's can replicate its concept with minor modifications abroad and train local personnel to conduct the well-defined steps involved. In contrast, a Japanese department store would find it difficult to replicate in other nations the high level of personal attention expected and provided at home. The German or French entrepreneur, similarly, would find it difficult to ''reduce'' the level of service characteristic of the home nation in order to allow replication of the concept in many other nations. Club Med, one of the few prominent French international service firms, competes in an industry segment where high levels of personal service are provided.

The success of U.S. and U.K. service firms abroad suggests that a segment of foreign markets is satisfied with systematized service delivery. This segment is typically a small, though growing, one in foreign markets, while the largest segment in the United States or United Kingdom. The Swiss success in services, in contrast to that of the United States and Britain, is often in business services where a high level of personal attentiveness and customer contact is necessary. Swiss home demand conditions support this sort of behavior.

The sophistication of a nation's home buyers confers an advantage on that nation's firms in service industries not amenable to the sort of standardization described earlier, provided home buyers have needs that mirror or anticipate those in other nations. The sophisticated home buyer provides the training ground for improving a service and a spur to introduce new services that will ultimately be demanded abroad. Denmark has a leading international cleaning services company, International Service System (ISS), for example, in part because demand for industrial cleaning in Denmark has moved from just cleaning to total environmental management. This demand reflects a deep concern in Denmark with all aspects of the environment, manifested in regular and intense press coverage. Another good example is in financial services related to mergers, buyouts, and restructurings, where American investment banking companies are competing globally and often accelerating the adoption of such practices by foreign companies.

Where a nation has internationally competitive manufacturing and service industries, it frequently enjoys the most sophisticated demand for associated business services. Italy is world leader in design services, reflecting a strong position in fashion, furnishings, and other design-intensive products. The presence of the world's leading advertising agencies in the United States, along with the most advanced advertising media, has helped make the United States the leading nation in the world in many marketing-related services such as coupon processing and market research. Another example is in accounting, where American clients are sophisticated and demanding buyers because of the complexity of U.S. accounting standards, the far-flung locations of many companies, and the greater importance attached to financial reports in American capital markets than elsewhere. This is one of several reasons why U.S. accounting firms are world leaders. The first international accounting firms were British, reflecting Britain's early industrial dominance, and followed British multinationals abroad. Coopers & Lybrand, Price Waterhouse, and Deloitte Haskins and Sells of the former "Big Eight" have a strong British heritage.

Buyers for many business services come not from one or two industries but from many industries. In accounting and advertising, for example, clients are drawn from virtually every industry in a nation's economy. A broad base of competitive industries in a nation, as the United States has enjoyed, is of particular benefit in stimulating internationally competitive business services firms.

The Size and Timing of Service Demand. Nations vary a great deal in the intensity of demand for particular services. Earlier in this chapter, I described some of the most significant reasons for growth in service demand. Nations differ considerably in attributes such as household income, the extent of female participation in the workforce, the desire for convenience, and the propensity of firms to de-integrate service activities, that affect the timing of service demand. Affluent nations have high demand for services such as lawn care and fast food. Nations where a high proportion of women work have high demand for child care and many other personal services related to convenience.

Social and historical factors also play a role in the intensity of service demand. At a given income level, for example, Germans seem to consume fewer personal services than Americans. Greater frugality may play a role, growing out of a more recent history of deprivation than exists in America. Swiss citizens tend to be relatively risk averse, and the Swiss purchase more insurance per citizen than any other nation. In America, buying on credit is much more common than in all other advanced nations. Not surprisingly, American credit card companies such as American Express, Master-Card, VISA, and Diners Club are the dominant international competitors. American firms are also leaders in credit reporting and collection.

Differences in the local mix of industries and company strategies lead to substantial variations among nations in business service demand. For example, part-time workers are more typical in the United States than in many other nations. Demand for temporary help services is correspondingly large in the United States relative to its size. America also has unusually high demand as a percentage of GDP for services such as advertising and public relations, a function of American strength in consumer industries and local practices. Another important determinant of services demand is the willingness of firms to turn to outside service providers. Companies are more reluctant in some nations than others to de-integrate services to outside vendors. German companies, for example, are less likely to use outside service vendors in consulting, maintenance, and other fields than are companies in Britain and the United States, perhaps because of a greater tradition of central control.

Timing plays an important role in which nation's service firms become international. The United States has been the early market for many new services such as fast food, temporary help, hospital management, specialized health care services, management consulting, and financial services, all areas where the United States now has leading positions. Sweden, with an unusually high level of plant automation, developed an early need for sophisticated security services for unmanned facilities. Swedish firms are strong in providing consulting services in this area in other nations.

Service firms, like manufacturing firms, often turn to international markets when their home markets have been saturated. In hotels and fast food, for example, American firms moved overseas as they neared full coverage of the U.S. market. The presence of several large, multi-unit service firms in a nation in a particular field accelerates the saturation process.

The pattern of government involvement also shapes service demand. Nations differ in the range of services provided by governments as opposed to private firms. In the United States, for example, the health care system is largely private. This private system has allowed a myriad of new health care-related service industries to grow up in areas such as hospital management, home care, retirement living centers, ambulatory surgical clinics, and fitness testing clinics in advance of other nations. Some of these services are beginning to be delivered internationally by U.S. firms. In Sweden, Italy, and Germany, in contrast, government-owned entities are particularly prominent in service delivery and international activity is minimal.

Government regulation also directly influences the demand for some services, making national differences in regulation important. Pollution standards, for example, determine the need for hazardous waste disposal, cleanup services, and environmental testing services. The prevalence of leasing grows partly out of a nation's tax laws. Government policy may determine not only the amount but the timing and sophistication of demand for new services.

Internationalization of Domestic Service Demand. The internationalization of domestic demand is particularly important in many services for a number of reasons. Mobile home consumers, that travel frequently in significant numbers to other nations, provide a formidable advantage to the nation's service firms. Opportunities to establish overseas locations are quickly apparent and firms also enjoy a base of loyal buyers abroad. This effect is quite apparent in travel-related industries, where U.S. hotel, rent-a-car, and credit card firms have been the beneficiaries. It is also important in fast food and financial services (American Express, for example). As Japanese began traveling in larger and larger numbers, the first signs of significant foreign development by Japanese restaurants and hotels have become evident.

A similar set of arguments applies when a nation is home base for many multinationals. Particularly in the early years of operating abroad, multinationals often prefer to deal with service firms from their home country. There are benefits in terms of communication, mutual understanding, and reducing risk, giving homegrown service firms a base of foreign demand and, more importantly, an early stimulus to move abroad. This had an influence on American accounting firms, advertising agencies, public relations firms, and consulting firms, and, to a lesser extent, Swiss banks. Britain gained important and continuing benefits from the British Empire and the continued strong ties between Britain and such nations as Australia, Canada, Hong Kong, and South Africa. The pull-through effect of a large number of increasingly multinational Japanese firms is now benefiting Japanese banks and construction firms.

Mobile or multinational buyers take on particular significance in service industries because of widespread protectionism. Local service firms tend to be numerous and wield political power. If a nation's service firms have a base of loyal home customers in foreign countries, the odds of developing a viable competitive position abroad are greatly enhanced.

International sales by a nation's service firms are also facilitated if the nation can export its culture, practices, and regulations abroad. A good example is in the area of legal services. American law firms are the clear leaders in terms of international offices. Baker & McKenzie (United States) is the largest international law firm, with twenty-six foreign offices as of 1985. Five of the largest eight law firms are American, while two are British. Eleven of the top twenty are American and five are British. Part of the international success of U.S. and U.K. firms comes from following clients abroad.[16] However, a considerable part of their advantage lies in the fact that many international business and financial transactions are written under New York or English law.

RELATED AND SUPPORTING INDUSTRIES

The presence of national competitive advantage in related and supporting industries spawns other service industries, just as it does in manufacturing industries. A particularly important group of supporting industries to many services is that involving information technology. The United States, with world-class computer companies as well as a plethora of custom and packaged software vendors, is in an advantaged position because U.S. service firms have access to a wide variety of specialized tools to automate their operations.

National advantage in complementary manufactured goods or other services pulls through demand in some service industries. The presence of internationally competitive industries in a nation has a triple-barreled benefit for national advantage in related service industries: it provides sophisticated buyers at home, creates a base of demand abroad, and pulls through linked services.

Recently, related diversification by service firms has begun. The presence of large, internationally competitive service firms in nations such as the United States and the United Kingdom is beginning to spawn advantage in related fields. Established service firms enter new industries, bringing to them advantages in terms of systematization. The process of domestic industry consolidation speeds up. The next step is to expand abroad.

Marriott, for example, a leading international competitor in hotels, is also gaining a leading international position in airline catering and other food- and hospitality-related businesses. ISS (Denmark), with revenues over

$500 million, is moving from hospital cleaning services to an international position in such areas as industrial laundry. At this stage in the development of the services sector, the existence of already established large service firms in a nation is a strength.

FIRM STRATEGY, STRUCTURE, AND RIVALRY

Service firms in different nations enjoy some characteristic differences in organizational practices. Swiss firms do well where trust, discretion, and personalized attention are important, or complex negotiations among parties are essential (for example, trading). American firms do well in fields where systematic analytical techniques can be built (such as consulting) or rapid problem solving is necessary (for example, advertising).

The prestige of various service occupations varies markedly among nations. In some nations, heavy industry and technical occupations attract the best people, while services fall far down in the pecking order. In America, conversely, joining a consulting firm or working on Wall Street carries considerable prestige. Many of the brightest people are attracted into services. In the United Kingdom, services such as consultancy, auctioneering, and, recently, financial services are also socially acceptable, while taking a job in industry is still "not done" by many upwardly mobile or upper-class graduates.

Unimpeded, vigorous domestic rivalry creates a fertile environment in which to grow world-class service firms. The rivalry among the "Big Eight" American accounting firms, the numerous Swiss banks, and the many British insurance companies (Lloyd's of London itself consists of a large number of loosely affiliated but competing companies) provide good examples. Competition in most service industries involves attention to detail, constant introduction of new service variations, and the need for high levels of responsiveness to buyers. A group of domestic rivals provides an essential ingredient to success in this sort of industry environment.

Lack of effective domestic rivalry, conversely, means that a nation's service industry will rarely succeed abroad. In securities, for example, Japan's Big Four competitors (Nomura, Daiwa, Nikko, Yamaichi) enjoy sheltered positions in the home market because of regulations that limit entry and fix brokerage commissions. They earn extraordinary profits in the absence of the fierce domestic rivalry so typical in many Japanese industries. This, coupled with still relatively unsophisticated individual and corporate home buyers of financial services, has meant that these firms have still to make much headway in international competition despite favored access to Japanese companies' foreign business, low-cost capital, and the willingness to absorb large losses.

Service industries tend to grow out of small, entrepreneurial start-ups rather than large-scale entries. Nations gain a particular advantage in services when starting a new firm is easy and accepted. Also relevant is the availability of second-stage financing to transform the start-up into a multi-unit enterprise (initial capital requirements in many services are modest). The service sector is one of the areas that benefits most from active markets for venture capital and equity financing. The United States and the United Kingdom both enjoy this advantage.

The service sector, with its preponderance of smaller companies and fragmented industry structures, is particularly prone to government intrusion. Regulations that protect small businesses or otherwise influence small business activity are common. If these regulations retard the introduction of technology, delay or block the creation of new services, retard the consolidation of localized service industries into national ones, inhibit foreign competition, or mute domestic rivalry, they will all but eliminate the possibility that the nation will achieve international competitive advantage in the service industries affected.

Italy suffers from this problem in many service fields, despite a vibrant climate for new business formation. The numerous restrictions on opening new locations, hours of operation, and the like have severely retarded development of the Italian services sector. Also, Italian currency laws have restricted foreign direct investment that is essential in many services. German and Japanese firms face some similar, though less daunting, difficulties.

Conversely, a nation that provides its service industries with flexibility will benefit. One of the major reasons Britain is a world leader in certain forms of insurance is that Lloyd's of London is perhaps the least regulated insurance entity in the world when it comes to products. Its freedom to set rates and write new kinds of insurance, while foreign firms were tied up in meeting local standards and gaining regulatory approvals, has made Lloyd's the innovative force in the industry for decades.[17] Similar flexibility has been a benefit to Swiss traders. International success in services requires a local environment that exposes firms to international competition and facilitates rather than inhibits international activity.

A heavy direct government role in a service industry is usually a reliable indication that a nation will have a modest international presence. Those nations with the greatest government involvement in providing services, such as Italy, Germany, and Sweden, are among the weakest nations in terms of international service positions.

CLUSTERING AND SERVICE INDUSTRIES

Service industries are an integral part of clusters. Competitive service industries help spawn or upgrade supplier and buyer industries. Competitive manufacturing industries also stimulate international success in linked services.

Italy's design services firms, which design cars, footwear, apparel, and many other products for foreign clients, grew out of Italy's strong manufacturing industries in these fields.

A good example illustrating a service industry embedded in a national cluster is the specialty shipping industry. Swedish firms are among the leaders in the world in car carriers, or specialized ships that transport cars between Europe, North America, and Asia. Sweden's success in this industry has its roots in, and has been reinforced by, its presence in a number of other international Swedish industries. Swedish shipyards possess sophisticated technology and have increasingly focused on specialized vessels as a way of coping with Asian competition. Sweden has a long tradition in merchant shipping, and shipping firms have had to move into more specialized fields because of high Swedish labor costs. The final part of the equation is the presence in Sweden of two internationally successful car and truck manufacturers, Volvo and Saab-Scania, who were early exporters to many other nations. Swedish car carrier firms were early and aggressive investors in new, specialized vessels, and became industry leaders. The other leading nation in car carriers is, not surprisingly, Japan.

Another good example of clustering involving services is the U.S. advertising industry. America is a leader in advertising-intensive consumer packaged goods, making its consumer goods firms sophisticated buyers of advertising services. American advertising agencies followed U.S. packaged goods companies abroad after World War II. The United States also has a long tradition of innovation in media; it was the first place where television was introduced, for example, and an early site for telemarketing. The private ownership of media, their sophistication, and the early ability to advertise freely on TV and radio also reinforced the position of U.S. agencies.

Clusters of service industries are often geographically concentrated, just as in the case of manufacturing. The City of London is a good example in financial services and related industries, while Boston illustrates a unique concentration in many forms of consulting and software. In services as in manufacturing, clusters tend to be associated with specialized schools or concentrations of strong university programs in a field.

SERVICES AND NATIONAL ECONOMIC DEVELOPMENT

There is some controversy about whether international success in services is as valuable to a nation as international success in manufacturing, particularly in services characterized by Type 3 competition in which many jobs are overseas. This question anticipates the discussion of public policy (Chapter 12), but in a word the answer is a resounding "yes." Many services offer prospects for high levels of productivity and rapid productivity growth.

Many international service industries employ highly skilled workers and managers at home in fields tied to modern technology. Custom software, consulting, and engineering services are just a few examples. Many services (such as nondestructive testing) operate at the frontiers of technology and are essential to success in other high-technology industries. International success in services also leads to an inflow of foreign profits on a base of modest foreign direct investment compared to manufacturing.

Services are integral to the clustering process so central to creating national competitive advantage. Service firms provide needed skills, technologies, and support to many other industries. A nation without a favorable position in services will increasingly forfeit national income as well as benefits to the competitive position of other industries. The character and internationalization of many service industries have changed markedly in the postwar period, and any stereotype of services as low technology and domestic is long since obsolete.[18]

Conversely, a widespread lack of competitive advantage in a nation's service industries can be a serious drag on national productivity and productivity growth, as it is in nations such as Japan and Sweden. Services represent a substantial share of employment in virtually all nations, especially in advanced ones. Low productivity in services, because of muted rivalry, restrictive regulations, government ownership, or other causes, represents a constraint to per capita income. Opening service industries to domestic and international competition is essential not only to spur productivity improvement but to free up scarce human resources that can be deployed in other, more productive industries. Sweden, for example, faces labor shortages which are preventing competitive manufacturing firms from expanding in Sweden while human resources are locked in a relatively inefficient services sector.

CASE STUDIES IN THE DEVELOPMENT OF COMPETITIVE SERVICE INDUSTRIES

Many of the principles of international competition in services can be illustrated by case studies of particular service industries. Engineering and construction, among the largest traded services, provide excellent examples. Auctioneering, much smaller but highly visible, illustrates other important lessons.

ENGINEERING AND CONSTRUCTION[19]

The engineering services industry is engaged in the design of industrial process plants and other industrial and public projects. Engineering firms also often supervise construction. The construction services industry is engaged in actual building projects. Sometimes, both engineering and construction services are provided by the same firm, but in many cases there are different service firms involved.

A good deal of engineering services, and the majority of construction, involve relatively simple projects such as small plants, warehouses, offices, and residential dwellings. There is little international competition in these market segments. In large-scale projects and sophisticated industrial facilities, however, there has been a high degree of internationalization of competition since World War II.

American firms have historically been the dominant international competitors in both the engineering and construction industries. Even in 1987, U.S. firms accounted for 24.5 percent of the international contracting awards reported by the top 250 international contractors, ahead of Japan (13.4 percent), Italy (12.4 percent), France (11.6 percent), the United Kingdom (10.7 percent), Germany (8.0 percent), Korea (2.8 percent), the Netherlands (1.9 percent), Switzerland (1.6 percent), and Turkey (1.1 percent).[20]

Large U.S. engineering and construction firms grew up in the 1930s, primarily by building domestic projects. Demand conditions in the United States were extremely favorable for both the engineering and construction industries. The presence in the United States of nearly every resource extraction industry as well as a large number of internationally competitive manufacturing industries exposed American engineering and construction firms to the most sophisticated projects and the world's most demanding buyers of many types of facilities. Climate, terrain, and other building conditions were highly variable within the United States, providing a broad range of conditions from which to learn. Heavy wartime activity led to rapid growth in firm size and sophistication.

By the end of World War II, several large American firms such as Bechtel, Fluor, Kellogg, and others were skilled in the design, management, and construction of large projects of many kinds. After the war, they drew from a large pool of engineering graduates and men from the Navy Seabees and Army Corps of Engineers. Rivalry among American firms was fierce, in contrast to the greater accommodation and even collusion present in other nations.

The early postwar period provided a boom to American engineering and construction companies abroad. The U.S. industrial base was largely intact, while many nations in Europe and Asia faced large-scale reconstruction. With local engineering and construction firms either small or fully occupied, American firms gained a window of opportunity to enter foreign markets. Possessing the best process technology as well as sophisticated construction management skills, U.S. companies quickly dominated the list of international engineering and construction firms.

American firms also designed and built many overseas projects for other U.S. companies, who were rapidly internationalizing in part because of the same surge in foreign demand. American mining and forest products firms, for example, were heavy foreign investors. The large U.S. foreign aid program undoubtedly helped as well, because aid was tied in some cases to contracts for U.S. firms. American engineering and construction firms, in turn, stimulated international sales of many manufactured goods, including Caterpillar bulldozers, Otis elevators, and Carrier air-conditioning equipment.

American dominance in engineering and construction extended into the 1960s and early 1970s. By the 1960s, however, firms from other nations began to reach significant size and sophistication. With their local markets beginning to saturate as reconstruction ran its course, firms from Italy, Germany, France, and Scandinavia began to look to export markets. The best of them began achieving some degree of international success.

Japanese engineering and construction firms began to play a significant role in international markets in the 1970s. They drew on advanced process technologies that had been developed in Japanese process industries such as steel. Many of the overseas projects were either built for Japanese companies or were projects in which Japanese companies provided financing and/ or had partial ownership. In this period, many overseas projects were initiated by Japanese companies to secure raw material access.

Firms from Germany, Italy, Japan, and Scandinavia did well in segments where home demand conditions were favorable: local buyers were internationally competitive and/or local needs were unusually stringent. Scandinavian firms, for example, did well in paper plants, dams, bridges, ports, and hydroelectric power generation facilities. Italian firms did well in road and infrastructure projects, drawing on experience in coping with difficult and varied Italian terrain. German firms did well in constructing chemical and metallurgically based process plants. Japanese firms were successful in the construction of steel plants, shipyards, earthquake-proof buildings, railways, subways and other mass transit systems, dams (Japan generates a significant amount of electricity from hydropower), and aquaculture facilities.[21]

The successful nations also drew on skilled personnel and other factors. For example, Italy had a strong tradition and educational system in civil engineering as well as in certain areas of chemical technology. Italian firms were particularly successful in African and Middle Eastern countries where geographic proximity and the fact that Italy was not viewed as a colonial nation had helped build foreign relations. Italian entrepreneurs were good negotiators, and the sometimes Byzantine Italian regulatory environment made them unusually skillful at dealing with the complexities of doing business in developing nations. Italians were more willing than other nationalities to live abroad in inhospitable places. Italian firms also benefited from a particularly aggressive use of foreign aid to the developing world to pull through demand for Italian products and services.

By the late 1970s, construction firms from developing countries such as Korea, the Philippines, and Taiwan began to play a role in the international construction industry. Korean firms were particularly aggressive. They got their start in domestic reconstruction after the Korean War, and learned from large projects involving U.S. military bases. Further work for the U.S. military in Vietnam was a stepping-stone to international markets. The point of entry of Korean and other developing country firms into international competition was basic factors: providing motivated but low-wage workers. Korean firms often worked as subcontractors to firms from developed nations. Gradually, some of them took over leadership roles on projects, though largely still on those involving relatively simple technology and relatively low levels of management complexity. The Middle East building boom, involving many simple infrastructure projects, was a boon to the Korean industry. The slowdown in the Middle East has particularly hurt Korean firms, which never progressed beyond basic factor advantages.

The engineering and construction industries illustrate the role of early demand, advanced local buyers, unusually stringent local needs, and demand surges in international success. They also illustrate the link between services and related manufacturing industries, and the energizing role of intense domestic rivalry in propelling a nation's service firms to international success. The role of factor conditions is also evident. Nations succeed in fields where they have well-developed educational systems in engineering. Factor costs do not seem decisive, however, except in the case of firms from low-wage countries. The vulnerability of those nations to slowing growth or to too great a dependence on low wages is very apparent in the depressed conditions that have prevailed recently. Conversely, American firms have sustained a strong position despite high factor costs, because of a favorable national "diamond." As firms from other nations (notably Japan) become the world-leading manufacturers in many industries, however, this raises a fundamental threat to U.S. competitive advantage.

AUCTIONEERING

While engineering and construction are huge industries with international sales rivaling almost any manufactured good, many services (and manufacturing industries) are more specialized. One interesting example, auctioneering, will provide another case of how national advantage in a service industry emerges. Auctioneers are involved in the sale of a wide variety of collectible items, ranging from paintings and other artwork to furniture, jewelry, and china. Some auctioneers buy goods for their own account and then sell them via the auction mechanism. Other auctioneers, including the leading British international firms, act solely as middlemen. Here, goods are auctioned on behalf of the seller, and the auctioneer typically earns a commission from both parties to the transaction. In return for the commission, the auctioneer prepares catalogs, advertises the auction, stores the goods and conducts the actual auction. Modern auctions involve not only those attending, but also bids placed in advance by buyers located all over the world, and telephone hookups to buyers while the auction is actually taking place.

British firms, or firms that developed and have home bases in Britain, dominate the world auctioneering industry. Sotheby's, Christie's, Phillips, and Bonhams are the four leading firms. Collectively, their turnover exceeds 1 billion pounds per year, the great majority involving foreign buyers. All are British-owned except Sotheby's, purchased from British owners by an American-led investor group (although the home base is still in Britain). Sotheby's, Christie's, and Phillips all operate offices and showrooms in other nations in addition to their London facilities and hold auctions all over the world. Bonhams operates only in London but attracts buyers and sellers from all over the world. There are smaller auctioneers operating domestically in other nations, but British firms represent the dominant force in the international auctioneering industry.

Britain was a nation of enormous wealth, where large collections of fine arts were amassed. Home demand size, however, does not explain the British dominance in auctioneering. France and Italy had arguably much stronger traditions in the arts, for example, while America quickly became the single largest force in art buying. Japanese buyers have become prominent buyers at international auctions in the late 1980s.

In Britain, there is a long tradition in auctioneering that dates back several centuries. More important, however, is the fact that the auction has long been an honorable, respectable way in Britain to buy and sell goods, while in some other countries it has historically been viewed with some suspicion.

This tradition meant that there were hundreds of auctioneers in Britain at the turn of the twentieth century. Partly because of active competition, the leading British auctioneers developed the practice of acting solely as middlemen. Auctioneers in many other countries, in pursuit of higher profits, often bought goods for their own account. The British approach, in addition to reducing capital requirements, created the best possible motives for the auctioneer from both the buyer's and seller's perspective.[22] British home demand for auctioneering services became increasingly sophisticated as goods were periodically put up for auction because of high local inheritance taxes.

The reputation of British auctioneers became one important reason why people consigned goods to Britain to be sold. Closely related was the far-flung British Empire that made London a market for exotic items from all over the globe. Added to these other advantages was Britain's relatively central location, near continental Europe and between America and Asia. This, combined with the attraction of London as a cosmopolitan center, helped reinforce the importance of London as the center of the international auctioneering world.

The auctioneering industry attracted highly educated people in Britain. Connected with the arts, auctioneering was respectable in a country where commerce was not a prestigious occupation. The British university system provides strong training in the arts, though it is lacking in more practical areas such as engineering and business. The huge infrastructure of museums and galleries in England provided a base of experts (and objects for comparison purposes) to be called on in authenticating and valuing items.

Also important to British success was a relatively less restrictive regulatory environment. In many nations, among them France and Italy, the flow of art objects into and out of the country was tightly controlled and often heavily taxed.[23] France has taken regulation one step further, making auctioneers quasi-state employees, separating auctioneering from the valuation of goods, and requiring French nationals to hold key jobs. French auctioneers have enjoyed a comfortable, protected existence but have not succeeded in international competition.

British regulation related to auctioneering, in contrast, has been among the least rigid in the world, with only modest administrative requirements for importing and exporting objects and no value-added tax on sales. The only exception is jewelry, which historically was taxed relatively heavily in Britain. Not surprisingly, the center of jewelry auctioneering became Switzerland, a low-tax country, and this situation has persisted. But the British auctioneers are still strong participants, operating from their Swiss offices.

Perhaps the most fundamental reason for sustained British success, however, is a long and active history of innovation in the British auctioneering industry. British houses pioneered such practices as estimated prices, international sales, flamboyant public relations, and heavy marketing. Underlying this innovation were highly skilled personnel, advanced local buyers who were sophisticated users of auctions, and the lack of restrictive regulation. Perhaps the greatest single influence, however, has been the intense rivalry among the "Big Four" London houses. Sotheby's and Christie's, particularly, have been aggressively trying to beat each other for decades. Innovations are copied rapidly and the competition among auctioneers for the right to sell large estates and collections is legendary. "Stodgy" Britain is far from stodgy in the auctioneering business.

Auctioneering illustrates the subtle role of factor conditions in services competition. Important factors of production in auctioneering are highly trained, specialized personnel attracted to the business, a cadre of art experts, a pool of art objects in museums and homes, and the location of Britain as a central point in the world that was desirable to visit. Demand conditions and the nature of domestic rivalry were also essential to British success.

The pervasive role of regulation and protection in influencing service firm operating practices and rivalry is well illustrated in auctioneering as well. The case of auctioneering, like many other services we studied including insurance and health care-related fields, shows that restrictive regulation and protection may serve legitimate national purposes but works against international competitiveness in services just as it does in manufacturing.

Finally, auctioneering is an industry where early mover advantages are particularly significant. By becoming established early, British auction houses developed the reputation for drawing the best buyers. This in turn provided access to sellers, who sought the top prices for their goods. While Britain's period of unique national wealth has passed, some industries that rose to prominence during this period retain strong international positions.

PART III

Nations

PART II

Nations

7

Patterns of National Competitive Advantage: The Early Postwar Winners

A close look at the economies of the industrialized nations reveals sharp differences in their patterns of national competitive advantage. Germany has long-standing leadership positions in chemicals, many types of production machinery, and high-performance cars; Sweden in specialty steel, heavy trucks, and mining equipment; Switzerland in trading, textile machinery, pharmaceuticals, and chocolate; Italy in wool fabrics, leather goods, and robots; and the United States in detergents, medical equipment, and airplanes. These differences are not new. Some national advantages have persisted for over a century.

If anything, the differences in national competitive advantage among nations have only become sharper. The growing internationalization of competition has exposed more and more industries to the world's best rivals, in manufacturing as well as in services. Over time, patterns of success and failure have become more defined.[1] National advantage has come to reside in particular industries and even increasingly in industry segments, not in entire sectors.

The pattern of success and failure in its economy will shed light on the fundamental determinants of productivity in the nations, because it bears on the capacity of a nation's industry to compete in sophisticated industries and segments. National economic prosperity depends not only on the pattern at any point in time, however, but even more so on the capacity of a nation's industry to *upgrade itself over time*. Upgrading an economy is the result of broadening and upgrading the competitive advantages of a nation's firms: the attainment of wider and more sophisticated competitive advantages in established industries, which leads to rising productivity, and the ability to compete successfully in more sophisticated new segments and entirely new industries. Upgrading in this way drives productivity growth while maintaining full employment. Failure to upgrade, in contrast, results in slow productivity growth in established industries and the loss of competitive position in some high-productivity fields without enough others to replace them. Inevitably, this leads to pressure on wages and faltering per capita income growth.

The period since World War II has seen especially large shifts in the pattern of competitive advantage in industrial nations. Despite devastation during the war, Germany has regained its position as an industrial powerhouse and has enjoyed sustained prosperity. Japan, also devastated by the war, has come to challenge America for leadership as the preeminent industrial nation. Italy has emerged as a vibrant force in international competition. Korea has enjoyed remarkable growth, and has almost, but not quite, made the leap that Japan successfully negotiated to advanced industrial status. Switzerland and Sweden, despite these shifting positions, continue their traditions of high per capita income and low unemployment dating back many decades, though neither economy is without challenges. The United States, once dominant in an extraordinarily wide range of advanced industries, has lost preeminence in a good number of them. The United Kingdom has had to contend with chronic difficulties in industry and lagging income growth.

Table 7–1 provides an overview of some of the most telling indicators of the economic performance of the nations we studied over the postwar period. These illustrate both sharp differences among nations and important shifts. They will provide a backdrop to my discussion of individual nations.

The shifting patterns of national competitive advantage challenge any simple notion of comparative advantage. The nations with the broadest successes in sophisticated industries, Japan and Germany, both began the postwar period in shambles. In both nations, capital was scarce, and salespeople attempting to sell products in foreign markets sometimes faced outright hostility. Yet Germany regained and sustained leading positions in many advanced industries. It has coped with high and rising labor costs, shortening workweeks, and a rising currency. Japan has become a premier industrial power despite almost no natural resources, an isolated location necessitating long supply lines, devastating Nixon (import surcharge) and yen shocks, and strained relations in its region.

Sweden and Switzerland continue as important trading nations and are

TABLE 7-1 Selected Measures of Economic Performance in the Postwar Period

Real Compound Annual Growth in Gross Domestic Product (1980 Prices), 1950–1987

Nation	1950–87	1950–55	1955–60	1960–65	1965–70	1970–75	1975–80	1980–85	1985–87
Korea	7.9%[1]	—	3.3%	6.5%	12.6%	8.8%	7.7%	7.6%	11.4%
Japan	7.2%[1]	—	8.5%	10.0%	11.0%	4.3%	5.0%	3.9%	3.4%
Germany	4.6%	9.4%	8.3%	4.8%	4.2%	2.1%	3.3%	1.3%	2.1%
Italy	4.5%	6.0%	6.6%	5.2%	6.2%	2.4%	3.8%	1.6%	3.0%
Denmark	3.2%	1.9%	4.6%	5.3%	3.7%	2.0%	2.5%	2.4%	1.1%
Switzerland	3.2%	4.9%	4.3%	5.2%	4.2%	0.8%	1.7%	1.4%	2.5%
United States	3.2%	4.4%	2.2%	4.8%	2.9%	2.3%	3.3%	3.0%	2.9%
Sweden	3.0%	3.3%	3.4%	5.2%	4.1%	2.6%	1.3%	1.8%	2.0%
United Kingdom	2.5%	3.0%	2.5%	3.2%	2.5%	2.1%	1.7%	1.8%	3.3%

Real Compound Annual Growth in Gross Domestic Product Per Capita (1980 Prices), 1950–1987

Nation	1950–87	1950–55	1955–60	1960–65	1965–70	1970–75	1975–80	1980–85	1985–87
Japan	6.2%[2]	—	7.5%	9.0%	9.8%	2.9%	4.0%	3.2%	2.9%
Korea	5.7%[2]	—	0.3%	3.6%	10.0%	6.8%	6.1%	6.0%	10.0%
Germany	4.0%	8.3%	5.7%	3.5%	3.6%	1.7%	3.4%	1.4%	1.9%
Italy	3.9%	5.3%	6.0%	4.2%	5.6%	1.8%	3.5%	1.4%	2.8%
Denmark	2.7%	1.1%	3.9%	4.5%	3.0%	1.4%	2.3%	2.5%	0.9%
Sweden	2.6%	2.6%	2.8%	4.5%	3.3%	3.2%	1.0%	1.7%	1.7%
Switzerland	2.2%	3.7%	2.8%	3.4%	3.1%	0.1%	1.8%	1.1%	2.0%
United Kingdom	2.2%	2.8%	2.1%	2.5%	2.0%	2.0%	1.6%	1.6%	3.0%
United States	1.9%	2.7%	0.4%	3.3%	1.7%	1.2%	2.2%	2.6%	1.9%

TABLE 7-1 (Continued)

Compound Annual Population Growth, 1950–1987

Nation	1950–87	1950–55	1955–60	1960–65	1965–70	1970–75	1975–80	1980–85	1985–87
Korea	2.0%	1.1%	3.0%	2.8%	2.4%	1.8%	1.6%	1.5%	1.2%
United States	1.3%	1.7%	1.8%	1.5%	1.1%	1.0%	1.1%	1.0%	0.9%
Japan	1.1%	1.4%	0.9%	1.0%	1.1%	1.5%	0.9%	0.7%	0.6%
Switzerland	0.9%	1.2%	1.5%	1.8%	1.1%	0.7%	−0.1%	0.2%	0.5%
Germany	0.7%	1.0%	2.4%	1.1%	0.7%	0.4%	−0.1%	−0.2%	0.1%
Denmark	0.5%	0.8%	0.6%	0.8%	0.7%	0.5%	0.3%	−0.1%	0.2%
Italy	0.5%	0.7%	0.6%	0.7%	0.6%	0.7%	0.4%	0.3%	0.2%
Sweden	0.5%	0.7%	0.6%	0.7%	0.8%	0.4%	0.3%	0.1%	0.3%
United Kingdom	0.3%	0.2%	0.4%	0.7%	0.5%	0.2%	0.0%	0.1%	0.3%

Overall Labor Productivity Growth, 1950–1987[3] (Compound Annual Growth in Gross Domestic Product per Employee)

Nation	1950–87	1950–55	1955–60	1960–65	1965–70	1970–75	1975–80	1980–85	1985–87
Japan	5.9%[4]	—	6.3%	11.0%	9.2%	3.8%	3.8%	3.0%	2.5%
Korea	5.8%[5]	—	—	—	8.8%	4.6%	4.6%	5.7%	6.6%
Italy	4.4%	6.1%	6.4%	5.7%	6.8%	2.1%	3.0%	1.4%	2.8%
Germany	3.8%	6.4%	5.2%	4.2%	4.4%	2.7%	3.0%	1.9%	1.2%
Denmark	2.4%[4]	—	3.2%	3.5%	3.6%	1.7%	1.7%	1.8%	−0.6%
Sweden	2.3%[6]	—	—	4.4%	3.5%	1.7%	0.6%	1.6%	1.7%
United Kingdom	2.2%	2.1%	2.1%	2.4%	2.8%	2.0%	1.7%	2.4%	2.0%
Switzerland	1.2%[7]	—	—	—	—	1.5%	0.7%	1.3%	1.8%
United States	1.4%	2.9%	1.2%	2.5%	0.9%	0.7%	0.5%	1.0%	0.5%

Manufacturing Productivity Growth, 1950–1987[8] (Compound Annual Growth in Output per Employed Person in Manufacturing)

Nation	1950–87	1950–55	1955–60	1960–65	1965–70	1970–75	1975–80	1980–85	1985–87
Japan	7.96%	12.03%	8.77%	6.93%	12.59%	4.10%	8.04%	5.68%	2.76%
Italy	5.14%	7.39%	4.84%	5.32%	6.85%	1.16%	5.84%	4.83%	4.83%
Germany	4.30%	7.58%	5.48%	4.65%	5.03%	3.07%	3.39%	2.71%	0.04%
Sweden	3.30%	1.69%	3.90%	5.71%	5.03%	2.78%	0.87%	3.95%	1.46%
Denmark	2.97%	1.34%	2.90%	4.76%	4.19%	5.64%	3.27%	0.50%	−1.14%
United Kingdom	2.81%	1.77%	2.16%	2.76%	3.25%	2.24%	0.88%	5.84%	4.99%
United States	2.63%	2.87%	0.77%	4.96%	0.46%	2.68%	1.82%	4.48%	3.79%

Unemployment Rates, 1951–1987 (Period Averages)

Nation	1951–87	1951–55	1956–60	1961–65	1966–70	1971–75	1976–81	1980–85	1986–87
Switzerland	0.3%	0.8%	0.4%	0.0%	0.0%	0.1%	0.4%	0.7%	0.8%
Japan	1.7%	1.3%	1.4%	1.3%	1.2%	1.4%	2.1%	2.5%	2.9%
Sweden	2.1%	2.4%	1.9%	1.5%	1.8%	2.2%	1.9%	3.0%	2.3%
Germany	3.5%	7.4%	2.9%	0.5%	0.8%	1.4%	4.1%	5.5%	6.8%
United Kingdom	4.7%	1.6%	1.8%	2.5%	2.9%	3.8%	6.1%	11.2%	10.7%
Korea	5.0%[9]	—	—	7.9%	5.5%	4.2%	4.0%	4.1%	3.5%
Italy	5.4%	9.6%	6.8%	2.9%	3.4%	3.4%	4.1%	5.5%	7.6%
United States	5.7%	3.9%	5.2%	5.4%	3.8%	6.0%	6.7%	8.2%	6.5%
Denmark	6.4%	9.8%	8.3%	2.8%	3.4%	4.0%	6.4%	9.7%	8.1%

Net National Investment (Gross Fixed Capital Investment—Consumption of Fixed Capital as Percentage of Gross Domestic Product), Period Averages[10]

	1951–87	1951–55	1956–60	1961–65	1966–70	1971–75	1976–81	1980–85	1986–87
Japan	17.6%	12.9%	16.7%	20.7%	20.2%	21.2%	18.5%	15.3%	14.4%
South Korea	14.7%[11]	—	5.6%	7.7%	18.0%	16.1%	21.8%	20.9%	—
Switzerland	13.7%	9.1%	12.6%	18.4%	15.3%	16.4%	11.0%	13.2%	14.7%
Germany	11.8%	10.5%	13.9%	16.1%	13.8%	12.7%	9.8%	8.0%	7%
Denmark	11.6%	9.9%	10.0%	13.1%	13.7%	13.4%	13.2%	8.0%	10.9%
Sweden	11.0%	11.1%	12.5%	13.4%	13.6%	11.7%	9.3%	7.2%	7.1%
Italy	10.9%	9.9%	12.6%	13.6%	11.4%	11.6%	9.4%	8.5%	9.0%
United Kingdom	7.7%	6.2%	7.8%	9.5%	10.3%	9.7%	7.1%	4.5%	5.2%
United States	7.1%	9.3%	7.9%	7.3%	7.8%	6.6%	6.8%	4.6%	5.1%

[1] 1955–87. [2] 1955–87. [3] Maddison's (1987) statistics show that total factor productivity comparisons are similar to these labor productivity comparisons for the nations he included.

[4] 1955–87. [5] 1963–87. [6] 1960–87. [7] 1970–87. [8] Data for other nations on this measure was unavailable. [9] 1961–87.

[10] Adjusting these data to eliminate investment in residential construction leaves the rank order of nations unchanged, but significantly lowers the percentages. In the 1980s, the U.S. rate of net investment falls to near zero and is negative in some years.

[11] 1955–85.

SOURCES: International Monetary Fund, International Financial Statistics Yearbook OECD, Economic Outlook and Historical Statistics United Nations, Statistical Yearbook, National Accounts, and Monthly Bulletin of Statistics U.S. Department of Labor, Comparative Real GDP Figures and Indexes of Output per Hour, Unpublished Data

home bases for a remarkable number of leading multinational firms, despite tiny home markets, high wages, and, in the case of Sweden, the closest thing to socialism (in terms of welfare benefits and income distribution) among the major industrialized countries. Italy has prospered despite an ineffective government bureaucracy, barely functioning infrastructure, and highly restrictive labor legislation. Korea is enjoying growing prosperity in spite of the burden of the Korean War, few national resources, a long period of Japanese occupation, and huge and continuing costs of national defense.

Postwar industrial history is not a story of exploiting abundance but of creating abundance. It is a story not of enjoying advantage but of coping with selective disadvantage. National adversity, when combined with the right underlying circumstances, has been an energizing force for innovation and change. Pressure and challenge, not "a quiet life," has led firms and nations to advance.

DESCRIBING NATIONAL ECONOMIES

My task in this part of the book is twofold. First, I will apply my theory to begin to explain the patterns of international success and failure in particular industries in a number of important national economies. For reasons of space, I will confine my discussion to eight of the ten nations we studied. Denmark and Singapore, though they appear in examples elsewhere in the book, will not be discussed except briefly in Chapter 10.[2]

Second, I will examine the extent to which a nation's industry has upgraded over the period and some of the reasons why. I will also, in tandem with Chapter 13, assess the nation's capacity to continue doing so. One important indication of the health of upgrading in an economy is how the pattern of international success and failure in industries and segments has evolved. A healthy pattern for national income growth is a shift toward more sophisticated and productive segments and expanding positions in industries involving more advanced technology and more skilled human resources. Rising national world export share can be a sign of upgrading, but the types of industries that are gaining and losing competitive position are more important than the average, as I discussed in Chapter 1.

In examining a nation, I will begin by presenting a profile of all the successful industries in its economy in 1985. We identified every industry in the nation in which there was evidence of international competitive advantage at three points in time: 1971, 1978, and 1985 (the most recent year for which data for all the nations were available). As I discussed in Chapter 1, the lack of complete data makes measuring the presence of international competitive advantage problematic. Also, government intervention sometimes supports firms that lack true competitive advantage.

The presence of competitive advantage in international terms is measured here by a significant and sustained share of world exports to a wide array of nations and/or foreign 'direct investment reflecting skills and strengths created in the home nation.[3] We generally found exports and substantial foreign investment to be closely related. The national profiles, in which clusters of competitive industries are identified and displayed, represent a good, albeit imperfect indication of the patterns of national competitive advantage in the economy (a fuller description of how the profiles were developed is contained in Appendix A).

In explaining the patterns of national advantage and how they have been changing, I draw on our case studies, extensive interviews, and my co-researchers in each nation. Care must be taken to avoid an overly macroeconomic view. A central premise of this book is that national advantage is best understood by examining particular industries and industry clusters. Yet there are hundreds of industries of consequence in every nation, and it is impractical to discuss every one. I will highlight those aspects of the nation's environment most important in influencing a range of industries, albeit in differing specific ways, though I will mention many particular industries. This approach runs the risk of seeming to emphasize cross-industry considerations in exploring a theory that is aggressively industry (and cluster) specific. There is no practical way around it, however. Each example reflects a more extensive study than I can do justice to here.

In the course of explaining the pattern of international success and failure in a nation's industry, I will especially seek to highlight its evolution. Of particular concern will be the capacity of the nation's industry to upgrade over time. A nation cannot and should not succeed in all industries, and loss of competitive positions is not in and of itself a cause for concern. What is more significant is the nature of positions lost and the reasons why. Of critical importance is the capacity of the nation's firms to achieve higher-order competitive advantages over time and successfully compete in new advanced industries in order to deploy national resources in increasingly productive ways.

This chapter will focus on the nations that emerged from World War II and the decade after with the most robust national competitive advantage. The United States, Switzerland, and Sweden were the earliest winners. All avoided destruction, and all had considerable strengths which made them well positioned to prosper in the early postwar period. Germany joined the early winners when, to the world's amazement, it was able to rebound from the war with astonishing speed.

My aim is not a definitive treatment of each nation, but a story which illustrates how the theory can integrate many of the disparate influences on competitiveness that have been proposed, as well as important additional ones, in order to shed some new light on the question. My discussion of each nation must necessarily be brief, and some elements of the story will inevitably be left out. All the data available to support the points I make cannot be cited, nor can all the salient literature possibly be reviewed and acknowledged. By presenting an overview, however, I hope to provide a new perspective on the nation's competitive position in industry and how it may be changing.[4]

AMERICAN POSTWAR DOMINANCE

The story of national competitive advantage in the decades immediately after World War II is a story in which the United States has the starring role. The economic strength of the United States after the war was unique in modern times. American firms had already established leading positions in many industries in the early 1900s, with the likes of Singer (sewing machines), Ford (automobiles), and Otis (elevators) holding dominant global positions. The breadth of industries in which U.S. firms were internationally competitive further widened in the 1950s and early 1960s. The average productivity of the American economy was the highest of any nation, reflecting a remarkably wide range of industries that were productive in international terms, even if they did not export. Indeed, a much lower percentage of American GDP was accounted for by exports and imports than any other advanced economy.

The United States enjoyed a unique combination of circumstances that spawned and sustained internationally competitive industries. American industry emerged unscathed from the war. The United States had a large, uniquely affluent home market. Modern plants and equipment, often built up to serve wartime needs, were poised to supply burgeoning international demand against little or no foreign competition. A huge defense program provided funding for research in core technologies and a market for advanced goods such as aircraft and electronics. The new technologies were readily adapted for civilian use. The Boeing 707, for example, was first an air force transport plane (the KC-135). The U.S. government also bought many of the first computers and electronic components.

However, these relatively conventional reasons only begin to explain U.S. dominance in postwar international competition. As will become apparent, a much broader set of forces was at work. American success, which may have been too great and have come too easily, was the result of a unique combination of circumstances that was self-reinforcing.

PATTERNS OF U.S. COMPETITIVE ADVANTAGE

One way to gain an initial understanding of the patterns of competitive success in U.S. industries is to examine the top fifty American industries in 1971 in terms of share of world exports, shown in Table 7–2 (I will

TABLE 7–2 **Top Fifty U.S. Industries in Terms of World Export Share, 1971**

Industry	Share of Total World Exports	Export Value ($ millions)	Import Value ($ millions)	Share of Total U.S. Exports
Soya beans	97.4	1,326,819	8	3.1
Natural phosphates	95.3	94,827	2,830	0.2
Coloring compounds	81.9	16,243	—	0.0
Aircraft	77.5	2,552,652	79,887	5.9
Radioactive elements	76.6	167,106	—	0.4
Rough sawn, veneer conifer logs	75.5	264,628	3,943	0.6
Office machine parts	55.9	927,810	121,151	2.1
Coal, excluding briquettes	53.4	901,598	569	2.1
Stable isotopes and compounds	50.4	68,555	73,239	0.2
Aircraft parts	49.3	852,619	257,888	2.0
Animal oils and fats	47.4	241,836	11,926	0.6
Organic chemicals	44.1	989,723	400,286	2.3
Rice	42.4	99,606	2	0.2
Vegetable oil residues	41.6	419,954	1,319	1.0
Nonchemical coal, petroleum wastes	41.2	183,918	39,673	0.4
Unmanufactured tobacco	41.1	466,135	88,724	1.1
Unmilled maize	39.6	746,415	7,693	1.7
Nondomestic refrigeration equipment	39.3	232,303	—	0.8
Anti-knock preparations	39.0	155,789	—	0.4
Sugar preparations	37.9	1,455	568	0.0
Meat and edible offals	37.7	9,094	—	0.0
Kraft paper, paperboard	37.2	283,110	10,322	0.7
Iron and steel scrap	37.1	215,761	13,551	0.5
Aircraft gas, jet turbines	36.8	381,077	35,405	0.9
Waste of textile fabrics	35.9	49,719	5,186	0.1
Unmilled wheat	35.8	1,004,729	648	2.3
Excavating, leveling, etc., machinery	35.6	711,140	—	1.6
Computers, accounting machines	35.2	462,382	196,190	1.1
Bovine, equine hides	34.5	133,176	4,852	0.3
Non-road tractors	34.2	417,783	87,172	1.0
Cigarettes	33.7	183,012	2,106	0.4
Photochemical products	33.7	23,339	—	0.1
Unmilled cereals	33.5	176,717	2,551	0.4
Soft fixed vegetables oils	33.1	326,749	22,457	0.8
Transistors, valves	32.7	480,147	259,160	1.1

TABLE 7–2 *(Continued)*

Industry	Share of Total World Exports	Export Value ($ millions)	Import Value ($ millions)	Share of Total U.S. Exports
Motor vehicle parts	32.3	2,175,245	1,070,173	5.0
Measuring, controlling instruments	32.0	463,004	61,750	1.1
Non-wheat meal and flour	30.8	15,271	—	0.0
Unworked iron, steel castings	30.7	96,086	9,405	0.2
Electronic measuring, control equipment	29.7	417,330	83,370	1.0
Margarine, shortening	29.6	52,092	—	0.1
Other telecommunication equipment	28.8	492,649	243,036	1.1
Copper scrap	28.1	73,832	13,143	0.2
Synthetic rubber	27.6	172,851	56,736	0.4
Horse meat, offals, poultry livers	27.4	79,024	8,476	0.2
Photo film	27.3	259,298	111,008	0.6
Nonelectrical power machinery	25.8	1,187,741	921,674	2.7
Aluminum oxide, hydroxide	25.7	77,659	160,070	0.2
Footwear with cork soles	25.6	11,127	11,185	0.0
Ignition, starting equipment	25.5	94,293	55,199	0.2
TOTAL				49.1

NOTE: No import data are reported if import value is less than 0.3 percent of the total trade for 1971.

discuss data for 1985 in Chapter 9). The top fifty industries in terms of world export share, which I will show for all eight countries studied, are those where the nation has the most commanding international position and, accordingly, an unusually strong international competitive advantage. Often, the top fifty account for a substantial fraction of the nation's exports. (I also present, in Table B–1, the top fifty industries in terms of export value. In all the nations, this list is dominated by industries that also have a significant world export share. It sometimes also includes a few large industries, such as petroleum or automobiles, where the nation has a minor position but frequently a negative trade balance.)

The top fifty U.S. industries in 1971 include a number heavily dependent on national resources, among which I classify many agricultural products. This will prove to be true in the economy as a whole. But the unusual competitive strength of the United States is suggested by the wide variety of other industries in the top fifty, such as aircraft, photographic equipment, computers, chemicals, various types of production machinery and components, and consumer packaged goods.

In order to illustrate better the patterns of national advantage in the United States and other nations and the ways in which they have been changing, I will use as a primary tool a chart like that shown in Figure 7–1.[5] I will refer to this as a *cluster chart*. Industries appearing on the chart have either a world export share greater than the nation's average share of world exports or an international position based on foreign investment that was estimated to be as significant. Industries whose world export share exceeds a nation's average typically account for two-thirds or more of the nation's *total* exports. Individual industries are displayed in different typefaces, depending on the strength of their international positions.

My theory assigns important roles to demand conditions and to vertical relationships among industries in stimulating competitive advantage. Accordingly, industries are grouped in the chart by end-use application. Across the top row of Figure 7–1 are broad sectors containing industries whose primary products are inputs to products in many other industries; they are termed *upstream sectors*. Semiconductors and computers, while a relatively new sector of the economy, are a modern category of products that are basic inputs to virtually every industry. Across the middle row are broad end-use sectors involving *industrial or supporting functions*. Most are related to particular end uses such as transportation or defense. The multiple business category contains industries such as measuring instruments and power tools, whose products are ancillary or supporting products used in many end-use sectors. Along the bottom row are end-use sectors most associated with *final consumption goods*. How the internationally successful industries in a nation are distributed by end-use sector and level in the chart will prove to be an interesting and widely differing feature of national economies.

Within each broad sector, internationally successful industries are grouped into primary goods, machinery (and other equipment) used in making them, specialized inputs to the goods, and services associated with the goods or their production. This allows an examination of the vertical relationships among successful industries and the depth of national clusters. At each vertical stage, successful industries are grouped into subcategories most closely related by end use in order to further expose the nature of clustering.

Often, related industries are found within the same broad sector. Passenger cars and trucks are both classified, for example, in the transportation sector. In all nations, however, there are linkages among groups of industries that extend beyond sectors. In the United States, for example, the position in semiconductors and computers is related to strength in defense. Some of the most important of these links in each nation will be illustrated by shading. While industry positionings on the chart are imperfect and limited in some cases by overly broad industry definitions in the international trade classification system, the charts provide an interesting profile of each nation's economy

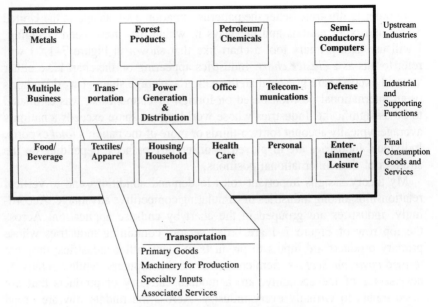

FIGURE 7-1 **The Cluster Chart**

and a tool for analyzing how they are changing. (A fuller description of how industries were identified and positioned on the cluster chart is contained in Appendix A.)

Figure 7-2 shows the results of this process for the United States in 1971. It gives a crude profile of all the industries in which there is evidence of U.S. international success in that year, its crudeness reflecting a much more aggregated industry classification system in 1971 than was introduced in 1976. All subsequent charts, including a more recent one for the United States in Chapter 9, will be based on 1985 data.

Figure 7-2 illustrates that the breadth of successful industries suggested by the top fifty list is genuine. The areas of U.S. strength during the first two decades after World War II are numerous, particularly given the stiff requirement that an industry's share of world exports was 13.8 percent or higher to appear on the chart at all. Among the strongest positions, some of which are poorly measured in the trade classification system, are semiconductors and computers, transportation equipment (automobiles, aircraft, materials handling machinery), consumer packaged goods, office equipment, power generation and distribution equipment, chemicals and plastics, telecommunications equipment, defense goods, entertainment and leisure products, timber and agriculture-related products, health care related products, and general business services. Indeed, in contrast to other nations, there are few sectors (notably textiles/apparel and housing/household) in which the United States is not significantly represented.

FIGURE 7-2 Clusters of Internationally Competitive U.S. Industries, 1971

	MATERIALS/METALS	FOREST PRODUCTS	PETROLEUM/CHEMICALS	SEMICONDUCTORS/ COMPUTERS
Primary Goods	IRON & STEEL Iron, simple steel blooms Iron, steel tube fitting *Iron, steel castings unworked* NONFERROUS METALS Aluminum plate, sheet, strip Nonferrous base metals Aluminum, zinc structures and parts# Refined copper Nickel, alloys worked OTHER MATERIALS Natural abrasives Other crude materials# WASTE & SCRAP *Iron & steel scrap* *Copper scrap*	WOOD PRODUCTS **Saw-, veneer-logs conifer** PAPER Coated printing paper ***Kraft paper, paperboard*** Coated, etc. paper nes, bulk	PETROLEUM PRODUCTS ***Nonchemical coal, petroleum wastes*** Coal, petroleum, etc., chemicals **Coal, excl. briquettes** INORGANIC CHEMICALS Other inorganic chemicals Inorganic elements, oxides# ORGANIC CHEMICALS *Organic chemicals* PLASTICS Products of condensation	*Transistors, valves* *Computers, accounting machines* Note: Few industries in this sector were isolated in the classification system in 1971. The U.S. was preeminent.
Machinery	Converters & welding appliances# Rolling mills and rolls Mineral crushing, etc. machinery		*Oilfield equipment***	
Specialty Inputs	Refractory building products Sulphur	Pulp and waste paper#		
Services	Mining*		*Oilfield services***	*Data processing***

FIGURE 7-2 *(Continued)*

	MULTIPLE BUSINESS	TRANSPORTATION	POWER GENERATION AND DISTRIBUTION	OFFICE
Primary Goods	EQUIPMENT Tools Pumps for liquids, etc. Pumps for gases, etc. Centrifuges, etc., nondairy Electric lamps, hand tools, etc.* *Electronic measuring, control equipment* INSTRUMENTS *Measuring, controlling instruments* OTHER Optical elements, medical instruments, cameras* Cocks, valves, etc., nes Shaft, crank, pulley, etc. Ball, roller bearings*	*Aircraft gas, jet turbines* **Aircraft, heavier than air** *Tractors, nonroad* Lifting, loading machines Forklift trucks, etc. Railway vehicles Buses, road tractors* Lorries, trucks Motor vehicles* *Excavating, leveling, etc. machinery* VEHICLE EQUIPMENT Ignition, starting equipment	Power machinery, nonelectrical* Switchgear, etc. Electric power machinery Electric insulating equipment*	**Office machine parts nes** Office supplies nes
Machinery	Nonelectric machines, nes* Powered tools, nes*			Printing, binding machinery
Specialty Inputs		*Synthetic rubber, etc.* Antiknock preparations Rubber articles* Materials of rubber *Motor vehicle parts, nes* *Aircraft parts*	**Radioactive elements** *Stable isotopes & compounds*#	
Services	Accounting• Advertising• Management consulting• *Commercial banking*	Service stations• Airlines•		

KEY

roman   13.8% world export share or higher, but less than 27.6% share
bold italics   27.6% world export share or higher, *but less than 55.3% share*
sans serif   **55.3% world export share or above**

\#   Calculated residuals
•   Added due to FDI
••   Upgraded due to FDI
•••   Added based on in-country research

	TELECOMMUNICATIONS	DEFENSE
Primary Goods	***Other telecommunications equipment**[†] Line telephone equipment*[*] Note: Few industries in this sector were isolated in the classification system in 1971. The U.S. was a leader.	War firearms, ammunition[***] Note: Relatively few industries in this sector were isolated in the classification system in 1971. The U.S. had a leading position.
Machinery		
Specialty Inputs		
Services		

FIGURE 7-2 (Continued)

Primary Goods	FOOD/BEVERAGES		HOUSING/HOUSEHOLD	TEXTILES/APPAREL
	BASIC FOODS	EDIBLE OILS	*Soap, polishes****	***Bovine, equine hides***
	Rice in husk or husked	**Vegetable oil residues**		Raw cotton, excl. linters
	Rice glazed or polished	***Margarine, shortening***		Cotton linters, waste#
	Flour of wheat, etc.	***Animal oils and fats***		Discontinuous synthetic fiber uncombed
	Meal and flour, nonwheat	***Fixed soft vegetable oils***		Cellulose derivatives#
	Dried fruit			***Waste of textile fabrics***#
	Fruit preserved, prepared			**Coloring compounds**#
	Soya beans			
	Meat & edible offals#			
	PROCESSED FOODS			
	Cereal, etc., preparations			
	Food preparations, nes			
Machinery	Milking & other agricultural machinery#	*Nondomestic refrigeration equipment*		
	Food machinery, nondomestic	Packaging, filling, etc. machines		
Specialty Inputs	Phosphatic fertilizers#	***Maize unmilled***		
	Insecticides, chemicals	***Cereals nes unmilled***		
	Natural phosphates#	Horsemeat, offals#		
	Wheat, etc., unmilled	***Sugar, preps., flavored or colored***#		
Services	Fast food*			
	Trading of agricultural commodities***			

KEY

roman	13.8% world export share or higher, but less than 27.6% share
bold italics	27.6% world export share or higher, but less than 55.3% share
sans serif	55.3% world export share or above

#	Calculated residuals
*	Added due to FDI
**	Upgraded due to FDI
***	Added based on in-country research

	HEALTH CARE	PERSONAL	ENTERTAINMENT/LEISURE
Primary Goods	Electromedical, X-ray equipment Medicinal, pharmaceutical products# Note: Relatively few industries in this sector were isolated in 1971. The U.S. was a leader.	Cigars & tobacco, manufactured# *Cigarettes*	*Photochemical products* Photo film, excl. developed cinema Developed cinema film Children's picture books, maps, etc.# Printed books, pamphlets Newspapers, printed music, postcards# Recording media, musical instruments
Machinery			
Specialty Inputs		*Tobacco, unmanufactured* Essential oil, perfume	
Services		*Secondary & university education****	*Hotels & hotel management** *Car rental & leasing** *Cinema film production** *Television program production**

A number of points should be kept in mind when considering Figure 7–2. First, the trade classification system in use in 1971 was a good deal more aggregated (and therefore less satisfactory) than an updated version which first appeared in 1976. A second important consideration is foreign direct investment (FDI). As of 1971, the extent of foreign investment by U.S. firms was extremely high compared to other nations. U.S. export shares understate U.S. international strength, particularly in consumer packaged goods and services. Where data allowed, I added additional industries reflecting areas of significant foreign investment. FDI data except at aggregate levels are scarce for 1971, however, and the FDI adjustments I could make for 1971 are less complete than were possible for 1985.

Figure 7–3 provides summary calculations of the share of the nation's exports represented by competitive industries (those exceeding the cutoff) in each broad cluster, with additional detail provided in Figure B–1. Also calculated is the share of total world cluster exports accounted for by competitive U.S. industries classified to the cluster. While these calculations are much less illuminating than those possible with more recent data, they do illustrate many of the areas of U.S. strength.

FACTOR CONDITIONS

The explanations for America's areas of success begin with factor conditions. The United States has been well endowed with natural factors of production, among them an exceptionally large supply of arable land, abundant forests, and indigenous deposits of many resources such as phosphate, copper, iron ore, coal, oil, and natural gas. America stands alone among nations, with the possible exception of Sweden, in possessing abundant natural resources *and* achieving a significant international position in sophisticated manufactured goods. Canada and Australia, other nations with abundant resources, have largely failed to move beyond them.

Though important then and still so today, however, the uniqueness of the United States has not only been its inherited resources. The mechanisms in place to create and upgrade factors were, with few exceptions, second to none. There were singularly large and sustained investments over decades in upgrading the quality of factors.

World War II represented an investment in factor creation of unprecedented scale, driven by the spur of a national emergency. The war stimulated a major research effort and breathtaking advances in many fields. Huge investments in core technologies such as electronics, aerospace, synthetic materials, health care, and nuclear energy marked a breakthrough for America in technology. This research effort, continued in the 1950s and 1960s, put the United States in the lead in many fields of basic science and technology that could be applied to many industries. The buildup also extended to infrastructure. The two combined to give the United States the world's premier engineering and construction industry by the end of the war.

Production technology was also pushed to new heights during the war under pressure to boost output. The United States emerged from the war well entrenched as the leader in mass production technology. The war effort also contributed to human resource development. Millions of military personnel learned discipline and were trained in important skills, among them aviation and electronics, and later entered industry.

A few examples will illustrate how investments in factor creation translated into leading industries. Bell Laboratories research, heavily funded by govern-

FIGURE 7–3 Percentage of 1971 U.S. Exports of Competitive Industries by Broad Cluster

Cluster	Share of Country Exports	Share of World Cluster Exports
UPSTREAM INDUSTRIES	**13.3**	**5.9**
Materials/Metals	2.9	3.1
Forest Products	2.1	7.1
Petroleum/Chemicals	6.1	6.4
Semiconductors/Computers	2.2	33.9
INDUSTRIAL AND SUPPORTING FUNCTIONS	**38.7**	**19.5**
Multiple Business	9.0	15.9
Transportation	21.1	20.9
Power Generation & Distribution	5.0	21.1
Office	2.5	25.3
Telecommunications	1.1	17.3
Defense	0.0	0.0
FINAL CONSUMPTION GOODS AND SERVICES	**20.9**	**7.5**
Food/Beverage	14.4	12.1
Textiles/Apparel	2.0	2.7
Housing/Household	0.2	0.9
Health Care	0.7	8.6
Personal	1.7	10.1
Entertainment/Leisure	1.9	1.3

▨ Identifies broad sectors in which the nation's international competitive positions are related.

ment, led to the development of the transistor in 1948. Tektronix, a world leader, along with Hewlett-Packard and other U.S. firms in test and measurement equipment for electronic products, was founded by two ex-military radio technicians. They saw a need for better measuring instruments to improve the ability to design sophisticated electronic gear. Timex, which was to become the world leader in unit sales of wristwatches by the end of the 1950s, applied new materials developed under government contracts during the war to design a revolutionary new watch that was accurate and reliable despite very low cost.

World War II (as World War I before it) yielded other benefits in terms of the nation's scientific base. The war spurred sectors such as chemicals and pharmaceuticals to new heights. Large-scale synthetic rubber and penicillin manufacturing processes were developed to meet wartime needs. Research expenditures in chemicals and pharmaceuticals increased dramatically. The quality of chemical education in the United States came to rival that of any other nation. American companies were able to enter foreign markets from which German companies were excluded. German assets (including GAF and the nucleus of the present Schering-Plough Company), patents, and trademarks were confiscated and sold to American firms.

In addition to patents and assets, the United States enjoyed an influx of some of the world's best minds in science, education, and many other fields. Many outstanding scientists came to the United States and went on to become U.S. citizens. Operation Paperclip, for example, was an air force program initiated in 1944 to bring German scientists into the United States. It later sought to specifically recruit aircraft engineers and scientists. One result was the F-86 Sabre Jet Fighter, which drew heavily on German designs. The United States continued to attract top talent during the postwar period, lured by economic opportunity, access to education, and favorable taxation.

Factor creation did not stop after the war. The GI Bill (legislation providing benefits to war veterans) paid the cost of further education and training for many millions of returning service personnel. Major investments in education occurred through the 1960s. The American education system was of high quality and set demanding standards. A mark of the quality of American education was the number of foreign students coming to the United States, especially at the university level. Sustained investment by government opened higher education to more and more people. The result was that U.S. workers, engineers, and managers were among the most skilled in the world. Education was widely viewed as essential to advancement. Parents worked hard so that their children could go to college.

Strong research universities, a tradition of federal investment in research, and numerous corporate research laboratories provided a strong scientific base. In agriculture, for example, a highly developed network of agricultural universities, an active research program, and effective technology diffusion mechanisms such as the Agricultural Extension Service underpinned sustained productivity growth.

A growing number of both private and public colleges and universities, all with government support, not only provided education but became the bedrock of U.S. research capability. Federal spending on basic research grew to be by far the largest of any nation in the world. The challenge of Sputnik and the cold war provided continuing stimulus to investment in research. They called forth not only major efforts to train more engineers and scientists, but a national commitment to master space. In 1973, the number of university degrees granted per capita in natural sciences and engineering, as well as doctoral degrees in these two areas, was significantly higher in the United States than in Germany, the nation that came closest to America in scientific and technical prowess.[6] Partly out of the national research effort, through unparalleled investment, came leading positions in such industries as aerospace, semiconductors, medical equipment, and computers.

The United States also enjoyed a well-developed infrastructure. Transportation and communications were advanced, a necessity in such a large, spread-out country. The fact that communications, power generation, and transportation companies in the United States were privately owned was a stimulus to investment and innovation. American infrastructure was arguably the most advanced in the world. Infrastructure continued to be developed to a high level, through such programs as the interstate highway system and large-scale investments by AT&T.

Finally, a huge pool of investment capital had accumulated in the United States, allocated by the world's most fluid capital markets. Capital was widely available. Large amounts of capital could be mobilized for promising investments. Interest rates were low. As shown in Tables 7–3 and 7–4, long-term interest rates were either the lowest of any of the nations we studied or a close second to Switzerland in the 1950s and early 1960s. A long-term perspective by investors was encouraged by the favorable tax treatment of long-term capital gains. Pension funds which traded actively were minor market participants. Financial instruments were uncomplicated.[7]

American firms did not face an entirely benign factor environment, and selective disadvantages served useful purposes. Scarcity or unavailability of materials had spurred breakthroughs in new materials during the war effort. The real wages of workers and managers in the United States were very high in the early postwar period compared to those in other nations. Wages grew rapidly throughout the 1950s and 1960s. U.S. firms moved aggressively to automate production and find ways of reducing labor content, building on traditional American strength in mass production that had been honed by production pressures during the war.

TABLE 7–3 Nominal Long-Term Interest Rates for Selected Nations,* 1950–1987

Nation	1950	1955	1960	1965	1970	1975	1978	1979	1980	1981	1982	1983	1984	1985	1986	1987
Denmark	4.53%	5.55%	5.76%	7.35%	10.57%	13.10%	14.54%	15.82%	17.66%	18.92%	20.39%	14.46%	13.93%	12.01%	10.76%	11.19%
Germany	—	—	6.40%	7.10%	8.30%	8.50%	5.80%	7.40%	8.50%	10.38%	8.95%	7.89%	7.78%	6.87%	5.92%	5.84%
Italy	5.73%	6.20%	5.01%	6.94%	9.01%	11.54%	13.70%	14.05%	16.11%	20.58%	20.90%	18.02%	14.95%	13.00%	10.52%	9.65%
Japan	—	—	—	—	7.19%	9.20%	6.09%	7.69%	9.22%	8.66%	8.06%	7.42%	6.81%	6.34%	4.94%	4.21%
Korea	—	—	—	—	—	21.10%	21.60%	25.20%	28.80%	23.60%	17.40%	13.10%	14.30%	13.60%	11.60%	12.40%
Sweden	3.11%	3.70%	5.19%	6.18%	7.39%	8.79%	10.09%	10.47%	11.74%	13.49%	13.04%	12.30%	12.28%	13.09%	10.26%	—
Switzerland	2.67%	2.93%	3.09%	3.95%	5.82%	6.44%	3.33%	3.45%	4.77%	5.57%	4.83%	4.52%	4.70%	4.78%	4.29%	4.12%
U.K.	3.00%	4.32%	5.77%	6.56%	9.22%	14.39%	12.47%	12.99%	13.79%	14.74%	12.88%	10.81%	10.69%	10.62%	9.87%	9.48%
U.S.	—	2.82%	4.12%	4.28%	7.35%	7.99%	8.41%	9.44%	11.46%	13.91%	13.00%	11.11%	12.52%	10.62%	7.68%	8.38%

SOURCE: *International Financial Statistics: Yearbook for 1988.*

* Yields on long-term government bonds. These are also a proxy for interest rates on other debt instruments.

TABLE 7–4 Real Long-Term Interest Rates for Selected Nations,* 1965–1987

Nation	1965	1970	1975	1978	1979	1980	1981	1982	1983	1984	1985	1986	1987
Denmark	−0.08%	2.06%	0.60%	4.26%	7.65%	8.71%	8.03%	8.89%	6.34%	7.83%	6.45%	6.30%	5.91%
Germany	3.38%	0.66%	2.37%	1.43%	3.26%	3.54%	6.12%	4.39%	4.48%	5.70%	4.55%	2.74%	3.75%
Italy	2.63%	2.01%	−5.08%	−0.15%	−1.59%	−3.76%	1.73%	4.06%	2.61%	3.24%	3.74%	2.79%	3.81%
Japan	—	0.22%	−0.34%	4.24%	5.45%	4.11%	4.12%	4.85%	5.41%	3.94%	2.63%	2.30%	0.17%
Korea	—	—	−2.82%	−0.01%	4.32%	2.83%	7.06%	10.11%	8.82%	10.10%	9.15%	8.72%	8.44%
Sweden	0.18%	1.96%	−4.56%	0.49%	2.34%	0.02%	3.68%	4.03%	2.36%	4.27%	5.94%	2.98%	—
Switzerland	0.15%	1.06%	−0.65%	−0.27%	1.43%	2.01%	−1.26%	−2.29%	1.16%	1.86%	2.02%	0.44%	1.60%
United Kingdom	1.37%	1.77%	−10.02%	1.05%	−1.32%	−4.85%	2.96%	4.93%	4.94%	6.13%	4.75%	6.06%	4.38%
United States	1.81%	1.43%	−1.71%	1.04%	0.47%	2.11%	4.06%	6.14%	7.48%	8.63%	7.70%	4.97%	5.17%

SOURCES: *International Financial Statistics: Yearbook for 1988;* OECD: National Accounts 1960–1987. The World Bank: World Tables 1988–89 Edition.

* Real interest rates are calculated by dividing the yield on long term government bonds by the annual change in the GDP price deflator. In the case of Korea the GNP price deflator was used.

This combination of circumstances gave the United States the broadest, deepest, and most advanced array of factors of production of any nation in the world. Sustained investment in factor creation by government, by industry, and by individuals led to a continued upgrading of the factor pool. The foundation for an equally continuous upgrading of American industry was laid.

As unique as they were, however, U.S. factor conditions did not explain the range of advanced industries in which the United States had national competitive advantage. The entire "diamond" favored the United States in the 1950s and 1960s and meant that the pool of factors was mobilized in innovative and productive ways.

DEMAND CONDITIONS

The role of factor conditions in the upgrading of U.S. industry was overshadowed in many ways in the 1960s by American demand conditions. Many have cited the size of the U.S. home market as a strength. Yet the sheer size of the U.S. market often deterred American companies from looking abroad, limiting international success.

More important than the size of the U.S. market was its composition, even before World War II. The United States was the first mass consumption society, at a time when Europe and Japan were still coping with scarcity and emphasizing necessities. With an orientation toward mass production, American companies pioneered the introduction of low-cost, standardized, mass-marketed products in many industries. A typical example is chocolate. While most foreign firms were relatively small and the leading Swiss firms emphasized quality and exclusivity, Hershey, M&M/Mars, Reese's, and Whitman's were mass-producing and mass-marketing mid-priced chocolate bars.[8] As early as the beginning of the twentieth century, Hershey had sought to produce chocolate in such high volumes as to lower its costs and make it accessible to every American.

This concept was taken one step further to produce products that were disposable. Americans were affluent and placed a high value on convenience. Products were created or popularized that could be thrown away after use— paper towels, pens, and even watches (Timex).

Affluence also meant that the United States was an early and advanced market for many other types of consumer goods.[9] The move to suburbia and the high penetration of single-family homes meant cutting-edge demand for new appliances, cars, air-conditioning, lawn care products, and countless others. Black & Decker, for example, achieved world leadership in power tools on the strength of low-priced, mass-marketed tools targeted at the do-it-yourself homeowner. Black & Decker pioneered this entire segment in Europe, where higher-priced tools designed for tradesmen had been the norm.

Affluence, shortening workweeks, and less concern with tradition meant that many products oriented toward convenience and enjoyment of leisure time were pioneered or popularized in the United States. Movies and records became major American exports. So did sports equipment and color television. Photographic equipment and supplies also were an area of U.S. strength, but especially in "point and shoot," mass-marketed products for amateur photographers.

America was a potent incubator for consumer service industries. With high incomes, a convenience-oriented lifestyle, and a consumer willingness to accept self-service and less personal attention, services in the United States were amenable to systematization and standardization (see Chapter 6). Multi-unit service companies emerged in fields such as fast food and convenience stores to spread new concepts nationwide and ultimately overseas. Branding and heavy advertising were applied to services to create the first real mass-marketed services of any nation.

America was also in the vanguard in the development of mass distribution channels. Their early emergence stimulated still further innovations in consumer products. America also pioneered a steady stream of new concepts in retailing. Many spread to other nations, but U.S. firms were the first to understand and respond to them.

Not only did demand for many new types and varieties of consumer goods originate in America, but many of the techniques of modern marketing were pioneered there as well. Privately owned mass media, including radio and television, were vehicles for the first truly large-scale mass advertising.[10] Commercial television, for example, was introduced in America twelve years before the next nation. The absence of restrictions on advertising, especially television advertising, fostered marketing innovation. American companies developed unique skills in image building for mass-consumed products, in industries such as soft drinks, detergents, toiletries, toothpaste, cosmetics, cleansers, and other consumer packaged goods. These skills were transferred abroad, and American brand names became household words around the world.

Demand advantages in the United States extended to industrial goods. American companies producing industrial or commercial products and services benefited from selling to many of the world's most sophisticated and advanced buyers, other U.S. companies. The breadth of the U.S. economy particularly benefited industries that served many other industries (multiple business on the cluster chart), such as business services and pumps. The United States, with its varied climate, terrain, and array of industries, exposed companies to a wide range of market needs and segments within the nation's borders. American firms gained skills in meeting the range of needs that would be encountered in many other nations.

American industrial demand was a forerunner of world demand in many industries. Automation, computerization, the introduction of electronics, new plastics materials, and many other cutting-edge developments first took place in the United States in the 1950s and early 1960s. Selling at home to the world's leading manufacturing companies, U.S. firms achieved international preeminence in many types of capital goods and production equipment sold to industry, among them machine tools, industrial process controls, and heating, ventilation, and cooling equipment.

Some examples of sophisticated U.S. industrial home demand are in the energy and construction sectors. Exploration for energy inside the United States was intensive because the industry had begun early in America and the nation had large energy needs. The continued search for oil in more difficult locations led to rapid advancements in technology. American oil companies and suppliers to the industry became world leaders. In construction, U.S. firms pioneered the large high-rise building and other innovations in building techniques. This, in turn, prompted innovations in air-conditioning, elevators, and other construction-related products and services, and frequently led to world leadership.

Sophisticated domestic demand also resulted from a well-funded health care system in which purchasing decisions were decentralized to the many independent U.S. hospitals and health care providers. This structure provided a fertile environment for innovation, in contrast to other nations where health care was government owned or heavily regulated. American firms became leaders in a wide variety of health-related fields.

Demand at home in a number of U.S. industries also benefited from the largely private ownership of telecommunications providers, electric and gas utilities, liquor and tobacco companies, and virtually all other important industries. Private owners, with independence and a profit motive, were often more forward looking and sophisticated buyers than the government monopolies typical in other nations. Finally, defense demand was an early stimulus to a range of important U.S. industries, among them semiconductors, computers, software, and aerospace.

Internationalization of U.S. Demand. Despite major advantages from home demand conditions, American firms could hardly be said to have pushed their way into international markets. Many were content to focus on the large home market. Instead, American firms were often *pulled* into foreign markets to fill the vacuum created after World War II by strong foreign demand coupled with the near absence of foreign competitors, who were just becoming established or preoccupied with rebuilding.

Growing international dominance of many important industries, coupled with lingering protectionism, led to a wave of large-scale foreign investment by American companies. Caterpillar, for example, initially moved to overseas production in the 1950s not to lower cost but because of tariffs and import restrictions. American companies soon became the world's largest foreign investors. In countries such as Germany and Britain, American overseas subsidiaries became leading industrial companies. Overseas subsidiaries boosted sales even further through establishing a local market presence. The international strength of U.S. multinationals was self-reinforcing. One U.S. industry pulled through demand for the products and services of other U.S. industries.

Affluent American tourists also traveled abroad in large numbers, as did American businesspeople. They provided a ready base of overseas postwar demand for U.S. companies in industries such as fast food, hotels, car rental, and numerous other services. The sheer numbers of Americans traveling (and living) abroad made this a significant advantage.

A final demand-side advantage of U.S. industry was the extent to which U.S. culture and values were transmitted abroad. The English language was solidified as the international business language. The weight of the U.S. economy was one important reason, as was the amount of technical and other literature written in English. Many foreigners were educated in the United States and brought back to their home countries a bias for U.S. goods. As discussed in Chapter 5, for example, an important benefit to U.S. health care firms was the large number of doctors trained in America. Finally, American movies, publications, television shows, and advertising agencies transmitted American styles, values, and needs abroad.

                              *   *   *

The cumulative effect of these demand conditions was an enormous source of competitive advantage in countless U.S. industries. Home demand was large, early, varied, and sophisticated. American needs often anticipated, if not defined, foreign demand. Internationalizing U.S. firms, mobile individuals, and the postwar demand/supply imbalance in foreign nations drew American companies into foreign markets. The base was laid for success in many of the industries in which American firms are still leaders. At the same time, unique demand conditions supported innovation and upgrading in established industries and the pioneering of new industries.

RELATED AND SUPPORTING INDUSTRIES

Widespread clustering of competitive industries was present throughout the United States economy. The presence of internationally successful end products, parts, machinery, and service industries could be found in fields such as automobiles, aircraft, energy, power generation, mining, and construction. Emerging and established clusters were often concentrated in one or two geographic areas: autos around Detroit, electronics in Silicon Valley, main-frame computers in Minneapolis and New York, minicomputers in Boston, oil field equipment and services in Houston, and pharmaceuticals and medical products in the corridor between New York and Philadelphia. American companies had to look no further than home to find technology and suppliers. While American firms were not notable in their working relationships with local suppliers and customers, the sheer breadth of world-class industries present in the United States was a major advantage in innovation and new business formation.

American industry also benefited from leading positions in a number of industries that, perhaps more than any others, touched many other industries. One was electronics. This important new technology was to have some impact on virtually every aspect of the economy. The large U.S. lead in electronics meant that American firms had access to not only technical interchange with the best suppliers but to a growing pool of trained personnel. Another important supporting industry was machine tools, where a lead in mass production technology and sophisticated home demand from industrial customers had made American firms the world leaders. A third important supporting industry was plastics, a new material used in countless other products. A final vital supporting industry that developed somewhat later was computers, along with its cousin software. The U.S. preeminence in this field also began to benefit countless other industries.

America also possessed an unparalleled set of supporting industries in modern marketing. American advertising agencies were at the cutting edge and became dominant world leaders. American media were the most advanced and least regulated. American companies rode marketing savvy to leadership in many industries, even if their products were not outstanding.

One symbol of clustering in the American economy is the industries producing products connected to defense. Consisting of industries in aero-space, electronics, communications, and transportation, this cluster has some-times been portrayed as sinister. At the time, however, it produced a dazzling array of innovative new products and services, and put men on the moon.

FIRM STRATEGY, STRUCTURE, AND RIVALRY

American companies became adept at creating standardized, mass-produced products and services, and marketing them aggressively. Leadership was won in many industries where products had previously been customized, production had previously been handcrafted, and marketing had previously been low-key. The techniques for managing large-scale enterprises were largely pioneered in the United States beginning in the late nineteenth century, with many new techniques developed in the 1940s, 1950s, and 1960s.

Companies drew on a large pool of talent that flowed into industry. Industry was an honorable and prestigious calling in postwar America. Outstanding people joined American corporations and started new ones.

Motivation among American workers and managers was high. Marginal tax rates were low compared to other nations. More importantly, American society was relatively open. Many who tried for betterment and were willing to take risks could succeed. The diversity of the American people, reflecting a large number of immigrants seeking to improve their lot, also encouraged risk taking; people who had uprooted themselves to come to America were risk takers.

Corporate goals reflected a sense of limitless opportunity. Interest rates were among the lowest of any nation, encouraging investment to boost productivity. (Massive wartime investments meant that many American industries had modern facilities.) Individuals owned the majority of corporate equities. The rate of trading was modest by modern standards, and most equity was committed for long periods. Bankers and large investors were more typical on corporate boards. Large amounts of capital were available and could be mobilized to fund companies with good ideas.

Underlying the goals of both individuals and companies was confidence. America had won the war and made many scientific breakthroughs. A "can do" attitude was a powerful force that propelled Americans to try new things and accept tough challenges.

Competition, combined with these goals and attitudes, was what in many ways most set America apart. America was built on competition. There was active domestic rivalry in most important U.S. industries. Several if not dozens of competitors contested the market and pushed each other to advance. American antitrust laws, particularly tough on monopolization, mergers, and price fixing, reflected a national consensus for competition.[11] American rivalry stood in stark contrast to cartelized Europe and undeveloped and protected Asia.

One result of American goals, values, and capital market conditions was an exceptional climate in the United States for new business formation. Honest failure was socially acceptable, part of the American sympathy for the underdog. Cultural diversity meant that there were many "outsiders" ready to challenge prevailing norms. Start-ups and spin-offs populated most industries, feeding rivalry even more. Internal development was the source of most new businesses, and the number of mergers and acquisitions was modest.

THE ROLE OF GOVERNMENT

Government policy in the United States reflected a nation with strong and growing national advantage. The extent of direct intervention in industry was among the lowest in the world. Public ownership was rare, in contrast to a more socialist orientation that especially characterized Europe.

Instead, the American government played a number of indirect roles in industry. One was that of factor creator. Investments in education, science, and infrastructure were heavy and continuous, and involved state and local governments as well as the federal government. Another important government role was as protector of competition. America maintained a vigorous antitrust policy, championed a free and open trading system, and took important steps to reduce cartelization and economic concentration abroad, especially in Germany and Japan.

The American government also set out aggressively and in some cases earlier than other nations to meet a series of challenges and in the process created important indirect benefits for industry: space exploration, equal opportunity, health care, and environmental protection. The U.S. government also sought to promote and defend American interests and democracy abroad. These roles, which would take on greater significance as the decades passed, would come to override the needs of industry.

Finally, a large defense program was instrumental in promoting science and in creating advanced home demand. In the 1940s, 1950s, and 1960s, defense research centered on core technologies such as electronics, computers, and aerospace. Commercial spin-offs were numerous and rapid. With a huge technological lead in fields serving defense and aerospace markets, U.S. companies often exploited their knowledge and experience to establish leading positions in civilian markets.

It may be most notable, however, that explicit American government attention to industry was modest. While government policy yielded benefits that flowed to industry, these were rarely the primary motivating force. Instead, American economic strength was used to advance other goals.

THE ROLE OF CHANCE

By far the most significant chance event affecting U.S. national advantage was World War II. While the United States was already an international leader in many industries (such as autos, steel, and electrical generating equipment) by 1920, it is hard to overstate the significance of the war in allowing U.S. industry to achieve widespread preeminence in international competition.

Wartime pressures led to massive levels of research in vital new technologies and to major advances in production methods. Some companies became established internationally through the war effort. Coca-Cola, for example, set up bottling operations around the world to supply American troops, in response to a request by General Eisenhower designed to boost morale. Caterpillar went international because machines used by American military engineers were left abroad when hostilities stopped. The demand for spare parts provided the initial impetus for what was to become a preeminent global strategy.

American industry was left intact after the war, while the industrial bases of other leading nations were devastated. More U.S. firms were pulled abroad, as pressing foreign demand overcame any hesitation in many companies to export and later invest overseas. While the rest of the world was preoccupied for some time with obtaining the most basic and necessary products and services, the United States was already the world's most sophisticated and affluent market.

THE UNITED STATES IN PERSPECTIVE

The United States in the early postwar period represented the continuation of a potent, self-reinforcing system for creating and upgrading competitive advantage in an enormous range of industries that had been put in place many years earlier. From an improving base of well-developed and advanced factors of production, and powered by cutting-edge demand conditions, competitive advantage in one U.S. industry begat competitive advantage in others. The American economy was truly a leading indicator of where the world economy was going and became the world's center of innovation. American firms reaped early mover advantages that would persist for decades. Upgrading of the economy was continuous, and foreign direct investment transferred lower-productivity activities overseas and led to a growing stream of repatriated profits from abroad.

The result was a high and rising standard of living, accumulating national wealth, low levels of unemployment, and the capacity to make large social investments in areas such as foreign aid, defense, space exploration, cultural life, and equal opportunity. These activities, in turn, stimulated yet more demand for new, cutting-edge goods and services.

As I have explored the reasons underlying the extraordinary American success, however, one question looms. Was it all too easy? America *began* the postwar period with a level of per capita income far above other nations. The war weighed so heavily in widening America's industrial success. The sheer scale of the United States and its breadth of industries conferred advantages with little need to develop them aggressively. The vacuum in overseas markets made American companies successful international competitors without any real opposition, except political. The technological breakthroughs resulting from the war, combined with high levels of postwar spending, conferred advantages in many U.S. industries that could be maintained even if new technology was slow to be commercialized. American plants were so modern that a low rate of investment was sufficient. American demand was so uniquely advanced that American companies gained early mover advantages that would preserve their competitive positions for decades through inertia. Finally, America's natural resource abundance was so great that it alone could support substantial exports.

The data I presented in Table 7–1 provide some important signs that all was not well in the upgrading of American industry. A low rate of net capital investment, disappointing productivity growth, and slow rate of growth in per capita income relative to other nations all date back to the 1950s.[12] Moreover, population growth greater than that in any other advanced nation fueled GDP growth without the need to rapidly increase productivity.

Was American confidence misplaced? Did America emerge from the 1960s as an environment in which many industries could renew and regenerate themselves? Were American companies too preeminent and too complacent? These questions will serve as a useful backdrop against which to examine the postwar economic development of other leading nations. I will return to them when I examine the American economy in the 1970s and 1980s in Chapter 9. More recent decades present a rather different story.

STABLE SWITZERLAND[13]

America was not the only success story, though it was the largest one. Switzerland and Sweden, both tiny by American standards, achieved remarkable prosperity and sophistication that challenged the United States in some industries.

Switzerland had been a poor nation as late as the nineteenth century. Among its major exports were mercenaries and emigrating citizens. By the early decades of the twentieth century, Switzerland had emerged as an industrial nation of importance far beyond its small size. In the postwar period, Switzerland was one of the richest of nations. By the 1960s, using some measures, Swiss per capita income was the highest in the world.

Swiss prosperity is the result of national competitive advantage in a surprisingly wide range of advanced manufacturing and service industries for a small nation. Industrial success has been enough to more than employ all available Swiss citizens at high wages (total Swiss unemployment in many years has been less than 200 people) as well as many guest workers. Swiss companies, among them Nestlé, Hoffmann-LaRoche, Sandoz, Ciba-Geigy, Schindler, Landis and Gyr, and Lindt and Sprüngli, are among the most global of any nation. The leading Swiss multinationals employ far more people outside of the country than in Switzerland. The Swiss case vividly illustrates how a small nation, without a large home market as in Japan or America, can nevertheless be a successful global competitor in many important industries. Switzerland is also an economy that has continually upgraded itself to support a rising standard of living.

PATTERNS OF SWISS COMPETITIVE ADVANTAGE

Table 7–5 lists the top fifty Swiss industries in 1985 in terms of world export share. The list includes a remarkably diverse set of industries for a small nation, though virtually none is dependent on natural resources.[14] The list includes both consumer and industrial goods, along with many types of machinery and instruments. A number of the industries, including precious stones, coins, and metals, appear on the list because of Switzerland's strong position in trading, not because of local production. The top fifty industries in terms of export share account for 42.4 percent of total Swiss exports. This figure falls to 37.6 percent if the traded goods are eliminated and the next ranking industries substituted. The figure is lower than nations such as Japan and Korea and is indicative of the wide range of Swiss market positions.[15]

In Switzerland, as in virtually all the nations, industries with high export share which signals the presence of competitive advantage account for the major part of export trade. Table B-2 shows the top fifty Swiss industries in terms of export value. Twenty-nine of the fifty leaders in terms of value are also among the top fifty in terms of export share, and nearly all the others have world export shares several times the Swiss cutoff. Only one industry that makes the top fifty value list falls below the cutoff in terms of world export share. I will concentrate on the export share data in my discussions of each nation, because it is more representative of the industries where the nation has a competitive advantage and these industries account for a large fraction of both trade and foreign investment.

The breadth of the Swiss economy is revealed more fully in Figure 7–4, a profile of all the internationally competitive industries in the Swiss economy in 1985. Figure 7–4 is the first of a series of cluster charts using 1985 data, a good deal more disaggregated to specific product areas and thereby more closely reflecting strategically distinct industries than data available in 1971. Figure 7–4 contains adjustments to reflect foreign investment and to incorporate competitive industries identified during the research that do not show up separately in the trade classifications, as described more fully in Appendix A.

For each nation, the detailed 1985 export data were used to make a number of summary calculations of the pattern of exports. The results of those for Switzerland are given in Figure 7–5 (more detailed data is shown in Figure B-2). Figure 7–5 shows the distribution by broad cluster of the exports of competitive Swiss industries (defined as those whose world

TABLE 7–5 **Top Fifty Swiss Industries in Terms of World Export Share, 1985**

Industry	Share of Total World Exports	Export Value ($ millions)	Import Value ($ millions)	Share of Total Swiss Exports
Rough, unsorted diamonds	89.3	303,694	15,548	1.10
Nongold, noncurrent coins	46.3	140,561	24,491	0.51
Weaving machines (looms)	45.1	361,864	11,671	1.32
Platen printing presses	37.2	15,586	537	0.06
Watches	34.1	1,413,763	47,464	5.14
Vegetable alkaloids and derivatives	32.0	152,366	8,588	0.55
Amide compounds excluding urea	26.6	321,689	34,613	1.17
Textured yarn, containing polyamide	25.9	212,011	36,925	0.77
Synthetic organic dyestuffs	25.3	664,318	211,208	2.42
Looms, knitting machines and parts	24.1	181,030	38,107	0.66
Precious metals, jewelry, pearls	23.9	230,464	65,241	0.84
Provitamins and vitamins	21.9	191,703	74,055	0.70
Herbicides	20.6	275,488	24,629	1.00
Fans, blowers, and parts	19.2	180,650	87,975	0.66
Electromechanical hand tools	17.6	228,209	48,674	0.83
Clocks with watch movements	17.3	151,578	89,838	0.55
Mixed perfume substances	17.2	194,333	22,396	0.71
Surveying instruments	16.2	79,018	13,637	0.29
Parts of textile processing machines	16.0	115,147	21,044	0.42
Hearing, orthopedic aids	15.9	151,006	37,710	0.55
Metalcutting machine tools	15.3	424,457	55,467	1.54
Precious, semiprecious stones	15.2	168,344	210,450	0.61
Paper product manufacturing machines	14.1	120,311	16,221	0.44
Heterocyclic compounds	14.0	696,186	245,601	2.53
Textile extruding, processing machines	13.9	79,438	4,542	0.29
Rolled platinum, platinum metals	13.6	158,800	90,900	0.58
Lace, ribbons, tulle	13.2	138,244	22,026	0.50
Clocks, clock and watch parts	13.0	210,745	83,206	0.77
Medicaments containing hormones	12.3	961,084	246,227	3.50
Metal reaming, etc., machines	12.3	109,340	30,852	0.40

TABLE 7-5 (*Continued*)

Industry	Share of Total World Exports	Export Value ($ millions)	Import Value ($ millions)	Share of Total Swiss Exports
Textiles for machinery	11.4	98,334	26,257	0.36
Meters and counters	11.1	52,761	9,145	0.19
Oxygen-function amino compounds	10.8	212,415	69,353	0.77
Typesetting, bookbinding machinery, parts	10.5	215,268	59,212	0.78
Hand paintings	10.3	169,447	121,838	0.62
Optical instruments	9.9	169,289	65,462	0.62
Oxygen-function acids, derivatives	9.6	84,020	25,579	0.31
Spinning, reeling, etc., machines	9.6	80,521	12,182	0.29
Cut, unset nonindustrial diamonds	9.6	585,833	909,277	2.13
Other metalworking machine tools	9.5	314,943	85,821	1.15
Steel, copper nails and nuts	9.4	66,542	12,083	0.24
Aluminum foil	9.3	115,170	26,552	0.42
Steam engines, turbines	9.1	117,114	12,752	0.43
Other organic, inorganic compounds	8.8	68,273	36,218	0.25
Refined petroleum products	8.7	58,789	5,533	0.21
Office supplies	8.6	65,019	25,245	0.24
Non-outboard marine piston engines	8.5	60,860	2,364	0.22
Glycosides, glands, sera	8.2	93,610	47,984	0.34
Precious metal jewelry	8.1	372,719	531,262	1.36
Pearls worked and unworked	8.0	27,662	256,697	0.10
TOTAL				42.44

NOTE: No import data are reported if import value is less than 0.3 percent of the total trade for 1985.

export share exceeds the average Swiss share of world exports). Also shown is the share that competitive Swiss industries represent of total world exports in the broad cluster. The latter is approximated by assigning all SITC industries to broad clusters (which we term the world cluster chart) and comparing Swiss exports to total cluster exports.[16] The figures in parentheses represent the changes since 1978. Note that these statistics do not cover all Swiss exports, but only those of competitive industries as I have defined them. While Switzerland may be competitive in some industries falling below

FIGURE 7-4 Clusters of Internationally Competitive Swiss Industries, 1985

	MATERIALS/METALS	FOREST PRODUCTS	PETROLEUM/CHEMICALS	SEMICONDUCTORS/ COMPUTERS
Primary Goods	IRON & STEEL Iron, other steel bars, hotrolled FABRICATED IRON & STEEL Iron, steel tubes, pipes Iron, steel tube fittings METAL MANUFACTURES **Steel, copper nails, nuts#** **Iron, steel nuts, bolts** Base metal manufactures# NONFERROUS METALS *Aluminum powders, tubes, pipes#* *Aluminum structures, parts* *Aluminum bars, wire* Aluminum plate, sheet, strip **Aluminum foil**	WOOD PRODUCTS *Reconstituted wood* PULP *Unbleached pulp** Bleached pulp, nondissolving· PAPER Paper & paperboard, tarred, coated#· Paper and paperboard#	ORGANIC CHEMICALS **Oxyacids, derivatives** *Amine compounds* **Oxyamino compounds** **Amide compounds** **Nitrogen compounds#** **Organosulphur compounds** **Other organic, inorganic compounds#** **Heterocyclic compounds** *Aldehyde compounds* Inorganic esters, organic chemicals# *Phenols, derivatives* OTHER Albuminoid substances, glues· **Reclaimed rubber#** POLYMERS *Copolymers vinylchloride#* *Products of condensation#*	
Machinery	*Foundry molds*	*Paper mill machinery, parts#*		
Specialty Inputs				
Services				

KEY
roman   1.6% world export share or higher, but less than 3.2% share
bold italics   **3.2% world export share or higher, but less than 6.3% share**
sans serif   **6.3% world export share or above**

·   Industries below cutoff in 1978
Calculated residuals
Added due to significant export value in a segmented industry

*   Added due to FDI
**   Upgraded due to FDI
***   Added based on in-country research

FIGURE 7-4 (Continued)

Primary Goods	MULTIPLE BUSINESS			TRANSPORTATION
	TOOLS & EQUIPMENT **Electromechanical hand tools*** *Machine tools for special industries* Other hand tools Central heating equipment# Pumps for liquids# **INSTRUMENTS** Optical instruments Meters & counters Surveying instruments *Measuring, drawing, etc., instruments*	*Measuring, drawing instrument parts#* Gas, liquid control instruments *Measuring, controlling instruments#* **TRADED GOODS** **Rolled platinum, platinum metals*** *Platinum alloys, unwrought* Natural abrasives Precious metal ores, waste *Pearls, synthetic stones#* *Rolled, semi-mfr. silver#*	**Precious metal jewelry** **Other precious jewelry#** **Diamonds, rough, unsorted** Diamonds, simply worked **Diamonds, cut, notset** **Precious, semiprecious stones** **Coins, nature collections** **Coin, nongold, noncurrent*** *Gold, nonmonetary* **Hand paintings, etc.** **Other works of art#**	**ENGINES** **Marine combustion engines#** **other than outboard** **Jet reaction engines** **VEHICLES** *Other railway vehicles#* *Aircraft 2,000–15,000 KG* **OTHER** *Elevators, escalators#* *Aluminum transport boxes#*
Machinery	*Machinery for special industries*# *Other mineral-working machines*# Lathes, metalworking *Converters, rolling mills#* *Metal-cutting machine tools*# Reaming machines, metalworking	**Metal-forming machine tools** **Other metalworking machine tools#** *Gas welders, brazers#* **Electric welders** *Gas generators, furnace burners#* Electric industrial furnaces	**Other nonelectric machinery, parts#** *Spraying machinery#* **Other electrical machines#** **Rubber, plastics-working machines** **Other nonelectric machinery, tools#**	
Specialty Inputs	*Gas, liquid filters* Cocks, valves *Shafts, cranks, pulleys*	*Glazes, driers, putty* *Rubber articles nes#* *Blades, tips for tools*	**Fans, blowers, parts** Mineral manufactures#	**PARTS** *Lifting, loading machinery, parts#* Parts of railway vehicles
Services	*Trading** *Commercial banking** *Money management**	*Reinsurance** *Tourism**** *Customs services****	Management consulting* Security services* Temporary help***	Airlines*** Airport terminal*** Logistics management***

	POWER GENERATION AND DISTRIBUTION	OFFICE	TELECOMMUNICATIONS	DEFENSE
Primary Goods	GENERATION **Steam engines, turbines** **Rotating electric plant**# *Nuclear reactors, parts* DISTRIBUTION *Inductors, etc.*# Liquid dielectric transformers' **Other electric transformers**# *Static converters* *Switchgear* Electric insulating equipment STORAGE Primary batteries, cells *Fixed, variable resistors*	**Trade advertising materials, catalogs** Office supplies# *Cash registers, accounting machines**		DEFENSE
Machinery		Printing, bookbinding machinery, parts# *Rotary printing presses* *Platen printing presses*# Paper product manufacturing machines		
Specialty Inputs		Other coloring matter#		
Services				

KEY

roman   1.6% world export share or higher, but less than 3.2% share

bold italics   *3.2% world export share or higher, but less than 6.3% share*

sans serif   **6.3% world export share or above**

.   Industries below cutoff in 1978

Calculated residuals

Added due to significant export value in a segmented industry

*   Added due to FDI

**   Upgraded due to FDI

***   Added based on in-country research

FIGURE 7-4 *(Continued)*

Primary Goods	FOODS/BEVERAGES	HOUSING/HOUSEHOLD	TEXTILES/APPAREL
	BASIC FOODS *Live bovine, breed*# PROCESSED FOODS **Cheese & curd** Sugar candy nonchocolate *Chocolate & products*** Edible products, preparations Cereals*** Other fancy packaged foods*** EDIBLE OILS Animal oil, fat# BEVERAGES *Nonalcoholic beverages*'	FURNITURE **Metal furniture** *Chairs, seats, parts*# *Furniture of other material*# OTHER HOUSEHOLD PRODUCTS **Cutlery** Soaps, polishes, creams# *Washing preparations*	FABRICS **Grey woven cotton fabric** *Woven cotton, bleached*# *Continuous regenerated weaves, nonpile* Silk fabrics, woven Woven card wool *Woven combed wool, combed fine hair** *Knit natural fabric*# Knit, etc., synthetic fabric' **Lace, ribbons, tulle** Plastic coated textiles OTHER **Textiles for machinery** APPAREL *Dresses, wool, etc.**
Machinery	*Food machinery, nondomestic* **Packaging, bottling machinery** Dairy, agricultural machinery#		*Sewing machines* Sewing machine needles, parts# **Textile extruding, processing machines**# Spinning, reeling machines Weaving machines (looms) Knitting, felt mfg. machines# *Other textile, leather machines*# Loom, knit machines, parts Parts of textile processing machines
Specialty Inputs	**Insecticides** **Herbicides** *Coffee extracts, essences*		FIBERS AND YARNS Discontinuous synthetic fiber, uncombed *Wool, hair yarn** *Other cotton yarn*# *Cotton yarn 40–80 KM/KG* *Cotton linters, waste** *Synthetic fiber waste*# Yarn, textured, containing polyamide *Discontinuous synthetic fiber blend yarn* OTHER **Synthetic organic dyestuffs** *Lub. for textiles*# Raw skins*
Services			

	HEALTH CARE	PERSONAL	ENTERTAINMENT/LEISURE
Primary Goods	PHARMACEUTICALS **Provitamins & vitamins** *Antibiotics in bulk* **Vegetable alkaloids & derivatives** Bulk hormones** Glycotides, glands, sera Medicaments, containing antibiotics** **Medicaments with hormones#** Pharmaceutical goods# MEDICAL EQUIPMENT *Medical instruments* **Hearing, orthopedic aids**	Cigarettes *Combustible products* **Mixed perfume substances** *Perfumery, cosmetics* **Watches** **Clocks with watch movements#** *Clocks, parts* *Fountain pens* *Pen nibs, pencils#*	Cinema cameras, projectors *Photo, cinema apparatus, equipment#* *Children's picture books, globes#*
Machinery			
Specialty Inputs			Photosensitized cloth Photo plates, film#
Services	Health services***	Secondary and university education***	

KEY

roman 1.6% world export share or higher, but less than 3.2% share
bold italics 3.2% *world export share or higher, but less than 6.3% share*
sans serif **6.3% world export share or above**

*	Industries below cutoff in 1978
#	Calculated residuals
##	Added due to significant export value in a segmented industry

*	Added due to FDI
**	Upgraded due to FDI
***	Added based on in-country research

FIGURE 7–5 Percentage of Swiss Exports of Competitive Industries by Broad Cluster

UPSTREAM INDUSTRIES

Materials / Metals
Share of Country Exports: 3.8 (0.1)
Share of World Cluster Exports: 0.7 (−0.0)

Forest Products
Share of Country Exports: 1.0 (0.3)
Share of World Cluster Exports: 0.6 (0.1)

Petroleum / Chemicals
Share of Country Exports: 8.0 (1.2)
Share of World Cluster Exports: 0.6 (0.2)

Semiconductors / Computers
Share of Country Exports: 0 (0.1)
Share of World Cluster Exports: 0 (−0.1)

Share of Country Exports: 12.8 (1.8)
Share of World Cluster Exports: 0.6 (−0.1)

INDUSTRIAL AND SUPPORTING FUNCTIONS

Multiple Business
Share of Country Exports: 28.1 (1.6)
Share of World Cluster Exports: 6.4 (−1.4)

Transportation
Share of Country Exports: 2.1 (−0.4)
Share of World Cluster Exports: 0.5 (−0.1)

Power Generation & Distribution
Share of Country Exports: 4.4 (−0.6)
Share of World Cluster Exports: 2.9 (0.1)

Office
Share of Country Exports: 2.3 (0.1)
Share of World Cluster Exports: 3.8 (−0.8)

Telecommunications
Share of Country Exports: 0 (−0.1)
Share of World Cluster Exports: 0 (−1.0)

Defense
Share of Country Exports: 0 (−0.7)
Share of World Cluster Exports: 0 (−4.3)

Share of Country Exports: 36.9 (0.1)
Share of World Cluster Exports: 2.1 (−0.6)

FINAL CONSUMPTION GOODS AND SERVICES

Food / Beverage
Share of Country Exports: 4.7 (0.1)
Share of World Cluster Exports: 0.6 (−0.0)

Textiles / Apparel
Share of Country Exports: 11.0 (−1.0)
Share of World Cluster Exports: 2.4 (−0.7)

Housing / Household
Share of Country Exports: 0.9 (0.1)
Share of World Cluster Exports: 0.6 (0.1)

Health Care
Share of Country Exports: 7.0 (0.2)
Share of World Cluster Exports: 7.2 (−3.4)

Personal
Share of Country Exports: 8.0 (−2.2)
Share of World Cluster Exports: 4.4 (−1.9)

Entertainment / Leisure
Share of Country Exports: 0.5 (0.1)
Share of World Cluster Exports: 0.2 (0.1)

Share of Country Exports: 32.0 (−2.7)
Share of World Cluster Exports: 1.7 (−0.4)

▨ Identifies broad sectors in which the nation's international competitive positions are related.
▧ Identifies broad sectors in which the nation's international competitive positions are related.

Note: Numbers in parentheses are changes between 1978 and 1985.
Exports are those of competitive industries, not all industries.

the cutoff due to positions in narrow segments, Swiss exports in many industries below the cutoff are likely to reflect border trade, government subsidies, or exports of foreign multinationals based in Switzerland and not Swiss-based competitive advantage. In practice, a large fraction of the trade of each nation is accounted for by competitive industries, and the effect on the shares of world cluster exports of including all industries is minor.

For a nation of only six million people, the range of industries in which Switzerland has a position is extraordinary. They fall into a series of clusters, the number and breadth of which are a good deal greater than in other small nations such as Sweden, Denmark, and Singapore. One of the most important is a cluster of health care related industries, including pharmaceuticals, hearing aids, orthopedic devices, medical instruments, various forms of related machinery, health care services, and health care consulting. Competitive Swiss industries hold a remarkable 7.2 percent of total world exports in this cluster, not to mention the fact that the large Swiss pharmaceuticals companies have extensive foreign investments. Another important cluster is a group of industries related to textiles, including textile fibers, yarns and fabrics, apparel (mostly specialty items), textile machinery, and synthetic dyes. A third important cluster is in internationally oriented general business services, including trading, banking, insurance, temporary help, logistical management, international headquarters, and human resources consulting. A fourth important cluster is highly processed metal products, tools, machine tools, and other equipment for multiple business applications. Another important cluster is in specialty chemicals. Switzerland's 0.6 percent share of world cluster exports in petroleum and chemicals is composed of a negligible share of petroleum-related industries and a 3.4 percent share of total world chemical cluster exports, fourth behind Germany, the United States, and the United Kingdom.

Other significant clusters include processed food products (such as chocolate, cheese, and others), mechanical and optical instruments, printed paper goods and associated machinery, and heavy electrical goods. Switzerland has weak positions in forest products, semiconductors and computers, telecommunications, entertainment and leisure (except tourism), and defense (though much Swiss defense trade, as well as that of other nations, is not captured by the UN statistics).

Swiss strength cuts across all three levels in the cluster chart, to a much greater extent than is the case in Sweden, Denmark, Italy, Korea, and Singapore. Its greatest strength is in the bottom two levels, however. By vertical stage, the Swiss position is unusually strong in machinery for production, which shows up clearly in Figure B-2. The composition of Swiss exports by cluster is quite stable between 1978 and 1985.

Some of the most important links among clusters are illustrated by the shading on Figure 7–5. The Swiss positions in textiles (dyes and synthetic fibers, for example), chemicals, and pharmaceuticals are all connected by history and chemical technology. Similarly, a variety of high-precision multiple business products and equipment are linked to watches, clocks, and other personal products.

The composition of the Swiss economy is like that of the German economy (see below) in a number of respects. Both have strength in chemicals, machinery, machine tools, precision mechanical goods, optical products, and textiles. Switzerland's position in these industries, however, tends to be more specialized and focused on the most sophisticated segments. German companies tend to offer broader lines, though they also usually compete via differentiation. Switzerland's position is much stronger than Germany's in services and in marketing-intensive consumer goods. Germany, in contrast, is strong in materials and transportation equipment where the Swiss position is minor. Both the similarities and differences between the Swiss and German economies are instructive for understanding the sources of national advantage.

SWISS FACTOR CONDITIONS

Switzerland has few natural resources, with the exception of sites for the generation of hydropower and a pleasant landscape that attracts many tourists. However, one natural factor of historical importance is location. Centrally located on major European trade routes, Switzerland became a trading, commercial, and financial center early on. This advantage, plus the early Swiss position in textiles (necessitating silk purchases, among other imports, from the Far East) gave Switzerland a strong position in trading that has never been lost. Banking and insurance also benefited from such a central location and from the Swiss position in trading. Switzerland's location, coupled with a stance of political neutrality, also allowed its firms to maintain commercial contacts with each of the major European power centers (France, Germany, and Great Britain), resulting in numerous benefits that will become apparent.

Switzerland has a highly educated and skilled pool of human resources, who have a positive attitude toward work. Absenteeism is extremely low. Swiss are unique in cultural sophistication and language skills. Because Switzerland is a country with German-, French-, and Italian-speaking areas, many Swiss speak multiple languages (including English) with relative fluency. Swiss banks, for example, take pride in the ability to serve customers in any of four languages from any bank branch. Accustomed to a society with multiple cultures and with a social philosophy of compromise and accommodation, Swiss employees and managers can work effectively inside and outside of Switzerland with people of many nationalities. In industries such as trading and those involving intricate foreign sales and service, these assets have carried considerable weight.

Switzerland has long had a high savings rate. It also has attracted foreign capital because of a strong currency, political stability, neutrality, and bank secrecy laws. The combination results in Swiss interest rates that are low and stable compared to all nations. As shown previously in Table 7–3, to which I will return again when discussing other nations, Swiss interest rates are consistently the lowest of the other nations we studied. As a result, Swiss companies are aggressive capital investors and use a low discount rate in evaluating investments. Switzerland is also a large net lender to the rest of the world.

Swiss infrastructure is well developed, especially in logistics-related fields such as airport services, roads, and railroads. There are some exceptions, however, notably in telecommunications. There, the state monopoly has proven to be a disadvantage due to high costs and its tendency to grant a guaranteed market to Swiss suppliers. The contrast between Switzerland and Sweden is instructive. Ericsson, the leading Swedish telecommunications supplier, was not guaranteed the home market and was forced to aggressively seek export sales. It has emerged as one of the world's leading companies in its industry. Hasler, the comparable Swiss company, had world-class capabilities but was protected. Today Hasler has virtually no international position and the Swiss home market is too small and benign to stimulate innovation and efficiency.

Factor Creation Mechanisms. Switzerland has been able to create specialized factors and upgrade them over time to support rising productivity in its industries. Prominent among the factor-creating mechanisms in Switzerland is the educational system. Public education is universal, has high standards, and is taken seriously by all segments of society. Teacher qualifications are unusually high compared to nations such as the United States and the United Kingdom. The courses offered reflect the composition of Swiss industry. For example, there are professors of banking at Zurich and St. Gall.

More important, in many respects, for specialized factor creation is the existence of a well-developed apprenticeship system, similar to that in Germany. The apprenticeship system covers all young people who do not go on to university.[17] It involves a combination of practical on-the-job training in a company and part-time classroom work at a local vocational school. Students are not only equipped to perform at high skill levels but to grow and develop throughout their careers. Swiss companies also devote significant resources to training. Employees in Swiss companies are thought of more as technicians than "blue collar" workers. In my experience, Swiss companies are unusually attuned to the welfare of their employees. At the Swiss textile equipment producer Stäubli, for example, it was understood that if the company were successful the employees would be well taken care of.

Also of importance to human resource development is compulsory military service in Switzerland. Many Swiss cite this as a strength for industry. Nearly all Swiss citizens receive some training and are taught discipline; they also establish a network of relationships that stay with them all their lives.

Switzerland has a strong tradition of university research and enjoys a world-class position in a variety of fields, among them chemistry and physics. The research links between universities and companies are well developed in many Swiss industries. World-leading capabilities in chemistry helped give rise to the Swiss pharmaceutical industry. A centuries-old tradition in medical education, research in health-related subjects centered in Basel, and social philosophy of universal health care have contributed to success in a wide variety of medically related products and services. Overall, Swiss national spending on R&D as a percentage of GDP, most of it by industry, is in the upper tier of nations (see Table 13–1).

Swiss companies are often led by technically trained executives, and there is a high degree of commitment to research. Swiss companies are also adept at sourcing specific technologies from other nations when there is no superior source in Switzerland. In many of our case studies, including surveying equipment, heating controls, pharmaceuticals, and hearing aids, Swiss companies developed close relationships with foreign research centers in specific technologies, and in many instances established research subsidiaries in foreign countries. The early establishment of research centers in the United States and the United Kingdom by the Swiss pharmaceutical companies, for example, has been vital to their output of innovative new drugs. The adeptness of Swiss companies at sourcing foreign technology, common to a number of nations that have been unusually successful in upgrading industry, seems to stem from a number of factors. The Swiss do not for a moment entertain the possibility that all technology can be developed in Switzerland, given its small size. The high skill level of Swiss scientists and engineers provides a foundation for assimilating foreign technology. Also, language and cultural skills make them particularly able to forge strong relationships abroad.

A final factor creation mechanism in Switzerland is immigration. Historically, Switzerland has been a home for talented foreigners who have gone on to play important roles in Swiss industry. The world wars were times when the inflow of talent into the country was particularly great, and it still occurs on a limited scale. Today, however, Switzerland's strict limits on immigration seem to have become a disadvantage. Swiss companies have great problems in bringing in skilled people in fields such as software and specialized finance that are necessary for continued upgrading of competitive advantage in important Swiss industries.

Information availability in Switzerland represents another weakness for the upgrading process. It lacks a well-developed business press, and most Swiss rely on foreign publications. Government statistics are nearly nonexistent. Few studies and reports are available to create an awareness of future competitive and technological developments. Each Swiss company and budding Swiss entrepreneur must create information to a far greater extent than in nations such as Japan and the United States.

Selective Factor Disadvantages. An essential motive force behind innovation and upgrading in Swiss industry has been selective factor disadvantages. Switzerland lacks most natural resources and must import most raw materials as well as energy. Swiss firms have been pressured to economize on raw materials and to find ways to create higher levels of differentiation in order to compete.

Switzerland was also perhaps the first nation to develop labor shortages after World War II. These provided an early impetus toward automation and to competing in more differentiated segments of the market.[18] High and rising wages have long prevailed in Switzerland. Economizing on labor and employing it in highly productive ways have been a persistent challenge facing Swiss firms. Shortages of highly skilled technical personnel have been another factor encouraging the sourcing of foreign technologies.

An important milestone in Swiss economic development was the move to floating exchange rates. Since 1973, the Swiss franc has risen steadily and has appreciated more than any other currency. Swiss firms have been pressured to enhance differentiation and boost productivity in order to compete, and also encouraged to produce less sophisticated product varieties outside Switzerland.

DEMAND CONDITIONS

While Swiss factor conditions are important, what most sets Switzerland apart from other nations in many ways are demand conditions. Swiss demand conditions have supported a remarkably broad base of competitive industries for such a tiny nation. This has made the Swiss economy very resilient and has meant that Swiss firms could operate in highly specialized industries and segments, involving high levels of productivity, while the economy maintained full employment.

One thing Switzerland does not have is a large home market, though its per capita consumption is quite high in some industries. Instead, most Swiss will cite the small home market as an important reason why Swiss companies have adopted an international outlook and set out very early to compete globally. The small home market has also led many Swiss companies to focus on narrow segments of the market, where they often place more attention than foreign firms and can sustain their position. The choice of segments frequently reflects unique Swiss demand conditions.

A surprisingly large number of Swiss industries trace their origins in some way to the textile industry, once dominant in the Swiss economy and still significant. (The textile and apparel cluster represented 11 percent of total Swiss exports in 1985, though Swiss positions today are concentrated more in machinery and specialty inputs than in end products.) Swiss quality and technical capability in textiles has long been high. Today, in part because of selective factor disadvantages (notably high wages), Swiss textile producers are highly focused on specialty or high-priced segments such as fine apparel, undergarments, lace, woven silk fabrics, and fine yarns.

The Swiss textile industry helped spawn a number of other competitive Swiss industries, including synthetic organic dyes, textile machinery, and trading. In each of these, Swiss firms are, or are among, the world leaders and have sustained competitive advantage for many decades. The sophistication of Swiss textile and apparel firms, coupled with the selective factor disadvantages they faced, have meant that there is continual pressure on Swiss suppliers to innovate. Switzerland is world leader in weaving machinery, for example, because it has consistently developed innovative new equipment.

Swiss geography and climate have played a significant role in determining those industries in which the Swiss home market is particularly sophisticated, as well as in the segment structure of home market demand. Switzerland has strength in tunnelling technology, for obvious reasons. The Swiss surveying equipment industry benefited from demanding local surveying needs. Also significant was the fact that surveyors in Switzerland are all independent contractors and not government employees. They choose their own equipment and depend on it for their livelihood, making them unusually demanding buyers. Geographic and climatic factors also play a role in such industries as heating controls (Switzerland has a cold but variable climate, very high energy costs, and there is great sensitivity to the working or living environment, all placing tough demands on controls) and railway equipment (Swiss trains must be able to handle rugged terrain and meet world-famous standards of reliability).

Swiss affluence has led its consumer goods firms into premium market segments and into industries that cater to upper-income individuals. Such firms as Bally (shoes), Rolex and Patek Philippe (watches), and Hanro and Zimmerli (clothing) are just a few examples. The high standard of living in Switzerland also means that the Swiss home market demand in premium segments anticipates that in many other nations. The influx of wealthy tourists into classy Swiss resorts reinforces this tendency.

The clustering of successful Swiss industries means that Swiss buyers of industrial goods are often internationally successful and sophisticated. Swiss firms must often confront needs at home that will eventually be felt elsewhere. One manifestation of this is in the area of environmental protection, where the Swiss have long established strict standards.

Social norms also play an important role in making Swiss home demand sophisticated in some industries. Swiss are demanding and critical, both as individuals and in their roles in industry. They expect good-quality, functional, and durable design, and prompt delivery. The risk aversion and care of the Swiss is reflected in, for example, very high per capita consumption of insurance, fire protection equipment, and banking services. Swiss are not known for their display of emotions, but do have their own distinctive passions for punctuality, precision, security, and permanence. These are reflected in successful Swiss industries from airline services to banking, insurance, and trading.

Because Switzerland is a mixture of multiple cultures, Swiss firms gain a unique window on evolving product needs. The Swiss company has buyers at home that reflect needs in several nations. Not surprisingly, the French part of Switzerland has unusual strength in consumer goods, while the German part is the home of many Swiss precision machinery and chemically related companies. Cultural diversity may account in part for the unusual breadth of advantage in Swiss industry compared to Sweden, which shares some important other characteristics with Switzerland but lacks this diversity.

Germany, France, and to a lesser extent Italy, are so closely linked to Switzerland both culturally and geographically as to nearly represent "home markets." Swiss firms deal fluidly in these nations that are often their first export markets. Because each country has demanding buyers for differing types of goods, the range of sophisticated buyers in close contact with Swiss industry widens. Moreover, Switzerland is prone to adopt German technical and environmental standards, because it does not itself have a national standards setting agency. Since German standards are tough, further beneficial demand side pressure is created in affected Swiss industries.[19]

The breadth of Swiss market positions, coupled with the close links with the French, German, and Italian markets, contribute to Switzerland's unusual success in the multiple business category, or equipment and products sold to many other industries. Such industries accounted for almost 30 percent of Swiss exports in 1985.

Swiss demand for services is also unusually advanced. High per capita income drives demand for personal services, while a large number of highly international firms (and regional headquarters of foreign firms, a Swiss service export) is a benefit to business services. Swiss service industries are most developed internationally in fields that relate to Swiss needs, such as insurance, personnel-related services such as temporary help (critical given the tight Swiss labor market), trading, logistical services, and international banking.

Swiss home demand works against international success in some industries, however. Demand for lower-quality, mass-produced consumer goods is low. Demand for entertainment and leisure products and services is rarely anticipatory in conservative Switzerland. The presence of state monopolies or intrusive regulation in a number of industries also undermines home demand quality.

RELATED AND SUPPORTING INDUSTRIES

The Swiss economy is extensively clustered. Competitive advantage grew out of supplier industries in several of the cases we studied. For example, hearing-aid producers drew on skills in precision mechanics as well as the availability of suppliers of parts and machinery for making miniature products. The watch industry and associated supplier industries were important sources of expertise for many of these firms. Swiss machinery manufactuerers are an important source of advantage to Swiss end-product producers in fields such as printed materials, textiles, and food products.

A number of important Swiss industries grew out of related industries, and some of the links I have already discussed. The Swiss pharmaceutical industry emerged out of the synthetic dye industry; drugs were first developed, almost by accident, when therapeutic effects of dyes were noticed. Specialty chemicals grew out of dyes as well. Herbicides, insecticides, and pesticides developed along with the pharmaceutical industry. Flavorings and fragrances tapped Swiss chemical expertise and a sophisticated home demand for processed foods. Strength in silk led to emphasis and success in those synthetic fibers most like silk.

Interchange within clusters that upgrades competitive advantage works unusually well in Switzerland for a number of reasons. First is the well-developed network of personal relationships among Swiss, due to the small size of the country, the relatively small number of universities, and the compulsory military service. Second is the unusual Swiss ability to work cooperatively and pragmatically with others. Swiss firms understand that their real challenge is to succeed internationally and that their Swiss buyers and suppliers are allies and not adversaries. Third, geographic proximity encourages working relationships between suppliers and customers. Finally, in some sectors such as chemicals, pharmaceuticals, machinery, and food, large Swiss firms have been important in extending clusters via internal diversification.

Switzerland was relatively slow to adopt television, and television advertising is limited. This and the size of the country have meant that few Swiss firms (with the notable exception of Nestlé) have been adept at mass consumer marketing. Instead, Swiss consumer goods companies rely on restrained marketing, stressing image and quality. Success is nearly always in premium market segments.

FIRM STRATEGY, STRUCTURE, AND RIVALRY

Swiss firms have a strategic orientation and operating philosophy that grows out of their national circumstances and culture: one element of this is to compete in relatively small industries and with relatively focused strategies, concentrating on highly differentiated, high-quality segments. Success in industries involving high-volume mass production is rare. This pattern is a function of a small home market, high wages, and an expensive currency. Swiss conservatism precludes the sort of large, risky R&D investments necessary in industries such as aircraft, semiconductors, and others. Pharmaceuticals is the exception, a function of very early Swiss entry and because Swiss firms gained the scale required to more than match American and German firms by globalizing more aggressively.

In most industries, Swiss firms succeed by seeking perfection through continuous improvement, driven by the technical background and orientation of many top managements and their long tenure in the industry. Progress is in small, steady steps and not in leaps and bounds.[20] Swiss firms do particularly well in industries where close contact with the buyer is required, either in complex selling, customization of products to particular buyers' needs, or extensive after-sale service and support. Fluency in languages, diplomacy, and high skill levels are some of the explanations. Swiss companies also have a remarkable ability to integrate disciplines such as mechanics, materials, electronics, and others.

Relations between Swiss firms and their employees are open and subject to few conflicts. There is a pragmatism to labor-management negotiations and an understanding of the need for Swiss firms to maintain competitiveness with foreign industry. Labor peace dates back to the 1937 agreement, known as *la paix du travail*, which stipulated that labor conflicts must be resolved through discussions and negotiations or, if necessary, binding arbitration.[21] Labor restrictions rarely impede innovation nor do they block automation.

Swiss companies are extremely open to internationalization; it comes as second nature. Language skills, multiple cultures, a small home market, and absence of government restrictions all contribute. The Swiss have a long history of trade and have long had a freely convertible currency, further reasons why the Swiss feel comfortable abroad. Another reason is the Swiss penchant for travel. In many of the industries we studied, key managers had studied and lived abroad before returning to Switzerland to found a company or take a management role.

Both human resources and capital in Switzerland have been highly committed to the business in which they are employed, especially through the 1970s. Swiss investors have a long time horizon. Low interest rates encourage a low time discount rate. As was evident in Table 7–1, Switzerland has had the highest rate of net fixed capital investment as a percentage of GDP of any nation we studied except Japan and Korea.

Widespread share ownership by banks and other institutions with a low proclivity for trading results in a governance structure in which investors have historically worked with management to renew companies rather than sell them or shut them down. Swiss accounting allows the establishment of generous reserves to tide companies over difficult periods.[22] Swiss firms can sustain huge losses for a period of years as they restructure. Unfriendly takeovers have been rare and made almost impossible in some companies by special classes of restricted stock and requirements for Swiss ownership.

Both workers and managers are highly skilled and seldom move between firms and professions. This slows down adjustment to a certain extent, but has been offset by the constant wage and currency pressure on Swiss industry that promotes upgrading. Swiss firms like to earn attractive profits, and adjustment has been continuous at least through the 1970s.

The extent of domestic rivalry in many of the successful Swiss industries is surprising. Switzerland's small size might lead one to expect that there was only one Swiss company in many industries. This is true mostly in those industries where Switzerland is *not* competitive. In many industries in which Switzerland is internationally successful, two or more competitors are engaged in active rivalry, often with similar strategies. Only a partial list of such industries includes banking (Union Bank, Credit Suisse, Swiss Bank Corporation), trading (Siber Hegner, André, Diethelm, Desco von Schulthess, Marc Rich, UHAG, UTC), chocolate (Nestlé, Jacobs-Suchard, Lindt and Sprüngli), pharmaceuticals (Sandoz, Ciba-Geigy, Hoffmann-La-Roche), premium watches (Rolex, Patek Philippe, and others), hearing aids (Phonak, Gfeller, and Rexton, now a subsidiary of Siemens), comfort controls (Landis and Gyr, Staefa, Sauter), and logistical services (Danzas, Panalpina). Even where Swiss rivals do not go head to head on price and product, they have been potential competitors and competed in other beneficial ways.

The combination of sophisticated demand, competition, and committed managers and investors worked well into the 1970s. However, there are growing signs that all is not well, and that the upgrading that has characterized Swiss industry may falter. Switzerland has long had a tradition of cartels, protected monopolies, and protected markets. Where these have been present (in brewing, for example), Swiss industry has either never succeeded internationally or its position has badly eroded. Innovation and change have been smothered. In the last decade, tendencies toward collaboration and accommodation in Swiss industry have, if anything, continued.

Lagging domestic competition has turned some of the advantages of Swiss industry into disadvantages. Huge hidden reserves, though positive in a dynamic company because they support a long-term perspective, have turned into a negative in some companies that have lost their dynamism by making it possible to avoid adjustment and innovation. Similarly, restrictions on share ownership are insulating poorly performing companies from the need to change. The electrical equipment manufacturer Brown Boveri is a good example; troubled for many years, it ultimately merged with ASEA. Recently, mergers among Swiss firms have become much more prevalent, reducing rivalry even further in favor of hoped-for scale economies. The implications for future competitive advantage are ominous. The Swiss case illustrates well how the entire "diamond" must be present in order to sustain advantage. If one determinant is lacking, especially if it is competition, others may have counterproductive effects.

The problem in Switzerland is compounded because Switzerland is not among the leading nations in its capacity for new business formation, though it ranks ahead of Sweden and probably Germany. While there was a surge of new companies formed after World War II, often by immigrants, there are impediments to new business formation today in Switzerland compared to such countries as the United States, Italy, and Japan. One is risk capital, for which sources are only just emerging. Swiss banks are conservative and entrepreneurs have had few places to obtain risky loans. More important is managers' aversion to risk. Failure is not acceptable in Switzerland, not unlike the situation in Germany. This deters many talented Swiss from starting new ventures. The process of developing new industries and new segments of existing industries is blunted. This same conservatism and risk aversion, a product also of prosperity and the tight Swiss labor market, has made managers of established companies slow to restructure and innovate.

THE ROLE OF GOVERNMENT

The Swiss government has historically had a benign or positive influence on national competitive advantage in Swiss industry. The Swiss federal system has guaranteed little intervention in most industries. Subsidies are low by international standards, and public spending is modest. Swiss companies have been free to internationalize, and government-business relations are generally pragmatic and oriented toward problem solving. The Swiss government at the various levels has had a good record in factor creation, particularly in the area of education.

Swiss neutrality and political stability have played a positive role in industry. Swiss companies are politically acceptable in nations where firms from other nations are not. Commercial contacts have always been possible with all three major European power centers (France, Germany, and the United Kingdom). Switzerland has attracted regional headquarters of foreign firms as well as international organizations and institutes such as the United Nations and CERN, the leading European center for nuclear research. These employ highly skilled people and create sophisticated home demand that is uniquely internationalizable for some products and services.

Competition policy is perhaps the single greatest weakness in Swiss government policy toward industry. In areas such as telecommunications, brewing, truck manufacture and others, protected local monopolies or sanctioned cartels have led to inefficiencies, lack of innovation, and sometimes large-scale failures (such as the low- and medium-priced watch industry and the leading truck producer, Saurer). Other cartels have artificially driven up the price of imported goods, and government has sanctioned or created standards and regulations that result in *de facto* protection for still other Swiss industries. The result, as in Japan, is a dual economy in which many competitive industries stand in stark contrast to a large group of inefficient and protected sectors.

Swiss government intrusion in banking has also had significant costs. The imposition of transaction taxes has driven away important markets from Switzerland in areas such as precious metals trading, Eurobonds, investment banking, and mutual funds. There is also a growing tendency for the Swiss government to regulate firms in areas such as environmental protection, labor, and social security. While some of these regulations will benefit Swiss industry by sensitizing Swiss firms to problems that will become important elsewhere, on balance the trend is ominous. Many Swiss regulations, such as restrictive labor regulations governing such things as overtime and night work, are creating rigidities that will blunt innovations and upgrading.

The Role of Chance

Swiss national competitive advantage benefited greatly from the two world wars. Switzerland's neutrality meant that its industry remained intact. It was in a position to satisfy demand when other nations could not. Switzerland benefited from an inflow of talent, dynamism, and funds. Many of its industries gained important advantages from the invalidation of German patents and because German industry was cut off from world markets, advantages made particularly significant by the similarities that already existed between successful Swiss and German industries. Some Swiss firms were also prompted to internationalize research and production to hedge their bets against German actions. This contributed to a Swiss head start in globalization. Finally, Swiss industry enjoyed a unique ability to be aware of what both sides in the war were doing, particularly in technology.

SWITZERLAND IN PERSPECTIVE

Swiss firms have been able to achieve and sustain competitive advantage in a remarkably broad range of industries. Drawing on unique home demand conditions and driven by the relentless pressure of high wages and appreciating currency, Swiss firms have sought out the high-quality, differentiated segments of industries. A pool of highly trained and highly skilled people have provided the capabilities to upgrade advantage over time. Swiss firms have had a unique capacity to internationalize in order to upgrade advantage even further.

Switzerland illustrates the success of an economy that has upgraded its competitive advantages over time. Swiss firms simply have no choice. While they have gone through painful periods, pragmatic though deliberate adjustment took place. At the same time, the unusually broad demand advantages for a nation of Switzerland's size have supported success in sophisticated segments in a wide range of industries. These absorb any employees freed up by productivity growth. The result is a high and rising standard of living for nearly all Swiss, without the pockets of disadvantaged citizens that plague so many other nations.

Yet Switzerland exhibits some disturbing tendencies. Per capita income growth has been modest since the 1970s, and productivity growth is not robust. Competition, long viewed in Switzerland with mixed feelings, seems to be waning. Companies in a number of industries have lost their dynamism. Emphasis has shifted in some quarters to protecting existing positions through artificial means rather than through continued innovation. Over forty years of sustained prosperity have taken their toll on motivation and risk taking.

That Switzerland has been losing world export share in most clusters is perhaps a symptom of these underlying problems. Figure 7–6 summarizes the number of competitive Swiss industries that gained or lost 15 percent or more world export share between 1978 and 1985, an analysis I will provide for each nation. The absolute number of industries is far less significant for national productivity growth than the specific character of the industries that are gaining and losing. Upgrading would be suggested by gains in new or more sophisticated industries and losses in those industries more sensitive to factor costs. The absolute number of industries gaining and losing in any category is also less important than the proportional change, since industries differ in size, the number of industries in each sector varies greatly because of the trade classification system, and country size plays a role in the number of industries represented. Finally, services are not included due to lack of data, though trade in them is important in some nations, including Switzerland.

With these caveats, however, it is evident that Switzerland's share gains in sophisticated industries are far outnumbered by its losses. More losses

FIGURE 7–6 Competitive Swiss Industries with Gains or Losses of World Export Share of 15 Percent or More Between 1978 and 1985*

Upstream Industries

	Materials/Metals			Forest Products			Petroleum/Chemicals			Semiconductors/Computers			UPSTREAM INDUSTRIES		
	Total Comp. Inds.	Share Gains	Share Losses	Total Comp. Inds.	Share Gains	Share Losses	Total Comp. Inds.	Share Gains	Share Losses	Total Comp. Inds.	Share Gains	Share Losses	Total Comp. Inds.	Share Gains	Share Losses
Primary Goods	11	3	5	5	4	2	15	3	11	0	0	1	31	10	19
Machinery	1	0	2	1	0	0	0	0	0	0	0	0	2	0	2
Specialty Inputs	0	0	0	0	0	0	0	0	0	0	0	0	0	0	0
Total	12	3	7	6	4	2	15	3	11	0	0	1	33	10	21

Industrial & Supporting Functions

	Multiple Business			Transportation			Power Generation & Distribution			Office			Telecommunications			Defense			INDUSTRIAL & SUPPORTING FUNCTIONS		
	Total Comp. Inds.	Share Gains	Share Losses	Total Comp. Inds.	Share Gains	Share Losses	Total Comp. Inds.	Share Gains	Share Losses	Total Comp. Inds.	Share Gains	Share Losses	Total Comp. Inds.	Share Gains	Share Losses	Total Comp. Inds.	Share Gains	Share Losses	Total Comp. Inds.	Share Gains	Share Losses
Primary Goods	29	8	20	6	1	4	11	2	7	3	1	3	0	0	2				49	12	37
Machinery	16	4	5	0	0	0	0	0	0	4	1	2	0	0	0				20	5	7
Specialty Inputs	8	0	4	2	0	1	0	0	0	1	1	0	0	0	0				11	1	5
Total	53	12	29	8	1	5	11	2	7	8	3	5	0	0	2				80	18	49

Final Consumption Goods & Services

	Food/Beverage			Textiles/Apparel			Housing/Household			Health Care			Personal			Entertainment/Leisure			FINAL CONSUMPTION GOODS & SERVICES		
	Total Comp. Inds.	Share Gains	Share Losses	Total Comp. Inds.	Share Gains	Share Losses	Total Comp. Inds.	Share Gains	Share Losses	Total Comp. Inds.	Share Gains	Share Losses	Total Comp. Inds.	Share Gains	Share Losses	Total Comp. Inds.	Share Gains	Share Losses	Total Comp. Inds.	Share Gains	Share Losses
Primary Goods	7	3	3	12	2	9	6	2	3	10	6	6	9	6	8	3	0	3	47	13	32
Machinery	3	1	1	9	1	4	0	0	0	0	0	0	0	0	0	0	0	0	12	2	5
Specialty Inputs	3	1	1	11	5	5	0	1	0	0	0	0	2	0	1	0	0	0	16	7	7
Total	13	5	5	32	8	18	6	3	3	10	6	6	11	6	9	3	0	3	75	22	44

*Gains and losses include industries exceeding the cutoff in either 1978 or 1985, including those that were competitive in 1978 but fell below the cutoff in 1985 or that had first achieved sufficient share to exceed the cutoff in 1985. The total number of competitive industries refers to 1985.

than gains are registered in machinery (14 to 7) and in advanced industries in areas of Swiss strength such as health care, power generation, personal products, and chemicals. Switzerland has also lost share in many multiple business industries, a warning sign of an economy experiencing a broad decline in competitive strength in which industrial demand sophistication is falling. Swiss share gains have occurred in relatively slow-growing industries while its losses are in much more rapidly growing ones, an indication of faltering new business formation (see Table B-3). While some of the export share losses may be accounted for by foreign investment, and Swiss competitive positions in services seem to have been maintained, the rate of upgrading in the Swiss economy shows unmistakable signs of slowing.

SWEDEN'S CHOICES[23]

Switzerland was joined by one other small nation, Sweden, in its early postwar prosperity. In some ways, the nations are quite similar: small size, high levels of education, strong language abilities, neutrality, and membership in the European Free Trade Association and not the European Community. Yet Sweden's patterns of national competitive advantage could hardly be more different than Switzerland's.

Sweden, like Switzerland, emerged from World War II with a strong base of international companies. For a small nation, Sweden is the home base of a striking number of large, global companies, among them such prominent firms as Volvo, Saab-Scania, Atlas Copco, SKF, and Electrolux. Of the nations we studied, Sweden's exports are the most concentrated in large firms, with the twenty largest multinationals accounting for more than 40 percent of total exports.[24] Sweden has been able to sustain national competitive advantage in a range of sophisticated industries, and its success in such industries as heavy trucks, cars, roller bearings, mining equipment, and others is remarkable. The economy has supported a very high standard of living and funded an enormous investment in public welfare for which Sweden is noted.

Swedish performance, while notable, has been less impressive in some respects than that of the Swiss. Per capita income is lower. Rising employment in the government sector has been essential to maintaining the low Swedish unemployment rate. In addition, successive currency devaluations (1976, 1977, 1981, and 1982) have been necessary to sustain exports in commodity industries such as pulp and paper, iron ore, and steel. Nevertheless, the striking number of truly global companies, and sustained positions in important industries make the Swedish case one that offers important insights into national competitive advantage.

Table 7–6 lists the top fifty Swedish industries in terms of world export

TABLE 7–6 Top Fifty Swedish Industries in Terms of World Export Share, 1985

Industry	Share of Total World Exports	Export Value ($ millions)	Import Value ($ millions)	Share of Total Swedish Exports
Kraft paper, paperboard	41.7	545,304	13,676	1.79
Kraft liner	31.7	378,772	—	1.24
Sawn conifer lumber	26.4	888,112	10,168	2.92
Iron, steel powders	24.1	52,549	4,991	0.17
High carbon steel heavy plate	22.9	147,522	7,066	0.48
Unmilled cereals	20.8	63,369	—	0.21
Nonelectric power handtools	20.8	166,970	14,088	0.55
Unbleached soda, sulphate woodpulp	18.7	53,711	624	0.18
Bleached sulphite woodpulp	17.6	101,983	14,984	0.34
Centrifuges	17.2	230,085	33,056	0.76
Unbleached chemical sulphite woodpulp	16.4	14,457	846	0.05
Bleached soda, sulphate woodpulp	15.5	818,021	16,369	2.69
Plastic coated paper	15.0	159,384	35,919	0.52
Power hand tool parts	14.6	44,111	8,323	0.14
Aircraft 2,000–15,000 kg	14.3	155,499	14,949	0.51
Iron, steel wire	14.2	100,133	9,712	0.33
Prefabricated builders woodwork	14.0	155,515	17,074	0.51
Iron, steel hoop, strip	13.5	134,529	17,135	0.44
High carbon steel medium plate	13.3	40,917	4,689	0.13
Nonoutboard marine engines	13.1	93,544	22,132	0.31
Other coated paper in bulk	12.6	328,646	64,447	1.08
Unrefined coppers	12.2	97,945	—	0.32
Motor vehicle chassis	11.1	113,780	—	0.37
Iron, steel wire rod	10.7	86,053	13,703	0.28
Dairy, other agricultural machinery	10.6	86,659	10,450	0.28
Zinc ores concentrates	10.0	97,415	4	0.32
Blades, tips for tools	9.9	337,832	89,082	1.11
Other pulp and waste paper	9.8	123,529	23,136	0.41
Line telephone equipment	9.3	515,615	41,080	1.69
Rubber articles	9.3	68,522	16,095	0.23
Worked copper alloys	9.1	72,569	27,544	0.24
Newsprint	8.9	514,813	—	1.69
Other furniture, parts	8.8	73,466	33,311	0.24
Other paper and paperboard	8.7	318,969	47,718	1.05

TABLE 7–6 (*Continued*)

Industry	Share of Total World Exports	Export Value ($ millions)	Import Value ($ millions)	Share of Total Swedish Exports
Uncombed discontinuous regenerated fiber	8.6	37,507	2,926	0.12
Raw mink skins	8.5	58,567	17,560	0.19
ADP equipment	8.4	565,341	655,235	1.86
High carbon steel bars	7.7	211,841	53,283	0.70
Iron ore agglomerates	7.7	142,702	74	0.47
Rough or split pulpwood	7.6	17,483	124,373	0.06
Paper mill machinery	7.6	124,793	116,673	0.41
Precious, semiprecious stones, pearls	7.4	25,826	4,706	0.08
Mineral crushing machinery	7.1	19,002	2,810	0.06
Uncoated writing paper	7.1	229,894	13,158	0.76
Centrifugal pumps	6.7	69,156	23,658	0.23
Ship derricks, cranes	6.6	70,167	32,784	0.23
Bread, biscuits, bakery products	6.4	13,186	6,859	0.04
Sinks, wash basins, bidets	6.2	24,759	4,260	0.08
Tankers	6.1	148,092	1,287	0.49
Textiles for machinery	6.1	52,440	47,841	0.17
TOTAL				29.53

NOTE: No import data are reported if import value is less than 0.3 percent of the total trade for 1985.

share in 1985. Looking down the list creates some immediate impressions that prove to be widely true. First, Sweden's list contains many natural resource-related industries, in stark contrast to Switzerland. Second, coexisting with the natural resource industries are a wide variety of machinery and mechanical industries. Third, the Swedish list is unique among the nations we studied in the paucity of consumer goods industries. Furniture, sinks and wash basins, and bakery products, all well down the list, are the only exceptions.[25]

Figure 7–7 profiles all the competitive industries in the Swedish economy, and Figure 7–8 and Figure B-3 provide summary calculations of the pattern of exports by competitive Swedish industries. The internationally competitive Swedish industries group into five large clusters. The largest cluster in terms of Swedish exports is in transportation and logistics, where competitive industries account for 20.5 percent of total exports. This includes vehicles such as passenger cars, trucks, and ships, along with engines, associated machinery, and specialized inputs. Also in this cluster are transportation services as well as products for material handling such as forklift trucks,

FIGURE 7–7 **Clusters of Internationally Competitive Swedish Industries, 1985**

	MATERIALS/METALS			FOREST PRODUCTS
Primary Goods	IRON AND STEEL **Iron, steel powders#** Iron, steel ingots# *Iron, steel blooms, slabs#* **Iron, steel hoop, strip#** *Iron, steel blooms* **Other steel wire, rod#** **High carbon steel bars#** Iron, other steel bars Iron, steel, other profile *Iron, steel heavy plate* **High carbon steel heavy plate#** **High carbon steel medium plate#** High carbon steel thin plate# *Iron, steel angles, shapes#*	Other iron, steel universal plate# *Stainless steel, thin plate* FABRICATED IRON AND STEEL **Other iron, steel wire#** *Iron, steel seamless tubes* NONFERROUS METALS Silver, unwrought **Coppers, unrefined'** **Other coppers, alloys, worked#** Copper plate, sheet Copper tubes, pipes *Lead, alloys unworked#* Lead, alloys worked# Aluminum bars, wire Nickel, alloys#	Other aluminum, alloys worked# *Casks, drums, etc., of aluminum#* METAL MANUFACTURES Other steel, copper nails, nuts# Structures, iron, steel' *Structures aluminum* Metal storage tanks* Wire cables, ropes' Hand tools* **Other hand tools** Other base metal manufactures# Blades, tips for tools Saws*** *Iron, steel chain* Iron, steel articles* **Ball, roller bearings**	WOOD PRODUCTS **Pulpwood, rough or split** Sawn conifer lumber *Lumber planed, conifer* *Reconstituted wood* *Other wood manufactures#* Other veneers, plywood# Pitprops, poles# PULP **Other pulp and waste paper#** Chemical woodpulp Unbleached soda, sulphate woodpulp Bleached soda, sulphate woodpulp
Machinery	*Construction, mining machinery*** Cemented carbide rock drills*** Mineral-working machinery# **Mineral-crushing machinery**	*Rolling mills#* *Roll-mill parts, rolls* Machine tools for special industries *Electric industrial furnaces*	Compressors*** Hydraulics***	**Paper mill machinery#** Soda recovery boilers*** Energy-saving equipment, pulp-plants*** Chainsaws***
Specialty Inputs	ORES *Iron ore, nonagglomerated* Iron ore agglomerates Copper ores' **Zinc ores concentrates**	MATERIALS Stone, sand, and gravel *Other petroleum, bitumen, coke#* OTHER **Prec., semiprecious stones, pearls#**		Chlorine*** Cellulose derivatives Wood waste#
Services				

	PETROLEUM/CHEMICALS	SEMICONDUCTORS/ COMPUTERS
Primary Goods		
	Unbleached chemical sulphite woodpulp#	
	Bleached sulphite soodpulp	
	PAPER	
	Other paper and paperboard#	
	Corrugated paper, bulk*	
	Newsprint	
	Uncoated writing paper	
	Coated writing paper	
	Kraft paper, paperboard#	
	Kraft liner, bulk	
	Other coated paper, bulk#	
	Plastic-coated paper	
	Paper containers**	
	Other paper articles#	
	Paper articles*	
	ORGANIC	
	Mineral tars	*Printed circuits**
	Acyclic alcohols	ADP equipment#
	Polyalcohols***	
	Nitrogen-function compounds#	
	INORGANIC	
	Chemical elements	
	Inorganic acids*	
	Sodium hydroxide*	
	Metal compounds of inorganic acids	
	Phosphite, phosphate	
	POLYMERS/OTHER	
	Plastic materials	
	Albuminoid substances	
	Copolymers vinylchloride	
Machinery		
Specialty Inputs		
Services		

KEY
roman 1.75% world export share or higher, but less than 3.50% share
bold italics *3.50% world export share or higher, but less than 7.00% share*
sans serif 7.00% world export share or above

. Industries below cutoff in 1978
\# Calculated residuals
\#\# Added due to significant export value in a segmented industry

* Added due to FDI
** Upgraded due to FDI
*** Added based on in-country research

FIGURE 7-7 (Continued)

TRANSPORTATION

Primary Goods	MULTIPLE BUSINESS		ENGINES	VEHICLE EQUIPMENT
	Other material of rubber#	Gas, liquid filters*	Motor vehicle piston engines	*Ship derricks, cranes*
	Other rubber articles	*Gas generators, furnace burners*#	**Marine engines, nonoutboard**	*Trailers*#
	Cork manufactures	Surveying instruments	Piston engines*	Railway braking equipment***
	*Other machinery, special industries***	Other measuring, control instruments#	VEHICLES	Offshore platforms***
	Centrifugal pumps	Central heating equipment	*Passenger motor vehicles***	MATERIALS-HANDLING EQUIPMENT
	Centrifuges*	Compaction equipment***	**Trucks***	**Forklift trucks***
	Pumps for gases*		Buses*	**Other mechanical handling equipment**#
			Other vehicles, not mechanically propelled#	CONSTRUCTION & MINING EQUIPMENT
			Aircraft 2,000–15,000 KG*	*Roadrollers, construction eqpt.*#
			Tankers of all kinds	
Machinery		Metal-forming machine tools		*Other nonelectric machinery*#
		Industrial robots***		Metal cutting mach. tools#
		Gas welders, brazers*		**Nonelectric power handtools**
		Electric welders		
Specialty Inputs		Fork lift truck parts#***		**Motor vehicle chassis**
		Radar apparatus		**Power hand tools, parts**#
		Parts of railway vehicles		Motor vehicle bodies, parts#
		Industrial gasses***		Aircraft, motorcycle tires#
		Parts of lifting, loading machines#		
Services	Civil engineering services***	Car carriers***		
	Contracting***	Reefer services***		
	Industrial cleaning***			
	Security services*			
	Building maintenance*			
	Equipment maintenance and repair*			

Primary Goods	POWER GENERATION AND DISTRIBUTION	OFFICE	TELECOMMUNICATIONS	DEFENSE
Primary Goods	GENERATION Steam boiler* *AC motors, excluding universal* Generator sets* *Nuclear reactors, parts#* *Wind, water engines* DISTRIBUTION ***Other electrical transformers**** ***Liquid dielectric transformers*** Switchgear* High voltage transmission*** Electric accumulators	***Cash registers, accounting machinery#*** Base metal office supplies* Office equipment*** Office supplies# ***Other printed matter#*** ***Duplicating, etc., mach.#***	***Other telecommunication equipment, parts#*** **Line telephone equipment** Telecommunication equipment* Mobile telephone networks***	Explosives, pyrotech products ***War firearms, ammunition***
Machinery	Environmental control equipment***	Rotary printing presses		
Specialty Inputs	Electrical carbons		Parts of telecommunications equipment***	
Services				

KEY

roman	1.75% world export share or higher, but less than 3.50% share
bold italics	*3.50% world export share or higher, but less than 7.00% share*
sans serif	**7.00% world export share or above**

*	Industries below cutoff in 1978
#	Calculated residuals
##	Added due to significant export value in a segmented industry

*	Added due to FDI
**	Upgraded due to FDI
***	Added based on in-country research

FIGURE 7-7 (Continued)

Primary Goods	FOOD/BEVERAGES	HOUSING/HOUSEHOLD	TEXTILES/APPAREL
	BASIC FOOD Pig meat, fresh, chilled Fish, fresh, chilled Bird eggs#* PROCESSED FOOD *Bread, biscuits, bakery products#* Chocolate and products Pastry, cakes* EDIBLE OILS *Sesame, mustard oils* Processed animal, vegetable oil	HOUSING COMPONENTS Wood-based panels* Wooden flooring*** **Builders woodwork, prefabricated** *Quicklime, asbestos, cement materials#* FURNITURE *Chairs and other seats* *Other furniture and parts#* Metal furniture Wood furniture APPLIANCE Sewing machines *Domestic refrigerators* Domestic electrical equipment*	OTHER HOUSEHOLD PRODUCTS Electrothermic apparel* *Other household-type equipment*** Vacuum cleaners*** Household, hotel glass Other base metal household equipment# *Lamps, fittings of base metals* *Sinks, wash basins, bidets#* Gardening equipment***	FABRICS/OTHER Other special textile fabrics, products#* Leather bovine, equine *Textiles for machinery*
Machinery	**Dairy, other agricultural machinery#** Dairy equipment*** Nondomestic refrigeration equipment *Packaging, bottling machinery*		Textile & leather prep. machinery#
Specialty Inputs	**Unmilled cereals#** Unmilled barley* **Chemical fertilizers#** *Parts of nondomestic refrigeration equipment#*	Other glass#	**Uncombed discontinuous regenerated fiber** Mink skins, raw
Services		Furniture retailing	

	HEALTH CARE	PERSONAL	ENTERTAINMENT/LEISURE
Primary Goods	MEDICAL EQUIPMENT Electromedical equipment X-ray apparatus Furniture for medical, etc., practice# Medical instruments *Hearing, orthopedic aids* PHARMACEUTICALS Medicinal, pharmaceutical products	**Combustible products"** Safety matches" Manufactured tobacco#	Color TV receivers *Yachts, sport vessels*
Machinery			
Specialty Inputs			
Services			

KEY

roman   1.75% world export share or higher, but less than 3.50% share

bold italics   *3.50% world export share or higher, but less than 7.00% share*

sans serif   **7.00% world export share or above**

*   Industries below cutoff in 1978

\#   Calculated residuals

\#\#   Added due to significant export value in a segmented industry

*   Added due to FDI

**   Upgraded due to FDI

***   Added based on in-country research

FIGURE 7–8 Percentage of Swedish Exports of Competitive Industries by Broad Cluster

UPSTREAM INDUSTRIES
Share of Country Exports: 35.1 (-2.9)
Share of World Cluster Exports: 1.7 (-0.4)

Materials / Metals
Share of Country Exports: 12.5 (-1.7)
Share of World Cluster Exports: 2.4 (-0.1)

Forest Products
Share of Country Exports: 17.9 (-2.5)
Share of World Cluster Exports: 10.5 (-1.3)

Petroleum / Chemicals
Share of Country Exports: 2.6 (0.5)
Share of World Cluster Exports: 0.2 (+0.0)

Semiconductors / Computers
Share of Country Exports: 2.1 (0.9)
Share of World Cluster Exports: 0.9 (-0.4)

INDUSTRIAL AND SUPPORTING FUNCTIONS
Share of Country Exports: 30.7 (-0.6)
Share of World Cluster Exports: 2.0 (-0.2)

Multiple Business
Share of Country Exports: 4.2 (+0.0)
Share of World Cluster Exports: 1.1 (-0.1)

Transportation
Share of Country Exports: 20.5 (-0.4)
Share of World Cluster Exports: 2.3 (-0.2)

Power Generation & Distribution
Share of Country Exports: 1.0 (-0.7)
Share of World Cluster Exports: 1.1 (-0.5)

Office
Share of Country Exports: 0.7 (-0.1)
Share of World Cluster Exports: 1.0 (-0.2)

Telecommunications
Share of Country Exports: 3.7 (0.6)
Share of World Cluster Exports: 5.5 (-1.5)

Defense
Share of Country Exports: 0.7 (-0.0)
Share of World Cluster Exports: 3.6 (-0.6)

FINAL CONSUMPTION GOODS AND SERVICES
Share of Country Exports: 10.6 (0.5)
Share of World Cluster Exports: 0.6 (0.1)

Food / Beverage
Share of Country Exports: 2.5 (0.1)
Share of World Cluster Exports: 0.4 (0.1)

Textiles / Apparel
Share of Country Exports: 1.1 (+0.0)
Share of World Cluster Exports: 0.3 (0)

Housing / Household
Share of Country Exports: 3.9 (+0.0)
Share of World Cluster Exports: 2.4 (0.2)

Health Care
Share of Country Exports: 2.5 (0.6)
Share of World Cluster Exports: 2.8 (0.1)

Personal
Share of Country Exports: 0.1 (+0.0)
Share of World Cluster Exports: 0.1 (+0.0)

Entertainment / Leisure
Share of Country Exports: 0.5 (-0.2)
Share of World Cluster Exports: 0.3 (-0.2)

Note: Numbers in parentheses are changes between 1978 and 1985. ▨ Identifies broad sectors in which the nation's international competitive positions are related. Exports are those of competitive industries, not all industries.

lifting and loading machines, and others. Also part of this cluster (and linked to metal fabrication as well) are welding machines, tools of various sorts, and robots. A second major cluster is in forest-related industries (where competitive industries account for 17.9 percent of Swedish exports). These include timber, pulp and paper, along with paper-making machinery and other related equipment and chemicals closely connected to pulp and paper. Also linked to the forestry cluster are finished goods such as prefabricated housing, hardwood flooring, and furniture. A third major cluster is in ferrous metals and fabricated metal products (12.5 percent of Swedish exports). Included in this cluster are equipment and other products related to mining, as well as electric furnaces, rolling mills and rolls, and other machinery and tools for metalworking. Other significant clusters are in health-related products (2.5 percent of Swedish exports and 2.8 percent of world cluster exports), and telecommunications. There is a pocket of strength in power generation and distribution, particularly in long-distance power transmission equipment. This cluster can be linked to Sweden's hydropower resources and to the metal and pulp and paper sectors that make heavy use of power.

In addition to these well-developed clusters, there are smaller clusters in food products and associated items, such as packaging and food-related machinery. Virtually all these industries are concentrated in the agriculturally intensive southern region of Sweden, Skåne, that abuts Denmark (Denmark's economy is heavily oriented toward food-related industries). Other clusters include household appliances and a group of products and services related to water treatment and other environmental control functions.

The shading on Figure 7–8 represents some of the important links between clusters. The Swedish position in transportation and related machinery is connected to the need for mining/harvesting, transport, and logistics in Sweden's resource-based metals and forest products industries. Power generation and distribution has also developed in part because of power needs in metal as well as pulp and paper processing.

Sweden's position in its principal clusters is remarkably stable. While the Swedish position is eroding slowly in resource-based industries, such as iron ore and forest products, its position in many other industries has been maintained over decades. World export share has increased significantly since 1978 in such disparate industries as kraft liner, automobiles, hearing and orthopedic aids, and lifting and loading machines.

Yet Sweden is as striking in what is missing in its economy as in where it is strong. Sweden's internationally competitive industries are largely in upstream and industrial sectors. Sweden has virtually no international position in consumer packaged goods of any type and a weak overall position in consumer goods—textiles and apparel, personal products, entertainment and leisure, and food and beverages are all weak. Appliances (Electrolux), furniture (IKEA, among others), and crystal (Orrefors, Kosta-Boda) are the only sectors where there are significant international positions.[26] Sweden also has almost no international strength in services, except in a few general business services, furniture retailing, and specialty shipping.[27] Other major gaps in the Swedish clustering chart are in chemicals and in semiconductors/computers.

Sweden's range of internationally competitive industries is quite narrow, in contrast to Switzerland, but its position in sectors is deep. The Swedish economy is heavily concentrated in a few areas. About 50 percent of total Swedish exports come from clusters of competitive industries in the materials and metals, forest products, and transportation sectors, as illustrated in Figure 7–8. Sweden is successful, like Switzerland, in a range of industries that are relatively specialized, though it also holds positions in a number of large, often resource-related sectors. Unlike Switzerland, Swedish firms tend to have wide product lines in many industries. Sweden also has a much weaker overall position in machinery than Switzerland. To understand this pattern of national advantage in the Swedish economy, we must examine Sweden's position vis-à-vis the "diamond" and how it has evolved over the postwar period.

SWEDISH FACTOR CONDITIONS

The origin of a great majority of Sweden's internationally competitive industries can be traced in some way to Sweden's natural resource endowment, strikingly different from that of Switzerland. Sweden possesses extensive forests, large deposits of low phosphorus iron ore, and derives about 30 percent of its energy from inexpensive hydroelectric power.[28] Sweden's resources are mostly located in the more remote northern regions of the nation, which are far from the major population centers around Göteborg and Stockholm (Sweden is almost 1,000 miles long from north to south).

Though many of Sweden's successful industries have their roots in natural resources, however, many fewer draw their principal competitive advantage from these resources today. (Sweden does, however, have an unusually large number of industries which are sensitive to factor costs, which is important to its future economic development). Sweden's iron ore deposits lost their unique advantage in the nineteenth century, with improvements in steel-making technology. Exports peaked in the early 1970s after which falling transportation costs and the opening of new deposits in countries such as Brazil and Australia broke Sweden's stranglehold of the nearby European market. Sweden's forests, though well managed, are much slower growing than those in many other countries because of climatic conditions. While the resulting variety of wood fiber leads to high pulp quality and provides advantages in some segments, almost 20 percent of the wood inputs to Swedish paper in 1987 were imported. Similarly, Sweden's electricity is low cost but not any lower cost than a number of other nations with similar water resources, such as Norway, Canada, and Brazil.

To understand Swedish patterns of advantage, however, we must look beyond factor endowment to other determinants, particularly those bearing on the upgrading process. Despite a loss of competitive advantage in natural factors, and in some cases because of it, Swedish firms moved into more sophisticated industries and industry segments such as specialty steels and fine paper, as well as into supplier, related or downstream industries such as roller bearings, rock drills, and fabricated steel products. In industries where upgrading could not be accomplished successfully, such as the once important textile industry, the result has generally been failure. Sweden was less successful than Switzerland in sustaining specialized positions in textiles, some of the reasons for which will become apparent later. Only a few remnants of international success in textiles remain, and these are largely in specialized machinery.

Sweden's success and failure in sustaining advantage and in upgrading competitive positions is a function of the unique national "diamond" in Sweden. One important area is Swedish human resource conditions. Sweden has an unusual wage structure. Its system of so-called *solidarity wages* is one in which wage differentials among skill levels and across industries are among the lowest in the world. This form of egalitarianism is also reflected in relatively low wages for managers (as well as in extremely high and progressive levels of personal taxation). Though the average wage level in Sweden is high, these policies actually result in Sweden having lower wages than some major competing nations in the automobile, truck, and heavy machinery industries which represent a competitive advantage.

Sweden has long had a universally high level of education. This, combined with a common language, common religion, and an identical school curriculum nationwide, yields a well-trained workforce with the ability to work closely together. Swedish education is particularly strong in engineering, where it has emulated the German model. Close ties first with Great Britain and later Germany have meant that many Swedes were educated in these nations and worked abroad for a time in their leading industries. Today, the focus has shifted to the United States. Swedes, like the Swiss, have a very high level of competence in foreign languages. Nearly all Swedes speak English, and many (especially older citizens) speak German.

Though strong in many fields, however, the Swedish educational system, nearly all public, has had difficulty keeping pace with rising standards and the changing skills needed by industry. An egalitarian system seems to have lowered standards and worked against advanced training in specialties. An educational bureaucracy that is slow to adjust has meant acute shortages of trained people in fields such as information technology and software.

The ability to achieve more sophisticated competitive advantages and compete in new industries has suffered.

Sweden has a number of excellent technical universities, and university research contributes to the local scientific and technical base, notably at the Chalmers Institute of Technology and the Royal Institute of Technology. There are also technical institutes connected to, and supported by, the major industries in Sweden. However, the extent of government or privately funded research institutes is less than one would find in the United States or Germany.

Most research is highly applied and takes place within the large Swedish companies, often in some type of collaboration with universities. Moreover, R&D cooperation within clusters is unusually strong in Sweden. Overall, R&D spending as a percentage of GDP in Sweden was the highest of any nation in 1987, partly reflecting a narrow economy unusually concentrated in R&D-intensive sectors and the heavy role of large companies which more fully report R&D spending.

Swedish companies have a long tradition of sourcing basic technology from around the world, often through licensing. Swedish firms were early licensees of the Bessemer patents in steel, the Krupp technology in cemented carbides, and diesel technology for automotive applications. After obtaining core technologies from abroad, Swedish firms often employ ingenious engineering to make numerous improvements and extend the range of applications. As in Switzerland, the ability of Swedish firms to source technology seems to reflect a highly international outlook, good language skills, strong technical training, and a relatively low dose of the "not invented here" syndrome.

Selective Factor Disadvantages. A major driver of innovation and upgrading in Swedish industry has been a number of important selective factor disadvantages. The first and foremost is high wages and benefits, which have been a potent force toward automation. Solidarity wages lead to rapid and early restructuring in more labor-intensive industries. Swedish restructuring in textiles, shipbuilding, and steel was faster and less painful than in many other nations. Restructuring was further speeded by the fact that wage rollbacks were not an option and domestic demand for the affected industries was relatively small, limiting policy options involving protection and subsidy.

High relative wages for lower-skill employees has also spurred intensive efforts to automate even low-skill jobs. This applies also to services, because Swedish service workers are paid about the same as manufacturing workers.[29] A chronic shortage of skilled labor, which continues, has also led to process innovation. For many of these reasons, penetration of robots has, until recent years, been the highest per capita and per manufacturing worker in Swedish industry than in any other nation. Automated warehousing and material handling is also advanced in Sweden.[30]

The long winters and cold climate (Sweden is on the same latitude as

Alaska) has led to the development of sophisticated technology in energy conservation and related products. The long distances between resources and cities, as well as the distance of Sweden from many markets, have led to great sophistication in logistics as well as Swedish presence in a number of transportation and logistics-related industries. In a number of the industries we studied, Swedish firms gained advantages from superior logistics. In newsprint, for example, Swedish firms pioneered highly specialized terminal facilities and the use of specialized ships.

Distance from markets is also one of several factors that have prompted Swedish firms to make early and heavy foreign direct investment. Swedish companies are some of the most global in the world, with far-flung networks of subsidiaries established very early compared to firms from other nations. Sandvik, for example, established its first foreign unit in 1865. Alfa Laval had U.S. plants before the turn of the century, while SKF established a German unit in 1910 and had plants in five countries by 1933.[31] Foreign sales account for more than 90 percent of total sales in many Swedish industries.

SWEDISH DEMAND CONDITIONS

Once established, the resource-based industries that were the early core of the Swedish economy became sophisticated buyers that begot many related and supporting industries. Even a cursory look at Figure 7–7 makes it clear how many internationally competitive Swedish industries today are in some way supporting industries for timber and paper products, iron ore mining, and iron and steel making and processing. In chemicals, for example, one of the few areas where Sweden is internationally competitive is in chemicals associated with pulp and paper processing. The clustered nature of the Swedish economy is striking. Buyer-supplier relationships among the internationally competitive Swedish industries are pervasive.

A variety of conditions make Swedish buyers demanding and sophisticated purchasers of industrial products. Given the long distances within Sweden as well as the need to ship goods to major foreign markets, early, intense, and sophisticated demand for all types of transportation equipment and services has long been present. High levels of automation in both manufacturing and materials handling have led to strong positions in robotics (ASEA, now ABB), specialized forklifts (Kalmar, BT), and automated guided vehicles (BT).

Sweden's harsh climate, rugged geography, and geological conditions all create unusually tough conditions for Swedish mining, transportation, and manufacturing companies. Swedish rock, among the hardest in the world, creates stringent demands on mining equipment. Swedish roads in the northern regions are rugged, and local demand is for hauling very heavy loads, often of timber. This local demand placed a premium on quality and durability, hallmarks of Swedish competitive advantage in heavy trucks. A number of core Swedish industries are major users of power, and hydro-power generated in the north has to be moved long distances. This has stimulated competitive success in a variety of power-generation and transmission industries. A number of Swedish electric power companies were private companies, and the Swedish public power company is quite sophisticated, both adding to the quality of home demand. The cold climate also creates strong demand for energy conservation equipment and services. Swedish firms are leaders in such industries as heat exchangers, cogeneration equipment, and the like.

Many of Sweden's natural resource-based industries faced growing disadvantages in natural factors of production in the postwar period and even before. These disadvantages created a strong need for advanced equipment and other assistance from their suppliers, an important benefit for supporting industries. Swedish firms in resource-based industries also tended to move into more sophisticated segments and into related industries, giving Swedish machinery and other input suppliers an edge in moving with them.

Sweden's position in prefabricated housing illustrates a number of these points. Participation in this industry is a forward integration move from Sweden's traditional position in sawn lumber. High wages for construction crews, a short building season, and the need for tight fit and high quality because of a harsh climate have all combined to create a fertile environment for success in this industry, which had to develop very high-quality products that could be rapidly assembled.

A number of other aspects of Swedish attitudes and culture also play an important role in the ability of Swedish firms to sustain higher-order competitive advantage in many industries. Sweden is a nation with an extraordinary level of concern for safety, environmental quality, and public welfare. These values are embedded in Swedish laws as well as in the mentality of Swedish managers and trade unions. They are reflected as well in the large size of the government sector. Swedish drivers must keep their headlights on at all times, for example, and Sweden was in the forefront of mandatory use of seat belts generally, of mandatory installation of three-point belts, and now of mandatory use of seat belts in the back seat. Volvo was the first car in the world with three-point seat belts as standard equipment.

These values have created advanced demand for a wide range of products and services in environmental protection and public welfare. Sweden has a strong international position in seat belts, to continue my example. Another example is in health care, where Sweden has a large position for a small nation. In products for handicapped people, for example, Swedish public support is far ahead of most countries, and Swedish firms are emerging as significant international players.

Swedish values are also reflected in unusually safe and environmentally friendly products, often an important competitive advantage for Swedish firms. Atlas Copco is known for quiet compressors and shock-absorbing devices for hydraulic drilling equipment, Volvo for safe cars and safety cabs on trucks, and AGA for safety valves that control the release of the industrial gases it sells.[32] These examples, and others, demonstrate the extent to which many aspects of Sweden's welfare society have represented anticipatory demand conditions with respect to other advanced nations.

The same values have not been without costs, however, in terms of demand conditions. Swedish demand for microwave ovens initially lagged behind that of other nations because of the intense consumer concern over radiation leakages. The nuclear industry, where Sweden has historical strength because of a relatively early and significant move to nuclear power, is in danger of losing position given the halting of domestic development. The Swedish defense sector has been seriously impeded by unusually strict limits on the nations to which Swedish companies can sell arms, a product of Swedish pacifism and neutrality.

More significant across a range of industries, however, is the enormous Swedish state sector (the public sector employs 31 percent of the workforce). Government monopolies control health care delivery, child care, and many other services. This sector has eliminated private demand for many services and is one of the reasons Sweden has few international service firms. The large public sector also means that government is a major buyer of many products. In some areas, Swedish government companies have worked well with industry and played the role of sophisticated buyer. In others such as health care, the rigidities of the state sector have taken their toll. Given the high level of expenditure, the Swedish health care sector could be a more fertile ground for innovation in products and services.

Demand conditions for consumer goods are also a serious disadvantage for Swedish industry. Sweden has high average wages, but income taxes are high and very progressive and have cut deeply into disposable income, particularly for high-income consumers. The marginal tax rate is 75 percent for annual income of SKr 200,000 and up (about U.S. $33,000), and there is also a value-added tax of 23 percent.[33] This reduces effective demand for goods and personal services, and slows product upgrading which is so useful as a demand stimulus. Swedish egalitarianism dampens demand for new and emerging products and services, many of which begin as luxuries. Conspicuous consumption is taboo in Sweden.

Sweden has allowed no television and radio advertising on the government-controlled channels.[34] As a result, Swedish firms have had to learn modern marketing abroad and not at home. Few have. Swedish retailing has also been relatively undeveloped, with a historically lower penetration of newer types of retail stores and chains. While Swedish demand is sophisticated or anticipatory in some consumer industries, these are few and far between.

RELATED AND SUPPORTING INDUSTRIES

The Swedish economy is in many ways an economy of related and supporting industries. Numerous Swedish industries emerged because of an initial Swedish position in a downstream industry. Among them are mineral crushing machinery (iron ore) and welding machines (shipbuilding). Sweden has international positions in many products connected to the pulp and paper industry, including pulp machines, paper machines, drying machines, boilers, conveyor systems, process instruments, wood-handling machines, and specialty trucks. A strong position in hard metals developed to meet needs in metalworking and mining equipment.

The reverse chain of causation is even more prevalent. Many competitive Swedish industries emerged from related and supporting industries. Specialty steel products, roller bearings, fabricated metal products, fine paper, and many others resulted from upstream positions or positions in related industries.

Today, the clustering of Swedish industries is very developed. The Swedish context, moreover, has made mechanisms that make interchange and information flow within clusters particularly effective. There is a striking frequency of cooperation and joint efforts among vertically or horizontally related Swedish companies. For example, Atlas Copco (mining and construction equipment) and Sandvik (rock drills) cooperated closely for over forty years on marketing and R&D, while Fläkt (dryers) and Götaverken (pulp recovery boilers) cooperate in international marketing of environmental control equipment. Informal collaboration is more common even than formal arrangements; in Sweden there is little need for formal contracts for such arrangements to work. Also, collaborative relationships exist between Swedish companies and some Swedish government entities such as the military and the state telephone company. Buyer-supplier relationships are unusually open and fluid, a strength in Swedish demand conditions.

One reason for the high levels of cross-industry collaboration is the ownership links among companies that grew out of the Wallenberg financial empire and other financial groups. It is quite common for the CEO of a major Swedish company to serve as a director of one or more related Swedish companies, sometimes even holding a position in management. Aside from ownership linkages, close collaboration reflects the Swedish culture and the backgrounds of Swedish executives. Swedish society values cooperation and being part of the group. Because Sweden is a relatively small country, many Swedish executives know each other, went to school together, or served in the military together. This cooperation among Swedes allows them to face competition with foreign firms and extends outside of Sweden. Foreign subsidiaries of Swedish companies in related and supporting industries frequently know each other well and collaborate abroad.

FIRM STRATEGY, STRUCTURE, AND RIVALRY

Swedish firms have organizational characteristics that fit well with competing in complex, technically sophisticated industries involving far-flung networks of subsidiaries. Swedes, like Japanese, are cooperative and loyal to the company. Swedish companies are characterized by conservatism, discipline, and trust. Leaders are nondirective but respected. Communications are open and organization is informal. Coordination in producing complex products and among far-flung widespread international subsidiaries takes place with more ease than in an American or Swiss firm, where managers desire independence. Many Swedish companies have established foreign subsidiaries by simply sending a manager abroad with complete autonomy to become established. Such trust and lack of supervision is extraordinary.[35]

Swedish firms are very open to internationalization, because of the relatively small home market for many of Sweden's specialized goods as well as the long distances to markets. Swedish neutrality and a long tradition of traveling also play a role. Working abroad is viewed as a normal and essential part of one's career. Many of the large Swedish companies date back to the latter part of the nineteenth century. They first began investing abroad at a time when transport costs were high and tariffs were stiff. Many of Sweden's successful industries (steel, paper, mining equipment) are also resource related and thereby politically sensitive, which creates greater-than-average pressures for local content and foreign investment.

Swedish companies typically operate in a large number of countries. Sandvik, for example, has production of rock drills in approximately thirty countries and sells in many more. Many of these are small countries, and firms find their way into out-of-the-way places. Swedish firms sometimes avoid nations with higher barriers to entry, such as Germany and Japan.[36]

Industry is a prestigious occupation in Sweden, and many of the best university graduates enter the large Swedish multinationals. Sweden's core industries have been particularly prestigious, and Swedish firms are characterized by highly committed employees. Many Swedish top managers have technical backgrounds, and are dedicated to finding solutions to company problems rather than abandoning traditional businesses.[37] The result is reinvestment to keep facilities modern, a matter of prestige for the managers involved. In the paper industry, for example, the United States and Canada have a mixture of modern and rundown plants, while Swedish plants have all been modernized.

Historically, the public capital markets have had little impact on the decisions of Swedish managers. Capital is invested for sustained periods and investments are rarely sold. Financial groups often own large fractions of company shares. Swedish accounting also allows untaxed reserves which give Swedish companies added flexibility in weathering hard times.[38] In recent years, financial market pressures have been growing. Swedish markets are becoming more efficient and sophisticated, and more Swedish companies have foreign shareholders. There is also a growing tendency toward mergers and toward holding financial assets instead of making corporate investments. Top management backgrounds in finance have become also more prevalent.

Sweden's competitive advantage resides in many relatively concentrated industries. In some notably successful industries, there is more than one Swedish competitor and relatively vigorous domestic rivalry. Volvo and Saab-Scania compete actively in cars and trucks. Sandvik and Fagersta compete in rock drills. There are a number of paper companies and specialty steel producers.

Yet Sweden is unique among the nations we studied in there being but one significant Swedish company in many international industries. Examples include car carriers, refrigerated ships, telecommunications equipment, roller bearings, mining machines, and a variety of others. Mergers have often led to domestic monopolies. Antitrust plays a role in domestic industries but is suspended in more international industries based on the view, also prevalent in Italy (and which I believe is erroneous), that greater scale at home is necessary to meet global competition.

There is also a tradition of cooperation among direct competitors in a variety of Swedish industries, such as steel and paper. Swedish paper companies, for example, collaborated for some time in export pricing. Accommodation among rivals is also exemplified by Sweden being among the first nations in the world to initiate restructuring in such industries as steel and shipbuilding. A cooperative solution, often involving the swapping of product lines, was worked out with minimum acrimony.

The roots of this behavior are in Swedish social structure and training. Swedes are taught to cooperate, not compete. This is beneficial in vertical relations and interactions with related industries, but eliminates the spark of conflict so necessary for some important types of innovation.

This mixed record in domestic rivalry is partly compensated for by other determinants. One is that Sweden is a small nation with citizens that have an unusually international outlook. Sweden is also a very open market, quite exposed to imports. Another important spur to dynamism is that most internationally competitive Swedish companies have very high levels of foreign direct investment. This means that they have long met foreign rivals head on in many foreign countries, often including the rivals' home nations.

Nevertheless, the mixed Swedish situation in terms of domestic rivalry has extracted its inevitable price. Sweden's range of competitive industries is narrow. It has lost ground in those industries where too much cooperation has replaced competition. Mergers have replaced innovation as a way to solve competitive problems. Sweden does not succeed in industries that demand rapid responsiveness and frequent product changes.

The general lesson is that it appears to be difficult to fully compensate for the absence of active domestic rivalry. Swedish firms do so partly through close interchange with sophisticated and demanding suppliers and buyers. However, the Swedish domestic competitive climate, when combined with the fact that individuals and companies are risk averse (in part because of a group orientation and few financial incentives due to high marginal taxation), limits sharply the range of industries in which the nation can successfully compete. Further upgrading in the Swedish economy is also threatened.

Exacerbating this problem is that the conditions in Sweden for new business formation are unfavorable. While large multinationals prosper, high personal taxation dampens the incentive for entrepreneurial risk taking. The group orientation of many Swedes also works against entrepreneurship. Cultural homogeneity means that there are few outsiders or individuals who will risk becoming outsiders by bucking established companies and practices. Few are prepared to leave their companies to do so. Societal values also scorn great personal wealth. Risk capital is scarce, another significant problem.

Many of the fledgling Swedish enterprises that are formed have sold out to large companies very early in their development rather than take the chance of further building the company. Yet becoming part of a large group is not the most fertile ground for innovation and entrepreneurship. The result is that few new companies of any size have developed in Sweden in the last two decades, and business closures have substantially exceeded start-ups.

The Role of Government

Government plays a substantial role in the Swedish economy through offering many public services, though its direct ownership of industry is not as high as in several other nations we studied. The Swedish government has engaged in extensive regulation of industry, reflecting a strong set of societal values. Many such regulations have served to create sophisticated standards and anticipatory Swedish buyer needs in areas such as safety and environmental protection. In some areas, however, Swedish values are so extreme as to make Swedish regulations out of synch with other nations and debilitating to industry.

The Swedish government has a very supportive relationship with industry, particularly the large, established Swedish multinationals. A major responsibility of the Swedish diplomatic corps is to assist industry. Effective corporate tax rates are low (often in the 20 to 30 percent range) in contrast to personal taxation. Industry is recognized as vital. Various government programs have served to help the large Swedish companies. Favorable tax rules spur the purchase of automobiles, for example, while electricity prices are kept low. Swedish government agencies have often played an unusually constructive role in the way they handle public procurement compared to those in other nations. They work cooperatively with Swedish suppliers but are demanding and buy sophisticated products that advance the state of the art.

Swedish government policy is not uniformly positive, however. It is heavily focused on large companies, and the problems of small enterprise receive little attention. Devaluation has been used as a prime policy tool, reflecting an overly macroeconomic view of competitiveness. Arguably, this approach has been a short-term salve but has worked against the long-term dynamism of Swedish firms. So have efforts to artificially hold down factor costs.

In addition, the Swedish government plays a very substantial direct role in the economy. Its heavy role in the service sector, and the costs of that role, have already been described. Government-owned or partially owned companies represent 8 percent of Swedish industrial employment and 9 percent of total Swedish exports, operating in industries such as mining, pulp, steel, forest products, shipbuilding, and shipping.[39] Government employment in Sweden is huge and characterized by relatively low levels of productivity at a time when Swedish companies are moving production abroad for lack of workers. The future role of government in Sweden raises significant issues for the development of the economy.

THE ROLE OF CHANCE

Sweden, like Switzerland, was a major beneficiary of World War II. Neutrality preserved Sweden's industrial base, and Swedish firms were able to gain important international positions in serving the postwar demand for industrial goods.

SWEDEN IN PERSPECTIVE

The Swedish economy has developed out of resource positions in forest products and mining. Today it is an economy with deep clusters in these upstream sectors as well as in a range of industrial and supporting sectors. The Swedish "diamond" has been a powerful machine for upgrading the established clusters of industry. Sophisticated demand, fluid buyer-supplier relationships, good technical and human resources, and well-managed large companies have partially offset a mixed record in domestic rivalry. Sweden has been able to sustain national competitive advantage where it has historically competed.

Yet there are significant challenges facing Swedish industry. Sweden remains sensitive to factor costs, and the regular use of devaluation threatens upgrading. So do home demand conditions and an unresponsive educational system. Individual motivation and risk taking is faltering, while domestic rivalry is a serious concern. All this bodes poorly for innovation and dynamism in Swedish industry. The penetration of robots in Swedish industry, for example, has begun to lag behind that of other nations.

The broader data I presented earlier in Table 7–1 contain cause for concern. The rate of net capital investment in Swedish industry has fallen off markedly since the mid-1970s. Productivity growth is moderate and per capita income growth relatively slow. Figure 7–9, which summarizes the competitive Swedish industries gaining and losing 15 percent or more market share, shows that Sweden has been losing share more often than gaining it. More significant are the specific industries in which gains and losses have occurred, which confirm a mixed record in upgrading. Sweden has, by and large, held its own in the clusters where it has traditionally been strong, especially outside of natural resource-intensive areas and in machinery and specialty inputs. However, losses in some of the more sophisticated products such as papermill machinery and some machine tools raise questions about upgrading, as does the fact that many share gains have come in commodities and less processed items. Foreign investment by Swedish firms is unlikely to account for all of the losses.

Figure 7–9 also highlights a second broad issue for Sweden, which is how to extend the clusters further and broaden the base of the economy into new clusters. While the Swedish context has been effective in upgrading established industries, it is not nearly so favorable for creating new advanced industries that are so necessary to continued improvement in national productivity and to maintaining full employment at high wages. The internationally successful portion of the Swedish economy is narrow. Figure 7–9 shows that Sweden has tended to lose position much more often than gain it outside of traditionally strong clusters such as materials/metals, transportation, health care, and household products. Losses also outnumber gains in power generation, office products, and telecommunications.

Demand conditions, the absence of important media, government dominance of services, and limits on new business formation place important constraints on widening the industries in which Swedish firms are successful.

FIGURE 7–9 Competitive Swedish Industries with Gains or Losses of World Export Share of 15 Percent or More Between 1978 and 1985*

UPSTREAM INDUSTRIES

	Materials/Metals			Forest Products			Petroleum/Chemicals			Semiconductors/Computers			UPSTREAM INDUSTRIES		
	Total Comp. Inds.	Share Gains	Share Losses	Total Comp. Inds.	Share Gains	Share Losses	Total Comp. Inds.	Share Gains	Share Losses	Total Comp. Inds.	Share Gains	Share Losses	Total Comp. Inds.	Share Gains	Share Losses
Primary Goods	38	10	18	23	5	12	11	4	1	2	0	1	74	19	32
Machinery	7	4	0	1	1	1	0	0	0	0	0	0	8	5	1
Specialty Inputs	6	4	3	2	1	1	0	0	0	0	0	0	8	5	4
Total	51	18	21	26	7	14	11	4	1	2	0	1	90	29	37

INDUSTRIAL & SUPPORTING FUNCTIONS

	Multiple Business			Transportation			Power Generation & Distribution			Office			Telecommunications			Defense			INDUSTRIAL & SUPPORTING FUNCTIONS		
	Total Comp. Inds.	Share Gains	Share Losses	Total Comp. Inds.	Share Gains	Share Losses	Total Comp. Inds.	Share Gains	Share Losses	Total Comp. Inds.	Share Gains	Share Losses	Total Comp. Inds.	Share Gains	Share Losses	Total Comp. Inds.	Share Gains	Share Losses	Total Comp. Inds.	Share Gains	Share Losses
Primary Goods	10	3	3	13	5	5	7	3	7	4	2	3	2	0	0	2	0	1	38	13	21
Machinery	0	0	0	6	3	3	0	0	0	1	0	1	0	0	0	0	0	0	7	3	4
Specialty Inputs	0	0	0	8	3	3	1	0	0	0	0	0	0	0	0	0	0	0	9	3	3
Total	10	3	3	27	11	11	8	3	7	5	2	4	2	0	0	2	0	1	54	19	28

FINAL CONSUMPTION GOODS & SERVICES

	Food/Beverage			Textiles/Apparel			Housing/Household			Health Care			Personal			Entertainment/Leisure			FINAL CONSUMPTION GOODS & SERVICES		
	Total Comp. Inds.	Share Gains	Share Losses	Total Comp. Inds.	Share Gains	Share Losses	Total Comp. Inds.	Share Gains	Share Losses	Total Comp. Inds.	Share Gains	Share Losses	Total Comp. Inds.	Share Gains	Share Losses	Total Comp. Inds.	Share Gains	Share Losses	Total Comp. Inds.	Share Gains	Share Losses
Primary Goods	8	4	4	3	1	0	13	6	5	6	2	2	3	1	0	2	1	1	35	15	13
Machinery	3	1	2	1	0	0	0	0	0	0	0	0	0	0	0	0	0	0	4	1	2
Specialty Inputs	4	3	1	2	2	1	1	0	1	0	0	0	0	0	0	0	0	0	7	5	3
Total	15	8	7	6	3	1	14	6	6	6	2	2	3	1	0	2	1	1	46	21	18

*Gains and losses include industries exceeding the cutoff in either 1978 or 1985, including those that were competitive in 1978 but fell below the cutoff in 1985 or that had first achieved sufficient share to exceed the cutoff in 1985. The total number of competitive industries refers to 1985.

Without doing so, job creation will continue to be sluggish and the government sector will remain chronically large. This, in turn, will lead to forces that make conditions more difficult for industry.

RENEWING GERMAN DYNAMISM[40]

America, Switzerland, and Sweden were immediate success stories in a range of industries after World War II, because of conditions existing long before the war coupled with the unique circumstances posed by the war itself. Since the true globalization of competition was just beginning in many industries in the 1950s and 1960s, it is hard to overestimate the early mover advantages that accrued to those nations who were in a position to exploit them in the early postwar years because their economies had not been damaged.

It did not take long after World War II, however, for West Germany (hereafter Germany) to reemerge as a nation with broad and deep national competitive advantage and a rapidly rising standard of living. Germany had strong competitive advantages in a wide range of industries dating back to the turn of the century, many of which were already global. It rebounded quickly. Germany has been perhaps the preeminent trading nation when considering the entire postwar period. Its share of world exports is higher than the share of the world economy represented by its GNP, unlike the United States and Japan.[41] Because overseas manufacturing by German firms is estimated to be as high or higher in percentage terms than it is for American companies, German export performance relative to the United States and Japan is all the more impressive (foreign manufacturing by Japanese companies is still modest, though increasing rapidly).

The breadth and depth of successful German industries can only be fully appreciated in historical context. Germany's position has been achieved or regained in the space of a few decades in spite of enormous problems. Germany was defeated in war for the second time in less than thirty years. Its industrial base was badly damaged. Germany lost about half its land area, notably that containing some of the most abundant natural resources as well as some of the most modern parts of the industrial base.[42] Many German patents were confiscated, as were foreign assets in a variety of industries. During the war, German firms were cut off from most world markets, a circumstance that often allowed the development of strong rivals based in such countries as America, Sweden, and Switzerland. Finally, German efforts to rebuild international market positions faced difficulties in obtaining export licenses from the Allies, who kept many German firms out of world markets until the early 1950s, as well as continued resentment by foreign buyers in some industries.

These circumstances were overcome, emphasizing that the conditions in Germany represented an incredible machine for generating national competitive advantage in a wide range of industries. The German economy also has had a remarkable ability to sustain advantage. Despite rising wages, shortening workweeks, and a rising currency, many German industries have been able to upgrade their advantage over decades. In a range of industries, German firms have been world leaders for a century or more through achieving higher and higher levels of differentiation and competing in more and more sophisticated segments.

Germany is not without problems; the relatively high unemployment rate and problems in competing successfully in new industries are symptomatic. Market positions are gradually slipping in many sectors. However, the German case will be a particularly interesting and important one to study.

PATTERNS OF SUCCESS IN GERMAN INDUSTRY

Table 7–7 shows the top fifty German industries in terms of world export share in 1985. It includes an unusually wide range of industries, spanning industrial and consumer goods; a striking number of industries (ten) are involved in making various types of production machinery. While German firms hold strong world export shares, they tend not to dominate industries as is the case in the United States and Japan.[43]

The true uniqueness of German industry can only be fully understood by examining the profile of the German economy in Figure 7–10 (Figures 7–11 and B–4 provide summary calculations). No country in the world, including Japan, exhibits the breadth and depth of industries with strong international positions. No less than 345 German industries had world export shares that exceeded 10.6 percent in 1985, Germany's average share of world exports. What is also unusual about Germany is that the top fifty industries in terms of export value (Table B–5) account for only 41.6 percent of German exports, compared to 51.6 percent in the United States, and 62.7 percent in Japan.

Germany does not have dominant positions in large industries but has strong positions in many, many industries. Of the 345 German industries that made the cutoff, only seven accounted for more than 1 percent of German exports.[44,45] The breadth means that German positions are in segments and relatively specialized industries characterized by high levels of productivity, and in which German firms usually compete with differentiation strategies. This characteristic of German industry, which will be discussed further, also makes Germany's economy quite robust in competitive terms.

The German economy is extensively clustered, and the number of clusters

TABLE 7–7 Top Fifty German Industries in Terms of World Export Share, 1985

Industry	Share of Total World Exports	Export Value ($ millions)	Import Value ($ millions)	Share of Total German Exports
Briquettes of coal, coke	70.4	121,397	1,373	0.07
Potassium sulphate	59.4	232,490	6	0.13
Reciprocating pumps	58.1	517,351	78,608	0.28
Steel high pressure conduit	55.4	491,786	1,488	0.27
Fresh milk and cream	54.5	450,280	42,272	0.25
Rotary printing presses	51.1	923,218	50,671	0.50
Iron, high carbon steel coil	49.8	360,894	458	0.20
Iron, steel ingots	49.5	82,015	8,660	0.04
Synthetic organic lumino-phores	47.1	190,485	30,882	0.10
Coke of coal, retort carbon	44.5	605,757	78,915	0.33
Spinning, reeling, etc., machines	42.7	358,730	18,924	0.20
Clothes dryers	41.3	50,744	14,384	0.03
Iron, simple steel hoop, strip	38.8	572,830	197,373	0.31
Aircraft over 15,000 kg	38.1	2,377,571	2,362,416	1.30
Paper product manufacturing machines	36.7	313,969	90,101	0.17
Jukeboxes	36.5	6,344	64	0.00
Alkyds in primary forms	36.3	471,898	170,370	0.26
Polyvinyl chloride plates, strip, etc.	35.9	422,424	153,213	0.23
Rubber, plastics working machines	35.5	849,798	107,651	0.46
Phenols, phenol alcohols, derivatives	35.3	251,675	96,054	0.14
Combine harvester-threshers	35.3	282,078	14,756	0.15
Trade advertising materials, catalogs	34.8	374,289	102,452	0.20
Other vehicles, not mechanically propelled	34.4	289,683	68,146	0.16
Packaging, bottling, etc., machines	34.1	802,409	125,408	0.44
Tractors for tractor–trailers	34.0	387,879	32,117	0.21
Woven cardigan wool, fine hair	34.0	156,152	200,866	0.09
Woodwaste	33.5	21,028	9,798	0.01
Sewing machine needles	33.2	110,580	26,019	0.06

TABLE 7–7 (*Continued*)

Industry	Share of Total World Exports	Export Value ($ millions)	Import Value ($ millions)	Share of Total German Exports
Vegetable alkaloids and derivatives	33.2	157,904	57,331	0.09
Trailers, semi-trailers	32.6	255,402	63,984	0.14
Synthetic organic dyestuffs	32.4	849,848	153,271	0.46
Parts of chairs, other seats	31.6	131,172	95,668	0.07
Lubricating preparations for textiles	31.6	130,637	30,674	0.07
Roasted coffee	31.4	185,108	11,727	0.10
Refractory bricks, etc.	31.0	240,897	54,938	0.13
Vending, weighing machines, etc., parts	30.7	518,447	148,074	0.28
Metal reaming, etc., machines	30.6	271,337	106,376	0.15
Other textile, leather machinery	30.4	695,398	106,094	0.38
Mustard, sesame oils	30.2	242,766	38,198	0.13
Other spinning, extruding machines	30.1	172,495	18,392	0.09
Shafts, cranks, pulleys	29.9	960,332	294,859	0.52
Cinema cameras, projectors	29.9	53,761	12,198	0.03
Zinc, iron, lead, etc., oxide	29.8	265,179	72,224	0.14
Knit, felt manufacturing machines	29.6	323,583	32,032	0.18
Acrylic polymers	29.6	279,107	103,243	0.15
Lead, alloys worked	29.6	19,340	2,562	0.01
Parts of textile processing machines	29.2	209,557	41,972	0.11
Copper foil, powders	29.2	232,449	82,947	0.13
Gas welders, brazers	29.2	56,125	8,981	0.03
Copper plate, sheet, strip	28.9	290,557	91,880	0.16
TOTAL				10.14

NOTE: No import data are reported if import value is less than 0.3 percent of the total trade for 1985.

is substantial. Perhaps the most dominant cluster is in the chemical field, where German firms are leaders in a vast array of chemical and related products, including plastics and specialties, as well as associated machinery and equipment such as pumps, liquid measurement and control equipment, and even services such as the engineering and construction of chemical plants.[46] If the petroleum and chemicals field is separated into petroleum-related and chemical-related industries, competitive German industries hold

FIGURE 7–10 Clusters of Internationally Competitive German Industries, 1985

	MATERIALS/METALS	FOREST PRODUCTS
Primary Goods	OTHER MATERIALS AND WASTE Other iron and steel scrap[#] IRON AND STEEL Pig iron, spiegeleisen *Iron, steel ingots[#]* Iron, simple steel blooms Iron, simple steel coils *Iron, high carbon steel coil for rerolling[#]* Iron, steel wire rod Other iron, steel universal, plate[#] Iron, simple steel heavy plate, rolled *High carbon steel heavy plate, rolled[#]* Iron, high carbon steel medium plate, rolled[#] Iron, simple steel thin plates Stainless steel plates Tinned plates, sheets *Iron, steel hoop, strip* *Iron, high carbon steel hoop, strip[#]* Iron, simple steel wire Other wire (excl. wire rod)[#] High carbon steel bars[#] Other iron, steel profiles[#] *Iron, steel castings, unworked* FABRICATED IRON AND STEEL Railway rails Cast iron tubes, pipes[#] Iron steel seamless tubes Iron, steel tubes, pipes' **Steel high pressure conduit** Iron, steel tube fittings Iron, steel cable, rope Other wire cables, ropes[#] NONFERROUS METALS *Copper bars, wire* *Copper plate, sheet* *Copper foils, powders[#]* *Copper tubes, pipes* Aluminum plate, sheet **Aluminum foil** *Other aluminum, alloys worked[#]* *Lead, alloys worked[#]* Unworked, partly worked silver[*] *Nickel, alloys worked[#]* *Tin, alloys worked[#]* METAL MANUFACTURES Structures, parts, iron, steel Struct., parts, alum. Steel storage tanks *Aluminum storage tanks[#]* Metal fencing, gauze Other steel, copper nails, nuts[#] Iron, steel nuts, bolts *Locksmith wares, etc.* Iron, steel chains, parts Other base metal manufactures[#]	WOOD MANUFACTURES *Pulpwood, rough, split* *Improved wood in sheets[#]* Reconstituted wood PAPER Printing paper, coated Plastic coated paper' Paper tarred, coated[#] Other paper, precut, articles[#] Other paper, paperboard[#] WASTE *Wood waste[#]*
Machinery	*Mineral-crushing machinery* *Other mineral-working machinery[#]* Foundry molds, etc. Converters, ladles, ingot molds[#] Rolling mills[#] *Gas generators, furnace burners[#]* Roll-mill parts, rolls *Industrial furnaces, electric* *Industrial furnaces, nonelectric*	Other paper mill mach.[#] *Paper prod. mfg. machines*
Specialty Inputs	**Briquettes[#]** **Coke of coal, retort carbon**	
Services		

FIGURE 7-10 (Continued)

Primary Goods	PETROLEUM/CHEMICALS		SEMICONDUCTORS/ COMPUTERS
	ORGANIC		Digital computers
	Halogen hydrocarbon deriv.	**Polyamides in plates, sheets**#	*Printed circuits and parts*#
	Acyclic alcohols, deriv.	Polyethylene in monofil, plates, waste#	
	Phenols, derivatives	Polypropylene	
	Monoacids and derivatives	**Polystyrene**	
	Polyacids and derivatives	Polystyrene, waste*	
	Oxy-acids, derivatives	**Polyvinyl chloride**	
	Amine-function compounds	**Polyvinyl chloride, monofil, waste**#	
	Oxy-func. amino compounds		
	Amide-function compounds	**Polyvinyl chloride, plates, strips**	
	Other nitro-function compounds#	Other poly. products#	
	Organo-sulphur compounds	**Acrylic polymers**	
	Other organic-inorganic compounds#	Other articles of plastic#	
	Heterocyclic compounds		
	Ethers, epoxides, acetals		
	Aldehyde-function compounds		
	Inorganic esters and organic chemicals nes#		
	Cyclic hydrocarbons		
	INORGANIC		
	Chemical elements'		
	Inorganic acids, etc.		
	Zinc, iron, lead oxide		
	Other inorganic bases#		
	Sodium hydroxide, solid		
	Metal comp. of inorg. acid		
	Metallic salts and peroxysalts#		
	OTHER		
	Glazes, driers, putty		
	Albuminoid substances, glues		
	Misc. chem. products#		
	Pet. jelly, pitch#		
	POLYMERS		
	Synthetic rubber'		
	Reclaimed rubber#		
	Other products of condensation#		
	Alkyds in primary forms		
	Polyamides		
Machinery			
Specialty Inputs			
Services			

KEY

roman	10.6% world export share or higher, but less than 21.2% share
bold italics	21.2% world export share or higher, but less than 42.4% share
sans serif	42.4% world export share or above

•	Industries below cutoff in 1978	Added due to FDI
#	Calculated residuals	:: Upgraded due to FDI
##	Added due to significant export value in a segmented industry	... Added based on in-country research

	MULTIPLE BUSINESS	TRANSPORTATION
Primary Goods	*EQUIPMENT* **Mach. tools for spec. ind.** **Reciprocating pumps** **Centrifugal pumps** Pumps for gases Pump, compressor parts **Other pumps, centrifuges#** Other pumps for liquids# **Spraying machinery** *PARTS* **Fans, blowers, parts** **Ball, roller bearings** Cocks, valves, etc., nes **Gaskets, other machine parts#** **Shaft, crank, pulley** *INSTRUMENTS* Optical instruments **Meters and counters** Surveying instruments Measure, draw instruments **Gas, liquid control instruments** Other measure, control instruments#	*ENGINES* Motor vehicle piston engines Marine piston engines, nonoutboard Piston engines *VEHICLES* **Passenger motor vehicles** Special motor vehicles Buses Nonmotor cycles, wheelchairs# **Trucks*** Other railway vehicles# **Aircraft over 15,000 KG** **Tractors** **Other vehicles, not mechanically propelled#** *VEHICLE EQUIPMENT* Tires, for cars Steel transport boxes Other metal transport boxes# **Ignition, starting equipment** Electric vehicle lighting equipment **Trailers, semitrailers#** Motor vehicle chassis *CONSTRUCTION EQPT.* Self-propelled shovels, excavators Roadrollers## *MATERIALS HANDLING EQPT.* Forklift trucks Other lifting, loading machinery# Ship derricks, cranes
Machinery	*Rubber, plastics-working machines* Vending, weighing, etc., machines and parts# Other machinery for special industries#	*Other handtools* Lathes, metalworking Reaming machines, metalworking *Metal-forming machine tools* Other metalworking machine tools# Other metal-cutting machine tools# *Gas operated welders, brazers#* Electric welders *Power handtools, nonelectric* Nonelec. power handtool parts# *Electromechanical handtools*
Specialty Inputs	Blades, tips for tools Gas, liquid filters Other mineral manufactures#	*Other materials of rubber#* Unhardened vulcanized rubber tubes Other rubber articles# Unhardened rubber products Asbestos, friction material Piston engine parts Motor vehicle parts, accessories# *Parts of railway vehicles* Lift, load mach. parts# Forklift truck parts#
Services	Engineering/architecture* Construction* Reinsurance*	Airlines*** Air cargo*** Airport terminal*** Port services***

FIGURE 7–10 (Continued)

	POWER GENERATION AND DISTRIBUTION	OFFICE	TELECOMMUNICATIONS	DEFENSE
Primary Goods	GENERATION Steam boilers, etc. *Steam engines, turbines* DC Motors, rotary converters** *AC motors* AC generators` *Nuclear reactors, parts* *Wind, water, etc., engines*  DISTRIBUTION Liquid, dielectric transformers Other electric transformers\*\* Static converters Inductors, elec. power machinery\*\* *Switchgear* Insulated wire, cable, etc. Elec. insulating eqpt. Primary batteries, cells` Electric accumulators Electric filament lamps Other electric lamps, bulbs** Electrical carbons Other electrical machinery**	*Electric typewriters* *Trade advtg. materials, catalogs* Other office supplies** Duplicating machines**		*Warships***
Machinery		*Other printing, bookbinding machinery*** **Rotary printing presses** Platen printing presses**		
Specialty Inputs		Other coloring matter and printing ink**		
Services		Other printing matter and printing		

KEY
roman   10.6% world export share or higher, but less than 21.2% share
bold italics   21.2% world export share or higher, but less than 42.4% share
sans serif   42.4% world export share or above

\`   Industries below cutoff in 1978
*   Calculated residuals
\#   Added due to significant export value in a segmented industry
*\ Added due to FDI
**   Upgraded due to FDI
***   Added based on in-country research

	FOOD/BEVERAGES	HOUSING/HOUSEHOLD
Primary Goods	BASIC FOODS Bovine, live breed# *Bovine meat with bone in* Milk and cream, fresh# Cocoa powder, unsweetened *Cocoa paste#·* Starch, inulin, gluten# EDIBLE OILS Margarine and shortening *Mustard and sesame oils#* Sunflower seed oil Processed animal, veg. oil *Animal oils, fats#* PROCESSED FOODS *Dry milk* Milk, preserved *Bread, biscuits#* Pastry, cakes, etc.· Sugar candy, nonchocolate· *Roasted coffee#* BEVERAGES Beer, ale, stout, porter	HOUSING Builders' woodwork, prefab Glass, surface-ground Other glass# Central heating equipment FURNITURE Lamps, fittings base metal Illuminating glassware# Chairs and other seats *Parts of chairs, other seats#* *Metal furniture* Wood furniture APPLIANCES Dom. heating, cooking app. *Domestic washing machines* *Clothes-drying machines#* Domestic refrigerators· Other household-type equipment# GLASSWARE AND CERAMICS Household, hotel glass Other glassware# *Porcelain, china houseware* Ceramic ornaments, etc. OTHER HOUSEHOLD PRODUCTS Soaps, polishes, and creams# *Washing preparations* Cutlery Basketwork, brooms *Varnishes, distempers* Other household equipment#
Machinery	AGRICULTRUAL EQUIPMENT Cultivating machinery· Lawn mowers, harvesting machines# *Combine harvester-thresher* Parts of harvesting and threshing machinery Dairy and agric. machinery# *Wheeled tractors* Handtools for agric.# FOOD PROCESSING EQPT. Food mach., nondom. *Packaging, bottling machines*	
Specialty Inputs	*Potassic fertilizer#* *Phosphites, phosphates* Insecticides Fungicides, disinfectants# Herbicides Glass bottles, nonvacuum *Paper containers* *Plastic pkg. cont., lids* Hay, bran· Coffee extracts, essences·	Cement, artificial stone products Insulating bricks and refractory cements# *Refractory bricks* Lime, construc. mat.# *Nonrefractory bricks#*
Services		

FIGURE 7-10 (*Continued*)

Primary Goods	TEXTILES/APPAREL		HEALTH CARE
	FABRICS	Other special tex. fabric#	MEDICAL EQUIPMENT
	Fur skins, tanned, dressed#	Plastic-coated textiles	*X-ray apparatus*
	Other woven cotton, bleached#	Textiles for machinery	Medical instruments
	Pile, etc., cotton fabrics	APPAREL	PHARMACEUTICALS
	Other woven syn. fiber fabric#	Dresses of synthetic fibers	*Provitamins and vitamins*
	Cont. regen. weaves nonpile	*Skirts*	*Veg. alkaloids and derivatives*
	Synthetic pile fabric		Hormones
	Woven cardigan wool		Medicaments cont. antibiotics
	Knit synthetic fabric		Medicaments cont. hormones, etc.#
	Other knitted fabrics#		

Machinery		
	Sewing machines	*Spin, reel mach. parts*
	Sewing machine needles#	*Knit, felt mfg. machines*#
	Extrud. and process. mach.#	*Loom, knit mach. parts*
	Spinning, reeling machinery#	*Other textile, leather mach.*#

Specialty Inputs		
	Synthetic organic dyestuffs	Waste of textile fabrics
	Dyes, tanning products	*Yarn, textured, polyamide*
	Synthetic, organic luminophores#	Yarn, nontextured polyamide
	Discontinuous synthetic fiber, uncombed	*Lubs. for textiles*#
	Other synthetic fibers to spin#	Cellulose derivatives
	Regenerated fiber to spin#	*Other synthetic fiber yarn*#
	Waste of synthetic fibers#	Yarn, of discon. synthetic fibers
		Discon. syn. fiber yarn
		Regenerated fiber yarn, monofilament

Services

KEY

roman	10.6% world export share or higher, but less than 21.2% share	*	Industries below cutoff in 1978
bold italics	*21.2% world export share or higher, but less than 42.4% share*	#	Calculated residuals
sans serif	42.4% world export share or above	##	Added due to significant export value in a segmented industry

•   Added due to FDI
::   Upgraded due to FDI
•••   Added based on in-country research

	PERSONAL	ENTERTAINMENT/LEISURE	
Primary Goods	Cigarettes· Mixed perfume substances· *Spectacle frames* Clocks, watch parts *Fountain pens* *Pen nibs, pencils#* Smallwares, toiletries Precious met. arts.#	Color TV receivers *Cinema cameras, projectors* Radiotelephonic receivers, TV cameras, parts## Other photo apparatus, equipment# Newspapers, periodicals Postcards, printed matter# Other musical instruments, parts#	Prep. sound rec. media Recorded discs, tapes *Jukeboxes#*
Machinery		Photosensitized cloth	
Specialty Inputs	Lenses, prisms unmounted#		
Services	Secondary and university education***		

KEY

roman   10.6% world export share or higher, but less than 21.2% share

bold italics   *21.2% world export share or higher, but less than 42.4% share*

sans serif   42.4% world export share or above

·   Industries below cutoff in 1978
\#   Calculated residuals
\##   Added due to significant export value in a segmented industry

·   Added due to FDI
::   Upgraded due to FDI
***   Added based on in-country research

FIGURE 7–11 Percentage of German Exports of Competitive Industries by Broad Cluster

	UPSTREAM INDUSTRIES	INDUSTRIAL AND SUPPORTING FUNCTIONS	FINAL CONSUMPTION GOODS AND SERVICES
Share of Country Exports:	21.2 (−0.5)	36.2 (−0.7)	17.1 (−1.0)
Share of World Cluster Exports:	6.3 (−1.9)	13.8 (−2.6)	6.8 (−0.7)

Materials/Metals
Share of Country Exports: 10.0 (−2.3)
Share of World Cluster Exports: 11.9 (−2.5)

Forest Products
Share of Country Exports: 2.0 (0.3)
Share of World Cluster Exports: 7.3 (2.6)

Petroleum/Chemicals
Share of Country Exports: 8.6 (1.2)
Share of World Cluster Exports: 4.6 (−0.7)

Semiconductors/Computers
Share of Country Exports: 0.6 (0.3)
Share of World Cluster Exports: 1.9 (−1.4)

Multiple Business
Share of Country Exports: 7.0 (0.4)
Share of World Cluster Exports: 10.8 (−1.1)

Transportation
Share of Country Exports: 23.7 (0.5)
Share of World Cluster Exports: 15.0 (−2.0)

Power Generation & Distribution
Share of Country Exports: 3.8 (−1.3)
Share of World Cluster Exports: 17.3 (−8.1)

Office
Share of Country Exports: 1.6 (−0.0)
Share of World Cluster Exports: 16.3 (−2.5)

Telecommunications
Share of Country Exports: 0.0 (−0.2)
Share of World Cluster Exports: 0.0 (−7.0)

Defense
Share of Country Exports: 0 (0)
Share of World Cluster Exports: 0 (0)

Food/Beverage
Share of Country Exports: 4.7 (−0.1)
Share of World Cluster Exports: 4.4 (0.2)

Textiles/Apparel
Share of Country Exports: 5.0 (−0.6)
Share of World Cluster Exports: 7.1 (−1.6)

Housing/Household
Share of Country Exports: 3.3 (−0.6)
Share of World Cluster Exports: 12.0 (−1.8)

Health Care
Share of Country Exports: 1.9 (0.3)
Share of World Cluster Exports: 13.9 (−2.2)

Personal
Share of Country Exports: 1.1 (+0.0)
Share of World Cluster Exports: 10.5 (−0.2)

Entertainment/Leisure
Share of Country Exports: 1.1 (−0.1)
Share of World Cluster Exports: 3.6 (−1.3)

Note: Numbers in parentheses are changes between 1978 and 1985.
Exports are those of competitive industries, not all industries.
▨ Identifies broad sectors in which the nation's international competitive positions are related.

16.0 percent of total world exports in the chemical cluster, well ahead of second-place United States and third-place United Kingdom (see Figure 9–9). A second major cluster is in the area of metals, metalworking and associated machinery along with the construction of metallurgical plants. Closely related is an extremely strong cluster in transportation equipment and related parts and machinery (23.7 percent of German exports and 15.0 percent of total world cluster exports). A fourth cluster revolves around printed materials and printing machinery. Another strong cluster is in health care-related products. Germany also has significant overall position in food-related products and textiles/apparel, though the real German strength in both cases is in machinery and specialty inputs rather than end products.

Some of the strongest links between clusters are represented by the shading in Figure 7–11. German positions in chemicals are associated with those in pharmaceuticals (health care) and dyes and synthetic fibers (textiles/apparel), as is the case in Switzerland. In addition, a number of Germany's multiple business industrial products are related to its strong position in chemicals (pumps, valves, and filters). Germany also has by far the leading position in machinery industries cutting across all clusters. However, its position in machinery is usually strongest in those areas where its position in the end product industries is also strong.

In addition to these more extensive clusters, Germany enjoys competitive advantage in optical-related products and in household goods, including certain segments of ceramic and porcelain-related products and equipment and segments of furniture and appliances.

German firms lack national competitive advantage in service industries of almost all types, semiconductors/computers, most electronic products or products heavily based on electronics, most final consumer goods except those with a high mechanical content such as upscale writing instruments, eyeglass frames, and appliances, telecommunications equipment, and defense goods.

Germany's positions in steel, coal, shipbuilding, and apparel have declined significantly in the last two decades (though textile inputs and machinery have recently made a comeback). While Germany has experienced major losses of position in relatively few industries, it should be noted that these are high-employment industries. Moreover, Germany has lost share of world cluster exports in nearly all the sectors since 1978, including significant losses in machinery, as I will discuss further later.

One can begin to understand this evolving pattern of national competitive advantage by examining Germany's position vis-à-vis the "diamond." Germany has generally been well positioned to upgrade its industry, though there are some disturbing developments.

GERMAN FACTOR CONDITIONS

Germany enjoys relatively few natural resources and almost none that have remained a significant advantage in international competition in recent decades. Iron ore and coal reserves were important to the formation of the steel industry. German coking coal deposits are among the finest in the world, and coke and related items represent the one German industry with a major export position that is closely tied to raw materials. The German chemical industry historically used coal as a feedstock, though it became the world leader while it still imported coal tar from Britain.

However, Germany's overall situation is one of disadvantages, not advantages, in natural factors. Many natural resources are not found in abundance, and arable land is in tight supply relative to domestic needs. Energy costs are relatively high. The northern regions of Germany with the greatest natural endowments are in economic decline. What is now East Germany contained some of Germany's most abundant resources. Yet Germany's loss of natural factors of production may have been a blessing in disguise. It created pressures to move into more technically advanced industries and segments.

While weak in natural endowments, Germany enjoys other advantages decisive to upgrading industry. One is a pool of high-wage but highly educated, skilled, and motivated workers. German workers take unusual pride in their work, particularly in producing quality goods.[47] Germany also enjoys a large number of qualified, white-collar personnel, especially in scientific and technical fields. It has a deep scientific and technical knowledge base, dating back to the late nineteenth century when Germany was the birthplace of modern science. Infrastructure is also well developed and of generally high quality, though not a compelling advantage in any industry.

Factor Creation Mechanisms. More significant than the available pool of factors is the quality and sheer depth of mechanisms in Germany for creating advanced and specialized factors. These are unmatched in any other nation we studied in their ability to upgrade factors in the fields in which Germany has historically had a strong position.

The German factor creation mechanisms begin with the public educational system, which is rigorous and of high quality.[48] Next comes an extensive system of universities and *Fachhochschulen*. The latter are technical colleges that are more practically oriented than universities and involve a somewhat shorter study period. These technical colleges are well regarded and of top quality, unlike those in the United States and the United Kingdom. In fact, in some fields, technical colleges are more prestigious than universities.

University and college education in Germany is the responsibility of the Länder, or state governments. They are close to local industry needs, unlike the case in more centralized systems. In Germany, individual universities and colleges tend to specialize in fields relating to the needs of local industries and develop strong capabilities in such areas.

German universities are outstanding in science and engineering and produce a large number of doctorates in scientific and technical fields. The number of doctorates granted per capita is well ahead of the United States, and the number has been growing at the same time as it has been shrinking in the United States. By the early part of the twentieth century, Germany was well ahead of any other nation in scientific and technical education. While the very best American universities now match or even exceed those in Germany in some technical fields, what is remarkable about Germany is the uniformly high standard that virtually all institutions of higher learning meet. An academic career is far more prestigious in Germany than in America or Britain, especially in sciences and in technical fields.

German university education is less effective in social sciences and management. Swiss management education is far better developed, for example, and Switzerland has three of Europe's leading graduate business schools (two of which are soon to merge). Germany has none. German programs in social science and management are highly theoretical, and German companies often hire foreigners in these fields. This may contribute to German weakness in many marketing-intensive consumer goods and business services.[49]

Another factor-creating mechanism in Germany whose importance is hard to overestimate is a well-developed and distinctive apprenticeship system.[50] Apprenticeships are sponsored by companies and the *Länder* (state) governments, and involve millions of students in all significant German industries. Graduates of intermediate school enter the program at about age sixteen, and the programs run for three to four years. Half the week is spent in the company getting practical training and half in a vocational school receiving further training in theory.[51] Apprenticeship programs lead to qualification in highly specialized areas; in optics, for example, a student can apprentice to become a *Feinoptiker* (precision optical instrument maker) or *Glaspresser* (glass maker). A large German optical equipment maker might offer apprenticeships in up to twelve different technical fields and up to five commercial fields.

As a result, German workers are not only better trained in specialized fields than workers in most countries, but have a better theoretical base from which to develop and enhance their skills. This supports the ability to produce goods of rising quality and sophistication. For example, the CEO of Zeiss, the leading German optical company, was quoted as saying that Zeiss was unable to shift production abroad because of the unavailability of specialized workers. Workers are viewed as technicians and command high respect. Some occupations that would be termed ''blue collar'' in

America enjoy high status in Germany. German companies also provide extensive and ongoing in-company training.

A final component of human factor creation in Germany is the tradition of generations of families tending to work in the same industry. This tradition, most similar to that in Italy of the nations we studied, means that expertise is passed along from family member to family member and reinforces formal training.

Combined with superb mechanisms for creating and upgrading human resources in technical and practical fields is perhaps the most effective overall structure for commercial research and development of any nation. Germany has a long tradition of world-class research, particularly in fields such as chemistry, physics, metallurgy, and medicine. Breakthroughs in important fields were the seeds of a number of German industries, notably in the chemical and optical sectors though far from limited to these fields (the X-ray tube and modern printing press were invented in Germany, for example).[52] Preeminence in science and technology in important fields gave German firms early mover advantages in a wide range of important industries. Through continual improvement, German firms have sustained advantage in many of them.

The world-famous Max Planck Gesellschaft is a group of research institutes funded both by government and industry that was founded around the turn of the century. They cover a variety of fields. Though there is substantial government funding, they are legally independent and maintain close ties with industry. Also important are a number of Fraunhofer Institutes, research centers with a more practical orientation. These conduct research under contract from industry. If they are successful in obtaining industry contracts, they receive public funds as well. There is also a system of federal laboratories in a number of fields. Young investigators can move from company laboratories to postings in government or quasi-private research institutes to upgrade their skills.

University research is important and well developed in Germany. German universities are supported by both *Länder* and federal governments, and there is a commitment to support university research by both levels of government. There has long been a similar commitment to support university research in those industries most connected to technology, and a widening range of others. Companies maintain close contacts with universities. For example, BASF has an entire staff devoted to university relations, which manages ongoing contact with many universities and research institutes.

Companies and industry associations sponsor university research and specialized research institutes. The printing-related institutes discussed in Chapter 6 are examples, as is the packaging machinery institute at the University of Dortmund. Universities have specialties in fields that are closely linked to the needs of local industries: Stuttgart, Hannover, and Braunschweig in automotive, Darmstadt and Karlsruhe in chemical engineering, and Aachen and Berlin in industrial and manufacturing engineering.

Finally, German companies themselves engage in active research, reflecting their strong technical orientation. Company research grew from DM 14.5 billion in 1975 to DM 36.5 billion in 1985, faster than the growth of university and public-supported research.[53] The net result of all this activity is that nondefense R&D grew in Germany from 1.9 percent of GNP in 1970 to 2.5 percent in 1985, compared to a rise from 1.7 percent to 1.9 percent in the United States.[54] Overall German R&D as a percent of GDP also exceeded that of the United States in 1987 despite the large U.S. defense R&D expenditure.

As strong as Germany is overall in research, however, it cannot match the United States in inventiveness in new industries nor Japan in the rapid commercialization of new products. Germany is the undisputed leader in improving and upgrading technology in fields in which its industry is established, but there are weaknesses in newer fields such as electronics, biotechnology, and new materials. German firms have been forced to establish overseas subsidiaries and collaborate with foreign firms to obtain such technologies, with mixed success.

Selective Factor Disadvantages. German success in sustaining and upgrading competitive advantage has been powered not only by active factor creation but by pressure from selective factor disadvantages. The chemical industry is a good example. Shortages or the absence of locally available raw materials stimulated breakthroughs in synthetic materials, starting as far back as around the turn of the century with synthetic dyes. "Chemistry rather than colonies" was a popular refrain in Germany, reflecting an orientation toward innovation to secure alternatives to natural raw materials. The two world wars only accelerated such efforts, as shortages were common.

Labor shortages and high German labor costs, combined with labor laws that make layoffs difficult, have long been important stimuli to innovation. They have pushed German firms to automate ahead of American companies in many industries, and have led to manufacturing labor productivity that is by some measures the highest in the world. High wage costs have also prompted German firms to stress quality so that they could command premium prices, as well as to move into more technologically sophisticated industry segments. The need to import many raw materials has placed a premium on sophisticated processing.

GERMAN DEMAND CONDITIONS

The domestic market in Germany is significant in size, the third largest in the free world in terms of GDP. Home demand is particularly large in many industrial goods. Yet saturation in the domestic market, particularly in the many specialized industries in which Germany competes, triggered efforts to sell overseas in many industries. Unlike Britain or France, Germany had no colonies to provide guaranteed export markets. German firms have always had to sell to tough foreign buyers and were forced to rebuild positions abroad after the two world wars. This has honed German strength.

German buyers, both in households and in industry, are sophisticated and extremely demanding. Quality is insisted upon, and no one is bashful about complaining if it is not delivered. Buyers in the United States are often early buyers of new products or services but are not particularly demanding by international standards. German buyers may be somewhat later, but are among the toughest in the world.

German household consumers, for example, tend to keep durable goods longer and maintain them better. Buying on credit is rare; Germans pay cash, and this seems to mirror a greater concern with durability and a tendency to buy higher-quality items in the product range. Credit card penetration per person over eighteen years of age was only 2 percent in Germany in 1987, the lowest of any major European nation.[55] Specialized retail channels supplement a sophisticated end consumer in forcing product improvements in such industries as drafting equipment and cutlery. German industrial workers and managers are highly trained and highly skilled, and this makes them demanding and sophisticated buyers. The extensive apprenticeship program for plastic molders, for example, makes German molders highly sophisticated users and buyers of plastic processing machinery.

The demanding home market is partly manifested by tough product standards, known as DIN (*Deutsche Industrie Norm*). DIN are consistently among the most stringent of any nation (within Germany their difficulty and level of detail is the subject of many amusing stories). Germany has also promulgated tough standards in terms of product safety. An example is the *Maschinenschutzgesetz,* an early and rigorous German law to prevent accidents from machine use. German environmental regulations are also today the most stringent in some fields, and spending on environmental protection is by far the highest in Europe. Germany is very early to set demanding standards and environmental regulations that other nations follow.

Because of the presence of clusters of world-class industries in Germany, the world's most sophisticated and demanding customers of German products are often other German firms. This is true for machinery as well as many industrial inputs, where the greatest German success is in fields in which there are strong domestic buyer industries. German auto companies, for example, are sophisticated buyers of plastics and rubber working machinery, machine tools, and measuring equipment. German firms are also world leaders in the design and construction of complex chemical and metal processing plants, one of the few services in which German firms are internationally successful.

Selective factor disadvantages faced by German buyer industries, such as high labor costs or resource disadvantages, have created further beneficial pressure for upgrading by German firms that supply them. A good example is in the agricultural field, where farmland is scarce and labor expensive. The result is a pressing need for high productivity, and Germany had the greatest number of combines per harvestable hectare in the European Community in 1983. German agriculture also placed a very early emphasis on fertilizers, as far back as the nineteenth century.

In the medical sector, German demand conditions are perhaps the most advanced in Europe. German spending on health care is over 10 percent of GNP, close to that of the United States and significantly higher than Japan's. Germany's social insurance program covers more than 90 percent of its citizens, but is administered through many private insurance companies, not only by government. Germans have free choice of their doctor, and this breeds competition among practitioners and hospitals that has encouraged innovation. German firms account for over 10 percent of total world exports in health care-related industries.

German demand conditions are limiting in some fields, however. For example, German consumers seem less persuaded by image marketing, and demand is slow to develop in German consumer and business services. Anachronistic legislation restricts store hours. Germany also has a relatively high degree of regulation and state ownership in fields such as telecommunications, transportation, electric power, and other areas which impedes the development of innovative new German industries in these fields and diminishes their quality as buyers. Finally, government procurement does not consistently stress competition and pressure firms to produce international competitive product varieties.

RELATED AND SUPPORTING INDUSTRIES

As Figure 7–10 makes clear, the German economy is extensively clustered. Germany is not only competitive in many chemicals and plastics but in pumps, liquid measuring and control instruments, plastics processing machinery, process controls, and heat exchangers, to name a few linked industries. German clusters are often geographically concentrated, though not as strongly as in Italy. Examples are tool making in Remscheid; locksmith wares in Velbert; medical products in Tuttlingen; and optics in Wetzlar (see Figure 4–7).

Some German clusters have developed sequentially, as is the case in Sweden. A strong supplier industry begets a strong downstream industry. For example, a variety of metal processing industries grew out of Germany's historical position in iron and steel. More often, however, suppliers and buyers have grown up in parallel and reinforced each other. In the many industries that Germany pioneered, such as optical goods and X-ray equipment, supplier industries also had to be created from scratch.

German buyers and suppliers work closely together, because of the technical orientation of German firms. This leads both buyers and suppliers to collaborate naturally on new products and on improving existing products. Geographic proximity of suppliers is also typical and reinforces working relationships.

Successful German industries have also emerged from related industries. The breadth of the positions in machinery and chemicals provides examples. German firms tend to practice closely related diversification, often through internal development. Most often it is based on technological connections. Widespread diversification (for example, by Daimler-Benz) is still the exception rather than the rule in Germany.

An area where Germany has serious weaknesses in terms of related and supporting industries is in the consumer sector. The historical lack of television and radio advertising (the major television channels can show advertising only about twenty minutes per day, with commercials all bunched together, and not on Sunday), coupled with the technical orientation of most German managers, means that image marketing skills are poorly developed. New and specialized marketing media and many new types of distribution channels are not well developed. It is rare that a German firm succeeds in an industry in which intangible brand images and mass communication are important to competitive success. This is in stark contrast to the case in America, Italy, or even Japan.

Germany's weakness in electronics and computing has also exposed related industries to foreign competition. In rubber and plastic working machines, for example, Japanese firms have been gaining market position as robotics becomes more important. In X-ray equipment, German firms retain strong positions but have never really become factors in electronics-based ultrasound diagnostic equipment, where American and Japanese firms hold strong positions.

FIRM STRATEGY, STRUCTURE, AND RIVALRY

While there is a mixture of large and small firms, German international success is built to a surprising extent on small- and medium-sized firms, something often not well understood by observers of the German economy.[56] German discipline and order is evident in the way firms are managed. The structure of companies tends to be hierarchical and patriarchal, characteristics often attributed to the German family. There is often a deep involvement by the owner in all aspects of the business, especially in technical areas, and a close and enduring relationship with employees.

German companies are particularly adept at complex production processes such as those required in chemical synthesis and in producing sophisticated machinery. Germany has succeeded in an enormous range of chemicals and in mechanical-related goods where complex products, processes, and service requirements are present or where high precision is required. Selling is often technical and not based on advertising or intangible appeals.

The customers in many of the industries in which Germany is successful are conservative and cautious about new products. Complex service requirements, combined with buyer loyalty, have led to early mover advantages for German firms. Yet these same company characteristics mean that German firms rarely succeed in industries with short product cycles (less than three to five years) or the need for aggressive marketing.

German labor is well organized. Historically, labor-management relations have not impeded productivity improvements or innovation. German unions historically adopted a pragmatic stance. The number of labor-management disputes has been low.

Yet labor-management relations have been undergoing a fundamental shift. German unions are increasingly a conservative force and are resisting change. The problem is not so much high wages and a short workweek but prohibitions on weekend work and other practices which undermine productivity and deter adjustment. The union role on boards is degenerating to one of acting as an adversary to management. This shift, which seems to stem more from union leadership than from the average worker, has disturbing implications for the ability of German firms to continue upgrading.

Pragmatism has characterized German management. Most German companies have been run by executives with technical or scientific backgrounds, and positions in these functions are often the highest paid positions in the firm. The technical orientation of most German firms is manifested in a stubborn desire for technical perfection, as well as a high level of concern for quality. Having the world's best-performing products is a matter of pride and prestige (and also a necessity because of high wage and material costs). German firms are prone to work closely with their customers to achieve this standard, particularly in the case of machinery.

This orientation leads German firms almost inevitably to compete on the basis of differentiation, not cost. They upgrade products continuously and almost invariably gravitate to the high-performance product segments, as in cutlery, cars, and printing presses. German emphasis is less on overall market share than it is in Sweden or Japan, and more on mastering and dominating sophisticated market segments and earning satisfactory profits. German firms are usually heavily focused on one or two core industries, in which they have a broad product line and often generations of technical experience. Unrelated diversification is extremely rare.

Most German firms have a very international orientation. In many specialized industries such as packaging machinery, global sales are necessary to achieve substantial volume. German firms have a history of seeking to export very early. The tendency to compete in sophisticated products and segments rather than in high-volume ones further necessitates an international outlook to reap the available economies of scale.

While Germany has extremely high export levels, German companies do not hesitate to invest abroad where necessary for cost or market access reasons. Foreign investment by German industry has grown significantly since the late 1970s. In 1985, for example, 22.9 percent of German automobile production and 32.7 percent of truck production was abroad.[57] German unions historically have not seriously stood in the way of foreign investment, nor has government.

National prestige in Germany rests in industry, particularly in sophisticated machinery and instruments, automotive-related fields, and chemicals. Outstanding people enter industry, and many of the best enter technical fields. The most popular field of study among male German university students is *Maschinenbau*, or mechanical engineering.[58] Prestige in science and technology in Germany dates back for a century. The world's first graduate schools, and doctoral dissertations requiring original research, were German inventions. (American universities, for example, adopted the German model beginning with Yale in 1861.)

German workers and managers have a high and sustained commitment to their industry. Workers and managers are extensively trained in their chosen field. The thought of leaving it is anathema. Workers and management are technically oriented and deeply involved in both the product and the production process. The commitment of workers and managers to a particular field, and to find solutions (usually technical ones) to problems rather than to abandon it, is manifested in a willingness to reinvest continually in the business. Widespread private and family ownership of companies is another contributing factor. These considerations make German firms unusually successful in industries and segments where there is a learning curve and the need for highly skilled and specialized employees. The nature of individual goals is less amenable to success in industries characterized by the need for entrepreneurship and risk taking.

Sustained commitment to the business is reinforced by the nature of the German capital markets. Many company shares are held by banks and other long-term holders, who often play a prominent role on boards. There is no tax on long-term capital gains. The concern for quarterly earnings, in preference to actions required to sustain the long-term position, has been all but absent, in contrast to the United States. In Germany, there has been no obligation even to publish interim (quarterly or semi-annual) financial reports.

Disturbing signs are appearing, however, which suggest that goals are shifting. In management, a tendency toward group decision making has retarded dynamism in some companies. Financial executives are moving in increasing numbers into top management positions (examples include

Daimler-Benz, Volkswagen, Veba, and Hoechst) and a financial orientation is creeping into boardrooms, moving investment decisions away from technical criteria and an unfailing commitment to preserve technical leadership in the industry. Large companies are issuing annual reports on a more timely basis, and more have started making interim financial reports. The prevalence of acquisitions and unrelated diversification are rising. A proposed change in the tax law will tax long-term capital gains and threatens to shorten investment horizons and trigger a wave of mergers.

Strong domestic rivalry is widespread in industries where Germany has national competitive advantage. Cars, trucks, chemicals, optical goods, writing instruments, and many other industries are characterized by at least three or four significant German competitors. German rivals actively compete not only for sales but, as importantly, for prestige, scientific and technical firsts, and the best recruits.[59] German domestic rivalry is often not on price but on technology, product performance, and service. Technological competition, arising from managers' orientation and goals, drives improvement even where the number of competitors is small. The level of import protection in Germany is also very low by international standards.

Yet competition is another area where there are grounds for concern. In numerous German industries there has been consolidation and a tendency toward high levels of collaboration, some of which date back to the interwar years. Mergers and alliances among leading German competitors, sometimes justified as preparing for a more unified European market, are proliferating (1,159 mergers were registered in 1988, up 63% from 1985). Almost none have been prohibited on antitrust grounds. The threat to German competitive advantage is palpable.[60] Another area of concern is German participation in alliances linking the leading competitors in a number of European nations. Overall, danger signals are appearing again in the area of domestic rivalry as they have several times in the past in Germany.[61]

In addition, there is significant state ownership in Germany compared to the United States, covering telecommunications, utilities, airline and rail transportation, and other important industries. As mentioned earlier, the German position in supplier industries to these sectors is, not surprisingly, rather weak.

Another area of enduring weakness in Germany in the post–World War II period is new business formation. The notion of a self-made individual has a negative connotation in Germany. Failure carries a very strong social stigma. Risk aversion is high, and there is an unwillingness to bet everything on a new venture, perhaps a legacy of the two world wars. There is also a poorly developed risk capital market. Investor protection laws limit investments in new companies by institutional investors. Labor laws, which impede layoffs, set common minimum wages, and are not suspended for small firms as in Italy, also tend to work against the formation of new companies.

So does the relative paucity of truly revolutionary new technology. There have been few spin-offs from German universities, partly because the great majority are public institutions where the faculty and staff are public servants, partly because professors are severely restricted in terms of outside activities, and partly because prestige lies in large established companies.

The role of new business formation in further upgrading the German economy is central. Without enough new jobs to cope with demographics and restructuring, unemployment has emerged as the economic Achilles heel. There are some signs of improvement, including some new venture capital funds, more new companies going public, and the creation of new centers for encouraging high-technology companies based around universities. Yet the pace of new business formation is still modest and many impediments remain.

THE ROLE OF GOVERNMENT

The German government has a relatively modest involvement in industrial policy compared to most European and Asian countries. For example, there is no foreign trade ministry in Germany, and Germans maintain that foreign trade is principally the role of firms, not government. Germany is among the most open markets in the world, and tariffs have historically been low. German industry has had to face foreign competition and has been strengthened in the process. Export financing is done on a commercial basis, not through a government agency that is subsidized. Direct government funding of corporate R&D is modest and declining.

The principal role of the German government, both federal and Länder, has been in factor creation, especially in education and in science and technology. The extensive array of mechanisms described earlier is heavily funded by government. Interestingly, though, direct government control is not exercised in many instances; a degree of independence is present even in government-funded technical institutes.

German regulation has tended to be demanding and has generally pressured innovation, not impeded it. German environmental standards are also stringent and lead the world in some fields, stimulating innovation in the industries affected. Yet German regulation has frozen the status quo in other areas. A notable example is in services, where a tangle of restrictions, licensing requirements, and standards has contributed to hindering the development of virtually any German service firms with the strength to compete internationally.

Despite its generally constructive role, the German government has also had a stubbornly persistent tendency to subsidize ailing sectors such as steel and shipbuilding, with little effect except to postpone adjustment. Deregulation has lagged behind many other nations, placing a drag on the advancement of the affected industries. The extent of state ownership in Germany is relatively high; privatization and the opening of industries to competition have also lagged. Moreover, the commitment to competition has seemed increasingly tentative. Finally, the tax changes I described earlier raise serious concerns for corporate goals, as well as, in the long term, for new business formation.

The Role of Chance

The two world wars had a major impact on the German economy. They had major and obvious negative effects in terms of the loss of markets, loss of territory, loss of human resources, loss of technology, loss of momentum, and loss of goodwill. Germany also lost many world-class minds who fled the country during the Third Reich.

Yet in a tragic and ironic way, as has been observed by others, the wars seem to have had so many positive effects that they have outweighed the negatives in determining Germany's success in postwar industrial competition. The national challenges that were created by both wars produced remarkable technological progress in synthetic materials and other fields. After the wars, recovering from defeat was an enormously important motivation for industrial success for a proud and educated population. The challenge of rebuilding foreign market positions created strong pressure to produce products that were truly superior. Loss of natural resources placed a premium on knowledge-based competition.

World War II brought a breakup of cartels that unleashed rivalry. Imposition of tough antitrust laws, courtesy of the Americans, was among the greatest gifts that could have been given from the perspective of the economy. The loss of patents, the destruction of production facilities, and the deportation of production machinery to victorious nations provided German firms with the necessity, actually a unique opportunity, to begin with a clean slate to improve old technologies, invent new ones, and build modern facilities. Finally, the new competition between East and West Germany may have provided a stimulus to prove that the West German system was superior.

Germany in Perspective

Germany has had unusual advantages in all the determinants of national competitive advantage, covering a range of industries that draw on technological ability in chemistry, mechanical engineering and physics. The economy is built on early mover advantages, mostly growing out of science and technology. Many German competitive positions were created by the turn of the century. What is particularly notable about Germany is the ability to sustain positions in these fields over long periods of time.

The unique strength of the German economy has been its capacity to upgrade its advantage by raising the quality of human and technical resources and improving product and process technology. In accomplishing this, German firms have moved into more and more sophisticated segments. The mutual reinforcement of the "diamond" has allowed German firms to sustain these positions as well as to extend clusters into a remarkably wide range of related industries. Decades of prosperity, like in Switzerland, are taking their toll.

Germany achieved premier industrial status around the turn of the century. The deep, systemic advantages it has long enjoyed allowed Germany to recover from two devastating wars. The wars may well have provided the setbacks, the hardships, and the pressures that have sustained German advantage for so long. Without them, Germany might have lost its dynamism decades ago. Germany's performance was much weaker after World War I than after World War II, perhaps reflecting the greater tendency toward cartels and monopoly during this period.[62]

The major historical weakness of the German economy is in its inability to create positions in new industries. Germany has not been able to replace the jobs lost in the few failed industries, or those jobs inevitably lost in the process of upgrading successful industries. More recently, a decline in the ability to make fundamental breakthroughs in new scientific fields, the growing militancy of unions, a tendency toward consolidation and more muted domestic rivalry, shifting managerial and investor goals, and demand-side limits raise real questions for the future.

These questions are reflected in the data I presented earlier in Table 7–1. Germany's productivity growth has slowed dramatically, as has its rate of net fixed capital formation. Per capita income growth is also lagging. The pattern of market share gain and loss between 1978 and 1985 is also troubling. Figure 7–12 shows that Germany has lost 15 percent or more world export share in far more industries than have gained. Losses far outnumber gains in important clusters such as transport, chemicals, power generation and distribution, office, and semiconductors/computers, though net losses occurred in every sector except food and beverages and defense. While some export share losses are the result of foreign investment, movement into advanced segments, or predictable losses of market position in factor cost-sensitive industries, the sheer number of losing industries and the fact that many produce sophisticated products such as instruments, switchgear, and computers raise serious concerns about the health of upgrading.

FIGURE 7-12 Competitive German Industries with Gains or Losses of World Export Share of 15 Percent or More Between 1978 and 1985*

UPSTREAM INDUSTRIES

	Materials/Metals			Forest Products			Petroleum/Chemicals			Semiconductors/Computers			UPSTREAM INDUSTRIES		
	Total Comp. Inds.	Share Gains	Share Losses	Total Comp. Inds.	Share Gains	Share Losses	Total Comp. Inds.	Share Gains	Share Losses	Total Comp. Inds.	Share Gains	Share Losses	Total Comp. Inds.	Share Gains	Share Losses
Primary Goods	50	13	18	9	2	2	44	6	23	2	0	4	105	21	47
Machinery	8	0	5	2	0	1	0	0	0	0	0	0	10	0	6
Specialty Inputs	2	0	3	0	0	0	0	0	0	0	0	0	2	0	3
Total	60	13	26	11	2	3	44	6	23	2	0	4	117	21	56

INDUSTRIAL & SUPPORTING FUNCTIONS

	Multiple Business			Transportation			Power Generation & Distribution			Office			Telecommunications			Defense			INDUSTRIAL & SUPPORTING FUNCTIONS		
	Total Comp. Inds.	Share Gains	Share Losses	Total Comp. Inds.	Share Gains	Share Losses	Total Comp. Inds.	Share Gains	Share Losses	Total Comp. Inds.	Share Gains	Share Losses	Total Comp. Inds.	Share Gains	Share Losses	Total Comp. Inds.	Share Gains	Share Losses	Total Comp. Inds.	Share Gains	Share Losses
Primary Goods	19	2	8	22	3	14	20	5	13	4	0	5	0	0	2	1	0	0	66	10	42
Machinery	3	0	1	11	0	5	0	0	0	3	0	2	0	0	0	0	0	0	17	0	8
Specialty Inputs	3	0	1	10	0	4	0	0	0	1	0	0	0	0	0	0	0	0	14	0	5
Total	25	2	10	43	3	23	20	5	13	8	0	7	0	0	2	1	0	0	97	10	55

FINAL CONSUMPTION GOODS & SERVICES

	Food/Beverage			Textiles/Apparel			Housing/Household			Health Care			Personal			Entertainment/Leisure			FINAL CONSUMPTION GOODS & SERVICES		
	Total Comp. Inds.	Share Gains	Share Losses	Total Comp. Inds.	Share Gains	Share Losses	Total Comp. Inds.	Share Gains	Share Losses	Total Comp. Inds.	Share Gains	Share Losses	Total Comp. Inds.	Share Gains	Share Losses	Total Comp. Inds.	Share Gains	Share Losses	Total Comp. Inds.	Share Gains	Share Losses
Primary Goods	18	8	4	14	5	8	25	2	10	7	1	3	8	1	6	9	2	8	81	19	39
Machinery	9	2	2	8	3	2	0	0	0	0	0	0	0	0	0	0	0	0	17	5	4
Specialty Inputs	10	5	5	16	4	7	5	1	2	0	0	0	1	0	1	1	0	1	33	10	16
Total	37	15	11	38	12	17	30	3	12	7	1	3	9	1	7	10	2	9	131	34	59

*Gains and losses include industries exceeding the cutoff in either 1978 or 1985, both those that were competitive in 1978 but fell below the cutoff in 1985 and those that had first achieved sufficient share to exceed the cutoff in 1985. The total number of competitive industries refers to 1985.

Our case studies confirmed loss of competitive advantage in a number of advanced industries. Of equal concern is the fact that Germany has lost 15 percent or more share in eighteen machinery industries but gained it in five. Finally, the industries in which Germany gained share over the 1978–85 period had the slowest average growth of any nation, while the industries in which it lost share had among the fastest (see Table B–3). How to renew the dynamism of the German economy is a challenge I will return to later. The promise of German unification, so unexpected until 1989, may provide the discontinuity needed to jar Germany off its present course and make the challenge more surmountable.

8

Emerging Nations in the 1970s and 1980s

As America, Switzerland, Sweden, and Germany were prospering in the 1960s, important developments were brewing in the pattern of national competitive advantage. Technological change, accelerating globalization of competition, and developments within nations themselves set the stage. A number of new nations emerged as advanced international competitors, supplanting others to achieve leadership in a range of industries. Japan is the most striking and visible success story. I will examine the much-discussed Japanese case from the perspective of my theory to seek new insights into what has happened there. Hardly less impressive in many respects is Italy, which has achieved vibrant competitive positions in a wide range of industries.

Still other nations had been, or are, in the process of becoming advanced industrial economies. The most prominent are several Far Eastern nations. I will discuss South Korea, which has, in my judgment, the best prospects of reaching true advanced status in the next decade of any of these nations. Japan, Italy, and Korea are the three nations we studied with the fastest growth of per capita income and productivity.

My task is to begin to understand the reasons why these nations have moved from positions lagging behind more established trading powers to create competitive advantage against the world's best rivals in increasingly advanced industries and segments. To do so, I must explain the pattern of success and failure in their industries and how this has been changing over time. I will also place particular emphasis on the circumstances which have supported the upgrading of their industry over time.

As in the previous chapter, I cannot hope to paint a complete picture of every sector of the economy in these three nations, nor mention and document every important consideration. Competitive advantage results from a combination of industry-specific, sector-specific, and more general national characteristics. Mention of the latter should not be confused with downplaying the former. The changing competitive patterns in these nations provide important lessons not only about the "diamond" but also how entire national economies advance.

THE RISE OF JAPAN[1]

Japan, the other large defeated nation in World War II, was not far behind Germany in becoming a world economic power. The achievement is all the more remarkable because Japan started behind even Germany in terms of natural resources. It also lacked Germany's historical positions in such important sectors as chemicals and machinery.

The story of Japan's economic success has been told many times in recent years. It is a story that usually assigns a starring role to government and emphasizes Japanese management practice. My own view of Japan's success is somewhat different. Like all nations, Japan has achieved national competitive advantage in some industries but has failed in many others. Whatever is happening in Japan clearly does not work equally well in all industries. Management practice alone cannot explain all it has been credited with.

The framework of previous chapters will provide a new vantage point from which to view the pattern of national competitive advantage in Japanese industry and the reasons underlying it. Of particular concern will be the forces that have allowed Japanese firms to upgrade their competitive advantages rapidly over time and to compete successfully in advanced new industries. There is a role for government in the process, but it has been a shifting role whose significance is rather different from what has emerged as the accepted view.

PATTERNS OF JAPANESE NATIONAL ADVANTAGE

Table 8–1 lists the top fifty Japanese industries in terms of share of world exports in 1985. The list contains a wide variety of industries, as do the comparable lists of Germany, Switzerland, and the United States. Notable are many electronic products, heavy equipment, and steel- and transportation-related industries. What is unique about the Japanese list is the extraordinarily high share of world exports that Japanese firms hold in many industries. The only comparable case is American export shares in some agricultural

TABLE **8–1 Top Fifty Japanese Industries in Terms of World Export Share, 1985**

Industry	Share of Total World Exports	Export Value ($ millions)	Import Value ($ millions)	Share of Total Japanese Exports
Motorcycles	82.0	2,092,416	16,684	1.19
TV image and sound recorders	80.7	6,622,119	9,924	3.77
Dictating machines	71.7	1,817,413	15,194	1.03
Calculating machines	69.7	660,432	11,294	0.38
Mounted optical elements	67.5	579,472	29,646	0.33
Photo and thermocopy apparatus	65.9	2,032,389	6,055	1.16
Still cameras and flash apparatus	62.2	1,608,936	82,174	0.92
Cash registers and accounting machines	62.0	351,522	1,626	0.20
Outboard marine piston engines	61.0	216,878	1,448	0.12
Electric gramophones	59.0	264,557	997	0.15
Microphones, loudspeakers, and amplifiers	55.7	981,176	51,602	0.56
Motorcycle parts and accessories	53.4	747,246	13,370	0.43
Track-laying tractors	51.8	295,286	9,427	0.17
Pianos, musical instruments, and parts	51.0	687,841	47,188	0.39
Self-propelled dozers	50.6	283,448	2,631	0.16
Color TV receivers	49.5	2,691,101	6,899	1.53
Portable radio receivers	48.4	1,171,209	31,718	0.67
Other radio receivers	47.9	575,146	9,443	0.33
Special-purpose vessels	46.8	635,608	13,555	0.36
Electric typewriters	45.0	498,134	5,214	0.28
Steam boiler auxiliary plants and parts	42.8	393,155	51,450	0.22
Motor vehicle radio receivers	42.5	908,083	3,052	0.52
TV picture tubes	42.2	709,509	35,503	0.40
Prepared sound recording media	41.5	1,589,513	96,184	0.90
Photo chemical products	41.5	346,817	26,170	0.20
Metalworking lathes	39.7	524,440	16,281	0.30
Coarse ceramic housewares	39.3	229,081	6,168	0.13
New bus or truck tires	39.1	860,530	4,411	0.49
Buses	38.7	592,138	6,926	0.34
Sewing machines	38.7	444,548	24,716	0.25
Iron, steel seamless tubes	38.7	2,227,632	6,587	1.27
Self-propelled shovels and excavators	38.4	964,654	—	0.55

TABLE **8–1** (*Continued*)

Industry	Share of Total World Exports	Export Value ($ millions)	Import Value ($ millions)	Share of Total Japanese Exports
ADP peripheral units	37.9	3,571,949	427,126	2.03
Lorries and trucks	37.5	7,956,271	16,969	4.53
Forklift trucks	36.9	612,440	—	0.35
Other electronic tubes	36.5	313,761	95,967	0.18
Metal cutting machine tools	36.5	1,009,629	111,274	0.57
Generating sets with piston engines	36.1	377,849	9,165	0.22
Other cargo vessels	35.7	4,399,729	216,601	2.50
Iron, simple steel rolled thin plate	35.2	1,893,459	84,656	1.08
Continuous synthetic weaves nonpile	34.7	1,456,391	31,808	0.83
Clocks, watch movements, cases	33.8	296,181	62,532	0.17
Rolling mill parts and rolls	33.4	203,563	3,487	0.12
Liquid dielectric transformers	33.4	210,792	—	0.12
Containers including road-rail	32.2	280,192	1,048	0.16
High carbon steel wire rod	32.0	258,370	1,029	0.15
Tankers	31.7	767,626	13,116	0.44
Passenger motor vehicles	30.8	25,402,210	538,683	14.46
Iron, steel tubes and pipes	30.6	1,437,337	17,006	0.82
Monochrome TV receivers	30.3	124,238	1,374	0.07
TOTAL				48.50

NOTE: No import data are reported if import value is less than 0.3 percent of the total trade for 1985.

and resource-based goods. High Japanese shares in manufactured goods reflect a number of elements of the Japanese environment that I will discuss further, among them the types of strategies typically adopted by Japanese firms, the nature of the goals they set, and the structure of many Japanese industries.[2]

Another unique characteristic of the Japanese top fifty list is the absence of anything approaching a natural resource-intensive industry. (The closest is seamless tubes of iron and steel, which in Japan are made with imported coal and iron ore.) The United States has the greatest number of natural resource-intensive industries among its top fifty. Sweden is next in the ranking, while Germany, Switzerland, and Italy each have some.

Figure 8–1 presents the Japanese cluster chart in 1985, and Figures 8–2 and B–5 provide summary statistics. The breadth of industries in which

FIGURE 8–1 Clusters of Internationally Competitive Japanese Industries, 1985

Primary Goods	MATERIALS/METALS			FOREST PRODUCTS
	IRON & STEEL		NONFERROUS METALS	Tarred coated paper[#]
	Pig iron, etc.[*]	*Iron, simple steel rolled thin plate*	Copper plate, sheet, strip	
	Iron, simple steel coils	*High carbon steel rolled thin plate*	Copper foil, powders, flakes, fittings[#]	
	High carbon steel coil[#]	*Stainless steel rolled thin plate*	Copper tubes, pipes, etc.	
	Iron, simple steel wire rod	*Tinned plates, sheets*	Aluminum plates, sheet, strip	
	High carbon steel wire rod[#]	Iron, simple steel hoop, strip	Aluminum foil[*]	
	High carbon steel bars, etc.[#]	*High carbon steel hoop, strip*[#]		
	Iron, other steel bars hotrolled		OTHER	
	Iron, steel profiles, etc.[#]	FABRICATED	Cement	
	Large U, I, H sections, etc.	*Iron, steel railway rails*		
	Other profiles hotrolled	Iron, simple steel wire		
	Iron, steel universal plates, sheets[#]	*High carbon steel wire*[#]		
	Iron, simple steel rolled heavy plate	*Cast iron tubes & pipes*[#]		
	High carbon steel rolled heavy plate[#]	*Iron, steel seamless tubes*		
	Iron, simple steel rolled medium plate	*Iron, steel tubes, pipes*		
	High carbon steel rolled medium plate[#]	Iron, steel tube fittings		
		Steel storage tanks		
		Iron, steel cable, rope		
		Iron, steel nuts, bolts		
		Iron, steel chain & parts		
Machinery	*Mineral crushing, etc. machinery*	Gas generators, furnace burners[#]		
	Rolling mills[*]	Electric industrial furnaces		
	Rolling mill parts nes, rolls	Nonelectric industrial furnaces		
Specialty Inputs				
Services				

FIGURE 8-1 (Continued)

	PETROLEUM/CHEMICALS	SEMICONDUCTORS/COMPUTERS
Primary Goods	ORGANIC CHEMICALS Coke of coal, retort carbon* Polyacids & derivatives Oxyamino compounds Heterocyclic compounds, etc. INORGANIC CHEMICALS Zinc, iron, lead oxide* Metal compound of inorganic acid PETROLEUM PRODUCTS Petrol. jelly, pitch# PLASTICS Alkyds, sheets, waste# Polystyrene PVC plates, strip Acrylic polymers *Polyamide sheets, waste**	Digital central processors* **ADP peripheral units*** *Other electronic tubes** Diodes, transistors, etc. Electronic microcircuits **Piezoelectric crystals#** ADP machine parts##
Machinery		*Semiconductor mfg. equipment****
Specialty Inputs		Ceramic packaging***
Services		

KEY

roman   10.12% world export share or higher, but less than 20.24% share
bold italics **20.24% world export share or higher, but less than 40.48% share**
sans serif 40.48% world export share or above

* Industries below cutoff in 1978
# Calculated residuals
Added due to significant export value in a segmented industry

• Added due to FDI
** Upgraded due to FDI
*** Added based on in-country research

	MULTIPLE BUSINESS	TRANSPORTATION		
Primary Goods	Other hand tools Blades, tips for tools' *Centrifugal pumps nes* *Pumps for gases, etc.* Fans, blowers, etc., parts *Ball, roller, etc., bearings* Cocks, valves, etc., nes Shaft, crank, pulley, etc. *Optical instruments* Meters & counters Surveying instruments Measuring, drawing, etc., instruments *Mineral manufactures#* Measuring, controlling instruments##	ENGINES Motor vehicle piston engines' **Marine piston engines, outboard#** ***Marine piston engines, other than outboard*** Piston engines nes VEHICLES **Track-laying tractors** Wheeled tractors' **Self-propelled dozers** *Self-propelled shovels, excavators*	***Fork lift trucks, etc.*** Lifting, loading machines nes# ***Passenger motor vehicles*** ***Lorries, trucks*** Special motor vehicles ***Buses*** **Motorcycles** ***Bicycles, wheelchairs#*** Railway vehicles# ***Tankers of all kinds***	***Other cargo vessels*** **Special purpose vessels** Civil engineering equipment## VEHICLE EQUIPMENT Ship derricks, cranes ***Containers, including road-rail***
Machinery	Machinery for special industries nes# Vending, weighing machines#*	***Rubber, plastics working machines*** ***Metal cutting machine tools#*** ***Metalworking lathes*** Reaming, etc., metalworking machines'	***Metal-forming machine tools*** Metalworking machine tools, parts# ***Converters, ladles, casting machines#***	Gas-operated welding, brazing, etc., machines#* ***Nonelectric power hand tools*** Electric welders, etc.' ***Electromechanical hand tools#*** ***Other electrical machinery#***
Specialty Inputs	Foundry molds nes Gaskets, nonelectric machine parts#*	Synthetic rubber Radar apparatus, etc.' Piston engine parts nes Tires for cars' ***New tires for buses or trucks*** Tires for aircraft, motorcycles# Rubber articles#	***Electric accumulators*** ***Ignition, starting equipment*** ***Electric vehicle lighting equipment*** ***Electrical condensers*** ***Electrical carbons***	Motor vehicle bodies, parts, accessories#* Primary batteries, cells Motor vehicle chassis **Motor cycle parts, accessories** **Motor vehicle radio receivers**
Services	Engineering/architecture' Trading''' Commercial banking' Reinsurance'	Shipping'''		

FIGURE 8–1 (Continued)

	POWER GENERATION AND DISTRIBUTION	OFFICE	TELECOMMUNICATIONS	DEFENSE
Primary Goods	GENERATION Steam boilers **Steam boiler auxiliary plants*** *Steam engines, turbines* DC motors, generators, rotary converters, parts* AC motors, incl. universal motors *AC generators* *Generating sets with piston engines* DISTRIBUTION *Liquid dielectric transformers* Other electrical transformers# *Static converters* Inductors, electric power machine# Switchgear *Fixed, variable resistors* Insulated wire, cable *Electric insulating equipment*	**Electric typewriters** Nonelectric typewriters, checkwriters# **Calculating machines** Cash registers, accounting machines* *Duplicating, other office machines*# Photo, thermocopy apparatus Dictating machines Base metal office supplies nes#	*Line telephone equipment* TV, radio transmitters *Radiotelephonic receivers, TV cameras, parts*#	
Machinery		Rotary printing presses* *Platen printing presses*#		
Specialty Inputs				
Services				

KEY
roman   10.12% world export share or higher, but less than 20.24% share
bold italics   20.24% world export share or higher, but less than 40.48% share
sans serif   40.48% world export share or above

*   Industries below cutoff in 1978
\#   Calculated residuals
\##   Added due to significant export value in a segmented industry

•   Added due to FDI
••   Upgraded due to FDI
•••   Added based on in-country research

	FOOD/BEVERAGES	HOUSING/HOUSEHOLD	TEXTILES/APPAREL
Primary Goods	BASIC FOODS Fish prepared, preserved *Fish oils, fats#* BEVERAGES *Other fermented beverages#*	HOUSEHOLD CERAMICS *Porcelain, china housewares* *Coarse ceramic housewares* Ceramic ornaments DOMESTIC APPLIANCES Heating, cooking apparatus' *Air-conditioners* Domestic washing machines' *Domestic refrigerators'* *Other domestic appliances#* OTHER *Cutlery* Synthetic carpet#	FABRIC Woven cotton bleached# *Continuous synthetic weaves nonpile* Woven synthetic fiber fabrics# *Continuous regenerated weaves nonpile* Synthetic knit nonelastic fabric ACCESSORIES Nonknit textile accessories#
Machinery	Hand tools for agric., horti., or forestry# Nondomestic refrigeration equipment' Nondomestic refrigeration equipment parts nes# Harvester, thresher#		Spinning, extruding machine parts Weaving machines *Knitting, felt mfg, etc., machines#* Loom, knitting machine parts nes' *Sewing machines* *Sewing machine needles, parts#* Textile processing machines# *Spinning, reeling machines*
Specialty Inputs	Fungicides, disinfectants#'	Glass#'	FIBERS & YARN Discontinuous synthetic fiber uncombed Discontinuous synthetic fiber combed# *Discontinuous regenerated fiber uncombed* Discontinuous regenerated fiber combed#
		Glass inners for vacuum flasks#'	*Nontextured continuous polyamide fiber* Discontinuous synthetic fibers Regenerated fiber yarn, monofilament OTHER Lub. for textiles#'
Services			

FIGURE 8–1 (Continued)

	HEALTH CARE	PERSONAL	ENTERTAINMENT/LEISURE
Primary Goods	PHARMACEUTICALS Provitamins & vitamins MEDICAL EQUIPMENT *Electromedical equipment* X-ray apparatus, etc. Medical instruments	Watches **Clocks, watch movements, cases#** *Fountain pens, etc.* *Pen nibs, pencils#* *Combustible products, etc.* Smallwares, toiletries Pearls* *Spectacles#* *Gold, silverware#*	CONSUMER ELECTRONICS **Color TV receivers** *Monochrome TV receivers* *Portable radio receivers* Other radio receivers Electric gramophones TV image. sound recorders Microphones, loudspeakers, amplifiers PHOTOGRAPHIC **Still cameras, flash apparatus** Cinema cameras, projectors, etc. *Photo & cinema apparatus & equipment nes#* **Photo chemical products#** *Photo film flat unexposed* *Photo film roll unexposed* Photo sensitized cloth OTHER ENTERTAINMENT **Prepared sound recording media** Baby carriages, sporting goods# Toys, dolls# *Indoor game equipment* Pianos, musical instruments, parts#
Machinery			TV picture tubes Unmounted optical elements# Mounted optical elements Electric filament lamps Discharge lamps, flashbulbs#
Specialty Inputs		*Clocks, clock, watch parts*	
Services			Hotels*

KEY

roman   10.12% world export share or higher, but less than 20.24% share
bold italics   *20.24% world export share or higher, but less than 40.48% share*
sans serif   **40.48% world export share or above**

*   Industries below cutoff in 1978
\#   Calculated residuals
\#\#   Added due to significant export value in a segmented industry

*   Added due to FDI
**   Upgraded due to FDI
***   Added based on in-country research

FIGURE 8-2 Percentage of Japanese Exports of Competitive Industries by Broad Cluster

UPSTREAM INDUSTRIES

Materials/Metals
Share of Country Exports: 9.6 (-6.4)
Share of World Cluster Exports: 10.8 (-1.7)

Forest Products
Share of Country Exports: 0.2 (+0.0)
Share of World Cluster Exports: 1.0 (0.3)

Petroleum/Chemicals
Share of Country Exports: 1.3 (-0.5)
Share of World Cluster Exports: 1.0 (-0.2)

Semiconductors/Computers
Share of Country Exports: 4.7 (3.6)
Share of World Cluster Exports: 11.3 (6.3)

UPSTREAM INDUSTRIES
Share of Country Exports: 15.6 (-3.3)
Share of World Cluster Exports: 4.6 (-0.4)

INDUSTRIAL AND SUPPORTING FUNCTIONS

Multiple Business
Share of Country Exports: 3.7 (0.1)
Share of World Cluster Exports: 5.5 (0.9)

Transportation
Share of Country Exports: 36.9 (1.0)
Share of World Cluster Exports: 22.6 (4.2)

Power Generation & Distribution
Share of Country Exports: 3.3 (-0.6)
Share of World Cluster Exports: 14.6 (1.0)

Office
Share of Country Exports: 3.5 (0.5)
Share of World Cluster Exports: 28.0 (8.5)

Telecommunications
Share of Country Exports: 3.4 (1.4)
Share of World Cluster Exports: 28.1 (8.8)

Defense
Share of Country Exports: 0.0 (-0.1)
Share of World Cluster Exports: 0.3 (-0.1)

INDUSTRIAL AND SUPPORTING FUNCTIONS
Share of Country Exports: 50.8 (2.3)
Share of World Cluster Exports: 17.4 (3.5)

FINAL CONSUMPTION GOODS AND SERVICES

Food/Beverage
Share of Country Exports: 0.7 (-0.1)
Share of World Cluster Exports: 0.7 (0.2)

Textiles/Apparel
Share of Country Exports: 3.2 (-1.5)
Share of World Cluster Exports: 4.9 (-0.5)

Housing/Household
Share of Country Exports: 2.3 (0.4)
Share of World Cluster Exports: 8.2 (3.4)

Health Care
Share of Country Exports: 0.7 (0.3)
Share of World Cluster Exports: 4.7 (1.9)

Personal
Share of Country Exports: 1.6 (-0.4)
Share of World Cluster Exports: 5.3 (0.3)

Entertainment/Leisure
Share of Country Exports: 11.8 (2.4)
Share of World Cluster Exports: 32.7 (8.4)

FINAL CONSUMPTION GOODS AND SERVICES
Share of Country Exports: 20.3 (1.0)
Share of World Cluster Exports: 6.9 (2.0)

Note: Numbers in parentheses are changes between 1978 and 1985. ▨ Identifies broad sectors in which the nation's international competitive positions are related. Exports are those of competitive industries, not all industries.

Japan has strong positions is extremely wide, rivaled only by Germany and, to a lesser extent, the United States. The vertical depth of Japanese positions within clusters is somewhat less than in other highly advanced nations, notably Italy, Germany, and Sweden. The deepening of Japanese clusters into machinery and, to a lesser extent, in components, however, has been significant since 1978.

The most significant clusters of competitive industries in the Japanese economy are in transportation equipment and related machinery, office machines, entertainment and leisure (notably consumer electronics), steel and fabricated metal products, electronic components and computing equipment, and optical-related products (including cameras and film). Japanese firms also have strong or emerging positions in printing equipment, telecommunications equipment (mostly hardware), ceramics-related products, household appliances, electrical goods, personal mechanical or electronic products such as pens, watches, and clocks, and a growing array of general business inputs such as fans, pumps, and tools. Many of these clusters are themselves related.

Some of the stronger links between clusters are indicated by the shading in Figure 8–2. Semiconductors and electronics technology unite a number of clusters. Japan's position in semiconductors grew out of earlier positions in consumer electronics and telecommunications. Office machines and computers emerged later out of the previous three. Japan's position in health care is heavily skewed toward electronics-related equipment.

Japan exhibits little national competitive advantage in forest products or related fields, chemicals and plastics (many of the positions Japan holds are declining except in a few areas I will discuss), food and beverages, packaged consumer personal products such as detergents or toiletries, and defense-related goods. Japan is also weak internationally in services of nearly all types and in home furnishings. Positions in health care and textiles/apparel (except machinery) are also modest.

Indeed Japan, more so than perhaps any other nation, is a study in contrasts. On the one hand, it contains some of the most competitive firms and industries in the world, that have powered remarkable national economic progress. On the other hand, however, there are large portions of the Japanese economy that not only fail to measure up to the standards of the best worldwide competitors but fall far behind them. The continued existence of these sectors is both a reflection of the complicated balance of Japanese policy and a growing constraint to future Japanese prosperity.

To understand this pattern of national competitive advantage as well as how it has evolved and upgraded over time, it is necessary to examine how Japan has been situated vis-à-vis the "diamond." I will concentrate here on those industries in which Japan has achieved international competitive advantage, and treat the industries in which Japan is uncompetitive more briefly. There is a unique ability in Japan for the "diamond" to function as a system. In no country we studied was the self-reinforcement among the determinants more pronounced, though Italy was a close second.

JAPANESE FACTOR CONDITIONS

The starting point for assessing Japan's factor conditions is the nation's paucity of natural resources or other natural factors such as arable land or a location close to markets. Japan does enjoy relatively favorable circumstances for hydroelectric power generation because of its mountainous terrain, and a large share of electric power in the 1950s and1960s came from hydroelectric sources. This conserved foreign exchange and benefited early Japanese export industries such as steel.[3]

With the exception of an abundance of natural ports, however, Japan by and large faces systematic disadvantages in natural factors of production. Its absence of natural endowments has precluded any significant international success in areas such as forest products, mining, and agriculture. As we will see, however, Japan's natural resource disadvantages have played a considerable role in the process of creating and upgrading competitive advantage in a wide range of industries and in rapidly rising productivity.

Another weakness in factors of production was that of capital. Japan emerged from World War II with very limited capital resources. The breakup of the *zaibatsu* (giant holding companies) system also weakened the financial structure.

Human resources, in contrast, were an area where Japan brought some advantages. With a long tradition of respect for education that borders on reverence, Japan possessed a large pool of literate, educated, and increasingly skilled human resources. Japanese are disciplined, hardworking, and willing to cooperate with the group. Japanese also assign very high status to teachers and authority figures.[4] Small living quarters and shared multipurpose central rooms also demand cooperation and mutual respect.[5]

Like Germany, Japan has benefited from a large pool of trained engineers. Japanese universities graduate many more engineers per capita than universities in the United States. A growing number of Japanese are also being educated abroad, particularly in technical fields. In 1987–1988, more than 18,000 Japanese were studying in U.S. universities, and Japan ranked sixth on this dimension, well ahead of the United Kingdom, Germany, and Italy.[6]

The scientific base in Japan after World War II did not rival that of America or Germany but was significant in a range of fields. Japan's wartime industrial achievements bear witness to considerable capabilities in aviation, communications, shipbuilding, and machinery. An intense national effort was devoted in wartime to making progress in these fields. Japanese benefited from cooperation with German researchers during World War II in industries such as optical instruments.

Factor Creation Mechanisms. Any notion that Japan began its ascendance with nothing misses the mark by a wide margin. Only in the area of human resources, though, did Japan enjoy any real factor advantages. More important than the availability of factors is that Japan was able to create and upgrade needed factors at a rate that arguably far exceeded that of all other nations. Japanese industry was also able to circumvent shortages in other factors, and to deploy available factors faster and more aggressively than firms from other nations.

While Japan began the postwar period with little capital, capital accumulation took place rapidly, due to an extraordinarily high savings rate. The savings habit was partly cultural and partly a reflection of government policies, among them the absence of social security, a low housing stock which made the purchase of a home difficult for many, and impediments to placing capital abroad. To compensate for weak financial institutions, the Japanese government instituted a financial investment policy (*zaisei-to-yushi*) that involved encouraging savings and deploying it in priority fields. Individuals were given tax incentives to deposit savings in the postal savings system (*yubin chokin*), banks, and securities companies. The postal system was widely used because of the plethora of conveniently located post offices throughout Japan.[7] In the early postwar period, scarce capital collected through the postal savings system was allocated under government guidance through the Japanese Development Bank and other government institutions at low interest rates to firms in particular sectors such as steel and shipbuilding. Through this process, Japan was able to achieve international success in a number of capital-intensive industries despite capital scarcity relative to other advanced nations. By the 1970s, sustained high savings combined with growing competitive success meant that capital had ceased to be a constraint to Japanese industry.[8] The resulting low interest rates have contributed to a high rate of capital investment (as was evident in Table 7–1) and to many Japanese companies adopting capital-intensive strategies involving aggressive investments in large-scale facilities. So effective is capital creation that Japan is now awash with capital without enough to spend it on (a potential threat to the economy, see Chapter 13).

The process for creating capital was not the only impressive Japanese factor creation mechanism. More significant was the rapid and continual upgrading of human resources, which supported a growing sophistication of competitive positions. A first-rate primary and secondary educational system in Japan operates based on high standards and emphasizes math and science. Primary and secondary education is highly competitive, and family involvement, especially the mother's, in education is the highest of any nation I studied with the possible exception of Korea.[9] While Americans often claim (with some justification) that a lack of creativity results from Japan's rigid system, Japanese education provides most students all over Japan with a sound foundation for later education and training. A Japanese high school graduate knows as much math as most American college graduates.

Japan's universities are numerous and provide an adequate education, particularly in technical areas. In 1986, there were 465 four-year and 548 two-year universities in Japan. Yet, Japanese universities are not up to par when compared to those in Germany, the United States, Switzerland, or Sweden, especially in social sciences and humanities. Though high school students take rigid national entrance exams to compete for admission to university (many take extracurricular cram courses starting in grade school to prepare for them), once admitted, the norm is more play and less work in the nontechnical fields. In engineering and science, the curriculum is better developed and training is more rigorous.

What is unique about Japan's postsecondary educational system is the education and training that is provided both for workers and managers in Japanese companies. Japanese knowledge creation has taken place in companies much more than in other institutions. In-company training is rigorous and essential for advancement. Managers in many Japanese companies actually have to pass tests to advance to the next level. Companies such as NEC Corporation provide training for employees even at the postdoctoral level. In-company training is continuous and focused on the specific skills and fields relevant to the industry involved. Most of the Japanese students studying abroad are sent by their companies and are fully supported by them. Employees accumulate specialized skills throughout their careers, underpinning the continuous upgrading of competitive advantages.

Japanese companies are also the principal engine of research and development in Japan. University research is limited, and interchange between companies and universities is modest compared to a number of other nations. There is a series of national laboratories in Japan connected to the various Japanese ministries, and these have had some role in research and development. Many of the best science graduates, however, choose positions in the research laboratories of major Japanese companies. It is here that most of the important research in Japan takes place.

Japanese companies have also had unusual skill in sourcing technologies from abroad, as have the Swiss and the Swedes. Japanese have a long tradition of adopting parts of other cultures. There is a high level of respect in Japanese companies for strong rivals and a lack of technical arrogance or concern over authorship. The pragmatic search for better technology is also driven by intense domestic competitive pressure. Japanese companies have long invested heavily in attending foreign conferences, visiting friendly overseas companies, studying the literature, and licensing good technologies rather than attempting to duplicate them.

As technological capability has grown in Japan, companies have increased the rate of spending on more and more basic research. Today, Japanese government statistics show that Japan is a net exporter of technology measured in terms of new research contracts or agreements. The overall level of R&D spending in Japan has risen from 1.9 percent of GNP in 1971 to 2.8 percent in 1987, along with Germany and Sweden the highest of any advanced nation. Virtually all of Japanese R&D is in areas other than defense. Government funds a modest 21 percent of national R&D (compared to 47 percent in the United States) and more than 80 percent of Japanese government-funded R&D is in general science and energy (see Tables 12–1 and 13–1).

Much has been said about the Japanese practice of cooperative research, in which a group of companies under the leadership of a government agency, often the Ministry of International Trade and Industry (MITI), conduct joint research in an area of broad importance. Some government money is involved in these programs, but most of the funds and personnel come from the participating companies. Many have argued that cooperative research avoids waste and duplication and has been a significant source of Japanese national advantage in the industries in which it has been practiced.

My view is rather different. I see the principal role of cooperative research as a signaling device to indicate important areas for long-term research attention, and as a stimulus to proprietary company research. Japanese companies typically spend far more internally on private research in the same field than they contribute to the cooperative venture. The cooperative projects are established as independent entries in which most industry participants have access, minimizing the threat to competition. Companies jealously guard their best ideas and do not necessarily contribute their best people. Yet the existence of the cooperative project signals emerging technologies, highlights a field in which competitors will also be working, and often helps company research directors extract larger budgets from senior management. Fierce rivalry makes it a point of honor for a company to become involved in new, high-profile technologies. All this is extremely beneficial for technical progress but not for the reasons typically supposed.

Another important area of factor creation in Japan, and in some ways the most critical, is in the area of information. Every Japanese company and Japanese citizen is inundated with economic information. Data are available in profusion in Japan (about market shares, company developments, technical trends, and so on) in those industries and product areas in which Japan has a position. Prime-time news shows provide heavy coverage of economic issues. (Since many Japanese executives are still at work, some tape the news as well as the frequent specials on current economic issues with their VCRs.) Information is made available by the media, government agencies, industry associations, and countless other organizations, which crank out report after report and book after book. There is a constant stream of books about Japanese companies and by leading Japanese executives, which often figure prominently on Japanese best seller lists.

This pool of economic information, unrivaled even in the United States, is an important part of the process of rivalry among Japanese companies. It confronts them with the need to be forward looking and constantly measure progress against their rivals. Interestingly, market share rankings are accorded much more significance than financial rankings.

Selective Factor Disadvantages. Japanese national competitive advantage is rarely due to basic factor advantages. It often stems partly from the mechanisms in place to create specialized factors relevant to particular industries. As important as factor creation, however, is the stimulus provided by selective factor disadvantages that face Japanese firms.

Japan started out with a large pool of unemployed workers after World War II. By the late 1960s, however, there were labor shortages, especially in the rapidly growing automobile and electronics industries.[10] These and rapidly rising wages created pressures to automate. Adding to these pressures was the practice in larger companies of permanent or lifetime employment, making Japanese companies very careful about hiring and prone to try instead to improve productivity with the existing workforce.[11] The ironic result of these circumstances was that many Japanese companies automated away one of their early advantages vis-à-vis Western companies, cheap labor. Labor costs were also no help in competing with what were typically many Japanese rivals; this, too, promoted automation.

Disadvantages in natural factors of production were also stimuli to innovation and upgrading in Japanese industry. At the broadest level, Japanese children are taught at an early age that Japan can only survive through *kakō-bōeki*, or exports based on imported materials. The concept of upgrading is implanted early. At a more concrete level, absence of natural resources translated into innovation in many Japanese industries. A lack of indigenous metals and other raw materials led to an intense interest in reducing the material content in products, as well as in using advanced new materials.[12] Japanese firms are world leaders in ceramics, composites, and carbon fibers, for example, and there is brisk and advanced demand for new materials in Japanese industry.

The high level of dependence on foreign energy beginning in the 1960s has meant high domestic energy prices and an intense concern with energy conservation. For example, energy utilization in Japanese steel companies is believed to be the most efficient in the world. The two oil crises hit Japan particularly hard and galvanized the attention of Japanese industry even more toward energy conservation, prompting many innovations.[13] For example, many companies switched to solid-state technology right after the first oil shock, first and foremost to reduce power consumption. This unlocked other benefits such as greater reliability, fewer components, and ease of automation, and catapulted Japanese firms into leadership in such industries as television sets and audio equipment. The oil shocks caused every nation to become more concerned with energy costs, but historically high Japanese energy costs gave Japanese firms a head start.

The long distance between Japan and many markets (and supply sources) has also stimulated innovations in logistics. Containerization came early to Japan, as did the usage of specialized cargo vessels. Distances have also prompted concern for reliability to minimize service requirements. Japan's location has also had another effect: it allows relatively unimpeded access to Asian markets that were not emphasized or well served by Western firms. In many industries, the first Japanese exports were within Asia, in contrast to Korean and Taiwanese industries whose first major exports have been almost invariably to the West (and in particular the United States).

Another pervasive selective factor disadvantage in Japan is the extremely high cost of land, due to a shortage of usable land. Population density is high relative to other nations even counting Japan's total land area (see Table 1–1), but seventy-five percent of Japan is mountainous and poorly suited for homes or factories. Space pressures not only affect demand conditions (favoring compact and space-efficient goods) but have also led Japanese companies to shorten production lines, avoid unnecessary storage space and inventory, and combine production operations. Japanese firms, for example, pioneered space-saving just-in-time production.

A final potent selective disadvantage was the rise of the yen beginning in 1973 but particularly the upward revaluation of the yen beginning in the mid-1980s. Revaluation led to feverish activity in Japanese companies to compensate. Improving productivity through automation, shifting to more sophisticated product segments, and globalizing production are three typical responses, all extremely beneficial to the long-term sustainability of Japanese advantage. Under intense domestic competitive pressure, the response to revaluation has been fast and has led to the rapid upgrading of Japanese industry.[14]

Each of the shocks (the Nixon shock involving the imposition of an import surcharge by the United States, the oil shocks, the yen shock) was in fact a powerful spur to progress and innovation in Japanese industry. Each had a disproportionate impact on Japan. Greeted with widespread alarm and pessimism, each of the shocks exposed Japanese industry to strong stimuli that triggered waves of innovation. If they had not occurred, it would have been to Japan's advantage to invent them.

As in Switzerland, Germany, and Sweden, selective disadvantages triggered innovation and not paralysis or harvesting because of other parts of the "diamond," especially the intense commitment of Japanese firms to their industry and fierce domestic rivalry. Japan has been truly unique, however, in the extent to which the other determinants made the response to selective disadvantages particularly positive. Japan's rebound from the oil shocks, for example, took place with remarkable speed.

DEMAND CONDITIONS

Factor conditions suggest some generalized advantages available to Japanese industry, while selective factor disadvantages begin to point to particular fields where Japanese industry would excel. Yet, to understand fully the patterns of Japanese success, we must look elsewhere in the "diamond." Demand conditions prove to be one of the most important of the determinants of national competitive advantage in Japanese industry. In a remarkable number of the industries in which Japan achieved strong positions, the nature of domestic demand characteristics provided a unique stimulus to Japanese companies. The domestic market, not foreign markets, led industry development in the vast majority of Japanese industries. Only later did exports become significant.[15]

Any discussion of Japanese demand conditions must begin with the recognition that the Japanese home market is quite large, with about 120 million people and a vast number of companies packed into a relatively small land area. Moreover, the Japanese people are culturally and ethnically very homogeneous, which serves to concentrate purchasing power even further.

In the 1950s and 1960s, Japan's home market demand was growing rapidly in industries in which other nations' markets had begun to level off. This produced some significant advantages. During the postwar period, international Japanese successes such as sewing machines, steel, shipbuilding, and motorcycles, for example, began when booming home demand gave firms the conviction to invest aggressively in large, efficient facilities with the latest technology at a time when U.S. and European competitors were incrementally adding to existing, less efficient older plants. The war facilitated this, by forcing many industries to start again from scratch. So did the "scrap and build" mentality that was common in industry and encouraged by government. The orientation was to tear down old, inefficient facilities and replace them with large, modern ones. The resulting higher productivity often yielded major advantages for Japanese competitors.

Many of the industries in which Japan succeeded benefited from a disproportionately large home market, reflecting unusually intense Japanese demand. The industries I noted earlier are all examples: steel (Japan was rebuilding), ships (Japan has huge shipping needs, given its remote location and need to import oil and other raw materials), motorcycles (used for basic transportation), and sewing machines (1.1 million out of 1.7 million sewing machines in Japan were destroyed in the war; many citizens used sewing machines to make their own clothes in the early postwar years and apparel was also a booming export industry).

As the Japanese economy grew and broadened, disproportionately large industrial home demand aided such industries as robotics, copiers, ceramics, and semiconductors. In memory chips and integrated circuits, for example, Japan has unusual home demand because of the strength of the Japanese consumer electronics, watch, camera, and office machine industries, all heavy chip users.[16] Invariably, however, the large home market is carved up among several if not dozens of Japanese companies. For this and other reasons, Japanese firms do not become bloated feasting on the large home market but are pushed to innovate and ultimately to internationalize.

The rates of market penetration (and saturation) in Japan are very high. In consumer goods, rapid information flow, desire for the latest model for status reasons, and cultural homogeneity all contribute to a strong bandwagon effect in purchasing. Among industrial buyers, intense domestic rivalry in their industries and a strong tendency toward imitation cause other companies to follow quickly if one important company buys a new product or service. One result of rapid penetration is explosive domestic growth. This often leads Japanese companies in pursuit of market share to make large investments all at once in efficient scale capacity.

The mirror image of rapid penetration is early saturation. Since the late 1960s, the Japanese home market for a product generation is often maturing while markets in other countries are still growing. Early and rapid home market saturation leads to intense efforts by Japanese competitors to come up with new models or features. Pressures are also intense to shorten the time required to develop new products and models. The Japanese market becomes a leading indicator of conditions that will prevail elsewhere.

Domestic saturation is also invariably the impetus for a major export drive, as companies scramble to replace lost domestic volume and fill excess capacity. In nearly every Japanese industry we studied, exports increased substantially *only* when the domestic market became mature.

More significant than the size and growth pattern of the home market is the segment structure of Japanese demand. Japan, like the United States, has a wide range of climatic and geological conditions. It also has a curious combination of advanced and backward infrastructure, yielding what might be called a dual demand structure. These circumstances expose Japanese firms to multiple segments, often in interesting combinations. In trucks, truck and bus tires, and forklifts, for example, the poor Japanese roads, a strong user tendency toward overloading, and tight space constraints made products built for the Japanese home market well suited for sales to developing countries, notably elsewhere in Asia. Japanese producers have been very successful in such markets.

Unique local demand conditions focused particular attention on some product attributes. Because of crowded conditions and limited living space, Japanese demand was for compact, portable, quiet, and multifunctional products. In home audio, for example, Japanese firms had concentrated on small, compact units which embodied multiple functions. Consumers ranked compactness and sound quality ahead of power for their small, thinly-walled apartments. Another good example is electronic keyboards, where Japanese firms dominate. Electronic keyboards are much smaller than pianos, can be put away after use, and can also be used with headphones to limit the noise to which others are exposed.

The profusion of relatively small companies, small offices, small plants, and small warehouses has also skewed Japanese demand toward smaller, compact products in numerous industries such as lift trucks, machine tools, and office machines. A great deal of mountainous terrain and a number of major islands have led to a long-standing focus on microwave and satellite communications systems. In textiles, Japanese firms are strong in synthetic textile fibers and fabrics which come close to simulating silk, where Japanese home demand is unusually great.

These and other attributes of Japanese home demand directed Japanese firms to segments of the market that were ignored or underserved elsewhere, and only later emerged as global segments. Demand, skewed toward compactness, lightness, and multifunctionality, was also a leading indicator of broader trends in world demand. Japanese companies thus gained undefended routes for foreign market entry in such industries as cars, light trucks, radios, TV sets, copiers, motorcycles, programmable controllers, numerically controlled machine tools, and lift trucks where the compact segment was initially unimportant in advanced nations. This, coupled with the fact that many Japanese firms started their export drives in a time of rapid world economic expansion, helps in understanding why competitive retaliation by foreign firms was often light and why protectionism was limited.

Japanese success is not only in industries where the segment structure of home demand leads to greater attention but also in those where needs at home are unusually stringent or buyers are particularly sophisticated. Copiers and facsimile machines, for example, are a pressing need because Japanese companies have a penchant for documentation yet the use of *kanji* (with some 60,000 Chinese characters), *hiragana,* and *katakana* characters make typewriters (and carbons or stencils) as well as telex machines impractical. Prior to the advent of word processors, most documents in Japan were handwritten, and copiers and facsimile machines were essential to disseminating information. Both copiers and facsimile machines are industries in which Japanese firms are world leaders due to both early and sustained attention and investment.[17] The rapid shift in Japan to word processors, which can handle the Japanese language, is also easy to understand for similar reasons.

The Japanese written language also leads to unusually stringent and sophisticated demand in Japan for pens and pencils. Handwriting is an important sign of education and culture in Japan, and precise and well-functioning writing instruments take on unusual importance. Another product area in which there is sophisticated home demand is cameras, where the Japanese love of photography is legendary. Cameras have long been used to record family events, and in the early postwar years many Japanese spent three times their monthly salaries to buy a German-made camera. Now, of course, Japanese firms are world leaders.

Consumer durables, in particular, are important status symbols among Japanese. With limited living space, little spare time, and an inability to consume conspicuously on housing, Japanese conspicuously consume such products as cars, cameras, consumer electronics, and compact appliances. This heightens buyer concern with having the latest model or the most up-to-date features. Japanese buyers are willing to replace products frequently to get newer and better models. Japanese manufacturers respond with frequent model changes and microsegmentation of the market through numerous product varieties. The combination of status needs and cultural homogeneity results in a large number of product varieties within a relatively narrow range. The demands on production created by such strategies have, in turn, pushed Japanese firms to early introduction of flexible manufacturing technology while Western firms were still employing traditional forms of automation. Japanese firms do particularly well in industries where frequent new model introduction is important to competitive advantage.

Pressure from demanding and sophisticated buyers is widespread in Japanese consumer industries. Japanese consumers will reject a product because of a small surface defect, one reason for the attention of Japanese companies to "fits and finishes." Consumers demand high quality and superior service. Japan has a visual culture, in which the presentation, and the packaging, are as important as the product. Japanese consumers are also fickle in comparison to those in most other nations. They will readily switch brands if a quality difference is noticeable. The sophistication of Japanese buyers is reinforced by an extreme abundance of product information.

Sophisticated and demanding Japanese buyer behavior for industrial products initially grew out of the same attitudes. Japanese firms expect a great deal from their suppliers. The role of salespeople in Japan creates reinforcing pressures for product innovation. Salespeople require new models to provide an acceptable way to initiate customer contact. Because of the value placed on long-term relationships, purchasers in Japan tend to be less prone to switch suppliers simply for a short-term price break, though they will switch for a quality improvement at the same time as they entreat their traditional supplier to match it. The result is even more pressure for innovation, because the only way to win new customers is through real improvements.

As Japanese industry has developed, the quality of home demand has been upgraded even further. In a growing number of industries, the world's most sophisticated buyers of industrial goods are other Japanese firms who represent the cutting edge of buyer needs. This has benefited the supplier industries. Good examples are in robotics, automotive components, advanced materials, and many types of electronic components. The importance of sophisticated industrial demand is perhaps even better illustrated by Japan's pockets of strength in the chemical sector, an area where Japanese firms are generally weak internationally. The most significant world export shares occur in precursor materials to synthetic fibers, where Japan has a significant competitive position, and in types of plastics used heavily in the electronics and automobile industries. The breadth of Japan's competitive industries is also beginning to have the same effect it had in the United States decades earlier—growing success in the multiple business category, or products that are sold to many other industries (such as pumps and tools).

Domestic demand conditions also help to explain the areas in which Japan has, by and large, not succeeded internationally. There is virtually no home market for defense goods, a legacy of the constitution written under the supervision of U.S. occupation forces. Home market demand in the food sector (with heavy dependence on rice, fresh fish, and other distinctive dishes) is sufficiently out of synch with most other important nations as to disadvantage Japanese firms abroad (but keep out foreign firms except in fast food, where American chains are popular). Differences in taste and in living space are disadvantages in home furnishings such as furniture.

In consumer packaged goods, Japanese demand took off too late. American, British, Swiss, and other foreign firms became well established in Japan through foreign direct investment. Fragmented and poorly developed retail and wholesale channels in food and other packaged goods also impede the development of competitive advantage in Japanese industries that sell through them. Japanese firms have succeeded abroad in industries such as watches and consumer electronics, where close relationships with fragmented and diverse channels are important. This is partly because of well-honed skills in dealing with complex channels at home. They are less successful, however, in products sold through supermarkets, drug stores, and other mass channels where home market experience is lacking. Even in consumer electronics, Japanese firms have often had to employ channel approaches different from those used at home.

Interestingly, some Japanese consumer packaged goods companies such as Kao and Shiseido are beginning to internationalize their strategies. The demanding Japanese consumer, well-developed mass media, growing affluence, and intense local rivalry have led to cutting edge developments in some packaged good product categories such as disposable diapers, and are likely to produce more. A poorly developed distribution system, however, will remain a daunting impediment.

In health care, the Japanese system is socialized and quite homogeneous.

Doctors all receive similar training, and there is central control over approved procedures and treatments. Hospitals have little reason to change. Japanese doctors are primarily compensated not for their time and services but through reimbursement for the drugs they prescribe. This makes Japanese per capita drug demand the highest in the world, but it is not quality demand from the perspective of international competition. Japan provides a poor environment for innovation in health-related fields. Except in medical equipment heavily based on electronics technology (such as ultrasound and CT scanners), Japan has a weak international position.

The Japanese weakness in services is a function of a number of factors. One is that the standard of personal service in Japan is very high, involving large numbers of people. It does not lend itself to systemization and standardization as does the American or British approach (see Chapter 6) and is too costly to replicate abroad. The Japanese weakness in the English language is another major impediment, because international services tend to involve extensive personal communication. It is also important that a range of significant Japanese service industries (such as financial services) are regulated by the Japanese government, blunting competition and impeding innovation. Finally, Japanese manufacturing companies have only recently begun to make extensive foreign direct investments. Japanese business services firms are just beginning to enjoy the base of foreign demand that is so crucial to U.S., British, and Swiss firms.

RELATED AND SUPPORTING INDUSTRIES

The role of related and supporting industries in Japanese national competitive advantage is among the most striking aspects of the Japanese economy. Successful Japanese industries have often grown out of other related Japanese industries. The table below illustrates just a few examples:

TABLE 8–2 **Origins of Successful Japanese Industries**

Industry	Industry(s) From Which It Grew
Typewriters	Sewing machines
Lift trucks	Trucks, construction machinery
VCRs	TV sets, home audio
Copiers	Cameras
Facsimile	Copiers
Robotics	Machine tools, motors
Synthetic textile fibers (filament type)	Natural textile fibers (silk)
Carbon fibers	Synthetic textile fibers

When they diversify, Japanese firms almost exclusively pursue related diversification.[18] Prevailing norms against acquisitions, substantial share ownership by long-term minded institutions, and high price-earnings multiples sharply limit mergers. Most diversification is via internal development. The predominance of internal development, in turn, makes closely related diversification almost a necessity. The driving force in internal diversification is often to redeploy people and facilities. The net result is efficient skill transfer from industry to industry, which facilitates upgrading.

A related industry is often born or invigorated when the base industry matures, and competitors face pressures from excess capacity. To protect employment and continue growth, many if not all of the competitors from the base industry will enter the related industry almost simultaneously (remember the strong tendency of Japanese companies to imitate each other). Because there is sometimes more than one industry related to a new industry and every Japanese industry usually has many competitors, the result is a flood of new entrants. In facsimile, for example, some entrants came from cameras (Canon, Ricoh, Minolta, Konica), some from office machines (Matsushita, Sharp, Toshiba), and some from telecommunications (NEC, Fujitsu, Oki). New entrants bring skills from different fields, further stimulating innovation as each firm strives to apply its existing skills and acquire those it lacks.

The role of supporting industries in creating competitive advantage in Japanese industries is also pervasive. Forward and backward integration is common, driven by the same forces that spur diversification. Japanese air-conditioning firms became world-leading suppliers of compressors, for example. Over time, the result is that many of the most competitive Japanese industries are those in which there are also world-class Japanese suppliers.

Larger Japanese firms frequently have networks of many small- and medium-sized subcontractors and suppliers (called *shita-uke*). With firms and their suppliers typically located close to each other, information flows freely, service is superb, and change is rapid. Larger firms sometimes have equity stakes in their suppliers, opening information flow further. At the same time as they cooperate with their suppliers, however, Japanese companies bargain vigorously, and supplier profitability is modest.

Japan also has the important advantage of leading positions in a variety of industries that in the 1980s were essential supporting industries to many others. Notable are semiconductors, machine tools, robotics, and advanced materials. These positions, some won from the United States, create favorable conditions for upgrading competitive advantages in established industries and developing new ones.

Strong forces, then, lead to clustering in the Japanese economy. Japanese companies are uniquely able to exploit its benefits. They stress cooperative long-term relationships with buyers and suppliers instead of opportunism.

The principal function of the *keiretsu* (groups of companies affiliated by shareholdings) and *shita-uke* structures is to facilitate interchange among related companies (the role of the *keiretsu* in strategy formulation and financing is greatly overstated in most Western accounts). Companies loosely linked in Japanese groups look to each other for guidance and input on new products, new processes, and new businesses. Japanese trade associations also promote the links between suppliers and buyers, by collecting information and sponsoring studies. Japanese trade associations often span a variety of supplier, buyer, and related industries, promoting the working of clusters. Cultural homogeneity and physical proximity also play a role in the effective functioning of clusters. So does a strong social tradition of affiliation to groups, which leads to a desire to maintain close personal relationships such as those between members of the same graduating class in high school and university.

Supporting industries are significant in two other areas that deserve mention. The first is the Japanese trading companies. These huge firms, with well-developed worldwide networks, helped many Japanese companies penetrate foreign markets. They still play an important role in marketing to smaller and developing countries and are important sources of information to Japanese companies that lack overseas personnel or that are smaller and less sophisticated in international operations.

Another vital supporting industry to many others is the media. Unlike Sweden and Germany, Japan has long had commercial radio (1951) and television (1953). Half a dozen national newspapers (for example, *Asahi, Mainichi, Nikkei*) are sold throughout the nation, and all have morning and evening editions. There is a proliferation of weekly and biweekly magazines.

Mass media and mass advertising, then, are well developed in Japan, and Japan ranks second in the number of television advertising minutes per day behind the United States. This was a major benefit as Japanese durable consumer goods companies sought to penetrate foreign markets such as those of the United States and the United Kingdom that demanded mass marketing expertise. Unlike German and Swedish firms, Japanese firms have been able to learn mass marketing skills at home.

FIRM STRATEGY, STRUCTURE, AND RIVALRY

Japanese firms are hierarchical and disciplined, a reflection of social history, the Japanese educational system, and the practice of lifetime employment in the larger Japanese firms. At the same time, however, cooperation and subordination of the individual to the group are the norm, and there is a unique ability to coordinate across functions. Project teams are frequently used to move an important project out of the hierarchical structure. All this leads to short new product introduction times and products that are designed with the needs of manufacturing and marketing in mind.

Relationships between labor and management are respectful and strikes are rare. This was not always true, because labor disruptions occurred in Japan in the 1930s and again in the early 1950s. Good relationships are not culturally determined but were forged through secured employment, inviting union leadership onto boards, and an attitude of mutual respect. Company-based unions also fostered a cooperative attitude between the union and the company.[19] The Japanese labor-management relationship creates few barriers to innovation or change due to work rules or other rigidities.

Many of the most talented people in Japan flow to industry.[20] While the hot industries and companies to join change over time, they have always been major industries and usually manufacturing industries. After World War II, many of the best engineers joined textile and later steel companies. Then the flow shifted to consumer electronics companies such as Sony and Matsushita. Today, companies such as NEC Corporation and FANUC lead the list.

Engineers are at the helm of many of the leading Japanese manufacturing companies, and a technical orientation is pervasive. A strong belief in R&D and in the most modern facilities and equipment is nearly universal. The chief executives of many of the leading companies are also still the entrepreneurs who founded or built them after the war. This generation of managers, many of them visionaries, has had an intense commitment to build global companies that mastered the technologies of the future. As this generation of leaders retires, the goals of Japanese firms may well shift in ways that slow the rate of innovation.

Japanese companies almost invariably adopt a strategy of standardization and mass production. In many industries, among them cameras, lift trucks, pianos, and television sets, firms gained competitive advantage initially by producing relatively standard models in large volumes and transforming the production process from craft or batch production to assembly line techniques. Higher and higher levels of automation were sought and achieved over time. Such an approach led to Japanese industry leadership or to dominance of more standardized industry segments.

Part of the ability of Japanese firms to accomplish this in the 1960s and 1970s was a rapid agreement on domestic and international standards, while firms from many other nations were still squabbling to preserve their own varieties. The government pushed early standardization in a number of industries, including sewing machines, memory chips, and facsimile machines. The Japan Industrial Standards (JIS) have continued to help standardize components and parts. Standardization removed uncertainty on basic features and meant that firms began competing on other features and on productivity

in manufacturing. More recently, as Japanese firms have become technological leaders, they have become more prone to resist standards. The controversy
over VCR and video camera standards are two examples. MITI continues
to play an active role in pressuring firms to agree to standards in order to
stimulate further industry development.

Japanese firms solidify their positions by creating a steady stream, or
even a flood, of new models. Typically, these are relatively standard products
embodying a wide range of options or additional features, often produced
with flexible manufacturing technology. The result is microsegmentation
and sometimes excessive product proliferation. This is partly due to the
demand-side pressures I described earlier, partly due to the role of the
salesperson in Japan, and partly due to the desire to redeploy people and
capacity.

Hand in hand with standardization and mass production is an extreme
emphasis on product quality. In fact, standardization and automation are
seen by many Japanese companies as the only way to achieve very high
quality levels. Demand-side pressures motivate an intense concern for quality.
Also important was a national program in the 1950s and 1960s to upgrade
product quality to overcome the previous image of ''cheap'' Japanese goods.
The bad image of Japanese goods abroad was turned into an energizing
force for Japanese industry. The quality mentality is etched into the minds
of all Japanese and institutionalized in the prestigious Deming Prize for
quality excellence, awarded annually.

Japanese firms often define their goals in terms of volume and market
share. This reflects the desire to maintain employment (making labor costs
fixed), a strong belief in the advantages of scale, and an intense desire to
outdo rivals. Production and market share data are readily available for
almost every Japanese industry, unlike in the United States and other nations
where such information is spotty. Companies compare themselves in terms
of market share on a continuous basis, and loss of share is cause for embarrass-
ment and a strong response. Workers define their status in no small part
based on how well their company is doing along this variable. Market
share is a principal goal unless a company is suffering losses; then companies
will take strong steps to preserve the continuity of the enterprise.

Japanese labor and capital have sustained commitments to the company
and the industry. Ownership of companies is predominantly held in institutions (and to some extent by other companies) that seek long-term appreciation
and do not often trade the shares. Japanese interest rates are low, reducing
the cost of capital and promoting investment. Banks and other institutions
that hold equity in companies are active in corporate governance. Both
major investor and management concern for stock price is minimal compared
to ensuring sustained company prosperity. Management compensation is

not closely tied to short-run results. Problems are confronted. Selling off or closing a business unit is rare, though it is becoming more common.

Workers and managers are also committed to their company, and vice versa. There is a mutual investment in upgrading skills. This, plus norms of cooperation, lead to unusual success in industries requiring accumulated learning. Less success is typical in businesses where individual achievement and internal competition is of paramount importance.

Another characteristic I observed in Japanese companies, bearing on motivation, is a certain pessimism and insecurity. Nearly all Japanese managers could recite a list of their company's dozen most pressing problems at a moment's notice; eliciting a list of strengths was like pulling teeth. This is yet another force that works against complacency in Japanese industry.

Japanese companies adopt an international outlook, but this is less from the pull of foreign markets (as in the United States) or an international tradition (as in Sweden or Switzerland) than from the *push* of conditions at home. While there is a large domestic market, intense (and crowded) domestic rivalry and excess capacity are frequently the spur to international sales. The market share orientation is extended to encompass the share of world production.[21] The Japanese case illustrates why language skills can be an effect instead of a cause of exports. Japanese have difficulty learning Western languages, but an intense desire to export has led to great efforts to do so.

As leading Japanese companies established international networks, the globalization process for newer industries became more rapid. Until very recently, however, Japanese global strategies involved relatively low levels of foreign direct investment and were based almost solely on export. This is an important reason why Japanese shares of world exports are so high. Concentration of production at home, however, has been a barrier to success in those industries where extensive foreign investment is a necessity for competitive advantage, such as consumer packaged goods, services, and heavily engineered or customized products.

These tendencies in the structure and management philosophy of firms lead Japanese firms toward particular types of industries or industry segments. Japanese firms do not do well, by and large, in industries or segments involving high degrees of customization to individual buyers, narrow applications, heavy after-sale support, and small lot sizes.

While these other areas I have discussed are important, however, perhaps the single greatest determinant of Japanese success, based on our research, is the nature of domestic rivalry. While the *zaibatsu* structure concentrated economic power in prewar Japan, its breakup by the Allies unleashed a level of competition that is unmatched in any nation. Virtually every significant industry in which Japan has achieved international competitive advantage is populated by several and often a dozen or more competitors (see Table 8–3, which appeared earlier as Table 3–2).[22] Many of the reasons for this have already been described.

The proliferation of domestic rivals, coupled with demand-side pressure and goals heavily oriented toward market share, creates a tinderbox of innovation and change. Competition tends to be among equals or near equals, in contrast to a more stable situation in which there is a leader and clear followers. The intense competition for market share, strong commitment to the industry, and sophisticated and demanding consumers combine to work against stable oligopolies.[23]

Competitors are studied carefully, and moves are rapidly matched. Companies invest aggressively in large-scale capacity additions, often all at the same time. Industry leadership shifts frequently. There have been three different market share leaders in the facsimile industry in the last three years, for example, and two different leaders in cameras. Hit products produce major swings in domestic market share in short periods of time, because of the desire of Japanese consumers for the latest and best model. A success by one firm kicks off vigorous responses by others.

Rivalries are intensely personal. Emotion and face-saving seem to play a central role. Everyone in the organization focuses on besting the key competitors, and the company's market share is a matter of pride. In parts of Sony, for example, a popular slogan is BMW which means "beat Matsu-

TABLE **8–3 Estimated Number of Japanese Rivals in Selected Industries**

Air conditioners	13	Motorcycles	4
Audio equipment	25	Musical instruments	4
Automobiles	9	Personal computers	16
Cameras	15	Semiconductors	34
Car audio	12	Sewing machines	20
Carbon fibers	7	Shipbuilding**	33
Construction equipment	15*	Steel***	5
Copiers	14	Synthetic fibers	8
Facsimile machines	10	Television sets	15
Lift trucks	8	Truck and bus tires	5
Machine tools	112	Trucks	11
Mainframe computers	6	Typewriters	14
Microwave equipment	5	Videocassette recorders	10

SOURCES: Field interviews; *Nippon Kōgyō Shinbun, Nippon Kōgyō Nenkan,* 1987; Yano Research, *Market Share Jiten,* 1987; researchers' estimates.

* The number of firms varies by product area. The smallest number, ten, produced bulldozers. Fifteen firms produce shovel trucks, truck cranes, and asphalt paving equipment. There are twenty companies in hydraulic excavators, a product area where Japan is particularly strong.

** Six firms had annual production in excess of 10,000 tons.

*** Number of integrated companies.

shita whatever.'' In this environment, domestic margins are sometimes far below those of international markets (good examples are in tires and automobiles before the recent boom in home market demand for high-end models).[24] Competition is not always on price, especially in consumer goods where competitors each have their own exclusive distribution system, but rivalry in virtually all dimensions remains fierce. For Japanese companies, competing with foreign rivals often seems a relief.

A number of important other benefits flow from the presence of a number of fierce Japanese domestic rivals. One is that any basic factor advantages such as low labor cost or cheap steel are nullified, forcing Japanese companies toward automation, higher technology, and new products to outdo other Japanese competitors. Japanese companies trade up from basic factor advantages to more sustainable sources of competitive advantage. Another benefit of domestic rivalry is the stimulation of supporting industries as well as competition in recruiting and human resource development.

While domestic rivalry is intense in virtually every industry in which Japan is internationally successful, however, it is *all but absent in large sectors of the economy*. In fields such as construction, agriculture, food, paper, commodity chemicals, and fibers, there are cartels and other restrictions on competition, some sanctioned by government. Almost none of these (and other similar) industries have ever achieved international success. Yet the existence of restraints on domestic competition in such industries has misled many outside observers into thinking that all Japanese industries are cartelized. The absence of effective competition in large sectors of the economy is a danger signal and represents a serious challenge to continued Japanese economic advancement, as I will discuss further below.

New business formation in Japan is dynamic, largely taking place through internal diversification by established companies. Because of a desire to redeploy workers, diversification is usually highly related and rarely through acquisition. The result is a continuous widening and deepening of clusters.

The climate for forming entirely new companies in Japan is favorable and improving, though it is not yet at the level of the United States. Most of the best educated and most skilled Japanese still want to join larger companies that have the highest status. Spin-offs from university research are comparatively rare, as are managers leaving large companies to set up their own. Venture capital for independent start-ups is relatively scarce, and the ''venture capital'' subsidiaries of Japanese financial services firms are risk averse, reluctant to invest in unproven new companies. They are more accurately seen as financiers of smaller but established companies.

Yet many new companies are being founded in Japan, especially in services. The willingness of individuals to take risk appears greater in Japan than in Switzerland or Germany. In addition, larger companies are creating highly autonomous subsidiaries in some emerging industries such as software.

Ventures are also sometimes spun out of large companies. FANUC was once a unit within Fujitsu. Japan, as a result, is successful in both fragmented and concentrated industries where other favorable conditions in the "diamond" are present.

THE ROLE OF GOVERNMENT

The Japanese government has played a rapidly changing and often subtle role in the industries in which Japan has achieved national competitive advantage. After World War II, its role was relatively heavy-handed. It directed the flow of capital and scarce resources (such as steel) into particular sectors, limited foreign entry, negotiated licenses of foreign technology, held down exchange rates, and provided various kinds of assistance in exporting.

In the early Japanese successes, such as steel, shipbuilding, and sewing machines, this sort of government role was constructive. Price was important to competitive position in the segments in which Japanese firms competed. Many of the industries were capital intensive. Competitive advantage depended on having modern, large-scale facilities. Government's levers at this stage were powerful ones. Important Japanese industries were able to move beyond reliance on basic factor costs.

In these early successes, however, government was not working in isolation. Japan also had advantages in other determinants such as demand conditions (ships, steel, and motorcycles) or related and supporting industries (sewing machines) that contributed to success, along with vigorous domestic competition. It is also important to recognize that in other large and significant industries such as chemicals and plastics, aerospace, aircraft, and software, in which Japan brought no other advantages to the industry, aggressive efforts by government to develop the industry have largely failed to produce true international competitors.

In a number of industries, the government erroneously attempted to limit the number of Japanese competitors.[25] Examples include steel, autos, machine tools, and computers. The unwillingness of Japanese companies to abide by government consolidation plans proved to be a blessing, and intense domestic rivalry contributed to international success. In the 1980s, MITI has become more aware of the importance of domestic rivalry though a tendency to limit competition is a continuing problem, as I have discussed.

Overall, what has most separated Japanese policy from French "Indicative Planning" and other past efforts at national economic planning is a much greater stress on competition. The large number of aggressive Japanese rivals, pressuring each other to compete globally, is perhaps the most essential underpinning of Japanese success. This contrasts with policies built around "national champions" that have an implicit focus on static efficiency. The protection of Japanese industry would not have resulted in world-class competitors without keen local rivalry. A crucial aspect of Japanese protection was also that foreign rivals were often gradually let into industries, based on concrete timetables for liberalization known in advance. This approach stimulated major efforts at upgrading within the Japanese industry. A good example is the approval of Caterpillar's joint venture with Mitsubishi, which in many ways led to the renaissance of Komatsu, at the time a low-quality, inefficient producer of construction equipment.

Japanese government policy has recognized demand-side factors to an unusual degree. In facsimile machines, for example, the industry benefited from early approval of facsimile transmission of legal documents and early approval for hooking facsimile machines to ordinary telephone lines. Buyer incentives and other devices (for example, leasing companies to eliminate the need to purchase outright) have been provided to stimulate early demand in important industries such as robotics.

Government policy has forced rapid standardization in such products as cameras and sewing machines, leading to intense rivalry on product and feature improvement. The government has been a major early buyer in some industries (for example, all public schools purchased pianos for use in music classes). Government procurement has been unusually oriented toward upgrading the technology offered by suppliers. The multifaceted campaign to boost quality, exemplified by the Deming Prize and bolstered by the inspection of exports in the early postwar period, was another important effort to pressure firms to meet stringent demand.

Japanese policy has also been notable in its emphasis on related and supporting industries. Beginning with the Temporary Measures Law for Machinery and Electronics, 1971–1978, emphasis was placed on parts and production machinery. This has contributed to deep clustering in many sectors.

Another unique dimension of Japanese policy, dating back many years, is the Japanese government's role in signaling. Through high-visibility government reports, joint industry, academic and government committees, highly publicized campaigns, cooperative research projects that called attention to emerging technologies, and the like, MITI in particular has sought to nudge and influence innovation and change in companies. The effect is to raise aspirations and highlight challenges that industry must overcome, while prodding companies to act on them. A good example is the program to call attention to energy efficiency. The effect is to promote improvement and upgrading by industry.

The Japanese government has shifted the mix of policies as the economy advanced (many descriptions of the Japanese "model" are out of date by a decade or more). Direct intervention has substantially decreased. Demand conditions have received growing attention. The signaling role has become, in the last decade, the most prominent role of government in Japan. Many of MITI's formal powers have lapsed, though it still exercises substantial influence. This is appropriate, not only because of the world outcry against Japanese targeting but more importantly because the old model simply does not work at Japan's level of development (more on this in Chapter 10). Today's emerging Japanese successes are sensitive not to factor cost but to rapid innovation and a willingness to invest.

As successful as Japan has been, it is important to understand that Japanese government policy has undermined competitive advantage in some important areas of the economy. The regulation and central control of health care, for example, has dampened innovation. Educational policy has reduced the responsiveness of schools and universities to the needs of industry and constrained the important benefits of university research.

Most importantly, government policy in a range of industries has had the effect of undermining competition and sheltering inefficient competitors, lowering the overall productivity of the Japanese economy. Regulations in retailing and distribution, for example, have blocked the creation of efficient enterprises and have also led to a situation in which the Japanese home market is out of step with most other nations. The Law Concerning the Adjustment of Retail Operations in Large-Scale Retail Stores limits the ability of large retailers to open locations and compete with small shops. Protection in tobacco and agriculture has led to inefficiency in these industries as well as in supporting industries.

Limits on competition in one form or another have also led to inefficiency in a wide range of other fields, some of which were mentioned earlier. MITI-sanctioned "recession" and "rationalization" cartels, which suspend rivalry and involve *de facto* protection, have preserved unproductive firms in dozens of other industries. Only a handful of the more than sixty industries involved have subsequently achieved significant international success.

Japan, then, is characterized by some of the fiercest domestic rivalry of any nation juxtaposed with large areas of little or no rivalry. These and other examples suggest the complex balance of political power, which leads to intervention in some industries at the expense of consumers. They also suggest that policy makers may be giving up traditional roles too slowly. Both are danger signals for the future.

THE ROLE OF CHANCE

Chance, and associated good timing, have played an important role in Japanese success in a variety of industries. World War II was a seminal event. Occupation forces began breaking down the *zaibatsu* structure, unleashing rivalry in the economy. As in Germany, the importance of this unfreezing of competition is hard to overestimate.

The aftermath of World War II also brought an inflow of technology from the United States and created the opportunity and the necessity to build industries from scratch. Because Japanese domestic demand began to accelerate later than in other advanced nations, Japanese companies were often in the position of investing in more modern facilities than foreign rivals. An early government policy in some industries (notably steel) that required old facilities to be scrapped in order to build new efficient ones encouraged modernization.

The Korean War was a major stimulus to the Japanese economy. The Korean War helped rescue the Japanese truck industry, for example, providing some of its first foreign orders. The 1964 Tokyo Olympics marked another major milestone, raising Japanese visibility in world markets. Many Japanese companies geared major technical efforts to produce new products to show at the Olympics. For example, Hattori-Seiko, the leading Japanese watch manufacturer, credits the fact that it won the right to be official timekeeper at the Olympics with providing a major impetus for internal progress as well as wide visibility abroad. Major infrastructure improvements were also undertaken for the Olympics.

Another major precondition for Japanese ascendency in many industries was the broad technological trends toward electronics and modern manufacturing technologies. When Japanese companies were scrambling for a way to gain an advantage over foreign (and domestic) rivals, these major structural change agents provided the lever time and time again. Foreign rivals, often better established and with facilities and experience geared to older technologies, could be leapfrogged.

A final series of chance events that benefited many Japanese industries was the series of "shocks" beginning with the Nixon shock and moving through the oil shocks to the mid-1980s yen shock.[26] Each of these produced major and anticipatory adjustments in Japan that bolstered national advantage. Given intense domestic rivalry and some of the other circumstances I have described, Japanese industries were uniquely aggressive in responding.

JAPAN IN PERSPECTIVE

The Japanese success story is built on dynamism. Japanese firms have been pressured into rapid and continual innovation that has often anticipated world market needs. Companies have relentlessly upgraded their competitive advantages rather than resting on them.[27] The Japanese economy has formed competitive clusters and upgraded its mix of industries.

The high rate of capital investment, rapid productivity growth, and rapidly rising income per capita (shown in Table 7–1) are some of the many overall indicators that the process of upgrading is occurring. Equally striking evidence is found in the pattern of export share gains and losses between 1978 and 1985 in competitive Japanese industries, summarized in Figure 8–3. Japan had world export share gains of 15 percent or greater in more than twice as many industries as losses. The plurality of gains over losses is particularly striking in advanced industries such as semiconductors/computers, transportation, office products, entertainment and leisure products, and household appliances (including air conditioning). Strong gains in multiple business products are signs of an economy reaching a breadth and depth of positions in sophisticated industries. So is the fact that Japan gained share in twenty-nine machinery industries and lost it in only two. Japan's gains in world export share on average have occurred in the largest industries of any of the nations and in industries that are growing more rapidly, compared to those in which share was lost (see Table B–3). Share losses in Japanese industries have been predominantly in less sophisticated and factor cost-sensitive items such as basic steel products, fish products, black and white television, and textiles. Japan has also lost more positions than it has gained in chemicals, an area of continuing weakness.

Japanese industry is perhaps the most vivid example of the determinants of national competitive advantage working as a system. In the industries where Japan has succeeded, advantages all around the "diamond" are self-reinforcing. (Where Japan has not succeeded, important determinants were missing.) Many industries grow out of related and supporting industries. Once established, domestic market growth attracts numerous other entrants. Sophisticated and demanding local buyers help further stimulate innovation and intense competition.

Rapid domestic saturation intensifies rivalry and leads to major pressures to export. The segment structure of home demand channels Japanese firms to undefended segments through which they can penetrate foreign markets. Relentlessly intense domestic rivalry powers continued rapid innovation and broadening of product lines. Basic factor advantages are replaced by advantages in advanced and specialized factors that have been created largely within firms, coupled with growing advantages drawn from global strategies.

Market saturation, intense rivalry, and the desire to preserve employment lead to closely related internal diversification into new industries. As many rivals pour into upstream, downstream, or horizontally related new fields, intense competition spills over industry boundaries. The infusion of different skills into new industries often leads to innovations that alter the bases of competition.

Over time, this self-reinforcing process has made the Japanese economy more and more clustered. For reasons I have discussed, Japanese companies are often uniquely able to exploit the benefits of clustering, which enhances

FIGURE 8-3 Competitive Japanese Industries with Gains or Losses of World Export Share of 15% or More Between 1978 and 1985*

UPSTREAM INDUSTRIES

Materials/Metals

	Total Comp. Inds.	Share Gains	Share Losses
Primary Goods	38	9	16
Machinery	6	3	2
Specialty Inputs	0	0	0
Total	44	12	18

Forest Products

	Total Comp. Inds.	Share Gains	Share Losses
Primary Goods	1	1	0
Machinery	0	0	0
Specialty Inputs	0	0	0
Total	1	1	0

Petroleum/Chemicals

	Total Comp. Inds.	Share Gains	Share Losses
Primary Goods	13	8	11
Machinery	0	0	0
Specialty Inputs	0	0	0
Total	13	8	11

Semiconductors/Computers

	Total Comp. Inds.	Share Gains	Share Losses
Primary Goods	0	6	0
Machinery	0	0	0
Specialty Inputs	0	0	0
Total	0	6	0

UPSTREAM INDUSTRIES

	Total Comp. Inds.	Share Gains	Share Losses
Primary Goods	52	24	27
Machinery	6	3	2
Specialty Inputs	0	0	0
Total	58	27	29

INDUSTRIAL & SUPPORTING FUNCTIONS

Multiple Business

	Total Comp. Inds.	Share Gains	Share Losses
Primary Goods	13	6	1
Machinery	2	2	0
Specialty Inputs	2	2	0
Total	17	10	1

Transportation

	Total Comp. Inds.	Share Gains	Share Losses
Primary Goods	22	17	4
Machinery	12	12	0
Specialty Inputs	17	11	1
Total	51	40	5

Power Generation & Distribution

	Total Comp. Inds.	Share Gains	Share Losses
Primary Goods	15	10	6
Machinery	0	0	0
Specialty Inputs	0	0	0
Total	15	10	6

Office

	Total Comp. Inds.	Share Gains	Share Losses
Primary Goods	8	7	0
Machinery	2	2	0
Specialty Inputs	0	0	0
Total	10	9	0

Defense

	Total Comp. Inds.	Share Gains	Share Losses
Primary Goods	0	0	1
Machinery	0	0	0
Specialty Inputs	0	0	0
Total	0	0	1

Telecommunications

	Total Comp. Inds.	Share Gains	Share Losses
Primary Goods	3	3	0
Machinery	0	0	0
Specialty Inputs	0	0	0
Total	3	3	0

INDUSTRIAL & SUPPORTING FUNCTIONS

	Total Comp. Inds.	Share Gains	Share Losses
Primary Goods	61	43	12
Machinery	16	16	0
Specialty Inputs	19	13	1
Total	96	72	13

FINAL CONSUMPTION GOODS & SERVICES

Food/Beverage

	Total Comp. Inds.	Share Gains	Share Losses
Primary Goods	3	0	3
Machinery	4	4	0
Specialty Inputs	2	2	1
Total	9	6	4

Textiles/Apparel

	Total Comp. Inds.	Share Gains	Share Losses
Primary Goods	6	3	6
Machinery	8	6	0
Specialty Inputs	8	2	4
Total	22	11	10

Housing/Household

	Total Comp. Inds.	Share Gains	Share Losses
Primary Goods	10	6	0
Machinery	0	0	0
Specialty Inputs	1	1	0
Total	11	7	0

Health Care

	Total Comp. Inds.	Share Gains	Share Losses
Primary Goods	4	3	1
Machinery	0	0	0
Specialty Inputs	0	0	0
Total	4	3	1

Personal

	Total Comp. Inds.	Share Gains	Share Losses
Primary Goods	9	5	1
Machinery	0	0	0
Specialty Inputs	1	1	0
Total	10	6	1

Entertainment/Leisure

	Total Comp. Inds.	Share Gains	Share Losses
Primary Goods	19	11	3
Machinery	0	0	0
Specialty Inputs	5	3	0
Total	24	14	3

FINAL CONSUMPTION GOODS & SERVICES

	Total Comp. Inds.	Share Gains	Share Losses
Primary Goods	51	28	14
Machinery	12	10	0
Specialty Inputs	17	9	5
Total	80	47	19

* Included were industries exceeding the cutoff in either 1978 or 1985, including those that were competitive in 1978 but fell below the cutoff in 1985 or that had first achieved sufficient share to exceed the cutoff in 1985.

the rate of innovation and change. Selective factor disadvantages (notably in energy, space, labor shortages, labor costs, and recently currency) have accelerated the process of upgrading industry and globalizing strategies. The presence of active domestic rivalry, commitment to employees, and a long-term perspective has meant that the response to selective disadvantage was innovation and selective globalization rather than abandonment of industries and wholesale outsourcing.

The system of determinants prevalent in Japan does not work for every industry. Home demand conditions, management practices, or compelling factor disadvantages sometimes do not fit. In other industries, the problem is simply that foreign firms have early mover advantages that have been extremely difficult to overcome. Another large group of industries has been sheltered from competition for one reason or another and lacks the dynamism to compete abroad. Yet the self-reinforcing system in Japan has produced major competitive advantages in a wide range of industries, coupled with the ability to sustain them over long periods of time.

There is little sinister in the process by which Japanese firms gained national competitive advantage. Westerners have tended to create fantasies to explain Japanese success: Japan, Inc., neomercantilism, and national goals which are not centered on raising the standard of living. Though Japan has protected, and still continues to protect, its home market more than many other advanced nations (increasingly a constraint to further Japanese economic upgrading), this is far from the heart of Japanese national competitive advantage. Japan's is an economy driven by firms, not government. Manufactured imports into Japan, including cars, have been rapidly rising. The attention in Japan to working hours, housing, pollution, and other constraints to rising living standards is going through a predictable cycle for a nation at Japan's state of development.

Aggressive domestic rivalry, demanding buyers, cooperative suppliers, and rapid upgrading of factors of production are the more decisive advantages. Japanese advantage is truly systemic, a term to which my theory hopefully provides a clearer meaning. "Cultural" factors are often derived instead from the "diamond." The different goals of Japanese firms sometimes seem unfair (particularly) to U.S. rivals. These goals are a reflection of the Japanese environment and capital market conditions and not a creation of Japanese government. The time horizon and lower profit targets of Japanese firms are similar to the conditions found in other advanced nations such as Germany and Sweden. Americans must learn to see the United States as the exception in this regard, not Japan.

When viewing Japan, moreover, it is important not to overlook the failures and the substantial sectors where productivity is low that have fallen outside the Japanese miracle. Japan today is in many ways two economies. One economy is vibrantly competitive and characterized by rapid upgrading and productivity growth. Side by side is another economy in which there is little true competition and widespread inefficiency. Overall, the productivity of the Japanese economy (as well as the Japanese standard of living) is still far behind that of the United States.

There are also signs of shifting goals in industry, and signs that government entities are too slowly relinquishing control and allowing adjustments to new circumstances. Some observers have argued that the Japanese "model" supersedes the model based on free trade and open competition that has underpinned postwar efforts at trade liberalization. Instead, the Japanese case starkly illustrates the importance of competition and the need for any policy model to evolve if a nation is to continue advancing. I will return to these issues in the concluding chapter.

SURGING ITALY[28]

Italy rejoined the ranks of advanced nations in the last two decades. Italian exports grew briskly relative to domestic production, and the Italian share of world exports increased from less than 3.2 percent in 1960 to over 5.2 percent in 1986. Italy's overall growth in world export share is second only to Japan among leading nations. Its growth in productivity and per capita income is behind only Japan and Korea among the nations we studied.

The case of Italy is particularly interesting for a number of reasons. Italy is not generally known as a nation whose firms have competitive advantage in many industries. Its image is more of chaotic government, poor telephone and other public services, inefficient state-owned enterprises, and pervasive subsidy. Italy is also yet another important nation with few advantages in inherited factors of production. It imports most of its energy and raw materials and is even a net importer of food.

Yet Italy developed a remarkable dynamism and a capacity to successfully upgrade competitive advantage in industries. In the early postwar period, Italy was a nation where most industries had competitive advantage based on low-cost labor. By the early 1980s, many Italian industries achieved advantage based on segmentation, differentiation, and process innovation. The Italian case, like that of Japan, illustrates the power of a growing alignment between national circumstances and the shifting demands of modern global competition.

Italy remains, however, a study in contrasts. Its national characteristics produce striking advantage in many industries but failure in many others. Further upgrading of the Italian economy is beginning to confront limits that will not be easily overcome.

PATTERNS OF ITALIAN COMPETITIVE ADVANTAGE

Table 8–4 lists the top fifty Italian industries in 1985 in terms of world export share. The presence on the list of such industries as wine, footwear, and wool cloth is perhaps not surprising. More interesting is the presence of domestic appliances and a range of machinery industries. The top fifty industries in terms of world export share account for only 27 percent of Italian exports, low in comparison to the nations as a group (the same is true for the proportion of total exports accounted for by the top fifty Italian exports by value, shown in Table B-7).[29]

The patterns of national advantage in the Italian economy are illustrated much better in Figure 8–4 and the summary statistics in Figures 8–5 and B-6. What is immediately striking about Italy is the sheer number of exporting industries and the fact that no small number of industries dominates exports. Yet the successful industries are highly clustered. The most important cluster to Italian trade is related to textiles and apparel (for example, footwear, fabrics, clothing, handbags, travel goods), along with specialized inputs and associated machinery. The next most significant cluster is in the area of household products, including appliances, furniture, lighting, ceramics-related products (for example, ceramic tiles, ornaments), sinks and wash-basins, housewares, natural and artificial stone products, and associated machinery (for example, woodworking machines, marble-cutting machines) and inputs. Another important cluster is in food and beverages, including wine, olive oil, pasta, processed vegetables (notably tomatoes), though Italy is overall a net importer in food, especially unprocessed food. The Italian position in the food and beverage area is as strong in machinery and equipment (for example, wine-making equipment, small agricultural implements) as it is in the end products.

Another important cluster is in personal products, particularly jewelry but also eyeglass frames, pens, and toilet articles. Italy also has strong positions in a number of relatively specialized metal fabricated goods and specialty materials, along with associated machinery. Italy's position is often in too narrow a category to show up separately in trade statistics (as indicated by the strong position in "machine tools for special industries").

Italy holds a moderate (and overall declining) position in the transportation sector, though its strongest positions are more in machinery and components (Pirelli, for example) and specialty vehicles (Ferrari, Lamborghini, Maserati) than in the large vehicle industries. Fiat's real strength is in small compact cars, the only category in which it holds more than a small percent of the European market. Fiat has been protected from Japanese competition in the Italian home market where its position is dominant.[30]

The clusters of successful Italian industries are concentrated in final consumption goods, those along the bottom row of the cluster chart. Competitive

TABLE 8–4 Top Fifty Italian Industries in Terms of World Export Share, 1985

Industry	Share of Total World Exports	Export Value ($ millions)	Import Value ($ millions)	Share of Total Italian Exports
Groats, meal, and pellets of wheat	69.5	159,765	3,631	0.20
Worked building stone	62.2	701,208	5,319	0.89
Other wine of fresh grapes (aperitifs)	58.1	75,754	513	0.10
Glazed ceramic sets	56.6	866,879	16,437	1.10
Precious metal jewelry	49.6	2,288,256	19,978	2.90
Fresh stone fruit	45.5	247,385	10,159	0.31
Rubber and plastic footwear	41.9	452,469	20,402	0.57
Fabrics of combed wool	41.8	278,003	34,861	0.35
Domestic washing machines	38.2	396,595	32,123	0.50
Steel high pressure conduit	35.9	319,193	11,271	0.40
Sweaters of synthetic fibers	34.0	631,213	5,419	0.80
Handbags	33.7	343,408	3,978	0.43
Woolen sweaters	33.1	499,221	55,460	0.63
Leather footwear	32.8	3,285,427	178,156	4.16
Other woven textile fabric	32.3	510,145	48,634	0.65
Woven silk fabrics	31.7	215,629	53,632	0.27
Cement, artificial stone products	31.2	124,617	4,224	0.16
Chairs and other seats	30.6	685,124	29,894	0.87
Textile clothing accessories	27.8	251,618	24,303	0.32
Fresh grapes	27.8	235,494	7,105	0.30
Domestic deep freezers	26.8	80,738	3,379	0.10
Women's outerwear	26.2	491,478	50,159	0.62
Domestic refrigerators	26.1	314,900	16,353	0.40
Wood furniture	25.5	1,026,911	40,390	1.30
Machine tools for wood, ceramics	24.7	485,500	35,141	0.61
Leather	24.6	452,233	266,542	0.57
Other sweaters, pullovers	24.5	641,799	16,830	0.81
Coke and semi-coke of lignite	24.2	323	1,159	0.00
Unbleached sulphite woodpulp	23.3	20,576	36,907	0.03
Footwear components	23.0	198,785	11,270	0.25
Olive oil	22.4	131,742	283,534	0.17
Furniture and parts	22.3	186,395	14,522	0.24
Men's suits	22.2	145,837	17,341	0.18
Spectacle frames	22.2	164,124	30,899	0.21
Knitted clothing accessories	22.2	186,366	25,954	0.24
Metal furniture	21.5	174,076	11,804	0.22
Wine of fresh grapes	20.7	803,915	75,121	1.02

TABLE **8–4** (*Continued*)

Industry	Share of Total World Exports	Export Value ($ millions)	Import Value ($ millions)	Share of Total Italian Exports
Bulk antibiotics	20.5	321,442	228,622	0.41
Ceramic ornaments	20.3	114,451	23,432	0.14
Nontextured yarn containing polyamide	20.3	97,411	64,949	0.12
Packaging, bottling machines	19.8	464,507	55,063	0.59
Men's overcoats	19.8	435,710	99,379	0.55
Sinks, washbasins, bidets	19.5	77,117	3,781	0.10
Domestic heating, cooking apparatus	19.5	199,544	27,309	0.25
Foliage, branches and other parts of plants	19.3	26,045	2,750	0.03
Lamps, fittings of base metal	19.1	275,239	26,915	0.35
Other textile specialized leather machinery	18.6	425,736	100,203	0.54
Solid sodium hydroxide	18.3	35,690	1,711	0.05
Woven synthetic fiber fabric	18.1	753,426	189,393	0.95
Plastic coated textiles	18.0	157,913	30,376	0.20
TOTAL				27.16

NOTE: No import data reported if import value is less than 0.3 percent of the total trade for 1985.

industries in final consumption goods represent a remarkable 47.5 percent of all Italian exports. Italy is actually the world's leading exporter in the textile/apparel sector, the household sector, and the personal products sector, and third among the nations we studied in the food and beverage sector.

Italian clusters tend to be very deep. Most contain final products (apparel), competitive industries producing intermediate products (woven cloth, tanned leather), other inputs (synthetic fibers), specialized machinery associated with the cluster (leather-working machinery, spinning machines), and occasionally supporting services (notably design services). Italian firms are often world export leaders in machinery or inputs related to the cluster that are too specialized to get their own trade classification. Groups of closely related industries that are all competitive are common (leather footwear, ski boots, après-ski boots).

As the shading on Figure 8–5 indicates, there are links among some important clusters. Textiles/apparel, housing/household products, and personal products are related by a heavy orientation toward fashion, style, and design. Individual Italian positions in these sectors are self-reinforcing and draw on some common supporting industries.

FIGURE 8–4 Clusters of Internationally Competitive Italian Industries, 1985

	MATERIALS/METALS	FOREST PRODUCTS
Primary Goods	IRON & STEEL *Other iron, steel bars*# *Iron, other steel bars hot rolled* *Other profiles hot rolled* Iron, simple steel thin plate' Iron, simple steel heavy plate' Iron, simple steel wire' Stainless steel thin plate FABRICATED IRON & STEEL **Steel high-pressure conduit** Iron, steel castings unworked' *Iron, steel tube fittings* Iron, steel tubes, pipes Iron, steel seamless tubes *Iron, steel cable, rope*	NONFERROUS METALS Other copper, alloys worked'* Copper plate, sheet, strip' Aluminum bars, wire, etc. *Aluminum foil* Structures, parts of aluminum METAL MANUFACTURES Structures, parts iron, steel **Steel storage tanks** *Metal fencing, gauze* *Iron, steel nuts, bolts* Blades, tips, etc. for tools' Other base metal manufactures# *Locksmiths wares* Iron, steel chains, parts	WOOD MANUFACTURES *Wood manufactures*# *Wood panels*# PAPER *Printing paper, coated, impregnated, etc.* Paper, etc., containers' PULP **Unbleached sulphite wood pulp**'
Machinery	*Other mineral-working machinery*# Mineral-crushing, etc., machinery' Rolling mills'*	Roll-mill parts, rolls' Industrial furnaces, electric'	Paper, etc., mill machinery and parts#
Specialty Inputs	*Foundry molds* **Coke, semi coke of lignite#**		
Services			

FIGURE 8–4 (Continued)

	PETROLEUM/CHEMICALS	SEMICONDUCTORS/ COMPUTERS
Primary Goods		Small computers***
	PETROLEUM PRODUCTS	
	Jet fuel (spirit)*	
	Kerosene including jet fuel	
	Lubricants (high petroleum content)	
	ORGANIC CHEMICALS	
	Phenols, phenol alcohols, derivatives	
	Polyacids and derivatives	
	Oxy-function acids, derivatives	
	Oxygen-function amino compounds	
	Amide-function compounds, excluding urea*	
	Esthers, epoxies, acetals*	
		Metal compounds of inorganic acid
		Other inorganic bases·*
		Other inorganic chemicals*·*
		PLASTICS
		Other polyamides#
		Other polymerization products#
		Polyvinyl chloride in primary forms
		Polyvinyl chloride, plates, strip etc.
		Fabricated plastic products***
	INORGANIC CHEMICALS	
	Sodium hydroxide, solid	
Machinery		
Specialty Inputs		
Services		

KEY

roman   4.6% world export share or higher, but less than 9.1% share

bold italics   9.1% world export share or higher, but less than 18.2% share

sans serif   **18.2% world export share or above.**

·	Industries below cutoff in 1978	·	Added due to FDI
#	Calculated residuals	··	Upgraded due to FDI
··	Added due to significant export value in a segmented industry	···	Added based on in-country research

TRANSPORTATION

	MULTIPLE BUSINESS	TRANSPORTATION		
Primary Goods	*Rotary, other pumps#* *Pumps for gases* Gas, liquid filters' *Cocks, valves* Shaft, crank, pulley' Gas, liquid control instruments## Measure, control instruments##	ENGINES Piston engines nes' VEHICLES Motor cars, racing' Special motor vehicles' *Tractors for tractor trailers#* *Bicycles, wheelchairs#*	Trucks## Small passenger motor vehicles## CONSTRUCTION EQUIPMENT *Self-propelled dozers* Self-propelled shovels, excavators	VEHICLE EQUIPMENT Containers, incl. road-rail Transport containers# Trailers, other vehicles, not mechanically propelled# Ship derricks, cranes Steel transport boxes Other metal transport boxes#
Machinery	Spraying machinery Conveyors, elevators# *Other nonelectric machinery#*	*Other metalworking machine tools#* Other metal-cutting machine tools# Lathes, metalworking *Metal reaming machines* Metal-forming machine tools Converters, ladles, ingot molds#	Gas welders# *Electric welders, etc.* Power hand tools, nonelectric' *Factory automation equipment (including robotics)###* *Rubber, plastics working machines*	
Specialty Inputs	Pump, compressor parts Fans, blowers, parts'	*Parts, accessories of motorcycles, cycles* *Parts of railway vehicles'* *Electric vehicle lighting equipment* Electric accumulators, parts# Motor vehicle bodies, parts, accessories##	*Other materials of rubber#* *Unhardened vulcanized rubber tube* *Tires new for motor cars##* *Tires new, bus or lorry##* Unhardened rubber products *Radar apparatus* Gaskets, machinery parts# Glass surface-ground	
Services	*Construction/engineering###*	*Design###*		

FIGURE 8-4 (Continued)

	POWER GENERATION AND DISTRIBUTION	OFFICE	TELECOMMUNICATIONS	DEFENSE
Primary Goods	*AC motors, incl. universal motors* AC generators' Other electric transformers# Insulated wire, cable *Electrical carbons*	*Electric typewriters, normal* Other office supplies* Printed books, pamphlets Trade advertising material, catalogs Office, ADP machine parts##	Radiotelephonic receivers, TV cameras, parts##	*Aircraft 2,000–15,000 KG* Small arms*** Aircraft parts##
Machinery		*Paper, etc., product manufacturing machines* Typesetting, bookbinding machinery, parts# *Platen printing presses#*		
Specialty Inputs				
Services				

KEY

roman   4.6% world export share or higher, but less than 9.1% share

bold italics   *9.1% world export share or higher, but less than 18.2% share*

sans serif   18.2% world export share or above.

*   Industries below cutoff in 1978
\#   Calculated residuals
\##   Added due to significant export value in a segmented industry

'   Added due to FDI
''   Upgraded due to FDI
'''   Added based on in-country research

	FOOD/BEVERAGES	FRUITS/VEGETABLES	BEVERAGES
Primary Goods	BASIC FOODS Pig meat dried, salted, smoked *Meat and edible meat offals#* *Rice milled unbroken* Flour of wheat or meslin PROCESSED FOODS Pastry, cakes' Chocolate products *Pasta, breakfast cereal#* *Vegetables preserved, prepared* *Jams, preserved fruit#*	Other vegetables fresh, simply preserved# *Fresh potatoes* *Other fruit, nuts, fresh, dried#* Oranges, fresh or dried' Lemons, grapefruit *Fresh apples* *Fresh grapes* Edible nuts **Fresh stone fruit**	Wine of fresh grapes **Other wine of fresh grapes#** *Fruit or vegetable juice#* Distilled alcohol# EDIBLE OILS **Olive oil** Sunflower seed oil' Animal oils, fats#
Machinery	*Cultivating machinery* Combine harvester-thresher *Other harvesting, etc., machines#* *Wheeled tractors*	Dairy, wine-making, and other machinery#* *Refrigeration equipment, nondomestic*	*Nondomestic refrigeration equipment parts#* **Packing, bottling machinery** *Food machinery, nondomestic*
Specialty Inputs	**Groats, meal and pellets of wheat#** *Meal fodder#* *Durum wheat unmilled* Urea'	Nitrogen-phosphate-potassium fertilizer Phosphites, phosphates Potassium-sulphate fertilizer# *Glass bottles, etc., nonvacuum#*	*Other articles of plastics#* Plastic packaging containers, lids Parts of harvesting machines, threshers' Glass inners for vacuum flasks#*
Services			

FIGURE 8-4 (Continued)

HOUSING/HOUSEHOLD

Primary Goods	FURNITURE			

Primary Goods

FURNITURE
- **Chairs and other seats**
- *Parts of chairs*
- **Metal furniture**
- **Wood furniture**
- **Furniture of other materials***
- **Lamps, fittings base metal**
- **Other lighting equipment**

GLASS, CERAMICS, AND STONE PRODUCTS
- **Glazed ceramic sets, etc.**
- **Other bricks, etc., nonrefractory**#
- **Cement, artificial stone products**

- **Building stone, worked**
- *Other lime, cement, building products**
- *Household, hotel, etc., glass*
- Coarse ceramic housewares
- **Ceramic ornaments**
- **Sinks, wash basins, bidets***

HOUSEHOLD EQUIPMENT/APPLIANCES
- **Other base metal household appliances***
- **Domestic heating, cooking apparatus***
- Air conditioners`

- **Domestic washing machines**
- **Clothes drying machines***
- **Domestic refrigerators**
- **Deep freezers, household***
- *Central heating equipment*
- *Other household type equipment**

OTHER HOUSEHOLD PRODUCTS
- Basketwork, brooms
- Cutlery
- Cut flowers
- **Foliage, branches***
- Electric filament lamps

Machinery
- *Marble-cutting machinery****
- *Gas generators, furnace burners**
- Machinery, for wood, glass#

- *Industrial furnaces, nonelectric*
- Machine tools for wood, ceramics, etc.

Specialty Inputs
- *Stone, sand, gravel*
- Glazes, driers, putty
- Other glass#

Services
- Design***

KEY

roman	4.6% world export share or higher, but less than 9.1% share
bold italics	*9.1% world export share or higher, but less than 18.2% share*
sans serif	**18.2% world export share or above.**

•	Industries below cutoff in 1978	••	Added due to FDI
#	Calculated residuals	•••	Upgraded due to FDI
##	Added due to significant export value in a segmented industry	•••	Added based on in-country research

Primary Goods	TEXTILES/APPAREL		
	FABRICS		LUGGAGE
	Pile, etc., cotton fabrics	Plastic coated textiles	Handbags
	Continuous synthetic weaves nonpile	Textiles for machinery	Travel goods, briefcases, etc.#
	Continuous regenerated weaves nonpile	Other textile articles#	ACCESSORIES
	Synthetic pile, etc., fabric'	Linens, etc.	Artificial fur products#
	Other woven textile fabrics#	APPAREL	Industrial leather articles#
	Other synthetic woven fiber fabrics#	Men's overcoats#	Textile fabrics, clothing accessories#
	Silk fabric woven	Men's suits	Clothing accessories, etc.
	Woven cardigan wool, fine hair	Men's trousers, breeches#	knitted hosiery
	Fabrics of combed wool#	Cotton trousers	Other headgear, nontextile clothing#
	Other knitted fabrics#	Women's suits#	Leather clothes, accessories
	Knit synthetic fabric nonelastic	Wool, cotton dresses#	
	Special textile fabrics#	Skirts	Jerseys of wool, hair
		Cotton blouses#	Jerseys of synthetic fibers
		Cotton outergarments	Other women's dresses
		Other jerseys, pullovers#	Other outergarments, accessories#
			Other undergarments knitted#
			Undergarments of cotton nonelastic'
			Other unknit undergarments#
			Men's shirts, other fibers#
			FOOTWEAR
			Footwear components
			Rubber, plastic, footwear
			Leather footwear
			Après-ski boots'''
Machinery	Textile, leather preparation machinery#	Other spinning, extruding, etc., machines#	Other weaving, etc., machines#
	Sewing machines	Spinning, reeling, etc., machines'	Weaving machines'
	Sewing machine needles#	Parts of textile processing machines'	Loom, knit machine, etc., parts
Specialty Inputs	Synthetic, organic dyestuffs'	Yarn, nontextured, continuous polyamide	Regenerated fiber yarn, monofilament
	Cellulose derivatives	Yarn of discontinuous synthetic fibers	Leather bovine, equine
	Other synthetic fibers to spin#	Discontinuous synthetic fiber blend yarn	Wool, hair yarn#
	Discontinuous synthetic fiber uncombed		Cotton yarn#
	Yarn, textured, continuous polyamide		Other leather#
Services	Design'''	Specialty stores'	

FIGURE 8–4 (*Continued*)

	HEALTH CARE	PERSONAL	ENTERTAINMENT/LEISURE
Primary Goods	PHARMACEUTICALS **Antibiotics in bulk** *Medicaments containing antibiotics*	JEWELRY Imitation jewelry Other precious jewelry# **Precious metal jewelry** Other articles of precious metal# OTHER **Spectacle frames** ***Spectacles, goggles#*** *Fountain pens* ***Smallwares, toiletries*** Watch movements, cases# Carvings, umbrellas#	Cinema cameras, projectors, etc.· ***Developed cinema film*** Newspapers, periodicals Specialty magazines··· Other printed matter# Children's picture books, maps, globes# Toys, indoor games# Baby carriages, sporting goods# ***Yachts, sports vessels*** Musical instruments, parts# **Ski boots**··· **Premium bicycles**··· **Disco lights**···
Machinery			TV picture tubes
Specialty Inputs			
Services			Tourism···

KEY	
roman	4.6% world export share or higher, but less than 9.1% share
bold italics	9.1% world export share or higher, but less than 18.2% share
sans serif	18.2% world export share or above.

· Industries below cutoff in 1978
Calculated residuals
Added due to significant export value in a segmented industry

· Added due to FDI
·· Upgraded due to FDI
··· Added based on in-country research

FIGURE 8-5 Percentage of Italian Exports of Competitive Industries by Broad Cluster

	UPSTREAM INDUSTRIES
Materials / Metals	Share of Country Exports: 12.3 (−1.2)
Share of Country Exports: 8.5 (−1.9)	Share of World Cluster Exports: 1.6 (−0.4)
Share of World Cluster Exports: 4.2 (−0.4)	

Forest Products	**Semiconductors/ Computers**	**Petroleum/ Chemicals**
Share of Country Exports: 1.0 (+0.0)	Share of Country Exports: 0.4 (+0.0)	Share of Country Exports: 2.5 (0.6)
Share of World Cluster Exports: 1.9 (0.1)	Share of World Cluster Exports: 0.4 (−0.5)	Share of World Cluster Exports: 0.6 (+0.0)

			INDUSTRIAL AND SUPPORTING FUNCTIONS
			Share of Country Exports: 12.7 (−5.3)
			Share of World Cluster Exports: 3.3 (−1.1)

Multiple Business	**Power Generation & Distribution**	**Office**	**Telecom- munications**	**Defense**
Share of Country Exports: 3.5 (0.4)	Share of Country Exports: 0.8 (−0.4)	Share of Country Exports: 1.0 (−0.4)	Share of Country Exports: 0.5 (−0.0)	Share of Country Exports: 0.3 (−0.2)
Share of World Cluster Exports: 2.4 (0.1)	Share of World Cluster Exports: 4.0 (−0.9)	Share of World Cluster Exports: 3.6 (−1.5)	Share of World Cluster Exports: 1.9 (−0.8)	Share of World Cluster Exports: 7.4 (−3.3)

	FINAL CONSUMPTION GOODS AND SERVICES
	Share of Country Exports: 43.7 (1.8)
	Share of World Cluster Exports: 6.7 (0.6)

Food/ Beverage	**Textiles/ Apparel**	**Housing/ Household**	**Health Care**	**Personal**	**Entertainment/ Leisure**
Share of Country Exports: 8.8 (0.1)	Share of Country Exports: 19.6 (2.0)	Share of Country Exports: 9.5 (−0.5)	Share of Country Exports: 0.6 (0.1)	Share of Country Exports: 4.3 (0.6)	Share of Country Exports: 0.9 (−0.5)
Share of World Cluster Exports: 3.5 (0.5)	Share of World Cluster Exports: 12.0 (1.2)	Share of World Cluster Exports: 13.8 (1.1)	Share of World Cluster Exports: 1.8 (−0.3)	Share of World Cluster Exports: 6.6 (1.4)	Share of World Cluster Exports: 1.3 (−1.0)

Note: Numbers in parentheses are changes between 1978 and 1985. ▨ Identifies broad sectors in which the nation's international competitive positions are related. Exports are those of competitive industries, not all industries.

Internationally successful Italian industries tend to be characterized by medium- and small-sized firms that compete primarily through export, with only limited foreign direct investment. Individual firms tend to be specialized in relatively narrow product areas.[31] Large firms, some of which have restructured in recent years, account for a modest share of overall Italian trade. Of the leading Italian industries in terms of export value, only one out of the top five, and five out of the top twenty, involve large firms.[32] While there are successful large firms in Italy, they are not generally in the industries where Italy is most successful.

Another striking feature of successful Italian industries is geographic concentration, in which many if not hundreds of firms in one industry are located in a single town. Two small regions in Italy, Valenza Po and Arezzo, for example, account for a $2 billion trade surplus in precious metal jewelry and nearly half of total world jewelry exports. A further illustration of concentrated Italian industries was shown in Figure 4–6.

The cluster chart (Figure 8–4) also reveals many sectors in which Italian industry has little or no national competitive advantage. Italian industry has little or no position in semiconductors and computers,[33] telecommunications, defense (except small arms), and forest products. The glaring weaknesses in final consumer goods are in consumer electronics and health care-related items. The strong Italian position in antibiotics reflects the fact that Italy did not recognize pharmaceutical patents until comparatively recently. Italian companies copied foreign developments and competed on cost. While Italian process skills are well developed, the Italian position reflects historical accident rather than true national advantage.

Italy is also quite weak in power generation and distribution and office equipment (with the exception, in some product areas, of Olivetti). The number of industries where Italian firms are strong in chemicals and materials are few compared to the leading nations in these sectors.[34] Heavy subsidies distort the impression gleaned from trade statistics. ENICHEM (chemicals) and Finsider (steel) are state-owned companies which have shown chronic losses and are at best marginally profitable. Italian participation in capital-intensive industries is often via state-owned firms (state-owned enterprise, many of whose industries are part of the IRI group, represents a significant fraction of the Italian economy). Few have competitive advantage in international terms.

Italy has a generally weak position in services, with the notable exception of design services. Italian firms, among them Memphis and Artemide (furniture design); Sotsass and Bonetto (industrial design); Pininfarina, Bertone, Italdesign (automotive design); and Armani, Valentino, Versace, and Bellini (fashion design) are international leaders in design services. These are closely related to and often grow out of Italian export industries such as clothing, furniture, jewelry, and premium automobiles. One estimate places Italian exports of design services at $10 billion annually.[35]

Italian firms also have a solid, though not leading, international position in engineering and construction, with 12.4 percent of international contract awards in 1987.[36] Italy also has a significant trade surplus in tourism. Outside of these areas, however, Italian service firms are domestically oriented and lack advantages when compared to foreign firms. In financial services, for example, Italian banks and insurance companies are notably weak.

Figure 8–4 shows that Italian exports have become more skewed toward the successful clusters since 1978. There has also been a deepening of successful clusters, especially in terms of machinery and in some cases specialty inputs.

ITALIAN FACTOR CONDITIONS

Italy draws relatively few advantages from inherited or socially created factors of production. There are few unique natural resources (marble is an exception). Growing conditions are favorable for some crops, and Italy exports a number of agriculturally related products (such as wine and pasta), though Italy is nowhere near self-sufficient in food because a large proportion of its land is not arable.

Italy has a large pool of high school-educated workers. Low Italian wages were a significant advantage in the early postwar period. However, a major jump in wages occurred beginning in 1969. Complex and, some would say, onerous labor regulations, which regulate working hours and working conditions while making it very difficult to lay off employees, were enacted about the same time. Italy has the highest social benefit costs compared to wages (86 percent) of any nation in the OECD.[37] Some observers believe that effective Italian labor costs are today on a par with other leading European nations. They are well above those of firms from the newly industrialized countries (NICs) and less developed European nations (such as Spain and Portugal) which have emerged as competitors of Italian firms in many industries.

The traditional view of Italian labor is of powerful unions and a poor work ethic. While this is true in the very large and particularly the state-owned companies, neither represents the essence of Italian international success. Unionization is less prevalent in small- and medium-sized firms, and militancy of unionized employees in such companies is far different. Small companies (less than fifteen employees) are also exempt in large part from labor regulations.[38] Italians do not like to work for an anonymous company but want to feel that they are part of a familylike organization where they will be recognized. If they do belong to such an organization, they work extremely hard and work very long hours like the Japanese. The internationally successful Italian companies frequently have this sense of an extended family and often are led by a founder or a descendant of the founder. These characteristics have a strong impact on the nature of the industries in which Italian companies succeed.

Capital was and still is an Italian disadvantage. The problem is not so much with the pool of capital, because Italians are very high savers (19.6 percent of household disposable income in 1985 versus 16 percent in Japan and 7.32 percent in the United States), but in the drain of a huge public debt and in the poorly developed mechanisms for allocating capital. Large government deficits have absorbed a large fraction of savings and made Italian real interest rates high for extended periods, especially for smaller companies. With tax-free interest rates on government bonds and treasury bills of consistently over 14 percent, investors had little incentive to put capital at risk.[39]

A public equity market has been all but nonexistent until recently, due to regulation and the absence of pension funds or a concentration of other institutional investors. The market is small, thin, and inefficient. Few firms are listed, and the proportion of shares traded is relatively small. Volatility is high, and spectacular crashes scare away investors. A lack of insider trading laws and the ability of a few large investors to strongly influence the market also made it a poor vehicle for financing growing companies. Italian family firms have been unwilling in most cases to sell equity because of fears about the market and a desire to maintain control, though this was changing somewhat in the 1980s.

Italian banks have not taken up the slack. Commercial banks are prohibited by law from holding equities and from making long-term loans. They have not played the same constructive role in funding industry as they have in Japan or Germany.[40] Most Italian banks are directly or indirectly controlled by the state and are extremely conservative. The great majority of bank capital flows to the large companies, to government projects or state-owned firms, and to funding the enormous national debt. Venture capital is also largely nonexistent in Italy.

Private capital in Italy is concentrated in a relatively small group of individuals who mobilize it to create large groups of companies with partial interlocking ownership and effective control (the Fiat group, the de Benedetti group, the Ferruzzi group, and the Pirelli group). These few groups wield enormous influence in the capital markets, and, through coalitions, are sometimes the only ones beside the government that can mobilize large amounts of funds.

This financial market structure is not an efficient mechanism for funding and nurturing independent companies. The majority of Italian entrepreneurs want no part of it: Most firms in Italy have financed entry and growth out of private savings, profits, and rolling short-term loans. The nature of the capital markets means that Italian firms rarely succeed in capital-intensive industries. The great majority of successful Italian industries, such as textiles, shoes, tiles, jewelry, specialized machinery, and even appliances, are characterized by low capital requirements for entry. In capital-intensive industries, Italian participants are frequently state-owned or *de facto* local monopolies controlled by one of the large financial groups which have access to capital. Few have competitive advantage in global terms.

With the exception of roads, Italian infrastructure is almost always a genuine weakness as well. Telecommunications and postal service have been poor, financial services slow and archaic,[41] and transportation and logistics often a nightmare. A web of regulations and state-owned monopolies in most infrastructure services makes getting things done in Italy extremely difficult. Public services are especially prone to strikes, which disrupt transportation and other infrastructure areas.

Factor Creation Mechanisms. Italy succeeds as much through informal as formal factor creation. Italian high schools provide a good basic education. The *Liceo scientifico* and *Liceo classico,* in particular, are highly selective and demanding, though laboratory and other facilities have much room for improvement. Training in computers remains substandard.

The real uniqueness of Italy, however, is the out-of-school learning process in particular industries. There is a long tradition in many of the internationally successful industries such as textiles and furniture. Highly specialized knowledge and skills are passed within families and from generation to generation.

The process of factor creation in ceramic tiles, described in Chapter 5, is typical. Italian companies have a very strong family orientation, and there is a strong tendency for the family to live in one area. This facilitates the process of skills transfer. As or more important is the striking geographic concentration of Italian industries, where many firms are all located in a single town. Geographic concentration speeds the accumulation and diffusion of knowledge. In some fields, such as jewelry, there are long formal apprenticeship programs.

There are some excellent departments in Italian universities. Engineering is a prestigious occupation in Italy with a long tradition. The title *Ingegnere* is used in the same way "Doctor" is in the United States. Schools of engineering are highly selective, and programs involve an extra year compared to other degrees. Italian engineers have an unusual ability to combine aesthetic and technical elements, attributed by some Italians to a humanistic tradition and great interest among Italians in art, architecture, and philosophy. Even in engineering, however, formal master's and doctoral programs are relatively weak.

Overall, Italian university education does not rank near the top in European or world terms. The Italian university system is heavily state run (the only three entirely private universities are Bocconi and Cattolica in Milan, and LUISS in Rome). Departments are concentrated in traditional fields, and there are chronic shortages of places in newer fields such as computing and electronics. Facilities are in need of upgrading. Programs lack rigor, quality is uneven, and updating is slow. Master's-level programs are weak, and there is little doctoral-level training available. Italians go abroad for training, but Italy is well behind all the other nations we studied in this respect in per capita terms. Only 2,200 Italians were studying in America at the postsecondary level in 1987–88, for example, compared to 4,870 Singaporeans.[42]

Italian companies provide little formal training, nor do they actively support the universities. Hence advanced training in Italy is like other training, informal and on the job. Italy does well in industries where this approach is suitable; it does poorly where human resources with advanced formal training are necessary (such as computers and aerospace).

Italy is also relatively weak in formal research, either in universities, government laboratories, or firms. Italian universities lack doctoral programs that are usually the core of much university research.[43] Funding is modest for university research and government laboratories. Pockets of research excellence exist in Italy, but they benefit few industries. Formal research inside companies tends to be modest, specialized, and highly applied in character.[44] Italian firms are rarely on the frontiers of technology or basic product performance.

Yet it would be a mistake to conclude that Italian firms are not strong in technology. Indeed, Italian firms in many industries are masters at artfully adapting foreign technologies and applying them to particular end-use applications. Technological prowess is not only in products but in processes. Surging international success in a range of Italian industries can be traced to process breakthroughs and the application of modern flexible manufacturing technology to traditional products.

Italian companies are very willing and able to seek and apply foreign technologies. Through extensive travel and a network of personal relationships, Italian managers are often quite sensitive to the pulse of technological change. Broader advances are rapidly translated to a more specialized use, often growing out of close contact with customers.

It should be clear from what I have already said that the most effective factor creation in Italy occurs at the level of the particular firm or industry. The geographic concentration of firms leads to very rapid accumulation and diffusion of knowledge. The industry is the constant subject of discussion, and intense rivalry leads to rapid imitation of good ideas and the constant search for new competitive edges. Local *Istituti Tecnici* (technical high schools) and universities often adapt their courses and research to the needs of the local industry, and develop corresponding fields of unusual strength. Companies contribute to industry associations that play a broader role than in most countries, related to the modest size of many Italian exporting firms. Associations sponsor technical institutes, gather and disseminate information, promote exports, stimulate the upgrading of infrastructure, and deal with government.

Selective Factor Disadvantages. Rapid innovation and adaptation within Italian firms is partly driven by selective factor disadvantages. The minimill (Chapter 3) and ceramic tile (Chapter 5) cases provide extended Italian examples. Many Italian firms confront expensive energy, lack domestic raw materials, and face a complex labor environment and burdensome regulations. The ability of Italian firms to upgrade by overcoming these problems is impressive, whether it is through innovation, automation, or organization into small units to take advantage of exceptions granted in labor and tax laws.

In wool textiles, for example, Italian firms faced significant cost and quality disadvantages in sourcing raw materials compared to wool-producing countries such as the United Kingdom and United States. Prato-area firms pioneered the use of recycled wool and a number of other innovations such as blending recycled wool with man-made fibers (where Italy has a solid international position). Another example is in appliances, where labor circumstances led to the creation of small factories focused on single models. In many industries, this focused nature of Italian firms has often facilitated automation and high levels of productivity compared to broader-line foreign plants. Even in an industry such as automobiles, however, Italian labor conditions have led to perhaps the most automated plants in the world.

The difficult Italian environment, with its poor public services and complex regulatory tangle, has spawned a curious sort of advantage. Italian firms are intensely pragmatic, undeterred by obstacles, and adept at adaptation and improvisation. They manage constraints rather than succumb to them. Many observers cite Italian success in marketing in Africa, the Middle East, and other developing nations, for example, as a product of years of coping with the Italian bureaucracy.

The real upgrading of the Italian economy was triggered by selective factor disadvantages. In the 1950s and 1960s, Italian firms were content to compete on price based on cheap labor. Beginning in 1969, new laws pushed wages and social benefit costs much higher and made it very difficult to fire workers. Italian wage structures were also affected, leading to few job categories and wage compression that translated into high wages for relatively unskilled workers. In response to these pressures, Italian firms began moving into sophisticated and higher-priced industry segments. They also began upgrading process technology and automating production. The end of a policy of devaluing the lira, beginning in the late 1970s, provided the final impetus for upgrading in many industries. The Italian rate of productivity growth in manufacturing has been especially remarkable compared to other nations since the mid-1970s (see Table 7–1).

Instead of floundering, Italian firms prospered in the face of selective factor disadvantages in industries where other favorable conditions in the "diamond" were present, notably sophisticated demand, high levels of motivation, and intense domestic rivalry. By the early 1980s, Italian industry had upgraded advantage significantly. Selective disadvantages in basic factors forced Italy to a more advanced stage of development.

ITALIAN DEMAND CONDITIONS

If inherited and socially created factor conditions are among Italy's greatest weaknesses, demand conditions are among its greatest strengths. In virtually every consumer goods industry in which Italy has national competitive advantage, Italian buyers are among the, if not the, world's most sophisticated, advanced buyers (this is true in apparel, shoes, jewelry, furniture, lighting, ceramic tiles, food products, wine, and many others). Some of these are well-known Italian passions.

Italian consumers are on the cutting edge of taste and style. Some observers attribute this to an unusual interest in design and the arts, a function perhaps of living among masterpieces. Italians are very sensitive to new trends and are among the first to adopt new designs and features. Italians spend more per capita on items such as clothes, accessories, and shoes than citizens of any other nation.[45] Industry executives state that Italians buy fewer individual items but ones of much higher average quality compared to consumers in other nations. Sophisticated and picky demand for household items reflects, among other things, the fact that Italy has the highest percentage of home ownership of any major European country.[46]

The sophistication of Italian consumers in areas such as clothing, footwear, tiles, and furniture is reinforced by the presence of sophisticated distribution channels in Italy for these products. Italian retailers are almost invariably smaller and more specialized in particular products than foreign retailers. They are intimately familiar with their business and represent an extremely knowledgeable and demanding intermediate buyer for the products involved. Italian firms must constantly come up with new models to secure and maintain distribution. As a result, the product variety available in Italy is enormous. In furniture, for example, there is a profusion of stores, many highly specialized in such areas as bathrooms, kitchens, and office furniture. These represent demanding intermediate buyers of such products as built-in appliances, ceramic tiles, lighting, and office furnishings. Italy is a powerful illustration of the self-reinforcing effects of sophisticated consumers, channels, and companies all interacting with each other in close proximity.

In some industries, the segment structure of consumer demand has worked to the benefit of Italian industry. Fiat is most successful in small, economical cars. Another example is in appliances, where local demand is for relatively compact units where Italy has or had its initial international success. More recently, Italy has led in built-in appliances as well as in appliances closely integrated with furniture. Active demand reflects the strong propensity of Italians to renovate their homes and apartments. (New construction is relatively difficult today in Italy because of regulations.)

Finally, unusual local conditions make Italian consumption unusually high in a range of industries where Italy is internationally successful. Good examples are stone and tile (because of taste and climate), pasta, espresso machines (reflecting a profusion of small bars which feature espresso), and dance club lighting (reflecting social norms).

Italian success extends well beyond consumer goods themselves, as Figure 8–4 makes clear. The industrial products in which Italian firms are internationally competitive are almost always inputs or machinery sold to successful Italian consumer goods industries, a manifestation of the depth of Italian clusters. Good examples are tanned leather, footwear parts and leather-working machinery, fabrics and textile machinery, kilns for ceramic tiles, olive oil manufacturing machines, stone cutting machinery, and many other varieties of specialized equipment. In these industries, Italian end-product firms play the role of advanced and highly demanding buyers for other Italian firms. They compete on the basis of frequent product changes and want to stay on the cutting edge of style and technology. Emerging NIC competitors have pressured Italian firms to reduce cost and speed up innovation, leading Italian firms to step up demands on their suppliers. For similar reasons, Italy is also the home of world-leading design firms, many of which were listed earlier.

The strategies and organizational structures of firms in many Italian industries provide a unique segment structure of demand for inputs and machinery. Populated by hundreds of firms and competing with frequent model changes, Italian industries demand highly customized inputs and machinery.[47] In agricultural machinery, for example, Italy does well in products that relate to small Italian farms and the specialized crops where Italy is an important producer. Italian suppliers do well whenever a desire for small scale, flexibility, and rapid model changes is present.

Italy has also achieved international success in a number of other industries where industrial buyers have unusually stringent or intense needs. Geological conditions make Italy a complicated country in which to build, for example, contributing to Italian international success in the engineering of infrastructure projects. Italian construction techniques make heavy use of cement structures instead of metal ones. Italian private steel producers, in turn, are highly competitive internationally in concrete reinforcing bars and in a range of tubular and bar products. Italian labor laws place a high premium on avoiding layoffs and on eliminating jobs that have a high minimum labor cost. Italian machinery firms and other suppliers produce products sensitive to these unusually intense but universal needs. Factory automation equipment, for example, has emerged as a major Italian industry.

Italian industries benefited, as did Japan, from a later takeoff in the Italian economy compared with other European nations, which meant that the Italian economy was rapidly growing when others were slowing to a more moderate rate. This fueled widespread entry and more aggressive investment in new facilities. Italian export success in many industries began when the domestic market leveled off. Italian appliance firms became aggressive exporters, for example, after the postwar capital spending boom ended in 1963–64. Footwear exports took off in the 1960s, while construction/engineering exports followed the falloff in domestic infrastructure construction in the early 1970s.

Italian exports have also benefited through the internationalization of Italian style and taste. This has occurred through Italian (and non-Italian) design and fashion magazines, design firms, and the pull-through effect of related industries. Italian furniture benefits Italian lighting, for example, while Italian clothing benefits Italian jewelry. Internationalization of demand also occurs through tourism, as many visitors to Italy are exposed to Italian products under favorable circumstances. One industry executive estimated, for example, that tourists purchased 10 percent of the shoes sold in Italy. This is not reflected in Italian trade statistics, which understate Italian market share.

Areas in which Italy is weak also reflect demand conditions. Italian firms are strikingly unsuccessful internationally *in any industry in which the government is a significant buyer.* Notable examples are telecommunications, power generation and distribution, health care, much transportation equipment, and many services.

Italian firms also rarely succeed in products sold to industries in which Italian firms are uncompetitive. Also rare is success in products that are sold to a wide range of other industries. The mix of industries in Italy is sufficiently unusual that Italian positions in the "multiple business" category are modest in comparison to Germany, Switzerland, Japan, the United States, and the United Kingdom.

RELATED AND SUPPORTING INDUSTRIES

Deep clusters of related and supporting industries are characteristic of the Italian economy, as I have already noted. Figure 8–6 illustrates just one of many examples. Italy has a strong international position in all the industries shown.

As Figure 8–6 illustrates, vertical relationships between successful Italian industries are the most pronounced. Horizontal relationships are based most typically on commonalities in consumer demand or distribution channels and are rarely based on technology, as is the case in Germany or Japan. A wide range of successful Italian industries is related through what might be termed the Italian fashion and furnishing complex.

Entire clusters of Italian industries are often tightly concentrated in a particular geographic region or regions. Italian suppliers provide superb and rapid service to their Italian customers. New machinery and other inputs are invariably tested and first made available in Italy, and intense home market competition means that Italian buyers sometimes receive better prices.[48] Italy, as a result of such clustering, is surprisingly strong in machinery industries.

Fluid interchange within Italian clusters is facilitated by proximity, by the strong family or familylike ties that connect many Italian firms with their suppliers and related firms, and by community spirit. Italy is in many ways still not a nation but a series of towns (once city states) with which citizens closely identify. Dealings with suppliers and customers are heavily based on personal relationships and are characterized by continuity over long periods of time. Interchange with suppliers and customers is virtually instantaneous. The geographic area becomes a self-contained and self-reinforcing economic system.

Levels of vertical integration in Italian firms tend to be very low. Firms often perform just a few activities in the value chain, contracting out others to firms that are often located down the street. Benetton, the well-known Italian clothing company, is a notable example. The result is a high degree of specialization, the ability to reap economies of scale in those activities where they are significant, and great fluidity in adjusting capacity to demand and in changing product varieties.

Clusters often stimulate investments in factor creation as well as investments in joint activities, frequently through industry associations. Italy has well-developed trade fairs in many of its leading industries. In the Rimini area, home of the greatest concentration of Italian dance clubs as well as the dance club equipment industry, the annual SIB/MAGIS exhibition of dance club equipment is an important international event. It is just one of many.

Another good example of the cluster's role in factor creation is the Prato area (wool cloth). Through five industry associations in different but related fields, there is joint research on new technologies, construction of a central depurator (purifier), cooperation in the purchases of services, raw materials, and equipment, operation of a general warehouse, and an ongoing effort to influence local infrastructure. Competition among Prato firms is extraordi-

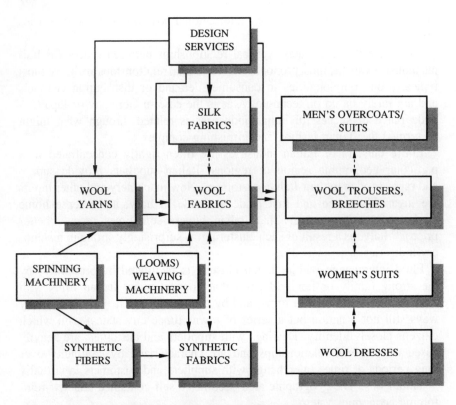

NOTE: Solid lines represent supplier relationships. Broken lines signify related industries.

FIGURE **8–6 Related and Supporting Italian Industries to Wool Textiles**

narily intense, but the concentration of firms in the area has led to important joint, as well as local government, investments in factors.

As one would suspect, given the prevalence of consumer goods among the industries in which Italy has national advantage, the Italian media is also well developed. Private television is extensive, with six private national channels and numerous regional channels.[49] Italian magazines such as *Amica, Grazia, Domus,* and *Casa Bella* also have worldwide circulations and are major voices shaping trends in fashion, furnishings, and other fields in which Italy is strong. Fashion designers and design firms are also world class in areas such as footwear, fashion, furniture, industrial styling, and even automobile design.

Absence of important related and supporting industries contributes to some areas of Italian weakness. A notable example is in consumer electronics, where the absence of a major electronics cluster places potential Italian competitors at a significant disadvantage vis-à-vis foreign rivals. Olivetti's success in some electronics-related industries is both remarkable and isolated.

Olivetti built its international position as a pioneer and innovator in mechanical typewriters, and established a strong brand name and distribution channels that have been transferred to electronic products.

FIRM STRATEGY, STRUCTURE, AND RIVALRY

Most Italian firms that are successful in international competition are small- and medium-sized firms by international standards. Many of the large firms, especially in capital-intensive industries, are state owned and domestically oriented. The large private firms tend to dominate their home market. Comparatively few, such as Pirelli, Olivetti, Fiat, and Montedison, are internationally active. In their industries, Italy holds only a modest share of world markets. In contrast, Italian industries composed of many medium-sized and small firms are often world leaders.

The reasons that Italy has greater international success in medium and small firms are several. An important one has already been discussed, and that is poorly developed capital markets. Another is the management style and organizational approach that is characteristic of Italian companies. Italians do not usually function well in hierarchies and aspire to working in their own or a close-knit company. Firms are often managed by a commanding leader involved in virtually all of the firm's activities. Below the leader the organization is often fluid, relatively unstructured, and, some would say, chaotic. There are exceptions in some larger companies, but my experience has been that even larger Italian companies have this character. Managers desire independence and their own areas of responsibility instead of working in groups. There is interpersonal competition that would be very unusual in Sweden or Japan. Professional management structures and systems necessary in large companies are rare. Managers are resourceful improvisers and able to adjust to changes, to circumvent constraints, and to adapt to new rules of the game.

Italian firms tend to be highly specialized and compete through constant model changes and innovation. In industrial products, such as machinery and specialized inputs, Italian firms work hand in hand with their customers to produce highly customized products that offer superior price/performance in a particular application, though they may lack some of the technological sophistication of German or Swiss goods. Italian firms also deal with customers based on familylike and personal relationships. A typical Italian shoe company, for example, will produce only one type of shoe (such as children's shoes) and sell to only one or two countries via channels with whom the owner has a long relationship.

While superior product design may be part of the equation, however, Italian firms are also imaginative innovators in process technology. Process technology, in fact, is the principal source of competitive advantage in many Italian industries, partly due to the labor pressures I described earlier.

The strategies and organization style I have described mean that many industries in which Italy exhibits national competitive advantage are highly segmented, specialized, or fragmented. Italian firms are not often successful where standardization, high-volume mass production, or heavy investments in fundamental research are involved.

Large enterprises in Italy must confront powerful unions, a social structure that is uncomfortable with large, disciplined organizations, and capital markets ill-equipped to fund capital-intensive businesses except in a small circle of financial groups. Large companies also become entangled with government. They may benefit through subsidy and protection, but political maneuvering and an inward focus on Italy blunt or distract the drive for international success. Innovation is stifled.

While successful Italian firms are extremely international in outlook, foreign direct investment is comparatively rare. The Italian position abroad is largely won through exports. Foreign marketing channels are often informed and heavily based on personal relationships. This structure means that the destination of Italian exports fluctuates markedly over time as entrepreneurs respond opportunistically to market trends. This is both a cause and a reflection of the types of industries in which Italy successfully competes. Where foreign production is essential to international success, Italian firms are rarely important competitors. Also significant is the fact that until recently there were strict government currency controls which made foreign investment difficult. Foreign investment is growing, often in response to barriers to market access as the Italian position has become more significant.

The goals of Italian workers, managers, and capital holders are an important source of Italian advantage. Since most Italian companies are privately owned, the entire family may be on the payroll. Italian entrepreneurs do not want outside shareholders, in order to maintain total control and independence, to avoid the need to clearly separate company and family finances, and because of a well-founded suspicion of the public capital markets.

Owners, managers, and workers are closely attached to the industry and often to a particular region where the industry is located. The company itself is often like an extended family, where employees are known and feel important. These conditions lead to a very long-term orientation in Italian companies and a commitment to sustained investment. When problems arise, Italian owners will pour all they have into new machinery or make whatever changes necessary to preserve the business. To exit voluntarily is unthinkable. One cannot close down the family. Low margins or even no margins for a time are far preferable.

Business is front-page news in Italy and a magnet for talented individuals. Leading business executives are highly visible and part of the folklore.

Aspirations to become like them add to the commitment and motivation in Italian companies.

The real driver of Italian success in many industries (as in Japan), however, is extraordinary rivalry. Almost every internationally successful Italian industry has several if not hundreds of domestic competitors. Frequently, they are all located in one or two towns (see Figure 4–6). Rivalry is personal and emotional. The interpersonal competition that is prevalent in Italy feeds rivalry.

The effect of this competition is constant innovation and specialization. Innovations and ideas diffuse with amazing speed. A network of suppliers, usually located nearby, fans the flames. Market positions change frequently. At the same time, local associations exist to perform limited joint functions such as export promotion.

Where domestic rivalry is absent, Italian firms rarely succeed internationally. This is true for the majority of the state-owned companies and also helps explain why many of the large Italian private firms are not stronger internationally. Through financial clout and political influence, they gain dominant positions in the Italian home market and are often very profitable. Yet the dynamism necessary to achieve real competitive advantage in foreign markets is too often lacking.

Entrepreneurship thrives in Italy, feeding rivalry in existing industries and the formation of clusters.[50] Italians are risk takers. Many are individualistic and desire independence. They aspire to have their own company. They like to work with people they know well, as in the family, and not as part of a hierarchy. Spin-offs to start a new company at the first possible opportunity are common in Italy, either in the same industry or a closely related one. The result is a constant succession of new products and forays into new segments, upstream industries, or related businesses. Recently, the entrepreneur has become celebrated in Italy, and a number of business magazines are full of nothing but profiles of successful entrepreneurs. The rate of business failure is also high, as one might suspect. Yet the family seems to provide a safety net to cushion failure.

The Role of Government

The Italian case suggests quite clearly that government policy is not a *sine qua non* of national competitive advantage. The Italian government, at the national level, has created far more disadvantages than advantages. Government services and state-owned companies tend to be inefficient. Italian firms are rarely internationally successful when government is an important buyer or the provider of significant inputs. Government investment in factor creation is low and poorly managed. Public support for research is low. Much government aid has been funneled not into factor creation but into rescues, subsidies, and promoting development in the South. Regional policy, based not on building clusters but attracting isolated plants to the South with heavy subsidies, is widely perceived as a failure. A misguided effort to build up "high technology" industries suffered from Italian weakness in many determinants and missed the fact that nearly all industries in the 1980s involve high tech.

Government policy is heavily influenced by the large Italian companies. There is a strong bias toward the use of preferential loans or subsidies, administered in a cumbersome fashion. Fiscal policy, in such forms as tax incentives, is rarely employed. Italy lacks antitrust laws, allowing the larger firms to achieve commanding positions in the domestic market, especially in capital-intensive industries because potential competitors have difficulty raising capital. Trade barriers also limit foreign rivals. Government policy has too often favored *de facto* domestic monopolies, working against innovation and international success in the affected industries.[51] In industries with low capital barriers to entry, the lack of antitrust laws is irrelevant given the vibrant new business formation in Italy.

Numerous, short-lived governments, the political power of the large firms, a predilection toward state-ownership, and politically powerful labor unions have made Italian policy an impediment to, rather than a promoter of, firm innovation. Public institutions have not worked well in Italy and are seen as constraints that must be bypassed. In a range of Italian industries, the disadvantages created through government policy have undermined competitive advantage. Italy has succeeded largely where it has been possible to minimize, circumvent, or avoid these government-induced disadvantages.

One of the few areas in which the Italian government has created advantages is in its aggressive use of aid to developing nations to pull through Italian goods. Italy has unusually good relationships with developing countries and has positioned itself as a bridge between them and the developed world. Most other positive government programs have sought to minimize disadvantages created by other programs; for example, *cassa integrazione,* a compensation system whereby government pays employees dismissed by companies 80 to 90 percent of their normal wage for varying periods to overcome government-legislated restrictions on layoffs.

Local governments in Italy are more constructive than the national government. Successful Italian industries are usually concentrated in particular regions and towns. Local governments take an intense interest, sometimes becoming involved in funding specialized university programs and providing assistance through locally owned banks, infrastructure investments, and other factor-creating investments. Local government intrusion in company activities was not a factor in any of the cases we studied, even where the government in the area was controlled by the Italian Communist Party.[52]

There is major scope for changes in government policy that would improve

Italian competitiveness (see Chapter 13). Many believe there is only modest hope that such changes will be forthcoming.

THE ROLE OF CHANCE

Italy benefited in some industries from its relatively late postwar boom and because it was somewhat behind other advanced European nations in development. Its situation is not unlike that of Japan. The result was the ability to leapfrog generations of process technology and penetrate emerging segments unhindered by past investments. In appliances, for example, Italian demand continued to grow rapidly after other nations had reached higher levels of saturation.

ITALY IN PERSPECTIVE

Italy has emerged with a vibrant economy in the last two decades. Its history, which I will touch on briefly in Chapter 10, provided some important underpinnings for its success. Until the 1970s, however, Italian industry still depended on low labor costs, devaluations, pervasive subsidies, and trade distortions for international success. These were a trap for long-term development.

Italian industry upgraded when pressure built to jolt it from this path. Wage escalation, a rising lira, the threat of the low-wage NICs, and globalization forced Italian industries to seek more sophisticated forms of competitive advantage. Where other determinants were favorable (for example, human resources, demanding buyers, and numerous rivals), this pressure was translated into international advantage.

The Italian case, like that of Japan, illustrates again the self-reinforcing nature of the "diamond": sophisticated demand, world-class suppliers, deep personal commitment to an industry, and intense domestic rivalry (fed by active new business formation) create an irresistible force for innovation, all inside a concentrated geographic region. This structure of industry consisting of a dynamic, geographically concentrated group of rivals has been well recognized in Italy. What many Italians may not recognize is that internationally successful industries in every nation take on this character, though often without quite so many rivals.

The Italian economy is also a vivid illustration of clustering. While success was often initially in end products, such as ceramic tiles or shoes, world-class input and machinery industries emerged to serve them. At the same time, Italian success broadened to related industries, for example, home and office lighting to dance club lighting, machine tools to robotics. Cluster formation is particularly rapid in Italy because of the prevalence of spin-offs and other mechanisms for new business formation. As Figure 8–7 illustrates, Italian clusters are vibrant and self-reinforcing.

Italian success is interesting also because it often comes in sectors that could be termed traditional, such as shoes, apparel, and furniture. Italian industry demonstrates how "traditional" industries can be transformed and how competitive advantages can be upgraded. Italian firms rapidly adapted new technology and marketing techniques to such industries. That Italy did not succumb to low-wage, developing countries in such industries is a testament to its firms' ability to innovate and change.

Italian success is far broader than traditional industries, however. It encompasses sophisticated machinery often connected to traditional consumer sectors, which represents nearly 10 percent of total Italian exports. Italy is also achieving advantage in a range of new fields such as factory automation

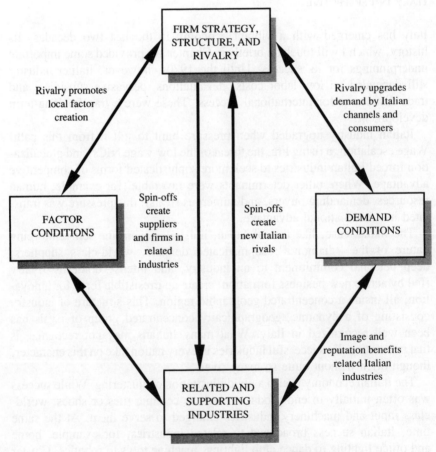

FIGURE 8–7 Dynamics of Italian Clusters

equipment and specialized materials. Any image of Italy which focuses too strongly on shoes and furniture is a flawed one.

Italy benefited from a number of important trends in the world economy. One trend is the shift from standardized, mass-produced products toward more customized, higher-styled, higher-quality goods. Another is the movement of production technology away from inflexible, scale-sensitive processes toward those with more flexibility that are suitable for, and adaptable to, small production runs. It would be a serious mistake to ascribe Italy's success in industries only to style and design. In many of the industries, style was combined with aggressive investments in state-of-the-art production equipment to support segmented and rapidly improving product lines while containing cost.

The pattern of gains and losses in world export share between 1978 and 1985, summarized in Figure 8-8, makes clear the upgrading of the Italian economy. Italy has had 15 percent or greater gains in share in comfortably more industries than those experiencing losses, a sign that the upgrading of competitive advantage is occurring when combined with other indicators. The plurality of gains over losses is particularly striking in the strong Italian clusters: food and beverages, housing and household, and textiles and apparel. Most significant is that losses have tended to occur in factor cost-sensitive or less processed products, while many gains are in sophisticated industries. Italy has gained share in twenty-eight machinery industries (compared to Japan's twenty-nine) and lost share in only two, verifying the deepening of clusters. An upgrading economy is also indicated by substantial gains in the multiple business sector.

Yet the Italian environment creates limits. Italy's national advantage is largely in particular industry structures: fragmented, frequent product changes, consumer oriented, or supplier industries that serve consumer industries. Italian strength is greatest along the bottom row of the cluster chart. Italian firms compete with characteristic strategies such as a focus on a specialized variety or small industry segment. Both reflect the Italian environment.

Large areas of the Italian economy lack international advantage because of the government's role, the nature of financial markets, the absence of domestic competition, and labor-management relations, to name just some of the problems described earlier. Figure 8-8 shows that Italy has experienced more share losses than gains in areas such as power generation, office equipment, and chemicals where it has had some historical position. Its ability to hold share in transportation-related equipment, except for production machinery, is mixed. Italy has gained world export share, on average, in industries growing relatively slowly and lost it in industries growing more rapidly, a sign of mixed success in newer industries (Table B-3).

Italian firms have succeeded where these problems were not present or

FIGURE 8–8 Competitive Italian Industries with Gains or Losses of World Export Share of 15% or More Between 1978 and 1985*

Upstream Industries

	Materials/Metals			Forest Products			Petroleum/Chemicals			Semiconductors/Computers			UPSTREAM INDUSTRIES		
	Total Comp. Inds.	Share Gains	Share Losses	Total Comp. Inds.	Share Gains	Share Losses	Total Comp. Inds.	Share Gains	Share Losses	Total Comp. Inds.	Share Gains	Share Losses	Total Comp. Inds.	Share Gains	Share Losses
Primary Goods	26	12	13	5	2	3	17	10	13	0	0	0	48	24	29
Machinery	5	3	0	1	0	0	0	0	0	0	0	0	6	3	0
Specialty Inputs	2	0	2	1	0	0	0	0	0	0	0	0	3	0	2
Total	33	15	15	7	2	3	17	10	13	0	0	0	57	27	31

Industrial & Supporting Functions

	Multiple Business			Transportation			Power Generation & Distribution			Office			Telecommunications			Defense			INDUSTRIAL & SUPPORTING FUNCTIONS		
	Total Comp. Inds.	Share Gains	Share Losses	Total Comp. Inds.	Share Gains	Share Losses	Total Comp. Inds.	Share Gains	Share Losses	Total Comp. Inds.	Share Gains	Share Losses	Total Comp. Inds.	Share Gains	Share Losses	Total Comp. Inds.	Share Gains	Share Losses	Total Comp. Inds.	Share Gains	Share Losses
Primary Goods	7	5	1	12	5	7	5	5	3	4	1	4	0	0	0	1	1	1	29	15	19
Machinery	3	2	0	10	3	2	0	0	0	3	2	0	0	0	0	0	0	0	16	7	2
Specialty Inputs	2	1	0	10	5	4	0	0	0	0	0	0	0	0	0	0	0	0	12	6	4
Total	12	8	1	32	13	13	5	5	3	7	3	4	0	0	0	1	1	1	57	28	25

Final Consumption Goods & Services

	Food/Beverage			Textiles/Apparel			Housing/Household			Health Care			Personal			Entertainment/Leisure			FINAL CONSUMPTION GOODS & SERVICES		
	Total Comp. Inds.	Share Gains	Share Losses	Total Comp. Inds.	Share Gains	Share Losses	Total Comp. Inds.	Share Gains	Share Losses	Total Comp. Inds.	Share Gains	Share Losses	Total Comp. Inds.	Share Gains	Share Losses	Total Comp. Inds.	Share Gains	Share Losses	Total Comp. Inds.	Share Gains	Share Losses
Primary Goods	25	12	8	57	15	22	30	13	13	2	0	1	10	2	6	10	3	6	134	45	50
Machinery	9	7	2	9	7	0	9	5	4	0	0	0	0	0	0	0	0	0	23	18	0
Specialty Inputs	12	7	2	13	7	1	5	0	1	0	0	0	2	0	0	1	0	0	37	15	5
Total	46	26	10	79	29	23	44	18	18	2	0	1	12	2	6	11	3	7	194	78	55

*Included were industries exceeding the cutoff in either 1978 or 1985, including those that were competitive in 1978 but fell below the cutoff in 1985 or that had first achieved sufficient share to exceed the cutoff in 1985.

they could be circumvented or avoided. For instance, small firms avoided regulations, and in some cases, taxation. Success is often in industries that do not require access to efficient capital markets. "Small is beautiful" has been a popular phrase in Italy. It is an apt phrase because the Italian environment has skewed success toward industries in which large scale is not important to competitive advantage. On average, Italy has gained world export share in smaller industries and lost it in larger industries, as Table B-3 illustrates.

Progress has been made in the mid- and late 1980s in restructuring some large Italian companies, both private and state owned. Because of such widely publicized turnarounds and anticipation of greater European integration in 1992, there is much recent emphasis in Italy on large companies and on increasing company size through mergers. As I will discuss in more detail later, such an emphasis is more likely to harm than benefit Italian competitive advantage. Many large Italian companies still lack true competitive advantage in global terms though they may have reduced their disadvantages. Their profitability still depends heavily on the domestic market and on sectors in which government intervention is significant. For many reasons, small- and medium-sized firms facing active domestic competition are likely to remain the principal source of dynamism in the Italian economy.

Further development in established Italian industries, and especially extension of success into new industries, demands important changes from both firms and government. Some of these changes will require a rebalancing of power and the roles of industry and government in Italy. I will return to these issues in Chapter 13.

EMERGING KOREA[53]

While Japan and Italy were relatively advanced before World War II, a group of Asian NICs has emerged as forces in international competition in only the last decade. Of these, South Korea (hereafter Korea) is the nation with perhaps the best prospects for reaching advanced status and developing national advantage in a range of important industries. Korean industry has rapidly upgraded its competitive advantage in the last two decades and is enjoying rapid growth in productivity and per capita income (see Table 7–1).

Yet Korea is still far from achieving a fully advanced economy. Nearly all Korean industries compete on cost, and Korea has yet to build the demand-side advantages and related and supporting industries necessary to compete on innovation and differentiation.

TABLE 8–5 Top Fifty Korean Industries in Terms of World Export Share, 1985

Industry	Share of Total World Exports	Export Value ($ millions)	Import Value ($ millions)	Share of Total Korean Exports
Iron, steel wire	57.0	45,666	25	0.15
Monochrome TV receivers	52.4	215,041	347	0.71
Off-line data processing equipment	41.8	238,310	73,350	0.79
Men's shirts of synthetic fibers	40.9	292,283	—	0.97
Men's jackets, blazers	39.4	417,910	233	1.38
Other cargo vessels	36.9	4,545,449	3,296,174	15.01
Containers including road-rail	32.2	279,798	11,815	0.92
Jukeboxes	31.9	5,531	9,225	0.02
Women's coats, jackets of synthetic fibers	31.8	212,399	—	0.70
Leather clothes, accessories	26.7	539,989	862	1.78
Travel goods, satchels	24.6	337,005	1,264	1.11
Sweaters of synthetic fibers	24.2	448,201	—	1.48
Nonpile continuous synthetic weaves	21.1	885,906	69,888	2.93
Railway sleepers	20.5	17,050	18,640	0.06
Women's blouses of synthetic fibers	16.4	149,778	—	0.49
Frozen fish, excluding fillets	15.7	260,784	58,225	0.86
Cotton yarn, 40–80 km/kg	15.4	128,634	353	0.42
Woven silk fabrics	15.4	104,845	35,892	0.35
Men's cotton shirts	15.0	211,624	—	0.70
Articles of furskin	14.7	161,287	994	0.53
Iron, steel structures and parts	14.4	700,826	28,280	2.31
Leather footwear	14.3	1,436,334	—	4.74
Knitted clothing accessories	14.2	119,430	1,000	0.39
Tankers	14.1	342,319	17,381	1.13
Knit undergarments of wool, fibers	13.7	283,956	677	0.94
Imitation jewelry	13.1	101,207	6,935	0.33
Handbags	13.1	133,056	—	0.44
Discontinuous synthetic fiber yarn	12.6	128,440	23,843	0.42
Iron, steel cable, rope	12.5	124,856	8,178	0.41
Nitrogen-phosphate fertilizer	12.0	136,588	9,509	0.45
Men's overcoats, outerwear	11.9	261,603	160	0.86
Other radio receivers	11.9	142,529	9,432	0.47
Dresses of synthetic fibers	11.7	68,662	—	0.23
Sweaters of cotton, fibers	11.4	299,388	512	0.99
Textile articles	11.2	186,546	2,054	0.62

TABLE **8–5** (*Continued*)

Industry	Share of Total World Exports	Export Value ($ millions)	Import Value ($ millions)	Share of Total Korean Exports
Men's suits	11.1	72,771	109	0.24
Toys, indoor games	10.8	475,254	7,283	1.57
Men's shirts of other synthetic fibers	10.6	20,507	519	0.07
Steel and copper nails, nuts	10.1	71,652	2,162	0.24
Men's trousers, breeches	9.9	82,255	173	0.27
Steam boilers	9.9	36,391	17,118	0.12
Non-electric stoves, heating apparatus	9.8	185,942	12,278	0.61
Shellfish prepared, preserved	9.7	82,820	2,424	0.27
TV picture tubes	9.7	162,286	41,177	0.54
Aircraft, motorcycle tires	9.6	249,212	3,175	0.82
Synthetic pile fabric	9.0	38,567	4,128	0.13
Women's dresses of wool, cotton	8.8	57,102	103	0.19
Cutlery	8.8	109,536	2,833	0.36
Motor vehicle radio receivers	8.6	182,887	5,368	0.60
Woven cotton fabric	8.6	122,745	2,730	0.41
TOTAL				52.53

NOTE: No import data are reported if import value is less than 0.3 percent of total trade for 1985.

PATTERNS OF KOREAN COMPETITIVE ADVANTAGE

Table 8–5 lists the top fifty Korean industries in terms of world export share in 1985. Compared to the other nations I have discussed, the range of these industries is relatively narrow. Most are final consumer goods, while the balance are resource-dependent industries (such as fish products), basic materials, and a smattering of industrial manufactured goods. The top fifty Korean industries in terms of world export share account for 52 percent of Korean exports, a higher proportion than in Switzerland and Japan, and much higher than in Germany, Sweden, Italy, the United Kingdom, and the United States. Exports in Korea are relatively concentrated.[54]

Figure 8–9 profiles all the competitive industries in the Korean economy (summary statistics are shown in Figures 8–10 and B-7). By far the most important cluster is in textiles and apparel-related industries, where competitive industries account for nearly 30 percent of total Korean exports. A second significant cluster is in transportation equipment, including ships

FIGURE 8–9 Clusters of Internationally Competitive Korean Industries, 1985

	MATERIALS/METALS	FOREST PRODUCTS
Primary Goods	IRON & STEEL Pig iron˙ *Iron, simple steel blooms˙* *Iron, simple steel coils˙* Iron, simple steel wire rod˙ Iron, steel bars, etc.˙* *Iron, other steel bars hotrolled* *Iron, steel profiles, etc.*˙ Large u, i, h sections, etc.˙ Iron, steel universal plate, sheet# *Iron, simple steel rolled heavy plate* *Iron, simple steel rolled thin plate* Iron, simple steel wire Iron, steel castings unworked FABRICATED IRON & STEEL Railway rails˙	**Iron, steel tubes, pipes** **Iron, steel structures, parts** *Steel storage tanks, etc.˙* Iron, steel cable, rope **Iron, steel wire, barbed or not#** **Steel, copper nails, nuts, etc.*˙** Iron, steel nuts, bolts˙ NONFERROUS METALS Tungsten ore, concentrate Copper plate, sheet, strip˙ Aluminum bars, wire, etc. BUILDING MATERIALS Stone, sand & gravel *Cement* *Building stone, etc., worked*	**Railway sleepers*˙** Wood panels# PAPER Plastic coated paper˙
Machinery			
Specialty Inputs			
Services			

	PETROLEUM/CHEMICALS	SEMICONDUCTORS/COMPUTERS
Primary Goods	PLASTICS Polypropylene· Polystyrene· *Polyvinyl chloride·* PETROLEUM PRODUCTS Kerosene incl. jet fuel· Spirit jet fuel#· Pet. jelly, pitch, coke#· ORGANIC CHEMICALS Oxyamino compounds	**Off-line data processing equipment·** *Diodes, transistors, etc.* *Electronic microcircuits* ADP machine parts##
Machinery		
Specialty Inputs		
Services		

KEY

roman   1.74& world export share or higher, but less than 3.48% share

bold italics   *3.48% world export share or higher, but less than 6.96% share*

sans serif   **6.96% world export share or above**

·   Industries below cutoff in 1978

\#   Calculated residuals

\#\#   Added due to significant export value in a segmented industry

·   Added due to FDI

··   Upgraded due to FDI

···   Added based on in-country research

FIGURE 8–9 (Continued)

	MULTIPLE BUSINESS	TRANSPORTATION	POWER GENERATION AND DISTRIBUTION	OFFICE
Primary Goods	Optical instruments Optical elements mounted˙ Rubber articles#	*VEHICLES* Forklift trucks, etc.˙ *Aircraft nes over 15,000 KG#* **Tankers** Other cargo vessels *Trawlers, ships & boats#* *Tugs, floating structures#* *Special-purpose vessels* *Bicycles, wheelchairs#* Passenger motor vehicles##	*GENERATION* **Steam boilers˙** AC motors, incl. universal motors˙ **Wind, water engines˙** *DISTRIBUTION* *Liquid dielectric transformers˙* *Other electrical transformers#* Electrical condensers Insulated wire, cable *STORAGE* Electric accumulators˙	Calculating machines *Dictating machines, etc.* Pen nibs, pencils#
Machinery				
Specialty Inputs		*PARTS* Forklift trucks, etc. parts#˙ **Containers inc. road-rail** *Tires for cars˙* *Tires for bus or lorry* **Tires for aircraft, motorcycles#**		
Services	Engineering/architecture˙ Construction			

	TELECOMMUNICATIONS	DEFENSE
Primary Goods	Line telephone, etc., equipment˙ TV radio transmitters Telecomm. eqpt., parts#	
Machinery		
Specialty Inputs		
Services		

KEY

roman	1.74& world export share or higher, but less than 3.48% share
bold italics	***3.48% world export share or higher, but less than 6.96% share***
sans serif	**6.96% world export share or above**

.	Industries below cutoff in 1978	·	Added due to FDI
#	Calculated residuals	::	Upgraded due to FDI
##	Added due to significant export value in a segmented industry	···	Added based on in-country research

FIGURE 8–9 (Continued)

Primary Goods	FOOD/BEVERAGES	HOUSING/HOUSEHOLD
	BASIC FOODS Mutton fresh, chilled, frozen Fish fresh, chilled, ex. fillets **Fish frozen, ex. fillets** *Fish fillets, frozen* *Fish (ex. cod) dried, salted* *Shellfish fresh, frozen* Fish prepared, preserved **Shellfish fresh, frozen** Fish prepared, preserved **Shellfish prepared, preserved** Vegetable, fresh# **PROCESSED FOODS** Refined sugar, etc. *Edible products*	CERAMICS **Coarse ceramic housewares** *Ceramic ornaments, etc.* APPLIANCES *Domestic refrigerators* *Dishwashers, shavers,* *appliances#* OTHER Cutlery **Base metal household** **appliances#** **Electric filament lamps** **Basketwork, brooms, etc.** *Foliage#* Linoleum, rugs#
Machinery	*Hand tools#*	
Specialty Inputs	*Crude vegetable materials#* Nitro-phospate-potassium fertilizer **Nitro-phospate fertilizer** *Nitro-potassium fertilizers#•*	
Services		

TEXTILES/APPAREL

Primary Goods			
FABRICS			
Grey woven cotton fabric	Women's dresses of wool, cotton*	Women's dresses of synthetic fibers, knit	
Pile, etc., cotton fabrics	Women's dresses of synthetic fibers, nonknit	Knitted undergarments of wool, fibers#	
Continuous synthetic weaves nonpile	Women's skirts	Undergarments, of cotton nonelastic	
Woven synthetic fiber fabric#	Women's blouses of cotton, other fibers#	Articles of furskin	
Continuous regenerated weaves nonpile'	Women's blouses of synthetic fibers	ACCESSORIES	
Synthetic pile, etc., fabric	Other women's outerwear of synthetic fibers	Textile clothing accessory#	
Silk fabric, woven	Men's cotton shirts	Knitted clothing accessories	
Lace, ribbons, tulle	Men's shirts of synthetic fibers#	Leather clothes, accessories	
Woven combed wool*	Men's shirts of other fibers#	Plastic, rubber accessories, headgear#	
Special textile fabric, products#	*Men's & women's undergarments#*	FOOTWEAR	
Plastic coated textiles'	*Jerseys, pullovers of wool, fine hair*	*Prepared parts of footwear*	
Textile articles#	*Jerseys, pullovers of cotton fibers#*	Rubber, plastic, footwear	
APPAREL	Jerseys, pullovers of synthetic fibers	Leather footwear	
Men's overcoats, outerwear#	*Women's dresses, of wool, cotton, fibers#*	*Footwear, wood, cork#*	
Men's suits		LUGGAGE	
Men's trousers, breeches#		Handbags nes	
Men's jackets, blazers		Travel goods, satchels#	
Women's coats, jackets of wool, cotton#		OTHER	
Women's coats, jackets of synthetic fibers		Industrial leather, saddlery, etc.#	
Women's suits, costumes#			

Machinery			

Specialty Inputs			
FIBERS & YARN			
Discontinuous synthetic fiber uncombed•	*Wool, hair yarn#*	Discontinuous synthetic fiber yarn	
Cotton yarn#	Cotton yarn, 40–80 KM/KG	Discontinuous synthetic fiber blend yarn	
	Synthetic fiber yarn, bulk, monofil##•		

Services			

KEY

roman	1.74& world export share or higher, but less than 3.48% share	•	Industries below cutoff in 1978	· Added due to FDI
bold italics	*3.48% world export share or higher, but less than 6.96% share*	#	Calculated residuals	·· Upgraded due to FDI
sans serif	6.96% world export share or above	##	Added due to significant export value in a segmented industry	··· Added based on in-country research

FIGURE 8-9 (Continued)

Primary Goods	HEALTH CARE	PERSONAL	ENTERTAINMENT/LEISURE		
				CONSUMER ELECTRONICS	OTHER
		Spectacle frames˙		Color TV receivers	*Prepared sound recording media*
		Spectacles#		Monochrome TV receivers	Toys, indoor games#
		Watches		Motor vehicle radio receivers	Hand paintings, etc., nes˙
		Imitation Jewelry		Portable radio receivers	*Pianos, musical instruments,*
		Carvings, umbrellas, mfrd.		Other radio receivers	*parts#*
		goods nes#		TV image, sound recorders˙	Zoo animals, pets, etc.
		Combustible products, etc.		*Microphones, loudspeakers,*	Coin nongold, noncurrent
		Baby carriages, parts#		*amplifiers*	
		Pearls, precious, semiprecious		Jukeboxes#	
		stones#			
				PHOTOGRAPHY	
				Developed cinema film˙	
Machinery					
Specialty Inputs		Tobacco unstripped, virginia type●	PARTS		
		Tobacco stripped, virginia type	TV picture tubes●		
		Tobacco stripped, non-virginia			
		type#			
Services					

FIGURE 8–10 Percentage of Korean Exports of Competitive Industries by Broad Cluster

UPSTREAM INDUSTRIES

Cluster	Share of Country Exports	Share of World Cluster Exports
Materials/Metals	9.6 (1.8)	1.8 (1.0)
Semiconductors/Computers	3.8 (0.9)	1.6 (−0.2)
Petroleum/Chemicals	1.8 (1.4)	0.2 (0.1)
Forest Products	0.2 (−4.0)	0.4 (−1.2)

Share of Country Exports: 15.4 (0.1)
Share of World Cluster Exports: 0.8 (0.2)

INDUSTRIAL AND SUPPORTING FUNCTIONS

Cluster	Share of Country Exports	Share of World Cluster Exports
Defense	0.0 (0.0)	0.0 (0.0)
Telecommunications	0.7 (0.3)	1.0 (0.5)
Office	0.5 (−0.6)	0.7 (−0.3)
Power Generation & Distribution	1.5 (0.5)	1.1 (0.6)
Multiple Business	0.3 (−0.2)	0.2 (+0.0)
Transportation	20.0 (10.4)	2.1 (1.5)

Share of Country Exports: 23.0 (10.4)
Share of World Cluster Exports: 1.4 (0.9)

FINAL CONSUMPTION GOODS AND SERVICES

Cluster	Share of Country Exports	Share of World Cluster Exports
Entertainment/Leisure	8.0 (1.6)	3.8 (1.7)
Personal	2.1 (−1.5)	1.4 (0.1)
Health Care	0.0 (+0.0)	0.1 (0.1)
Housing/Household	2.6 (−0.0)	1.6 (0.7)
Textiles/Apparel	29.4 (−10.6)	6.6 (1.3)
Food/Beverage	4.3 (−4.3)	0.7 (0.0)

Share of Country Exports: 46.3 (−14.9)
Share of World Cluster Exports: 2.7 (0.7)

Note: Numbers in parentheses are changes between 1978 and 1985. Exports are those of competitive industries, not all industries.

■ Identifies broad sectors in which the nation's international competitive positions are related.
▨ Identifies broad sectors in which the nation's international competitive positions are related.

and more recently a growing position in cars. Another important cluster is in consumer electronics products and related items such as recording tape. A fourth significant cluster is in iron and steel. Other sectors with pockets of strength are in semiconductors (mostly memory chips), food (fish products), cement, and international construction services. Other more isolated positions exist in a range of final goods such as toys and games, pianos, baby carriages, cutlery, ceramic products, and electrical transformers.

Korean firms have virtually no position in health care, chemicals and plastics, forest products, most areas of food and consumer packaged goods, all services except construction,[55] and most multiple business products. The Korean position in defense products is too small to show up yet as important, but it is rapidly growing. Telecommunications and office equipment are also sectors with little strength as of 1985, but where Korean position is growing in some industries and segments.

Some of the most important links among clusters are shown by the shading in Figure 8–10. Korea's emerging position in semiconductors and computers has grown out of its strength in consumer electronics. Transportation (shipbuilding and automobiles) has developed in parallel with metals (largely steel).

Korean strength is largely along the bottom of the cluster chart, with competitive industries in final consumption goods and services clusters representing 46 percent of total Korean exports. The breadth of successful clusters is rather narrow, even more so than in Sweden.[56] Even more striking is Korea's lack of vertical depth. Success is almost exclusively in end products, with few specialty input industries and virtually no machinery industries or services (Korea ranks last among the eight nations in both). This profile of national competitive advantage in the Korean economy, a manifestation of its state of national economic development (Chapter 10), reflects important aspects of the Korean environment.

FACTOR CONDITIONS

Korea, like most of the other successful nations I have described, is weak in natural resources. It has many natural ports, significant deposits of tungsten, locally available raw materials for cement production, and some modest fishing grounds. However, it lacks any significant reserves of most minerals, energy, or timber. Because of its mountainous terrain, Korea is also short on arable land. The Korean cement industry has achieved a significant international position, and tungsten has long been a Korean export. However, virtually all of Korea's other competitive industries depend heavily on foreign raw materials. Fish products, which might seem resource-related, are predominantly caught in deep international waters off Alaska, Africa, and in the

Pacific, using capital-intensive methods. Articles of fur, where Korean firms (notably Jindo) have built a strong international position, are made from imported pelts.

In contrast to Korea's thin endowment of natural resources is a large pool of human resources. The Korean workforce numbers 17 million. While Korea has relatively low labor costs, what is more unique about the nation is that Koreans are unusually disciplined and hardworking. In the past few decades, Korean employees have also been distinguished by a high average level of education. In industries such as shipbuilding and construction, for example, the quality of the labor force translates into uniquely fast building times and deliveries often ahead of schedule. In shipbuilding, for example, a very large crude carrier takes about thirty months to build by international standards, but Korean yards can complete the task in eighteen.

These attributes of Korean workers are a function of a number of factors. One is the homogeneity of the population, in terms of race, language, and the absence of class distinctions. Another important consideration is that almost everyone must spend three years in military service. The older generation is motivated by the memory of deprivation and hard times under Japanese occupation and during the Korean War. Both the older and younger generations are energized by a sense of national economic competition with North Korea, more intense than but similar to the West German rivalry with East Germany. Koreans also view Japan as a competitor to be bested to settle old scores. A final important underpinning of motivation and discipline is the Confucian culture that puts a high value on education, hard work, respect for authority, and achieving success in life through moving up the social hierarchy.

Factor-creating Mechanisms. The Korean people, companies, and government have made major investments in factor creation, well beyond those of most other Asian NICs and other developing countries. This is a principal reason why Korea has been able to upgrade its economy and compete in more and more advanced industries. One of the most striking and important attributes of Korea is the commitment of Koreans to education. This commitment, the strongest I observed in any nation we studied, is the top priority of all Korean parents. A survey performed by the Economic Planning Board in 1987 found that 84.5 percent of Korean parents wanted to provide their children with a college level education.[57]

Koreans have a high level of literacy and a high average level of education, with nearly universal education up to the high school level. Between 300,000 and 400,000 students enter college each year (36 percent of high school graduates in 1987). The university system is extensive, and particularly aggressive investments have been made in engineering. The system for higher education includes well over one hundred technical colleges as well as more than one hundred regular universities and colleges. It sets Korea apart from virtually all other developing nations.

Supplementing the local educational system are a large number of students who train abroad. Particularly in technical fields, many Koreans earn advanced degrees from top American universities. Table 8–6 illustrates that Korea leads the nations we examined in students studying in the United States at the postsecondary level, and its lead is particularly great at the graduate level.

The Korean government and Korean companies have provided generous funding for such studies. While some students do not return home after graduation and stay on to work in the United States, many eventually return to Korea, bringing knowledge and contacts with them from their work experience. Overall, educational spending represented 20.8 percent of the total government budget in 1987.

Korean companies above a certain size, as a matter of law, are required to provide training for their employees.[58] It is typical for a large Korean group to invest $25 to 30 million in training facilities alone. A typical employee goes through one to two weeks of training every year. Executive programs offered by major Korean universities have ten applicants for each place, a reflection of the demand for business education.

The striving for education extends into the management ranks as well. Many senior managers in Korea have advanced degrees, and doctorates in technical fields are common at the upper management levels in the larger companies. Holding a doctorate from a leading American university is an important status symbol. The high level of technical education among senior executives is essential to understanding Korean attitudes toward technology

TABLE 8–6 **Foreign Postsecondary Students in the United States by Nationality, 1987–1988**

Nation	Number of Students	Overall Rank among Nations in Number of Students	Percent of Students in Graduate Programs	Number of Students in the United States per 10,000 Inhabitants
Korea	20,520	4	72.8	5.0
Japan	18,050	6	23.6	1.5
United Kingdom	6,600	12	38.5	1.2
Germany	5,730	17	45.8	0.9
Singapore	4,870	20	21.6	18.7
Italy	2,200	32	N/A	0.4
Sweden	1,600	49	N/A	1.9
Switzerland	1,040	61	N/A	1.6
Denmark	670	N/A	N/A	1.3

SOURCE: Zikopoulos (ed.) (1988).

as well as the ability of Korean companies to develop their own technology.

The pool of scientific and technical resources in the country is still modest, but rapidly growing. University research is modest by Western standards but is increasing. Academic research is supplemented by a whole range of specialized research institutes funded in whole or part by government, such as the Korean Advanced Institute of Science and Technology, the Korean Electronics and Telecommunications Research Institute, the Korean Automotive Systems Research Institute, and the Korean Biogenetics Research Institute. The mission of these institutes is almost exclusively focused on industry. They are closely allied to universities, and have both government and industry funding and input.

Major Korean companies also invest heavily to upgrade their technical capability compared to companies from other developing countries. High rates of R&D/sales are typical. With doctoral-level engineers trained at the best universities in the world and an aggressive orientation toward pursuing licenses and other agreements in order to acquire foreign technology, Korean firms are unique among firms from NICs in their commitment to developing their own product models and to investing in state-of-the-art process technology. Korean firms are much less likely to be content to be mere production sites for foreign-designed products than is the case in other Asian NICs.

Since the 1960s, with the implementation of a series of five-year economic plans, there has also been a massive Korean investment to create a sophisticated infrastructure. Korean infrastructure is the match of most advanced nations. Infrastructure remains a high priority, and the Seoul Olympics triggered a new wave of investment. Infrastructure investments have just begun in the western part of the Korean peninsula in the hope that normalizing diplomatic relations with China and eventually North Korea will spur trade.

Korea emerged from the Korean War with virtually no capital. American aid was crucial in the early years and funded massive trade deficits into the early 1960s. After that, however, much of the capital used for Korean development came from foreign loans. Once Korea was able to demonstrate progress, and foreign investors gained confidence, foreign capital poured in. All loans went directly or indirectly to the Korean government, which channeled capital at heavily subsidized interest rates to selected industries. The Korean case starkly illustrates that abundance of capital is not required for international success in capital-intensive industries if there are institutional mechanisms to channel available capital into productive investments.

In the 1980s, a rapidly rising savings rate has led to rapid domestic capital formation; Koreans saved 32 percent of their income in 1987, second in the world behind Taiwan. Korea was expected to become a net creditor nation in the early 1990s after a string of mounting trade surpluses. However, Korea has yet to develop efficient public capital markets, an important constraint to further development. High real interest rates, by far the highest in the 1980s of the nations we studied, constrain the investment required to broaden and deepen the economy.

Selective Factor Disadvantages. Korea is just beginning to face the rising wages, labor shortages, and other pressures for automation and movement toward more productive segments that helped catalyze advancement in other nations. However, its lack of raw materials and its distance from markets have long led to an emphasis by Korean industry on producing final manufactured goods of increasing sophistication. Ironically, many of the natural resources on the Korean peninsula are located in what is now North Korea and were cut off by the Korean War.[59]

Korea was fortunate in not being tempted to depend on natural resource industries, a trap for many developing countries. Its economy very early showed a higher proportion of manufacturing to GNP than most nations at its state of development.[60] Where selective disadvantages have been combined with strong domestic rivalry, rapid upgrading of competitive position has resulted. There has been a tendency for government to intervene in factor and currency markets, however, which will only limit the rate of advancement in a nation that has reached Korea's level (I will discuss this issue further in Chapters 10 and 12).

DEMAND CONDITIONS

Korea represents a significant home market, with 42 million inhabitants populating a relatively small land area. Many of the industries in which Korea enjoys national competitive advantage draw on substantial local demand. Shipbuilding has very old roots in Korea, and the nation depends heavily on shipping for trade. The international construction industry developed from a base of substantial domestic construction activity, beginning with contracts to participate in the building of U.S. military bases in Korea just after the Korean War. The reconstruction of Korea after the war, coupled with large-scale investments in domestic infrastructure, created an experience base and a group of strong Korean construction companies that eventually moved abroad. Interestingly, U.S. military contracts in Vietnam provided some of Korea's first overseas construction business. The cement, iron, and steel industries have also been fed by booming domestic demand. These have developed into viable export industries.

More recently, the defense industry has been growing rapidly as an export industry. It has benefitted from years of heavy domestic investment in defense and the threat of hostilities with North Korea, making the home market unusually sophisticated and demanding. In consumer goods, pianos are an industry where Korea has developed a strong international position. A strong musical tradition is present in Korea, and parents are eager for their children to learn to play the piano and other musical instruments. Korea also has an unusual number of internationally famous performers, contributing to the sophistication of home demand.

In many of Korea's export industries, home demand represents a tiny share of production. Nevertheless, Korea's per capita income, location, terrain, culture, and mix of industry often provided some demand-side influences. Korean companies naturally focus on small cars, basic appliance models, and other product segments that reflect local conditions. As many Japanese companies have moved upmarket while the yen has appreciated and trade barriers have been erected against Japanese products, these segments of international markets have opened to Korean firms. In semiconductors, Korean emphasis on standard memory chips is a result of the fact that the predominant local chip demand is in consumer electronics. Similar demand-side influences are typical.

It is fair to say, however, that demand conditions to date play a less significant role in Korea than in any of the other nations I have described so far. The modest role of demand conditions reflects the earlier state of development of Korean industry, something I will discuss in later chapters. Demand has played some role in determining what industries Korea has entered, but it rarely provides an advantage beyond the simple size and growth of the home market. There are few industries in which Korean buyers are sophisticated and advanced, though this is changing. This lack of sophisticated domestic demand is reflected in the thinness of Korean clusters where there is capability to export in only limited segments and industries.

Korean companies are heavily driven by export demand and are less sensitive to domestic demand. Indeed, they often seem to ignore the home market even though it has the potential to be significant. With a lack of sophisticated home demand and a location far from important foreign markets, Korean firms have difficulty making product innovations and serving emerging industry segments. Whether and how the demand side can develop into an advantage for Korean industry represent among the most important questions in Korean economic development.

RELATED AND SUPPORTING INDUSTRIES

As in every nation, there is clustering in the Korean economy. One competitive industry has frequently developed out of another. International construction is linked to cement and steel. Korea's many apparel and textile businesses are connected. So are the many consumer electronics industries, which have led to a position in semiconductors and in turn to emerging positions in office machines and telecommunications.

Many of Korea's successful industries benefited from the presence of the large Korean general trading companies. These enterprises, huge in developing-country terms, have well-established international networks of offices and helped Korean manufacturers penetrate foreign markets. The trading companies also diversified through affiliated companies into a wide array of other businesses to become the large Korean groups, the *chaebol*.

Yet Korean clusters are still shallow in comparison to those of more advanced nations, representing a major vulnerability in national competitive advantage. Korea has few positions in components, tools, and production machinery. The absence of sophisticated local parts and machinery manufacturers makes it difficult to compete in differentiated industry segments or to keep up with process innovation. Product and process technology in Korean industries is often a generation or two behind the world leaders. Thus far, Korean firms are relying on strategies that are difficult to sustain.

FIRM STRATEGY, STRUCTURE, AND RIVALRY

Most Korean companies are production oriented and follow strategies heavily based on achieving low production costs. Mass production of standardized products is the predominant approach. The focus is on the more price-sensitive industry segments, and Korean products are usually a generation behind those of quality and performance leaders. Low-cost, highly productive workers are combined with large-scale, modern facilities employing the best available foreign technology to yield a significant cost advantage. Major investments are made in training personnel so they are capable of operating state-of-the-art facilities. The rate of capital investment is extremely high and capacity expansion is often breathtaking, which serves to preempt the market. Korean firms do well where this strategy fits well, such as in consumer electronics, shipbuilding, computer peripherals, and even deep-sea fishing.

Korean companies are characterized by extremely strong chief executives, who wield enormous power within their organizations. Many firms are still run by their founders or the entrepreneur who built them. Leaders are highly charismatic and intimately involved in all company affairs as well as in civic activities. They are bold and willing to invest aggressively. Employees and top management work extremely long hours. Companies are hierarchical and characterized by rigid discipline.

Korean firms move quickly to export, driven by their growth orientation, intense domestic rivalry, and government pressures. Larger companies exhibit a growing internationalization of strategies, though still primarily through export. Many companies are suppliers of completed products to other manufacturers who sell them under their own name (original equipment manufacturers or OEMs), and most companies still depend on OEM sales for the majority of their business.

However, a unique feature of many Korean companies is their early effort to develop their own product models and to market abroad under their own brand names. In contrast to companies from such nations as Taiwan and Hong Kong, Korean companies are less OEM-oriented and more willing to invest in international marketing and in-house technology. This investment has been vital to their ability to upgrade and sustain competitive advantage. It reflects, among other things, the high state of technical education among both managers and employees as well as avid study of management theory. The case of Sony, for example, which in its early years turned down a huge order to make transistor radios for RCA, is famous in Korea as an example of the importance of developing a company's own brand. Korean firms have also been extraordinarily early to establish foreign plants, when compared to Japanese firms or those from other Asian NICs. In industries such as videotape and consumer electronics, for example, foreign plants are already in place. Even more striking is that Hyundai, the leading car manufacturer, opened its first foreign assembly plant in Canada in 1989 less than a decade after commencing significant foreign sales.

Perhaps the most unique feature of Korean companies, however, is an awesome willingness to take risk. Companies rush into industries and are prepared to make huge investments in equipment and plants in advance of any substantial orders. In shipbuilding, for example, Hyundai and Daewoo built huge yards without the orders to fill them. In videotape, all four of the leading Korean firms (Sachan, SKC, Lucky-Goldstar, and Kolon) have recently doubled capacity despite having *already* achieved about 25 percent of the world market. The mentality is not unlike the shoot'em-up cowboys of the early American West.

The sources of this willingness to take risk are several. An important theme is found in Korean history. The Japanese occupation, the Korean War, and the continued division of the nation, created anger and a level of deprivation that touched all Koreans. Everyone had to start from scratch, motivated by a sense of crisis, a lingering resentment of the Japanese, and the feeling that there was nothing to lose. The competitive spirit that has resulted is perhaps the single greatest source of advantage that Korean companies have possessed. It has led not only to risk taking by established companies but to vibrant new business formation. It has also led to many bankruptcies and reorganizations, as might be expected.[61]

Korean companies are managed less for profitability than for growth. Company size is the key source of social recognition and the driving force for entrepreneurs. A growth mentality skews entry toward large end-product industries such as TV sets, ships, cars, and memory chips. One sees little of the competition in specialized businesses so characteristic of Switzerland, Italy, or even Germany. A thirst for volume leads to willingness to price aggressively, and cash flow to fund growth is more important than profitability.

The ownership of most companies is predominantly private, though many of the leading entrepreneurs have donated large blocks of company shares to foundations to ensure keeping control of the company over generations. For example, Hyundai has the Asan Foundation and Daewoo the Daewoo Foundation. There is little or no financial market pressure on companies. The commitment of personnel to the company, and the willingness to risk everything to preserve it, is distinctive in Korea with the possible exception of Italy.

Another unique feature of Korean industry is the importance of the large groups, the *chaebol*. Companies such as Hyundai, Daewoo, Samsung, and Lucky-Goldstar, each with $10 to $15 billion in sales, account, along with the other *chaebol*, for a major fraction of Korean exports and a major fraction of GNP, as much as 50 percent of exports by some estimates.[62] The top four *chaebol* alone represented 30 percent of total Korean exports in 1987 and 32 percent in 1988.

The *chaebol* have been favored and heavily supported by government.[63] They command the capital and clout to make huge investments in industries such as shipbuilding and semiconductors. Each is prone to enter every important Korean industry, especially if one of the others does so. Each also aggressively uses profits from some businesses to subsidize new entry and growth in others. The incentives to mobilize resources and take risk are much greater than is typical of firms in most developing countries, where there may be only one or two large groups that feel little competitive pressure.

The Korean groups have diversified using class portfolio management strategies. Using their access to capital, management talent, and clout with government, the groups entered any industry that looked promising or which government targeted, irrespective of its relationship to the rest of the group. This approach is in stark contrast to the strategies of leading firms from most other nations such as Germany and Japan. It has led to firms that are widely diversified in unrelated fields but still managed with a high degree of central control. It is important not to confuse the Korean *chaebol* with the Japanese *keiretsu*, whose members have informal ties and partial interlocking ownership but are managed with great independence.

The strategies of the large groups have fit the Korean environment thus far. Aggressive managers, heavy government-backed capital investment, and low-cost labor are their principal sources of advantage. However, there are real questions about whether this corporate structure, and the concentration of economic power that goes with it, will benefit Korean national competitive advantage in the future.

A final and essential underpinning of Korean competitive advantage is the fierce and even cutthroat rivalry that characterizes every successful Korean industry. At least four or five companies compete in every significant industry, often including a subsidiary of each of the leading *chaebol*. A pioneer makes the initial entry but other competitors soon follow. Table 8-7 illustrates this for some of the major industries.

The notable exception to the pattern of numerous domestic rivals is in steel, where the state-owned company, Pohang Steel (POSCO), is the only fully integrated iron and steel producer through the efforts of its politically powerful chairman. But POSCO, though the exception, proves the rule.

TABLE **8–7 Estimated Number of Korean Rivals in Selected Industries**

Automobiles[1]	3	Television sets	
Capacitors	45	Black and white	14
Cathode ray tubes	3	Color	12
Cement	9	Synthetic fibers	13
Computers	31	Cotton spinning	23
Construction[2]	480	Worsted spinning	26
Footwear[3]	221	Woolen spinning	55
Motor vehicle radio and		Fabrics	2,046
cassette receivers	18	Garments	3,270
Pianos	3	Dyeing and finishing	144
Printed circuit boards[4]	200	Tires	5
Semiconductors[5]	21	Travel goods	328
Shipbuilding[6]	250	Video cassette tapes	4
Steel[7]	13	Wigs	25

[1] 3 Korean firms (Hyundai, Daewoo, and Kia) produced passenger cars. One firm, Daewoo Motor Co., has a 50:50 joint venture with General Motors. Daewoo retained most of the management rights.

[2] Number of firms licensed as general contractors.

[3] 26 firms with more than 5 production lines accounted for 51.5% of the total.

[4] 7 firms accounted for about 70% of the market.

[5] 13 firms were domestic and 8 firms were joint ventures. There were also 8 majority-owned foreign subsidiaries.

[6] 4 firms (Hyundai, Daewoo, Samsung, and KSEC) accounted for 90% of the nation's total production capacity.

[7] POSCO is the only integrated iron and steel mill in Korea.

SOURCE: Field interviews; Korea Development Bank, *Industry in Korea,* 1988; Korea Federation of Textile Industries, *The Textile Industries in Korea,* 1988; Bank of Korea, *Yearbook of Economic Statistics,* 1988; researchers' estimates

The chairman has defined the company's mission in truly national terms, as providing low-cost steel to Korean industry as well as contributing to Korean exports. Aggressive risk taking and investment by the company, reflecting a sense of national purpose and priority, have stood in stark contrast to the behavior of state monopolies in most developing nations.

Given the goals and attitudes of Korean managers, it should not be surprising that rivalry is so intense and emotional. Because most Korean firms compete with similar cost-based strategies, they meet head-to-head not only in the Korean market but abroad. This competition creates continued pressure to invest, improve productivity, and introduce new products. The presence of committed Korean rivals mitigates any tendency for firms to compete solely on the basis of low Korean labor costs.

The rivalry among Korean companies is so fierce that the Korean government on occasion has intervened to prevent "destructive" competition. In automobiles, for example, the Automobile Industry Rationalization Measure of 1981 was introduced in response to a worldwide recession. The law reduced the number of passenger car producers from three to two (Hyundai, Daewoo) and forced Kia to concentrate on trucks. The measure was reversed in 1983, allowing Kia to enter car production, but a new law in 1986 has limited competition again.

These episodes threaten the long-term success of the industries involved. In automobiles, for example, repeated intervention will eventually diminish domestic rivalry and limit investment and upgrading. Fierce domestic and international competition among Korean firms has been essential to Korean success and is one of the things that has set Korea apart.[64] The tendency to intervene in rivalry is a dangerous one.

THE ROLE OF GOVERNMENT

The Korean government has played a relatively heavy and important role in the economy. Governments have enjoyed unusual power and continuity in Korea and have been blessed with a national consensus for decades about the importance of economic growth.[65] This has provided a capacity to carry out sustained programs in slow-to-change areas such as education that is unmatched in any nation we studied with the possible exception of Japan. Some aspects of the role of the Korean government have been unqualified successes. Most significant were a series of actions that laid the foundation for upgrading. Substantial investments in education and infrastructure, efforts to promote exports (through such tools as export insurance, tax credits, help in financing), and the elevation of international competitive success to the level of a national priority have been important stimuli to Korean industry. So have government investments in a range of industry-related

R&D institutes, as well as the effort to encourage clustering through the establishment of industrial centers in particular fields, built around technical and educational facilities. The electronics center in Kumi is a good example. During the period when Korean firms were able to compete only in unsophisticated segments and industries, devaluations of the Korean *won* aided price competitiveness in foreign markets, helping to establish momentum.

As in Japan, some of the most important influences of the Korean government have been symbolic and informational. Studies and plans nudged companies to deal with trends in international competition. Beginning in the 1960s, export success was established as an explicit and highly touted national priority. Many awards and ceremonies were created to recognize success in trade. The president of Korea was personally involved, making frequent visits to companies and attending monthly export meetings. Success in international competition was elevated to a patriotic duty, not just a way of earning a living. An example of a more recent program to stimulate upgrading in the industry was the designation in 1986 of ten consumer product areas where Korea had potential to achieve the world's highest quality within three years.[66] While primarily designed to spur industry's own efforts, the program includes some funds for technology development and for image-building in international markets.

The proclivity of the Korean government to intervene directly in individual industries has a more mixed record. The role of the Korean government in channeling capital was vital when the nation was short of it. Subsidies and loans targeted to particular industries were common in the 1960s and 1970s. Protection of the domestic market from both imports and foreign investment was common. However, domestic rivalry was so fierce that protection did not usually dull incentives. The Korean government also sought to secure the best terms on foreign technology licenses in chosen industries, which lowered the cost of obtaining technology and speeded up the process by which Korean firms developed their own technical capability.

Yet Korean targeting has been as often wrong as right. A major focus on chemicals, plastics, and machinery industries consumed large amounts of scarce resources with modest results. Government's selection of areas for cooperative R&D projects has had a mixed record as well. Government targeting distorts private expectations and incentives, and can obscure the sectors with true underlying prospects for competitive advantage. Targeting has been heavily concentrated in a relatively small number of mostly end-product industries, and has resulted in a narrow economy with very shallow clusters. Heavy reliance on the widely diversified *chaebol* as a primary engine of economic development only accentuated these problems.

One of the great historical strengths of Korean government policy, however, has been its capacity to adjust and evolve. Much of the direct intervention in individual industries is in the process of being phased out. Protection is declining. Support to the large *chaebol* has been scaled back. Government is playing a different and diminished role. Nevertheless, an elite and powerful bureaucracy is still in place. The tendency for meddling, a continuation of past modes of intervention, and intrusion into competition all represent threats to further Korean development.

THE ROLE OF CHANCE

The pattern of competitive advantage in Korean industry was heavily influenced by chance. The Korean War divided the nation into two parts. The natural resources and hydroelectric power potential of the North was lost to the South, eliminating any hope of building a national economy on resource endowments alone. War also provided its own peculiar advantages. After the Korean War, American aid was vital to getting the economy started. The Vietnam War was an important stimulus to early Korean industries, such as international construction and cement. Later, the shipping boom that accompanied the growing world dependence on Middle Eastern oil provided the initial window of opportunity for Korean shipbuilding, as Japanese shipyards were swamped with orders and were forced to quote long delivery times. The Middle East construction boom, in the wake of OPEC price increases, powered the growth of the Korean construction industry.

The first oil shock proved a turning point to the Korean economy. In 1974, as the world economy went into recession, the Korean government was compelled by political pressures to press for and support continued heavy investments by Korean industry while other nations cut back. Korean firms were able to acquire technology at bargain basement prices and had the capacity in place to serve the rebounding world economy in 1975 and 1976. Exports boomed.

Perhaps the most important chance events in shaping the Korean economy, however, were developments affecting Japan. Trade friction and resulting import restraints (such as orderly marketing agreements) opened up opportunities for Korea to penetrate a number of Japanese-dominated industries, including consumer electronics, cars and, recently, semiconductors. Korean firms benefited from these restraints on Japan and from the move upmarket by Japanese firms. More recently, the large rise in the value of the yen has helped Korean companies undercut Japanese rivals.

These developments affecting Japan have influenced which industries Korean firms entered. Perhaps as important though more intangible has been a strong sense of rivalry with Japan, born out of history and proximity. When talking with Korean executives, Japan is never far from the surface. Industries in which Japan is successful are always viewed as prime targets for entry.

Koreans hope that the 1988 Seoul Olympics will prove to have been the next external stimulus to the Korean economy. As was the case in Japan in the 1960s, the Olympics were seen as a vehicle to upgrade Korea's image and a catalyst to further internationalize Korean industry. Only time will tell if the desired effect will be achieved.

KOREA IN PERSPECTIVE

Korea provides a striking example of a rapidly upgrading economy. Its competitive advantage has thus far rested largely on basic factor conditions (principally human resources), investment-oriented company and managerial goals, and fierce domestic rivalry. Korea's uniqueness as a nation comes from its rapidly improving talent base, the presence of the large *chaebol*, the willingness to take risk, and the intensity of competition. The combination of skilled and productive labor with aggressive investment to acquire technology and build modern, large-scale facilities has created low-cost positions in a variety of industries and industry segments. Korea's rate of net capital investment has been the highest percent of GDP of any nation we studied since the mid-1970s (Table 7–1).

The particular industries in which Korea has succeeded reflect local circumstances and the emulation of Japan. But they are almost all industries or industry segments characterized by standardized, mass-produced products, relatively low requirements for customer contact or after-sale service, and the availability of product and process technology on international markets from independent machinery suppliers or faltering Western competitors willing to license their technology. Successful Korean industries mostly produce final products made with mostly imported components using imported machinery.

This pattern is reflected in Figure 8–11, which summarizes the industries in which Korean firms have gained and lost 15 percent or more of world export share between 1978 and 1985. Korea's rapid upgrading is manifested by the far greater number of industries gaining export share than losing it, and especially by the nature of the industries involved. Many of the losses are in factor cost or resource-sensitive industries (fish products, tobacco, fertilizers, stone, cement, wood products, textiles, and apparel). Gains are strong in the industrial and supporting sectors along the middle of the cluster chart, a sign of an increasingly sophisticated economy. Yet Korea still holds relatively few competitive positions in machinery (seven) and in specialty inputs, and the numbers of share gains and losses in these types of industries are comparable, a clear indication that Korea is still not a full-fledged advanced nation.

Korea's ability to sustain and extend national competitive advantage is

FIGURE 8–11 Competitive Korean Industries with Gains or Losses of World Export Share of 15% or More Between 1978 and 1985*

UPSTREAM INDUSTRIES

	Materials/Metals			Forest Products			Petroleum/Chemicals			Semiconductors/Computers			UPSTREAM INDUSTRIES		
	Total Comp. Inds.	Share Gains	Share Losses	Total Comp. Inds.	Share Gains	Share Losses	Total Comp. Inds.	Share Gains	Share Losses	Total Comp. Inds.	Share Gains	Share Losses	Total Comp. Inds.	Share Gains	Share Losses
Primary Goods	27	24	6	3	2	6	7	6	1	3	1	3	40	33	16
Machinery	6	0	0	0	0	0	0	0	0	0	0	0	6	0	0
Specialty Inputs	0	0	0	0	0	0	0	0	0	0	0	0	0	0	0
Total	**33**	**24**	**6**	**3**	**2**	**6**	**7**	**6**	**1**	**3**	**1**	**3**	**46**	**33**	**16**

INDUSTRIAL & SUPPORTING FUNCTIONS

	Multiple Business			Transportation			Power Generation & Distribution			Office			Telecommunications			Defense			INDUSTRIAL & SUPPORTING FUNCTIONS		
	Total Comp. Inds.	Share Gains	Share Losses	Total Comp. Inds.	Share Gains	Share Losses	Total Comp. Inds.	Share Gains	Share Losses	Total Comp. Inds.	Share Gains	Share Losses	Total Comp. Inds.	Share Gains	Share Losses	Total Comp. Inds.	Share Gains	Share Losses	Total Comp. Inds.	Share Gains	Share Losses
Primary Goods	3	3	1	8	5	2	8	8	1	3	0	0	3	2	1	0	0	0	25	18	5
Machinery	0	0	0	0	0	0	0	0	0	0	0	0	0	0	0	0	0	0	0	0	0
Specialty Inputs	0	0	0	5	4	2	0	0	0	0	0	0	0	0	0	0	0	0	5	4	2
Total	**3**	**3**	**1**	**13**	**9**	**4**	**8**	**8**	**1**	**3**	**0**	**0**	**3**	**2**	**1**	**0**	**0**	**0**	**30**	**22**	**7**

FINAL CONSUMPTION GOODS & SERVICES

	Food/Beverage			Textiles/Apparel			Housing/Household			Health Care			Personal			Entertainment/Leisure			FINAL CONSUMPTION GOODS & SERVICES		
	Total Comp. Inds.	Share Gains	Share Losses	Total Comp. Inds.	Share Gains	Share Losses	Total Comp. Inds.	Share Gains	Share Losses	Total Comp. Inds.	Share Gains	Share Losses	Total Comp. Inds.	Share Gains	Share Losses	Total Comp. Inds.	Share Gains	Share Losses	Total Comp. Inds.	Share Gains	Share Losses
Primary Goods	11	4	7	48	27	19	10	7	4	0	0	0	8	7	4	15	12	4	92	57	39
Machinery	1	1	0	0	0	1	0	0	0	0	0	0	0	0	0	0	0	0	1	1	1
Specialty Inputs	4	2	4	7	5	3	0	0	0	0	0	0	3	1	3	1	1	0	15	9	10
Total	**16**	**7**	**11**	**55**	**32**	**23**	**10**	**7**	**4**	**0**	**0**	**0**	**11**	**8**	**7**	**16**	**13**	**4**	**108**	**67**	**50**

*Included were industries exceeding the cutoff in either 1978 or 1985, including those that were competitive in 1978 but fell below the cutoff in 1985 or that had first achieved sufficient share to exceed the cutoff in 1985.

still in doubt. It depends heavily on whether the other two determinants in the "diamond," demand conditions and related and supporting industries, can be brought into play. It also depends on Korea's capacity to sustain vigorous rivalry. The strategic orientation of Korean companies, the level of sophistication of home demand, and the pattern of clustering within the economy are significantly different from the case of Japan. The experience of Japan provides no assurance that the Korean economy can continue to upgrade, deepen, and broaden.

9

Shifting National Advantage

The same forces working to enhance national advantage in Japan, Italy, and Korea created pressures on national advantage in other nations in the 1970s and 1980s. The United Kingdom suffered. The erosion of competitive advantage, which had begun many years earlier, continued in a wide range of British industries. The result has been that the British standard of living has lagged behind, in relative terms, that of other advanced nations.

The United States also encountered in the late 1970s its first real economic challenges in many decades. American competitive advantage in many industries began to erode. While this is partly the inevitable result of other advanced nations catching up after the unique circumstances caused by World War II, the problems experienced by U.S. industry are more than that. Advanced industries in which the competitive advantage of U.S. firms has grown significantly in the last decade are relatively scarce, yet cases of diminished advantage are widespread. Overall, the rate of net investment in industry, the rate of productivity growth, and the rate of per capita income growth have been among the lowest of the nations we studied. The United States has become a less favorable environment for competitive advantage in a number of important respects.

Both Britain and the United States share the characteristic of being studies in contrasts. They each contain some of the most competitive industries of any nation. However, these are juxtaposed with many cases of declining advantage over the postwar period. Both Britain and the United States provide fascinating settings in which to explore further the nuances of national advantage, how it is gained and, particularly, how it is lost.

After discussing Britain and revisiting the United States to examine the experience of recent decades, I will conclude the chapter by presenting data that compare all the nations. The experience of the eight nations, taken as a group, will provide an empirical base from which to extend my theory further.

THE SLIDE OF BRITAIN

Britain has been losing competitive advantage in industry since well before the second world war. From a position of industrial dominance in the nineteenth century, Britain began a long slide that only recently shows signs of being arrested. Britain has been plagued in the postwar period with high unemployment and pressure on living standards. As Table 7–1 illustrated, the growth in productivity and per capita income in Britain have, along with that of the United States, been at the bottom of the nations we studied. Unlike the United States, however, Britain was not far ahead of the other nations to start with. One by one, most advanced nations have overtaken or passed her.

Yet Britain possesses national competitive advantage in a range of industries and enjoys a vast pool of accumulated wealth. The contrast between the wealth and sustained success of parts of the British economy and eroding positions in so many core manufacturing industries is a striking one.

The story of Britain's decline has been told numerous times.[1] Many of these accounts contain important insights, and I agree individually with many of them. What is perhaps lacking is a way of seeing the many discrete problems identified from a broader and more integrated perspective. It is also important to recognize that Britain is a mixture of both success and failure, a point easily lost in focusing on the problem areas. Viewing Britain through the lens of my theory, this mixture of success and failure is both explicable and suggestive of a somewhat different view of British competitiveness than is sometimes held.

It is also important to note that Britain is a nation in the midst of considerable change. I will concentrate in this section on explaining the patterns of success and failure in British industry during the postwar period, as well as the reasons why the upgrading of British industry has faltered. I will conclude by noting some of the most important recent changes, returning to an evaluation of them in Chapter 13.

PATTERNS OF BRITISH COMPETITIVE ADVANTAGE

Table 9–1 lists the top fifty British industries in 1985 in terms of world export share. While the list is not fully representative of the international

TABLE 9–1 Top Fifty U.K. Industries in Terms of World Export Share, 1985

Industry	Share of Total World Exports	Export Value ($ millions)	Import Value ($ millions)	Share of Total U.K. Exports
Whiskey	77.7	1,294,923	9,993	1.28
Aircraft 2,000–15,000 kg	56.5	615,942	67,163	0.61
Aircraft reaction engines	44.5	922,434	550,747	0.91
Pig or cast iron scrap	44.0	29,757	—	0.03
Engravings, antiques	39.8	479,984	293,430	0.47
Sorted, rough, simply worked diamonds	37.1	1,471,103	1,209,695	1.45
Hand paintings	31.3	513,459	480,170	0.51
Woven cardigans of wool, fine hair	28.4	130,385	23,598	0.13
High carbon steel blooms, slabs	27.0	174,727	27,599	0.17
Developed cinema film	24.9	49,973	19,149	0.05
Unwrought platinum alloys	23.5	273,581	62,350	0.27
Duplicating machines	22.6	159,698	74,961	0.16
Amine compounds	22.2	280,104	119,207	0.28
Glass inners for vacuum flasks	21.6	4,477	131	0.00
Coarse ceramic housewares	21.2	123,709	18,703	0.12
Regenerated fiber to spin	21.2	99,814	34,242	0.10
Amide compounds	20.6	249,366	110,023	0.25
Live animals for food	19.4	285,065	137,919	0.28
Aircraft parts	19.1	1,912,422	858,464	1.89
Printed books, pamphlets	18.5	609,928	338,993	0.60
Spirits and distilled alcoholic beverages	18.5	182,208	92,707	0.18
Antiknock preparations	18.5	369,613	84,342	0.36
Soap, polishes, and creams	18.4	119,500	34,762	0.12
Unexposed photo film roll	18.1	318,230	276,774	0.31
Precious metal articles	17.9	55,095	15,906	0.05
Worked nickel alloys	17.8	102,488	61,390	0.10
Polyacids and derivatives	17.4	331,110	60,641	0.33
Aircraft engines, motors, and parts	17.1	1,010,906	730,433	1.00
Cigarettes	16.7	541,417	98,558	0.53
Wheeled tractors	16.6	573,576	190,964	0.57
Cider, mead	16.6	6,538	4,024	0.01
Woven combed wool	16.5	109,924	31,208	0.11
Unmilled barley	16.4	414,202	32,818	0.41
Knit outerwear of wool	16.4	247,858	88,949	0.24
Typesetting, bookbinding machinery, parts	16.1	328,878	273,553	0.32

TABLE **9–1** (*Continued*)

Industry	Share of Total World Exports	Export Value ($ millions)	Import Value ($ millions)	Share of Total U.K. Exports
Insecticides	16.1	208,179	26,257	0.21
Children's books, maps, and globes	15.9	20,862	16,209	0.02
Medicaments containing antibiotics	15.9	213,860	46,236	0.21
Acrylic polymers	15.4	206,248	73,393	0.14
Herbicides	15.4	144,736	91,662	0.20
Porcelain, china housewares	15.3	109,214	27,658	0.11
Digital central processors	15.2	775,895	1,016,452	0.77
Petroleum coke	15.2	170,058	40,441	0.17
Unwrought platinum, alloys	15.1	142,275	28,178	0.14
Other wool, animal hair	15.1	130,886	178,960	0.13
Nonchocolate sugar candy	15.1	131,629	56,210	0.13
Radioactive elements	15.1	471,301	426,915	0.47
Other iron and steel scrap	14.5	411,429	12,738	0.41
Monoacids and derivatives	14.5	328,590	226,470	0.32
Cards and printed matter	14.5	251,861	138,210	0.25
TOTAL				17.88

NOTE: No import data are reported if import value is less than 0.3 percent of total trade for 1985.

position of the British economy because of its success in services and in industries with high foreign investment, it already suggests certain generalizations. Many strong British positions are in consumer goods of various sorts. British strength is also significant in trading, reflected by entries in diamonds and platinum. Along with these successes are a wide smattering of other industries that range broadly across the economy, including chemicals, engines, and textiles. The top fifty industries account for 17.9 percent of British exports (17.0 percent after eliminating traded goods), very low in comparison to the nations we studied. This reflects the breadth of the British economy, the relatively specialized positions British firms often now hold, and the importance of exports of oil, gas oil, fuel oil, aviation oil, and motor oil (19.25 percent of total British exports in 1985), where the British share does not place the industry in the top fifty industries.[2]

The profile of British national competitive advantage is better reflected in Figure 9–1 and the summary statistics in Figures 9–2 and B-8. The largest concentration of British competitive advantage is in consumer packaged goods, including alcoholic beverages, food such as confectionery products and biscuits, personal products such as cigarettes, cosmetics, and perfume,

FIGURE 9–1 Clusters of Internationally Competitive U.K. Industries, 1985

	MATERIALS/METALS	FOREST PRODUCTS	PETROLEUM/CHEMICALS
Primary Goods	IRON & STEEL **High carbon steel blooms, slabs**# Iron, steel powders# High carbon steel bars# High carbon steel med. plate#* Large u, i, h sections' **Hotrolled profiles, etc.** Stainless steel sheets' Iron, steel castings unworked Tinned plates, sheets FABRICATED IRON & STEEL Iron, steel tube fittings Iron, steel structures, parts High carbon steel wire#* Cast iron tubes, pipes# Iron, steel chain and parts Steel storage tanks, etc. Iron, steel railway rails NONFERROUS METALS *Other crude minerals*#* Zinc, iron, lead oxide ***Copper alloys, unwrought***# ***Nickel, alloys worked***# METAL MANUFACTURES Copper bars, wire, etc. Copper foil, powders & fittings# Aluminum structures, parts Aluminum storage tanks#* Other mineral manufactures# SCRAP *Other iron and steel scrap*# Pig or cast iron scrap' Copper waste and scrap Other nonferrous metal scrap nes#*		RAW MATERIALS Coke, retort carbon' *Crude petroleum*#* ***Motor, aviation spirit*** Gas oils Liquefied propane, butane' **Petroleum coke** Petroleum jelly, pitch coke# ORGANIC CHEMICALS Acyclic hydrocarbons' Halogen derivatives of hydrocarbons Acyclic alcohols, derivatives ***Monoacids and derivatives*** ***Polyacids and derivatives*** Oxyacids, derivatives ***Amine compounds***
Machinery	Other mineral-working machinery# Mineral-crushing machinery Rolling mill parts nes, rolls Electrical industrial furnaces	Pulp making mach. & parts#	Centrifugal pumps nes Rotary & other pumps for liquids, parts# Pumps for gases, etc. Gas, liquid filters
Specialty Inputs	*Radioactive elements, etc.* Other radioactive & associated materials#		
Services			*Service stations'*

FIGURE 9–1 (*Continued*)

	SEMICONDUCTORS/ COMPUTERS
Primary Goods	*Digital central processors'* **Office, ADP machine parts, accessories**
	Oxyamino compounds *Amide compound* **Other nitrogen compounds*** Heterocyclic compounds Other misc. chemical products# INORGANIC CHEMICALS Sodium hydroxide, solid Metal compound of inorganic acid Other inorganic chemicals, etc.* Phosphites, phosphates PLASTICS Polyamides *Acrylic polymers, etc.* Plastic material nes
Machinery	*Pump, compressor parts* *Generators, centrifuges, parts,* *etc.** Custom software''' Information'''
Specialty Inputs	
Services	

KEY

roman	5.8% world export share or higher, but less than 11.6% share
bold italics	**11.6% world export share or higher, but less than 23.2% share**
sans serif	23.2% world export share or above

•   Industries below cutoff in 1978
\#   Calculated residuals
\#\#   Added due to significant export value in a segmented industry

'   Added due to FDI
''   Upgraded due to FDI
'''   Added based on in-country research

	MULTIPLE BUSINESS	TRANSPORTATION
Primary Goods	TRADED GOODS Tin, alloys worked[#] *Rolled silver, unworked, partially worked[#]* **Platinum, alloys unwrought, partially worked[#]** Tin, alloys, unwrought* *Platinum, alloys unwrought* Diamonds, sorted, rough, simply worked	Precious, semiprecious stones nes INSTRUMENTS Optical instruments Meters and counters nes Surveying instruments Gas, liquid control instruments *Measuring, controlling instruments[#]* Glass articles[#]	VEHICLE EQUIPMENT Steel transport boxes Ship derricks, cranes ENGINES ***Piston engines nes*** **Jet aircraft reaction engines** Marine piston engines other than outboard
Machinery	Machinery for special industries nes[#] Nonelectric power hand tools[#] Spraying machinery	Blades, tips, etc., for tools Cocks, valves, etc., nes Gaskets & nonelectric machine parts[#] Fans, blowers, etc., parts	Reaming, etc., machines, metalworking Metalworking machine tools[#]
Specialty Inputs	*Glass* Unmtd. polarizing sheets[#]		Radar apparatus, etc. Other rubber articles[#] Synthetic rubber, etc. Other materials of rubber[#] LUBRICANTS Lubricants (high petroleum content), etc. Other lubricating preparations[#]
Services	*Specialty stores* *Advertising* Engineering/architectural* Construction* Contract research* Industrial laundry/apparel supply* *Public relations* Security services* Building maintenance services*	*Trading* *Reinsurance* Accounting* Management consulting* Commercial banking* Merchant/investment banking* *Money management* Leasing* Legal*	Airport terminal*** Airlines***

FIGURE 9–1 (Continued)

	VEHICLES	POWER GENERATION AND DISTRIBUTION		OFFICE
		GENERATION	DISTRIBUTION	
Primary Goods	Special motor vehicles *Forklift trucks, etc.* *Wheeled tractors nes* Bicycles, wheelchairs# Tugs, special vessels# Other civil engineering equipment, etc.# Self-propelled shovels, excavators Aircraft nes 2,000–15,000 KG·	*Steam boilers, etc.*· Steam boiler aux. plants & parts# Steam engines, turbines Generators, rotary converters & parts# *AC generators* *Generating sets with piston engines* Wind, water, etc., engines·	Liquid dielectric transformers Insulated wire, cable Electric insulating equipment *Other electrical machinery nes*· Primary batteries, cells	*Office supplies nes*# *Duplicating machines*# *Printed books, pamphlets* *Cards & printed matter*#
Machinery				*Other printing, bookbinding machinery, parts*#
Specialty Inputs	*Antiknock preparations* Asbestos manufactures, friction material PARTS Piston engines parts nes *Forklift truck parts*# Lifting, handling, loading eqpt parts# Motor vehicle chassis Motor vehicle bodies & parts, accessories# *Aircraft parts nes* *Jet engines and motors, parts*# Railway vehicle parts Unhard vulcanized rubber tubes New tires for motor cars New tires, bus or lorry			*Other coloring matter, printing ink*#
Services				

KEY

roman	5.8% world export share or higher, but less than 11.6% share	·	Industries below cutoff in 1978	· Added due to FDI
bold italics	*11.6% world export share or higher, but less than 23.2% share*	#	Calculated residuals	:: Upgraded due to FDI
sans serif	23.2% world export share or above	##	Added due to significant export value in a segmented industry	*** Added based on in-country research

	TELECOMMUNICATIONS	DEFENSE
Primary Goods	*TV, radio transmitters*	Explosives, pyrotechnics *War firearms, ammunition*
Machinery		
Specialty Inputs		
Services		

FIGURE 9–1 (Continued)

	FOOD/BEVERAGES	HOUSING/HOUSEHOLD
Primary Goods	**BASIC FOODS**	**PACKAGED GOODS**
	Live animals for food#	*Soap, polishes & creams#*
	Dry milk	Washing preparations, etc.
	Bovine meat with bone in	**FURNISHINGS**
	Jams, marmalades***	*Knotted carpets of wool or fine hair*
	Mutton, etc., fresh, chilled, frozen	*Porcelain, china houseware*
	Fish fresh, chilled excl. fillets*	*Coarse ceramic houseware*
	Sunflower, sesame oils**	Lamps, fittings base metal
	Barley unmilled	**OTHER**
	Breakfast cereal, pasta#	Cutlery
	Malt inc. flour	**APPLIANCES**
	BEVERAGES	*Clothes dryers#*
	Spirits & distilled alcoholic beverages#	
	PROCESSED FOODS	
	Whiskey	
	Sugar candy, nonchocolate	Flavored carbonated waters*
	Chocolate & products*	*Tea***
	Bread and other baker's wares#	*Cider, mead#*
	*Pastry, biscuits, cakes***	
Machinery	Food machinery, nondomestic	
Specialty Inputs	*Insecticides*	Heat-insulating bricks#
	Fungicides, disinfectants#	Refractory bricks, etc.
	Herbicides	Varnishes, distempers
	Glass inners for vacuum flasks#	*Glazes, driers, putty*
		Refractory building products#
Services		

KEY	
roman	5.8% world export share or higher, but less than 11.6% share
bold italics	*11.6% world export share or higher, but less than 23.2% share*
sans serif	**23.2% world export share or above**

•	Industries below cutoff in 1978
#	Calculated residuals
##	Added due to significant export value in a segmented industry

*	Added due to FDI
**	Upgraded due to FDI
***	Added based on in-country research

TEXTILES/APPAREL

Primary Goods		
FABRICS		
Hides, skins*#		Knit outerwear of wool
Other raw fur skins#		Knit dresses of synthetic fibers
Raw mink skins*		ACCESSORIES
Leather#		Artificial fur articles#
Fur skins fanned, dressed		
Textiles for machinery		
Knitted fabrics#		
APPAREL		
Womens coats, jackets#		
Womens dresses, skirts of synthetic fibers		

Machinery

Spinning, reeling machine parts

Specialty Inputs

DYES	Other synthetic fibers#
Synthetic organic dyestuffs	Wool tops
Synthetic organic luminophores#	Nontextured synthetic polyamide yarn
FIBERS & YARNS	Woven cardigan wool, fine hair
Regenerated fiber to spin#	Woven combed wool*
Wast of synthetic fibers#	Other textile yarn#
Cellulose derivatives, etc.	Other wool, hair#
Other wool, hair yarn#	

Services

FIGURE 9–1 (Continued)

	HEALTH CARE	PERSONAL	ENTERTAINMENT/LEISURE	
Primary Goods	PHARMACEUTICALS Provitamins and vitamins' **Bulk antibiotics** Hormones' *Medicaments containing antibiotics* *Medicaments containing hormones*# **Pharmaceutical goods**#*** MEDICAL EQUIPMENT Medical instruments nes	Cigars & other tobacco, manufactured** **Cigarettes** *Mixed perfume substances* *Perfumery, cosmetics* *Precious metal articles*#	*Photo film roll unexposed* *Photo-sensitized cloth* **Developed cinema film** *Indoor game equipment* *Recorded discs, tapes* Zoo animals, pets, etc. Newspapers, periodicals' *Children's books, maps, globes, etc.* **Mail, not classified**	*Hand tools for agric., horti., & forestry*# Yachts, sports vessels Saddlery, leather articles# AUCTIONS **Hand paintings, etc., nes** **Engravings, antiques**# Coins, nature collections
Machinery				
Specialty Inputs				
Services	Health care***	Secondary & university education***	**Auctioneering***** Television programs*** Hotels'	

KEY

roman   5.8% world export share or higher, but less than 11.6% share

bold italics   *11.6% world export share or higher, but less than 23.2% share*

sans serif   **23.2% world export share or above**

•   Industries below cutoff in 1978

\#   Calculated residuals

\#\#   Added due to significant export value in a segmented industry

*   Added due to FDI

**   Upgraded due to FDI

***   Added based on in-country research

FIGURE 9–2 Percentage of U.K. Exports of Competitive Industries by Broad Cluster

UPSTREAM INDUSTRIES

Materials / Metals	**Forest Products**	**Petroleum / Chemicals**	**Semiconductors / Computers**	Share of Country Exports: 32.4 **(15.7)**
Share of Country Exports: 4.0 **(−1.6)**	Share of Country Exports: 0.1 **(−0.1)**	Share of Country Exports: 24.8 **(15.0)**	Share of Country Exports: 3.5 **(2.4)**	Share of World Cluster Exports: 5.5 **(2.1)**
Share of World Cluster Exports: 3.3 **(−0.4)**	Share of World Cluster Exports: 0.7 **(−0.1)**	Share of World Cluster Exports: 6.9 **(3.6)**	Share of World Cluster Exports: 6.3 **(−0.6)**	

INDUSTRIAL AND SUPPORTING FUNCTIONS

Multiple Business	**Transportation**			Share of Country Exports: 22.8 **(−8.6)**
Share of Country Exports: 6.3 **(−2.4)**	Share of Country Exports: 12.1 **(−5.3)**			Share of World Cluster Exports: 5.4 **(−1.9)**
Share of World Cluster Exports: 6.1 **(−2.1)**	Share of World Cluster Exports: 4.6 **(−1.9)**			
	Power Generation & Distribution	**Office**	**Telecommunications**	**Defense**
	Share of Country Exports: 2.0 **(−0.5)**	Share of Country Exports: 1.6 **(−0.2)**	Share of Country Exports: 0.3 **(−0.1)**	Share of Country Exports: 0.6 **(−0.1)**
	Share of World Cluster Exports: 7.2 **(−0.8)**	Share of World Cluster Exports: 8.3 **(−0.7)**	Share of World Cluster Exports: 3.9 **(−2.2)**	Share of World Cluster Exports: 10.3 **(−2.7)**

FINAL CONSUMPTION GOODS AND SERVICES

Food / Beverage	**Textiles / Apparel**	**Housing / Household**	**Health Care**	Share of Country Exports: 14.7 **(−7.7)**
Share of Country Exports: 4.1 **(−1.2)**	Share of Country Exports: 2.6 **(−1.7)**	Share of Country Exports: 1.3 **(−1.4)**	Share of Country Exports: 2.1 **(0.1)**	Share of World Cluster Exports: 3.4 **(−1.0)**
Share of World Cluster Exports: 2.5 **(−0.0)**	Share of World Cluster Exports: 2.6 **(−1.1)**	Share of World Cluster Exports: 4.2 **(−1.7)**	Share of World Cluster Exports: 8.8 **(−1.3)**	
		Personal	**Entertainment / Leisure**	
		Share of Country Exports: 1.2 **(−2.9)**	Share of Country Exports: 3.3 **(−0.6)**	
		Share of World Cluster Exports: 2.4 **(−4.7)**	Share of World Cluster Exports: 6.0 **(−1.9)**	

Note: Numbers in parentheses are changes between 1978 and 1985. Exports are those of competitive industries, not all industries.

☒ Identifies broad sectors in which the nation's international competitive positions are related.

and household products such as toothpaste, soaps, and cleaning preparations. Another consumer-related cluster is in the area of household furnishings including porcelain, ceramic housewares, and carpets. Related to this strength in consumer goods is a strong position in many areas of consumer goods retailing. Another important cluster is in financial or financially related services such as insurance, auctioneering, trading (Jardines, Inchcape, Unilever), money management, and international legal services.[3] Another important cluster, looming large in export volume, is petroleum and chemicals, including paint (where ICI and Courtaulds are world leaders).

Significant clusters are also present in pharmaceuticals, entertainment and leisure products (such as movies, records, games, coin and nature collections), publishing and other information products, aircraft, defense goods, motors and engines, and textiles (largely fibers). Other pockets of advantage lie in radio transmitters and radar apparatus, electrical generation equipment, glass, and scrap metal. Britain's position in semiconductors/computers is heavily dependent on the subsidiaries of American companies.

Britain lacks national competitive advantage in forest products, most areas of textiles/apparel, office products, telecommunications equipment, consumer electronic products, most transportation equipment, and mechanically based consumer goods such as watches. Britain also lacks a strong position in most machinery industries, ranking sixth among our nations after Italy, Switzerland, and the three leading industrial powers.

Figure 9–1 illustrates that Britain maintains some position in a large number of industries (third after Germany and Japan). The range of these industries is broad given the size of the economy. Another manifestation of the breadth (or former breadth) of competitive British industries is a substantial representation in products and especially services sold to a wide range of other industries (classified in Multiple Business).

Few British positions, however, are unusually strong ones. There are scarcely any industries with the high shares that characterize leading Japanese, American, and German industries. Moreover, British clusters are shallow, with few strong positions in specialty input businesses and even fewer in machinery industries. The vertical depth of clusters is less than in nations such as Italy, Sweden, or even Switzerland.

Analysis of changes in world export share between 1978 and 1985 contains grounds for concern about the path of development of the economy (see Figure 9–3). Far more competitive industries in Britain have lost world export share than have gained it. Yet the pattern of gains and losses is what is most ominous. Some gains have occurred in chemicals, health care products, and computers, all areas of British strength.[4] Many of the gains, however, have been in petroleum and related products and in relatively unprocessed metal products. Net losses have been experienced in most clusters and involve many sophisticated industries. Transportation has been especially

FIGURE 9–3 Competitive U.K. Industries with Gains or Losses of World Export Share of 15% or More Between 1978 and 1985*

UPSTREAM INDUSTRIES

	Materials/Metals			Forest Products			Petroleum/Chemicals			Semiconductors/Computers			UPSTREAM INDUSTRIES		
	Total Comp. Inds.	Share Gains	Share Losses	Total Comp. Inds.	Share Gains	Share Losses	Total Comp. Inds.	Share Gains	Share Losses	Total Comp. Inds.	Share Gains	Share Losses	Total Comp. Inds.	Share Gains	Share Losses
Primary Goods	29	11	22	0	0	1	26	12	17	2	2	4	57	25	44
Machinery	4	0	1	1	0	0	6	2	2	0	0	0	11	2	3
Specialty Inputs	2	1	1	1	0	0	0	0	0	0	0	0	3	1	1
Total	35	12	24	2	0	1	32	14	19	2	2	4	71	28	48

INDUSTRIAL & SUPPORTING FUNCTIONS

	Multiple Business			Transportation			Power Generation & Distribution			Office			Telecommunications			Defense			INDUSTRIAL & SUPPORTING FUNCTIONS		
	Total Comp. Inds.	Share Gains	Share Losses	Total Comp. Inds.	Share Gains	Share Losses	Total Comp. Inds.	Share Gains	Share Losses	Total Comp. Inds.	Share Gains	Share Losses	Total Comp. Inds.	Share Gains	Share Losses	Total Comp. Inds.	Share Gains	Share Losses	Total Comp. Inds.	Share Gains	Share Losses
Primary Goods	13	4	7	13	1	15	12	3	8	4	2	3	1	0	1	2	0	1	45	10	35
Machinery	7	1	4	2	0	5	0	0	0	1	1	0	0	0	0	0	0	0	10	2	9
Specialty Inputs	2	1	2	19	1	16	0	0	0	1	0	0	0	0	0	0	0	0	22	2	18
Total	22	6	13	34	2	36	12	3	8	6	3	3	1	0	1	2	0	1	77	14	62

FINAL CONSUMPTION GOODS & SERVICES

	Food/Beverage			Textiles/Apparel			Housing/Household			Health Care			Personal			Entertainment/Leisure			FINAL CONSUMPTION GOODS & SERVICES		
	Total Comp. Inds.	Share Gains	Share Losses	Total Comp. Inds.	Share Gains	Share Losses	Total Comp. Inds.	Share Gains	Share Losses	Total Comp. Inds.	Share Gains	Share Losses	Total Comp. Inds.	Share Gains	Share Losses	Total Comp. Inds.	Share Gains	Share Losses	Total Comp. Inds.	Share Gains	Share Losses
Primary Goods	15	5	9	12	2	11	8	1	12	7	2	4	5	0	2	15	2	11	62	12	49
Machinery	1	0	6	1	0	7	0	0	0	0	0	0	0	0	0	0	0	0	2	0	13
Specialty Inputs	4	4	2	13	2	12	5	1	4	0	0	0	0	0	0	0	0	0	22	7	18
Total	20	9	17	26	4	30	13	2	16	7	2	4	5	0	2	15	2	11	86	19	80

*Included were industries exceeding the cutoff in either 1978 or 1985, including those that were competitive in 1978 but fell below the cutoff in 1985 or that had first achieved sufficient share to exceed the cutoff in 1985.

hard hit. Large net losses in machinery (five gains and twenty-six losses), specialty inputs (ten gains and thirty-seven losses), and in industries serving many other industries (the multiple business category had six gains and thirteen losses) signal an inability to upgrade, a shrinkage of clusters, and a narrowing of competitive industries in the economy.

FACTOR CONDITIONS

Britain has never enjoyed an abundance of natural factors of production, with the exception of, importantly, North Sea oil and coal deposits (which lost competitiveness compared to other nations decades ago). North Sea oil and gas have provided an enormous windfall to the British economy ($16.7 billion in exports in 1985) and maintained export volume. They have also contributed to British positions in petroleum products and some commodity chemical industries. If anything, however, the discovery of oil has been more of a disadvantage than an advantage. It delayed important policy shifts to revitalize the economy.

Britain enjoys a large pool of capital and a favorable geographic location. Centuries of investment and wealth have been focused in London, centrally located in world terms and an attractive place to visit as well. This is an important asset in a number of service industries, among them financial services, auctioneering, and airport services. British infrastructure, though once ahead or comparable to that of other nations, is today mostly a disadvantage. This has been particularly noticeable in telecommunications and in other public facilities and services such as ports and railroads which need continual reinvestment.

Britain was among the first nations to develop a skilled, industrial workforce and to enjoy a high level of literacy. The English language also became the world business language, because of Britain's historical strength and colonial ties. More important until the late 1800s, however, was a premier capability in technology, the essential driving force behind the ascendance of British industry.

British inventiveness is well recorded and shows up early in the history of many of the industries we studied. Perhaps because of the highly individualistic university educational system for the upper tier of students, top British graduates long had a creativeness and inventiveness that comes from independent thinking. Interestingly, however, skilled tradesmen were important in adapting technology and applying it to the needs of industry. Many of the entrepreneurs who founded British industries were not university educated.

Strength in scientific research is still present in Britain, though many top British minds have gone abroad where the conditions for applying their talent are better. British companies succeed in a number of industries closely connected to science and technology such as chemicals and pharmaceuticals. Many foreign companies have also located research laboratories in Britain. The inability of the British economy to support a rapidly rising standard of living has meant that the salaries of skilled scientists and other highly educated personnel in Britain are well below those in other advanced nations. This cost advantage in advanced human resources contributes to indigenous success in a number of British industries that depend on them (consultancy, publishing, advertising, and pharmaceuticals, for example). It has also attracted substantial foreign investment in these industries as well as others such as computers.

Factor Creation Mechanisms. Where Britain has fallen down is not so much in the starting pool of factors but in the mechanisms to create and upgrade them. The result has been a major barrier to upgrading and even to sustaining competitive advantage in industry. The British educational system has badly lagged behind that of virtually all the nations we studied. Access to top-quality education has been limited to a few, and a smaller percentage of students go on to higher education than in most other advanced nations. Education for the elite has stressed humanities and pure science in favor of more practical pursuits, and many talented people in Britain have avoided practical disciplines such as engineering.[5] Consequently, the proportion of university students in technical areas is lower than in other advanced nations. Even engineering has been treated in a theoretical way at the leading universities.

The more serious problem is the education of the average student. British children are taught by teachers less qualified than those in many nations, receive less training in math and science, put in fewer hours, and drop out more. The thrust of educational reform until the Thatcher years was to make the system more egalitarian rather than competitive.[6] Standards have fallen and the performance of British children with them. The educational system has also both reflected and reinforced British tendencies toward noncompetitiveness in personal terms. British people tend to downplay their accomplishments. Moreover, once they are out of secondary school the alternatives are thin. Technical colleges still have low status, and there is no well-developed apprenticeship system as in Germany. The government-supported Youth Training Scheme, still poorly linked to the needs of industry, has not compensated.

The result of such an educational system is a study in contrasts. On the one hand, there is a pool of outstanding people well qualified for professional services, consultancy, software, publishing, and the like. The upper tier of the human resource pool remains well trained and low cost compared to other nations. Outstanding thinkers and scientists continue to graduate from the top British universities. On the other hand, there is a serious problem confronting the bulk of industry. The British workforce is well behind in education and skills compared with that of many other advanced nations. Managers in Britain are also much less likely to have college or university degrees than are those in other advanced nations. There is a shortage of managers trained in technology entering manufacturing industries, and a technical background has been uncommon in top management.

Most British companies have done little in-house to offset a weak educational system. Investment in training by industry is estimated at far less than one percent of revenues (.15 percent in 1980) in Britain, compared to 2 percent in Germany and 3 percent in Japan.[7] The pool of human resources that starts out more poorly educated only falls further behind. The net result is that Britain has lagged badly in upgrading the average quality of human resources. This is in many ways the most fundamental problem for the nation's economy, as it has come to be in the United States.

Britain makes a significant investment in research. Most of it is oriented toward pure science and especially to defense. Much of British public R&D spending has been defense-related. In 1987, for example, 50 percent of government R&D was for defense purposes compared to about 12 percent in Germany, 5 percent in Japan, and 34 percent in France.[8] As in the United States, this has had limited benefit for industry and sometimes distracted British firms from commercial opportunities. Public R&D spending in all fields has long been under pressure because of a chronic need to reduce government expenditure.

British companies have been aggressive investors in R&D in some industries, such as chemicals and pharmaceuticals. Here, they have established close links with university researchers in related fields. In most industries, however, British companies have been outspent by foreign rivals. Many firms have lacked organized R&D.[9] Overall, private sector R&D spending in Britain as a percentage of GDP (1.19 percent in 1986) is well behind Japan (2.19 percent), Germany (1.60 percent), and Sweden (1.71 percent).[10] Total British nondefense R&D spending as a percentage of GDP, at 1.8 percent in 1986, compares unfavorably with 2.8 percent in Japan, 2.6 percent in Germany, and similar figures in several other advanced nations.[11] Numerous industries have gradually lost technical position. The pace of decline accelerated with the advent of electronics, new materials, and advanced manufacturing techniques.

Selective Factor Disadvantages. Selective factor disadvantages were once a principal driver of innovation in the British economy. Britain was a relatively small island nation that depended on many raw materials from abroad. This helped propel Britain initially to become a great trading nation. British firms established a far-flung trading system, including associated industries in finance, shipping, and insurance. Later, British scientists and engineers created many advanced product and process technologies to upgrade imported raw materials and create new, advanced goods.

As British prosperity grew, rising wages led to pressures for process innovation that fueled technological leadership in many British industries. Many new forms of automation were pioneered. Britain originated and developed strong positions in many machinery industries.

In the postwar period and before, however, the process has been working in reverse. Until the development of North Sea oil and gas, devaluations took pressure off industry. As British wages have lagged behind, the impetus to innovate and automate declined compared to nations such as Germany, Switzerland, Italy, and Sweden. Union restrictions on work practices have further blunted change. Over time, many British manufacturing industries drifted toward competing on price with obsolete or lower-quality products and processes. Instead of overcoming selective disadvantages, British firms have slowly harvested market position.[12]

DEMAND CONDITIONS

Britain was once on the cutting edge of world demand in both consumer and industrial goods. In the consumer sector, Britain's early industrialization, a high level of education, rising incomes, and rapidly accumulating wealth ensured that Britain was a leading market for many advanced goods and services. British tastes and culture were exported throughout the Empire. The Empire reinforced the tendency toward high-end or luxury demand. Expatriates served as the elite administrators of British colonies and defined the tastes of those abroad with the wealth to buy imported goods.

In the industrial sector, the presence of national advantage in a wide range of industries led to advanced demand for many of the products and services they consumed. The breadth of British industrial strength, like that of America, helped create national advantage that still partly remains in ''multiple business'' products and services (industries that sell to a wide range of other industries). Britain's trade stimulated demand in trade-related industries such as insurance, law, and banking. The overseas presence of British multinationals, and the far-flung British Empire, pulled British goods into world markets.

Many of the industries in which Britain still has competitive advantage today are related to luxury, leisure, entertainment, and wealth. Early and advanced demand often provided the initial seed. Britain has been able to sustain advantage in such industries for a number of reasons. First, many of them are industries in which early mover advantages are particularly important. In such industries as cigarettes, porcelain, alcoholic beverages, woolens, and toiletries, to name a few, established international brand names and distribution channels that resulted from early home demand are hard to overcome. Where Britain has sustained advantage, technological change has often not been significant enough to provide newcomers with a lever to supplant British firms, especially in the high-end segments that are not price-sensitive and where buyers often value traditional methods. Britain also retains a domestic consumer base for luxury and wealth-related goods, especially around London. In addition, many foreigners are attracted to London because of theaters, museums, and other manifestations of long-accumulated wealth. Wealthy foreigners buy products in London and also provide a base of foreign demand.

Britain's broad strength in services partly reflects historical and current demand conditions. In business services, a combination of skilled human resources, the language, and early and broad industrial strength have given British firms a solid position in many industries such as accounting, consultancy, and engineering. In retailing, strength in high-end consumer goods and a sophisticated demand base in London have been important. Among the international British retailers are Burberry's, Conran's, Laura Ashley, and Aquascutum.

Continuing British national advantage in some other industries outside of services is a reflection of unusually sophisticated home demand or a peculiar segment structure of home demand. British consumers have the highest per capita sugar consumption of any nation, for example, a long-standing stimulus to the confectionery industry. This same sweet tooth and the tea time tradition benefit Britain in biscuits and cakes. The passion for gardening is reflected in a strong international position in garden tools. The reluctance of the British consumer to spend time in the kitchen (in contrast to consumers in France, Italy, and Germany) benefited British strength in chilled and processed foods.

More often than not, however, British firms have faced growing disadvantages in local demand conditions. A falling relative standard of living has made the *average* British consumer increasingly out of synch with needs in other advanced nations. Some observers characterize the British consumer as more price conscious than consumers in the more prosperous nations. This directs British firms to segments of the market that are less profitable and more vulnerable to competition from less advanced countries. Such a process is one of the important ways in which a nation in decline creates conditions that reinforce the decline, as I will discuss in the next chapter.

The average British consumer today has become a less demanding buyer than consumers in many other nations, and more resigned to poor service or substandard quality. Wartime and its aftermath may well have played a role. Rationing lasted into the 1950s, and utilitarian products of mediocre quality became widely accepted. The same attitude has extended to industrial products, where a certain number of defects is accepted, and poor quality and service are tolerated. A foreigner notices immediately how loath British people are to complain openly. Unfortunately, a stiff upper lip is not good for upgrading an economy. Poorly trained workers and managers have also contributed to lack of sophistication in industrial purchasing.

British demand conditions were also undermined by a history of widespread state ownership and regulation. The British health service, for example, is underfunded and bureaucratic. It lacks the resources to deploy the latest technology and procedures on a large scale. Other important industries, such as airlines, railroads, and telecommunications, have been state-owned. Their funds have been constrained and they have not played the role of sophisticated buyers of the many products and services that are sold to them. The recent moves toward privatization represent a hopeful sign of change, though the implementation of privatization has left some to be desired as I will discuss further.

A lack of demand-side pressure also extended to Britain's traditional overseas markets for many goods. Until the last decade or so, many British firms exported principally to former British colonies, the bulk of them developing countries. Such nations are usually not the most demanding and sophisticated buyers of consumer and industrial goods. British goods were frequently accepted out of tradition if not political and economic necessity. Even today, the British trade balance is much more favorable with developing nations than it is with advanced countries such as Germany, Sweden, and Italy. Not only is demand quality low in Britain's traditional markets but their potential to buy British goods has lagged behind as well. Growth in trade among advanced countries has exceeded that of trade with developing countries, hurting the United Kingdom.

British demand conditions were also undermined by the thinning of clusters. As some British industries became uncompetitive, they were increasingly poor buyers for other British industries. The spiral continued downward, cushioned only by long tradition and the remnants of technological innovation. For example, many British manufacturing companies lagged behind those of other advanced nations in process technology and in their willingness to invest in new plants and equipment, undermining competitive advantage in industries producing manufacturing equipment such as machine tools, lift trucks, and process controls.

RELATED AND SUPPORTING INDUSTRIES

Britain once enjoyed the fruits of clustering, as one sophisticated British industry spawned and reinforced others. British goods pulled British services into overseas markets and vice versa. British multinationals served as a loyal market abroad. Britain's strong cluster of financial services and trade-related industries was highly self-reinforcing.

In industrial businesses, however, there has been a gradual unwinding of clusters, in which only pockets of competitive advantage remain. British firms rely heavily on foreign inputs and machinery. In cars, for example, competitive advantage has been lost in end products outside of a small luxury niche (for example, Jaguar, Rolls Royce), and positions in a wide variety of automotive components have eroded with it. The same is true to an even greater extent in consumer durables such as appliances and consumer electronics.

Those areas where British firms have sustained competitive advantage partly owe it to related and supporting industries. In consumer goods and services, a vibrant retail sector has created pressures to innovate. Marks and Spencer, for example, has been a major force in the upgrading of British suppliers in food and apparel. Britain was among the first to allow advertising on television. Many would rank British advertising agencies first in the world in advertising creativity, ahead of the Americans. This environment has been a fertile one for British firms in which to build greater skills in modern consumer marketing.

The City of London illustrates another sector where British strength is a classic illustration of clustering. Britain's considerable international position in financial services (for example, in trading, investment management, insurance, and parts of banking) is concentrated in the City, along with countless related and supporting industries such as information and telecommunications services (such as Reuters), financial journalism and publishing, financial printing, legal services, and financial advertising and public relations. The dynamism of the cluster has attracted firms from all over the world to locate there, and London is solidifying its position as Europe's financial center.

FIRM STRATEGY, STRUCTURE, AND RIVALRY

British firms have, too often, a management culture that works against innovation and change. A penchant for tradition, a narrow definition of responsibility, and a high level of concern for form and order are characteristic. That something is "not done" has been a frequently heard phrase in British industry.

Combined with such managerial attitudes has been a debilitating relationship between labor and management. An atmosphere approaching class warfare has frozen the status quo. Unions have had great power to negotiate restrictive practices, which have inhibited innovation and retarded productivity. There are often a number of separate unions representing different groups of workers in the same factory or office, further complicating negotiations and restricting improvements.

An often noted but highly significant observation about Britain is that the best talent has, by and large, avoided industry. Social norms have meant that certain occupations were acceptable and others were simply "commerce." The exceptions are often the British success stories. Top graduates have entered industries with a heavy scientific orientation such as chemicals and pharmaceuticals, fields that were seen as creative or socially relevant such as publishing, motion pictures, and television, and other areas distanced from the factory like law and accountancy. More recently, talent has flowed into service industries such as finance, consultancy, advertising, and software. The flow of outstanding minds has contributed significantly to the areas in which Britain has achieved international success.

The motivation of workers and managers in Britain has traditionally been low in many industries. Working too hard, or striving to earn a great deal of money, is viewed with suspicion in Britain. Punitive personal tax rates contributed to dulled incentives. In addition, Britain is one of the few countries that has taxed capital gains, discouraging long-term investment. Absenteeism has been rampant. One study found that in 1983 an average of 12 percent of workers were absent, far higher than other advanced nations. [13]

The structure of the British capital markets has contributed to corporate goals that do not support investment and innovation. Britain's structure is similar to America's. Institutional investors have become dominant. Unlike Germany, Japan, and Switzerland, however, they have not viewed themselves as permanent investors. There are no universal banks to play the dual role of debt and equity holders. The result is the same type of market behavior typical in America. With institutional equity holders primarily concerned with share price appreciation and dividends, the result is heavy trading, intense concern by managements with share prices, a persistent tendency toward harvesting, and an explosion of acquisitions and takeovers. While takeovers often lead to substantial cost cutting and rationalization of facilities, a good thing, the pattern of low reinvestment is continued. The rate of net fixed investment in British industry over the postwar period has ranked near the bottom of the nations we studied, along with that of the United States.

Domestic rivalry in Britain has long been "gentlemanly." Traditionally, the goal has been satisfactory rather than outstanding performance. Companies lacked the strong profit orientation of the Americans or the market-share orientation of the Japanese. Merging rather than competing was a common choice or perceived necessity. In the automobile industry, for example, Austin and Morris were merged to create British Motor Corporation, and then a merger with Leyland created British Leyland. Such moves often had a predictable result, perpetuating the lack of dynamism and further eroding market position.

A noncompetitive orientation is reinforced in Britain by social norms and the educational system, discussed earlier. A concern with protocol and form sometimes creates hesitancy to act. Competition is viewed as distasteful and even vulgar.

The aim of avoiding competition surfaced repeatedly in the histories of industries we studied. The typical pattern was for a British firm to attempt to block exports of a new type of machinery or to protect a British monopoly. The inevitable result was that firms in other nations were forced to develop their own technology, or entrepreneurs left Britain to set up shop elsewhere. In textile machinery, for example, the Swiss and German industries (now the world leaders) were founded when exports of British machinery were restricted.

Lacking strong pressure from buyers or rivals, many U.K. companies settled into a comfortable pattern of slow decay in market position. Demand eroded slowly because of buyer loyalties. Outside of high-end consumer goods, products gravitated toward price-sensitive segments and buyers. Underinvestment resulted in acceptable financial performance, but the underpinnings of competitive advantage were ebbing away.

Rivalry has also been limited by a slow rate of new business formation. Some of the same factors that have shaped career choices and goals in established companies have also sapped entrepreneurship in Britain. Building a business to accumulate wealth has not been the stuff of the upper classes or those that strive to be part of them. New business formation has been further stunted in Britain by the attitude that failure is unforgivable. Many companies and industries have been founded by entrepreneurs who were "outsiders." Some had lower-middle-class backgrounds. Others, such as Lord Beaverbrook, Ian MacGregor, and more recently Rupert Murdoch, Robert Maxwell, and the Saatchi brothers, came to Britain from other nations and were unencumbered by prevailing attitudes and norms. Viewed by some with dismay, entrepreneurs such as these have often been the most aggressive competitors and have shaken up stodgy domestic industries. Unfortunately, however, many entrepreneurs who achieved success sought to adopt upper-class norms and distance themselves from industry.

THE ROLE OF GOVERNMENT

The British government traditionally adopted a laissez-faire attitude toward the development of the economy, in many ways comparable to that of the American government. The dominant view for many decades was that there was no competitiveness problem, or that market adjustments would inevitably address any difficulties. Control of aggregate demand, and interest rate management to influence inflation and the exchange rate, were the principal British policy tools, a reflection of an orientation toward macroeconomic and not microeconomic policy. The Treasury was the dominant force in economic policy, and building competitive strength in industry was not a major objective. The discovery of North Sea oil and gas, while breaking the cycle of devaluation and creating pressures through a stronger currency to upgrade British industry, further delayed painful adjustments in public policy. Yet the difficulties in industry and chronic unemployment created fiscal pressures that constrained spending for education, infrastructure, and other areas of factor creation, making the long-term problem worse.

Where government did attempt to aid industry, the approaches taken were often inappropriate and rarely sustained. Direct intervention, subsidy, consolidation, and protection reflected a flawed model of competition. The Industrial Reorganization Corporation established by the Wilson government in the 1960s, for example, operated under the faulty theory that encouraging British companies to merge would create world-class competitors. Consolidation of steel, automobiles, machine tools, and computers all led to notable failures. A program of research support for industry, one of the few genuine government responses to growing concerns over industrial decline, proved disastrous. The British government tried to choose promising technologies and give direct grants to firms to develop them. Most of the choices were failures. The underlying conditions for national advantage were not present. Even if technical successes were achieved, few commercial successes resulted. Regional policy was similarly unsuccessful, as subsidies to attract investments in depressed regions ignored whether a favorable "diamond" was present to make them viable in the long run. Few of the operations that were established ultimately survived.

Sharp policy reversals have accompanied new governments. Conservative governments have been beset by labor strife until the Thatcher government began to reverse the trend. Labor governments tended to accommodate labor union programs but these created inflexibility. Bouts of state ownership undermined competition and dynamism in affected and linked industries. The dramatic differences between the two parties made it even less likely that firms would commit for the long term. Why should one invest for tomorrow when tomorrow might bring high taxes or even nationalization?

In a number of industries, mostly services, British government policy was, by dint of its absence, a notably positive factor. Unusually low levels of regulation in some service industries have avoided disadvantages faced by other nations and allowed innovation and change. I have described how British firms escape constraints imposed on foreign firms in auctioneering, and a similarly low level of regulation also occurred in trading and insurance. British firms in these industries have been among the most innovative in the world.

Britain in Perspective

British industry has for many decades lacked dynamism and the ability to upgrade its competitive advantage. Britain declined because of growing disadvantages in each part of the "diamond." Most significant in my judgment have been weaknesses in human resources, low motivation, the lack of rivalry, and eroding demand conditions.

Britain illustrates the negative reinforcement of the determinants particularly well. Problems in one industry hurt others. Falling competitiveness reduced living standards and in turn made consumer demand less sophisticated and advanced. Pressures on government revenues led to cutbacks and short-cuts in factor creation and in social services, undermining still more industries. The British case also illustrates why it is so hard to turn around an economy once it begins to erode. There was no shock or jolt to reverse the cycle; indeed, a victory during the war bolstered confidence, and lingering market positions and customer loyalties may have allayed a sense of urgency about the need to change.

Britain sustains competitive advantage in industries that draw advantages from pure science, the fact that Britain has an upper tier of highly educated people whose wages are relatively low in world terms, a long tradition that has created early mover advantages, a well-established infrastructure in finance, trading, and the arts, and unusual or high-end demand. Such industries—luxury consumer goods and services, finance, information, general business services, and others—many of them concentrated around London, illustrate vividly the self-reinforcing effects of geographic concentration. The problem is that they do not create enough well-paying jobs to employ all of Britain's citizens, and lack of success elsewhere in Britain has meant that regional disparities have become greater and greater.

Signs of Change

There are signs in Britain that important elements of the equation are beginning to change, catalyzed by a shift in political leadership. A controversial government initiative is seeking to improve education, and there are signs that company investment in training is on the rise. Attitudes toward work, standards for work hours, and pay are beginning to rise. Falling tax rates and the possibility of higher incomes have boosted motivation. A decline in union power, partly because of legislation by the Thatcher government, has improved labor-management relations, made restructuring more possible, and created a spurt of productivity growth. Consumer demand is becoming more advanced and picky in the prosperous London and South East regions. Cutting-edge retailers are stimulating the development of new consumer products. Exchange controls, lifted in 1979 after many decades, have created new pressures on British firms to compete for capital.

The distress of many British companies in the 1970s and early 1980s finally made it clear that the choice was to compete or go under. A flurry of takeovers has shaken up staid companies and led to more aggressive managements. Privatization has created more competition in some industries such as telecommunications and electric power generation. Deregulation is increasing competition in others such as financial services where Britain's competitive advantage will benefit. Competing aggressively is becoming more socially acceptable, and rivalry shows signs of being on the rise.

Entrepreneurship is increasing, and the Thatcher government has sought to celebrate the entrepreneur. A venture capital industry has developed that ranks well ahead of the rest of Europe. Finally, foreign investment in assembly facilities, much of it in distressed areas, is creating welcome new jobs. The recent experience of Britain illustrates the change in climate that accompanies a series of vigorous policy shifts which triggers responses and counterresponses throughout an economy.

Yet Britain is far from assured of broad-based industrial success that will support a sustained increase in its standard of living. Human resource skills still lag far behind other advanced nations, and factor creation remains anemic. Much of the foreign investment is being driven by low wages, a fact that limits its benefits for upgrading the economy. Some of the newly privatized government firms are still protected monopolies, albeit within a regulatory framework. Demand conditions for goods aimed at the average consumer, and those for many industrial products, are still a serious disadvantage. Investor, corporate, and individual goals are still not well aligned with innovation and long-term success. The rate of investment in industry still lags. Rivalry is hesitant, and calls for subsidy and protection are common. The spurt in productivity growth due to restructuring may prove to be unsustainable. I will return to some of these concerns in Chapter 13.

CROSSCURRENTS IN AMERICA

Beginning in the late 1960s, broad segments of American industry began to lose competitive advantage. America's balance in merchandise trade went into deficit for the first time in the twentieth century in 1971. Trade problems widened even though the dollar fell in the latter 1970s. Real wages, after decades of growth, flattened and began declining in 1973. Productivity growth, while long only moderate, became anemic. Looking at the postwar period as a whole, American productivity growth and per capita income growth are at the bottom of the eight nations.[14] So is its rate of net capital investment in industry (see Table 7–1).

Yet, national competitive advantage in American industry is a study in contrasts. The average productivity in American industry as a whole is still at or near the top compared to any nation. The United States retains competitive advantage in a range of manufacturing industries, including new and important ones such as computers, packaged software, and biotechnology. America is still strong in consumer packaged goods, and it is still dominant in services. American companies are the leaders, or among the leaders, in most business and consumer service industries in which there is international competition, except shipping and tourism (where Americans still travel more than foreigners visit). America's international position, if anything, is becoming more significant in services as more and more service industries begin to internationalize. (Higher relative productivity in the services sector, which represents a large fraction of GDP, is an important reason why the average productivity in the United States is so high compared to nations such as Japan.) Finally, the United States maintains a strong position in agriculture and related industries.

Because of the particular pattern of American national advantage, the merchandise trade figures are only a partial measure of U.S. competitive strength. In many industries in which the United States leads, such as services and consumer packaged goods, international competition is heavily based on foreign direct investment and not on exports. Also, many American companies already had extensive foreign manufacturing or established it in the heady decades after World War II. Export position, as a result, understates the true U.S. international market position in a variety of industries.

Overall, however, there has been a significant loss of competitive advantage in a wide range of sophisticated U.S. manufacturing industries, including automobiles, trucks, machine tools, semiconductors, consumer electronics, and many, many others. The upgrading of the economy has been faltering.

CHANGING PATTERNS OF AMERICAN COMPETITIVE ADVANTAGE

Table 9–2 shows the top fifty American industries in terms of world export share in 1985. For many Americans, accustomed to thinking of the United States as an advanced industrial nation, this list may come as a surprise. Of the top twenty-five industries, fifteen are heavily based on natural resources (as are twenty-two of the top fifty).[15] Table 9–3 compares the extent of

TABLE 9–2 Top Fifty U.S. Industries in Terms of World Export Share, 1985

Industry	Share of Total World Exports	Export Value ($ millions)	Import Value ($ millions)	Share of Total U.S. Exports
Cotton seed oil	82.4	124,770	3,047	0.06
Unexposed, undeveloped photo film	81.9	885,712	630,695	0.42
Petroleum coke	80.3	760,981	19,522	0.36
Commercial aircraft and helicopters[1]	79.4	8,823,833	1,806,783	4.14
Rough sawn, veneer logs	75.8	1,170,516	17,408	0.55
Other manufactured fertilizers	69.6	1,272,439	992	0.60
Beet pulp, bagasse	69.5	549,301	7,585	0.26
Unmilled maize	69.5	5,335,039	20,588	2.50
Aircraft internal combustion piston engines and parts	67.4	383,483	9,766	0.18
Soya beans	67.1	3,749,941	976	1.76
Unmilled sorghum	65.8	769,266	13	0.36
Coal, lignite, and peat	64.4	4,399,776	135,986	2.06
Analog, hybrid DP machines, storage units	64.3	4,323,864	4,116,526	2.03
Fresh fish	63.5	664,102	631,303	0.31
Aircraft gas turbine engines	62.8	1,229,403	1,254,813	0.58
War firearms, ammunition	62.7	2,888,887	203,863	1.36
Fats of bovine, sheep	60.3	554,747	—	0.26
Measuring, drawing, instrument parts	60.0	104,473	23,586	0.05
Nitrogen-phosphate fertilizer	57.3	649,698	30,129	0.30
Radioactive materials	57.1	980,118	1,399,330	0.46
Aircraft parts	56.6	5,674,001	1,793,513	2.66
Whey	54.2	199,938	—	0.09
Warships and boats	53.1	278,283	—	0.13
Clay	52.4	310,053	3,246	0.15
Green groundnuts	51.3	209,987	463	0.10
Piezoelectric crystals	50.7	3,019,250	1,100,923	1.42
Measuring, drawing, etc., instruments	48.4	600,200	177,534	0.28
Regenerated fiber to spin	48.0	226,088	2,018	0.11
Typewriters, checkwriters	47.8	167,562	375,209	0.08
Wholly or partly stripped tobacco	47.7	129,913	177,163	0.06
Iron pyrites	47.2	240,557	556,954	0.11
Electromedical equipment	46.6	865,609	524,326	0.41
Dissolving chemical wood pulp	45.3	299,445	62,012	0.14
Raw bovine, equine hides	45.3	1,021,116	30,670	0.48

TABLE 9–2 *(Continued)*

Industry	Share of Total World Exports	Export Value ($ millions)	Import Value ($ millions)	Share of Total U.S. Exports
Cyclic alcohols	44.5	154,502	22,238	0.07
Glycosides, glands, sera	44.5	505,183	201,777	0.24
Footwear with soles of cork, wood	44.4	80,675	173,548	0.04
Edible offal	43.1	298,577	7,063	0.14
Rolling mills	42.5	77,911	11,642	0.04
Roadrollers/civil engineering equipment, etc.	42.2	4,091,920	1,937,088	1.91
Pharmaceuticals other than medicaments	41.8	806,956	52,058	0.38
Aircraft engines and motor parts	41.6	2,451,731	1,202,089	1.15
Track-laying tractors	40.5	230,718	69,695	0.11
Fungicides, disinfectants	40.3	788,551	116,851	0.37
Kraft liner	40.3	481,920	—	0.23
Polyethylene in rods	39.9	647,607	151,409	0.30
Polyvinyl chloride in rods	39.1	262,736	98,344	0.12
Artificial fur products	38.9	8,697	—	0.00
Motor vehicle chassis	37.7	386,818	968,789	0.18
Office, ADP machine parts, accessories	37.1	7,816,542	5,326,652	3.70
TOTAL				33.80

[1] Commercial aircraft is estimated to account for $5.5 billion of exports in this category.
NOTE: No import data are reported if import value is less than 0.3 percent of total trade for 1985.

natural resource-dependent exports in the three leading industrial nations. An estimated 24.2 percent of total U.S. exports are natural resource intensive, far higher than in Germany and Japan. Removing resource-dependent industries, Germany with 61 million people has an equivalent share of world exports to America with 240 million people. Japan actually has a higher world export share in non-resource dependent industries.

Because American exports are heavily based on natural factors of production, U.S. trade is sensitive to factor costs and the value of the dollar.[16] Between 1978 and 1985, as the dollar rose, resource-intensive exports fell from 28 percent of total U.S. exports to 24 percent. The recent fall in the dollar has boosted resource-dependent exports, but competitive advantage in these types of industries is notoriously unstable.

At the same time as resource-intensive goods make up an important fraction of America's competitive industries, the list of top fifty industries shows

TABLE **9–3** **Natural Resource-Dependent Exports, 1985**

	Share of Nation's Exports			Nation's Share of World Exports			Share of Total World Exports
	U.S.	Ger-many	Japan	U.S.	Ger-many	Japan	
INDUSTRIES DEPENDENT ON NATURAL RESOURCES	24.2%	12.4%	2.7%	8.3%	3.7%	0.8%	36.7%
INDUSTRIES *NOT* DEPENDENT ON NATURAL RESOURCES	75.8%	87.6%	97.3%	15.1%	14.9%	16.1%	63.3%
TOTAL	100%	100%	100%	12.6%	10.8%	10.4%	100%

SOURCE: Author's estimates. Natural resource-dependent industries are defined as those involving agricultural goods, minerals, or other natural or cultivated commodities where the level of processing is relatively low and goods are not packaged or branded. The classification of SITC industries by natural-resource dependency is available from the author.

that the United States has retained some strong positions in industries such as defense goods, aircraft, computers, air-conditioning equipment, and electromedical equipment. While cigarettes show up as the sole consumer packaged good on the top fifty list, American firms have extensive foreign direct investments in many other consumer goods that make exports an understatement of competitive strength.

Figure 9–4 profiles America's competitive industries in 1985, and Figures 9–5 and B-9 present summary statistics. The United States has strong positions in forest products and especially in agriculturally related goods (the United States holds a wide lead in overall food/beverage cluster exports). The U.S. position in agriculture includes products, machinery, specialized inputs, and services, notably trading. Increased production in foreign nations, however, seems likely to limit future U.S. agricultural export growth. The United States also has a commanding position in defense, aerospace, and related fields. The shading on Figure 9–5 illustrates that the American positions in defense, transportation (aircraft), and computers are linked through the role of government spending.

The American position in health care-related products is also extremely strong and strengthening. Another world-leading cluster is in computers and software (though the position in semiconductors is eroding). Other strong U.S. clusters are in entertainment and leisure (the United States is extremely strong outside of consumer electronics), consumer packaged goods (both food and nonfood), consumer services, and business services such as finan-

FIGURE 9-4 Clusters of Internationally Competitive U.S. Industries, 1985

	MATERIALS/METALS	FOREST PRODUCTS
Primary Goods	FABRICATED METAL PRODUCTS Blades, tips, etc., for tools Copper, alum. wire cables# *Steel, copper nails, nuts*# NONFERROUS METALS **Clay** Copper alloys# Tin, alloys worked# *Rolled silver*# OTHER MATERIALS & WASTE ***Aluminum***· ***Molybdenum, niobium, etc., ores***· Metaliferrous nonferrous waste· Copper waste & scrap ***Other nonferrous metal scrap*#** Precious metal ores, waste	WOOD PRODUCTS ***Pulpwood chips, particles*** **Rough sawn, veneer, logs** Improved wood#· PULP Waste paper, wood pulp# *Chemical woodpulp dissolving* PAPER **Kraft liner in bulk** Plastic-coated paper
Machinery	*Rolling mills*# Electric industrial furnaces Mineral working machinery#·	
Specialty Inputs	Refractory bricks, etc., nes *Iron pyrites*#	
Services	Mining·	

	PETROLEUM/CHEMICALS		SEMICONDUCTORS/ COMPUTERS
Primary Goods	RAW MATERIALS **Coal, lignite, & peat***#* **Petroleum coke***#* *Crude petroleum** ORGANIC CHEMICALS*#* Other cyclic hydrocarbons*#* Chemically pure xylenes Halogenic hydrocarbon derivatives *Cyclic alcohols, etc.** Monoacids & derivatives *Polyacids & derivatives* Amine compounds Ethers, epoxides, acetals Inorganic esters & other organic chemicals*#*	Nitrogen-fn compounds*#* Misc. chemical products*#* INORGANIC CHEMICALS Inorganic acids, etc. Phosphites, phosphates* *Other inorganic chemicals, etc.** PLASTICS *Alkyds, poly in plates**#* **Polyethylene in rods***#* *Polypropylene*** Plastic material nes *Engineering plastics** *Polyamides in plates** *Polystyrene in plates** *PVC in rods**#	**Analog & hybrid, digital storage units***#* *Digital computers* Digital central processors Office, ADP machine parts, accessories Other electronic tubes **Piezoelectric crystals***#* Printed circuits & parts*#* *Electronic microcircuits**
Machinery	*Oilfield equipment****		*Semiconductor mfg. equipment****
Specialty Inputs			
Services	*Oilfield services**** Service stations*		*Custom software**** *Network services**** *Information processing**** **Information*****

KEY
roman	12.3% world export share or higher, but less than 24.6% share	
bold italics	*24.6% world export share or higher, but less than 49.2% share*	
sans serif	**49.2% world export share or above**	

•	Industries below cutoff in 1978	*	Added due to FDI
#	Calculated residuals	**	Upgraded due to FDI
##	Added due to significant export value in a segmented industry	***	Added based on in-country research

FIGURE 9–4 *(Continued)*

Primary Goods	MULTIPLE BUSINESS		TRANSPORTATION	
	EQUIPMENT	INSTRUMENTS	ENGINES	VEHICLES & EQUIPMENT
	Elevators, escalators*# Air-conditioning machinery* Other electrical machinery (traffic control eqpt., security devices, etc.)* Rotary and other pumps for liquids, parts* Pumps, compressor parts Gas, liquid filters	Lightbulbs* Measuring, drawing, etc., instruments Measure, draw, etc., instruments parts* Gas, liquid control instruments Measuring, controlling instruments*	Piston engines nes* Aircraft internal combustion piston engines and parts* Aircraft gas turbine engines Marine piston engines, other than outboard **VEHICLES & EQUIPMENT** Special motor vehicles	Motor vehicles* Helicopters & commercial aircraft nes# Railway vehicles & associated equipment* Tracklaying tractors** Roadrollers & civil eng. eqpt.*** Motor vehicle chassis Tugs, floats**
Machinery	Machinery for special industries*# Spraying machinery	Vending, weighing machines#	Gas welders#	Aircraft engines & motors nes parts# Aircraft parts nes Forklift truck parts# Motor vehicle bodies, parts, accessories# Railway vehicles and associated equipment parts
Specialty Inputs	Unhard rubber products Nonelectric power hand tool parts# Unmounted polarizing sheets#		Synthetic rubber Asbestos, friction materials Radar apparatus Antiknock preparations Tires* **PARTS** Piston engine parts nes	
Services	Accounting* Advertising* Management consulting* Legal* Engineering/architectural* Construction* Contract research* Temporary help* Building maintenance* Security services* Industrial laundry/apparel supply* Industrial cleaning*	Commercial banking* Merchant/investment banking* Money management* Consumer finance* Equipment leasing & rental* Credit reporting* Waste management* Corporate training* Charge/credit card* Convenience stores* Public relations*	Airlines*** Air cargo***	

	POWER GENERATION AND DISTRIBUTION	OFFICE	TELECOMMUNICATIONS	DEFENSE
Primary Goods	GENERATION Steam boilers & auxiliary plants# Steam engines, turbines' Nuclear reactors, parts DISTRIBUTION Electric insulating equipment	**Large, high-volume photocopiers**··· *Nonelectric typewriters,* *checkwriters*#·	TV, radio transmitters	**War firearms, ammunition** *Military aircraft*··· *Military electronics*··· **Warships**#
Machinery				
Specialty Inputs	**Radioactive, etc., material**#·			
Services			*Satellite launching*···	

KEY

roman   12.3% world export share or higher, but less than 24.6% share
bold italics   *24.6% world export share or higher, but less than 49.2% share*
sans serif   **49.2% world export share or above**

·   Industries below cutoff in 1978
Calculated residuals
Added due to significant export value in a segmented industry

·   Added due to FDI
··   Upgraded due to FDI
···   Added based on in-country research

FIGURE 9-4 (Continued)

	FOOD/BEVERAGES	HOUSING/HOUSEHOLD
Primary Goods	BASIC FOODS	Soap, polishes***
	Live, bovine bread#	
	Live animals for food*	Whey#
	Fresh fish*	Breakfast cereal, pasta#
	Poultry	Edible products, preparations nes
	*Fish, salted, dried, smoked**·	Meat offal, dried*#
	Rice in husk or husked	*Maté*#
	Rice milled unbroken	*Lemons, grapefruits*
	Flour of wheat or meslin	Dried raisins*#
	Other cereal meals, flour	Edible nuts
	Soya beans	**Green groundnuts**
	Leguminous vegetables, dry	*Edible offal*·
	Oranges, fresh or dried	EDIBLE OILS
		BEVERAGES
		Flavored carbonated
	EDIBLE OILS	**beverages***
	Fats of bovine, sheep	
	Soya bean oil	
	Cottonseed oil	
	Sunflower seed oil·	
	PROCESSED FOODS	
	Frozen foods·	
Machinery	Cultivating machinery	Lawn mower, harvesting, etc.,
	Combine harvester-thresher	machinery#
	Parts for harvesting machinery	Nondomestic refrigeration
	Nondomestic food machinery	equipment
		Nondomestic refrigeration
		equipment parts#
Specialty Inputs	*Metal cans***	Natural calcium phosphates,
	Beet pulp, bagasse, etc.	unground
	Hay, animal feeds#	Insecticides
	*Seeds, etc., for planting**·	*Fungicides, disinfectants*#
	Unmilled wheat, etc.	
	Unmilled maize	**Unmilled sorghum**
		Oilcake & other residues
		AGRICULTURAL CHEMICALS
		**Other mfr fertilizers*#
		Nitrogen-phosphate fertilizer
		nes
Services	*Fast food*·	
	Food service/vending·	
	Trading of agricultural	
	commodities*	

	TEXTILES/APPAREL	HEALTH CARE	PERSONAL	ENTERTAINMENT/LEISURE
Primary Goods	FABRICS Special textile fabrics# *Footwear with wood soles#* *Artificial fur & arts.#*	PHARMACEUTICALS *Bulk hormones* *Glycosides, glands, sera* *Medicaments with hormones**** *Pharmaceuticals other than medicaments#* MEDICAL EQUIPMENT *Electromedical equipment* Medical instruments nes *Hearing, orthopedic aids* Syringes*** Contact lens*** *Surgical furniture, etc.#*	Cigars, cheroots, tobacco manufacture#* **Cigarettes****	**Cinema cameras, projectors, etc.***** Photochemical products*** **Photo film & plates, exposed#*** *Developed cinema film* Newspapers, periodicals** *Hand paintings, etc., nes* Recorded discs, tapes *Jukeboxes#* Photo apparatus# Discharge lamps, bulbs#
Machinery	Textile-processing machine parts **Buttonholing machines*****			
Specialty Inputs	Lub. prep. of textiles#* *Bovine, equine hides, raw* Other furskins, raw# FIBERS & YARNS *Raw cotton, excl. linters* Disc. syn. fiber, uncombed *Regenerated fiber to spin#* Waste of syn. fibers# *Waste of textile fabrics* Cellulose derivatives *Synthetic fiber yarns#**		*Tobacco wholly or partly stripped* Tobacco refuse#* *Tobacco virginia type, flue-cured*	
Services		*Health care** *Hospital management**	*Secondary & university education**** *Graduate education****	*Hotels & hotel management** *Car rental & leasing** *Cinema film production**** *Television program production****

KEY

roman   12.3% world export share or higher, but less than 24.6% share
bold italics   *24.6% world export share or higher, but less than 49.2% share*
sans serif   **49.2% world export share or above**

*	Industries below cutoff in 1978	*	Added due to FDI
#	Calculated residuals	**	Upgraded due to FDI
##	Added due to significant export value in a segmented industry	***	Added based on in-country research

FIGURE 9-5 Percentage of U.S. Exports of Competitive Industries by Broad Cluster

UPSTREAM INDUSTRIES

Materials/Metals	Forest Products	Petroleum/Chemicals	Semiconductors/Computers
Share of Country Exports: 1.5 (−0.6)	Share of Country Exports: 1.3 (−0.3)	Share of Country Exports: 6.3 (1.8)	Share of Country Exports: 8.8 (4.5)
Share of World Cluster Exports: 2.6 (−0.3)	Share of World Cluster Exports: 5.9 (−0.7)	Share of World Cluster Exports: 4.1 (0.6)	Share of World Cluster Exports: 20.5 (−8.9)

Upstream Industries — Share of Country Exports: 17.9 (5.4); Share of World Cluster Exports: 5.7 (0.7)

INDUSTRIAL AND SUPPORTING FUNCTIONS

Multiple Business	Transportation	Power Generation & Distribution	Telecommunications	Defense
Share of Country Exports: 9.4 (2.0)	Share of Country Exports: 18.4 (0.5)	Share of Country Exports: 0.8 (0.2)	Share of Country Exports: 0.2 (0.2)	Share of Country Exports: 1.5 (0.1)
Share of World Cluster Exports: 18.2 (3.2)	Share of World Cluster Exports: 13.4 (−1.1)	Share of World Cluster Exports: 13.8 (1.7)	Share of World Cluster Exports: 6.2 (−0.2)	Share of World Cluster Exports: 55.0 (−0.1)

Office
Share of Country Exports: 0.1 (−0.0)
Share of World Cluster Exports: 7.3 (−0.0)

Industrial and Supporting Functions — Share of Country Exports: 30.4 (2.9); Share of World Cluster Exports: 14.5 (0.2)

FINAL CONSUMPTION GOODS AND SERVICES

Food/Beverage	Textiles/Apparel	Housing/Household	Health Care	Personal	Entertainment/Leisure
Share of Country Exports: 10.8 (−5.0)	Share of Country Exports: 2.2 (−0.5)	Share of Country Exports: 0.0 (−0.1)	Share of Country Exports: 2.4 (0.8)	Share of Country Exports: 0.8 (−1.0)	Share of Country Exports: 1.3 (−0.1)
Share of World Cluster Exports: 12.1 (−2.1)	Share of World Cluster Exports: 3.7 (−0.5)	Share of World Cluster Exports: 0.3 (−0.3)	Share of World Cluster Exports: 19.2 (4.2)	Share of World Cluster Exports: 6.4 (−2.9)	Share of World Cluster Exports: 5.7 (−1.0)

Final Consumption Goods and Services — Share of Country Exports: 17.5 (−5.6); Share of World Cluster Exports: 7.9 (−1.4)

Note: Numbers in parentheses are changes between 1978 and 1985. ▨ Identifies broad sectors in which the nation's international competitive positions are related. Exports are those of competitive industries, not all industries.

cial services, management consulting, and accounting. The past and present breadth of the U.S. economy is reflected in strength in multiple business products and especially services. The American position in chemicals is also strong, but not leading except in plastics.

Many industries in which America retains competitive advantage are in the most politically sensitive fields. Aerospace, defense, computers, agriculture, and many services, for example, are heavily subsidized or protected in other nations, a constraint to international success. The potential for trade disputes is unusually great.

America's position is weak or weakening in transportation-related goods and services, machinery of many types, machine tools, office products and equipment other than computers, consumer electronics, consumer durables of all types, apparel and related products, steel and other materials, and telecommunications equipment (except large central-office switches and fiber optics, which are areas of strength).

The most striking changes between 1971 and 1985 are in highly visible industries such as steel, automobiles, machine tools, consumer electronics, and office equipment. Yet the declining competitive advantage of American companies is widespread and apparent in many of our case studies. While the rising dollar of the early 1980s certainly did not help, the dollar had fallen through the 1970s and, except for a brief period, did not rise above a level at which the United States had achieved balance in manufacturing trade in the 1960s.[17] The erosion of U.S. position began many years before the dollar's rise. American firms, in industry after industry, lost leadership in product and process technology.

How could a position of such consistent strength in sophisticated, high-productivity fields turn into one where competitive advantage was eroding in so many advanced industries and per capita income growth was the slowest of any of the nations we studied in the postwar period? Why has the upgrading process in the American economy been faltering? In order to answer these questions, I must revisit the determinants of national competitive advantage as they bear on the United States. It is here that the reasons for the problems in some industries, and continued prosperity in others, are to be found.

FACTOR CONDITIONS

The United States maintains a relative abundance in natural factors of production. Some industries, such as aluminum and copper, have lost position because of dwindling reserves, high electric power costs, and/or the opening up of new, low-cost foreign deposits. However, American agricultural and forest products-related industries maintain strong competitive positions through continued productivity improvement, though production is growing in other countries.

America remains preeminent in scientific research, particularly in more fundamental disciplines. That American firms have sustained advantage in defense and aerospace industries and in science-based industries such as medicine and biotechnology is no accident. This is where the technical resources flow.

Yet the technological lead is all but gone in many more established industries. American firms have been slow to adopt new process technologies, slow to upgrade facilities, and slow in introducing new products and features. Japan, in particular, is filing a growing share of patents, including those important patents that are frequently cited. Overall, non-Americans were awarded 47.1 percent of all U.S. patents awarded in 1988, the highest in history. Japanese firms are technological leaders in such important fields as advanced manufacturing technology, new materials, and important areas of electronics. America still creates much science and technology but lags in translating it into competitive U.S. industries. The problem is not in services or packaged goods, where technological complexity is modest and product and process changes are relatively rapid. The difficulties arise in industries such as automobiles, machine tools, or printing machines, where innovation requires sustained R&D investment, where introducing new products and processes is complicated and time consuming, and where complex coordination among disciplines is required.

Factor Creation. The causes of America's dwindling lead in innovation are important and touch on the entire "diamond." First, America has fallen down badly in factor creation. America's overall rate of investment in factor creation and upgrading has slowed down since the 1960s, at the same time as it has risen significantly in other nations, particularly as it applies to established industries. Perhaps the single most important reason for faltering commercialization of technology is the eroding quality of human resources relative to other nations. While its overall rate of spending on education as a fraction of GDP is among the highest, America's educational system is faltering badly.

The top schools and universities are second to none, and many foreign students come to America for training especially at the graduate level. High quality at the top, however, masks grave problems everywhere else. The average American university is not up to the standard of the average German or Swiss university, and the percentage of students majoring in technical fields is lower.

Even more serious is the educational system for the average worker. American schools set low standards and are weak in discipline. American high school graduates are well behind those in other advanced nations in training in vital areas such as math, science, and languages. Japanese firms building U.S. plants have found, for example, that the statistical techniques involved in statistical process control, which can be understood by most Japanese high school graduates, are a mystery to many American college graduates. School years are short, absenteeism is high, hours spent on homework are low, and competition among students has been de-emphasized. America has not yet sorted out how to provide access to education for disadvantaged groups and still maintain excellence. Teaching has lost prestige, pay has not kept up with other opportunities, and the average quality of teachers has fallen. Military service, once an important developer of human resources, is playing a diminished role.

The result is an extraordinary rate of functional illiteracy in the American workforce. Many workers and managers lack the educational foundations for further training and the skills necessary to improve productivity. In-company training is growing but has not been able to compensate. Training by American companies lags far behind that in Japan and Germany.

University research in the United States continues to be uniquely strong. However, research spending by the federal government has not kept up with inflation. Long skewed toward defense-related research, it has become more so (67 percent in 1988). Unlike the 1940s and 1950s, however, defense R&D is less on core technologies and more on highly specialized defense needs. American spending on *non*defense research is about 1.9 percent of GDP, compared to 2.8 percent in Japan and 2.6 percent in Germany. Even overall American R&D spending, including defense, is now lower as a percentage of GDP than that in Japan, Germany, and Sweden.[18] Research spending by U.S. companies lagged in the 1970s at a time when spending levels by firms in other nations increased.

The discussion of the decisive importance of specialized factors for competitive advantage in Chapter 3 suggests, however, an arguably more significant problem. While the United States has some effective mechanisms for creating generalized factors such as leading universities and a large science establishment, it often lacks the mechanisms present elsewhere to create advanced and specialized factors for particular industries. Generalized factor creating mechanisms are *necessary but not sufficient.* There is no well developed apprenticeship system, no strong vocational school system, no Italian-style tradition of working in an industry for generations, and no Japanese-style emphasis on in-company training. Specialized research institutes and joint university-private research programs are still comparatively rare.

Factor creation has also lagged in the area of capital. A low and declining rate of household savings has limited the pool of investable capital. In the 1980s, large federal budget deficits have absorbed much of private savings and led to huge net foreign borrowings. Real interest rates have risen from among the lowest of any nation in the 1950s to among the highest in the 1980s.

Diminished Pressure To Upgrade. Selective factor disadvantages have also ceased to be a unique spur to American industry. Wage growth has been slower in the United States than in the majority of other advanced nations, reducing pressure to improve productivity. American wages are now no longer the highest in the world.

A large pool of available labor entered the American labor force in the 1970s and 1980s, a function of the postwar baby boom, more women working, and immigration. With many new employees available, American firms did not face the same pressure to automate and move into more sophisticated segments as did those in most other advanced nations. The necessity was lacking for firms to invest in improving the skills or the employees they had, because a ready supply of new employees was available. While many new jobs were created, the rate of upgrading in the American economy was set back. At the same time, economic growth could occur despite sluggish growth in productivity.[19]

As important as lack of pressure along some dimensions has been the nature of the response to pressures in others. Because of a lack of sustained commitment to core businesses and faltering domestic rivalry, many American companies reacted to the rising dollar in the 1980s by ceding market position, selling out, sourcing abroad, or seeking protection, instead of innovating. The same circumstances mean that the large drop in the dollar has eased the pressure to boost quality and raise productivity.

The labor shortages that are emerging in some fields, however, foreshadow demographic changes that could be very beneficial to American industry. Tight labor supplies will create pressure for upgrading advantage. A maturing population is likely to save more. However, changes elsewhere in the "diamond" (such as factor creation, goals, and rivalry) must occur if these developments are to bear full fruit.

DEMAND CONDITIONS

A less apparent but equally serious problem for American national advantage is an erosion in demand conditions. No longer is America the nation that always foreshadows the world market. No longer is America so consistently the home of the world's most sophisticated buyers. The American consumer and the American industrial buyer, then, no longer represent as great a strength as they once did.[20] The result is an inability of American firms to keep pace in innovation and with the differentiation strategies of foreign rivals. The upgrading of American industries then falters.

American consumers are often no longer the most affluent. They are certainly not the most demanding. They tolerate products and services that no Japanese or German would.[21] This observation was made time after time in our interviews with executives, frequently American executives. It is confirmed by buyer behavior in industries ranging from shampoo to automobiles.

There has been a subtle evolution in buyer needs in many industries that is moving them away from a strategy that American companies largely invented. With a large home market, American companies tend to produce standardized goods that are mass produced, mass marketed, and even disposable. This requires compromises in product design, quality, and service. The symbol of this approach for me is Wonder Bread, so refined to allow mass production and distribution that it has lost its taste and nutritional value (except for that which is added back using synthetic vitamins). Such a "Wonder Bread" mentality has been typical of many U.S. industries, not only in consumer packaged goods but in consumer durables and industrial goods.

Japan upset this equation beginning in the 1970s by introducing standardized products with dramatically higher levels of quality. Driven by domestic rivalry, however, Japanese firms then began to introduce new models and new features at a rate unheard of in American industry. Product variety proliferated and Japanese firms learned how to produce wide lines efficiently using flexible automation.

Today, demand is moving toward even higher levels of quality, customization, segmentation, and service content. While the American mass market was once a strength, evolving competition has rendered it a weakness. Those firms most attuned and responsive to needs in particular segments, because of their national circumstances, become world leaders. German firms have growing strengths in premium kitchen appliances, for example, while Italians do well in the compact segment and Japan in segments such as microwaves that are heavily based on electronics.

Another reason America has lost some of its uniqueness in demand is institutional. Other nations have begun to catch up in terms of modern media, chain stores, and other institutions of modern marketing. These once gave American companies an edge in predicting future trends. The penetration of chain stores in food and other forms of retailing, for example, is now actually greater in a number of European nations. U.S. retailing, moreover, has moved strongly toward discount stores providing little consumer information or service. This reinforces the tendency toward standardized goods and makes American retailers less sophisticated and anticipatory buyers.

Buyer needs are also shaped by a growing concern in many industries for safety, health, environmental quality, and a better work environment. By and large, U.S. firms are behind those of advanced European nations in their exposure to those values. Of the nations we studied, a higher level of social concern is typical in Denmark, Sweden, and Germany. It is also increasingly present in Japan, a result of crowded conditions and a love of nature. In trucks, for example, Japanese and Swedish firms were leaders in improving the operator's environment. In power tools, Japanese and European firms led in designing tools sensitive to ergonomics and balance.

In consumer goods, the effect of these changes first surfaced in durables, where quality, dependability, and features are vital. In cameras, for example, American firms did well in simple point-and-shoot cameras and instant cameras with modest picture quality but have virtually no position in more sophisticated 35mm cameras, which now have become more compact and laden with electronic controls. Threats are just beginning to be apparent in some consumer packaged goods, long an area of American strength. While Germany and Sweden have poor demand conditions for consumer packaged goods, Italy, Switzerland, and Britain are contenders. Japan represents a long-term threat in these industries because it has advanced media combined with busy, affluent, and demanding consumers and intense domestic rivalry. While U.S. industry should hold its own, the fact that many U.S. consumer packaged goods industries have consolidated down to a few dominant competitors means that continued U.S. leadership is by no means assured.

In industrial and commercial products, American demand conditions have eroded because the United States is no longer the home for many industry leaders. In automobiles, for example, the most advanced buyers of parts and other inputs are German and Japanese. As one American industry loses competitive advantage, its quality as a buyer lessens for its suppliers. American companies are not necessarily the most advanced buyers of many types of machinery and modern materials, because the world-class manufacturing companies today are often not American. Penetration of advanced manufacturing equipment, for example, is slower in America than in Japan, Sweden, Germany, and parts of Italy. The innovators who first employ new materials are also not American in many industries. Japanese firms are leaders in employing ceramics and German firms are challenging Americans in plastics. Other nations also gain the pull-through effects as their multinationals succeed abroad.

The quality of U.S. firms as industrial buyers is also affected by the training and skills of human resources. The American worker is frequently less educated and less trained than a German or Japanese. In printing, for example, Germans undergo a three-year formal apprenticeship program while most Americans learn on the job. With less sophisticated workers, and often less technically trained managers as well, American firms will no longer represent the most advanced and cutting-edge needs. American workers were not capable in a number of industries we studied of using the most sophisticated foreign-made equipment.[22] Special, simpler models had to be created for the American market.

Regulation has played a mixed role in affecting the quality of U.S. demand.

Deregulation of competition has and will continue to unleash innovation in such industries as transportation services and telecommunications, a major strength for the industries that serve them. Yet the United States has been backing off from its strong commitment to health, safety, the environment, and working conditions. For example, fuel efficiency standards on automobiles were reduced by the Reagan Administration. The strictest regulations in many of these areas are first introduced abroad. Foreign companies learn to deal with stricter standards before American firms, giving them an advantage when U.S. regulations catch up.

Another problem for U.S. innovation is the extremes to which product-liability litigation has progressed. While a strict liability system is a beneficial discipline for industry, the United States illustrates how moving to extremes compared to other nations converts an advantage into a disadvantage. The risk of lawsuits is so great, and the consequences so potentially disastrous, that the inevitable result is for more caution in product innovation than in other advanced nations.

It is important to recognize, however, that American demand conditions are still advanced in many areas. High female participation in the workforce has continued to fuel the desire for convenience that has long been a part of the American mentality. Americans celebrate entertainment and leisure, a function of traditionally high incomes, short work hours, and the distinctively American mass popular culture. (Japanese have been too busy for leisure time until very recently.[23]) Other high-income nations are more conservative and tradition bound, limiting or slowing down the rate of innovation in entertainment and leisure activities. Britain is the only real U.S. competitor in these fields, and the dominance of English as the world language is certainly also a contributing factor.

The United States and Britain also lead overall in financial services. Due to less regulation and greater home buyer sophistication, American and British firms lead in many complex financial services, including asset management, underwriting of new forms of securities, and services related to corporate restructuring.[24] The historical dominance of these nations as industrial powers has clearly been a contributing factor, as has been the creation of large pools of wealth that have been passed along over several generations. Other historical and even cultural factors also play a role. American companies are still dominant internationally in credit cards, consumer finance, and credit reporting, for example, all a function of an advanced and insatiable home demand for credit. The preoccupation in the United States and the United Kingdom with managing wealth, however, is an important sign foreshadowing economic decline, as I will discuss in the next chapter.

The United States also continues to have uniquely favorable demand conditions for many services. In business services, U.S. companies were well ahead of firms from other nations in de-integrating service functions that historically were performed internally (see Chapter 6). This, coupled with the prestige of jobs in business services and a fertile environment for start-ups and for taking service companies public, have led to continuing American success. Early saturation of demand for services within the United States has prompted aggressive foreign entry by U.S. service companies.

Another area where U.S. demand is still the most sophisticated and advanced is defense, a strength for the industries that produce defense-related goods and services. The United States still leads, for example, in specialized electronic gear and semiconductors produced to high military specifications, though it has lost preeminence in more standardized items. Yet even here a traditional U.S. strength has become less potent. As theory would predict, Israel has emerged as a significant competitor under the pressure of a real national threat and in a nation where participating in national defense carries the highest prestige. The Israeli military may well be the most sophisticated and demanding buyer in some areas.

As defense needs become increasingly specialized, however, defense demand is no longer always a strength. The huge defense market has distracted American firms from segments with greater importance for international competition. In machine tools, for example, the focus of U.S. industry was on the large and early markets for numerically controlled tools in defense and aerospace. Japanese firms took over the market for machines sold to medium-sized manufacturing companies that is the heart of the global industry. In advanced materials such as carbon fibers and ceramics, American firms have been preoccupied with exotic defense and aerospace demand, while Japanese firms have gained a substantial lead in widespread applications.

American demand conditions, then, are a mixed bag. America remains on the cutting edge of demand in a variety of industries. It is still the place where some trends are popularized. Running shoes, casual leather shoes, and blue jeans are good examples, and American companies are leaders in these industries. Yet, the widespread demand advantages that powered early postwar American innovation and upgrading have diminished to a significant degree.

RELATED AND SUPPORTING INDUSTRIES

The clusters of competitive industries in the U.S. economy are thinning, particularly in machinery and specialized inputs. One uncompetitive U.S. industry has often undermined others. Many U.S. companies stayed with domestic steel suppliers, for example, at a time when foreign-made steel was of equal or better quality and much lower in cost. The same story could be told about many other industrial inputs. Uncompetitive supplier industries not only penalize other U.S. manufacturers directly but become less valuable partners in stimulating innovation.

Despite extensive industry clustering in the United States, U.S. firms have also been less effective in taking advantage of the benefits of clusters to speed up innovation compared to firms in other nations. Relationships with buyers and suppliers have tended to be opportunistic and at arm's length. The sort of vertical interchange so vital to innovation has been more the exception than the rule in American industry. Skill transfer and sharing of market insights takes place only sporadically.

This did not preclude competitive advantage through the 1960s when American companies possessed a compelling technological lead and when segmentation and rapid new product innovation were less essential. Today, however, competitive advantage draws heavily on these qualities, and arm's-length vertical relationships are a serious weakness. While there is increasing emphasis on working with suppliers and customers, American firms are still behind.

More broadly, the whole concept of strengthening the national cluster is not truly understood in America. The focus of U.S. firms is still largely parochial. They rarely invest in building up suppliers, sponsoring specialized research institutes at universities, or working to improve the pool of human resources available to them and their entire domestic industry. U.S. industry associations are little help to their members compared to associations in other nations. They rarely see their role as that of factor creation, which is perhaps the most important role an association can play. With a more international outlook, U.S. industry associations would work to further the common interests of their members, as foreign associations do.

FIRM STRATEGY, STRUCTURE, AND RIVALRY

In the last several decades, changes have occurred in American companies that sapped the rate of innovation and upgrading. One is a steadily diminishing number of senior managers with technical backgrounds. German, Swedish, and Japanese executives have usually been engineers or scientists. They are committed to modern technology as a matter of professional pride. American managers, often without technical backgrounds, have had more difficulty understanding the benefits of technology for products and processes. They sometimes lack the confidence and conviction to invest in it.

There is a diversion of top talent in America away from industry. Top graduates have flocked into law, medicine, and finance, not into technical fields. The best minds entering industry have chosen glamorous areas such as packaged goods, entertainment, real estate, services, and computers. Not surprisingly, these are areas of American strength.

American companies also suffer from poorly trained employees who lack the essential skills to assimilate modern techniques. Management structures impede coordination across functional lines. Another barrier to innovation has been rigid work rules.

Changing motivations of employees and managers have also contributed to a faltering rate of innovation. Employees are often not committed to their profession or to their company, partly because they have invested less in training for their profession and partly because their company is not committed to them. Growing affluence has also led to declining motivation to work and greater attention to other pursuits. The result is less investment in upgrading skills and a slower accumulation of product and process learning within companies.

Company goals have also shifted in ways that undermine the upgrading of industry. In the early postwar period, American capital markets served up mountains of cheap capital. Money flowed into new enterprises and ventures of every conceivable sort. With low interest rates, access to equity capital, and millions of former military personnel seeking careers in industry amid an atmosphere of optimism, innovation flourished.

By the 1970s, however, corporate goals had shifted. Real interest rates that were higher than those in most other advanced nations contributed to a lower rate of investment. More significant, however, has been shifting goals of major investors. The proportion of stock owned by institutions rose dramatically, much of it held in pension funds whose investment earnings are exempt from taxation. Unlike institutional investors in nearly every other advanced nation, who view their shareholdings as nearly permanent and exercise their ownership rights accordingly, American institutions are under pressure to demonstrate quarterly appreciation. Pension consultants have grown up that collect fees by assisting funds in changing asset managers whose recent performance is deemed inadequate. Asset managers, in turn, reward their employees based on the appreciation of their portfolio in the last quarter or year. With a strong incentive to find companies whose shares will appreciate in the near term and incomplete information about long-term prospects, portfolio managers turn to quarterly earnings performance as perhaps the single biggest influence on buy/sell decisions. The result of this institutional structure is a high rate of trading, which the absence of taxes only accentuates. Share prices of companies who report disappointing earnings in a period are penalized. Share prices of companies that have steady earnings growth, or who are involved in doing "deals" to create investor excitement, are rewarded.

Even those investors subject to tax have no incentive to seek companies with attractive long-term prospects and that are reinvesting profits instead of paying dividends. America is also one of the few advanced nations in the world that has taxed capital gains at all, and the Tax Reform Act of

1986 led to equal taxes on capital gains and ordinary income.[25] The same tendencies as those of institutional investors are created.

The influence of these shifting goals of investors is accentuated by the process of corporate governance in public companies. Investors exercise little real influence on managements, and are rarely represented on boards of directors. The only mechanism left to discipline poorly performing managements is takeovers or mergers, which are welcomed by institutional investors because they lead to an immediate capital gain. Managers have become preoccupied with heading off takeovers through boosting near-term earnings or restructuring. While restructuring has often led to beneficial sales of underperforming assets, cost cutting, and sometimes the weeding out of poor managements, the completion of restructuring starts the same pressures running again. The taking on of substantial debt in the course of restructuring, with proceeds paid to shareholders instead of invested in the business as was the case in highly leveraged Japanese companies, often leads to risk aversion and a slowing of true strategic innovation.

The third strand in the interconnected web of influences on corporate goals in public American companies is the incentives of managers. Senior executives in many companies receive a large part of their compensation in the form of bonuses based on annual results. With relatively short tenures in office, managers have little incentive to reduce this year's bonus for the uncertain prospect of a higher one in future years. Instead, investments with long-term payouts are deferred in favor of high reported earnings to raise bonuses and the stock price.

The results of this set of circumstances are unfortunate for competitive advantage. In American companies, rate-of-return targets used to screen investment opportunities are the highest of any nation we studied. Harvesting of market positions is common. American companies flee tough competition with foreign rivals rather than fight them.[26] The prevailing way in which capital budgeting systems operate only accentuates the problem, by not including in many cases the contribution of an investment to the underlying competitive advantage of the business. Techniques that are designed to choose among discretionary investments are used to screen out non-discretionary investments required to stay competitive, leading to harvesting of market positions.

Finally, and significantly, American companies have turned more than perhaps any other nation's to mergers and alliances, a quick way to grow and create stock market excitement.[27] (With managerial compensation often based as much or more on size as rate of return on investment, further incentives to merge are created.) Unfortunately, little of the capital involved in acquisitions goes into new plants, new products, and new technology that create competitive advantage. Internal diversification, far more beneficial for national competitive advantage than acquisitions, has been out of favor.

A great deal of merger activity in the U.S. has been in support of unrelated diversification. Much of this has failed—my own research shows that well over half of the acquisitions made by a sample of leading U.S. companies were divested.[28] In the process of buying and selling largely unrelated companies, competitive advantage has been undermined in countless American industries. The experience of the patient monitoring equipment industry that I described in Chapter 5 is typical. Little innovation or competitive advantage results from such a process, only the illusion of activity.[29] There is little commitment to newly acquired businesses nor skills to bring to them. Underinvestment is common to offset the large premium over book value paid for the acquisition.

A final change of fundamental importance affecting American industry has been an ebbing of domestic rivalry. A dry rot crept into many American industries. After decades of success, industries such as autos and steel settled into comfortable oligopolies in which competition was restrained and innovation blunted.

In America (and Europe), there were many new enterprises formed after the war, and a belief in competition was reinforced by seeing its fruits. Founders were at the helm of many companies. As time passed, memories faded, and professional managers took over. Reinforced by changes in capital markets, emphasis often shifted toward defending and away from innovating. More recently, mergers among leading competitors have consolidated many American industries, made possible by a drastic relaxation of antitrust restraints on mergers by the Reagan administration.

American companies, faced with international competitive problems, have chosen bad responses. They have resorted to merging, downsizing, cutting overhead, and paring back excess capacity. With pressures to maintain earnings and a lack of appreciation of the importance of the national cluster, many have also moved to source sophisticated components and entire products abroad. While this activity has boosted short-term profitability, it has rarely led to competitive advantage. The innovation and upgrading necessary to restore true competitive advantage have yet to occur.

Instead, American companies have learned to head to Washington to seek protection and complain about dumping, and this activity continues in spite of the drastic fall in the value of the dollar. Though having a stated policy of free trade, America has in fact frequently turned to protectionism in recent years. A web of "orderly marketing agreements" of one sort or another divides up markets in many industries. Semiconductors, automobiles, and machine tools are just a few examples. Rivalry is undermined and domestic buyers are disadvantaged.

America remains a nation uniquely suited for starting new companies. Without this, the American economy would be in serious difficulty. While American firms do well in new industries, however, the problems I have discussed mean that too few new companies are becoming serious international competitors.

THE ROLE OF GOVERNMENT

The American government has wavered from a number of long-term policy directions that were crucial to American national advantage. The first is a priority on education. Though rhetoric has recently begun to reemphasize education, attention to raising educational standards has lagged. A reduced commitment to education extends beyond government to include students and parents.

The second break with American tradition is in the area of competition. Antitrust enforcement was drastically curtailed in the vital area of mergers between competitors. A permissive attitude toward cooperation and alliances among direct competitors has also developed. The response to trade difficulties has been to erect a myriad of protectionist barriers and special agreements, and there are pressures for still more.

Coupled with these shifts have been fiscal deficits in the 1980s of immense proportions that have absorbed needed investment capital and driven up relative real interest rates, stunting the rate of investment in industry. At the same time, capital gains tax incentives for investors and some other investment incentives were eliminated to raise tax revenue, making the problem worse.

Deregulation of competition has been largely a positive development, though the extent of regulation was already relatively low in the United States. The breakup of AT&T, for example, has led to dramatic improvements in service and a rapid rate of innovation, and the same is true in other industries such as trucking.

Unfortunately, however, deregulation of competition and the appropriateness of lessening regulation in other areas were confused. The United States relaxed environmental, safety, and other standards under the Reagan administration. Tough and forward-looking standards once encouraged U.S. firms to innovate in ways that gave them advantages in sophisticated product segments. Today, other nations are often out front in such areas, giving their firms an edge in winning foreign markets.

The truth is, however, that in the postwar period U.S. government policy has largely ignored industry. The emphasis has been on the social agenda and on national security. The needs of industry were often sacrificed in pursuit of other goals. For example, trade laws were not enforced to help other nations develop, and exports of American goods were embargoed for geopolitical reasons. American policy was based on the assumption that U.S. industry had a commanding position. Today, for often self-inflicted reasons, this assumption is a shaky one.

AMERICA IN PERSPECTIVE

American firms have diminished competitive advantage in a wide range of industries. The fundamental problem is a lack of dynamism. American industry, in too many fields, has fallen behind in the rate, character, and extent of improvement and innovation. The rate of upgrading has slowed down. American industry is on the defensive, preoccupied with clinging to what it has instead of advancing.

Many have begun to speak about the American weaknesses in "commercializing" technology as if it were a technology problem. But the causes of the commercialization problem are much broader, and involve the entire "diamond:" inadequate factor creation, eroding demand quality, lack of competitive supplier industries, counterproductive goals, and ebbing rivalry.

There are some who argue that trade statistics do not accurately portray America's competitive position because a good portion of U.S. imports come from the foreign affiliates of U.S. companies, and American firms have extensive production abroad. This does not imply that American industry is sound. Imports from their affiliates are frequently advanced goods for which quality and productivity, not factor costs, are the determining reasons why they are produced abroad. Xerox, for example, imports virtually all the small copiers it sells in the United States from its Japanese affiliate, Fuji-Xerox, because Xerox was unable to design and manufacture a competitive small copier in America. Full design and production responsibility rests in Japan. This story is repeated in many other companies. Foreign affiliates effectively became the home base for American-owned companies. Foreign acquisitions by U.S. firms are run as independent entities. American ownership is not an indicator of where products and processes are developed.

Conversely, American companies are being acquired in increasing numbers by stronger foreign firms. When acquired companies are left largely intact, foreign ownership has little influence on the rate of innovation and productivity growth in American industry. When many of the acquired companies become largely marketing arms and the effective home base shifts elsewhere, however, this is a sign that all is not well. The implication is *not* to restrict foreign investment, but that the environment for innovation in America is in need of improvement.

American unemployment is low relative to nations such as Germany and Britain (though not compared to Japan, Korea, Sweden, and Switzerland). New job creation has absorbed the baby boom generation and women moving into the workforce. Start-ups as well as American demand for services and strength in service industries are at the root of this success. Yet pressures for automation and upgrading of labor skills have been reduced by the ready availability of labor. Wages have been falling in real terms, and long-term productivity growth has been anemic in American industry.

The pattern of gains and losses in world export share between 1978 and 1985, summarized in Figure 9–6, provides further evidence that the upgrading of American industry is faltering. The overall gain or loss in world export share is less significant than the particular industries in which the gains or losses are occurring. Net gains are strongest in health care and chemicals, areas of U.S. strength. While there are gains in other advanced industries, however, many gains have occurred in natural resource-sensitive industries. Conversely, losses in advanced industries are widespread and have been especially heavy in transportation, food (especially machinery), and such important industries as semiconductors and computers. Losses in machinery industries are almost twice as frequent as gains, an important danger signal for the upgrading process. Overall, the number of U.S. industries capable of a significant export share is far behind that of Germany and Japan.

America is no repeat of the British story and is in little danger of losing its status as a major power. America's size, natural resources, and breadth of industries effectively preclude that. The determinants of national advantage remain favorable in many industries, and American companies retain many strong positions. The balance between gains and losses is less adverse than in several other nations. The capacity to start new companies remains strong.

Yet what is at risk is the ability to continue to advance the American standard of living. The economy is showing clear signs of drift. Factor creation is faltering, and wage pressures affecting the less skilled have led to widening disparities in income. Ebbing rivalry and underinvestment have slowed innovation and upgrading. International success is increasingly concentrated in science/spending-based industries, those connected to leisure/wealth demand, and to industries depending on inherited natural resources. The sharp fall in the value of the dollar is not a cure for these underlying problems, but in some respects will make them worse.

Productivity growth has spurted in recent years, but its fall back leads to the suspicion that it reflects the one-shot restructuring and downsizing that has taken place in many industries. The still chronically low rate of net investment in industry, and the continued evidence of competitive pressures facing many sophisticated industries despite the lower dollar, raises serious questions about the sustainability of the improvement. While exports have grown rapidly since the dramatic fall in the value of the dollar, falling real wages and the importance of natural resource-intensive exports suggest a worsening mix of trade which will erode the American standard of living. The sharp increase in investment by foreign companies in the United States

FIGURE 9–6 Competitive U.S. Industries with Gains or Losses of World Export Share of 15% or More Between 1978 and 1985*

UPSTREAM INDUSTRIES

	Materials/Metals			Forest Products			Petroleum/Chemicals			Semiconductors/Computers			UPSTREAM INDUSTRIES		
	Total Comp. Inds.	Share Gains	Share Losses	Total Comp. Inds.	Share Gains	Share Losses	Total Comp. Inds.	Share Gains	Share Losses	Total Comp. Inds.	Share Gains	Share Losses	Total Comp. Inds.	Share Gains	Share Losses
Primary Goods	12	8	8	7	2	3	23	13	6	7	2	3	49	25	20
Machinery	3	2	1	0	0	1	0	0	0	0	0	0	3	2	2
Specialty Inputs	2	0	1	0	0	0	0	0	0	0	0	0	2	0	1
Total	17	10	10	7	2	4	23	13	6	7	2	3	54	27	23

INDUSTRIAL & SUPPORTING FUNCTIONS

	Multiple Business			Transportation			Power Generation & Distribution			Office			Telecommunications			Defense			INDUSTRIAL & SUPPORTING FUNCTIONS		
	Total Comp. Inds.	Share Gains	Share Losses	Total Comp. Inds.	Share Gains	Share Losses	Total Comp. Inds.	Share Gains	Share Losses	Total Comp. Inds.	Share Gains	Share Losses	Total Comp. Inds.	Share Gains	Share Losses	Total Comp. Inds.	Share Gains	Share Losses	Total Comp. Inds.	Share Gains	Share Losses
Primary Goods	11	6	5	11	3	9	4	4	3	1	1	1	1	0	0	2	1	1	30	14	19
Machinery	3	1	0	1	0	1	0	0	0	0	0	0	0	0	0	0	0	0	4	1	4
Specialty Inputs	3	0	3	10	2	3	1	1	1	0	0	0	0	0	0	0	0	0	14	3	5
Total	17	7	8	22	5	13	5	5	4	1	1	1	1	0	0	2	1	1	48	18	28

FINAL CONSUMPTION GOODS & SERVICES

	Food/Beverage			Textiles/Apparel			Housing/Household			Health Care			Personal			Entertainment/Leisure			FINAL CONSUMPTION GOODS & SERVICES		
	Total Comp. Inds.	Share Gains	Share Losses	Total Comp. Inds.	Share Gains	Share Losses	Total Comp. Inds.	Share Gains	Share Losses	Total Comp. Inds.	Share Gains	Share Losses	Total Comp. Inds.	Share Gains	Share Losses	Total Comp. Inds.	Share Gains	Share Losses	Total Comp. Inds.	Share Gains	Share Losses
Primary Goods	27	10	14	3	2	1	1	0	0	8	4	1	2	1	1	10	5	7	51	22	29
Machinery	7	2	5	1	0	0	0	0	0	0	0	0	0	0	0	0	0	0	8	5	5
Specialty Inputs	13	6	7	10	5	3	0	0	0	0	0	0	3	2	2	0	0	0	26	13	12
Total	47	18	26	14	8	4	1	0	0	8	4	1	5	3	3	10	5	7	85	38	46

*Gains and losses include industries exceeding the cutoff in either 1978 or 1985, including those that were competitive in 1978 but fell below the cutoff in 1985 or that had first achieved sufficient share to exceed the cutoff in 1985. The total number of competitive industries refers to 1985.

is also a danger signal, as I have suggested, that the upgrading of technology and productivity in American firms is lagging.

By achieving economic dominance so completely and so easily, American firms and policy makers may well have failed to understand the underpinnings of this success. America's traditional confidence, which contrasts starkly with German and Japanese circumspection, is one indication of this. The inability in the United States to gain consensus even that U.S. industry faces problems in international competition, much less on solutions, is in many ways the most disturbing sign of all.

POSTWAR DEVELOPMENT IN PERSPECTIVE

Each of the nations I have discussed has a unique mix of successful industries and has reached its current position through a unique historical process for reasons I have begun to explain. The cluster charts for each nation reveal substantial and often striking interconnections among the industries in which it is internationally successful. These links provide support for my theory. I believe that the clusters would be even sharper if more detailed and complete data were available. Such data would likely illuminate even clearer connections between a nation's machinery, input, and end-use industries, because machinery and input categories tend to be more aggregated. In addition, nations would hold higher shares in narrower industries and industry segments now lumped into broader categories.

Figure 9–7 compares the eight nations in terms of the percentage of their exports accounted for by internationally competitive industries in each broad sector.[30] Sectors encompass entire clusters including machinery and specialized inputs, not just end products. While these summary statistics are only one crude indication of the competitive position of national economies, the differences among nations are striking. Sweden relies heavily on materials/metals, forest products, and transportation; Switzerland on multiple business, textiles and apparel, health care, and personal products; Japan on entertainment and leisure, transportation, and materials/metals; Italy on apparel, food, and household goods; and Britain on petroleum and chemicals.

More striking in many ways is Figure 9–8, which summarizes the share of world cluster exports accounted for by the nation's competitive industries in each broad sector. (Figure 9–9 presents separate shares for petroleum and chemicals because of particularly significant differences in national position.) America has the leading position in food, health care, defense, and semiconductors/computers. Germany leads in chemicals and materials/metals; Japan in entertainment/leisure, office products, telecommunications, power generation and distribution, and transportation; and Italy in textiles/ apparel, housing/household goods, and personal products.

FIGURE 9-7 Share of Country Exports of Competitive Industries by Broad Cluster, 1985

Materials / Metals

Sweden	12.5	(−1.7)
Germany	10.0	(−2.3)
Korea	9.6	(−1.8)
Japan	9.6	(−6.4)
Italy	8.5	(−1.9)
U.K.	4.0	(−1.6)
Switzerland	3.8	(0.1)
U.S.A.	1.5	(−0.6)

Forest Products

Sweden	17.9	(−2.5)
Germany	2.0	(0.3)
U.S.A.	1.3	(−0.3)
Switzerland	1.0	(0.3)
Italy	1.0	(+0.0)
Japan	0.2	(+0.0)
Korea	0.2	(−4.0)
U.K.	0.1	(−0.1)

Petroleum / Chemicals

U.K.	24.8	(15.0)
Germany	8.6	(1.2)
Switzerland	8.0	(1.2)
U.S.A.	6.3	(1.8)
Italy	2.5	(0.6)
Sweden	2.6	(0.5)
Korea	1.8	(1.4)
Japan	1.3	(−0.5)

Semiconductors / Computers

U.S.A.	8.8	(4.5)
Japan	4.7	(3.6)
Korea	3.8	(0.9)
U.K.	3.5	(2.4)
Sweden	2.1	(0.9)
Germany	0.6	(0.3)
Switzerland	0.0	(0.1)
Italy	0.4	(+0.0)

UPSTREAM INDUSTRIES

Sweden	35.1	(−2.9)
U.K.	32.4	(15.7)
Germany	21.2	(−0.5)
U.S.A.	17.9	(5.4)
Japan	15.6	(−3.3)
Korea	15.4	(0.1)
Switzerland	12.5	(1.8)
Italy	12.3	(−1.2)

Multiple Business

Switzerland	28.1	(1.6)
U.S.A.	9.4	(2.0)
Germany	7.0	(0.4)
U.K.	6.3	(−2.4)
Japan	3.7	(0.1)
Sweden	4.2	(+0.0)
Italy	3.5	(0.4)
Korea	0.3	(−0.2)

Transportation

Japan	36.9	(1.0)
Germany	23.7	(0.5)
Korea	20.4	(10.4)
Sweden	20.5	(−0.4)
U.S.A.	18.4	(0.5)
U.K.	12.1	(−5.3)
Italy	6.7	(−4.8)
Switzerland	2.1	(−0.4)

Power Generation & Distribution

Switzerland	4.4	(−0.6)
Germany	3.8	(−1.3)
Japan	3.3	(−0.6)
U.K.	2.0	(−0.5)
Korea	1.5	(0.5)
Sweden	1.0	(−0.7)
U.S.A.	0.8	(0.2)
Italy	0.8	(−0.4)

Office

Japan	3.5	(0.5)
Switzerland	2.3	(0.1)
Italy	1.0	(−0.4)
U.K.	1.6	(−0.2)
Germany	1.6	(−0.0)
Sweden	0.7	(−0.1)
Korea	0.5	(−0.6)
U.S.A.	0.1	(−0.0)

Telecommunications

Sweden	3.7	(0.6)
Japan	3.4	(1.4)
Korea	0.7	(0.3)
Italy	0.5	(−0.0)
U.K.	0.3	(−0.1)
U.S.A.	0.2	(0.2)
Switzerland	0.0	(−0.1)
Germany	0.0	(−0.2)

Defense

U.S.A.	1.5	(0.1)
Sweden	0.7	(−0.0)
Italy	0.3	(−0.2)
U.K.	0.6	(−0.1)
Germany	0.0	(0.0)
Korea	0.0	(−0.1)
Switzerland	0.0	(−0.7)

INDUSTRIAL AND SUPPORTING FUNCTIONS

Japan	50.8	(2.3)
Switzerland	36.9	(0.1)
Germany	36.2	(−0.7)
Sweden	30.7	(−0.6)
U.S.A.	30.4	(2.9)
Korea	23.0	(10.4)
U.K.	22.8	(−8.6)
Italy	12.7	(−5.3)

Food / Beverage

U.S.A.	10.8	(−5.0)
Italy	8.8	(0.1)
Germany	4.7	(−0.1)
Switzerland	4.7	(0.1)
U.K.	4.1	(−1.2)
Korea	4.3	(−4.3)
Sweden	2.5	(0.1)
Japan	0.7	(−0.1)

Textiles / Apparel

Korea	29.4	(−10.6)
Italy	19.6	(2.0)
Switzerland	11.0	(−1.0)
Germany	5.0	(−0.6)
Japan	3.2	(−1.5)
U.K.	2.6	(−1.7)
U.S.A.	2.2	(−0.5)
Sweden	1.1	(+0.0)

Housing / Household

Italy	9.5	(−0.5)
Sweden	3.9	(+0.0)
Germany	3.3	(−0.6)
Korea	2.6	(−0.0)
Japan	2.3	(0.4)
U.K.	1.3	(−1.4)
Switzerland	0.9	(0.1)
U.S.A.	0.0	(−0.1)

Health Care

Switzerland	7.0	(0.2)
Sweden	2.5	(0.6)
U.S.A.	2.4	(0.8)
U.K.	2.1	(0.1)
Germany	1.9	(0.3)
Japan	0.7	(0.3)
Italy	0.6	(0.1)
Korea	0.0	(+0.0)

Personal

Switzerland	8.0	(−2.2)
Italy	4.3	(0.6)
Korea	2.1	(−1.5)
Japan	1.6	(−0.4)
U.K.	1.2	(−2.9)
Germany	1.1	(+0.0)
U.S.A.	0.8	(−1.0)
Sweden	0.1	(0.0)

Entertainment / Leisure

Japan	11.8	(2.4)
Korea	8.0	(1.6)
U.K.	3.3	(−0.6)
U.S.A.	1.3	(−0.1)
Germany	1.1	(−0.1)
Italy	0.9	(−0.5)
Switzerland	0.5	(0.1)
Sweden	0.5	(−0.2)

FINAL CONSUMPTION GOODS AND SERVICES

Korea	46.3	(−14.9)
Italy	43.7	(1.8)
Switzerland	32.0	(−2.7)
Japan	20.3	(1.0)
U.S.A.	17.5	(−5.6)
Germany	17.1	(−1.0)
U.K.	14.7	(−7.7)
Sweden	10.6	(0.5)

note: Numbers in parentheses are changes between 1978 and 1985. Exports are those of competitive industries, not all industries.

FIGURE 9–8 Share of World Cluster Exports of Competitive Industries by Nation, 1985

Materials/Metals

Nation	Share	Change
Germany	11.9	(–2.5)
Japan	10.8	(–1.7)
Italy	4.2	(–0.4)
U.K.	3.3	(–0.4)
U.S.A.	2.6	(–0.3)
Sweden	2.4	(–0.1)
Korea	1.8	(+1.0)
Switzerland	0.7	(–0.0)

Forest Products

Nation	Share	Change
Sweden	10.5	(–1.3)
Germany	7.3	(+2.6)
U.S.A.	5.9	(–0.7)
Italy	1.9	(+0.1)
Japan	1.0	(+0.3)
U.K.	0.7	(–0.1)
Switzerland	0.6	(+0.1)
Korea	0.4	(–1.2)

Petroleum/Chemicals

Nation	Share	Change
U.K.	6.9	(+3.6)
Germany	4.6	(–0.7)
U.S.A.	4.1	(+0.6)
Japan	1.0	(–0.2)
Italy	0.6	(+0.0)
Switzerland	0.6	(+0.2)
Korea	0.2	(+0.1)
Sweden	0.2	(+0.0)

Semiconductors/Computers

Nation	Share	Change
U.S.A.	20.5	(–8.9)
Japan	11.3	(+6.3)
U.K.	6.3	(–0.6)
Germany	1.9	(–1.4)
Korea	1.6	(–0.4)
Sweden	0.9	(–0.4)
Italy	0.4	(–0.5)
Switzerland	0.0	(–0.1)

UPSTREAM INDUSTRIES

Nation	Share	Change
Germany	6.3	(–1.9)
U.S.A.	5.7	(+0.7)
U.K.	5.5	(+2.1)
Japan	4.6	(–0.4)
Sweden	1.7	(–0.4)
Italy	1.6	(–0.4)
Korea	0.8	(0.2)
Switzerland	0.6	(–0.1)

Multiple Business

Nation	Share	Change
U.S.A.	18.2	(+3.2)
Germany	10.8	(–1.1)
Switzerland	6.4	(–1.4)
U.K.	6.1	(–2.1)
Japan	5.5	(+0.9)
Italy	2.4	(+0.1)
Korea	1.1	(–0.1)
Sweden	0.2	(+0.0)

Transportation

Nation	Share	Change
Japan	22.6	(+4.2)
Germany	15.0	(–2.0)
U.S.A.	13.4	(–1.1)
U.K.	4.6	(–1.9)
Italy	3.5	(–1.5)
Sweden	2.3	(–0.2)
Korea	2.1	(+1.5)
Switzerland	0.5	(–0.1)

Power Generation & Distribution

Nation	Share	Change
Germany	17.3	(–8.1)
Japan	14.6	(+1.0)
U.S.A.	13.8	(+1.7)
U.K.	7.2	(–0.8)
Italy	4.0	(–0.9)
Switzerland	2.9	(+0.1)
Korea	1.1	(+0.6)
Sweden	1.1	(–0.5)

Office

Nation	Share	Change
Japan	28.0	(+8.5)
Germany	16.3	(–2.5)
U.K.	8.3	(–0.7)
U.S.A.	7.3	(–0.0)
Switzerland	3.8	(–0.8)
Italy	3.6	(–1.5)
Sweden	1.0	(–0.2)
Korea	0.7	(–0.3)

Telecommunications

Nation	Share	Change
Japan	28.1	(+8.8)
U.S.A.	6.2	(–0.2)
Sweden	5.5	(–1.5)
U.K.	3.9	(–2.2)
Italy	1.9	(–0.8)
Korea	1.0	(+0.5)
Germany	0.0	(–7.0)
Switzerland	0.0	(–1.0)

Defense

Nation	Share	Change
U.S.A.	55.0	(–0.1)
U.K.	10.3	(–2.7)
Italy	7.4	(–3.3)
Sweden	3.6	(–0.6)
Germany	0.0	(0.0)
Switzerland	0.0	(–4.3)
Korea	0.0	(0.0)
Japan	0.3	(0.0)

INDUSTRIAL AND SUPPORTING FUNCTIONS

Nation	Share	Change
Japan	17.4	(+3.5)
U.S.A.	14.5	(+0.2)
Germany	13.8	(–2.6)
U.K.	5.4	(–1.9)
Italy	3.3	(–1.1)
Switzerland	2.1	(–0.6)
Sweden	2.0	(–0.2)
Korea	1.4	(+0.9)

Food/Beverage

Nation	Share	Change
U.S.A.	12.1	(–2.1)
Germany	4.4	(+0.2)
Italy	3.5	(+0.5)
U.K.	2.5	(–0.0)
Japan	0.7	(+0.2)
Korea	0.7	(0.0)
Switzerland	0.6	(–0.0)
Sweden	0.4	(+0.1)

Textiles/Apparel

Nation	Share	Change
Italy	12.0	(+1.2)
Germany	7.1	(–1.6)
Korea	6.6	(+1.3)
Japan	4.9	(–0.5)
U.S.A.	3.7	(–0.5)
U.K.	2.6	(–1.1)
Switzerland	2.4	(–0.7)
Sweden	0.3	(0.0)

Housing/Household

Nation	Share	Change
Italy	13.8	(+1.1)
Germany	12.0	(–1.8)
Japan	8.2	(+3.4)
U.K.	4.2	(–1.7)
Sweden	2.4	(+0.2)
Korea	1.6	(–0.7)
Switzerland	0.6	(+0.1)
U.S.A.	0.3	(–0.3)

Health Care

Nation	Share	Change
U.S.A.	19.2	(+4.2)
Germany	13.9	(–2.2)
U.K.	8.8	(–1.3)
Switzerland	7.2	(–3.4)
Japan	4.7	(+1.9)
Sweden	2.8	(–0.1)
Italy	1.8	(–0.3)
Korea	0.1	(+0.1)

Personal

Nation	Share	Change
Germany	10.5	(–0.2)
Italy	6.6	(+1.4)
U.S.A.	6.4	(–2.8)
Japan	5.3	(+0.3)
Switzerland	4.4	(–1.9)
U.K.	2.4	(–4.7)
Korea	1.4	(+0.1)
Sweden	0.1	(+0.0)

Entertainment/Leisure

Nation	Share	Change
Japan	32.7	(+8.4)
U.K.	6.0	(–1.9)
U.S.A.	5.7	(–1.0)
Korea	3.8	(+1.7)
Germany	3.6	(–1.3)
Italy	1.3	(–1.0)
Sweden	0.3	(–0.2)
Switzerland	0.2	(+0.1)

FINAL CONSUMPTION GOODS AND SERVICES

Nation	Share	Change
U.S.A.	7.9	(–1.4)
Japan	6.9	(+2.0)
Germany	6.8	(–0.7)
Italy	6.7	(+0.6)
U.K.	3.4	(–1.0)
Korea	2.7	(+0.7)
Switzerland	1.7	(–0.4)
Sweden	0.6	(+0.1)

note: Numbers in parentheses are changes between 1978 and 1985
Exports are those of competitive industries, not all industries

Share of Country Exports

Petroleum and Related Products   **Chemicals**

United Kingdom	19.9	(14.5)
Germany	5.1	(0.8)
United States	3.4	(1.5)
Italy	2.6	(–0.4)
Switzerland	1.9	(0.5)
Korea	1.7	(1.5)
Sweden	1.5	(0.3)
Japan	0.5	(0.1)

Switzerland	6.1	(0.5)
Germany	4.3	(0.8)
United Kingdom	3.9	(0.9)
United States	2.9	(0.5)
Italy	1.4	(0.8)
Sweden	1.1	(0.3)
Japan	0.8	(–0.1)
Korea	0.1	(–0.1)

Share of World Cluster Exports

Petroleum and Related Products   **Chemicals**

United Kingdom	6.3	(4.3)
Germany	2.9	(–0.6)
United States	2.3	(0.5)
Italy	0.6	(–2.1)
Japan	0.3	(0.1)
Korea	0.2	(0.2)
Switzerland	0.2	(0.0)
Sweden	0.1	(0.0)

Germany	16.0	(–2.2)
United States	12.7	(–1.9)
United Kingdom	8.1	(0.8)
Switzerland	3.4	(–1.4)
Japan	2.8	(–0.3)
Italy	2.3	(1.9)
Sweden	0.7	(0.1)
Korea	0.1	(0.0)

NOTE: Numbers in parentheses are changes between 1978 and 1985.

FIGURE **9–9 Breakdown of Petroleum and Chemical Exports of Competitive Industries by Nation, 1985**

Sweden's strong positions are concentrated in the upstream and industrial levels of the cluster charts, while Italy's are highly skewed toward final consumption goods. Japan is strongest along the middle of the chart. Switzerland, Germany, and the United Kingdom are represented more equally at all levels.

The patterns of competitive success in any nation are not static, and the eight nations I discuss are no exception. Figure 9–10 summarizes one partial manifestation of the evolving nature of competitive advantage, a summary tabulation of the number of competitive industries that gained or lost 15 percent or more world export share over the 1978 to 1985 period. The changes are classified by broad sector and by vertical stage within sectors. The specific industries that have gained and lost are far more important than the number because of the indication they provide about whether or not the economy is upgrading in a healthy way. I have discussed the nature

FIGURE 9–10 Competitive Industries with Gains or Losses of World Export Share of 15% or More Between 1978 and 1985 by Nation*

Materials/Metals

	Gns	Ls
Korea	24	6
Italy	15	15
United States	10	10
Sweden	18	21
Switzerland	3	7
Japan	12	18
United Kingdom	12	24
Germany	13	26

Forest Products

	Gns	Ls
Switzerland	4	2
Japan	1	0
Germany	2	3
Italy	2	3
United Kingdom	0	1
United States	2	4
Korea	2	6
Sweden	7	14

Petroleum/Chemicals

	Gns	Ls
United States	13	6
Korea	6	1
Italy	10	13
Japan	8	11
Sweden	4	1
United Kingdom	14	19
Switzerland	3	11
Germany	6	23

Computers/Semiconductors

	Gns	Ls
Japan	6	0
Italy	0	0
United States	2	3
Sweden	0	1
Switzerland	2	4
United Kingdom	1	3
Korea	1	3
Germany	0	4

PRIMARY GOODS

	Gns	Ls
Korea	108	60
United States	95	53
Japan	59	68
Italy	84	98
Sweden	47	66
Switzerland	35	88
Germany	50	128
United Kingdom	47	128

Multiple Business

	Gns	Ls
Japan	10	1
Italy	8	1
Korea	3	1
Sweden	3	3
United States	6	8
United Kingdom	6	13
Germany	2	10
Switzerland	12	29

Transportation

	Gns	Ls
Japan	40	5
Korea	9	4
Italy	13	13
Sweden	11	11
Switzerland	1	5
United States	5	13
Germany	3	23
United Kingdom	2	36

Power Generation/Distribution

	Gns	Ls
Korea	8	1
Japan	10	6
United States	4	5
Italy	3	6
Sweden	3	7
United Kingdom	3	8
Switzerland	2	7
Germany	5	13

Office

	Gns	Ls
Japan	9	0
Korea	3	3
Italy	1	1
United States	3	4
United Kingdom	0	1
Switzerland	3	5
Sweden	2	4
Germany	0	7

Defense

	Gns	Ls
United States	1	1
Italy	1	1
Korea	0	0
Germany	0	0
Japan	0	1
Sweden	0	1
United Kingdom	0	1
Switzerland	0	1

Telecommunications

	Gns	Ls
Japan	3	0
Korea	2	3
Italy	0	0
United States	0	0
United Kingdom	0	1
Germany	0	5
Sweden	0	4
Switzerland	0	7

UPSTREAM INDUSTRIES

	Gns	Ls
Korea	33	16
United States	27	23
Japan	27	29
Italy	27	31
Switzerland	10	21
Sweden	29	37
United Kingdom	28	48
Germany	21	56

MACHINERY

	Gns	Ls
Japan	29	2
Italy	28	7
Sweden	9	7
Korea	1	1
United States	6	11
Switzerland	7	14
Germany	5	18
United Kingdom	4	25

INDUSTRIAL/SUPPORTING FUNCTIONS

	Gns	Ls
Japan	72	13
Korea	22	7
Italy	28	25
Sweden	19	28
United States	17	28
Switzerland	18	49
Germany	10	55
United Kingdom	14	62

Food/Beverage

	Gns	Ls
Germany	15	11
Italy	12	8
Sweden	12	8
Japan	6	4
Switzerland	5	5
Korea	7	11
United States	18	26
United Kingdom	9	17

Housing/Household

	Gns	Ls
Italy	18	8
Japan	7	0
Sweden	6	6
Switzerland	3	3
United States	0	1
Korea	7	4
Germany	3	12
United Kingdom	2	16

Textiles/Apparel

	Gns	Ls
Korea	32	3
Italy	29	23
United States	8	4
Japan	11	10
Sweden	3	1
United Kingdom	12	17
Germany	8	18
Switzerland	4	30

Health Care

	Gns	Ls
United States	4	3
Japan	3	1
Sweden	2	2
Korea	0	1
Italy	3	1
United Kingdom	2	4
Germany	1	3
Switzerland	0	6

Personal

	Gns	Ls
Japan	6	1
Korea	8	7
Sweden	1	1
United Kingdom	0	1
Switzerland	6	9
United States	3	7
Italy	1	3
Germany	2	6

Entertainment/Leisure

	Gns	Ls
Japan	14	3
Korea	13	4
Sweden	1	1
United States	5	7
Switzerland	0	3
Italy	3	7
Germany	2	9
United Kingdom	2	11

FINAL CONSUMPTION GOODS AND SERVICES

	Gns	Ls
Japan	47	19
Italy	78	55
Korea	67	50
Sweden	21	18
United States	38	46
Germany	34	59
Switzerland	22	44
United Kingdom	19	80

SPECIALTY INPUTS

	Gns	Ls
Japan	22	6
Italy	21	11
Sweden	13	10
Korea	13	12
United States	16	18
Switzerland	8	12
Germany	10	24
United Kingdom	10	37

*Gains and losses include industries exceeding the cutoff in either 1978 or 1985, including those that were competitive in 1978 or that had first achieved sufficient share to exceed the cutoff in 1985.

of the gaining and losing industries in my treatment of each nation. The ratio of gainers to losers is also more meaningful for comparison than the absolute numbers, which are sensitive to the disaggregation of the trade classification system in the particular sectors where a nation is competitive as well as to the nation's size. While highly imperfect, these data nevertheless illustrate broad patterns that are generally confirmed by more detailed examination.

Japan, Italy, and Korea are the nations most clearly improving and upgrading market positions in international competition. The health of Italian and Japanese upgrading is manifested in the strong improvement in machinery and specialty input industries, and confirmed by the particular industries in which share gains and losses are occurring. Gains have been registered by many advanced industries, while losses in many cases are in industries sensitive to factor costs or natural resources. Korea's strong net gains are almost exclusively in primary goods, but they are goods of rising sophistication. One sign of Korean upgrading is a high ratio of gains to losses in industrial and supporting sectors, where advantage normally depends on a strong base of industry and considerable technological strength.

The other five nations have all lost share in more industries than gained it. The United States and Sweden are closest to balance. Sweden has held its own in the clusters where it has traditionally been strong, especially in machinery and specialty inputs, but is generally losing position in sectors where it has been weak. The United States shows a less attractive pattern, as I have just described. While the ratio of gains to losses is highly favorable in health care and chemicals, America has lost share much more often in machinery than gained it. In addition, many of the U.S. share gains are in natural resource-intensive or commodity goods in the materials and metals, food and beverage, and petroleum and chemical sectors.

Switzerland, Germany, and the United Kingdom had the worst ratios of gains to losses. In Switzerland and Germany, there are expected gains in some sophisticated industries and expected losses in factor cost or resource-sensitive industries. However, there are also many losses in both nations that represent clear signs that the upgrading process may be faltering. Both Germany and Switzerland have negative ratios of gains to losses in machinery. Germany has large net losses in chemicals and transport equipment (both partly due to foreign investment) and in semiconductors/computers. Switzerland had no gains and six losses in health care, an important area of strength, and significant net losses in power generation and distribution and personal products. These are hard to rationalize in terms of upgrading.

The United Kingdom had net losses across the board, and the pattern of gains and losses was the least encouraging. The United Kingdom registered a greater relative erosion in machinery and specialty input industries than in primary products. The most gains occurred in petroleum-related industries and in relatively unprocessed materials and metals. Some gains in computers (and a net gain in total world computer cluster export share) are positive, as is the British strength in international service competition, but the challenge of restarting the upgrading process in British manufacturing is palpable.

I have begun the process of explaining these dynamics. In order to bring them more fully into view, however, it is necessary to extend the theory further. The basic unit of analysis for understanding national advantage is the industry and industry cluster. However, the same principles can help explain the process by which entire national economies advance or fall behind.

10

The Competitive Development of National Economies

I have explored, one by one, the pattern and evolution of industrial success in a number of leading trading nations. What is clear is that, like industries, national economies are anything but static. There have been striking changes in the pattern of internationally successful industries in many nations since World War II. Upgrading in an economy is the movement toward more sophisticated sources of competitive advantage and toward positions in higher-productivity segments and industries. Such a process supports rapid overall productivity growth. Some national economies have shown a remarkable rate of upgrading. Other nations have experienced greater difficulty in sustaining the upgrading process, and their productivity growth has languished. As one examines the postwar development of the nations as a group, some basic forces seem to have been propelling change. At the same time, some characteristic impediments to upgrading reappear.

My purpose here is to extend my theory to consider the national economy as a whole, and provide some ways of thinking about how entire national economies progress in competitive terms. While the basic unit of analysis in understanding national advantage is the industry and industry cluster, the nature of competitive advantage achieved by many of a nation's industries tends to evolve together. This occurs for reasons I will describe.

Nations can be seen as differing in the stage of competitive development in international terms achieved by their industry. The stages represent one way of abstracting the upgrading process in a national economy. Each stage

involves different industries and industry segments as well as different company strategies. The stages also differ substantially in the appropriate array
of government policies toward industry.

The stages will provide a framework with which we can examine the
postwar development of the nations as a group. They serve as one means
of interpreting the considerable amount of information about each nation
that I have presented. The stages, and the requirements of moving among
them, will also serve as a useful foundation for my discussion of company
strategy and government policy.

ECONOMIC DEVELOPMENT

It is a considerable understatement to observe that there has been a great
deal written on economic development and the broad question of how an
economy progresses. The literature emphasizes such questions as how an
economy moves from agrarian to industrial to postindustrial, and the changing
attitudes and institutions that accompany such development.[1]

My concern here is with a different and somewhat narrower set of questions.
Economic prosperity depends on the productivity with which national resources are employed. The level and growth of productivity are a function
of the array of industries and industry segments in which a nation's firms
can successfully compete, and the nature over time of the competitive advantages achieved in them. Economies progress by *upgrading* their competitive
positions, through achieving higher-order competitive advantages in existing
industries and developing the capability to compete successfully in new,
high-productivity segments and industries. Trade, in which exports from
productive industries allow imports of products that could be produced in
the nation only at lower productivity, is essential to the upgrading process.
So is foreign direct investment that shifts less productive activities abroad
or that allows high productivity industries to better penetrate foreign markets.

A nation's industries are either upgrading and extending their competitive
advantages or are falling behind. The mutual reinforcement of industries
within clusters means that the upgrading process tends to spread. Attaining
higher-order competitive advantage in one industry often helps other industries upgrade. Part and parcel of the upgrading process is *loss of position*
in price-sensitive segments and in products involving less sophisticated skills
and technology.

Yet the process also works in reverse. The inability to improve and
innovate fast enough to sustain position in advanced industries and segments
can undermine position in others. When a nation's firms begin falling behind
in quality, features, and process technology, then there is a cause for concern
that the upgrading of industry is faltering. National economies are always
in a fluid state, reflecting the balance of these forces.

The ability to upgrade an economy depends heavily on the position of a nation's firms in that portion of the economy exposed to international competition. This is the part of the economy that I focus on here. It contains many of the industries and industry segments where there is potential for achieving high and rising levels of productivity. Without the ability to export (and sustain position against imports) in a range of such industries, national productivity growth will be stunted. The capacity to export in advanced industries, which allows imports in less productive fields, is also fundamental to the upgrading process.

Widespread global competition has made the portion of leading economies subject to international competition more and more decisive to national economic prosperity. As was evident in Table 1–1, the sum of imports and exports account for over half of GDP in some nations. Even where actual trade is a lower percentage of GDP, as in the United States, a large part of the economy is exposed to trade or to foreign competition in the form of subsidiaries of foreign firms. The ability to sustain a level of national prosperity becomes increasingly at risk.

STAGES OF COMPETITIVE DEVELOPMENT

National economies exhibit a number of stages of competitive development reflecting the characteristic sources of advantage of a nation's firms in international competition and the nature and extent of internationally successful industries and clusters.[2] The stages address a nation's position in those industries subject to international competition, though they also capture the state of competition in many purely domestic industries.[3] It is *not* inevitable that nations pass through the stages.

The stages do not purport to explain everything about a nation or its development process. Some important concerns in development are inevitably left out, and no nation will fit a stage exactly. Instead, the stages are an effort to highlight those attributes of a nation's industry most important to rising economic prosperity.

Any national economy contains a range of industries with widely different sources of competitive advantage. Even in advanced nations such as the United States and Germany there are industries whose competitive position derives almost solely from natural resources, even though the competitive advantages of most successful industries are much broader and more sophisticated.

Despite the diversity of most economies, we can identify a predominant or emergent pattern in the nature of competitive advantage in a nation's firms at a particular time. The pattern is reflected in the industries and segments in which the nation's firms can successfully compete as well as

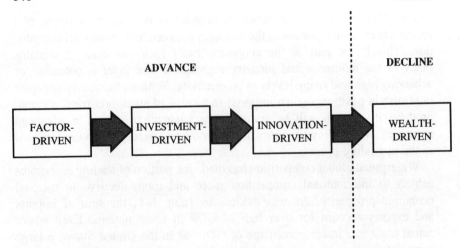

ADVANCE   DECLINE

FACTOR-DRIVEN → INVESTMENT-DRIVEN → INNOVATION-DRIVEN → WEALTH-DRIVEN

FIGURE 10–1 **Four Stages of National Competitive Development**

the types of strategies they employ. This is because the state of the "diamond," or determinants of national advantage, is similar across a range of industries in the nation though the specific conditions in each industry are unique. A central tendency in the nature of competitive advantage is also present because clustering serves to make groups of industries in a nation develop and upgrade in somewhat parallel ways. Moreover, the quality of factors often develops in parallel across industries because factor pools (such as skilled human resources) span groups of industries, and factor-creating mechanisms develop in tandem (partly because of demonstration effects). Approaches to competing, as well as prevailing norms and values, also spread from industry to industry.

My theory suggests four distinct stages of national competitive development: factor-driven, investment-driven, innovation-driven, and wealth-driven. They are illustrated schematically in Figure 10–1. The first three stages involve successive upgrading of a nation's competitive advantages and will normally be associated with progressively rising economic prosperity. The fourth stage is one of drift and ultimately decline. These stages, though broad schematics, provide one way of understanding how economies develop, the characteristic problems faced by a nation's firms at different points in time, and the forces that propel the economy to advance or cause it to falter.

FACTOR-DRIVEN

In nations at this initial stage, virtually all internationally successful industries in the nation draw their advantage almost solely from *basic* factors of production, whether they are natural resources, favorable growing conditions for certain crops, or an abundant and inexpensive semi-skilled labor pool. In the "diamond," only factor conditions are an advantage (Figure 10–2).This source of competitive advantage limits sharply the range of industries and industry segments in which the nation's firms can successfully compete in international terms.

A nation's indigenous firms in such an economy compete solely on the basis of price in industries that require either little product or process technology or technology that is inexpensive and widely available. Technology is sourced largely from other nations and not created. This occurs in some industries through imitation or more often the acquisition of foreign capital

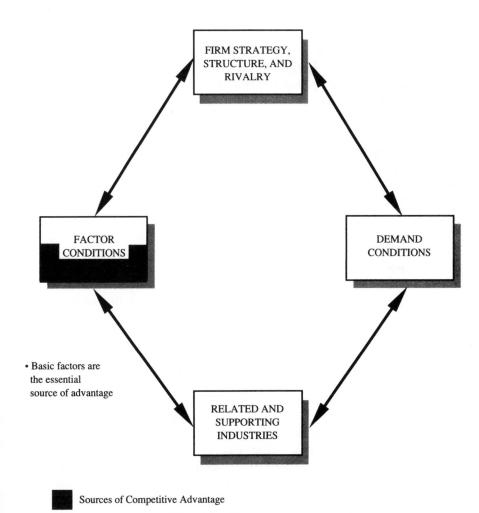

• Basic factors are the essential source of advantage

Sources of Competitive Advantage

FIGURE 10–2 **The Factor-Driven Economy**

goods. More advanced product designs and technologies are obtained through passive investments in turn-key plants or are provided directly by foreign firms that operate production bases in the nation or have OEM arrangements with local producers. Very few of a nation's firms at this stage have direct contact with end users. Foreign firms provide most of the access to foreign markets. Domestic demand for exported goods may be modest or even non-existent.

In this stage, an economy is sensitive to world economic cycles and exchange rates, which drive demand and relative prices. It is also vulnerable to the loss of factor advantage to other nations and to rapidly shifting industry leadership. While the possession of abundant natural resources may support a high per capita income for a sustained period of time, a factor-driven economy is one with a poor foundation for sustained productivity growth, as I will discuss later.

The factor-driven stage is one that has characterized virtually all nations at some point in time. Nearly all developing nations are at this stage, as are virtually all centrally planned economies. Some prosperous nations with bountiful resources such as Canada and Australia are also at this stage.

Few nations ever move beyond the factor-driven stage. The mix of domestically oriented industries in a factor-driven economy may widen over time through import substitution, which is often the result of protecting the home market from foreign competition. However, import-substituting domestic industries lack competitive advantage in international terms and, if protection is widespread, may actually reduce national productivity due to their inefficiency.

INVESTMENT-DRIVEN

In this stage, national competitive advantage is based on the willingness and ability of a nation and its firms to invest aggressively. Firms invest to construct modern, efficient, and often large-scale facilities equipped with the best technology available on global markets. They also invest to acquire more complex foreign product and process technology through licenses, joint ventures, and other means, which allows competing in more sophisticated industries and industry segments. Such technology is typically a generation behind international leaders, who are usually unwilling to sell the latest generation. In this stage, however, foreign technology and methods are *not just applied but improved upon.* The ability of a nation's industry to absorb and improve foreign technology is essential to reaching the investment-driven stage, and is a crucial difference between the factor- and investment-driven stages. Foreign technology and methods are mastered in-house, and firms from the nation begin developing their own refinements including their own product models. Passive investment in turn-key plants is insufficient.

Nations, their citizens, and firms all invest in an investment-driven economy to upgrade factors from basic to more advanced and create a modern infrastructure. Increasingly skilled workers and a growing pool of technical personnel, still paid relatively low wages, operate the sophisticated facilities and provide the internal capability to assimilate and improve technology. A nation's firms establish at least some international marketing channels of their own as well as direct contact with buyers, to supplement OEM or sourcing relationships with foreign firms. Intense domestic rivalry in the industries in which the nation competes propels firms to invest continuously to push down costs, improve product quality, introduce new models, and modernize processes. The presence of corporate goals that support investments in technology and capital assets is also an important condition. Essential to achieving this stage is that the nation's firms are risk takers, and that new entry leads to the presence in many industries of a number of domestic rivals that compete fiercely.

In the investment-driven stage, competitive advantages are drawn from improving factor conditions as well as firm strategy, structure, and rivalry (see Figure 10–3). While a nation's firms still retain advantages in basic factor costs, competitive advantages widen to include low-cost but more advanced factors (for example, university-trained engineers) and the presence of well-functioning mechanisms for factor creation, such as educational institutions and research institutes, though the nation's factor pools are still relatively generalized ones. More sophisticated and better assimilated technology and modern facilities allow the nation's pool of factors to be employed much more efficiently at this stage.

The investment-driven stage, as its name indicates, is one where the ability and willingness to invest is the principal advantage rather than the ability to offer unique products or produce with unique processes. At this stage, firms still compete in the relatively standardized, price-sensitive segments of the market, and product designs often reflect foreign market needs. Product designs are at least one generation behind the world's most advanced ones. Process technologies are near the state of the art but do not advance it. Yet the range of industries and industry segments in which the nation's firms can successfully compete is broader than in the factor-driven stage, and the industries have much higher entry barriers. Some industries in the economy inevitably take the lead in upgrading to investment-driven advantage, and then the process spreads to others.

Home demand at this stage is largely unsophisticated, because the standard of living is modest though improving and because there exists only a narrow and still emerging base of sophisticated industrial firms. In some industries, home demand for exported goods may be all but absent. A nation upgrades

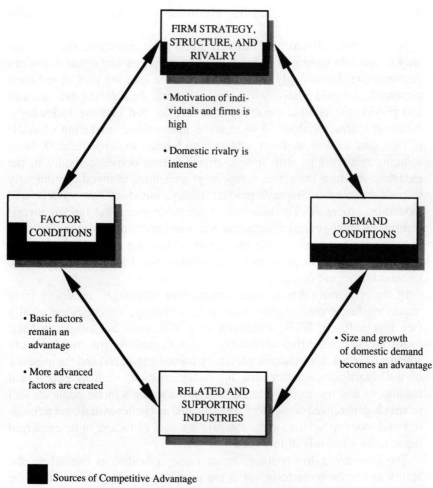

FIRM STRATEGY,
STRUCTURE, AND
RIVALRY

• Motivation of indi-
viduals and firms is
high

• Domestic rivalry is
intense

FACTOR
CONDITIONS

DEMAND
CONDITIONS

• Basic factors
remain an
advantage

• More advanced
factors are created

• Size and growth
of domestic demand
becomes an advantage

RELATED AND
SUPPORTING
INDUSTRIES

Sources of Competitive Advantage

FIGURE **10–3 The Investment-Driven Economy**

competitive advantage in this stage more from supply push than demand
pull.

However, the industries in which a nation is most likely to be successful
in the investment-driven stage are those where its home market demand is
relatively large due to local circumstances (such as shipbuilding in Japan
and then Korea, where each nation had unusually large water transportation
needs given its location), or where home market needs are heavily weighted
toward segments that have been ignored elsewhere (such as Japan in small
black and white TV sets). Hence the partial shading of demand conditions
in Figure 10–3.

Related and supporting industries are largely undeveloped in the nation
at this stage. Production is almost solely based on foreign technology, foreign

equipment, and even foreign components. As a result, process technology is modern but behind that of global leaders, and dependence on foreign suppliers constrains the pace of innovation.

The investment-driven route to competitive advantage is only possible in a certain class of industries: those with significant scale economies and capital requirements but still a large labor cost component, standardized products, low service content, technology that is readily transferable, and where there are multiple sources of product and process technology.[4] The advantages a nation can bring to bear in this stage (low labor costs, large, modern facilities) are most significant in these types of industries. Typically, industries are relatively mature and produce either end products, basic components, or undifferentiated materials. In mature industries, foreign competitors' plants may well be obsolete, providing opportunities for a nation's firms to gain an advantage because of greater willingness to invest in modern assets.

While it is often said that technology travels freely worldwide, this is only partly true. Firms in an investment-driven economy are only able to obtain and absorb technology in some industries. These are mature enough to have multiple sources of technology, and involve relatively discrete models and production processes so that accumulated experience and highly specialized human resources are not required. Usually, some firms from other nations must be under competitive stress to cause them to be willing to sell technology.

The investment-driven stage is characterized by rapid gains in employment and the bidding up of wages and factor costs. Loss of competitive position in the most price-sensitive industries and segments begins. The economy becomes less vulnerable to global shocks and to movements in exchange rates than in the factor-driven stage, but it remains fragile. Failures in some industries and abrupt loss of advantage in others are inevitable, because of the uncertainties involved in selecting viable foreign technology, building large-scale plants, and supplanting firms from more advanced nations.

The proper role of government in the investment-driven stage reflects the sources of competitive advantage in such an economy. Given that competition still rests heavily on factors and the willingness to invest, government's role can be substantial. It can be important in such areas as channeling scarce capital into particular industries, promoting risk taking, providing temporary protection to encourage the entry of domestic rivals and the construction of efficient scale facilities, stimulating and influencing the acquisition of foreign technology, and encouraging exports. Government, at this stage, must also usually take the lead in making investments to create and upgrade factors, though firms must begin to play a growing role as well.

The investment-driven model requires a national consensus that favors investment and long-term economic growth over current consumption and income distribution. Such a consensus was explicit, for example, in both Japan and Korea.[5] Effective policy making in this stage seems to require a political process that allows disciplined and tough decisions as well as a long time horizon. Sustained commitments to improve factor quality and invest in other preconditions for competitive upgrading are required. Some industries may be favored over others. Powerful corporate interests must often be resisted to ensure adequate domestic rivalry. Protection must be temporary despite inevitable pressures to make it permanent, in order to spur improvement and innovation. Political pressures often mean that, despite good intentions, some of the important elements of the investment-driven model are not put in place, leading to failure to progress beyond the factor-driven stage. A politically secure government, continuity in government officials, and the ability to counteract special interests seeking favors are all highly desirable to support advancement.

The investment-driven stage has long been possible. Substantial capital flows among nations are not new, nor is the sourcing of foreign technology and even personnel. In the nineteenth century, for example, British and French technology was carefully studied and engineers were imported to upgrade a number of the German industries we examined. The American economy also went through this stage. However, the investment-driven stage may well have become navigable more quickly in the postwar period than ever before. It has become more accessible because of the greater globalization of markets for inputs, technology, and capital, and because of more aggressive national industrial policies.

Very few developing nations ever make the jump to this stage. In the postwar period, only Japan and more recently Korea have succeeded. Taiwan, Singapore, Hong Kong, Spain, and to a lesser extent Brazil are showing signs of achieving this stage. Each, however, is still lacking important elements, whether they are capable indigenous firms, in-house abilities to improve product and process technology, international marketing channels controlled by the nation's firms, sufficiently advanced factors, or the presence of real domestic rivalry. There are many pitfalls in moving to the investment-driven stage that I will return to when I discuss government policy. Not all nations which set out in this direction succeed.

INNOVATION-DRIVEN

In the innovation stage, the full "diamond" is in place in a wide range of industries. As shown in Figure 10–4, all the determinants are at work and their interactions are at their strongest.

The mix of industries and segments in which the nation's firms can success-fully compete broadens and upgrades, though the specific industries and

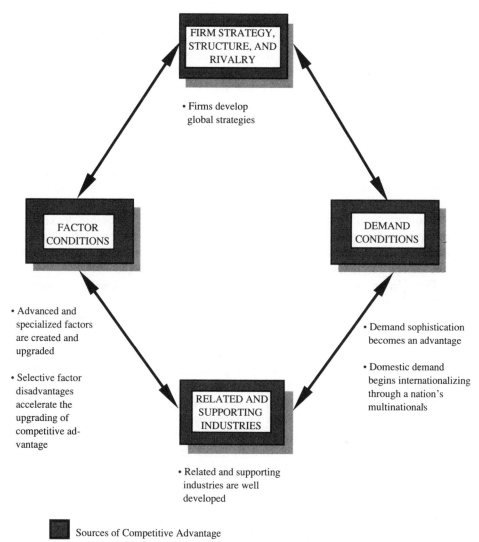

FIGURE **10–4 The Innovation-Driven Economy**

clusters will reflect the nation's particular environment and history. Consumer demand becomes increasingly sophisticated because of rising personal incomes, higher levels of education, increasing desire for convenience, and the invigorating role of domestic rivalry. The growing competitive strength of the nation's firms in a range of industries also leads to the emergence at home of sophisticated industrial customers. New entry feeds vibrant domestic rivalry in many industries, accelerating improvement and innovation. World-class supporting industries develop in the important clusters. New competitive industries emerge out of related industries.

Competitive advantage due to factor costs becomes more and more rare, as growing success in many industries puts upward pressure on factor costs and the value of the currency. Instead of factor cost advantages, selective factor disadvantages stimulate innovations that advance product and process technology. The sophistication of established universities, research facilities, and infrastructure grows. New mechanisms emerge to create advanced and specialized factors and to continually upgrade them, increasingly tied to particular industries. Industry "diamonds" become self-reinforcing, as do entire industry clusters.

This stage is called innovation-driven because firms not only appropriate and improve technology and methods from other nations but *create* them. A nation's indigenous firms push the state of the art in product and process technology, marketing, and other aspects of competing. Favorable demand conditions, a supplier base, specialized factors, and the presence of related industries in the nation allow firms to innovate and to sustain innovation. The capacity to innovate opens up yet more new industries.

Firms in an innovation-driven economy compete internationally in more differentiated industry segments. They continue to compete on cost but where it depends not on factor costs but on productivity due to high skill levels and advanced technology. Price-sensitive, less sophisticated segments are gradually ceded to firms from other nations.

Firms compete with self-contained global strategies and possess their own international marketing and service networks along with growing brand reputations abroad. Foreign manufacturing develops in those industries whose structure favors a dispersed value chain either to reduce cost or to enhance marketing effectiveness in other nations. The innovation-driven stage, then, marks the onset of significant foreign direct investment. A nation in the innovation-driven stage is enjoying the full fruits of self-reinforcement within the "diamond" in a growing number of industries.

The innovation-driven stage encompasses nations at varying levels of advancement. Some industries initially take the lead in the shift to the innovation-driven stage by achieving higher-order competitive advantages. Upgrading then spreads to others. Early in this stage, a vertical *deepening* of established industry clusters occurs. Competitive end product industries lead to competitive supplier industries (including machinery) or vice versa. These initially serve the domestic industry, but in a healthy economy they increasingly begin to compete globally. Deep clusters, often emanating from industries that began with factor- or investment-driven advantage, are a sign that the economy has achieved a moderate level of innovative capacity.

A more advanced and dynamic economy is capable of *widening* (horizontally) the range of successful industries and of spawning entirely new clusters. Both depend on a healthy process of new business formation either by established firms or through start-ups. The process of upgrading national productivity benefits when a nation has market positions capable of expansion in a broad range of industries, instead of depending on exports from a few. This reduces the dislocation that results from structural change in a few industries, from specialization by firms in more and more productive market segments, and from shifting abroad of less productive activities. At the same time, the presence of firms in a wide array of industries provides many possible avenues for improvement and innovation that raise productivity. Breadth creates more potential for the spillovers and cross-fertilization among industries that are so essential to the upgrading process.

A growing international position in sophisticated services is also characteristic of an innovation-driven economy, a reflection of the upgrading competitive advantages in industry. Factor- and investment-driven nations are rarely successful in international service industries except those dependent on labor costs (for example, general cargo shipping and some segments of international construction). In an innovation-driven economy, more advanced firms develop increasingly sophisticated service needs, such as in marketing, engineering, and testing. At the same time, more skilled human resources and other factors needed for sophisticated services such as engineering and advertising have developed. In addition, a nation's service firms may be pulled abroad by its growing pool of global manufacturing firms. Consumers, with higher incomes and rising education and skill levels, also begin consuming sophisticated services. This home demand may be the basis for the creation of international positions.

All innovation-driven economies will have a higher *domestic* service component than nations at earlier stages because of their sophistication and affluence. Whether an innovation-driven nation develops broad-based *international* strength in services, however, is another matter and depends on considerations I have discussed elsewhere. The United States and Switzerland, for example, have done so, while Germany and Italy have largely not.

The innovation-driven stage is most resistant to macroeconomic fluctuations and exogenous events, especially when the nation gains the capacity to widen clusters. Industries are less vulnerable to cost shocks and exchange rate movements because they compete on technology and differentiation. Globalization of firm strategies also provides a buffer against such fluctuations. The proliferation of successful industries reduces dependence on any one sector.

Government's appropriate role in this stage is markedly different from the previous one. The appropriate philosophy of intervention and types of intervention changes. Allocation of capital, protection, licensing controls, export subsidy, and other forms of direct intervention lose relevance or effectiveness in innovation-based competition. The impetus to innovate, the skills to do so, and the signals that guide its directions must come largely from the private sector. As an economy broadens and deepens, government cannot hope to keep track of every existing and new industry and all the linkages among them. Increasingly prosperous and international firms are also less amenable to guidance. Instead, government's efforts are best spent in *indirect* ways such as stimulating the creation of more and more advanced factors, improving the quality of domestic demand, encouraging new business formation, preserving domestic rivalry, and other areas I will discuss in Chapter 12. Firms must increasingly take a leading role in factor creation themselves.

Britain achieved the innovation-driven stage in the first half of the nineteenth century. America, Germany, and Sweden did so in the decades before or soon after the turn of the twentieth century. Italy and Japan have achieved (or in the case of Italy possibly re-achieved) the innovation-driven stage only in the 1970s. The northern regions of what is now Italy had arguably reached the innovation-driven stage in the twelfth century, though the industrial context of the times was wholly different.

WEALTH-DRIVEN

Nations pass through the first three stages of competitive development if they can sustain a dynamic process of upgrading national advantage. This involves the move to more sophisticated competitive advantages and the widening of the range of industries in which firms can successfully compete. In the process, positions in less advanced, lower productivity segments are lost.

The wealth-driven stage is, in contrast, one that ultimately leads to decline. The driving force in a wealth-driven economy is the wealth that has *already* been achieved. The problem is that an economy driven by past wealth is not able to maintain its wealth. This is because, most importantly, the motivations of investors, managers, and individuals shift in ways that undermine sustained investment and innovation, and hence upgrading. New goals are set, often including some socially laudable ones, that supplant those that have sustained progress in the economy.

In the wealth-driven stage, firms begin to lose competitive advantage in international industries for a variety of reasons. Ebbing rivalry, a result of more attention to preserving position than to enhancing it, declining corporate motivation to invest, and the ability of powerful firms to insulate themselves by influencing government policy, is often at the root of the problem.[6] Stewards ascend to senior management positions in place of entrepreneurs and company builders. Belief in competition falls not only in companies but in unions, which both lose the taste for risk-taking. The compulsion to innovate diminishes as the willingness to violate norms and bear disapproval falls. Employees lose motivation as they reach high levels of income and their aspirations broaden. Management-labor relations harden as each side strives to preserve the status quo and its entitlement: This strains the ability of productivity improvements to keep up with rising wages.

The prestige of working in industry may fall in favor of other careers. The striving for a practical education diminishes. Educational standards fall as societal and parental attention wanes. The rate of factor-creating investments will tend to decline and shift toward areas less beneficial for industry. A tendency to tax wealth as nations become highly prosperous reduces the incentive to invest in industry. Overall, chronic underinvestment in industry is an ironic manifestation of a wealth-driven economy.

The growing pool of investable capital that accompanies past success may also trigger shifts in the nation's capital markets. Goals of investors may move from capital accumulation to capital preservation. A slowing of innovation in the economy leads to a decline in attractive investment opportunities in industry. Investment in financial assets supplants investment in real assets.

A symptom that may accompany a move to the wealth-driven stage is widespread mergers and acquisitions. Companies, with cash flow in excess of internal needs, seek rapid growth without risking start-ups. Mergers may also reflect an increasing desire to reduce rivalry and increase stability. Mergers create the illusion of progress without creating new businesses or enhancing competitive advantage fundamentally in existing businesses. They often slow down innovation further. The wealth-driven stage is illustrated in Figure 10–5.

The tangible signs that an economy has moved into the wealth-driven stage may be slow to appear, because of the momentum created by customer loyalties and established market positions. Once the loss of advantage in some high-productivity industries and segments begins, however, it spreads to others through a declustering process. Industries that are no longer innovating become poor buyers for the industries that supply them, and lose the ability to contribute to or catalyze innovation in the industries they serve. The economy narrows, losing competitive advantage first in basic industries and final products, later in components, and then machinery. Spotty competitive advantage may persist where the nation has particularly unique demand or is well established in particular related industries. Foreign firms that more and more possess the true competitive advantage begin to acquire the nation's firms and integrate them into global strategies with the home base elsewhere. Alternately, foreign firms establish subsidiaries in the nation which result in an eroding share for domestic competitors.

As firms lose higher-order competitive advantages, many domestic industries downsize and resort to competing on price. Sluggish wage and job growth and rising unemployment further blunt incentives to improve productivity, and these contribute to the loss of other market positions. Personal income begins to fall behind that in other advanced nations, eroding the

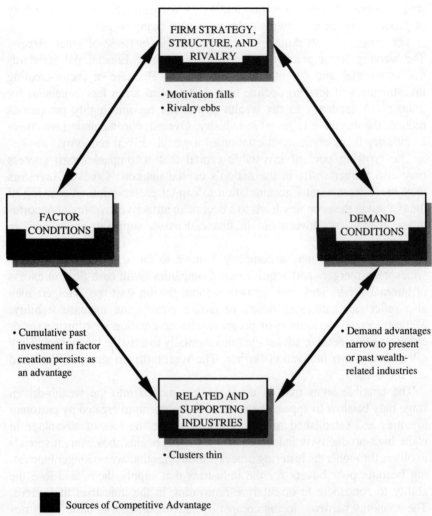

FIRM STRATEGY,
STRUCTURE, AND
RIVALRY

• Motivation falls
• Rivalry ebbs

FACTOR
CONDITIONS

DEMAND
CONDITIONS

• Cumulative past
investment in factor
creation persists as
an advantage

• Demand advantages
narrow to present
or past wealth-
related industries

RELATED AND
SUPPORTING
INDUSTRIES

• Clusters thin

Sources of Competitive Advantage

FIGURE 10–5 The Wealth-Driven Economy

quality and sophistication of home demand. Ironically, the nation may preserve position in some industries dependent on skilled personnel because their wages fall below those of other advanced nations. Under increasing pressure, labor-management relations deteriorate further and undermine innovation even more. At the same time, firms become defensive and defeatist, and there are rising calls for government support and intervention that blunt dynamism still further.

While the innovation-driven stage is one where the capacity to innovate and sustain competitive advantage is relatively widespread, the wealth-driven stage is marked by a narrowing of the range of industries in which firms can sustain competitive advantage to four broad categories. The first is industries in which the nation retains sophisticated and advanced demand because of accumulated wealth, in the form of accumulated personal assets, high incomes, or luxury needs (examples are financial services, convenience-oriented packaged goods, and entertainment). A second category is industries in which competitive advantage results from cumulative investment over a long period of time in basic science, the arts, highly specialized forms of higher education, pools of highly trained individuals in narrow fields, or other forms of social spending such as for defense or health care. These are all manifestations of a long history of national wealth (examples of industries where such advantages are important are biotechnology, educational services, space, and defense goods). A third category is industries where competitive position is retained due to early mover advantages (based on historical national success) that are particularly durable. Typical of such industries are those where there is strong brand loyalty (for example, cigarettes) or where there has been an absence of discontinuous product or process change. The fourth category of retained industries is that where the nation retains basic factor advantages, or inherited wealth. Reflected in all four categories of industries, then, is that wealth is the driving force in such an economy.

Since competition in many service industries is multidomestic or takes place via foreign subsidiaries, the services share of GDP is less vulnerable to international competition than manufacturing. Hence the loss of manufacturing positions in a wealth-driven economy often means that services account for a rapidly rising share of national income. The nation's position in a range of services (and some areas of manufacturing) may even expand because wealth creates favorable home demand conditions. The growing role of services in all advanced economies, however, complicates any generalizations about the share of GDP represented by services in different stages. International success in services is *not* a signal of incipient decline. The particular service industries in which a nation is successful are a better indication of the stage of the nation's economy.

The wealth-driven stage is a stage of drift and ultimate decline because the range of industries in which competitive advantage can be sustained becomes inadequate to employ the workforce in productive jobs and support a rising standard of living. A nation in this stage becomes a study in contrasts. On the one hand, it is a "rich" nation with some cash-rich companies and some wealthy citizens enjoying the fruits of the successful industries and accumulated past national investment. It is often a nation with lofty social goals. Outbound foreign direct investment may be substantial despite underfunding of home-based industries. The nature of foreign investment changes, however, from investments that transfer know-how or extend home-based positions (typical of the innovation-driven stage) to purely financial investments. Firms may also use their resources to acquire foreign companies with competitive advantage, but these are managed autonomously by foreign management.

On the other hand, the wealth-driven stage is one where malaise and an eroding sense of purpose may set in. As it progresses, many companies become troubled, unemployment or underemployment pressure is persistent, and the average standard of living is declining. Social programs begin to outstrip the ability of the economy to pay for them. Taxation of wealth in addition to income may come to be seen as the only way to make ends meet, diminishing incentives even further. The resulting decline can be very protracted until something jars the economy out of it.

The United Kingdom is a nation whose economy moved some time ago to the wealth-driven stage, and several other nations have either reached this stage or were close to it in the late 1980s, as I will explore later.

PRECONDITIONS FOR COMPETITIVE ADVANCEMENT

A nation's industry progresses through the first three stages because forces are present that create the potential for higher-order competitive advantages and put pressure on industry to seek and achieve them. A systemic upgrading of the "diamond" takes place.

Some of the most telling conditions necessary for a nation to progress to more advanced stages are the following:

· *Factor creation mechanisms:* The competitive potential of an economy is limited by the quantity and especially the quality of its factors of production. Well-functioning mechanisms that create and upgrade factors provide the foundation for higher-order advantage, because each of the first three stages requires more advanced and more specialized factors.

· *Motivation:* Progressing from stage to stage requires workers and managers who are motivated to work long hours, earn higher wages, seek greater profits, start new companies, and create larger companies. Vital to sustaining motivation is that citizens believe that they will be rewarded for hard work and good ideas. Holders of capital must also be motivated to make sustained investments.

· *Domestic rivalry:* Vigorous rivalry among domestic competitors in a wide range of industries is necessary to drive innovation and the upgrading of competitive advantage. Rivalry overcomes inertia through creating the fear of failure. Active rivalry among domestic firms also has important spillover effects on the other determinants.

· *Demand upgrading:* Upgrading the quality of demand creates the potential for success in more sophisticated segments and in more advanced industries. Demanding buyers also pressure improvement. Demand upgrades as the presence of one competitive industry creates a sophisticated buyer for others. It also upgrades as incomes rise and as citizens become busier and more educated. Rising social aspirations, and investment in areas such as health care and environmental protection, create demand-side stimulus for yet other new industries.

· *Selective factor disadvantages:* Selective disadvantages in less advanced factors furnish the impetus to increase productivity as well as to upgrade competitive advantages to higher-order types, provided there is appropriate motivation and vigorous domestic rivalry.

· *Capacity for new business formation:* Moving to a more advanced stage requires that there be effective mechanisms in place to create new businesses either through start-ups or internally by established firms. New business formation is essential to healthy rivalry, to movement into new and more sophisticated industry segments, to the development of suppliers and related industries, and, ultimately, to the development of clusters.

These forces are not only individually necessary but constitute a virtuous circle in which one reinforces another. Upgrading requires factor conditions that are increasingly advanced and specialized. But deploying factors in more productive ways depends on improving demand conditions, the impetus from selective disadvantages, and the presence of sophisticated supporting industries. Yet these will not actually lead to upgrading unless goals motivate sustained investment and rivalry forces it. But rivalry and the development of both supporting and related industries necessary for upgrading depend on active new business formation. The mutual dependency of the process of upgrading means that all these forces must be present.[7] A nation's rate of progress is constrained by its weakest link.

Nations vary widely in the strength of the forces and the length of time they can be sustained as the national economy develops. The strength of the forces depends on national circumstances that have been discussed earlier. Government plays a role through its policy choices, as do firms in their choice of strategies. If government policy and company strategies do not adapt as an economy progresses, this will hold back individual firms and the nation from advancing.

Chance is often a trigger allowing a nation's economy to move rapidly ahead. Major discontinuities such as wars, large adjustments in currency value, input price shifts, and demand surges provide the openings for well-positioned nations to advance rapidly in a range of industries. Discontinuities and disruptions can also unfreeze domestic industry structures and create new motivation for firms and individuals. The two world wars, for example, have been important to both American and German economic dynamism (see Chapter 7). In Japan, the breakup of the *zaibatsu* unfroze entrenched and powerful positions.

Nations falter or fall backward in their economic development when the forces lose strength. This happens when government policy holds back or prevents the forces from working (for example, through holding down wage increases, taxing away most of disposable income), the hopes and expectations of citizens are blunted, the ability or willingness to make social investments is lost, or special interests freeze the status quo, to list just some of the possibilities.

Until nations reach a certain level of income and accumulated wealth, the risk is not moving into the wealth-driven stage but sliding backward. Falling rivalry, lagging factor creation, declining motivation, and eroding demand quality are all causes of a slowing rate of improvement and innovation. Denmark is a good example of a nation facing this risk. As positions in advanced industries and segments are lost, eventually there is downward pressure on wages and the standard of living. It can take many years for this to become apparent, however, because of inertia, government intervention, and the like.

Nations that have enjoyed great prosperity evolve into the wealth-driven stage for some of the same reasons. Declining motivation and ebbing rivalry are the two most important causes. These not only directly undermine competitive advantage in many industries, but also work to reduce private and social investments in factor creation and redirect them to forms less beneficial for industry.

The Process of National Economic Development

Each nation goes through its own unique process of development. The mix of industries and trajectory by which the economy passes (or does not pass) through the stages is a reflection of each nation's unique circumstances with respect to the "diamond." The nation's history plays an important role, by shaping such things as the base of skills that have been created, the prevailing values and norms of behavior, the needs, tastes, and preferences that will underpin demand patterns, and the challenges that have been set or confronted.

The particular industries that provide the starting point for development are heavily dependent on the nation's natural endowment. Resource-rich nations, such as Sweden and the United States, begin the upgrading process from a position of international success in resource-based industries such as iron and steel, forest products, and agriculture. Clusters form around these fields and ultimately the economy broadens to new industries if the forces needed to spur upgrading are present. Resource-poor nations, such as Japan, Korea, Switzerland, and Italy, have started from a position of international success in labor-intensive final consumer goods industries such as textiles and apparel, housing and household products, and whatever agricul-

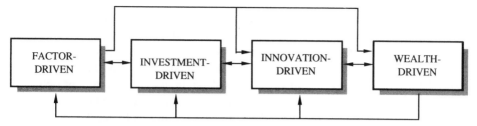

FIGURE 10–6 **Processes of National Competitive Development**

tural or food-related products can be produced locally. These industries become the basis for clusters, and competitive advantage is extended into related industries or into other industries where home demand conditions are favorable.

Economies first begin upgrading on the top (upstream industries) or the bottom (final consumption goods and services) level of the cluster chart. Strong positions in industrial and supporting functions, or the middle of the cluster chart, will emerge only late in the investment-driven or early in the innovation-driven stage. Achieving competitive advantage in the industrial and supporting sectors requires a pre-existing base of strong indigenous companies and higher levels of technological capability. Korea has only emerging positions in such sectors in the 1980s, for example, while Japan has for some years been registering strong gains in them. The ability to compete in a wide range of machinery industries, first domestically and then globally, is a reliable indicator of the innovation-driven stage, because it signals the capability for process innovation. Competitive success in the multiple business category and sophisticated general business services is a sign of achieving truly broad and advanced innovation-driven competitive advantage. These industries depend on having sophisticated home-based companies in a wide range of industries as buyers. Widespread competitive success in health care, personal products, and entertainment/leisure is also a sign of an advanced economy with sophisticated technology and high income consumers.

The process of moving through the stages can take many paths, and there is no single progression (see Figure 10–6).[8] Development often seems to occur in bursts of rapid upgrading, followed by periods of less perceptible change. This reflects the powerful reinforcement that takes place within the "diamond" both inside and across clusters. Competitive success in one industry, for example, triggers upgrading or new entry in several others. Demonstration effects, by which approaches, norms, and values diffuse, serve also to foster rapid advancement.

Nations do not inevitably progress. Many nations never move beyond factor-driven or investment-driven, for reasons I have sketched earlier. Indeed, my theory suggests far more formidable challenges facing developing nations than those that arise from a model of development in which improvements in factor quantity and quality are the principal concern. The nation that has advanced most rapidly in the postwar period, Japan, has passed through each of the first three stages. The investment-driven stage, though fraught with challenges and difficulties, has been a means to accelerate the development process in some nations. However, national economies seem to be able to move directly from factor-driven to innovation-driven over a long time period, skipping any noticeable transition through the investment-driven stage. A good example is Italy, whose attempts at the investment-driven model failed as I will describe later. The ability to forego the investment-driven stage and still advance rapidly requires a long history of industrial activity which leaves behind a legacy of human resources, educational institutions, and the like.

Economic prosperity will tend to rise as a nation moves through the first three stages, because upgrading leads to increasing national productivity. A nation with unusually abundant natural resources for its size, however, can enjoy high national income despite a position in the factor-driven stage, though it is not likely to be sustainable indefinitely. Good examples would be Kuwait and Saudi Arabia, which may enjoy high income per capita for decades because of an abundance of oil. Canada is another nation whose remarkable natural resource endowment has long supported a high standard of living though few industries outside of resource-intensive areas possess international competitive advantage.

Eventually, however, dependence on natural resources will leave a nation vulnerable to depletion, new foreign sources, or technological changes that reduce or eliminate resource needs. Abundant natural resources also create more subtle problems. They provide a satisfactory or even high level of national income without the need to upgrade the "diamond." But this makes it difficult to move beyond advantage based on resources or to replace it. At the same time, the level of wages supported by abundant resources precludes competing in the types of industries that serve as the foundation for new clusters, such as electronic goods or industrial apparatus and components of intermediate levels of sophistication. Where resource abundance is great enough, a nation may move directly from the factor-driven stage to the wealth-driven stage. Diminishing competition, adversarial labor-management relations, and protection may arise as attention in the economy shifts towards preservation of the *status quo*. Nations such as Canada and Norway face this risk.

Resting on factor-driven advantage, then, does not provide a solid foundation for sustained productivity growth or for expanding the range of internationally successful industries. Few nations with truly abundant natural resources have achieved sustained prosperity in this century of knowledge-based international competition. The United States, with its historically unique belief in competition and waves of immigrants providing fresh motivation, is perhaps the only real exception.

The wealth-driven stage, if it occurs, will eventually lead to a slow decline in economic prosperity. It may be decades before aggregate data reflect the underlying loss of competitive advantage, because inertia and early mover advantages mean the nation's positions persist in many industries. Leisure and luxury demand may even trigger some new industries. In fact, in the transition period from innovation to wealth-driven, company profitability and the standard of living may still be *rising,* as companies harvest (underinvest in) market positions, and as managers and employees obtain wage increases that begin moving ahead of productivity improvements.

It is possible that a nation mired in the wealth-driven stage will revert all the way back to the factor-driven stage. As positions are lost in the higher productivity industries within the economy, wages and other factor costs may eventually fall so far in relative terms that a nation regresses to competing on factor costs. Britain, for example, has seen an erosion of relative wages to the point that foreign investment is now being attracted to the nation by low wage costs. Italy, the dominant commercial power in the twelfth and thirteenth centuries, seems to have made the full cycle from innovation-driven, to wealth-driven, to factor-driven, to innovation-driven.[9] However, the decline of a wealth-driven economy can be arrested through policy changes, major discontinuities, or shifts in social values.

THE STAGES AND THE POSTWAR ECONOMIES OF NATIONS

The stages provide a framework to revisit the nations I have discussed from an additional perspective. Each nation is in a somewhat different stage of national competitive development and is on its own unique development path. Revisiting the eight nations, as well as briefly considering Singapore and Denmark which I have not discussed in detail, will provide new understanding of their economic progress as well as further insight into the stages concept. Doing so will also serve as a starting point for identifying the issues each nation will face in the future, the subject of Chapter 13.

Figure 10–7 estimates the position of each nation in the stages of competitive development and approximates the evolution in national advantage that has occurred in the postwar period. The position of each nation is intended only as indicative. It reflects my view of the shifting patterns of national advantage and the strength of the forces at work to upgrade the nation's industry. A brief discussion of the position of each nation will serve as a review of the previous three chapters.

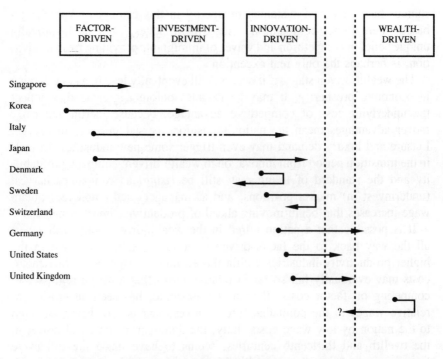

FIGURE 10–7 **Estimated Evolution of National Competitive Development During the Postwar Period**

Singapore, a nation I have not discussed in detail, became an independent republic in 1965. While it has made substantial progress since its formation, Singapore remains a factor-driven economy. Singapore is largely a production base for foreign multinationals, attracted by Singapore's relatively low-cost, well-educated workforce and efficient infrastructure including roads, ports, airports, and telecommunications. Indigenous companies have yet to develop to a significant extent, nor have they been given much emphasis in economic policy. Singapore's improvement in living standards has come from upgrading the quality of human resources and infrastructure in order to upgrade the quality of jobs. Singapore's exceptional performance in these areas has been what sets it apart from its peers. It has by far the greatest number of students per capita studying in the United States, for example (see Table 8–9). Yet Singapore is still a foreign production site, not a real home base. Singapore's approach to economic development, built mostly on foreign multinationals, has produced rapid progress and is lower risk than Korea's. Until Singapore becomes a home base, however, its upside potential will be capped.

Korea began the 1950s in the factor-driven stage. Its international success was largely in apparel and resource-dependent goods. In contrast to Singapore and all other Asian NICs including Taiwan, however, Korea fully achieved the investment-driven stage by the 1980s. The Korean government and Korean firms adopted the more risky course of limiting the role of foreign multinationals, seeking to establish indigenous industry, and borrowing heavily from abroad to finance aggressive investment. The result is the potential for the sustained upgrading of industry and far greater long-term prosperity.

Korea, indeed, provides a striking example of the investment-driven stage. Through sourcing foreign technology, aggressive capital investment in large-scale, modern facilities, risk taking, and vigorous domestic rivalry, Korea has achieved international positions in a range of moderately advanced industries. Korean companies compete largely in price-sensitive segments and with cost-based strategies. Product and process technology is modern but not state of the art. Competitive advantage results from still low wages for skilled and highly productive labor combined with modern, efficient facilities. The Korean government has played a heavy role thus far, directing scarce capital, limiting foreign investment, assisting in foreign technology licensing, and protecting the home market. Like Singapore, Korea has invested aggressively to upgrade human resources and infrastructure. Unlike Singapore, Korean development is based heavily on Korean companies though multinationals have some role. To a much greater extent than Singapore, Korean firms and the Korean government have also begun investing in research.

What most sets Korea apart, in addition to fierce domestic rivalry, is its ability both to fully assimilate and to improve upon foreign technology. In-house technological capabilities in Korean companies are rising rapidly. Companies are also developing their own international marketing channels and international brand names. A group of Korean multinationals has emerged with the beginnings of global strategies. However, Korea still lacks the demand conditions and related and supporting industries necessary for achieving innovation-based competitive advantage. It competes largely in end products, though these are of growing sophistication. The Korean market position is improving in industrial and supporting industries, a sign of upgrading. Yet product designs are still largely from abroad, and products are made from foreign components with foreign machinery. Home demand is rarely advanced and sophisticated enough to support true innovation. The challenge facing Korean industry is how to continue upgrading to reach the innovation-driven stage.

Denmark, the other nation we studied but that I have not discussed extensively, achieved innovation-driven national advantage by the 1960s. Danish firms have created and sustained positions primarily in large industry clusters related to agriculture and food, household products, and health care. Yet dynamism in the Danish economy is lagging behind that of many of the other nations. Faltering motivation, too little competition, and a looming state influence are some of the most pressing problems. The rate of upgrading of factor quality in Denmark also fails to match that of other advanced nations. As shown in Table 7–1, Danish productivity growth is weak overall and especially disturbing in manufacturing. If present long-term trends continue, Denmark will depend more and more on factor costs and the subsidiaries of foreign multinationals for its economic prosperity, which is likely to be limiting.

Italy has surged in the postwar period from factor- to innovation-driven national advantage. Its extent of upgrading is second only to Japan. Italy emerged from the war with a badly damaged economy, and competitive advantage in Italian firms was largely based on low labor cost. Yet sophisticated home demand, entrepreneurship, and vibrant domestic rivalry led to Italian positions in more sophisticated segments and in a widening array of industries. Clusters deepened into components and into a broad range of machinery industries. The self-reinforcing connections between buyers, suppliers, and machinery makers led to rapid upgrading. Substantial wage increases beginning in 1969, and an end to a regime of lira devaluation in 1978, were final catalysts for many Italian industries to upgrade their competitive advantages. The Italian economy was transformed to the innovation-driven stage by the 1980s.

Italy did not noticeably pass through the investment-driven stage so characteristic of Japan and Korea. It evolved directly over a period of decades from factor-driven to innovation-driven, drawing on centuries of industrial history, a pool of skilled people, a rich scientific and cultural tradition leading to sophisticated demand, a base of wealth, and an initial standard of living higher than in Asia. Italy's success has largely been in industries that are not scale-sensitive and where high levels of capital investment were not required. When Italian potential was combined with high levels of motivation, pressures from selective disadvantages, and fierce rivalry, the result was rapid upgrading in industry.

In the early 1970s, there were large investments in steel, autos, chemicals, and energy, among other sectors, in the Italian government's effort to implement the investment-driven model. Yet the great majority of these efforts were unsuccessful, a function of a lack of effective domestic competition and disadvantages in other determinants such as home demand, infrastructure, and appropriate skills. The Italian government, unstable and prone to political pressures, also proved ineffective in taking the steps required. Italy illustrates how success at the investment-driven model is by no means assured. Fortunately, outside of the industries in which government intervention was significant, Italy possessed the underpinnings of the innovation-driven stage.

The Italian economy has shown a remarkable capacity to upgrade itself. Competitive advantage in many Italian industries has shifted increasingly to segmentation and differentiation. Advanced production technology has been introduced. Deep clusters have formed in fashion, furnishings, food, and other sectors.[10] Italy has registered significant improvements in market position in machinery and specialty input industries, and its extent of gains is matched only by Japan. Overall, Italy is still enjoying positive momentum, though its development is approaching limits unless both company strategies and government policies evolve.

Sweden emerged from World War II at the innovation-driven stage, achieved in the decades after the turn of the century. Sweden has long had a large portion of its economy dependent on natural resources. Soon after the war, however, Sweden was to enjoy a rapidly rising standard of living as Swedish firms extended competitive positions beyond resource industries into transportation equipment, machinery, and other advanced industries linked to established clusters. Sophisticated home demand, unusual interchange within clusters, and high and rising human resource quality supported upgrading. Strong pressures from selective factor disadvantages, because Sweden's natural resource positions were under pressure from new sources, led to a rising level of technology and a move to more sophisticated segments. Heavy investments in health care and other social services also created advanced demand for new products.

Sweden has sustained and even enhanced advantage in many of its traditional industries in recent decades, and its rate of productivity improvement in manufacturing has continued. Yet Sweden runs the risk of a slowing rate of upgrading for a variety of reasons. One is a policy of periodic devaluation, which reinforces price competition and has retarded further moves away from factor-driven industries. A low level of individual incentives, faltering domestic competition, and a slow rate of new business formation are some other question marks limiting Swedish success in established and new industries. Another is a large state sector, which absorbs trained human resources in relatively low productivity activities at a time when Swedish firms are moving production out of Sweden for want of skilled labor. Sweden has been losing net position outside its established large clusters. Overall productivity growth in the economy is slow. While Sweden's egalitarian philosophy means that a move into the wealth-driven stage is unlikely, its rate of progress may slow. Maintaining the Swedish standard of living in relative terms, under these circumstances, may become increasingly difficult.

Japan has been the premier postwar success story. It began the period with factor-driven national advantage, competing primarily based on low labor cost in textiles and other unsophisticated industries. Many preconditions were in place in terms of human and technological resources, however, to support rapid upgrading. Japan moved rapidly to the investment-driven stage, achieving success in such industries as shipbuilding, steel, radios, small cars, and tires. Aggressive acquisition of foreign technology, capital investment in large, modern facilities, and fierce rivalry combined with still low labor cost to yield potent cost advantages in such industries. Unlike Korea, however, Japanese firms were able to gain foreign market penetration comparatively easily in segments reflecting home demand but ignored by foreign rivals. Japanese exports normally took off only after the domestic market saturated. Thus demand conditions became an advantage quite early, accelerating the rate of upgrading in the economy.

Japan achieved the innovation-driven stage by the late 1970s. Factor conditions kept rapidly upgrading. Internal diversification led to entry into related, supporting, and downstream industries. Japan's greatest net gains in export share since 1978 have been in machinery and specialty inputs. Selective factor disadvantages such as high energy costs and labor shortages fostered automation and innovation. Clusters formed and widened, and Japanese home demand became the world's most sophisticated in a growing range of industries. Intense domestic rivalry led to rapid improvement. At the same time, market positions have eroded in resource-sensitive and less sophisticated industries.

The extent and speed of Japan's evolution is unparalleled in modern competitive history. The dramatic appreciation of the yen since 1986, combined with shifting company strategies and government policy, were upgrading the economy even further in the late 1980s. Japanese firms have become technological leaders and differentiators in a growing number of industries. Japan also enjoys leading international positions in a group of industries that will support further upgrading of many others, such as semiconductors, robotics, and advanced materials. Continued modifications in policy and company strategy will be necessary, however, if Japan is to sustain continued advancement.

Three other nations, Switzerland, Germany, and the United States, have long been in the innovation-driven stage and have enjoyed prosperity in the postwar period. Each, to varying degrees, however, shows signs of a transition to the wealth-driven stage. Since 1978, all three nations have lost international position in more advanced industries than have gained it. If these trends continue, the result will be an eventual slippage in relative standard of living.

Switzerland, which entered the innovation-driven stage before World War II, has a very broadly based economy for a nation of its size, a reflection of the fact that it competes only in the most sophisticated segments of many industries. Numerous advantages have promoted the continual upgrading of Swiss industry over time such as rising human resource skills, a strong technological base, sophisticated demand, and relentless pressures from high wages. Sustained investment has been encouraged by low interest rates and supportive investor goals.

However, Switzerland has lost world export share in many more industries than has gained it, including advanced industries such as instruments and machinery. Many Swiss industries that have sustained advantage are linked to luxury demand or wealth. Of growing concern is a lack of domestic rivalry coupled with a financial structure that blunts dynamism. Decades of uninterrupted prosperity have taken their toll on motivation and risk taking. Whether enough new business formation sufficient to stimulate rivalry and support rising productivity will take place is also uncertain.

Germany achieved the innovation-driven stage around the turn of the century, primarily on the strength of its preeminence in science and technology. German success has been uniquely self-reinforcing, as strong positions in machinery grew out of strength in user industries. One competitive industry often led to several others. Unparalleled mechanisms for upgrading human and technological resources have been present. A favorable "diamond" allowed Germany to twice recover innovation-driven advantage after world wars.

Yet Germany also shows signs of movement into the wealth-driven stage. Market share losses far outnumber gains. Like Switzerland, they include many advanced industries in machinery, instruments, transportation equipment, and even chemicals, along with more predictable losses in resource-sensitive and less sophisticated industries. Evolving financial markets and a new breed of financially oriented managers are shifting investor and company goals. Unions are increasingly a force retarding dynamism. Domestic rivalry is showing unmistakable signs of waning. The inability to successfully enter new industries is of concern, made pressing by substantial unemployment.

The United States achieved the innovation-driven stage in the decades before the turn of the century, though it maintains a large proportion of trade based heavily on natural resources. The breadth and depth of American competitive positions grew markedly from World War II through the 1960s. America provided a unique environment for innovation-driven advantage in many industries: heavy investment in factor upgrading, trendsetting demand conditions, strong individual motivation, an intense belief in competition, and leadership in important supporting industries such as electronics, plastics, machine tools, and advertising are just some of the many strengths I discussed in Chapter 7.

Since then, however, America has experienced an equally troubling loss of competitive advantage as Switzerland or Germany. The United States is losing advantage in the wrong industries and segments, and many gains are in resource-sensitive and relatively unprocessed goods. The range of industries that can support substantial exports is low for a nation of America's size. The United States is being out-innovated. While American firms sustain many competitive positions and new business formation remains healthy, there are clear signs that upgrading of the U.S. economy is faltering.

The industries where the United States retains competitive advantage are often connected to leisure, mass consumption, the management of wealth, substantial cumulative investment in universities and on basic research, the immense defense budget, and natural resources. Other signs of movement toward the wealth-driven stage include rising accommodation and diminishing competition, rising protectionism, and investor and managerial goals that seem to have led to sustained underinvestment in industry. These and other changes, coupled with a rate of improvement of human resource skills that lags far behind that of other nations, constitute serious threats to the dynamism of the American economy and its capacity to further advance.

Britain is a nation that has been caught for decades in the wealth-driven stage. It had by far the worst ratio of export share losses relative to share gains of the nations we studied. As a result of the economy's slow rate of upgrading, the British standard of living has been losing ground relative to other advanced nations for many decades. Yet, as is characteristic of the wealth-driven stage, Britain has many wealthy individuals and enjoys prosperity in a range of sectors even though much of the nation is left behind.

Britain entered the wealth-driven stage as declining motivation combined with eroding human resource quality led to a slowing rate of innovation. Gentlemanly rivalry and forgiving home (and colonial) buyers led to little pressure to improve. The top talent often did not enter industry. With no effective shareholder governance, managerial complacency and lack of pressure led to a slow rate of improvement as well as underinvestment in capital equipment, technology, and skills. These problems only reinforced themselves.

The patterns of success and failure in British industries represent a vivid illustration of a wealth-driven economy. A remarkable number of industries on the list of internationally successful British industries have something to do with past wealth, leisure, entertainment, upscale consumer goods, and the management of wealth. These range from cigarettes, whiskey, and spirits to auctioneering, movies, records, books, fine home furnishings, premium apparel, financial services, business services, and upscale retailing. Industries such as pharmaceuticals, chemicals, and consultancy draw on a long history of investment in infrastructure, science, and a small but elite pool of human resources. Many international British industries, including a good number of the consumer industries, reflect past industrial success sustained through early mover advantages. Because of lagging salaries of skilled scientists and other highly educated personnel, a consequence of a long period as a wealth-driven economy, Britain has become a low-cost location for research and for competing in such skill-intensive industries as publishing, consultancy, and advertising. Finally, a significant proportion of British exports are also the result of inherited natural resources, notably oil and gas.

Britain's competitive advantage in most basic manufacturing industries and intermediate goods has eroded. The loss in British share of world cluster exports has been greatest in such industries. British firms have also lost position in many mass-produced consumer goods and in machinery.

Britain illustrates the self-reinforcing downward spiral of the wealth-driven stage. Position lost in one industry has spread to affect others. Pressures on employment have grown. A shortage of government revenues has led to budgetary pressures that have limited spending on education, R&D, and infrastructure. Falling relative average income levels have made consumer demand conditions less advanced except for the lingering luxury segment.

Recent developments in Britain are encouraging, and productivity growth has risen as restructuring and downsizing take place in industry. Yet a long-term turnaround is still far from certain. Of fundamental concern today for the development of the British economy are the continually eroding skills of the average worker relative to other nations, the absence of sophisticated domestic demand in many industries, and inadequate rivalry. The momentum created when a nation enters the wealth-driven stage takes decades or longer to halt and reverse.

POSTWAR ECONOMIC PROGRESS IN PERSPECTIVE

The most successful nations in the postwar period have faced pressures and adversity. They have possessed few obvious advantages. Germany, Japan, and Italy were all defeated powers. Germany and Korea were politically divided, losing resource-rich territory in the process. The greatest labor shortages, the sharpest wage increases, the highest energy costs, and the fewest inherited resources have often been associated with the most rapid upgrading and the most significant advances. This was true as long as human resource skills and the scientific base were high or rapidly improving, employees, managers, and investors were motivated to make sustained investments, and active domestic rivalry was present to pressure continual improvement.

Whatever its postwar performance, however, each of the nations I have discussed faces challenges if it is to maintain and improve its economic prosperity. The challenges confront both companies and governments. Companies must modify their strategies if competitive advantages are to be created and sustained in the face of improving international competitors. Government policy at the local, state, and national levels must create an environment conducive to more sophisticated competitive advantages. Policies must evolve to reflect the shifting competitive position of a nation's industry.

Company strategy and government policy will be the subjects of the next two chapters. Having set forth the principles, I will return in the final chapter to the nations to illustrate my theory further by highlighting some of the most important issues facing their firms and governments.

PART IV

Implications

11

Company Strategy

Companies, not nations, are on the front line of international competition. They must increasingly compete globally. Yet globalization does not supersede the importance of the nation. We have seen how its home nation plays a central role in a firm's international success. The home base shapes a company's capacity to innovate rapidly in technology and methods and to do so in the proper directions. It is the place from which competitive advantage ultimately emanates and from which it must be sustained. A global strategy supplements and solidifies the competitive advantage created at the home base; it is the icing, not the cake.[1]

However favorable the national circumstances, though, success is not ensured. Some firms from a nation prosper while others fail. Though America has world leadership in computers and IBM, Digital, and Cray have been superb performers, for example, countless other American computer companies have failed or faded. Japanese firms are dominant in small copiers. Yet Canon and Ricoh are more successful than a long list of other Japanese copier competitors. Having a home base in the right nation helps a great deal but does not ensure success. Having a home base in the wrong nation raises fundamental strategic concerns.

The most important sources of national advantage must be actively sought and exploited, unlike low factor costs obtainable simply by operating in the nation. Internationally successful firms are not passive bystanders in the process of creating competitive advantage. Those we studied were caught up in a never-ending process of seeking out new advantages and struggling with rivals to protect them. They were positioned to most benefit from their national environment. They took steps to make their home nation

577

(and location within the nation) an even more favorable environment for competitive advantage. Finally, they amplified their home-based advantages and offset home-based disadvantages through global strategies that tapped selectively into advantages available in other nations. Competitive advantage ultimately results from an effective combination of national circumstances and company strategy. Conditions in a nation may create an environment in which firms can attain international competitive advantage, but it is up to a company to seize the opportunity.

The actions required to create and sustain competitive advantage in international terms are challenging and often intensely uncomfortable. There are other ways to achieve profitability, such as seeking government protection, harvesting market position through underinvestment, and avoiding global industries altogether. A number of large Italian companies are highly profitable today, for example, because of government intervention that has eliminated effective rivalry. In a world of increasing global competition, however, such alternatives have their own perils. In Italy, for example, the reduction of internal European market barriers will be a grave threat to companies that have prospered through political and not economic strategies.

The premise in this chapter is that a firm must set its sights on creating and sustaining competitive advantage measured against the best worldwide competitors. I also presume that the firm is prepared to sacrifice an easy life to seek true international advantage, and that it aspires to sustained success rather than mere survival or the temporary profits of harvesting market position. Many of the principles I describe here will be equally important to companies in purely domestic industries.

COMPETITIVE ADVANTAGE IN INTERNATIONAL COMPETITION

Our study has involved a detailed look at the histories of well over a hundred industries. The particular strategies employed by the successful firms were diverse in every respect. Yet every firm (and national industry) that enjoyed sustained competitive advantage manifested certain underlying modes of behavior. Though the strategies differed, their character and their trajectory over time were remarkably similar, echoing themes I introduced in Chapter 2. There was a pervasive mentality and attitude toward competing within the national industry that set it apart from rivals. While essential to domestic competition, these principles are made even more important by global competition.

1. *Competitive advantage grows fundamentally out of improvement, innovation, and change.* Firms gain advantage over international rivals because they perceive a new basis for competing, or find new and better means to

compete in old ways. Sony was the first to transistorize the radio. Boeing pioneered the concept of an airliner family and was the first in its industry to compete aggressively on a global basis. Yamaha discovered how to automate the production of previously hand-built pianos. Sandvik and Atlas Copco pioneered the "Swedish method" of mining. The history of virtually every global leader reveals such insights and accomplishments.

Innovation, in strategic terms, is defined in its broadest sense. It includes not only new technologies but also new methods or ways of doing things, that sometimes appear quite mundane. Innovation can be manifested in a new product design, a new production process, a new approach to marketing, or a new way of training or organizing. It can involve virtually any activity in the value chain.

In international markets, innovations that yield competitive advantage anticipate not only domestic but foreign needs. Some innovations create competitive advantage when a firm perceives an entirely new buyer need or serves a market segment that rivals have ignored. Advantage results because foreign competitors are often slow to respond effectively. Japanese firms, for example, gained advantage in many industries through emphasis on smaller, compact, lower-capacity product varieties that foreign competitors disdained as less important and less profitable. Innovations that lead to competitive advantage are also frequently based on new methods or technology that render existing assets and facilities obsolete. Rivals fail to respond because of fear of speeding up the obsolescence of their past investments.

The home nation is integral to the process of perceiving the opportunity for innovation and successfully implementing it. One of the essential challenges of any firm is to position itself so that it is able to improve and innovate. Part of the task is to take best advantage of the national environment to help discern possibilities for innovation and overcome organizational inertia in pursuing them.

2. *Competitive advantage involves the entire value system.* The value system is the entire array of activities involved in a product's creation and use, encompassing the value chains of the firm, suppliers, channels, and buyers. Close and ongoing interchange with suppliers and channels is integral to the process of creating and sustaining advantage. Competitive advantage frequently comes from perceiving new ways to configure and manage the entire value system. Firms restructure or integrate their activities with suppliers, modify the strategies of channels, and recombine or integrate activities with buyers.

A good example is the Italian clothing company, Benetton. Production takes place through a network of owned and independent manufacturing facilities, connected closely to franchised retailers using state-of-the-art information systems. All through the value system, Benetton redesigned and recombined activities to minimize inventory, ensure rapid delivery, and allow rapid responsiveness to fashion trends. For example, garments are first manufactured and only later dyed, after color trends are better established. In order to control inventory and speed up delivery, retailers can order only fixed assortments of merchandise. Different retail store configurations have been franchised to address different market segments, including the children's market.

The importance of the entire value system to competitive advantage is manifested by the prevalence of clustering. The presence of world-class suppliers and users in a nation is an important asset, and is associated with international advantage in countless industries. The strongest competitive advantages often emerge from clusters that are geographically localized.

Firms must compete in ways that take advantage of the presence of the national cluster. To sustain advantage, firms must often create or extend these clusters by stimulating the formation of suppliers, improving the sophistication of customers, or encouraging entry into related industries.

3. *Competitive advantage is sustained only through relentless improvement*. There are few competitive advantages that cannot be imitated. Korean firms have matched the ability of Japanese firms to mass-produce standard color TV sets and VCRs. Brazilian firms have technology and designs comparable to Italy in casual leather footwear.

Firms (and national industries) that remain a stationary target are eventually overtaken by rivals. Sometimes entrenched competitive positions can be held for years or decades once improvement stops, on the strength of early mover advantages such as established customer relationships, scale economies in existing technologies, and the loyalty of distribution channels. Yet more dynamic rivals eventually find a way around these advantages by discovering better or cheaper ways of doing things. British and then American firms lost almost century-old positions in machine tools in the space of a decade, for example, when foreign rivals took advantage of new computer technology. German firms lost leadership in cameras for comparable reasons, when Japanese firms moved more aggressively to develop single lens reflex technology and to introduce electronics. In shipbuilding, it was Japanese firms that gave up a substantial share when improvement slowed and Korean firms replicated their strategies with cheaper labor.

Advantage once gained is only sustained by a continual search for different and better ways of doing things and through ongoing modifications in firm behavior within an overall strategic context. The firm competing with a differentiation strategy, for example, must find a stream of new ways to add to its differentiation, or, minimally, improve its effectiveness in differentiating in old ways. Yet the need for continuous innovation runs counter to organizational norms in most companies. Firms would rather not change. Particularly in a successful firm, powerful forces work against modifying strategy. Past approaches become institutionalized in procedures and management controls. Specialized facilities are created. Personnel are trained in one mode of behavior. Self-selection attracts new employees who believe in the existing ways of doing things and are particularly suited to implementing them. The strategy becomes almost like a religion, and questioning any aspect is regarded as bordering on heresy. Information that would challenge current approaches is screened out or dismissed. Individuals who challenge established wisdom are expelled or isolated. As an organization matures, its need for stability and security seems to rise.

It takes strong pressures to counteract these forces. Rarely do these come exclusively from within an organization. Companies seldom change spontaneously; the environment jars or *forces* them to change. A company must expose itself to external pressures and stimuli that motivate and guide the need to act. It must create the impetus for change. How a company chooses to position itself within its home nation, and elsewhere, is an important tool for doing so.

The difficulty of innovation means that it is often ''outsiders'' to the firm, the industry, the established social structure, or based in other nations, that are the catalysts for innovation. Outsiders can perceive changes that go unnoticed or contradict conventional wisdom. Outsiders are neither wedded to past strategies nor worried about upsetting industry or social norms. How a company and its management can behave like ''outsiders'' represents an interesting challenge. Whether the role of outsider can be played by firms from *within* the nation instead of those from other nations will have much to do with whether a nation's industry will advance.

4. *Sustaining advantage demands that its sources be upgraded.* A company's competitive advantage can grow out of any activity in the value chain, from product development to after-sale service. Sources of advantage differ in sustainability. Basic factor costs, company procedures involving little proprietary technology, and one-time design concepts represent easy-to-replicate advantages. Higher-order, more durable advantages are such things as established brand names resulting from years of marketing effort or proprietary process technology. Korean electronics firms, for example, have yet to develop sustainable advantages. They compete principally based on labor cost using Japanese production equipment and Japanese and American parts. American large-scale computer companies, in contrast, have much more sustainable advantages including economies as a result of large accumulated R&D investments, proprietary software development capability, established service networks whose cost is amortized by the presence of many machines already in place, and user loyalties created by substantial costs of switching because of a need for compatibility.

Lower-order advantages tend to be static and passive. They can be replicated by simple imitation. Factor costs shift rapidly. In global competition, factor cost advantages can also be readily nullified when foreign companies locate or source in a firm's home nation. Foreign competitors imitate procedures and buy the same manufacturing equipment. Not only are factor cost and other lower-order advantages unsustainable, but they usually imply competing on price in price-sensitive industry segments. Such segments are often especially vulnerable to new entrants. The Korean construction industry, for example, is facing tough rivalry from Thailand and the Philippines because of its inability to progress rapidly enough beyond labor-intensive infrastructure projects to more technologically involved projects and process plants.

More durable competitive advantages usually depend on possessing advanced human resources and internal technical capability. They demand ongoing investment in specialized skills and assets, as well as continuous change. For these reasons, differentiation strategies involving high product quality, advanced features, high levels of service, and a stream of new product innovations are usually more sustainable than cost-based strategies, even those resting on economies of scale or large initial capital investments. These can be replicated by competitors who purchase the latest equipment and facilities.

Sustaining advantage requires that a firm continually move *earlier* than rivals to widen its sources of advantage and especially to upgrade them. Having more sources of advantage means that the imitator has more to match. Upgrading the sources means that the imitator faces a greater challenge in matching each one.

Resting on less sophisticated advantages, conversely, is risky. A national industry that stops progressing to more advanced forms of competitive advantage is likely to be overtaken. Italian appliance producers, for example, were very successful competing on cost in selling midsize and compact appliances produced in Italy on an OEM basis through large chains. They may well have rested on this strategy too long. German competitors have been gaining position based on creating more differentiated products and strong brand identities.

Creating more sustainable competitive advantages may well require that a company make its less sustainable advantages obsolete even while they are still advantages. For example, by automating away much of the advantage of relatively low-cost and productive labor and competing in differentiated product varieties while still successful in standardized, low-priced ones, Japanese firms have been able to sustain advantage in many industries.

Sustaining competitive advantage demands that a firm practice a form of what Schumpeter called "creative destruction" on itself. It must destroy its old advantages by creating new ones. If not, some competitor will do so.[2]

Upgrading advantage confronts even more acutely the organizational challenges I described earlier. The difficulty of organizational change, particularly that which supplants previous approaches, means that rising factor costs, a strong home currency, or other selective factor disadvantages can be blessings in disguise. They prod an organization into productivity improvements, product upgrading, and globalization of strategy. The result is a more sustainable competitive position. This is the lesson of dozens of Swiss and German industries, where firms have migrated to advanced segments and/or automated complex manufacturing processes to offset high labor costs.

A company's leader must create a context in which widening and upgrading advantage is viewed as normal and expected. For example, the norm should be to move early to address factor cost pressures, rather than passively hoping that government policy will reverse them. In practice, such an orientation toward change is hard to accomplish from within. A leader must create an atmosphere that highlights the need for upgrading and demands that it take place. Competitive positioning should make it easier to sense and respond to possibilities to upgrade competitive advantage.

5. *Sustaining advantage ultimately requires a global approach to strategy.* A firm cannot sustain competitive advantage in international competition in the long run without exploiting and extending its home-base advantages with a global approach to strategy. A global approach supplements home-base advantages and helps nullify home-base disadvantages. German chemical companies employ extensive foreign production and worldwide marketing networks to solidify their leadership, as do Swiss pharmaceutical companies, Swedish truck manufacturers, and Japanese consumer electronics firms.

A global approach to strategy involves a number of important elements that I discussed in Chapter 2. First, it clearly means selling worldwide, not just in the home market. However, international sales are viewed not as incremental business but as integral to strategy. The firm builds an international brand name and establishes international marketing channels it controls. Second, a global strategy involves locating activities in other nations in order to capture local advantages, offset particular disadvantages, or to facilitate local market penetration. Third, and most importantly, a global strategy involves coordinating and integrating activities on a worldwide basis in order to gain economies of scale or learning, enjoy the benefits of a consistent brand reputation, and serve international buyers. Simply operating internationally does not equate to a global strategy unless this sort of integration and cooperation takes place. Advantages drawn from the global network add to home-based advantages and make them more sustainable. The scale from selling globally, for example, may allow a higher rate of R&D spending to take advantage of sophisticated home buyers and suppliers.

A company must move toward a global strategy as soon as its resources and competitive position allow if it is competing in a global industry. A high domestic cost of capital, high domestic factor costs, and a strong currency are no excuse in global competition. With a global strategy, these sorts of disadvantages can be circumvented. Yet competing globally is not a substitute for improvement and innovation at home. As we will see later, too much reliance on activities in other nations threatens the sustainability of a firm's competitive advantage.

THE CONTEXT FOR COMPETITIVE ADVANTAGE

These imperatives of competitive advantage constitute a mindset that is not present in many companies. Indeed, the actions required to create and sustain advantage are unnatural acts. Stability is valued in most companies, not change. Protecting old ideas and techniques becomes the preoccupation, not creating new ones.

The long-term challenge for any firm is to put itself in a position where it is most likely to perceive, and best able to address, the imperatives of competitive advantage I have described. The challenge is not an easy one, because the bias toward continuing past modes of behavior is strong. One problem is to expose a company to new market and technological opportunities that may be hard to perceive. Another is preparing for change by upgrading and expanding the skills of employees and improving the firm's scientific and knowledge base. Ultimately, the most important challenge is overcoming complacency and inertia to *act* on the new opportunities and circumstances.

The challenge of action ultimately falls on the firm's leader. Much attention has rightly been placed on the importance of visionary leaders in achieving unusual organizational success. Our study uncovered many examples of visionaries who had a large impact on their companies and industries. Some of the names might be familiar (Thomas J. Watson, Jr., Willis Carrier, Akio Morita, Koji Kobayashi, Carl Duisberg, Robert Bosch, Emil Barell, and Robert Sulzer), while others might be less familiar (Gaetano Barbieri, Henry Wild, and Friedrich Koenig).

But where does a leader get the vision and how is it transmitted to cause organizational accomplishment? Great leaders are influenced by the environment in which they work. Innovation takes place because the home environment stimulates it. Innovation succeeds because the home environment supports and even forces it. The right environment not only shapes a leader's own perceptions and priorities but provides the catalyst that allows the leader to overcome inertia and produce organizational change.

Great leaders emerge in different industries in different nations, in part because national circumstances attract and encourage them: visionaries in consumer electronics are concentrated in Japan, chemicals and pharmaceuticals in Germany and Switzerland, and computers in America. Leadership is important to any success story, but is not in and of itself sufficient to explain it. In many industries, the national environment provides one or two nations with a distinct advantage over their foreign competitors. Leadership often determines which particular firm or firms exploit it.

More broadly, the ability of any firm to innovate has much to do with the environment to which it is exposed, the information sources it has available and consults, and the types of challenges it chooses to face. Seeking safe havens and comfortable customer relationships only reinforces past behavior. Maintaining suppliers who are captive degrades a source of stimulus, assistance, and insight. Lobbying against stringent product standards sends the wrong signal to an organization about norms and aspirations.

Innovation grows out of pressure and challenge. It also comes from finding the right challenges to meet. The essential role of the firm's leader is to create the environment that meets these conditions. One essential part of the task is to take advantage of the national "diamond" that is currently present for competing in the industry.

PRESSURES FOR INNOVATION

A company should actively seek out pressure and challenge, not try to avoid them. Part of the task is to take advantage of the home nation in order to create the impetus for innovation. Some of the ways of doing so are the following:

Sell to the most sophisticated and demanding buyers and channels. Some buyers (and channels) will stimulate the fastest improvement because they are knowledgeable and expect the best performance. They will set a standard for the organization and provide the most valuable feedback. Sophisticated and demanding buyers and channels need not be the firm's only customers, and exclusive focus on them may unnecessarily diminish long-term profitability. However, serving a group of such buyers, chosen because their needs will challenge the firm's particular approach to competing, must be an explicit part of any strategy.

Seek out the buyers with the most difficult needs. Buyers who face especially difficult operating requirements (such as climate, maintenance requirements, or hours of use), who confront factor cost disadvantages in their own businesses that create unusual pressures for performance, who have particularly tough competition, or who compete with strategies that place especially heavy demands on the firm's product or service, are buyers that will provide a laboratory (and the pressure) to upgrade performance and extend features and services. Such buyers should be identified and cultivated. They become part of a firm's R&D program.

Establish norms of exceeding the toughest regulatory hurdles or product standards. Some localities (or user industries) will lead in terms of the stringency of product standards, pollution limits, noise guidelines, and the like. Tough regulatory standards are not a hindrance but an opportunity to move early to upgrade products and processes. Older or simplified models can be sold elsewhere.

Source from the most advanced and international home-based suppliers. Suppliers who themselves possess competitive advantage, as well as the insight that comes from international activities, will challenge the firm to improve and upgrade as well as provide insights and assistance in doing so.

Treat employees as permanent. When employees are viewed as permanent instead of to be hired and fired at will, pressures are created that work to upgrade and sustain competitive advantage. New employees are hired with care, and continuous efforts are made to improve productivity instead of adding workers. Employees are trained on an ongoing basis to support more sophisticated competitive advantages. They are transferred to new functions instead of laid off. Ideas for new products and related diversification are stimulated in order to redeploy skilled people.

Unions, for their part, must also change their attitudes. Impediments to productivity improvement, job movement, and advancement on merit must be eliminated.

Establish outstanding competitors as motivators. Those competitors who most closely match a company's competitive advantages, or have exceeded them, must become the standard of comparison. Such competitors can be a source of learning as well as a powerful focal point to overcome parochial concerns and motivate change for the entire organization. They become the common enemy to be bested. Komatsu (Japan), for example, has long seen Caterpillar (United States) this way, and the goal of beating Caterpillar has energized remarkable improvements in Komatsu's product quality, productivity, and relationship with distribution channels.

The implication is not that a firm should imitate such competitors, because imitative strategies rarely succeed. Komatsu competes differently from Caterpillar in important respects. Nevertheless, outstanding competitors should serve as benchmarks and motivators. Instead, companies have a tendency to compare themselves with competitors that make them look good. This only reinforces complacency and inertia.

These prescriptions may seem counterintuitive. The ideal would seem to be the stability growing out of obedient customers, captive and dependent suppliers, and sleepy competitors. Such a search for a quiet life, an understandable instinct, has led many companies to buy direct competitors or form alliances with them. In a closed, static world, monopoly would indeed be the most comfortable and profitable solution for companies.

In reality, however, competition is dynamic. Firms will lose to other firms who come from a more dynamic environment. Good managers are always running a little scared. They respect and study competitors. An attitude of meeting challenges is part of organizational norms. An organization that values stability and lacks self-perceived competition, in contrast, breeds inertia and creates vulnerabilities. Some companies maintain only the myth that they believe in competition. Success grows out of making the myth a reality.

If competition were purely domestic, confronting powerful customers and tough competitors might seem to result in lower company profitability, because of high buyer power and intense rivalry. Even in domestic competition, however, gaining competitive advantage allows a firm to outperform its industry. A firm need not exclusively serve demanding buyers nor should it compete head on with any rival. The aim in seeking pressure and challenge is to create the conditions in which competitive advantage can be preserved. Short-term pressure leads to long-term sustainability.

In global competition, the pressures of demanding local buyers, capable suppliers, and aggressive domestic rivalry are even more valuable and necessary for long-term profitability. These drive the firm to a faster rate of progress and upgrading than international rivals, and lead to sustained competitive advantage and superior long-term profitability. A tough domestic industry structure creates advantage in the international industry. A comfortable, easy home base, in contrast, leaves a firm vulnerable to rivals who enjoy greater dynamism at home.

A home base with demanding buyers, stringent needs, and able competitors, then, is a distinct advantage to a firm. A firm must actively position itself to capture the benefits, however. If a firm lacks the pressures for improvement and innovation, it must create them.

PERCEIVING INDUSTRY CHANGE

Beyond pressure to innovate, one of the most important advantages an industry can have is early insight into needs, environmental forces and trends that others have not noticed but will be important elsewhere. Japanese firms had an early and visible warning about the importance of energy efficiency. American firms have often gotten a jump in seeing demand for new services, giving them a head start in many service industries. Better insight and early warning signals lead to competitive advantages. Firms gain competitive position before rivals perceive an opportunity (or a threat) and are able to respond.

Perceiving possibilities for new strategies more clearly or earlier comes in part from simply being in the right nation at the right time. Yet it is possible for a firm to more actively position itself to see the signals of change and act on them. It must find the right focus or location within the nation, and work to overcome the filters that distort or limit information flow.

Identify and serve buyers (and channels) with the most anticipatory needs. Some buyers will confront new problems or have new needs before others, because of their demographics, location, industry, or strategy. Teaching hospitals see the most difficult medical cases, for example, and usually experiment first with new medical procedures and equipment. Customers facing the most acute labor shortages will be unusually attuned to new automation equipment or labor-saving business services.

Buyers with anticipatory needs should be identified, designated as priorities, and cultivated. Managers in all functions, as well as the chief executive, should have direct contact with them regularly.

Investigate all emerging new buyers or channels. It is new types of buyers or channels that often provide the opportunity for shifts in competitive position. The early emergence of the suburban market in the United States, for example, created opportunities in numerous industries for new products such as do-it-yourself tools that later penetrated foreign markets.

Find the localities whose regulations foreshadow those elsewhere. Some regions and cities will typically lead others in terms of their concern with social problems such as safety, environmental quality, and the like. Instead of avoiding such areas, as some companies do, they should be sought out. A firm should define its internal goals as meeting, or exceeding, their standards. An advantage will result as other regions, and ultimately other nations, modify regulations to follow suit.

Discover and highlight trends in factor costs. Increases in the costs of particular factors or other inputs may signal future opportunities to leapfrog competitors by innovating to deploy them more effectively or avoid the need for them altogether. A firm should know which markets or regions are likely to reflect such trends first.

Maintain ongoing relationships with centers of research and the sources of the most talented people. A firm must identify the places in the nation where the best new knowledge is being created that is relevant to the industry or might be relevant. Equally important is to identify the schools, institutions, and other companies where the best specialized human resources needed in the industry are trained. Investment in time, money, and ongoing contact is necessary to ensure access to people and research. Regularly recruiting personnel from the top schools, or other training grounds, is a good way to introduce new ideas and skills into the company.

Study all competitors, especially the new and unconventional ones. Rivals sometimes discover new ideas first. Innovators are often smaller, more focused, competitors that are new to the industry. Alternatively, they are firms led by managers with backgrounds in other industries not bound by conventional wisdom. The difficulty of change I spoke of earlier means that "outsiders," with fewer blinders to cloud their perception of new opportunities and fewer perceived constraints in abandoning past practices, are frequently the innovators in industries. A firm should designate the most forward-looking or unconventional competitors for particular study, including foreign competitors who may enjoy the benefits of a very different home base. The aim is as much to *learn* from competitors as to develop strategy to counter them.

Bring some outsiders into the management team. The incorporation of new thinking in the management process is often speeded by the presence of one or more "outsiders"—managers from other companies or industries or from the company's foreign subsidiaries. While internal development of most management is desirable for accumulating skills, the regular effort to introduce a new management perspective will benefit the innovation process.

INTERCHANGE WITHIN THE NATIONAL CLUSTER

A firm gains important competitive advantages from the presence in its home nation of world-class buyers, suppliers, and related industries. They provide insight into future market needs and technological developments. They contribute to a climate for change and improvement, and become partners and allies in the innovation process. Having a strong cluster at home unblocks the flow of information and allows deeper and more open contact than is possible when dealing with foreign firms. Being part of a cluster localized in a small geographic area is even more valuable.

Buyers, Channels, and Suppliers. The first hurdle to be cleared in taking advantage of the domestic cluster is attitudinal, or recognizing that home-based buyers and suppliers are allies in international competition and not just the other side of transactions. A firm must pursue the types of interchange with other industries in the cluster that I described in Chapters 3 and 4:

- Regular senior management contact
- Formal and ongoing interchange between research organizations
- Reciprocity in serving as test sites for new products or services
- Cooperation in penetrating and serving international markets

Working with buyers, suppliers, and channels involves helping them upgrade and extend *their own* competitive advantages. Their health and strength will only enhance their capacity to speed the firm's own rate of innovation. Open communication with local buyers or suppliers, and early access to new equipment, services, and ideas, are important for sustaining competitive advantage. Such communication will be freer, more timely, and more meaningful than usually possible with foreign firms.

Encouraging and assisting domestic buyers and suppliers to compete globally is one part of the task of upgrading them. A company's local buyers and suppliers cannot ultimately sustain competitive advantage in many cases unless they compete globally. Buyers and suppliers need exposure to the pressures of worldwide competition in order to advance themselves. Trying to keep them "captive" and prevent them from selling their products abroad is ultimately self-defeating.

It might seem that internationally active buyers and suppliers might run the risk of becoming closer to foreign firms. These sorts of concerns, while understandable, reflect a static and overly narrow view of competitive advantage. Competitive advantage grows out of ongoing improvement and innovation. Worrying about protecting today's secrets is less important than creating tomorrow's.

Attempting to prevent local suppliers from selling the current generation of equipment outside the nation looks backward instead of forward toward the next source of competitive advantage. It will encourage efforts to protect old advantages rather than create new ones, ultimately leading to a loss in position. This happened many times in the history of British industry. The result was always the same, foreign suppliers were spurred to enter the market and innovate while British suppliers became uncompetitive. Hesitation in encouraging local buyers to sell and even produce abroad is equally backward-looking. It is far better to face the pressure of more sophisticated local buyers and to develop the capability to also serve them in foreign nations. Home buyers and suppliers with a global scope and outlook will provide better insight into international and not just domestic needs and technological possibilities. Buyers and suppliers who are not captive will also challenge the firm to improve and upgrade, the only way to sustain competitive advantage.

An orientation toward closer vertical relationships is only just starting to take hold in many American companies, though it is quite typical in Japanese and Swedish companies. Interchange with buyers, channels, and suppliers always involves some tension, because there is inevitably the need to bargain with them over prices and service. In global industries, however, the competitive advantage to be gained from interchange more than compensates for some sacrifice in bargaining leverage. Interchange should not create dependence but interdependence. A firm should work with a group of suppliers and customers, not just one. As the Japanese case illustrates (Chapter 8), working closely with suppliers does not imply a reduction in bargaining power.

Related Industries. Industries that are related or potentially related in terms of technology, channels, buyers, or the way buyers obtain or use products, are potentially important to creating and sustaining competitive advantage. The presence in a nation of such industries deserves special attention. These industries are often essential sources of innovation. They can also become new suppliers, buyers, or even new competitors.

At a minimum, senior management should be visiting leading companies in related industries on a regular basis. The purpose is to exchange ideas about industry developments. Formal joint research projects, or other more structured ways to explore new ideas, are advisable where the related industry holds more immediate potential to affect competitive advantage.

Locating Within the Nation. A firm should locate activities and its headquarters at those locations in the nation where there are concentrations of sophisticated buyers, important suppliers, groups of competitors, or especially significant factor-creating mechanisms for its industry (such as universities with specialized programs or laboratories with expertise in important technologies). Geographic proximity makes the relationships within a cluster closer and more fluid. It also makes domestic rivalry more valuable for competitive advantage.

SERVING HOME BUYERS WHO ARE INTERNATIONAL AND MULTINATIONAL

To transform domestic competitive advantage into a global strategy, a firm should identify and serve buyers at home that it can also serve abroad. Such buyers are domestic companies that have international operations, individuals who travel frequently to other nations, and local subsidiaries of foreign firms. Targeting such buyers has two benefits. First, they can provide a base of demand in foreign markets to help offset the costs of entry. More important, they will often be sophisticated buyers who can provide a window into international market needs.

Examples of firms and industries that benefited from such pull-through effects could be cited in virtually every nation we studied. As I discussed in Chapter 9, for example, an important part of Britain's and later America's international success was built on the foundation of serving home buyers' needs abroad. A nation's international and multinational buyers are an important asset to the industries that serve them.

IMPROVING THE NATIONAL COMPETITIVE ENVIRONMENT

Sustaining competitive advantage is not only a function of making most of the national environment. Firms must work actively to improve their home base by upgrading the national "diamond." A company draws on its home nation (for example, factor pools, local suppliers, demand conditions) to extend and upgrade its own competitive advantages. The firm has a stake in making its home base a better platform for international success.

Playing this role demands that a company understand how each part of the "diamond" best contributes to competitive advantage. It also requires a long-term perspective, because the investments required to improve the home base often take years or even decades to bear fruit. What is more, short-term profits are elevated by foregoing such investments, and by shifting important activities abroad instead of upgrading the ability to perform them at home. Both will diminish the sustainability of a firm's competitive advantages.

Firms have a tendency to see the task of ensuring high-quality human resources, infrastructure, and scientific knowledge as someone else's responsibility. Another common misconception is that because competition is global the home base is unimportant. Of the nations we studied, the perspective of improving the home base is least common today in the United States, Britain, and Sweden. Too often, U.S. and British companies, especially, leave investments in the national "diamond" to others or to the government. The result is that companies are "well managed" but lack the human resources, technology, and access to capable suppliers and customers needed to succeed against foreign rivals.

THE FIRM'S ROLE IN FACTOR CREATION

Advanced and specialized factors of production, such as highly skilled personnel, industry-specific infrastructure, and local scientific expertise in particular fields, are *sine qua nons* of competitive advantage. The level of competitive advantage that a nation's firms can achieve is set by the quantity and especially the quality of factors. Yet they are not inherited by a nation but created. While government has a constructive and important role in creating factors, it cannot be left to government alone.

In nearly every competitive industry we studied, no matter what the nation, leading firms took explicit steps to create factors or ensure that institutions were established or influenced to do so. Companies did not accept the status quo of factor development in the nation but sought to upgrade it. Italian industry associations invest in marketing information, process technology, and common infrastructure in such industries as wool cloth, ceramic tiles, and lighting equipment. Swiss and German firms widely participate in apprenticeship programs. In Britain, successful industries such as chemicals and pharmaceuticals are characterized by close ties with universities and government research institutes, even though such collaboration in Britain is the exception rather than the rule.

Company Investments in Factor Creation. Firms must invest directly in factor creation through their own training, research, and infrastructure building. Internal efforts at factor creation lead to the most specialized, and often most important, factors. The competitive firms we studied usually had well-developed internal training programs and, compared to their rivals, set aside more than average resources for R&D. Leading Japanese companies, for example, often have their own schools and are rapidly building basic research capability in company laboratories. International leaders also often pioneered or were major driving forces behind improvements in infrastructure as well. Yamaha, for example, faced a shortage of skilled piano technicians in Japan. It founded its own educational program that is now highly regarded internationally for acoustics training. The benefits flow to Yamaha as well as the entire Japanese industry. Companies' own investments in factor creation need not be made entirely in-house, and can take advantage of external resources such as schools to which company personnel are sent or contract research establishments.

The typical argument against company investments in factor creation, often heard in America, is the so-called *free rider* problem. Firms hesitate to make such investments because trained employees leave, technology is copied, and infrastructure cannot be kept proprietary. Though this argument has a ring of truth, it is another vestige of a static conception of competition. Few of the most competitive firms we studied acted as if they believed it. Trained personnel do leave innovative, successful firms, but rarely in large numbers. Turnover is itself a function of the investments companies make in factor creation. Companies that invest in their personnel and have an orientation toward innovation and change usually have low turnover of key personnel. Departing personnel may benefit the national industry by ending up at suppliers or customers.

Even more important, however, is that regular and rapid technological *progress,* not one-shot breakthroughs, is the secret to retaining competitive advantage. A firm that bases its strategy on free riding on another's investments will ultimately lose because it will always be behind. Technology is inevitably diffused in most national industries, and eventually imitated by foreign rivals. Diffusion of innovations within the nation, however, benefits the national industry through stimulating further progress and upgrading; so do spin-offs from established firms.

Failing to invest in factor creation is a fatal error in international competition. While a firm's investments will always benefit competitors to some extent, the short-term cost of leakage is usually outweighed by the faster rate of innovation such investments make possible. Investments in factor creation have a medium- to long-term payback. It takes sustained investment over a number of years to see the return. Stop and start patterns of investment are often ineffective.

Compared to the United States, the lower rate of personnel turnover in nations such as Japan and Germany certainly makes it easier for firms in these nations to see the benefits of human resource investments. However, one can point to numerous U.S. companies that prove the rule by being exceptions. IBM, DuPont, Hewlett-Packard, and others illustrate that sustained investment in technology and human resources can yield high returns in terms of international success.

One way to foster the right orientation toward factor creation among both managers and employees, that I discussed earlier, is for a company to make the commitment to maintain permanent employment to the maximum extent possible. Viewing employment as permanent creates the best incentives both for the company and its employees to invest in upgrading skills.

Industry or Cluster Programs for Factor Creation. As important, in many ways, as a firm's own internal efforts at factor creation is the pool of specialized factors available in the nation. Firms can influence these through industry or cluster-wide (sectoral) programs. Firms can invest in information, training schools, infrastructure, and research that benefits the entire national industry in a variety of ways. One is through trade associations. In the Italian apparel, shoe, ceramic tile, and furniture industries, for example, industry associations played a role in improving communications and logistical facilities, investigating process technology, and holding trade fairs. Firms in these industries compete fiercely but recognize the need to upgrade the pool of factors from which they all draw. In Japan, umbrella trade associations often cover many distinct industries within a sector and sponsor factor-creating investments that benefit the cluster. In America, the Electronics Industry Association has taken an active role in working with schools and universities.

Trade associations are often primarily lobbying organizations, especially in the United States. This squanders their most important potential benefit. When management recognizes that the pool of national factors is essential to success vis-à-vis firms from other nations, the view taken toward the role of trade groups is often profoundly altered.[3]

Firms can employ other institutional mechanisms to invest in industry or clusterwide factor creation. However, cooperative R&D among direct competitors is a risky approach. Notwithstanding the practical management problems, it runs the risks of dulling incentives to innovate and eliminating experimentation with alternative approaches, both necessary for sustained advancement. I discuss cooperative R&D and other forms of cooperation, and their proper role in company strategies, in the next chapter.

Influencing and Participating in Government/Community Factor Creation. Firms can influence factor creation through active involvement in the efforts of government entities, educational institutions, and the local community. Firms have a responsibility, not to mention a self-interest, in influencing the type and character of degree programs, research directions, and public services. A concentrated effort by a firm or group of firms can make a difference. Nestlé, for example, founded and supported Geneva-based IMI, which has become a leading European business school.[4] Nestlé has benefited from a steady flow of talented management and a vehicle for ongoing management training. German chemical companies have established relationships with all the major German universities and sponsor institutes devoted to chemical research, contributing to the rate of upgrading in the industry.

Firms can shape factor creation in educational institutions in many ways. One is by sponsoring students or sending personnel from the firm to study. Others include playing an active role in helping institutions identify the needs of the industry, planning curriculum, placing graduates, and providing financial support for equipment and facilities, faculty positions, scholarships, and recognition programs for outstanding teachers and students. Firms can establish working relationships with faculty in disciplines of interest to help such faculty understand the needs of industry and advise students accordingly.

The research program in fields relevant to an industry can also be improved in many ways. A firm must maintain regular contact with all centers of research that bear on its activities, through sponsoring visits by faculty to the firm's research facilities, creating programs in which company researchers spend time in university laboratories and vice versa, and participating in corporate sponsorship programs.

The firm can sponsor the creation of new university departments or research institutes in technological fields important to the industry. Research by leading investigators can be funded through specific research contracts in areas of company interest. A firm can provide financial support for research facilities and endowed research positions. Finally, companies can play an active advisory role in shaping research agendas and priorities. Private-sector time and the attention of outstanding people are as important as money to educational institutions and governmental entities.

High levels of corporate participation in such activities are typical in Germany and Switzerland, an important reason why these nations have been able to upgrade factors and sustain innovation in industries for many decades. In Germany, for example, virtually every significant company participates in apprenticeship programs involving local technical schools, maintains close contacts with local university departments, and sponsors research at independent research institutes. In Japan, advanced factor creation is mostly within firms, and contacts with schools and universities are less significant, which represents a weakness. In America, such efforts are often seen as community service or something firms should do as "social responsibility."

In these as well as industrywide efforts at factor creation, companies tend to view their self-interest too narrowly. They fail to contribute to university research programs because they cannot gain exclusive access to the results. They hesitate in establishing vocational training schools because competitors can also draw on them. This attitude reflects a narrow and inappropriate view of how competitive advantage is created. A firm has a stake in the pool of available factors, even (and especially) if they also benefit suppliers, customers, and competitors.

Forming and Upgrading the National Cluster

The presence of world-class suppliers, buyers, and related industries in the home nation is particularly valuable to a firm's competitive advantage. Firms can and should play an active role in the formation of clusters. One aspect of this is to help domestic buyers upgrade their competitive position and become international. This includes encouraging them to invest abroad and awarding them overseas as well as domestic business. Having internationally successful industrial buyers at home not only makes them more sophisticated and more anticipatory of foreign needs, but also means they will be larger customers. Consumer goods firms will also benefit in the long run from efforts to make home demand more sophisticated. Japanese musical instrument manufacturers, led by Yamaha and Suzuki, have widened and upgraded home demand (and later, foreign demand) by establishing music schools.

Firms should work actively to stimulate the establishment of local suppliers of important inputs (including services) if they are not already present, assist them in upgrading their capabilities, and encourage them to compete internationally. Developing domestic suppliers is better for sustaining competitive advantage in the long run than relying solely on foreign suppliers, though a firm must deal with both. Having world-class suppliers at home speeds the innovation process and the sophistication and sustainability of competitive advantage. For example, IBM recognizes this in its continuing efforts to assist U.S. semiconductor companies and semiconductor manufacturing companies. Firms should also do what they can to stimulate related industries in the nation that could provide local sources of new technology.

In some cases, firms may find it necessary and desirable to *enter* upstream and related industries to speed their development. I described earlier how the German pioneer in printing presses, Koenig & Bauer, entered the paper manufacturing industry to ensure a supply of high-quality paper when the industry was developing in the nineteenth century. NEC Corporation, now the world leader in semiconductors, entered that industry to provide high-quality chips needed for its telecommunications products. Corning, a leader in fiber optic cable, was an important early participant in optical connectors and photodiodes, both important to overall fiber optic system performance.

In some cases, such as Koenig & Bauer and Corning, firms eventually exited upstream or related industries once the domestic industry was well developed. Their entry, however, was an important tool for upgrading local industries and attracting more competitors.

Firms are often hesitant to help their local customers and suppliers, or encourage them to become international, for several reasons. One is the fear they will buy elsewhere or sell their technology or services to foreign rivals. A second issue is that of protecting proprietary technology. In the Italian ceramic tile industry, for example, I spoke with a number of manufacturers who were dismayed that Italian equipment producers were selling abroad. I discussed earlier why both these concerns are ill-founded. A third source of hesitancy in making investments to upgrade local suppliers is that it will depress short-term financial results. While moving completely to a foreign supplier may seem more profitable, however, the experience of many industries suggests that it may well undermine long-term competitive advantage.

Home-based but international suppliers, buyers, and related industries carry a final important benefit. I discussed earlier the dangers of a cluster becoming insular. The risks are diminished if firms in many industries in the cluster have global strategies and activities abroad.

The mandate to build and upgrade the domestic cluster does not mean that foreign customers and suppliers should receive no attention or be discriminated against. They remain important. What is implied instead is that local buyers and suppliers should receive full attention and support, even if they are initially smaller or less sophisticated.

A concern with the health of home-based customers, suppliers, and related industries reflects not economic nationalism but the realities of how improvement and innovation take place. Protection of customers and suppliers is inappropriate. Foreign customers and suppliers are also integral to strategy, as I will discuss later.

THE IMPORTANCE OF DOMESTIC RIVALRY

Companies have a vested interest in having capable, home-based competitors. Part of what makes a nation successful in an industry is vigorous domestic rivalry. Rarely do firms gain and sustain competitive advantage internationally without tough competition at home. I have also discussed how important domestic rivalry is to the entire national "diamond," in areas such as factor creation, supplier development, and demand sophistication.

While tough domestic rivalry is a national asset, there is a tendency to view it as a liability. Companies complain about excessive competition. Merging with domestic rivals is viewed as beneficial to international success.

This has become particularly prevalent in the United States, and also recently in Europe as a response to potential liberalization of trade within the EC. The logic is that a greater domestic market share will lead to a critical mass and allow companies to reap economies of scale.

This perspective, while understandable, reflects an incomplete view of competitive advantage. What is most important to competitive advantage is not static efficiency but a firm's dynamism. Firms will not be served by eliminating domestic rivalry. It is better to gain scale by expanding internationally than to dominate the domestic market. Foreign acquisitions are preferable to domestic acquisitions of leading competitors for the same reason. They also speed the process by which a company globalizes its strategy to supplement home-based advantages or offset home-based disadvantages.

The Japanese case illustrates particularly well how a group of active domestic rivals, many of whom compete globally, can not only each achieve the necessary scale but can establish strong international positions. The presence of active domestic rivalry helps in sustaining international success. Buying domestic competitors is the easier solution, but not often the right one.

INFLUENCING GOVERNMENT POLICY

Firms have an important role to play in shaping government policy, and in placing their weight and support behind constructive government programs. Unfortunately, firms sometimes do not perceive their long-run interests clearly when it comes to government policy. In fact, they are sometimes their own worst enemies. Companies often lobby for quick fixes that undermine the prospects of gaining long-run competitive advantage: protection, guaranteed government procurement, relaxation of regulatory standards, subsidized capital and energy, permission to merge with competitors, and so on. It will become clear from the next chapter that these instincts are unfortunate ones.

Firms should be championing government policies that enhance the national "diamond" in their industry, such as investments in factor creation and assistance in gaining foreign market access. The most serious mistake is to support policies that will undermine true competitive advantage, reduce the impetus to improve and innovate, and create an attitude of dependence on government.

WHERE AND HOW TO COMPETE

A firm's home nation shapes where and how it is likely to succeed in global competition. Germany is a superb environment for competing in printing equipment but not a very conducive one for international success in heavily advertised consumer packaged goods. Italy represents a remarkable setting for innovation in fashion and furnishing, but a poor environment for success in industries that sell to government agencies or infrastructure providers.

Within an industry, a nation's circumstances also favor competing in particular industry segments and with certain competitive strategies. Given local housing conditions, for example, Japan is a good home base for competing globally in compact models of appliances and in appliances that are inherently compact (such as microwaves) but a poor home base for competing in full-sized refrigerators. Within compact appliances, the Japanese environment is particularly conducive to differentiation strategies based on rapid new model introduction and high product quality. Korea, without advanced local demand and far from major markets, is an environment that favors low-cost strategies in relatively standardized product segments. Korean home demand conditions also mean that firms almost invariably compete in compact, smaller-size models.

The national "diamond" becomes central to choosing the industries to compete in as well as the appropriate strategy. The home base is an important determinant of a firm's strengths and weaknesses relative to foreign rivals.

ANALYZING INTERNATIONAL COMPETITORS

Understanding the home base of foreign competitors is essential in analyzing them. Their home nation yields them advantages and disadvantages. It also shapes their likely future strategies.[5] The "diamond" serves as an important tool for competitor analysis in international industries.

I have provided an overview of the patterns of national advantage in a number of nations in Chapters 7, 8, and 9. These chapters can serve as a starting point for industry and company-specific studies of competitors based in these nations. Some areas of particular importance in analyzing international competitors are the following:

Goals. The goals of companies differ substantially in different nations, due to such diverse factors as capital market conditions, ownership and corporate governance structures, management backgrounds, the nature of domestic rivalry, and the degree of commitment to the industry and to the local area. Many Korean firms are preoccupied with growth and volume. German firms frequently frame goals in technical terms and emphasize profitability in differentiated segments over market share. Japanese firms have patient institutional holders of equity and place particular weight on market share as the measure of where they stand. Each particular competitor based in a nation will have its own unique goals, but the national environment is always an important influence.

Competitive Advantages and Disadvantages. The "diamond" provides a framework for assessing important areas of competitive strength and weakness. The following are only a few examples:

Factor conditions: International rivals will differ in the mix and cost of available factors and the rate of factor creation. Swedish automobile firms, for example, benefit from the solidarity wage system that makes the wages of Swedish auto workers closer to those of other Swedish industries but relatively lower than the wages of auto workers in other advanced nations.

Demand conditions: Competitors from other nations will face differing segment structures of home demand, differing home buyer needs, and home buyers with various levels of sophistication. Demand conditions at their home base will help predict foreign competitors' directions of product change as well as their likely success in product development, among other things.

Related and supporting industries: Competitors based in other nations will differ in the availability of domestic suppliers, the quality of interaction with supplier industries, and the presence of related industries. Italian footwear firms and leather goods producers, for example, have early access to new tanned leather styles because of the world-leading Italian leather tanning industry.

Firm strategy, structure, and rivalry: The environment in their home nation will strongly influence the strategic choices of foreign rivals. Italian packaging equipment firms, for example, reflect their Italian context. They are mostly small and managed by strong paternal leaders. Owners of firms have personal relationships with significant buyers. This makes them unusually responsive to market trends and provides the ability to custom-tailor machinery to buyer circumstances.

Predicting Probable Behavior. National characteristics provide important clues to probable foreign competitor behavior. Each of the determinants contains insights into future moves. A partial set of questions that must be answered is listed in Table 11–1.

CHOOSING INDUSTRIES AND STRATEGIES

A firm's home base does not provide an equal chance for international success in all industries. We have seen how a Japanese firm is more likely to achieve world-class status in writing instruments, advanced materials, or facsimile than it is in food and beverages, aerospace, or furniture. A Swiss firm is more likely to succeed in climate control or processed foods

TABLE 11-1 Predicting the Behavior of Foreign Rivals

FIRM STRATEGY, STRUCTURE, AND RIVALRY

- How will the goals of firms shape strategies, time horizons, and target segments?
- How will the nature of domestic rivalry pressure firms to change?

FACTOR CONDITIONS	DEMAND CONDITIONS
• What is the direction of industry-related research in the nation and the types of training received by new employees?	• Which industry segments are likely to be emphasized because of their importance domestically?
• How will pressures from selective factor disadvantages modify strategies?	• What trends in domestic buyer needs will shape competitor perceptions of new product directions?

RELATED AND SUPPORTING INDUSTRIES

- How will developments in local supplier industries skew the direction of technical development?
- How will entry from related industries redefine the nature of domestic rivalry or pressure firms to change?

than in movies or computers. American firms will do better in industries involving frontier technology that draw on university research and funding by venture capitalists than in mature industries requiring high levels of ongoing investment that have volatile profits (for example, machine tools or steel).

The same applies to the choice of strategies. American footwear and apparel producers usually fail against international rivals in relatively standardized products, but many have succeeded by focusing on upscale designer clothing (Ralph Lauren) or on particularly American segments such as running shoes (Nike, New Balance), blue jeans (Levi's, Farah), and casual leather shoes (Timberland, Topsiders, Bass). German optical firms struggle in mass consumer products but prosper in specialized industrial segments.

The likelihood that a firm can achieve breakthroughs or innovations of strategic importance in an industry is also influenced by its home nation. Innovation and entrepreneurial behavior is partly a function of chance. However, I have discussed how it depends to a considerable degree on the environment in which the innovator or entrepreneur works. The "diamond" has a strong influence on which nation (and even on which region within the nation) will be the source of an innovation. Important innovations in

Denmark, for example, have occurred in enzymes for food processing, in natural vitamins, in measuring instruments related to food processing, and in drugs isolated from animal organs (insulin, the anti-coagulant heparin). These are hardly random in a nation whose exports are dominated by a large cluster of food- and beverage-related industries. A firm or individual has the best odds of succeeding in innovation, or in creating a new business, where the national "diamond" provides the best environment.

A firm's home base defines, in part, its competitive advantages and disadvantages in global industries. Korean firms in the automobile and apparel industries enjoy a large pool of dedicated, disciplined workers who still earn moderate wages. Yet firms lack sophisticated local demand and must import many parts and most machinery because domestic suppliers are poorly developed. American medical equipment firms face relatively high wages and pressure to report high levels of profitability, yet they benefit from the world's most advanced buyers, rapid and specialized factor creation both in medical science and human resources, and a pull-through effect from medical personnel trained in the United States who practice abroad.

The national circumstances most significant for competitive advantage depend on a firm's industry and strategy. In a resource- or basic factor-driven industry, the most important national attribute is a supply of superior or low-cost factors. In a fashion-sensitive industry, the presence of advanced and cutting-edge customers is paramount. In an industry heavily based on scientific research, the quality of factor-creating mechanisms in human resources and technology, coupled with access to sophisticated buyers and suppliers, are decisive.

Cost-oriented strategies are more sensitive to factor costs, the size of home demand, and the conditions that favor large-scale plant investments. Differentiation strategies tend to depend more on specialized human resources, sophisticated local buyers, and world-class local supplier industries. Focus strategies rest on the presence of unusual demand in particular segments or on factor conditions or supplier access that benefit competing in a particular product range.

As competition globalizes, and as developments such as European trade liberalization and free trade between the United States and Canada promise to eliminate artificial distortions that have insulated domestic firms from market forces, firms must increasingly compete in industries and segments where they have real strengths. This must increasingly be guided by the national "diamond." A firm can raise the odds of success if it is competing in industries, and with strategies, where the nation provides an unusually fertile environment for competitive advantage. The questions in Table 11–2 are designed to expose such areas. Of major importance is a *forward-looking* view in answering these questions. The focus must be on the nature of evolving competition, not the past requirements for success.

TABLE 11–2 Choosing Industries and Segments for Which the Nation Is a Favorable Home Base

FIRM STRATEGY, STRUCTURE, AND RIVALRY

- Does the style of management and prevailing types of organizational structures in the nation match industry needs?
- What types of strategies exploit national norms of organization?
- Does the industry attract outstanding talent in the nation?
- Do investor goals fit the competitive needs of the industry?
- Are there capable domestic rivals?

FACTOR CONDITIONS

- Does the nation have particularly advanced or appropriate factors of production? In what segments? For what strategies?
- Does the nation have superior factor creation mechanisms in the industry (for example, specialized university research programs, outstanding educational institutions)?
- Are selective factor disadvantages in the nation leading indicators of foreign circumstances?

DEMAND CONDITIONS

- Are the nation's buyers for the industry's products the most sophisticated or demanding? In what segments?
- Does the nation have unusual needs in the industry that are significant but will likely be ignored elsewhere?
- Do buyer needs in the nation anticipate those of other nations?
- Are the distribution channels in the nation sophisticated, and do they foreshadow international trends?

RELATED AND SUPPORTING INDUSTRIES

- Does the nation have world-class supplier industries? For what segments?
- Are there strong positions in important related industries?

Ricola, the Swiss herbal candy company, provides a good example of the choice of a segment that exploits national advantages. Ricola became successful when it focused its product line (out of the hundreds of possible segments) on herbal candy and cough drops (*Kräuterzucker*). Herbal medicine has a long tradition in Switzerland and fits with the Swiss concern for health. In this segment, Swiss buyers are a good proving ground for marketing appeals. Ricola moved aggressively to reap scale economies in its narrow product line through efficient production and worldwide sales. It took advantage of the Swiss position in related industries by piggybacking on Tobler's (chocolate) international distribution channels to penetrate foreign markets. It also took advantage of the Swiss reputation for high standards of purity in its international marketing campaign. Ricola succeeded by carefully choosing a segment where Switzerland provided home-base advantages. It would have had little prospects for success in other segments.

PENETRATING FOREIGN MARKETS

The same principles I have described also bear on the best way to penetrate foreign markets. A firm should select segments where its home base provides advantages but which are modest or emerging segments in foreign nations. Local firms or international rivals based in other nations will often have placed their attention elsewhere and be ill-prepared to fight.

Another guideline for penetrating foreign markets is to follow home-based multinationals. This not only provides a foothold but leads to segments where local firms may be disadvantaged.

DIVERSIFICATION

While diversification is part of company strategy in virtually every nation, its track record has been mixed at best. Widespread diversification into unrelated industries was rare among the international leaders we studied. They tended instead to compete in one or two core industries or industry sectors, and their commitment to these industries was absolute. For every widely diversified Hitachi or Siemens, there were several Boeings, Koenig & Bauers, FANUCs, Novo Industris, and SKFs, who are global competitors but heavily focused on their core industry.

It is *internal* diversification, instead of acquisition, that has resulted in leading international market positions to a striking degree. Sandvik's move from specialty steel into rock drills, the diversification of Swiss pharmaceuticals companies from dyes, and Canon's evolution from cameras to calculators to copiers to facsimile are just a few examples. Where acquisitions were involved in international success stories, the acquisitions were often modest or focused ones that served as an initial entry point or reinforced an internal entry. Hewlett-Packard's acquisition of Sanborn in patient monitoring equipment, for example, was a springboard for applying HP's marketing, technological, and international marketing skills to a new industry. Whenever a firm began broad-ranging diversification, it was generally a sign that competitive advantage was about to fade. Where the diversification took place through a series of major acquisitions, the sign was even more reliable.[6]

The reasons for this track record in diversification are not hard to understand when viewed in light of my theory. Improvement and innovation are at the heart of competitive advantage. They grow out of focus, commitment, and sustained investment in an industry. Diversification within a cluster, or which extends the cluster, is prone to stimulate new ways of competing as complementary skills and resources are brought to bear. Internal diversification facilitates the transfer of skills and resources, quite difficult to accomplish when acquiring an independent company with its own history and way of operating. Internal entry tends to increase the overall rate of investment in factor creation. There is also an intense commitment to succeed in diversification into closely related fields, because of the benefits that accrue to the base business and the effect on the overall corporate image.

Unrelated diversification, particularly through acquisition, makes no contribution to innovation. Unrelated diversification almost inevitably detracts from focus, commitment, and sustained investment in the core industries, no matter how well-intentioned management is at the outset. Acquired companies, where there is no link to existing businesses, often face short-term financial pressures to justify their purchase price. It is also difficult for corporate managers of a diversified firm to be forward-looking in industries they do not know. The process of innovation and change is undermined. In a number of U.S. industries we studied, for example, the acquisition of competitors by widely diversified firms diminished the rate of innovation and investment. Examples include syringes, patient monitoring equipment, oil field equipment, and machine tools. This pattern is widespread.

The nations in which unrelated diversification has been the most popular and acquisitions are the easiest to make today are America and Britain. In both nations, diversification seems to have contributed to competitive problems. In continental Europe and Japan, many of the strongest international companies are either not diversified or have diversified into closely related businesses, often through internal development. There are disturbing signs, however, that unrelated diversification is on the rise in both these areas.

In Korea, unrelated diversification has been consistent with investment-driven competitive advantage. The ability of the *chaebol* to mobilize capital and management talent into new fields was a benefit as long as Korea was a nation with scarce capital and limited technical and managerial resources (see Chapter 8). In the future, however, this pattern of diversification threatens to undermine further national progress. The major *chaebol* are moving into too many unrelated industries because of misplaced self-confidence, and the prospects for gaining competitive advantage in such disparate businesses are dim. I will discuss these issues further when I turn to the agendas facing individual nations.

The implications of my theory for diversification strategy are as follows:[7]

- New industries for diversification should be selected based on those where a favorable national "diamond" is present or can be created. Diversification proposals should be screened for the attractiveness of the home base.
- Diversification is most likely to succeed when it follows or extends clusters in which the firm already competes.
- Internal development of new businesses, supplemented by small acquisitions, is more likely to create and sustain competitive advantage than the acquisition of large, established companies.
- Diversification into businesses lacking common buyers, channels, suppliers, or close technological connections is not only likely to fail but will also undermine the prospects for sustaining advantage in the core businesses.

TAPPING SELECTIVE ADVANTAGES IN OTHER NATIONS

In modern international competition, a firm cannot rely solely on its national circumstances to sustain its competitive advantage. A firm must selectively add to its advantages or offset home-based disadvantages through activities in other nations. This is what a global strategy is all about.

In theory, it might appear that a multinational company could reap all the advantages of every nation through establishing foreign subsidiaries. In practice, it rarely works that way. Gaining the benefits of a home base requires insider status within the national "diamond." This is difficult to achieve unless another nation is truly the home base. A firm must become part of the culture, feel the local competitive pressure, and break completely into the network represented by the national cluster.[8] Not only is it difficult for a foreign subsidiary to become a true insider, but it is even more difficult for it to substantially influence the parent's global strategy at a distance from headquarters and the core research base.[9]

Indeed, the more a foreign subsidiary becomes an insider in one nation, the more difficult it is for the subsidiary to influence global strategy set at another home base. The subsidiary becomes viewed as "captive" to its nation and loses credibility at headquarters. The more integrated a subsidiary is into a global strategy driven from another home base, conversely, the less likely it is to become an insider in the nation. It lacks a full complement of manufacturing and research facilities.

A firm can only have one true home base for each distinct business or segment. If it attempts to have several, it will divide strategic authority, fragment technology development, and forego the synergistic benefits of concentrating the critical skills. Most importantly, it will sacrifice the dynamism that arises from true integration in a national "diamond."

The goal of a global company should not be to replicate home-base advantages of other nations. This will require moving its home base (see below). Instead, the goal is to tap selectively into sources of advantage in other national "diamonds" to supplement its own.

A global strategy, however, is not a substitute for a weak home base. Sustaining competitive advantage in the long run is difficult unless most of the underpinnings of innovation are present at home. Innovating to offset local factor disadvantages leads to more sustainable advantage than outsourcing. Developing domestic suppliers and buyers is better for improvement and innovation than relying solely on foreign ones. The aim should always be to upgrade domestic capabilities in order to make the foreign activities only selective and supplemental to overall competitive advantage.[10] A global strategy can minimize or offset disadvantages. Rarely can it create competitive advantage if the home base is unsound. Some Swedish and Swiss companies are risking their capacity to maintain positions as innovators, for example, by failing to invest in their home environments in a desire to "go global."

SERVING SOPHISTICATED BUYERS AND MARKETS

To sustain competitive advantage in global industries, a firm must sell to all significant country markets. Particularly important are nations that contain advanced and demanding buyers. All of the most advanced and sophisticated buyers are rarely located at home, even under the best of circumstances. Identifying sophisticated buyers in other nations will help the firm understand the most important new needs and create pressures that stimulate rapid progress in products and services. Nations with sophisticated buyers may well be where leading international competitors are based, making it all the more challenging to penetrate them.

Benetton, the leading Italian apparel producer, followed this principle very early in its development as an international company. The words of the chief executive, Luciano Benetton, describe the process:

"We have always thought it essential, since 1969 in fact, that we expand our activities outside Italy. We opened our first shop in Paris in 1969 and that was a major challenge for us. It was not easy to go into the French market. I felt like a schoolboy taking a tough exam when I decided to try and bring Italian fashion to Paris. We started out by trying to satisfy the Parisian consumer, a very demanding client indeed," he recalls, adding that once Benetton was successful in Paris he realized "we could make it anywhere."[11]

The Swiss printing press firm Wifag provides another good example. It placed great emphasis on penetrating the German market, home of not only sophisticated customers but also the majority of the world's competitors.

Among its proudest achievements is selling a press in Augsburg, hometown of MAN, a leading German producer. This mentality is part of what enables Wifag to remain a leading international competitor.

A firm must begin by identifying those nations where advanced buyers have their home base and invest to gain access. In telecommunications, for example, the United States is a highly advanced market due to the private ownership of telecommunications service providers, active rivalry between AT&T, MCI, and Sprint, and the presence of many large, spread-out buyers of telecommunications services with complex information needs. NEC, the leading Japanese telecommunications equipment company, recognized many years ago that it had to compete in the United States. If it could succeed there, NEC reasoned, it would gain advantages that would allow it to succeed elsewhere. NEC embarked on a long and often frustrating process of gaining access to the U.S. market. The results to date are a qualified success when measured in terms of U.S. profitability. However, the benefits to NEC's global position are incalculable.[12]

Gaining access to sophisticated and demanding buyers in other nations often requires a sequence of steps over a considerable period of time, and it always demands investment. Sometimes access is as easy as establishing a marketing presence. In other cases, the only way to gain initial access is through subcontracting or private-label sales. Typically, a subsequent move is to supply relatively simple items in the product line, or products targeted at underserved niches. Investment in some local production may be a further step along the path. Where there is protection or high entry barriers, gaining access may require targeted alliances with local firms.

Once a firm has access to demanding buyers, it must actively exploit the benefits. One such benefit is the ability to test new products or services in the most advanced market. For example, Procter & Gamble tests new varieties of disposable diapers in Japan, not only in the United States. The Japanese consumer is among the world's most demanding for diapers, and Procter & Gamble has started to expose itself to this discipline in product development. Montblanc (Germany) similarly seeks extensive input from Japanese customers when developing new pen models. It views Japanese buyers today as the world's most sophisticated.

GLOBAL PRODUCTION

A firm should conceive of its production system in global terms (see Chapter 2). Hewlett-Packard has substantial assembly activity in Singapore, for example, while world-leading Swedish and German truck manufacturers assemble in a variety of nations. Particular activities in the value chain should be dispersed to whatever country enjoys advantages. There is no excuse for accepting basic factor disadvantages. Dispersing selected production activities also facilitates foreign market access and signals greater commitment to foreign buyers. Process knowledge should also be sourced wherever good ideas arise, by coordinating among international production sites.

Performing activities abroad, however, or sourcing foreign process technology, does not imply ceding responsibility for the activities involved. If this occurs, the firm will undermine its possibilities for competitive advantage and risk always being one step behind foreign rivals. The knowledge and capability to design and upgrade the product and to improve and operate the complete production process *must* be maintained at home. Foreign activities should be viewed as selective. At the same time, continual efforts should be made to upgrade capabilities inside the firm and within the national cluster.

FOREIGN SOURCING

A firm must be willing to source products or equipment from foreign firms if they are superior, at the same time as it works to upgrade local suppliers. Access to the world's best inputs is necessary to sustain competitive advantage. Loyalty to domestic suppliers, for its own sake, is ultimately self-defeating. By not buying cheaper foreign steel, for example, U.S. automobile companies did not really help the U.S. steel industry in the long run and undermined their own competitive position.

The best form of loyalty to domestic suppliers is to confront them in no uncertain terms with the need to match their foreign competitors in quality and productivity in order to retain the business. Domestic suppliers should be given some leeway to allow time for adjustment, and be provided with active technical help and other assistance in upgrading. But domestic suppliers cannot be guaranteed the business. Unless they are taking aggressive action to upgrade quality, boost productivity, and globalize their own strategies, supporting domestic suppliers is to no one's ultimate gain.

TECHNOLOGY DEVELOPMENT ABROAD

A firm aspiring to competitive advantage must be aware of, and ideally have some access to, *all* the important scientific work going on in the world that is related to its industry. No matter how favorable the home base, useful research is likely to be taking place outside the home country. Today, a firm seeking competitive advantage should question its strategy if it does not have at least one foreign technology monitoring or research site. Such sites should be in nations with the best national "diamond," not just the ones with a top laboratory.

To get the benefit of tapping foreign technology development, the quality of personnel stationed abroad must be sufficient to understand and interpret local research directions. A critical mass of effort in a nation is also necessary to be accepted by the local scientific community. Some level of reciprocity is always required. A firm must be willing to invest money and personnel in local universities and in local industry efforts, as well as provide some access to its own ideas, in order to get something in return. If the firm conceives of its competitive advantage as resulting from continuous improvement instead of protecting today's secrets, it will be much more comfortable with this kind of interchange.

A good example of a firm that is pursuing such an approach is Novo Industri of Denmark. Novo has identified Japan and America as the places outside Denmark where world-class biotechnology research is taking place, a crucial technology for Novo's insulin and enzyme businesses. Novo has made substantial investment in research facilities in both countries. Such examples are numerous in the industries we studied. Swiss pharmaceutical firms have long had research centers in the United Kingdom and the United States. Swedish companies develop software in America, as do Swiss and German companies. Japanese companies have long been active investors in foreign technology development centers, not only using them as listening posts but also tapping into the best sources of scientific talent in the world in specialized fields.

A firm can only tap *selectively* into foreign technology development, however. If it lacks domestic technical capability, a domestic supplier base, and a knowledge base at home in core technologies, it will be difficult to access foreign developments completely enough to ensure competitive advantage. Moving the home base for competing in the industry may be required.

A strategy of seeking to rapidly achieve self-sufficiency in technology is characteristic of many global industry leaders. In the Japanese automobile industry, for example, Toyota sought from the beginning to be self-sufficient in car technology while other Japanese firms were forming joint ventures or licensing technology from foreign firms. Toyota's more rapid improvement both in product and in process technology, where it invented, among other things, the *kanban* system (just-in-time delivery of parts), meant that Toyota emerged as the leader among a group of strong Japanese competitors.

MEETING THE BEST FOREIGN COMPETITORS

A firm must meet the best rivals in the marketplace in order to sustain and upgrade its advantage. Capable rivals provide the benchmark for measuring competitive advantage. They are also the best stimulus for innovation and change. Ultimately, a firm must find a way to gain advantages over the best rivals in order to assure its market position. Another reason to meet the best rivals in all the important markets is to deny them profits in safe markets that can be used to cross-subsidize low profits in contested markets.[13]

Ideally, the most capable rivals are at home. Competing with them will lead to many self-reinforcing benefits for the entire national industry. However, a firm must meet the best rivals in other nations as well.

Korean companies, for example, view Japanese rivals as their prime competitors both for strategic and historical reasons. The result is that there is little danger that Korean firms will fall into the classic trap of firms in low labor cost countries, that of resting on labor costs as their sole advantage. They are setting out to challenge their Japanese rivals in terms of product sophistication, process technology, and foreign marketing presence. This is another example of how sustaining advantage requires that a firm create pressure, not avoid it.

A more specific example of the effort to meet the best foreign rivals is the move of the leading Spanish ceramic tile producer, Porcelonosa, to establish a commercial subsidiary in Sassuolo, Italy. Spain is the second-leading ceramic tile-producing nation behind Italy. Porcelonosa's subsidiary, in the midst of the world's most dynamic national "diamond" in the industry, provides an important conduit for information and challenge.

LOCATING REGIONAL HEADQUARTERS

The principles I have described carry implications for the choice of where to locate regional headquarters that are responsible for managing a firm's activities in a group of nations. Regional headquarters are best placed not for administrative convenience but in the nation with the most favorable national "diamond." Of special importance in choosing the location is to expose the firm to significant needs and pressures lacking at home. The purpose is to learn as well as raise the odds that information passes credibly back to the home base. DuPont, for example, moved its European headquarters in agricultural chemicals from Geneva to Paris, to take advantage of a better-developed national cluster. France is the world's second-largest market for crop protection after the United States, and is a highly sophisticated one.

SELECTIVE FOREIGN ACQUISITIONS

Foreign acquisitions can serve two purposes. One is to gain access to a foreign market or to selective skills. Here the challenge of integrating the acquisition into the global strategy is significant but raises few unusual issues. The other reason for a foreign acquisition is to gain access to a highly favorable national "diamond." Sometimes the only feasible way to tap into the advantages of another nation is to acquire a local firm, because an outsider is hard-pressed to penetrate such broad, systemic advantages. The challenge in this latter type of acquisition is to preserve the ability of the acquired firm to benefit from its national environment at the same time as it is integrated into the company's global strategy.

There is frequently a trade-off. Success in making foreign acquisitions of this type usually implies moving in one of two directions. The first is to make the acquired firm the new global home base for the company in the industry or its particular segment, and to subordinate other units to it. The other approach is to identify those particular activities in which the acquired company can contribute the most to overall global position, and focus its efforts exclusively there. For example, the newly acquired foreign company may be given responsibility for one item in the product line or for one stage of the production process, where its national "diamond" is superior.

The intermediate case, that of maintaining the acquired unit as a stand-alone company while attempting to integrate it into the global strategy, runs the grave risk of not succeeding at either. Extensive integration of an acquired firm into a global strategy may well compromise its position in the national cluster by distancing it from strategy formulation and stripping it of full R&D capability. Such a solution precludes the sensitive and rapid response to local conditions that is so necessary to reap national advantage. Assigning the unit a selective role, and giving it wide autonomy, appears to be a better course. However, the ability of the acquired firm to maintain its position in the national cluster and respond fluidly to national circumstances is not assured.

The Role of Alliances

Alliances, or coalitions, are a final mechanism by which a firm can seek to tap national advantages in other nations. Alliances are long-term agreements between firms from different nations that go beyond normal market transactions but stop short of merger. They take many forms, including joint ventures, licenses, cross licenses, sales agreements, and supply agreements. They have become prominent in international competition, because they can speed the process of globalizing strategy, reap economies of scale, gain access to technology or markets, and achieve other benefits without giving up corporate independence or requiring an expensive merger.[14] They are particularly common in industries undergoing structural change, especially when many firms feel threatened.

Alliances are a tempting solution to the dilemma of a firm seeking the home-base advantages of another nation without giving up its own. Unfortunately, alliances are rarely a solution. They can achieve selective benefits, but they always involve significant costs in terms of coordination, reconciling goals with an independent entity, creating a competitor, and giving up profits. These costs make many alliances temporary and destined to fail. They are often transitional devices rather than stable arrangements.

Alliances do not shift true competitive advantage unless the best home base for competing in the industry shifts. Here, firms from the new nation frequently use alliances to speed the process of gaining international position. Japanese firms, for example, have employed alliances to more rapidly penetrate a range of industries where they have ultimately prevailed.

No firm can depend on another independent firm for skills and assets that are central to its competitive advantage. If it does, the firm runs a grave risk of losing its competitive advantage in the long run. Alliances tend to ensure mediocrity, not create world leadership. The most serious risk of alliances is that they *deter the firm's own efforts at upgrading*. This may occur because management is content to rely on the partner. It may also occur because the alliance has eliminated a threatening competitor.

The best alliances are highly selective, involving particular activities in the value chain or specific product lines or markets. They seek a specific technology or access to a particular market. Participants often view them as temporary. If a broader alliance is necessary to gain the advantages necessary for competitive success, the firm faces a more fundamental problem. It must question its choice of segment or strategy in the industry. It must also question whether its home base is a viable one for competing globally. Ultimately, the alliance partner may have to be acquired (or acquire the firm) to yield a sustainable international position.

LOCATING THE HOME BASE

Some nations are far better home bases than others for competing in particular industries, particular segments, or with particular strategies. The argument that home base is irrelevant, on the premise that a global firm can enjoy the benefits of many home bases, is rarely true as I have described. The role of the nation in international success is much more subtle than factor costs. The national "diamond" is dauntingly hard to penetrate or replicate from afar (not to mention even from within the nation) unless a nation is indeed the place where strategy is set, products and processes are ultimately created, and the firm seeks to be an insider in a national cluster.[15] If a firm tries to have many "home bases," the chances are that it will fail to reap the benefits of any.

The more competition becomes global, ironically, the more important the home base becomes. In Europe, for example, nations have maintained positions in many industries not because the nation was a good home base but because of protection and impediments to trade. As such barriers fall, as they may in coming years, the home base will become even more important.

If it is to succeed in global competition, a firm may have to move its home base for competing in a particular industry or for competing in particular segments. If the circumstances in the home nation do not support the innovation required for competitive advantage and cannot be improved, a firm must shift its home base to a nation that better catalyzes and provides the needed tools for international success. This implies that the management team must be relocated and perhaps replaced. It also means that the primary R&D and marketing resources must move as well. Note that a firm can have different home bases for different distinct businesses.[16]

The same considerations imply that a firm may choose different nations as home bases for competing globally in different industry *segments*. This implies that the nations involved have full strategic responsibility worldwide and control over core technical, production, and international marketing resources.

Some international firms have established worldwide business unit headquarters outside of the home nation. Philips's C. H. F. Müller (Germany), for example, has worldwide responsibility for X-ray tubes, X-ray generators, and computer systems for nuclear medicine. Philips also moved its headquarters for major appliances from Holland to Italy, a nation that has been a highly competitive location for the appliance industry. Other examples illustrate that designating a home base outside the home country of the parent company is not a new phenomenon. Sandvik (Sweden), for example, has located its home base in conveyor systems in Stuttgart, Germany, since the 1950s. Germany was where the most sophisticated customers and related machine tool industries were based.

The incidence of such examples is still relatively low, but we detected a noticeable increase in their frequency. Siemens is making a major investment to establish the United States as the center of some of its medical equipment operations, taking advantage of the United States's role as the world's most advanced market (see the discussion of patient monitoring in Chapter 5). Xerox has assigned worldwide responsibility for small copiers to its Fuji-Xerox joint venture in Japan. Japan is both the world's most advanced home market for small copiers as well as the location of the preeminent cluster of small copier competitors, supplier industries, and related industries such as facsimile. Xerox found that it could not compete globally in small copiers from a U.S. home base.

As competition globalizes, every firm must take a hard look at its choice of home base for each distinct business. More firms must be prepared to shift the home base, perhaps the ultimate act of global strategy. Shifting the home base requires that the new nation truly becomes the center for the worldwide strategy in an industry. The personnel left in the old home base must be given new incentives in order that they are motivated to adopt a supporting role. Corporate management from the home country must avoid the tendency to interfere in strategic management.

THE ROLE OF LEADERSHIP

What I have described in this chapter is a concept of corporate leadership. Leaders believe in change. They possess an insight into how to alter competition, and do not accept constraints in carrying it out. Leaders energize their organizations to meet competitive challenges, to serve demanding needs, and, above all, to keep progressing. They find ways of overcoming the filters which limit information and prevent innovation. They harness and even create external pressures to motivate change.

Leaders have a broad view of competition in which their national environment is integral to competitive success. They work hard to improve that environment and to encourage appropriate (though sometimes painful) government policies. As a result, leaders are often seen as statesmen, though few would describe their own actions that way. Leaders also think in international terms, not only in measuring their true competitive advantage but in setting strategy to enhance and extend it.

This concept of leadership has been lost in many companies. Too many companies and too many managers misperceive the true bases for competitive advantage. They become preoccupied with improving financial performance, soliciting government assistance, and seeking stability through forming alliances and merging with competitors. These sorts of steps are not good for companies or for nations. Today's competitive realities demand more.

12

Government Policy

Government plays a prominent role in international competition, but it is a different one than is commonly supposed. My purpose here is to examine the implications of my theory for government policy. At one extreme, some view government as at best a passive participant in the process of international competition. Because the determinants of national advantage are so deeply rooted in a nation's buyers, its history, and other unique circumstances, it could be argued that government is powerless. Its proper role would then be to sit back and let market forces work. My theory, and the evidence from our research, does not support this view. Government policy does affect national advantage, both positively and negatively, as has been clear in much previous discussion.

While the role of government in creating and sustaining national advantage is significant, however, it is inevitably *partial*. Without the presence of underlying national circumstances that support competitive advantage in a particular industry, the best policy intentions will fail. Governments do not control national competitive advantage; they can only influence it. A more subtle, and thoughtful, role for policy makers is indicated.

The central goal of government policy toward the economy is to *deploy a nation's resources (labor and capital) with high and rising levels of productivity.*[1] As I have discussed earlier, productivity is the root cause of a nation's standard of living. To achieve productivity growth, an economy must be continually upgrading. This requires relentless improvement and innovation in existing industries and the capacity to compete successfully in *new* industries. New business formation is necessary to create jobs for new persons entering the workforce, to replace any jobs freed up by productiv-

617

ity gains in other successful industries, and to replace jobs lost in less productive industries that become uncompetitive.

The proper role for government policy toward a nation's industry is to stimulate such dynamism and upgrading. Government's aim should be to create an environment in which firms can upgrade competitive advantages in established industries by introducing more sophisticated technology and methods and penetrating more advanced segments. Government policy should also support the ability of the nation's firms to enter new industries where higher productivity can be achieved than in positions ceded in less productive industries and segments.

One manifestation of an upgrading economy is the movement of less productive jobs to other nations via foreign investment and foreign sourcing. This is a healthy process if it is indeed the less productive jobs that are moving overseas. If high-productivity jobs are lost to foreign rivals, as has been the case in a number of U.S., German, and British industries in the past decade, long-term economic prosperity is compromised.

Defining national economic goals in terms other than long-term productivity growth is a fundamental error that leads to inappropriate policies. No nation can achieve net exports in every industry, as I discussed in Chapter 1. Efforts to preserve all industries will lower the national standard of living. Balancing trade is not in and of itself an appropriate goal, nor is attempting to boost ''competitiveness'' through forcing down the value of the currency. If policies are always measured in terms of their effects on dynamism and sustained productivity growth, however, the chances of working at cross-purposes to true economic progress are much less.

If the first prerequisite for sound policy toward industry is the appropriate goal, the second is a proper model of the underpinnings of competitive success. Many policy makers approach the task with a faulty one. If competitive advantage is seen as driven largely by macroeconomic factors or factor costs, the wrong tools may well be used to attempt to benefit industry. As I have sought to illustrate, the determinants of national advantage bear on the capacity of a nation's firms to innovate and upgrade and go far beyond wage rates, interest rates, and the exchange rate. As we will see, many of the actions governments take to ''help'' industry from the perspective of a narrow, static view of competitive advantage can actually hurt in the long run. Also, actions that seem appropriate when considering a single policy area such as R&D, taxation, or regulation in isolation become questionable when seen in a more complete and integrated framework.

My theory suggests a different and far more varied role for government, even parts of government that appear far removed from economic policy. A consistent program is needed in a wide range of areas, because seemingly discrete policies are often interdependent. The effect of choices in one policy area frequently depends on those made in others (in view of the systemic character of the "diamond," this might be expected). The most potent influences of government in advanced nations are often slow and indirect.

Each of the many policy areas that can influence national advantage is a subject unto itself. I cannot hope to provide an exhaustive treatment here, nor to raise all the considerations that bear on individual policy choices. Instead, the purpose is a more modest one, which is to sketch how the theory can be used to shed light on discrete policy alternatives as well as a nation's overall approach to economic policy.

Governments in nearly all nations today are taking steps designed to improve competitiveness. Some of the most prominent and common policy thrusts are the following: devaluation, deregulation, privatization, relaxation of product and environmental standards, promotion of interfirm collaboration and cooperation of various types, encouragement of mergers, tax reform, regional development, negotiation of voluntary restraint or orderly marketing arrangements, efforts to improve the general education system, expansion of government investment in research, government programs to fund new enterprises, and a more proactive role for defense and other forms of government procurement. My theory will provide a yardstick against which these initiatives can be measured.

PREMISES OF GOVERNMENT POLICY TOWARD INDUSTRY

Government at the local, state, or national level can influence competitive advantage in an industry if its policies influence one or more of the four determinants. At the broadest level, a number of premises must guide government policy if it is to enhance national competitive advantage rather than detract from it. These premises will resonate throughout my discussion of specific policy areas and provide a set of benchmarks against which to evaluate any government initiative toward the economy.

1. *Firms compete in industries, not nations.* A nation's firms themselves must ultimately create and sustain competitive advantage compared to rivals from other nations. Governments have been notably unsuccessful in managing firms and in responding to the fluid market changes that characterize international competition. Even when staffed with the most elite civil servants, governments make erratic decisions about the industries to develop, the technologies to invest in, and the competitive advantages that will be the most appropriate and achievable. Examples of tendencies toward shadow corporate decision making by governments can be drawn from Japan, Korea, Singapore, the United Kingdom, France, and many other nations. Government simply cannot be as in tune with market forces as industry participants,

nor can it practically isolate its decisions from political forces that distort them.

Government cannot create competitive industries, firms must do so. Government's role in competition is inherently partial, because many other characteristics of a nation bear on it. Government can shape or influence the *context* and *institutional structure* surrounding firms, however, as well as the *inputs* they draw upon. Government policies that succeed are those that create an environment in which firms can gain competitive advantage rather than involve government directly in the process, except in nations at early stages of competitive development. Government's most powerful roles are indirect rather than direct ones.

Government's proper role is to unleash and even amplify the forces within the "diamond." This creates opportunities, and pressures, for continued innovation. The Japanese government, at its best, understands this like no other. By stimulating early demand, confronting industries with the need for frontier technology through symbolic cooperative projects, establishing prizes to highlight and reward quality, encouraging rivalry, and other policies, the pace of innovation and upgrading is accelerated. At their worst, though, Japanese bureaucrats attempt to manage industry structure (by limiting entry or encouraging mergers), protect the home market too long, and yield to political pressure in insulating inefficient retailers, distributors, farmers, and industrial firms in a range of industries from competition. Industries that ignore this government "assistance" succeed, while those that rest on it drag down national productivity.

Government should involve industry in determining what factors are created, and encourage firms to play a prominent role in factor creation themselves. The decisive factors are specialized and anticipate the emerging needs of industry. Government cannot pick the right factors or create them very effectively by itself. In R&D policy, Germany has a good record in upgrading technology, for example, because most government-funded research takes the form of joint projects with research institutes involving firms, partial funding of research contracts between firms and universities, or incentives for company research. Conversely, Britain and France have had highly mixed results in funding R&D because elite staffs at the ministry level sought to select projects to support. In the United States, a huge federal research program has had only coincidental benefits to competitive advantage in recent decades because in most instances the spending is largely unconnected to industry.

Governments should play a direct role only in those areas where firms are unable to act (such as trade policy) or where externalities cause firms to underinvest. Externalities occur where the benefits to the nation as a whole exceed those accruing to any single firm or individual, so that private entities will tend to underinvest in such areas from the perspective of the nation. Good examples are general education, environmental quality, and some types of R&D that can boost productivity in many industries.

2. *A nation's competitive advantage in industry is relative.* Many discussions of national advantage are intensely inward-looking. Yet standards for competitive advantage are set not within a nation but by firms in other nations. The skill and motivation of workers elsewhere define what is required at home. Absolute levels of growth in productivity are much less important than relative productivity compared to firms in other nations.[2] The standards have been rising continuously, particularly since the 1960s. In the United Kingdom, the United States, and Denmark, the problem is not so much that industry does not improve at all but that it has not improved fast enough.

International standards set the minimum policy targets if a nation is to upgrade its economy. In setting policy toward engineering education, for example, Japanese and German norms for the number of graduates and the training they receive are the appropriate targets. Incremental improvement over a nation's own historical performance is not enough.

3. *Dynamism leads to competitive advantage, not short-term cost advantages.* National competitive advantage grows out of the capacity of a nation's firms to improve and innovate relentlessly. Old advantages are eventually duplicated or obsoleted by firms from some other nation.

Policies that convey static, short-term cost advantages but that unconsciously undermine innovation and dynamism represent the most common and most profound error in government policy toward industry. In a desire to help, it is all too easy to adopt policies such as sanctioning joint projects that avoid "wasteful" R&D, or approving mergers that allow efficiencies in corporate overhead but eliminate domestic competition. These sorts of policies, and many others that governments have adopted, usually defer, delay, or eliminate the perceived need to improve and innovate, or send the wrong signals about where to innovate. Even a 10 percent cost saving through economies of scale, which is rarely achievable through a domestic merger or cooperative effort, is nullified quickly by rapid product and process improvement and the pursuit of volume in global markets—dynamism that such policies undermine.

Pressure and a sense of urgency are part and parcel of national competitive advantage. Italian firms progressed to advanced industry segments, for example, not when the lira was cheap but when a rising lira in the 1970s forced them to upgrade products and introduce modern technology. Only if the conditions for innovation are fertile (demanding buyers, intense domestic rivalry, for example), can policies such as those described ever be justified, except in nations early in their development process (factor-driven or early investment-driven).

4. *National economic prosperity demands that industries upgrade.* Some bases for competitive advantage lead to higher national productivity (and

are more sustainable) than others. Competitive advantage based on such sources as abundant natural resources, low cost labor, a devalued currency, or even a single new product idea, is often associated with lower productivity and is notoriously unstable. Basing competitive advantage on such sources leads firms to price-oriented strategies and price-sensitive market segments. History shows that such strategies are especially vulnerable, not only to challenge by firms from other nations but also to protectionism. Firms competing on the basis of low prices invite charges of dumping and are most sensitive to tariffs. Easy imitation by firms from developing nations or large-scale government subsidies can also nullify such advantages.

The highest-order advantages, associated with high levels of productivity, are those that accrue from a steadily rising level of technology, a stream of new models, investments in building close customer relationships, and economies of scale growing out of a global market presence. The most sustainable strategies are those that widen and upgrade the market rather than simply take business away from foreign firms. Nations whose competitive advantages depend on swamping other nations' markets are vulnerable to foreign government response. Where a nation's firms enjoy superior differentiation and target previously unserved market segments, these risks are diminished.

Government policy must be concerned with laying the foundation for upgrading competitive advantage in a nation's industry and prodding firms to do so. Too often, however, policies are addressed toward preserving old advantages and actually deter the upgrading process.

5. *A nation's competitive advantage in industries is often geographically concentrated.* I have illustrated with many examples that internationally successful industries and industry clusters frequently concentrate in a city or region, and the bases for advantage are often intensely local. Geographic concentration is important to the genesis of competitive advantage, and it amplifies the forces that upgrade and sustain advantage. While the national government has a role in upgrading industry, the role of state and local governments is potentially as great or greater.

Discussions of policy to encourage competitiveness are preoccupied with the national government and with overarching national circumstances. As much or more attention is necessary at the regional and local level, in areas such as university education, infrastructure, local regulations, local research initiatives, and information. In our research, government initiatives in regions such as Baden-Württemberg (Germany) and individual Italian towns had arguably a more significant influence on competitive advantage than any national policy initiatives.

6. *Competitive advantage in a nation's industries is created over a decade or more, not over three- or four-year business cycles.* Competitive advantage is created through a long process of upgrading human skills, investing in

products and processes, building clusters, and penetrating foreign markets. Japanese car producers began exporting in the 1950s, for example, only to achieve strong international positions in the 1970s.

Yet a decade is an eternity in politics. Much of economic policy in virtually every nation is preoccupied with short-term economic fluctuations. Governments' focus on improving the aggregate trade balance through wage controls, currency intervention, controlling inflation, and other steps, may affect many industries on the margin but is far from decisive in shaping long-term competitive advantage in any industry. Governments are also prone to choose policies with easily perceived short-term effects, such as subsidies, protection, and arranged mergers. Such actions will dampen innovation and erode average productivity in the economy.

Many of the most beneficial policies within the purview of government, such as factor creation, competition policy, and upgrading demand quality, are slow and patient ones. Many desirable policies also carry short-term negatives. For example, deregulating a protected industry is unsettling and may lead to bankruptcies. Such consequences, as well as the long time horizon for desirable policies, put a premium on having a political system that allows continuity and offers some resistance to the pressures of special interests. Japan benefits, for example, from a governmental system in which career bureaucrats strongly influence if not determine policy choices. The political majority has also stayed the same in the postwar period, providing a stable policy environment. Italy and the United States represent the other extreme, with frequent changes in key policy-making positions and political systems unusually susceptible to influence by special interests.

7. *Nations gain advantage because of differences, not similarities.* Each nation has a unique array of competitive industries, and no nation is, or can be, competitive in everything. Competitive success results from the match between a nation's unique environment and the sources of competitive advantage in particular industries. The Italian success in fragmented industries and in competing with highly focused strategies, for example, draws on unique attributes of the Italian environment. Most commentators on the Italian economy have persistently underestimated Italy, because they have applied American, German, or Japanese norms to an economy with a very different structure. National differences (in demand, skills, suppliers, and fields of educational excellence) are valuable and often essential to competitive advantage.

While there are some broad principles and policies that will benefit almost any national economy, it is a mistake for any nation to follow too closely a model of economic development created for another nation. Emulating another nation's model for national advantage—the same industries, the same strategies, the same government programs—will allow a nation to reach only a certain state of development. The task for any government is to understand the underlying principles of national advantage and translate them into policy initiatives that reflect the nation's particular circumstances. Good policies in one nation may well be bad policies in another.

8. *Many categorizations used to distinguish or prioritize industries have little relevance.* In an effort to foster economic development, there is a temptation to classify a nation's industrial base into categories such as high tech and low tech, sunrise and sunset, growing and mature, manufacturing and service, and labor (or capital) intensive and knowledge intensive. The implication drawn from such distinctions is that some categories are better than others—typically the high-tech, sunrise, growing, manufacturing, and knowledge-intensive ones. Much is made of such distinctions in evaluating an economy and in choosing policies.

This line of thinking does not withstand close scrutiny. Italy has supported buoyant economic growth and a rising standard of living by achieving robust national advantage in many "traditional" and "mature" industries such as textiles, apparel, furniture, and footwear. It has done so by introducing modern process technology and dramatically increasing the knowledge content in terms of design, new materials, and rapid innovation. Productivity has increased substantially. Germany, Sweden, and Switzerland have generated large positive trade balances and supported a high standard of living based in no small part on sustaining advantage in a range of "mature" industries such as cars, trucks, textile and other machinery, and mining equipment.

Most industries are, or will become, high-technology or knowledge-intensive industries. Electronics, advanced materials, information systems, and other manifestations of modern technology are changing the product and the value chain in virtually every industry.[3] One nation's mature industry is another nation's growth industry if its firms are dynamic. Manufacturing is not "better" than services, because the two are inextricably tied and because many services involve sophisticated technology and high levels of productivity.

Government policy must provide an environment in which *any* industry can prosper if firms are innovative and achieve high productivity. A diversified economy has room for a range of industries that can provide employment to human resources with different skills and aspirations.[4] Conversely, few industries are so indispensable that a nation should guarantee the market to unproductive indigenous competitors. The most important distinction among industries (and segments) is productivity, because of its link to the standard of living. Industries and technologies that affect the potential productivity of many other industries do deserve special attention, though the number of these is limited. Policies to upgrade such industries must address the premises I have described, however, and not seek to guarantee firm profits or ensure foreign market shares through quotas.

9. *The process of sustaining advantage may be intensely uncomfortable for firms and those who work in them.* Sustaining advantage involves constant pressure and challenges, requires constant improvement, and demands sustained investment. Many firms would prefer more stability and an environment in which prosperity is guaranteed rather than continually having to be re-earned.

This quite understandable tendency is manifested in a number of ways. One is pressure on government to attempt currency devaluation in order to take the pressure off prices. Another is a desire for protection from foreign rivals, usually justified by citing the "unfair" advantages they possess. Another is a desire to cool off "excessive" domestic rivalry, either through cartels (relatively prevalent in Switzerland) or American- and Scandinavian-style mergers among leading competitors. Yet another tendency is diversification to escape tough problems in the base industry instead of investing to address them.

Each of these tendencies, and others like them, dooms a national industry in the long run. Many firms, employees, and labor leaders succumb to human nature and lose sight of what really gives them competitive advantage. They propose and support policies that are not really in their long-term interest. Such actions postpone change, dampen innovation, cut off firms from the benefits of clustering, and work in exactly the wrong direction from those necessary for competitive advantage. Postponing change will only work if the domestic market continues to be protected. This puts off change even longer, and harms the nation's consumers as well as other industries that rely on the protected industry.

The broad lessons for government policy are twofold. First, firms (and unions) will not change if they believe that government "assistance" will allow them to avoid the need to do so. Direct government "assistance" in one firm or industry also has a strong tendency to create forces that cause it to spread and multiply. Second, selecting only policies that please local firms may well be counterproductive. Government officials must be sympathetic to the legitimate concerns, fears, and uncertainties faced by industry. Yet choosing policies based on unanimity of corporate or union support, as politicians under short-term pressure for reelection or reappointment are prone to do, may do as much harm as good.[5]

GOVERNMENT POLICY AND NATIONAL ADVANTAGE

There is a wide range of government policies that bear in some way on national advantage in some industry or group of industries. Education policy, tax policy, health care policy, antitrust policy, regulatory policy, environmental policy, fiscal and monetary policy, and many others are all relevant.

This is one of the major challenges of policy making toward industry—the agenda of nearly every government agency and legislative committee touches national competitive advantage in some way. Yet it is the principal agenda of few bodies in most governments. The issue cuts across traditional ways of organizing the social and economic policy agenda. All of the nations we studied suffered to some degree from overlapping authority and inconsistent policies toward industry in different parts of government.[6]

Many treatments of government policy toward competitiveness are organized around policy areas such as tax policy, education, or regulation. This is not, I believe, the best approach. Government policy is significant not for its own sake but via its influence on the "diamond." Broad policy areas such as regulation affect competition in many different ways. Regulation of product standards affects demand conditions, for example, while regulation of industry structure affects the nature of domestic rivalry. Relaxing regulation may be appropriate in some cases while tightening it is in others.

More illuminating is to examine government policies as they affect each determinant in the "diamond." This exposes the underlying mechanisms through which each policy affects national advantage. Since the array of policies that can affect each determinant are numerous, I can concentrate here on only the most common and most important ones. It is also impractical to discuss all the nuances and specific program options available in each area—many would justify an entire book of their own.

GOVERNMENT'S EFFECT ON FACTOR CONDITIONS

The potential rate of upgrading in an economy is set by the rate at which the quantity and especially the quality of factors improve. To achieve high productivity, firms must have access to an improving pool of advanced and specialized human resources, scientific knowledge, economic information, infrastructure, and other factors of production. Factor conditions must also encourage firms to upgrade their competitive advantages over time. Government policy has a role in each of these areas.

FACTOR CREATION

Among the most important, and most traditional, roles of government is creating and upgrading factors, whether they are skilled human resources, basic scientific knowledge, economic information, or infrastructure. Nations gain advantage not as much from the factors available today as from the presence of unique institutional mechanisms to upgrade them continually.

The standards for factors are inexorably rising. For example, a workforce with only basic literacy today no longer represents a real advantage.

Government is often seen as the principal engine of factor creation. It does bear responsibility for important areas such as the primary and secondary education systems, basic infrastructure, and research in areas of broad social concern such as health care. Government's role in factor creation in such areas is justified by externalities or benefits to the economy that exceed those to any individual participant, especially significant where factors can be deployed in a range of industries. A nation's industry will be at a disadvantage if government does not meet these responsibilities well, as American problems with workforce literacy and basic skills attest.

Yet government factor-creating mechanisms are rarely in themselves a source of competitive advantage. Government's direct efforts at factor creation are appropriately in generalized areas, yet the most significant factors for competitive advantage are advanced and specialized and inevitably tied to industries or groups of industries. In the industries we studied, the most important factor creation involved firms, though sometimes in collaboration with government entities. Mechanisms included specialized apprenticeship programs, research efforts in universities connected with the industry, trade association activities, and most important, the private investments of firms themselves. Domestic rivalry, clustering, and geographic concentration all proved to be vital to the rate of factor upgrading because they multiplied the centers of initiative, drew a critical mass of attention and effort, and stimulated the investments of public institutions.

Governmental efforts at creating specialized factors run the risk of creating the wrong factors at the wrong time. Government educational bureaucracies have been years late in many nations in sensing and responding to needs for new types of training or for training in new fields such as information technology, despite pressing needs in industry. Both government *and* industry must invest in factor creation. The process of factor creation benefits greatly from the proximity of clear economic interest. Without it, the factors created are insufficient, inappropriate, too late, or too generalized.

Factor creation is the most vibrant and effective in nations where there is widespread understanding of the importance of factor creation to economic prosperity and consensus about the need for sustained investment. Education and training, research, and infrastructure are viewed as vital in Germany, Japan, Korea, and Singapore. The issues have largely been given lip service in America and are still being debated in Britain. In Italy, historical aversion to the central government has stunted factor creation and put limits on the potential to upgrade competitive advantages in industry.

Education and Training. Achieving more sophisticated competitive advantages and competing in advanced segments and new industries demands human resources with improving skills and abilities. The quality of human resources must be steadily rising if a nation's economy is to upgrade. Not only does achieving higher productivity require more skilled managers and employees, but improving human resources in other nations sets a rising standard even to maintain current competitive positions.

There is little doubt from our research that education and training are decisive in national competitive advantage. The nations we studied that invest the most heavily in education (Germany, Japan, and Korea) had advantages in many industries that could be traced in part to human resources. What is even more telling is that in every nation, those industries that were the most competitive were often those where specialized investment in education and training had been unusually great. In Britain, for example, the chemical and pharmaceutical industries draw on disciplines and skills where British universities are strong, though the education system generally leaves something to be desired. In Sweden, mechanical engineering training is outstanding and many successful industries depend on this discipline. In the United States, aerospace and pharmaceuticals are examples of industries where firms and universities work closely together, and both are areas of strength.

Education and training constitute perhaps the single greatest long-term leverage point available to all levels of government in upgrading industry. Improving the general education system is an essential priority of government, and a matter of economic and not just social policy. At the same time, however, the general education system is insufficient to ensure national advantage. As important is setting policies that link the educational system to industry and encourage industry's own efforts at training.

The effectiveness of an educational system is partly a function of the rate of spending. As or more important, however, is the approach taken. The appropriate policies toward education and training must reflect each nation's particular circumstances, but the following characteristics of sound educational policy emerge from our research.

1. *Educational standards are high.* The educational and training system must demand high performance, and students must have to compete for advancement. Many nations, including the United States, Britain, Sweden, and Germany, went through a period in the 1970s of relaxing educational standards and/or eliminating grades. The fact is that world standards for workers, technical personnel, and managers are high and rising. No nation will prosper unless its citizens meet them.

High standards are difficult to achieve without some national or state involvement, and standards setting is an important role of government. Rigorous national standards are set in Japan, Korea, and Switzerland, and *Länder* standards are set in Germany. In the United States and United Kingdom, there have been protracted debates about standards, and local control has contributed to uneven standards that too often drift to the lowest common denominator. The United Kingdom has initiated a controversial program to raise standards in the late 1980s, which I will discuss in Chapter 13.

High standards for education and training are not inconsistent with open access to them. Access is better opened in other ways besides reducing standards, such as by providing generous financial support to students from all economic backgrounds and preadmission programs to raise student preparation.

2. *Teaching is a prestigious and valued profession.* Quality education is simply not possible without a cadre of well-prepared and competent teachers at all levels, up through postgraduate work. In the United States, teaching has not been seen as an attractive occupation especially up through the secondary level. Qualifications are relatively low, pay lags well behind industry, and many faculty positions (especially in science and engineering) are unfilled or underfilled. In Japan and Korea, conversely, teaching at all levels is prestigious, and faculty positions are staffed with outstanding people.[7] The same was true in Germany through the 1970s, but the prestige of teachers up through secondary school has fallen in the 1980s.

3. *The majority of students receive education and training with some practical orientation.* Students must be equipped with the skills necessary to be meaningful participants in the economy. While some will find a place in the arts or in other fields outside of industry, most will not. The majority of students must be given the foundations that will allow them to be trained in industry or on the job. Math, computing, writing, basic sciences, and languages are particularly vital. The minimum standards necessary have been rising continuously as technology advances.

The training of a significant proportion of the outstanding students in a nation in science and engineering seems to provide the greatest benefit to an upgrading economy. Such a pool of talent not only contributes to innovation and upgrading as employees but also, as importantly, as managers.

4. *There are respected and high-quality forms of higher education besides the university.* Most students do not go on to advanced degrees or to careers in academia and research. Yet an economy cannot upgrade rapidly unless these students gain the skills required for continued personal development as well as the specialized skills needed in particular industries. Technical universities and vocational schools are respected alternatives to university training in a number of nations such as Germany and Korea. In some fields, German technical universities are more prestigious than regular universities. In Japan, companies themselves play a heavy role in postsecondary education.

Conversely, in the United Kingdom, a nation with human resource problems, the greatest value has been attached to studying liberal arts and pure sciences rather than engineering or vocations. A similar pattern exists in the United States. A high percentage of students who attend university is not necessarily a sign of the most effective human resource development. A system for vocational, technical, and specialized industry training is a central priority in any advanced economy.

5. *There is a close connection between educational institutions and employers.* Many of the most successful industries we studied in every nation had established strong ties with universities and technical schools. The German (and Swiss) apprenticeship system is an extraordinary example of a system in which millions of young people combine education with on-the-job training over a period of about three years.

Close ties between educational institutions and employers are enhanced if individual schools, colleges, and universities have the flexibility to adapt to the specialized needs of their local industries, as is the case in Germany. Rigid central control, while beneficial in maintaining standards, may work against the specialized factor creation in geographically concentrated industries so vital to upgrading competitive advantage.

6. *Firms invest heavily in ongoing in-house training through industry associations or individually.* Successful firms accept and play their own role in education and training. In Japan, companies view one of their principal roles as providing continuing education. Employees must pass examinations to move to the next level. Trade associations provide another mechanism with which firms can offer training in critical skills needed by the entire industry, and programs organized by trade associations were common in the industries we studied. Associations provide a way to achieve a critical mass even if individual firms are small.

Government policy must not unwittingly discourage firm or trade association investments in human resource development through policies such as taxing training benefits or labor laws that discourage employer training initiatives. The need for actual incentives for company training is less clear, however, because firms in nations such as Japan and Germany invest as a matter of competitive necessity not because of government inducement. Subsidies for training, as is the case in subsidizing research and development, are often unnecessary if firms and employees have a sustained commitment to their business and are facing vigorous competition.

7. *Immigration policies allow the movement of personnel with specialized skills.* Inward migration of skilled personnel is a feature of many of the successful industries we studied. Countries such as the United States, that have relatively open policies toward skilled personnel, have benefited. Nations with restrictive policies, such as Switzerland, are working at cross-purposes with industry.

Science and Technology. An upgrading economy demands a steadily rising level of technology. Improvements in technology, broadly defined, are integral to improving efficiency, commanding higher prices through better quality, and penetrating new industries and segments, the underpinnings of productivity growth. Stimulating improvements in science and technology is a widely acknowledged role of government. Research and development cannot be left solely to firms because the benefits to the national economy exceed those to individual firms due to spillovers. Technological progress not only benefits a firm but often raises the rate of advancement in the entire national industry as well as linked industries. This is particularly true in basic research and in fields with applications in numerous industries such as advanced materials, information technology, flexible manufacturing systems, health sciences, environmental sciences, and energy.

Virtually every advanced nation, including all of those we studied, has policies designed to encourage research. To varying degrees, governments also participate directly in conducting research in government laboratories. A few examples drawn from my earlier discussion will illustrate the range of approaches. Italy provides tax incentives for installing approved types of factory automation equipment. Germany partially funds research projects in firms and underwrites (along with industry) a series of Fraunhofer and Max Planck Institutes that conduct research in a variety of important fields. The United States conducts billions of dollars worth of research in federal laboratories such as the National Institutes of Health, funds university research through the National Science Foundation, and mounts a huge research effort in defense-related fields. In Japan, some research is conducted in laboratories connected to ministries, and MITI and other government agencies sponsor and partly fund cooperative research projects involving firms in various fields, though only a modest amount of university research is funded by government.

The overarching principle in addressing science and technology should be to create an *innovation policy* and not just a science and technology policy. Science and technology cannot be decoupled from its commercial application in seeking to enhance national advantage. Policy to stimulate commercial innovation must go beyond science and technology and include policy toward competition, regulation, and other areas bearing on the "diamond."

In the particular area of science and technology, some characteristics of effective policy are as follows:

1. *A match between science and technology policy and the patterns of competitive advantage in the nation's industry.* The appropriate policy toward science and technology must be consistent with a nation's mix of competitive industries, its stage of competitive development, and the capacity of its firms and research universities. Basic research in computing is unlikely to be beneficial or necessary in Denmark, for example, but an active biotechnol-

ogy program will be because of the influence of this technology on many of Denmark's agriculturally based industries. Programs should concentrate on technologies that affect many (old or new) industries or which are important to deepening or upgrading national industry clusters.

2. *Emphasis on research universities instead of government laboratories.* Upgrading in an economy is most encouraged if government investments in R&D are heavily oriented toward research universities, either directly or via partial government funding of corporate research contracts with universities. University research offers a number of benefits in stimulating a rising level of productivity in an economy. First, new generations of scientists and technicians are trained in state-of-the-art problems as a natural by-product of conducting research. Second, diffusion of research is facilitated by the relative openness of the university setting. Third, university research institutes and laboratories are fertile incubators of new businesses, as professors and particularly students see ideas with commercial potential and form new companies or take them to established companies. The research university system is the great strength of the United States and accounts for much of American success in new businesses. The lack of well-developed university research will be one of the hurdles facing Japan in upgrading its economy further.

Directing a major share of government research funds to government laboratories, as takes place in some European countries, is less likely to benefit industry. Research in government labs is often far removed from commercial applications, diffusion is difficult, and researchers are less prone to understand market needs or think entrepreneurially.

3. *Principal emphasis on commercially relevant technologies.* Research with direct relevance to industry has particularly strong leverage in an economy. A much higher percentage of total government research spending is on industrial research in Japan, Germany, and Sweden than it is in the United States and the United Kingdom, as shown in Table 12–1. Defense-related research accounted for 68 and 49 percent respectively, of total government R&D in the year reported in the United States and the United Kingdom.[8] Defense R&D cannot be relied upon as the backbone of a nation's technological strategy. It is no longer centered on core technologies as was the case in the 1930s, 1940s, and 1950s. While it can lead to commercial spin-offs, many observers see the needs of defense and industry as diverging.[9] I have also already discussed how defense demand can distract firms from industry segments that will be important commercially (and globally).

4. *Strong links between research institutions and industry.* Whatever the institutional setup for conducting R&D, it works best in those settings where research institutions have tangible connections to industry. While every nation pays lip service to this goal, in reality the connections are often distant. In America, for example, the national laboratories are only just

TABLE 12–1 **Estimated Distribution of National R&D Spending by Category (latest year available)**

	Percentage of National R&D Spending Accounted for by Private Sector	Percentage of National R&D Spending Accounted for by Government	Percentage of Government R&D Spending on Defense	Percentage of Total National R&D Spending on Non-Defense Fields
Denmark (1985)	55.7	44.3	0.5	99.9
Germany (1987)	59.1	40.9	12.5	94.8
Italy (1987)	43.7	56.3	7.8	95.3
Japan (1986)	78.8	21.2	3.5	99.3
Sweden (1987)	58.4	41.6	26.9	88.7
Switzerland (1986)	87.2	12.8	17.2	97.9
United Kingdom (1986)	49.2	50.8	49.2	74.8
United States (1988)	53.5	46.5	68.1	68.3

SOURCE: Organization for Economic Cooperation and Development, *Main Science and Technology Indicators,* 1989.

NOTE: For additional R&D data, see Figure 13–1.

beginning to have meaningful interchange with firms and to diffuse their research results.

Links can be forged through a variety of mechanisms:

· *Specialized research institutions focused on industry clusters or crosscutting technologies.* One of the strong findings from our research is the frequency with which internationally leading national industries are associated with specialized research institutes or university departments, often located in close proximity. The Hollywood film schools and the Dutch flower growing and handling research institutes that I have already discussed are just a few of many similar examples. Such institutions, in which both industry and government can contribute money and scientific talent, create a natural focus for solving industry problems and prompting more vigorous individual company research efforts. For example, the German cutlery industry, long internationally prominent, is centered in Solingen. For many years, the city has operated a materials testing institute catering to the industry. Trade associations play an important role in many nations in funding and even creating such specialized research institutions.

· *Research contracts.* Research contracts between firms and government research institutions or universities introduce some market discipline and facilitate more fluid interchange. Government can provide matching funds or otherwise partially underwrite the cost. Encouraging industry to seek such research contracts is a particularly good way to support research in small- and medium-sized companies.

· *Explicit dissemination mechanisms.* Research at government laboratories and government-sponsored university research will not diffuse without explicit mechanisms. In Denmark, for example, a well-developed system of government-paid agricultural consultants is a major force for disseminating new agricultural technology. In the United States, NASA has taken constructive steps to encourage diffusion of its technologies, unusual in American federal research programs.

5. *Encouragement of research activity within firms.* By far the most important influence on innovation comes from the R&D efforts of firms. Firms themselves must apply technology to the needs of their industry. As Table 12–1 illustrates, the private sector's contribution to national R&D varies significantly by nation. It is lowest in Italy and the United Kingdom and highest in Japan and Switzerland. In nations such as Japan, firms have needed only modest encouragement to invest aggressively in research in many industries because of their goals and the presence of active domestic rivalry. In other nations, more encouragement may be necessary until research becomes an ongoing element of company strategy.

Means of stimulating research in firms vary from nation to nation. In some countries, such as Germany, Denmark, and the United Kingdom, government has provided *direct research grants or subsidies to firms.* This approach is questionable, and experience with it has been largely unsatisfactory. It is difficult enough under the best of circumstances to evaluate the true commercial prospects of a research project. Without having to bear the financial risk, firms often propose bad projects or do not manage them well. They also use government funds to pay for projects they would have conducted anyway, or overstate the amount of research actually performed. Both Germany and the United Kingdom have quite rightly moved away from this approach.

Another approach is providing *tax credits* to firms to encourage company R&D spending, as has been the case in the United States. While there is little concrete evidence about the success of tax credits, I believe that they do not address the most significant determinants of successful research and development activity. Many advanced nations (such as Germany and Sweden) have no such special R&D incentives and yet their firms are aggressive investors in R&D.

Other parts of the "diamond" are more decisive than R&D incentives in shaping the innovative activity of a nation's firms. Policies that ensure vigorous domestic rivalry, raise the sophistication of home demand, enhance the amount of market and technical information in the nation, and promote appropriate corporate goals offer the best approaches for advancing science and technology in the nation as a whole as well as stimulating R&D in firms. I will discuss the important role of *policies to stimulate early and advanced demand* later in this chapter.

The most effective means to encourage industry R&D directly seem to be partial funding of specialized research institutes connected to industry clusters, partial subsidization of research contracts between firms and research institutions, particularly for small firms, and generous support of universities. These were all important to competitive success in a range of the industries we studied.

6. *Primary emphasis on speeding the rate of innovation rather than slowing diffusion.* Protection of intellectual property rights is a legitimate part of insuring adequate incentives for R&D. However, there is a balance to be struck. What sustains competitive advantage and bolsters national productivity growth is ongoing and vigorous innovation. Active rivalry within the national cluster is integral to successful innovation. Long patent lives and broad copyright protection serve to protect past ideas but impede the process of creating new ones. The emphasis in R&D policy should be in promoting more rapid innovation and not slowing diffusion. Firms (and nations) rarely sustain position very long merely by protecting yesterday's secrets.

7. *A limited role for cooperative research.* Much attention has been directed in recent years to cooperative research as a means to bolster the rate of innovation in industry. An important reason for this interest is the prevalence of MITI-sponsored cooperative research projects in Japan. There are three principal arguments for cooperative research: independent research by a number of firms is "wasteful and duplicative"; economies of scale in R&D are reaped through collaborative efforts; and firms acting individually will underinvest in R&D because they cannot appropriate all the benefits. In the United States, antitrust laws have been explicitly modified to allow more cooperative R&D. A variety of European cooperative research projects are underway or under consideration, while a number of large megaprojects on core technologies (for example, the project on information technology known as ESPRIT) now involve firms from several countries.

The Japanese case, in the context of our research in ten nations, is more the exception than the rule. Firms are prospering in countless technologically sophisticated industries without cooperative research. Moreover, a close look at Japanese cooperative R&D projects suggests that they have often been widely misinterpreted.

Japanese firms participate in such projects out of a desire to cooperate with MITI, to maintain their corporate image, and to hedge the risk that competitors will benefit. Firms do not necessarily contribute their best scientists and engineers to such projects. Company representatives communicate almost daily with in-house laboratories to feed ideas into proprietary research projects. Firms typically spend much more on their own private research in the same field than they do on the cooperative project, and they compete fiercely to bring their own proprietary technologies to market. The government's own financial contribution is typically modest.

The most important role of Japanese cooperative research is to *signal* the importance of emerging technical areas and *stimulate proprietary firm research,* not to achieve efficiencies in R&D. MITI believes that Japanese firms are not always forward-looking and need highly public and visible stimuli to investigate new fields. Cooperative projects do this and enhance internal R&D spending because firms know their competitors are investigating a field as well. Executives have told me, for example, that the existence of a cooperative project is a good lever for corporate R&D executives to use in persuading top management to invest in a field. Cooperative projects also sometimes aid the process of agreeing on basic technical standards. As I will discuss later, this is often important to speeding the rate of innovation in an industry.

In the industries we studied, competition among a group of firms was by far the most powerful force for stimulating innovation that resulted in competitive advantage. Any duplication of effort is more than offset by greater pressures to innovate, the exploration of multiple technical approaches which serve to raise the likelihood and increase the rate of technological progress, and the spillovers that occur when a number of firms within a domestic industry cluster are engaged in R&D which also speed progress.

Firms facing strong competitive pressure are forced to invest in improving technology, so that others do not gain an edge that will allow them to improve market position. Even though innovations are imitated, diffusion is incomplete and occurs with a lag. The innovator often reaps durable gains in reputation.[10] Moreover, as innovations diffuse inside the domestic cluster, the entire national industry progresses faster than foreign rivals.

Cooperative projects are only beneficial under certain conditions. First, they should be in areas of more basic product and process research or to catch up to the state of the art, not on subjects closely connected to firms' proprietary sources of advantage. Second, cooperative efforts should constitute only a *modest portion* of firms' overall research in a field. If a significant portion of firms' R&D takes place through cooperative projects, this hedges the risk that any firm will fall behind in the technical race and will slow the rate of progress in the industry. Moreover, if cooperative projects become the focus of R&D, there is a real chance that other aspects of rivalry will be dulled.

Third, cooperative research should only be indirect, taking place through *separate* and independent entities to which the majority of industry participants have access. Examples include university laboratories, centers of excellence such as those being established in engineering by the American National Science Foundation, and other quasi-independent research institutes (a common model in Germany). Such a structure lessens management problems and minimizes the risks to rivalry. Cooperative projects among firms are also notoriously hard to manage, because participants face complex motives.

Whether they actually lead to efficiencies in R&D is questionable. Fourth, the most useful cooperative projects often involve fields that impinge on a number of industries and that require a substantial R&D investment. In Japan, for example, an Automated Sewing System project has been created involving firms from the textile, chemical, sewing machine, software, and retailing industries. The purpose is to work toward automating the labor-intensive garment manufacturing process.

All cooperative R&D should include a number of firms which are active rivals rather than be restricted to a few dominant or favored firms. Ideally, several competitors from a nation should be involved even if firms from other nations are participating. Without the participation of active rivals, cooperative R&D is unlikely to stimulate private innovation in the national cluster. The European consortia, which in many cases involve only one dominant and often protected firm from each nation, may play a role in catching up in areas of basic technology but have uncertain prospects for creating and successfully commercializing new technology.

The case of cooperative research illustrates well the needed alignment between a nation's particular industrial environment and the policies it adopts. Japanese firms face a disadvantage because university research and research institutes are not well developed. A mechanism is needed to compensate. Cooperative projects succeed in Japan because they involve technologies directly related to industry concerns, the cooperative project is only a small part of firms' overall research effort, powerful and neutral representatives from the ministries mediate conflicts, and intense domestic rivalry in Japan ensures little threat to competition.

Infrastructure. Upgrading a nation's industry depends on a modern and improving infrastructure. This is particularly true in advanced transportation, logistics, and telecommunications, all integral to introducing modern technologies and to competing in international markets. Both firms and governments have a role in creating and upgrading infrastructure. Governments have historically played the major role in most nations. Increasingly, privatization is taking place and groups of firms and even private vendors have made investments in specialized facilities.

Of the nations we studied, Japan, Korea, and Singapore have adopted the most aggressive posture toward infrastructure investments, to their benefit. Britain and Italy have clearly underinvested. It is interesting to note, however, that in those Italian industries where there is competitive advantage, industry associations and local government bodies have frequently cooperated to improve or establish their own specialized infrastructure where the national government has failed. In the Prato region, for example, telephone service is better than elsewhere in Italy. This is another one of the benefits of clustering.

Though infrastructure is rarely a source of national competitive advantage, except highly specialized infrastructure tailored to particular industries, it can well be a disadvantage. In the 1980s, infrastructure is more than just roads and telephones. Also important are cultural and recreational activities that attract talented individuals to a place to live and work. In the highly successful German *Länder* of Baden-Württemberg, for example, these sorts of investments play a prominent role in economic policy.

Capital. The upgrading of an economy requires that ample capital is available at low real cost and is allocated efficiently through the banking system and other capital markets to investments with the highest productivity. A low cost of capital not only encourages the high levels of investment necessary to improve productivity, but also supports sustained investments by lowering the time discount rate. High interest rates do not preclude sustained investment if other determinants of national advantage are favorable, as the cases of Italy and Korea illustrate. Despite periods of high real interest rates, both nations have high rates of net national investment that have supported upgrading. In both nations, however, the ability to develop the economy further will be constrained unless access to low cost capital improves and broadens (see Chapter 13).

Government has a role in affecting both the supply and cost of capital as well as the markets through which it is allocated. A nation's supply of capital is most influenced by the personal savings rate, the size of the government surpluses or deficits, and foreign capital flows. Government policy can affect all three. In Singapore, for example, there is a program of forced savings tied to the social security system. This has generated an enormous pool of capital that is beyond the ability of the Singaporean economy to deploy. Tax policy is another prominent tool for encouraging or retarding savings. Until recently, Japan has encouraged private savings through tax-free interest on postal savings accounts and by limiting alternative investment vehicles. The United States, conversely, has historically discouraged savings and encouraged consumption by allowing the deductibility of personal interest expense (though this is now being phased out), allowing home mortgage interest deductions, and fully taxing interest income.

Controlling government deficits that are not being used to finance productivity-enhancing investments in the economy is perhaps the most direct way in which government can influence the pool of investable capital. In Italy and more recently the United States, government deficits have not reflected investments in infrastructure or other areas supporting productivity growth. With no compensating benefit, they have only served to elevate real interest rates to industry. The globalization of capital markets is working in the direction of making real capital costs more equal among nations, but national differences remain significant and will persist.

Efficient mechanisms for allocating capital are as important to economic upgrading in many ways as the availability of capital. Successful emerging companies must have open and fair access to a nation's pool of capital in order to fund growth and the pursuit of higher-order competitive advantages. Nations such as Italy and Korea are being hampered in further advancement by poorly developed capital markets. Korea, like Japan, progressed to the investment-driven stage through a system where government borrowed and channeled scarce capital, at subsidized rates, to selected industries. However, a direct role for government in allocating capital will only support the upgrading of industry to a certain level. Beyond that, market mechanisms must take over. I will discuss below some of the desirable characteristics of capital markets for economic advancement.

Information. The amount and quality of information available in a nation is of growing importance in modern international competition. Information is a means to overcome inertia and create a sense of urgency in firms. It is integral to the upgrading of competitive advantage in established industries and to competing successfully in new industries. Information about markets, technology, and competition shapes the decisions of firms. It highlights new needs and opportunities and exposes threats.

The stock of information in a nation is created by a myriad of sources. Company documents, technical publications, patent records, private information providers, and the popular press are just a few. Government plays a prominent role in most nations in expanding the stock of information available to firms, through such things as government statistics and other publications as well as disclosure regulations. Equally important to creating information is disseminating it. Government policy to boost dissemination through clearinghouses such as the National Technical Information Service (United States) and other mechanisms supports the upgrading of industry.

One of the most important roles of government is *signaling,* in which government highlights information and issues of importance to firms. This role is best illustrated today by MITI in Japan. MITI conducts or commissions countless study groups, industry committees, and reports concerned with new technologies, trends in international competition, and future issues. These are conducted with the input of the best Japanese experts, academics, high-level industry representatives, and government officials. The reports are broadly disseminated and publicized and are widely covered in the press.

The major function of such studies is to awaken firms to emerging trends and problems, and cajole them into responding. Companies are free to respond in any way they choose. By widely disseminating such studies in industry, however, firms are put on notice that their competitors have seen them. This stimulates added internal study and response.

Direct Subsidy. Providing direct subsidies to firms has been a prominent tool used by governments to attempt to influence factor cost and otherwise shape competitive advantage. Subsidized capital, subsidized research, subsidized raw materials, subsidized exports, and direct grants are employed by nearly every nation in one industry or another. The aim is to tilt advantage in a nation's favor.

Subsidy is rarely associated with true competitive advantage. We found many instances, in contrast, where it was associated with chronic failures— German and Swedish shipbuilding, American shipping, and Italian aerospace are just a few examples. The reasons are clear in the context of the "diamond." Subsidy delays adjustment and innovation rather than promoting it. Most forms of subsidy come with explicit or implicit strings attached, such as limits on where plants can be located or the number of jobs that can be eliminated. These limit flexibility and dampen innovation.

Ongoing subsidies dull incentives and create an attitude of dependence. Government support makes it difficult to get industry to invest and take risk without it. Attention is focused on renewing subsidies rather than creating true competitive advantage. One subsidized industry propagates its noncompetitiveness to others. Once started, subsidy is difficult to stop. What is worse, subsidies to one ailing industry encourage others to seek them.

As a general rule, tax incentives are better vehicles than subsidies to promote upgrading of industry because they force firms to undertake projects only when they see the prospect of an economic return. Direct subsidies are only beneficial if they cover just a modest fraction of the cost involved, and if they are used as *signals* of directions for appropriate corporate behavior. Japanese cooperative research projects and Italian incentives to purchase advanced manufacturing equipment are two examples.

Indirect subsidies, in areas such as education, research universities, and advanced infrastructure, are a much better investment of government funds from the perspective of improving the competitive position of a nation's industries. Similarly, providing incentives to buyers is often a better way of stimulating the development of advanced new products than giving support to firms directly.

Policies Toward Factor and Currency Markets

Macroeconomic and microeconomic policies designed to control factor costs and the exchange rate through intervention in factor and currency markets are a prominent part of many nations' efforts to improve the competitiveness of industry. Fiscal and monetary policy, regulation of energy markets, and policies to influence the collective bargaining process are prominent tools to influence wage levels, energy costs, and exchange rates. The rationale is that lower factor costs or a lower exchange rate will help firms compete more effectively in international markets. The Reagan administration, for example, made much of dollar devaluation as a solution to the U.S. merchandise trade deficit.

Such policies are based on an incomplete view of the determinants of competitive advantage and of the process of upgrading that determines economic prosperity. Nations such as Germany, Switzerland, and in the last decade, Japan, have experienced rising wages, high-priced energy, and strong currencies but have sustained or increased competitive advantage in industry. Japan's case is particularly instructive. The Nixon shock, energy shocks, and most recently the yen shock triggered a strengthening and upgrading of competitive advantage in Japanese industry, not a weakening of position. Such pressures from selective factor disadvantages not only affect industries directly but feed back to encourage innovation by suppliers of machinery and inputs. Conversely, a history of devaluations or artificially low input prices failed, in nations such as Britain, Sweden, and Italy, to make much of a difference to long-term industry success.

If all other things remained equal, a reduction in factor costs or foreign prices would indeed benefit industry. The problem is that factor costs are decisive to competitive advantage only in those industries where technology is unsophisticated and easily accessible and basic factor costs make up the majority of cost.[11] In most industries with the potential for high productivity, however, competitive advantage is based on innovation. What is beneficial in a static view of competition undermines competitive advantage in a dynamic one. Artificially restricting the rise of factor costs or intervening to push down exchange rates removes pressures for innovation and upgrading and steers firms to price- and cost-sensitive market segments where competitive advantage is ultimately less sustainable. Instead of improving quality, introducing more sophisticated new models, and lowering manufacturing costs through automation, firms breathe a sigh of relief and collect profits. As other nations' firms innovate faster, the result is a long-term loss of national position. In the U.S. auto industry, for example, the response to higher Japanese prices due to the falling dollar against the yen was to raise prices (and earn high profits) rather than win back market position. Meanwhile, Japanese auto producers have been frantically improving productivity and upgrading product features and technology.

The implication for policy is not that government should endeavor to drive up factor costs or the exchange rate, but that upward movements reflecting market forces should not be resisted and no efforts should normally be made to push them down. The following more specific considerations for policy emerge:

1. *Devaluation.* The value of a nation's currency is a function of a wide range of influences, among them budget deficits and interest rates. Provided foreign and domestic goods are not perfect substitutes, devaluation works

to raise exports and lower imports, improving the balance of trade. The extent of devaluation necessary to restore balanced trade is a function of the broad state of competitive advantage of a nation's industry, which determines how much of a price change is necessary to induce enough domestic and foreign buyers to switch from foreign goods. Devaluation is an undesirable means of balancing trade, however, because it works to lower a nation's standard of living. It makes foreign goods more expensive and discounts a nation's own products in foreign markets.[12]

The more serious problem with devaluation, however, is its effect on the process of upgrading in an economy. The expectation of a lower exchange rate leads firms toward a dependence on price competition and toward competing in price-sensitive segments and industries. Automation and other forms of innovation that improve productivity slow down, and the shift to higher-order competitive advantages is retarded.[13] Devaluation, then, may well lead to pressures for further devaluation. The experience of nations in the postwar period is that devaluation rarely leads to long-term productivity growth. The best case for devaluation is for nations relatively early in the stages of competitive development (factor-driven or investment-driven). Even here, however, an overreliance on policies that artificially hold back currency appreciation will ultimately block advancement.

There is a balance to be struck. Currency pressures need to be strong enough to promote upgrading but not so great as to run ahead of factor quality and other preconditions for upgrading to succeed. A strong currency is most beneficial in the upgrading process if other parts of the "diamond" are favorable (such as healthy domestic rivalry and access to skilled human resources). An exchange rate that rises steadily, reflecting normal market forces, is most likely to encourage upgrading. However, the Japanese case illustrates how a currency shock can be a source of dynamism provided that the nation's industry has strong advantages throughout the "diamond." It is appropriate for government to seek to reduce an artificially high exchange rate, but only to purchasing power parity.

2. *Input prices*. The upgrading of competitive advantage is served if a nation's domestic input costs are moving somewhat in advance of those in other nations, to give firms early warning of trends that will affect international competition. Government must avoid the temptation to seek to hold down input prices artificially. This was the case with U.S. energy prices. American industry was not helped in the long run, as U.S. firms fell behind in energy conservation and other nations' firms were able to gain market position.

3. *Wages*. Policies to retard wage growth are often misguided. Wages should be allowed to rise with or slightly ahead of productivity growth. This creates beneficial pressures to seek more advanced sources of competitive advantage and compete in more sophisticated industries and segments. Rising wages also lead to increasing purchasing power for more and better-quality

goods, improving demand conditions. Wage increases well ahead of productivity growth for a sustained period, however, are a cause for concern.

4. *Workforce growth.* Rapid growth in the available workforce fuels economic growth because new employees require goods and services and they expand purchasing power. However, rapid workforce growth may slow the upgrading of an economy. With a ready supply of employees, pressures to boost productivity, upgrade skills, and seek more advanced forms of competitive advantage are eased. A similar effect occurs when there is large-scale immigration of unskilled workers as was the case in Germany and Switzerland, though immigration may well be desirable on humanitarian grounds. (Free movement of skilled personnel, conversely, is generally beneficial to the upgrading process.) Part of lagging productivity growth in American industry may be due to population growth more rapid than that of most nations (Table 7–1) coupled with a higher rate of immigration of low skilled workers and a greater propensity for women to enter the workforce.

Similar considerations partly explain the persistence of unemployment. A high rate of unemployment reduces incentives for productivity growth and upgrading. Where competition is international, this may lead to more unemployment.

*   *   *

The considerations I have described are inevitably partial. Each of these policy areas is influenced by a range of variables that go well beyond the competitive position of a nation's industry, and each has broader effects. Yet, it is important to note that the policy most beneficial to upgrading industry is often the reverse of that which may initially seem appropriate, especially in nations seeking to compete in advanced industries. What appears beneficial in a static conception of competition retards innovation in a dynamic one.

The posture toward factor and currency markets most beneficial to economic upgrading is apt to be unpopular with industry and to cause short-term discomfort. Despite political pressures, however, resisting the temptation to intervene in factor markets is necessary. A better policy approach is to make *responding* to factor cost or currency shifts a national priority, as has happened repeatedly in Japan.

As I discussed in Chapter 3, selective factor disadvantages will not lead to the desired effect if there are substantial barriers to innovation. Other determinants (notably factor quality, goals, and domestic rivalry) must support it because the forces leading to the upgrading of competitive advantages are an independent system. This makes policies toward industry mutually dependent, and dependent on the overall stage of competitive development in a nation's industry.

To be sure, factor disadvantages must be selective if they are to motivate and not discourage. Factor costs far out of line with those in other nations of comparable economic advancement are a cause for concern, and policy should work to bring them into proximity. Yet seeking lower factor costs is not the appropriate target.

GOVERNMENT'S EFFECT ON DEMAND CONDITIONS

The upgrading of competitive advantage in a nation's industry requires advanced and sophisticated home demand. Government policy to affect demand has traditionally focused on influencing the overall quantity of domestic demand through government spending or manipulating the availability or cost of credit. Such efforts are a fixture of macroeconomic policy. In Japan, for example, much attention is being placed today on increasing domestic demand to substitute for exports.

My theory suggests a different and much broader role for policies affecting demand. The greatest significance of home demand for competitive advantage rests not in aggregate demand but in demand conditions in particular industries. Government affects these in many often unintentional and counterproductive ways because it has an incomplete view of what determines competitive advantage. Worse yet, nations attempting to follow an "export-driven" model of development ignore home demand altogether, which limits advancement.

The principal aim of demand-side policies should be to improve the *quality* of domestic demand. Demand quality, whose dimensions I discussed in Chapter 3, plays a central role in the process of upgrading. Government has a surprising number of levers to elevate demand quality if it perceives the significance of doing so.

GOVERNMENT PROCUREMENT

The most direct effect of government on demand conditions is via its role as a buyer of many goods and services. Government agencies or state-owned companies are the principal buyers in defense-related industries, industries connected with infrastructure (for example, state-owned airlines, electric utilities, or telephone companies), and of many other products and services as well.

Government procurement can work for or against national competitive advantage. It works against it if, as happens all too often, government purchases become a guaranteed market. The German *Bundespost,* the state-owned telecommunications monopoly, is a notorious example. In the United States, there are "buy American" laws that affect some types of procurement;[14] similar laws or *de facto* exclusion of foreign suppliers are common in other nations as well. Domestic firms, in such a setting, view government demand as a birthright. The government market becomes the focus of attention, and domestic firms lobby for unusual product standards or other regulations to freeze out international rivals.

Exclusion of foreign suppliers is supposed to help domestic firms. In fact, the result in most industries is that innovation and upgrading by domestic firms slow down. Their products and services diverge in quality, features, and cost from those demanded internationally. Domestic firms are then unable to compete in international markets, and even more blatant favoritism at home becomes necessary to support them.

Government procurement can be a positive force for upgrading national competitive advantage under the following circumstances:

• *Early demand.* Government procurement should provide early demand for advanced new products or services, pushing its local suppliers into new areas.

• *Demanding and sophisticated buyers.* Government agencies should set stringent product specifications and seek sophisticated product varieties rather than merely accept what domestic suppliers offer.

• *Procurement reflecting international needs.* Government specifications should be set with an eye to what will be valued in other advanced nations, rather than reflecting only the nation's idiosyncratic needs. Ideally, government specifications will anticipate needs elsewhere.

• *Procurement processes that facilitate innovation.* Government procurement that makes innovation easier works to the benefit of a nation's industry. In Denmark, for example, the national health service provides free clinical testing in Danish hospitals for new products. It also keeps careful data on all patients, allowing providers of health care products to identify populations of patients with very specific characteristics for research and testing purposes. This sort of behavior is one of the reasons why tiny Denmark does well in the health care sector.

• *Competition.* Government procurement must include a strong element of competition if it is to upgrade the local industry. In Japan, for example, Nippon Telephone and Telegraph (NTT) has played its role as a government buyer better than most state telecommunications monopolies (NTT was privatized in 1985). It has typically ordered the next-generation systems rather than what Japanese suppliers currently produced. Most importantly, NTT has maintained a number of suppliers for each product, ensuring domestic competition for its business. Despite the high entry barriers into foreign telecommunications markets, Japanese firms have done well overseas in areas where Japanese domestic demand is particularly stringent (such as microwave equipment) and hence Japanese equipment is sophisticated.

In the long run, foreign vendors must be allowed at least some access to the home market to stimulate further innovation by domestic firms. NTT has moved too slowly in this regard. If domestic firms are weak, the best solution is to award foreign vendors some business and force domestic firms to upgrade their positions against a timetable in order to retain a large share of the business. Shutting out foreign firms altogether and guaranteeing domestic firms the business will most likely mean that domestic firms will remain domestic.

Defense Procurement. Defense procurement represents a substantial part of demand in some nations such as Britain and the United States. It is widely regarded as beneficial to national advantage. It represents a major, and early, market for some types of sophisticated goods.

Yet, defense demand is a decidedly mixed blessing, as I have discussed earlier. Defense needs for many products are quite different from civilian needs. In the years before and after World War II, defense needs stimulated fundamental research on core technologies—aerospace, electronics, and synthetic materials. The spin-offs were substantial. As defense technology has progressed, however, defense and civilian needs have often grown apart. Defense needs today are highly specialized. Moreover, where defense and civilian needs do overlap, the appropriate performance versus cost tradeoffs are usually quite different. Firms that are defense contractors, the ones most prone to perceive and implement technology spin-offs, have had a notably mixed record in competing in commercial businesses because the determinants of competitive advantage are so different.

In nations where defense spending is a significant fraction of the GNP, the defense market represents a major market segment in many industries. Domestic firms are prone to concentrate on this segment, not only because it is large but because it is often early to develop. The result can be that firms succeed in the defense market but fail to develop the product varieties and cost position needed to serve the commercial market, which is a much bigger international market. Foreign rivals, with little or no defense demand to distract them, concentrate on the commercial market all along. American machine tool suppliers had this difficulty in computer numerically controlled machine tools. While defense demand is an important advantage in a few industries, where there are very substantial economies of scale and defense applications represent a large fraction of the overall market (notably aerospace), it is more of a disadvantage in other industries because it sends the wrong signals about market needs.

The defense establishment is also a questionable instrument for developing a national economy.[15] Not only is defense demand often distracting, but the goals of a defense agency diverge from those best suited to upgrade industry. From a purely national defense perspective, it would be desirable to have ample domestic capacity in every significant industry. Defense agencies are prone, as a result, to try to support and preserve domestic firms rather than introduce real competition into procurement and act as demanding and sophisticated customers. National commercial advantage is undermined and not enhanced by such actions, and productivity growth is slowed. It should also be noted that large defense expenditures may well detract from investments in factor creation in areas such as education, research, and infrastructure, which also slows the upgrading of an economy.[16]

REGULATION OF PRODUCTS AND PROCESSES

Government affects demand conditions through regulations that affect product standards and the processes by which products are made, such as those governing product performance, product safety, environmental impact (such as those covering noise, pollution, reclamation, and visual impact), energy efficiency of products, and the operating practices of firms (such as working conditions for employees). Not only does government set regulatory standards directly, but many nations have national or regional standards-setting organizations such as Germany's *Deutscher Normenausschuss* (Deutsche Industrie Norm or DIN), America's Underwriters Laboratory, and Japan's Japanese Industrial Standards (JIS). These standards are frequently incorporated into laws.

The last decade produced a backlash against all forms of regulation, nowhere stronger than in the United States. Regulation can be divided into two broad types, that relating to *standards* of one type or another, such as those I have described, and that relating to *competition*. Regulation of competition includes such practices as restrictions on entry, rules for pricing, and laws governing other aspects of industry structure or the ways firms can compete.

Regulation of competition influences the process of domestic rivalry and new business formation, subjects I will discuss later. Regulation of standards has an important influence on demand conditions. It might seem that regulation of standards would be an intrusion of government into competition that undermines competitive advantage.[17] Instead, the reverse can be true in many circumstances.

Stringent standards for product performance, product safety, and environmental impact contribute to creating and upgrading competitive advantage. They pressure firms to improve quality, upgrade technology, and provide features in areas of important customer (and social) concern. Japan, for example, established tough quality standards for export goods in the 1950s and 1960s. These were a stimulus to improve quality in Japanese industry. Germany's DIN standards are also well known for their toughness and detail. While sometimes attacked as protectionist, foreign firms dislike them in no small part because they are hard to meet. Industry-level standards can also pressure upgrading. The Solingen Law established in 1938, for example, set rigid standards for the quality of cutlery and the right to use the Solingen name (the city where the German cutlery industry is concentrated). The law, a response to practices that were causing product quality to deteriorate, has proved to be an important device for preserving German differentiation.

Particularly beneficial are stringent regulations that *anticipate* standards that will spread internationally. These give a nation's firms a head start in developing products and services that will be valued elsewhere. Social concerns such as the environment are increasingly differentiating factors in advanced markets, and regulation influences the response of a nation's firms to them. Sweden's tough standards for product safety and environmental protection, for example, have been a significant source of competitive advantage in a variety of industries. Atlas Copco, for example, produces quiet compressors that can be used in urban areas with minimal disturbance to residents. Another example is the Japanese Energy Conservation Law of 1979. This law set tough standards for energy usage in air-conditioning equipment, refrigerators, and automobiles, leading to many product improvements that have enhanced international position.

Tough standards also encourage the start-up of specialized manufacturing and service firms to help address them, which can develop strong international positions. American firms have historically led in the export of pollution control equipment and services, reflecting advanced domestic standards. As Germany, Sweden, and Denmark have moved ahead of the United States in standards governing a number of aspects of environmental quality, their firms in these areas are increasingly supplying world markets.

Firms, like governments, are often prone to see the short-term cost of dealing with tough standards and not their longer-term benefits in terms of innovation. Firms point to foreign rivals without such standards as having a cost advantage. Such thinking is based on an incomplete view of how competitive advantage is created and sustained. Selling poorly performing, unsafe, or environmentally damaging products is not a route to real competitive advantage in sophisticated industries and industry segments, especially in a world where environmental sensitivity and concern for social welfare are rising in all advanced nations. Sophisticated buyers will usually appreciate safer, cleaner, quieter products before governments do. Firms with the skills to produce such products will have an important lever to enter foreign markets, and can often accelerate the process by which foreign regulations are toughened. Old models can be offered to buyers in markets with lax regulation or to developing nations unable to afford newer ones.

Regulation undermines competitive advantage, however, if a nation's regulations *lag* behind those of other nations or are *anachronistic*. Such regulations will retard innovation or channel the innovations of domestic firms in the wrong directions. An electric code based on twenty-year-old technology, for example, will work against the competitive advantage of all the industries in a country that are affected by it. Limits on biotechnology research in some nations, such as Germany, threaten industries such as agrochemicals and pharmaceuticals where this technology is important. Similarly, the practice of using idiosyncratic local regulations to protect a domestic industry will only work to ensure that its competitive success is domestic. It is not always easy to decide which regulations are forward-looking and which are backward-looking. This is nowhere more clear than in the field of nuclear energy. Yet in most areas, the principle of setting regulations that are forward-looking can be practically applied.

A prominent example of an area where regulatory policy can work for or against national advantage is *product liability*. Product liability laws can benefit competitive advantage by acting like a sophisticated buyer to encourage the development of better products. In the United States, however, product liability is so extreme and uncertain as to retard innovation. The legal and regulatory climate places firms in constant jeopardy of costly and, as importantly, lengthy product liability suits. The existing approach goes beyond any reasonable need to protect consumers, as other nations have demonstrated through more pragmatic approaches.

A final important distinction in evaluating regulatory standards, suggested by my product liability example, is between the *content* of standards and the *process* of administering them. The two are often confused. National advantage is enhanced by stringent standards that are *rapidly, efficiently, and consistently applied*. These play the same role as a demanding buyer.

Slow or uncertain application of standards, conversely, both wastes resources and undermines innovation. A good example is aseptic food packaging. The technology was quickly approved in Switzerland and Germany, while U.S. approval came more than a decade later. Consequently, foreign firms, with far greater experience with the technology, became the dominant suppliers in the U.S. market when U.S. approval came.[18] Tough standards combined with an effective process of enforcement represent the best combination for national advantage.[19]

BUYER INDUSTRY STRUCTURE

Government regulation and policies toward state ownership affect the structure of industries that are important buyers of other products and services, in fields such as health care, electric power, and telecommunications. Regulation or state ownership is beneficial to supplier industries if it encourages an industry to act as a more sophisticated buyer with more stringent and advanced needs. It works against local suppliers if it retards innovation and introduces conservatism into purchasing decisions.

In most instances, private ownership and exposure to competitive pressure create the best environment leading industries to play the role of demanding and anticipatory buyers. These lead to greater incentives for rapid innovation in industries and less intrusion of political and bureaucratic constraints on purchasing. Some state-owned monopoly firms act as sophisticated buyers, but this is the exception rather than the rule. The health care sector provides a good example. In the United States, the largely private and decentralized health care system, characterized by substantial competition, has been perhaps the single biggest source of advantage to American suppliers of health-related goods and services. In most other nations, partially or completely government-owned health care systems slow down innovation. Many new products, procedures, and services have penetrated first or much faster in the United States, among them cardiac pacemakers, disposable syringes, and patient monitoring equipment.

One area where government policy frequently affects the structure of buyer industries is in retailing and distribution. Many nations have regulations that protect small independent wholesalers and retailers against the growth of large chains, or other restrictions on forming modern distributive structures. While anti-chain store laws were abandoned decades ago in the United States, they persist in various forms in such nations such as Japan and Italy.

While such laws may serve some social purposes and represent a form of protection because fragmented channels are harder for foreign competitors to penetrate, restrictions on modern distribution channels have a double negative effect on the upgrading of competitive advantage. First, they artificially elevate costs and reduce labor productivity in retailing and wholesaling, stunting national productivity growth. Second, however, they serve to block the development of sophisticated and cutting-edge channels in a nation, undermining in the long run the competitive advantages of all the industries that serve them or sell through them. A nation's firms are forced to learn how to deal with advanced and sophisticated channels abroad instead of at home. The inefficient and anachronistic Japanese distribution and retail sector, for example, will become increasingly limiting to Japanese firms.

American firms, in contrast, have gained important advantages from the fluidity of innovation at home in retailing and distribution.[20] The broad principle in this and many other aspects of government policy is that a nation benefits if its circumstances are in sync with and even ahead of those in other nations.

STIMULATING EARLY OR SOPHISTICATED DEMAND

Government has the ability to encourage early or sophisticated demand in a variety of other ways that promotes the upgrading of industry. In robotics, for example, I described earlier how the Japanese government provided incentives for firms to purchase approved types of robots, and created a leasing company to aid in financing them.[21] Even more significant incentives for purchasing advanced manufacturing equipment exist in Italy.

Such programs lead a nation's buyers to become early purchasers of advanced new products and services and encourage firms to innovate in order to be able to supply them. Just as important, however, is that such programs *reduce the risk perceived by firms* that demand will fail to materialize. Explicit or implicit assurances of future demand encourage investment both in R&D and efficient scale productive assets.

Stimulating early and sophisticated demand (or its promise) provides an advantage as long as the demand is for product varieties suitable for other nations. Moreover, there must be active domestic competition in supplying the early demand, or it will be a drug that tranquilizes domestic suppliers instead of energizing them.

A policy of providing incentives to buyers to be early purchasers of sophisticated products is often more beneficial to innovation and to competitive advantage than directly subsidizing firms. A focus on buyers preserves the discipline on firms of having to meet buyer needs. Competitive rivalry among firms is stimulated. Such a policy also clearly helps *buyers* upgrade as well, and hence encourages the mutually reinforcing process in which a nation's buyers become more sophisticated and in turn stimulate local suppliers.

There are many specific mechanisms by which government policy can create early, intense, or sophisticated demand for products and services. The Nordic mobile telephone program, for example, was a cooperative effort of the Scandinavian nations to establish mobile telephone systems in each nation well before they were common elsewhere. It led to an international position in this industry for such Scandinavian equipment suppliers as Nokia of Finland.

Sometimes early or intense demand is a by-product of a nation's commitment to social programs. In Sweden, for example, equal access for handicapped persons is given unusual priority. The advanced level of support for the handicapped has led to an active Swedish industry supplying products for handicapped persons. In Denmark, an early decision by government to pay for hearing aids for those who needed them was an important reason for the international success of Danish firms in this industry. In Japan, a decision to provide widespread music education led to the purchase of a piano by every public school. This benefited the Japanese piano industry not only through creating demand but by focusing industry attention on developing inexpensive, mass-produced pianos since foreign pianos were too costly for schools. The resulting product and process innovations laid the groundwork for an internationally successful industry (Yamaha and Kawai are leaders). An early commitment to environmentally friendly wind power also spawned an internationally active Danish windmill industry.

Laws that aim to be forward-looking can also stimulate early demand. In Japan, for example, one of the spurs to facsimile demand was a decision by the Ministry of Justice that facsimile documents were acceptable for legal purposes. Also potentially significant to demand sophistication are policies that govern the use of credit.[22]

It is clear from this and earlier discussion that there are many parts of government with some ability to influence domestic demand conditions. Agencies as diverse as a national health service, environmental protection agency, department of education, transportation department, and defense department all have a role, through their own purchasing or through the way they regulate or influence other domestic buyers. Many of these agencies and departments rarely see themselves as affecting national competitive advantage, however, but define their roles largely in social or public welfare terms. This neglects an important leverage point for upgrading the national economy.

BUYER INFORMATION

Government policy can improve demand quality by providing accurate and complete information to buyers or requiring that firms provide such information. Information allows better and more sophisticated choices and pressures firms to upgrade performance. Complaint systems, particularly if they are publicized, are an added stimulus for improvement.

TECHNICAL STANDARDS

Government policy affects the rate of innovation and upgrading in industry through its role in setting technical standards. In many fields (for example, television sets, facsimile, and data transmission), standards are necessary to allow compatibility of equipment or services. Where the process of setting standards is long and drawn out and the basic technological parameters remain in doubt, the process of innovation slows down. Conversely, when basic standards are set, firms then turn their attention to rapidly developing and improving products and processes to meet them.[23]

Government policy encourages the upgrading of competitive advantage if it supports early adoption of technical standards that embody a high overall level of technology. In the United States and often in Europe, the process of reaching technical standards is frequently protracted as firms jockey for their individual positions. In Japan, conversely, MITI has frequently applied significant pressure on firms to set basic standards, pushing them to move on to the next stage in the innovation cycle. In sewing machines, for example, standards were established for parts in the early post–World War II period. This spawned numerous parts suppliers, lowered entry barriers into sewing machine assembly, and speeded up attention to new features and quality. In television sets, facsimile, and other products, relatively rapid agreement on standards benefited Japanese industry in progressing to the rapid introduction of new models and features.[24]

FOREIGN AID AND POLITICAL TIES

Government influences demand conditions for its firms through foreign aid that is explicitly or implicitly tied to the purchase of the nation's goods and services. Historically, colonial ties had an even stronger effect. While colonies are rare today, special buying, trade, and political relationships between nations are not. Traditional colonial ties remain a remarkably persistent influence today because of large expatriate communities, historical influences on social norms and products standards, and many other residual influences.

Foreign aid and special buying relationships create, in effect, an extension of the domestic market. The result is "captive" markets for a nation's firms. While the pragmatic use of foreign aid can benefit a nation's industry, there are two important cautions.[25] The first is that any "captive" market has a tendency to distract firms from adopting a more global market outlook. As discussed in Chapter 9, for example, British firms have been too oriented toward serving present and former parts of the Empire. Conversely, Sweden and Switzerland, without any former colonies, gained an early orientation toward broad-based foreign market penetration.

A second problem with markets created by foreign aid or special relationships is that they are rarely advanced and demanding markets. If a nation's firms focus on them, their capabilities may not be developed to meet the more stringent needs of other advanced countries. This has been a problem for both British firms serving former colonies and American firms focusing on Latin America. The implication for government policy is not that foreign aid should be avoided, but that it should not be viewed as a primary instrument of policy toward industry.

GOVERNMENT'S EFFECT ON RELATED AND
SUPPORTING INDUSTRIES

Government policy has a role in shaping the breadth and international success of related and supporting industries in a nation, integral to the competitive upgrading of other industries. The same policies that I have described which enhance competitive advantage in industry generally will benefit particular related and supporting industries. Policies in Japan toward the semiconductor industry, for example, have benefited many other industries because the semiconductor industry is an important supplier.

There are a number of policy areas that have particular significance because they influence industries that are related to or support many other industries or the formation of clusters. A number of these are discussed below.

POLICIES TOWARD THE MEDIA

The media, for our purposes, is defined as all the means through which firms can communicate to buyers about their products and services. It includes television, radio, magazines, newspapers, direct mail, and telemarketing.

The presence of advanced and innovative media in a nation is a source of national advantage. Such media expose the nation's firms to the most sophisticated marketing channels and leads to innovations in marketing in the nation that serve as advantages elsewhere. For example, U.S. policy provides for private ownership of media and places relatively few restrictions on advertising and other marketing practices. As a result, important media such as television emerged first in America, and American firms have often been at the cutting edge of marketing technology. This has contributed to unusual American strength in consumer packaged goods and services, where mass marketing rather than unique products or services has often been the key to competitive success.

Other nations have had a tendency to place more constraints on the use of media, particularly television and radio networks. In Sweden, an extreme case, no advertising is allowed on television and radio. While there are legitimate social reasons for such policies, their indirect effect on industry is often overlooked. Government policies which restrict consumer access to information in some forms, for whatever social reasons, extract a subtle price in terms of a nation's international success. A nation's firms that cannot practice advanced marketing at home rarely master it. Swedish firms, for example, have rarely been internationally successful in consumer packaged goods and service industries involving mass marketing.

Nations can be arrayed on a spectrum in terms of the availability of media and the sanctions and limits on their use. There is a striking correlation between this and competitive advantage in mass-marketed consumer goods and services. Japan and Britain, both with advanced commercial media and allowing significant advertising time on television, are the only real competitors of American firms in such industries.

CLUSTER FORMATION

National advantage resides as much in clusters as in individual industries. The presence of world-class buyer, supplier, and related industries in a nation triggers self-reinforcing benefits in upgrading competitive advantage in industry. Government policy has an important role in nurturing and reinforcing clusters.

Clusters often emerge and begin to grow naturally. Government policy had little to do with the beginning of Silicon Valley or the concentration of mechanical firms around Modena, Italy. Once a cluster begins to form, however, government at all levels can play a role in reinforcing it. Perhaps the most beneficial way is through investments to create specialized factors, such as university technical institutes, training centers, data banks, and specialized infrastructure. In Germany, for example, local governments often become actively involved in supporting educational institutions and other projects closely tied to concentrations of local firms. In the United States, efforts to support clusters are becoming more common, particularly at the state and local level. The Research Triangle, in North Carolina, provides a good example. Because of the powerful role of geographic concentration in national advantage, the state and local role is an essential one in cluster formation.

In addition to reinforcing or widening existing clusters, some nations have set out to spawn new ones. In Korea, for example, the government has established a special industrial region in the Kumi area for electronics-related companies. By providing specialized infrastructure and technical centers, the hope is to attract a variety of companies whose geographic concentration will be self-reinforcing. In Japan, a similar though less focused effort to create a "technopolis" is taking place in Tsukuba. New clusters are most effective if they are built around a concentration of specialized expertise, such as a university department or a group of sophisticated hospitals. Industrial zones that place no constraints on the types of firms that can utilize them, conversely, will offer limited benefits.

Government policy will be far more likely to succeed in reinforcing an existing or nascent industry cluster than in trying to promote an entirely new one, however tempting it might be for national prestige. A nation such as Denmark, for example, is better off building on existing clusters in health and environmental management than it would be if it attempted to establish an aircraft industry. Most regions will have something to build on. A central government policy toward cluster formation is best directed toward encouraging and supporting many localized efforts rather than a few centrally chosen ones.

Governments have a poor track record in selecting sectors where the subtle conditions for national advantage are present. The presence of an established cluster signals the presence of some favorable determinants of competitive advantage, raising the odds that governmental investments will bear fruit. Being preoccupied with "new" industries also obscures the fact that clusters always represent a mix of traditional and new industries. Even "mature" industries involve new technologies. A "mature" industry, such as food processing, can lead into many related new fields ranging from biotechnology to process instrumentation.

In setting policies to upgrade or enhance clusters, buyers, suppliers, and related industries often need to develop in parallel in order to best promote competitive advantage.[26] Establishing a technical institute to benefit machine tool firms will not achieve maximum impact unless there are sophisticated local manufacturers able to use the equipment who can participate in the development process. More broadly, all parts of the "diamond" must progress if true competitive advantage is to result. Government policy must recognize the interconnectedness of industries in creating competitive advantage. The Japanese Automated Sewing System project, an effort to develop automated garment manufacturing, involves a wide range of end-product and supplier industries. It is a good example of a policy initiative which marshals efforts across an entire cluster. The project, if it succeeds, will upgrade competitive advantage in a whole range of linked industries.

REGIONAL POLICY

National economies rarely develop evenly. Some regions or cities outpace others in economic prosperity. In Britain and Germany, the depressed areas are in the north, while in Italy they are in the south. The reasons for these differences can be explained by the same considerations as those captured in the "diamond": factor conditions, demand conditions, the presence of supporting industries, and so on.

To stimulate economic development in those areas that are relatively depressed, many nations practice regional policy of one sort or another. Regional policy has rarely been effective, because it usually involves generalized subsidies to induce or "bribe" firms to locate plants or other facilities in a region. Britain and Italy provide typical examples. Subsidies to induce firms to locate activities where they would prefer not to is hardly a way to foster a solid economic base or create competitive advantage. The depressed area does not become a true home base, necessary for one firm to reinforce competitive advantage in others and to stimulate new business formation.

Regional policy will be more effective if it follows the principle of building on clusters. Magnets for clusters, in the form of universities, research laboratories, specialized infrastructure, or trained labor pools, are much more effective than subsidies. The best regional policy identifies cores of industry strength and builds on them, to encourage geographically concentrated clusters. One industry creates sophisticated demand or inputs for others. This is by far superior to encouraging a diverse and random group of firms to establish feeder plants or distribution centers in a location that they will never develop and upgrade further.

GOVERNMENT'S EFFECT ON FIRM STRATEGY, STRUCTURE, AND RIVALRY

Government policy has many influences on the ways firms are created, organized, and managed, their goals, and how they compete. Government policy in these areas is undergoing change in many nations in the late 1980s, not always for the better.

INTERNATIONALIZATION

Sustaining and enhancing competitive advantage requires that a nation's firms take a global approach to strategy. Government policy plays a role in this process, through mechanisms such as regulations on foreign direct investment, exchange and import controls, and the like. Government policy should actively encourage an international outlook and exports. One way is through the provision and dissemination of foreign market and technical information. Japan's JETRO (Japan External Trade and Research Organization) is perhaps the most prominent example, with numerous foreign offices and a staff dedicated to assisting Japanese exporters. Such export promotional activities are most effective when closely connected to industries and industry clusters. Government policy should also seek to avoid currency restrictions, restrictions on foreign investment, and restrictions on the inflow and outflow of skilled personnel that impede internationalization.

The internationalization of a nation's firms is sometimes viewed with suspicion. Some see an inevitable dichotomy between the needs of the nation (and its citizens) and the needs of firms. If firms invest abroad or outsource, this is taken as evidence of harming or abandoning the nation. Licensing of technology abroad is seen as giving away the nation's secrets.

These sorts of arguments have emotional appeal. However, the dichotomy between the interests of the nation and the interests of its firms is often a false one in the long run. Globalization of strategy and the sourcing of less sophisticated products and components from abroad is integral to the process of making competitive advantages more sophisticated and upgrading an economy. In an upgrading economy, internationalization does not threaten domestic jobs but raises their productivity. Internationalization also makes an economy less sensitive to exchange rates. In Japan, for example, there was much public debate about the rapid globalization of strategies in the immediate aftermath of the major rise in the value of the yen beginning in 1986. However, Japanese exports and economic growth are robust in the late 1980s as companies have employed global strategies to solidify foreign market positions.[27]

The dichotomy between the firm and the nation's long-term interests *is* real when firms internationalize or outsource not the less-productive activities but the highly productive ones. This occurs when the national "diamond" is not healthy, such as when firms have goals that do not support the sustained investments required to upgrade their domestic activities or there is too little competitive pressure to innovate. Alternatively, sending the wrong jobs overseas may reflect inadequate factor creation, weaknesses in crucial supporting industries, or other disadvantages.

Nations do not benefit from this type of internationalization, nor do firms themselves in the long run. As I discussed in the previous chapter, innovation at home usually yields more sustainable competitive advantage than shifting most of production and control over process technology abroad. Developing domestic suppliers produces more sustainable advantage than relying solely on foreign suppliers.

Yet even when internationalization takes forms which are counterproductive, attempting to block it is not appropriate policy. Policies that impede the process of internationalization may preserve a few jobs today but usually eliminate the possibility of saving them tomorrow except through subsidy. Preventing firms from internationalization is not the answer. Instead, policy should deal with the underlying reasons why firms are failing to upgrade.

GOALS

Both firms and the individuals that work in them must have goals that encourage hard work and sustained commitment to their industry if national advantage is to be widespread. Such goals are necessary if firms are to improve and innovate and if new businesses are to be formed. Goals reflect a wide variety of circumstances in a nation, many of which lie outside the direct influence of government policy. Social attitudes toward wealth, aspirations for upward mobility, and the social status of business are significant influences and reflect a nation's history, religious affiliations, social structure, and existing level of prosperity. Yet government policy can have an important effect on goals as well.

Individuals' Goals. The goals of individuals are most affected by government in several ways. The first is through tax policy. Tax policy must encourage effort, not tax away its fruits through high marginal tax rates. Recently, there have been efforts in some nations to use tax incentives to encourage practices that link pay closer to performance. While this aim is a desirable one in a broad sense, to motivate greater commitment and effort, some approaches to achieving it may be counterproductive. If tax incentives work to make employee compensation heavily linked to current profits or current share prices, long-term investment and innovation may suffer.

Another influence of government on the goals of individuals is through policies that affect the nation's labor markets. The operation of labor markets is a subject far beyond the scope of this book. However, what is clear from theory as well as the industries we studied is that rapidly mobile labor is not necessarily the ideal for upgrading a national economy. Human resources must move out of inherently unproductive industries, but employees need a commitment to their profession and their firm if upgrading of competitive advantage is to occur. Productivity in an industry is not a given or fixed, as many discussions of labor mobility seem to assume, but can be enhanced through the right types of individual and corporate behavior. The Italian and Japanese cases are instructive, because both involve relatively immobile labor but high rates of productivity growth.

The commitment of workers and managers to their firms and industries involves mutuality. From the perspective of both individuals and firms, a policy of permanent employment except in emergencies creates the incentive to hire carefully, train and upgrade workers, and redeploy rather than terminate them (which encourages closely related diversification). The Japanese case is instructive in demonstrating such behavior. Policies that encourage mutual commitment, whether they involve labor laws, the tax treatment of training benefits, and the like are desirable ones. Policies to encourage labor mobility are inappropriate, except in structurally declining, distressed industries.

Government can also influence the motivation of individuals through policies that provide citizens with *access to advancement based on merit*. The importance of this for economic upgrading is hard to overstate. Most entrepreneurs in America have not come from the upper strata of society. In Britain, most successful companies were created not by the upper classes but by individuals from middle- and lower-middle-class backgrounds, as discussed in Chapter 9. The possibility of personal achievement based on merit encourages investment in building skills, risk taking, and unusual effort. It comes from such policies as an open educational system, financial aid for education and training for deserving individuals, and strict policies against discrimination.

Company Goals. The goals of firms are also influenced by government, most importantly through policies that affect the goals of investors, the nature of corporate governance, and the goals of senior managers. Competitive advantage demands sustained investment in an industry. Investors must not discourage such behavior by management, as they do when stock prices fall in response to short-term earnings fluctuations reflecting investments in new products, new facilities, or other underpinnings of competitive advantage.[28] Nations such as Japan and Germany, where the institutional structure is one where investors hold shares for long-term appreciation and who rarely trade, have enjoyed a significant advantage. Nor must the incentives of managers work against investment and taking the risks needed to upgrade productivity.

Some forms of investment, notably sustained company investments in R&D, new facilities, and training, have greater benefits to the national economy than others. They underpin productivity growth in industries and create beneficial spillovers to other related and supporting industries. They contribute not only to returns to investors but to rising wages for employees. Government has a legitimate role in encouraging such investments in preference to others which have a lower social return, even though the private return may be equivalent. This is especially true in nations in which investor goals diverge most from long-term capital appreciation because of the institutional structure. Ironically, reductions in the transaction costs of investing, which make financial markets more ''efficient,'' contribute to a rise in trading to profit from short-run price swings and may discourage corporate investment. The goal of policy is not overinvestment that dissipates national resources. Though there is a socially optimal rate of investment that will most advance national productivity, however, the problem in most economies is underinvestment in desirable forms, not overinvestment.

One policy to encourage high and sustained rates of capital investment in industry is favorable tax treatment of long-term capital gains on equity investments in firms. This provides investors with a motivation to invest in or form companies whose shares will perform well over a long period of time because of improving competitive advantage.[29] Many leading nations have no capital gains taxes at all. Of those that do, most tax short-term gains much higher than long-term gains, a desirable approach. In the United States, capital gains tax rates are the highest of any nation except Britain and have been the same as taxes on ordinary income since the 1986 tax reform. Pension funds, exempt from any taxes, have even greater incentives to seek current income instead of long-term appreciation. There is a trend in other nations toward equalizing tax rates for income and capital gains. Britain has already done so. Such policies are based on an overly narrow view of financial market efficiency and are likely to be counterproductive for a nation's industry.[30]

Investor and managerial behavior is also affected by the process of corporate governance. If shareholders have no influence on management except to sell their shares, trading and takeovers are encouraged and management will be prone to underinvest to prop up stock prices to avoid them. While takeovers can be beneficial by stimulating cost reduction, selling of underperforming assets, and greater motivation of new private owners, they are a second best solution. The first best solution is investors with more appropriate goods and a governance process that provides proper management incentives. Takeovers require a company to service high levels of debt the proceeds of which *have not been invested in the business* to support an improving competitive position. The resulting pressure on current cash flow runs the risk of slowing the rate of true innovation. The new owners may also be more interested in reselling the company rather than building a world leader.

Governance structures in which boards represent the interests of investors, and large investors have a role in management (such as when institutional equity holders are represented on boards), tend to lead to more emphasis on building long-term shareholder value. This benefits long-term productivity growth and hence the nation's standard of living. Regulations that support a meaningful role of shareholders in corporate governance are desirable. Allowing debt holders to hold equity, as is common in nations such as Germany and Japan, may also promote a more sustained commitment to building competitive position instead of preoccupation with debt coverage and security.

The goals of senior managers also play a role in company goals. Compensation based on short-term results discourages investment and innovation, while basing it on long-term success has the opposite effect. Government policy can influence compensation methods through their tax treatment. Equating tax rates on ordinary income and long-term capital gains, for example, works against the use of long-term stock ownership and in favor of annual bonuses. Stock options, because they do not involve the risk of actual ownership, are not as powerful a motivator as owning shares. Long-term stock options can be beneficial incentives, however, and tax regulations should not discourage them.

Another policy that affects company goals is the accounting rules governing the use of reserves (untaxed deductions from income) that lower reported profitability but increase capital. In nations such as Japan, Germany, Sweden, and Switzerland, firms can establish generous reserves to tide them over difficult periods. Reserves can help avoid the need to overreact in order to protect short-term financial results. The danger in such policies, evident in Switzerland, is that a lack of effective competition will transform reserves into barriers to restructuring and innovation.

DOMESTIC RIVALRY

Few roles of government are more important to the upgrading of an economy than ensuring vigorous domestic rivalry. Rivalry at home is not only uniquely important to fostering innovation, but benefits the national industry and cluster in many other ways that I have described and illustrated. Maintaining vigorous domestic competition is also important to ensure that a nation's firms gain advantages from other parts of the "diamond" such as demanding buyers and selective factor disadvantages instead of harvesting market positions, seeking government assistance, or outsourcing high-productivity manufacturing abroad.

The importance of domestic rivalry for national advantage has strong implications for antitrust policy, particularly policy toward mergers and alliances. Yet the need for antitrust has been questioned because of the globalization of industries and the view that domestic firms must merge to gain economies of scale. The prospects for greater European unification have set off a flurry of such activity in Europe, for example, which seems to reappear every few decades. Managers are often the first and loudest voices for easy approval of mergers or alliances, because eliminating domestic rivals is a tempting way to raise short-term profits.

In fact, creating a dominant domestic competitor rarely results in international competitive advantage. Firms that do not have to compete at home rarely succeed abroad. Economies of scale are best gained through selling globally, not through dominating the home market (see Chapters 3 and 4.)

The national champion theory, or the idea that domestic firms will be more efficient if they merge into one or two large national competitors, fails the test of logic (see Chapter 3) and history. Every nation has its examples. In Britain, for example, British Leyland, ICL, and Alfred Herbert provide vivid illustrations of how consolidating a national industry rarely succeeds.[31] In contrast, active domestic rivalry is strongly associated with international success, as previous chapters have amply demonstrated.

Practical political reasons also make the national champion approach a policy nightmare. With only one or two domestic firms, there is a strong tendency for special deals and favored treatment by government that dull incentives. Product standards that are *de facto* protectionist are established. Government purchases are guaranteed without any competition from foreign (or domestic) rivals. The government bullies other domestic companies into purchasing the national champion's inferior products. A lack of domestic rivalry leads the dominant domestic firm to rely on local factor costs instead of upgrading competitive advantage. As innovation slows, the extent of government support tends to rise as more aid is necessary to prop up the firm's position. A policy by government to encourage mergers also tends to become self-reinforcing. Encouraging one merger frequently leads to a series of other mergers.

Leniency toward cartels is also a trap. It is hard to find examples of true competitive advantage in industries where there are cartels. In Switzerland, which still lacks strong cartel laws, cartels have undermined national competitive advantage in such industries as watches and beer. Cartels dampen or suspend the self-reinforcing process of upgrading that grows out of domestic rivalry. A cartel may maintain profits for a time, but usually it marks the beginning of the end of international success.

A strong antitrust policy, especially in the area of horizontal mergers, alliances, and collusive behavior, is essential to the rate of upgrading in an economy. Mergers, acquisitions, and alliances involving industry leaders should be disallowed. (Acquisitions of smaller domestic rivals by a firm in a related industry seeking to transfer skills are more potentially beneficial to competitive advantage and should be permissible.) The same standards towards mergers and alliances should apply to domestic and foreign firms in order to prohibit acquisitions that significantly threaten domestic rivalry. A strong policy bias should favor internal entry, both domestically and abroad, instead of acquisition.[32] Direct interfirm collusion should be illegal. Cooperative ventures involving direct collaboration between competitors must pass strict guidelines such as those I describe elsewhere in this chapter.

Leniency toward mergers and alliances (and monopolies) has become counterproductive in such nations as the United States, Italy, Sweden, Switzerland, and Germany. These policies are part of a disturbing trend toward viewing competition as "wasteful" or "excessive" that has gained currency during the last decade, as it did in the 1930s. "Wasteful" and "excessive" competition is, in fact, the essence of national advantage. The only consistent case for suspending competition in selected instances is to encourage the flow of resources out of structurally declining industries.

While antitrust should be tough on horizontal cooperation and mergers, policies that protect inefficient or lagging competitors should be abolished. Such uses of antitrust have occurred in most nations. In Japan and Italy, for example, small retailers are protected from more efficient chains. In the United States, Eastman Kodak was sued repeatedly when its introductions of new products disadvantaged established and potential competitors. Company behavior that leads to innovation and productivity growth, such as aggressive capital investment and new product introduction, should not be deterred even if rivals lose market share as a result.

Antitrust laws must also not be a barrier to vertical collaboration between suppliers and buyers that is so integral to the innovation process. Vertical activities should not be generally impeded unless they unduly exclude other competitors from access to customers, channels, or suppliers. Similarly, antitrust policy should not interfere with trade association activities connected with factor creation such as training, infrastructure, and research as long as they are not exclusionary. American antitrust laws toward trade associations have been especially counterproductive and have contributed to the ineffectiveness of most associations in enhancing national advantage. With nothing else to do, too many associations spend all their energy on lobbying.

Regulation of Competition. Regulation of competition, through such policies as maintaining a state monopoly, controlling entry, or fixing prices, usually works against the upgrading of competitive advantage in an economy. It has double negative consequences. The first is in stifling rivalry and innovation. Without open competition, firms lose dynamism and become preoccupied with dealing with regulators and protecting what they have.

Regulation of competition also frequently makes the industry a less desirable buyer or supplier, as I have already discussed. Lack of dynamism and innovation in the industry is reflected in less advanced and sophisticated needs for inputs, and results in the provision of less innovative new products or services to domestic customer industries.

The nation in which competition itself was least regulated was often the international leader in the industries we studied. In insurance, for example, Britain's *laissez faire* policies have allowed an unusual degree of innovation. London has sustained its position as the international insurance capital. While regulation to protect consumers, workers, or the environment is desirable, impeding new products and processes through restricting competition often is not.

Deregulation of competition and privatization of state monopolies are usually spurs to national advantage. They will stimulate rivalry and have ripple effects on linked industries. Telecommunications services are a hotbed of improvement and innovation in America today after the breakup of AT&T, for example, despite some misplaced early concerns. Yet deregulation and privatization will not succeed without active *domestic rivalry*. A strong antitrust policy is necessary to ensure the desired effect. The deregulation and privatization efforts in Britain and the United States have been hampered by inconsistent attention to competition.

In addition to eliminating the regulation of industry structure, government restrictions on practices associated with innovation should be eliminated. Examples include labor legislation that impedes job redefinition and restrictions on firms' choice of location. Such restrictions erode the underpinnings of sustained national advantage. Other and better approaches must be found to address the social concerns that such policies reflect.

Protection and Domestic Rivalry. Protection, in its various forms, insulates domestic firms from the pressure of international competition. Protection is practiced in all nations, including the United States.[33] It is typically justified in terms of either nurturing emerging local industries[34] or providing "breathing space" to allow an established industry to adjust. While both imply short-term protection, the result is often long-term protection. The evidence from our research is that protection does not work in the vast majority of circumstances.

Infant industries. Protection of infant industries can be effective in nations lacking well-established competitors in an industry in which strong foreign rivals are present. By delaying the entry of foreign competition, a number of domestic rivals may become established and trigger the self-reinforcing process that extends and upgrades the national "diamond." The infant industry justification for protection is legitimate only in developing nations without a strong base of industries, in industries where foreign competitors are already well established.

Yet protection even when it can be justified is a risky policy that does not often succeed.[35] It works only under three conditions. The first is the presence of effective domestic rivalry. Intense domestic rivalry substitutes for international competitive pressure. Competition at home, combined with home market saturation, turns attention to foreign markets. Given this domestic structure, protection does not dull incentives for innovation and upgrading.

Protecting a dominant local firm will rarely result in true competitive advantage. Without competition, the protected industry will never emerge at all to become internationally successful. Protection has enjoyed some success in the developmental processes of Japan and Korea only because it involved domestic rivalry. In both nations, the protected industries that achieved competitive advantage invariably had numerous, substantial rivals. This was the case, for example, in autos, steel, machine tools, electronics, and numerous other Japanese industries. Ironically, MITI tried to limit entry into a number of important industries because it was inappropriately concerned about achieving economies of scale and avoiding excessive rivalry. Fortunately for Japan, firms repeatedly refused to listen to MITI's guidance.[36] In Korea, most significant export industries are populated by several if not all four of the major industrial groups. The vigorous battle among these archrivals has been essential to their rapid innovation and their success abroad, as I have discussed.

The second requirement for successful protection is the presence in the nation of the potential for a favorable national "diamond." A national industry will usually fail to compete abroad unless it enjoys appropriate demand conditions, specialized factor pools, and other circumstances at home which encourage the development of sustainable advantages.

The third condition for successful protection is that it is *limited in duration*. All protected industries eventually suffer from the lack of full competition. Protection becomes an addictive drug. It also usually carries a price in terms of political IOUs and restraints on the actions of domestic firms. The attention of firms is drawn toward the domestic market.

In both Japan and Korea, industries that have succeeded are usually those whose protection was, or is to be, eliminated. Firms were put on notice in advance that this would occur, and the pledge was carried out. The onset of entry by foreign rivals frequently set off a new burst of innovation. In construction equipment, for example, Komatsu dominated the home market while it was protected, but it had poor-quality products and inefficient manufacturing. When Caterpillar was allowed to form a joint venture with Mitsubishi to compete in Japan, Komatsu entered a period of intense innovation and upgrading that has made it a viable global competitor.[37]

The process of removing protection can reinforce industry upgrading if less sophisticated segments are opened somewhat before others. In Japan, for example, restrictions on imports of machine tools were first lowered for manual varieties, encouraging (along with other policies) a move toward numerically controlled tools. Such an approach will only succeed, however, when other parts of the "diamond" support upgrading.

Carrying out a policy of temporary protection requires unusual independence and continuity in government, along the lines I described earlier. In many nations, "temporary protection" is an oxymoron.

Breathing space. Protection to allow established industries to adjust rarely succeeds. There were few examples in the industries we studied where competitive advantage once lost was regained. The best outcome in practice was that an industry shrank to a core that was sustainable.

Protection to allow breathing space does not address the real causes of industry decline, which reside in an unfavorable "diamond." Protection often delays, instead of encourages, the process of restructuring to areas of true competitive advantage. It allows firms to stay in segments where they lack real strength. It postpones the wrenching changes necessary to restore competitive advantage after years of drift. Firms are loath to adjust if they believe adjustment can be avoided with government help. Protection linked to an adjustment plan is usually impractical, because an adjustment plan crafted through a political process will not include the bankruptcies and drastic capacity reduction that are really needed.

Protection is likely to persist in overt as well as in more subtle forms long after it was supposed to end. The U.S. auto industry provides a vivid example. It still lacks significant competitive advantage, and profits still depend heavily on "voluntary restraint" by the Japanese. The U.S. semiconductor industry is moving down the same disturbing path: first, an orderly marketing agreement to protect against imports; next, the sanctioning and government subsidy of Sematech, a cooperative industry project in manufacturing technology; more recently, an effort to form a consortium of firms to actually produce memory chips under an exemption from the antitrust laws. Japan illustrates the point even more vividly. MITI has instituted dozens of "restructuring cartels" and "recession cartels." Few have resulted in an internationally competitive industry.

Interfirm Cooperation. There is a growing interest in interfirm cooperative ventures of various sorts to enhance competitiveness, usually justified in terms of avoiding duplication of effort and reaping economies of scale. While some forms of cooperation are beneficial, many are not. Direct competitor to competitor cooperation usually undermines competitive advantage in the long run. It reduces incentives and saps rivalry, ultimately slowing progress. It limits the exploration of alternative approaches. Cooperation presages mergers. It fosters calls for protection. Direct cooperation is not only dangerous for public policy but is often bad strategy (see Chapters 2 and 11). Joint production by leading competitors should be prohibited, as should most other forms of direct cooperation between leaders.

Indirect cooperation, where joint efforts involving competitors take place through independent entities, can be beneficial in some circumstances. I discussed earlier the conditions under which cooperative R&D through independent entities is appropriate. Cooperation through trade associations for the purpose of factor creation is also desirable, in forms such as training centers, operation of specialized infrastructure, and sponsoring university research centers. As with cooperative R&D, such efforts should take place through an independent entity to which the majority of firms have access. There is also a role for industry-wide projects to organize trade fairs and conduct other forms of foreign market promotion. Effective trade association efforts in factor creation and market development are common in Germany, Italy, Japan, and elsewhere. The best structure is one in which cooperative activities are managed independently and have precise charters, so that participants face no mixed motives in being involved. At the same time, companies must compete vigorously on product development, pricing, and other aspects of strategy.

Finally, vertical cooperation (buyer-supplier) is beneficial to national advantage, as long as no one or two firms form relationships that preclude all others. Vertical cooperation is integral to the innovation process. Joint production, however, is generally detrimental to competitive advantage because it limits investment in both capacity and process technology and has a tendency to hold back rivalry on other dimensions.

NEW BUSINESS FORMATION

New business formation is integral to the process of upgrading competitive advantage in an economy. Start-up competitors employ new technologies, serve new segments, supply needed inputs, or provide specialized services. Related diversifiers, who enter a new business from a base in another one, bring new skills and resources to bear on industry competition that often spur innovation. New business formation is essential to the mutual reinforcement of the national "diamond" and the formation of clusters.

New business formation is not only essential to the upgrading process in an economy, but also mitigates some dangerous forces that undermine economic progress. New business formation is necessary to replace jobs freed up in established industries and segments as they improve productivity. If new business formation falters, new job prospects can become bleak and workers and their unions became more strident. With an abundance of labor and slowing wage increases, firms are less prone to invest in improving workforce skills and boosting productivity. Government is pressured into bad policies that protect jobs in the short term at the expense of long-term competitive advantage. Investment abroad to globalize strategies is discouraged, subsidies flow to threatened sectors, and established industries start to be successful in securing protection from foreign competition.

Government policy influences new business formation indirectly through its effect on goals, discussed earlier. Perhaps the single greatest determinant of entrepreneurial activity is the willingness to take risk. This is not only a matter of rewards to success but of attitudes toward failure. The United States and Italy are blessed with the fact that failure is not a stigma. In Germany, Switzerland, the United Kingdom, and Singapore, however, failure is likely to be viewed as a personal catastrophe. Government can play only a partial and patient role in shaping such attitudes.

New business formation cannot flourish without a strong commitment to competition. Policies that protect established competitors should be eliminated. Internal entry must be favored over mergers.

Another essential ingredient in new business formation is ideas. Sustained investment by government at all levels in technical schools and in colleges and universities, as well as in university research efforts connected to such institutions, can play an important role in seeding new firms and industries. Rules governing treatment of patents and faculty activities in universities should not discourage this process. In Japan, for example, guidelines for the activities of faculty members are onerous compared to other nations, and start-ups resulting from university research are comparatively rare.

Yet another important element in new business formation is capital. Government's direct provision of venture capital or subsidies for new enterprises is usually ineffective. Bureaucratization and an inability to select good projects lead to bad choices. Encouraging private venture capital through tax incentives for long-term capital gains is a far better solution, because a market test is more likely to be applied. The availability of venture capital will not lead to successful new business formation; however, other parts of the national "diamond" are favorable.

Finally, government policy must be sensitive to the realities of actually starting a new business. Regulations and requirements can place an especially onerous burden on small firms. Streamlined regulations for new companies and assistance in finding infrastructure are desirable.

TRADE POLICY

National competitive advantage will not be fully reflected in rising productivity unless a nation's firms have access to foreign markets. A pressing goal for government is to pursue open market access vigorously in every foreign nation. Trade policy should not just passively respond to complaints or to those industries that can muster the most political clout, but must seek to open markets wherever a nation has competitive advantage. Similarly, negotiations should not require a history of injury or be biased toward industries in distress but be equally concerned with emerging or incipient problems.

The aim of trade policy should be to open markets and eliminate unfair practices, not protect domestic competitors. Standards for intervention should be based on demonstrated unfair practices or a distorted pattern of trade compared to other similar nations. Poor financial performance by domestic firms is an insufficient test, because it can reflect a lack of innovation and dynamism rather than unfair foreign competition.

Remedies should be concentrated on the dismantling of barriers, not on directly regulating exports or imports. Orderly marketing or voluntary restraint agreements, by dividing up and often effectively cartelizing markets, are dangerous, ineffective, and often enormously costly to consumers.[38] So are other specific quantitative targets for exports or imports, which have the effect of guaranteeing a market for inefficient firms rather than promoting innovation in the nation's industry.

Dumping remedies are also fraught with danger. Too often, as is increasingly occurring in the United States, they are used to blunt price competition and protect inefficient firms. Dumping penalties should only be instituted as a result of sustained selling at below variable cost.

There is a growing tendency in some advanced nations to practice "managed" trade, in which quantitative targets are employed to divide up markets. The export success and low imports of Japan are the principal justification. Managed trade is cartelized trade, and slows the upgrading of industries and economies. Japan's imports are rapidly rising, and continued pressure on Japan to speed up imports through other approaches is far superior.

Compensatory tariffs that penalize firms from the offending nation, no matter where goods are actually produced, are a far better remedy for unfair trade practices than quantitative restrictions. Another remedy, of growing relevance as competition becomes more global, is restricting firms from the offending nation from investing in the nation either in the form of acquisitions or production facilities. This prevents the offending nation's firms from translating unfair trading practices into a position in the nation which is largely immune from sanctions.

Any of these remedies to unfair trade runs the risk of backfiring, however. It is hard to craft remedies which avoid reducing the incentives for domestic firms to innovate and to export, and which avoid at least temporarily harming domestic buyers. The aim of remedies, then, is not that they become permanent but that they result in adjustments that allow them to be quickly removed. Each remedy should contain a process for its own demise, to mitigate the political pressures to make it permanent.

To successfully negotiate in the complex world of international trade, a nation must have top-quality personnel who know their subject intimately. Japan and Korea send their elite, while the United States sends a new appointee every two years. There must also be a single point of responsibility for trade negotiations that speaks for the chief executive of the nation, as there is in most countries besides America. Trade laws should be designed to provide maximum negotiating power to the nation's representatives. Access to a nation's own markets is the only real bargaining lever in trade negotiation, and this lever must be selectively used. The political realities in foreign nations mean that credible threats are essential.

Foreign Investment in the Nation

Policy toward investment by foreign firms in a nation has long been an issue for governments. It raises concerns about national sovereignty and the effects on a nation's industry. Foreign investment is a manifestation of global competition and the need for global strategies; it can be part of the process by which an economy upgrades productivity. Foreign investment involving largely passive ownership of a nation's firms raises few issues for policy. Here, the nation is still the home base, and nationality of ownership *per se* has little impact on economic upgrading.[39] Where foreign investment takes the form of production facilities or acquisitions of domestic firms that are transformed into marketing or production arms, this is a sign that foreign firms possess competitive advantage in the industry. Here, the foreign investment will still raise national productivity by stimulating improvements by domestic firms and supplanting the less efficient rivals.

In advanced nations, intervention in foreign investment should occur only in two circumstances. The first is where it threatens the health of rivalry, such as when a significant foreign competitor acquires a leading domestic firm. The second is where market access in the industry is restricted in the foreign firm's home nation or where the nation engages in unfair trade practices or investment under international rules. Where there are trade distortions, restricting the ability of foreign firms to invest will not only penalize them but also encourage them to help to eliminate the offending practices, a desirable outcome.

While intervention to restrict foreign investment in a nation is usually not justified, widespread foreign investment may carry an important message. Except when it is largely passive, widespread foreign investment usually indicates that the process of competitive upgrading in an economy is *not entirely healthy* because domestic firms in many industries lack the capabilities to defend their market positions against foreign firms. Britain, for example, has enjoyed a foreign investment boom in the late 1980s. However, much of it is in less sophisticated activities such as assembly facilities, attracted by low wages. Though the jobs created will contribute to the British economy, the extent of foreign investment is a sign that the rate of upgrading of British industry is lagging behind that of other advanced nations. Though less extreme, the same concerns can be voiced about the United States.

Inbound foreign investment is never the solution to a nation's competitive problems. While intervention is counterproductive, except in the circumstances noted, widespread foreign investment is a sign that policy initiatives toward industry must receive high priority.

GOVERNMENT POLICY AND THE STAGES OF COMPETITIVE DEVELOPMENT

The appropriate government policy toward industry shifts as nations progress to successive stages of competitive development. The mix of policies at any one time must be mutually consistent and reflect the nature of competitive advantage in a nation's industry.

Government has the greatest *direct* influence on national advantage in the factor- and investment-driven stages. The tools at its disposal, such as capital, subsidies, and temporary protection, are most powerful at these stages in a nation's competitive development. In the early stages, government also must take the lead in factor creation: encouraging savings or foreign borrowing to accumulate capital, upgrading education and infrastructure, and beginning the development of a technological base.

Government at this stage can play an important role in such areas as channeling scarce capital into selected industries, promoting risk taking through implicit or explicit guarantees of assistance, stimulating and influencing the acquisition of foreign technology, and employing temporary protection to foster entry leading to domestic rivalry and the construction of modern facilities. Government's role in challenging and exhorting industry to upgrade is also a vital one, as the Japanese and Korean cases illustrate. Devaluation, or intervention to hold down currency appreciation, will also only be beneficial in the early stages, when a nation's firms still depend on price competition to penetrate foreign markets. Government is often a prime mover early in the development process, though it will not succeed without active domestic rivalry and corporate and individual goals that support investment, as I have discussed earlier.

As the nation aspires to move beyond early investment-driven to the innovation-driven stage, however, firms must increasingly become the prime movers. They must dominate choices about new businesses to enter and have the freedom to compete globally. Firms and educational institutions acting independently must also play an increasing role in factor creation. At the same time, public capital markets and an independent and competitive banking system must move to center stage in allocating capital, to ensure that capital flows widely and efficiently to promising sectors.

Government's role must shift to almost exclusively an *indirect* one. Its early tools lose effectiveness and may well become counterproductive. Devaluation, for example, may forestall the process of upgrading. Temporary protection of firms that are already well-established may encourage dependence and become permanent, almost guaranteeing that the economy will not progress. Needed factors are highly specialized. Strict central control in areas such as education and research may stifle responsiveness and tailoring to individual industry and local requirements.

Government's essential task at the innovation-driven stage is to create an environment in which firms are and continue to be innovative and dynamic. Its role must shift from actor and decision maker to facilitator, signaler, and prodder. Intervention must decrease substantially. Government's most significant influences at this stage are in creating advanced factors, upgrading demand conditions (such as through setting stringent standards and raising aspirations in areas such as health care and environmental quality), deconcentrating economic power, ensuring competition, and signaling. Antitrust, which may have been less necessary when domestic rivals were scrambling to become established, becomes essential.

A nation's international success itself eliminates some of the tools available to government in earlier stages. Gaining foreign market access eventually requires reciprocal behavior, limiting the possibilities for temporary protection. International citizenship demands other new standards for behavior. At the same time as a nation's firms become larger and more global, they become less affected by domestic macroeconomic factors and less amenable to government persuasion. Finally, the sheer breadth and complexity of the economy and the interdependencies among industries preclude a success-ful effort at micromanagement.

Unless national policy toward industry shifts as a nation moves to the threshold of a more advanced stage, the upgrading of industry will be retarded or blocked. This principle has been violated by many national governments, who are either unwilling to give up their power and influence on industry or fail to understand how earlier policies become counterproductive when firms seek higher-order competitive advantages. The protection-devaluation-subsidy cycle is a hard one to break.

Government policy must evolve so as to anticipate the needs of an upgrad-ing economy. In many ways, government must be *ahead* of most firms to allow and stimulate firms to advance. Political pressures are strong, however, to continue old policies because firms have adjusted to (and many have prospered under) them.

TARGETING

I have so far addressed a wide range of policy areas related to industry but have not mentioned a prominent subject of debates about industrial policy in recent years: targeting. Targeting is the practice of singling out particular industries for support and development. This contrasts with the notion that the role of government is to create an environment in which any firm in any industry has the opportunity to prosper. Japan, Korea, and other countries are frequently said to practice targeting, made explicit by national economic plans that identify particular industries as important priori-ties.

Targeting is not a single policy, but typically involves a group of policies often including subsidies, selective protection, and channeling capital. How-ever, one nation's targeting and another nation's targeting are frequently different. Targeting that involves government white papers, investments in specialized educational institutions, university research capabilities, and sponsoring trade fairs might be called *indirect targeting*. It is a far cry from *direct targeting*, involving intervention in the form of subsidies, protec-tion, and brokered market division or mergers.

Every nation practices implicit targeting of some kind, whether it will admit to it or not. Government programs are inevitably skewed toward some industries and not others. In the United States, for example, federal defense research provides *de facto* assistance to some industries and not others. The issue, then, is less whether targeting is taking place than how a nation is going about it.

Targeting distorts market signals by altering the incentives of private firms to compete in an industry. Through providing capital, boosting local demand, and the like, government policy improves the expected returns. Targeting also signals government's confidence in the future prospects in the industry as well as government's implicit promise to support it. This often attracts private capital from banks and other sources. The mere act by government of identifying an industry as a priority industry may be enough to skew private incentives, even without any direct government aid.

Whether targeting is sensible depends on the specific mix of policies it involves. Such steps as persistent subsidies, protection without domestic rivalry, and guaranteed government procurement of unsophisticated domestic goods will fail. These are simply inappropriate policy approaches no matter what the stage of development of a nation's industry.

The appropriateness of targeting also depends on the industries chosen and the stage of national competitive development. Explicit targeting is risky because it implies that the reallocation of resources to the chosen industries will benefit the economy as a whole. This is by no means assured. Korean targeting, for example, has skewed resources toward a few large industrial groups and thereby inevitably constrained entrepreneurship in many promising industries.

Explicit targeting also requires the selection of industries where the underlying determinants of national competitive advantage are present or can be developed. The record of even the most successful practitioners of targeting is mixed at best. Korea, for example, has fared poorly in nearly all chemical and machinery industries though these were singled out in national economic plans. In these industries, government policy levers were unimportant to competitive advantage, which was more dependent on highly specialized technology, knowledge of sophisticated users' applications, and customer relationships. Labor costs were relatively unimportant and international competitors already had world-scale efficient plants. In contrast, Korean targeting has been more successful in industries such as shipbuilding and steel, where low labor costs and large-scale investment in modern plants provided decisive advantages, given the labor intensity of these industries and the obsolete capacity of American and European competitors. Japan also has a mixed record in targeting, as I have discussed.

When government distorts market signals, especially through direct targeting, it cannot rely on firms to invest only in fundamentally sound industries. This places the burden on government planners to understand the subtle conditions for national advantage. Since many governments base these choices on the wrong model, one dominated by factor costs or economies of scale, the results are all too predictable. One nation after another crowds into the same industries and into the same price-sensitive market segments, building huge, subsidized plants, and creating additional excess capacity.[40] Another problem with direct targeting is that, once started, it is hard to stop. Industries become accustomed to assistance and want to keep it. This is particularly likely in nations where the political process allows special interests to wield significant power.

Direct targeting is only likely to succeed during the stage when a nation has investment-driven national advantage. The policies involved in targeting, implemented properly, can significantly influence the bases of competitive advantage at this stage in well-chosen industries. Targeting in its most direct form will fail to move an economy to innovation-driven advantage, however, because it does not address the true determinants of advantage. Policy must shift to much more indirect forms of government assistance designed to support efforts by *any* industry to upgrade its demand conditions, human resources, and scientific expertise. Government also has a legitimate and important role in encouraging the development of particular skills or technologies that are important to upgrading in a *substantial number of industries*. Japanese policy has already largely made this shift at a time when many observers still use it as an example of how direct targeting is successful.

GOVERNMENT POLICY IN DEVELOPING NATIONS

While my focus has been on relatively advanced nations, the principles can be applied to developing nations as well. There is a large body of thought on the subject, and I cannot provide a complete or exhaustive treatment here. What follows should be viewed as some general observations that are illustrative of the implications of my theory for the earlier stages of the development process. My focus here will be on developing nations that have achieved a basic level of development and are seeking more advanced status.

The central task facing developing countries is to escape from the straitjacket of factor-driven national advantage (Chapter 10). Competitive advantage in developing countries tends to be almost exclusively in industries where natural resources, cheap labor, locational factors, and other basic factor advantages provide a fragile and often fleeting ability to export. Dependence on such industries, where exports are invariably sensitive to price, leaves the nation vulnerable to exchange rate and factor cost swings. Many of these industries are also not growing, as the resource intensity of advanced economies falls and demand becomes more sophisticated.

Finally, competing in such industries means that developing countries suffer most from protectionist policies in the developed world. By lifting trade restrictions in such sectors as textiles and agriculture, which contain many industries that should be the early export industries for a developing nation, advanced nations would probably do more good than all the foreign aid programs combined.[41]

To progress, the developing nation faces the daunting task of upgrading all four parts of the national "diamond" sufficiently to reach the threshold necessary to compete in advanced industries. Indeed, my theory contains a much more daunting challenge for a developing nation than a model based heavily on factor cost, factor quality, and economies of scale. The mutual dependency of the determinants that I have emphasized means that the weakest one will constrain development. Creation of advanced factors is perhaps the first priority. Education, local technical capability, an information base, and modern infrastructure are prerequisites. The investment-driven stage provides an approach to accelerating development that has been successful in Japan and Korea.[42]

Yet sophisticated home demand and supporting industries are necessary for continued development. Nations such as Japan, Italy, and Korea have long-standing cultures and histories that provide a basis for demand-side advantages that are hard to envisage in most developing nations. The changes in technology that I have described earlier threaten the traditional role of developing nations in providing goods that have heretofore been human and natural resource intensive.

There are two hopeful contemporary changes for developing nations. One is the emergence of dramatic new technologies such as electronics and new materials which promise to proliferate products and industries. Second is the slowing or even negative population growth in the advanced nations which means that human resource constraints will create opportunities in the developing world.

While this is not the setting for a fuller treatment of the policies to guide developing nations, some important issues emerged from my theory. Many of the same considerations can also be readily applied to the problem of a state or region seeking to upgrade its economy.

MARKET VERSUS PLANNED ECONOMIES

The determinants of national advantage lead to pessimism about the prospects of centrally planned economies. They lack many of the most important elements of the "diamond." There are few mechanisms for creating specialized factors. Restrictions on buyer choice remove sophisticated demand pressure. The lack of competition eliminates most interchange with related and supporting industries. Lack of motivation and the restricted flow of information blunt upgrading. Most importantly, effective domestic rivalry is absent.

Centrally planned economies will almost be relegated to competing on price competition and in standardized segments. National advantage will almost exclusively be factor-driven. Exceptions will be those special circumstances where some of the forces in the "diamond" are allowed to work. Wholesale economic restructuring is necessary to support advancement.

DEVELOPMENT PRIORITIES

In moving beyond factor-driven national advantage, a number of important choices deserve special mention. One is the industries and sectors on which to concentrate. Given limited resources, developing nations cannot do everything. There particularly needs to be some focus in factor creation. Generalized factors, while a prerequisite for developing advanced factors, do not themselves provide an advantage in modern international competition.

One school of thought is that nations should pursue import substitution. This involves the establishment of core industries in the nation such as steel and basic chemicals. The idea is that freed-up foreign exchange can be used for more advanced purchases, feeding the process of upgrading industrial skills.

The principles reflected in the "diamond" raise questions about this approach.[43] Import substitution tends to draw a nation into unattractive industries or industries where it has little prospect of gaining a competitive advantage. While protection can guarantee the home market, a nation's firms will lack advantage in international markets. Fragile positions will be vulnerable to economic cycles and currency shifts.

Similar questions can be raised about a development strategy based solely on identifying industries where the nation has only basic factor advantages. This basis for advantage is not sustainable and may limit the potential standard of living. Norway has fallen into this trap by stressing its low-cost electric power supplies (from hydroelectric generation) as a lever for entering a range of power-intensive industries, and by depending heavily on North Sea oil. Canada, Australia, and New Zealand, with national advantage primarily in resource industries, have a similar problem. In a sense, a nation *without* abundant natural factors has a sort of advantage in economic development. It avoids the temptation of relying too much on natural advantages.

A better model for setting development priorities is the principle of clustering. A nation will be most likely to be successful not in isolated industries but in building whole clusters. As a starting point, a nation must identify those industries where its factor advantages today provide some competitive advantage but where *other* determinants of national advantage are also actually, or potentially, present. The questions provided in Chapter 11 can serve as an initial set of criteria for doing so. Such industries become initial centers of development. Import substitution will succeed if the determinants are present. However, a nation must move quickly to upgrade its advantages in these industries beyond basic factor costs.

With these industries as a base, the next step is to stimulate the development of upstream, downstream, or related industries in which advantage is less factor sensitive. Investments in education, research, and infrastructure should concentrate on these clusters. Indigenous companies should be encouraged to become multinationals, to acquire technology and skills, and to gain direct access to foreign markets.

In addition to building outward in clusters from factor-driven industries, the theory suggests a parallel stream of development based on demand. Government and local firms should identify those industries (or more likely, industry segments) in which its demand conditions are favorable. These will be industries where there are sophisticated buyers or where local needs are distinctive. In Singapore, for example, this may be products for use in tropical climates or products and services related to shipping and logistics. Such segments may well be ignored by firms from other countries and may provide an entry strategy for establishing a broader international position. Products designed explicitly to meet needs in other developing countries (such as equipment for use with low-quality fuel or simple home appliances) also represent a target of opportunity likely to be ignored by firms from advanced nations.[44] However, upgrading home demand conditions so as to allow penetration of *advanced* foreign markets is a daunting task that ultimately constrains the extent of development.

An important caveat in any effort to set development priorities, no matter how well intentioned, is the difficulty of government organizations to conduct the required analysis. Bureaucratic structures and political pressures create a setting ill-suited to objective choices.

INDIGENOUS COMPANIES VERSUS FOREIGN MULTINATIONALS

Another important issue for developing countries is whether to build the economy largely through indigenous companies or encourage widespread investments in the nation by foreign multinationals. Foreign multinationals provide some obvious attractions. They can rapidly create jobs, bring welcome technical resources, train local citizens, and avoid the need to risk scarce local capital. Ireland and Singapore, for example, have been extremely successful in attracting responsible foreign multinationals. These nations have enjoyed rapid economic progress since the early 1970s, though some problems have emerged in the 1980s.[45]

Foreign multinationals are an important part of the process of economic development, particularly in its early stages. They cannot ultimately be the *sole* engine for creating national advantage in advanced industries, however. Multinationals locate activities in the value chain in foreign nations as part of integrated global strategies (see Chapter 2). Such investments are usually made because of factor cost considerations or in order to open up protected markets.

Though these investments will sometimes be expanded and upgraded, it is rarely in a multinational's interest to make a developing country a major center for producing sophisticated components or for conducting core R&D. These are activities, first and foremost, for either the multinational's home base, nations with markets large enough to justify significant concessions to local governments, or nations with attributes (such as demand conditions) that make locating in them important to innovation. In addition, foreign subsidiaries do not necessarily breed managers with an orientation toward exports and international competition.

A development strategy based solely on foreign multinationals may doom a nation to remaining a factor-driven economy. If reliance on foreign multinationals is too complete, the nation will not be the home base for any industry. At the same time, multinationals can relocate when factor costs shift or if wages get too high. The result of not developing more advanced forms of competitive advantage is a *cap* on economic development; rapid progress can be made, but it only goes so far.

The growth of indigenous companies is a much slower, and in many ways riskier, process than attracting foreign multinationals. Yet if it succeeds, the result can be the means to move beyond factor-driven advantage, as Japan and more recently Korea have demonstrated. Indigenous firms view the nation as the home base. They energize the process of creating advanced and specialized factors. If the conditions described in Chapter 4 are met, they upgrade competitive advantages beyond basic factors. Provided government does not interfere, they eventually develop global strategies that make competitive advantage more sustainable and upgrade it further. Eventually as the nation develops, factor cost-sensitive activities are shifted abroad, raising national productivity.

Foreign multinationals should be only *one component* of a developing nation's economic strategy, and an evolving component. At some stage in the development process, the focus should shift to indigenous companies. In Singapore and Ireland, my view is that the shift has been too little and too late. Neither nation has truly committed to the slow process of developing a broader base of indigenous firms.

Foreign multinationals should be wooed that operate in industries within those broad sectors in which the nation's firms might themselves eventually gain competitive advantage. Here multinationals can seed a cluster. They can act as sophisticated home buyers, and spur indigenous entry into supporting industries or new segments. Several multinationals in an industry should be sought instead of only one, to encourage rivalry that will spill over to benefit the nation and to stimulate supporting or related industries. Government should encourage the formation and upgrading of indigenous companies in related and supporting industries to those in which multinationals operate, not solely with an eye toward import substitution but ultimately as international competitors. This will not take place, however, without parallel development of human resource skills, a scientific base, and infrastructure in those fields to support higher-order competitive advantages.

Multinationals should also be cultivated whose rationale for locating in a nation goes beyond basic factor considerations. If a multinational is locating in a nation solely because of cheap labor, the stability of the investment is ultimately suspect. If the nation represents a good location for a regional production and distribution center, or if local conditions make it a desirable product development center in a particular segment, however, then the multinational will have more enduring reasons for investing in the nation and upgrading that investment over time. The ideal is to make the nation almost a "home base."

OEM SUPPLIER VERSUS GLOBAL COMPETITOR

Another strategic choice facing both governments and firms in developing nations is whether to pursue a strategy of being an OEM supplier to foreign firms or to seek to develop a global strategy. In practice, most nations pursue some combination of the two, but the relative weights can vary markedly. Korean policy, for example, is more oriented toward encouraging companies to develop global strategies. Leading Korean groups are attempting to create internationally known brand names, establish foreign distribution organizations, and even build foreign plants, despite the fact that Korea's major advantage has been low labor costs. Taiwanese firms, in contrast, are pursuing more the pure OEM route. Many of Taiwan's exports are private-label goods; even most of the leading Taiwanese companies have still made only nominal investments in developing foreign marketing channels of their own.

To achieve sustained national advantage that transcends basic factor endowment, the global competitor route is more desirable. Global strategies not only themselves create new sources of competitive advantage, but provide a better foundation for proactive innovation instead of passive response to foreign OEM customer requests. Taiwan's development will be constrained until its companies move aggressively to modify their strategies.

THE ROLE OF GOVERNMENT

Many treatments of national competitiveness assign government the preeminent role. Our study of ten nations does not support this view. National competitive advantage in an industry is a function of underlying determinants that are deeply rooted in many aspects of a nation. Government has an important role in influencing the "diamond" but its role is ultimately a partial one. It only succeeds when working in tandem with the determinants.

Government's proper role in enhancing national advantage is the reverse of what is often supposed. Many see government as a helper or supporter of industry. Yet many of the ways in which government tries to "help" can actually hurt a nation's firms in the long run (for example, subsidies, domestic mergers, supporting high levels of cooperation, providing guaranteed government demand, and artificial devaluation of the currency). These sorts of policies mean that firms will fail to take the steps necessary to create sustainable competitive advantage and will slow the upgrading of the economy. Too much government support also makes it difficult to persuade industry to invest and take risk without it. At the same time, helping creates the demand for more helping.

Government's proper role is as a *pusher and challenger*. There is a vital role for pressure and even adversity in the process of creating national competitive advantage. These are drives that government, by providing too much assistance, undermines. Government's role should be to transmit and amplify the forces of the "diamond" as well as help upgrade the determinants themselves. Sound government policy seeks to provide the tools necessary to compete, through active efforts to bolster factor creation, while ensuring a certain discomfort and strong competitive pressure. Government's proper role is to encourage or even push firms to raise their aspirations and move to a higher level of competitive prowess even though this may be an unsettling and even unpleasant process.

At the broadest level, one of government's most essential roles is signaling. It can influence how firms compete by identifying and highlighting the important priorities and challenges they face. Government leaders have a stage from which they can define issues of national importance and shape attitudes toward particular problems in industry. A good example is the campaign of the Japanese government to elevate national attention to quality and overcome the stigma of "cheap" Japanese goods. One of the most visible elements of the program was the establishment of the Deming Prize. This prize carries enormous prestige and sends a strong signal to all Japanese firms about the requirements for competitive success.

Some nations enjoy a built-in national consensus about the importance of economic success. This tends to occur in nations that have faced difficulties or feel vulnerable, such as Germany, Japan, and Korea. In nations that have enjoyed long periods of prosperity, such as Britain and the United States, competitive challenges have often been instinctively seen as manifestations of unfair foreign competition rather than indications of problems to be solved at home. Government leaders have a role to play in creating or elevating the national priority placed on competition.

The most powerful levers available to government for influencing national competitive advantage are *slow-acting* ones such as creating advanced factors, encouraging domestic rivalry, shaping national priorities, and influencing demand sophistication. Many of the most important levers may well be unpopular, such as stimulating new entry and creating pressures to upgrade by allowing factor costs to rise. The quick, easy roles of government (subsidy, protection, macroeconomic management) are either insufficient or counterproductive. The long time horizon and uncomfortable nature of the most effective policies raise difficult challenges in nations where special interest groups wield political power or where the national consensus for industrial development is not strong.

There is a dangerous tendency to think that with enough business-government collaboration and enough cooperation among firms within and across nations, all firms and industries can win. As I have discussed, too much cooperation can ensure that few of a nation's industries ever really win. Governments and firms must recognize the reality that this hope is a false one.

Government policy toward industry must recognize that the "diamond" is a system, which makes policies in many areas interdependent. The weakest link constrains the development of an economy, so that progress is needed on each determinant. At the same time, policies to improve one aspect of the national environment will often have unintended consequences if others are not addressed as well. Greater domestic rivalry may accelerate the outsourcing of jobs, for example, if human resource quality is inadequate and corporate goals do not support sustained investment.

Government should not overstate or overplay its role in national competitive advantage. If it does, it will create an economy of dependent, backward-looking, and ultimately unsuccessful firms. At the same time, government must recognize those areas in which it has a legitimate influence in creating the conditions for economic prosperity. These areas are different, and broader in many ways, than those which preoccupy much contemporary policy debate.

National competitive advantage is not a zero-sum game. One nation's firms need not succeed only at the expense of another's. With a narrow view of national competitive advantage centered on factor costs and economies of scale, it is all too easy for policy debates to degenerate into "us versus them."[46] In fact, a much broader set of forces is at work. The underlying cause of sustained national advantage is improvement and innovation. All nations' firms can innovate faster and upgrade the productivity of labor and capital. World economic prosperity depends on rapid innovation by advanced nations, which creates new products and cedes relatively less productive activities to developing nations. If the rate of innovation slows because an "us versus them" attitude leads to subsidy, protection, and consolidation that blunts incentives, the consequences for advanced and less advanced nations alike are severe.

13

National Agendas

W hat of the future? The central economic concern of every nation should be the capacity of its economy to upgrade so that firms achieve more sophisticated competitive advantages and higher productivity. Only in this way can there be a rising standard of living and economic prosperity. The process of upgrading requires that the nation's firms continuously improve their capabilities and technology and evolve their strategies if they are to achieve and sustain competitive advantages against ever-improving international competitors. The role of the nation's government is to set policies that will provide the foundation of human resources, science and technology, and infrastructure to allow upgrading. As importantly, government must encourage, challenge, and even pressure its firms to advance.

Every nation, no matter what its current position, faces challenges in moving to a higher level of competitive prowess and productivity. These challenges may be said to constitute the national economic agenda. The agenda is a function of the stage of national competitive development a nation's industry has achieved. The issues for Korean companies and the Korean government are utterly different from those facing Sweden or Italy, because the mix of industries, the nature of existing competitive advantages, and the strategies through which they are achieved reflect very different national environments. Nations at the investment-driven stage aspire to innovation-driven status. Nations that have achieved innovation-driven advantage must guard against the drift toward a wealth-driven economy.

The issues for each nation, as well as the ways of best addressing them, are unique. Each nation has its own history, social structure, and institutions which influence its feasible options. Emulating company strategies or government policies from another nation may be appropriate in the early stages of the development process, but will rarely succeed in propelling a nation's industry to leading positions in advanced industries. I have described in some detail the different company and government policies in each nation; it is the differences that have often been decisive. It is equally clear that both company strategies and government policy in a nation must evolve as a nation progresses.

My purpose here is to illustrate how to use my theory to identify the important long-term issues facing a nation's firms and government in upgrading competitive advantage in industry and in the national economy as a whole. To do this, I will briefly revisit the nations we studied and highlight some of the constraints that I believe must be overcome if further upgrading is to take place over coming decades. Since the issues facing a national economy are fundamentally different at each stage of competitive development, I will use Figure 13–1, reproduced from Chapter 10, to guide my discussion and determine the order in which I treat the nations.

My aim is not to presume to suggest policy but to raise issues. The appropriate mix of policies to address these issues must be sensitive to a nation's unique circumstances, and will demand a careful balance of political, social, and economic choices that no outsider should attempt; nations can only upgrade industry within their own context. My focus is on economic prosperity, but there are also trade-offs to be resolved with other national goals. Ultimately, only a nation's citizens have the right to choose how, and how quickly, to act.

The treatment here must necessarily be selective, for I cannot hope to discuss every relevant issue. I am mindful of the controversial nature of some of the issues, and I am aware of the risk that too much attention may be focused here rather than on the theory of the competitive advantage of nations which is my real purpose. Nevertheless, some consideration of the future of each nation is a fitting way to complete my story, and to stimulate discussion in companies and among policy makers about the choices which lie ahead.

Every nation can improve its economic prosperity if it succeeds in relaxing the constraints to upgrading its industry. There has been a tendency in recent years to see national competitiveness as a contest that some nations win at the expense of others.[1] This, like so many other aspects of the competitiveness debate, reflects a static view of competition. As I have discussed, national competitive advantage is not a zero-sum game. New industries are constantly being created and there are new needs to be served in existing ones. Rising productivity in all industries is made possible by advancing technology. Innovation and change make the pie bigger. Progress in many nations will widen the breadth of economic activity and improve the overall living standards in the world economy.

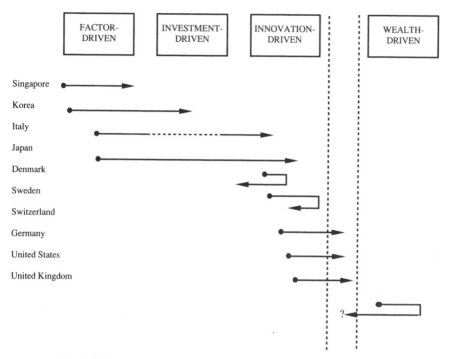

FIGURE 13-1 **Estimated Evolution of National Competitive Development During the Postwar Period**

THE AGENDA FOR KOREA

Korea represents a remarkable success story. It has achieved what no other developing nation has in the postwar period—development to the threshold of innovation-driven status. Korean industry has set itself apart from that of other Asian Newly Industrializing Countries (NICs) with which it is often compared. The other Asian NICs, even to a significant extent Taiwan, are deriving national competitive advantage largely from basic factors of production. They are competing in foreign markets via sourcing arrangements with Japanese or Western firms. Products are mostly foreign designed.

Korea has moved beyond factor-driven national advantage to investment-driven advantage. Korean firms have aggressively invested in modern process technology and in large-scale production. They have made early and vigorous efforts to develop their own product technology, drawing on a growing pool of highly trained Korean engineers and scientific personnel. They have also moved early to begin establishing their own brand names and international marketing channels, a *sine qua non* of higher-order advantage. Foreign production sites are being established.[2]

Korean industry has yet to make the transition to the innovation-driven stage, however. Korean firms still compete essentially on price. They lag behind the leading nations in product and process innovation. There is potential, without more fundamental change, for continued growth and some further widening of industries in which Korea is successful. Yet Korean industry must evolve in significant respects if the nation is to take its hoped-for place next to Japan. There are some signs that firms and the government are resisting changes necessary to advance further.

Korea provides a good illustration of the changes in policy and company strategy necessary to move from the investment-driven to the innovation-driven stage. The following illustrate some of the issues facing Korean firms and the Korean government:

Investment in Advanced Factors. Korea enjoys a good start in human resources and a scientific base, vital underpinnings of innovation and of upgrading its economy. The task is to seek even higher levels of training, skill, and local scientific activity that is increasingly specialized to particular industries. Korean firms must create and support high-quality institutions for specialized factor creation and take on growing responsibilities for training and technology development internally. Korean firms will not move beyond low price segments until their human and technical abilities approach those of Japanese or Western firms.

Upgrading Pressures. Nations that enjoy rapidly upgrading industry face inevitable upward pressures on factor costs and the value of the currency. Both firms and government in many nations have a tendency to attempt to hold back these forces because of the perceived short-term costs they involve. Yet rising wages and a rising currency support, rather than impede, true economic development. They encourage the right kind of innovations as well as a desirable reorientation of firm strategies. Selective factor disadvantages also feed back to upgrade supplier industries by making Korean companies more demanding buyers for machinery and inputs.

Rising wages have other systemic benefits. Not only do they create pressure for innovation, but they also work toward improving the quality of consumer demand by shifting demand to more advanced segments and widening consumption into new industries. Finally, rising wages spread prosperity to workers and sustain their motivation to improve their skills, speeding the rate at which companies can improve.

Korea is no exception to the general tendency to intervene in markets to hold back wages and other factor costs as well as to resist revaluation of the currency. In the area of wages, for example, the Korean government and Korean firms seem to have had an implicit understanding to hold the line. The unrest in the Korean workforce today over wages and working conditions is one manifestation of the dangers of continuing to be preoccupied with factor costs. While the adjustment of wages and the value of currency should ideally be gradual, such adjustments are part of the way in which the Korean economy will advance further.

An Efficient Capital Market. Further upgrading of the Korean economy demands that the capital markets develop and become much more efficient mechanisms for allocating funds to promising companies. This is how rivalry is sustained and new industries are formed. Korean real interest rates have been by far the highest of any of the nations we studied (see Table 7–3). The Korean government has historically directed most investment capital through subsidized loans, much of it through the large Korean *chaebol.* Outside of areas favored by government, however, capital costs have been prohibitive and stunted the development of competitive companies.

As Korea becomes a net creditor nation and its high rate of private savings leads to rapid capital accumulation, funds must be drawn into efficient capital markets to drive down interest rates and create a pool of equity capital. Government can no longer effectively play the capital allocation role as the economy diversifies. Markets must widen access to capital to all promising companies, not just the *chaebol.* Appropriate rules and institutional structures need to be established to ensure confidence in the market by investors and entrepreneurs.

Demand-Side Advantages. Achieving innovation-driven status in any nation requires that it develop the entire "diamond" of determinants. An important missing element in Korea is favorable demand conditions. Korean firms will have difficulty in truly innovating without more sophisticated home demand in a wider range of industries. Their distance from markets, both in miles and in the nature of buyer needs, will make it difficult to anticipate new needs or create new market segments.

In industrial goods and services, home demand is most likely to become advanced and sophisticated in those industries where Korean firms are significant international competitors themselves. The suppliers to these industries are prime candidates for future competitive advantage.

Among consumers, achieving sophisticated home demand will require a rising level of affluence and higher levels of consumer information (including news of developments in foreign countries). Korean buyers must become aware of and be exposed to the best products and services available. This implies the need to allow imports as well as local production of foreign goods and services.

Developing sophisticated domestic demand must become an important priority for both Korean firms and government, which have both had a tendency to ignore it in favor of export markets. Government should take steps to stimulate advanced, early home demand, such as those I described in the previous chapter. It should avoid taxation that dampens demand for high-end or advanced product models. In cars, for example, Korean firms will have a hard time competing in middle- and high-priced segments until punitive taxation at home on such models is eased (some steps have begun in this regard).

Deepening of Clusters. The other vital missing link in the Korean economy, and any economy in the investment-driven stage, is the presence of related and especially supporting industries. Clusters of industries must form and deepen if the Korean economy is to progress to the next stage. While many observers have noted the dependence of Korean firms on imported parts and machinery, few have understood the real significance. The problem is not the cost of inputs or currency exposure, but the effects on the innovation process. Without fluid relationships with capable domestic suppliers, Korean firms will remain behind in process technology and will lack the inputs required to serve new product segments.

Machinery and other supplier industries should ideally be independent of the large Korean *chaebol*. Otherwise, guaranteed sales to other group companies will dull incentives. The establishment of positions in supplier industries inside the groups will also limit rivalry in the domestic industry and reduce the market available to other domestic suppliers, which will prove harmful to innovation. The large role the groups play in the Korean economy makes these concerns especially important.

There are some signs, in industries such as cars and shipbuilding, of upgrading in domestic machinery and other supplier industries. Yet corporate commitment in most Korean firms is still to end products. Companies show little of the emphasis on building their own production equipment that characterized Japanese industry, for example. Success in input and machinery industries in Korea will require a mastery of new and specialized technologies, as well as the forging of vertical relationships among Korean firms that are as yet unformed and untested.

Reorientation of Competitive Strategy. Part and parcel of a shift to innovation-driven advantage is that companies broaden their strategies away from cost competition. Cost competition in price-sensitive segments is frequently unprofitable. Such strategies are always vulnerable to the next low labor cost nation, or to the next nation such as Malaysia or Thailand willing to subsidize construction of large, modern plants.

Korean firms now invariably compete with cost-based strategies. They must upgrade their competitive advantages and learn to compete on differentiation, a process that may require decades. This will demand true innovation, not imitation of Japanese and other competitors' products and processes. Korean firms must also increasingly distinguish their strategies from those of other Korean competitors. In the past, there has been a strong tendency for all Korean firms to emulate each other and compete on price in the same segments. This slows' the creation of more sustainable competitive advantages.

Patterns of Diversification. The Korean *chaebol* have become unwieldy conglomerates. Their further development as international competitors will require a shift from unrelated diversification to more integrated corporate strategies. Each group must identify a narrower range of fields, related by technologies, channels, or customers, in which it seeks to become a world leader.

Selling off businesses peripheral to these core fields will allow the focusing of company resources on improving technology, developing brand awareness, mastering production skills, and solidifying foreign distribution channels. These steps are all essential to moving from cost-based competitive advantage to innovation- and differentiation-based advantage. This shift in corporate strategy will not only benefit each group but the Korean economy as a whole. Japan prospered after the *zaibatsu* were disbanded. Shifting strategies by the Korean *chaebol* will benefit Korean national advantage in many of the same ways.

Deconcentration of the Economy. The Korean economy has benefited thus far from the presence of the *chaebol*. They have mobilized resources, taken risk, and spearheaded success in a range of industries. Their vigorous competition with each other has been essential to Korean dynamism.

At this stage, however, the groups' role in the economy must not only change but become less central if rapid advancement is to continue. The presence of more independent companies, that are more focused on particular fields of specialty, will foster innovation and be a force for upgrading competitive advantage. More centers of initiative, more potential buyers for new products and services, and less political clout in the hands of a small group of firms will be essential to further Korean economic development. This is particularly true in machinery, specialized inputs, intermediate goods, consumer packaged goods, and services.

Domestic Rivalry. As is true in any rapidly advancing economy, the vigor of domestic rivalry has been essential to Korean industrial success to date. It has fostered dynamism and set Korea apart from other developing nations that attempted to upgrade their economies via state-owned firms or protected monopolies.

There are inevitable pressures in Korea to curb domestic rivalry. In addition, the ability of large groups to discourage entry is considerable, given their size and relationship with government. It is important for the Korean government to resist the tendency to focus on the short-term "inefficiency" of domestic rivalry and miss its fundamental significance for dynamic progress. Strong antitrust laws need to be established, as well as an orientation to prevent too much concentration in Korean industries. Mergers that consolidate an industry to one or two firms should be prohibited.

Korea instituted the Monopoly Regulation and Fair Trade Law in 1981, a promising effort to deal with pricing abuses and other barriers to open competition. Implementation has been proceeding far too slowly, however, and is threatened by special interests. Korea's resolve to maintain and widen free competition will represent an important determinant of future Korean development.

A Shifting Role for Government. Another prerequisite to making the transition to the innovation-driven stage will be a reorientation in the role of the Korean government. Direct intervention in individual industries, reliance on the *chaebol* as a prime development tool, widespread protection, emphasis on basic factors, and directing capital through government decisions were appropriate in earlier stages, as I discussed in Chapters 10 and 12. But such policies must give way to a new set of priorities if Korean industry is to progress further.

Moving to the next stage requires that economic decision making be decentralized into a growing number of private sector hands. The prime role of government must shift from direct intervention to providing the resource foundations for upgrading and creating a more challenging environment in which firms compete. Rule setting and signaling need to replace a direct role in decisions. Efforts to stimulate investment in advanced and specialized factors, upgrade home demand, institute world-class product and environmental standards, deconcentrate economic power, and preserve rivalry are prime government roles in moving to the innovation-driven stage. The job of factor creation must increasingly fall to industry as well as to universities and research institutes with close ties to industry.

It is hard for any government accustomed to an activist role to make these changes. The capacity of the Korean government to do so is yet to be determined. It must be said, however, that Korean government policy has been evolving, which bodes well for the nation's future.

THE AGENDA FOR ITALY

Italy has moved from an economy dependent on low wages, pervasive subsidies, and widespread protection to an innovation-driven economy with many uniquely dynamic industries in the space of a few decades. Catalyzed by rising wages and labor inflexibilities that spurred innovation, and the end of a policy of lira devaluation, Italian firms were forced to upgrade product and process technology, and did so.

Italian industry has shown a remarkable ability to innovate in products as well as to incorporate state-of-the-art manufacturing and other technologies in relatively small and medium-sized firms. Sophisticated and advanced home buyers and the development of world-class Italian supplier industries have contributed to the process. Intense and often personal domestic rivalry, coupled with goals that are decidedly long-term in orientation, energize rapid change. A potent environment for starting new firms in Italy leads to continued segmentation of industries and extension into related fields.

The Italian environment has produced striking success in a range of industries, but has also created limits. It places constraints on further upgrading of competitive advantage in established industries and has limited unnecessarily the types of industries in which Italian firms are internationally successful. There are substantial areas of the economy that are unproductive and uncompetitive which limit Italian prosperity and absorb public funds. Upgrading and extending Italian competitive positions is needed to reduce still relatively high unemployment and to allow further productivity growth.

The potential liberalization of European markets only raises the stakes. Large sectors of the Italian economy will benefit from liberalization because of their dynamism. Others, however, are gravely threatened because they lack real competitive advantage and will lose protection. A shift in the traditional accommodation among big business, labor, and politicians has been next to impossible in Italy. Particularly for Italy, European liberalization provides the necessity, and thus an opportunity, for a new order. Significant changes in Italian policy, however, have yet to occur.

Italy illustrates the constraints to further advancement posed by a nation whose government has not performed its responsibilities well and where company strategies have had to work around it. The following illustrate some of the issues facing both Italian firms and the Italian government if the Italian economy is to further advance:

Human Resource Development. Italian industry has succeeded more on a foundation of informal rather than formal education and training. Expertise is built in families and through diffusion of skills within localized Italian industries in such clusters as textiles, apparel, furnishings, and machinery.

The ability to upgrade existing industries will require a stronger and better-trained human resource foundation. To keep progressing and learning on the job, Italians must have better skills in mathematics, computing, and other basic fields. In order to extend Italian success into new fields, a more formally educated human resource pool will be a prerequisite. Better-trained engineers and scientists are a requirement, as are skills in other advanced specialties.

Continued progress in Italian industry will demand a major commitment to upgrading Italian public education, and perhaps the creation of new private universities such as those being formed in Japan and Germany. The Italian educational system has much opportunity for improvement at the university and postgraduate levels. There are fine schools and departments in Italy, but not enough of them. University programs lack consistent quality and are too slow in reflecting new learning and new fields. Masters' programs are undeveloped, and doctoral programs are almost nonexistent. Crucial skills are in short supply.

Human resource development cannot be left only to government, however. Italian companies must take a greater role in investing in and supporting the improvement of public and private education. They must also create more internal training programs to supplement the role of the schools. Public education is most effective in more generalized disciplines. Corporate training and efforts of trade associations must address the narrow fields and specialties necessary in particular industries.

Research and Development. Italy has among the lowest rates of spending on R&D as a percentage of GDP of any advanced nation. It is well below, for example, that of Germany, France, the United Kingdom, Sweden, and the Netherlands (see Table 13–1). Italian success has generally been in industries (and segments) not requiring large R&D outlays. Adaptation and improvement of established technologies by Italian firms has been aggressive and successful.

To allow continued upgrading of competitive advantage and competing successfully in new industries, however, more formal R&D will be required in companies and other institutions. Clever adaptation of foreign technologies will only take Italian industry so far. It will need the capacity to innovate in more fundamental ways as well as the technological foundation to enter new industries.

Italy's research establishment is underfunded and underdeveloped compared to that of other advanced nations. University research is spotty. Facilities are not up to world standards. Public research investment falls behind that of other nations. Top Italian scientists often go abroad to work.

More support for research, especially in universities, is a pressing need in Italy. It would be a mistake to try to concentrate on research in so-called "high-technology" fields such as semiconductors, supercomputers, or biotechnology, a course of action advocated by some Italians. This would fall into the trap of emulating other nations and failing to recognize the Italian context. Pan-European megaprojects are not the answer either, as I discussed in Chapter 12.

The Italian economy will be better served by increasing the overall level of technological capacity in all industries. A better focus is on applied

TABLE 13–1 Estimated Total National R&D Spending as a Percentage of National Product in Selected Nations, 1975–1987

	1975	*1977*	*1979*	*1981*	*1983*	*1985*	*1987*
Sweden	1.7	1.8	1.9	2.2	2.5	2.8	3.0
Japan	2.0	2.0	2.3	2.6	2.8	2.9	
		42.1					
Germany	2.2	2.1	2.4	2.4	2.5	2.7	2.8
United States	2.3	2.3	2.3	2.4	2.7	2.8	2.6
United Kingdom	2.2	n/a	n/a	2.4	2.3	2.2	2.4**
France	1.8	1.8	1.8	2.0	2.3	2.3	2.3
Switzerland	2.4	2.3	2.4	2.3	2.3	n/a	n/a
Netherlands	2.0	1.9	1.9	2.0	2.0	2.1	n/a
Norway	1.3	1.4	1.4	1.3	1.4	1.5	1.9
Finland	0.9	1.0	1.0	1.2	1.3	1.5	1.7
Belgium	1.3	1.3	1.4	n/a	1.5	n/a	n/a
Italy	0.9	0.9	0.8	1.0	1.1	1.4	1.5
Canada	1.1	1.1	1.1	1.2	1.3	1.4	1.4**
Austria	0.9	n/a	n/a	1.2	1.2	1.3	1.3
Denmark	1.3	1.0	1.0	1.1	1.2	1.3	n/a
Australia	n/a	n/a	n/a	1.0	1.0	1.1	n/a
Ireland	0.8	0.8	0.7	0.7	0.7	0.8	n/a
Spain	0.4	n/a	0.4	0.4	0.5	0.5*	n/a
Korea	n/a	n/a	n/a	n/a	1.1	n/a	n/a
Singapore	n/a	n/a	n/a	n/a	n/a	0.5*	n/a
Taiwan	n/a	n/a	n/a	n/a	n/a	1.1	n/a
OECD TOTAL	1.9	1.8	1.9	2.0	2.2	2.4	
EEC TOTAL	1.6	1.6	1.6	1.8	1.8	1.9	

SOURCE: *International Science & Technology Data Update 1988.* Washington, D.C.: National Science Foundation, forthcoming. OECD/STIID Data Bank, April 1987.

 * Data for 1984.

 ** Data for 1986.

NOTE: National product refers to GDP for some countries and GNP for others. In practice, the differences between the two are not great and do not significantly affect international R&D comparisons.

research in crosscutting fields: software, information systems, new materials, and advanced manufacturing technologies. Active university research programs in such fields will also stimulate entrepreneurship, as students and faculty form new companies. An Italian research strategy will also contribute most to industrial upgrading if it places central emphasis on technologies relevant to existing clusters of successful Italian industries. The creation of programs in fields such as automated apparel production and control systems for production machinery, for example, will leverage and upgrade established Italian positions.

Italian firms, if they are to achieve more sustainable competitive advantage, will also need to make a growing commitment to research. Government-funded R&D in Italy lags behind other advanced nations as a percentage of GDP, but it is the highest percentage of total national R&D of the advanced nations we studied (Table 12–1) because the private sector's contribution is so low. Private sector R&D as a percentage of GDP is 2.6 times higher than Italy in the United States, about three times higher in Germany and Sweden, and almost four times higher in Japan. Italian firms will require the capacity to master new technologies early to hold position against improving competitors from Asia, Spain, and elsewhere. Companies must create more formal internal research programs, supplemented by research institutes sponsored by industry associations and research contracts with universities. Bureaucratic restrictions that now limit relationships between university research institutes and industry should be removed.

Infrastructure. Italian infrastructure has stood in the way of greater competitive advantage in many industries. Poor ports, poor airports, poor telecommunications, and an archaic financial payments system benefit no one. Frequent strikes make vital services uncertain. Companies' costs are needlessly elevated. Success in industries requiring efficient logistics and other infrastructure is made difficult.

Italian economic progress will depend in part on a consensus in Italy to change this state of affairs. Part of the solution is greater investment. A multibillion-dollar agreement with AT&T to upgrade the Italian telephone system, signed in 1989, is a promising step, and such efforts can be widened. Achieving rapid improvement in infrastructure will also benefit from moves to introduce more competition. New entrants will challenge and push state-owned firms. Italian entrepreneurs will rapidly improve the situation if allowed to do so, as the case of television broadcasting has illustrated. The new private television networks have not only benefited the consumer but pushed the state network to improve.

Privatization of state-owned firms may also be necessary in some infrastructure fields to produce meaningful improvement. It is particularly important for Italians to understand, however, that privatization will not yield the full benefits unless it is carried out in a way that ensures competition.

Financial Markets. While there is a large pool of capital in Italy, the structure of Italian financial markets places a serious constraint on the further upgrading of Italian industry. The Milan equity market is poorly developed and inefficient. Stock prices can be influenced by a few large investors and market imperfections favor a few financial groups. Most Italian entrepreneurs want nothing to do with the public markets and their companies remain private. Medium-sized Italian companies have difficulty raising the resources to extend their competitive advantages, invest abroad, or diversify into related fields requiring significant capital.

Poorly developed financial markets not only constrain progress in existing fields but also limit success in newer capital-intensive industries that could absorb labor freed up by rising productivity and loss of position to NIC competitors. Only government firms and a few financial groups are able to mobilize the resources necessary to enter such industries. The result is that Italian competitors, if they are present in capital-intensive industries at all, tend to have dominant and protected domestic positions and are rarely dynamic enough to achieve international success.

The Italian banking system is equally in need of improvement. Most Italian banks are prevented from significant long-term lending. Most debt capital is short term. A combination of regulation, protection from foreign competition, and government ownership all but eliminates competition among banks and has led to glaring inefficiency, not to mention a lack of innovation. The international position of Italian banks is correspondingly weak, and their likelihood of future international success will remain modest without real home market competition. Italian banks tend to be risk averse, and most bank capital flows to government projects or the large groups. The availability of long-term capital to the most dynamic Italian firms is circumscribed.

Italy is also woefully short of venture capital. Venture capital markets are young and well behind those in the United States and Britain. Much of the available venture capital is not invested in new businesses at all because of risk aversion.

Italy's few large corporations, financial holding companies such as the Fiat group, the DeBenedetti group, and the Ferruzzi group, have become conglomerates, diversified into many unrelated businesses. Buying and selling of positions in companies takes place among a relatively small circle of business leaders, and is subject to little broader shareholder scrutiny. The groups, as currently structured, are too diversified to contribute much competitive advantage to their subsidiaries, except access to capital.

Italy will have difficulty advancing to an economy with broader and more sophisticated competitive advantages unless its financial markets develop further. Access to capital needs to be expanded, and capital allocated through a more open and rational process. Bank regulations should permit more long-term lending. Competition among banks should be stimulated *before* European markets liberalize if Italian banks are to have a chance of maintaining, much less strengthening, their positions. The Italian stock market needs to be transformed in an efficient market, extending and accelerating recent changes. Mutual funds and other means to widen share ownership need to be liberalized. Disclosure requirements, insider trading laws, and stricter supervision by the Securities Commission (CONSOB) are needed to protect investors and attract entrepreneurs. Venture capital availability needs to be expanded beyond government sources through providing incentives for private venture capital investors.

A more open, better supervised, and less concentrated equity market will fund a new generation of medium-sized and large Italian companies. Such changes will also protect well-managed Italian companies from takeover, and promote more rational diversification. European liberalizations may make it easier for large Italian companies to source capital outside of Italy. However, a better-functioning capital market at home will be invaluable to funding the small and medium-sized firms so important to Italy's economic progress.

Supply of Capital. Further upgrading of Italian industry will be constrained by the relatively high cost of capital in Italy, especially to smaller and medium-sized firms. They have faced much higher real interest rates than large firms with far better access to the banking system. An opening of Italian capital markets will help lower the cost of capital to industry. However, progress will be hamstrung without a commitment to reduce the public deficit. Funding the deficit and servicing the huge Italian public debt draws funds into government bonds and treasury bills and offsets Italy's high rate of private savings. The corporate bond market is small and accessible only to a few large companies. Deficit reduction is essential to free up capital that could be better deployed in raising the productivity of industry.

Government Ownership. Italian industry is not internationally successful in virtually any industry in which the Italian government is a significant buyer, supplier, or producer. A significant fraction of the Italian economy is state-owned or state-operated. The problems with infrastructure and government services have already been described. In the state-owned manufacturing sector, few firms have true competitive advantage in international terms. Government ownership in manufacturing has often been the result of taking over failing companies, which rarely results in competitive advantage.

State ownership has three important costs. The first is lower efficiency and lack of dynamism in the industries involved. The productivity of the Italian economy is depressed. The second is the effect of inefficient state activities on the Italian industries that must buy from them. The third cost of state ownership is through the role of state-owned companies as buyers. Italian industry is rarely internationally successful in industries in which the Italian government is a significant buyer, such as health-related products and services, transportation equipment, power generation and distribution, telecommunications, and defense. State-owned firms and Italian authorities often violate the principles of a good buyer—they are too slow to innovate, specifications and requirements lag behind other nations, there is a large political influence on purchase decisions, and too much purchasing takes place without competition.

Reducing the size of the Italian state sector will be necessary for the economy to advance rapidly. Privatization should be implemented in ways that create healthy domestic competition instead of replacing a public monopoly with a private monopoly. This means that Italian state-owned firms should not be sold to competitors or to firms that will dismember them for sale to competitors. Where state ownership is retained, modifying procurement practices along the lines I outlined in Chapter 12 will lead to important benefits for other Italian industries.

Regulation. Regulation in Italy creates unnecessary costs and impedes innovation. The irony is that despite high levels of regulation, Italian products are not safer, the Italian environment is not better protected, and Italian consumers do not get better services and more choice. Too often, regulations reduce competition and lead to temptations for favoritism.

Italian regulations will be more effective if they shift toward setting high standards in areas of social concern and create incentives for corporate compliance, moving away from direct intrusion into corporate behavior. Regulations that unleash innovation and competition, instead of protecting existing products and producers, will have the greatest benefits. Regulatory bodies need statutory authority which preserves some independence from the Italian political process. Regulatory enforcement needs to be streamlined and speeded up.

Competition. Italy provides a striking illustration of the importance of domestic rivalry for international success. Italy is highly competitive in those industries where there are numerous domestic competitors and local rivalry is intense—ceramic tiles, shoes, apparel, cloth, furniture, pasta, and many others. Italy rarely succeeds in international terms where there is either no domestic rivalry or where competition is highly constrained by government policies or informal agreements, such as in the state sector and banking. Firms in such industries may be profitable because of protected domestic circumstances or a dominant Italian market position, but most lack true competitive advantage in international terms.

Italian industry will have difficulty developing further until competition is extended. Italy is one of the few advanced nations without antitrust laws. Such laws are an important priority today, as is the elimination of regulations that limit entry or lead to *de facto* cartels. Mergers among leading Italian companies should be prohibited. Privatization of state-owned firms should be accomplished in a way that enhances competition rather than eliminates it. When Alfa Romeo was sold to Fiat, for example, dynamism in the Italian industry was threatened.

There is a real risk that Italian policy will move in the direction of making the problem worse and not better. As industries have globalized and as greater European integration begins to look more likely, many in Italy are arguing that Italian firms need greater scale to compete. This is being used to justify mergers among leading Italian companies. For reasons I have discussed earlier, *domestic* mergers which eliminate effective competition in Italy are a serious mistake. The better solution is for Italian firms to gain scale by expanding *abroad,* and foreign acquisitions represent one tool for doing so. Vigorous domestic rivalry among competitors who compete globally creates the most powerful and sustainable competitive advantages.

Regional Policy. Many nations face regional disparities in economic prosperity, and Italy is no exception. A long history of regional policy, involving substantial public resources, has sought to narrow the gap between the north and the south. With few exceptions, Italian regional policy has not succeeded. It has been based on the use of subsidies to entice Italian firms to locate facilities in the south. Emphasis has been placed on large industries such as autos, chemicals, and steel. Isolated plants and other facilities, unconnected to established industry clusters and lacking local availability of the right types of human resources, infrastructure, and suppliers, have had little chance of ever achieving competitive advantage.[3]

A more effective approach to spawning and stimulating industry in the south is to build on clusters. Successful industries grow out of existing and emerging concentrations of companies, skills, and related and supporting industries. There are potential clusters in the south around food-related industries and tourism, to name just two possibilities. Government support should take such forms as specialized educational institutions, research institutes in local universities, specialized infrastructure, and export promotion. Suppliers and related industries can be given incentives to locate nearby.

Italian government policy will also be more effective if it moves from outright subsidies to *tax incentives* that depend on making profits. Too often, subsidies have gone to enterprises with little prospect of ever doing so.

Company Strategy and Structure. Italian companies will need to evolve their strategies and approaches to management if their competitive advantages are to be preserved and extended, in addition to making a greater commitment to human resources development and research as I have described earlier. Past management styles have worked well in small and medium-sized companies. A high level of commitment to the business, a familylike orientation, and flexibility need to be preserved and supplemented by more professional management structures. The introduction of better-trained managers, modern information technology, and better controls will allow Italian companies to move beyond the scale and complexity that one charismatic leader can personally supervise. Without a more professional management structure, Italian companies have been unable to grow or have faced severe difficulties when they strayed from their core businesses. Such structures can make Italian entrepreneurs more effective.

Italian companies will need to adopt more global strategies. In many industries, well-developed foreign distribution channels and, in some cases, foreign manufacturing will be necessary to sustain and extend competitive advantages. Alliances with foreign firms, a tempting option for many Italian companies because they limit the required investment, are not in themselves the long-term answer. Italian firms must control their own destinies and develop internally the critical assets and skills that are necessary for competitive advantage, or they will never sustain it. Alliances can be a good transitional step, or can be used to achieve highly specific purposes, but are not in themselves a sufficient long-term strategy.[4]

Finally, Italian firms face a risk of repeating the mistakes of firms from other nations in diversification. Unrelated diversification has proved to be a dismal failure in the long run. The inefficiency of the Italian capital markets and artificial restraints on competition have made conglomerates viable in the past. But times are rapidly changing. The Italian financial groups must shift from being conglomerates to concentrating on a few tightly related core businesses where they can achieve world-class positions. Size for its own sake is not important to competitive advantage. In pursuing new businesses, medium-sized Italian companies must concentrate on closely related fields and resist the temptation to enter unrelated industries, no matter how rapidly they are growing. For example, Benetton's move into financial services and Berlusconi's entry into retailing from a base in television programming are questionable. In contrast, Ferruzzi's/Montedison's moves to pare back diversity and compete globally in core industries provide a better model for Italian industry.

THE AGENDA FOR SWEDEN

Sweden began to emerge as an innovation-driven economy when technological breakthroughs around the turn of the century set the stage for more sophisticated competitive advantages and entry into more advanced industries. Productivity has risen steadily, especially in manufacturing, and with it prosperity. The Swedish economy is highly clustered, and Swedish firms have been able to sustain their competitive positions in many industries. Research and development investment is substantial. Far-flung global networks yield robust advantages for the unusual number of large Swedish multinationals. Restructuring of industries sensitive to factor costs has been rapid compared to many nations.

Yet the Swedish economy is caught in a kind of trap. It is narrow compared even to other small countries such as Switzerland, with Sweden holding a weak position in consumer goods, international services, and other large sectors. The mechanisms for broadening the economy, so important to rising productivity growth, are sputtering. Few new international firms of any size have been formed since World War II. The process of innovation in Sweden is slow and restricted to a relatively narrow range of fields—Swedish firms rarely succeed in industries with short product life cycles. The large public sector impedes private-sector development in large and important fields.

Sweden's traditional industries are not growing, and some of its resource-based industries are shrinking. Sweden's economy has an unusual dependence on factor costs for an advanced nation. Devaluation has slowed down the erosion of exports in the more commodity-oriented basic industries. Government employment has absorbed jobs freed up by industrial restructuring. However, this equation threatens to come out of balance. Overall productivity growth is anemic.

Sweden illustrates a nation in which some deliberate policy choices and some national values may be becoming inconsistent with the imperatives of further economic advancement. Sweden's challenge is to avoid a drift that may lead eventually to a lower relative standard of living. The following illustrate some of the issues for Swedish firms and the Swedish government:

The Policy Framework. Devaluation has been one of the prime tools to improve the international position of Swedish industry, and it has buoyed exports in some industries. Debate on competitiveness in Sweden is also preoccupied with wages and electricity prices. Focus on these areas, however, reflects too narrow a model of national competitive advantage, based too heavily on factor costs. While this is understandable given the heavy role of resource-based industries in the Swedish economy, it will slow the process by which Sweden both widens and upgrades its economic base. Both government and industry must mount a broader program to enhance and extend competitive advantage. Without it, the pressures on Swedish industry will only continue.

Investment in Factor Creation. An advanced nation such as Sweden cannot maintain its relative economic prosperity unless the quality of its factor pool rises as fast as that of other advanced nations. The pace of investment in Sweden must rise. The educational system may no longer be superior enough to provide an advantage, given the progress of other nations. More specialization in training is also needed, as is a higher priority given to vital fields that affect many industries such as software, computing, and new materials. Shortages of highly skilled workers and technical personnel are holding back the upgrading of the economy.

The Swedish government cannot by itself be the solution to the problem, yet it has a tendency to seek too large a role. More public research funds need to be channeled into universities instead of disbursed through government-administered programs. Swedish firms need to continue to raise their own rate of investment in human resource development and technology. Joint investments in factor creation involving buyers, suppliers, and related industries should also be increased.

Demand Conditions. New business formation in Sweden will be stunted without improvements in demand conditions for consumer goods and services. Tax policy, which reduces effective purchasing power for advanced consumer goods, is holding back advanced local demand in such industries. So is a looming government role in the services sector, which constrains consumer choice and blocks new enterprise formation. Also limiting are prohibitions on advertising and other modern marketing techniques.

Sweden has some potential advantages in business and consumer services, including language skills, neutrality, a good record in automating service functions, and a group of large Swedish multinationals to provide a base of foreign demand. Ikea, the international furniture retailer, illustrates that Sweden can succeed internationally in services and gain pull-through benefits in manufacturing. With an upgrading of domestic demand conditions and a better climate for new business formation (see below), the base of the Swedish economy could expand.

The Role of the Public Sector. Given the Swedish consensus for a large public sector, it is unrealistic to expect wholesale privatization of public activities. Instead, the challenge in Sweden is to improve the performance of state activities and ensure that they provide the maximum overall benefit to Swedish industry. Each Swedish public body, in addition to its normal functions, must be guided by a mandate to operate in a way that stimulates innovation and dynamism in industry. For example, health procurement must place important emphasis on encouraging new Swedish medical products and services.

Boosting productivity in state-provided services and other areas will be necessary to support productivity growth in the Swedish economy. A move in the direction of privatization is the only way in the long run to ensure that productivity enhancement and internationalization of activities now controlled by the state are encouraged. In this regard, the recent move to partially privatize Procordia, the Swedish government-owned conglomerate, is a positive step. So is the very existence of the debate taking place within the

Social Democratic Party about privatization and other modifications in the role of the public sector.

There is another pressing reason to diminish the size of the state sector. Swedish firms are moving production out of Sweden for lack of educated employees at a time when a large fraction of the Swedish workforce is deployed in state activities with relatively low levels of productivity. This state of affairs not only holds back current national productivity, but threatens the ability to increase it. Resources must be redeployed away from the public sector if the Swedish economy is truly to advance.

Motivation. The goals of individuals and firms in Sweden are shaped by an environment that encourages modest economic aspirations. Tax rates have been extremely high, and social norms have discouraged the creation of wealth through entrepreneurship. Workers and managers are disciplined, skilled, and effective, but they sometimes lack the willingness to take risk and open new territory so necessary to creating and upgrading competitive advantage.

Tax policy is the easiest part of the equation to change, and a constructive dialogue in Sweden is beginning. Reducing the size of the government sector is important in part to allow the reduction of tax rates. Greater use of profit sharing in industry, and a greater linkage of pay to individual skills and accomplishment, are other possible but more difficult steps. The move in some Swedish companies to sell bonds convertible into equity to employees, so far opposed by many Swedish unions, is a positive development. Another sign of progress is a discussion about limiting untaxed reserves, which would provide greater pressure for performance in Swedish firms.

Competition. Perhaps the single greatest deterrent to upgrading Swedish industry is a slow disappearance of domestic competition. While an open home market and global strategies are partial substitutes for domestic rivalry in some industries, Swedish dynamism has suffered. The pace of innovation and upgrading in Swedish industry is hardly likely to rise without a reversal of the drift toward local monopolies and cooperation among rivals. There is too much tolerance in Sweden of mergers, swapping of product lines, and tacit coordination. There is a sense in Sweden that with enough collaboration all will benefit. Industry is taking the easy solution of buying local competitors rather than beating them through innovation, which would improve the entire national industry (through more rapid factor creation, development of suppliers, and other benefits described in Chapters 3 and 4).

Antitrust in Sweden is applied to local industries, but suspended in international industries in the name of allowing Swedish companies to gain scale for competing in global markets. I believe this is a mistake for the nation and for Swedish firms. The national champion concept is flawed, even in a small nation. Sweden will benefit from preserving domestic rivalry and from opening up sheltered domestic sectors such as services.

New Business Formation. Another important challenge to Swedish industry is new business formation, both by new firms and by established Swedish companies. Sweden must widen the range of industries in which international success is achieved. Without new industries, and the job creation they bring, Sweden's prosperity will eventually suffer.

In order to invigorate entrepreneurship, Swedish tax policy needs to be seriously reexamined. The level of after-tax return available is insufficient to induce entrepreneurs to take the risk of starting new companies, particularly in light of the lack of social prestige ascribed to such activities. Taxation rules make it difficult for entrepreneurs to build personal wealth by building a company, and prompt emerging Swedish companies to sell out too quickly to large firms.

Government policy must focus on the needs of small and not just large businesses. Incentives are necessary, for example, to launch a true private venture capital market. The current venture capital system, administered largely through government bodies, tends to be bureaucratic and ineffective. A campaign by business and government leaders to educate the public on the vital role of new industry will help to shift the perceptions of prestige in the nation and encourage more entrepreneurship. There are some signs that recent university graduates in Sweden today are becoming more interested in entrepreneurship. This encouraging development should be reinforced so that social pressures do not halt it, and budding entrepreneurs do not seek opportunities outside Sweden.

Company Strategies. Swedish firms are extremely international, and this has served them well in sustaining competitive advantage in international markets. Yet there is a growing risk that, in their enthusiasm for globalization, Swedish companies will neglect their home base. Global strategies supplement and extend competitive advantage, but rarely create it. Innovation depends on a healthy home environment.

Partly because of a shortage of skilled personnel (discussed earlier), firms are showing signs of moving abroad and not investing in upgrading Sweden. The result will be diminished innovative capability and further constraints on new business formation. A firm needs a true home base in order to retain dynamism. It is important for Sweden that its leading companies remain Swedish-based though highly international.

The Choice of Values. I recognize that changes such as these may run counter to some deeply rooted Swedish national values: redistribution of income, egalitarianism, a profound concern with social welfare, cooperation instead of competition, and a major role for the state. These values have been consistent so far with rising economic prosperity. Increasingly, however, developments in the international economy may force the Swedish people to choose between preserving these values in every respect and the maintenance of the Swedish standard of living.

Swedish values minimize the risk that Sweden will drift to the wealth-driven stage, a serious concern in nations such as the United States, Germany, and Switzerland. Yet they are blunting the dynamism necessary to maintain relative position as an innovation-driven economy. Some national values, such as concern for safety and the environment, will remain strengths in international competition. Others, such as income redistribution, egalitarianism, and a continued heavy state role in services, may limit further development. Sweden is showing some intriguing signs of change, and prospects for a new period of advancement in Swedish industry have brightened.

THE AGENDA FOR JAPAN

Japan has made a remarkable transition from the factor-driven to the innovation-driven stage in the postwar period. Its companies have evolved from competing on price to competing on advanced products and processes. Japan illustrates the process of upgrading industry as no other nation does. The system of determinants in Japan leads to extraordinary dynamism and innovation in many industries. Japan is enjoying the positive reinforcement effects of the "diamond," as one competitive industry begets another and demand conditions upgrade. Momentum is widening the base of successful industries.

The recent appreciation of the yen has prompted even further upgrading of the sources of competitive advantage in Japanese industry. More and more companies are competing on differentiation, advanced product technology, and improved productivity. More significant, perhaps, is that the yen shock has finally accelerated the adoption by Japanese companies of truly global strategies, an area where many had moved too slowly. Foreign direct investment is proceeding rapidly in many internationally successful Japanese industries, and will boost productivity by shifting less sophisticated activities elsewhere. This will not only help deal with protectionism but will make the Japanese economy less vulnerable to domestic factor costs. It will also allow Japanese firms to be better able to compete in a range of industries when local proximity is important.

Personal incomes in Japan are rising. Domestic demand for many goods has also been limited by housing conditions and little leisure time. Working hours are already falling in major Japanese companies with the encouragement of government, and this change will fuel substantial growth in leisure-related industries.[5] Growth in the number of second homes, coupled with a boom in remodeling existing homes and apartments (in Japan this is termed "rehousing''), will create new demand for furnishings and household products. There are more than ample opportunities, then, to create enough jobs to soak up any employment freed by foreign investment, greater imports, and domestic productivity growth. The rate of direct intervention by government in the economy has fallen markedly, as it should.

Given such a positive foundation, the continued health of the Japanese economy in the medium term is not in doubt. The most pressing immediate challenge for Japan is dealing with the large portion of the economy that is unproductive and has fallen outside the Japanese miracle and holds back national productivity. In the long run, the challenge for a nation like Japan is even more fundamental—how to retain dynamism and avoid a drift toward a wealth-driven economy. As profits accumulate, debt is repaid, and the pool of wealth grows, forces are set in motion which produce consequences that are seen in the economic histories of nations such as Germany, the United States, and Britain. The rate of productivity growth overall and in manufacturing has already slowed markedly in the Japanese economy.

Japan provides an illustration of the agenda facing a highly successful nation seeking to preserve the foundations of that success and continue the upgrading process. Some challenging issues facing Japan include the following:

Education. Upgrading an economy demands that human resources upgrade as well. The secondary and especially the vocational and university education systems must be improved. While the educational system has served Japanese industry well so far, the future will bring the need for more and more skilled workers, demands for new types of skills to compete in new industries, and growing globalization. Japanese employees and managers must develop greater skills in software, computers, international business, languages, marketing, and other foundations of future industry. In the area of computers, for example, only 14 percent of elementary schools and 36 percent of junior high schools had more than one computer in 1987, compared to 85 percent and 92 percent in the United States and 99 percent and 100 percent in Britain in 1984.[6]

Company training, while of vital and continuing importance, covers only *a portion* of the workforce that is employed in larger organizations. It cannot substitute for first-rate universities or for post-secondary vocational training to fill the gap in training in specialized disciplines to meet the needs of industry.

Rigid central control and standardization at all levels of the Japanese educational system have served the nation thus far, but will increasingly hold back further economic progress. Curriculum must become more flexible and tailored to student and local industry needs. A good base of universities exists, but standards for performance at universities must rise, the quality of teaching must improve, and course work must broaden and upgrade, especially in nontechnical areas. There is an especially acute need to improve university curriculum in the computer field. Vocational schools in Japan are also still early in their development, and attendance is growing rapidly. They provide a vital role in creating the specialized skills needed for particular industries, and can be more responsive than public education to market needs. Efforts to develop and substantially upgrade the quality of vocational education should receive high priority.

University Research. Strength in basic research and research in emerging new fields is increasingly necessary for continued progress as an economy becomes more advanced. Japan's R&D system must broaden substantially, away from its dependence on the large corporations. The missing link is the university research program. A pool of basic research will increasingly be necessary in order for corporate research to continue its advance and for fundamental innovativeness to rise. University research can also serve as a potent incubator of new enterprises, and a place where top researchers are trained for industry.

Japanese companies need to make an even stronger commitment to building linkages with universities. Joint research with universities is rare. Contributions of money and talent will be a necessary supplement to public funds. Research linkages are beginning (such as the TRON [The Real-Time Operating system Nucleus] computer project, thus far not successful), and universities such as Tokyo University are establishing company-sponsored courses. Such efforts must proliferate.

Part of the process of upgrading both university educational programs and research activities will be an easing of the often tight restrictions on the permissible activities of government universities and their faculties. The Ministry of Education, like MITI, needs to learn to play a more flexible and less intrusive role. At the same time, the development of private universities with freedom to experiment and innovate should be encouraged and supported.

Demand Conditions. Demand conditions lead the development of advanced economies. Japan's growing affluence will itself spur economic development by creating and widening the demand for advanced goods and services. Government has a role in removing any barriers to this process. Growth in leisure time is already stimulating the development of new products and services. Both firms and government should move to capitalize on these positive developments. Progress on improving housing is particularly important because it will unleash demand for many new industries that may develop into tomorrow's international success stories (for example, home electronic controls and space-saving bathroom units). Deploying resources toward improving the quality of life has a dual benefit. Capital investments in such areas as transportation, telecommunications, health care, cultural institutions, and others will not only improve people's lives but trigger innovations in industries supplying them.

Other constraints on Japanese demand conditions are the following:

The Distribution System. Japan's anachronistic wholesale and retail distribution system will increasingly represent a barrier to international success in the industries that are affected by it. Japanese companies, in industries such as consumer packaged goods, must be able to learn world-class marketing at home. Japan will have difficulty innovating in industries that depend heavily on distribution channels that are not world class. Artificial restrictions on the modernization of the wholesale and retail distribution system should be eliminated. This will improve national productivity directly, and also encourage greater imports which can have the same effect.

Health Care. Japan's health care system is structured in such a way as to dampen the rate of innovation in products and services. This huge sector is important for public welfare and for national productivity, and will be increasingly so because Japan faces among the most acute aging problems of any advanced nation. Japan will compete at a disadvantage in this huge sector until procurement and service delivery practices become more efficient, flexible, and diversified. Central control should diminish. Only then will suppliers understand the leading-edge needs that foster international competitive advantage.

Services. Part of the process of continuing development in advanced nations is a growing international role in services. Many service industries in Japan are well developed domestically, but most lack significant positions in international markets. This will restrict the deepening of industry clusters and limit the potential upgrading of the economy. Japanese service firms enjoy growing potential advantages due to the presence abroad of many Japanese citizens and Japanese multinationals. Those Japanese service industries that have capitalized on this, such as banking and trading, have been slow to aggressively develop non-Japanese customers.

International success in services will not only require a determined effort to serve non-Japanese buyers but also better language skills, more systemization of service functions, more sophisticated use of information technology (where Japan lags), and extensive investment in overseas locations and the hiring/training of qualified personnel.

In addition, governmental or other restrictions that are blunting competition and dynamism in distribution, construction, financial services, and other domestic service industries must be eased, or they will prevent international success. The same principle applies in services as in manufacturing. Without active rivalry and freedom to innovate at home, Japanese service firms will have little chance of succeeding abroad.

Unproductive Sectors. Japan is in many ways two economies, as I have discussed earlier. While it has some of the most productive industries of any nation with the capacity to upgrade rapidly, it also contains large sectors where productivity is low. Distribution and retailing have already been mentioned. Many other services also have lagging productivity, among them the huge construction sector. In construction as well as many other services, cartels and other restraints to competition are common.[7]

But the problem is not confined to services. In a range of agricultural and manufacturing industries, Japan also falls far behind the world's best competitors in productivity and/or quality. Many of these industries are insulated from domestic and international competition in some way. Examples are petroleum and related products, aluminum smelting, tobacco, food, paper products, fibers, and bulk chemicals. In many of these industries, "recession" and "rationalization" cartels sanctioned by MITI have allowed the survival of inefficient competitors and effectively blocked imports. Very few of the many industries in which such cartels have been allowed have ever subsequently achieved a significant international market position.

Such large areas of subpar productivity pull down the overall productivity of the Japanese economy. In the economy as a whole, average productivity is well behind such nations as the United States and Germany. In the manufacturing sector, one study estimates that Japan's average output per man hour was 32 percent less than the United States in 1985.[8] The drag of unproductive sectors is increasingly a constraint that rapid upgrading in internationally competitive sectors will be unable to overcome. As Table 7-1 illustrated, Japan's overall rate of productivity growth has slowed. Japan's standard of living growth will eventually suffer.

Opening unproductive sectors to competition (see below) is one essential remedy. Another is trade. Japan must import more if vibrant productivity growth is to continue. As I discussed in Chapter 1, imports both stimulate productivity improvements in domestic industries and free up resources (labor and capital) to allow the expansion of more productive sectors. Japan's imports as a percentage of GDP were 6.9 percent in 1987, the *lowest* of any nation we studied including the United States (9.5 percent). The penetration of imports in Japan has remained about the same for decades though it has risen significantly in other nations. A higher rate of imports will be essential not only to deal with trade problems, as I will discuss later, but to assure continuing improvement in Japan's economic prosperity. While imports have begun rising in the late 1980s, there are deep-seated attitudes and beliefs in Japan that imports are undesirable. Overcoming these is one of the prerequisites to further upgrading of the Japanese economy.

Goals. A seemingly inevitable tendency in successful nations is shifting goals of individuals, investors, and companies that threaten dynamism in industry. The risk of such a shift, caused in no small part by success itself, will increasingly be an issue for Japan.

Rising incomes and a rapidly accumulating pool of wealth in Japan threaten to change the motivation of individuals. Many Japanese point to a declining willingness of young people to do factory work or make commitments to their company. Mid-career job mobility is rising. A recent survey of university graduates in science and engineering found that a declining percentage wanted careers in manufacturing, but the proportion wanting to go into finance, insurance, and real estate has doubled since 1986.[9] Individuals may also become preoccupied with maximizing existing wealth instead of creating new wealth, and a liberalization of the investment options open to individuals will only encourage such a shift. For all these reasons, motivation in the workplace may begin to fade.

A new generation of managers is taking the helm in Japanese industry. They are replacing, in many cases, the founders and entrepreneurs who built up companies after the war. The risk is that vision and institution building may be replaced by stewardship and conservatism.

Companies may also find it easier to make money in the stock market, speculate in real estate, and buy companies than create new products and processes. Indeed, a recent survey found that 55 percent of the 1,010 firms listed on the first section of the Tokyo stock exchange reported profits through what the Japanese call "money games," a record high.[10] Such a shift will stunt productive investment and innovation. A large pool of wealth tends to increase risk aversion in an economy. Yet wealth must be deployed productively if any economy is to continue advancing.

Evolution in the Japanese capital markets, partly driven by broader worldwide financial market changes, could have profound effects on the goals of Japanese investors and, in turn, of companies. Institutional investors without a voice in management are gaining a growing influence in the Japanese equity market. After decades of passivity, they will come under increasing pressure to earn higher investment yields. The "Big Four" Japanese securities firms (Nomura, Daiwa, Nikko, and Yamaichi) account for 80 percent of trading volume on the Tokyo stock exchange. Their interests are much more centered on trading (to generate commissions) than are those of banks and insurance companies. The buying and selling of equity stakes by institutional investors is showing some signs of increasing.

So far, a rising Japanese stock market has led to attractive equity returns. However, evolution in the Japanese capital markets, combined with the growing foreign holdings of Japanese corporate equities, may lead to less commitment to sustained investment in Japanese companies.

Capital market regulations must avoid creating the same bias toward

short-term price appreciation and mergers driven solely by financial considerations that have come to dominate markets in America. Tax policy must
also ensure that investors have appropriate incentives. A move to tax long-
term capital gains in Japan may be counterproductive.

Company Strategy. Japanese companies have already begun to shift from
cost to differentiation strategies and toward higher levels of technological
innovation. Their next challenge will be to move to the next generation of
global strategies. The first stage is exporting from a production base at
home. The next stage is to disperse activities, including less sophisticated
production, to foreign sites. Catalyzed by the upward shift in the value of
the yen, Japanese companies have begun this process in earnest. The risk
is that once foreign subsidiaries are established, they will evolve into highly
autonomous units. This is what happened to many European and American
multinationals. The challenge instead is to coordinate and integrate the activities of subsidiaries.

Another crucial area in strategy will be future moves toward diversification.
Japanese industry has been uniquely able to grow through *internal* diversification into related industries, which offers the best prospects for creating
competitive advantage. There are signs, however, that a predictable combination of circumstances is beginning to alter this pattern.

Japanese firms are accumulating large pools of cash that exceed their
ability to build new businesses internally. Dividend payout in Japanese
companies is small, because reinvestment of profits has been necessary for
funding growth. If payout does not increase (and little pressure to increase
dividends is now apparent because of attractive gains in share prices), slowly
but surely the need to deploy capital means that unrelated (conglomerate)
forms of diversification will begin to appear. This is already occurring in
large Japanese companies. Sony entered life insurance, for example, while
New Nippon Steel entered catalog selling. At the same time, mergers and
acquisitions are becoming more common. Mergers among Japanese companies have risen from 140 in 1984 to 223 in 1988, while Japanese acquisitions
of foreign firms have increased from 44 to 315 over the same period.[11]

If this movement becomes widespread, as it has in the United States
since the 1970s, experience suggests that it will begin to slow the rate of
innovation in the Japanese economy. Emphasis will shift to buying and
selling assets rather than the investments required to create competitive
advantage. Evidence is growing that the great majority of unrelated diversification, of whatever nationality, fails. Both the Japanese examples I cited
above were failures, and predictable ones.

Competition. The intense rivalry that characterizes the internationally
successful sectors of the Japanese economy is more fragile than it may

seem. At the same time, companies used to international success and accumulating substantial resources and power may begin to lose a taste for competing. Companies facing mature markets may pressure government for relief. As mergers become more common and stock market pressures grow, industries may begin to consolidate. The merger between Mitsui Bank and Taiyo Kobe Bank to create Japan's second-largest bank, announced in 1989, could well foreshadow future developments. At the same time, other large parts of the economy, as I have discussed, have grown accustomed to insulation from competition and will resist change.

The vigorous rivalry that has been typical in many Japanese industries has made enforcement of antitrust laws seem relatively unimportant. It should not be assumed this will always be the case. It was not that long ago that the Japanese economy was effectively cartelized by the large industrial groups. It was even more recently that the Japanese government attempted to limit entry or foster consolidation in important industries. MITI is still prone to attempt to control entry and to sanction ''recession cartels'' that preserve inefficient competitors. The evidence is clear that such policies have little chance of leading to productive industries, not to mention international success.

The antitrust laws that have been on the books in Japan since World War II, especially those regarding mergers, are important ones. Restraints to competition in manufacturing and services need to be eliminated. Breaking down governmental and other barriers to imports will also be essential to maintaining industrial vitality. Preserving and extending competition in light of past success is perhaps the single greatest challenge facing Japan.

Trade. Japan's export success has led to trade frictions in a variety of industries. A prevalent solution to these problems has been to negotiate ''orderly marketing agreements'' or other restraints on exports with individual nations. Typically, quotas for Japanese exports into a foreign nation are set based on historical market shares.

Such an approach to dealing with trade friction is flawed. It freezes the status quo and tends to blunt rivalry in Japanese industries. As such deals proliferate, the vitality of *Japanese* competition is threatened. At the same time, Japan's still relatively closed markets—not formally protected sometimes making simple comparisons of trade barriers misleading—make Japan vulnerable to a more unified Europe and more aggressive United States.

The best approach to reducing trade friction is for Japan to import. This not only eases protectionist pressures, but it is essential to upgrading the productivity of the Japanese economy as I have already discussed. While the impediments to importing are complex, the most unfortunate one is a perception in Japan that imports are required only to appease foreigners. At this stage in Japan's economic development, the stakes are much higher.

Japan has enacted in the late 1980s, or is considering, unprecedented moves to build imports such as Japanese Export-Import Bank Financing for imports and tax incentives for buying imported goods. Such measures take on high priority.

*   *   *

The Japanese environment has so far made policy initiatives in a number of these areas unnecessary. Competition has flourished in important sectors of the economy. Investors have been permanent holders of stock. Managers have all but ignored short-term stock price movements in favor of sustained investments to build their companies. It cannot be taken for granted that these blessings will continue.

Japanese have come to *assume* much about their competitive system. Americans made the same kinds of assumptions and have been slow to respond to a cumulation of important changes both within the nation and in the international competitive environment. It is certain that the state of Japanese industry will continue to evolve. Company strategy and government policies must evolve with it.

THE AGENDA FOR SWITZERLAND

Switzerland has enjoyed prosperity for decades, growing out of a long history as an innovation-driven economy. It brings many strengths to international competition. Switzerland's breadth of market positions is a stabilizing force in the economy, as is the extensive globalization of many Swiss firms which allows them to respond to factor cost and exchange rate shifts.

Swiss firms enjoy advantages in demand conditions that are likely to continue. The home market is both sophisticated and anticipatory of trends in other advanced nations. As worldwide buyer needs become more segmented and as the desire for quality, customization, and service rises, these will play to Swiss strengths. Growing international concern with the environment and with employee welfare will find Swiss firms already able to cope. The right kind of selective factor disadvantages will continue to pressure change earlier in Switzerland than in many nations. Management-employee relations remain positive and flexible.

Yet there are some disturbing signs that the dynamism of Swiss industry is slackening. Too many companies seem to be intent on defending what they have rather than creating new advantages. Change is being resisted or avoided through compromise. Mergers are concentrating important industries. Motivation is slackening. Risk taking and entrepreneurship seem to be waning. Per capita income and productivity growth are slow.

Switzerland is showing signs of a drift toward the wealth-driven stage that will ultimately limit national prosperity. As the prospect of European liberalization grows, increasing the pace and intensity of competition and conferring advantages on nations in the EC, Swiss industry may begin to fall behind and lose out to German or Italian firms for European business.

Switzerland is a nation that illustrates many of the risks of sustained prosperity. The following are some of the issues constraining further Swiss development:

Human Resources. Swiss success hinges on the ability to upgrade industry and compete in sophisticated and highly differentiated industry segments. This depends fundamentally on Switzerland having among the most skilled and specialized human resources in the world, even more so than Sweden because of the absence of natural resources.

A tradition of investment in upgrading human resources is well established in Switzerland. What is less clear is whether the Swiss educational system, with the rigidities that afflict most government bureaucracies, is adjusting rapidly enough in new fields such as information technology, new materials, modern manufacturing technology, and telecommunications.

Also cause for concern are strict limits on the immigration of skilled personnel in Switzerland, at the same time that immigration of ''seasonal'' unskilled workers has been heavy. This has the perverse effect of constraining the process of upgrading at the same time as it reduces the pressures to boost productivity by economizing on unskilled labor.

Technological Infrastructure. Swiss government spending on R&D is the smallest percentage of GDP of any of the advanced nations we studied. While companies should shoulder the major R&D burden, the basic scientific infrastructure in Switzerland is not keeping pace with other advanced nations. This may not only contribute to slow technological development in new fields but also fail to produce enough upcoming scientists and engineers that can move into industry.

Public Infrastructure and Services. Switzerland faces a growing burden from the state sector. This not only lowers national productivity, but soaks up scarce human resources that are badly needed in industry.

Another consequence of a large state role is that Switzerland suffers from high costs and a slow pace of innovation in telecommunications, and transportation and other public services also labor under a heavy state role. There is a need to reexamine the state role. Allowing private-sector entry, and movement toward privatization of state companies, should not only improve service but also boost the quality of domestic demand.

Regulation. There is a growing tendency for regulations in Switzerland to slow innovation and upgrading, partly a reflection of a desire for stability and the legacy of sustained prosperity. Notable examples are restrictive labor regulations that limit overtime or night work and set a low retirement age, transaction taxes in financial services that are driving business outside of Switzerland, and price controls. A return to the Swiss tradition of non-intervention is a pressing priority.

Domestic Competition. Switzerland has a tradition of weak cartel laws, a tolerance for monopoly, and a tendency toward other forms of "cooperation" in industry such as so-called "gentlemen's agreements." Closely related is the practice of erecting nontariff barriers that effectively protect Swiss domestic industries from international competition, and guaranteeing public procurement to Swiss firms. Recently, mergers that create dominance in the Swiss industry are on the rise, such as Sulzer's acquisition of Rüti and Saurer in textile machines and the merger between Wild and Kern in surveying equipment. All these threats to competition work against the long-term interests of the nation and Swiss firms. The rate of innovation is slowed and productivity improvement is dampened.

A new attitude toward competition policy will pay large dividends in Switzerland. The idea that cartels and mergers work, even in a small country, is not supported by the evidence. Swiss firms must learn to welcome healthy rivalry as necessary for their long-term success in international terms. This will be increasingly necessary as European competition grows.

Goals. The goals of Swiss companies seem to have been shifting in the last decade away from building and toward defending and protecting. Swiss investors and managers have had a long time horizon and a commitment to investment to build market positions, in part because of the role of banks and other institutional investors in corporate governance. With so much prosperity and ebbing competition, however, a long time horizon has turned into paralysis. Large off-balance sheet reserves and restricted shares have become weaknesses as rivalry slackens. They give Swiss management a false sense of security and impede real change.

The first priority is to reinvigorate competition. However, Swiss dynamism would also benefit from a reduction in the protection offered by restricted shares, and from requiring that firms include reserves in the capital base when reporting earnings. The sort of capital market structure characteristic of the United States and the United Kingdom is *not* the goal. Nevertheless, an increase in investor pressure on management would benefit Swiss industry.

Individual motivation has also been waning, as a tight labor market and more leisure have diminished commitment and risk taking in industry. Lower marginal tax rates, pay more linked to performance (Swiss managers have among the highest fixed salaries involving little or no bonus) and greater opportunities for rapid advancement based on merit would increase the dynamism of Swiss industry.

New Business Formation. Switzerland lacks an environment for new business formation that compares to that of other important nations such as the United States, Japan, Italy, the United Kingdom, and Korea. One problem is the lack of risk capital. Conservative Swiss banks have not been a source of risk capital, and an independent venture capital industry has been slow to develop. Another potentially more serious problem is risk aversion, partly a function of how prosperous most Swiss already are. This deters the Swiss from taking chances that might lead to failure.

Without a better record in new business formation, Switzerland will not be able to continue net job creation, bolster domestic competition, and lay the foundation for future industries. Both business and government in Switzerland must find Swiss ways of unleashing more entrepreneurship.

THE AGENDA FOR GERMANY

Germany became an industrial powerhouse in the late nineteenth century when it achieved world-class status in science and technology. It has been an innovation-driven economy ever since. The enormous breadth of industries in which Germany has competitive advantage has made the German economy a robust one in international competition. German companies usually compete on the basis of differentiation instead of cost. They enjoy early mover advantages due to an installed base of sales, well-developed foreign sales and service networks, and an international manufacturing presence in many industries. The dynamism of German industry has been continually stimulated by a rapid rate of factor creation, selective factor disadvantages, and demand-side pressures.

Yet there are some real threats to German dynamism. Germany has enjoyed more than three decades of uninterrupted prosperity and has what, by some measures, is among the highest standards of living in the world. While the breadth of German industry is substantial, and positions in most established German industries have been sustained, many more industries are losing world share than gaining it. The creation of new businesses in Germany is inadequate to deal with a stubbornly high unemployment rate. Major commercial and scientific breakthroughs by German firms have become rarer. Germany is at the cutting edge of few new consumer product or service industries.

At the same time, the beginnings of a shift in goals shows signs of occurring. Workweeks are shortening as other dimensions of life are emphasized. Investors and managements appear to be increasingly concerned with share prices and mergers. Rivalry shows signs of waning. Complacency in companies may be creeping in. Some examples begin to suggest a pattern. German camera companies were slow to respond to Japanese rivals. Pen and pencil firms have lost the innovation initiative.

Along with signs of complacency are growing barriers to change. The world wars were disruptive to the German economy. Yet they provided motivation, broke up existing structures, and stimulated much innovation to cope with the fact that Germany was cut off from the rest of the world. After decades of success, German tendencies toward accommodation and concentration that were evident in the interwar years are reappearing. Furthermore, sustained prosperity is taking its toll on the attitudes of German unions. Unions have become more preoccupied with preserving the status quo as if the rest of the world did not exist, and creating barriers to change. Furthermore, the decision-making process in German boardrooms is facing growing gridlock as the labor-management consensus breaks down.

All these indicators signal the possibility of a national economy moving toward the wealth-driven stage. The statistics in Table 7–1 show slow per capita income growth, slow productivity growth, and a diminished rate of capital investment in the German economy in the 1980s. These are disturbing signs of a slackening of dynamism. The following areas illustrate some of the issues facing German firms and the German government if continued upgrading of industry is to occur in the coming decades:

Factor Creation in New Sciences. A genuine threat to many German industries will be the inability to remain innovative due to lack of skills and expertise in new sciences such as semiconductors, computers, software, and bioengineering. While many German firms have been able to acquire these skills abroad and apply them to their specialized fields, a major national investment will be required in both education and basic research in these areas if new industries are to be created and German companies are to move from a defensive to an offensive mode.

New sciences need attention and prestige to overcome the decades of influence on German thinking and German companies of mechanical engineering and physical sciences. The case of biotechnology is symbolic of how the mind-set toward new sciences lags behind other nations. German laws for biotechnology research are so strict that BASF and Hoechst are conducting their research programs in their U.S. subsidiaries, while other German firms are basing their programs in the United Kingdom.

Large government-sponsored R&D megaprojects built around dominant firms are unlikely to succeed, based on the experience of other nations and the lessons of Germany's own history. Neither are pan-European collaborative efforts likely to be effective. The best approach is active competition among a number of German firms, working closely with universities and independent research institutes.

Services. The state of development of international services in Germany is stunted, a function of domestic demand for services that seems to lag other nations, a tendency toward performing service functions in-house, and problems in new business formation (see below). Also significant is the relative weakness of education in social sciences and management, as well as the presence of a large state service sector that impedes private initiative.

Without a healthy service sector in which German firms in a range of industries have competitive advantage in international terms, the upgrading of the German economy will be slowed.

Supporting Industries. German firms will have great difficulty achieving higher levels of differentiation and succeeding in advanced consumer goods and services until the tools of modern marketing and distribution are available at home. German firms are behind in sophisticated market research, consumer behavior measurement, and other marketing techniques. Part of the problem is the weakness in social science and management training in universities. Also, television advertising, long store hours, efficient parcel delivery, and other advances are limited or blocked by regulations that sometimes have legitimate purposes but slow the advancement of the German economy.

Motivation. The motivation and sustained commitment to invest of German employees, managers, and investors is showing signs of decline. If this continues, it represents a fundamental threat to the ability of German industry to continue upgrading. After decades of prosperity, there are indications that emphasis is shifting toward maintaining instead of improving. The change is most noticeable in the attitudes of German unions, that have fallen into the unfortunate role of becoming barriers to innovation and a force to preserve the status quo. German workers are also opting for the shortest workweek of any nation, a sign of prosperity but a challenge to future productivity growth.

German managers and investors are also showing signs of less commitment to core businesses. Sensitivity to short-term stock prices is rising. Financial executives are taking the helm in more companies. Diversification through acquisition, sometimes in unrelated areas, is on the rise. The AEG case, where a number of disparate companies were merged, illustrates that unrelated diversification will be no more successful in Germany than it has been elsewhere.

While these changes have been under way for some time, a change in the German tax law is a new factor that raises concerns for future investor and corporate goals in Germany. As of January 1, 1990, the tax exemption on long-term capital gains is to be eliminated. The time horizons of investors will shorten. The proposed shift has already triggered the sale of some privately owned German companies, and the number of mergers is likely to grow. The shift from private to public ownership may lower the rate of investment and reduce commitment to core businesses. The venture capital and initial public offering markets may be set back. Instead of raising capital gains taxation, a better policy to increase revenue to pay for a reduction in income taxes would be to raise the tax on short-term capital gains, eliminate deductions in order to boost taxable income, and reduce the size of the state sector.

Rivalry. German industry, especially the portions of it involving larger firms, exhibits a disturbing tendency toward cooperation and accommodation that is reminiscent of U.S. industries before and during the stagnation of recent decades. A process of consolidation has also created tight oligopolies in important German industries. German firms are sometimes taking the lead in mergers or alliances that threaten competition in the entire European industry. Another issue is raised by German boards. Each of the large German banks often has representatives on the supervisory boards of all large German companies in an industry. No matter how well intentioned, an important role for the same banks in decision making in so many important companies cannot help but raise questions for domestic rivalry. Such a role also reinforces the tendencies toward mergers and the financial orientation I spoke of earlier. Management representation on the boards of competitors also raises concerns.

A fading culture of competition is among the fastest ways that German industry could lose its international position. Both government officials and company executives must recognize the dangers. The strong antitrust laws instituted after World War II should not be relaxed, and recent discussion of tightening should be encouraged. Some standards for interlocking ownership and directorships among competitors should be instituted. Artificial restraints on imports, where they are present, should be eliminated. Mergers and alliances among leading domestic competitors should be prohibited, and merger standards tightened. Laws that allow cartels under certain circumstances should be modified. As I discussed in Chapter 12, domestic monopolies will not improve German competitiveness. Finally, Germany should oppose EC Commission tendencies toward cooperation and concentration in advanced technology industries.

Deregulation and Privatization. One tool for unleashing competition in existing German industries and creating competition in new industries is deregulation and privatization. While there has been progress in privatization, there is more to be done in a variety of German industries such as telecommunications and transportation. This will not only invigorate rivalry in these industries directly, but will also have positive ripple effects on other industries for which these industries are suppliers or buyers. Public firms, however, should not be sold to leading competitors.

New Business Formation. New business formation in Germany has been faltering. Few important German companies have been started since the postwar boom. Like Switzerland, part of the problem is attitudes toward risk. Failure is unacceptable in Germany, and a secure job in an established company is the preferred path. There is little of the desire for independence that energizes Italian entrepreneurship, or the sense of unlimited opportunity that has been so vital in the United States. What is more, the prevailing philosophy since the 1970s modified the public perception of the entrepreneur from someone who is a driving force in the economy to one who is ''expropriating'' wealth from others. Another part of the problem is the lack of well-developed risk capital markets, either in venture capital, initial public offerings, or the banking system, partly because of investor protection rules that unduly constrain institutions from investing in new companies.

Another constraint is the paucity of breakthrough scientific work in new fields. German firms are awesome improvers of technology in existing fields, but not enough are pushing the state of the art in new fields. The spin-offs that are so important to new enterprise formation are becoming rare. A higher rate of investment in new sciences will pay dividends not only in existing industries but in new business formation.

In the last several years, a venture capital market has begun developing in Germany, a promising sign. Centers for encouraging new technology companies have been established close to leading universities. Broadening these initiatives and extending them in other fields is among the highest priorities for Germany. Yet there is by no means a turnaround. Laws and regulations that limit risk capital investment should be eliminated. Top incentives for long-term capital gains should be restored.

The will to deal with this agenda, and restore German dynamism, may come from an unexpected source. The moves toward German unification, arising from momentous political changes in 1989, are both an invigorating and an unsettling force for the economy. The need to assimilate new workers, meet new market demands, and contend with companies liberated from central planning could provide German industry and workers with a new and more constructive mission. What will prove decisive is whether Germany opts for a new era of individual initiative and open competition instead of seeking to avoid disruption and discontinuity through intervention, economic concentration, and accommodation.

THE AGENDA FOR BRITAIN

Britain has been caught in the wealth-driven stage for some time. Its relative living standards have suffered accordingly, particularly for the average worker. The loss of competitive advantage created its own momentum.

One industry's weakness spread to others. Falling income eroded demand quality. Pressure on government revenues led to underinvestment in factor creation, infrastructure, and public services, undermining competitive advantage further. This momentum, once created, is hard to arrest.

There are some signs of renewal in British competitive advantage. Positions in chemicals, oil, pharmaceuticals, software, publishing, financial services, and consumer goods are being sustained. Along with these is growing strength in retailing and signs of a rebound in manufacturing companies. Productivity growth and investment have improved.

An important catalyst for change has undeniably been the Thatcher government. Given the enormous momentum created in economic drift, it is instructive to note that only a government with Mrs. Thatcher's longevity in office and political power has shown signs of deflecting it. Yet other forces are also at work in Britain which have helped. Economic necessity, changing social norms, and the takeover and turnaround of stodgy companies have also contributed to the new wave of energy sweeping across many British firms and industries.

However, the renewal of British industries appears fragile and spotty. A large pool of unemployed persists. Renewal is also confined, in many industries, to one-shot restructuring and cost cutting, made possible in some cases by a new balance of power between unions and management. Mergers are prevalent, but the benefits to real competitive advantage are less clear. Especially in manufacturing, British firms have undone some past sins, but most have yet to create the basis for future advantage. This requires new products and new processes; it requires innovation.

A good deal of the growth in British employment has come from investments by foreign firms. Much of this, however, is driven by factor costs. Foreign investments are largely in assembly facilities taking advantage of low-wage, mostly unskilled labor. While foreign investment provides some welcomed benefits to British industry, an economy whose growth depends on assembly outposts of foreign companies will be constrained in terms of productivity growth.

Britain demonstrates the problems facing a nation attempting to restart the upgrading process. The following illustrate some of the issues that must be faced in Britain for sustained advancement to take place:

Human Resources. While hardly an original observation, it must be emphasized that Britain will not regain innovation-driven status without a world-class educational and training system encompassing all socioeconomic and ability levels. The rate of social investment must rise substantially, standards must be raised and enforced, and technical fields must be stressed. This is perhaps the most pressing issue facing Britain and the area in which current policies provide the least comfort.

Educational policies under the Thatcher government are seeking to raise standards. The Educational Reform Act of 1988, which centralized educational standards and instituted a core curriculum, is a bold step. A group of proposed city technology colleges is aimed at upgrading technical education, though only one is now in operation.

Yet the real thrust so far seems to have been in gaining control over decision making. Funding for education has been cut, perhaps because greater spending is seen as inappropriate before a new structure is in place. Yet this does nothing to deal with woefully inadequate facilities and threatens to drive away good teachers and permanently reduce the quality of both research and teaching. The need to rebuild British education is urgent.

The agenda facing British companies is also great. They must understand that without a broader pool of trained human resources their competitive advantage will be constrained. This includes the ranks of management, where British firms have far fewer university graduates than other advanced nations. British companies will benefit by working closely with local universities in developing curricula, sponsoring research in closely allied fields, and recruiting graduates. Company investments in universities are still minimal. Support for the new city technology colleges, for example, is patchy. Companies also need to accept greater responsibility for internal training of all employees, where little progress has yet been made compared to that in other advanced nations.

Not only must the quality of human resources be improved but also the way they are managed. British labor-management relations still work against both sides. Mutual suspicion, too many unions in a single company, and absenteeism are just some of the barriers to improvement and innovation that hold back British industry.

Research and Development. The United Kingdom falls behind other leading nations in the share of GDP allocated to research. Government investment in R&D is among the highest as a percentage of GDP of any of the nations we studied, but half goes for defense and has questionable benefits for industry. Government investment should be maintained, but funds should be channeled through universities and specialized research institutes and not into direct subsidies.

More troubling in many ways than the government R&D program is the low rate of overall R&D spending in firms. A reallocation of both government and company attention toward commercial R&D will be necessary for successfully restarting the upgrading process.

Demand Conditions. Without demanding and sophisticated buyers, innovation and dynamism will be stunted in British industry. Britain enjoys demand-side advantages in luxury and leisure-related goods. The challenge

is to upgrade British consumer and industrial demand and broaden the areas
in which British companies benefit from challenging and well-informed
buyers. Improving the education and training of workers and managers will
contribute to this aim.

The prosperous London and South East markets can be the cutting edge
of new British consumer demand conditions. Elimination of state-sanctioned
monopolies and regulations which restrict consumer choice will also create
more demand-side pressure.

Financial Markets. The London financial markets have contributed to
the renewal of British industry by providing a vehicle to fund new companies
and to restructure old ones. Yet the time is rapidly approaching when they
may become a barrier instead of a benefit to British competitive advantage.

As in the United States, institutional investors seem to have little commitment to companies nor do they have a meaningful role in corporate governance. Tax laws governing the treatment of goodwill encourage mergers.
Corporate goals revolve around short-term financial results. A group of
large British conglomerates has emerged which buys and sells unrelated
companies, but whose financial orientation does little in the long run to
upgrade true competitive advantage in British industry. Some of them, such
as BAT and Lonrho, have come under fire.

In 1988, long-term capital gains tax rates (adjusted for inflation) were
equalized with those on ordinary income, removing the incentive for investors
to make sustained commitment to companies. The result of all of this is
that American-style earnings pressures threaten to dominate British management thinking. A long-term bias is in the interests of the national economies.
Policies should be adjusted to create one.

Regulation and Government Ownership. British industry (like that in
many other nations) has been undermined by monopoly companies and
protective regulations in important fields such as telecommunications, ports,
and health care, to name a few. Innovation in these fields is stunted and
they also undermine competitive advantage in the industries that depend
on them as well as those that supply them.

Privatization has proceeded quickly in Britain, a very positive sign. However, there is still a tendency to leave monopoly positions, or obstacles to
competition, intact.[12] In the case of airlines, for example, British Airways
and British Caledonian were allowed to merge.

Privatization without effective competition defeats much of the economic
purpose of the policy change. Fortunately, the Thatcher government is showing signs of grasping this point; British Airways has been forced to cede
some routes to competitors, and the recent privatization of the electricity
industry has sought to introduce competition in power generation by creating

two separate companies. Nevertheless, a more consistent concern with competition is necessary.

Competition. A reversal of decades-old corporate complacency in Britain can only be accomplished through vigorous domestic rivalry. Where there are only one or two British firms in an industry, pressures for intervention and protection are irresistible. The wave of mergers and takeovers today threatens to go too far in consolidating British industry. The U.S. model is a poor one to follow.

A strong orientation toward antitrust is increasingly necessary in Britain. While efforts underway in 1989 to introduce more competition into areas such as the legal profession and health care are positive steps, albeit with some implementation problems, a more serious concern is the state of competition in the core of British industry. GEC and Siemens, for example, were recently permitted to divide up Plessey and eliminate effective British rivalry.

New Business Formation. British economic prosperity will not be complete without a faster rate of new business formation, to make headway in reducing British unemployment. Revitalization of established industries will often lead to fewer employees, not more. New business formation depends on skills and ideas, on appropriate motivation and goals, on active competition, and on access to capital. One of the urgent reasons to upgrade British education, especially in universities, is to contribute to seeding new ventures. Britain cannot rely on foreign investment for job creation.

THE AGENDA FOR THE UNITED STATES

The United States has entered a period during which its future economic prosperity may well be set for many decades. The economy has been drifting for at least the last decade toward the wealth-driven stage. Positions in many advanced industries have eroded. Goals of firms and investors have turned away from sustained investment. Competition has slackened. The gap in standard of living between the highly educated and skilled employees and those with less training is becoming more apparent. Companies are turning to government for help in suspending competitive pressures that create appetites for more help. The orientation has turned from offensive to defensive.

The recent improvements in productivity growth and exports, while encouraging, are not yet a sign of fundamental change. Productivity growth reflects in no small part a one-shot restructuring and downsizing in many industries, and recent figures show that the period of growth above historical norms may be short-lived. Net investment still lags behind other nations despite the fact that industry is operating at near capacity. Export growth reflects a sharp devaluation of the dollar and real wage declines, both of which reduce the long-run standard of living. The bases of renewed sustained productivity growth are still not in place.

There are many areas of underlying advantage in the United States, such as top universities, unique demand conditions in some fields, the capacity for risk taking, and vibrant new business formation. There are also demographic forces which will create pressures for rising productivity growth and a higher rate of savings. The rapid pace of change in technology promises to provide many opportunities for American inventiveness and entrepreneurship. These create the potential for the United States to enter a period of sustained prosperity. At the same time, however, the erosion of U.S. position over the last two decades signals some strong constraints to further advancement.

A debate is taking place about whether America will remain a great power, with strong proponents on both sides.[13] This debate is about the wrong question. That America will remain a great power is not in doubt, because of its sheer size, resources, and the strengths I have explored earlier. The issue instead is whether the American economy has the dynamism to maintain or raise the American standard of living, or whether the nation will slowly lose ground in relative terms. The question is whether America will restore its ability to compete in sophisticated segments or industries or whether trade problems will be "solved" through continued devaluation, real wage sacrifices, and exports of natural-resource-intensive goods.

American firms and the American government have important choices to make. The nation is teetering between a renewed commitment to traditional American values and a retreat to consolidation, protection, and defensiveness. Some of the most important choices include those that follow:

The Policy Model. American policy in recent decades has often seemingly been based on the implicit premises that the value of the dollar, the intrusion of government, and unfair practices by foreign nations are the cause of any difficulties facing U.S. industry. Such a view of national advantage is, to say the least, incomplete. It has led to policies such as relaxing regulatory standards and allowing horizontal mergers, which usually undermine instead of help U.S. industry. More importantly, acceptance of this model has delayed steps in many important policy areas that fall outside of it.

It may be even more accurate to say that there has been no real consensus on a policy model at all. Much energy has been spent debating whether there are problems in U.S. industry, when the vast majority in U.S. industry agree there are. Both American firms and the U.S. government need a new and richer view of the underpinnings of national advantage. Both firms and governments must understand that improvement and innovation are at the core of national success, not low wages, loose regulation, or easy mergers.

Human Resources. America cannot regain preeminence in innovation without human resources at least on a par with those in other advanced nations. While there is great strength at the highest educational levels, the *average* quality of human resources is lagging behind that of other advanced nations. As competition has internationalized and become increasingly based on knowledge, workers without skills are finding their livelihoods more and more threatened by the lower wages in developing nations.[14] A fundamental commitment to upgrading human resources is necessary.

America spends more as a fraction of GNP on public education than most other advanced countries (6.8 percent in 1987 versus 5.0 percent in Japan and 4.5 percent in Germany).[15] The problem is less money than quality. There is the need for higher standards for educational quality that match or exceed those of other advanced nations. Hours of schooling need to be increased. New programs are necessary to boost teacher pay, prestige, and competence. A new national effort to upgrade technical and vocational schools, which are a vital link in developing specialized human resources for industry, must begin immediately. While education should remain a state and local responsibility, a federal role in education is not only legitimate but vital at a time when state and local efforts are incomplete. National standards will help rapidly raise performance targets. Federal resources are required to catalyze improvements in facilities and the quality of teaching.

Yet improving the general education system in the United States is *not* enough. What is required for competitive advantage is specialized skills tailored to particular industries. American companies must understand more clearly that human resources will be what really determine their long-term competitive position relative to international rivals, not capital costs or the value of the dollar. There is a need for firms to play a greater role in the training and continual upgrading of their workforce. American companies must work more closely with the educational institutions in their regions, as well as with those elsewhere in the nation that have high-quality programs with relevance to their industry. Joint programs with local institutions (both schools and universities) improve the quality of programs and their relevance to industry. Trade associations must also increasingly see their role as human resource development, through creating training centers and working with educational institutions.

There are grounds for optimism. American industry, with a rapidly growing labor force in recent decades, has been largely able to ignore the problem of human resources quality. Pressures to upgrade skills in order to improve the productivity of employees have been blunted. In the decades ahead, however, labor force growth will slow dramatically, and much of the growth will come in minorities and immigrants well down the skill ladder. Labor shortages are already apparent.

These forces promise to mobilize the private sector in America to finally tackle the human resources problem. Companies may begin investing more in their employees and viewing them as assets, thinking that has been prevalent in other nations where workers are scarce. At the same time, the children of baby boom parents will be entering the public schools. When these parents, many of them products of public education, encounter the current state of American schools, a force will be set in motion to improve them. Parents and companies have the opportunity to transform American human resources development in coming decades. Government must do its part to encourage and support these efforts.

Research and Development. The United States has an unequalled university system and a substantial public investment in R&D. The problem is not so much the size of public investment or the quality of the institutions, but the direction, rate, and priorities of U.S. activity. While the United States spends heavily on research, it cannot rely on defense R&D as the engine of research and development in the United States. In 1988, federal support for civilian R&D in real terms was 14 percent below 1980 levels.[16]

More emphasis is needed on stimulating demand for innovative new products in addition to efforts to encourage greater R&D in firms. As experience in other nations has demonstrated, providing domestic buyers with incentives to purchase advanced goods is a powerful stimulus to innovation in the industries that supply them. Selective investment tax credits for purchases of advanced factory and office automation equipment, and rapid regulatory approval of new products, are just two of the approaches employed elsewhere that hold promise.

The core of the American public R&D system should be the universities. This is an area of unique strength, and universities are also a potent source of new business formation. University research funding in real terms is the same as it was twenty years ago, and research facilities are particularly in need of renewal because funding for facilities has been cut drastically. More of the federal R&D money in the United States should go through the National Science Foundation (NSF) to universities instead of to government laboratories. This increases the diffusion rate compared to research in federal laboratories. At the same time, however, more projects should address the development of technologies vital to industry. The traditional focus of NSF has been heavily skewed toward pure science.

A much higher level of interchange between companies and universities is necessary, in part to stimulate more applied research. A suspicion of university-industry collaboration is deep-seated in the academic community, out of concern for independence and academic freedom. The German and

Swiss cases suggest that such collaboration can be positive for both sides.

American university research represents an important potential source of competitive advantage for U.S. companies. Despite the benefits of proximity, however, American companies often seem to lag behind foreign firms in taking advantage of it.[17] American companies must identify and cultivate the important centers of research on technologies important to their industry, and be willing to invest to gain preferential access. Jointly funded research institutes at universities, or research institutes sponsored by trade associations and accessible to all members, are good approaches. Widespread cooperative R&D projects between competitors are *not* the answer, as I have described in Chapter 12.

The real key to a faster rate of innovation in American industry, however, is the behavior of American companies. The rate of investment in innovation must increase if companies are to sustain competitive advantage. Instead, the rate of R&D spending in American companies has been growing more slowly than that in other advanced nations, and preliminary data show a fall in real spending in 1989.

Unfortunately, American firms and the American government are showing signs of being more concerned about yesterday's innovations than about creating tomorrow's. Efforts to extend the life of patents, bills designed to limit severely the imitation of product designs and features, and widespread paranoia about the transmission of American technology abroad through licenses all reflect a lack of confidence and a desire to blunt the force of competition. History shows that this is no way to sustain competitive advantage. While there must be adequate incentives to innovate, the evidence from other nations and from the history of U.S. industry suggests that there are ample incentives without the need for such measures that block the diffusion of technology. A rapid rate of technological advancement, combined with diffusion of technology within national clusters, represents the best combination for productivity growth and sustained economic prosperity. Active rivalry, goals that support sustained investment in industry, and improving human resource quality will be most important ways to achieve it.

National Savings. A low rate of private savings and a large public deficit have pushed up U.S. interest rates and held down stock prices, deterring investment by U.S. companies. One reason why U.S. companies lose market position is that only by harvesting can they achieve profit targets much higher than those in Germany, Japan, and virtually every other nation we studied.

Boosting private savings is difficult because the causes of the savings rate are incompletely understood, but efforts to do so through tax policy (such as further limiting the deductibility of interest expense, raising margin requirements on credit purchases, and providing tax incentives for long-term forms of saving) and other means should continue. Reduction of the government deficit is also essential, because it absorbs savings that could instead lower interest rates, boost stock prices, and stimulate investment. Many observers view deficits principally as a drag on the economy and a problem for future generations. They have equally serious consequences for the incentives of industry.

Demand Conditions. Demand conditions in the United States must improve if American industry is to regain the knack of innovation. The following represent some of the more pressing areas for attention:

Regulation. The United States has backed away from advanced and stringent standards in areas such as product safety, environmental quality, energy efficiency, and working conditions, based on the erroneous view that these "hurt" industry. A good example was the Reagan administration's move to relax federal gas mileage standards, at a time when energy imports are substantial and the burning of gasoline is creating major environmental problems. (The Bush administration's review of this unfortunate policy as well as its new initiatives in the environmental area are encouraging.) Without advanced regulations in areas of legitimate social concern, U.S. industry will lose the innovation race in the affected industries and U.S. products will not sell well to sophisticated customers abroad. Stringent standards for products, environmental quality, and the like not only benefit the social agenda but are vital to the economic agenda.

Regulatory requirements at all levels of government also need to be set with greater attention to their effect on the process of innovation. Regulations should encourage demand for emerging new technologies and products. Too often, their effect is the opposite.

As important as regulatory standards, however, is the *process* by which they are created and enforced. Delays and uncertainty in deciding on standards and in approving or disapproving products and practices waste time and resources and represent a needless drag on innovation in industry. The United States needs a thorough review and overhaul of the process of regulation, including the rules governing how regulations are established, how they are enforced, the product approval process, the right and process of review, and the opportunity for judicial intervention. The regulatory process can contain adequate safeguards while making standards less arbitrary, shortening the time to establish new standards and approve products against them, and limiting redundant reviews and challenges. Legally mandated timetables, and allowing only one legal challenge at the conclusion of regulatory proceedings, are promising approaches.

The same is true in the area of technical standards. The possibility for legal challenges at every step of the process compounds the problem. A more rational and timely approach to establishing standards would help competition advance beyond parochial squabbles over basic technical parameters. It would speed product improvement and upgrading, as well as U.S. entry into foreign markets.

Defense Procurement. There have been recent proposals that the Department of Defense (DoD) take a more active role through its procurement in bolstering industry. While a greater concern in defense procurement with the needs of industry is desirable, and I have described some guidelines for appropriate procurement in the previous chapter, DoD is not an instrument that should be relied upon too heavily. The goals of DoD are skewed toward preserving domestic competitors. This has the danger of leading to protection and to the blunting of rivalry. In addition, defense needs are not the same as civilian needs in most industries. Too much of a role for DoD can be a distraction.

Product Liability. It is time for a systematic overhaul of the U.S. product liability system. Making companies accountable for product liability is beneficial to obtaining high-quality goods and services. However, the ease of filing lawsuits in the United States, often with little merit, combined with huge and uncertain damage awards, goes well beyond the point of benefiting the consumer or U.S. industry.

The effect of the current system is often stifling to innovation, as the patient monitoring industry discussed in Chapter 5 illustrated. There, a promising avenue of innovation into "closed loop" or self-regulating monitoring systems has been all but foreclosed to U.S. firms. Other nations have product liability systems which protect the consumer without tying innovation up in knots. Rapid screening of lawsuits, reasonable caps on damage awards, and mandated resolution procedures short of a full trial would be promising steps.

Goals. Among the most important issues facing American industry are the goals of investors, managers, and employees. All three have been changing in ways that work against upgrading American industry. Investor goals have been reshaped by changes in the American financial markets. Institutional investors dominate ownership but have little influence on corporate governance. Institutions are motivated through the way their own performance is measured to buy and sell positions rather than make sustained commitments to building companies. Current earnings growth is a principal determinant of stock prices. Takeovers are welcomed and encouraged as the only means to deal with entrenched management. A trend toward a greater role for

TABLE 13–2 **Capital Gains Taxation in Leading Nations, 1988**

	Maximum Long-Term Rate	Maximum Short-Term Rate
United States[1]	33%[1]	33%
United Kingdom	40%[2]	40%
Sweden	0%[3]	70%
Canada	17.51%	17.51%
France	16%	16%
Germany	Exempt[4]	56%
Belgium	Exempt	Exempt
Italy	Exempt[5]	Exempt
Japan	Exempt	Exempt
Netherlands	Exempt	Exempt
Hong Kong	Exempt	Exempt
Singapore	Exempt	Exempt
Korea	Exempt	Exempt
Taiwan	Exempt	Exempt
Malaysia	Exempt	Exempt

SOURCES: *The Wall Street Journal,* March 8, 1988; author's additions and corrections.

[1] Rates are the same as those on ordinary income. Many states and some cities also tax capital gains.

[2] Maximum long-term and short-term rates were raised on April 6, 1988 to 40 percent, equal to the maximum rate on ordinary income. Capital gains are indexed for inflation.

[3] The rate reaches 0 percent after five years for many types of assets.

[4] Capital gains rates are planned to be pegged to the ordinary income rate. The highest short- and long-term rates will reach 53 percent by 1990.

[5] Italy is also planning to introduce taxes on capital gains.

institutional investors in corporate governance is centered, ironically, on removing barriers to takeover erected by management and not to influencing the long-term strategy of companies.

Investors have seen rising taxes on capital gains. Most advanced nations do not tax long-term capital gains at all, encouraging investments with long time horizons that carry important social as well as private benefits (see Table 13–2).

Managers, compensated by bonuses based on annual results and holding their positions only a few years, focus on yearly performance. To build the company, they have been increasingly turning to mergers, which require no sacrifice of current profitability. Since compensation is often more correlated with size than profits, mergers are made even more attractive. Attention to stock price has been increasingly driven by the fear of takeover. The sustained investment and risk taking required to build competitive advantage are often not forthcoming.

Employees also are themselves less and less committed to their company or profession. Individuals and families do not invest enough in education and training. Advancement occurs through shifting companies and positions instead of investing in skills. Companies, on their side, are often not committed either. They hire and fire with impunity and underinvest in human resource development.

All this must begin to change if the rate of innovation and upgrading in American industry is to rise. To modify corporate and managerial goals, takeovers are not the best overall solution, as I discussed in the previous chapter. A tax incentive for long-term (over five years) capital gains on equity investments in companies would be a positive step. No similar incentive is needed or justified on bonds, real estate, or other types of assets. Long-term capital gains incentives must be extended to cover not only ordinary investors but also institutions such as pension funds whose investments are now tax exempt. The marginal tax rate on very short-term capital gains (less than twelve months) of both individuals and companies can be raised to further encourage sustained investment and offset any lost tax revenue.

Also needed is a new approach to corporate governance in which the long-term prosperity of the company is made a central concern. Relaxation of the limits on bank ownership of equity shares, for example, represents one potential way to promote a more constructive role by capital providers who could develop deeper long-term relationships with companies. However, no restrictions on takeovers are appropriate because they remain a useful discipline on management.

Company Strategy. American companies, more often losing than gaining position in international markets, must examine their approaches to strategy. The biggest problem is a lost focus on investment and innovation. Instead of investing, companies merge. Instead of innovating, they source products and components abroad that could be made more efficiently using improved technology at home. Instead of investing to improve their domestic suppliers and their local schools and universities, they lobby for tougher trade laws to protect against foreign competitors. Instead of developing skills and capabilities internally, they turn to alliances as an easy "solution."

In the area of corporate strategy, the attraction of diversification remains irresistible in American industry. Despite decades of evidence that most are unprofitable, unrelated mergers continue. Instead of creating businesses internally through taking advantage of company skills, companies make acquisitions that prove impossible to assimilate.

A reorientation is needed in many American companies if they are to achieve true competitive advantage. I have outlined some of the needed steps in Chapter 11. More than anything, a new sense of challenge will be required.

Competition. Nothing has contributed to the drift in American industry more than ebbing rivalry. A long period during which American firms faced little challenge from foreign rivals led to sleepy oligopolies where domestic rivalry was muted. Beginning in the 1960s, mergers began consolidating many industries. Relaxation of antitrust enforcement in the area of mergers has allowed leading competitor to buy leading competitor. Recently, such transactions are being justified, ironically, as enhancing competitiveness. Alliances between leading competitors are also on the rise and are rarely challenged.

A backing away from antitrust enforcement in the area of mergers has also undermined some of the positive developments that have taken place in the area of deregulation. Mergers have led to the creation of *de facto* regional monopolies in the airline industry, for example, despite the fact that deregulation led initially to substantial new entry and a surge of innovation.

At the same time as domestic rivalry has ebbed, U.S. trade policy shifted in the 1970s and 1980s toward protection. International markets have been divided through all sorts of special agreements and deals. The 1988 trade bill has unfortunately made it easier for any industry facing competitive distress to seek protection whether or not unfair trade practices are involved. The result has been further reduction in domestic rivalry and the blunting of competitive pressure from abroad, slowing the process of innovation and upgrading in U.S. industries. In semiconductors, for example, an agreement with Japan has led to rising prices, improving Japanese profits, and chip shortages in U.S. industry.

A renewed commitment to competition is a pressing need. Domestic rivalry is even more important in an era when global markets make sleepy domestic industries vulnerable to challenge. Mergers and alliances among leading competitors should be prohibited. The same standards for mergers among U.S. companies should be applied when approving acquisitions of U.S. companies by foreign firms. Foreign investment in the United States via acquisition should be prohibited if it undermines competition. Direct cooperation among leading competitors should be discouraged and cooperative R&D approved only under the conditions outlined in the previous chapter. Relaxation of antitrust to allow joint production by leading competitors is inappropriate. At the same time, antitrust constraints on the activities of trade associations and on vertical cooperation should be loosened, with safeguards for cases where the aim is collusion or monopolization.

Trade Policy. American trade policy has failed to deal with the real protectionism and intervention violating international rules that does exist in many nations. At the same time, it has moved in the direction of "orderly marketing agreements" which undermine the very essence of competition.

This approach to dealing with trade difficulties is fundamentally flawed, as I have discussed. Any effort to guarantee sales by U.S. firms in any nation or to preserve a set share of the U.S. market will slow innovation in the long run. Managed trade is cartelized trade, and not a real solution. "Temporary" protection to provide the opportunity for adjustment rarely succeeds, as I discussed in Chapter 12.

Trade policy must focus on unfair subsidies and trade barriers, and counter them with compensating tariffs and restrictions on industry investment in the United States by the nation's competitors until foreign practices are modified. At the same time, antitrust scrutiny must guard domestic competition. To make effective trade policy, there must be a clearer voice for U.S. trade. Relative to most nations, the United States has a cumbersome structure for formulating and implementing trade policy. Too many federal agencies, with inconsistent goals, are involved. Trade policy is usually *ad hoc*, set through responding to individual cases. Trade laws have too often become a tool for companies to gain protection and avoid the difficult steps required to be truly competitive. Instead, a more integrated trade policy is needed, along the lines I discussed in Chapter 12.

A Renewed Philosophy. What is in many ways most necessary in the United States is a philosophical shift. Defensiveness and a loss of confidence have crept into American industry and government. The mind-set has developed that devaluation, relaxation of regulations, removal of antitrust, cooperation among leading competitors, policies that create a monopoly in particular technologies, and "temporary" protection will help U.S. industry. These policies, as appealing as they may seem in the short run, will only make further loss of competitive advantage more likely. There is a growing tendency to turn to government to solve competitive difficulties, which, once it starts, is self-perpetuating and ultimately self-defeating. A return to some neglected historical values, of individual initiative, education, competition, long-term investment, tough regulation, and free trade, is long overdue.

NATIONAL AGENDAS IN PERSPECTIVE

Each nation faces its own unique set of issues as well as its own opportunities and constraints in dealing with them. Yet there are clear themes that emerge from our look at each of the nations in turn. The rate of factor creation and upgrading determines the potential rate at which a national economy can advance. The intensity of domestic competition has a great deal to do with whether this potential is achieved. Preserving competition is a continual challenge which becomes greater as a nation's prosperity persists. So is creating and maintaining appropriate goals for firms and employees. Improving demand conditions are also necessary so that firms perceive new buyer needs and are challenged to meet them.

Company strategies must continually evolve. The lure of unrelated diversification is difficult to resist. A well-functioning capital market, combined with investors who make sustained commitments to firms and are active in their governance, must be created and nurtured if firms and a national economy are to prosper. Yet the growing "efficiency" of capital markets in many nations carries paradoxical risks of reducing the rate of investment in companies. Finally, government policy must be constantly shifting, to create the foundation for a more advanced economy. Yet evolution of policy is inevitably retarded by political pressures and special interests that have prospered under the previous rules. It is also held back by the assumption that the same formula will always work even though the nature of international competition and the position of a nation's industry have changed.

As my discussion of the eight nations has illustrated, there is no shortage of issues. There is always the temptation to avoid them through protection or isolation. There is always the false allure of stability and economic concentration. Whether the world economy advances, and what the fate of individual nations will be, will have much to do with whether nations are able to resist these tendencies.

Epilogue

This study has attempted to present a broad and organic view of how firms, industries, and national economies advance and to illustrate its practical application. My hope, more than anything else, is to begin to reshape the perspective with which firms and governments view the true underpinnings of competitive success. Much of what guides company strategy and government policy today is based on flawed premises that must be revised. Companies and economies flourish because of pressures, challenges, and new opportunities, not a docile environment or outside "help" that eliminates the need to improve. Progress comes from change, not from a preoccupation with stability that obstructs it.

My theory is intensely optimistic, providing all firms and nations with the opportunity to prosper, though not all will. Firms themselves hold the power to determine their long-term competitive success. National economic prosperity is not a zero-sum game in which one nation's gain is at the expense of others. A healthy process of economic upgrading can allow all nations to enjoy a rising standard of living. The choices required to act on the prerequisites for economic success, or not to act, will ultimately fall to each nation, and to each company. Yet company strategy and national policy cannot be set by just responding to today's problems; they demand a comprehensive view of competition, and I have tried to provide one here.

My theory highlights and reinforces the importance of differences in nations and of differences in national character. Many contemporary discussions of international competition stress global homogenization and a diminished role for nations. But, in truth, national differences are at the heart of competitive success.

Nations prosper in industries that draw most heavily on unique elements of their histories and characters. Firms can increasingly source labor, materials, components, and even basic product and process technology in global markets. As competition has become more knowledge-intensive, the influence of the national environment has become even more vital. It shapes the way opportunities are perceived, how specialized skills and resources are developed, and the pressures on firms to mobilize resources in rapid and efficient ways. It is the creation of knowledge and the capacity to act, which are the result of a process that is highly localized, that determines competitive success. Regions within nations will also differ markedly in economic prosperity as a result of the same forces. The relative decline of resource-rich regions is another manifestation of the new order.

Some resist open international competition out of a desire to preserve national identity. Instead of submerging national character, however, the removal of protectionism and other distortions to free and open international competition will arguably make national character more decisive. Globalization makes nations more, not less, important.

Dominant nations at a point in time tend to export their culture and character to other nations, as Britain once did through the Empire and America has done in this century via its media, its political and military power, and its companies. Such a process reinforces the exporting nation's competitive advantage through creating foreign demand for the nation's products. Yet the British and American examples illustrate that the national characters of other nations remain intact, and that the power to export culture is no guarantee of sustained economic success.

This study, in a way I could not anticipate, has led me to a conviction that incentives, effort, perseverance, innovation, and especially competition are the source of economic progress in any nation and the basis for productive, satisfied citizens. I am mindful that this may seem to reflect a set of implicit values or perhaps even an ideology that many do not share. But I am not proposing an ideology. This study demonstrates that whatever the system of values or ideology at home, firms meet in global competitive markets whose workings I have sought to describe. My description of their behavior is ideologically neutral; it simply reflects how the world works.

I acknowledge that my conception of economic progress may be uncomfortable to some. The individual incentives and competition I have stressed run counter in some ways to the egalitarianism and group norms present in Sweden or the aversion to fierce competition often seen in Britain. I am convinced, however, that, in the long run, the ability to realize any set of national values today depends on a healthy economy and on having skilled, productive people. As global competition becomes sharper, nations may increasingly have to make choices between maintaining certain values and continued national well-being. In Sweden, for example, environmental sensitivity reinforces national advantage while extreme income redistribution will increasingly detract from it. Japan's protection of farmers and small shopkeepers, and Germany's aversion to advertising, will similarly be more and more costly.

This book comes at a time of remarkable changes in the fundamental precepts that guide some national economies. Socialist nations such as those in Eastern Europe and Asia are openly admitting to themselves that some of their fundamental assumptions have been obstacles to their economic well-being. They are moving haltingly toward economic structures with increased competition and incentives based on performance, whose importance to national competitive advantage this study has demonstrated. Some capitalist nations such as Britain and Sweden that have been most enamored with principles such as state ownership and redistribution are now beginning to modify them.

One might almost feel a sense of relief at this economic convergence. How comforting to imagine a world in which nations, regardless of home ideologies, could compete effectively and peacefully for world markets. One might only hope the world becomes that simple.

As I have demonstrated in earlier chapters, there are disquieting signs that important Western nations, reflecting decades of prosperity, are themselves retreating from some of the very values that the socialist world is now hesitantly embracing. In once vigorous capitalist nations, one sees efforts to blunt competition, to freeze markets, to preserve and protect entrenched positions, and to shorten horizons. Firms and nations move to protect old technology instead of moving on to develop new technology. Euphemisms such as cooperation, alliances, and business-government collaboration are the words of the day. But these slow down the process of competition and make it seem that all can prosper irrespective of skills and initiative.

Such developments leave hanging in the balance the exciting prospects in Europe. The possibility of eliminating restrictions on trade and investment within Europe provides the opportunity and the pressures for a burst of innovation and dynamism that has not been seen for decades. Yet a surge of mergers, alliances, and consortia threatens to eliminate effective European competition in important industries. We learn, for example, that quotas on imports of Japanese cars are to remain, and local content rules have crept into "dumping" investigations and are being used to restrict imports of American television programming. If these tendencies gain the upper hand, the 1990s will prove to be the wrong kind of turning point in European economic history.

The United States runs the risk of succumbing to the same forces. Through calls for relaxing antitrust, encouraging cooperation, managing trade, using dumping rules to block price competition, and limiting the diffusion of technology, America is retreating from competition. The false fears of Americans about Japan, and the false arguments justifying protection and other forms of intervention, are sadly reminiscent of mistaken European concerns about American domination in the 1960s.

Dismaying as this may be, it should not be surprising. In all processes involving great effort and the need for disruptive change, there is a strong and perhaps inevitable desire to stop the process when the initial goals have been met. Once this occurs, both individuals and nations seem to prefer to consume and live off the interest on their wealth and stop creating new wealth.

Closely related to this phenomenon are efforts by nations that have achieved prosperity to guide and cushion the process of structural change and upgrading, but such efforts run a grave risk of stifling it. Social intervention is not conducive to experimentation and innovation, and it blunts productivity growth. Too much government support also eliminates the willingness of the private sector to invest and take risks.

We need not accept these tendencies. Companies and nations have the power to choose between the false allure of concentration, collaboration, and protection, and the reaffirmation of an economic order based on innovation, competition, and rewards for effort. The latter choice is our best hope for sustained economic prosperity.

This is a time for political and business leaders, not stewards. Slow population and workforce growth in all the advanced nations is providing the need to achieve new levels of human skill and contribution. The slow growth of population in the advanced nations also offers the heartening prospect of a brighter economic future for developing nations, which have abundant labor. Revolutionary new technologies (information systems, bioengineering, new materials, superfast microchips, and others) provide the opportunity for an era of innovation and improving productivity in virtually all industries that may well be unprecedented in industrial history. We have only to accept the challenge and act upon it.

Appendix A

Methodology for Preparing the Cluster Charts[1]

Data used to prepare the cluster charts came from a number of sources. The basic source was the *United Nations International Trade Statistic Yearbook*. Other sources included national data on foreign direct investment and services trade, trade association data, and field interviews.

Each nation's chart was constructed by identifying all the industries (both product and service) in which the nation has achieved success in international competition. Industries were defined narrowly and were based as closely as possible on strategically distinct businesses (such as farm tractors) rather than broad sectors (such as agricultural machinery). International success was measured by the presence of significant exports or foreign direct investment drawing on strengths or skills created in the home country (in contrast with portfolio investment abroad).

These measures seek to proxy the existence of true competitive advantage in international terms in an industry. Domestic profitability is not a reliable measure of international success because of the existence of protection. There are also differences in reporting requirements, accounting conventions, rules covering unreported reserves, and the availability of data that make direct profitability comparisons highly suspect. Finally, diversification means that it is not possible to compile profitability by industry.

The starting point for preparing the charts was the UN trade statistics. All three-, four-, and five-digit SITC industries were identified in which the nation's share of the world market economy exports in the industry equalled or exceeded the nation's average share of world trade in the year (referred to as the nation's cutoff). In the case of Japan, for example, the cutoff was 10.1 percent of world exports for 1985. The use of this cutoff is equivalent to selecting those industries in which the nation has a revealed comparative advantage, in the parlance of the literature on international trade.

We included relevant industries at the lowest level of aggregation for which data were published. To eliminate double counting, the four-digit industry was excluded where there were five-digit industries published. Where some of the five-digit industries in a four-digit category were not published, a residual was calculated by subtracting the included five-digit industries from the four-digit industry and calculating its export share. Where the residual exceeded the cutoff, it was included. Industry names were created for the residual industries based on the SITC classification manual definitions. The same procedure was used to eliminate three-digit industries where four-digit industries were published.

This list of industries provided the basic raw material for the cluster chart. The first step in preparing the clustering was to eliminate those industries from the list for which the balance of trade was negative, unless the nation's share of world exports in the industry was two or more times its average share. The rationale for this procedure was that a negative trade balance raised serious questions about the strength of the nation's indigenous competitive advantage in the industry, unless its share of world exports was quite high. In the latter case, the explanation was most likely that the nation had a strong position in one or more segments of the industry (as defined in the SITC classification), though a weak position in others. Including the industry was therefore justified. The choice of two times the cutoff share was arbitrary.

The second rationale for excluding industries was where the nation's exports were believed to be dominated by foreign companies who produced in the nation as part of global manufacturing strategies. Because disaggregated data on foreign investment is scarce, relatively few industries were excluded for this reason. Suspected cases were footnoted.

We also excluded a few industries from the list when their trade was almost exclusively with neighboring nations. For example, U.S. automobile chassis exports are heavily skewed toward Canada. A preponderance of trade with neighbors indicated that the nation's competitive advantage was not significant in international terms and trade solely reflected geographic proximity, unless we had indications of significant foreign direct investment by the nation's firms in the industry. In the latter case, the industry was left on the list.

The list of industries emerging from the UN trade data was supplemented in a number of ways. First, industries were added where available data indicated that the nation's firms had made substantial foreign direct investments, if the investments were based on skills and strengths developed in the nation. We found few instances in the manufacturing and agricultural sectors where there was significant foreign investment and not *also* a significant export share. Exports and foreign investment occur together, and complement each other in global strategies.

Service industries were also added to the cluster chart, using national data on invisible trade, other published sources, and interviews. Finally, a variety of other specific industries were added to the list, often as subcategories of broader industries that showed up in the trade data. We included industries where there was a clear indication of substantial competitive strength. In each case, available data and our judgment was used to classify the strength of the nation's position in the industry. Each industry added to the cluster chart based on other sources is marked with an asterisk after its name.

In a number of industries, the strength of the nation's position in an industry measured by exports was upgraded. This occurred primarily in industries where the nation had substantial foreign direct investment in an industry in which it also had a significant share of world exports. In such cases, a double asterisk appears after the industry listing.

We also added industries to the chart whose export value was in the top fifty industries in the nation and whose trade balance was positive to modestly negative, even if the nation's share of world exports fell below the cutoff. The presence of such substantial exports for the nation was taken as an indication of competitive advantage in one or more industry segments, unless we had some evidence of substantial subsidies or other trade distortions.

Choosing the industries to include or upgrade in competitive strength calculated from the UN trade data necessarily required judgment on the part of the researchers. Since data on foreign investment and services trade are highly incomplete, there was no choice but to make judgments based on inputs from many sources. The alternative, to leave out all industries not showing up in the UN trade statistics, was deemed unacceptable because large groups of important industries in some nations would be ignored.

Our posture in including industries not reflected in the trade data was conservative. We required a strong indication of competitive strength to add an industry to the chart. Nonetheless, there are no doubt errors or omissions that remain. It is unfortunately not feasible to list the sources used to add each industry. The sources can be obtained by contacting the author.

THE CLUSTER CHART

The cluster chart represents an effort to display all the industries in which a nation has competitive advantage in a way that highlights the pattern of competitive industries and the connections among them. Because my theory places strong emphasis on demand conditions as well as on the vertical linkages among industries, the basic classification system in the chart, illustrated in Figure A-1, is based on end-use application. Its rationale is described in Chapter 7.

Within broad end-use categories, the chart highlights the vertical connections among industries. The primary goods themselves are listed first, divided

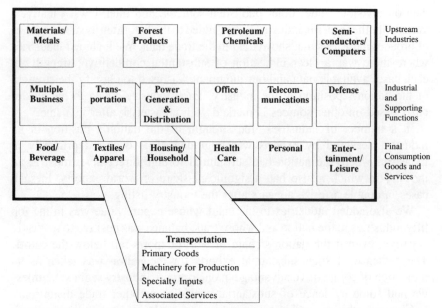

as appropriate between self-contained components and end products. Then the machinery used to make the primary goods is listed. Next, any specialized inputs that go into them are displayed. Finally, any service industries that are closely connected are indicated. Where its end-use application was not clearly linked to one of the broad sectors, the industry was assigned to the Multiple Business heading.

Industries are positioned on the chart using the best judgments of the researchers, given an extensive knowledge of the nation involved. Placements were reviewed by experts from the nation in most cases.

The same industry might be placed at a different location on the chart in different nations if the researchers' judgment was that this best reflected the segments of relative strength. For example, pumps might be classified as machinery used in chemical production in one nation if the researchers had information that the nation's pump manufacturers were strong in that particular end use. In another nation, pumps might be classified in the Multiple Business category if the nation's pump producers were competitive in supplying broad lines of pumps to many industries.

Certain conventions were followed for positioning certain industries. In the Foods/Beverages sector, foods sold in their initial form were subclassified under Basic Foods while foods which underwent a transformation process were subclassified under Processed Foods. Food products not for human consumption, usually animal feed, were listed as Specialty Inputs. In the Textile cluster, fibers and yarns were listed as Specialty Inputs; in the Transportation cluster, parts were designated as Specialty Inputs. Industries listed in the Multiple Business cluster were industries that produced goods for industrial purposes but were not classifiable as any particular industry.

To indicate visually those industries with particularly strong positions, industries were listed on the cluster charts in three different typefaces. Industries with a world export share from the cutoff value to *twice* the cutoff value are listed in roman type. Industries with export shares from *two to four* times the cutoff are listed in bold italics. Industries with shares of *more than four times* the cutoff are listed in a bold sans serif face. Asterisks are used to signify industries that were added or upgraded.

The basic classification system in the chart cannot possibly capture all the connections among industries, particularly those between horizontally related industries. Shading has been employed for each nation to signify some of the most important of these connections.

The cluster charts for each nation reveal substantial and often striking interconnections among the industries in which it is internationally successful. Based on our industry research, I believe that the clusters would be even sharper if more detailed and complete data were available. Such data would likely illuminate clearer connections among machinery, inputs, and end-use industries, because machinery and input categories tend to be more aggregated. In addition, nations would hold higher shares in narrower industries and segments now lumped in broader categories.

Each cluster chart is necessarily an approximation, and legitimate disagreements are possible about the headings, subheadings, and classification of particular industries. Nonetheless, I believe that the cluster chart represents an accurate and hopefully useful overall picture of the economy of the nations included in the study. Others can supplement and improve the charts in subsequent research.

CHANGES IN POSITION

Cluster charts were prepared for 1985, 1978, and 1971. Most of the analysis of changes in position employed the comparison between 1978 and 1985 data. This is because 1978 was the first year in which the new, more detailed trade classification system (SITC Rev. 2) was in use. Data for 1971, much less satisfactory, were examined for broad trends only, except for the United States.

In addition to the shifting composition of the cluster charts, we examined the change in world export share by industry. The pattern of such changes by type of industry and cluster was analyzed.

Given the scarcity of data, detailed analysis was not possible on changing position in services nor for those industries characterized by significant FDI. Qualitative impressions of the changes in position of such industries that could be gleaned from our field research are discussed.

Computations of Trade Patterns

In analyzing trade patterns, a number of measures were used to compare a nation's relative position in a given industry or cluster. The first is *export share*, or the nation's share of world market economy exports in the industry. For example, Switzerland's 34.1 percent export share in watches signifies that the Swiss exported just over a third of the total value of watch exports in 1985.

The second measure was *share of total country exports*, which is the absolute share of a nation's total exports represented by a given industry or industry cluster. The third measure calculated was the *share of world cluster exports*. To do so, a cluster chart including all industries was constructed for the world market economy. Industries were classified based on the end use most common in most countries. Each nation's position in each broad cluster was compared with the world cluster in terms of its share of exports, change in position, and size. Occasionally, a nation's cluster might contain industries not appearing on the world cluster chart because of the particular target markets of firms in that nation.

The share of world cluster exports compared the nation's exports to total world exports of industries in the cluster. For example, a 17.9 percent share of world cluster exports in Food/Beverages specialty inputs for the United States indicates that the United States accounted for 17.9 percent of total world exports of all specialty inputs related to food and beverages. Because the classification of industries to clusters occasionally varied among countries, the world exports in the cluster were adjusted to make the universe of industries comparable for calculation purposes.

Our comparative analysis within and across nations began with a look at changes in these basic measures over time. As with the cluster charts, our benchmark years were 1978 and 1985. We analyzed changes in the export share in an industry to discern the patterns. We were also particularly interested in how different vertical stages were either gaining or losing position as well as the changing positions of industries at the three levels in the overall cluster chart.

Natural Resource Dependence

Since it is important based on my theory to distinguish between competitive advantage based on inherited factors and that due to other sources, we analyzed the exports of selected nations to measure their dependence on natural resources. We identified some 264 industries that relied heavily on natural resources (including agricultural land) and where there was limited further processing by the exporting nation, based on industry definitions and general knowledge of the industries themselves. The resulting summary statistics are given in Chapter 9.

Appendix B

Supplementary Data on National Trade Patterns

TABLE B–1 Top 50 U.S. Industries in Terms of World Export Value, 1971

Industry	Share of Total World Exports	Export Value ($ thousands)	Import Value ($ thousands)	Share of Total U.S. Exports
Aircraft	77.5	2,552,652	79,887	5.9
Motor vehicle parts	32.3	2,175,245	1,105,072	5.0
Soya beans	97.4	1,326,819	8	3.1
Passenger motor vehicles	8.8	1,188,933	5,296,466	2.7
Nonelectrical power machinery	25.8	1,187,741	921,674	2.7
Unmilled wheat	35.8	1,004,729	648	2.3
Organic chemicals	44.1	989,723	400,286	2.3
Office machine parts	55.9	927,810	121,151	2.1
Coal, excluding briquettes	53.4	901,598	569	2.1
Aircraft parts	49.3	852,619	257,888	2.0
Unmilled maize	39.6	746,415	7,693	1.7
Excavating, leveling machinery	35.6	711,140	0	1.6
Other nonelectric machines	17.5	697,413	255,299	1.6
Raw cotton	25.1	583,162	6,568	1.3
Lorries, trucks	16.3	542,259	437,840	1.2
Lifting, loading machines	25.0	497,138	74,704	1.1
Other telecommunications equipment	28.8	492,649	243,036	1.1
Transistors, valves	32.7	480,147	259,160	1.1
Unmanufactured tobacco	41.1	466,135	88,724	1.1
Measuring, controlling instruments	32.0	463,004	61,750	1.1
Accounting machines, computers	35.2	462,382	196,190	1.1

TABLE **B-1** (*Continued*)

Industry	Share of Total World Exports	Export Value ($ millions)	Import Value ($ millions)	Share of Total U.S. Exports
Medical instruments, optical apparatus	18.5	431,410	319,364	1.0
Chemicals	18.0	423,826	95,342	1.0
Vegetable oil residues	41.6	419,954	1,319	1.0
Nonroad tractors	34.2	417,783	87,172	1.0
Electronic measuring, control equipment	29.7	417,330	83,370	1.0
Electrical machinery	16.8	400,778	241,468	0.9
Aircraft gas, jet turbines	36.8	381,077	34,505	0.9
Electric power machines	18.1	344,630	145,792	0.8
Switchgear	17.2	339,748	116,900	0.8
Soft fixed vegetable oils	33.1	326,749	22,457	0.8
Products of polymerization	12.4	322,943	0	0.7
Kraft paper, paperboard	37.2	283,110	10,322	0.7
Machine tools for metalworking	12.8	272,179	90,302	0.6
Buses, road tractors	22.3	267,935	28,540	0.6
Rough sawn, veneer conifer logs	75.5	264,628	3,943	0.6
Photo film	27.3	259,298	111,008	0.6
Pumps for liquids	24.2	242,221	53,321	0.6
Animal oils and fats	47.4	241,836	11,926	0.6
Medicinal and pharmaceutical products	17.7	233,247	109,457	0.5
Nondomestic refrigeration equipment	39.3	232,303	0	0.5
Pumps for gases	23.9	230,507	74,165	0.5
Petroleum jelly, mineral wastes	10.4	224,011	57,113	0.5
Powered tools	19.8	219,113	73,257	0.5
Metal manufactures	13.2	217,831	207,767	0.5
Cocks, valves	18.6	215,762	57,436	0.5
Iron and steel scrap	37.1	215,761	13,551	0.5
Products of condensation	16.4	211,217	0	0.5
Tools	16.4	210,428	97,774	0.5
Pulp and waste paper	24.6	207,933	119,656	0.5
TOTAL				63.9

NOTE: No import data are reported if import value is less than 0.3 percent of the total trade for 1985.

FIGURE B-1 Percentage of Exports by Cluster and Vertical Stage, United States, 1971

Materials/Metals, Forest Products, Semiconductors/Computers, Petroleum/Chemicals, Upstream Industries

	Materials/Metals SCE	SWCE	Forest Products SCE	SWCE	Semiconductors/Computers SCE	SWCE	Petroleum/Chemicals SCE	SWCE	UPSTREAM INDUSTRIES SCE	SWCE
Primary Goods	2.2	3.0	2.1	7.5	2.2	33.9	6.1	6.4	12.6	4.0
Machinery	0.5	23.0	—	0.0	—	—	—	—	0.5	13.7
Specialty Inputs	0.2	1.1	—	—	—	—	—	—	0.2	1.1
Total	2.9	3.1	2.1	7.1	2.2	33.9	6.1	6.4	13.3	5.9

Multiple Business, Transportation, Power Generation & Distribution, Office, Telecommunications, Defense, Industrial and Supporting Functions

	Multiple Business SCE	SWCE	Transportation SCE	SWCE	Power Generation & Distribution SCE	SWCE	Office SCE	SWCE	Telecommunications SCE	SWCE	Defense SCE	SWCE	INDUSTRIAL AND SUPPORTING FUNCTIONS SCE	SWCE
Primary Goods	6.9	18.3	13.1	18.2	4.4	19.4	2.2	27.0	1.1	17.3	—	0.0	27.7	18.7
Machinery	2.1	12.7	0.0	0.0	—	—	0.3	17.5	—	—	—	—	2.4	2.8
Specialty Inputs	—	0.0	8.0	28.0	0.6	66.5	—	—	—	—	—	—	8.6	27.0
Total	9.0	15.9	21.1	20.9	5.0	21.1	2.5	25.3	1.1	17.3	—	0.0	38.7	19.5

Food/Beverage, Textiles/Apparel, Housing/Household, Health Care, Personal, Entertainment/Leisure, Final Consumption Goods and Services

	Food/Beverage SCE	SWCE	Textiles/Apparel SCE	SWCE	Housing/Household SCE	SWCE	Health Care SCE	SWCE	Personal SCE	SWCE	Entertainment/Leisure SCE	SWCE	FINAL CONSUMPTION GOODS AND SERVICES SCE	SWCE
Primary Goods	7.2	9.4	0.1	0.3	0.2	1.1	0.7	8.6	0.5	8.6	1.9	5.9	10.6	6.2
Machinery	1.1	18.9	—	0.0	—	—	—	—	—	—	—	—	1.1	7.0
Specialty Inputs	6.1	16.6	1.9	6.4	0.0	0.0	—	—	1.2	10.9	—	0.0	9.2	0.8
Total	14.4	12.1	2.0	2.7	0.2	0.9	0.7	8.6	1.7	10.1	1.9	5.3	20.9	7.5
													73.0	10.3

Note: Totals may not add due to rounding
Key: SCE   Share of country's total exports 1985
SWCE   Share of world cluster exports 1985

TABLE B–2 Top Fifty Swiss Industries in Terms of Export Value, 1985

Industry	Share of Total World Exports	Export Value ($ millions)	Import Value ($ millions)	Share of Total Swiss Exports
Watches	34.1	1,413,763	47,464	5.14
Medicaments with hormones	12.3	961,084	246,227	3.50
Measuring, controlling instruments	4.9	775,446	335,890	2.82
Heterocyclic compounds	14.0	696,186	245,601	2.53
Synthetic organic dyes	25.3	664,318	211,208	2.42
Switchgear	5.4	613,595	275,710	2.23
Cut unset nonindustrial diamonds	9.6	585,833	909,277	2.13
Machinery for special industries	5.0	474,241	132,651	1.73
Metal cutting machine tools	15.3	424,457	55,467	1.54
Precious metal jewelry	8.1	372,719	531,262	1.36
Weaving machines (looms)	45.1	361,864	11,671	1.32
Amide compounds	26.6	321,689	34,613	1.17
Other metalworking machine tools	9.5	314,943	85,821	1.15
Rough, unsorted diamonds	89.3	303,694	15,548	1.10
Herbicides	20.6	275,488	24,629	1.00
Phenoplasts	6.2	263,147	236,642	0.96
Electrical machinery	5.1	253,299	137,625	0.92
Cheese and curd	6.2	236,760	68,825	0.86
Precious metal jewelry, pearls	23.9	230,464	65,241	0.84
Electromechanical hand tools	17.6	228,209	48,674	0.83
Bleached woven cotton	5.1	224,392	77,982	0.82
Copolymers of vinyl chloride	5.2	216,765	487,505	0.79
Typesetting, bookbinding machinery, parts	10.5	215,268	59,212	0.78
Oxygen-function amino compounds	10.8	212,415	69,353	0.77
Textured yarn, containing polyamide	25.9	212,011	36,925	0.77
Clocks, clock and watch parts	13.0	210,745	83,206	0.77
Base metal manufactures	2.9	204,132	170,143	0.74
Miscellaneous chemical products	2.5	201,124	214,703	0.73
Cocks, valves	3.7	200,934	135,124	0.73
Mixed perfume substances	17.2	194,333	22,396	0.71
DC motors, rotary converters	6.4	192,597	152,555	0.70
Provitamins and vitamins	21.9	191,703	74,055	0.70
Articles of plastic	2.8	182,566	233,626	0.66
Loom, knitting machine parts	24.1	181,030	38,107	0.66
Fans, blowers, and parts	19.2	180,650	87,975	0.66
Packaging, bottling, machines	7.7	179,912	85,955	0.65

TABLE **B–2** (*Continued*)

Industry	Share of Total World Exports	Export Value ($ millions)	Import Value ($ millions)	Share of Total Swiss Exports
Hand paintings	10.3	169,447	121,838	0.62
Optical instruments	9.9	169,289	65,462	0.62
Radiotelephonic receivers, TV cameras, parts	1.2	168,583	156,930	0.61
Precious, semiprecious stones	15.2	168,344	210,450	0.61
Nonmonetary gold	2.2	165,753	102,666	0.60
Edible products, preparations	4.7	165,002	59,652	0.60
Blades, tips for tools	4.8	161,881	93,149	0.59
Gas generators, furance burners	3.9	161,457	84,255	0.59
Rolled platinum, platinum metals	13.6	158,800	90,900	0.58
Medical instruments	3.7	153,235	77,915	0.56
Alkaloids and derivatives	32.0	152,366	8,588	0.55
Clocks with water movements	17.3	151,578	89,838	0.55
Hearing, orthopedic aids	15.9	151,006	37,710	0.55
Aircraft reaction engines	6.8	141,765	49,331	0.52
TOTAL				55.34

NOTE: No import data are reported if import value is less than 0.3 percent of the total trade for 1985.

FIGURE B-2 Percentage of Exports by Cluster and Vertical Stage, Switzerland

Upstream Industries

	Materials/Metals SCE	ΔSCE	SWCE	ΔSWCE	Forest Products SCE	ΔSCE	SWCE	ΔSWCE	Semiconductors/Computers SCE	ΔSCE	SWCE	ΔSWCE	Petroleum/Chemicals SCE	ΔSCE	SWCE	ΔSWCE	UPSTREAM INDUSTRIES SCE	SWCE
Primary Goods	3.6	0.2	0.9	+0.0	0.8	0.3	0.5	0.1	0.0	+0.0	0.0	-0.1	8.0	1.2	0.7	-0.2	12.5	0.6
Machinery	0.2	-0.1	1.3	-0.1	0.2	+0.0	2.1	-0.0	—	—	—	—	—	—	—	—	0.4	0.7
Specialty Inputs	—	—	—	—	—	—	—	—	—	—	—	—	—	—	—	—	—	—
Total	3.8	0.1	0.7	-0.1	1.0	0.3	0.6	0.1	0.0	+0.0	0.0	-0.1	8.0	1.2	0.6	-0.2	12.8	0.6

Industrial & Supporting Functions

	Multiple Business SCE	ΔSCE	SWCE	ΔSWCE	Transportation SCE	ΔSCE	SWCE	ΔSWCE	Power Generation & Distribution SCE	ΔSCE	SWCE	ΔSWCE	Office SCE	ΔSCE	SWCE	ΔSWCE	Telecommunications SCE	ΔSCE	SWCE	ΔSWCE	Defense SCE	ΔSCE	SWCE	ΔSWCE	INDUSTRIAL & SUPPORTING FUNCTIONS SCE	SWCE
Primary Goods	16.0	0.9	5.0	-1.4	1.6	-0.4	0.2	-0.1	4.4	-0.6	3.4	-1.1	0.6	-0.2	1.7	-0.8	0.0	-0.1	0.0	-1.0	0.0	-0.7	0.0	-4.3	22.6	1.8
Machinery	8.9	0.9	8.8	-0.2	—	—	—	—	—	—	—	—	1.6	0.1	11.0	-2.7	—	—	—	—	—	—	—	—	10.4	7.8
Specialty Inputs	3.3	-0.2	16.7	-7.2	0.4	+0.0	0.1	-0.1	—	—	—	—	0.2	0.2	7.1	1.0	—	—	—	—	—	—	—	—	3.9	1.2
Total	28.1	1.6	6.4	-1.4	2.1	-0.4	0.5	-0.1	4.4	-0.6	2.9	0.1	2.3	0.1	3.8	-0.8	0.0	-0.1	0.0	-1.0	0.0	-0.7	0.0	-4.3	36.9	2.1

Final Consumption Goods & Services

	Food/Beverage SCE	ΔSCE	SWCE	ΔSWCE	Textiles/Apparel SCE	ΔSCE	SWCE	ΔSWCE	Housing/Household SCE	ΔSCE	SWCE	ΔSWCE	Health Care SCE	ΔSCE	SWCE	ΔSWCE	Personal SCE	ΔSCE	SWCE	ΔSWCE	Entertainment/Leisure SCE	ΔSCE	SWCE	ΔSWCE	FINAL CONSUMPTION GOODS & SERVICES SCE	SWCE
Primary Goods	2.1	-0.0	0.5	-0.0	2.6	-0.2	1.0	-0.4	0.9	0.1	0.6	-0.0	7.0	0.2	7.2	-3.4	8.0	-2.2	6.3	-5.5	0.3	0.1	0.1	+0.0	20.8	1.6
Machinery	1.1	-0.1	2.1	-0.1	3.9	-0.6	12.5	-2.4	—	—	—	—	—	—	—	—	—	—	—	—	0.0	-0.1	2.1	-0.7	5.0	5.5
Specialty Inputs	1.5	0.2	0.6	+0.0	4.5	-0.2	3.1	-0.5	—	—	—	—	—	—	—	—	—	—	—	—	0.2	+0.0	0.6	-0.1	6.2	1.2
Total	4.7	0.1	0.6	-0.0	11.0	-1.0	2.4	-0.7	0.9	0.1	0.6	0.1	7.0	0.2	7.2	-3.4	8.0	-2.2	4.4	-1.9	0.5	0.1	0.2	0.1	32.0	1.7

Grand Total: 81.8 / 1.4

Note: Totals may not add due to rounding

Key:
SCE — Share of country's total exports 1985
ΔSCE — Change in share of country's exports 1978–1985
SWCE — Share of world cluster exports 1985
ΔSWCE — Change in share of world cluster exports 1978–1985

TABLE B–3 Comparative Profile of Competitive Industries That Gained and Lost World Export Share by Nation

		Average Total World Exports in the Industry (000) 1985	Average Nation's Exports in the Industry (000) 1985	Weighted Average Change in Industry World Exports 1978–85	Weighted Average Change in Nation's Industry Exports 1978–85
Japan	Increases	$2,981,099	$732,956	55.24%	136.22%
	Decreases	1,667,419	267,516	36.00	(11.48)
Korea	Increases	1,932,087	159,706	44.71	287.93
	Decreases	1,587,293	55,700	64.57	(12.44)
Sweden	Increases	2,632,655	119,379	42.86	78.24
	Decreases	1,983,637	93,831	50.64	0.73
Switzerland	Increases	1,391,817	91,146	29.35	95.36
	Decreases	2,006,804	108,865	54.84	(3.28)
United States	Increases	1,777,908	562,672	55.74	148.69
	Decreases	1,481,673	255,086	47.70	(14.57)
Germany	Increases	917,058	212,003	21.26	59.83
	Decreases	2,283,197	345,330	59.31	7.77
Italy	Increases	1,388,338	174,093	26.68	82.58
	Decreases	3,023,434	168,382	60.87	(4.20)
United Kingdom	Increases	4,923,368	545,550	63.53	314.94
	Increases*	1,837,540	248,035	70.73	170.91
	Decreases	1,798,914	130,998	46.57	(18.37)
Averages	Increases*	1,857,313	287,499	43.32	132.47
	Decreases	1,979,046	178,214	46.63	(5.55)

* Excluding crude petroleum, motor and aviation spirit, and liquefied propane and butane (United Kingdom only)

Averages weighted by the size of the industries in each group.

SOURCE: Computations from *United Nations Trade Statistics.*

TABLE **B–4** Top Fifty Swedish Industries in Terms of Export Value, 1985

Industry	Share of Total World Exports	Export Value ($ millions)	Import Value ($ millions)	Share of Total Swedish Exports
Passenger motor vehicles	2.6	2,101,624	986,086	6.90
Trucks	4.4	938,790	169,263	3.08
Motor vehicle bodies, parts, accessories	2.2	893,713	722,476	2.94
Sawn conifer lumber	26.4	888,112	10,168	2.92
Bleached soda, sulphate woodpulp	15.5	818,021	16,369	2.69
Telecommunication equipment, parts	4.7	644,128	210,783	2.12
ADP equipment	8.4	565,341	655,235	1.86
Kraftpaper, paperboard	41.7	545,304	13,676	1.79
Gas oils	3.2	539,714	737,835	1.77
Newsprint	8.9	514,813	—	1.69
Line telephone equipment	9.3	489,513	31,043	1.61
Roadrollers/civil engineering equipment	4.8	460,792	81,504	1.51
Medicinal, pharmaceutical products	2.6	405,469	31,178	1.33
Kraft liner	31.7	378,772	—	1.24
Copolymers vinychloride	2.0	361,300	50,013	1.19
Measuring, controlling instruments	2.3	360,963	352,025	1.19
Fuel oils	1.4	359,659	484,837	1.18
Blades, tips for tools	9.9	337,832	89,082	1.11
Other coated paper in bulk	12.6	328,646	64,447	1.08
Other paper and paperboard	8.7	318,969	47,718	1.05
Machinery for special industries	3.0	287,183	205,891	0.94
ADP machine parts	1.3	277,463	444,782	0.91
Switchgear	2.2	244,509	331,298	0.80
Articles of precut paper	5.9	232,765	90,981	0.76
Centrifuges	17.2	230,085	33,056	0.76
Uncoated writing paper	7.1	229,894	13,158	0.76
Wood furniture	5.7	229,668	64,997	0.75
Nonagglomerated iron ore	4.4	215,835	2,464	0.71
High carbon steel bars	7.7	211,841	53,283	0.70
Iron, steel seamless tubes	3.5	202,930	52,413	0.67
Spirit jet fuel	2.4	200,072	405,689	0.66
War firearms, ammunition	4.2	191,485	56,473	0.63
Other cargo vessels	1.6	191,154	193,445	0.63
Articles of plastic	2.8	183,461	192,980	0.60

TABLE **B–4** (*Continued*)

Industry	Share of Total World Exports	Export Value ($ millions)	Import Value ($ millions)	Share of Total Swedish Exports
Coated writing paper	5.8	182,844	30,696	0.60
Ball, roller bearings	5.6	180,596	111,955	0.59
Lifting, loading machine parts	4.7	179,081	98,858	0.59
Planed conifer lumber	5.5	174,783	251	0.57
Other base metal manufactures	2.5	173,840	173,259	0.57
Motor vehicle piston engines	2.9	172,944	48,699	0.57
Other household type equipment	2.6	168,162	124,305	0.55
Gas generators, furance burners	3.9	163,838	93,459	0.54
Nonelectric power hand tools	19.8	159,776	14,088	0.52
Plastic coated paper	15.0	159,384	35,919	0.52
Builders woodwork, prefabricated	14.0	155,515	17,074	0.51
Aircraft 2,000–15,000	14.3	155,499	14,949	0.51
Tankers	6.1	148,092	1,287	0.49
High carbon steel heavy plate	22.9	147,522	7,066	0.48
Miscellaneous chemical products	1.8	147,521	179,345	0.48
Iron ore agglomerates	7.7	142,702	74	0.47
TOTAL				59.09

NOTE: No import data are reported if import value is less than 0.3 percent of the total trade for 1985.

FIGURE B-3 Percentage of Exports by Cluster and Vertical Stage, Sweden

UPSTREAM INDUSTRIES

	Materials/Metals				Forest Products				Petroleum/Chemicals				Semiconductors/Computers				UPSTREAM INDUSTRIES	
	SCE	ΔSCE	SWCE	ΔSWCE	SCE	ΔSCE	SWCE	ΔSWCE	SCE	ΔSCE	SWCE	ΔSWCE	SCE	ΔSCE	SWCE	ΔSWCE	SCE	SWCE
Primary Goods	9.9	-1.8	2.8	0.1	17.4	-2.4	11.0	-1.4	2.6	0.5	0.2	+0.0	2.1	0.9	0.9	-0.4	32.0	1.6
Machinery	0.6	-0.0	1.8	0.4	0.4	-0.1	5.8	-1.6	—	—	—	—	—	—	—	—	1.0	2.6
Specialty Inputs	2.0	0.1	1.7	-0.2	0.1	-0.0	2.1	-0.2	—	—	—	—	—	—	—	—	2.1	1.7
Total	**12.5**	**-1.7**	**2.4**	**-0.1**	**17.9**	**-2.5**	**10.5**	**-1.3**	**2.6**	**0.5**	**0.2**	**+0.0**	**2.1**	**0.9**	**0.9**	**-0.4**	**35.1**	**1.7**

INDUSTRIAL & SUPPORTING FUNCTIONS

	Multiple Business				Transportation				Power Generation & Distribution				Office				Telecommunications				Defense				INDUSTRIAL & SUPPORTING FUNCTIONS	
	SCE	ΔSCE	SWCE	ΔSWCE	SCE	ΔSCE	SWCE	ΔSWCE	SCE	ΔSCE	SWCE	ΔSWCE	SCE	ΔSCE	SWCE	ΔSWCE	SCE	ΔSCE	SWCE	ΔSWCE	SCE	ΔSCE	SWCE	ΔSWCE	SCE	SWCE
Primary Goods	4.2	+0.0	1.5	-0.2	14.7	-0.3	2.3	-0.2	0.9	-0.7	1.2	-0.5	0.5	-0.1	1.1	-0.2	3.7	0.6	5.5	-1.5	0.7	-0.0	3.6	-0.6	24.7	2.3
Machinery	0.0	0.0	0.0	0.0	1.3	-0.2	12.5	-2.2	—	—	—	—	0.2	-0.0	1.2	-0.4	—	—	—	—	—	—	—	—	1.5	1.5
Specialty Inputs	0.0	0.0	0.0	0.0	4.5	+0.0	1.7	-0.2	0.1	0.0	0.5	-0.0	0.0	0.0	0.0	0.0	—	—	—	—	—	—	—	—	4.6	1.5
Total	**4.2**	**+0.0**	**1.1**	**-0.1**	**20.5**	**-0.4**	**2.3**	**-0.2**	**1.0**	**-0.7**	**1.1**	**-0.5**	**0.7**	**-0.1**	**1.0**	**-0.2**	**3.7**	**0.6**	**5.5**	**-1.5**	**0.7**	**-0.0**	**3.6**	**-0.6**	**30.7**	**2.0**

FINAL CONSUMPTION GOODS & SERVICES

	Food/Beverage				Textiles/Apparel				Housing/Household				Health Care				Personal				Entertainment/Leisure				FINAL CONSUMPTION GOODS & SERVICES	
	SCE	ΔSCE	SWCE	ΔSWCE	SCE	ΔSCE	SWCE	ΔSWCE	SCE	ΔSCE	SWCE	ΔSWCE	SCE	ΔSCE	SWCE	ΔSWCE	SCE	ΔSCE	SWCE	ΔSWCE	SCE	ΔSCE	SWCE	ΔSWCE	SCE	SWCE
Primary Goods	1.0	0.2	0.2	0.1	0.6	0.1	0.2	+0.0	3.6	0.1	2.7	0.2	2.5	0.6	2.8	0.1	0.1	0	0.1	-0.0	0.5	-0.2	0.3	-0.2	8.3	0.7
Machinery	0.8	-0.4	1.9	-0.3	0.2	+0.0	0.9	0.2	—	—	—	—	—	—	—	—	0.0	0.0	0.0	0.0	0.0	0.0	0.0	0.0	1.0	1.5
Specialty Inputs	0.7	0.3	0.3	0.2	0.3	-0.1	0.3	-0.0	0.3	-0.1	1.0	0.1	—	—	—	—	—	—	—	—	0.0	0.0	0.0	00.0	1.3	0.3
Total	**2.5**	**0.1**	**0.4**	**0.1**	**1.1**	**+0.0**	**0.3**	**0.0**	**3.9**	**+0.0**	**2.4**	**0.2**	**2.5**	**0.6**	**2.8**	**0.1**	**0.1**	**0.0**	**0.1**	**+0.0**	**0.5**	**-0.2**	**0.3**	**-0.2**	**10.6**	**0.6**
																									76.4	**1.4**

Note: Totals may not add due to rounding

Key:
SCE   Share of country's total exports 1985
ΔSCE   Change in share of country's exports 1978–1985
SWCE   Share of world cluster exports 1985
ΔSWCE Change in share of world cluster exports 1978–1985

TABLE **B–5** **Top Fifty German Industries in Terms of Export Value, 1985**

Industry	Share of Total World Exports	Export Value ($ millions)	Import Value ($ millions)	Share of Total German Exports
Passenger motor vehicles	23.2	19,118,000	4,344,396	10.42
Motor vehicle bodies, parts, accessories	15.5	6,341,841	2,134,554	3.46
Measuring, controlling instruments	15.8	2,484,492	1,382,339	1.35
Switchgear	21.4	2,427,723	984,522	1.32
Aircraft over 15,000 kilograms	38.1	2,377,571	2,362,416	1.30
Trucks	9.9	2,089,820	449,741	1.14
Miscellaneous chemical products	24.5	1,997,810	964,465	1.09
Machinery for special industries	18.9	1,781,181	637,921	0.97
Office, ADP machine parts	7.9	1,661,001	2,063,364	0.91
ADP peripheral units	15.3	1,443,513	1,499,948	0.79
Articles of plastic	19.8	1,274,569	653,337	0.69
Medicaments with hormones	16.1	1,258,691	678,727	0.69
Piston engine parts	14.5	1,207,932	296,223	0.66
Base metal manufactures	16.4	1,163,157	586,727	0.63
Cocks, valves	21.1	1,156,869	487,103	0.63
Iron, steel seamless tubes	19.9	1,145,710	176,128	0.62
Radiotelephonic receivers, TV cameras, parts	8.0	1,109,642	807,686	0.61
Products of condensation	25.9	1,094,911	505,275	0.60
Other household type equipment	15.8	1,012,347	474,679	0.55
Roadrollers/civil engineering equipment	10.4	1,010,463	287,696	0.55
Shafts, cranks, pulleys	29.9	960,332	294,859	0.52
Gas generators, furance burners	22.2	927,559	218,586	0.51
Rotary printing presses	51.1	923,218	50,671	0.50
Gaseous petroleum gases	8.1	922,456	5,914,597	0.50
Iron, simple steel thin plate	16.7	896,142	514,027	0.49
Motor vehicle piston engines	14.5	872,278	754,087	0.48
Medical instruments	20.9	859,792	343,001	0.47
Synthetic organic dyes	32.4	849,848	153,271	0.46
Rubber, plastic working machinery	35.5	849,798	107,651	0.46
Metalworking machine tools	24.6	815,380	267,162	0.44
Aircraft parts	8.1	811,723	1,177,712	0.44
Wheeled tractors	23.5	810,339	94,275	0.44
Packaging, bottling, machines	34.1	802,409	125,408	0.44
Wood furniture	19.8	797,212	526,253	0.43
Ball, roller bearings	24.3	782,989	417,090	0.43

TABLE **B–5** (*Continued*)

Industry	Share of Total World Exports	Export Value ($ millions)	Import Value ($ millions)	Share of Total German Exports
Articles of precut paper	19.6	774,632	387,527	0.42
Other lifting, loading machinery	19.2	731,961	135,819	0.40
Electronic microcircuits	5.9	720,432	1,323,628	0.39
Acyclic alcohols	21.5	713,425	381,830	0.39
Heterocyclic compounds	14.3	712,932	496,440	0.39
Textile, leather machinery	30.4	695,938	106,064	0.38
Woven cotton, bleached	15.5	681,016	355,560	0.37
Polymerization products	16.2	679,882	352,908	0.37
Blades, tips for tools	19.9	677,492	404,001	0.37
Bovine meat with bone in	22.3	672,096	222,944	0.37
Iron, steel, plate, sheet	13.6	658,354	279,951	0.36
Aluminum plate, sheet, strip	20.1	654,541	317,370	0.36
Electrical machinery	13.0	653,247	434,304	0.36
Locksmiths wares	26.0	646,838	204,307	0.35
Insulated wire, cable	12.2	646,668	377,144	0.35
TOTAL				41.62

NOTE: No import data are reported if import value is less than 0.3 percent of the total trade for 1985.

FIGURE B-4 Percentage of Exports by Cluster and Vertical Stage, Germany

UPSTREAM INDUSTRIES

	Materials/ Metals				Forest Products				Petroleum/ Chemicals				Semiconductors/ Computers				UPSTREAM INDUSTRIES	
	SCE	ΔSCE	SWCE	ΔSWCE	SCE	ΔSCE	SWCE	ΔSWCE	SCE	ΔSCE	SWCE	ΔSWCE	SCE	ΔSCE	SWCE	ΔSWCE	SCE	SWCE
Primary Goods	8.4	−1.0	13.7	−0.9	1.6	0.3	6.2	1.0	8.5	1.3	4.5	−0.7	0.6	0.3	1.9	−1.4	19.1	6.1
Machinery	0.9	−0.4	16.5	−2.9	0.4	+0.0	25.9	−4.8	0.2	−0.0	21.3	−3.1	—	—	—	—	1.4	18.6
Specialty Inputs	0.6	−0.9	5.1	−6.6	0.1	+0.0	24.2	4.8	—	—	—		—	—	—	—	0.7	5.3
Total	10.0	−2.3	11.9	−2.5	2.0	0.3	7.3	2.6	8.6	1.2	4.6	−0.7	0.6	0.3	1.9	−1.4	21.2	6.3

INDUSTRIAL & SUPPORTING FUNCTIONS

	Multiple Business				Transportation				Power Generation & Distribution				Office				Telecommu- nications				Defense				INDUSTRIAL & SUPPORTING FUNCTIONS	
	SCE	ΔSCE	SWCE	ΔSWCE	SCE	ΔSCE	SWCE	ΔSWCE	SCE	ΔSCE	SWCE	ΔSWCE	SCE	ΔSCE	SWCE	ΔSWCE	SCE	ΔSCE	SWCE	ΔSWCE	SCE	ΔSCE	SWCE	ΔSWCE	SCE	SWCE
Primary Goods	7.0	0.4	14.8	−2.3	19.3	1.8	19.2	0.7	3.8	−1.3	19.7	−8.7	0.8	−0.1	12.3	−3.0	0.0	−0.2	0.0	−7.0	0.0	0.0	0.0	0.0	30.9	16.9
Machinery	0.0	0.0	0.0	0.0	3.7	−1.3	22.7	−8.1	—	—	—		0.8	0.1	36.7	−2.2	—	—	—		—	—	—	—	4.4	13.6
Specialty Inputs	0.0	0.0	0.0	0.0	0.8	−0.1	1.8	−0.5	0.0	0.0	0.0	0.0	0.1	0.0	6.7	−2.3	—	—	—		—	—	—	—	0.9	1.7
Total	7.0	0.4	10.8	−1.1	23.7	0.5	15.0	−2.0	3.8	−1.3	17.3	−8.1	1.6	−0.0	16.3	−2.5	0.0	−0.2	0.0	−7.0	0.0	0.0	0.0	0.0	36.2	13.8

FINAL CONSUMPTION GOODS & SERVICES

	Food/ Beverage				Textiles/ Apparel				Housing/ Household				Health Care				Personal				Entertainment/ Leisure				FINAL CONSUMPTION GOODS & SERVICES	
	SCE	ΔSCE	SWCE	ΔSWCE	SCE	ΔSCE	SWCE	ΔSWCE	SCE	ΔSCE	SWCE	ΔSWCE	SCE	ΔSCE	SWCE	ΔSWCE	SCE	ΔSCE	SWCE	ΔSWCE	SCE	ΔSCE	SWCE	ΔSWCE	SCE	SWCE
Primary Goods	1.9	0.1	2.9	0.4	1.8	−0.3	4.4	−1.4	3.0	−0.4	14.1	−2.2	1.9	0.3	13.9	−2.2	1.1	+0.0	15.3	−5.0	0.6	−0.2	1.9	−1.6	10.3	6.3
Machinery	1.5	−0.2	19.1	−0.4	1.3	−0.1	27.0	−0.4	0.3	−0.2	26.3	−3.7	—	—	—		—	—	—		+0.0	−0.0	29.9	16.5	3.1	22.3
Specialty Inputs	1.3	0.0	4.0	0.2	1.9	−0.3	8.7	−1.2	0.0	0.0	0.0	0.0	—	—	—		0.0	0.0	0.0	0.0	0.5	0.2	12.4	1.6	3.7	5.2
Total	4.7	−0.1	4.4	0.2	5.0	−0.6	7.1	−1.6	3.3	−0.6	12.0	−1.8	1.9	0.3	13.9	−2.2	1.1	+0.0	10.5	−0.2	1.1	−0.1	3.6	−1.3	17.1	6.8
																									74.4	8.7

Note: Totals may not add due to rounding
Key:
SCE Share of country's total exports 1985
ΔSCE Change in share of country's exports 1978–1985
SWCE Share of world cluster exports 1985
ΔSWCE Change in share of world cluster exports 1978–1985

TABLE B–6 Top Fifty Japanese Industries in Terms of Export Value, 1985

Industry	Share of Total World Exports	Export Value ($ millions)	Import Value ($ millions)	Share of Total Japanese Exports
Passenger motor vehicles	30.8	25,402,210	538,683	14.46
Lorries, trucks	37.5	7,956,271	16,969	4.53
TV image, sound recorders	80.7	6,622,119	9,924	3.77
Motor vehicle bodies, parts, accessories	12.8	5,227,670	187,706	2.98
Other cargo vessels	35.7	4,399,729	216,601	2.50
Radiotelephonic receivers, TV cameras, parts	28.6	3,945,888	302,334	2.25
ADP peripheral units	37.9	3,571,949	427,126	2.03
Color TV receivers	49.5	2,691,101	6,899	1.53
Electronic microcircuits	19.9	2,415,252	699,618	1.37
Iron, steel seamless tubes	38.7	2,227,632	6,587	1.27
ADP machine parts	10.0	2,105,665	501,908	1.20
Motorcycles	82.0	2,092,416	16,684	1.19
Photo, thermocopy apparatus	65.9	2,032,389	6,055	1.16
Iron, simple steel rolled thin plate	35.2	1,893,459	84,656	1.08
Switchgear	16.5	1,877,891	34,619	1.07
Dictating machines	71.7	1,817,413	15,194	1.03
Still cameras, flash apparatus	62.2	1,608,936	82,174	0.92
Prepared sound recording media	41.5	1,589,513	96,184	0.90
Measuring, controlling instruments	9.3	1,459,409	924,601	0.83
Nonpile continuous synthetic weaves	34.7	1,456,391	31,808	0.83
Iron, steel tubes, pipes	30.6	1,437,337	17,006	0.82
Iron, steel universal plates, sheets	29.3	1,419,903	11,577	0.81
Other domestic appliances	21.8	1,401,394	72,247	0.80
Line telephone equipment	26.2	1,378,545	57,018	0.78
Machinery for special industries	14.3	1,349,143	290,643	0.77
Piston engine parts	15.9	1,320,517	45,806	0.75
Portable radio receivers	48.4	1,171,209	31,718	0.67
Other electrical machinery	20.3	1,014,478	427,359	0.58
Metal cutting machine tools	36.5	1,009,629	111,274	0.57
Watches	24.0	997,512	160,139	0.57
Microphones, loudspeakers, amplifiers	55.7	981,176	51,602	0.56
Self-propelled shovels	38.4	964,654	—	0.55
Motor vehicle radio receivers	42.5	908,083	3,052	0.52

TABLE **B–6** (*Continued*)

Industry	Share of Total World Exports	Export Value ($ millions)	Import Value ($ millions)	Share of Total Japanese Exports
Truck tires	39.1	860,530	4,411	0.49
Piezoelectric crystals	14.0	835,800	43,896	0.48
Motor vehicle piston engines	13.5	813,915	25,749	0.46
Hotrolled iron, other steel bars	24.1	811,754	—	0.46
Tankers	31.7	767,626	13,116	0.44
Roadrollers/civil engineering equipment	7.8	754,372	56,111	0.43
Motorcycle parts, accessories	53.4	747,246	13,370	0.43
TV picture tubes	42.2	709,509	35,503	0.40
Insulated wire, cable	13.3	700,607	58,421	0.40
Iron, simple steel coils	18.5	695,106	337,018	0.40
Gas generators, furnace burners	16.7	694,773	107,846	0.40
TV, radio transmitters	29.8	692,249	14,810	0.39
Pianos, musical instruments, and parts	51.0	687,841	47,188	0.39
Pumps for gases	24.1	686,437	63,585	0.39
Woven synthetic fiber fabrics	16.0	668,946	77,921	0.38
Calculating machines	69.7	660,432	11,294	0.38
Iron, simple steel rolled heavy plate	25.1	653,184	210,305	0.37
TOTAL				62.74

NOTE: No import data are reported if import value is less than 0.3 percent of the total trade for 1985.

FIGURE B-5 Percentage of Exports by Cluster and Vertical Stage, Japan

UPSTREAM INDUSTRIES

Materials/Metals

	SCE	ΔSCE	SWCE	ΔSWCE
Primary Goods	8.9	-5.7	14.2	-1.3
Machinery	0.7	-0.7	11.3	-2.1
Specialty Inputs	0.0	0.0	0.0	0.0
Total	9.6	-6.4	10.8	-1.7

Forest Products

	SCE	ΔSCE	SWCE	ΔSWCE
Primary Goods	0.2	+0.0	1.1	0.3
Machinery	0.0	0.0	0.0	0.0
Specialty Inputs	—	—	—	—
Total	0.2	+0.0	1.0	0.3

Petroleum/Chemicals

	SCE	ΔSCE	SWCE	ΔSWCE
Primary Goods	1.3	-0.5	1.0	-0.2
Machinery	—	—	—	—
Specialty Inputs	—	—	—	—
Total	1.3	-0.5	1.0	-0.2

Semiconductors/Computers

	SCE	ΔSCE	SWCE	ΔSWCE
Primary Goods	4.7	3.6	11.3	6.3
Machinery	—	—	—	—
Specialty Inputs	—	—	—	—
Total	4.7	3.6	11.3	6.3

Upstream Industries

	SCE	SWCE
Primary Goods	15.0	4.8
Machinery	0.7	11.3
Specialty Inputs	—	—
Total	15.6	4.6

INDUSTRIAL & SUPPORTING FUNCTIONS

Multiple Business

	SCE	ΔSCE	SWCE	ΔSWCE
Primary Goods	2.6	-0.4	5.2	-0.1
Machinery	0.9	0.3	5.8	3.2
Specialty Inputs	0.2	0.1	7.0	2.8
Total	3.7	0.1	5.5	0.9

Transportation

	SCE	ΔSCE	SWCE	ΔSWCE
Primary Goods	27.1	-0.9	23.7	3.5
Machinery	2.7	0.7	22.4	10.4
Specialty Inputs	7.1	1.2	15.2	4.1
Total	36.9	1.0	22.6	4.2

Power Generation & Distribution

	SCE	ΔSCE	SWCE	ΔSWCE
Primary Goods	3.3	-0.6	16.6	1.4
Machinery	0.0	—	—	0.0
Specialty Inputs	0.0	0.0	0.0	0.0
Total	3.3	-0.6	14.6	1.0

Office

	SCE	ΔSCE	SWCE	ΔSWCE
Primary Goods	3.3	0.4	35.5	10.7
Machinery	0.2	0.1	9.1	6.2
Specialty Inputs	0.0	0.0	0.0	0.0
Total	3.5	0.5	28.0	8.5

Telecommunications

	SCE	ΔSCE	SWCE	ΔSWCE
Primary Goods	3.4	1.4	28.1	8.8
Machinery	—	—	—	—
Specialty Inputs	—	—	—	—
Total	3.4	1.4	28.1	8.8

Defense

	SCE	ΔSCE	SWCE	ΔSWCE
Primary Goods	0.0	-0.1	0.3	-0.1
Machinery	—	—	—	—
Specialty Inputs	—	—	—	—
Total	0.0	-0.1	0.3	-0.1

Industrial & Supporting Functions

	SCE	SWCE
Primary Goods	39.7	19.0
Machinery	3.8	12.9
Specialty Inputs	7.3	13.7
Total	50.8	17.4

FINAL CONSUMPTION GOODS & SERVICES

Food/Beverage

	SCE	ΔSCE	SWCE	ΔSWCE
Primary Goods	0.3	-0.2	0.4	-0.1
Machinery	0.3	0.2	3.9	2.9
Specialty Inputs	0.1	-0.1	0.4	+0.0
Total	0.7	-0.1	0.7	0.2

Textiles/Apparel

	SCE	ΔSCE	SWCE	ΔSWCE
Primary Goods	1.8	-0.8	4.2	-0.7
Machinery	0.8	-0.2	16.0	2.6
Specialty Inputs	0.6	-0.5	4.1	-0.3
Total	3.2	-1.5	4.9	-0.5

Housing/Household

	SCE	ΔSCE	SWCE	ΔSWCE
Primary Goods	2.0	0.3	8.7	3.3
Machinery	—	—	—	—
Specialty Inputs	0.3	0.1	6.1	3.5
Total	2.3	0.4	8.2	3.4

Health Care

	SCE	ΔSCE	SWCE	ΔSWCE
Primary Goods	0.7	0.3	4.7	1.9
Machinery	—	—	—	—
Specialty Inputs	—	—	—	—
Total	0.7	0.3	4.7	1.9

Personal

	SCE	ΔSCE	SWCE	ΔSWCE
Primary Goods	1.3	-0.4	6.6	-1.5
Machinery	—	—	—	—
Specialty Inputs	0.3	-0.1	2.6	1.1
Total	1.6	-0.4	5.3	0.3

Entertainment/Leisure

	SCE	ΔSCE	SWCE	ΔSWCE
Primary Goods	10.9	2.6	35.8	9.9
Machinery	—	—	—	—
Specialty Inputs	0.9	-0.2	15.8	-0.7
Total	11.8	2.4	32.7	8.4

Final Consumption Goods & Services

	SCE	SWCE
Primary Goods	17.0	8.3
Machinery	1.1	8.3
Specialty Inputs	2.2	3.2
Total	20.3	6.9

86.7   9.2

Note: Totals may not add due to rounding

Key:
SCE — Share of country's total exports 1985
ΔSCE — Change in share of country's exports 1978–1985
SWCE — Share of world cluster exports 1985
ΔSWCE — Change in share of world cluster exports 1978–1985

TABLE **B–7** Top Fifty Italian Industries in Terms of Export Value, 1985

Industry	Share of Total World Exports	Export Value ($ millions)	Import Value ($ millions)	Share of Total Italian Exports
Leather footwear	32.8	3,285,427	178,156	4.16
Precious metal jewelry	49.6	2,288,256	19,978	2.90
Motor vehicle bodies, parts, accessories	4.0	1,644,122	865,691	2.08
Passenger motor vehicles	2.0	1,638,791	3,669,976	2.08
Wood furniture	25.5	1,026,911	40,390	1.30
Glazed ceramic sets	56.6	866,879	16,437	1.10
Machinery for wood, glass industries	8.8	831,627	275,187	1.05
Wine of fresh grapes	20.7	803,915	75,121	1.02
ADP peripheral units	8.4	786,775	928,607	1.00
Jet fuel, other light oils	6.4	781,320	674,639	0.99
Woven synthetic fiber fabric	18.1	753,426	189,393	0.95
Cocks, valves	13.2	726,767	205,779	0.92
Worked building stone	62.2	701,208	5,319	0.89
Trucks	3.3	694,554	535,189	0.88
Office, ADP machine parts	3.3	692,904	760,634	0.88
Chairs and other seats	30.6	685,124	29,894	0.87
Other sweaters, pullovers	24.5	641,799	16,830	0.81
Articles of plastic	9.8	632,351	271,758	0.80
Sweaters, etc., of synthetic fibers	34.0	631,213	5,419	0.80
Base metal manufactures	8.7	616,699	260,504	0.78
Gas oils	3.3	553,334	1,649,392	0.70
Wheeled tractor	14.9	514,936	43,309	0.65
Gas generators, furnace burners	12.3	514,691	91,237	0.65
Other woven textile fabric	32.3	510,145	48,634	0.65
Switchgear	4.4	502,573	487,539	0.64
Woolen sweaters	33.1	499,221	55,460	0.63
Women's outerwear	26.2	491,478	50,159	0.62
Fuel oils	1.9	490,142	3,116,200	0.62
Household type equipment	7.6	485,888	188,573	0.62
Machine tools for wood, ceramics	24.7	485,500	35,141	0.61
Packaging, bottling machines	19.8	464,507	55,063	0.59
Bovine, equine leather	17.4	454,579	290,265	0.58
Rubber, plastic footwear	41.9	452,469	20,402	0.57
Leather	24.6	452,233	266,5421	0.57
Men's overcoats	19.8	435,710	99,379	0.55
Vegetables preserved, prepared	17.1	430,238	126,441	0.54

TABLE B–7 (*Continued*)

Industry	Share of Total World Exports	Export Value ($ millions)	Import Value ($ millions)	Share of Total Italian Exports
Measuring, controlling instruments	2.7	426,624	814,429	0.54
Other textile, leather machinery	18.6	425,736	100,203	0.54
Kerosene including jet fuel	9.2	410,426	—	0.52
Radiotelephonic receivers, TV cameras, parts	3.0	410,425	346,499	0.52
Iron, steel structures and parts	8.4	409,784	29,403	0.52
Domestic washing machines	38.2	396,595	32,123	0.50
Digital central processors	7.7	389,930	448,014	0.49
Aircraft part	3.8	384,641	300,101	0.49
Iron, steel seamless tubes	6.4	370,376	115,942	0.47
Pumps for gases	12.6	360,249	133,105	0.46
Motor, aviation spirit	4.3	358,507	52,938	0.45
Other metalworking machine tools	10.8	358,400	90,504	0.45
Other polymerization products	8.5	358,211	236,037	0.45
Miscellaneous chemical products	4.3	354,530	615,330	0.45
TOTAL				42.90

NOTE: No import data are reported if import value is less than 0.3 percent of the total trade for 1985.

FIGURE B-6 Percentage of Exports by Cluster and Vertical Stage, Italy

UPSTREAM INDUSTRIES

	Materials/Metals				Forest Products				Petroleum/Chemicals				Semiconductors/Computers				UPSTREAM INDUSTRIES	
	SCE	ΔSCE	SWCE	ΔSWCE	SCE	ΔSCE	SWCE	ΔSWCE	SCE	ΔSCE	SWCE	ΔSWCE	SCE	ΔSCE	SWCE	ΔSWCE	SCE	SWCE
Primary Goods	6.7	-1.9	4.7	-0.5	0.7	-0.0	1.6	+0.0	2.5	0.6	0.6	+0.0	0.4	+0.0	0.4	-0.5	10.3	1.5
Machinery	1.7	-0.0	13.3	3.58	0.3	+0.1	8.1	1.7	—	—	—	—	—	—	—	—	2.0	12.3
Specialty Inputs	0.1	-0.0	0.3	-0.0	—	—	—	—	—	—	—	—	—	—	—	—	0.1	0.2
Total	**8.5**	**-1.9**	**4.2**	**-0.4**	**1.0**	**+0.0**	**1.9**	**0.1**	**2.5**	**0.6**	**0.6**	**+0.0**	**0.4**	**+0.0**	**0.4**	**-0.5**	**12.3**	**1.6**

INDUSTRIAL & SUPPORTING FUNCTIONS

	Multiple Business				Transportation				Power Generation & Distribution				Office				Telecommunications				Defense				INDUSTRIAL & SUPPORTING FUNCTIONS	
	SCE	ΔSCE	SWCE	ΔSWCE	SCE	ΔSCE	SWCE	ΔSWCE	SCE	ΔSCE	SWCE	ΔSWCE	SCE	ΔSCE	SWCE	ΔSWCE	SCE	ΔSCE	SWCE	ΔSWCE	SCE	ΔSCE	SWCE	ΔSWCE	SCE	SWCE
Primary Goods	3.1	0.4	2.1	-0.0	2.2	-3.0	2.2	-1.4	0.8	-0.4	4.5	-0.9	0.7	-0.4	3.7	-2.1	0.5	-0.0	1.9	-0.9	0.3	-0.2	7.4	-3.3	7.7	3.0
Machinery	0.2	0.1	0.5	0.2	2.4	+0.2	12.6	2.3	—	—	0.0	0.0	0.2	+0.0	3.2	0.1	—	—	—	—	—	—	—	—	2.7	4.7
Specialty Inputs	0.2	0.0	2.4	-0.3	2.1	2.0	3.7	-2.6	0.0	0.0	0.0	0.0	0.1	+0.0	3.0	2.1	—	—	—	—	—	—	—	—	2.3	3.4
Total	**3.5**	**0.4**	**2.4**	**0.1**	**6.7**	**-4.8**	**3.5**	**-1.5**	**0.8**	**-0.4**	**4.0**	**-0.9**	**1.0**	**-0.4**	**3.6**	**-1.5**	**0.5**	**-0.0**	**1.9**	**-0.9**	**0.3**	**-0.2**	**7.4**	**-3.3**	**12.7**	**3.3**

FINAL CONSUMPTION GOODS & SERVICES

	Food/Beverage				Textiles/Apparel				Housing/Household				Health Care				Personal				Entertainment/Leisure				FINAL CONSUMPTION GOODS & SERVICES	
	SCE	ΔSCE	SWCE	ΔSWCE	SCE	ΔSCE	SWCE	ΔSWCE	SCE	ΔSCE	SWCE	ΔSWCE	SCE	ΔSCE	SWCE	ΔSWCE	SCE	ΔSCE	SWCE	ΔSWCE	SCE	ΔSCE	SWCE	ΔSWCE	SCE	SWCE
Primary Goods	0.6	-0.1	3.6	0.5	15.2	0.7	14.6	-0.2	8.8	-0.2	17.2	0.8	0.6	0.1	1.8	-0.3	4.3	0.6	9.7	-0.3	0.9	-0.4	1.5	-1.1	35.4	7.9
Machinery	2.5	0.2	13.5	3.3	1.3	0.3	11.9	3.8	0.5	-0.3	7.6	-0.9	—	—	—	—	0.0	0.0	0.0	0.0	—	—	—	—	4.3	12.0
Specialty Inputs	0.6	-0.1	0.9	-0.0	3.1	1.1	6.6	2.5	0.2	0.0	2.0	0.4	—	—	—	—	0.0	0.0	0.0	0.0	0.0	-0.0	0.5	-0.1	3.9	2.4
Total	**8.8**	**0.1**	**3.5**	**0.5**	**19.6**	**2.0**	**12.0**	**1.2**	**9.5**	**-0.5**	**13.8**	**1.1**	**0.6**	**0.1**	**1.8**	**-0.3**	**4.3**	**0.6**	**6.6**	**1.4**	**0.9**	**-0.5**	**1.3**	**-1.0**	**43.7**	**6.7**
																									68.7	**3.7**

Note: Totals may not add due to rounding

Key:
SCE   Share of country's total exports 1985
ΔSCE   Change in share of country's exports 1978–1985
SWCE   Share of world cluster exports 1985
ΔSWCE Change in share of world cluster exports 1978–1985

TABLE B–8 **Top Fifty Korean Industries in Terms of Export Value, 1985**

Industry	Share of Total World Exports	Export Value ($ millions)	Import Value ($ millions)	Share of Total Korean Exports
Other cargo vessels	36.9	4,545,449	3,296,174	15.01
Leather footwear	14.3	1,436,334	—	4.74
Nonpile continuous synthetic weaves	21.1	885,906	69,888	2.93
Electronic microcircuits	6.3	760,213	261,271	2.51
Iron, steel structures, parts	14.4	700,826	28,280	2.31
Leather clothes, accessories	26.7	539,989	862	1.78
Passenger motor vehicles	0.6	518,789	—	1.71
Toys, indoor games	10.8	475,254	7,283	1.57
Sweaters of synthetic fibers	24.2	448,201	—	1.48
Men's jackets, blazers	39.4	417,910	233	1.38
Iron, steel tubes, pipes	8.1	381,006	40,035	1.26
Color TV receivers	6.9	376,049	5,626	1.24
Tankers	14.1	342,319	17,381	1.13
Travel goods, handbags	24.6	337,005	1,274	1.11
Fuel oils	1.1	300,988	271,955	0.99
Sweaters of cotton fibers	11.4	299,388	512	0.99
Iron, simple steel coils	7.8	293,666	280,343	0.97
Men's shirts of synthetic fibers	40.9	292,283	—	0.97
Knit undergarments of wool, fibers	13.7	283,956	677	0.94
Containers including road-rail	32.2	279,798	11,815	0.92
Men's overcoats, outerwear	11.9	261,603	160	0.86
Frozen fish, excluding fillets	15.7	260,784	58,225	0.86
Aircraft, motorcycle tires	9.6	249,212	3,175	0.82
Spirit jet fuel	2.0	242,708	158,076	0.80
Off-line data processing equipment	41.8	238,310	73,350	0.79
Dishwashers, shavers, appliances	3.6	233,057	16,371	0.77
Prepared sound recording media	6.0	231,939	20,412	0.77
Fresh, frozen shell fish	4.4	223,669	17,582	0.74
Woven synthetic fiber fabric	5.3	219,732	119,297	0.73
Aircraft over 15,000 kilograms	3.5	215,745	204,617	0.71
Monochrome TV receivers	52.4	215,041	347	0.71
Women's coats, jackets of synthetic fibers	31.8	212,399	—	0.70
Men's cotton shirts	15.0	211,624	—	0.70
Hotrolled iron, other steel bars	6.3	210,964	—	0.70

TABLE **B–8** (*Continued*)

Industry	Share of Total World Exports	Export Value ($ millions)	Import Value ($ millions)	Share of Total Korean Exports
Telecommunication equipment, parts	1.5	209,727	368,652	0.69
TV image, sound recorders	2.5	206,562	12,745	0.68
Iron, simple steel rolled thin plate	3.8	202,556	49,701	0.67
Baby carriages, parts	7.3	188,476	50,826	0.62
Textile articles	11.2	186,546	2,054	0.62
Non-electric stoves, heating apparatus	9.8	185,942	12,278	0.61
Motor vehicle radio receivers	8.6	182,887	5,368	0.60
Portable radio receivers	7.2	174,489	1,023	0.58
TV picture tubes	9.7	162,286	41,177	0.54
Articles of furskin	14.7	161,287	994	0.53
ADP machine parts	0.7	157,694	133,357	0.52
Diodes, transistors	5.2	154,821	74,388	0.51
Women's blouses of synthetic fibers	16.4	149,778	—	0.49
Iron, simple steel rolled heavy plate	5.5	144,248	140,708	0.48
Other radio receivers	11.9	142,529	9,432	0.47
Gas oils	0.8	139,262	—	0.46
TOTAL				65.67

NOTE: No import data are reported if import value is less than 0.3 percent of the total trade for 1985.

FIGURE B-7 Percentage of Exports by Cluster and Vertical Stage, Korea

Upstream Clusters

	Materials/Metals SCE	ΔSCE	SWCE	ΔSWCE	Forest Products SCE	ΔSCE	SWCE	ΔSWCE	Petroleum/Chemicals SCE	ΔSCE	SWCE	ΔSWCE	Semiconductors/Computers SCE	ΔSCE	SWCE	ΔSWCE	UPSTREAM INDUSTRIES SCE	SWCE
Primary Goods	9.6	1.8	2.5	1.5	0.2	−4.0	0.4	−1.3	1.8	1.4	0.2	0.1	3.8	0.9	1.6	−0.2	15.4	0.8
Machinery	0.0	0.0	0.0	0.0	0.0	0.0	0.0	0.0	—	—	—	—	—	—	—	—	—	—
Specialty Inputs	0.0	0.0	0.0	0.0	—	—	—	—	—	—	—	—	—	—	—	—	—	—
Total	**9.6**	**1.8**	**1.8**	**1.0**	**0.2**	**−4.0**	**0.4**	**−1.2**	**1.8**	**1.4**	**0.2**	**0.1**	**3.8**	**0.9**	**1.6**	**−0.2**	**15.4**	**0.8**

Industrial & Supporting Clusters

	Multiple Business SCE	ΔSCE	SWCE	ΔSWCE	Transportation SCE	ΔSCE	SWCE	ΔSWCE	Power Generation & Distribution SCE	ΔSCE	SWCE	ΔSWCE	Office SCE	ΔSCE	SWCE	ΔSWCE	Telecommunications SCE	ΔSCE	SWCE	ΔSWCE	Defense SCE	ΔSCE	SWCE	ΔSWCE	INDUSTRIAL & SUPPORTING FUNCTIONS SCE	SWCE
Primary Goods	0.3	−0.2	0.2	+0.0	17.6	10.7	2.6	2.0	1.5	0.5	1.2	0.7	0.5	−0.6	1.0	−0.3	0.7	0.3	1.0	0.5	0.0	0.0	0.0	0.0	20.5	1.7
Machinery	0.0	0.0	0.0	0.0	0.0	0.0	0.0	0.0	—	—	—	—	0.0	0.0	0.0	0.0	—	—	—	—	—	—	—	—	—	—
Specialty Inputs	0.0	0.0	0.0	0.0	2.4	−0.3	0.9	0.2	0.0	0.0	0.0	0.0	0.0	0.0	0.0	0.0	—	—	—	—	—	—	—	—	2.4	0.8
Total	**0.3**	**−0.2**	**0.2**	**+0.0**	**20.0**	**10.4**	**2.1**	**1.5**	**1.5**	**0.5**	**1.1**	**0.6**	**0.5**	**−0.6**	**0.7**	**−0.3**	**0.7**	**0.3**	**1.0**	**0.5**	**0.0**	**0.0**	**0.0**	**0.0**	**23.0**	**1.4**

Final Consumption Goods & Services Clusters

	Food/Beverage SCE	ΔSCE	SWCE	ΔSWCE	Textiles/Apparel SCE	ΔSCE	SWCE	ΔSWCE	Housing/Household SCE	ΔSCE	SWCE	ΔSWCE	Health Care SCE	ΔSCE	SWCE	ΔSWCE	Personal SCE	ΔSCE	SWCE	ΔSWCE	Entertainment/Leisure SCE	ΔSCE	SWCE	ΔSWCE	FINAL CONSUMPTION GOODS & SERVICES SCE	SWCE
Primary Goods	3.3	−3.4	0.8	0.0	27.3	−10.0	9.6	1.3	2.6	−0.0	1.9	0.9	0.0	+0.0	0.1	0.1	1.9	−1.0	1.7	0.1	7.4	1.1	4.2	1.7	42.5	3.6
Machinery	+0.0	−0.0	0.1	+0.0	0.0	−0.1	0.1	−0.1	—	—	—	—	—	—	—	—	—	—	—	—	—	—	—	—	+0.0	0.1
Specialty Inputs	0.9	−0.9	0.5	0.0	2.1	−0.5	1.6	0.6	0.0	0.0	0.0	0.0	—	—	—	—	0.3	−0.6	0.5	−0.0	0.5	0.5	1.6	1.5	3.8	0.9
Total	**4.3**	**−4.3**	**0.7**	**0.0**	**29.4**	**−10.6**	**6.6**	**1.3**	**2.6**	**−0.0**	**1.6**	**0.7**	**0.0**	**+0.0**	**0.1**	**0.1**	**2.1**	**−1.5**	**1.4**	**0.1**	**8.0**	**1.6**	**3.8**	**1.7**	**46.3**	**2.7**

Overall total: **84.7** **1.6**

Note: Totals may not add due to rounding
Key:
SCE — Share of country's total exports 1985
ΔSCE — Change in share of country's exports 1978–1985
SWCE — Share of world cluster exports 1985
ΔSWCE — Change in share of world cluster exports 1978–1985

TABLE B–9 Top Fifty U.K. Industries in Terms of Export Value, 1985

Industry	Share of Total World Exports	Export Value ($ millions)	Import Value ($ millions)	Share of Total U.K. Exports
Crude petroleum	9.8	16,715,740	5,457,394	16.50
Office, ADP machine parts, accessories	13.1	2,749,948	1,890,312	2.71
Motor vehicle bodies, parts, accessories	6.1	2,511,869	2,124,648	2.48
Measuring, controlling instruments	12.7	2,004,327	1,622,250	1.98
Aircraft parts	19.1	1,912,422	858,464	1.89
Passenger motor vehicles	2.1	1,737,123	5,367,945	1.71
Sorted, rough, simply worked diamonds	37.1	1,471,103	1,209,695	1.45
Whiskey	77.7	1,294,923	9,993	1.28
Gas oils	7.4	1,246,235	392,256	1.23
Medicaments with hormones	14.1	1,105,672	439,318	1.09
Aircraft engines and motors, parts	17.1	1,010,906	730,433	1.00
Motor, aviation spirit	11.8	984,500	153,973	0.97
Aircraft reaction engines	44.5	922,434	550,747	0.91
Electronic microcircuits	7.4	894,693	1,169,129	0.88
ADP peripheral units	8.8	826,208	1,975,888	0.82
Digital central processors	15.2	775,895	1,016,452	0.77
Machinery for special industries	8.1	769,269	573,807	0.76
Switchgear	6.6	748,891	790,277	0.74
Other electrical machinery	14.4	720,408	367,991	0.71
Civil engineering equipment	7.3	710,585	26,180	0.70
Miscellaneous chemical products	8.2	672,666	533,826	0.66
Aircraft 2,000–15,000 kilograms	56.5	615,942	67,163	0.61
Printed books, pamphlets	18.5	609,928	338,993	0.60
Liquefied propane, butane	7.1	597,260	102,674	0.59
Wheeled tractors	16.6	573,576	190,964	0.57
Radiotelephonic receivers, TV cameras, parts	4.0	558,027	648,966	0.55
Fuel oils	2.1	554,542	3,180,750	0.55
War firearms, ammunition	12.0	551,806	269,708	0.54
Cigarettes	16.7	541,417	98,558	0.53
Base metal manufactures	7.6	537,902	582,973	0.53
Hand paintings	31.3	513,459	480,170	0.51
Piston engine parts	5.8	485,606	321,299	0.48
Engravings, antiques	39.8	479,984	293,430	0.47
Radioactive elements	15.0	471,301	426,915	0.47
Cocks, valves	8.5	465,290	436,710	0.46
Perfumery, cosmetics	13.5	456,565	304,587	0.45

TABLE **B–9** (*Continued*)

Industry	Share of Total World Exports	Export Value ($ millions)	Import Value ($ millions)	Share of Total U.K. Exports
Aircraft over 15,000 kilograms	7.3	454,719	1,058,329	0.45
Articles of plastic	6.7	429,940	531,499	0.42.
Heterocyclic compounds	8.6	427,414	408,179	0.42
Unmilled barley	16.4	414,202	32,818	0.41
Other iron and steel scrap	14.5	411,429	12,738	0.41
Iron, steel structures, parts	7.9	381,679	126,174	0.38
Medical instruments	9.3	381,457	270,380	0.38
Trucks	1.8	376,243	628,097	0.37
Lubricants (high petroleum content)	10.4	374,451	361,588	0.37
Antiknock preparations	18.5	369,613	84,342	0.36
Insulated wire, cable	6.9	365,374	294,587	0.36
Gasoline and other light oils	2.8	345,303	719,599	0.34
Polyacids and derivatives	17.4	331,110	60,641	0.33
Typesetting, bookbinding machinery, parts	16.1	328,878	273,553	0.32
TOTAL				54.47

NOTE: No import data are reported if import value is less than 0.3 percent of the total trade for 1985.

FIGURE B-8 Percentage of Exports by Cluster and Vertical Stage, United Kingdom

UPSTREAM INDUSTRIES

	Materials/ Metals				Forest Products				Petroleum/ Chemicals				Semiconductors/ Computers				UPSTREAM INDUSTRIES	
	SCE	ΔSCE	SWCE	ΔSWCE	SCE	ΔSCE	SWCE	ΔSWCE	SCE	ΔSCE	SWCE	ΔSWCE	SCE	ΔSCE	SWCE	ΔSWCE	SCE	SWCE
Primary Goods	3.1	-0.9	3.7	+0.0	0.0	-0.1	0.0	-0.2	23.8	15.3	6.9	3.8	3.5	2.4	6.3	-0.6	30.4	5.7
Machinery	0.3	-0.4	5.1	-1.2	0.1	+0.0	4.5	0.8	1.0	-0.3	9.1	-0.6	—	—	—	—	1.4	7.0
Specialty Inputs	0.6	-0.3	1.6	-1.0	—	—	—	—	—	—	—	—	—	—	—	—	0.6	1.6
Total	4.0	-1.6	3.3	-0.4	0.1	-0.1	0.7	-0.1	24.8	15.0	6.9	3.6	3.5	2.4	6.3	-0.6	32.4	5.5

INDUSTRIAL & SUPPORTING FUNCTIONS

	Multiple Business				Transportation				Power Generation & Distribution				Office				Telecommu- nications				Defense				INDUSTRIAL & SUPPORTING FUNCTIONS	
	SCE	ΔSCE	SWCE	ΔSWCE	SCE	ΔSCE	SWCE	ΔSWCE	SCE	ΔSCE	SWCE	ΔSWCE	SCE	ΔSCE	SWCE	ΔSWCE	SCE	ΔSCE	SWCE	ΔSWCE	SCE	ΔSCE	SWCE	ΔSWCE	SCE	SWCE
Primary Goods	4.4	-1.7	5.3	-2.5	3.8	-3.4	2.3	-1.6	2.0	-0.5	8.2	-0.8	1.1	-0.2	7.8	0.5	0.3	-0.1	3.9	-2.2	0.6	-0.1	10.3	-2.7	12.2	4.1
Machinery	1.8	-0.6	9.0	-1.0	0.3	-0.3	11.4	-7.8	—	—	—	—	0.3	-0.0	8.5	-1.4	—	—	—	—	—	—	—	—	2.4	9.2
Specialty Inputs	0.1	-0.0	5.0	-1.0	7.9	-1.6	10.0	-2.6	0.0	0.0	0.0	0.0	0.2	+0.0	12.7	-0.9	—	—	—	—	—	—	—	—	8.2	9.2
Total	6.3	-2.4	6.1	-2.1	12.1	-5.3	4.6	-1.9	2.0	-0.5	7.2	-0.8	1.6	-0.2	8.3	-0.7	0.3	-0.1	3.9	-2.2	0.6	-0.1	10.3	-2.7	22.8	5.4

FINAL CONSUMPTION GOODS & SERVICES

	Food/ Beverage				Textiles/ Apparel				Housing/ Household				Health Care				Personal				Entertainment/ Leisure				FINAL CONSUMPTION GOODS & SERVICES	
	SCE	ΔSCE	SWCE	ΔSWCE	SCE	ΔSCE	SWCE	ΔSWCE	SCE	ΔSCE	SWCE	ΔSWCE	SCE	ΔSCE	SWCE	ΔSWCE	SCE	ΔSCE	SWCE	ΔSWCE	SCE	ΔSCE	SWCE	ΔSWCE	SCE	SWCE
Primary Goods	3.4	-0.9	3.1	0.0	1.1	-0.6	1.8	-0.7	0.9	-1.0	3.9	-1.6	2.1	0.1	8.8	-1.3	1.2	-2.9	3.6	-10.1	3.3	-0.6	7.1	-2.4	11.9	3.9
Machinery	0.2	-0.3	3.1	-1.1	0.1	-0.4	3.8	-2.6	—	—	—	—	—	.	—	—	—	—	—	—	0.0	0.0	0.0	0.0	0.2	3.4
Specialty Inputs	0.6	0.1	1.2	0.3	1.5	-0.8	4.0	-1.2	0.5	-0.4	5.8	-1.9	—	—	—	—	0.0	0.0	0.0	0.0	0.0	0.0	0.0	0.0	2.6	2.1
Total	4.1	-1.2	2.5	-0.0	2.6	-1.7	2.6	-1.1	1.3	-1.4	4.2	-1.7	2.1	0.1	8.8	-1.3	1.2	-2.9	2.4	-4.7	3.3	-0.6	6.0	-1.9	14.7	3.4
																									70.0	4.8

Note: Totals may not add due to rounding

Key: SCE   Share of country's total exports 1985
ΔSCE   Change in share of country's exports 1978–1985
SWCE   Share of world cluster exports 1985
ΔSWCE   Change in share of world cluster exports 1978–1985

TABLE **B–10** Top Fifty U.S. Industries in Terms of Export Value, 1985

Industry	Share of Total World Exports	Export Value ($ millions)	Import Value ($ millions)	Share of Total U.S. Exports
Motor vehicle bodies, parts, accessories	25.6	10,476,330	9,669,742	4.92
Commercial aircraft and helicopters	79.4	8,823,833	1,806,783	4.14
Office, ADP machine parts	37.1	7,816,542	5,326,652	3.67
Passenger motor vehicles	7.5	6,153,653	39,088,930	2.89
Aircraft parts	56.6	5,674,001	1,793,513	2.66
Unmilled maize	69.5	5,335,039	20,588	2.50
Measuring, controlling instruments	28.1	4,422,593	1,883,423	2.07
Coal, lignite, and peat	64.4	4,399,776	135,986	2.06
Analog, hybrid DP machines, storage units	64.3	4,323,864	4,116,526	0.20
Roadrollers/civil engineering equipment	42.2	4,091,920	193,708	0.19
Soya beans	67.1	3,749,941	976	1.76
Piezoelectric crystals	50.7	3,019,250	1,100,923	1.42
War firearms, ammunition	62.7	2,888,887	203,863	1.36
Aircraft engines and motors parts	41.6	2,451,731	1,202,089	1.15
Machinery for special industries	22.5	2,121,790	1,681,149	1.00
Piston engine parts	24.9	2,069,649	1,431,972	0.97
Trucks	9.8	2,069,200	7,489,290	0.97
Radiotelephonic receivers, TV cameras, parts	15.0	2,066,605	4,647,997	0.97
Fuel oils	7.2	1,889,673	7,652,369	0.89
Switchgear	15.6	1,775,540	1,794,662	0.83
Electronic microcircuits	13.8	1,678,027	4,421,879	0.79
Raw cotton	34.2	1,634,779	15,773	0.77
Digital central processors	30.4	1,548,476	—	0.73
Digital computers	35.8	1,519,395	—	0.71
Nonmonetary gold	17.4	1,322,441	2,690,974	0.62
Electrical machinery	25.9	1,298,038	1,641,469	0.61
Other manufactured fertilizers	69.6	1,272,439	992	0.60
Gas turbines	62.8	1,229,403	1,254,813	0.58
Motor vehicle piston engines	20.1	1,209,376	1,904,459	0.57
Cigarettes	36.6	1,183,792	21,863	0.56
Rough sawn, veneer logs	75.8	1,170,516	17,408	0.55
Miscellaneous chemical products	14.2	1,155,456	395,435	0.54
Raw bovine or equine hides	45.3	1,021,116	30,670	0.48
Medicaments with hormones	12.7	997,437	816,088	0.47
Radioactive materials	57.1	980,118	1,399,330	0.46

TABLE **B–10** *(Continued)*

Industry	Share of Total World Exports	Export Value ($ millions)	Import Value ($ millions)	Share of Total U.S. Exports
Articles of plastic	14.9	962,927	1,670,496	0.45
Bleached, nondissolving pulp	17.8	937,298	1,225,127	0.44
Line telephone equipment	17.2	906,005	2,099,325	0.43
Other inorganic chemicals	30.4	904,765	341,823	0.42
Unexposed, undeveloped photo film	81.9	885,712	630,695	0.42
Oilcake & residues of soya	21.7	870,651	—	0.41
Electromedical equipment	46.6	865,609	524,326	0.41
Medical instruments	20.1	828,165	524,589	0.39
Insulated wire, cable	15.5	820,142	1,420,983	0.38
Pharmaceuticals other than medicaments	41.8	806,956	52,058	0.38
Fungicides, disinfectants	40.3	788,551	116,851	0.37
Unmilled sorghum	65.8	769,266	13	0.36
Pumps for liquids	25.9	761,027	625,712	0.36
Petroleum coke	80.3	760,981	19,522	0.36
Air-conditioners	35.4	751,041	309,924	0.35
TOTAL				51.59

NOTE: No import data are reported if import value is less than 0.3 percent of the total trade for 1985.

FIGURE B-9 Percentage of Exports by Cluster and Vertical Stage, United States, 1985

Upstream Industries

	Materials/Metals SCE	ΔSCE	SWCE	ΔSWCE	Forest Products SCE	ΔSCE	SWCE	ΔSWCE	Petroleum/Chemicals SCE	ΔSCE	SWCE	ΔSWCE	Semiconductors/Computers SCE	ΔSCE	SWCE	ΔSWCE	UPSTREAM INDUSTRIES SCE	SWCE
Primary Goods	1.1	-0.5	3.0	-0.3	1.3	-0.3	5.8	-0.7	6.3	1.8	4.1	0.6	8.8	4.5	20.5	-8.9	17.5	6.0
Machinery	0.2	-0.1	4.2	-0.2	0	-0.0	7.0	-1.3	—				—				0.2	4.8
Specialty Inputs	0.2	-0.0	0.9	-0.1	—				—				—				0.2	0.9
Total	1.5	-0.6	2.6	-0.3	1.3	-0.3	5.9	-0.7	6.3	1.8	4.1	0.6	8.8	4.5	20.5	-8.9	17.9	5.7

Industrial & Supporting Functions

	Multiple Business SCE	ΔSCE	SWCE	ΔSWCE	Transportation SCE	ΔSCE	SWCE	ΔSWCE	Power Generation & Distribution SCE	ΔSCE	SWCE	ΔSWCE	Office SCE	ΔSCE	SWCE	ΔSWCE	Telecommunications SCE	ΔSCE	SWCE	ΔSWCE	Defense SCE	ΔSCE	SWCE	ΔSWCE	INDUSTRIAL & SUPPORTING FUNCTIONS SCE	SWCE
Primary Goods	7.9	1.7	20.5	3.1	7.6	-1.3	7.4	-3.0	0.4	0.1	12.0	1.3	0.1	+0.0	7.3	0.8	0.2	0.2	6.2	-0.2	1.5	0.1	55.0	-0.1	17.6	11.6
Machinery	1.3	0.3	10.6	3.3	0.0	-0.1	21.2	-5.0	—				0.0	-0.1	10.6	-3.8	—				—				1.3	11.7
Specialty Inputs	0.3	-0.0	19.2	-2.9	10.7	1.8	27.9	3.3	0.5	0.1	27.2	3.3	0.0	0.0	0.0	0.0	—				—				11.4	26.8
Total	9.4	2.0	18.2	3.2	18.4	0.5	13.4	-1.1	0.8	0.2	13.8	1.7	0.1	-0.0	7.3	-0.0	0.2	0.2	6.2	-0.2	1.5	0.1	55.0	-0.1	30.4	14.5

Final Consumption Goods & Services

	Food/Beverage SCE	ΔSCE	SWCE	ΔSWCE	Textiles/Apparel SCE	ΔSCE	SWCE	ΔSWCE	Housing/Household SCE	ΔSCE	SWCE	ΔSWCE	Health Care SCE	ΔSCE	SWCE	ΔSWCE	Personal SCE	ΔSCE	SWCE	ΔSWCE	Entertainment/Leisure SCE	ΔSCE	SWCE	ΔSWCE	FINAL CONSUMPTION GOODS & SERVICES SCE	SWCE
Primary Goods	4.6	-2.7	8.4	-2.1	0.2	-0.0	0.6	-0.1	0.0	-0.1	0.4	-0.4	2.4	0.8	19.2	4.2	0.6	-0.2	8.4	-2.6	1.3	-0.1	6.7	-1.3	9.2	6.2
Machinery	0.7	-0.6	14.6	-3.4	0.1	-0.0	1.3	0.1	—				—				—				0	0	0	0	0.8	9.7
Specialty Inputs	5.4	-1.7	18.5	-2.3	2.0	-0.4	10.9	-0.5	0.0	0.0	0.0	0.0	—				0.2	-0.8	2.2	-5.2	—				7.6	11.9
Total	10.8	-5.0	12.1	-2.1	2.2	-0.5	3.7	-0.5	0.0	-0.1	0.3	-0.3	2.4	0.8	19.2	4.2	0.8	-1.0	6.4	-2.9	1.3	-0.1	5.7	-1.0	17.5	7.9

Grand Total: 65.8 / 9.0

Note: Totals may not add due to rounding

Key:
- SCE — Share of country's total exports 1985
- ΔSCE — Change in share of country's exports 1978–1985
- SWCE — Share of world cluster exports 1985
- ΔSWCE — Change in share of world cluster exports 1978–1985

Notes

Preface

1. President's Commission on Industrial Competitiveness (1985).

2. Funding for the Danish study was provided by the National Agency of Industry and Trade, Denmark Employees Capital Pension Fund, Advisory Council of Research Policy and Planning, Danish Society of Chemical, Civil, Electrical and Mechanical Engineers, and the *Børsen Daily*.

Chapter 1

1. Throughout this book I will use Korea and Germany to refer to South Korea and West Germany, respectively.

2. In the 1950s, 1960s, and even 1970s, much literature sought to explain why the United States was so competitive and the pattern of U.S. trade. This was a reflection of the commanding position that U.S. firms enjoyed in so many industries. Today, attention has shifted to Japan and to explaining its success. Newer models examine Japanese-style policies such as temporary protection.

3. See Yoshino (1968), Athos and Pascale (1981), Ouchi (1981), and Abernathy and Hayes (1980) for discussions of the virtues of Japanese management and the shortcomings of America's. Servan-Schreiber (1968) is among the best known of the works about the superiority of American management.

4. The annual ranking of competitiveness prepared by the European Management Foundation, based on a large number of such measures, is interesting but begs the question of what a competitive nation is. Its many measures also lack an explicit theory to justify and integrate them.

5. The term *productivity* here refers to real productivity, with output adjusted for inflation.

6. Many discussions of productivity use the term more narrowly to refer to efficiency.

7. Many discussions of competitiveness stress "high-value-added" industries because these are seen as contributing most to economic prosperity. Value-added

is the difference between revenue and the cost of purchased inputs. Value-added *per se* is only incidentally related to labor and capital productivity. Value-added per worker or other more direct measures of labor and capital productivity are far better and more precise indicators.

8. At the margin, the productivity of resources deployed in all industries is equalized by market forces. Crucial for national economic prosperity, however, is achieving an equilibrium in which the resulting *average* productivity of resources is as high as possible. This depends on raising the quality of factors and increasing the level of technology, broadly defined, with which factors are deployed. The opportunity to do so varies by industry and industry segment, and the productivity differences between firms in given industries and segments can also be substantial because of differences in skills and technology. A central focus of this book is the process by which the skills and techniques that underpin high average productivity are created.

9. Clearly, the capacity to improve productivity in all major sectors of an economy, not just manufacturing, is important to economic prosperity.

10. The role of growing export sectors in bidding up wages and pushing up the exchange rate is sometimes called the Dutch disease because of the popular example of the effect of natural gas exports on Dutch manufacturing. See Corden and Neary (1982). In Holland, however, export success was due to a natural resource windfall rather than to sustainable productivity increases in industry. The windfall was used to finance a bloated social welfare system rather than the education, research, or infrastructure necessary to boost future productivity. Eventually, even the natural resource windfall could not finance social spending.

11. The total value of goods, services, and financial assets a nation sells to the rest of the world must necessarily equal what it buys. This means that a positive imbalance of trade, which must be compensated for by accumulating foreign debt or foreign assets, creates self-limiting forces.

12. Purely domestic industries are also significant to national economic prosperity because their productivity contributes to or detracts from national productivity. Any nation in which many purely domestic industries, making up a significant fraction of any economy, are inefficient will face a constraint on its standard of living, as is the case in Italy and Japan. The leverage of international industries for national productivity is normally higher, however, because of their capacity to export and thereby expand output beyond local needs. Achieving high productivity in such industries thus allows greater positive effect on national productivity.

13. The loss or shrinkage of market positions to imports and foreign investment involves especially significant adjustment costs. The shareholders, managers, and workers in less productive firms and industries face economic losses and dislocation. Government comes under political pressure to intervene.

Upgrading an economy works best when needed shrinkage occurs gradually in a range of industries rather than abruptly in a few industries, because this minimizes the social and economic adjustment costs and the likelihood of counterproductive intervention.

In part because of these adjustment costs, the process of upgrading national productivity benefits when a nation has market positions capable of expansion in a broad range of industries, instead of depending on exports from a few. This reduces the dislocation that results from structural change in a few industries and from specialization by firms in more and more productive market segments and shifting abroad of less productive activities. At the same time, the presence of firms in a wide array of industries provides many possible avenues for improvement and innovation that raise productivity. In addition, breadth creates more potential for spillovers and cross-fertilization among industries. As will become clearer in subsequent chapters, the interconnections among related industries are essential to the upgrading process. Switzerland is a nation that illustrates how an economy with a broad array of international market positions has been able to upgrade continuously for decades, while Sweden, with an economy much more concentrated in a few sectors, has experienced greater difficulty and has had to resort to periodic devaluations.

14. The evidence is compelling, moreover, that the cost of such intervention both to the national treasury and to the nation's consumers is extremely high per job saved. See OECD (1984).

15. Trade (the sum of imports and exports) represents a significant fraction of national output in all advanced economies (about 15 percent in the United States, 25 percent in Japan, and 55 percent in Germany). An even greater proportion of national economies are *exposed* to international competition. Industries and segments of industries that involve sophisticated technology and skilled employees, and thus offer the greatest potential for high productivity, tend to be more exposed to trade than most industries. A wide range of activities, from production to R&D, can also readily be performed abroad.

16. A nation's terms of trade are affected by shifting exchange rates if domestically produced and foreign goods are differentiated and not perfect substitutes, a realistic assumption.

17. We will examine these issues further for individual nations in Part III.

18. See Maddison (1987) and Nelson (1981) for surveys.

19. Most efforts to investigate the patterns of national success in industries have examined broad industry sectors such as transportation equipment, food and beverages, and machinery. The picture at this level is often hazy, because the larger nations have some exports in virtually all sectors. In fact, a much-noted finding in the literature on international trade has been the prevalence of so-called intra-industry trade, or trade between nations in similar goods. For the most comprehensive treatment, see Grubel and Lloyd (1975).

20. Governmental distortions are prevalent in such industries as apparel, agriculture, automobiles, aircraft, and telecommunications, not to mention many others. Protection and administrative regulations, for example, have significantly distorted the patterns of national advantage in Europe. The onset of 1992 in Europe, if real barriers to trade decline, will mean that national economies are likely to become more concentrated in those industries where they have true competitive advantage.

21. Use of the term *comparative advantage* today has become considerably looser. Nations are sometimes said to have a comparative advantage in an industry if the industry is a successful exporter. This *ex post* interpretation of comparative advantage, of course, explains nothing at all.

22. Modern versions of Ricardian theory have assumed one factor of production (labor) and that countries differ in the amount of labor required to produce a good. See Dornbusch, Fisher, and Samuelson (1977).

23. For the seminal statement, see Ohlin (1933). Ohlin's elegant book noted many of the complexities of actual competition in the course of focusing on factors. Later treatments, of increasing mathematical rigor, became more stylized.

24. The factors of production relevant to comparative advantage are normally defined in broad terms such as labor, natural resources, capital, and the like. There have been many efforts to sharpen and extend the theory, as well as to use it to explain statistically the broad patterns of trade among nations. For a survey of the theory and evidence, see Jones and Kenen (1984).

Much of the literature on comparative advantage takes the form of mathematical models used to derive propositions about the composition of trade and the effect on trade of changes in parameters such as the number of goods, countries, and factors of production. These models are based on assumptions that make no claim to match the richness of actual competition: for example, labor and capital are frequently the only factors of production, the products produced in all countries are assumed to be identical, and production functions (and hence productivity) are assumed constant.

Empirical tests of comparative advantage have been difficult, because of the challenges of constructing tests which derive rigorously from the theory in light of its aggregate nature. Recent examples are Harkness (1983), Sveikauskas (1983), and Leamer (1984). Empirical tests are generally confined to broad groupings of industries such as labor-intensive industries or skill-intensive industries. The results have been mixed but generally supportive of some of the broad propositions of the theory, though they do not explain much of the variation in trade patterns among countries.

Refinements of the theory have introduced the role of skilled labor, and human and physical capital as it relates to labor. More recently, efforts have been made to relax certain key assumptions in the theory, such as the absence of economies of scale, as I will discuss further later.

25. See, for example, Zysman and Tyson (1983).

26. Leontief's (1954) famous paradox, in which the capital-rich United States was exporting labor-intensive goods, is just one salvo in a long debate on whether the Heckscher-Ohlin-Samuelson model (Samuelson made important later contributions) explained which countries had comparative advantage in particular products. See Hindley and Smith's (1984) assessment. Leamer (1980) is credited by many as having resolved the paradox, by arguing that the United States was a net exporter of both labor and capital services in the period Leontief studied.

27. Relaxing this assumption to allow the mobility of factors eliminates the rationale for trade. Despite the growing mobility of factors, however, trade has continued to increase.

28. See Helpman and Krugman (1985) for a critique. The theory also predicts the equalization of factor prices (for example, wages) among nations, which clearly has not occurred.

29. Nations can create such modern infrastructure in a matter of decades, as countries such as Singapore and Korea have demonstrated. Newly developing nations, by skipping intermediate generations of technology, can even improve on the infrastructure of long-advanced nations, as is evident to anyone who compares a phone call in Singapore to one in many parts of Europe.

30. Dutch capital helped finance the British Industrial Revolution, for example, while American railroads and other industries were financed with the help of British capital.

31. While for some nations this may be the best they can hope for, the point is that factor cost-based competitive advantage is not a desirable long-run target.

32. A new paradigm will raise daunting challenges for developing nations, as I will explore in Chapters 10 and 12.

33. See Helpman and Krugman (1985). A growing literature on the relationship between imperfect competition and trade investigates the role of these and other market imperfections in determining trade. The basic theme is that virtually every market imperfection creates a rationale for trade even if factor costs are equal across nations. Market imperfections also create a role for strategy. Left indeterminate is the central issue that concerns us here, the specific patterns of trade.

A related literature, sometimes called "strategic trade theory," investigates the implications of market inperfections for government policy. The thrust of this literature is normative, and it shows how government intervention in the presence of market imperfections can influence trading patterns through influencing firm commitments. The models explored are stylized, however, and the results of the various models are highly sensitive to which of a range of plausible specific assumptions about firm behavior is chosen. See, for example, Brander and Spencer (1983), Krishna (1984), and Krugman (1986). Dixit (1984) provides a critique.

34. This observation has been made by Deardorff (1984) and others.

35. Similarly, protecting the home market is no guarantee of reaping available scale economies in global markets. Increasing returns to scale have been used to justify protection, because if production enhances a nation's position in industries with increasing returns, this will increase national welfare. See Graham (1923).

36. For a survey, see Wells (1972).

37. The original reference is Vernon (1966).

38. Other threads of research on the role of home demand are discussed in Chapter 3.

39. The view that there are different explanations for international success that apply to different industries has led some authors to divide industries into groupings such as traditional, knowledge intensive, resource intensive, scale or mass production sensitive, and high technology (or science based). One such taxonomy is due to Pavitt (1984). The aim of such categories is to reflect the varying determinants of competitive success in different industries. See, for example, Arndt and Bouton (1987).

The problem with such generalizations is that technological change and the globalization of strategy have blurred the categories. Given flexible manufacturing, information systems, and other technological developments, nearly every industry in the 1980s is knowledge intensive. "Traditional" industries such as apparel and furniture are being revolutionized by new production and distribution methods. Economies of scale are generally falling in production, though rising in marketing and distribution. No simple division of industries can capture the diversity of sources of competitive advantage and how they are achieved. As we will see, a richer theory cuts across them.

40. For surveys, see Hood and Young (1979), Dunning (1981), and Caves (1982). Dunning's (1989) paper updates his so-called "eclectic" theory.

41. Trade and foreign investment are generally employed together in the expansion of successful firms (for evidence, see Blomström, Lipsey, and Kulchycky [1988]). The same types of assets and skills create the potential for both.

42. The concept of home base refers to a particular industry. A diversified multinational may have home bases for competing in different industries in different nations.

43. Some observers see firms becoming competitive at the expense of their nation when they source parts, manufacture, or develop products abroad. Policies by a nation to prevent its firms from manufacturing or sourcing offshore, though tempting, are self-defeating. Blocking such actions will only undermine the ability to sustain advantage in an industry. The only real solution is to alter national circumstances so that firms will choose to do more at home. See Chapter 12.

44. In X-ray equipment, for example, C. H. F. Müller is owned by Philips (Holland). Yet the German subsidiary retains full strategic control and, along with Siemens, it has a strong position in the global X-ray equipment industry. Germany is home base despite foreign ownership.

45. Not only trade theory but much of growth theory is based on this view. See Romer (1987).

46. My fundamental perspective is more Schumpeterian (1934, 1942) than neoclassical. Entrepreneurship and innovation prove central to national advantage. Why some firms and individuals innovate in particular industries, and why they are based in particular nations, will be the focus of much of what follows.

47. A stream of literature has reached this conclusion. See the famous work of Solow (1957) and Denison (1962).

48. Factors are still scarce at a given point in time, but my research suggests that the possibilities for upgrading their quality or deploying them more productively are numerous and that the gains are substantial.

49. These advanced nations have had varying degrees of success in sustaining advantage. See Chapters 7 through 9.

50. The study was limited to relatively developed nations because of its focus on competition in relatively sophisticated industries. Though no less developed countries (LDCs) were examined, however, the study explored the determinants of competitive success in those industries in which LDCs aspire to compete. I believe the study carries many implications for firms and governments in developing nations. See Chapter 10.

51. Notable examples are Vogel (1985), McCraw (1986), and Prestowitz (1988).

52. See Chapters 8 and 12.

53. Trade patterns were measured at the five-digit level in the Standard International Trade Classification (SITC).

54. Most empirical studies of national competitiveness or the patterns of trade have been based on statistical tests of trading patterns at one point in time. Limits in available data have meant that only a sample of industries in a nation has been investigated. Industries are defined broadly, and explanatory variables are few. Most statistical studies have investigated trade and foreign investment separately. Results for the relationship between trade and foreign investment range from neutral to complementary.

55. An industry was designated as competitive if its share of world exports

exceeded the nation's average share of world exports and the industry had a positive trade balance, with certain other conditions discussed in Appendix A. The industries that met these conditions typically accounted for two-thirds or more of a nation's total exports. We added industries based on evidence of significant outbound foreign investment, provided it was not of a passive, portfolio nature or involved acquisitions of independently managed foreign companies. A good example of portfolio investment would be the substantial Japanese investment in U.S. real estate. Similarly, the international position of a firm such as Thompson CSF (France) in television sets, consisting largely of acquired foreign companies that have been left intact, was not taken as a sign of robust French competitive advantage in international terms.

We excluded industries where there was evidence that exports were due to foreign production subsidiaries located in the nation. We also excluded industries whose international success was primarily in neighboring countries, and those in which there were chronic subsidies or chronic losses with no reasonable prospect of future profits. These were industries where international position did not reflect underlying competitive advantage. In the later phase of the research in which we investigated detailed case studies, the presence of competitive advantage could be assessed more directly.

56. These years were selected to provide the longest time period available, given changes in the Standard International Trade Classification (SITC) system. The bulk of our attention was concentrated on the 1978 and 1985 data, because we had available the less aggregated industry classification system (SITC Revision II) introduced in 1978 which was more representative of actual industries.

57. To supplement the statistical sources, interviews were used to identify successful industries and segments and to help exclude industries where success was a reflection of foreign investment or other anomalies.

58. We also conducted interviews in each nation with senior government officials, bankers, leading industrialists, and other observers with a broad perspective on the economy, supplemented by library research. Our purpose was to gain an understanding of each nation's institutional context, attitudes toward industry, and social, political, and economic structure. Of particular interest were such areas as government policy toward industry, the nature of the health care, educational, and financial systems, the institutional structure of R&D, and the pattern of local demand for goods and services.

59. The industry histories were based on historical sources, primary company documents, and interviews with current and former industry participants, industry observers, and trade association personnel. Case studies were circulated in draft form to industry participants to solicit comments and additions. In some instances, case studies were also reviewed by experts from firms based in other nations.

Chapter 2

1. While much has been written on all these subjects, a basic level of understanding for all readers is necessary to set the stage for subsequent chapters. My theory of competitive strategy and competitive advantage is presented most fully in Porter (1980, 1985, and 1986). What follows here condenses that theory and adds some new elements relevant to a broader theory of the dynamics of competition.

2. These concepts apply equally to products and services. I will often just use the term product to avoid repetition.

3. Indeed, entry barriers, which make an industry attractive for existing competitors, at the same time make it difficult for a new entrant to attain a good position.

4. In many consumer goods and some industrial products, there is both an immediate buyer (for example, a retailer) and an end user (for example, the household). The bargaining power of the immediate buyer determines profitability, but the end user's power and price sensitivity strongly influences that of the intermediate buyer.

5. For a complete discussion, see Porter (1980).

6. The conditions are described in Porter (1985), Chapter 1.

7. The distinction between a segment and an industry is sometimes a matter of degree, and can lead to endless discussions among managers. The essential issue, which firms must not lose sight of, is competitive advantage. The appropriate industry and segment definitions are those that highlight differences in the essential sources of competitive advantage. When in doubt, it is best to err on the side of narrow industry and segment definitions, though setting strategy with an eye to the interrelationships with other segments and industries.

One test of the appropriate definition is competitor behavior. Where none of the competitors in one segment overlap with the competitors in other segments, that segment may have sufficiently different sources of competitive advantage to constitute a strategically distinct industry.

8. There are some common (though not universal) differences in the choice of scope in many industries. German, Japanese, Swedish, and American companies tend to offer relatively wide product lines, while Italian, Swiss, and Korean companies are more likely to focus on segments. Japanese firms, in addition to having broad product lines, tend to compete in an array of related industries. These differences in scope are something that I will explore in subsequent chapters. They bear on patterns of national success in different industries.

9. These linkages, while suggesting the need for coordination with suppliers and channels, do not alter the fact that a firm must bargain with them over how profits are divided. Achieving coordination does not preclude hard bargaining; in fact, part of hard bargaining is persuading suppliers and channels to modify activities so that greater coordination is achieved. Contrary to popular assertion, Japanese companies, known for cooperative supplier relationships, maintain multiple suppliers for important inputs and bargain aggressively. Suppliers to leading Japanese companies usually earn lower returns than the firms to which they sell.

10. I discuss the structural determinants of cost relative to competitors, which I term cost drivers, in Porter (1985), Chapter 3.

11. Merely imitating competitors and basing advantage on cheap labor or raw materials, a strategy often employed by firms from developing nations, is possible in less sophisticated industries and industry segments but is rarely sustainable nor the basis for economic development beyond a certain level.

12. An innovation in my parlance is a new way of doing things (termed an invention by some authors) that is *commercialized*. The process of innovation cannot be separated from a firm's strategic and competitive context.

13. My theory and findings stress incomplete information and organizational

barriers to perceiving and acting on new ways of competing. Recent research on technological innovation, with a somewhat narrower focus, illustrates a growing recognition that great uncertainty surrounds new technology, that firms in the same industry pursue widely varying technological approaches, and that much technical knowledge involves learning by doing, which is proprietary and difficult to transfer (see Nelson [1981] and Dosi [1988] for surveys). These characteristics apply even more to innovation in broader, strategic terms.

14. Investment in such specialized assets is sometimes termed *commitment* in the literature of industrial economics. Ghemawat (forthcoming) has expanded this notion to shed much light on some dynamic aspects of strategy.

15. For an interesting study of sustainability in a sample of one hundred companies, see Ghemawat (1986).

16. When the architect of the original strategy is still present, change may be virtually impossible. Richard Tedlow (forthcoming, 1990) has described, for example, how Henry Ford and Robert Woodruff (Coca-Cola) both lived to a ripe old age and blocked needed strategy changes in their companies.

17. Schumpeter's (1934, Chapter 2) marvelous description of the entrepreneur and of leadership highlights some of these issues.

18. Sometimes the geographic scope of competition is regional (for example, European) and not fully global. The basic strategic issues, however, are the same.

19. Many of the issues here are treated in more detail in Porter (1986). That book contains extensive references to relevant literature for the interested reader.

20. For another useful treatment of the relationship between activities and global strategy, see Kogut (1984, 1985).

21. For example, governments may desire national autonomy in decision making, or to gain the spillover effects of domestic R&D and the training of skilled workers.

22. Further discussion of these organizational issues is found in Bartlett and Ghoshal (1989), Keegan (1989), and Prahalad and Doz (1987).

23. Just as the pattern of globalization can differ by industry segment, it can also differ by group of countries. There are frequently groups of countries among which the advantages of a global or regional strategy are particularly strong; for instance, countries with similar climatic conditions have similar product needs. Other relevant groupings can be based on language, state of economic development, extent of government intervention in competition, and historical or current political ties.

24. For a fuller treatment of alliances, see Porter (1986).

25. These attributes are quite different from, and often independent of, the considerations entering into neoclassical comparative advantage.

Chapter 3

1. In view of the important role of innovation in international competition among nations, the literature on R&D and technological innovation contains many useful insights. I will cite a few selected examples in this chapter and treat the literature as a whole in note 33 in Chapter 4.

2. What is required is a theory of disequilibrium, not one that assumes a fixed set of resources and a constant technology within which firms optimize. By adopting

these assumptions, much neoclassical economic theory, including growth theory, has assumed away what must be explained. In fact, technology is constantly evolving and resources are being continuously created and upgraded. The payoff is not in optimizing within existing constraints but in changing the constraints.

3. Recent developments in trade theory, by embodying market imperfections, have made a promising beginning. As I discussed in note 33 in Chapter 1, however, newer models still fall short of explaining why nations are able to export in particular industries.

4. Related industries are those where firms can share activities in the value chain across industries (for example, distribution channels, technology development) or transfer proprietary skills from one industry to another. An example of three related industries is cars, light trucks, and forklift trucks (used for material handling inside and outside factories and warehouses).

5. While globalization makes differential access to classical factors of production less likely and less significant, information is traded much less efficiently in markets, especially if it is specialized and embodied in personnel and procedures. For an interesting study which stresses the role of differential information and rate of learning on competitive success in operations management, see Jaikumar and Bohn (1989).

6. The determinants are observable characteristics of a nation. Each has informational characteristics, bears on available resources or skills (including organizational capabilities), influences the goals of various participants (in a broad sense) in industry competition, and has a role in pressuring firms. Though it is possible to recast the theory around these four attributes, such an approach is less operational and less intuitively clear.

7. In terms familiar to an economist, the operation of the determinants and the interactions among them lead to powerful external economies within the nation, often within in a particular city or region, that are difficult to tap from another home base.

8. The systemic character of the "diamond" sometimes blurs cause and effect, a subject to which I will return.

9. An important distinction in the theory, which I noted in Chapter 1, is between absolute and comparative advantage. Absolute advantage reflects a factor endowment which makes the nation the world's low-cost producer of a good. Relative advantage is a weaker condition in which the nation exports those goods which use its relatively abundant factors intensively. It nonetheless leads to gains from trade, because it reflects the opportunity cost to the nation of deploying resources in alternative uses. A nation may import a good for which it has absolute advantage if it can deploy the factors more productively elsewhere.

10. Less aggregated accounts divide labor into a few skill classes and include a few other categories such as infrastructure. One of the least aggregated trade studies, Leamer (1984), includes capital, three types of labor, four types of land, coal, minerals, and oil. But even this level of aggregation is far too broad to capture the differences among nations that lead to competitive advantage.

11. Standard trade theory, in which technology is constant (and fixed) among nations and products are undifferentiated, puts aside these issues.

12. Mobility of skilled people and technical knowledge is far from new. Our industry case studies revealed repeated examples as far back as early in the nineteenth

century. British engineers and technicians, for example, were often hired to help establish industries in other nations.

13. Some observers, citing the diminished role of basic factors and the fact that the multinational firm can tap them anywhere, argue that this eliminates a role for the nation altogether in international competition. See, for example, Reich (1989), who argues that the American economy has ceased to exist. Yet this is like throwing the baby out with the bathwater. While basic factors such as low-skilled labor are not sources of competitive advantage and will not command high returns, the growing importance of innovation, skills, and rapid change in competition that is increasingly knowledge-intensive has made the nation arguably more important.

14. Such a pool exists in the United States and to a lesser extent Britain. In continental Europe and Japan, most software firms produce custom software under contract and not general-purpose packaged software which requires sustained start-up investment for product development.

15. If advantages in advanced and specialized factors are nullified, basic factors may become decisive, though advantages in them are unstable. In shipbuilding, for example, Scandinavian design expertise and building techniques were diffused to the Far East through licensing to the extent that they could not offset the vastly lower wages of Asian workers whose skills where rising. Thus the cost of semiskilled labor, a basic factor, became decisive to competitive advantage outside of specialized segments. Japan enjoyed a labor cost advantage for a time, but the labor cost advantage shifted to Korea.

16. New financial instruments are being invented, for example, which allow finer tailoring of risk/return to the nature of the investment opportunity, and which package investments to allow funding in public markets where wealthy private investors were once the only funding source.

17. In classical and neoclassical trade theory, the stock of factors in a nation is taken as fixed. Firms optimize within the constraints of this fixed pool in deploying factors in particular industries.

A number of authors have pointed out that factors can be created, dating at least back to Friedrich List (1856). For more recent statements, see Zysman and Tyson (1983) and Scott and Lodge (1985). What is less well understood is where, how, and in what forms factor creation takes place and its link to national competitive advantage.

18. Factor creation is cumulative; one generation inherits those factors created by the previous generation.

19. Specialized factor-creating institutions are difficult to replicate, while proximity facilitates ongoing interchange with a nation's firms.

20. Where the abundance of a factor leads to its inefficient utilization, a firm is especially vulnerable to shifts in factor costs.

21. I will discuss the role of the exchange rate in economic upgrading in Chapter 12.

22. In some instances, the resources required to innovate around factor disadvantages exceed the long-term benefits. Here, basic factor disadvantages will prevent the achievement of competitive advantage. However, this very dependence on basic factors means that such industries are likely to be characterized by low or modest productivity and hence will be less important to economic upgrading.

23. A body of research has investigated the theory of induced innovation, in which firms innovate around the relatively expensive factors. This work is concerned with the role of factor costs in the direction of technological change and has rarely been linked to national competitiveness. For surveys, see Davidson (1976) and David (1975). For early studies, see Rothbart (1946) and Habakkuk (1962). Rosenberg (1976) coined the useful term "focusing devices" to refer to inducements to innovation.

There is some controversy in the literature about whether factor costs should have an impact. Some authors argue that a firm will always make profit-maximizing choices about investing in innovation to reduce factor intensity regardless of relative factor cost. This school of thought takes an overly narrow view of innovation and its causes, and makes what I believe to be a faulty assumption about the information available to firms regarding the payoffs to particular investments in innovation and their incentives and ability to innovate. Under more realistic assumptions, the role of cross-national factor differences is an important one.

Mention of factor-saving innovation appears in the literature on international business. See Vernon (1966), who discusses labor-saving innovation by American firms, and Franko (1976), who highlights the prevalence of labor-saving innovations in Europe as a result of labor shortages.

Finally, the literature on innovation contains an important thread of work on stimuli or inducements to innovation, including some akin to factor disadvantages. A particularly insightful example is Rosenberg (1976).

24. Technological possibilities may mean that selective factor disadvantages cannot be offset or overcome at all, or not overcome economically. Swedish shipbuilders, facing high labor costs, innovated to automate the shipbuilding process. However, the Swedish firms were unable to eliminate a significant labor content. Labor cost remained a large proportion of cost, and the Swedish innovations were soon copied and improved upon by Japanese yards. The result was a loss of competitive position.

25. For an account, see Danielson (1988).

26. Airfreight is so efficient from Schipol Airport that the region has attracted other delivery-sensitive industries.

27. Vernon's product cycle theory of trade (1966) rests in part on demand-side influences. Another interesting Danish study that confirms empirically some influence of home market demand on trade patterns is that of Andersen, Dalum, and Villumsen (1981).

28. The role of home demand characteristics in trade is stressed by the insightful work of Staffan Linder (1961). Linder argues that there must be local demand for a product before a nation will export that product, because local demand is necessary to allow local firms to learn how to succeed in the industry. He goes on to observe that trade will be greatest between nations with similar demands, because the experience gained by local firms will result in goods that these nations will value. Linder argues that similarity in per capita income is the best proxy for similarity in demand, and hence that trade will be most intense between nations with similar per capita income.

Linder's theory contains important elements of truth. Since many nations have similar per capita incomes and similar demands in Linder's broad terms, however, the effect of these variables in determining patterns of trade may be somewhat less compelling today than when Linder was writing in the late 1950s and early 1960s. Moreover, similarity in per capita income is no longer as good a predictor of similarity of demand as it once was. Globalization of competition, rapid and fluid international communications, and the desire of developing nations to have the most advanced goods all mean that broad similarities in demand exist in many nations.

Linder's theory highlights the importance of local demand to trade, and that broad demand similarities are necessary for trade. Yet this does not predict the direction of trade or expose the specific attributes of local demand that allow one nation to gain advantage in a particular industry. It is specific *dissimilarities*, in demand among nations, within broadly overlapping demand structures, that are crucial to achieving competitive advantage.

29. Many studies of new product innovation document the importance of an acute understanding of buyer needs to competitive success. Understanding market needs, the timing of product introductions, and the approach taken to marketing are always at the top of the list of causes of successful and unsuccessful new products. All are variations of the same theme. For one survey, see Cooper (1986). What is less clear from past studies is *why* some firms are able to perceive needs better than others. This is the issue I stress here.

30. This influence is especially decisive when a firm is first getting established and initially creating a competitive advantage.

31. Becoming a true "insider" in another nation requires a long presence, management by local nationals, and a good deal of local autonomy. But these circumstances diminish the influence of the foreign subsidiary on the developments of global product varieties.

32. Foreign needs are dealt with through features or modification but not through altering the core product.

33. This was the conclusion of important early work on Belgium by Drèze (1961). He argued that small countries with ethnic and cultural diversity, such as Belgium, were unable to attain the scale to be competitive in style- and design-sensitive goods because local segments were too small. Instead, he argued, Belgium specialized in the production of varieties more standardized in world markets.

Grubel and Lloyd (1975) also emphasize this fact in their valuable work on intra-industry trade, or trade among nations in similar goods. They argue that such trade is difficult to explain with conventional trade theory. Where there are economies of scale in producing individual product varieties, Grubel and Lloyd reason that nations will specialize and trade among themselves.

34. Ethier (1979) argues, based on such a view, that national scale is unimportant.

35. Sophisticated and demanding buyers are frequently associated with rapid penetration of improved products and short product life cycles.

36. The role of demanding buyer can also be played to some extent by subsidiaries of foreign firms located in a country. Singapore has a very high concentration of the world's leading electronics companies that use Singapore as a manufacturing base. These represent a unique asset that Singapore has yet to exploit.

37. See, for example, Scott and Lodge (1985) and Wells (1972).

38. The reference to Japan is curious given the large relative size of the Japanese home market, the second largest in the world. I will have more to say later about why Japanese firms export.

39. While his focus is narrower, Schmookler (1966) contains an illuminating discussion of the role of market size and growth in stimulating technological innovation.

40. The advantage of early demand in a nation has been discussed by a number of authors. Vernon's product cycle of international trade (1966) is a prominent example. The United States, as the most advanced country, was seen as having the earliest demand for advanced goods. As Vernon himself has recognized, however, early demand does not necessarily occur today in the United States.

41. Where firms from a nation are already internationalized in other product lines, saturation at home is less necessary to encourage overseas sales of new products and models.

42. Hirschman (1958), in his insightful book on economic development, emphasizes the importance of complementarities and linkages among industries to the development process, primarily through providing a volume of demand for one another's products. I broaden the nature of such linkages, and assign them an important role not only to the composition of the domestic economy but to the industries in which a nation can succeed internationally.

43. Locating subsidiaries in a supplier's home nation suffers from similar problems in reverse.

44. New entry is also often stimulated, an important influence I will treat in the next chapter.

45. See, for example, Lieberman (1988).

46. There have been some efforts to measure international differences in management practices, a task fraught with complexities. I cannot hope to provide a complete framework here, but our research highlights the importance of such differences and their relevance to a complete theory of national advantage. The important point stressed here is that the prevailing management practices in a nation will be an advantage in some industries and a disadvantage in others.

47. Chandler's (forthcoming) historical research on the rise of the multinational firm, which has proceeded in parallel to my own, stresses the development of internal skills and managerial capabilities in the growth of successful international competitors. My stress is more on the environment surrounding firms, and how this influences the creation of strategy, skills, organizational arrangements, and success in particular fields.

48. Chandler's research provides further illustrations of the role of social factors and tradition on the way in which firms are managed and their *modus operandi*. In Britain, for example, Chandler's research has shown that British firms were more likely to resist the adoption of managerial hierarchies than firms in Germany and the United States. In the end, this constrained their competitive advantage in some industries as competition became more complex and global. See Chandler in Porter (1986) and Chandler (forthcoming).

49. While much economic theory views goals as identical among firms and frames them in terms of profit or utility maximization, in practice goals are much more complex. Involved are such questions as time horizon, required rate of return,

perceived prestige, and the amount of effort expended. The sorts of considerations embodied in Leibenstein's notion of X-efficiency are quite important. See Leibenstein (1966) and Franz (1988).

50. I will use this term to refer to companies whose shares are owned by private individuals and other corporations and are traded on public capital markets. Private firms refer to those that are closely held by a few individuals. State-owned corporations are those owned by government.

51. Leveraged buyouts (LBOs), which have proliferated in the 1980s in America, are seen as a solution to the faulty incentives of managers. By offering substantial ownership to managers and removing the pressures of the public capital market, LBOs provide accountability and motivation. Other things being equal, LBOs will tend to improve motivation and lead to the sale of underperforming assets. Because the firm takes on high levels of debt whose proceeds are not invested in the business, however, the pressure to generate short-term cash flow is severe. The potential impact on investment and risk-taking may mean that the LBO cure is worse than the disease. A better overall solution for national competitive advantage would be to shift the goals of public investors and improve the governance process.

52. See Ravenscraft and Scherer (1987). A supporting perspective is found in Porter (1987).

53. The trend, reflecting these views, is to relax constraints on mergers and cooperative agreements among domestic rivals. These policies are often a serious mistake, as will be discussed further in Chapter 12.

54. Local rivals may not necessarily compete head-on in every segment but are potential entrants into one another's product segments. In the Italian machinery industry, for example, one or two firms tend to be strong in each specialized segment, but many others could potentially take their place.

55. It is interesting to note that in Japan, some of the most dramatic successes (such as autos, steel, and machine tools) occurred in industries where government actively attempted to limit entry but failed.

56. For a survey and discussion of the ample evidence that national champions usually fail in international competition, see Adams and Brock (1988).

57. The literature on the economics of innovation contains strong empirical and theoretical support for the idea that competition is associated with greater rates of innovation. See Arrow's (1962) early theoretical demonstration and the excellent review by Scherer (1980). An interesting recent study of the pharmaceutical industry by Thomas (1989) finds that both greater domestic rivalry and strict national regulation speeds up the rate of innovation by one nation's firms relative to others.

58. The rapid mobility of technology across nations has been emphasized in recent years. As I will discuss further, this is true primarily in less sophisticated segments and does not threaten competitive advantage in industries where the home environment supports continued innovation. Much innovation also involves learning that is specific to particular segments and strategies and is slower to diffuse than technology embodied in product designs or manufacturing equipment.

59. Schumpeter (1942), while stressing the importance of innovation, argues that a large firm with market power will be the more innovative, not a group of rivals. The literature on innovation does not support this view, nor was it borne

out in the industries we studied. Innovation is not undertaken because of stability and only with ample resources, as Schumpeter argued, but because of pressures and challenges. A minimum scale threshold is necessary for R&D to be effective, varying by industry, but it is smaller firms and "outsiders" who are the real engines of creative destruction.

60. In an industry such as central office telephone switches, for example, economies of scale (principally in R&D) are huge. Japan has several competitors as does the United States, but small nations such as Sweden (Ericsson) and Canada (Northern Telecom) have just one.

61. Economic theory stresses the incentives to innovate due to appropriability, which are diminished by the presence of many rivals. While such incentives are necessary, in imperfect competition a firm has the incentive to innovate if it can gain sustainable advantage in its narrow target market segment, even though others imitate or adopt the innovation to compete in different segments. The first mover in innovation also gains advantages that justify innovation though others follow. An incentive to innovate is also created by the penalty of *not* innovating if others do, something not stressed in many treatments. This negative incentive, in our research, is as or more important than positive incentives in determining the rate of innovation because of the inertia and complacency of many companies.

My theory, moreover, suggests that domestic rivalry and its impact on the national "diamond" make investment in innovation more effective. Even discounting the arguments made above, greater effectiveness of investments in innovation where there is domestic rivalry may outweigh lower appropriability and lead to greater innovative effort. See, for a careful discussion, Enright (1990).

Many discussions of appropriability also have an implicit domestic focus. In global competition, a group of national competitors who collectively innovate more rapidly than foreign rivals can *all* earn profits through exporting, especially if they each compete in somewhat different segments.

62. Cartels and extensive cooperation among direct rivals will be consistent with sustaining competitive advantage only in the rare case where vigorous rivalry on important variables, notably technology, can be preserved.

63. The likelihood of spin-offs is usually greatest during early phases of industry development, or when structural changes in markets or technology occur.

64. Occasionally, established firms acquire smaller companies and develop them, creating effective new business formation. This approach to acquisitions, while benefiting national advantage, is the exception and not the rule. Empirical evidence (Ravenscraft and Scherer [1987], for example) and our own case studies confirm that many acquisitions are not a beachhead for growth but are milked for cash. In the process, innovation slows.

65. These may be partly influenced by local conditions.

66. This point has also been stressed by Olson (1982), who focuses on the disruptive effect of wars on cartels and coalitions that freeze change. I believe the effect of wars is much broader and will explore some of the reasons why in Chapters 7 and 8.

67. Government's role is frequently overstated because the economic underpinnings of success are not examined in studies that set out to examine the influence of government. Most studies also have focused on a few large, highly visible industries such as steel, shipbuilding, automobiles, and semiconductors, where government

attention is inevitable. Such industries are far from a representative sample of any nation's economy. Most studies also examine only one or two countries, selected because government seems important. Our sample of industries and nations seeks to be more representative.

Chapter 4

1. The size and quality of public investments in generalized factors can be and are influenced by the attitudes of the business community and private citizens.

2. In Europe, professorships are few in number, and a department will often have only one professor who supervises numerous other faculty. The mix of professorships by specific field varies among nations and is often an interesting indicator, with a lag reflecting the pace of academic institutions, of the areas where factor creation is most developed.

3. Investments in factor creation are subject to public good or externality problems, in which firms are unable to capture all the benefits. Domestic rivalry, however, helps shape the institutional structure to overcome such problems, because it influences the formation and behavior of independent institutions as well as the incentives of outside actors considering factor-creating investments.

4. Each firm, through its many contacts with outside parties, transmits information about itself and its industry. One large firm will not attract double the attention of two smaller ones whose sizes exceed some minimum threshold, so that multiple rivals will normally lead to more effective signaling.

5. The economic theory of location shows how firms will locate close to each other to gain access to the broadest array of customers. The rationale here is similar.

6. This point dates back to Adam Smith (1776). See Stigler (1951) for a more recent treatment.

7. In this way, a group of rivals helps reduce transactional failures.

8. For example, see Marshall ([1890] 1920).

9. To state the point more technically, domestic rivalry has signaling benefits, reduces transactional failures, and improves the incentives of individuals, suppliers, and factor creating institutions.

10. For supporting data, see Jerusalem Institute of Management (1987).

11. Leamer (1984), in the process of creating aggregates of traded commodities with which to test trade models, discovered "clusters" of commodities with highly correlated exports. Leamer noted that trade models are hard-pressed to explain the phenomenon.

12. A number of French writers (see Toledano [1978]) have coined the term *filières* to refer to families of technologically interdependent sectors. Their importance is seen in the fact that technological interdependencies may mean that technological strength in one sector is dependent on strength in another. The notion of *filières* is a valuable precursor to the broader notion of clustering. It highlights one reason why clusters might occur, because technical connections are close, and why presence in related sectors in a nation might be necessary for their mutual advantage.

Other literature on innovation, though not addressing international competitiveness, is also suggestive of clustering by stressing technological interdependencies among industries. See, for example, Abernathy and Utterback (1978) and Rosenberg (1979).

Other useful antecedents to the notion of clusters appear in literature by Swedish writers. This reflects, in part, the structure of the Swedish economy in which the activities of the large Swedish multinationals are often closely connected. An early contribution is Dahmén's (1950, 1988) concept of development blocks. Dahmén stresses the necessary link between the ability of one sector to develop and progress in another. In his examples, Dahmén often also talks of stages or vertical activities within a given industry. This interesting work is suggestive that connections among industries can be important to achieving advantage.

A more recent line of work is that by Lars Gunnar Mattsson (1987). He has charted networks or relationships among firms and some of their characteristics. This work is suggestive of the interchange among firms within clusters.

Finally, recent empirical research on diversification patterns within nations provides evidence that diversification often follows the input-output matrix, or between industries with supplying and buying relationships. This is consistent with the mechanisms that lead to clusters. See Lemelin (1982) and MacDonald (1985).

13. It is important to note at this point that the process also works in reverse. The uncompetitive industry can undermine other industries through its role as a buyer.

14. External economies, which I described earlier, extend within clusters and not just within individual national industries. The presence of clusters helps mitigate some of the public good problems that constrain factor creating investments.

15. Part of the problem is also what economists call "impacted information," or information which is blocked from being credibly transmitted to another entity because there is no way for the holder of the information to convince the other entity that the information is valuable without disclosing it.

16. These ease transactional difficulties in the parlance of Williamson (1975, 1985).

17. These also encourage greater information exchange.

18. Large groups also present in such nations as Belgium and France are less beneficial for competitive advantage, because they are primarily financial holding companies.

19. Lars Gunnar Mattsson's (1987) interesting work on "networks" involving independent firms is a reflection of interchange within clusters. Working in Sweden, it is perhaps not surprising that his attention was drawn to them.

20. Sabel, a student of Italian industry, has highlighted the importance of regionalized "industrial districts" and argued for their increasing importance based on falling scale economies. See Sabel (1987) and Piore and Sabel (1983).

21. See Marshall ([1890] 1920).

22. Geographic proximity of rivals raises interesting questions about whether a city or region instead of the nation is the proper unit of analysis. There are significant differences in economic prosperity between regions in many nations, and resource-rich regions are declining relative to resource-poor ones. I will explore this question further below.

23. A long tradition of work in location theory and economic geography contains useful parallels. Weber (1929) set forth a theory in which the objective of industrial location was to minimize total costs including transportation. Lösch (1954) developed a stylized model in which spatial supply and demand considerations entered into optimal location. Economic geographers identify "agglomeration econo-

mies'' of concentrated plants in a region, which stress economies of specialization. See O'Sullivan (1981) and Lloyd and Dicken (1977).

Related literature on regional development in high technology industries also contains useful insights. The Silicon Valley phenomenon has been particularly investigated. See, for example, Hall and Markusen (1985).

My theory sees geographic concentration as part of the more general process by which advantage is created and sustained. While economic geography has not been seen as a core discipline in economics, my research suggests that it should be. Enright's (1990) doctoral dissertation takes a deep look at the phenomenon of geographic concentration both through formal modeling and expirical work.

24. Geographic proximity also has important reputational effects which limit opportunistic behavior. This facilitates vertical interchange within clusters (see Enright 1990). Lundvall (1985, 1988) has stressed the interdependence between users and suppliers in a region or country as important to technological innovation.

25. These arguments also help explain why external economies are most significant within a nation (or region within a nation) and not across nations.

26. The work of Jacobs (1984) appropriately highlights the important role of cities in economic development. Cities or regions are often the locus of competitive advantage in an industry. I have described how the city, as a locale for a given industry, is part of the process of competition. Trade between a city or region and others within the nation plays a parallel role to international trade in affecting local productivity.

27. The impact of new technologies such as information systems in even ''mature'' industries represents a fundamental threat to the normal role of nations in the developing world, who have competed in traditional and mature industries. Yet these same technologies are widening the potential range of industries in the world economy and hence the overall size of the pie, and slow population growth in the advanced nations is constraining the pool of human resources and thus the extent of industries in which such nations can participate. Which forces prove to be stronger will be important to future prosperity in developing nations. See Chapter 12.

28. Olson (1982) provides a fascinating description of this process. See also Etzioni (1985).

29. The Swiss premium watch competitors have sustained position all along.

30. I am grateful to Richard Tedlow for suggesting this term.

31. For a description, see Lazonick (1983).

32. Rising factor costs and upgraded pressure on the nation's currency help to shift resources to higher-productivity industries.

33. The literature on technological innovation contains many insights for understanding international competition though it has been developed largely in a domestic context. It has identified individually the role of users, suppliers, and firms themselves as innovation sources. See, for example, von Hippel's (1988) interesting book as well as classics by Schmookler (1966), Abernathy and Utterback (1975), Rosenberg (1976), Freeman (1982), Nelson and Winter (1982) and others. An extended debate has pitted ''demand pull'' against ''technology push'' explanations.

My theory integrates these sources and others into a broader framework. Innovation cannot be decoupled from its strategic and competitive context. Much innovation does not involve technology in the narrow scientific sense but improvements in ways of doing things. The environment surrounding a firm is as or more important to innovation than what goes on inside. Exposure to and interpretation of information is central to the innovation process. Innovation is an unnatural act in firms that results only from pressures on unusual motivation. My theory shows how a range of determinants all interact to shape the innovation process. Demand pull and technology push are both necessary, as is the proper competitive environment and access to appropriate factors.

34. The "diamond" also provides a broader view of the determinants of investment. Investment is influenced by capital costs, but Korea and Italy illustrate that the causes of investment are much broader. Rivalry, demand-side pressures, corporate and managerial goals, and other influences have an arguably more important role.

35. This same theme emerges from studies of social progress in a range of disciplines. Max Weber wrote about the motivation arising from the Protestant ethic. David McClelland's (1969) work on achievement motivation contains this notion. What I have attempted to do here is to make it concrete in the context of industrial competition.

36. The local "diamond" bears centrally on the learning and diffusion process in a national industry. The spread of information through the diamond feeds back to affect the directions of technology development.

37. In this respect, the framework here generalizes a theme that has begun to appear in other work. Spence (1983) stresses the effects of history in industrial organization. A number of authors have stressed the "path dependence" of industry development for products that are part of networks or must be compatible with other products. An initial lead in such a market often creates substantial entry barriers because of the importance of the installed base. See Saloner (1986).

38. In some respects, the situation is similar to recent "chaos" theories, in which the path is predictable though the initial conditions are unknown.

Chapter 5

1. A collection of other selected case studies is available in Porter and Enright, *Studies in National Advantage,* forthcoming.

2. Research for this case was conducted by Claas van der Linde, St. Gall Graduate School of Business, Switzerland.

3. Japan was second with a 19.1 percent share of world exports.

4. All figures are converted from deutsche marks at early 1988 exchange rates.

5. Wolf (1981).

6. This was typical in Germany at the time, due to the strong desire of Germans for higher education.

7. Wolf (1981).

8. Ibid.

9. The two machines were installed secretly to prevent unrest among the many printers who were made redundant. See Goebel (1956).

10. Wolf (1981).

11. Koenig, F. G., letter of November 1816, quoted in Ibid.

12. Goebel (1956).

13. Wolf (1981) is the basic reference for much of this section.

14. Company documents.

15. Koenig & Bauer AG, *Details and Facts on the Development and Structure of the Enterprise,* company history.

16. Industry source, May 18, 1987.

17. Wolf (1981).

18. VDMA (1986).

19. Manufacturing efficiency had also received a boost after World War II. Most German factories needed to be rebuilt, and German firms designed and built the world's most advanced production facilities.

20. Industry source, May 18, 1987.

21. Wolf (1981).

22. Bundesverband Druck, *Annual Report 1985* (Wiesbaden, 1986), p. 33.

23. *Frankfurter Allgemeine Zeitung,* June 7, 1988.

24. Wolf (1981).

25. BASF was estimated to hold a 14 percent share of the European printing ink market and 17 percent of the U.S. market. Foreign sales accounted for about 80 percent of total sales.

26. Industry source, September 9, 1988.

27. Harris was acquired in 1988 by Heidelberg for $300 million.

28. Industry source, September 9, 1988.

29. Research for this case study was conducted by Research Assistant William M. McClements.

30. In 1987, exports represented approximately 10 percent of total domestic production, estimated at about $650 million.

31. A doctor in Australia developed a similar idea at the same time, but the practice took off first and fastest in the United States.

32. Interview with industry executive, August 25, 1988.

33. Frost and Sullivan (1984).

34. Germany was one of the most sophisticated European health care markets, as were Sweden and Denmark.

35. Interview with industry executive, April 22, 1988.

36. Interview with industry executive, September 8, 1988.

37. This case was prepared by Michael J. Enright with the assistance of Paolo Tenti.

38. In 1987, Italy produced some 29 percent of the world's ceramic tiles by quantity (350 million square meters), well ahead of second-place Spain's 15 percent and Brazil's 14 percent (Assopiastrelle estimates). Italian share of world exports (by value) reached 59 percent in 1986, compared to second-place Spain with 11 percent and third-place Germany with 10 percent. United Nations (1988).

39. In 1987, the Emilia-Romagna region accounted for 85 percent of Italian production and 79 percent of Italian employment in the industry. The overwhelming majority of firms was located in a very small area in the provinces of Modena and Reggio Emilia, which extended for roughly 10 kilometers (6 miles) from the epicenter of Sassuolo.

40. Interview with Giorgio Saltini, June 25, 1986; interview with Antonio Camellini, July 22, 1986.

41. Banca Nazionale del Lavoro (1973).

42. In the years following World War II, it was easy to sell tiles without regular invoices. The small size of many of the firms involved made it difficult for the government to trace these transactions. For a time, firms benefited from this additional form of tax avoidance.

43. Interview with Graziano Sezzi, July 22, 1986.

44. Bursi (1984).

45. Interview with Mauro Poppi, July 22, 1986.

46. Saltini; Camellini.

47. Home demand was boosted by the availability of good tile installers in Italy at a relatively low cost. Italian tile manufacturers gave seminars and provided detailed instructions for tile installation. All this was a function of the size and sophistication of Italian demand.

48. Based on data contained in Sezzi (1979).

49. Camellini; interview with Pedro Riaza, October 26, 1988.

50. Estimates based on a sample of 152 firms and 500 retailers. See CRESME (1986).

51. CRESME (1986).

52. CRESME (1986).

53. Camellini.

54. These estimates reflect recent conditions but are indicative of earlier ratios. (The average was 35 percent for all U.S. manufacturing establishments.) Lukes (1983).

55. Utili (1983).

56. Prodi (1966).

57. Databank (1985).

58. Utili (1983). Firing times of forty minutes were common by 1987.

59. Based on Assopiastrelle data.

60. Interview with Luciano Galassini, October 20, 1988.

61. *Business Week,* October 15, 1984.

62. *Il Giornale,* September 19, 1988.

63. Bursi (1984).

64. Based on Assopiastrelle data (April 1988).

65. Baccarani (1985) used a similar taxonomy.

66. Roncaccioli (1986).

67. Databank (1985). By September 1988, *cassa integrazione* represented some 2.4 percent of total employment.

68. Lukes (1983).

69. Interview with Pedro Riaza, October 26, 1988.

70. Nomisma (1983).

71. Ibid.

72. This section is based on a case study prepared by Associates Fellow

Michael J. Enright, in collaboration with a research team at Hitotsubashi University.

73. This figure used a broad definition of a robot.

74. Sadamoto (1981).

75. Ibid.

76. Ibid.

77. Interview with industry expert, February 27, 1987.

78. Automatic printed circuit board insertion machines were included in the total.

79. Taken from Yonemoto (1987).

80. Sadamoto (1981).

81. United Nations Economic Commission for Europe (1985).

82. Robotics producers from other nations had entered into such arrangements as well.

83. U.S. Department of Commerce (1987).

84. Ibid.

85. Databank (1986).

Chapter 6

1. See United States Office of Technology Assessment (1986). The statistical problems in measuring services trade are numerous. Many international service transactions go unmeasured, because there are no goods crossing borders to inspect and count. Transactions involving both goods and services are typically assigned to the goods sector. Much foreign activity of service firms takes place through foreign affiliates. This activity is lumped under broad categories such as license fees or repatriated profits in national accounts. For a discussion of some of the measurement problems in services trade, see Sapir (1982) and Schott (1983).

2. Many service industries involve a tangible element or component, for example, an accountant who delivers a chart of accounts.

3. Many authors have debated the precise definition of what is or is not a service, and how services can be distinguished from manufactured goods. There are indeed many shades of grey in defining services, but these are not particularly important for my analysis.

4. A body of research has documented the typical pattern of growth in the service sector as economies develop. For the standard reference, see Chenery and Syrquin (1975). Services grow in importance as a nation develops for similar reasons to those I discuss here. Our interest here is in *international* competition in services, not the role of services in the domestic economy. But the particular role of individual services in the economy is linked to the capacity to compete internationally.

5. A positive association between the percentage of total employment in a nation represented by the service sector and per capita income and urbanization is demonstrated by Thompson and Stollar (1983).

6. Many of the same forces that lead to the de-integration of services are also tending to reduce the extent of vertical integration in many manufacturing industries.

7. Theodore Levitt has termed this mass production the "industrialization" of services. See Levitt (1976).

8. In Sweden, interestingly, there have been some efforts to export "bureaucracy," such as systems for issuing drivers' licenses and management of health care institutions. While foreign sales have occurred, however, most have been to third world nations and have been comparatively minor.

9. Other taxonomies of international service competition, which overlap to varying degrees with mine, are given in Riddle (1986), Sapir (1982), and Gray (1983), among others.

10. An international company has discretion about where it places warehouses, sales and service offices, and regional headquarters to serve a group of countries. Singapore, for example, is actively competing to attract such regional sales and distribution centers to serve Southeast Asia. Switzerland has a strong position in European headquarters, as does Belgium (Brussels).

11. See Sölvell (1979).

12. Government sources are highly aggregated, lumping together many service industries into each category. Data on services trade also normally include license fees, repatriated profits, and other financial flows that often have little to do with services. Data on foreign investment in service industries are essentially absent.

13. There has been relatively little theoretical or empirical work on comparative advantage in service industries. Most authors argue that conventional trade theory largely applies to services; see Sapir (1982) and Katouzian (1970). Sampson and Snape (1985), among others, point out that mobility of factors and buyers, prevalent in services, complicates the problem. The efforts to apply conventional trade theory to services are a start, but the problems I identified in Chapter 1 remain.

14. For a review of the literature on social differences that may bear on services, see Riddle (1986).

15. The whole notion of standardized products (some would say to a low common denominator), disposability, mass production, and mass marketing are deeply embedded in American demand patterns. See Chapter 7.

16. International Financial Law Review (1985).

17. Particularly important is regulatory freedom to develop new services and to operate internationally. Regulations to ensure capital adequacy or to protect against fraud, on the other hand, enhance instead of inhibit genuine innovation and rivalry.

18. The role that services play as a national economy develops is discussed in Chapter 10.

19. This section draws on project case studies including William McClements, *The U.S. Engineering and Construction Industry*, Paolo Tenti, *The Italian Engineering and Construction Industry*, and Dong-Sung Cho, *The Korean Heavy Construction Industry*.

20. *Engineering News-Record*, July 7, 1988, and *International Construction Week*, July 11, 1988.

21. See Nukazawa (1980).

22. While buying goods tied up capital, serving purely as a middleman did not. Instead, it created incentives for moving a large volume of goods.

23. With less indigenous art from the United Kingdom, tight restrictions to protect national treasures were less likely.

Chapter 7

1. The international division of labor has become more specialized, in the parlance of trade theory.

2. For a preliminary report of the research on Denmark, see Pade and Møller (1988).

3. Domestic profitability is not a good indication of true international competitive advantage for three important reasons. First, government intervention can impede international competition and artificially support domestic profits. In Italy, for example, some large firms are highly profitable because they have *de facto* local monopolies and are protected in some way from foreign competition, yet they lack competitive advantage in international terms. Second, in an industry or economy where many firms are following harvesting strategies, firms may maintain profitability though they are losing competitiveness. Finally, differences in accounting standards in preparing financial statements make cross-national comparisons in profitability problematic, as does the lack of systematic data in many countries.

4. It should be noted that all the nations I will discuss are important trading nations with considerable strengths when compared to the total community of nations. That I will be noting many advantages does not imply that many nations possess them.

5. The cluster chart has some similarities to Leontief's input-output tables because it seeks to represent vertical flows among industries. The ways in which industries are grouped and displayed, however, has broader purposes.

6. National Science Foundation (1986).

7. See McCraw (1986).

8. Interestingly, the other nation with international success in mass-produced confectionery products was the United Kingdom (for example, Cadbury's and Rowntree's). Some of the reasons why will become apparent in Chapter 9.

9. That the United States was an early market for advanced goods has been emphasized in many accounts and is the basis for Vernon's life cycle theory of international trade. See Vernon (1966).

10. In most advanced nations, electronic media was government owned or controlled, and advertising was absent or limited. In nations such as Germany and Sweden, severe restrictions on television advertising continue today, though changes are under way.

11. Some aspects of U.S. antitrust policy such as the Robinson-Patman Act (covering resale price maintenance), it must be noted, were less helpful and tended to protect inefficient competitors rather than preserve competition.

12. Maddison's (1987) survey of historical growth and productivity data concludes that the United States passed the United Kingdom around 1890 and its performance was strong until 1950, slowing markedly thereafter.

13. Michael J. Enright and Professor Silvio Borner contributed significantly to this section.

14. Aluminum products and chemicals are made from imported raw materials.

15. The top fifty Swiss industries in terms of export value account for 51.2 percent of total Swiss exports after elimination of traded goods, also relatively low compared to Japan, Korea, and Sweden.

16. These data necessarily cover only exports, and not the sales of overseas

production subsidiaries either in industries with high export shares or in low export share industries added to the cluster chart because of substantial foreign direct investment.

As discussed in Appendix A, industries were occasionally classified differently on the cluster chart in different nations, based on the segments in which the nation's firms competed. In cases such as this, the world cluster chart was adjusted by adding or subtracting industries before calculating the nation's export share. The resulting figures are approximations but in practice represent a good indication of each nation's position in clusters.

17. Interestingly, the percentage of Swiss who do go to university is lower than that of many other advanced nations.

18. Labor shortages were so severe that Swiss firms began employing migrant workers for less skilled jobs. This practice was a drag on productivity improvement, in the long run, and may have been as much a detriment as a benefit to Swiss industry.

19. In some important consumer-related industries, in contrast, standards have been established at the behest of Swiss trade associations and trade unions that represent nontariff barriers to imports. These sap innovation and Swiss firms in such industries are not internationally successful.

20. The only exception is perhaps the pharmaceutical industry, where the Swiss have won a number of Nobel Prizes in recent years.

21. Danthine and Lambelet (1987).

22. Adjusting for these reserves, many Swiss companies with apparently modest profits are actually quite profitable.

23. My co-researcher in Sweden, Örjan Sölvell, has contributed significantly to this section.

24. The seventeen largest Swedish multinationals also accounted for one-third of Swedish industrial employment and 60 percent of industrial R&D spending. *Regeringens Proposition* (1986–1987).

25. Table B-4 gives the top fifty Swedish industries by export value. Sweden has large absolute exports of cars and trucks though modest world export shares. Foreign production by Swedish firms in trucks is significant. Exports of petroleum products are also large, but the Swedish trade balance is significantly negative. Only two industries made the top fifty value list that did not exceed the Swedish export share cutoff to qualify as a competitive industry. Both have negative trade balances.

26. There are only three significant consumer goods manufacturers among the large Swedish companies: Electrolux (appliances, vacuum cleaners, garden implements); Wasabröd (hard rye bread, acquired by Sandoz [Switzerland]), and Mölnlycke (diapers and sanitary napkins, linked to forest products). Volvo and Saab produce passenger cars, but their other businesses are industrial. Swedish Match produces some consumer goods (matches and lighters) but is more linked to forest products.

27. Sweden once had a positive trade balance in services due to a large general cargo shipping industry.

28. Sweden also generates about 40 percent of its electricity from nuclear power, the highest in the world. However, due to strong environmental and safety concerns, a hallmark of Sweden, a plan has been put in place to phase out nuclear power by

2010. This not only is likely to raise Swedish energy costs but may lead to a loss of the existing Swedish position in nuclear power generation equipment. The Swedish position in nuclear generating equipment provides yet another illustration of the role of home demand.

29. Automated gas stations, automated payment systems in parking garages, and automated banking machines are common in Sweden, for example.

30. Devaluations have brought Swedish unit labor costs to a relatively low level compared to other advanced OECD countries. The move to devaluation has contributed to a slowing up of these beneficial pressures for upgrading. It has likely contributed, for example, to a lagging rate of penetration of robots in recent years.

31. Vahlne (1986).

32. Volvo sends a team to investigate every major truck accident in Sweden, for example.

33. This marginal rate combines federal and local taxes. A proposal in early 1989 would lower the marginal tax rate for low- and moderate-income families.

34. Television advertising is just beginning to make some inroads into Sweden via satellite dishes and cable systems that receive foreign programming.

35. One problem of this structure is that Swedish multinationals often have autonomous "country kings" that make global integration of strategy more difficult.

36. See Sölvell (1987).

37. There has been a trend toward top managers coming more from nontechnical backgrounds, a danger signal in the context of the other nations we studied because goals may shift away from technical advancement toward financial results. See Carlson (1986).

38. The pressures of a relatively open market have led to these reserves serving a more constructive purpose in recent years than in Switzerland. Yet some of the same risks are present.

39. *Regeringens Proposition* (1986–1987).

40. Claas van der Linde, my co-researcher in Germany, and Michael J. Enright contributed significantly to this section.

41. Germany's location undoubtedly helps, bordered by several other nations. Yet trade with neighboring countries does not account for Germany's remarkable export intensity for a large country. Its industries typically export to a very large number of nations.

42. During the pre–World War II industrial buildup, attention had been focused on the eastern part of Germany for security reasons.

43. Table B-5 shows the top fifty German industries in terms of export value. Only seven of fifty fail to make the German cutoff, of which four have substantial negative trade balances. Trucks (where there is heavy FDI), roadrollers, TV cameras, and radiotelephonic receivers are segmented industries in which German firms have significant advantages. These industries have been included on the cluster chart.

44. The only individual German industries accounting for more than 2 percent of German exports are related to passenger cars. Cars represented 10.4 percent of German exports in 1985, while auto parts were 3.5 percent. Other industries accounting for more than 1 percent were trucks, switchgear, measuring and controlling instruments, miscellaneous chemical products, and aircraft over 15,000 kilos.

45. The lack of dominant positions in large industries contributes modestly to the number of German industries that exceed Germany's average share of world products. But an absolute cutoff in terms of world export share reveals the same conclusion relative to other nations.

46. The German share of world exports in this sector is held down by extensive foreign investment.

47. Germans do not have just a job, but a *Beruf*, a term with a meaning akin to having a calling.

48. Compulsory public education began in Germany. Large governmental investments in general and technical education date back to the nineteenth century. See Landes (1969).

49. The student movement beginning in the late 1960s has led to a growing gridlock in decision making within German universities. Some top professors are leaving German universities to take jobs in other nations or to enter other fields, a matter of concern.

50. The Swiss system is modeled after Germany's.

51. Recently, the system has been modified so that the apprentice spends a couple of months in the company and then a couple of months in school.

52. Today, such breakthroughs are rarer. Innovations are steady but more incremental, an area of weakness, in part because Germany is not a leader in a number of newer technical fields such as semiconductors, computing, and biotechnology.

53. Figures in historical prices. Statistisches Bundesamt (1982, 1987).

54. National Science Foundation (1986).

55. MAC Group (1988). The use of consumer credit is rapidly rising in Germany, one of a number of indications of changing German attitudes that I will discuss later.

56. Of the nations we studied, Germany was most like Italy in the importance of family firms.

57. Measured in units. Verband der Automobilindustrie (1986).

58. Electronics, computer science, physics, and chemistry are also high on the list. Interestingly, economics is far down the list, the major field of less than 2 percent of German university students.

59. An apprentice with one firm would rarely join another. Most employees are jealously loyal to their companies.

60. Monopolkommission (1988); *Frankfurter Allgemeine Zeitung*, June 14, 1989, page 17.

61. There have been some efforts in the German government to tighten antitrust enforcement (see Adams and Brock [1988]), but leniency toward mergers persists. Cartels are permitted under certain conditions and the federal minister of economics can override a cartel office merger prohibition with no court challenge. Ministerial override was used in the Daimler-Benz-MBB merger.

62. See Maddison (1987).

Chapter 8

1. Hirotaka Takeuchi, my co-researcher in Japan, has contributed significantly to this section. Michael J. Enright also made numerous suggestions.

2. Japan's top fifty industries in terms of export value are shown in Table B–6. Only two fail to make the Japanese cutoff: measuring and controlling instruments and road rollers. Both are segmented industries in which Japan's trade balance is positive, and so they have been added to the cluster chart (Figure 8–1). There is a large overlap of industries on the export value and the export share lists.

3. Today, about 15 percent of electric power is generated from hydroelectric sources, down from about 50 percent as late as 1960. Nuclear power represents a growing percentage.

4. Confucian teachings, which stress education, self-betterment, hard work, and reverence for family, were influential in the pre-World War II period. They have been less important to the postwar generation, and are more influential in the 1980s in nations such as Korea and Taiwan.

5. Japan's cooperative farming heritage, in contrast to the individualistic hunting tradition in countries such as Germany, is also cited by some observers as explaining the willingness to cooperate. See Lodge and Vogel (1987).

6. Zikopoulos (ed.) (1988). It was estimated that there were only 800 U.S. citizens studying in Japanese universities in 1987.

7. In many developing countries, capital is not available for industry due to capital flight and because savings are not deposited in institutions where they can be redeployed but are kept "under the mattress."

8. The tax break for postal savings was eliminated on April 1, 1988.

9. Japanese mothers are sometimes called "education mamas," or *kyōiku-mama*.

10. Unlike other nations such as Germany and Switzerland, government policy has precluded the importation of workers. In 1985, registered foreign workers and managers represented 0.7 percent of the population, compared to 14.5 percent in Switzerland and 7.2 percent in Germany. The effect has been to create even greater pressures to boost productivity, instead of using foreign workers to fill low-productivity jobs. Korean workers who came to work in Japan during the Japanese occupation of Korea were classified as registered aliens and not granted Japanese citizenship.

11. Part-time work, a further boost to productivity, developed quite early in Japan for similar reasons.

12. Facing shortages of materials, machinery, or other needed items, Japanese companies have also been adept at sourcing raw materials, components, and machinery from anywhere in the world where it was cost effective.

13. A high dependence on imported oil also meant that the oil shocks led to a depreciation of the yen.

14. The positive response of Japanese industry to revaluation has depended on strengths in other determinants, notably factor upgrading, goals that lead to intense commitment by firms to their industries, and intense domestic rivalry. In other nations without these conditions, revaluation can lead to stagnation and pressures for government intervention, which in turn dampen adjustments.

The intense domestic rivalry in Japan also meant that the periods of devaluation led to no slacking of innovation.

15. Even today, exports represent less than 15 percent of Japanese GDP, compared with 28 percent in Germany and 40 percent in Switzerland.

16. American semiconductor firms have maintained a strong position in complex logic chips, such as microprocessors, where U.S. strength in computers, aero-

space, and defense creates large home demand, but not in ordinary memory chips.

17. While U.S. firms were early competitors in both industries, market penetration was faster in Japan than in the United States. In copiers, for example, intense need led to greater adoption in Japan of the messy, smelly diazo copying process, a forerunner of plain paper copying.

18. There are exceptions, such as Yamaha's (originally a musical instrument product) entry into motorcycles. Yet other elements of the "diamond" were at work. Yamaha's home base is located in Hamamatsu, near Honda. Suzuki is based in Hamamatsu as well. Honda's success in motorcycles convinced Yamaha that it could also succeed in the industry.

19. The Japanese case raises interesting questions about the future of Korean labor-management relationships, now in a period of unrest.

20. The most elite jobs in Japan are in the ministries, the most prestigious of which are the Ministry of Finance and MITI.

21. Japanese (and German) company handbooks routinely include the export ratio for each company, a statistic not typical in U.S. publications.

22. Statistical evidence suggests that concentration in Japanese industries decreased at least through the 1960s and 1970s and that Japanese industry is less concentrated overall than that in the United States. See Caves and Uekusa (1976) and Iguchi (1987).

23. The exceptions tend to be in older industries such as musical instruments, where Yamaha has a large share advantage over Kawai and others.

24. Some observers have pointed to lower prices in the United States than in Japan in industries such as cameras and copiers as evidence of domestic collusion. This view is incorrect. Prices are sometimes lower in the United States than in Japan because of the inefficient multistage Japanese distribution system and during periods of intense scramble for U.S. share. Exchange rate swings also lead to a "grey market."

25. When this occurred, companies were at least chosen on the basis of competitiveness. The number of Japanese competitors allowed to export was also restricted in some industries; again, the criterion was domestic strength and efficiency. Some incentives for improvement and upgrading were preserved.

26. Many other smaller chance events have affected individual industries.

27. Shinohara (1982) rightly focuses on the ability of Japanese industry to transform itself.

28. Paolo Tenti, my co-researcher in Italy, has contributed substantially to this section, as has Michael J. Enright.

29. Twelve of the top fifty Italian industries in terms of value had export shares that fell below the cutoff. Six had negative trade balances, while three others had marginal trade surpluses. Italy's problems in large industries will be discussed below. Trucks are included in the cluster chart because of significant FDI which increases Italy's true position. Passenger cars and parts are also included, though Italy's position in larger cars benefits from domestic protection and subsidies.

30. In Class A vehicles, the smallest size category, Fiat held 35 percent of the European market outside of Italy in 1987 and 87 percent of the Italian market. Fiat holds over 50 percent of the total Italian market. DRI-McGraw-Hill (1987).

31. Piore and Sabel (1983) were early foreign observers of the distinctive structure and performance of Italian industry.

32. See Table B-7.

33. The exception is Olivetti's European position in personal computers.

34. Onida (1985) has demonstrated the dependence of successful Italian producers on imported chemicals and electronic components.

35. *Business Week* (October 15, 1984).

36. *Engineering News Record* (July 7, 1988).

37. European Management Foundation (1986).

38. Such companies are important participants in many Italian exporting industries.

39. In 1988, a 12.5 percent tax was instituted on government bond and treasury bill interest, but the interest rate has adjusted to keep the net yield the same.

40. Mutual funds were only allowed to buy government bonds in a limited way in Italy in 1983. Italian banks have been prevented from holding corporate equity and making extensive long-term loans since the 1933 bank panic. Long-term loans are the province of special credit institutions who lend principally to large companies and the government.

41. Few Italians use checks, for example, because they are slow to clear. Italy has only 0.3 bank accounts per capita, compared to 0.8 in Belgium and France, 0.9 in Germany and the Netherlands, and 1.8 in the United Kingdom. Britain's strength in financial services is reflected by these figures, which illustrate the role of domestic rivalry in boosting home demand. See Eurostat Dafsa (1988).

42. Zikopoulos (ed.) (1988).

43. A recent move to award research doctorates is embryonic.

44. Survey evidence suggests that formal research is heavily oriented to products. See Sirilli (1984, 1987).

45. For one source, see *Advertising Age* (1985). This view was universally held among industry observers.

46. MAC Group (1988).

47. Italian firms who supply them almost invariably compete themselves in specialized niches or in providing highly customized machinery and other inputs.

48. Though Italian firms complained to us that their Italian suppliers made the latest technology available overseas, in practice it was apparent that a special relationship was present within Italy, particularly in technological and idea exchange.

49. The leading Italian television entrepreneur, Berlusconi, exploited a loophole in Italian law prohibiting direct competition with government-owned stations.

50. A strong entrepreneurial and competitive spirit dates back at least to the intense competition between the republics (such as Genoa, Pisa, and Venice) that predates the unification of Italy.

51. For example, when government-owned Alfa Romeo was recently privatized, it was sold to Fiat despite strong interest from Ford.

52. While socialist in orientation, it should be noted that the Italian Communist Party is a far cry from what most would identify as communist.

53. Dong-Sung Cho, my co-researcher in South Korea, has contributed substantially to this section.

54. The top fifty exports by value account for 65 percent of Korean exports (see Table B-8). All but five exceed the Korean export share cutoff, with three having negative or minor trade balances. One industry, passenger cars, has been added to the cluster chart because its exports are significant and rapidly growing, and Korea holds a strong position in its segment.

55. Korea's large general trading companies are successful but are almost exclusively involved in trade in and out of Korea. They have not yet achieved the truly global status of the Swiss, Dutch, and some Japanese trading companies that are involved in substantial amounts of trade not involving the home nation.

56. Another indication is that Korea is represented by 178 industries which meet the cutoff, of which 76 are either iron and steel or textiles and apparel. In contrast, Switzerland is represented by 189 industries, and no one sector is close to dominant.

57. Economic Planning Board (1987).

58. Some executives state that the law is unnecessary because companies would engage in training of their own volition.

59. *De facto* division took place before the war.

60. See Mason et al. (1980).

61. The Korean government has been willing to step in to assist some of those who failed.

62. Seok Ki Kim (1987).

63. For example, the *chaebol* received the lion's share of export incentives, subsidized loans, and investment licenses. They also were asked to take over ailing or state-owned enterprises on favorable terms.

64. Outside observers of Korea have also had a tendency to see the excess capacity caused by competitive investments as wasteful, instead of the impetus for upgrading by Korean industries.

65. For a discussion see Mason et al. (1980).

66. The ten products are pianos, athletic footwear, microwave ovens, eyeglass frames, fishing rods, travel goods, toys, porcelain, color TV sets, and VCRs.

Chapter 9

1. See, for example, Barnett (1987) and Lazonick and Elbaum (1986).

2. Table B-9 shows the top fifty British industries in terms of export value. Appearing on this list, in addition to petroleum-related industries, are modest British positions in a number of large industries such as cars and computer equipment in which foreign direct investment in Britain is substantial. Of the fifty leading British export industries in terms of value, all but five exceed the U.K. export share cutoff, and all of these have a large negative trade balance. Field research suggests that subsidiaries of foreign firms account for a significant part of British exports.

3. Positions in a number of other industries, such as precious metals, precious stones, and paintings, are a function of strength in the auctioneering and trading industries, not of goods produced in Britain.

4. British gains in computer-related industries are heavily influenced by American foreign investments in the United Kingdom.

5. Engineering is looked down upon as "applied" rather than pure science in

Britain. There is no national certification or licensing system for engineers, so anyone can take that title. In nations such as Italy, Germany, Sweden, and Japan, the title of engineer is an official and prestigious one.

6. These characteristics of British education have a long history. See Weiner (1981).

7. Clutterbuck and Crainer (1988).

8. National Science Foundation (1988).

9. See Pavitt (1980).

10. Organization for Economic Cooperation and Development (1989).

11. *Ibid.* (1988).

12. British industry often lacked the force of competition as well, as I will discuss further later.

13. *The Economist*, May 20, 1989.

14. America's relative standard of living fares better in comparisons that attempt to adjust for purchasing power parity, but its relative position is declining none-theless.

15. The top fifty U.S. industries in terms of export value, shown in Table B-10, shows a lower proportion of resource-intensive industries (thirteen of fifty). Only three industries in the top fifty export value list fail to make the U.S. export share cutoff, and all have large negative trade balances.

16. While comparable figures cannot be calculated because of changes in the trade classification system, our best estimate is that natural resource-dependent exports represented approximately 29 percent of total U.S. exports in 1971.

17. See Dornbusch, Krugman, and Park (1989).

18. See Table 13–1.

19. Research by Jorgenson (1987) has shown that American economic growth in recent decades has been largely a function of growth in factors and not improving technology. This conclusion, in striking contrast to studies by Solow and Denison covering earlier periods, supports a declining rate of innovation and upgrading in American industry and is troubling indeed.

20. American consumers buy large quantities of imported goods, as do British consumers. Some observers take this as an indication that they are sophisticated and demanding. In fact, American and British buyers are finally discerning what foreign buyers have long recognized. Confronted with obvious differences in quality and features, they are buying foreign products that were accepted earlier in their home nation.

21. One interesting fact that may bear on attitudes toward product quality and durability is the prevalence in the United States of purchases on credit. In Japan and Germany, consumers pay cash, which seemed from our interviews to reinforce a desire for high quality.

22. This illustrates why simply spending more on modern equipment is not the solution to quality and productivity problems in American industry.

23. Given the picky and trend conscious Japanese consumer, I would expect that growing leisure time in Japan will translate into a very high rate of innovation in such industries. Japan may well become an exporter in these fields.

24. The international success of Japanese financial services firms is thus far

almost exclusively in those fields where access to low-cost capital is the principal basis of competitive advantage. They have achieved little penetration in sophisticated financial services and with non-Japanese clients.

25. See Table 13–2 for supporting data. Britain adopted a similar policy in April 1988, and Germany has announced plans to do so as well.

26. Some recent examples are General Electric's swap of its lagging consumer electronics business with Thompson (France) in return for Thompson's medical instruments division, and Firestone's sale of its tire operations to Bridgestone (Japan).

27. Because most stock in the United States is held by investors with little loyalty to the company (unlike the case in Germany or Japan), mergers are comparatively easy to accomplish. Nearly every U.S. company is "in play."

28. See Porter (1987).

29. All these developments have contributed to uniquely advanced and sophisticated demand for financial services, and U.S. firms, not surprisingly, are world leaders in providing many of them. American financial service firms pioneered large-scale mergers and acquisitions practices, junk bonds, leveraged buyouts, and many new types of securities and financial investments. American industry, however, has paid a profound price in terms of competitive advantage.

30. Data to make less aggregated comparisons can be found in the individual country tables in Appendix B. They show differences among nations in the pattern of competitive success that are even more striking than these broad comparisons.

Chapter 10

1. It should be stressed that the development literature is suggestive of some of the issues that I discuss here and elsewhere in the book. The hope is that my somewhat different starting point and frame of reference will provide a useful additional perspective.

2. Rostow's (1971) stages model seeks to characterize economies more broadly and is concerned principally with earlier stages in the development process.

3. The state of competitive advantage in international industries tends to mirror that in purely domestic industries because of parallel developments in demand sophistication, factor conditions, supporting industries, and other national circumstances across industries. There are also externalities in factor creation, demand, technology transfer, and other areas that I discussed in Chapter 4 that span industries, as well as the role of clustering. Domestic industries must also compete for human resources and capital, and thus must achieve productivity sufficient to pay wages that attract and retain human resources and earn acceptable returns on capital. Without the discipline of having to meet foreign competition, however, the efficiency of deploying human resources and capital in domestic industries may be less than in other nations. This constrains national productivity and imposes higher costs on a nation's consumers and firms.

4. In Chapter 4, I discussed the types of industries in which the full "diamond" was not required for competitive advantage.

5. For an excellent discussion of the Japanese consensus, see Yamamura in Krugman, ed. (1986).

6. Mancur Olson's (1982) insightful book on the decline of nations stresses

some of the geneses of such rigidities. He links them to the formation of "distributional coalitions" or quasi-cartels in which firms and employees seek to bargain away a bigger share of the economic pie rather than expand it.

7. Research on productivity growth has emphasized three sources: technological change, accumulation of capital, and improving education or skill levels. Nelson's excellent survey (1981) identifies these and makes the important point that they are both complementary and reinforcing (see also Lindbeck [1983]). I view technological change and capital accumulation as endogenous, and seek to model them as the result of the "diamond" in which investment in skills plays a role. It is the mutual reinforcement among these variables, as Nelson's insight suggests, that determines productivity growth.

8. A problem with many stage models, including Rostow's (1971), is a sense of inevitability about progressing through them.

9. For an interesting account of Italian development, see Baumol (1985).

10. Italy and Denmark have important similarities in the mix of industries in which they compete. Both nations are strong in food and furnishings and compete in many fragmented industry structures. Italy is far more successful because of much greater dynamism. Denmark lacks the aggressive domestic rivalry and the high levels of individual and family motivation so essential to Italy's success.

Chapter 11

1. I have shared the view of many others about the importance of global strategy. See, for example, Porter (1986). Yet my research on this book has made it clear that globalization does not eliminate a powerful role for the home nation. The role of location, particularly of the home base, is far greater than I once supposed.

2. Schumpeter's theory (1942) posited that new firms would inevitably overcome past leaders. While this risk is indeed present, firms that are able to maintain dynamism, usually because of a dynamic national environment, can sustain leadership for many decades.

3. If trade associations degenerate into cartels, they can sap the competitive position of the national industry and harm consumers. Antitrust authorities in the United States, because of this risk, have adopted a suspicious view of trade association activities, one of the reasons that most U.S. trade associations are principally involved in lobbying and collecting industry statistics instead of more important activities such as training or the encouragement of university technical efforts.

Where the primary role of trade associations is factor creation, they should raise few antitrust concerns and their activities will benefit the national industry. The participation of suppliers and customers in trade associations is a useful check against abuses as well as a way of widening the potential benefits.

4. IMI is soon to merge with IMEDE, another Swiss-based business school.

5. I have described how to analyze competitors in general terms in Porter (1980), Chapter 3.

6. These conclusions are consistent with those I reached in research within the United States. See Porter (1987).

7. For additional discussions about how to diversify successfully, see Porter (1987).

8. Ohmae (1985) is on the right track when he talks about becoming an insider in all three major regions of the world. While a firm can tap selective advantages of foreign nations through acquisitions, alliances, and local subsidiaries, however, every firm has only the one true home base in a particular industry.

9. Part of the difficulty a multinational faces in gaining the benefits of a foreign nation's environment via a subsidiary is what are commonly called transactional failures (see Williamson [1975]), involving such things as the difficulty of credibly communicating information. Yet it should be clear that the impediments are much broader than this.

10. This view, which may appear nationalistic, is not based on chauvinism but only on the realities of sustaining competitive advantage.

11. *Financial Times*, July 4, 1988.

12. Ericsson (Sweden) was also early to employ a similar approach, which has since been followed by others.

13. This point is often overlooked by American companies who view "international competition" as competing with foreign firms trying to penetrate the American market, rather than meeting foreign competitors in foreign markets.

14. For a fuller discussion of the strategic rationale for alliances and some evidence on where they are most prevalent, see Porter (1986).

15. The home base need not represent the country of ownership or the place where the preponderance of investors reside, as I described in Chapter 1.

16. Cases of companies whose home base seems ambiguous, such as Royal Dutch Shell, can often be resolved by making the distinction between the corporation as a whole and individual business units. In Shell, for example, the home base for many upstream operations is in Holland while that for downstream activities is in Britain.

Chapter 12

1. As I described in Chapter 1, productivity refers to the revenue generated by employees per unit of time (which determines wages) and the return generated by capital. These are the two sources of national income.

2. See Dahmén (1982) for an interesting demonstration of the flaws of using such indices in interpreting Swedish industrial performance.

3. Protectionist policies that bar imports in these industries run grave risks of hurting a whole range of other industries that depend on them.

4. Supporting a local industry in the name of national security, and at the same time insulating it from the pressure to innovate, is another trap into which many nations have fallen.

5. Here again, nations such as Japan, where most policy is actually made by civil servants with long tenures, have a built-in advantage. The United States represents the other extreme, where nearly all officials in important policy positions must be re-elected frequently or are appointed and turn over rapidly with each new administration.

6. The myriad of ways in which government can affect national advantage makes the concept of a national economic strategy an abstraction. No nation we studied has one. None consciously and coherently manages all the policies that

bear in some way on industry, not even Japan. Doing so is probably not feasible nor necessarily desirable. It takes a nation down the path of substituting government for management which deters innovation and slows the upgrading of a nation's industry.

7. For a discussion of Korea, see Snodgrass in Mason et. al (1980).

8. National Science Foundation (1988).

9. A recent study of Israel, with a large defense sector, illustrates the paucity of defense spin-offs. See Jerusalem Institute of Management (1987).

10. Many treatments of cooperative research focus on problems of appropriability of the gains of R&D (see, for example, Ouchi and Bolton [1988]). Unless a firm can reap profits from the innovation, it is argued, it will underinvest in R&D. Cooperative R&D is recommended because it improves appropriability.

What is neglected is that avoidance of loss is an equally if not more potent incentive to invest in R&D. The fear of loss overcomes the organizational inertia that plagues the innovation process, and this is one reason why domestic rivalry is so important in innovation. In addition, innovations involve much specialized learning that is tailored to a firm's particular strategy and diffuses more slowly and incompletely than is often supposed, so that technological leads persist and also enhance the reputation of the innovator. For further discussion of this issue, see Chapter 3.

11. This condition is most closely met in commodities and other natural resource-based industries such as timber, aluminum, and unprocessed agricultural goods. Even in such industries, though, the technological differences among nations can be substantial, partly or wholly offsetting factor cost differences.

12. Indeed, downward pressure on a nation's currency is a sign that there are productivity problems in its industry.

13. There is an asymmetry between firm response to a rising currency value and a falling one because firms' efforts at innovation and improvement are heavily influenced by pressure and challenge.

14. Many Americans, not aware of such laws, may be unintentionally hypocritical in condemning foreign nations for restricting government procurement to local firms (such as the complaints to Japan about procurement for the Kansai Airport near Kyoto).

15. In the United States, some have proposed that the Defense Department should be used as an explicit tool to strengthen industrial competitiveness. As I will discuss further in Chapter 13, such an approach is fraught with difficulties.

16. Kennedy's (1987) thesis linking defense and economic prosperity stresses this point.

17. Many forms of regulation are aimed at dealing with important social problems where private decision making simply does not work. Safety and environmental regulations, for example, reflect social standards that firms cannot be expected to set independently. One can question the specific ways such regulations are implemented but not their basic legitimacy.

18. Another example is in nuclear power, where the United States was once a major exporter of nuclear reactor technology. Uncertain and slowly applied safety regulations created demand conditions that have brought the development of nuclear equipment in the United States to a halt. The United States has lost substantial exports in the sector, and other nations are becoming the technological leaders.

19. In the United States, there has been too little attention to the regulatory process and too much attention to eliminating or watering down standards. The business community has also failed to contribute enough to improving the regulatory process. In pharmaceuticals, for example, Merck gets very rapid approvals because it works hard to make its applications easier for the Food and Drug Administration to review. Too many companies, both American and non-American, react instinctively that all regulation is bad. This undermines their true competitive advantage.

20. As distribution channels in a nation become more sophisticated, their initial response is often to purchase more from abroad if foreign suppliers are more competitive. This may hurt domestic suppliers in the short term, at the same time as it sets in motion the basis for competitive advantage in the long term by promoting supplier upgrading provided other elements of the "diamond" are in place.

21. A similar leasing company, JECC, was established earlier for computers. To qualify, the buyer had to purchase a latest-generation machine.

22. Government policy that influences the use of credit purchases has traditionally been a means of stimulating or retarding the size of aggregate demand. More interesting for long-term national advantage, and more speculative, is the effect of credit purchases on the quality of demand. A different mentality seems to be present in those nations where most buyers pay cash, such as Germany and Japan. Choices are made carefully, and quality and durability loom large in making them. While it might seem that credit would allow more price-quality tradeoffs, in practice there seems to be a positive association between cash purchases and how demanding buyers are in the nations we studied. This is an area that deserves further study.

23. For a supporting discussion, see Ergas (1984).

24. My theory raises some interesting questions about the movement to unify standards in the European market. The motivation is to make Europe one large market. Yet the size of "home" demand does not unambiguously favor national competitive advantage.

National competitive advantage usually grows out of *differences* between local demand conditions and those in other nations, in areas such as segment structure, sophistication, or timing. If the possibility for such differences is eliminated or standards are reduced to the lowest common denominator, it could be more difficult for any European firm to gain advantage. Conversely, tariff reductions and elimination of frictional impediments to trade within Europe are unambiguously beneficial to productivity growth.

25. Nations such as the United States and the United Kingdom can learn a lot in this respect from nations such as Italy and Japan, which are more aggressive in linking foreign aid to purchases from domestic firms.

26. This is an important insight in Hirschman's (1958) notion of linkages in the development process, as well as in Dahmén's (1950) work on "development blocs."

27. Studies in Sweden and Switzerland have examined the question of whether foreign investment by a nation's firms costs jobs at home. In both cases, the conclusion was negative. In these nations, a consensus has supported internationalization, perhaps because of the small size of their home markets. See Borner (1986) and Vahlne (1986).

28. Freely mobile capital is desirable only if technology is constant and the return on capital is taken as a given. In reality though, patient investment and strong incentives to innovate can *alter* the level of technology and dramatically improve a firm's long-term rate of return.

29. Trading of shares will still occur but based more on investors' differing views of long-term prospects.

30. There is little reason, much less economic justification, for favorable taxation of capital gains on non-equity corporate investments such as real estate, artwork, and bonds because these do not have the same influence on productivity growth. Capital gains on bonds, for example, arise mostly from swings in interest rates rather than improved corporate prospects.

31. This failure to incorporate domestic competition has been the principal failing of French "indicative planning," which stresses consolidation of French industries. However, French policy is noteworthy for its attention to developing clusters, a constructive approach.

32. Policies to reshape firms' goals in the direction of sustained high rates of investment also take on great significance in eliminating the bias toward acquisition.

33. A partial list of protected U.S. industries includes automobiles, shipbuilding, machine tools, and semiconductors.

34. For a classic statement, see List ([1856] 1922).

35. For supporting arguments, see Zysman and Tyson (1983).

36. MITI has since become more prone not to tamper with competition, though its tendency to intervene in counterproductive ways is not entirely curbed as I will discuss later.

37. The requirement that Caterpillar form a joint venture was itself a milder form of protection. However, it represented a movement toward opening competition, and the partnership with Mitsubishi made Caterpillar more of an insider in the home market.

38. For a supporting discussion, see Zysman and Tyson (1983). A report by the OECD (1984) documents the economic costs of orderly marketing agreements in a number of cases.

39. Of course, foreign ownership means that profits flow back to the nation of ownership, eliminating a potential source of national income.

40. Direct targeting has a chance of success only when one or two nations are practicing it in a particular industry, but the tendency of nations today to imitate each other makes this comparatively rare.

41. I am grateful to Michael J. Enright for emphasizing this point.

42. I have described the process of moving to investment- and innovation-driven advantage in Chapter 10. Each of the specific policy areas and how they can best be implemented have been treated earlier in this chapter.

43. Shinohara (1982) has raised similar concerns in his interesting book about Japanese economic development.

44. Selling to developing nations confronts the dual problem of limited foreign exchange and a tilt toward protectionism. Yet bilateral trade among developing nations, under the principle of reciprocity, can circumvent such problems.

45. Canada and Australia are other nations heavily dependent on foreign multinationals.

46. Such an orientation is an unfortunate fallout of "strategic trade theory," which shows how one nation can benefit at the expense of others under some assumptions through intervention in competition. The models are based on a partial and stylized concept of international competition and the results are highly sensitive to small changes in assumptions, as their authors recognize. A case for widespread intervention has not been established. See Krugman (1986).

Chapter 13

1. Such views have recurred regularly for centuries.

2. As I illustrated in Chapter 8, Korean firms have moved faster to globalize strategies than many Japanese firms did. This reflects a more protectionist world marketplace in the 1980s than in the 1970s, making exports more difficult, and also a higher level of risk-taking by Korean firms.

3. The targeted industries also involved large-scale plants, the management of which is even more difficult in the south than in the rest of Italy because of, among other things, the lack of an industrial tradition which leads to more frequent labor-management difficulties.

4. For a fuller discussion of alliances, see Chapter 11.

5. Work on Saturday, once universal in Japanese companies, is being curtailed in the larger companies with the encouragement of government.

6. Japan Information Processing Development Center (1988).

7. The average productivity of the U.S. economy benefits, in contrast, from much greater efficiency in most services, which represent a large fraction of GNP in any advanced economy.

8. Japan Productivity Center (1988).

9. Industrial Structure Council Machinery Industry Committee (1989). Between 1986 and 1988, the proportion of students seeking jobs in manufacturing fell from 45 percent to 32 percent, while those interested in finance, insurance, and real estate rose from 6.3 percent to 12.2 percent.

10. *Asahi Shinbun*, June 10, 1989.

11. OS Publications (1989).

12. For one discussion critical of British privatization, see Vickers and Yarrow (1988).

13. For leading statements, see Kennedy (1987) and Huntington (1988). Huntington coins the term "declinists" to refer to those who doubt continued American preeminence, itself a commentary on the debate.

14. The rise in the 1980s of the working poor reflects these considerations. When competition was more sheltered, wages of less skilled workers reflected domestic circumstances.

15. Council on Competitiveness (1989).

16. See Council on Competitiveness (1988).

17. A 1989 $85 million agreement between Shiseido (Japan) and Harvard Medical School's Department of Dermatology covering skin research is just one example of more aggressive pursuit of university relationships by foreign firms.

Appendix A

1. Cheng Gaik Ong played the leading role in compiling and analyzing the cluster charts, with the assistance of Thomas P. Lockerby. Researchers from individual countries were also instrumental in preparing and refining the charts for their nations.

References

ABERNATHY, WILLIAM J., AND HAYES, ROBERT H. "Managing Our Way to Economic Decline," *Harvard Business Review*, July–August 1980, 67–77.

ABERNATHY, WILLIAM J., AND UTTERBACK, JAMES M. "Patterns of Industrial Innovation," *Technology Review*, Volume 80, Number 7, June–July 1978, 40–47.

ADAMS, WALTER, AND BROCK, JAMES W. "The Bigness Mystique and the Merger Policy Debate: An International Perspective," *Northwestern Journal of International Law and Business*, Volume 9, Number 1, Spring 1988, 1–48.

Advertising Age. "Feeding Italians' Hunger for Fashion," Volume 56, Number 26, April 4, 1985, 22–25.

AGMON, TAMIR, AND KINDLEBERGER, CHARLES P. *Multinationals From Small Countries*. Cambridge, Mass.: MIT Press, 1977.

ALEXANDER, ALBERT N. "Services Exports: Brightening the 80's," *Business America*, October 20, 1980, 25–26.

ANDERSEN, ESBEN S.; DALUM, BENT; AND VILLUMSEN, GERT. *International Specialization and the Home Market: An Empirical Analysis*. Institut for Produktion, Aalborg Universitetscenter, Denmark, December 1981.

ARNDT, SVEN W., AND BOUTON, LAWRENCE. *Competitiveness: The United States in World Trade*. Washington, D.C.: American Enterprise Institute for Public Policy Research, 1987.

ARROW, KENNETH J. "The Economic Implications of Learning by Doing," *Review of Economic Studies*, June 1962, Volume 29, 155–173.

ARTHUR, W. BRIAN. "Competing Techniques and Lock-in by Historical Events. The Dynamics of Allocation Under Increasing Returns," IIASA, Luxembourg, 1983, revised edition, Center for Economic Policy Research, Stanford University, 1985.

———. "Industry Location and the Importance of History," Center for Economic Policy Research, paper number 43, Stanford University, 1986.

—— "Competing Technologies: An Overview," in Dosi, ed., 1988.

ATHOS, ANTHONY, AND PASCALE, RICHARD. *The Art of Japanese Management*. New York: Simon & Schuster, 1981.

AUJAC, H. "La Hiérarchie des industries dans un tableau d'échanges industriels," *Revue Economique,* Volume 2, Number 2, 1960, 169–238.

BACCARANI, CLAUDIO. *Profilo di maturità di un settore: struttura e strategie*. Padova: CEDAM, 1985.

BALDWIN, WILLIAM L., AND SCOTT, JOHN T. *Market Structure and Technological Change*. Chur, Switzerland and New York: Harvard Academic Press, 1987.

Banca Nazionale del Lavoro (Ufficio Studi). *Ceramiche per pavimenti e rivestimenti*. Rome, April 1973, 22.

BARNETT, CORRELLI. *The Pride and the Fall: The Illusion and Reality of Britain as a Great Nation*. New York: The Free Press, 1987.

BARTLETT, CHRISTOPHER A. "Multinational Structural Evolution: The Changing Decision Environment in the International Division." DBA dissertation, Harvard Graduate School of Business Administration, 1979.

BARTLETT, CHRISTOPHER A., AND GHOSHAL, SUMANTRA. *Managing Across Borders: The Transnational Solution*. Boston: Harvard Business School Press, 1989.

BAUMOL, WILLIAM J. "Rebirth of a Fallen Leader: Italy and the Long Period Data," *Atlantic Economic Journal,* Volume 13, September 1985, 12–26.

BELASSA, BELA. "A 'Stages Approach' to Comparative Advantage," in *National and International Issues,* edited by Irma Adelman. London: Macmillan, 1979, 121–156.

BENZ, STEPHEN F. "High Technology Occupations Lead Growth in Services Employment," *Business America,* Volume 7, September 3, 1984, 19–21.

BHAGWATI, JAGDISH N. "Splintering and Disembodiment of Services and Developing Nations," *The World Economy,* Volume 7, Number 2, June 1984, 133–144.

BLAUG, MARK. *Economic Theory in Retrospect*. Cambridge: Cambridge University Press, 1985 (4th edition).

BLOMSTRÖM, MAGNUS; LIPSEY, ROBERT E.; AND KULCHYCKY, KSENIA. "U.S. and Swedish Direct Investment and Exports." In *Trade Policy Issues and Empirical Analysis,* edited by Robert E. Baldwin. Chicago: University of Chicago Press, 1988.

BORNER, S. *Internationalization of Industry: An Assessment in the Light of a Small Open Economy* (Switzerland). Berlin: Springer, 1986.

BORNER, S., AND WEHRLE, F. *Die Sechste Schweiz: Überleben auf dem Weltmarkt*. Zurich and Schwäbisch Hall: Orell Füssli, 1984.

BOUBLIL, ALAIN. *Le Socialisme industriel*. Paris: Presses Universitaires de France, 1977, 322.

BRANDER, JAMES A., AND SPENCER, BARBARA J. "Tariffs and the Extraction of Foreign Monopoly Rents Under Potential Entry," *Canadian Journal of Economics,* Number 14, November–February 1981, 371–389.

————. "International R&D Rivalry and Industrial Strategy," *Review of Economic Studies,* Volume L(4), Number 163, October 1983, 707–722.

BRUGGER, ERNST A., AND STUCKEY, BARBARA. "Regional Economic Structure and Innovative Behavior in Switzerland," *Regional Studies,* Volume 21, Number 3, 1987, 241–254.

BUCKLEY, PETER J., AND CASSON, MARK C. *The Future of the Multinational Enterprise.* London: Holmes and Meier, 1976.

BURSI, TIZIANO. *Il settore meccano-ceramico nel comprensorio della ceramica: struttura e processi di crescita.* Milan: Franco Angeli, 1984.

Business America. "Switzerland's Service Oriented Economy Offers Growing Markets for Wide Range of Computers and Peripheral Equipment," Volume 5, June 14, 1982, 20–21.

————. "Service Industries," Volume 8, October 15, 1985, 13–14.

Business Week. "The Next Trade Crisis May Be Just Around the Corner," Foreign Edition, March 19, 1984, 48–56.

————. "Why Italian Design Is Sweeping the World," October 15, 1984, 170.

BUZZELL, ROBERT D. "Can You Standardize Multinational Marketing?" *Harvard Business Review,* November–December 1968, 102–113.

CAMPBELL, NIGEL. "Sources of Competitive Rivalry in Japan," *Journal of Product Innovation Management,* Volume 4, 1985, 224–231.

CARLSON, SUNE. "A Century's Captains of Industry," *Scandinaviska Enskilda Banken Quarterly Review,* Number 2, 1986, 52–60.

CASSON, MARK C. "Transaction Costs and the Theory of the Multinational Enterprise." In *New Theories of the Multinational Enterprise,* edited by Alan Rugman. London: Croom Helm, 1982.

CAVES, RICHARD E. *Multinational Enterprise and Economic Analysis.* Cambridge: Cambridge University Press, 1982.

CAVES, RICHARD E., AND JONES, RONALD W. *World Trade and Payments.* Boston: Little, Brown, 1985 (4th edition).

CAVES, RICHARD E., AND UEKUSA, MASU. *Industrial Organization in Japan.* Washington, D.C.: Brookings Institute, 1976.

CHANDLER, ALFRED. " 'The Evolution of Modern Global Competition.' " In *Competition in Global Industries,* edited by Michael E. Porter. Boston: Harvard Business School Press, 1986.

————. *Scale and Scope: The Dynamics of Western Managerial Capitalism.* Cambridge, Mass.: Harvard University Press, forthcoming.

CHANG, WINSTON W. "Production Externalities, Variable Returns to Scale, and the Theory of Trade," *International Economic Review,* Volume 22, Number 3, October 1981, 511–525.

CHENERY, HOLLIS, AND SYRQUIN, MOISES. *Patterns of Development.* London: Published for the World Bank by Oxford University Press, 1975.

CLUTTERBUCK, DAVID, AND CRAINER, STUART. *The Decline and Rise of British Industry*. London: Mercury, 1988.

COOPER, RICHARD N. *Economic Policy in an Interdependent World*. Cambridge, Mass.: MIT Press, 1986.

CORDEN, MAX, AND NEARY, J. PETER. "Booming Sector and De-industrialisation in a Small Open Economy," *Economic Journal*, Volume 92, December 1982, 825–848.

COUNCIL ON COMPETITIVENESS. *Picking Up the Pace*. Washington, D.C., September 1988.

CRESME. *Caratteristiche distributive e di mercato delle piastrelle di ceramica*. Rome: Printed for Assopiastrelle, 1986, 55.

DAHMÉN, ERIK. *Entrepreneurial Activity and the Development of Swedish Industry, 1919–1939*. Stockholm: Industriens utredningsinstitut, 1950.

———. "A Neo-Schumpeterian Analysis of the Recent Industrial Development of Sweden," in *Economics in the Long View: Applications and Cases*, Volume 3, edited by Charles T. Kindleberger and G. De Tella. London: Macmillan, 1982.

———. "Development Blocks in Industrial Economics." Paper presented at workshop on New Issues in Industrial Economics, Case Western Reserve University, Ohio, June 1988. Forthcoming in *Scandinavian Economic Review*.

DANIELSON, RICHARD RENNER, JR. "Formulation of a Strategy for Dutch Cut-Flower Exports to the United States," unpublished master's thesis, Nijenrode, The Netherlands, February 1988.

DANTHINE, JEAN-PIERRE, AND LAMBELET, JEAN-CHRISTIAN. "The Swiss Case," *Economic Policy*, Volume 5, October 1987, 149–179.

Databank. *Competitors Report on Ceramic Tiles*. Milan, 1985, 18.

———. *Data e analisi: robotics*. Milan, 1986.

DAVID, PAUL A. *Technical Choice, Innovation and Economic Growth*. Cambridge: Cambridge University Press, 1975.

DAVIDSON, WILLIAM H. "Patterns of Factor Saving Innovation in the Industrialized World," *European Economic Review*, Volume 8, 1976, 207–217.

DEARDORFF, ALAN V. "Testing Trade Theories and Predicting Trade Flows," in Jones, Ronald W., and Kenen, Peter B., eds. 1984, 467–517.

DE BERNIS, DESTANNE. "Industries industrialisantes et contenu d'une politique d'intégration régionale," *Economie Appliquée*, Volume 19, Number 3–4, 1966, 415–473.

DENISON, EDWARD. *The Sources of Economic Growth*. Committee for Economic Development, Washington, D.C., 1962.

Dentsu Japan Marketing. "The Service Economies of Japan and Other Major Countries—An International Comparison," 20–25.

DIXIT, AVINASH K. "International Trade Policy for Oligopolistic Industries," *Economic Journal*, Supplement to Volume 94, December 1984, 1–16.

DORNBUSCH, RUDIGER; FISHER, STANLEY; AND SAMUELSON, PAUL A. "Comparative Advantage, Trade and Payments in a Ricardian Model with a Continuum of Goods," *American Economic Review,* Volume 67, December 1977, 823–839.

DORNBUSCH, RUDIGER; KRUGMAN, PAUL; AND PARK, YUNG CHUL. "Meeting World Challenges: U.S. Manufacturing in the 1990s," Eastman Kodak Company, Communications and Public Affairs, Rochester, N.Y., 1989.

DOSI, GIOVANNI, ED. *Technical Change and Economic Theory,* London and New York: Pinter Publishers, 1988.

DOSI, GIOVANNI; PAVITT, KEITH; AND SOETE, LUC. *The Economics of Technical Change and International Trade,* Brighton: Wheatsheaf, forthcoming.

DOZ, YVES. "National Policies and Multinational Management." DBA dissertation, Harvard Graduate School of Business Administration, 1976.

DRÈZE, JACQUES. "Les exportations intra-C.E.F. en 1958 et la position Belge," *Recherches Economiques de Louvain,* Volume 27, Number 8, 1961.

DRI/McGRAW-HILL. *World Automotive Forecast Report.* London: DRI Europe, 1987.

DRUCKER, PETER F. *The Frontier of Management: Where Tomorrow's Decisions Are Being Shaped Today.* New York: Truman Tally Books, 1986.

DUNNING, JOHN H. *International Production and the Multinational Enterprise.* London: Allen & Unwin, 1981.

―――. "The Eclectic Paradigm of International Production: A Restatement and Some Possible Explanation," Graduate School of Management, Rutgers University Working Paper 87–006, June 1987.

DUNNING, JOHN, AND McQUEEN, MATTHEW. "The Eclectic Theory of International Production: A Case Study of the International Hotel Industry," *Managerial and Decision Economics,* Volume 2, December 1981, 197–210.

The Economist, Business in Britain Survey, May 20, 1989.

Economic Planning Board, *Social Indicators in Korea,* Seoul, Korea, 1987.

Engineering News-Record, July 7, 1988.

ENRIGHT, MICHAEL J. "Geographical Concentration and Industrial Organization," unpublished PhD dissertation, Harvard University, 1990.

ERGAS, HENRY. "Why Do Some Countries Innovate More Than Others?" Center for European Policy Studies paper number 5, Brussels, 1984.

ETHIER, WILFRED J. "Internationally Deceasing Costs and World Trade," *Journal of International Economics,* Volume 9, 1979, 1–24.

ETZIONI, AMITAI. "The Political Economy of Imperfect Competition," *Journal of Public Policy,* Volume 5, Part II, May 1985, 169–186.

European Management Foundation, *Report on International Competitiveness,* Geneva, 1986.

Eurostat Dafsa, "Le secteur bancaire en Europe," Special Report, Paris, 1988.

Financial Times. "Benetton 'To Gain Nothing,' " July 4, 1988, Italian Industry Section, 2.

FLAHERTY, THERESE M.; GHOSHAL, SUMANTRA; AND STOBAUGH, ROBERT B. "Competitive Advantage versus Global Competition: The Effects of R&D Intensity on U.S. Trade," Harvard Business School Working Paper, October 1984.

FRANKEL, H. "Industrialization of Agricultural Countries and the Possibilities of a New International Division of Labor," *Economic Journal,* Volume 53, June–September 1943, 188–201.

———. "Obsolescence and Technological Change in a Maturing Economy," *American Economic Review,* Volume 45, Number 3, May 1956, 94–112.

Frankfurter Allgemeine Zeitung. "Voith hatte noch nie so viele Aufträge für Papiermaschinen," June 7, 1988, 15.

———. "Die gedruckte Information bleibt das wichtigste Medium," August 23, 1988, 12.

———. "Das Flaggschiff des MAN-Konzerns hat nochmals an Fahrt gewonnen," December 11, 1988, 15.

FRANKO, LAWRENCE G. *The European Multinationals: A Renewed Challenge to American and British Big Business.* Stamford, Conn.: Greylock, 1976.

FRANZ, ROGER S. *X-Efficiency: Theory, Evidence and Applications.* Boston: Kluwer, Dordrecht, 1988.

FREEMAN, CHRISTOPHER. *The Economics of Industrial Innovation,* second edition, London: Francis Pinter, 1982 (1st edition, Penguin, 1974).

FROST & SULLIVAN. *The European Market for Patient Monitoring Equipment.* New York: Frost & Sullivan, May 1984, 63.

GHEMAWAT, PANKAJ. "Sustainable Advantage," *Harvard Business Review,* Volume 64, September–October 1986, 53–58.

———. *Commitment: The Dynamic Theory of Strategy,* forthcoming.

GIARINI, ORIO. *The Emerging Service Economy.* Oxford: Pergamon Press, 1987.

GOEBEL, THEODOR. *Friedrich Koenig und die Erfindung der Schnellpresse.* Reprinted Würzburg: Schnellpressenfabrik Koenig & Bauer AG, 1956 (1883).

GRAHAM, FRANK D. "Some Aspects of Protection Further Considered," *Quarterly Journal of Economics,* Volume 37, 1923, 199–227.

GRAMMA, S.P.A. *Il management d'impresa nelle aziende italiane: comparazione Italia-USA-Giappone di strategia e organizzatione.* Milan, June 1988.

GRAY, PETER H. "A Negotiating Strategy for Trade in Services," *Journal of World Trade Law,* Volume 17, September–October 1983, 337–388.

GRUBEL, HERBERT G., AND LLOYD, P. J. *Intra-industry Trade: The Theory and Measurement of International Trade in Differentiated Products.* London, New York: Macmillan (distributed in the United States by Halsted Press), 1975.

GRUBER, WILLIAM; MEHTA, DILEEP; AND VERNON, RAYMOND. "The R&D Factor in International Trade and Investment of United States Industries," *Journal of Political Economy,* Volume 75, Number 1, February 1967, 20–37.

HABAKKUK, H. J. *American and British Technology in the Nineteenth Century.* Cambridge: Cambridge University Press, 1962.

HALL, PETER, AND MARKUSEN, ANN, EDS. *Silicon Landscapes.* Boston: Allen & Unwin, 1985.

HAMEL, GARY, AND PRAHALAD, C. K. "Do You Really Have a Global Strategy?" *Harvard Business Review,* Number 4, July–August 1985, 139–148.

HANNAN, MICHAEL T., AND FREEMAN, JOHN. "Structural Inertia and Organizational Change," *American Sociological Review,* Volume 49, Number 2, April 1984, 149–164.

HARKNESS, JON. "The Factor-Proportions Model with Many Nations, Goods and Factors: Theory and Evidence," *Review of Economics and Statistics,* Volume 65, Number 2, May 1983, 298–305.

HAYES, ROBERT H.; WHEELWRIGHT, STEVEN C.; AND CLARK, KIM B. *Dynamic Manufacturing: Creating the Learning Organization.* New York: The Free Press, 1988.

HELPMAN, ELHANAN, AND KRUGMAN, PAUL R. *Market Structure and Foreign Trade: Increasing Returns, Imperfect Competition, and the International Economy.* Cambridge, Mass.: MIT Press, 1985.

HINDLEY, BRIAN, AND SMITH, ALASDAIR. "Comparative Advantage and Trade in Services," *The World Economy,* Volume 7, Number 4, December 1984, 369–390.

HIRSCH, SEEV. "The United States Electronics Industry in International Trade," *National Institute Economic Review,* Number 34, November 1965; also in Wells (1972).

———. "Technological Factors in the Composition and Direction of Israel's Industrial Exports." In *Technological Factors in International Trade,* edited by Raymond Vernon. New York: National Bureau of Economic Research, 1970.

HIRSCHMAN, ALBERT O. *The Strategy of Economic Development.* New Haven: Yale University Press, 1958.

HIRSCHMEIER, JOHANNES, AND YUI, TSUNCHIKO. *The Development of Japanese Business 1600–1980.* London: George Allen Unwin, 1981 (2nd edition).

HLADIK, KAREN. "International Joint Ventures: An Empirical Investigation into the Characteristics of Recent U.S.-Foreign Joint Venture Partnerships." Ph.D. dissertation, Business Economics Program, Harvard University, 1984.

HOOD, NEIL, AND YOUNG, STEPHEN. *The Economics of Multinational Enterprise.* London: Longman Group, 1979.

HOUT, THOMAS; PORTER, MICHAEL E.; AND RUDDEN, EILEEN. "How Global Companies Win Out," *Harvard Business Review,* September–October 1982, 98–108.

HUNTINGTON, SAMUEL P. "The U.S.—Decline or Renewal?," *Foreign Affairs,* Volume 67, Number 2, 1988, 76–96.

HYMER, STEPHEN H. "The International Operations of National Firms: A Study of Direct Foreign Investment." Ph.D. dissertation, Massachusetts Institute of Technology, 1960. Published Cambridge, Mass.: MIT Press, 1976.

IGUCHI, TOMIO. "Aggregate Concentration, Turnover, and Mobility Among the Largest Manufacturing Firms in Japan," *Antitrust Bulletin,* Volume 32, Number 4, 1987, 939–965.

Il Giornale. Ceramic Tile Industry Supplement to Number 35, September 19, 1988, 4.

International Construction Week, July 11, 1988.

International Financial Law Review. "Lawyers Question Foreign Offices," October 1985, 7–11.

JACOBS, JANE. *Cities and the Wealth of Nations: Principles of Economic Life.* New York: Random House, 1984.

JAIKUMAR, RAMCHANDRAN, AND BOHN, ROGER E. "The Dynamic Approach: An Alternative Paradigm for Operations Management," paper presented to Manufacturing International '88 ASME Conference Proceedings, April 1988.

JAPAN INFORMATION PROCESSING DEVELOPMENT CENTER. *Informatization White Paper for 1988 edition.* Tokyo: JIPDEC, 1988.

Japan Productivity Center. "International Comparison of Labor Productivity," Tokyo, February 1988.

Jerusalem Institute of Management. *Export-led Growth Strategy for Israel.* Tel Aviv: Jerusalem Institute of Management, 1987.

JOHANSON, JAN, AND MATTSSON, LARS GUNNAR. "Internationalisation in Industrial Systems—A Network Approach." In *Strategies in Global Competition,* edited by Neil Hood and Jan-Erik Vahlne. London: Croom Helm, 1988.

JOHNSON, CHALMERS. *MITI and the Japanese Miracle: The Growth of Industrialized Policy, 1925–1975.* Stanford, Calif.: Stanford University Press, 1982.

JONES, RONALD W., AND KENEN, PETER B., EDS. *Handbook of International Economics.* Amsterdam, New York: North-Holland (distributed in the United States and Canada by Elsevier Science Publishing Company), 1984.

JORGENSON, DALE W.; GOLLOP, FRANK M.; AND FRAUMENI, BARBARA M. *Productivity and U.S. Economic Growth.* Cambridge, Mass.: Harvard University Press, 1987.

KATOUZIAN, M. A. "The Development of the Service Sector: A New Approach," *Oxford Economic Papers,* Volume 22, Number 3, November 1970, 362–382.

KEEGAN, WARREN J. *Global Marketing Management.* Englewood Cliffs, N.J.: Prentice-Hall, 1989 (4th edition).

KENNEDY, PAUL. *The Rise and Fall of the Great Powers.* New York: Random House, 1987.

KIM, SEOK K. "Business Concentration and Government Policy." DBA dissertation, Harvard University, 1987.

KINDLEBERGER, CHARLES P., AND AUDRETSCH, DAVID B. *The Multinational Corporation in the 1980s.* Cambridge, Mass.: MIT Press, 1983.

KNICKERBOCKER, FREDERICK T. *Oligopolistic Reaction and Multinational Enterprise.* Cambridge, Mass.: Harvard University Press, 1973.

KOGUT, BRUCE. "Normative Observations on the International Value-Added Chain and Strategic Groups," *Journal of International Business Studies,* Volume 15, Number 3, Fall 1984, 151–167.

———. "Designing Global Strategies: Comparative and Competitive Value-Added Chains," *Sloan Management Review,* Volume 26, Number 4, Summer 1985, 15–28.

KRISHNA, KALA. "Trade Restrictions as Facilitating Practices," Woodrow Wilson School, Princeton University Discussion Paper in Economics Number 55, 1984.

KRUGMAN, PAUL R. "Scale Economies, Product Differentiation, and the Pattern of Trade," *American Economic Review,* Volume 70, Number 5, December 1980, 950–959.

———, ed. *Strategic Trade Policy and the New International Economics.* Cambridge, Mass.: MIT Press, 1986.

LAFAY, BRENDER, AND CHEVALLIER. "Trois expériences de spécialisation internationale: France, Allemagne, Japon." *Statistiques et Etudes Financières,* Série Orange, Number 30, 1977, 23–41.

LANDAU, RALPH. "U.S. Economic Growth," *Scientific American,* Volume 256, Number 6, June 1988, 44–52.

LANDES, DAVID S. *The Unbound Prometheus.* Cambridge: Cambridge University Press, 1969.

LANTNER, R. *Théorie de la dominance économique.* Paris: Dunod, 1974, 315.

LAWRENCE, PAUL R., AND LORSCH, JAY W. *Organization and Environment.* Boston: Division of Research, Harvard Graduate School of Business Administration, 1967.

LAZONICK, WILLIAM. "Industrial Organization and Technological Change: The Decline of the British Cotton Industry," *Business History Review,* Volume 52, Number 2, Summer 1983, 195–236.

LAZONICK, WILLIAM, AND ELBAUM, BERNARD. *The Decline of the British Economy.* Oxford, New York: Clarendon, 1986.

LEAMER, EDWARD E. "The Leontief Paradox Reconsidered," *Journal of Political Economy,* Volume 88, 1980, 495–503.

———. *Sources of International Comparative Advantage: Theory and Evidence.* Cambridge, Mass.: MIT Press, 1984.

LEIBENSTEIN, HARVEY. "Allocative Efficiency vs. X-Efficiency," *American Economic Review,* Volume 56, June 1966, 392–415.

LEIGH, BRUCE. "The Italians: The Best Europeans?" *International Management,* Volume 42, Number 5, May 1987, 24–31.

LEMELIN, ANDRE. "Relatedness in the Patterns of Interindustry Diversification," *Review of Economics and Statistics,* Volume 64, November 1982, 646–657.

LEONTIEF, WASSILY. "Domestic Production and Foreign Trade: The American Capital Position Re-examined," *Economica Internazionale,* Volume 7, February 1954, 3–32.

LEVITT, THEODORE. "The Industrialization of Services," *Harvard Business Review,* September–October 1976, 63–74.

———. "The Globalization of Markets," *Harvard Business Review,* May–June 1983, 92–102.

LIEBERMAN, MARVIN. "Learning, Productivity, and U.S.-Japan Industrial Competitiveness." In *Managing International Manufacturing,* edited by Kasra Ferdows. North-Holland, 1988.

LINDBECK, ASSAR. *Swedish Economic Policy.* Berkeley and Los Angeles: University of California Press, 1974.

———. "The Recent Slowdown of Productivity Growth," *Economic Journal,* Volume 93, 1983, 13–34.

LINDER, STAFFAN. *An Essay on Trade and Transformation.* New York: John Wiley, 1961.

LIST, FRIEDRICH. *The National System of Political Economy.* 1856. Translated by Sampson S. Lloyd. Reprinted London: Longman's, 1922.

LITTLE, JANE SNEDDON. "Intra-Firm Trade: An Update," *New England Economic Review,* May–June 1987, 46–51.

LLOYD, PETER E., AND DICKEN, PETER. *Location in Space.* London: Harper & Row, 1977.

LODGE, GEORGE C., AND VOGEL, EZRA F., EDS. *Ideology and National Competitiveness: An Analysis of Nine Countries.* Boston: Harvard Business School Press, 1987.

LÖSCH, AUGUST. *The Economics of Location.* New Haven: Yale University Press, 1954.

LUKES, JAMES J. *Competitive Assessment of the U.S. Ceramic Floor and Wall Tile Industry.* Washington, D.C.: Department of Commerce, 1983, 45–49.

LUNDVALL, BENGT-AKÉ. *Product Innovation and User-Producer Interaction.* Aalborg: Aalborg University Press, 1985.

———. "Innovation as an Interactive Process: User-Producer Relations," in Dosi ed., 1988.

MAC Group, "The Effects of 1992 on Financial Services in the EEC," Special Report, March 1988.

MACDONALD, JAMES M. "R and D and the Directions of Diversification," *Review of Economics and Statistics,* November 1985, Volume 67, Number 4, 583–590.

MADDISON, ANGUS. *Phases of Capitalist Development.* New York: Oxford University Press, 1982.

———. "Growth and Slowdown in Advanced Capitalist Economies: Techniques of Quantitative Assessment," *Journal of Economic Literature,* Volume 25, June 1987, 649–698.

MALMGREN, HARALD B. "Negotiating International Rules for Trade in Services," *World Economy,* Volume 8, Number 2, March 1985, 11–26.

MARIOTTI, SERGIO, AND CAINARCA, GIAN CARLO. "The Evolution of Transaction

Governance in the Textile-Clothing Industry," *Journal of Economic Behavior and Organization,* Volume 7, Number 4, December 1986, 351–374.

Marketing News. "Puerto Rico Service Firms with Tax Breaks," Volume 18, October 12, 1984, 24–25.

MARSHALL, ALFRED. *Principles of Economics.* 1890. Reprinted London: Macmillan, 1920 (8th edition).

MASON, EDWARD S., et al. *The Economic and Social Modernization of the Republic of Korea.* Cambridge, Mass.: Harvard University Press, 1980.

MATTHEWS, KENT, AND MINFORD, PATRICK. "Mrs. Thatcher's Economic Policies, 1979–87." *Economic Policy,* Volume 2, Number 2, October 1987, 57–101.

MATTSSON, LARS GUNNAR. "Management of Strategic Change in a 'Markets-as-Networks' Perspective." In *The Management of Strategic Change,* edited by Andrew M. Pettigrew. Oxford, New York: Basil Blackwell, 1987.

McADAM, BRUCE M. "The Growing Role of the Service Sector in the U.S. Economy," *U.S. Industrial Outlook,* 1985, 38–43.

McCLELLAND, DAVID C. *Motivating Economic Achievement.* New York: The Free Press, 1969.

McCRAW, THOMAS K., ED. *America Versus Japan.* Boston: Harvard Business School Press, 1986.

MEADE, JAMES E. "External Economies and Diseconomies in Competitive Situations," *Economic Journal,* Volume 62, March 1952, 54–67.

MONOPOLKOMMISSION. Die Wettbewerbsordnung erweitern. Hauptgutachten 1986/1987. Baden-Baden, 1988.

National Science Foundation. "The Science and Technology Resources of West Germany: A Comparison with the United States," Special Report Number 86–310, Washington, D.C., March 1986.

———. "International Science and Technology Data Update 1988, NSF89–307, Washington, D.C., 1988.

NELSON, RICHARD R. "Research on Productivity Growth and Differences: Dead Ends and New Departures," *Journal of Economic Literature,* Volume 19, Number 3, September 1981, 1029–1064.

NELSON, RICHARD R., AND WINTER, SIDNEY G. *An Evolutionary Theory of Economic Change,* Cambridge, Mass.: Belknap Press of Harvard University Press, 1982.

The New York Times. "Chip Makers Will Seek U.S. Aid to Spur Output," September 10, 1988, 37.

NOMISMA, S.P.A. *L'industria delle piastrelle di ceramica nel mondo.* Sassuolo: EdiCer, 1983.

NUKAZAWA, KAZUO. *Implications of Japan's Emerging Service Economy.* Tokyo: Keidanren, 1980.

OHLIN, BERTIL. *Interregional and International Trade.* Cambridge, Mass.: Harvard University Press, 1933.

OHMAE, KENICHI. *Triad Power: The Coming Shape of Global Competition.* New York: The Free Press; London: Collier Macmillan, 1985.

OLSON, MANCUR. *The Rise and Decline of Nations: Economic Growth, Stagflation, and Social Rigidities*. New Haven: Yale University Press, 1982.

ONIDA, FABRIZIO, ED. *Innovazione, competitività e vincolo energetico*. Bologna: Il Mulino, 1985.

Organization for Economic Cooperation and Development, "Competition and Trade Policies: Their Interaction," 1984.

———, "Main Science Technology and Indicators," 1988.

———, "Main Science Technology and Indicators," 1989.

OS Publications. *All About M&A*, Tokyo, 1989.

O'SULLIVAN, PATRICK. *Geographical Economics*. London: Macmillan, 1981.

OUCHI, WILLIAM G. *Theory Z: How American Business Can Meet the Japanese Challenge*. Reading, Mass.: Addison-Wesley, 1981.

OUCHI, WILLIAM G., AND BOLTON, MICHELE K. "The Logic of Joint Research and Development," *California Management Review*, Volume 30, Number 3, Spring 1988, 9–33.

PADE, HENRIK, AND MØLLER, KIM. *Industrial Success*. Gylling, Denmark: Samfundslitteratur, 1988.

PALMER, JOHN D. "Consumer Service Industry Exports: New Attitudes and Concepts Needed for Neglected Sectors," *Columbia Journal of World Business*, Volume 20, Spring 1985, 69–74.

PAVITT, KEITH. *Technical Innovation and British Economic Performance*, London: Macmillan, 1980.

———. "Sectoral Patterns of Technical Change: Towards a Taxonomy and a Theory," *Research Policy*, Volume 13, December 1984, 343–373.

———. "Technological Accumulation, Diversification and Organization in UK Companies, 1945–83," DRC Discussion Paper, SPRU, University of Sussex, Brighton, 1988.

PERLMUTTER, HOWARD V. "The Tortuous Evolution of the Multinational Corporation," *Columbia Journal of World Business*, Volume 4, Number 1, January–February 1969, 9–18.

PERROUX, F. "L'effet d'entraînement: de l'analyse au repérage quantitatif," *Economie Appliquée*, Number 2–3–4, 1973, 647–674.

PETERS, THOMAS J. *Thriving on Chaos: Handbook for a Management Revolution*. New York: Knopf, 1987.

PIORE, MICHAEL J., AND SABEL, CHARLES F. "Italian Small Business Development: Lessons for U.S. Policy." In *American Industry in International Competition, Government Policies and Corporate Strategies*, edited by John Zysman and Laura Tyson. Ithaca, London: Cornell University Press, 1983.

PORTER, MICHAEL E. *Competitive Strategy: Techniques for Analyzing Industries and Competitors*. New York: The Free Press, 1980.

———. *Competitive Advantage: Creating and Sustaining Superior Performance.* New York: The Free Press, 1985a.

———. "Beyond Comparative Advantage." Working Paper. Harvard Graduate School of Business Administration, August 1985b.

———, ED. *Competition in Global Industries.* Boston: Harvard Business School Press, 1986.

———. "From Competitive Advantage to Corporate Strategy," *Harvard Business Review*, May–June 1987, 43–59.

PORTER, MICHAEL E., AND ENRIGHT, MICHAEL J. *Studies in National Advantage,* forthcoming.

PORTER, MICHAEL E., AND MILLAR, VICTOR E. "How Information Gives You Competitive Advantage," *Harvard Business Review*, Number 4, July–August 1985, 149–160.

PRAHALAD, C. K. "The Strategic Process in a Multinational Corporation." DBA dissertation, Harvard Graduate School of Business Administration, 1975.

PRAHALAD, C. K., AND DOZ, YVES. *The Multinational Mission: Balancing Local Demands and Global Vision.* New York: The Free Press; London: Collier Macmillan, 1987.

President's Commission on Industrial Competitiveness, *Global Competition: The New Reality,* the report of the President's Commission on Industrial Competitiveness, Volumes I and II, Washington, D.C.: U.S. Government Printing Office, January 1985.

PRESTOWITZ, CLYDE V. *Trading Places: How We Allowed Japan to Take the Lead.* New York: Basic Books, 1988.

PRODI, ROMANO. *Modello di sviluppo di un settore in rapida crescita.* Milan: Franco Angeli, 1966, 123–127.

PRYOR, MILLARD H. "Planning in a Worldwide Business," *Harvard Business Review*, January-February 1965, 130–139.

RAVENSCRAFT, DAVID J., AND SCHERER, FREDERICK M. *Mergers, Sell-offs, and Economic Efficiency.* Washington, D.C.: Brookings Institution, 1987.

Regeringens Proposition. "Näringspolitik infor 90-talet," Volume 74, 1986–1987.

REICH, ROBERT. "As the World Turns," *The New Republic*, May 1, 1989, 23–28.

Republic of Korea, Economic Planning Board, *Social Indicators in Korea,* 1987.

RIDDLE, DOROTHY I. *Service-Led Growth: The Role of the Service Sector in World Development.* New York: Praeger, 1986.

ROMER, PAUL M. "Capital Accumulation in the Theory of Long-Run Growth," in *Modern Business Cycle Theory,* edited by Robert J. Barro. Cambridge: Harvard University Press, 1989.

RONCACCIOLI, ANGELA. *Un' analisi empirica dell' imprenditorialitá: l'industria delle piastrelle di ceramica.* Padova: CEDAM, 1986.

RONSTADT, ROBERT C. "International R&D: The Establishment and Evolution of Research and Development Abroad by Seven U.S. Multinationals," *Journal of International Business Studies,* Volume 9, Number 1, Spring-Summer 1978, 7–23.

ROSENBERG, NATHAN. *Perspectives on Technology.* Cambridge: Cambridge University Press, 1976.

———. "Technological Interdependence in the American Economy," *Technology and Culture,* Volume 20, Number 1, January 1979, 25–49.

ROSTOW, WALT W. *The Stages of Economic Growth.* Cambridge: Cambridge University Press, 1971 (2nd edition).

ROTHBART, ERWIN. "Causes of the Superior Efficiency of USA Industry as Compared with British Industry," *Economic Journal,* Volume 56, September 1946, 383–390.

SABEL, CHARLES F. "The Reemergence of Regional Economies: Changes in the Scale of Production," paper prepared for the Social Science Research Council, Western European Committee, August 1987.

SADAMOTO, KUNI, ED. *Robots in the Japanese Economy.* Tokyo: Survey Japan, 1981.

SALONER, GARTH AND FARRELL, JOSEPH. "Installed Base and Compatibility: Predation, Product Preannouncements and Innovation," *American Economic Review,* Volume 76, Number 5, 1986, 940–955.

SAMPSON, GARY P., AND SNAPE, RICHARD H. "Identifying the Issues in Trade in Services," *The World Economy,* Volume 8, Number 2, June 1985, 171–182.

SAPIR, ANDRÉ. "Trade in Services: Policy Issues for the Eighties," *Columbia Journal of World Business,* Volume 17, Fall 1982, 77–83.

SCHERER, FREDERICK M. *Industrial Market Structure and Economic Performance.* Chicago: Rand McNally College Publishing Company, 1980.

———. "Inter-Industry Technology Flows in the United States," *Research Policy,* Volume 2, Number 4, August 1982, 227–245.

SCHMOOKLER, JACOB. *Invention and Economic Growth.* Cambridge: Harvard University Press, 1966.

SCHOTT, JEFFREY J. "Protectionist Threat to Trade and Investment in Services," *World Economy,* Volume 6, Number 2, June 1983, 195–214.

SCHUMPETER, JOSEPH A. *The Theory of Economic Development.* Cambridge, Mass.: Harvard University Press, 1934.

———. *Capitalism, Socialism and Democracy.* New York: Harper & Row, 1942.

SCOTT, BRUCE R.; LODGE, GEORGE C.; AND BOWER, JOSEPH L., EDS. *U.S. Competitiveness in the World Economy.* Boston: Harvard Business School Press, 1985.

SEZZI, GRAZIANO. *Struttura e tendenza dell'industria italiana delle piastrelle di ceramica.* Sassuolo: Assopiastrelle, 1979.

SHELP, RONALD K. *Beyond Industrialization: Ascendancy of the Global Service Economy.* New York: Praeger, 1981.

————. "A Service Economy," *The Journal of the Institute for Socioeconomic Studies,* Autumn 1983, Volume 8, 26–38.

SHINOHARA, MIYOHEI. *Industrial Growth, Trade and Dynamic Patterns in the Japanese Economy.* Tokyo: University of Tokyo Press, 1982.

SIRILLI, GIORGIO. "The Innovative Activities of Researchers in Italian Industry," *Research Policy,* Volume 13, Number 2, April 1984, 63–83.

————. "Patents and Inventions: An Empirical Study," *Research Policy,* Volume 16, Number 4, August 1987, 157–174.

SMITH, ADAM. *An Inquiry into the Nature and Causes of the Wealth of Nations.* 1776. New York: The Modern Library, 1937.

SOLOW, ROBERT. "Technological Change and the Aggregate Production Function," *The Review of Economics and Statistics,* Volume 39, Number 3, August 1957, 312–320.

SÖLVELL, ÖRJAN. "Swedish Technical Consultants: The Spearhead Effect," unpublished paper, Institute for International Business, Stockholm School of Economics, 1979.

————. "Entry Barriers and Foreign Penetrations: Emerging Patterns of International Competition in Two Electrical Engineering Industries." Ph.D. dissertation, Institute for International Business, Stockholm School of Economics, 1987. Published Stockholm: Gotab, 1987.

SPENCE, A. MICHAEL, AND KREPS, DAVID M. "Modelling the Role of History in Industrial Organization and Competition," Working Paper #992, Harvard Institute of Economic Research, July 1983.

Statistisches Bundesamt, Statistisches Jahrbuch 1982 für die Bundesrepublik Deutschland. Wiesbaden, 1982.

Statistisches Bundesamt, Statistisches Jahrbuch 1987 für die Bundesrepublik Deutschland. Wiesbaden, 1987.

STIGLER, GEORGE J. "The Division of Labor Is Limited by the Extent of the Market," *Journal of Political Economy,* Volume 59, Number 3, June 1951, 185–193.

STOBAUGH, ROBERT B., et al. *Nine Investments Abroad and Their Impact at Home: Case Studies on Multinational Enterprise and the U.S. Economy.* Boston: Harvard Business School Division of Research, 1976.

STOPFORD, JON J., AND WELLS, LOUIS T., JR. *Managing the Multinational Organization of the Firm and Overlap of Subsidiaries.* New York: Basic Books, 1972.

SVEIKAUSKAS, LEO. "Science and Technology in United States Foreign Trade," *Economic Journal,* Volume 93, September 1983, 542–554.

SWEDENBORG, BIRGITTA. *The Multinational Operations of Swedish Firms: An Analysis of Determinants and Effects.* Stockholm: Industrial Institute for Economic and Social Research, 1979.

SYLOS LABINI, PAOLO. *Oligopoly and Technical Progress.* Cambridge: Harvard University Press, 1984 (2nd edition).

TEDLOW, RICHARD. *Creating Mass Markets.* New York: Basic Books, 1990, forthcoming.

TEECE, DAVID J. "Multinational Enterprise: Market Failure and Market Power Considerations," *Sloan Management Review,* Volume 22, Number 3, September 1981, 3–17.

―――. "Transaction Cost Economics and the Multinational Enterprise: An Assessment," Working Paper IB-3, Business School, University of California at Berkeley, January 1985.

Telesis Consultancy Group. "A Review of Industrial Policy," National Economic and Social Council, 1982, Dublin: TCG, 1983.

THARAKAN, P. K. MATHEW, ED. *Intra-Industry Trade: Empirical and Methodological Aspects.* The Netherlands: Elsevier Science Publishers, 1983.

THOMAS, LACY G. "Spare the Rod and Spoil the Industry: Vigorous Competition and Vigorous Regulation Promote Global Competitive Advantage: A Ten-Nation Study of Government Industrial Policies and Corporate Pharmaceutical Competitive Advantage," Columbia Business School working paper, October, 1989.

THOMPSON, G. RODNEY, AND STOLLAR, ANDREW J. "An Empirical Test of an International Model of Relative Tertiary Employment," *Economic Development and Cultural Change,* Volume 31, Number 4, July 1983, 775–785.

TOLEDANO, JOELLE. "A propos des filières industrielles," *Revue d'Economie Industrielle,* Volume 6, Number 4, 1978, 149–158.

United Nations. *U.N. International Trade Statistics Yearbook, 1986.* New York: United Nations, 1988.

United Nations Center on Transnational Corporations. *Salient Features and Trends in Foreign Direct Investment.* New York: United Nations, 1984.

United Nations Economic Commission for Europe. *Production and Use of Industrial Robots.* New York: United Nations, 1985.

United Nations Office of Economic Cooperation and Development, Science Resources Newsletter, Number 7, Paris, 1983.

United States Department of Commerce. *A Competitive Assessment of the U.S. Robotics Industry.* Washington, D.C., 1987, 16–17.

United States Office of Technology Assessment. "Trade in Services: Exports and Foreign Revenues," September 1986.

UTILI, GABRIELLA. *Transformazione e sviluppo dell'industra italiana delle piastrelle di ceramica.* Sassuolo: EdiCer, 1983.

UTTERBACK, JAMES M., AND ABERNATHY, WILLIAM J. "A Dynamic Model of Product and Process Innovation," *Omega,* Volume 3, 1975, 639–656.

VAHLNE, JAN-ERIK. *Multinationals: The Swedish Case.* London: Croom Helm, 1986.

VERBAND DER AUTOMOBILINDUSTRIE (VDA). *Annual Report 85/86.* Frankfurt, 1986, 85.

VERBAND DEUTSCHER MASCHINEN UND ANLAGENBAU (VDMA). *Fachgemeinschaft Druck-und Papiertechnik* (brochure). Frankfurt, 1986, 11.

VERNON, RAYMOND. "International Investment and International Trade in the Product Cycle," *Quarterly Journal of Economics,* Volume 80, Number 2, May 1966, 190–207.

———. "The Location of Economic Activity." In *Economic Analysis and the Multinational Enterprise,* edited by John H. Dunning. London: George Allen & Unwin, 1974.

VICKERS, JOHN S., AND YARROW, GEORGE K. *Privatization and the Natural Monopolies.* London: Public Policy Center, 1988.

VOGEL, EZRA F. *Comeback, Case by Case: Building the Resurgence of American Business.* New York: Simon & Schuster, 1985.

VON HIPPEL, ERIC. *Sources of Innovation.* New York: Oxford University Press, 1988.

WATERMAN, ROBERT H., JR. *The Renewal Factor: How the Best Get and Keep the Competitive Edge.* Toronto, New York: Bantam Books, 1987.

WEBER, ALFRED. *Theory of the Location of Industries.* Translated by Carl J. Friedrich. Chicago: University of Chicago Press, 1981.

WEINER, MARTIN J. *English Culture and the Decline of the Industrial Spirit, 1850–1950.* Cambridge: Cambridge University Press, 1981.

WELLS, LOUIS T., JR., ED. *The Product Life Cycle and International Trade.* Division of Research, Graduate School of Business Administration, Harvard University, Boston, 1972.

WILLIAMSON, OLIVER E. *Markets and Hierarchies.* New York: The Free Press, 1975.

———. *The Economic Institutions of Capitalism: Firms, Markets, Relational Contracting.* New York: The Free Press; London: Collier Macmillan, 1985.

WIND, YORAM; DOUGLAS, SUSAN P.; AND PERLMUTTER, HOWARD V. "Guidelines for Developing International Marketing Strategies," *Journal of Marketing,* Volume 37, Number 2, April 1973, 14–23.

WOLF, HANS-JÜRGEN. *Schwarze Kunst: Eine Illustrierte Geschichte der Druckverfahren.* Frankfurt: Deutscher Fachverlag, 1981.

YONEMOTO, KANJI. "Robotization in Japan," *Japan Industrial Robot Association,* February, 1987.

YOSHINO, MICHAEL Y. *Japanese Management System: Tradition and Innovation,* Cambridge, Mass.: MIT Press, 1968.

ZIKOPOULOS, MARIANTHI, ED. *Open Doors: 1987/1988 Report on International Educational Exchange.* New York: Institute of International Education, 1988.

ZYSMAN, JOHN, AND TYSON, LAURA, EDS. *American Industry in International Competition, Government Policies and Corporate Strategies.* Ithaca, N.Y., London: Cornell University Press, 1983.

Index